The Divine Drama
The Old Testament as Literature

John Dancy

D0733423

The Lutterworth Press
Cambridge

The Lutterworth Press
P. O. Box 60
Cambridge
CB1 2NT

website: www.lutterworth.com
e-mail: publishing@lutterworth.com

British Library Cataloguing in Publication Data:
A catalogue record is available from the British Library

ISBN 0 7188 2987 5

Printed in Great Britain by IBT Global, London

The imagination fuses hitherto isolated beliefs into strongly unified systems.
These, if they are filled with sufficient energy and force of will –
and, it may be added, fantasy, which is less frightened by the facts
and creates ideal models in terms of which the facts are ordered –
sometimes transform the outlook of an entire people.

Isaiah Berlin, reviewing the first
volume of Winston Churchill's
History of the Second World War, 1949

CONTENTS

The Old Testament Apocrypha

Appendices

REFERENCES AND ABBREVIATIONS

References to passages within the Bible are made as follows:

1.15, 18	Chapter 1, verses 15 and 18
15ad	verse 15, lines one and four (of poetry)
+/++ *or* f./ff.	with the following chapters, verses or pages
[ ]	passages of the OT not printed in this selection

Sigla   * see Glossary

• marks beginning of verse where the text does not make it clear

Abbreviations

Am	Amos	KJV	*see* AV
ANE	Ancient Near East(ern)	Lev	Leviticus
ANET	*Ancient Near Eastern Texts* edited by J.B. Pritchard, (Princeton, 3rd edn, 1969)	LXX*	The Septuagint or Greek text of the OT
		M *or* Macc	Maccabees
AV	Authorised (or King James) Version	Mic	Micah
		ms(s)	manuscript(s)
C	Century, e.g. C7th=seventh century	MT*	Masoretic or Hebrew text of the OT
D *or* Dt	Deuteronomy	*NERT*	*Near Eastern Religious Texts relating to the OT* (SCM Press, 1978)
Dan	Daniel		
DtH	The deuteronomic historian *or* history (Jos-2 K)		
		NJB	*New Jerusalem Bible* (1985)
E *or* Eccl	Ecclesiastes (Qoheleth)	NRSV	*New Revised Standard Version* (1989)
Ecclus	Ecclesiasticus (ben Sira)		
Esd	Esdras (1 and 2)	NT	New Testament
Est	Esther	Num	Numbers
Ex *or* Exod	Exodus	OT	Old Testament
Ez	Ezekiel	P	The 'Priestly' writers of the OT
Gen	Genesis		
Gk	Greek	PNTW	*The Psalms: a new translation for worship* (Collins, 1977)
Heb	Hebrew		
Hos	Hosea		
Is	Isaiah	Prov	Proverbs
I¹	'First' Isaiah	Ps(s)	Psalm(s)
I²	'Second' Isaiah (Chs 40-55)	REB	*Revised English Bible* (1989)
J	The 'Yahwistic' writers in the Pentateuch		
		RSV	*Revised Standard Version* (1952)
Jer	Jeremiah		
Jg	Judges	RV	*Revised Version* (1886)
Jon	Jonah	S *or* Sam	(Books of) Samuel
Jos	Joshua	Wisd Sol	Wisdom of Solomon
K	(Books of) Kings	Zech	Zechariah

ACKNOWLEDGEMENTS

English translations of the Old Testament:

Extracts from the *Authorized Version* of the Bible (The King James Bible), the rights of which are vested in the Crown, are reproduced by permission of the Crown's Patentee, Cambridge University Press

Revised English Bible © Oxford University Press and Cambridge University Press, 1989

The Revised Standard Version, 1952 and the *New Revised Standard Version*, 1989: to the National Council of the Churches of Christ in the United States of America

The New Jerusalem Bible, 1985: to Messrs Darton, Longman and Todd

The Psalms, a New Translation for Worship, David L. Frost, John A. Emerton and A. Macintosh, 1977: to HarperCollins Publishers

Other books:

Ancient Near Eastern Texts relating to the Old Testament, ed. James Pritchard, third edition with supplement, 1969, third printing, 1974: to Princeton University Press

Myths from Mesopotamia, Stephanie Dalley, 1989: to Oxford University Press

Near Eastern Religious Texts relating to the Old Testament, ed. Walter Beyerlin, ET John Bowden, 1978: to SCM Press

Rituals of Kinship among the Nyakusa, Monica Wilson, OUP, 1957: to the International African Institute

The Art of Biblical Poetry, Robert Alter, 1985: to Basic Books Inc., NY

The Epic of Gilgamesh, Andrew George, 1999: to Penguin UK

The Song of Songs and the Egyptian Love Poetry, M.V. Fox, 1985: to the University of Wisconsin Press

PREFACE

This book aims to rescue the Old Testament from the long list of the great unread. The thinking behind it is laid out in the next section, on Purpose, Plan and Principles. Here a few personal remarks are in order.

I originally conceived the idea some forty years ago when I first had to 'teach' the OT to intelligent sixth-formers as part of a religious studies course. That experience started as misery for me as well as for them. But over the years it changed, at least for me, into something to look forward to each week. It did so gradually, as I came to formulate two principles. First, don't ever expect anyone to read a *whole* book at one gulp, except for Ruth and Jonah: none of them, not even Job, can sustain it. Second, having excerpted the 'best', treat it as the great literature it undoubtedly is. Most sixth-formers nowadays know what it is to read a serious work of English literature: let them read the OT in the same way.

But what matters is the text itself: all else is secondary. Hence the layout on the pages of this book, with the commentary in every sense inferior. References, which are the hallmark of scholarly works, are kept to a minimum, most of them being cross-references within the OT itself. Where literary parallels are quoted, they are all from the ancient literatures of the Near East or of Greece, those two flanking bodies of literature between which that of ancient Israel occupies a middle position not only in place but in spirit.

As to modern works of OT scholarship, whether books or articles, I hope not to have missed much of what has been accessible in the UK up to 1998, but I give no references and no bibliography.

A book so long in gestation leaves many debts to pay. Long ago Dr Colin Roberts taught me papyrology and Sir Isaiah Berlin attempted to teach me philosophy. Both often later gave me the kind of encouragement that revives the spirit: the book is needed, they said, and *you* must write it. More technical help has been freely given by the Reverend Professors Chris Bryan and Roy Porter.

In another category a grant from the British Academy enabled my research to range more widely. Finally I owe a great deal to three Trusts – the Binks Trust, the Farmington (Dulverton) Trust and the Kirby Laing Charitable Foundation – and to Mr Dov Gottesman of Geneva. Each of them gave generous financial support designed to reduce the selling price of what otherwise would have been a very expensive book.

But my first debt is to my pupils at Winchester, Lancing and Marlborough, whose critical responsiveness set me on my way. And my last must be to my wife Angela. Her unfailing loyalty over the decades has in these last years been tested almost to destruction by the absence of her husband in libraries and the presence in her drawing room of an adolescent computer demanding constant maternal attention.

Mousehole, 2000

PURPOSE, PLAN AND PRINCIPLES

The aim of this book is to help restore the OT to the reading list of the general educated public. For a century now it has been the case that the Bible is 'the world's least read best-seller'. What is true of the Bible is even more true of the OT: few except scholars and believers read it for pleasure.

And there are good reasons for this state of affairs. Chief of them is that about half the OT is not *worth* reading by any but scholars or believers. Much of the other half is superb; but a reader has to know the way about the whole field before being able to unearth the pearls buried in it. As things stand, the best suffers from the presence of the rest.

Secondly, the text of the OT as traditionally presented is far from easy on the eye. True, some more recent translations are more attractively set out. But even then the *full* text is so long as to leave no adequate room on the page for the notes needed to explain it. The *New Jerusalem Bible* makes a gallant attempt to solve the problem but is defeated by sheer bulk.

In any case, thirdly, the notes provided rarely tell the general reader what he or she wants to know. Many of them are historical. Since the OT is a useful source for the ancient history of the Near East, such a concern is entirely valid; but it is of little general interest. Many others are theological. Again this is perfectly proper in itself. But unfortunately the theological standpoint (Jewish, Catholic or Protestant) is often too narrow to be of general appeal. Christians here are the worst offenders: how Jews must resent having their Bible patronized as a failed approximation to subsequently revealed truth!

Not that the Hebrew Bible is identical in coverage with the Old Testament – which is why this edition uses the latter title rather than the former. The OT includes all the books in the Hebrew Bible, but also some others. Christians call these other books apocryphal or deuterocanonical. Most of them were originally written in Hebrew, but hardly anything survives of that Hebrew text beyond fragments: the only complete text of them is preserved in the Greek translation of the OT, the Septuagint*. Christians treat these other books with a greater respect than Jews do, if less than they accord to the canon* of the OT.

From this analysis derive the principles governing this edition. First, it offers selections – approximately 30% of the OT and 15% of the Apocrypha. And the chief criterion of selection is readability: whether such and such a passage is capable of holding the attention of the general educated reader. This is primarily a literary criterion, and I explain below what I mean by it. But the OT is of interest also to many people for non-literary reasons. Therefore some passages have been included for their importance to specialists of one kind and another: students of history, theology, anthropology, law, Jewish traditions, etc.

Within passages I have also cut: sometimes in order to clarify, where the text offered by the mss is either incoherent or so obscure as to need a tedious explanation; sometimes to abbreviate where it is piously repetitive. Where the text can be confidently ascribed to different written sources, I have usually followed the sources in making the cuts; and I confess to a predilection for the oldest or 'original' text where it is recoverable. I have however resisted the temptation to transpose: the order of the excerpts is virtually always that of the King James Version.

I am aware that this selective approach will seem misguided or even offensive to some. I believe I can rebut such special criticisms, and I do so in Appendix C. But I must draw the general reader's attention to one point. This selection does not seek to preserve the *balance* of the OT. Certain kinds of content are under-represented here, especially lists (genealogies and dynasties) and ritual provisions. The same goes for certain attitudes, especially the complaining (which soon becomes monotonous, even in the psalms), the condemnatory (especially frequent in the prophets) and the vindictive.

The passages chosen have been taken from a variety of different translations. Translations fall into two groups. First there is the King James or *Authorized Version* (1611) and its relatives the *Revised Version* (1886), the *Revised Standard Version* (1952) and the *New Revised Standard Version* (1989). For verbal fidelity to the Hebrew and for literary quality – especially in its diction and rhythm – the KJV/AV remains unsurpassed. Coleridge said of it that 'intense study of the Bible will keep any writer from being *vulgar* in point of style'. But its archaisms can be an obstacle to a modern reader, and its scholarship has inevitably been superseded in many places. Hence the popularity of NRSV, which 'revises' AV somewhat in both respects.

I wish I could have used AV more. But time and again when I have sought to do so I have been defeated. Sometimes it misses a nuance, often it mistranslates. There is, I know, a sophisticated argument by which the accuracy of a translation is irrelevant. If the AV has printed, in a famous passage of Job (19.26), 'yet in my flesh shall I see God', then that is a text in its own right, irrespective of any connection with a Hebrew original. Against that I can only declare the principle, that the text I am concerned with is a Hebrew and/or Greek text of the first millennium BC, not an English one of the second millennium AD.

Recently however we have had a spate of new translations of the Bible. Three of these stand out as generally reliable: the RC (French) *New Jerusalem Bible*

(1985), already referred to, and two Protestant versions, the *Revised English Bible* (1989) and the American *New Revised Standard Version* (1989). The translations given by these versions are often a clear improvement, for various reasons. One reason is that the translators have been able to supplement or correct the text of the medieval Hebrew mss (MT*) not only by that of the C4th-6th AD mss of the Greek translation (LXX*) but also by the recently discovered Hebrew Dead Sea Scrolls of C2nd BC - 1st AD. All three of these translations have however their occasional weaknesses – a flatness of rhythm, a banality of tone, or a loss of sinew by paraphrase. REB is also liable to obscure a cross-reference or echo by varying its translation of a Hebrew word, even within brief compass.

Moreover all of them have created literary problems for themselves by a resolve to avoid linguistic sexism, including the use of the word 'man' in its generic sense of 'human being'. The resolve is virtuous but the English language is recalcitrant. This is particularly awkward in contexts where the central theme is the relation between God and man/men. Modern translators who are determined not to use generic 'man' have to choose between two unhappy alternatives. The formulation 'God and mortals' is theologically inept: 'mortals' belong with 'immortals', a pagan concept alien to the Bible. Locutions like 'human beings' or 'humankind' are shapeless abstractions unsuited to the concrete language of the OT. It is NRSV which carries this principle furthest. Take for example the highly evocative picture of universal peace in Micah 4.4, where AV gave a literal rendering: 'they shall sit every man under his own vine and under his own fig tree'. REB and NJB both swallowed hard and kept 'each man' (though they lost the overtones of 'Everyman'). NRSV however stickles – 'they shall all sit under their own vines and under their own fig trees' – and thus blurs the sharp pictorial focus of the Hebrew.

Had it not been for this, I should have been tempted to use NRSV throughout. As it is I have chosen for each passage that translation which on balance seems most appropriate. For the Psalms see also p.415.

The actual excerpts from these translations form the main part of this book. If the object of the selection is to render the text readable, that of the commentary is to make it *more* readable. Specifically it aims (i) to provide necessary background information and (ii) 'to observe those excellences which should delight a reasonable reader' (Dryden). In pursuit of those aims I have drawn on the work of very many scholars. When quoting, I have normally given the author's name but not the specific reference, so as to avoid cluttering the commentary. By the same token, no space is devoted to scholarly controversy nor to lists of alternative interpretations.

The standpoint of the commentary is thus again primarily that of literary criticism. An English critic has written that in looking at a work of literature we need to consider 'what it says, how it says it, and why what it says is important to us' – though 'it is only for purposes of analysis that we separate what is [there] not separate'. Since about 1970 the insights of literary criticism have been increasingly applied to the Bible, particularly by scholars like Luis Alonso-Schökel, Northrop Frye, Robert Alter and John Barton. Literary terms used in the commentary are explained in the Glossary.

I must here warn that I am not using the term literary criticism in the private sense in which biblical scholars have traditionally used it, i.e. as equivalent to what general critics call 'source criticism'. Nor however am I using it in the academic sense appropriate to modern literary analysis at university level. Any reader who wants to be up to date at that level should perhaps get Alter and Kermode, *The Literary Guide to the Bible* (1987), with the warning that its contributory essays are of uneven quality. Both these are legitimate senses of 'literary' and necessary forms of scholarship. I hope to have acquired from them that which will illuminate the general reader. In structuralism, however, and in some later critical approaches, I have found little or no illumination.

Each age has its own preferred literary patterns. My own experience in teaching the OT leads me to think that the pattern currently preferred, at any rate by the young, is the dramatic, particularly the tragic, doubtless because it best reflects the ambiguity of contemporary life and thought. Such a preference is particularly suited to the OT, which contains a great deal of drama. Adam is only the first of the dramatis personae – 'un homme, une femme, une pomme, un drame'. Not only he but Moses, Saul, David and Job can be seen as tragic heroes in the classical sense. The books of Jonah, Esther, Ruth and Susanna are all nearer to the drama than to the novel. Most dramatic of all perhaps is the book of Jeremiah, whose agonised poetry is interwoven with the account of his own suffering and that of his country.

One could indeed go further and see the whole history of the Jews down to the deportation to Babylon as one long tragic drama – or perhaps, in the light of subsequent history, one should say rather the first of a series of tragic dramas in which that nation has played the central role. If one considers the whole history of civilization, ancient and modern, no people has contributed more than the Jews; yet few if any have suffered more. Many of these sufferings have been at the hands of Christians. This book is a drop in the ocean of due redress.

THE HEBREW LANGUAGE

Compared with modern European languages, biblical Hebrew has four main distinguishing features.

First, it is very **highly inflected**. What in English is a whole clause or sentence may in Hebrew be expressed in a single word, e.g. 'When I saw them' or 'I caused him to hate me'. In these cases the main verbal ideas – 'see' and 'hate' respectively – have prefixes and suffixes added to them which play the part of the other words present in the English. Students of classical languages are familiar with the process, but it is carried much further in Hebrew. The result is that Hebrew is built up of few but substantial words. If one takes a passage of Hebrew poetry together with its English translation, there will be roughly the same number of syllables in each language but two or three times as many words in English.

Secondly, the root idea of the verb is expressed in three consonants. (This **triliteral root** is the key feature of *all* Semitic languages, whether dead, like Akkadian*, Phoenician, Ugaritic* and Aramaic, or living like Hebrew and Arabic.) These consonants normally remain unchanged except for an occasional doubling. The inflexions are expressed either by the prefixes and suffixes already mentioned or by variations in the vowels between the consonants. To some extent we are familiar with this in English. The vowel change is seen e.g. in 'sit', 'sat', 'set'. 'Set' is an example of a vowel change used to make the verb 'sit' into a causative: 'set' = make to sit. This is much commoner in Hebrew, where most verbs have a causative mood of that kind. Another English example is 'begin', 'began', 'begun'. Here the 'be' is a prefix, and we could add a suffix also, to make 'beginning'. In that case one of the root consonants is doubled, though we do not pronounce it as double in English.

Because these vowel changes followed a regular pattern, written Hebrew could omit the vowels without risk of serious misunderstanding. (The same can actually be done in English, though less safely because so many English words have only one or two consonants.) And indeed the main Hebrew text of the OT was handed down for many centuries without special signs for the vowels: the modern vowel 'pointing' was not added until well into the Christian era.

One result of this is that, though we have a fair idea how the consonants were pronounced in ancient Hebrew, we are altogether less sure of the vowels. This uncertainty is particularly damaging to our appreciation of Hebrew poetry. For example, the commonest vowel in Hebrew, as in Sanskrit, is one which we traditionally pronounce as a long 'a', as in French 'âme', English 'calm'. But in ancient times it was probably sounded like the 'a' in 'fall'. At any rate it does not appear to have any particular associations with grief, such as we would expect of a long 'a', e.g. it is no more frequent in the speeches of Job than in those of his 'comforters'.

But if we do not know for certain how the language was pronounced at any one time, that does not prevent us from recognising assonance; and assonance is much commoner in an inflected language, particularly one which employs parallelism* of clauses. Thus the four lines which compose Isaiah 14.11 are, literally translated, as follows:

Brought down to the grave is this *pomp of-yours*,
the sound of these *harps-of-yours*;
beneath-you strewn are maggots,
and-covering-you worms.

The words in italics all end in -*ēkah* because that is the suffix meaning 'your'. In the first two lines those words come at the end, in the last two at the beginning. So the structure of the sound is plain to see, even if we cannot be sure how the 'ē' in the suffix was pronounced.

That instance shows up a difference of taste between us and the Hebrews. We follow Vergil, whose ear never allowed him to juxtapose e.g. a noun and an adjective agreeing with each other and both ending in -orum. But the Hebrews showed no such reluctance, doubtless because the assonance served to underline the parallelism which was the basis of their high style.

The third difference between biblical Hebrew and modern tongues lies in its **vocabulary**. The classical Hebrew vocabulary is small. Only about 5,000 words are used in the OT, probably nearer to 4,000 if you exclude the book of Job. This is so few that it would have been hard to get by on it in everyday life. It seems that the OT was written in an artificially limited high style, like the French of Racine. One result of this limitation was to offer ancient writers great scope for word-echoes within or between passages, a scope which however can lead to over-interpretation by modern critics.

The vocabulary of Hebrew is also differently distributed from modern languages. The force of the sentence is usually conveyed in the verb – and a transitive verb at that. Moreover the Hebrew verb is very flexible, as has been suggested, with a wide range of moods and tenses. Second to verbs in importance and frequency are nouns, again usually concrete nouns. Abstract concepts are represented, where possible, by parts of the body e.g. 'power' by 'hand', 'speed' by 'legs', 'anger' by 'nose', 'thoughts' by 'heart'. A very poor third come adjectives and modal adverbs. The relative lack of adjectives is not such a handicap as it would appear. For example, although there is no adjective in Hebrew meaning 'good', there is a verb (tōb) meaning 'to good', a verb which existed in English until the C17th. And a language which says 'God goods' may be worse at listing

God's qualities but better at expressing his activity.

Adjectives and adverbs are also used for emphasis in English. In Hebrew that emphasis is obtained by repetitions, especially in parallel. Thus, the English sentence 'A mighty wind will carry you off irresistibly' might be expressed in Hebrew by saying: 'a wind will carry you off, a storm will scatter you'. Or conversely we might find in Hebrew:

> that men may see and know
> that the hand of the LORD has done this,
> the Holy One of Israel has created it.
>
> (Is 41.20)

An English rendering of those lines might take this form:

> that you may be utterly convinced that it is God himself who has brought this about with irresistible power.

The fourth distinguishing feature of biblical Hebrew is its **syntax**. This is chiefly a matter of the build-up of sentences. In OT Hebrew, as in Homeric Greek, there are relatively few subordinate clauses: most clauses are coordinate, linked by the undifferentiated conjunction *waw* which, like the Homeric *de*, can vary its meaning according to context between 'and', 'but', 'for' and 'therefore'. The language, like that of Homer, had not developed far enough for conjunctions to have emerged with fixed and specialised meanings corresponding to those English words. It is consequently rare in OT Hebrew to find a long and intricate sentence like that of Genesis 24.14 or 28.6. The usual sentence is built up of short units loosely joined together, a structure which is clearly better suited to some kinds of writing than to others.

A subsidiary feature of the syntax is the omission of words. Thus the definite article (i.e. 'the'; Hebrew has no indefinite article) is often omitted. So is the relative pronoun 'which', e.g. in [Ps 118.22], where the Hebrew reads 'the stone the builders rejected'. For this we have an excellent parallel in English, where we readily omit 'which' as object, though no longer as subject. More interestingly Hebrew, like Ugaritic, boasts a compressed noun-clause, which adds great vividness to descriptions in prose or poetry. So in 2 Sam 18.14, where Abner 'picked up three stout sticks and drove them against Absalom's chest while he was held fast in the tree and still alive', the Hebrew sentence ends '. . . against Absalom's chest – he still alive in the midst of the tree'. Other forms of compression include a straight asyndeton (absence of connecting particles), used for speed e.g. in Judges 5.27 and throughout Ps 93. Finally Ezra [10.13] may be quoted as containing a phrase which is typically Hebrew in its concreteness: 'the time is rain', where we should say 'it is the rainy season'.

These features all point in one direction. Biblical Hebrew is a language ideally suited for saying relatively simple things concretely, succinctly and above all forcefully. That is to say that it is suited to narrative, to poetry and to aphorisms.

When it comes to translation into English, the problems are those which arise wherever an inflected language is being translated into an uninflected one. The latter finds it hard to match the concision or the weight of the original, but it has the advantage of flexibility in everything except word-order.

A special case is the translation of Hebrew *poetry*. The free rhythm of the Hebrew and (except for the problem of word-order) its parallelism are easily enough preserved in English – more easily, in fact, than either the strict rhythms of Greek and Latin poetry or the typical modern European end-rhymes. It is Barr's view that 'there is rather less lost . . . in translating Hebrew poetry into English than in translating Greek or Latin poetry'. But that judgement must be suspended until other features of Hebrew poetry have been considered.

Note on the transliteration of Hebrew

There are many competing methods of transliterating Hebrew into English. The method used here does not correspond to any of them. It is designed *ad hoc* to be intelligible to the general English reader. The following signs are the only ones that need explanation:

- **ch** to be pronounced as in Scottish 'loch'
- **q** is a harder 'k'
- **'** between vowels is a glottal stop, to be pronounced like tt in Cockney 'butter' or t in American 'Clinton'
- **–** over a vowel marks it as long, i.e.
    - **ā** as in English 'fall'
    - **ē** as in English 'fail'
    - **ī** as in English 'ravine'
    - **ō** as in English 'pole'
    - **ū** as in English 'true'

HEBREW STORY-TELLING

1. Kinds of Story

The stories of the OT are among the great stories of world literature. The word 'story' is used here rather than anything more technical. For critical purposes different kinds of story can be distinguished, but there is no hard and fast line between them. All of them were originally oral. All of them lose a little of their nature when they come to be written down.

The **basic story-units** in the OT are quite unlike those in the better-known literatures of Europe. The closest parallels to them are to be found in the medieval Icelandic sagas which, though written down, still seem close to their oral origins. An Icelandic scholar describes their features – shared with many OT stories: 'their economy of phrasing, the brevity with which the incidents and speeches are conveyed, the restriction of all commentary to the least available compass' (Ker). That principle of economy excludes ornamental adjectives, descriptions of nature and psychological comment: 'thoughts are practically never revealed, except in speeches – and not always then.'

A typical story in the OT shares not only content but also form with those in the Icelandic sagas. It falls into three parts. First (i) is a fairly brief introduction, setting the scene, identifying the characters and explaining or hinting at the tension whose resolution will constitute the main action of the story. Sometimes the opening summary will reveal so much that to our ears it seems to spoil the suspense e.g. the first 'he blessed him' in the story of Jacob and Esau (Gen 27.23; another example is Jon 3.5). But where the audience knew the end of the story already, such an anticipatory mention could actually increase the pleasure of listening. And when the audience did not know the story, the warning helped them to follow it and gave the author scope for dramatic irony.

The main scene (ii) is told more fully and slowly: indeed 'telling time' may here be almost as long as 'action time'. It centres round very few people – preferably not more than three – of whom only two are 'on stage' at any given time (though a third may be listening e.g. Gen 18.10; 27.5). One of them is the main character, the other(s) subordinate, and the main character often has a contrasting foil in one of the others. The narrative sequence is straightforward, though the author is at pains to introduce suspense, often by the pattern of two (or three) unsuccessful attempts before the hero is 'third (or fourth) time lucky'. Speeches play an important part, and may form the climax of the narrative.

Finally (iii) there is a brief conclusion. The tension is now resolved and e.g. the characters go their separate ways. Often the conclusion will frame* the story by echoing the introduction. At its simplest the echo consists of a repeated key-word e.g. the name of a person or place. Sometimes it extends to a whole sentence repeated almost word for word.

But that very spare treatment – 'concentrate of story' as one might term it – was not the only style at the disposal of Hebrew writers. A more elaborate treatment is often found, with more characters, fuller detail and longer speeches. The narrator may begin to obtrude himself, offering psychological, and sometimes also theological, comments (e.g. Gen 24.21).

Gradually, with the passage of time, single stories came to be grouped round some notable person. Such a **story-cycle**, as it is known, is a loose string, with little articulation of incident (i.e. plot) or development of character. There are many such cycles in the OT e.g. those of

Abraham, Isaac, Lot, Samson, Elijah and Elisha.

In this process a single story may be found in two different versions known as doublets. A doublet may occur twice within a single cycle (e.g. 1 Sam 24 and 26) or once in each of two cycles (e.g. a healing story told both of Elijah, more simply, in 1 K 17 and of Elisha, more elaborately, in 2 K 4) or even twice in one cycle and once in another (see Gen 12). There is also a curious phenomenon whereby the two versions are knitted together, as in Gen 37 or Ex 14.

Doublets are in fact only one form of the basic structural principle of all OT writing, both prose and poetry, viz. repetition-with-variation. The principle is most clearly visible in the parallelism* of the Hebrew poetic couplet. But for narrative the OT, unlike other ANE literatures, hardly ever uses parallelism. Instead it uses various forms in which sometimes the repetition dominates, sometimes the variation.

Repetition dominates where e.g. one character relays another's speech (as in Gen 24) or a written narrative is followed by an oral report of it (as in Gen 41) – though even in such cases an experienced reader will discern subtle variations. Conversely where variation predominates a reader may discern a basic similarity, as between the punishments awarded by God to Adam and Eve in Gen 3 and to Cain in Gen 4. The variation may even go so far as to create a contrast or reversal (as in Gen 27.39f.). In one particularly sophisticated form, the details in the first half of the story, i.e. up to the climax in the central scene, are answered in reverse order in the second half. This structure, sometimes called pedimental*, is used e.g. for both the healing stories referred to above, being especially suited to the rise and fall of an illness. It is also much used in poetry e.g. Is 14.4-21.

This principle of repetition-with-variation clearly made a deep appeal to the OT writers. In poetry it satisfied their aesthetic sense. In prose narrative it also reflected their sense of a pattern in events. And when the scale of those events becomes large enough, the literary principle comes to express a theology of history.

But in reading the OT it is helpful to distinguish three specialised kinds of story in addition to the basic kind so far described. They are **myth, legend and folk-tale**, of which the most interesting is myth. The simplest definition of a **myth** is 'a story of the gods'; but that will not do for the OT, if only because no other gods are recognised in it. A more comprehensive definition is that of Malinowski: 'These stories . . . are the assertion of an original, greater and more important reality, through which the present life and work of mankind are governed.' A structuralist definition by Leach says much the same thing in more formal terms: a myth is 'a logical model by means of which the human mind can evade unwelcome contradictions' of certain pairs of opposites e.g. death and immortality. In that broad sense, it is obvious that the story of the Garden of Eden is a myth; and so, a little less obviously, is the Flood. In fact these two are the only complete myths which the OT contains; but it contains many references to, and motifs from, other myths, especially those from Ugarit*.

A **legend**, as the term is normally used of the OT, is a story about religious (i.e. cultic) people or places or activities. Though it may have a historical basis, it often contains fantastic or miraculous elements: there is a good deal of such legendary matter in the stories of the prophets, running from Moses through Elijah and Elisha to Isaiah and Jonah. Sometimes, as in stories about the origins of religious names, the legend may be the work of pure fantasy.

Most people know what a **folk-tale** is from their childhood reading. Like a myth, it is a story not limited by every-day reality; unlike a myth, it does not aspire to say anything profound about the world. Its favourite themes are love and adventure, the test and the quest, ingenious devices and evasions. The only pure folk-tale identified in the OT is the story of Solomon and the two mothers, which seems to come from India. But there are countless folk-tale motifs* in other stories, e.g. those of Jacob, Samson, David, Esther, Tobit, Jonah.

2. Larger Compositions

So far we have considered short stories of various kinds, and also the collections of stories known as cycles. Such material lasts until there comes the creative mind which weaves it into a larger **composition** i.e. a coherent design linked by a system of ideas. In the case of early Greece, we know that creative mind as Homer's. For the OT we have no corresponding name: we can but speak of the 'author'* or the 'editor'* (see Glossary for the use of these terms and also for the 'narrator'*) of e.g. Genesis or the Pentateuch.

But of what kind is the resultant composition? In particular, should we read it as history or fiction? Once again, modern categories are too stark. If pressed, one might take refuge in a hybrid term like 'historical fiction', which can convey a whole range of writing according to whether the emphasis is on the adjective or the noun. Sometimes in the OT a concern for fact predominates, as in the lists of names or laws or cult-objects. More often the story-teller's concern predominates, as in 'reports' of conversations which cannot possibly have been recorded or even overheard. Such 'privileged' conversations are a feature of the most highly developed stories such as the Court History of David (2 Sam 9-1 K 2). Without them the author of that work could not have achieved what he has viz.

a sequential development not only of incident but of character. With them, however, he must forfeit, at least in the eyes of an austere critic, the title sometimes claimed for him of being the world's first historian. Only at the very end of the OT do we come across a book (1 Maccabees) which could be called historical in a more austere sense.

The OT also contains many excellent narratives which make no serious historical claims at all: history, though present as a setting for the plot, is more or less cavalierly treated. But there is a plot in these narratives, such that the component stories will not stand on their own; and there is often some psychological development on the part of the main character. The term for such a narrative is **romance** or **novella**. Examples in the OT are the romances of Joseph (Gen 37-45), Ruth, Esther, Tobit, Judith. More is said about them on p349.

This classification of OT stories must not be taken to imply that 'historical' writing represents a higher stage in a linear process. 'A view of the world in terms of the family or as a stage for heroes has as much to say for it as the chronicling of historical fact' (Koch). What matters is that the story should, at its deepest level, be true to life. With that proviso, 'a simple tale, told at the right moment, transforms a person's life with the order which its pattern brings to incoherent energies' (Ted Hughes).

And OT stories are in general outstandingly true to life. There is no love of the fabulous for its own sake, as in e.g. Egyptian stories. The legendary and the miraculous play a minor role. There is less of the supernatural (ghosts, omens, dreams) in the OT than in Herodotus' histories or Shakespeare's tragedies. The predominant tone is matter-of-fact – sometimes deliciously used to set off the violence which is never far below the surface. Outside the romances the heroes are a richly realistic mixture of strength and weakness, virtue and vice.

But finally, we misjudge the stories of the OT if we read them simply as good stories well told. In fact the stories are inextricably bound up with the **theology**: each is essential to the other.

One way round, this is obvious. Whatever the origin of the stories, they have now been edited and placed within an intricate theological setting. True, we can sometimes prise them out of their setting, but in doing so we risk damaging them. Providence in the OT is like the red thread which Goethe said was 'woven into all the ropes of the [English] royal fleet in such a way that it cannot be taken out without unravelling the rope'. And the hand of providence is visible not only in the content but in the structure of the stories.

In the romances the movement of the plot follows the axis of comedy, from (virtuous) unhappiness to (merited) happiness. In the main body of OT narrative it is otherwise. If happiness is achieved, it may well be undeserved. The commoner movement is along the axis of tragedy, from ignorance to knowledge. In either case the preferred OT method of pointing the moral is the use of structural irony, particularly the irony of pretensions exposed. This is seen at its delicate best in the stories of Adam and Eve, Nathan and David, Naaman and Elijah, more crudely in the fates of Haman and Holophernes. And the reversal is often underscored by the stylistic devices of chiasmus* and pedimental* structure.

But the converse is equally true: the theology needs the stories. Biblical theology is centred not upon timeless abstractions but upon the relationship between God and human beings, specifically between YHWH* and the people of Israel. That relationship is seen as a developing one: it has its own grand story. But the grand story is made up of countless little stories. The subjects of these are a cross-section of humanity, warts and all, and the most fully realised of the characters also develop in the course of their story. Change over time is the essence of a good story and the hallmark of *biblical* theology.

HEBREW POETRY

1. Poetry and Prose

Our distinction between poetry and prose was unknown to the Old Testament, as it was to the whole of the ANE. The nearest Hebrew equivalent to our word 'poetry' was 'songs' (*tehillim*), which was the Hebrew title of the Psalter. Modern readers recognise a number of other Old Testament books as poetry, but they would be wrong to classify the rest automatically as prose. It is not just that prose and poetry are found juxtaposed within a single book, as in Shakespeare, nor even that there is a single intermediate category of 'poetic prose'. Rather what we have is a continuum. The characteristics of what it is still convenient to call poetry are highly marked in certain places and not marked at all in others; and there is every shade in between. What are those characteristics?

It is easiest to begin by saying what they are *not*. First, there is no systematic use of rhyme (end-rhyme) in Hebrew. Of course any highly inflected language will have natural rhymes in the word endings, especially of its verbs, e.g. in French if *we* do something the verb usually ends in *-ons*; if *you*, in *-ez*. But Hebrew poets made only occasional use of this, as in Jg 16.24. Assonances of other kinds however they exploited to the full.

Next there is metre. That too, in the classical sense of a fixed number of syllables and a fixed relationship between the stressed and the unstressed (or the 'long' and the 'short'), has not been found in Hebrew poetry. In its place is a looser, more flexible rhythm, based on the stressed syllables only. A line had anything from two to five such stressed syllables, each usually accompanied by some unstressed ones. A line of three stresses, which was the commonest, might then consist of three words but ten syllables; but, since Hebrew words were often long, and long words tended to have a subsidiary stress, such a line could end up sounding like a line of Shakespearean blank verse, with all and more of Shakespeare's flexibility of rhythm.

2. Parallelism

Assonance and rhythm are essential features of all poetry. But the most characteristic mark of Hebrew poetry is something which at first sight is alien to us, namely parallelism. The basic principle of parallelism is that 'lines' come not singly but in pairs (or sometimes threes), of which the second (or third) takes up the thought expressed in the first and completes it. The completion may take a variety of forms, of which the most basic is a re-statement in syntactically parallel words – hence the term 'parallelism' or, as it is sometimes called, 'thought-rhyme'. For example:

> Can-you-bind the-clusters-of the-Pleiades
> or-loose the-belt-of Orion? (Job 38.31)

Each line here consists of three Hebrew words, and each Hebrew word has one stressed syllable (as in the English translation) plus some unstressed. We therefore say the couplet is in 3:3 rhythm.

Parallelism of this kind is found in literatures from all over the world, and it was the essential basis of poetic structure throughout the ANE. It marked the high style both in Egypt and Babylon, and dominated Ugaritic* as it later dominated Hebrew poetry. This for example is an extract from the Ugaritic *Keret* epic (c.1400 BC):

> In a bowl of silver he poured wine,
> honey in a bowl of gold.
> He went up to the top of a tower,
> bestrode the top of the wall. (ANET 144)

Even this short extract illustrates the difficulty of using parallelism in narrative.

The first couplet is successful, because the two parallel actions help to build up atmosphere. The second couplet however is a failure: the two actions blur each other and retard the movement of the story. Wisely therefore the OT writers tended to avoid parallelism for simple narrative. Almost all the great Hebrew poetry is speech, and heightened speech at that. In the psalms man speaks to God, in the prophets God to man, in Job man and God to each other, in the Song of Songs two lovers.

But even in speech parallelism can become monotonous. This happens in the OT, not just in the Wisdom literature but also sometimes in the psalms and prophecy. The greater poets however had various ways of avoiding monotony, some of them inherited from their Ugaritic predecessors.

One prime source of monotony is the end-stopping of lines, as in the *Keret* passage. To avoid this, the first line of the couplet can be left incomplete in sense or syntax and then picked up and carried on by the second. It may be picked up either by a repetition of an original word or, less dramatically, by a synonym. The device is familiar to us from Yeats: 'I will arise and go now / and go to Innisfree.' It is used to magnificent effect in the Song of Deborah, which is as near as the OT ever gets to narrative poetry (Judges 5 esp. vv.19 and 27).

Ugaritic and Hebrew poets both favoured a form of this device where the same word was repeated twice or even three times on either side of a parenthesis e.g. a vocative. For an Ugaritic example see the last three lines of the longer extract from *Keret* quoted on p. 772. Modern scholars have given this pattern the name of 'stairlike parallelism' and noted that it was especially used for dramatic openings e.g. Ps 29:

> Ascribe to the LORD, you sons of heaven,
> ascribe to the LORD glory and might.

In fact Ps 29, like the Song of Deborah, contains many other variations of this pattern and, partly for that reason, they are thought to be among the oldest poems in the Bible. But the pattern crops up also in unexpected places, e.g. the famous opening of Ecclesiastes.

Ugaritic poets also realised the advantage of the triplet in place of the couplet, especially to round off a poem, like the Alexandrine at the end of a sequence of heroic couplets. This device was much favoured by Isaiah and Job: see most notably Job 39.25. Second Isaiah also used what might be called 'a triplet within the couplet' e.g.:

> Scarcely are they planted, scarcely sown,
> scarcely has their stem taken root in the
>   earth.   (40.24; cp. 41.10; 42.2 etc.)

These and other formal devices help the Hebrew poets to avoid monotony in their use of parallelism. But what really ensures the liveliness and variety of their verse is a matter not of form but of thought. In their hands the thought of the second line rarely just repeats that of the first: rather it heightens, sharpens, strengthens it in a whole host of ways. For example:

> With their faces to the ground they will
>   bow to you
> and lick the dust of your feet.   (Is 49.23)

> They waited for me as for the rain,
> and they opened their mouths as for the
>   spring rain.   (Job 29.23)

> Therefore will we not fear though the earth
>   be moved
> and though the mountains are shaken in
>   the midst of the sea.   (Ps 46.2)

Sometimes indeed the poet abandons all formal parallelism. To take two well-known examples:

> Man is born to trouble
> as the sparks fly upward.   (Job 5.7 AV)

> The LORD is my shepherd;
> I shall lack nothing.   (Ps 23.1)

What can be said of couplets like these? It would not be enough to say that the second line answers or balances the first. We must go further and say that it rounds it off or completes it. If we follow the usual convention and call this a form of parallelism, then it is clear that the fundamental ingredient in it is not that which gave it its name but its roundedness or completion. It must be in that broader sense that Hopkins said that 'the artifice of poetry reduces itself to the principle of parallelism'.

Such are some of the more frequent variations of basic parallelism. All except the last of these involve – and many depend upon – pairs of words which are more or less synonymous. Many of these word-pairs are also to be found in Ugaritic, including some of the commonest e.g. cup/goblet, tent/dwelling, wine/beer, mountain/hill, hear/understand.

These stock word-pairs point to a literary tradition which goes back not only behind Hebrew to Ugaritic but also behind written to oral composition, to the days when poets improvised upon a theme. The word-pairs then fulfilled the same function as the metrical formulae in Homer, like 'Agamemnon king of men' or 'rosy-fingered dawn appeared'. An oral poet needs to have at his disposal a stock of words which help him to compose and his audience to follow. In Homeric poetry the formula must fit exactly into the hexameter line. In Hebrew poetry the poet needs a repertoire of word-pairs which can answer each other within the couplet.

And just as the word-pairs point backwards in time, to the days of oral improvisation, so they also point forward, to the later development of prose. Hebrew prose-writers made much use of them. Sometimes they lent emotional colour, e.g. 'the poor and needy', sometimes dignity, e.g. 'he lifted up his voice/eyes and wept/saw'. Sometimes, as in 'ox and ass', they stand for a whole class of objects for which the language may not even possess a word. (The extreme case of this is the usage known as merismus*.)

Parallelism too had a lasting influence upon certain kinds of Hebrew prose – not so much in straight narrative as in legal or ritual contexts, where it lends solemnity e.g. Num 5.12-13:

> When a married woman goes astray
> and is unfaithful to her husband
> by having sexual intercourse with another man,
> and this happens without the husband's knowledge,
> and without the woman being detected,
> because, though she has been defiled,
> there is no direct evidence against her
> and she was not caught in the act. . . .

It could indeed be said that parallelism was the dominant influence upon Hebrew writing throughout the great period: directly upon the poetry, indirectly upon the prose. But some time after 300 BC it began to decline. The apocalyptic writers, who are the natural heirs of the prophets, devoted their poetical energies rather to the elaboration of imagery. The later Wisdom writers continued to employ the form of parallelism, but lost the spirit. Where parallelism is still used in the old way, it represents a conscious effect on the part of the author, as in the psalms inserted into the narrative of Judith and Tobit. The last effective use of it in the OT is made by the learned Alexandrian Jew who wrote the Wisdom of Solomon in the first century BC.

But among ordinary Jews by this time the very conventions of it had ceased to be understood, as the text of Matthew 21.6f. suggests. The evangelist quotes the prophecy of Zechariah 9.9: 'See, your king is coming to you, humble and mounted on a donkey, on a colt, the foal of a donkey', and then records its fulfilment: 'The disciples . . . brought the donkey *and her foal*; they laid their cloaks on *them* and Jesus mounted.'

The understanding of parallelism, which was already lost to ordinary people by the end of the first century AD, was soon lost also to scholars, both Jewish and Christian. It was obscured, first, by Greek notions of poetry as essentially based on syllabic quantities, and then subsequently by the spread of rhyme, which came to dominate poetry not only in Europe but among the Arabs too. Only in the C18th was parallelism 'rediscovered' by scholars, of whom the most distinguished was Bishop Lowth – a discovery which had important consequences for the Romantic Movement.

3. The Poem as a Unit

So far we have considered only the couplet or triplet. The couplets however did not stand alone, except for the aphorisms of books like Proverbs. They were organised into poems as in any other language. The most obvious poems are the psalms, which have always been printed as distinct units. But the prophets also wrote many poems, of the same sort of length as the psalms, and they too are distinguished in the layout of this edition.

Within a poem the author felt free to vary his rhythms i.e. the number of stresses to the line. But certain rhythms go better together than others. There are three main groups of rhythms favoured by the Hebrew poets. One is the 3:3 of Job, with its occasional 3:3:3. This fits well with 4:2, 2:4 and 2:2:2, since all the groups add up to six. The second is the 2:2 of the prophets, with its occasional 2:2:2, which obviously goes with 4:4, 4:2 and 2:4. The last of the common rhythms is 3:2, which was used particularly, but not only, in dirges and laments. This fluidity of rhythm is one of many factors which often make it hard to tell where one poem ends and the next begins.

Sometimes a poem can be seen to have a structure additional to its rhythmic structure. Quite a few poems have refrains. Every verse in Ps [136] has the refrain 'for his mercy endureth for ever'. In Pss 42-43 a single refrain is repeated three times, twice in Ps 42 and once in Ps 43; which is why we can be sure they were composed as one psalm. In these and similar cases it is noticeable that the component sections are of unequal length. It is therefore uncertain how far we are justified in speaking of strophes or even of stanzas. Rather a Hebrew poem is like an ode of Keats or Pindar: a whole, which may or may not fall into sections.

A few poems derive a structure from the initial letters of their couplets. These are known as acrostic poems. The best known of them is Ps [119], each of whose twenty sections has every couplet beginning with the same letter. Something similar but less artificial is found in the structure of Job 31.7-40, where fourteen verses begin with an 'if', used by Job to deny a list of possible offences against morality; or (more simply) Jeremiah 4.23-26 where four successive verses begin 'I looked'. Other poems are built round a key-word, e.g. 'the LORD' in Ps 29. This last principle however was also used by the editors who later arranged poems in collections, and it is often difficult to tell whether such a link is the creation of the poet or the editor.

There is however one kind of echo which we can confidently ascribe to the author: that is the echo of a word or group of words between the beginning and the end of a section or a whole poem or indeed a unit of narrative. It is found in all literatures and is known by many names, of which framing* is the least technical. There are countless examples of it in the OT, whether in short passages, e.g. the words 'darkness, not light' in Amos 5.18-20, or in long ones, e.g. 'Bless the LORD, O my soul' in Ps 103. (Similarly in the NT the words 'in heaven' frame the first section of the LORD's prayer.) Often the author uses it to make a theological point, that the whole action is following God's plan. To a modern reader it gives the further clue that the passage or the poem is now concluded.

The same principle is extended also to cover the whole structure of a section or poem. Thus in Isaiah 23.1-14 we find a sequence of eleven proper names arranged in what might be called a concentric pattern. This pattern is one of the most important principles of arrangement in Hebrew literature. Other good examples of it can be seen in Isaiah 14.4-21 and 60.1-3. The pattern has also been discovered in prose e.g. 2 K 5.18, and the whole book of Ruth has been analysed along these lines. Be that as it may, there is no doubt of its importance in Hebrew poetry. A particular use of it is to throw emphasis upon the central section or unit. In that form it is sometimes called pedimental*.

4. Imagery

The imagery of the OT has in its time received extremes of praise and blame, the one scarcely more convincing than the other. For almost all the usual criteria of imagery are subjective. They vary according to the taste of the individual or the conventions of a culture.

Bishop Lowth in his Oxford lectures claimed that the greatest glory of Hebrew poetry is its use of images which are 'bold without obscurity and familiar without lack of dignity'. That judgement, though substantially fair, was made in terms of Greek poetic conventions. Since the time of Lowth two things have happened. First, our own conventions have changed: we no longer talk as if everyday images were inappropriate to 'the sublime'. Second, we now have some knowledge of the ANE tradition within which OT poetry developed, and can begin to distinguish between what the Hebrew poets inherited and what they created.

In the matter of imagery it is Babylonian poetry which throws most light on the OT. From before 2000 BC we find Babylonian authors delighting in bold, familiar and simple similes, not only in poetry but in unlikely kinds of prose. Their most frequent context is one of defeat and destruction. Thus royal inscriptions typically liken the king to a lion or a wild bull, his armies to locusts, his crushed enemies to rats or butterflies or pots. For some examples of these see commentary on Is 10. The same sets and kinds of images are also used in curses, in prophecies (always of victory) and in laments. Some of the similes are arresting. For example, the gods of the enemy 'roll over like tired donkey foals before him'. In Sumerian laments for Ur we find that 'dead bodies melted away like fat placed in the sun'. There are also more tender images e.g. that of Ur looking for its goddess Ningal 'like a child wandering in the devastated streets'. Such similes are rarely elaborated but often piled up e.g. in a curse:

> May he moan like a dove in a hole,
> may he thrash about like a swallow in its
>   cranny,
> may he scurry about like a dove in terror.
>   (*ANET* 650)

Sometimes one finds these similes borrowed. Thus the famous boast of Sennacherib, that he shut up Hezekiah in Jerusalem 'like a bird in a cage', had been used in inscriptions of his predecessor Tiglath-Pileser III. Nor is this at all surprising when such inscriptions – and much of the 'official' literature – were the work of scribes who had been taught in the royal schools. In certain social contexts a conventional image is actually preferred by reader as well as writer.

All this throws much light on the imagery of the OT, whether in prophecy or in psalms or even in historical narrative. We are not surprised when God says 'I will wipe away Jerusalem as when a man wipes his plate and turns it upside down' [2 K 21.13] – though we note already the beginning of elaboration.

Clearly the Hebrew writer did not share the Greek view that certain topics are too low for the high style (see p.783). Nor are we surprised by the piling up of similes [in e.g. Dt 32.2] – though we sit up a bit when Hosea in three successive verses says that Israel is 'a cake half-baked', 'a silly senseless pigeon' and 'unaware [that] his grey hair [has] turned white'. Some poets are evidently more adventurous than others.

It is indeed natural that the psalmists, whose aim is above all to reassure, should on the whole prefer the strong simple simile of the ANE tradition (see p.413). Psalm 23 is unusual in elaborating two images next door to each other: God as shepherd and God as host. But the images there are so reassuring, and their juxtaposition so skilful, that most readers scarcely notice the transition.

Conversely it is natural that the Hebrew prophets, whose aim (unlike that of ANE prophets) was to shock, should use the whole resources of language, and press imagery to its limits. Hosea [10.4] is also master of the single striking simile:

> Litigation spreads like a poisonous weed along the furrows of the field

– where what strikes is less the 'weed' than the 'litigation'. Amos [3.12] knows how to use the vivid detail:

> As a shepherd rescues out of the jaws of a lion
> two shinbones or the tip of an ear. . . .

Isaiah however is the first to elaborate his images systematically: a conquest likened to the robbing of a bird's nest (10.14); unreliable support likened to a cracked wall (30.13-14); and the two waters compared (see [8.6-8], quoted in § 5 below). The next logical step in this development is the parable of the vineyard in Is 5.1-6.

Later prophets carried the process still further but without corresponding gain. Ezekiel's lengthy allegories in which nations are compared to birds or trees (Chs [17], [19], 31) mostly collapse under their own verbiage. With the apocalyptists* the imagery luxuriates even further, until it becomes uncertain which is image and which is reality: this is the case even in a powerful passage like Joel 2.

There remain two poetical works which deserve special mention. The imagery of Job is among the most remarkable in any literature. In the speeches of his friends it is relatively conventional, to suit their views, but Job himself ransacks heaven and earth in his attempt to express his spiritual agony. The poet is consciously seeking special effects (see e.g. the elaborate detail of 6.15-20), and it is astonishing how often he succeeds.

The Song of Songs belongs in quite a different category. It is clearly composed in the tradition of Egyptian secular love poetry, of which enough has now been found to illuminate the Song. No longer do we speak dismissively, as Lowth's critics spoke, of 'oriental extravagance'. It is true that the songs and their images are different in kind from the rest of the OT. In responding to this difference, we may start by remembering the element of competitive playfulness that is present in all exchanges between lovers. We may have to end by admitting that love poetry too is conventional, and that other people's conventions are not always accessible. (See p. 502).

Lowth divided OT images into those derived from nature and those from everyday life. A division which is poetically and theologically more fruitful is that into what might be called 'black' and 'white' images. In opposing black to white I am opposing war to peace, death to life, uncleanness to purity, chaos to order etc. OT images often fall into similar pairs of opposites, e.g. night to day, wolf to sheep, thistle to fig, salt water to sweet and so on. These pairs can be used to represent all stages in the rise and fall of civilization, which in turn can be correlated with the loyalty or disloyalty of the people to God. Consequently any of these images, especially in pairs, have enormous potential resonance, e.g. 'the wolf will lie down with the lamb'.

The same is true of certain images which are ambivalent. For example, fire both refines and destroys, a rock both protects and causes to stumble. Such images offer much scope for irony. But of all the ambivalent images in the OT the most powerful, and also the most remote from us, is water.

For with a material element like water, history and geography are bound to influence the way in which it is seen by different peoples. Experience of the sea has not changed much over time: anyone who knows it knows its dangers. But sweet water – rain and rivers – is a different matter. To English speakers, rain implies repetition ('the rain it raineth every day') and rivers are symbols of ceaseless movement ('the river of time'). To the Hebrews, the rain could cease and the rivers dry up, in each case with disastrous effect. But the really important difference lies in the annual experience which the Mesopotamian peoples had with the Tigris and Euphrates. Each spring, when the snows melted, a torrent of water came down the valleys, which could flood the land and carry away whole towns built on its banks: 'like a flood-storm it destroys the cities', in the words of a Sumerian lament. Something very similar could happen in Syria (Ugarit) with the Orontes and in Palestine with the Jordan, as well as with lesser 'torrents' (wadis) after a heavy storm. Mesopotamian experience of flood-water was readily intelligible to Canaanites and Jews (see e.g. Job 9.23).

5. Myth and Image

This periodical catastrophe was the subject of very ancient and important ANE myths. Some time after 1750 BC the Babylonian creation myth related how the god Marduk had primevally vanquished Tiamat, who represented the flood-water of chaos, and so created (i.e. established the order of) the world. The myth spread to Hittite and Ugaritic mythology. The Ugaritic myth of the conflict of Baal and the waters tells how Baal, the sky god, fought against an enemy variously described as 'the sea', 'the mighty waters' or the dragon Leviathan and, having defeated it, gained control of fertility.

This myth in its various forms had a deep influence upon Hebrew literature, if not upon Hebrew religion. There are very many references to it in the OT, mostly oblique but some not so oblique, e.g. the mention of Leviathan in Is 27.1 and elsewhere. Later on the myth rose up, as it were, from the national subconscious to form one of the most powerful symbols of apocalyptic* writing.

In the interval the imagery had been demythologised in various ways. The most important way was to transfer it to certain 'historical' events in the nation's past, notably the crossings of the Reed Sea and of the River Jordan. That is why all rationalistic explanations of these two crossings really miss the point. In defeating the 'mighty waters', God was once again bringing order out of chaos. Hence the note of triumph which pervades the Song of Miriam (Exod 15), the story in Joshua 3, and Ps 114 which brings them both together.

As a result of all this, water imagery in Hebrew poetry is deeply ambivalent. It has four aspects which can be analysed as follows:

A Destructive
1. Leviathan (or Tiamat) representing primitive chaos out of which order was brought
2. storm or flood, representing a return from order to chaos

B Benevolent
1. natural flowing water (in Hebrew 'water of life') viz. steady rain or perennial springs or flowing rivers
2. static water, e.g. a cistern.

This pattern can be used in any sequence. For example, B1 could be contrasted by Jeremiah (2.13) with B2 or by Isaiah [8.6-8] with A2:

> Because this nation has rejected
> the waters of Shiloah, which run softly and
>   gently . . . ,
> therefore the LORD will bring up against it
> the strong, the flooding waters of the
>   Euphrates . . .
> it shall sweep through Judah in a flood,
> pouring over it and rising shoulder-high.

Conversely, to the later prophets and apocalyptists (e.g. Is 24.1+) the *present* time is one of chaos; order will be restored with the advent of God's kingdom, an advent symbolised negatively by a second slaying of Leviathan (Is 27.1) or positively by fresh-water springs (Is 35.7) or a mythical River of God (Ps 46.4).

That is why water imagery has the widest scope of any in the OT. Water can symbolise almost anything – except aesthetic beauty, in which the Bible is not interested – and it holds together many of the other great symbols such as the desert in Second Isaiah and the garden in the Song of Songs.

Other so-called nature imagery in the OT likewise contains 'dead' mythology. When the psalmists speak of thunder as the voice of God (29.3) and the clouds as his chariot (104.3), they are drawing on two of the regular epithets of Baal in Ugaritic myth. Again when we find a dramatic exchange between God and the elements, we may descry a mythic background. Not only does God command the sea:

> Thus far may you come but no further;
> here your surging waves must halt.

(Job 38.11)

He also calls the stars by name (Is 40.26) and speaks to the lightning, which responds obediently 'I am ready' [Job 38.35]. Literary topoi* like this derive from another common ANE myth, in which the stars (like the Greek Titans) once upon a time attempted to rebel but were overthrown and restored to obedience. In the OT there is only one reference to their original rebellion (Is 14.13f.), but many to their subsequent obedience.

Another literary borrowing from Ugaritic myth is the personification of Death in Job 28, where see commentary. But in general Hebrew poetry does not personify abstractions unless they are attributes of God himself. The outstanding example of such personification is Wisdom in Prov 9. Hebrew writers were undeterred by the resemblance of Wisdom to the Egyptian deity Ma'at, for Ma'at (unlike Leviathan) represented the principle of cosmic order. Other attributes of YHWH* such as mercy and righteousness could be semi-personified in Hebrew poetry e.g. Ps 85. But mythical beings from other religions had to be demythologised in one way or another. For the OT could not admit any serious threat to the sovereignty of YHWH.

ARCHAEOLOGY AND THE OLD TESTAMENT

1. The Early History of Israel

Much earth has been dug, and much ink spilled, during the last century or so, in the hope of answering the question: how reliable is the historical information carried by the OT? The question has sometimes been answered by classifying certain books as 'historical' (down to 2 Kings, or even to [2 Chronicles], with 1 and 2 Maccabees), and the rest as something else. But the reality is more complicated, and more interesting, than that.

In establishing the historicity of any ancient text, scholars use various criteria. Of these the 'hardest', i.e. the least subjective, is archaeology. During the twentieth century, and especially during its second half, the soil of Israel has been intensively dug – more so, probably, than any area of equal size in the world. The findings of the archaeologists are impressive. Nevertheless they have limitations.

One is that certain sites – most notably Jerusalem – cannot be dug with any thoroughness, because of modern occupation. Another is that excavation can answer some questions better than others. Suppose, for example, that we can securely identify the modern equivalent of a biblical site (which in practice we cannot always do), and that a dig shows that site to have been destroyed at the end of the Bronze Age, we shall still find it difficult to establish a date more precise than +/- 100 years, and impossible to say who, i.e. what people, destroyed it or even who occupied it before. The evidence of excavations therefore cannot be simply read off: it needs interpretation.

But there are other findings of archaeology which, to those seeking corroboration of the OT, look more promising. They may be stone-cut inscriptions recording Egyptian or Assyrian invasions of Israel, or incised tablets of baked clay carrying literary or historical texts. What light do they throw on the historicity of the OT? Here is a list of 'first' references.

1. The first mention of *Israel* outside the OT, and the only one before c.850 BC, is the tantalizing stele* of Pharaoh Merneptah dated c.1215 BC.
2. The first Hebrew name which is certainly mentioned both in the OT and outside is that of *Omri* king of Israel c.850 BC.
3. The first certain mention of YHWH* outside the OT is in a Moabite inscription, the Mesha stele* c.830 BC.
4. The first person from the kingdom of Judah to be certainly mentioned both in the OT and outside it is *Ahaz* king of Judah c.735 BC.

These four inscriptions provide a very slender scaffolding for the early history of Israel. But we must do the best with what we have, starting with the background to the Merneptah stele.

The land of Canaan* (which in this context can be taken as including Israel) had been part of the Egyptian empire since c.1500 BC. Down to 1350 the control of the Pharaohs was tight. Like the later Assyrians, they moved populations around at will, e.g. they deported some inhabitants of Gezer to Egyptian Thebes c.1400, and in another town they settled some Hapiru in place of those deported. To maintain control they imposed puppet princes, whose sons they took as hostages to be brought up at court.

These Hapiru were destined to play quite a part, over the next two or three centuries, in loosening Egyptian control of the Levant. They comprised a wide range of stateless people who scraped a semi-nomadic living on the fringes of settled society: brigands and runaway slaves, landless peasants and refugees. They were a permanent nuisance to the puppet princes. A prince of Jerusalem c.1350 BC even wrote to the Pharaoh that 'all the lands of the king are lost to the Hapiru'.

But a century or so later Egypt had to face a much more serious threat. This was a revolt of her Libyan subjects, supported by bands of sea-raiders from elsewhere in the Mediterranean. Pharaoh Merneptah hit back. In his fifth year (1220 or 1209 – the date is uncertain) he claimed a victory over all his enemies. Later he celebrated it in a long inscription, ending with a hymn of which this is the relevant extract:

> The princes are prostrate, saying 'Mercy!'
> Plundered is the Canaan with every evil,
> Carried off is Ashkelon, seized upon is Gezer . . .
> Israel is laid waste, his seed is not . . .
> Everyone who was restless [e.g. the Hapiru], he has been bound.
> (*ANET* 378)

Now the inscription has a sign before the word Israel which shows that it is not a town like Ashkelon or Gezer but a land or people; and the full sequence of place-names shows further that 'Israel' is somewhere near its later historical location. Merneptah therefore claimed to have re-asserted his authority over Canaan, including the region known as Israel, though we need not take literally such a phrase as 'laid waste'.

The late C13th BC saw many other crises than those which befell Egypt: it was a 'time of troubles' for the whole ANE. About 1200 BC two long-lasting empires, those of the Mycenaeans in Greece and the Hittites in what is now Turkey, came to an abrupt end, as did a number of smaller kingdoms including Ugarit*. Historians seeking a cause for all those catastrophes look to some widespread natural calamity, most likely a prolonged drought leading to famine.

One response to famine is to bring new land under cultivation, and that is what happened in Canaan. Excavations show that round about 1200 BC a substantial number of farmers moved up into the previously unoccupied central highlands of Israel, i.e. the line of hills running down west of the Jordan from Jezreel to Beersheba. With the aid of two inventions known before but not exploited, water cisterns and terracing, these farmers settled successfully in the highlands. There they were probably joined by other groups: on the one hand some Hapiru; on the other their fellow-Canaanites evicted from the coastal strip to the west.

For c.1190 BC a new nation appears on that coast, the Philistines. They were originally Cretans (the tradition preserved in Amos [9.7] is entirely plausible), probably mercenaries who had helped Egypt in her wars and were now rewarded with land on the coast of Canaan. Although Indo-Europeans by race, they soon adopted Canaanite culture; but their superior technology gave them an advantage over the locals, and in the long run over the Egyptians too. By 1150 the writ of the Pharaohs had ceased to run in Canaan.

We are now nearly in a position to consider the historicity of two traditions which play such a large part in the OT, the exodus from Egypt under Moses and the conquest of the holy land under Joshua. But there is one more set of archaeological findings to be fed in first. Sad to say, it shows conclusively that the 'conquest' cannot be historical.

For according to the OT the Israelites in the course of the conquest destroyed some twenty Canaanite cities. But most of those have now been identified and excavated, and it is clear that only two of them (Bethel and Hazor) have any archaeological claims to destruction between say 1300 and 1100 BC. The rest were either continuously occupied or continuously unoccupied. The walls of Jericho in particular had 'come tumbling down' before 1500 BC.

The same point can be put more positively. Archaeologists who have studied the material culture of that highland region are confident that throughout those two centuries it remained one and the same. There was no outside invasion, and no distinction can be made between Israelite culture and the Canaanite culture all round it. In other words the Israelites were there all the time. Historians therefore now talk not of the conquest of Canaan but of the emergence of Israel.

Where then does that leave the story of the exodus? There are plenty of parallels to its general setting viz. deportees put to work on public buildings in Egypt (see p.115f.). If REB's translation of Exod 1.11 is accepted, the Hebrews could have been taken there by Merneptah after his campaign c.1210 BC, together perhaps with Moses to be brought up at the court. Their subsequent escape c.1180 would then fall in a time of Egyptian weakness, and their return c.1150 to the highland villages of Israel would not show up as an alien intrusion in the archaeological record.

But there is still one piece to be fitted into the jigsaw – the master piece – YHWH* himself. As far as can be seen, YHWH was originally a Midianite deity. The Midianites were early Arabic speakers, with a settled civilization just east of Sinai (see map 1), but also with a nomadic fringe which extended into the peninsula. The close connection of Moses with the Midianites is clear from Exod Chs 2 and 18. Jethro, the Midianite whose daughter he married, is presented as a priest of YHWH, whose worship the Moses group adopted at Mount Sinai and took with them on their journey.

It was that fierce worship which then gave to the emergent Israelites the cohesion which their subsequent history attests and the distinctiveness upon which the biblical authors insist. Archaeology has revealed the steady growth of those highland villages in the period 1200-1000 BC. Their population and prosperity increased, and their social organization became more complex. Anthropological parallels tell us what to expect

next: first small-scale leaders, then a chieftain, finally a hereditary kingship. The OT adds the names: first the Judges, then Saul, finally David and Solomon. None of these names is corroborated outside the Bible (with the possible exception of David – see commnetary on 2 K 9) but we may accept them as historical, without necessarily accepting everything the OT says about them.

Curiously, it appears that four neighbouring states were 'emerging' at the same time along similar lines. Reading from north to south, they were: Aram, Ammon, Moab and Edom. In this way the political map of the ANE came to settle down in its new shape after the 'time of troubles'.

According to the OT, all these four states were conquered by David and paid tribute to him (2 Sam 8), though Solomon lost Aram and Edom (1 K 11), if not the others. Actually no trace has been found of Israelite influence in any of them at this time, so the whole notion of a Davidic 'empire' is questionable.

David and Solomon are also presented in the OT as ruling a united kingdom of Israel and Judah. (Confusingly, the term Israel is used in two senses in the OT. Sometimes its denotes the *whole* of the central highlands, sometimes only the northern *part*, viz. the territory of Saul and, later, Jeroboam.) But some scholars question the historicity of this too: even the text of 2 Sam suggests that David's hold over the northern part was weak. Archaeology also throws doubt on the ability of Jerusalem to function at that time as capital of any such 'united kingdom'. No buildings have yet been found in it which can safely be attributed to David or Solomon, and the city itself seems to have been too small to be of consequence until after the fall of Israel in 721 BC. On this hypothesis, the chroniclers of Judah rewrote history in order to claim for Judah the primacy which properly belonged to Israel. There may be echoes of that claim in the predilection of Genesis for the theme of the younger brother preferred.

Be that as it may, it was certainly Israel which first came to the notice of the outside world. Assyrian inscriptions c.850 onwards speak with respect of 'the house of Omri' (see 1 K 16), and excavations of his capital Samaria confirm the wealth of Israel at that time. Not until a century later does Jerusalem come into similar prominence – and by then there were only 150 years to run before the exile in Babylon.

2. Religion and Nationhood

There is one other field in which archaeology has illuminated Hebrew history. That is religion. In this field however the spade has not so much corrected the book as supplemented it, by drawing attention to a feature which the OT has played down. This feature is the persistent syncretism between Yahwism and the older Canaanite religion.

By syncretism is meant not just that e.g. El was worshipped alongside YHWH, but that the two deities were treated as identical. Such syncretism was the normal practice in the ancient world, and it had one great advantage. When two religions met, instead of fighting, they could agree on an equivalence between their various deities, and say e.g. that Jupiter is simply the Latin name of the Greek Zeus.

This kind of hospitable syncretism was bound to occur between Yahwism and Canaanite religion. After all, Israel had sprung from Canaan, so it was natural that, when YHWH arrived, he should be identified with the supreme deity of the Canaanite pantheon, El. Nowhere does the OT raise any objection to the use of El as a designation of YHWH, or as a component of names like Eli and Ezekiel – or, for that matter, Israel. Perhaps El was seen as a philosophical

concept rather than a person, and therefore no threat to YHWH. The acceptability of El extended to two other Canaanite deities, Elyon and Shaddai, who came to be treated in the OT as titles of El and thus equivalents of YHWH.

But when it came to YHWH and Baal, the OT took a different line. It may have been all right at the time for Saul's son to be named Ishbaal and his grandson Mephibaal, but the later copyists of the OT text tried to avoid the offending name. In its place they inserted an expletive meaning 'abomination', creating Ishbosheth and Mephibosheth. A century after Saul, Jeroboam set up the 'golden calf', a symbol of Baal, for his people to worship. The text of 1 K 12 hints, and the excavations of Tell Dan confirm, that he was not trying to *replace* the worship of YHWH by that of Baal but rather to *identify* YHWH with Baal. But the distinction would not have averted the wrath of the OT, which regularly refers to him as the king 'who made Israel to sin'.

What archaeology has done is to show that 'Yahwism in ancient [i.e. pre-exilic] Israel was *far* more syncretistic than the idealized portrait in the Hebrew Bible would have us believe' (Dever). It is probable even (though not all scholars agree about this) that YHWH was sometimes worshipped together with a consort. One excavated shrine of c.800 BC contained offerings inscribed ' for YHWH and his Asherah'. Asherah was the wife of El in the Canaanite pantheon.

The extent of this syncretism goes some way to explain the vehement denunciations it attracts in the pages of the OT, particularly in 'the law and the prophets'. But it goes only *some* way: it does not explain the thinking behind the denunciations. For that, archaeology cannot help; but perhaps anthropology can.

For the issue here is that of national identity or self-definition. Part of the identity of any nation is expressed negatively: thus the ancient Greeks defined themselves by religion and language, but also by *not* being what they called barbarians. In nations which are much smaller than their neighbours, the negative may even preponderate (e.g. modern Cuba). Anthropologists will then speak of a counter-identity.

And that is the concept which best explains the mind-set of OT orthodoxy. The national identity, on that interpretation, depended above all on the *differences* between the Jews and their neighbours. There are over 400 explicit references in the OT to these differences. Two notable ones are put into the mouths of foreigners. The Jews are 'a people that dwells apart, that has not made itself one with the nations' (the friendly Balaam in Num 23.9), and 'a people whose laws are different from those of every other people' (the hostile Haman in Est 3.8). The book which lays greatest stress on this distinctiveness is Deuteronomy with 50 references to it. And it is the deuteronomic tradition which is most insistent upon the central symbol of it viz. the opposition between YHWH and Baal.

Other symbols reinforce that one, and vary somewhat according to circumstance. Endogamy i.e. not marrying foreigners was usually important (but not always – see e.g. Gen 41.50+). Circumcision rose to prominence in the exile, because the Babylonians and Persians did not practise it, whereas Canaanites did. Later still, when the Greeks ruled the ANE, Jews must not participate in Greek activities like the gymnasium and the theatre, and they must not eat with gentiles.

But this separatism did not go unchallenged, even though we have to wait until the very end of the OT to hear the story of a challenge and its repercussions. 'We should go and make an agreement with the gentiles round about', said certain leading Jews c.200 BC; 'nothing but disaster has been our lot since we cut ourselves off from them' (1 Macc 1.11). The upshot was epoch-making. Those who shared that view, branded by 1 Macc as 'renegades', told the Greek King Antiochus of their desire to join the mainstream. He was delighted: his empire could do without that sore thumb. So he let them build their gymnasium in Jerusalem, and the young Jews flocked to it, even 'removing their marks of circumcision'. So far, it might seem, so good.

But then Antiochus went too far. He erected in the Temple of Jerusalem a syncretistic cult-object. It was meant to unify all his subjects, who could worship it under any name they wished, as Zeus or Baal or YHWH. The others were content, but to the Jewish people it was anathema. They rose up, drove out the 'renegades', destroyed the cult-object and achieved independence for the first time in four centuries. And when their scribes came to record the events, they once again replaced the name of Baal with an expletive, the one which AV translated 'the abomination of desolation' (Dan 11.31).

The story throws much light on the whole history of Israel – right down to the present day. (See also commentary on Est 3 and Ecclus 24.)

NAMES OF GOD AND OF MEN

1. Names and Titles of God

In the ancient world it was widely believed that any personal name carried both meaning and power. For someone else to know the name gave power over its owner, and to utter it could exercise that power.

To the Jews the personal name of God, YHWH, was so fraught with this power that to utter it gradually became taboo. Strictly, it might be spoken only once a year, by the high priest on the Day of Atonement. To avoid the blasphemy of speaking it on any other occasion, resort was had to numerous devices. They ranged from titles like 'the LORD' or 'the Almighty' to circumlocutions like 'the Holy Name' or even just 'He'. The same principle is at work among Christians who feel more comfortable using the *title* Christ (i.e. the Messiah) than the *name* Jesus. Even secular idiom says 'heaven only knows'.

Consequently one of the most numinous moments in the whole OT is when God reveals his personal name to Moses (Ex 3.15). Unfortunately its effect is obscured by a convention of printing the text of the Bible which was begun in the Hebrew mss and then carried through to most Christian translations. In early Hebrew mss words were written without vowels, and the name of God in Ex 3.15 and elsewhere was given as YHWH – shortened to YH in many psalms. But when such passages came to be read aloud in synagogues the reverent reader would utter, in place of the personal name of God, one of two alternatives: usually *adōnay*, meaning 'lord', but sometimes *elōhim,* meaning 'god'. And to prompt him in the appropriate direction, Hebrew scribes employed a curious convention. To the four consonants YHWH they added the three vowels of either *adōnay* or (less commonly) *elōhim.* The former created what is strictly a non-word

Yahowah. That non-word went through various forms until it emerged in Tyndale's Bible of 1530 as Jehovah. Until recently, English bibles have used Jehovah in that verse and in a few others, but elsewhere have rendered the Holy Name by LORD or GOD in small capitals. This book uses such capitals in all excerpts from the text of the OT.

The commentary however often uses YHWH, especially where God takes part in the action as a *dramatis persona.* The name is probably to be pronounced Yahweh, and that is how the NJB and other modern scholarly translations print it. Here YHWH is preferred, as a mark of respect for Jewish tradition. For the meaning of the name see on Ex Ch.3.

The name YHWH then was regularly used in the earlier books of the OT – histories, psalms and prophecy. But alongside it, often in the same context, are four other words for God. First and commonest is Elohim. Elohim is not a name but a plural noun meaning simply 'god' with a small 'g'. The plural form is the 'plural of majesty' (cp. our 'royal we'), and the word can be variously used. It may designate gods (pagan) in general, or a specific god (whether pagan or not), or (the) god of Israel. In the OT generally, Elohim is more objective and remote, YHWH more subjective and personal; see e.g. Exod 19.3, where both are used in the same verse, and contrast Jg 13.3 with 13.6.

Next commonest is El. El had been the name of the senior deity of the Ugaritic pantheon, with whom it was evidently unobjectionable to identify YHWH. Some ancient critics took El as the singular of Elohim, and linguistically it is related to 'Allah'. In English bibles it is generally translated 'God'.

Alongside El is Elyon. This is another Canaanite word, a title of El taken over from the earlier inhabitants of Jerusalem

[Gen 14.18+]. It is found particularly in the psalms, either on its own or joined with El. The usual English translation of it is 'Most High'.

Finally there is Shaddai. This seems to be another title, since it is sometimes joined with El, and so it is translated 'The Almighty'. It is most frequent in Job, who uses Shaddai as often as El, but never both together. Ps 91.1 however uses Elyon, Shaddai, YHWH and Elohim all in the one verse.

A rabbinic commentary on the book of Jonah suggests that the Hebrew Bible uses the different names and titles for God to denote different aspects of the divine activity. Thus:

> When I judge the creation I am called Elohim,
> When I wage war against the wicked I am called Sabaoth [Engl. 'of hosts'],
> When I suspend judgement for sins I am called El Shaddai,
> When I show mercy to my world I am called YHWH.

The generalization is not infallible, but in places it is illuminating e.g. Gen 22.

2. Names of Men and Women

Throughout history human parents have given their children theophoric names i.e. those which included the name, and thus secured the protection, of a god. In the OT such names typically end in -yah (English -iah) or -el or begin Yo- (English Jo-, as in Joshua, Jonathan). Other Semitic peoples might incorporate their own form of Baal e.g. the Phoenician Hannibal or the Babylonian Belshazzar. The Jews accepted Bel, as in Zerubbabel, but came to be uncomfortable with Baal; see Introd. to Deuteronomy.

More rarely, a father would give his children names chosen to signify his own policy. Hosea [1] and Isaiah [8] both did this. Similarly adults would be given new names to signify a change of policy, as Jacob-Israel (Gen 32).

One cannot however really suppose that any parents would actually give their children names meaning 'twister' (Jacob) or 'fool' (Nabal). In such a case, the name just suits the story, as the narrator makes clear of Nabal: 'As his name is, so he is' (1 Sam 25.25).

Biblical narrators are also careful in the locutions they use for their characters. Women are often referred to only by their relationship to a man. 'Jepthah's daughter' is never given a name, and Samson's mother is just 'wife' to Manoah (Jg 11 and 13). Michal does have a name, but it makes a great difference whether she is also referred to as 'Saul's daughter' (1 Sam 18 and 2 Sam 6) or 'David's wife' (1 Sam 19). Similarly it is a bad omen when Saul refers to David as 'the son of Jesse' (1 Sam 20.27).

It should not be thought that any of these beliefs and practices were peculiar to the Jews or other Semitic peoples. There are parallels to them all in many places, including ancient Greece. Most of them also have an attenuated afterlife even in our own day and place.

THE
OLD TESTAMENT

Genesis 1.1-5, Leningrad Codex

The Leningrad Codex was copied, according to a note by its scribe Samuel ben Jacob, in Cairo in the year 4770 of the creation of the World=AD 1010. (Unusually, ben Jacob wrote not only the consonants and the vowels but also the marginal notes or Masora, from which the Masoretic Text (MT*) gets its name.)

The Masora are for the most part a kind of concordance. For example, on Gen 1.1 they record the five other places where the word translated 'in the beginning' occurs in the Hebrew Bible. The purpose of such notes was to preserve and authenticate every word – indeed every letter – of the sacred text.

The Leningrad Codex is the basis of all modern editions of the Hebrew Bible.

INTRODUCTION TO THE PENTATEUCH

The first five books of the Bible (Genesis to Deuteronomy) are in English usually referred to by the Greek word Pentateuch, which means five volumes. To Jews they are known as the Torah, a name with more resonance. Torah i.e. 'instruction' can mean anything from legal texts to stories of God's dealing with Israel – kinds of writing which together constitute most of the Pentateuch. A brief summary of the five books is as follows:

down the narrative further, let us call it a national epic. It tells the story of the formation, under providence, of a people. As far as that goes, its closest parallel is a much later work, Vergil's *Aeneid*. In each of them the ancestors of a nation set out to travel to a land promised by God. On their way they meet dangers from nature and from human enemies, which they overcome by force or guile. Finally they wage a successful war against the previous inhabitants and take

Genesis	1 - 11	Prehistory: mankind before Abraham
	12 - 50	The patriarchs: in four generations, from Abraham to Joseph, the family moves from Mesopotamia via Canaan to Egypt
Exodus	1 - 18	Moses leads the escape from Egypt
	19 - 40	Laws given to Moses on Mt Sinai
Leviticus	1 - 27	ditto (cont.)
Numbers	1 - 9	ditto (cont.)
	9 - 36	The journey from Sinai to the east bank of Jordan
Deuteronomy	1 - 34	A further collection of laws; the death of Moses

What sort of a work is the Pentateuch? Already from that summary two features of it are clear. First it has a narrative framework. In modern terms, therefore, it falls somewhere in the triangle marked out by epic, history and fiction. As such, it has analogies in well-known works of European literature which can throw light upon it. But secondly it contains a good deal of material of a different kind, especially laws. Moreover that other material comes in great chunks: it is neither completely digested by the narrative nor entirely separate from it. To the laws we have good parallels in ANE legal codes, but there is nothing anywhere like the *mixture* which constitutes the Pentateuch.

In this selection the focus is almost entirely on the narrative; comparatively little of the legal, and virtually none of the cultic, material is included. To pin

possession of their new homeland themselves. (That successful conclusion has to wait, in the OT, for the next book, Joshua; which is why people sometimes treat the first six books as the unit rather than the first five.)

Vergil himself was consciously following Homer. Homer's two epics tell of the Trojan War (the *Iliad*) and the wanderings after it of Odysseus (the *Odyssey*); that is to say, the war and the wanderings come in the reverse order from that of the *Aeneid* and the OT. The Homeric poems played a role in the national consciousness of the ancient Greeks as great as the role played by the Pentateuch for the Jews. In this respect the Pentateuch, which reached its final shape between Homer (c.700 BC) and Vergil (*fl.*20 BC), is more like Homer.

Another similarity between the Pentateuch and the Homeric poems is their use of certain other kinds of writing beside epic. One major kind is myth. In the Pentateuch the mythical material, which is mostly to be found in the first eleven chapters of Genesis, includes some of the best-known stories in the OT. Myths treat of origins – the origin of anything from the universe and humanity down to the love of man and woman or the separation of different languages.

Other forms of writing which explain origins are aetiologies* of customs, etymologies of names, and genealogies of families. Genealogies, which are even commoner in Genesis than in the *Iliad*, have other functions too. They supply the continuity between earlier and later personalities, flattering and legitimizing a contemporary house or dynasty. They also provided a chronological framework of events before regnal years came to be used.

Myths, aetiologies and genealogies all furnish upholstery for a national epic. They reinforce its hidden message, that the features which distinguish the nation in the present were there from the beginning, and that the whole of its history, from then until now, has been under the hand of providence.

In view of all this, it is not surprising that modern scholarship has run a similar course in its study of the two works. For most of the last two centuries, scholars have been asking two questions in particular, first about the *Iliad* and then (a little later) about the Pentateuch: how far can they be regarded as history, and how did they come to be in the form they now have?

In the case of the Pentateuch, its ancient authors would doubtless have claimed it as history, and that is how it was read until fairly recently. But the evidence of archaeology, as set out on pp.29++, has finally made such a reading impossible. Unless one wishes to invent a separate category of 'sacred history', it is most appropriately read as epic. That does not mean that there is *no* historically reliable material to be found in it.

For example, tablets from Nuzi etc., corroborate the marriage customs ascribed to the patriarchs (see on Gen 16 etc.), and the Egyptian papyri fit the picture of the oppression of the Hebrews in Exodus; i.e. the local colour in each case is convincing. Moreover many of the cultic and legal provisions and some of the individual stories may well represent ancient traditions, though antiquity in such matters is no guarantee of reliability. Conclusions like these about the historicity of the Pentateuch are very close to those which Homeric scholars have reached about the *Iliad*.

The second question asked by scholars of these two works is: how and when did the material come together in its present form?

This question is easier to answer for the *Iliad*, because the poem is much more of a unity. Its material was the common property of a school of bards, who polished and recycled it in oral improvisation over many centuries. Eventually there came along the man we call 'Homer' who put together the *Iliad* essentially as we have it. The stamp of his genius, coupled with the reintroduction of writing (from Phoenicia c.750 BC), guaranteed that it changed little thereafter.

For the Pentateuch there is no clear evidence of oral composition, though it is inherently likely that some of the stories in it circulated originally by word of mouth. Some scholars have even claimed to detect a complete oral epic lying behind Genesis. If such a thing ever existed, it would have been more like the *Odyssey* than the *Iliad* i.e. less of a unity and much less 'heroic' – for the patriarchs were normally unarmed. But what we have now is a number of different written ingredients woven together. The main strands are those already distinguished, viz. (i) the narrative framework and (ii) what might be called the constitutional material: laws, lists and cultic provisions. Those two strands can be distinguished not only by subject matter but by style and vocabulary. Scholars have therefore come to think in terms of two different authors (or perhaps 'schools' of authors) known respectively as J and P.

J is the master story-teller, responsible for almost all the best-known stories of the Pentateuch. His title 'J' derives from his preference for referring to God by his name of YHWH ('J' is used rather than 'Y' because it was a German scholar who first worked this out, and German uses j, as in 'ja', for the consonantal y which it does not possess). J's style is light and easy. He tells a story sometimes with great economy, sometimes more expansively, but he knows when to throw in the telling detail, and his characters come quickly to life. He is also a considerable theologian. His picture of YHWH is attractively humane, though far above Homeric indignities.

P stands for the Priestly writer. He is the antiquarian, and his style conforms to his interests. At its best it is clear and stately, at its worst fussy and verbose. He is not a natural story-teller (see e.g. Jos Ch.6 – for P continues beyond the Pentateuch), and his narratives have mostly been omitted from this selection. From time to time, however, he rises to the occasion, notably in his account of creation in Genesis 1. P's theology also differs from J's. His preferred title for God is Elohim, on the significance of which see p.34.

In fact the first three chapters of Genesis show each author not only at his best but also at his most distinctive. Moreover the contrast between the two lends a magnificent stereoscopic quality. It is a fine composition, either by one of the two or, more probably, by a later editor. Elsewhere the Pentateuch contains instances of less successful editing. For example the chapter on Tamar (Gen 38) is out of place in the middle of the Joseph story which it interrupts. Similarly the Flood story in Gen 6-9 contains passages of P spliced into a J narrative in such a way as to defeat all attempts to read it as a single coherent whole.

For completeness, one other literary strand in the Pentateuch must be mentioned. Known as 'D', it is represented by most of the book Deuteronomy. But its influence upon the four earlier books is sporadic, except perhaps for the Sinai narrative in Exodus, so consideration of it is held over to the Introd. to Deuteronomy.

The Pentateuch thus consists of these two main bodies of material, put together with other smaller units, and edited into a reasonably coherent whole by one or more people or groups at one or more subsequent dates. There is no agreement among scholars about absolute dates (anything from 800 to 300 BC is canvassed for the period of composition), nor even about the order of the stages. For example, until recently it was thought that J was older than P; now there is doubt.

But as with the *Iliad*, so with the Pentateuch, more recent interest has tended to move on from the analysis of origins and components towards the final form of the work as a whole. In that form, the Pentateuch is bound together by a number of themes. Some of them are to be found in all national epics (see above). Others are peculiar to it. The latter derive from its theological slant, and may be summarized as follows. The chosen people recognize only one god, YHWH. He has made a covenant or contract with them. If they worship him alone and follow his commandments, he will treat them as his 'peculiar treasure'. Specifically, he will fulfil the blessings he promised to their ancestors viz. a large posterity, a land of their own and victory in battle.

Now the most interesting feature of this theology is its general similarity to the universal beliefs of the ancient world, whether Greco-Roman or ANE. Every nation recognised its own special god with whom it had an understanding: in return for his preferred sacrifices, he would bestow various favours, including success in war. What is it then which renders the Pentateuch in the last resort so *un*like the *Iliad*?

There is one difference of content. YHWH's demands were both more extensive and more exclusive than those of other national gods. But more fundamental is the *tone* which the Pentateuch adopts in speaking of them. It is the tone of one who possesses the truth and expects allegiance to it. The Pentateuch does not seek to entertain. Fortunately for the reader, however, it does hope to persuade, and in that hope it does not disdain the arts of some of the world's great story-tellers.

The Pentateuch then, as finally edited, probably in or after the exile, has a clear shape and thrust. It records a gradual movement towards the realization of the promises made to the patriarchs. Already by the beginning of Exodus the 'posterity' is secured. By the end of Deuteronomy some battles have been won (under Moses) and 'the land' is in sight. But for the successful 'occupation' of the land (under Joshua), and the full establishment of the nation as a military power (under David), we have to wait for the second half of the national epic, i.e. the books from Joshua to 2 Kings, known to scholars as the deuteronomic history, or DtH for short. Those books, finished in or after the exile, carry a message complementary to that of the Pentateuch. It is in effect a call to obedience. The obedience which advanced, and the sins that delayed, their ancestors' possession and development of the land will once again advance or delay their own repossession and redevelopment of it.

That combined work, Pentateuch and DtH together, is an achievement of remarkable scope, covering as it does the whole course of events from the origin of the cosmos down to the contemporary history of a single nation. The only known parallel to it in the ancient world is a Babylonian work of c.300 BC. Written in Greek by a priest Berossus, the *Babyloniaca* unfortunately survives only in fragments. Scholars however suppose that Berossus was following an earlier Babylonian work, now lost. This work would have been the predecessor both of the single Hebrew narrative Genesis-2 Kings and of its composite equivalent in Greek literature, viz. the writings of various independent authors from Homer through Hesiod to Hecataeus. What all these bodies of literature have in common is a flood myth marking the transition from myths of origin to narratives of the heroic and historic periods.

GENESIS

The Creation of Heaven and Earth

The OT begins with the Priestly (P) account of the creation of everything visible. It is an account of a special kind viz. a myth (for the term see p.18).

Virtually all peoples have their creation myths, ascribing the world as it is to some god or gods. There is much in common between them, partly because they are mostly accounting for the same phenomena, and partly because they travel, at least within their own 'culture-circle'. The culture-circle of the Hebrews included Mesopotamia, Egypt and Greece, and we have many creation myths from those countries, almost all of which were written before this of P. None of them is very close to the biblical account (closest is the Babylonian, of which some extracts are quoted below), though most of the individual motifs* here have their parallels somewhere in the ANE. There are two general differences between the biblical story and the others.

First, other cosmogonies* usually begin with a theogony, i.e. a narrative of the creation and descent of the gods. Anything such is conspicuously absent here. Not only was there nothing before God (v.1); it is emphasised that God himself made the sun and the moon, who were regarded as gods everywhere else in the ANE but are not so much as named here (v.16). The author spares no pains to assure us that what happens happens all and only in accordance with the will of the one god.

Secondly, many other creation-myths have a cultic function as well. That is, they were composed not to give a detached explanation of how things came to be ordered as they are, but to help in keeping them ordered. When recited at the festival of the relevant god, they served not just to praise him for favours past but to secure his co-operation in the future. In the biblical account there is no hint of a cultic use, nor is there even any explicit praise of god. But we cannot miss the implicit notes of praise in v.1 and of thanksgiving in the repeated 'God saw that it was good'. Indeed, though there is little parallelism* here, the prose is rhythmic, repetitive and patterned enough for the chapter to be printable in verses or sung antiphonally.

The pattern is provided in two ways. In each verse, i.e. each separate act of creation, God is the subject of one or more of six important verbs: said, made/created, separated, called/blessed. And most acts have one or both of the refrains: (i) *it was so*, answering to *God said*, and (ii) *God saw that it was good* – not to mention the concluding *evening and morning*. There are altogether eight 'acts', which fit imperfectly into the six days P could spare. The table below shows the pattern.

It should be said at this point that the idea of 'days' of creation has not yet been found elsewhere, and may be P's own contribution. It does indeed fit his approach: it brings order into a time sequence which is otherwise vague or mythical ('Once upon a time', 'at that time', 'When . . . not yet'). It also helps to demythologise the story.

act	verses	day	object	verbs	refrain
1	3 - 5	1	light	said, separated, called	(there was light)/was good
2	6 - 8	2	sky/waters	said, made, separated	it was so
3	9 -10	3	earth/sea	said, (gathered), called	it was so
4	11 -13	3	vegetation	said, (brought forth)	it was so/was good
5	14 -19	4	stars	(to separate), made	it was so/was good
6	20 -23	5	birds/fishes	said, created, blessed	was good
7	24 -25	6	animals	said, (bring forth), made	it was so/was good
8	26 -31	6	man	said, created, blessed	it was so/was very good

The Creation of Heaven and Earth

1. 1   In the beginning God created the heavens and the earth. • The earth was without form and void, and darkness was upon the face of the deep; and the Spirit of God was moving over the face of the waters.

    • And God said, 'Let there be light'; and there was light. • And God saw that the
5   light was good; and God separated the light from the darkness. • God called the light Day, and the darkness he called Night. And there was evening and there was morning, one day.

    • And God said, 'Let there be a firmament in the midst of the waters, and let it separate the waters from the waters.' • And God made the firmament and separated the waters which were under the firmament from the waters which were above the firmament. And it was so. • And God called the firmament Heaven. And there was evening and there was morning, a second day.   ▸

The Creation of Heaven and Earth (cont.)

Verses 1–2 are an overture. V.1 is best taken as a kind of summary, answered by the conclusion in 2.4a. The Hebrew word for *created* is a special one: it always has God as its subject in the OT, and it is never used of making one thing out of another. If one asks what there was before creation, the answer can only be 'chaos'. The Hebrew phrase translated *without form and void* has curiously been preserved by the French as 'un tohu-bohu' – meaning a shambles. Darkness is a regular feature of chaos in creation myths. The last clause of v.2 is difficult: the translation *Spirit of God* seems to imply a kind of reconnaissance.

For with v.3 the mighty orchestra crashes into life. The six Hebrew words that make it up have been much praised. They were the subject of a unique tribute by a Greek literary critic of the first century AD. In his book *On the Sublime* he quotes them as an example of grandeur of style, ascribing their authorship to 'the Jewish law-giver' (viz. Moses), whom he calls 'no ordinary man'. The French critic Boileau, agreeing, observed how the sublimity would be lost by re-wording: 'le souverain arbitre de la nature d'une seule parole forma la lumière'. Part of the effect is due to the use, here only, of the full *and there was light* instead of the flatter formula 'and it was so'. Among modern languages English has further advantages, in the assonance of 'let' with 'light'

and in the bright blade of the word 'light' to end with. The light of v.3 is the direct creation of God, unlike the indirect light of vv.14–18. It comes first because it is the precondition of the rest. Creation by command is one of the two main modes in ANE cosmogonies. P uses it in every case (see table on p.41), usually with the formula expressing exact compliance, but he often adds the other mode, viz. 'he made'. Separation and naming are crucial concepts in P, as in other ANE cosmogonies. To separate i.e. to distinguish is already to create order (cosmos) out of chaos; and to call or give a name is to distinguish in words. *The darkness* is now part of the established order, but it is not called good, because the night still threatens chaos. The sequence *evening and morning* in the formula for a day may be due to the fact that for cultic purposes the Jewish day began at sunset.

The second act of creation is unfamiliar to us. The *firmament* (6) is the dome or vault of the sky, which was believed to be strong and solid, except for apertures in it through which the rain descended from *the waters above. Heaven* means no more than sky: it has no theological overtones. Although we then conclude the second day, the formula *saw that it was good* is held up, because the ordering of the waters is not yet complete. The vertical separation has to be followed in the third act by the horizontal separation,

The Creation of Heaven and Earth (cont.)

• And God said, 'Let the waters under the heavens be gathered together into one place, and let the dry land appear.' And it was so. • God called the dry land Earth, and the waters that were gathered together he called Seas. And God saw that it was good. • And God said, 'Let the earth put forth vegetation, plants yielding seed, and fruit trees bearing fruit in which is their seed, each according to its kind, upon the earth.' And it was so. • The earth brought forth vegetation, plants yielding seed according to their own kinds, and trees bearing fruit in which is their seed, each according to its kind. And God saw that it was good. • And there was evening and there was morning, a third day.

• And God said, 'Let there be lights in the firmament of the heavens to separate the day from the night; and let them be for signs and for seasons and for days and years, • and let them be lights in the firmament of the heavens to give light upon the earth.' And it was so. • And God made the two great lights, the greater light to rule the day, and the lesser light to rule the night; he made the stars also. • And God set them in the firmament of the heavens to give light upon the earth, • to rule over the day and over the night, and to separate the light from the darkness. And God saw that it was good. • And there was evening and there was morning, a fourth day.

• And God said, 'Let the waters bring forth swarms of living creatures, and let birds fly above the earth across the firmament of the heavens.' • So God created the great sea monsters and every living creature that moves, with which the waters swarm, according to their kinds, and every winged bird according to its kind. And God saw that it was good. • And God blessed them, saying, 'Be fruitful and multiply and fill the waters in the seas, and let birds multiply on the earth.' • And there was evening and there was morning, a fifth day.

The Creation of Heaven and Earth (cont.)

which creates earth and sea. By now we have established the framework of order: two dimensions of space and one of time.

The similarities and differences between biblical and ANE cosmogonies are shown by the opening lines of the closest parallel viz. the Babylonian creation myth of c.1750 BC. It uses the negative formula common in such literature, which is found in the Bible in the opening of J's account of creation in Gen. 2.4b–5.

> When skies above were *not yet* named,
> nor earth below pronounced by name,
> Apsu, the first one, their begetter,
> and maker Tiamat, who bore them all,
> had mixed their waters together,
> but had *not* formed pastures . . .
> then gods were born within them [i.e. in
>   the waters].
>
> (Dalley 233, italics added)

The fourth act in Genesis is the creation of vegetation, roughly classified into plants and trees. Then we go back in the fifth act to finish the inanimate creation. The heavenly bodies in general determine the divisions of time. A clearer translation of v.14 is NJB's 'let them indicate festivals, days and years'. In particular sun and moon are to rule night and day as man later will *have dominion over* living creatures.

The sixth act concerns creatures which live in sea or air i.e. not on land. *Sea monsters* of a supernatural kind played quite a part in a number of ANE cosmogonies, but these here are natural ones. The recurrent phrase *according to their kinds* again betrays an interest in classification. The blessing (22) consists in the command to *be fruitful and multiply*. This is the first appearance of what will

The Creation of Heaven and Earth (cont.)

• And God said, 'Let the earth bring forth living creatures according to their kinds: cattle and creeping things and beasts of the earth according to their kinds.' **1.** 25 And it was so. • And God made the beasts of the earth according to their kinds and the cattle according to their kinds, and everything that creeps upon the ground according to its kind. And God saw that it was good.

• Then God said, 'Let us make man in our image, after our likeness; and let them have dominion over the fish of the sea, and over the birds of the air, and over the cattle, and over all the earth, and over every creeping thing that creeps upon the earth.' • So God created man in his own image, in the image of God he created him; male and female he created them. • And God blessed them, and God said to them, 'Be fruitful and multiply, and fill the earth and subdue it; and have dominion over the fish of the sea and over the birds of the air and over every living thing that moves upon the earth.' • And God said, 'Behold, I have given you every plant yielding seed which is upon the face of all the earth, and every tree with seed in its 30 fruit; you shall have them for food. • And to every beast of the earth, and to every bird of the air, and to everything that creeps on the earth, everything that has the breath of life, I have given every green plant for food.' And it was so. • And God saw everything that he had made, and behold, it was very good. And there was evening and there was morning, a sixth day.   ▸

The Creation of Heaven and Earth (cont.)

be one of P's call-signs throughout the Pentateuch. Seventh come the land animals: *beasts of the earth* (i.e. wild animals) and *cattle*. The expected blessing of them was presumably omitted when animals and humans were run together in the same day of creation.

The eighth and final act is appropriately given the fullest treatment by P. It has been the subject of endless discussions among scholars, of which the probable conclusions are given here. The plural *Let us* refers to God's heavenly council, an idea which is surprisingly common in the OT (e.g. Gen 3.22; 1 K 22.19; Ps 82.1). *Image and likeness* probably describes man's status, as a kind of divine representative on earth. Strangely, the idea of man made in the image of God, which has haunted the mind of Europe, is not referred to again in the Hebrew Bible, except for Gen 9.6 which is an ex-

press reference to this passage. (*Man* in 26 is of course collective: as 27–28 show, God is as much – or as little – female as male.) Man's *dominion* over the animals differs from the *rule* of 16 in implying responsibility. That in turn implies restricting his diet to the vegetable kingdom; only after the Flood will animal food be permitted (9.2f.). Here we meet the only hint in P of the paradise motif which is such a feature of J's account of creation. The *very good* of 31, which refers to the whole work of creation, is the nearest thing to emotion that P allows himself; for the rest the total absence of qualitative adjectives – or indeed of any descriptive colour – is remarkable. Gen. 2.1 properly belongs with 1.31; the chapter divisions, which are medieval, cannot always be relied on – nor indeed can the verse divisions, as is shown by 2.4.

The story is completed by the event

The Creation of Heaven and Earth (cont.)

• Thus the heavens and the earth were finished, and all the host of them. • And on the seventh day God finished his work which he had done, and he rested on the seventh day from all his work which he had done. • So God blessed the seventh day and hallowed it, because on it God rested from all his work which he had done in creation.

• These are the generations of the heavens and the earth when they were created.

(RSV)

The Creation of Heaven and Earth (cont.)

of 2.2–3. *Finished* would be more helpfully translated 'pronounced complete'. The idea of a creator's rest is common enough in ANE cosmogonies. It was not just that the creator had earned a rest, so to speak (the word for *work* is the ordinary human word), but that, since his work was perfect, he should withdraw and not tinker with it. To P however this rest had much more significance, for it provided advance justification for the institution of the sabbath. The seventh day is *hallowed* i.e. set aside as holy, not ordinary – the final instance of separation in the story. Gen. 2.4a is a second conclusion: it uses P's favourite formula *these are the generations*, which is now more commonly translated 'this is the story'.

This story of creation in Genesis is not intended as a scientific account (indeed the author would not have understood the phrase), and it is pointless to try to reconcile it with any such e.g. by interpreting the 'days' of creation as aeons. At most it can be called proto-scientific. It is concerned to stress that it was an action or word of *God* which has brought *order* (cosmos) out of chaos.

And every possible means is used by the author to emphasise these two themes. *God*'s position is unchallenged. Not only is there no other god, there is no opposition of any kind, and therefore, after the first two verses, no dramatic tension. Nor is any comment made on the work, except by God himself: the author does not obtrude. The theme of *order* is brought out in many ways. The vocabulary is starkly simple, with many monosyllables. The sentences largely consist of main verbs joined by 'and'. Detail is built up, brick upon brick, with architectural precision. Rhythmic progression is marked by solemn repetition and, though there is little parallelism of clauses, many of the building-blocks are made by equal division into balanced pairs: heaven and earth, night and day, male and female etc. In a word the hieratic style is exactly fitted to the subject matter. Elsewhere often pedantic, P here rises to 'lapidary greatness' (Gunkel).

Genesis Chs 2–3

The story recounted in Chs 2 and 3 of Genesis is perhaps the best known in the whole Hebrew Bible, though not directly referred to anywhere else in it – Ezekiel [Ch.28] comes nearest. It has also been the most widely misunderstood, sometimes with tragic consequences. So let it be said plainly that, although it is in story form, it is not history. Nor does it sustain what was for many centuries the official Christian interpretation, which ran roughly as follows: that the first ancestors of mankind once (in time) lived in a happy state of innocent nature in paradise; that Satan tempted them to (an original) sin; that as a result of their fall all their descendants are guilty until somehow saved. The words paradise, Satan and fall are indeed absent from the story and have been read into it.

But one must go on immediately to say that there is no alternative single or

Genesis Chs 2–3 (cont.)

simple reading of the story. Stories like this, especially when told by a great artist like J, have the porosity of myths, in that, though some meanings can be ruled out, many others can legitimately be found. There are various reasons for this. One is that the tellers of them are careful to keep their time and place indeterminate (here 2.5 and 2.8 respectively). Another is that such stories are often made up from free-floating material, whether narratives or motifs*, which carried associations now lost and which, when woven together, created tensions and ambiguities even for their first hearers. Such motifs in Genesis 2–3 include the garden of the gods, the tree of life, the serpent and 'being like gods', all of which are to be found in earlier ANE writings. Not that we know of any single ANE myth that could have served as a model for the Genesis story. There is however one Babylonian work of literature which contains all these motifs, and which therefore may have light to throw on the interpretation of the whole (see note at end of section).

The Creation of Man and Woman

2. 4,5 When the LORD God made the earth and the heavens, • there was neither shrub nor plant growing on the earth, because the LORD God had sent no rain; nor was there anyone to till the ground. • Moisture used to well up out of the earth and water all the surface of the ground.

• The LORD God formed a human being from the dust of the ground and breathed into his nostrils the breath of life, so that he became a living creature. • The LORD God planted a garden in Eden away to the east, and in it he put the man he had formed. • The LORD God made trees grow up from the ground, every kind of tree pleasing to the eye and good for food; and in the middle of the garden he set the tree of life and the tree of the knowledge of good and evil.   ▸

The Creation of Man and Woman

The change of style and tone from P to J is sharp. Stylistically, it is as if we are moving from a slow processional march into a lively if somewhat disorderly dance. Theologically, the movement is from transcendence (God above) to immanence (God among) – though the editor has tried to soften the transition by combining, for these two chapters only, the name YHWH and the title Elohim. Significantly the order of creation in 1.1 (heaven and earth) is reversed in 2.4b, so that the focus is now upon earth. And there are other changes of sequence. Since there had been *no rain* (5), the earth was desert and there were no plants: they now come after man (2.8, contrast 1.11f.).

There are many parallels to the idea of God creating man by fashioning his body from the earth and then animating it by the kiss of life. J adds an etymology* to underline the close symbiotic relationship between man (*ādām*) and earth (*adāmāh*) which is one important theme of these two chapters. The Hebrew word *ādām* means man as distinct from God or animals, not from woman; hence REB's translation *a human being* and Alter's 'human from the humus'. From v.8 on it is regularly used with the definite article, which shows it is not a proper name, and is translated *the man*.

The garden has mixed ancestry. On one side it is the garden of the gods, known in many myths, and often lying vaguely in the east. To it belong magic trees and talking animals; and *Eden*, its location here, means 'luxuriance' in Hebrew. Our familiar term 'paradise' is taken from a Greco-Persian word used

The Creation of Man and Woman (cont.)

• The LORD God took the man and put him in the garden of Eden to till it and look after it. • 'You may eat from any tree in the garden', he told the man, • 'except from the tree of the knowledge of good and evil; the day you eat from that, you are surely doomed to die.' • Then the LORD God said, 'It is not good for the man to be alone; I shall make a partner suited to him.' • So from the earth he formed all the wild animals and all the birds of the air, and brought them to the man to see what he would call them; whatever the man called each living creature, that would be its name. • The man gave names to all cattle, to the birds of the air, and to every wild animal; but for the man himself no suitable partner was found.

• The LORD God then put the man into a deep sleep and, while he slept, he took one of the man's ribs and closed up the flesh over the place. • The rib he had taken out of the man the LORD God built up into a woman, and he brought her to the man. • The man said:

'This one at last is bone from my bones,
     flesh from my flesh!
She shall be called woman,
     for from man was she taken.'

• That is why a man leaves his father and mother and attaches himself to his wife, and the two become one. • Both were naked, the man and his wife, but they had no feeling of shame.

The Creation of Man and Woman (cont.)

here in the LXX* text; originally it meant just a walled garden with no mythical overtones, i.e. it belongs to the other side of the ancestry. For this garden contained ordinary as well as magic fruit trees, and it still had to be tilled by the man (15). In this idyllic but not idle scene, there is only one source of unease, the mysterious *tree of the knowledge of good and evil* (9 and 17), whose fruit is forbidden on pain of death. REB's (and NJB's) translation *you are doomed to die* is tendentious. The Hebrew phrase here is the same as that used in OT laws which impose the death penalty, and is correctly translated by NRSV, following AV, as 'you shall surely die'. There is therefore a problem which the text never answers: why did God threaten a punishment which he did not implement? Another loose end in the story is the *tree of life*. It is not mentioned at all in vv.16–17, still less forbidden, and looks like an afterthought in v.9.

There is also one thing missing: God in J (but not in P, see 1.27) had overlooked *a partner* for the man. AV here translated 'an help meet for him'; from that came first the English 'helpmeet' and later the bastard 'helpmate'. But we need the broader word 'partner' here. For God first tries to find him a partner from the animal kingdom. The man however contents himself with giving the animals their names, a sign of dominion, even perhaps friendship, but not of partnership. The idea of *woman* formed out of man's *rib* has no clear parallel elsewhere. It may derive from the bone-carving of human figurines, as v.7 out of clay-modelling. The man's jubilant welcome of his new partner – n.b. the *at last!* – adapts the common Hebrew phrase 'my own flesh and blood', and also contains a naming which links her (*ishāh*, female) with him (*ish*, male).

In v.24 the author uses the rib motif to give his own aetiology* of the power of sexual love. The Hebrew reads 'the two become one flesh', which older English translations follow. They thus preserved

The Creation of Man and Woman (cont.)

what REB has lost, viz. the secondary reference to the loving fit of human bodies, unlike those of animals. One may compare Plato's myth in the *Symposium*, where human couples originally made a single body, which was sliced down the middle by Zeus to prevent them from challenging the gods.

Man's First Disobedience

3. 1 The serpent, which was the most cunning of all the creatures the LORD God had made, asked the woman, 'Is it true that God has forbidden you to eat from any tree in the garden?' • She replied, 'We may eat the fruit of any tree in the garden, • except for the tree in the middle of the garden. God has forbidden us to eat the fruit of that tree or even to touch it; if we do, we shall die.' • 'Of course you will not

5 die,' said the serpent; • 'for God knows that, as soon as you eat it, your eyes will be opened and you will be like God himself, knowing both good and evil.' • The woman looked at the tree: the fruit would be good to eat; it was pleasing to the eye and desirable for the knowledge it could give. So she took some and ate it; she also gave some to her husband, and he ate it. • Then the eyes of both of them were opened, and they knew that they were naked; so they stitched fig-leaves together and made themselves loincloths.

• The man and his wife heard the sound of the LORD God walking about in the garden at the time of the evening breeze, and they hid from him among the

10 trees. • The LORD God called to the man, 'Where are you?' • He replied, 'I heard the sound of you in the garden and I was afraid because I was naked, so I hid.' • God said, 'Who told you that you were naked? Have you eaten from the tree which I forbade you to eat from?' • The man replied, 'It was the woman you gave to be with me who gave me fruit from the tree, and I ate it.' • The LORD God said to the woman, 'What have you done?' The woman answered, 'It was the serpent who deceived me into eating it.'   ▸

Man's First Disobedience

J often begins a new scene by introducing a new character. Here it is *the serpent*, commonly regarded in folklore as clever and sinister. Being a *creature made* by *God*, he is not to be identified with Satan. The innocent woman is no match for his worldly wisdom. His seemingly naive question gets under her guard straight away. Defensively, she overstates the prohibition, in which originally there was no mention of *touch*ing the fruit. The serpent comes back confidently, drawing upon the common belief in the envy of the gods. The woman could see already that the fruit was tasty and pretty, as God planned (2.9). Now she learns that it would also give knowledge. Having eaten it, she and the man immediately fulfil the serpent's words: their *eyes were opened*. That is to say, they became self-conscious and embarrassed. In Israel, unlike Greece, nakedness was improper.

Then they hear *the LORD God* – not his voice (AV) but his footfall – and run to hide. When questioned, *the man* gives the game away; his nakedness is now more than physical, and for that he is not just embarrassed but guilty. Then when accused he blames *the woman* – and God! The woman shifts the blame onto *the serpent*; but God does not cross-question animals. Instead, having established the guilt, he launches into the first of three judicial sentences. They are given in the reverse order to that of the interrogation, which is J's usual way of underlining retribution.

Man's First Disobedience (cont.)

Then the LORD God said to the serpent:
> 'Because you have done this
>> you are cursed alone of all cattle and the creatures of the wild.
>
> On your belly you will crawl,
>> and dust you will eat all the days of your life.

5
> I shall put enmity between you and the woman,
>> between your brood and hers.
>
> They will strike at your head,
>> and you will strike at their heel.'

6 To the woman he said:
> 'I shall give you great labour in childbearing;
>> with labour you will bear children.
>
> You will desire your husband,
>> but he will be your master.'

17 And to the man he said:
> 'Because you have listened to your wife
>> and have eaten from the tree which I forbade you,
>> on your account the earth will be cursed.
>
> You will get your food from it only by labour
>> all the days of your life;
>> it will yield thorns and thistles for you.
>
18
> You will eat of the produce of the field,
>
19
>> and only by the sweat of your brow will you win your bread
> until you return to the earth;
>> for from it you were taken.
>
> Dust you are, to dust you will return.'

Man's First Disobedience (cont.)

First the serpent is *cursed*. This is a straightforward aetiology, in the tradition of the *Just So Stories*, explaining both the serpent's motion and its running fight with men. Next comes the woman. She is not cursed (use of 'the curse' for menstruation is another misinterpretation) any more than her husband is. Only the serpent and the earth are cursed, and these are the only curses uttered by God in the whole of the OT. Instead she is to be treated in a way that is so appropriate that it ranks more as consequence than as punishment. Her new 'knowledge' will bring pain along with the pleasures. Unlike the animals, her *childbearing* will be *with labour*; unlike the former partnership (2.18, 24), her marriage will be one of inequality.

Similarly the man will find his fundamental relationship to *the earth* (2.15) disturbed. Work, which previously was pleasant as well as necessary, will now be back-breaking – *labour* for him too. And this will last to the very end of his life. Then, almost as a merciful release, he *will return* at the end to the *dust* from which he came at the beginning of the story (2.7). These two 'sentences' on the man and his wife are also aetiologies, but of a vastly more weighty kind. They purport to explain the origin of suffering and discord in the basic circumstances of life. By inculpating humans, the story exculpates God: indeed, it says, he tried to save humans from it, but they insisted on *knowing good and evil* and have only themselves to blame.

Man's First Disobedience (cont.)

3. 21   • The LORD God made coverings from skins for the man and his wife and clothed them. • But he said, 'The man has become like one of us, knowing good and evil; what if he now reaches out and takes fruit from the tree of life also, and eats it and lives for ever?' • So the LORD God banished him from the garden of Eden to till the

24   ground from which he had been taken. • When he drove him out, God settled him to the east of the garden of Eden, and he stationed the cherubim and a sword whirling and flashing to guard the way to the tree of life.   (REB)

Man's First Disobedience (cont.)

Of the remaining verses the essential one is 23. Expulsion from the garden, and from close contact with God, rounds off the story which began with God's creating it and placing man in it. The making of the clothes in v.21 is a typical J touch showing that God's care will follow them even so. The *cherubim* were Babylonian winged monsters, far removed from the associations of our word 'cherubic', and the divine *sword* is also an ANE motif.

There remains *the tree of life*, which makes another superfluous appearance at the end of the story. God has already grounds enough for expulsion in the eating of the forbidden fruit, without adding his *fear* that they *might* eat of another tree whose fruit he had permitted (2.16). Perhaps the latent idea is that, whereas the possession of knowledge or wisdom makes men *resemble* gods, the possession of immortality would enable them to pose a *threat*. That was, of course a pagan notion, found for example in the Platonic myth quoted above, and too blasphemous to be tolerable in the OT. But it lies close to the surface in the Tower of Babel story, where Gen 11.6 has the same shape as 3.22. 'Look what these men have done', say the gods in effect: 'who knows what they may not do next?'

The Interpretation of Genesis Chs 2 and 3

Ch. 2 portrays a state of innocence. It has two sides. Collectively, the relationships are all naturally harmonious: God cares for humans, who obey him; the animals are treated like domestic pets; man and woman are one flesh. Individually, humans do not know good and evil. In particular, they are innocent in the sense of being unselfconscious: they are naked and do not know it (contrast 2.25 with 3.7).

Ch. 3 describes how, being tempted, they 'fell' from innocence through experience into self-consciousness and thereby into alienation. The lure was powerful: nothing less than the knowledge of good and evil. But that phrase, which is central to the story, is not as simple as it seems. For 'good and evil' in Hebrew can mean either 'right or wrong' or 'pleasant and painful'.

At this point we may turn for illumination to the ANE work which offers the closest parallel to Gen Chs 2–3. It is the Babylonian *Epic of Gilgamesh*, a work found in many versions, one of which was certainly known to J. The epic includes the story of the hero's friend Enkidu, who is a 'child of nature'. Created from 'a pinch of clay', he

> knows not a people, nor even a country.
> Coated in hair like the god of the animals,
> with gazelles he grazes on grasses.

In order to civilise him, Gilgamesh sends a harlot to seduce him. She does so, lying with him 'for six days and seven nights'.

But afterwards

> the beasts of the field shied away from his presence . . .
> Enkidu was weakened, could not run as before,
> but now he had reason (?) and wide understanding . . .
> Then to the harlot's words he listened intently . . .
> 'You are handsome, Enkidu, you are just like a God!
> Why with the beasts do you wander the wild?
> Come, I will take you to Uruk-the-Sheepfold . . .
> where Gilgamesh is perfect in strength'.
> (George 7–9)

Eventually on his deathbed Enkidu was first moved to curse the prostitute, and then persuaded by a god to call back the curse. The ambiguous status of knowledge is unresolved.

His friend being now dead, Gilgamesh then sets out to search for a way of securing everlasting life. He learns of a 'mystery of the gods', a plant which will guarantee eternal youth. He finds the plant, but loses it again, to a serpent who 'snatched it away'. This time there is no ambiguity. Immortality is not negotiable.

Clearly the *Gilgamesh* epic contains a number of the ingredients of the Genesis story. They are put together differently, but two of them in particular are illuminating. First is the sexual motif which is prominent in both. *Gilgamesh* is explicit: it was sexual experience which gave Enkidu 'wide understanding' and even made him 'like a god'. Genesis is more guarded. It does not suggest that Adam and Eve had abstained from love-making before they ate the fruit. Indeed it implies the opposite in 2.23–4, as Milton perspicaciously if polemically insisted (*Paradise Lost* 4.741+). But to anyone familiar with *Gilgamesh* the connection between sex and wisdom is obvious in Genesis too. Nor is this surprising. For sexual experience does mark the watershed, both physically and psychologically, between immaturity and maturity. And sexual love gives 'knowledge of good and evil' in both senses of the phrase. The same Hebrew verb 'know' is indeed the normal word used in the OT for sexual intercourse.

Secondly, the story of Enkidu draws attention to the social-historical aspect of the myth. The growth of civilization is symbolised in Genesis by the progression nakedness → fig-leaves → skins. The knowledge that enables that growth is bought at a high price. It disrupts the relationships of innocence. This is true ecologically. Man becomes alienated from the soil, though he was originally almost its son (2.7). He also becomes, like Enkidu, the enemy of his former brothers (2.19) the animals: first the serpent (3.15) but later all of them (9.2). It is true also of his closest human relationship, with his wife: the equality of one flesh is replaced by the dominance of the male, and the pleasures of parenthood have their painful corollary. It is true finally of his relationship with God, where trusting obedience is replaced by suspicion, resentment and alienation.

But the Genesis story may finally be interpreted on an individual level. The movement from innocence to experience is made by each of us as we grow up. Adults know that life is ambiguous, with pleasures and pains inseparable. At times they wish their children could remain innocent, and they themselves forbid the fruit, even with dire penalties. When the inevitable happens, the children leave home, but the parents equip them to do so (cp. 3.21) and follow them with love. The rest of J's work does indeed record how God followed this pair of errant children and their descendants with parental care.

Cain and Abel

4.1 Now the man knew his wife Eve, and she conceived and bore Cain, saying, 'I have produced a man with the help of the LORD.' • Next she bore his brother Abel. Now Abel was a keeper of sheep, and Cain a tiller of the ground. • In the course of time Cain brought to the LORD an offering of the fruit of the ground, • and Abel for his part brought of the firstlings of his flock, their fat portions. And the LORD had
5 regard for Abel and his offering, • but for Cain and his offering he had no regard. So Cain was very angry, and his countenance fell. • The LORD said to Cain, 'Why are you angry, and why has your countenance fallen? • If you do well, will you not be accepted? And if you do not do well, sin is lurking at the door; its desire is for you, but you must master it.'

  • Cain said to his brother Abel, 'Let us go out to the field.' And when they were in the field, Cain rose up against his brother Abel, and killed him. • Then the LORD said to Cain, 'Where is your brother Abel?' He said, 'I do not know; am I my
10 brother's keeper?' • And the LORD said, 'What have you done? Listen; your brother's blood is crying out to me from the ground! • And now you are cursed from the ground, which has opened its mouth to receive your brother's blood from your hand. • When you till the ground, it will no longer yield to you its strength; you will be a fugitive and a wanderer on the earth.' • Cain said to the LORD, 'My punishment is greater than I can bear! • Today you have driven me away from the soil, and I shall be hidden from your face; I shall be a fugitive and a wanderer on the earth,
15 and anyone who meets me may kill me.' • Then the LORD said to him, 'Not so! Whoever kills Cain will suffer a sevenfold vengeance.' And the LORD put a mark on Cain, so that no one who came upon him would kill him. • Then Cain went away from the presence of the LORD, and settled in the land of Nod, east of Eden.

(NRSV)

Cain and Abel

'Man's first disobedience' is followed immediately by man's first act of violence against his *brother* i.e. his fellowman. The story of Cain and Abel, famous as it is, presents many problems of interpretation, and indeed seems only half finished.

It starts with the relationship between the pair of brothers. The balance between them is shown by the chiastic* use of their names in vv.1–5, culminating in a double chiasmus for the crisis in v.5: *The LORD had regard for Abel, but for Cain he had no regard.* No reason is given for the preference of Abel, any more than it is for the many such preferences of younger brothers which cause enmity later in Genesis. Verse 7 is obscure. Certainly God is warning Cain. The general tenor seems to be that Cain is a fair-weather sailor: when things go his way he is fine (REB translates 'you hold your head up'), whereas a moment of failure is a moment of danger, with his quick temper like a demon lurking to pounce at a threshold. But the text is uncertain, and no light is thrown by the remarkable fact that the end of v.7 in Hebrew echoes the exact words which ended 3.16.

The events of vv.8–16 also follow closely the dramatic sequence of Ch. 3. God himself arraigns the guilty party, and his first question, *Where is Abel?* corresponds to 3.9 *Where are you?* His sentence is expressed in the form of a curse relating to the soil, and is accompanied by banishment. He also intervenes to soften the effects of the sentence (cp. 3.21). But there are some important differences as well. In answer to God's question, Cain offers not only evasion but a downright lie salted with flippancy. God however cannot be deceived: the very *blood* cries out to him *from the ground*.

The final twist is surprising. Cain realises his extreme vulnerability and complains. God thereupon offers him protection, first by a solemn threat of vengeance and secondly by *a mark*. The mark, presumably a tattoo, was not for shame (as in the English idiom) but for protection. Here again, the exact interpretation is uncertain, beyond the fact that God continues in spite of all to act as Cain's *keeper*.

Introduction to the Flood

The story of a primeval flood is perhaps the most widespread of all myths. Almost every part of the ancient world had its version, whether primitive or sophisticated. Most relevant to Genesis are two Babylonian versions, to be found in the epics of *Atrahasis* and *Gilgamesh*. In *Atrahasis* the flood is the climax, in *Gilgamesh* it is a later insertion which is not integral to the story. *Gilgamesh* is the closer to the OT, and there follows a summary of it, with parallel motifs italicised.

Atrahasis however contains details not in *Gilgamesh*, including the reason why the gods sent the flood in the first place. It is a surprising one. The population of the earth had increased to the point where the noise they made prevented the supreme god Enlil from getting to sleep. He therefore called the gods into council, and they decided to send the flood in punishment. But the plan of the gods was revealed to the hero by his personal god Ea. Ea advised him to build an ark and to board it with his family and the animals; and he drew a design of it on the ground.

At this point the *Gilgamesh* version takes over. The narrator is now the hero himself, named Utnapishtim. He describes in detail how he *built the boat*, with the *reeds* and the *pitch*, and *boarded it* with *cattle* and *wild beasts* and *all his kith and kin*. Then came *the storm*.

Even the gods took fright at the Deluge
. . .
The Mother-goddess cried out like a woman in childbirth . . .
'How could I speak evil in the gods' assembly?
It is I who give birth, these people are mine!
And now, like fish, they fill the ocean!

On the seventh day *the storm subsided*, Utnapishtim *opened a hatch* and saw the boat *aground on a mountain*. After seven more days he *let three birds in succession go* – a dove, a swallow and a raven. *The first two returned, the third did not.* Then Utnapishtim offered a sacrifice. The *gods smelled the sweet savour* and gathered like flies.

Then at once the Mother-goddess arrived
. . .
'All the gods shall come to the incense,
but to the incense let Enlil not come
because he . . . delivered my people to destruction.'
(George 88+)

Enlil's reaction was to complain that any of the mortals had escaped: 'No man was meant to survive.' But the gods as a whole regretted the flood, on the grounds that it destroyed the innocent along with the guilty. Enlil was outvoted, and sent to touch the foreheads of Utnapishtim and his wife so as to make them immortal.

The similarities of this to Genesis are striking – and not just in detail, e.g. the birds. For in *Gilgamesh*, as in all sophisticated versions, the myth is theologised. In most it is connected with the creation. Sometimes the flood comes even before the creation; where it comes after, it is regularly seen as a punishment for the human race, from which however the gods decide to save one family. So the chief difference between the biblical version and the others is also theological: the punishment and the compassion cannot be distributed between the gods, but must be reconciled within the heart of the LORD.

This is indeed one of the two underlying themes which are inter-

Introduction to the Flood (cont.)

woven in the biblical story of the Flood. The personal theme was what interested J, while P was more concerned with the impersonal sequence: creation (cosmos) – flood (chaos) – re-creation. The editor of our present text of Genesis retained the two stories of J and P almost complete – more so than elsewhere in the Pentateuch. Unfortunately the editing is not very skilful. It leaves not only such redundancies as four separate lists of the animals that went into the ark, but also contradictions: in one version (7.2) there were *seven pairs* of each clean animal and bird, in the other there is only *one pair* [6.19 etc.]. There is also a more serious contradiction in the chronology (see below).

There remains the question why the flood myth should be so widespread. It is certainly at home in Mesopotamia, where regular flooding of the Euphrates valley is attested by archaeology as far back as the fourth millennium BC. But most peoples have enough experience of floods to respond to a story told with the power of *Gilgamesh* or Genesis.

The Building of the Ark

6. 1 The human race began to increase and to spread over the earth and daughters were born to them. • The sons of the gods saw how beautiful these daughters were, so they took for themselves such women as they chose. • But the LORD said, 'My spirit will not remain in a human being for ever; because he is mortal flesh, he will live only for a hundred and twenty years.' • In those days as well as later, when the sons of the gods had intercourse with the daughters of mortals and children were born to them, the Nephilim were on the earth; they were the heroes of old, people of renown.

5 • When the LORD saw how great was the wickedness of human beings on earth, and how their every thought and inclination were always wicked, • he bitterly regretted that he had made mankind on earth. • He said, 'I shall wipe off the face of the earth this human race which I have created – yes, man and beast, creeping things and birds. I regret that I ever made them.' • Noah, however, had won the LORD's favour.   ▸

The Building of the Ark

Prefixed to the flood story is a puzzling fragment of J (6.1–4), even less finished than the story of Cain and Abel. It consists of three verses of pagan mythology, into which J has inserted a comment. The myth explains giants (Heb. *Nephilīm*) or heroes as sprung from intercourse between gods and mortals. More familiar to us in its Greek version about the Titans, the myth is found in many countries; but the nearest reference in the OT is in Ecclus [16.7]: 'God did not pardon the giants of old who, confident in their strength, had rebelled' (NJB). Here it is interrupted by God's imposition of a limit of 120 years' life on *human beings*. Presumably, in this context, that actually means on the giants, as in Ps 82.6f. where the 'sons of God' are told: 'you shall die like men.'

The relevance of this fragment as a prologue to the flood has to be inferred from cognate myths. The implication is that the *increase* of population (v.1, cp. *Atrahasis* quoted above) and the *wickedness* of human beings (5) were both seen as part of an aspiration to the status of God; this brings the flood into line with the eating of the fruit (3.5) and the Tower of Babel (11.6). Interpreted so, the fragment is part of J's introduction to his version of the flood story. We hear his own voice, and must attach due weight to his programmatic statement in vv.5–7.

The Building of the Ark (cont.)

3 • God said to Noah, 'I am going to bring the whole human race to an end, for because of them the earth is full of violence. I am about to destroy them, and the earth along with them. • Make yourself an ark with ribs of cypress; cover it with

5 reeds and coat it inside and out with pitch. • This is to be its design: the length of the ark is to be three hundred cubits, its breadth fifty cubits, and its height thirty cubits. • You are to make a roof for the ark, giving it a fall of one cubit when complete; put a door in the side of the ark, and build three decks, lower, middle,

22 and upper.' • Noah carried out exactly all God had commanded him.   (REB)

The Building of the Ark (cont.)

The flood then was sent as a punishment for the wickedness of men. But how could YHWH the creator also prove the destroyer? In *Gilgamesh* the Mother-goddess is creator, Enlil destroyer. This solution is not available to a Hebrew author. Hence *the* LORD*'s bitter regret* which led him to make an exception of Noah. Paradoxically, the LORD's transcendence makes him the more human.

The Hebrew word translated *ark* is found only in this story and in that of Moses' 'basket' in Exod 2. It was made partly of reeds, like the boats of ancient Egypt which Thor Heyerdahl recreated to sail across the Pacific. The ark's displacement (15) has been calculated at 43,000 tons! Noah's obedience in v.22 is expressed in a typical P formula, familiar from Ch. 1. From beginning to end of the story Noah remains silent – quite unlike Utnapishtim in *Gilgamesh*.

The Rise and Fall of the Waters

7.1 The LORD said to Noah, • 'Go into the ark, you and all your household; for you alone in this generation have I found to be righteous. • Take with you seven pairs, a male and female, of all beasts that are ritually clean, and one pair, a male and female, of all beasts that are not clean; • also seven pairs, males and females, of every bird – to ensure that life continues on earth. • For in seven days' time I am going to send rain on the earth for forty days and forty nights, and I shall wipe off the face of the earth every

5 living creature I have made.' • Noah did all that the LORD had commanded him.

• So to escape the flood Noah went into the ark together with his sons, his wife,

10 and his sons' wives. • At the end of seven days the water of the flood came over the earth. • In the year when Noah was six hundred years old, on the seventeenth day of the second month, that very day all the springs of the great deep burst out, the windows of the heavens were opened, • and rain fell on the earth for forty days and

16 forty nights. • That was the day Noah went into the ark. • And the LORD closed the door on him.   ▸

The Rise and Fall of the Waters

This section is chiefly P, with additions from J and elsewhere. Typical of J is the delightful touch at the end of 7.16, not found in any of the extant ANE flood myths. Typical of P is the precision of dating (7.11, cp. 8.4f. and 13) and the great age ascribed to Noah: *600 years* was a basic unit of time in Babylonian chronology. P's description of the coming of the waters (7.11) reverses the narrative of creation. Then the waters were divided and put in their respective places, above and below the earth, thus producing order. Now the *great deep* breaks through from below and the rain pours down from above. The idea of the *windows of the heavens* is as old as the Ugaritic* Baal-epic.

The Rise and Fall of the Waters (cont.)

7. 17 • The flood continued on the earth for forty days, and the swelling waters lifted up the ark so that it rose high above the ground. • The ark floated on the surface of the swollen waters as they increased over the earth. • They increased more and 20 more until they covered all the high mountains everywhere under heaven. • The water increased until the mountains were covered to a depth of fifteen cubits. • Every living thing that moved on earth perished: birds, cattle, wild animals, all creatures that swarm on the ground, and all human beings. • Everything on dry land died, everything that had the breath of life in its nostrils. • God wiped out every living creature that existed on earth, man and beast, creeping thing and bird; they were all wiped out over the whole earth, and only Noah and those who were with him in the ark survived.

8. 1 • God took thought for Noah and all the beasts and cattle with him in the ark, and he caused a wind to blow over the earth, so that the water began to subside. • The springs of the deep and the windows of the heavens were stopped up, the downpour from the skies was checked. • Gradually the water receded from the earth, and by the end of a hundred and fifty days it had abated. • On the seventeenth day of the 5 seventh month the ark grounded on the mountains of Ararat. • The water continued to abate until the tenth month, and on the first day of the tenth month the tops of the mountains could be seen.

• At the end of forty days Noah opened the hatch that he had made in the ark, • and sent out a raven; it continued flying to and fro until the water on the earth had dried up. • Then Noah sent out a dove to see whether the water on the earth had subsided. • But the dove found no place where she could settle because all the earth was under water, and so she came back to him in the ark. Noah reached out and 10 caught her, and brought her into the ark. • He waited seven days more and again sent out the dove from the ark. • She came back to him towards evening with a freshly plucked olive leaf in her beak. Noah knew then that the water had subsided from the earth's surface. • He waited yet another seven days and, when he sent out the dove, she did not come back to him. • So it came about that, on the first day of the first month of his six hundred and first year, the water had dried up on the earth, and when Noah removed the hatch and looked out, he saw that the ground was dry.

➤

The Rise and Fall of the Waters (cont.)

The primeval chaos returns, to last until 8.2. The addition of P to J here is effective in representing the apparently endless *swelling* of the *waters* in 7.17–20 and the obliteration of all other life in 21–3.

The turning point of the whole story is marked in 8.1 with the formal expression of God's care *for Noah*, which extends also to the animals (cp. the last words of the book of Jonah). The *wind* helped to dry the land, but the reference to it also echoes the wind in Gen 1.2: creation is beginning again. For *Ararat*, which is strictly a region, see map 1; the highest peak there is over 5,000 metres. The motif of the birds is found in almost all the ANE versions of the flood, no doubt because such test-flights were a standard way in which ancient navigators looked for a landfall. In the other versions there are either three separate birds or one bird three

The Rise and Fall of the Waters (cont.)

And God spoke to Noah. • 'Come out of the ark together with your wife, your sons, and their wives,' he said. • 'Bring out every living creature that is with you, live things of every kind, birds, beasts, and creeping things, and let them spread over the earth and be fruitful and increase on it.' • So Noah came out with his sons, his wife, and his sons' wives, • and all the animals, creeping things, and birds; everything that moves on the ground came out of the ark, one kind after another.

(REB)

The Rise and Fall of the Waters (cont.)

times. Here the three-fold release of the *dove* is clearly from J: witness Noah's loving care in 9 and the vivid 'lo in her mouth' of 11 (lost in REB). The more impersonal mention of the *raven* in 7 is typical of P. Verse 13 also shows the two different styles: P gives the legal dating of the event, then J the human story.

There is an irreconcilable contra-diction between the chronologies adopted by J and P for the Flood. In J the rain lasts 40 days (7.4 etc.). In P 'the water increased over the earth for 150 days' [7.24], and its end falls on a New Year's Day [8.13], thus marking a new creation. P's processional hymn in 8.15–19 likewise recalls the stately movement of creation as he sang it in Gen 1.

The Aftermath of the Flood

20   Then Noah built an altar to the LORD and, choosing from all the clean animals and all the clean birds he presented burnt offerings on the altar. • The LORD smelt the pleasing smell and said to himself, 'Never again will I curse the earth because of human beings, because their heart contrives evil from their infancy. Never again will I strike down every living thing as I have done.

22   As long as earth endures:
             seed-time and harvest,
             cold and heat,
             summer and winter,
             day and night
             will never cease.'

The Aftermath of the Flood

The last three verses of Ch. 8 conclude J's narrative of the flood. Noah's sacrifice, showing gratitude for escape, was the most natural thing in the (ancient) world. Even the reference to ritually *clean* animals here and in 7.2 is found in *Atrahasis*.

As in *Gilgamesh*, the Lord resolves never to repeat the flood. This resolution consciously echoes his deliberation at the beginning (6.5–7) and thus rounds the story off; the resolve *never again* to *curse the earth because of human beings* also echoes 3.17. The second *because* in v. 21 is better rendered 'even though', as in REB. Finally God makes a promise, not that the earth will last for ever, but that the orderly sequence of nature will never again be interrupted. He gives no reason for this, but one may recall the great words which Hosea (11.9) ascribes to him: 'I will not again destroy Ephraim, for I am God and not man.'

The Aftermath of the Flood (cont.)

9. 1 • God blessed Noah and his sons and said to them, 'Breed, multiply and fill the earth. • Be the terror and the dread of all the animals on land and all the birds of heaven, of everything that moves on land and all the fish of the sea; they are placed in your hands. • Every living thing that moves will be yours to eat, no less than the foliage of the plants. I give you everything, • with this exception: you must not eat

5 flesh with life, that is to say blood, in it. • And I shall demand account of your life-blood, too. I shall demand it of every animal, and of man. Of man as regards his fellow-man, I shall demand account for human life.

6   He who sheds the blood of man,
          by man shall his blood be shed,
      for in the image of God
          was man created.

7   Be fruitful then and multiply,
          teem over the earth and subdue it!'

• God spoke as follows to Noah and his sons, • 'I am now establishing my

10 covenant with you and with your descendants to come, • and with every living creature that was with you: birds, cattle and every wild animal with you; everything that came out of the ark, every living thing on earth. • And I shall maintain my covenant with you: that never again shall all living things be destroyed by the waters of a flood, nor shall there ever again be a flood to devastate the earth.'

• 'And this', God said, 'is the sign of the covenant which I now make between myself and you and every living creature with you for all ages to come: • I now set my bow in the clouds and it will be the sign of the covenant between me and the earth. • When I gather the clouds over the earth and the bow appears in the clouds,

15 • I shall recall the covenant between myself and you and every living creature, in a word all living things, and never again will the waters become a flood to destroy all living things. • When the bow is in the clouds I shall see it and call to mind the eternal covenant between God and every living creature on earth, that is, all living things.'

(NJB)

The Aftermath of the Flood (cont.)

Gen 9.1–16 gives P's different conclusion to the story. Here again the echoes are of P's own creation narrative in 1.27–29, e.g. God repeats the command to *multiply* etc. But whereas previously humans were to be vegetarians, now they are (reluctantly?) permitted to kill animals for food – provided that their flesh is not eaten with the *blood in it* (see Lev 17.10–14). When a man is killed, even to *shed* his *blood* must be requited. But animals are not made *in the image of god*, so their blood may be shed with impunity, though not eaten.

God then establishes a *covenant** with *Noah and his sons* and, somewhat surprisingly, with the animals. Not that this is a covenant in the full reciprocal sense; rather a unilateral promise, whose theme (as in 8.21) is *Never again*. And finally God gives a *sign* or token that his promise will last for ever. This is to be the rainbow, which marks the appearance of sunshine after rain. When God sees it, he will remember his promise. P's full and formal style is especially well suited to such a solemn declaration.

The Tower of Babel

1 There was a time when all the world spoke a single language and used the same words. • As people journeyed in the east, they came upon a plain in the land of Shinar and settled there. • They said to one another, 'Come, let us make bricks and bake them hard'; they used bricks for stone and bitumen for mortar. • Then they said, 'Let us build ourselves a city and a tower with its top in the heavens and make 5 a name for ourselves, or we shall be dispersed over the face of the earth.' • The LORD came down to see the city and tower which they had built, • and he said, 'Here they are, one people with a single language, and now they have started to do this, from now on nothing they have a mind to do will be beyond their reach. • Come, let us go down there and confuse their language, so that they will not understand what they say to one another.' • So the LORD dispersed them from there all over the earth, and they left off building the city. • That is why it is called Babel, because there the LORD made a babble of the language of the whole world. It was from that place the LORD scattered people over the face of the earth.   (REB)

The Tower of Babel

The story of the Tower of Babel looks straightforward enough. Men incur the displeasure of God and are punished. But there is an apparent asymmetry between sin and punishment. The final punishment (9) is clear: their languages are confused and they themselves scattered. And the story appropriately begins by saying that hitherto they had spoken *a single language*, and by illustrating the point in v.3: *they said to one another*. Yet to speak with one language is not a sin: at most it is, as it were, an accessory (6). The sin must lie in the *city* and the *tower*, built to secure a *name* (4). Of those, the only one which could merit punishment is the *tower with its top in the heavens*, and later tradition is correct in taking the tower as the title of the story. For many countries have myths about tall towers built so that giants or men may assault the gods. In those myths the gods usually topple the tower, e.g. in an Indian version older than Gen 11 the god Indra does so by pulling out just one brick. Here however that crucial event is missing: perhaps even J shrank from it.

Instead God *came down to see*, and for a moment we sense what is an undercurrent in the whole of J's early history, namely 'a primal awe vis-à-vis the colossal potentialities of mankind'

(von Rad). But God decides to intervene, and his intervention is decisive. It is also the centre of the pedimental* structure. On either side of it is an interior monologue, first by the men and then by God. There is no dialogue between them, but their *Come!* in v.3 (and also v.4, where REB omits it) is answered ironically by his in v.7. Taking the tower (*this* in v.6) as evidence of their aggressive designs, God defeats them by confusing their speech and then scattering them, so that they have to stop building the city. In the Hebrew text the retribution is brought out by the usual framing: the same words, 'the whole earth' close the story as opened it. The point is lost in the English translations.

In this narrative J has rolled together, not entirely successfully, a number of motifs. At the centre of them all is the city: this is where men assemble and speak a common language; this is also the setting of the tower. And what city could rival Babylon (called *Shinar* in v.2) as a setting for the resultant story? First, Babylon was always in the OT the city par excellence, with overtones of size and wealth and wickedness. Second, the name of Babylon, by a simple if false etymology, suggested the confusion of speech which is so happily rendered in REB.

The Tower of Babel (cont.)

Third, Babylon was the home of the most famous of all the temple towers or ziggurats. Verses 3 and 4 indeed seem almost to echo an inscription we have of king Nabopolassar, which reads:

> The lord Marduk commanded me concerning the ziggurat of Babylon, that I should make its foundations secure in the depth of the subsoil and build its top to rival the heavens. I caused baked bricks to be made ... (and) streams of bitumen to be brought.

The crucial phrase 'top to rival the heavens' was traditional in Babylon; so were the materials (3) in a land without stone, even if readers in Jerusalem had to have them explained.

The Tower of Babel fits into Genesis as follows. The story about the origin of languages, which in other mythologies is often linked with the flood and thus with creation, is rightly set in pre-history. But the motif of the tower belongs in the sequence of sin, punishment and reconciliation which binds together Gen Chs 2–11 – except that this time no reconciliation is even hinted at.

Introducing Abraham: His Call

11. 27 Now these are the descendants of Terah. Terah was the father of Abram, Nahor, and Haran; and Haran was the father of Lot. • Abram and Nahor took wives; the name of Abram's wife was Sarai, • Now Sarai was barren; she had no child. • Terah took his son Abram and his grandson Lot son of Haran, and his daughter-in-law Sarai, his son Abram's wife, and they went out together from Ur of the Chaldeans to go into the land of Canaan; but when they came to Harran, they settled there.

12. 1 • Now the LORD said to Abram, 'Go from your country and your kindred and your father's house to the land that I will show you. • I will make of you a great nation, and I will bless you, and make your name great, so that you will be a blessing. • I will bless those who bless you, and the one who curses you I will curse; and in you all the families of the earth shall be blessed.' • So Abram went, as the LORD had told him; and Lot went with him. Abram was seventy-five years old when he departed from Harran. ⬥

Introducing Abraham: His Call

With Abraham we move from mankind as a whole to a single family, which however in a sense represents *all the families of the earth* (12.3). The Priestly writer adds a full genealogy in [11.10–32] to link the two – ten generations from Noah to Abraham. The geography of his travels is straightforward: first from the ancient city of *Ur* near the mouth of the Euphrates to *Harran* 600 miles NW up the river; then another 350 miles SSW into *Canaan* – almost the whole length of the Fertile Crescent. As to chronology, P's system would imply something like 1450 BC. But that was some eight centuries before *Ur* was occupied by the *Chaldeans* – an early warning against treating the narrative as historical.

Abraham is portrayed above all as a figure of faith, a faith which is tested and established in various ways. First, he is ready to abandon all his roots at God's command and to move, initially to a country that is not even specified (*that I will show you* v.12.1), and many times later as well. In return God promises to *bless* him: implicitly with a *land*, explicitly with a large family which will grow into *a great nation* with a *great name* (note the echo of 11.4). Abraham's response, typically in this spare narrative, is recorded in a single word: silently, he *went*. For the importance of a blessing in the OT see p. 79.

Introducing Abraham: His Call (cont.)

• Abram took his wife Sarai and his brother's son Lot, and all the possessions that they had gathered, and the persons whom they had acquired in Harran; and they set forth to go to the land of Canaan. When they had come to the land of Canaan, • Abram passed through the land to the place at Shechem, to the oak of Moreh. At that time the Canaanites were in the land. • Then the LORD appeared to Abram, and said, 'To your offspring I will give this land.' So he built there an altar to the LORD, who had appeared to him. • From there he moved on to the hill country on the east of Bethel, and pitched his tent, with Bethel on the west and Ai on the east; and there he built an altar to the LORD and invoked the name of the LORD.   (NRSV)

Introducing Abraham: His Call (cont.)

The author is careful to record all the places where the patriarchs stopped, especially if they saw an appearance of the LORD (theophany) and/or built an altar. *Shechem* and *Bethel* (see map 2, B2) were important and long-lasting cult-centres. At Shechem God made explicit the promise hitherto implicit, that *this land* would belong (not to him but) to his descendants. Here again, Abraham responded in faith: he built an *altar* and, even more significant, *invoked the name of the LORD,* i.e. he addressed him by his name YHWH. But the reader has been warned by the mention of *the Canaanites* (6) that there are rocks ahead.

Abraham in Egypt

10 Now there was a famine in the land. So Abram went down to Egypt to reside there as an alien, for the famine was severe in the land. • When he was about to enter Egypt, he said to his wife Sarai, 'I know well that you are a woman beautiful in appearance; • and when the Egyptians see you, they will say, "This is his wife"; then they will kill me, but they will let you live. • Say you are my sister, so that it may go well with me because of you, and that my life may be spared on your account.'• When Abram entered Egypt the Egyptians saw that the woman was

15 very beautiful. • When the officials of Pharaoh saw her, they praised her to Pharaoh. And the woman was taken into Pharaoh's house. • And for her sake he dealt well with Abram; and he had sheep, oxen, male donkeys, male and female slaves, female donkeys, and camels. • But the LORD afflicted Pharaoh and his house with great plagues because of Sarai, Abram's wife. • So Pharaoh called Abram, and said, 'What is this you have done to me? Why did you not tell me that she was your wife? • Why did you say, "She is my sister," so that I took her for my wife? Now

20 then, here is your wife, take her, and be gone.' • And Pharaoh gave his men orders concerning him; and they set him on the way, with his wife and all that he had.

3.1 • So Abram went up from Egypt, he and his wife, and all that he had, and Lot with him, into the Negeb.

(NRSV)

Abraham in Egypt

This is one of the most remarkable of all the stories about the patriarchs, not least because versions of it are found in two other places in Genesis. In [Ch. 20] it is told of Abraham, Sarah and a Philistine king Abimelech; in [Ch. 26] of Isaac, Rebecca and Abimelech. The repetition shows the importance, or at least the popularity, of the story; similarly in the *Chanson de Roland* the hero's death is narrated three times. In this version J typically expresses no criticism of

Abraham in Egypt (cont.)

Abraham for sacrificing his wife's honour to save his own skin (a mere brother would not have to be killed by one who wanted Sarai). Yet *Pharaoh and his house* are visited by *great plagues* (in [Ch. 20], barrenness) as punishment for his taking her into his harem.

What then was the appeal of this story, which seems to us so discreditable, and why was it inserted here? Its appeal derives from its inclusion of some favourite national motifs: the beauty of Hebrew women, admired by gentiles (cp. Judith, Esther); the astuteness of Hebrew men in outwitting them (cp. Samson, David); and the protection given by God. The

placing of the story here is due to its combination with other motifs viz. (i) a move to Egypt to avoid famine, (ii) a defeat of Pharaoh through plagues and (iii) a return to Canaan. Placed at the very beginning of the patriarchal narrative, these motifs anticipate the book of Exodus.

The version in [Ch. 20] softens the story. Abraham explains that Sarah is genetically his half-sister, being daughter of the same father. Abimelech takes her into his harem but is warned by God not to touch her. The third version [Ch. 26] comes back to the story and gives it a humorous twist, again with no excuses made for the patriarch.

The Promise of the Land

13. 2,5 Now Abram was very rich in livestock, in silver, and in gold. • Lot, who went with Abram, also had flocks and herds and tents, • so that the land could not support both of them living together; for their possessions were so great that they could not live together, • and there was strife between the herders of Abram's livestock and the herders of Lot's livestock. At that time the Canaanites and the Perizzites lived in the land. • Then Abram said to Lot, 'Let there be no strife between you and me, and between your herders and my herders; for we are kindred. • Is not the whole land before you? Separate yourself from me. If you take the left hand, then I will go to the right; or if you take the right hand, then I will go to the left.'

10   • Lot looked about him, and saw that the plain of the Jordan was well watered everywhere like the garden of the LORD, like the land of Egypt, in the direction of Zoar; this was before the LORD had destroyed Sodom and Gomorrah. • So Lot chose for himself all the plain of the Jordan, and Lot journeyed eastward; thus they separated from each other. • Abram settled in the land of Canaan, while Lot settled among the cities of the Plain and moved his tent as far as Sodom. • Now the people of Sodom were wicked, great sinners against the LORD.   ▸

The Promise of the Land

The story of Abraham's parting from *Lot* is introduced to lead up to the events of Chs 18 and 19. It is plausible. The dispute over limited grazing-grounds, tactfully ascribed to the *herders*, is natural. From near *Bethel* it is indeed possible to see *the plain of the Jordan* down to the southern end of the Dead Sea – which we are to suppose did not yet exist. The fertility of the land is delightfully

compared both to paradise and to *Egypt*, and Lot made up his mind quickly. The narrative hints at the different characters of the two men: Abraham generous in giving his nephew the choice, Lot rash, first in choosing from so far away, and then in moving *his tent* near to *Sodom* the *wicked*. At the same time God's judgement is foreshadowed: Lot is doomed like Sodom, and his land will

The Promise of the Land (cont.)

• The LORD said to Abram, after Lot had separated from him, 'Raise your eyes now, and look from the place where you are, northward and southward and eastward and westward, • for all the land that you see I will give to you and to your offspring forever. • I will make your offspring like the dust of the earth; so that if one can count the dust of the earth, your offspring also can be counted. • Rise up, walk through the length and the breadth of the land, for I will give it to you.' • So Abram moved his tent, and came and settled by the oaks of Mamre, which are at Hebron; and there he built an altar to the LORD.   (NRSV)

The Promise of the Land (cont.)

fall to Abraham's side of the family. The promise in vv.15–17 repeats that of 12.7 and amplifies it on the ground. As we saw before, it is a double one: of *land* and *offspring*. To *walk through the length and breadth of* a piece of land was a standard ANE formality to mark its acquisition.

Abraham's Hopes of a Son

Abram's wife Sarai had borne him no children. She had, however, an Egyptian slave-girl named Hagar, • and Sarai said to Abram, 'The LORD has not let me have a child. Take my slave-girl; perhaps through her I shall have a son.' Abram heeded what his wife said. • He lay with Hagar and she conceived, and when she knew that she was pregnant, she looked down on her mistress. • Sarai complained to Abram, 'I am being wronged, you must do something about it. It was I who gave my slave-girl into your arms, but since she has known that she is pregnant, she has despised me. May the LORD see justice done between you and me.' • Abram replied, 'Your slave-girl is in your hands, deal with her as you please.' So Sarai ill-treated her and she ran away from her mistress.

• The angel of the LORD came upon Hagar by a spring in the wilderness, the spring on the road to Shur, • and he said, 'Hagar, Sarai's slave-girl, where have you come from and where are you going?' She answered, 'I am running away from Sarai my mistress.' • The angel of the LORD said to her:

'You are with child and will bear a son.
    You are to name him Ishmael,
        because the LORD has heard of your ill-treatment.
He will be like the wild ass,
    his hand will be against everyone
and everyone's hand against him,
    and he will live at odds with all his kin.'   (REB)

Abraham's Hopes of a Son

Abraham had been promised descendants, but Sarah still did not conceive. Instead of trusting God, the couple resorted to a procedure which was in itself perfectly respectable but which led to unexpected complications. The story thus serves to build up suspense as we wait for the fulfilment of the promise.

Documents from the ANE fill in the legal background. If a wife proved barren, she could give *her slave-girl* to her husband as his concubine. Any child born counted as the wife's: in the Hebrew phrase [Gen 30.3] it was born 'on the knees' of the wife. If the concubine then *looked down on her mistress*,

Abraham's Hopes of a Son (cont.)

she was reduced to the status of a slave and presumably returned to the possession of the wife.

Here too the arrangement is unsuccessful, and all three parties share the blame. Sarah is aggressive, blaming both God (2) and Abraham (5). *Hagar* is tactless (4) and defiant (8). Abraham shuffles uneasily between two strong women. The *son* so born cannot be the heir to the promise of the land, but God has another future for him. The Ishmaelites were a tribe of rough nomads who moved round the northern part of the Sinai peninsula between the C12th and C9th BC, and the story is able to provide an etymology for their name: *Ishmael* = God has heard. Can the reader perhaps detect a lurking note of admiration for them as for their untamed ancestress?

Circumcision as the Mark of the Covenant

17. 1 When Abram was ninety-nine years old, the LORD appeared to him and said, 'I am God Almighty. Live always in my presence and be blameless, • so that I may make my covenant with you and give you many descendants.' • Abram bowed low, and God went on, • 'This is my covenant with you: you are to be the father of many

8 nations. • As a possession for all time I shall give you and your descendants after you the land in which you now are aliens, the whole of Canaan, and I shall be their God.'

• God said to Abraham, 'For your part, you must keep my covenant, you and

10 your descendants after you, generation by generation. • This is how you are to keep this covenant between myself and you and your descendants after you: circumcise yourselves, every male among you. • You must circumcise the flesh of your foreskin, and it will be the sign of the covenant between us.'   (REB)

Circumcision as the Mark of the Covenant

Ch. 17 contains P's version of the promises to Abraham. It is in typical P style, i.e. full of legal repetitions, here pruned. But P introduces one crucial addition, namely the requirement of Abraham's *response* to the promise, thus constituting a *covenant** in the fuller sense. In putting the covenant so early, P is here running counter to the general thrust of the OT, whereby it was made not with Abraham but with Moses.

The outward sign of Abraham's response is to *be circumcised*. Circumcision was a common practice in the western part of the Fertile Crescent, as also in many other parts of the world. As well as the Canaanites, the Egyptians practised it; the Philistines were the odd men out in not doing so. Actually it does not feature much in the OT before the exile. Then, however, since it was not practised by Babylonians, it came to be the sign par excellence of loyalty to the LORD; and it is that period which is reflected in P's narrative.

P's chapter contains also one minor addition. In the course of it [vv. 5,15] he announces changes of names from Abram and Sarai to Abraham and Sarah. He gives these changes theological significance, but in fact they are no more than dialect variants.

The Promise of a Son to Sarah

1 The LORD appeared to him at the Oak of Mamre while he was sitting by the entrance of the tent during the hottest part of the day. • He looked up, and there he saw three men standing near him. As soon as he saw them he ran from the entrance of the tent to greet them, and bowed to the ground. • 'My lord,' he said, 'if I find favour with you, please do not pass your servant by. • Let me have a little water brought, and
5 you can wash your feet and have a rest under the tree. • Let me fetch a little bread and you can refresh yourselves before going further, now that you have come in your servant's direction.' They replied, 'Do as you say.'

   • Abraham hurried to the tent and said to Sarah, 'Quick, knead three measures of best flour and make loaves.' • Then, running to the herd, Abraham took a fine and tender calf and gave it to the servant, who hurried to prepare it. • Then taking curds, milk and the calf which had been prepared, he laid all before them, and they ate while he remained standing near them under the tree.

   • 'Where is your wife Sarah?' they asked him. 'She is in the tent,' he replied.
10 • Then his guest said, 'I shall come back to you next year, and then your wife Sarah will have a son.' Sarah was listening at the entrance of the tent behind him. • Now Abraham and Sarah were old, well on in years, and Sarah had ceased to have her monthly periods. • So Sarah laughed to herself, thinking, 'Now that I am past the age of childbearing, and my husband is an old man, is pleasure to come my way again?' • But the LORD asked Abraham, 'Why did Sarah laugh and say, "Am I really going to have a child now that I am old?" • Nothing is impossible for the LORD. I shall come back to you at the same time next year and Sarah will have
15 a son.' • Sarah said, 'I did not laugh,' lying because she was afraid. But he replied, 'Oh yes, you did laugh.'   (NJB)

The Promise of a Son to Sarah

One day, in the drowsy noontide haze, Abraham *was sitting* for coolness in the door of his tent when *he looked up and saw three men. We* know that in some mysterious way they represent the LORD. Abraham does not, at least to start with, though the MT* *My lord* allows a certain ambiguity of interpretation.

The scene that follows is delightfully told. Abraham is portrayed as hospitable but fulsome (compare his long speech with their curt reply), fussy (he scurries about himself and chivvies both Sarah and the servant) and somewhat unctuous (compare *a little water* and *a little bread* with the excellent meal which follows). The formalities are observed: Abraham stands waiting upon the visitors while Sarah remains hidden indoors, eavesdropping. The climax comes with her bitter, incredulous *laugh*: why, not only had she reached the menopause, but the couple had even ceased to make love! – matters to which God, in rebuking her, does not refer.

Sarah's laugh is what distinguishes this story from the many tales like it where gods visit mortals incognito, often to test their hospitality. In one Greek legend, three gods visit a childless peasant and in return for hospitality grant him a son. A pagan origin for the story of Ch. 18 would account for the feature which is otherwise unique in the OT, namely that YHWH actually *ate* with his host, both here and in the sequel (19.3).

Abraham Intercedes for Sodom

18. 16 Then the men set out from there, and they looked toward Sodom; and Abraham went with them to set them on their way. • The LORD said, 'Shall I hide from Abraham what I am about to do, • seeing that Abraham shall become a great and mighty nation, and all the nations of the earth shall be blessed in him? • No, for I have chosen him, that he may charge his children and his household after him to keep the way of the LORD by doing righteousness and justice; so that the LORD may bring 20 about for Abraham what he has promised him.' • Then the LORD said, 'How great is the outcry against Sodom and Gomorrah and how very grave their sin! • I must go down and see whether they have done altogether according to the outcry that has come to me; and if not, I will know.'

• So the men turned from there, and went toward Sodom, while Abraham remained standing before the LORD. • Then Abraham came near and said, 'Will you indeed sweep away the righteous with the wicked? • Suppose there are fifty righteous within the city; will you then sweep away the place and not forgive it for the fifty 25 righteous who are in it? • Far be it from you to do such a thing, to slay the righteous with the wicked, so that the righteous fare as the wicked! Far be that from you! Shall not the Judge of all the earth do what is just?' • And the LORD said, 'If I find at Sodom fifty righteous in the city, I will forgive the whole place for their sake.' • Abraham answered, 'Let me take it upon myself to speak to the LORD, I who am but dust and ashes. • Suppose five of the fifty righteous are lacking? Will you destroy the whole city for lack of five?' And he said, 'I will not destroy it if I find forty-five there.' • Again he spoke to him, 'Suppose forty are found there.' He 30 answered, 'For the sake of forty I will not do it.' • Then he said, 'Oh do not let the LORD be angry if I speak. Suppose thirty are found there.' He answered, 'I will not do it, if I find thirty there.' • He said, 'Let me take it upon myself to speak to the LORD. Suppose twenty are found there.' He answered, 'For the sake of twenty I will not destroy it.' • Then he said, 'Oh do not let the LORD be angry if I speak just once more. Suppose ten are found there.' He answered, 'For the sake of ten I will not destroy it.' • And the LORD went his way, when he had finished speaking to Abraham; and Abraham returned to his place.   (NRSV)

Abraham Intercedes for Sodom

This section is a skilful bridge-passage linking the story of Abraham with that of Lot. Courtesy required Abraham to set his three visitors on their way. This turns out to be down to the Jordan valley, which is in sight. As they walk, God reflects, in the light of his relationship to Abraham, upon what he is *about to do* to Sodom. His reflections reveal to us something new about that relationship. We knew that he had promised certain things to Abraham. We now learn that there was a condition attached to the promises, namely that Abraham should *do righteousness and justice*. And God

himself also has a problem of justice on his own hands. There is an *outcry against Sodom*, which needs investigation.

Two of the three men leave for that purpose, but YHWH remains standing. The MT* of v.22 contains a great rarity, a note recording that a scribe has changed the text. Originally it read 'YHWH still stood before Abraham'. But the Heb. word for 'stand before' could imply subservience, so the good scribe altered it – and owned up. Abraham himself shows the same anxious deference as before, but more steel in pushing against a limit which he knows must come. For, as the phrasing

Abraham Intercedes for Sodom (cont.)

of v.23 shows, what is uppermost in his mind is the fate of his nephew Lot.

But the LORD's concern is entirely general, and his responses judicially precise. Everywhere in the ancient world it was accepted that whole communities stood to be punished for the wrong-doing of some of their number. Abraham, naively assuming Lot and his family to be 'righteous', raises the question: how small can an innocent nucleus be and still affect the life – and so the just punishment – of the community? The dialogue is not a protest against the idea of collective responsibility. Elsewhere in the OT such protests were indeed made, but the nearest we get to one here is the hint at the very end of the story, that 'God took thought for Abraham by rescuing Lot' (19.29). God had evidently understood the subtext of Abraham's argument.

Perhaps the most notable feature of this dialogue is to be found in Abraham's question *Shall not the Judge of all the earth do what is just?* That even the gods are subject to justice is a thought which was familiar to the Greeks. But that a man should point this out to the Judge himself has an audacity which is peculiarly Hebrew.

Sodom is Destroyed, Lot Spared

.1 The two angels came to Sodom in the evening while Lot was sitting by the city gate. When he saw them, he rose to meet them and bowing low • he said, 'I pray you, sirs, turn aside to your servant's house to spend the night there and bathe your feet. You can continue your journey in the morning.' 'No,' they answered, 'we shall spend the night in the street.' • But Lot was so insistent that they accompanied him into his house. He prepared a meal for them, baking unleavened bread for them to eat.

• Before they had lain down to sleep, the men of Sodom, both young and old,
5 everyone without exception, surrounded the house. • They called to Lot: 'Where are the men who came to you tonight? Bring them out to us so that we may have intercourse with them.' • Lot went out into the doorway to them, and, closing the door behind him, • said, 'No, my friends, do not do anything so wicked. • Look, I have two daughters, virgins both of them; let me bring them out to you, and you can do what you like with them. But do nothing to these men, because they have   ▸

Sodom is Destroyed, Lot Spared

Of the three 'men' in Ch.18, one had stayed behind while the other two went on down into Sodom. The journey is 40 miles over rough country, but the arithmetic is irrelevant to such 'men'. In fact the two are here, for the first time, called *angels*. That is a term which in the earlier books of the Bible denotes not a special class of being but a human form in which God appears to men. Here as often the angel is eventually (21) revealed as God.

Lot's welcome (1–3) is clearly meant to be compared and contrasted with Abraham's. The busy townsman is found sitting where the elders sit in the evening, *by the city gate*, exchanging news and dispensing justice. His offer of hospitality is as formal as Abraham's, but the reality falls short: *unleavened* (3) implies ordinary. The visitors, as before, are curt.

The second episode which follows (4–11) is intentionally crude. The 'angels', whom we must suppose young and handsome, excited the lust of the Sodomites, who came *without exception* (cp.18.32). Lot, as host, has an overriding duty to protect his guests. But his offer of his *daughters* is vile by any standards. True, in some societies a host is expected to provide an unmarried daughter to warm

Sodom is Destroyed, Lot Spared (cont.)

19. 9   come under the shelter of my roof.' • They said, 'Out of our way! This fellow has
come and settled here as an alien, and does he now take it upon himself to judge us?
We will treat you worse than them.' They crowded in on Lot and pressed close to

10   break down the door. • But the two men inside reached out, pulled Lot into the
house, and shut the door. • Then they struck those in the doorway, both young and
old, with blindness so that they could not find the entrance.

• The two men said to Lot, 'Have you anyone here, sons-in-law, sons, or
daughters, or anyone else belonging to you in the city? Get them out of this place,
• because we are going to destroy it. The LORD is aware of the great outcry against
its citizens and has sent us to destroy it.' • So Lot went out and urged his sons-in-
law to get out of the place at once. 'The LORD is about to destroy the city,' he said.
But they did not take him seriously.

15   • As soon as it was dawn, the angels urged Lot: 'Quick, take your wife and your
two daughters who are here, or you will be destroyed when the city is punished.'
• When he delayed, they grabbed his hand and the hands of his wife and two
daughters, because the LORD had spared him, and they led him to safety outside the
city. • After they had brought them out, one said, 'Flee for your lives! Do not look
back or stop anywhere in the plain. Flee to the hills or you will be destroyed.' • Lot
replied, 'No, sirs! • You have shown your servant favour, and even more by your
unfailing care you have saved my life, but I cannot escape to the hills; I shall be

20   overtaken by the disaster, and die. • Look, here is a town, only a small place, near
enough for me to get to quickly. Let me escape to this small place and save my life.'
• He said to him, 'I grant your request: I shall not overthrow the town you speak of.
• But flee there quickly, because I can do nothing until you are there.' That is why
the place was called Zoar. • The sun had risen over the land as Lot entered Zoar,
• and the LORD rained down fire and brimstone from the skies on Sodom and

25   Gomorrah. • He overthrew those cities and destroyed all the plain, with everyone
living there and everything growing in the ground. • But Lot's wife looked back,
and she turned into a pillar of salt.   ▸

Sodom is Destroyed, Lot Spared (cont.)

the bed of a guest. This offer however goes
further. The crude language in which it is
expressed, and the sequel to it in vv.30–
36, show the narrator's disapproval.

For the rest, we may admire Lot's
courage in v.6, but there is something
comic in the way he has to be rescued by
his protégés (10). The Sodomites show
their contempt for him by speaking of him
in the third person (*this fellow*, 9), but they
too are last seen pathetically fumbling for
the front door (11). As often, comedy is
quite at home in Hebrew epic narrative.

This second episode is resolved, and
the tension lessened, by the miraculous

blinding of the assailants. But the guilt of
Sodom has now been established beyond
doubt (cp.18.21), and we await its
punishment. The third episode (12–22)
delays the climax and thus builds up the
tension again. The incredulity of the two
fiancés shows the complacency of Sodom.
Lot is pathetic: led by the *hand* like a child
(16) and flustered into wordiness (19–20),
with his small-mindedness symbolised by
his preference for *a place called Zoar*,
meaning precisely *small* (20).

The climax comes in the early
morning. Two verses suffice to record the
obliteration of the Cities of the Plain, but

Sodom is Destroyed, Lot Spared (cont.)

• Early next morning Abraham went to the place where he had stood in the presence of the LORD. • As he looked over Sodom and Gomorrah and all the wide extent of the plain, he saw thick smoke rising from the earth like smoke from a kiln. • Thus it was, when God destroyed the cities of the plain, he took thought for Abraham by rescuing Lot from the total destruction of the cities where he had been living.

• Because Lot was afraid to stay in Zoar, he went up from there and settled with his two daughters in the hill-country, where he lived with them in a cave. • The elder daughter said to the younger, 'Our father is old and there is not a man in the country to come to us in the usual way. • Come now, let us ply our father with wine and then lie with him and in this way preserve the family through our father.' • That night they gave him wine to drink, and the elder daughter came and lay with him, and he did not know when she lay down and when she got up. • Next day the elder said to the younger, 'Last night I lay with my father. Let us ply him with wine again tonight; then you go in and lie with him. So we shall preserve the family through our father.' • They gave their father wine to drink that night also; and the younger daughter went and lay with him, and he did not know when she lay down and when she got up. • In this way both of Lot's daughters came to be pregnant by their father.   (REB)

Sodom is Destroyed, Lot Spared (cont.)

their echoes are heard right through the Bible. The sin of Sodom is variously given in its later books: by no means always sodomy, sometimes no more than lack of hospitality. But the punishment is kept perennially present to the imagination by that stark and desolate landscape. The Dead Sea provides a natural location for the story, known in many forms in many parts of the world, of a city punished for its wickedness by earthquake or other disaster, of the few who were saved, and of the one who *looked back and* was *turned into* a rock or other well-known feature of the landscape.

But the location could well have a historical basis, preserved in folk-memory. The Dead Sea lies on a geological fault which extends right down to the Great Rift Valley in East Africa, and as such is especially liable to earthquakes. Below it lie reservoirs of oil and gas: when these are 'suddenly discharged, the gas explodes, carrying high up into the air masses of the oil which fall back in fiery rain and will float afire on water'. Given that the Dead Sea is also full of sulphur (brimstone), such an explosion would be exactly described by the phrase *fire and brimstone*, i.e. burning sulphur.

The final scene (27–28) rounds off the story brilliantly. It reintroduces Abraham, who looks silently down upon the valley as he had looked originally with Lot (13.10). All he can now see is destruction, but at his distance it brings to mind the peaceful image of a domestic craft. Even the addition in v.29 of P's flat summary of the whole story cannot spoil J's resolution of it.

The story of Lot and *his daughters* (30–36) is a postscript to the preceding narrative. It provides poetic justice in answer to his treatment of his daughters in 19.8. The roles of the protagonists are completely reversed between the two incidents. Lot switches from active to passive (his movement in v.30 continues the picture of his pusillanimity), but his actions are presented as morally ambiguous in both alike. The daughters switch from passive to active, and in the latter role they are evidently held up for admiration, like Tamar in Ch. 38, as women who will go to any lengths to preserve the stock.

The Birth of Isaac

21. 1 The LORD showed favour to Sarah as he had promised, and made good what he had said about her. • She conceived and at the time foretold by God she bore a son to Abraham in his old age. • The son whom Sarah bore to him Abraham named Isaac, • and when Isaac was eight days old Abraham circumcised him, as decreed by
5 God. • Abraham was a hundred years old when his son Isaac was born. • Sarah said, 'God has given me good reason to laugh, and everyone who hears will laugh with me.' • She added, 'Whoever would have told Abraham that Sarah would suckle children? Yet I have borne him a son in his old age.'

• The boy grew and was weaned, and on the day of his weaning Abraham gave a great feast. • Sarah saw the son whom Hagar the Egyptian had borne to Abraham
10 playing with Isaac, • and she said to Abraham, 'Drive out this slave-girl and her son! I will not have this slave's son sharing the inheritance with my son Isaac.' • Abraham was very upset at this because of Ishmael, • but God said to him, 'Do not be upset for the boy and your slave-girl. Do as Sarah says, because it is through Isaac's line that your name will be perpetuated. • I shall make a nation of the slave-girl's son, because he also is your child.'   (REB)

The Birth of Isaac

The narrative of Isaac's birth, when it comes, falls a little flat. Its chief source, P, likes to emphasise the literal fulfilment of God's promises and commands. The *name Isaac* implies '*laugh*' in Hebrew, and P here has Sarah pun upon it more innocently than J did in 18.12+.

The little story of *Ishmael* and Isaac seems merely to make explicit the demotion of the first-born son, a favourite motif in Genesis and already foreshadowed in Ch. 16. But it contains historical dynamite. For ever since the C1st AD there has been a tradition that the Arabs are descended from Ishmael, and Palestinian Arabs today claim on the strength of it that, by ancient inheritance law, they are entitled to a *double* portion of the land. Israelis however can point to this chapter in rejecting the claim.

The Testing of Abraham

22. 1 After these things God tested Abraham, and said to him, 'Abraham!' And he said, 'Here am I.' • He said, 'Take your son, your only son Isaac, whom you love, and go to the land of Moriah, and offer him there as a burnt offering upon one of the mountains of which I shall tell you.' • So Abraham rose early in the morning,   ▶

The Testing of Abraham

The story of the testing of Abraham is one of the finest – though also one of the blackest – in the whole of the OT. The opening words throw the emphasis of the whole story on to *Ha-Elohim*: it is *God* (with the definite article) who *tested Abraham*. This is the last and severest test of Abraham's faith. That information, given at the start (v.1), has two consequences. God is not presented as demanding human sacrifice; and the reader is to that extent spared the mental torture of Abraham. But God *is* presented as putting Abraham to that torture, and the normal reader's revulsion remains scarcely abated. Nor is it any help to say that the author's emphasis is all on Abraham's obedience, and that therefore we should not fuss about the circumstances.

The problem here is a theological one, and it is acute for a reader who believes

The Testing of Abraham (cont.)

5 saddled his ass, and took two of his young men with him, and his son Isaac; and he cut the wood for the burnt offering, and arose and went to the place of which God had told him. • On the third day Abraham lifted up his eyes and saw the place afar off. • Then Abraham said to his young men, 'Stay here with the ass; I and the lad will go yonder and worship, and come again to you.' • And Abraham took the wood of the burnt offering, and laid it on Isaac his son; and he took in his hand the fire and the knife. So they went both of them together. • And Isaac said to his father Abraham, 'My father!' And he said, 'Here am I, my son.' He said, 'Behold, the fire and the wood; but where is the lamb for a burnt offering?' • Abraham said, 'God will provide himself the lamb for a burnt offering, my son.' So they went both of them together.

The Testing of Abraham (cont.)

both in the goodness of God and in the authority of scripture. When Agamemnon had to sacrifice his daughter to placate Artemis, Aeschylus could present him as a man faced with an appalling dilemma; but no theological problem arose, because the gods were (i) plural and (ii) amoral. Later Judaism saw the problem posed by Gen 22 and was uncomfortable. Already in C2nd BC it was suggested that God had been tempted by Satan (as in Job) to test Abraham. By the time of Jesus it had been further suggested that Abraham had told Isaac of the command he had received and that Isaac went willingly to his fate. This latter idea appealed to Christians, who could see it as prefiguring the crucifixion. It was also incorporated in the Koran, which has Isaac saying: 'my father, do what you are bidden; if God please, you will find me patient' (Sura 37).

In these ways later Judaism softened the edges to help save God's goodness. Can we find anything similar in Genesis? Certainly the story is told with delicacy as well as power. God fully recognises what he is asking of Abraham. His first word *take* has a 'please' attached to it, which is very rare in a command of God; and he repeats the phrase *your son, your only*

son three times (2, 12, 16). The Hebrew word translated 'only' is not to be taken literally. It rather implies 'special': Isaac was not just the dear and unexpected son of his father's old age, he is also the heir to the promises. Of Abraham's thoughts we are told nothing, either now or later: typically they have to be gathered from his actions. So in v.3 his response is prompt: *early in the morning* is subjective time.

The journey itself is told quickly, but as they approach *the place* the tempo slows. With forced matter-of-factness Abraham sends away the men: he does not wish them to see, and he will not tell them, what is going to happen. So in the *Agamemnon* the chorus-leader says of the sacrifice of Iphigeneia: 'What happened next I neither saw nor tell.' He and Isaac then set off carrying the materials for the sacrifice. The oppressive silence between them on that last journey is broken only by Isaac's question (is it naive, or does he already fear?) and by Abraham's evasive reply (8), which means different things to him, to Isaac and to the reader. That ironical exchange is framed by a repeated sentence of unsurpassed poignancy: *So they went both of them together.*

	The Testing of Abraham (cont.)
22.9	• When they came to the place of which God had told him, Abraham built an altar there, and laid the wood in order, and bound Isaac his son, and laid him on the
10	altar, upon the wood. • Then Abraham put forth his hand, and took the knife to slay his son. • But the angel of the LORD called to him from heaven, and said, 'Abraham, Abraham!' And he said, 'Here am I.' • He said, 'Do not lay your hand on the lad or do anything to him; for now I know that you fear God, seeing you have not withheld your son, your only son, from me.' • And Abraham lifted up his eyes and looked, and behold, behind him was a ram, caught in a thicket by his horns; and Abraham went and took the ram, and offered it up as a burnt offering instead of his son. • So Abraham called the name of that place The LORD will provide; as it is said to this day, 'On the mount of the LORD it shall be provided.'
15	• And the angel of the LORD called to Abraham a second time from heaven, • and said, 'By myself I have sworn, says the LORD, because you have done this, and have not withheld your son, your only son, • I will indeed bless you, and I will multiply your descendants as the stars of heaven and as the sand which is on the seashore. And your descendants shall possess the gate of their enemies, • and by your descendants shall all the nations of the earth bless themselves, because you have obeyed my voice.' • So Abraham returned to his young men, and they arose and went together to Beersheba; and Abraham dwelt at Beersheba. (RSV)

The Testing of Abraham (cont.)

As the climax approaches (9–10) the pace slows even further. Each separate movement of the grief-stricken father is recorded in chilling detail as he steels himself to do what he has to do. Only at the very last moment (11) does God intervene. Down to v.10 it was Elohim or Ha-Elohim, but from v.11 on it is *the angel of the LORD* (i.e. YHWH) who speaks. The change fits exactly the schema proposed by the rabbinic scholar, that the Hebrew Bible uses Elohim when God is severe, YHWH when he is compassionate (see p.35).

In the concluding section (15–19) YHWH reaffirms the promises already made to Abraham, but this version is more emphatic and imposing than the previous ones. The rare introduction *By myself I have sworn* is new, and so is the reference to *possessing the gate of their enemies*. YHWH is fulsome in his language and in his reward, especially by contrast with the spare preceding narrative, as if to suggest that his conscience is uneasy.

When one observes that this last section is an addition to the main narrative (*a second time* in v.15 gives the game away), it does seem to be further evidence of an early disquiet about God's role in the story. The tradition itself was there, and must be transmitted. The author could not be as free with it as the Koran, but he did what he could to soften it. In doing so, he implied that God is capable of regret. Daring as this may seem, it is far from unique in the OT.

This narrative therefore raises many profound issues, only some of which have been touched on here. Politically, it has been of great importance both to Judaism and to Islam. Tradition from [2 Chron 3.1] onwards identified Mount *Moriah* with the rocky hill in Jerusalem on which Solomon built his temple. Now it is the site of the Muslim Dome of the Rock, within which the sacred rock is exposed to view. The story also forms the basis of Auerbach's famous comparison between Hebrew and Greek story-telling as between two different ways of representing reality (see p.783).

Abraham's Purchase of a Burial-plot

1 Sarah lived to be a hundred and twenty-seven years old, • and she died in Hebron in Canaan. Abraham went in to mourn over Sarah and to weep for her. • When at last he rose and left the presence of his dead one, he approached the Hittites: • 'I am an alien and a settler among you,' he said. 'Make over to me some ground among 5 you for a burial-place, that I may bury my dead.' • The Hittites answered, • 'Listen to us, sir: you are a mighty prince among us; bury your dead in the best grave we have. There is not one of us who would deny you his grave or hinder you from burying your dead.'

• Abraham rose and bowing low to the Hittites, the people of that region, • he said to them, 'If you have a mind to help me about the burial, then listen to me: speak to Ephron son of Zohar on my behalf, • and ask him to grant me the cave that belongs to him at Machpelah, at the far end of his land. In your presence let him make it over to me for the full price, so that I may take possession of it as a burial- 10 place.' • Ephron was sitting with the other Hittites and in the hearing of all who had assembled at the city gate he gave Abraham this answer: • 'No, sir; hear me: I shall make you a gift of the land and also give you the cave which is on it. In the presence of my people I give it to you; so bury your dead.' • Abraham bowed low before the people • and said to Ephron in their hearing, 'Do you really mean it? But listen to me – let me give you the price of the land: take it from me, and I shall bury 15 my dead there.' • Ephron answered, • 'Listen, sir: land worth four hundred shekels of silver, what is that between me and you! You may bury your dead there.' • Abraham closed the bargain with him and weighed out the amount that Ephron had named in the hearing of the Hittites, four hundred shekels of the standard recognized by merchants.   ▸

Abraham's Purchase of a Burial-plot

Ch. 23 offers a relaxation of tension after Ch.22, but the incident it records is important to the story. *A burial-place* for Sarah would provide a family tomb pending a more permanent settlement. But the plot must be acquired with full and public legal title, and that is what Abraham sets out to achieve.

The narrative is a delightful mixture of serious procedures with humorous 'oriental' bargaining and a great deal of expostulation – note the four-fold *listen to me* etc. in vv.6, 8, 13, 15. After ritual mourning for Sarah, Abraham approaches the community for formal permission to buy – though both he and they avoid the crude verb (Heb. *qānāh*) throughout the negotiations. The *Hittites* are pre-Semitic occupants of the country, from whom he as a resident *alien* can claim no property rights. They answer his modest self-description with an honorific address (thus putting the price up) and also offer to give him burial space for nothing (which puts it up further). But Abraham must buy: at last he names the cave and its owner, and asks the rest to bring pressure to bear on him to sell. *Ephron* repeats the offer of a gift, and brings in *the land* the cave was on – for which Abraham had not asked! Abraham, flustered (the translation of v.13 is uncertain), makes a final offer to buy. Ephron blandly names an exorbitant price, but *what is that between* friends? The bargaining over, we revert to legal formalities. The silver must be of the proper commercial *standard,* and the legal document be drawn up before witnesses in the regular terminology of

Abraham's Purchase of a Burial-plot (cont.)

23. 17   • So the plot of land belonging to Ephron at Machpelah to the east of Mamre, the plot, the cave that is on it, with all the trees in the whole area, became the • legal possession of Abraham, in the presence of all the Hittites who had assembled at the city gate.• After this Abraham buried his wife Sarah in the cave on the plot of land

20   at Machpelah to the east of Mamre, which is Hebron, in Canaan. • Thus, by purchase from the Hittites, the plot and the cave on it became Abraham's possession as a burial-place.

(REB)

Abraham's Purchase of a Burial-plot (cont.)

an ANE land register.

Abraham was later buried there alongside Sarah, and so were Isaac, Rebecca, Leah and Jacob. Centuries later a mosque was built over the traditional location of the cave.

Stories of the Patriarchs Isaac and Jacob: Genesis 24–36

A Wife for Isaac

24. 1   • Abraham was by now a very old man, and the Lord had blessed him in all that he did. • Abraham said to the servant who had been longest in his service and was in charge of all he owned, 'Give me your solemn oath: • I want you to swear by the Lord, the God of heaven and earth, that you will not take a wife for my son from the women of the Canaanites among whom I am living. • You must go to my own

5   country and to my own kindred to find a wife for my son Isaac.' • 'What if the woman is unwilling to come with me to this country?' the servant asked. 'Must I take your son back to the land you came from?' • Abraham said to him, 'On no account are you to take my son back there. • The Lord the God of heaven who took me from my father's house and the land of my birth, the Lord who swore to me that he would give this land to my descendants – he will send his angel before you, and you will take a wife from there for my son. • If the woman is unwilling to come with you, then you will be released from your oath to me; only you must not take my son back there.' • The servant then put his hand under his master Abraham's thigh and swore that oath.   ▸

A Wife for Isaac

This charming tale links the story-cycles of Abraham and Isaac. Its ceremonious length, its interest in human relationships within the family, and its relative lightness in theology all bring it close in tone to the story of Joseph (Chs 37–45).

There are four main characters in the tale. *Abraham* is nearing the end of his life. Verses 3–8 contain his last recorded wishes. He is concerned above all not to invalidate God's promise: for this reason *Isaac* must neither return to live in Mesopotamia (called *Aramnaharaim* in

v.10) nor marry a Canaanite woman. The complexity of the commission given by Abraham, coupled with the solemn nature of the *oath* he administers (explained in v.9), strongly suggests that these should be read as his deathbed instructions; and that is corroborated by the absence of any mention of him when the servant returns after completing the mission (vv.62–7).

The servant is no ordinary slave but a man in responsible position, careful to get his instructions right, and loyal and prudent in implementing them. His plan

A Wife for Isaac (cont.)

• The servant chose ten camels from his master's herds and, with all kinds of gifts from his master, he went to Aram-naharaim, to the town where Nahor lived. • Towards evening, the time when the women go out to draw water, he made the camels kneel down by the well outside the town. • 'LORD God of my master Abraham,' he said, 'give me good fortune this day; keep faith with my master Abraham. • Here I am by the spring, as the women of the town come out to draw water. • I shall say to a girl, "Please lower your jar so that I may drink"; and if she answers, "Drink, and I shall water your camels also," let that be the girl whom you intend for your servant Isaac. In this way I shall know that you have kept faith with my master.'

• Before he had finished praying, he saw Rebecca coming out with her water-jar on her shoulder. She was the daughter of Bethuel son of Milcah, the wife of Abraham's brother Nahor. • The girl was very beautiful and a virgin guiltless of intercourse with any man. She went down to the spring, filled her jar, and came up again. • Abraham's servant hurried to meet her and said, 'Will you give me a little water from your jar?' • 'Please drink, sir,' she answered, and at once lowered her jar on to her hand to let him drink. • When she had finished giving him a drink, she said, 'I shall draw water for your camels also until they have had enough.' • She quickly emptied her jar into the water trough, and then hurrying again to the well she drew water and watered all the camels.

• The man was watching quietly to see whether or not the LORD had made his journey successful, • and when the camels had finished drinking, he took a gold nose-ring weighing half a shekel, and two bracelets for her wrists weighing ten shekels, also of gold. • 'Tell me, please, whose daughter you are,' he said. 'Is there room in your father's house for us to spend the night?' • She answered, 'I am the daughter of Bethuel son of Nahor and Milcah; • we have plenty of straw and fodder and also room for you to spend the night.' • So the man bowed down and prostrated himself before the LORD • and said, 'Blessed be the LORD the God of my master Abraham. His faithfulness to my master has been constant and unfailing, for he has guided me to the house of my master's kinsman.' ▸

A Wife for Isaac (cont.)

(13–14) is shrewd. The village *well* was the one place where single girls could go unchaperoned in public, which is why so many romantic encounters took place there in the ancient world. The sort of wife Isaac needed would be not merely courteous, in giving the servant a *drink* himself, but also thoughtful and strong enough to *water* his *camels*. *Ten camels* would drink 1,000 litres at the end of a day's journey. The servant's formulation of the plan is cast in the form of a prayer, but it is a prayer not for any divine intervention but only for *good fortune* or (later) for *success*, terms which he uses five times in all.

His (and the reader's) hopes are soon answered. *Rebecca* not only meets his two requirements but is *beautiful* and chaste as well. The scene between them contrasts his mature calmness (21) with her youthful bustle: she is the subject of eleven verbs of action in vv.16–20, including the watering of the camels. All of this is very appropriate for the girl who will become 'the most potent of the matriarchs'.

The next moves are standard: he gives presents and enquires about her family; she offers hospitality – still not forgetting the camels (25) – and runs

A Wife for Isaac (cont.)

24. 28 • The girl ran to her mother's house and told them what had happened. • Rebecca had a brother named Laban, and, when he saw the nose-ring, and also the bracelets on his sister's wrists, and heard his sister Rebecca's account of what the man had said to her, he hurried out to the spring. When he got there he found the man still standing by the camels. • 'Come in,' he said, 'you whom the LORD has blessed. Why are you staying out here? I have prepared the house and there is a place for the camels.' • The man went into the house, while the camels were unloaded and provided with straw and fodder, and water was brought for him and his men to bathe their feet. • But when food was set before him, he protested, 'I will not eat until I have delivered my message.' Laban said, 'Let us hear it.'

35 • 'I am Abraham's servant,' he answered. • 'The LORD has greatly blessed my master, and he has become a wealthy man: the LORD has given him flocks and herds, silver and gold, male and female slaves, camels and donkeys. • My master's wife Sarah in her old age bore him a son, to whom he has assigned all that he has. • My master made me swear an oath, saying, "You must not take a wife for my son from the women of the Canaanites in whose land I am living; • but go to my father's home, to my family, to get a wife for him." • I asked, "What if the woman will not **40** come with me?" • He answered, "The LORD, in whose presence I have lived, will send his angel with you and make your journey successful. You are to take a wife for my son from my family and from my father's house; • then you will be released from the charge I have laid upon you. But if, when you come to my family, they refuse to give her to you, you will likewise be released from the charge."

• 'Today when I came to the spring, I prayed, "LORD God of my master Abraham, if you will make my journey successful, let it turn out in this way: • here I am by the spring; when a young woman comes out to draw water, I shall say to her, 'Give me a little water from your jar to drink.' • If she answers, 'Yes, do drink, and I shall draw water for your camels as well,' she is the woman whom the LORD intends for **45** my master's son." ' • Before I had finished praying, I saw Rebecca coming out with her water-jar on her shoulder. She went down to the spring and drew water, and I said to her, "Will you please give me a drink?" • At once she lowered her jar from her shoulder and said, "Drink; and I shall also water your camels." So I drank, and she also gave the camels water. • I asked her whose daughter she was, and she said, "I am the daughter of Bethuel son of Nahor and Milcah."   ◗

A Wife for Isaac (cont.)

on ahead. We learn by implication (53) that her father *Bethuel* is dead; *her mother* runs the house but she is under the care of her *brother Laban*. Laban's chief characteristic – in later chapters almost his only one – is greed (30). He presses the servant, whose blessings are so tangible, to enter and eat, but the latter loyally insists on delivering his *message* first. This he does at length, rehearsing in vv.37–48 what we have already been told in vv.3–27. But the

rehearsal is not verbatim: it includes a number of subtle variations. For example, when he comes to Abraham's interdiction upon Isaac's going to Mesopotamia, courtesy forbids him to repeat it to Laban.

His speech, like the rest of the narrative, combines the languages of God and Mammon. Having let Laban know that Abraham *has* already *assigned* his considerable wealth to Isaac, the servant hints that he may take

A Wife for Isaac (cont.)

Then I put the ring in her nose and the bracelets on her wrists, • and I bowed low in worship before the LORD. I blessed the LORD, the God of my master Abraham, who had led me by the right road to take my master's niece for his son. • Now tell me if you mean to deal loyally and faithfully with my master. If not, say so, and I shall turn elsewhere.'

• Laban replied, 'Since this is from the LORD, we can say nothing for or against it. • Here is Rebecca; take her and go. She shall be the wife of your master's son, as the LORD has decreed.' • When Abraham's servant heard what they said, he prostrated himself on the ground before the LORD.• Then he brought out silver and gold ornaments, and articles of clothing, and gave them to Rebecca, and he gave costly gifts to her brother and her mother. • He and his men then ate and drank and spent the night there.

When they rose in the morning, Abraham's servant said, 'Give me leave to go back to my master.' • Rebecca's brother and her mother replied, 'Let the girl stay with us for a few days, say ten days, and then she can go.' • But he said to them, 'Do not detain me, for it is the LORD who has granted me success. Give me leave to go back to my master.' • They said, 'Let us call the girl and see what she says.' • They called Rebecca and asked her if she would go with the man, and she answered, 'Yes, I will go.' • So they let their sister Rebecca and her maid go with Abraham's servant and his men. • They blessed Rebecca and said to her:

You are our sister,
may you be the mother of many children;
may your sons possess the cities of their enemies.

• Rebecca and her companions mounted their camels to follow the man. So the servant took Rebecca and set out.

• Isaac meanwhile had moved on as far as Beer-lahai-roi and was living in the Negeb. • One evening when he had gone out into the open country hoping to meet them, he looked and saw camels approaching. • When Rebecca saw Isaac, she dismounted from her camel, • saying to the servant, 'Who is that man walking across the open country towards us?' When the servant answered, 'It is my master,' she took her veil and covered herself. • The servant related to Isaac all that had happened. • Isaac conducted her into the tent and took her as his wife. So she became his wife, and he loved her and was consoled for the death of his mother.   (REB)

A Wife for Isaac (cont.)

his business *elsewhere* (41,49): whereupon Laban immediately makes a pious excuse to clinch the deal and receive the bride-price. The betrothal ceremony follows a pattern familiar from ANE texts: where a bride is given away by her brother, it is important that she shall explicitly declare her own agreement (58). The servant is now eager for the road – there is a hint that the atmosphere in Laban's household is corrupting – and the scene ends with a family blessing on Rebecca which arouses more than formal expectations.

Rapidly, the caravanserai returns home, to a final scene of welcome, in which *Isaac* at last appears in person. Though addressed by *the servant* as *my master*, he is even now allowed no speech. The closing words hint that he has exchanged the domination of *his mother* for that of *his wife*.

Jacob and Esau (i): Birth and Birthright

25. 21 Isaac prayed to the LORD on behalf of his wife, for she was barren. The LORD heard his prayer, and his wife Rebecca conceived. • But the children inside her struggled so much that she said, 'If this is the way of it, why go on living?' So she went to consult the LORD, • and the LORD said to her:

'There are two nations in your womb,
    your issue will be two rival peoples.
One nation will have the mastery of the other,
    and the elder will serve the younger.'

• When the time came for her confinement, there were indeed twins in her womb.

25 • The first to be born was red, altogether like a hairy cloak; so they named him Esau. • Then his brother was born, with his hand grasping Esau's heel; so they named him Jacob. Isaac was sixty years old at the time of their birth. • When the boys grew up Esau became a skilled hunter, a man of the open country. Jacob on the other hand was a quiet man, staying at home among the tents. • Isaac preferred Esau, for he had a taste for wild game; but Rebecca preferred Jacob.

• Once, when Jacob was cooking a stew, Esau returned from the countryside

30 exhausted. • Esau said to Jacob, 'Give me a mouthful of that red stuff there; I am exhausted' – hence the name given to him, Edom. • Jacob said, 'First, give me your birthright in exchange.' • Esau said, 'Here I am, at death's door; what use is a birthright to me?' • Then Jacob said, 'First give me your oath'. He gave him his oath and sold his birthright to Jacob. • Then Jacob gave him some bread and lentil stew; he ate, drank, got up and went away. That was all Esau cared about his birthright.   (NJB)

Jacob and Esau (i): Birth and Birthright

With Ch. 25 the story of the patriarchs spreads to a somewhat broader canvas. Since Ch. 12 the focus has been on the small family of Abraham, Sarah and the promised son Isaac. In Chs 25-36 the focus within the family is rather upon the relations between brother and brother, and at the same time the interest extends outside the family to include a wider society with its laws and customs, especially land-ownership and holy places. Appropriately also the composition of the narrative changes. From Chs 12–24 it was mostly made up of short units, each no longer than a chapter. From Chs.25–36 we find larger units of 2–3 chapters. Finally in Chs.37–45 we shall find a single story which links the fortunes of 'the' family to the international politics of the time.

The somewhat skeletal narrative of 25.21–34 provides an overture: it introduces the main theme of sibling rivalry, to be elaborated later in Chs 27 and 32–33. The tone is realistic, even comic. None of the four main parties comes out with credit.

Already in the womb the two brothers fought. *Rebecca*, who had waited twenty years to conceive, went to enquire at a local shrine about the omen. As often in such stories, the oracle treats the unborn children as ancestors of tribes or *nations*. There was indeed permanent hostility between the Israelites and the Edomites.

The popular etymology of *Jacob* in v.26 is of great importance to the story. His name *Ya'aqōb* is derived from *'āqē b*, meaning 'heel', and is given a special twist by the information that Jacob was grasping Esau's *heel*. Our word 'supplant' embodies the same idea: by catching someone's heel (Lat. *planta*) in a race one trips them up and so overtakes them (see 27.36).

Jacob and Esau (i): Birth and Birthright (cont.)

For *Esau* two separate etymologies are given. The Hebrew for *red* is *ādhom*, which fits *Edom* (30), though not Esau (25). The Hebrew for *hairy* (25) is *sāīr*, which puns on Seir, a mountain of the Edom region.

But the 'red' and 'hairy' have other connotations more important for the story. They represent not a tribe but a way of life, that of the *hunter* as opposed to the shepherd. The two differ in character to the point of mutual hostility and stereotyping: the 'boorish' hunter and the 'grasping' shepherd. And that is how the brothers behave towards each other. Jacob is clever but cold and legalistic. He drives

a hard bargain: his imperative *give* lacks the 'please' which is present in the Hebrew of Esau's request. Esau himself 'is all inarticulate appetite' (Alter), and in v.34 he is off again without a word. But most important is the short-sightedness which caused him to sell his *birthright* i.e. the two-thirds inheritance which in ANE law went to the elder of two sons.

The narrator is unusually free with his comments hereabouts. The final verdict is given against Esau (34): like Ishmael, he is not fit to inherit the promise to Abraham. But Jacob is not held up for admiration, and v.28 leaves little to be said for the parents either.

Jacob and Esau (ii): the Blessing

.1 When Isaac grew old and his eyes had become so dim that he could not see, he called for his elder son Esau. 'My son!' he said. Esau answered, 'Here I am.' • Isaac said, 'Listen now: I am old and I do not know when I may die. • Take your hunting gear, your quiver and bow, and go out into the country and get me some game. • Then make me a savoury dish, the kind I like, and bring it for me to eat so that I may give you my blessing before I die.'   ▶

Jacob and Esau (ii): the Blessing

This famous story is clearly and cleverly told. There are five scenes, of which the three main ones are those in the centre: between Rebecca and Jacob (6–17), Isaac and Jacob (18–30), and Isaac and Esau (31–40). The narrative sequence is generally smooth. The characters, except for Esau, are strongly drawn. In the case of Isaac and Rebecca, the hints of Ch. 25 are made explicit. *Isaac*, who has never been a dominant personality, is now old, blind and presumably on his deathbed (4). His concern for his food, mentioned in 25.28, is here repeated three times. *Rebecca*, eavesdropping like Sarah, sees her chance and seizes it. It is she who masterminds the whole scheme. She thinks up the plot, tells Jacob exactly what to do (*listen to me, my son* in vv.8 and 43, with a variant in v.14) and nerves him when he weakens. For most of their joint action she is the subject of the verbs

(15–17) as she was in 24.16–20. But *Jacob* is a worthy son of his mother. When under suspicion he saves himself with a bare-faced and blasphemous lie, adding an extra touch of treachery in speaking of *the* LORD *your God* (20). Weak-willed, cowardly (43), and treacherous now towards his father as well as his brother, he has only the one positive quality of quick-wittedness.

Fundamental to the whole story is the biblical concept of a *blessing* (and its opposite, a curse). The nearest concepts we have to it are those of an oath and a promise. Like them, it is what philosophers call a performative utterance i.e. the word is the action; and therefore it is irrevocable. So here in v.33 *the blessing will stand*; and a curse, even if intercepted (13), will still have its effect. But whereas an oath and a promise are specific, a blessing, especially the

Jacob and Esau (ii): the Blessing (cont.)

27. 5 • Now Rebecca had been listening as Isaac talked to his son Esau. When Esau went off into the country to hunt game for his father, • she said to her son Jacob, 'I have just overheard your father say to your brother Esau, • "Bring me some game and make a savoury dish for me to eat so that I may bless you in the presence of the LORD before I die." • Listen now to me, my son, and do what I tell you. • Go to the flock and pick me out two fine young kids, and I shall make them into a savoury

10 dish for your father, the kind he likes. • Then take it in to your father to eat so that he may bless you before he dies.' • 'But my brother Esau is a hairy man,' Jacob said to his mother Rebecca, 'and my skin is smooth. • Suppose my father touches me; he will know that I am playing a trick on him and I shall bring a curse instead of a blessing on myself.' • His mother answered, 'Let any curse for you fall on me, my son. Do as I say; go and fetch me the kids.' • So Jacob went and got them and brought them to his mother, who made them into a savoury dish such as his father

15 liked. • Rebecca then took her elder son's clothes, Esau's best clothes which she had by her in the house, and put them on Jacob her younger son. • She put the goatskins on his hands and on the smooth nape of his neck. • Then she handed to her son Jacob the savoury dish and the bread she had made.

• He went in to his father and said, 'Father!' Isaac answered, 'Yes, my son; which are you?' • Jacob answered, 'I am Esau, your elder son. I have done as you told me. Come, sit up and eat some of the game I have for you and then give me

20 your blessing.' • Isaac said, 'How did you find it so quickly, my son?' Jacob answered, 'Because the LORD your God put it in my way.' • Isaac then said to Jacob, 'Come close and let me touch you, my son, to make sure that you are my son Esau.' • When Jacob came close to his father, Isaac felt him and said, 'The voice is Jacob's voice, but the hands are the hands of Esau.' • He did not recognize him, because his hands were hairy like Esau's, and so he blessed him.

• He asked, 'Are you really my son Esau?' and when he answered, 'Yes, I am,'

25 • Isaac said, 'Bring me some of the game to eat, my son, so that I may give you my blessing.' Jacob brought it to him, and he ate; he brought him wine also, and he drank it. • Then his father said to him, 'Come near, my son, and kiss me.' • So he went ▸

Jacob and Esau (ii): the Blessing (cont.)

most solemn blessing on a deathbed, was general. The word refers to 'the inner strength of the soul and the happiness it creates' (Pedersen). Its concreteness is shown well in v.4: Isaac needs food to strengthen him so that (in Hebrew) 'my soul may bless you'. A similar idea is present where Jesus, on healing a woman, feels 'the power go out of him' (Mark 5.30).

The dramatic scene between Isaac and Jacob is riveting. There is nothing odd in Isaac's asking Jacob and Esau *which son* they were: we are not told how many sons he had in all, and even a sighted

sheikh has been known to ask the same question. Isaac's suspicions remain unallayed until the final, ironical kiss in v. 27. The audience however have been let into the secret by the anticipatory summary *he blessed him* in v.23; for this feature of Hebrew story-telling, see p.17. It was in the end *the smell of his clothes* that told – a typically biblical earthy motif which cleverly makes the transition to the blessing itself. This differs somewhat in its emphasis from previous patriarchal blessings. There is no mention here of children, but stress on the produce of the land (picking up the smell motif) and on

Jacob and Esau (ii): the Blessing (cont.)

7 near and kissed him, and when Isaac smelt the smell of his clothes, he blessed him
and said, 'The smell of my son is like the smell of open country blessed by the LORD.

8   God give you dew from heaven
        and the richness of the earth, corn and new wine in plenty!

9   May peoples serve you and nations bow down to you.
        May you be lord over your brothers,
        and may your mother's sons bow down to you.
    A curse on those who curse you,
        but a blessing on those who bless you!'

30 • Isaac finished blessing Jacob, who had scarcely left his father's presence when
his brother Esau came in from hunting. • He too prepared a savoury dish and brought
it to his father. He said, 'Come, father, eat some of the game I have for you, and
then give me your blessing.' • 'Who are you?' his father Isaac asked him. 'I am
Esau, your elder son,' he replied. • Then Isaac, greatly agitated, said, 'Then who
was it that hunted game and brought it to me? I ate it just before you came in, and
I blessed him, and the blessing will stand.' • When Esau heard this, he lamented
35 loudly and bitterly. 'Father, bless me too,' he begged. • But Isaac said, 'Your brother
came full of deceit and took your blessing.' • 'He is not called Jacob for nothing,'
said Esau. 'This is the second time he has supplanted me. He took away my right as
the firstborn, and now he has taken away my blessing. Have you kept back any
blessing for me?' • Isaac answered, 'I have made him lord over you and set all his
brothers under him. I have bestowed upon him grain and new wine for his sustenance.
What is there left that I can do for you, my son?' • Esau asked, 'Had you then only
one blessing, father? Bless me, too, my father.' Esau wept bitterly, • and his father
Isaac answered:
    'Your dwelling will be far from the richness of the earth,
    far from the dew of heaven above.
40   By your sword you will live,
    and you will serve your brother.
    But the time will come when you grow restive
    and break his yoke from your neck.'

Jacob and Esau (ii): the Blessing (cont.)

the superiority to your *brothers* (picking up 25.23).

In the scene of Isaac with Jacob the tension was in part comic; in that with Esau, it is tragic. There are few places where J portrays such strong emotions as here: on Isaac's part in v.33 (where NRSV's 'trembled violently' is preferable) and on Esau's twice (34 and 38). Esau's speeches open and close with the identical words, repeated in a neat chiasmus. There is a second chiasmus in v.36, which in the original reads: 'My

birthright (Heb. *bekōrāh*) he has taken away, and now he has taken away my blessing (Heb. *berākāh*).' Isaac's response to Esau is also well crafted. It starts with a parody of his blessing of Jacob, though there is no mention of God, since this is not a blessing. Verse 39bc answers 28ab, with a further chiasmus to emphasise the reversal of content. Verse 40 reverts to the tribal dimension which was present in Ch. 25. The Edomites, descendants of Esau, were regarded as savage and brutal (40a) by the Israelites. David subdued

Jacob and Esau (ii): the Blessing (cont.)

27. 41 • Esau harboured a grudge against Jacob because of the blessing which his father had given him, and he said to himself, 'The time of mourning for my father will soon be here; then I am going to kill my brother Jacob.' • When Rebecca was told what her elder son Esau was planning, she called Jacob, her younger son, and said to him, 'Your brother Esau is threatening to kill you. • Now, my son, listen to me. Be off at once to my brother Laban in Harran, • and stay with him for a while 45 until your brother's anger cools. • When it has died down and he has forgotten what you did to him, I will send and fetch you back. Why should I lose you both in one day?' (REB)

Jacob and Esau (ii): the Blessing (cont.)

them for a while (40cd), but in the time of Solomon they broke free – and this last is the best that Isaac can offer Esau in place of a blessing.

The final scene (41–5) reveals Esau as a man whose anger is violent but short-lived. Rebecca is still masterful and protective of Jacob: for Esau her only concern is self-centred (45), that if he has to die for the murder of Jacob *she* will be the loser. The episode also serves as a link to the Jacob-Laban cycle, which will

show that the period called *a while* in v.44 was actually twenty years.

The whole tale is typical of Hebrew story-telling. Formally the five scenes are each confined to two actors, and the pedimental* arrangement throws the light on the central one. The author passes no explicit moral judgement, though plenty of hints reveal his sympathies. And unlike a Greek writer, he is happy to combine the comic and earthy with the serious and even tragic.

Jacob's 'Ladder'

27. 46 Rebecca said to Isaac, 'The Hittite women sicken me to death. If Jacob were to marry a Hittite woman like these, one of the local women, what would there be left **28.** 1 in life for me?' • So Isaac summoned Jacob and blessed him; and he gave him this order: 'You are not to marry any of the Canaanite women. • Go off to the home of Bethuel your mother's father, and there choose a wife for yourself from the daughters of Laban your mother's brother. ▶

Jacob's 'Ladder'

The next task is to find a wife for Jacob. As with his father in Ch. 25, that means a return to Mesopotamia for a woman of his own family, not a *Hittite* or *Canaanite* (the two are treated as synonymous). The endogamy motif is even stronger here

than in Isaac's case. This, together with the flatter narrative, suggests the hand of P rather than J. The long journey to get her provides the thread for a variety of incidents which fill the next seven chapters of Genesis.

Jacob's 'Ladder' (cont.)

• Jacob left Beersheba and set out for Harran. • When he had reached a certain place, he stopped there for the night, since the sun had set. Taking one of the stones of that place, he made it his pillow and lay down where he was. • He had a dream: there was a ladder, planted on the ground with its top reaching to heaven; and God's angels were going up and down on it. • And there was the LORD, standing beside him and saying, 'I, the LORD, am the God of Abraham your father, and the God of Isaac. The ground on which you are lying I shall give to you and your descendants. • Your descendants will be as plentiful as the dust on the ground; you will spread out to west and east, to north and south, and all clans on earth will bless themselves by you and your descendants. • Be sure, I am with you; I shall keep you safe wherever you go, and bring you back to this country, for I shall never desert you until I have done what I have promised you.'

• Then Jacob awoke from his sleep and said, 'Truly, the LORD is in this place and I did not know!' • He was afraid and said, 'How awe-inspiring this place is! This is nothing less than the abode of God, and this is the gate of heaven!' • Early next morning, Jacob took the stone he had used for his pillow, and set it up as a pillar, pouring oil over the top of it. • He named the place Bethel, but before that the town had been called Luz. • Jacob then made this vow, 'If God remains with me and keeps me safe on this journey I am making, if he gives me food to eat and clothes to wear, • and if I come home safe to my father's home, then the LORD shall be my God. • This stone I have set up as a pillar is to be a house of God, and I shall faithfully pay you a tenth part of everything you give me.'   (NJB)

Jacob's 'Ladder' (cont.)

Without further authorial comment, the successful trickster of Ch. 27 is now awarded a personal vision of YHWH, in which his father's blessing is confirmed, or rather complemented. The promises of land and of posterity, as made to Abraham, are now repeated to Jacob (13–14), and a further promise is added in 15, specific to him. It is in response to this last that Jacob makes the *vow* of 20–21 – though we are left wondering what motivates him. Is it the old calculus of interest or a new sense of responsibility?

The narrative also has a cultic dimension. Like that of 32.22–32, it offers an aetiology* of a sacred site in a mysterious incident befalling Jacob on his travels. Bethel had been a holy place for a long time: indeed v.18 suggests that the Canaanite deity El was worshipped there in the form of a sacred *pillar* to which offerings of *oil* were made. The

etymology Beth-el = *house of God* is for once correct.

But the central feature of the story belongs to another religious tradition. The word translated *ladder* is found here only in the Bible. It properly means a ramp or staircase, such as led from bottom to top of the great temple-towers or ziggurats of Babylonia. The phrase *with its top reaching to heaven* in v.12 is that used of the Tower of Babel in 11.4. A ziggurat was a stepped tower with a ramp curling round up the outside: the bottom of it was in the precincts of the temple i.e. where the god met his worshippers; at the top was a small shrine (here called *the gate of heaven*) restricted to the god and his priestess. This feature has been hebraised, the staircase being used now for angels (not to be thought of as winged) carrying messages between earth and heaven.

A Wife for Jacob

29. 1 Continuing his journey, Jacob reached the Land of the Easterners. • And there, out in the open, he saw a well with three flocks of sheep lying beside it; this well was used for watering the flocks. Now the stone on the mouth of the well was a large one, • and only when all the flocks had collected there, did they roll the stone off the mouth of the well and water the sheep; then they would replace the stone over the mouth of the well. • Jacob said to the shepherds, 'Friends, where are you from?'

5 They replied, 'We are from Harran.' • He asked them, 'Do you know Laban son of Nahor?' They replied, 'We do.' • Then he asked them, 'Is he well?' 'He is,' they replied, 'and here comes his daughter Rachel with the flock.' • Then he said, 'But it is still broad daylight, not the time to round up the animals. Why don't you water the sheep and take them back to graze?' • To which, they replied, 'We can't, until all the shepherds have assembled to roll the stone off the mouth of the well; then we can water the sheep.'

• He was still talking to them, when Rachel arrived with her father's flock, for

10 she was a shepherdess. • As soon as Jacob saw Rachel, his uncle Laban's daughter, with his uncle Laban's flock, he went up and, rolling the stone off the mouth of the well, watered his uncle Laban's sheep. • Jacob then kissed Rachel and burst into tears. • He told Rachel he was her father's kinsman and Rebecca's son, and she ran to tell her father. • As soon as he heard her speak of his sister's son Jacob, Laban ran to greet him, embraced him, kissed him and took him to his house. Jacob told Laban everything that had happened, • and Laban said to him, 'You are indeed my bone and flesh!'

15 • After Jacob had been staying with him for a month, • Laban said to Jacob, 'Just because you are my kinsman, why should you work for me for nothing? Tell me what wages you want.' • Now Laban had two daughters, the elder named Leah, and the younger Rachel. • Leah had lovely eyes, but Rachel was shapely and beautiful, • and Jacob had fallen in love with Rachel. So his answer was, 'I shall work for you for seven years in exchange for your younger daughter Rachel.' • Laban replied, 'It is better for me to give her to you than to a stranger; stay with me.'   ▶

A Wife for Jacob

The events of Jacob's meeting with Rachel superficially resemble those of his father Isaac's meeting with her aunt Rebecca in Ch. 24. But the manner of telling is quite different in the two cases. Where the former was stately, this is rapid, even perfunctory.

The first scene is again set by a *well*. It is shared by a number of flocks with their taciturn *shepherds*. The precious water was protected by a huge *stone*, so heavy that it required the concerted strength of all of them to move it. Jacob however is inspired to move it all by himself (10), after which he greets his fair cousin, appropriately with kisses and *tears*. She invites him home, where her father *Laban* welcomes him – so far all of them on their best behaviour.

But Laban we already know from Ch. 24 as a man no less deceitful and grasping than Jacob, and much of the next three chapters is taken up by the attempts of each to outwit the other – with Rachel joining in later. Unlike Isaac, Jacob has brought no bride-price, but he offers a long period of labour in return for Rachel; and Laban's greedy eyes glint.

A Wife for Jacob (cont.)

• So Jacob worked for seven years for Rachel, and they seemed to him like a few days because he loved her so much. • Then Jacob said to Laban, 'Give me my wife, for my time is up and I should like to go to her.' • Laban gathered all the people of the place together, and gave a banquet. • But when night came, he took his daughter Leah and brought her to Jacob, and he slept with her. • (Laban gave his slave-girl Zilpah to his daughter Leah as her slave.) • When morning came, it was Leah! So Jacob said to Laban, 'What have you done to me? Did I not work for you for Rachel? Why then have you tricked me?' • Laban replied, 'It is not the custom in our place to marry off the younger before the elder. • Finish this marriage week and I shall give you the other one too in return for your working for me for another seven years.' • Jacob agreed and, when he had finished the week, Laban gave him his daughter Rachel as his wife. • (Laban gave his slave-girl Bilhah to his daughter Rachel as her slave.) • So Jacob slept with Rachel too, and he loved Rachel more than Leah. He worked for Laban for another seven years.   (NJB)

A Wife for Jacob (cont.)

When the time came, the bride escorted in veils to Jacob's house is the lack-lustre Leah. To Jacob's protest Laban gives a smooth reply (26) full of dramatic irony: for Jacob in Ch. 27 had put himself as *the younger before the elder*, and his own deception is now requited in a similar scene of close physical contact.

Jacob thus acquires two sisters to wife (an arrangement acccptable in early times), together with their two slave-girls. Should either of the wives at different times fail to conceive, she could offer her slave to her husband and count any children as her own. So there are born twelve sons, ancestors of the original twelve tribes of Israel. Rachel herself, the favourite, bore the favourites Joseph and Benjamin [35.22+]. The scene is set for the long tale of Joseph and his brothers in Chs 37–50.

Jacob then sets off for home with his family. The next section records the various ways in which Jacob and Laban cheat each other over the division of the flocks [Chs 30–31] and how Rachel and Leah join in the deception over their departure [31.19–35]. All parties are now on their worst behaviour and the narrative tension drops until the long-awaited encounter between Jacob and Esau.

The next two chapters (32 and 33) form a triptych. Its first and third scenes are businesslike narratives, almost two-dimensional by contrast with the second. The three together well exemplify Auerbach's contrast between the Homeric way of telling stories, 'uniformly illuminated', and the Hebrew way, 'fraught with background'. Yet the latter is not just inserted into the former: pains have been taken to weave it in, at least at the verbal level (see 32.20 and 33.10).

Jacob and Esau (iii): Jacob's Preparations for the Meeting

32. 1 Jacob sent messengers ahead of him to his brother Esau to the district of Seir in Edomite territory, • instructing them to say to Esau, 'My lord, your servant Jacob sends this message: I have been living with Laban and have stayed there till now. •

5 I have acquired oxen, donkeys, and sheep, as well as male and female slaves, and I am sending to tell you this, my lord, so that I may win your favour.' • The messengers returned to Jacob and said, 'We went to your brother Esau and he is already on the way to meet you with four hundred men.' • Jacob, much afraid and distressed, divided the people with him, as well as the sheep, cattle, and camels, into two companies. • He reasoned that, if Esau should come upon one company and destroy it, the other might still survive.

• Jacob prayed, 'God of my father Abraham, God of my father Isaac, LORD at whose bidding I came back to my own country and to my kindred, and who promised

10 me prosperity, • I am not worthy of all the true and steadfast love which you have shown to me your servant. The last time I crossed the Jordan, I owned nothing but the staff in my hand; now I have two camps. • Save me, I pray, from my brother Esau, for I am afraid that he may come and destroy me; he will spare neither mother nor child. • But you said, "I shall make you prosper and your descendants will be like the sand of the sea, beyond all counting." '

• After spending the night there Jacob chose a gift for his brother Esau from the herds he had with him: • two hundred she-goats, twenty he-goats, two hundred

15 ewes and twenty rams, • thirty milch-camels with their young, forty cows and ten young bulls, twenty she-donkeys and ten donkeys. • He put each drove into the charge of a servant and said, 'Go on ahead of me, and leave gaps between one drove and the next.' • To the first servant he gave these instructions: 'When my brother Esau meets you and asks who your master is and where you are going and who owns these animals you are driving, • you are to say, "They belong to your servant Jacob, who sends them as a gift to my lord Esau; he himself is coming behind us." ' • He gave the same instructions to the second, to the third, and to all

20 the drovers, telling each to say the same thing to Esau when they met him. • And they were to add, 'Your servant Jacob is coming behind us.' Jacob thought, 'I shall appease him with the gift that I have sent on ahead, and afterwards, when we come face to face, perhaps he will receive me kindly.' • So Jacob's gift went on ahead of him, while he himself stayed that night at Mahaneh.   (REB)

Jacob and Esau (iii): Jacob's Preparations for the Meeting

After twenty years' absence [31.41] Jacob was still extremely apprehensive about meeting his farouche brother again. When still 100 miles away, he sent men ahead with a message couched in the formulae of submission. His opening words *My lord, your servant* reverse the role-reversal which Jacob had achieved by trickery. The ambiguous intelligence brought back by his *messengers* (6) confirmed his worst fears. Like a prudent commander he took three steps. First, he split his company into two, to increase the chances of survival. Next he prayed for divine help. To God, as to Esau, he is humble enough (10); but neither here nor anywhere else in the whole story is there the least sign that he is penitent. Thirdly he plans to offer a rich gift: no less than five herds of different animals, which he craftily spaces out for greater effect. His instructions to the drovers emphasise his own submissiveness: four times we are told that the *gift* went on *ahead*, with the *servant* Jacob *behind*.

Jacob Wrestles at Peniel

2 During the night Jacob rose, and taking his two wives, his two slave-girls, and his eleven sons, he crossed the ford of Jabbok. • After he had sent them across the wadi with all that he had, • Jacob was left alone, and a man wrestled with him there till

5 daybreak. • When the man saw that he could not get the better of Jacob, he struck him in the hollow of his thigh, so that Jacob's hip was dislocated as they wrestled. • The man said, 'Let me go, for day is breaking,' but Jacob replied, 'I will not let you go unless you bless me.' • The man asked, 'What is your name?' 'Jacob,' he answered. • The man said, 'Your name shall no longer be Jacob but Israel, because you have striven with God and with mortals, and have prevailed.' • Jacob said, 'Tell me your name, I pray.' He replied, 'Why do you ask my name?' but he gave him his blessing there.

30 • Jacob called the place Peniel, 'because', he said, 'I have seen God face to face yet my life is spared'. • The sun rose as Jacob passed through Peniel, limping because of his hip.   (REB)

Jacob Wrestles at Peniel

At first sight the story of the encounter at the Jabbok is a version of a widespread folk-tale. The hero on his quest comes to an obstacle guarded by a god or other supernatural being. The two fight, and the hero has the deity at his mercy. The deity pleads for release: if he comes from the underworld, he has to be back there by sunrise, like Hamlet's father's ghost. The hero grants the plea only on condition that he learns the deity's name and/or receives a share of his power.

But if some such tale underlies our narrative, it has certainly suffered a sea-change. Part of the change was required in order for it to fit Hebrew monotheism. On the one hand the author could not recognise other deities; on the other, he could not easily accept the idea of the one God fighting with a man, still less being defeated. God's transcendence was such that, apart from Jacob here, Moses was the only man who saw God's face and lived. Hence, in some measure, the mysterious-ness of the account of the fight in Genesis. But there is more to it than that. The reader of a folk-tale expects the hero to have both a helper and an opponent, but is totally disoriented when helper and opponent become one. (The same thing, it is true, happens to Moses in Exod 4.24–6, but that incident is told too briefly to engage us.)

A few detailed points need explanation. The *Jabbok* (22; see map 2) flows through a deep gorge into the east bank of Jordan. Jacob is coming down from the north, Esau up from the south; the Jabbok was thus Jacob's Rubicon. The fight itself is here less important than its aftermath. The crafty Jacob extracts by force from the deity what he had extracted by guile from Isaac, namely his blessing. And the *blessing* is symbolised by a change of name, a re-baptism: he is no longer Jacob 'the cheat', but *Israel*, i.e. by a folk-etymology he who *has striven with God*. Henceforward the name will be proudly borne by his descendants, probably with the interpretation that God fights *for* his people. Jacob in turn gives a new name to the place: *Peniel* means 'the *face* of God'.

But there is one more layer to the story of the wrestling. Jacob's opponent is introduced as *a man*, and at the end he himself is said to have *striven with mortals* (AV 'men') as well as with God. The author's hint is strong. At this juncture of the narrative, the opponent must also represent the dreaded Esau. And the hint is made explicit by Jacob's words to him in 33.10, 'I have seen thy face as though I had seen (lit 'in seeing') the face of God, and thou wast pleased with me' (AV) – a clear cross-reference to 32.30.

Jacob and Esau (iv): the Reconciliation

33. 1 Jacob looked up and there was Esau coming with four hundred men. He divided the children between Leah and Rachel and the two slave-girls. • He put the slave-girls and their children in front, Leah with her children next, and Rachel and Joseph in the rear. • He himself went on ahead of them, bowing low to the ground seven times as he approached his brother. • Esau ran to meet him and embraced him; he threw 5 his arms round him and kissed him, and they both wept. • When Esau caught sight of the women and children, he asked, 'Who are these with you?' Jacob replied, 'The children whom God has graciously given to your servant.' • The slave-girls came near, each with her children, and they bowed low; • then Leah with her children came near and bowed low, and lastly Joseph and Rachel came and bowed low also. • Esau asked, 'What was all that company of yours that I met?' 'It was meant to win favour with you, my lord,' was the answer. • Esau said, 'I have more than 10 enough. Keep what you have, my brother.' • But Jacob replied, 'No, please! If I have won your favour, then accept, I pray, this gift from me; for, as you see, I come into your presence as into that of a god, and yet you receive me favourably. • Accept this gift which I bring you; for God has been gracious to me, and I have all I want.' Thus urged, Esau accepted it.

• Esau said, 'Let us set out, and I shall go at your pace.' • But Jacob answered him, 'You must know, my lord, that the children are small; the flocks and herds are suckling their young and I am concerned for them, and if they are overdriven for a single day, my beasts will all die. • I beg you, my lord, to go on ahead, and I shall move by easy stages at the pace of the livestock I am driving and the pace of the 15 children, until I come to my lord in Seir.' • Esau said, 'Let me detail some of my men to escort you,' but he replied, 'There is no reason why my lord should be so kind.' • That day Esau turned back towards Seir, • while Jacob set out for Succoth; there he built himself a house and made shelters for his cattle. Therefore he named that place Succoth.

• So Jacob arrived safely at the town of Shechem in Canaan and pitched his tent to the east of it. • The piece of land where he had pitched his tent he bought from the sons of Hamor, Shechem's father, for a hundred sheep.   (REB)

Jacob and Esau (iv): the Reconciliation

When Esau's company eventually came within sight, Jacob made one more precautionary disposition, of his immediate family. And this time he did go in front, approaching his brother with the *seven* obeisances used in a full submission. Esau's response is nobility itself. Like the father of the Prodigal, he takes the initiative in reconciliation. Jacob offers no apology, but Esau takes the offer of presents in lieu. The rules of courtesy are observed: Esau makes to decline the *gift* (with a little smile at its magnitude), but Jacob modestly insists. The scene ends remarkably. Having talked throughout of a gift (Heb. *minhāh*, a word implying 'tribute'), Jacob in v.11 finally nerves himself to utter the word of shame *berākāh*. AV alone preserves it in translation: 'Take, I pray thee, my blessing that is brought to thee.' Perhaps after all Jacob *has* come to self-knowledge and can face his own guilt.

Jacob and Esau (iv): the Reconciliation (cont.)

If so, he has not succeeded in mastering his fear. Esau's acceptance marks the final forgiveness. But Jacob still does not trust him. He makes various excuses to avoid going back with him to *Seir*: let Esau *go on ahead* as *lord*, again reversing the effect of Isaac's blessing. At the first opportunity Jacob breaks away and heads back across the Jordan. At one level of the story, of course, he has to do so. Esau has no share in the promise, and is heard of no more. Jacob's possession of it is officially confirmed by his purchase of *land* (19).

The Story of Joseph and his Brothers: Genesis 37–50

The last quarter of Genesis takes us to a new world in more senses than one. The story of Jacob and Esau already showed some articulation of incident and development of character. That of Joseph and his brothers has the same theme, of sibling rivalry. But (with the exception of Ch.38) it is an intricately structured story (technically a novella*), the longest in the Pentateuch. True, one can still detect from time to time two alternative versions of it. But whether the author juxtaposes the two or knits them together, he does it for the most part so skilfully as to add depth and colour to his tale. In style the narrative shows the humour and the psychological insight which marked previous chapters, together with a greater smoothness and sophistication. Sforzando has given way to legato.

The new world of the Joseph story is that of urban Egypt, not rural Palestine. No longer are we interested in parochial aetiologies, no longer do we disapprove of marriage with foreigners. The author was clearly fascinated with Egypt and brings in plenty of local colour. The specific milieu is that of the 'enlightened' upper classes, whose culture was exemplified in the international Wisdom* literature. Indeed the whole story of Joseph in Egypt is built upon a typical Wisdom tale, of the bright boy from a humble background who makes his way at court (cp. Moses and Daniel).

And the Wisdom tone is typically secular. The supernatural is admitted, but God is banished to the periphery. His role is that of providence, sending Joseph to Egypt (45.5) and giving him success there (see esp. Ch. 39), all with the ultimate object of preserving the family (45.7). He intervenes in person only once (46.3f.), and there his speech merely dramatises the providential purpose. The moral thrust of the story has more substance. In the opening chapter every member of the family is at fault, and its unity is broken. Events bring Joseph's brothers, unlike Jacob, to an admission of their guilt which Joseph overhears (42.21+), and his forgiveness is shown in deeds, not in words. But there is no great sign of change of heart except on the part of Judah, and the brothers are still lying to Joseph at the very end [50.16f.]. What they have done is to agree to work together for the greater good of the family.

Joseph Sold into Egypt

37. 2 When Joseph was a youth of seventeen, he used to accompany his brothers, the sons of Bilhah and Zilpah, his father's wives, when they were in charge of the flock, and he told tales about them to their father. • Because Joseph was a child of his old age, Israel loved him best of all his sons, and he made him a long robe with sleeves. • When his brothers saw that their father loved him best, it aroused their hatred and they had nothing but harsh words for him.

5 • Joseph had a dream, and when he told it to his brothers, their hatred of him became still greater. • He said to them, 'Listen to this dream I had. • We were out in the field binding sheaves, when all at once my sheaf rose and stood upright, and your sheaves gathered round and bowed in homage before my sheaf.' • His brothers retorted, 'Do you think that you will indeed be king over us and rule us?' and they hated him still more because of his dreams and what he had said. • Then he had another dream, which he related to his father and his brothers. 'Listen!' he said. 'I have had another dream, and in it the sun, the moon, and eleven stars were bowing

10 down to me.' • When he told his father and his brothers, his father took him to task: 'What do you mean by this dream of yours?' he asked. 'Are we to come and bow to the ground before you, I and your mother and your brothers?' • His brothers were jealous of him, but his father did not forget the incident. ▸

Joseph Sold into Egypt

The first three verses introduce all the main characters in the story, and reveal all the tensions in the family. Hatred between brothers was endemic, like the family curse of the house of Atreus, and parental favouritism fostered it. Joseph was the next-to-youngest son, if hardly a *child of his old age*. Jacob made Joseph a fancy coat – REB's translation *long robe with sleeves* is no more certain than AV's 'coat of many colours' – and the spoiled child *told tales* on his brothers. He was also smug (or naive) enough to tell them about his *dreams* of greatness, which made them even more jealous. In the first dream his naivety is further shown in the Hebrew by a thrice-repeated *hinneh* which AV alone keeps: 'behold, we were binding sheaves . . . lo, my sheaf

arose . . . behold, your sheaves stood.' The reference to *your mother* in 10 is a clear mistake. According to [35.15–20], Rachel had died in giving birth to Benjamin.

Dreams play an important part in the Joseph story, coming always in pairs. They do not, as in the rest of Genesis, convey messages from God: they simply foreshadow future events. Joseph's first dream was fulfilled when his control of the corn gave him power over his brothers; the second when the rest of his family too had to bow to him. When the brothers in v.19 describe him as *that dreamer* (the Hebrew means literally 'lord of dreams'), they intend the phrase contemptuously i.e. lord only in dreams; but Jacob suspects (11), and the reader knows, otherwise.

Joseph Sold into Egypt (cont.)

• Joseph's brothers had gone to herd their father's flocks at Shechem. • Israel said to him, 'Your brothers are herding the flocks at Shechem; I am going to send you to them.' Joseph answered, 'I am ready to go.' • Israel told him to go and see if all was well with his brothers and the flocks, and to bring back word to him. So Joseph was sent off from the vale of Hebron and came to Shechem, where • a man met him wandering in the open country and asked him what he was looking for. • 'I am looking for my brothers,' he replied. 'Can you tell me where they are herding the flocks?' • The man said, 'They have moved from here; I heard them speak of going to Dothan.' Joseph went after his brothers and came up with them at Dothan. • They saw him in the distance, and before he reached them, they plotted to kill him. • 'Here comes that dreamer,' they said to one another. • 'Now is our chance; let us kill him and throw him into one of these cisterns; we can say that a wild beast has devoured him. Then we shall see what becomes of his dreams.' • When Reuben heard, he came to his rescue, urging them not to take his life. • 'Let us have no bloodshed,' he said. 'Throw him into this cistern in the wilderness, but do him no injury.' Reuben meant to rescue him from their clutches in order to restore him to his father. • When Joseph reached his brothers, they stripped him of the long robe with sleeves which he was wearing, • picked him up, and threw him into the cistern. It was empty, with no water in it.

• They had sat down to eat when, looking up, they saw an Ishmaelite caravan coming from Gilead on the way down to Egypt, with camels carrying gum tragacanth and balm and myrrh. • Judah said to his brothers, 'What do we gain by killing our brother and concealing his death? • Why not sell him to these Ishmaelites? Let us do him no harm, for after all, he is our brother, our own flesh and blood'; his brothers agreed. • Meanwhile some passing Midianite merchants drew Joseph up out of the cistern and sold him for twenty pieces of silver to the Ishmaelites; they brought Joseph to Egypt. • When Reuben came back to the cistern, he found Joseph had gone. He tore his clothes • and going to his brothers he said, 'The boy is not there. Whatever shall I do?'   ◆

Joseph Sold into Egypt (cont.)

With v.12 things begin to move, though a slow introduction in vv.13–17 delays the fateful encounter. As to what happens then, we now run into a confusion which must be ascribed to the conflation of the two versions of the story. In one, where the name *Jacob* is preferred, *Reuben* proposes to save Joseph's life, and thus escape blood-guilt, by throwing him alive into an empty *cistern* (a large hole in the ground, designed to store winter rain for use in summer), from which later he would himself rescue him – though in the event he was found by *Midianites* and sold by them in Egypt (36). In the other version, which prefers the name *Israel*, *Judah* proposes to save him by selling him direct to *Ishmaelites*. Verse 28 is an attempt to reconcile the two by having the Midianites sell him to the Ishmaelites for the going rate of *twenty pieces of silver*.

Joseph Sold into Egypt (cont.)

37. 31 • Joseph's brothers took the long robe with sleeves, and dipped it in the blood of a goat which they had killed. • After tearing the robe, they brought it to their father and said, 'Look what we have found. Do you recognize it? Is this your son's robe or not?' • Jacob recognized it. 'It is my son's,' he said. 'A wild beast has devoured him. Joseph has been torn to pieces.' • Jacob tore his clothes; he put on sackcloth 35 and for many days he mourned his son. • Though his sons and daughters all tried to comfort him, he refused to be comforted. He said, 'No, I shall go to Sheol mourning for my son.' Thus Joseph's father wept for him. • The Midianites meanwhile had sold Joseph in Egypt to Potiphar, one of Pharaoh's court officials, the captain of the guard. (REB)

Joseph Sold into Egypt (cont.)

Fortunately the confusion is not too disastrous. One way or the other, the story coheres well enough. The caravan route from Syria to Egypt passed down the Jordan valley till it crossed over near *Dothan* (17, see map 2) to the coastal road. The merchants carried spices and medicinal herbs, used also for embalming, but they were not averse from slave-trading on the side.

In the last scene of the episode the brothers present themselves shiftily to their father: they let the *robe* do their lying for them, and avoid Joseph's name. The postscript (36) tells us he is safe, but as far removed as he could be from the fulfilment of his ambitions.

Judah and Tamar

38. 1 It happened at about that time that Judah left his brothers, to go down and settle with a certain Adullamite called Hirah. • There Judah saw the daughter of a Canaanite called Shua. He made her his wife and slept with her. • She conceived and gave birth to a son whom she named Er. • She conceived again and gave birth 5 to a son whom she named Onan. • Yet again she gave birth to a son whom she named Shelah.

• Judah took a wife for his first-born Er, and her name was Tamar. • But Er, Judah's first-born, offended the LORD, and the LORD killed him. • Then Judah said to Onan, 'Take your brother's wife, and do your duty as her brother-in-law, to maintain your brother's line.' • But Onan, knowing that the line would not count as his, spilt his seed on the ground every time he slept with his brother's wife, to avoid 10 providing offspring for his brother. • What he did was offensive to the LORD who killed him too. • Then Judah said to his daughter-in-law Tamar, 'Go home as a widow to your father, until my son Shelah grows up,' for he was thinking, 'He must not die like his brothers.' So Tamar went home to her father. ▸

Judah and Tamar

This intriguing tale was originally independent of the story of Joseph. It depends upon the same custom as the book of Ruth: the duty of a man's next of kin to take his widow and so to preserve the family line (see Dt 25.5 and Glossary s.v. 'Redeemer'). Verses 1–11 give the background. *Judah* took *a Canaanite* wife (this time without any editorial disapproval) and by her had three sons. The eldest took a wife *Tamar* but died prematurely without issue – an event described as an act of God (7). The next, Onan, took her as in duty bound, but for selfish reasons practised *coitus interruptus* (the English word onanism, derived from him, was used by misinterpretation to refer to the 'sin' of masturbation). When he too died prematurely,

Judah and Tamar (cont.)

2 • A long time passed, and then Shua's daughter, the wife of Judah, died. After Judah had been comforted he went up to Timnah for the shearing of his sheep, he and his friend Hirah the Adullamite. • When Tamar was told, 'Look, your father-in-law is going up to Timnah for the shearing of his sheep,' • she changed out of her widow's clothes, wrapped a veil around her to disguise herself, and sat down at the entrance to Enaim, which is on the way to Timnah; for she saw that, although Shelah was grown up, she had not been given to him as his wife.

5 • Judah, seeing her, took her for a prostitute, since her face was veiled. • Going up to her on the road, he said, 'Here, let me sleep with you.' He did not know that she was his daughter-in-law. 'What will you give me for sleeping with you?' she asked. • 'I will send you a kid from the flock,' he said. 'Agreed, if you give me a pledge until you send it,' she replied. • 'What pledge shall I give you?' he asked. 'Your seal and cord and the staff you are holding,' she replied. He gave them to her and slept with her, and she conceived by him. • Then she got up and left him and, taking off her veil, resumed her widow's weeds.

20 • Judah sent the kid by his friend the Adullamite, to recover the pledge from the woman. But he did not find her. He enquired from the men of the place, 'Where is the prostitute who was by the roadside at Enaim?' 'There has been no prostitute there,' they answered. • So returning to Judah he said, 'I did not find her. What is more, the men of the place told me there had been no prostitute there.' • 'Let her keep the things,' Judah said, 'or we shall become a laughing-stock.'

 • About three months later, Judah was told, 'Your daughter-in-law has played the harlot; furthermore, she is pregnant, as a result of her misconduct.' 'Bring her

25 out,' Judah ordered, 'and let her be burnt alive!' • But as she was being led off, she sent word to her father-in-law, 'It was the owner of these who made me pregnant. Please verify', she said, 'whose seal and cord and staff these are.' • Judah recognised them and said, 'She was right and I was wrong, since I did not give her to my son Shelah.' He had no further intercourse with her.   ▶

Judah and Tamar (cont.)

Judah remembered the folk-tale of the poison maiden (as e.g. in the book of Tobit), and said his third son was too young. But after a while it became clear that Judah, as head of the family, was just making an excuse; so Tamar, tired of passivity, sprang into action and set her cap at the next-but-one of kin, her father-in-law.

The story of her waylaying of Judah is told with marvellous circumstantial detail. Recently widowed, Judah needed feminine company again. A woman sitting by the roadside would be *a prostitute*, and he did not recognise her as Tamar behind the *veil* – indeed her anonymity is respected by the narrator throughout the incident. His eagerness is shown by his offer of two

precious properties as a *pledge*: his personal cylinder-*seal*, worn on its *cord* around his neck, and his stick with carved handle. Afterwards, these pledges had to be redeemed discreetly, so Judah sent his friend Hirah to find her. But she, not being a 'regular', could not be traced.

The denouement shows up Judah as an exponent of the double standard. Tamar, though living with her parents (11), was still under the jurisdiction of Judah as head of the family. In that capacity he decrees, in two brutal words, an unusually severe punishment. When revealed as the father, he behaves honourably enough (26). But Tamar is the heroine, and her courage and

Judah and Tamar (cont.)

38. 27   • When the time for her confinement came, there were twins in her womb! • During the delivery, one of them put out a hand, and the midwife caught it and tied a scarlet thread to it, indicating that this was the first to arrive. • Whereupon, he drew back his hand, and out came his brother. Then she said, 'What a breach you 30   have opened for yourself !' So he was named Perez. • Then his brother came out with the scarlet thread on his hand, so he was named Zerah.   (NJB)

Judah and Tamar (cont.)

resourcefulness are rewarded by the birth of *twins*, of whom *Perez* will be the ancestor of king David. The story ends with yet another instance of the 'younger preferred' motif which we know from Jacob and Esau.

Such is the story; but what on earth is it doing here, intruding into the Joseph-romance? Evidently it was too important to be omitted, dealing as it does with the powerful tribe of Judah. Chronologically it had to go somewhere between Ch. 37, while Judah is still working for his father, and Ch. 46 when the whole family moved to Egypt. In its present position it fills a

psychological gap while Joseph is, as it were, out of view, and provides a contrast between Tamar, the seductress who seems wanton and is virtuous, and Potiphar's wife of Ch. 39, the one who seems virtuous but is wanton. Finally, the editor has created a link with Ch. 37 in the motif of the token recognised: the denouement in each passage (37.32f. and 38.25f.) uses exactly the same formula – the request 'please identify' followed by the report 'he identified' – with the same Hebrew word used four times in all. English versions obscure this point by varying the word in translation.

Joseph in Potiphar's House

39. 1   Now Joseph had been taken down into Egypt. Potiphar the Egyptian, one of Pharaoh's officials and commander of the guard, bought him from the Ishmaelites who had taken him down there. • The LORD was with Joseph, and everything he undertook was successful. He lodged in the house of his Egyptian master, • and when his master saw how the LORD was with him and how the LORD made everything he undertook successful, • he was pleased with Joseph and made him his personal attendant; and his master put him in charge of his household, entrusting him with 5   all his possessions. • And from the time he put him in charge of his household and all his possessions, the LORD blessed the Egyptian's household out of consideration for Joseph; the LORD's blessing extended to all his possessions, both household and estate. • So he left Joseph to handle all his possessions, and with him there, concerned himself with nothing beyond the food he ate.   ♦

Joseph in Potiphar's House

Ch. 39, 'the most elegantly symmetrical in Genesis' (Alter), is made up of three sections, of which the first and third, preamble and conclusion, echo each other. The themes are (i) that *the LORD was with Joseph*, and so he was *successful* in *everything* (2, 3, 21, 23) and (ii) that (in consequence) he found favour with his master

Potiphar, who trusted him with everything (4, 6, 22) except his *food*, where the Egyptians feared ritual impurity (6, cp. 43.32) – and of course his wife.

And that is where the drama lies. Young men are frequently warned in the Wisdom literature (e.g. Prov 6.24), against temptation by married women, and this

---

Joseph in Potiphar's House (cont.)

7   Now Joseph was well built and handsome, • and it happened some time later that his master's wife cast her eyes on Joseph and said, 'Sleep with me.' • But he refused. 'Look,' he said to his master's wife, 'with me here, my master does not concern himself with what happens in the house, having entrusted all his possessions to me. • He himself wields no more authority in this house than I do. He has exempted nothing from me except yourself, because you are his wife. How could I do anything so

10   wicked, and sin against God?' • Although she spoke to Joseph day after day, he would not agree to sleep with her or be with her. • But one day when Joseph came into the house to do his work, and none of the men of the household happened to be indoors, • she caught hold of him by his tunic and said, 'Sleep with me.' But he left the tunic in her hand, took to his heels and got out. • When she saw that he had left the tunic in her hands as he ran out, • she called her servants and said to them, 'Look at this! My husband brought in a Hebrew to make a fool of me! He burst in on me, but

15   I screamed, • and when he heard me scream, he left his tunic beside me and ran out of the house.'

     • She kept his tunic by her until his master came home. • Then she told him the same tale, 'The Hebrew slave you brought to us burst in on me to make a fool of me. • But when I screamed, he left his tunic beside me and ran away.' • When his master

20   heard his wife say, 'This was how your slave treated me,' he became furious. • Joseph's master had him arrested and committed to the gaol where the king's prisoners were kept. • And there in gaol he stayed. • But the LORD was with Joseph. He showed him faithful love and made him popular with the chief gaoler. • The chief gaoler put Joseph in charge of all the prisoners in the gaol, making him responsible for everything done there. • The chief gaoler did not bother about anything put in his charge, since the LORD was with him, and the LORD made everything he undertook successful.

                                                                                              (NJB)

Joseph in Potiphar's House (cont.)

particular tale – the married woman scorned whose fury leads to an accusation of rape – is widespread: 'Potiphar's wife has many sisters.' Curiously, the oldest known version of it comes from Egypt c.1300 BC. But in that version husband and accused are brothers: accused persuades husband of his innocence, and husband kills wife. So there is no direct borrowing here, only the skilful adaptation of a well-known tale.

The theme *sleep with me* is repeated three times (7, 10, 12). Note the contrast at the start between her two-word proposition ('As Thomas Mann was to observe at great length, she must have said more than that' – Alter) and Joseph's verbose rejection of it. His reason is that it would be a betrayal of his master's trust. She

then sets him up with great cunning. The *tunic*, which was in fact a sign of innocence, is made into evidence of guilt; note the innuendo in the variation between *in her hands* (13) and *beside me* (15). The *scream* she claims to have uttered was the accepted evidence of a woman's innocence [Deut 22.24]. With the *servants* on her side, she quickly convinced her husband of *the Hebrew slave's* guilt. Joseph is now back at square one: out of the cistern into the prison. (The point is made in 40.15, where the Hebrew word translated 'dungeon' is not the normal word but the word used for the 'cistern' in Ch. 37.) But the punishment inflicted is astonishingly mild. Death would have been normal, even for a free man. It looks as though Potiphar had his doubts.

Joseph in Prison

40. 1 Some time after these events it happened that the king's cupbearer and the royal baker gave offence to their lord, the king of Egypt. • Pharaoh was displeased with his two officials, his chief cupbearer and chief baker, • and put them in custody in the house of the captain of the guard, in the guardhouse where Joseph was imprisoned. • The captain appointed Joseph as their attendant, and he waited on them.

5   They had been in prison in the guardhouse for some time, • when one night the king's cupbearer and his baker both had dreams, each with a meaning of its own. • Coming to them in the morning, Joseph saw that they looked dispirited, • and asked these officials in custody with him in his master's house, why they were so downcast that day. • They replied, 'We have each had a dream, but there is no one to interpret them.' Joseph said to them, 'All interpretation belongs to God. Why not tell me your dreams?' • So the chief cupbearer told Joseph his dream: 'In my

10 dream', he said, 'there was a vine in front of me. • On the vine there were three branches, and as soon as it budded, it blossomed and its clusters ripened into grapes. • I plucked the grapes and pressed them into Pharaoh's cup which I was holding, and then put the cup into Pharaoh's hand.' • Joseph said to him, 'This is the interpretation. The three branches are three days: • within three days Pharaoh will raise your head and restore you to your post; then you will put the cup into Pharaoh's hand as you used to do when you were his cupbearer. • When things go well with you, remember me and do me the kindness of bringing my case to Pharaoh's notice;

15 help me to get out of this prison. • I was carried off by force from the land of the Hebrews, and here I have done nothing to deserve being put into this dungeon.'

• When the chief baker saw that the interpretation given by Joseph had been favourable, he said to him, 'I too had a dream, and in my dream there were three baskets of white bread on my head. • In the top basket there was every kind of food such as a baker might prepare for Pharaoh, but the birds were eating out of the top basket on my head.' • Joseph answered, 'This is the interpretation. The three baskets are three days: • within three days Pharaoh will raise your head off your shoulders and hang you on a tree, and the birds of the air will devour the flesh off your bones.'

Joseph in Prison

Within the next two chapters (40 and 41) Joseph rises from the bottom to the top of Egyptian society. At the start he is lowest of the low: imprisoned himself and servant to two discredited prisoners. The *baker* and the *cupbearer* were officials, whose fall from favour had been as rapid as Joseph's rise was to be. Awaiting trial, each of them had a *dream* which he took as a pointer to his fate; but unlike Joseph's two dreams in Ch. 37 these were riddle-dreams which required *interpretation*. Dreams of this kind were a feature of Egyptian life and literature,

and successful interpreters of them rose to positions of influence. The absence of any such interpreter in prison increased the dejection of the prisoners. This was a heaven-sent opening for Joseph 'lord of dreams'. In a skilful phrase (8) he disclaimed divine inspiration for himself and claimed it for the interpretation which he proceeded to offer.

In spite of the surface similarity of the two dreams, Joseph spots a significant difference, viz. the *birds*, which in v.17 *were eating* what was meant for *Pharaoh*. On the basis of this he forecasts two

Joseph in Prison (cont.)

• The third day was Pharaoh's birthday and he gave a banquet for all his officials. He had the chief cupbearer and the chief baker brought up where they were all assembled. • The cupbearer was restored to his position, and he put the cup into Pharaoh's hand; • but the baker was hanged. All went as Joseph had said in interpreting the dreams for them. • The cupbearer, however, did not bear Joseph in mind; he forgot him.   (REB)

Joseph in Prison (cont.)

opposite fates. These however he formally reunites in a grim pun, using the same Hebrew phrase *raise your head* to mean *restore you* in v.13 and *hang you* in v.19.

Neither the two dreams in Ch. 39 nor their interpretation are of consequence to the main story. What matters to it is that Joseph interpreted them successfully, and so eventually came to the notice of Pharaoh. Joseph is impatient to exploit that success; but v.23 makes us all wait – for *two years*!

Joseph's Rise to Power

1 Two years later Pharaoh had a dream: he was standing by the Nile, • when there came up from the river seven cows, sleek and fat, and they grazed among the reeds. • Presently seven other cows, gaunt and lean, came up from the river, and stood beside the cows on the river bank. • The cows that were gaunt and lean devoured the seven cows that were sleek and fat. Then Pharaoh woke up.

5 • He fell asleep again and had a second dream: he saw seven ears of grain, full and ripe, growing on a single stalk. • Springing up after them were seven other ears, thin and shrivelled by the east wind. • The thin ears swallowed up the seven ears that were full and plump. Then Pharaoh woke up and found it was a dream.

• In the morning Pharaoh's mind was so troubled that he summoned all the dream-interpreters and wise men of Egypt, and told them his dreams; but there was no one who could interpret them for him. • Then Pharaoh's chief cupbearer spoke up. 'Now I must mention my offences,' he said: • 'Pharaoh was angry with his

10 servants, and imprisoned me and the chief baker in the house of the captain of the guard. • One night we both had dreams, each requiring its own interpretation. • We had with us there a young Hebrew, a slave of the captain of the guard, and when we told him our dreams he interpreted them for us, giving each dream its own interpretation. • Things turned out exactly as the dreams had been interpreted to us: I was restored to my post, the other was hanged.'

• Pharaoh thereupon sent for Joseph, and they hurriedly brought him out of the dungeon. After he had shaved and changed his clothes, he came in before Pharaoh,

15 • who said to him, 'I have had a dream which no one can interpret. I have heard ▶

Joseph's Rise to Power

The narrative of Pharaoh's dreams is also leisurely, delaying the long-awaited climax for another 40 verses. First, the dreams are once again paired, something for which Joseph offers an explanation in v.32. Then the narrator's description of them in vv.1–7 is repeated by Pharaoh himself in vv.17–24, with the addition of two subjective comments in vv.19b and 21b. In the interim Joseph has been released from prison and summoned to court. His change of position is marked as usual by a change of *clothes*, and also by shaving (14), a practice followed by Egyptians alone in the ANE. He then proceeds to defeat all the Egyptian

Joseph's Rise to Power (cont.)

41. 16 that you can interpret any dream you hear.' • Joseph answered, 'Not I, but God, can give an answer which will reassure Pharaoh.' • Then Pharaoh said to him: 'In my dream I was standing on the bank of the Nile, • when there came up from the river seven cows, fat and sleek, and they grazed among the reeds. • After them seven other cows came up that were in poor condition, very gaunt and lean; in all Egypt I

20 have never seen such gaunt creatures. • These lean, gaunt cows devoured the first cows, the seven fat ones. • They were swallowed up, but no one could have told they were in the bellies of the others, which looked just as gaunt as before. Then I woke up. • In another dream I saw seven ears of grain, full and ripe, growing on a single stalk. • Springing up after them were seven other ears, blighted, thin, and shrivelled by the east wind. • The thin ears swallowed up the seven ripe ears. When I spoke to the dream-interpreters, no one could tell me the meaning.'

25 • Joseph said to Pharaoh, 'Pharaoh's dreams are both the same; God has told Pharaoh what he is about to do. • The seven good cows are seven years, and the seven good ears of grain are seven years – it is all one dream. • The seven lean and gaunt cows that came up after them are seven years, and so also are the seven empty ears of grain blighted by the east wind; there are going to be seven years of famine. • It is as I have told Pharaoh: God has let Pharaoh see what he is about to

30 do. • There are to be seven years of bumper harvests throughout Egypt. • After them will come seven years of famine; so that the great harvests in Egypt will all be forgotten, and famine will ruin the country. • The good years will leave no trace in the land because of the famine that follows, for it will be very severe. • That Pharaoh has dreamed this twice means God is firmly resolved on this plan, and very soon he will put it into effect.

• 'Let Pharaoh now look for a man of vision and wisdom and put him in charge of the country. • Pharaoh should take steps to appoint commissioners over the land

35 to take one fifth of the produce of Egypt during the seven years of plenty. • They should collect all food produced in the good years that are coming and put the grain under Pharaoh's control as a store of food to be kept in the towns. • This food will be a reserve for the country against the seven years of famine which will come on Egypt, and so the country will not be devastated by the famine.' ▸

Joseph's Rise to Power (cont.)

interpreters (24), exactly as later Moses was to defeat all the Egyptian magicians.

The *cows,* i.e. water-buffalo, and the *ears of grain* together represent the produce of Egypt. The fact that the *lean* ones *devoured* the *fat* ones is taken to mean that the years of famine will obliterate the memory of the years of plenty. Having offered his interpretations, and presumably found them accepted, Joseph again goes on, this time without a break, to exploit his advantage. His advice to Pharaoh may be transparent (33) but is obviously wise. The *store*-cities of Egypt

were internationally renowned, and the author enjoys claiming them as a Hebrew invention.

We now come to the first climax of the story, and the colour is laid on thick. Joseph is promoted first to be *in charge of* Pharaoh's *household*, as he had been of Potiphar's, and then to be nothing less than Grand Vizier of all Egypt. He is invested with the *signet-ring* of office (the Vizier is referred to in Egyptian documents of this period as 'Sealbearer'), his new clothes are *of fine linen*, he wears a *gold chain*, and he rides in the Vizier's

Joseph's Rise to Power (cont.)

• The plan commended itself both to Pharaoh and to all his officials, • and Pharaoh asked them, 'Could we find another man like this, one so endowed with the spirit of God?' • To Joseph he said, 'Since God has made all this known to you, no one has your vision and wisdom. • You shall be in charge of my household, and all my people will respect your every word. Only in regard to the throne shall I rank higher than you.' • Pharaoh went on, 'I hereby give you authority over the whole land of Egypt.' • He took off his signet ring and put it on Joseph's finger; he had him dressed in robes of fine linen, and hung a gold chain round his neck. • He mounted him in his viceroy's chariot and men cried 'Make way!' before him. Thus Pharaoh made him ruler over all Egypt • and said to him, 'I am the Pharaoh, yet without your consent no one will lift hand or foot throughout Egypt.' • Pharaoh named him Zaphenath-paneah, and he gave him as his wife Asenath daughter of Potiphera priest of On. Joseph's authority extended over the whole of Egypt.

• Joseph was thirty years old at the time he entered the service of Pharaoh king of Egypt. When he left the royal presence, he made a tour of inspection through the land. • During the seven years of plenty when there were abundant harvests, • Joseph gathered all the food produced in Egypt then and stored it in the towns, putting in each the food from the surrounding country. • He stored the grain in huge quantities; it was like the sand of the sea, so much that he stopped measuring: it was beyond all measure.

• Before the years of famine came, two sons were born to Joseph by Asenath daughter of Potiphera priest of On. • He named the elder Manasseh, 'for', he said, 'God has made me forget all my troubles and my father's family'. • He named the second Ephraim, 'for', he said, 'God has made me fruitful in the land of my hardships'. • When the seven years of plenty in Egypt came to an end, • the seven years of famine began, as Joseph had predicted. There was famine in every country, but there was food throughout Egypt. • The whole world came to Egypt to buy grain from Joseph, so severe was the famine everywhere.   (REB)

Joseph's Rise to Power (cont.)

chariot. Finally he is given an Egyptian theophoric name (45) meaning 'God speaks, and he lives', and marries into the highest circles of the Egyptian nobility, which in a country where Pharaoh is God implies the priesthood. Thus, without any adverse comment from the author, Joseph is completely Egyptianised. True, he gives his children Hebrew names, but the etymologies offered imply a break, at least for the moment, with his past – though v.51 probably means only *all my troubles* arising from *my father's family*.

Joseph has now had part of his first dream fulfilled. He is also in some respects a changed man. From spoiled adolescent he has become in turn trusty servant and wise counsellor. His ambition may be satisfied, but he remains somewhat smug, and he can get on with everyone except his brothers. At this point we launch into the second act of the story. The linchpin of it is *the famine*, whose prospect has already brought Joseph to power, and whose realisation will now bring his brothers to Egypt.

The statement that *the whole world came to Egypt to buy grain* is corroborated from Egyptian sources, including this from an inscription of the C14th BC: 'certain of the foreigners who know not how they may live have come. Their countries are starving and they live like the beasts of the desert' (*ANET* 251).

The Brothers' First Visit to Egypt

42. 1 Jacob, seeing that there were supplies to be had in Egypt, said to his sons, 'Why do you keep staring at one another? • I hear', he said, 'that there are supplies in Egypt. Go down and procure some for us there, so that we may survive and not die.' • So ten of Joseph's brothers went down to procure grain in Egypt. • But Jacob did not send Joseph's brother Benjamin with his brothers. 'Nothing must happen to him,' he thought.

5 • Thus the sons of Israel were among the other people who came to get supplies, there being famine in Canaan. • It was Joseph, as the man in authority over the country, who allocated the rations to the entire population. So Joseph's brothers went and bowed down before him, their faces touching the ground. • As soon as Joseph saw his brothers he recognised them. But he did not make himself known to them, and he spoke harshly to them. 'Where have you come from?' he asked. 'From Canaan to get food,' they replied.

• Now when Joseph recognised his brothers, but they did not recognise him, • Joseph remembered the dreams he had had about them, and said to them, 'You are **10** spies. You have come to discover the country's weak points.' • 'No, my lord,' they said, 'your servants have come to get food. • We are all sons of the same man. We are honest men, your servants are not spies.' • 'Oh no,' he replied, 'you have come to discover the country's weak points.' • 'Your servants were twelve brothers,' they said, 'sons of the same man in Canaan, but the youngest is at present with our father, and the other one is no more.' • To which Joseph retorted, 'It is as I said, you **15** are spies. • This is the test you are to undergo: as sure as Pharaoh lives you shall not leave unless your youngest brother comes here. • Send one of your number to fetch your brother; you others will remain under arrest, so that your statements can be tested to see whether or not you are honest. If not, then as sure as Pharaoh lives you are spies.' • Whereupon, he put them all into custody for three days. ▸

The Brothers' First Visit to Egypt

With Ch. 42 we are back with all the tensions which have split Jacob's family. Jacob himself speaks first and last. At the start he shows his contempt for all his grown-up sons; when they return and tell him the results of their visit, he has nothing but criticism for them (36). He now cares only for the new favourite *Benjamin*, but the chief concern of this 'rhetorician of grief' (Alter) is for himself.

The main drama, however, unfolds in Egypt. At the very start (6) the brothers formally fulfilled the rest of Joseph's first dream (37.7) by bowing to him. But he wanted real humiliation, and set about a long game of cat and mouse with them. His first move was plausible enough. Egypt, as the granary of the ANE, was particularly sensitive on her north-eastern frontier, where a long canal backed by a row of fortresses had to make up for the lack of natural defences. Faced with the accusation of spying, the brothers became flustered. After the inadvertent irony of *We are all sons . . .* (11), they first of all annoy Joseph by the bland evasiveness of their reference to him (literally, he 'is not') and then, by mentioning a younger son, give him an idea. By demanding that they *fetch* Benjamin, he can *test* both the veracity of their story (20) and their attitude to the new youngest. Meanwhile all but one must remain in Egypt in prison – as surety, but also as requital for his own time in the cistern.

There follows a three-day interval, which allows time for reflection. Joseph reduces his demand to one brother as surety. The brothers have no alternative

The Brothers' First Visit to Egypt (cont.)

• On the third day Joseph said to them, 'Do this and you will live, for I am a man who fears God. • If you are honest men, let one of your brothers be detained where you are imprisoned; the rest of you, go and take supplies home for your starving families. • But you must bring your youngest brother back to me; in this way, what you have said will be verified, and you will not have to die!' And this is what they did. • And they said to one another, 'Clearly, we are being punished for what we did to our brother. We saw his deep misery when he pleaded with us, but we would not listen, and now this misery has come home to us.' • Reuben retorted to them, 'Did I not tell you not to wrong the boy? But you would not listen. Now comes the accounting.' • They did not know that Joseph understood, because there was an interpreter between them. • He turned away from them and wept. When he was able to speak to them again, he chose Simeon out of their number and had him bound while they looked on.

• Joseph gave the order to fill their panniers with grain, to put back each man's money in his sack, and to give them provisions for the journey. This was done for them. • Then they loaded their supplies on their donkeys and went away. • But when they camped for the night, one of them opened his sack to give his donkey some fodder and saw his money – there it was in the mouth of his sack. • He said to his brothers, 'My money has been put back; here it is, in my sack!' Their hearts sank, and they looked at one another in panic, saying, 'What is this that God has done to us?'

• Returning to their father Jacob in Canaan, they gave him a full report of what had happened to them, • 'The man who is lord of the country spoke harshly to us, accusing us of spying on the country. • We told him, "We are honest men, we are not spies. • We were twelve brothers, sons of the same father. One of us is no more, and the youngest is at present with our father in Canaan." • But the man who is lord of the country said to us, "This is how I shall know whether you are honest: leave one of your brothers with me. Take supplies for your starving families and be gone, • but bring me back your youngest brother and then I shall know that you are not spies but honest men. Then I shall give your brother back to you and you will be free to move about the country." '

• Then their father Jacob said to them, 'You are robbing me of my children; Joseph is no more; Simeon is no more; and now you want to take Benjamin. I bear the brunt of all this!' • Then Reuben said to his father, 'You may put my two sons to death if I do not bring him back to you. Put him in my care and I will bring him back to you.' • But he replied, 'My son is not going down with you, for now his brother is dead he is the only one left. If any harm came to him on the journey you are undertaking, you would send my white head down to Sheol with grief!' (NJB)

The Brothers' First Visit to Egypt (cont.)

but to accept. They also – and this is the first sign of grace – make the psychological connection and admit their own guilt (21). The reader now learns for the first time that Joseph had *pleaded with* them, and Joseph learns that *Reuben* had interceded for him; so in place of Reuben he retains the next oldest, *Simeon*. Joseph himself, moved by their repentance, weeps for the first of what will be three times. Then, with a new sense of family solidarity, he returns them their *money* without their knowledge. But their guilty consciences treat the gift as a trap (28), which causes them much anxiety and the reader much amusement.

The Brothers' Second Visit to Egypt

43. 1 But the famine in the country grew worse, • and when they had finished eating the supplies which they had brought from Egypt their father said to them, 'Go back and get us a little food.' • 'But', Judah replied, 'the man expressly warned us, "You will not be admitted to my presence unless your brother is with you." • If you are 5 ready to send our brother with us, we will go down and get food for you. • But if you are not ready to send him, we will not go down, in view of the man's warning, "You will not be admitted to my presence unless your brother is with you." ' • Then Israel said, 'Why did you bring this misery on me by telling the man you had another brother?' • They replied, 'He kept questioning us about ourselves and our family, asking, "Is your father still alive?" and, "Have you another brother?" That is why we told him. How could we know he was going to say, "Bring your brother down here"?' • Judah then said to his father Israel, 'Send the boy with me, and let us be off and go, if we are to survive and not die, we, you, and our dependants. • I will go surety for him, and you can hold me responsible for him. If I do not bring him back to you and produce him before you, let me bear the blame all my life. 10 • Indeed, if we had not wasted so much time we should have been there and back twice by now!'

• Then their father Israel said to them, 'If it must be so, then do this: take some of the country's best products in your baggage and take them to the man as a gift: some balsam, some honey, gum tragacanth, resin, pistachio nuts and almonds. • Take double the amount of money with you and return the money put back in the mouths of your sacks; it may have been a mistake. • Take your brother, and go back to the man. • May the Almighty move the man to be kind to you, and allow you to bring back your other brother and Benjamin. As for me, if I must be bereaved, 15 bereaved I must be.' • The men took this gift; they took double the amount of money with them, and Benjamin. They set off, went down to Egypt and presented themselves before Joseph. • When Joseph saw Benjamin with them he said to his chamberlain, 'Take these men into the house. Slaughter a beast and prepare it, for these men are to eat with me at midday.' • The man did as Joseph had ordered, and took the men to Joseph's house.   ▸

The Brothers' Second Visit to Egypt

As the denouement approaches, the progress of events is slowed still further. True, the journey itself passes, as often, in a flash (15). But the preparation for it (1–14) repeats much material from Ch. 42; the first scene in Egypt (18–25) is a diversion; and the final scene with Joseph (26–34) still scarcely advances the story. These three sections, consisting largely of conversation, deepen the psychology but retard the narrative, and thus aim to increase the tension.

The scene within the family (1–14) shows *Jacob* still fearful of losing Benjamin. Hitherto he has been prepared to sacrifice Simeon to save him, and even now he half hopes to keep *Benjamin* behind – hence, perhaps, *a little* in v.2. He is also, as before, inclined to pity himself and blame the brothers (6, 14). But *Judah*'s intervention represents an advance on Reuben's in 42.37: it is not only generous, but realistically so; it is also expressed with force, and it makes explicit the thinking which alone can unite this quarrelsome family (8).

The *gifts* (11) are part of normal Near Eastern courtesy even today; *honey* was especially prized before the discovery of sugar. The welcome announced in v.16

The Brothers' Second Visit to Egypt (cont.)

• The men were afraid at being taken to Joseph's house and said, 'We are being taken there because of the money replaced in our sacks the first time. They will set on us; they will fall on us and make slaves of us, and take our donkeys too.' • So they went up to Joseph's chamberlain and spoke to him at the entrance to the house. • 'By your leave, sir,' they said, 'we came down once before to get supplies, • and when we reached camp and opened our sacks, there was each man's money in the mouth of his sack, to the full. But we have brought it back with us, • and we have brought more money with us for the supplies. We do not know who put our money in our sacks.' • 'Set your minds at ease,' he replied, 'do not be afraid. Your God and the God of your father put treasure in your sacks for you. I received your money.' And he brought Simeon out to them.

• The man then took the men into Joseph's house. He offered them water to wash their feet, and gave their donkeys fodder. • They arranged their gift while they waited for Joseph to come at midday, for they had heard they were to dine there. • When Joseph arrived at the house they offered him the gift they had with them, bowing low before him. • He greeted them pleasantly, asking, 'Is your father well, the old man you told me of? Is he still alive?' • 'Your servant our father is well,' they replied, 'he is still alive,' and they bowed respectfully. • Looking about, he saw his brother Benjamin, his mother's son. 'Is this your youngest brother', he asked, 'of whom you told me?' And he added, 'God be good to you, my son.' • Joseph hurried out; so strong was the affection he felt for his brother that he wanted to cry. He went into his room and there he wept. • After washing his face he returned and, controlling himself, gave the order: 'Serve the meal.' • He was served separately; so were they, and so were the Egyptians who ate in his household, for the Egyptians could not take food with Hebrews; Egyptians have a horror of doing so. • They were placed facing him in order of seniority, from the eldest to the youngest, and the men looked at one another in amazement. • He had portions carried to them from his own dish, the portion for Benjamin being five times larger than any of the others. And they feasted with him and drank freely.   (NJB)

The Brothers' Second Visit to Egypt (cont.)

raises the reader's expectations, but the brothers take it quite otherwise. Fearing for the loss of everything (even their *donkeys!*), they launch into verbose exculpation. The chamberlain's reply (23) is lofty and a little mysterious – he clearly knows something they do not – but at least they are reassured by the release of *Simeon.*

And sure enough Joseph *greeted them pleasantly,* making no mention of spying or of the money-bags. He then sees *Benjamin,* who was only an infant when Joseph left home. The sight leads him to withdraw and weep for the second time, and this time we are given much circumstantial detail (31). *The meal* itself follows normal procedure. Herodotus confirms the Egyptian insistence on racial separation at table (32), a custom which has to be explained to Jewish readers. The host's gift of *portions from his own dish* (34) was and is another part of Near Eastern courtesy. But Joseph kept them guessing by seating them *in order* of age – how *could* he know? Only the wine relaxes them, alas too soon.

The Last Hurdle

44. 1 Joseph gave the steward these instructions: 'Fill the men's packs with food, as much as they can carry. • And put my goblet, the silver one, at the top of the youngest brother's pack.' He did as Joseph had told him. • At first light the brothers were allowed to take their donkeys and set off; • but before they had gone very far from the city, Joseph said to his steward, 'Go after those men at once, and when

5 you catch up with them, say, "Why have you repaid good with evil? • Why have you stolen the silver goblet? It is the one my lord drinks from, and which he uses for divination. This is a wicked thing you have done." ' • When the steward overtook them, he reported his master's words. • But they replied, 'My lord, how can you say such things? Heaven forbid that we should do such a thing! • Look! The silver we found at the top of our packs we brought back to you from Canaan. Why, then, should we steal silver or gold from your master's house? • If any one of us is found with the goblet, he shall die; and, what is more, my lord, the rest of us shall become

10 your slaves.' • He said, 'Very well; I accept what you say. Only the one in whose possession it is found will become my slave; the rest will go free.' • Each quickly lowered his pack to the ground and opened it, • and when the steward searched, beginning with the eldest and finishing with the youngest, the goblet was found in Benjamin's pack. • At this they tore their clothes; then one and all they loaded their donkeys and returned to the city.

• Joseph was still in the house when Judah and his brothers arrived, and they

15 threw themselves on the ground before him. • Joseph said, 'What is this you have done? You might have known that a man such as I am uses divination.' • Judah said, 'What can we say, my lord? What can we plead, or how can we clear ourselves? God has uncovered our crime. Here we are, my lord, ready to be made your slaves, we ourselves as well as the one who was found with the goblet.' • 'Heaven forbid that I should do such a thing!' answered Joseph. 'Only the one who was found with the goblet shall become my slave; the rest of you can go home to your father safe and sound.'   ▸

The Last Hurdle

For Joseph had one last trick up his sleeve. The motif of the *silver goblet* is used cleverly here. By telling the brothers that Joseph used it for *divination* (a practice like our reading the tea leaves) the steward increased (i) the value of the cup and the penalty for stealing it, (ii) the mysterious powerfulness of his master (cp. v.15) and (iii) the brothers' certainty that Joseph would find out the truth. Hence, at first, their extravagant protestation in v.7, equivalent to a self-curse 'May I die if. . .'. But the steward, briefed by Joseph, proposes a lighter penalty.

The plan is to set up a test where the brothers are tempted to sacrifice their father's favourite in order to go free themselves.

When the goblet is 'found', the brothers, in a final and most abject prostration (14), admit defeat. Judah as their spokesman still protests their innocence of the theft, but on the broader canvas admits that justice has finally caught up with them. He proposes a collective penalty (16), implying that the rest of them are ready to stand by Benjamin; but Joseph adheres to his planned test and turns the screw.

The Last Hurdle (cont.)

• Then Judah went up to him and said, 'Please listen, my lord, and let your servant speak a word, I beg. Do not be angry with me, for you are as great as Pharaoh himself. • My lord, you asked us whether we had a father or a brother. • We answered, "We have an aged father, and he has a young son born in his old age; this boy's full brother is dead, and since he alone is left of his mother's children, his father loves him." • You said to us, your servants, "Bring him down to me so that I may set eyes on him." • We told you, my lord, that the boy could not leave his father; his father would die if he left him. • But you said, "Unless your youngest brother comes down with you, you shall not enter my presence again." • We went back to your servant my father, and reported to him what your lordship had said, • so when our father told us to go again and buy food, • we answered, "We cannot go down; for without our youngest brother we cannot enter the man's presence; but if our brother is with us, we will go." • Then your servant my father said to us, "You know that my wife bore me two sons. • One left me, and I said, 'He must have been torn to pieces.' I have not seen him since. • If you take this one from me as well, and he comes to any harm, then you will bring down my grey hairs in misery to the grave." • Now, my lord, if I return to my father without the boy – and remember, his life is bound up with the boy's – • what will happen is this: he will see that the boy is not with us and he will die, and your servants will have brought down our father's grey hairs in sorrow to the grave. • Indeed, my lord, it was I who went surety for the boy to my father. I said, "If I do not bring him back to you, then you can blame me for it all my life." • Now, my lord, let me remain in place of the boy as my lord's slave, and let him go with his brothers. • How can I return to my father without the boy? I could not bear to see the misery which my father would suffer.'

(REB)

The Last Hurdle (cont.)

The crisis having come, Judah's response is magnificent. Although he knows Joseph's power is unlimited (18), he faces him with courage and diplomacy. The version he gives of the original conversation in Egypt (19–23) is the fullest we have had so far, held up so as to increase the emotional tension. Tactfully, Judah ascribes Joseph's original request to kindness; bravely he criticises Joseph's perseverance in it (22–23). Switching to the conversation in Canaan, he stresses Jacob's suffering (24–30), unconsciously striking the irresistible note, and even brings himself to quote the wounding words which showed the margin of Jacob's preference for his sons by Rebecca (27). Finally he refers briefly to his personal responsibility for Benjamin, and offers to stand in for him as Joseph's slave precisely *because* he is his father's favourite. The brothers would suffer *with* Benjamin, Judah will suffer *for* him. In their different ways they have passed the test set by Joseph, showing that they have not only learned but changed. This is the moral climax of the story.

The Recognition Scene

45. 1 Joseph was no longer able to control his feelings in front of all his attendants, and he called, 'Let everyone leave my presence!' There was nobody present when Joseph made himself known to his brothers, • but he wept so loudly that the Egyptians heard him, and news of it got to Pharaoh's household. • Joseph said to his brothers, 'I am Joseph! Can my father be still alive?' They were so dumbfounded at finding themselves face to face with Joseph that they could not answer. • Joseph said to them, 'Come closer to me,' and when they did so, he said, 'I am your brother

5 Joseph, whom you sold into Egypt. • Now do not be distressed or blame yourselves for selling me into slavery here; it was to save lives that God sent me ahead of you. • For there have now been two years of famine in the land, and there will be another five years with neither ploughing nor harvest. • God sent me on ahead of you to ensure that you will have descendants on earth, and to preserve for you a host of survivors. • It is clear that it was not you who sent me here, but God, and he has made me Pharaoh's chief counsellor, lord over his whole household and ruler of all Egypt. • Hurry back to my father and give him this message from his son Joseph:

10 "God has made me lord of all Egypt. Come down to me without delay. • You will live in the land of Goshen and be near me, you, your children and grandchildren, your flocks and herds, and all that you have. • I shall provide for you there and see that you and your household and all that you have are not reduced to want; for there are still five years of famine to come." • You can see for yourselves, and so can my brother Benjamin, that it is really Joseph himself who is speaking to you. • Tell my father of all the honour which I enjoy in Egypt, tell him all you have seen, and bring him down here with all speed.' • He threw his arms round his brother Benjamin and

15 wept, and Benjamin too embraced him weeping. • He then kissed each of his brothers and wept over them; after that his brothers were able to talk with him . . . ▸

The Recognition Scene

The emotional climax is marked by the last verse of Ch. 44, where Judah switches from formal to personal language, and the first three verses of Ch. 45. Now for the third and last time Joseph weeps, but this time in the presence of his brothers – and so loudly that he is overheard by the Egyptians, who have been sent out of the room especially so as to leave all twelve brothers on their own together for the denouement. Yet for ten of them anxiety is not yet over: fear is mixed with the incredulity which causes Joseph to repeat his identity, and his *come closer* creates a final frisson.

But quickly and generously he allays their anxiety (5). For Judah's magna-nimity has brought about a change in him too. Where the old Joseph would have explicitly and smugly forgiven them, the new one implicitly exonerates them by raising the story to a higher plane. They were not agents but instruments of God's providence, which was at work to preserve the family.

That preservation demands now that the family move to Egypt. They will live in *Goshen* (see map 1). Curiously, we have an Egyptian papyrus from c.1220 BC (*ANET* 259) in which a frontier official reports that he has permitted 'the Bedouin tribes of Edom' to settle in Goshen 'to keep them and their cattle alive'. Joseph therefore sends the

The Recognition Scene (cont.)

4   • He sent his brothers on their way, warning them not to quarrel among themselves on the road. • They set off, and went up from Egypt to their father Jacob in Canaan. • When they told him that Joseph was still alive and was ruler of the whole of Egypt, he was stunned at the news and did not believe them. • However when they reported to him all that Joseph had said to them, and when he saw the wagons which Joseph had provided to fetch him, his spirit revived. • Israel said, 'It is enough! Joseph my son is still alive; I shall go and see him before I die.'   (REB)

The Recognition Scene (cont.)

brothers back to Canaan to fetch the rest of the family. Relations are now so relaxed that he can tease them by telling them *not to quarrel on the road* (24). Nor is there any need for the brothers, on their return, to tell Jacob of the beginning of the whole story: for him *it is enough* that it has a happy ending.

The End of the Affair

.1   So Israel set out with all his possessions. Arriving at Beersheba, he offered sacrifices to the God of his father Isaac. • God spoke to Israel in a vision at night, 'Jacob, Jacob,' he said. 'Here I am,' he replied. • 'I am El, God of your father,' he said. 'Do not be afraid of going down to Egypt, for I will make you into a great nation there. • I shall go down to Egypt with you and I myself shall bring you back again, and Joseph's hand will close your eyes.'

28   • Israel sent Judah ahead to Joseph, so that Judah might present himself to Joseph in Goshen. When they arrived in Goshen, • Joseph had his chariot made ready and went up to Goshen to meet his father Israel. As soon as he appeared he threw his arms round his neck and for a long time wept on his shoulder. • Israel said to Joseph, 'Now I can die, now that I have seen you in person and seen you still alive.'

.29   • When Israel's time to die drew near he sent for his son Joseph and said to him, 'If you really love me, place your hand under my thigh as pledge that you will act with faithful love towards me: do not bury me in Egypt! • When I lie down with my ancestors, carry me out of Egypt and bury me in their tomb.' 'I shall do as you say,' he replied. • 'Swear to me,' he insisted. So he swore to him, and Israel sank back on the pillow.

.12   • His sons did what he had ordered them to do for him. • His sons carried him to Canaan and buried him in the cave in the field at Machpelah, facing Mamre, which Abraham had bought from Ephron the Hittite as a burial site of his own. • Then Joseph returned to Egypt with his brothers and all those who had come up with him to bury his father.   (NJB)

The End of the Affair

The excerpts here give the bare bones of events. Jacob's decision to go down to Egypt (45.28) is confirmed by a theophany (46.1–4). God promises not merely to *go down* with him but also to *bring* him *back*. The last phrase refers ostensibly to his burial in Canaan; but the exodus is already in view.

The place of *burial* was important because it was bound up with the promise of the land. So Jacob on his deathbed insists that Judah swears the most solemn oath (cp. 24.2). After his death the whole fraternity takes his body in procession to the ancestral tomb in *Machpelah* (see Ch. 23).

The End of the Affair (cont.)

50. 15   • Now that their father was dead, Joseph's brothers were afraid, for they said, 'What if Joseph should bear a grudge against us and pay us back for all the harm we did to him?' • They therefore sent a messenger to Joseph to say, 'In his last words to us before he died, your father gave us this message: • "Say this to Joseph: I ask you to forgive your brothers' crime and wickedness; I know they did you harm." So now we beg you: forgive our crime, for we are servants of your father's God.' Joseph was moved to tears by their words. • His brothers approached and bowed to the ground before him. 'We are your slaves,' they said. • But Joseph

20   replied, 'Do not be afraid. Am I in the place of God? • You meant to do me harm; but God meant to bring good out of it by preserving the lives of many people, as we see today. • Do not be afraid. I shall provide for you and your dependants.' Thus he comforted them and set their minds at rest.   (REB)

The End of the Affair (cont.)

But there is one last twist to come. The death of Jacob reawakened the anxieties of the brothers. So they found a face-saving way of repeating their apology to Joseph and ensuring his continued forgiveness. His reply ensures that Genesis ends with a reminder also of God's second promise, that of a large family. Yet there remains the hint that the enmity between the brothers may one day erupt again – as it did in the tensions between the two kingdoms of Israel and Judah.

EXODUS

Introduction

The story of the exodus is of central importance to the 'salvation history' of Jews and Christians. In the Bible, NT as well as OT, it is a prototype of all God's saving acts on behalf of his people. Jewish families have celebrated it every year throughout history in the solemn ritual of the Passover meal. And the oppressed of all nations still echo the refrain of the negro spiritual: 'Let my people go'.

But how far can the exodus story be regarded as historical in the ordinary sense of the word? There is plenty of evidence in support of its general setting viz. the presence in ancient Egypt of a colony of foreign workers, often prisoners of war, set to forced labour on public works for the Pharaohs, and finally making good their escape (see commentary on Ch.5). Jews in particular regularly used Egypt as something of a bolt-hole, and some of them settled there for good. But as to the more specific questions which interest modern historians, such as dates and numbers and sequences of causation, archaeology suggests that the narrative should be treated with great reserve (see p.30f.).

From a literary point of view Exodus is among the most uneven books in the OT. To a religious reader it offers the thrill of numinous encounters and the solemn ritual of the covenant. On the narrative plane the interest is aroused by the rumbling tensions between God and Moses and captured by the crescendo of the Great Escape. Against that, the magical element is more obtrusive than in any other book, and the ten plagues, even if removed from the realm of magic by rationalising interpretation, are simply too numerous to hold the attention. Moreover the actual story-telling is inferior to that of Genesis, especially from Ch. 16 on, where J seems to have been squeezed out by P and D.

Israel in Egypt

1.6 In course of time Joseph and all his brothers and that entire generation died. • The Israelites were prolific and increased greatly, becoming so numerous and strong that the land was full of them.

• When a new king ascended the throne of Egypt, one who did not know about Joseph, • he said to his people, 'These Israelites have become too many and too strong for us. • We must take steps to ensure that they increase no **10** further; otherwise we shall find that, if war comes, they will side with the enemy, fight against us, and become masters of the country.' • So taskmasters were appointed over them to oppress them with forced labour. This is how Pharaoh's store cities, Pithom and Rameses, were built. (REB)

Israel in Egypt

In the century since the death of Joseph, the group had grown in number, in accordance with the promise to Abraham, and is now known as *Israelites* collectively, with no special reference to Jacob (Israel) as an individual. They are also now for the first time referred to as *Hebrews*, a name of uncertain meaning. Etymologically it may be related to Hapiru, a people described in Egyptian texts as migrant foreigners. One such text is a letter of instruction to provide corn to 'the Hapiru who are transporting stone for the great gateway of . . . [Pharaoh] Rameses beloved of Amon'. That letter might have been written as a comment on v. 11f., for Rameses II (c.1280-1210 BC) built *Rameses* as his northern capital. *Pithom* has not been securely identified.

Israel in Egypt (cont.)

REB differs from most other translations in v.11b. The Hebrew reads 'And they built Pithom etc.', which most naturally means that the Israelites did the building. If they did, the exodus would have to be dated c.1250 BC. But 'they built' in Hebrew can also be used for the passive *were built*. This allows REB's rendering, which can bring the date of the exodus down to c.1170. Actually the half-verse 11b interrupts the sequence of thought, and may not be original anyway.

It was not absurd for the Egyptians to think that the Israelites might *side with the enemy*, as their settlement was in Goshen, astride the main route into the country.

The Birth of Moses

1.12 But the more oppressive the treatment of the Israelites, the more they increased and spread, until the Egyptians came to loathe them. • They ground down their Israelite slaves, • and made life bitter for them with their harsh demands, setting them to make mortar and bricks and to do all sorts of tasks in the fields. In every kind of labour they made ruthless use of them.

15 • The king of Egypt issued instructions to the Hebrew midwives, of whom one was called Shiphrah, the other Puah. • 'When you are attending the Hebrew women in childbirth,' he told them, 'check as the child is delivered: if it is a boy, kill him; if it is a girl, however, let her live.' • But the midwives were godfearing women, and did not heed the king's words; they let the male children live. • Pharaoh summoned the midwives and, when he asked them why they had done this and let the male children live, • they answered, 'Hebrew women are not like Egyptian women; they go into labour and give birth before the midwife arrives.'

20 • God made the midwives prosper, and the people increased in numbers and strength; • and because the midwives feared God he gave them families of their own. • Pharaoh then issued an order to all the Egyptians that every new-born Hebrew boy was to be thrown into the Nile, but all the girls were to be allowed to live.

2.1 A certain man, a descendant of Levi, married a Levite woman. • She conceived and bore a son, and when she saw what a fine child he was, she kept him hidden for three months. • Unable to conceal him any longer, she got a rush basket for him, made it watertight with pitch and tar, laid him in it, and placed it among the reeds by the bank of the Nile. • The child's sister stood some distance away to see what would happen to him.   ▸

The Birth of Moses

The story of Moses' birth is closer to folktale than to history. Even if the Pharaoh had wished to weaken his cheap labour force, the first two methods proposed in vv11-14 and 15-21 are intentionally absurd. The pair of *midwives*, whose names mean Beauty and Splendour, are members of a long line of Israelite women who outwit a (usually male) foreign oppressor. The third method, the edict of v.22, is obviously introduced as a lead-in to the story of Moses' birth, and the same probably goes for the story of the midwives. REB's phrase *check as the child is delivered* is a guess. The Hebrew is 'check the two stones', probably meaning the testicles.

The tale of the exposed child is found worldwide. A common version of it has a future ruler exposed in a chest or basket on water. In particular, a legend about Sargon I, king of Akkad* a thousand years earlier, contains the following lines:

The Birth of Moses (cont.)

5 • Pharaoh's daughter came down to bathe in the river, while her ladies-in-waiting walked on the bank. She noticed the basket among the reeds and sent her slave-girl to bring it. • When she opened it, there was the baby; it was crying, and she was moved with pity for it. 'This must be one of the Hebrew children,' she said. • At this the sister approached Pharaoh's daughter: 'Shall I go and fetch you one of the Hebrew women to act as a wet-nurse for the child?' • When Pharaoh's daughter told her to do so, she went and called the baby's mother. • Pharaoh's daughter said to her, 'Take the child, nurse him for me, and I shall pay you for it.'

10 She took the child and nursed him at her breast. • Then, when he was old enough, she brought him to Pharaoh's daughter, who adopted him and called him Moses, 'because', said she, 'I drew him out of the water.'   (REB)

The Birth of Moses (cont.)

My mother was a priestess (?), I do not know my father.
The priestess my mother conceived me and bore me in secret.
She laid me in a basket of rushes, sealed my covering with asphalt.
The river bore me to Akki, the drawer of water.
Akki, the drawer of water, (took me) as son and reared me.   (NERT 99)

The biblical version of the story has a number of special touches. The presence of Moses' *sister* (not here named as Miriam) shows the continuing care of the parents. The compassion of the *Pharaoh's daughter* is contrasted with the ruthlessness of her father: indeed there is a hint that she connived at Miriam's ruse about the wet-nursing. Ironically, Pharaoh will actually *pay* the child's own mother to *nurse* him in order to defeat the royal edict!

The princess could well have named him *Moses*, which is Egyptian for son. It is found, combined with the name of a God, in the name of many pharaohs e.g. Thutmose = son of Thut; and in many versions of the folk-tale the foundling does in fact become king. The Hebrew etymology* offered in v.10 is bogus, but an Egyptian name was unacceptable.

Moses Grows to Manhood

2.11 One day after Moses was grown up, he went out to his own kinsmen and observed their labours. When he saw an Egyptian strike one of his fellow-Hebrews, • he looked this way and that, and, seeing no one about, he struck the Egyptian down and hid his body in the sand. • Next day when he went out, he came across two Hebrews fighting. He asked the one who was in the wrong, 'Why are you striking your fellow-countryman?' • The man replied, 'Who set you up as an official and judge over us? Do you mean to murder me as you murdered the Egyptian?' Moses was alarmed and said to himself, 'The affair must have become known.'

15 • When it came to Pharaoh's ears, he tried to have Moses put to death, but Moses fled from his presence and went and settled in Midian.   ◢

Moses Grows to Manhood

Two brief stories, cleverly juxtaposed, carry the reader rapidly forward in the life of Moses. At the beginning he is a callow youth in Egypt, by the end a married man in *Midian**, poised for a crucial intervention. In both of them the powerful emotions involved have to be understood from action and speech. This compression, of which J was a master, invited commentary and interpretation (*midrash*) from later rabbis, and in the case of the first of these stories there are two such *midrashim*

Moses Grows to Manhood (cont.)

2.16 • As Moses sat by a well one day, • the seven daughters of a priest of Midian came to draw water, and when they had filled the troughs to water their father's sheep, • some shepherds came and drove them away. But Moses came to the help of the girls and watered the sheep. • When they returned to their father, he said, 'How is it that you are back so quickly today?' • 'An Egyptian rescued us from the shepherds,' they answered; 'he even drew water for us and watered the 20 sheep.' • 'Then where is he?' their father asked. 'Why did you leave him there? Go and invite him to eat with us.'

• So it came about that Moses agreed to stay with the man, and he gave Moses his daughter Zipporah in marriage. • She bore him a son, and Moses called him Gershom, 'because', he said, 'I have become an alien in a foreign land.'

• Years passed, during which time the king of Egypt died, but the Israelites still groaned in slavery. They cried out, and their plea for rescue from slavery ascended to God. • He heard their groaning and called to mind his covenant with 25 Abraham, Isaac, and Jacob; • he observed the plight of Israel and took heed of it.

(REB)

Moses Grows to Manhood (cont.)

easily accessible in the New Testament (Acts 7.23-9, Heb 11.24-7).

Moses is here already revealed as protector and rescuer. But his first exploit is a failure. His caution (12) is ineffective, his intervention unwelcome (14), and he has to flee the country. The scene at the well is the counterpart of the previous incident. Moses successfully rescues the girls from their own countrymen, and the whole family responds with gratitude.

The romantic encounter at the well is one of J's favourite type-scenes (see Gen 24 and 29). This is much the shortest of them, though it contains all the typical ingredients. Alter observes that 'it holds Moses the man at a distance' – indeed

throughout Exodus the reader is 'excluded from the intimacy of domestic observation' of him. Even the folk-element of the *seven* daughters serves to distance us. The same may be said of the emphasis on Moses as a displaced person: see v.22 and *an Egyptian* of v.19. So in 11-15 he is neither Egyptian nor Hebrew. This sets the tone for a life spent as an alien and a wanderer. Even in personal terms he can never be certain where he stands either with his fellow-Israelites or with God.

The last three verses of Ch.2 constitute a bridge passage. The death of another Pharaoh in v.23 forms a frame with 1.8, while the statement that *God heard* the Israelites' complaints looks forward.

The Call of Moses

3. 1 While tending the sheep of his father-in-law Jethro, priest of Midian, Moses led the flock along the west side of the wilderness and came to Horeb, the mountain of God. • There an angel of the LORD appeared to him as a fire blazing out from a bush. Although the bush was on fire, it was not being burnt up, • and Moses said to himself, 'I must go across and see this remarkable sight. Why ever does the bush not burn away?' • When the LORD saw that Moses had turned aside to look, 5 he called to him out of the bush, 'Moses, Moses!' He answered, 'Here I am!' • God said, 'Do not come near! Take off your sandals, for the place where you are standing is holy ground.' • Then he said, 'I am the God of your father, the God of Abraham, Isaac, and Jacob.' Moses hid his face, for he was afraid to look at God.   ▸

The Call of Moses (cont.)

• The LORD said, 'I have witnessed the misery of my people in Egypt and have heard them crying out because of their oppressors. I know what they are suffering • and have come down to rescue them from the power of the Egyptians and to bring them up out of that country into a fine, broad land, a land flowing with milk and honey, the territory of Canaanites, Hittites, Amorites, Perizzites, Hivites, and Jebusites. • Now the Israelites' cry has reached me, and I have also seen how hard the Egyptians oppress them. • Come, I shall send you to Pharaoh, and you are to bring my people Israel out of Egypt.' • 'But who am I', Moses said to God, 'that I should approach Pharaoh and that I should bring the Israelites out of Egypt?' • God answered, 'I am with you. This will be your proof that it is I who have sent you: when you have brought the people out of Egypt, you will all worship God here at this mountain.'

• Moses said to God, 'If I come to the Israelites and tell them that the God of their forefathers has sent me to them, and they ask me his name, what am I to say to them?' • God answered, 'I AM that I am. Tell them that I AM has sent ⟩

The Call of Moses

The call of Moses is a crucial moment in the Bible. It is introduced by a condensed narrative (2-4) typical of Hebrew story-telling. First the narrator tells us that *an angel of the LORD appeared to him*. This, if we know the convention, gives the game away, since the angel is none other than God. Moses however is still in the natural world, impelled by no more than scientific curiosity – though his phrase *this remarkable sight* already hints at something more. Any doubts are finally resolved when God himself speaks, calling Moses twice (the usual formula) by name. To remove one's shoes was a common mark of respect, still practised by Muslims on entry to a mosque.

YHWH's next sentence contains an unexpected phrase, *the God of your father* (sing.). Since Moses's own father was not even named in 2.1, the reference is probably to *his father-in-law Jethro*, who is important enough to be the frame of the whole narrative (3.1 and 4.18).

The rest of the section is a conversation between God and Moses. From the point of view of the exodus narrative and the story of Moses, the following are the main points. God confirms that he has *heard* the cry of the Israelites and is going to *rescue* them from Egypt. He calls Moses to be

his agent both in negotiating with *Pharaoh* and in leading the *people*. Moses' response is guarded – not surprisingly, in view of the immensity of the task. He has two reservations. First is that the people will not believe him when he says God has sent him. To this God's initial answer is obscure to us (what is the *proof* in v.12?) and does not meet Moses' point. When he presses the point, Moses draws the response of v.14 – momentous but not easy to interpret.

For the strange convention which results in the name YHWH being translated 'Jehovah' see p.34. What matters here is the name and, more particularly, its meaning. About the original meaning scholars are uncertain. But the biblical writers all connected it with the Hebrew verb for 'to be' – a verb which is not static but dynamic, implying not mere existence but being alive and active both now and in the future. That is the sense of 'being' in which YHWH's name means 'he is' or 'he who is', and in which he says of himself, in vv.12 and 14, *I AM*.

But that still leaves an uncertainty about the cryptic phrase in 14, *I AM that* (i.e. who/what) *I am*. Probably it is intentionally enigmatic, not in the crude sense that God is unwilling to reveal it – for he does precisely that in the next verse – but

3.15
4.10

16

> **The Call of Moses (cont.)**
>
> you to them.' • He continued, 'You are to tell the Israelites that it is the LORD, the God of their forefathers, the God of Abraham, Isaac, and Jacob, who has sent you to them. This is my name for ever; this is my title in every generation.'
>   • 'But, LORD,' Moses protested, 'I have never been a man of ready speech, never in my life, not even now that you have spoken to me; I am slow and hesitant.' • The LORD said to him, 'Who is it that gives man speech? Who makes him dumb or deaf? Who makes him keen-sighted or blind? Is it not I, the LORD? • Go now; I shall help you to speak and show you what to say.' • Moses said, 'Lord, send anyone else you like.' • At this the LORD became angry with Moses: 'Do you not have a brother, Aaron the Levite? • He will do all the speaking to the people for you; he will be the mouthpiece, and you will be the god he speaks for.'
>   • Moses then went back to Jethro his father-in-law and said, 'Let me return to Egypt and see whether my kinsfolk are still alive.' Jethro said, 'Go, and may you have a safe journey.'   (REB)

The Call of Moses (cont.)

because any further attempt to pin down the godhead in words would be more likely to mislead than to illuminate. God lives and acts; he *gives man speech* (11) and himself speaks with him. But he may not be defined.

Moses' second reservation, in Ch. 4, that he is not *a man of ready speech*, is altogether more lightweight, and God seems uncertain how to respond to it. His lofty rhetorical questions in 11 fail to allay the anxiety of Moses, whose sulky rejoinder in v.13 makes God *angry* but enables him to introduce *Aaron*. The remarkable analogy

he draws with pagan practices, where a prophet was *the mouthpiece* of *the god*, can only be read as a tease. Altogether it is no wonder that Moses felt insecure.

Aaron son of Levi is only a fringe character in the Pentateuch. He is of especial interest to P, who presents him as the prototype high priest. Outside P he is Moses' shadow, the typical Helper of folk-tales. Astonishingly (in view of this passage) he hardly ever speaks, and comes alive only on two important occasions when he acts in opposition to Moses, in Exod 32 and Num 12.

4.20

24

> **God's Assault on Moses**
>
> Moses took his wife and children, mounted them on a donkey, and set out for Egypt with the staff of God in his hand. • On the journey, while they were encamped for the night, the LORD met Moses and would have killed him, • but Zipporah picked up a sharp flint, cut off her son's foreskin, and touched Moses' genitals with it, saying, 'You are my blood-bridegroom.' • So the LORD let Moses alone. It was on that occasion she said, 'Blood-bridegroom by circumcision.'   (REB)

God's Assault on Moses

This is one of the most mysterious incidents in the Bible. Some things seem clear. First God tried to kill Moses. That in itselcp.s astonishing enough; the nearest parallel to it is Jacob's wrestling with God in Gen 32. No explicit reason is given, though one may suppose it was because

he was uncircumcised. Second, *Zipporah* saved Moses by circumcising her son and then simulating a *circumcision* of Moses. Third, someone linked circumcision with marriage. This suggests that at one time it was a marriage or puberty rite, later transferred (like Christian baptism) to infancy

God's Assault on Moses (cont.)

as the sign of membership of the nation. The fact that flints were used points to a Neolithic origin for the custom. But much remains obscure about this primitive story and whatever lies behind it – not only to us but also probably to the narrator here.

Moses' First Approach to Pharaoh

1 After this, Moses and Aaron came to Pharaoh and told him, 'These are the words of the LORD the God of Israel: Let my people go so that they may keep a pilgrim-feast in my honour in the wilderness.' • 'Who is the LORD,' said Pharaoh, 'that I should listen to him and let Israel go? I do not acknowledge the LORD: and I tell you I will not let Israel go.' • They replied, 'The God of the Hebrews confronted us. Now we request leave to go three days' journey into the wilderness to offer sacrifice to the LORD our God, or else he may attack us with pestilence or sword.' • But the Egyptian king answered, 'What do you mean, Moses and Aaron, by

5 distracting the people from their work? Back to your labours! • Your people already outnumber the native Egyptians; yet you would have them stop working!'

• Pharaoh issued orders that same day to the people's slave-masters and their foremen • not to supply the people with the straw used in making bricks, as they had done hitherto. 'Let them go and collect their own straw, • but see that they produce the same tally of bricks as before; on no account reduce it. They are lazy, and that is why they are clamouring to go and offer sacrifice to their God • Keep these men hard at work; let them attend to that. Take no notice of their lies.' ▸

Moses' First Approach to Pharaoh

This section records Moses' first and highly unsuccessful attempt to achieve the people's release, which is marked as the theme by the framing words *let* them *go* in 5.1 and 6.1. It falls clearly into three parts, the first and last of which involve Moses and God.

Moses starts off aggressively, using the standard formula of the prophets, more familiar in the AV translation: 'Thus saith the LORD', followed by an imperative. A pilgrim-feast is in Hebrew *hāg*, the same word as Arabic *haj*, the Muslim pilgrimage to Mecca. The object of the exercise was to get out of Egypt for long enough to escape for good. Pharaoh responds (2) with equal force: as a god himself, he feels entitled to repudiate a competitor. Moses then tries an argument based on the normal behaviour of ANE gods. Pharaoh counters with one based on the normal behaviour of ANE workers. His suspiciousness is supported by sur-viving Egyptian work journals of the C15th-13th BC. Mention is made in them of strikes, desertion and absenteeism. Men regularly went absent 'to offer to their god', and gangs might be idle for eight or even fourteen days at a time because of religious holidays.

The story of the punishment is also convincing, both historically and psychologically. Bricks in Egypt were made of sun-dried mud mixed with chopped straw to hold it together. (The word *adobe* is derived indirectly from the ancient Egyptian word for brick.) The punishment was not, as the English idiom mistakenly has it, to make bricks *without* straw, but to *collect their own straw*, and thus to work longer hours to achieve the same quota of bricks. Again Egyptian documents corroborate. One official mentions a daily quota of 65 bricks a man, while another complains that 'there are neither men to make bricks nor straw in the neighbour-

Moses' First Approach to Pharaoh (cont.)

5. 10 • The slave-masters and foremen went out and said to the people, 'Pharaoh's orders are that no more straw is to be supplied. • Go and get it for yourselves wherever you can find it; but there is to be no reduction in your daily task.' • So the people scattered all over Egypt to gather stubble for the straw they needed, • while the slave-masters kept urging them on, demanding that they should complete, day after day, the same quantity as when straw had been supplied. • The Israelite foremen were flogged because they were held responsible by Pharaoh's slave-masters, who demanded, 'Why did you not complete the usual number of bricks yesterday or today?'

15 • The foremen came and appealed to Pharaoh: 'Why does your majesty treat us like this?' they said. • 'We are given no straw, yet they keep telling us to make bricks. Here are we being flogged, but the fault lies with your people.' • The king replied, 'You are lazy, bone lazy! That is why you keep on about going to offer sacrifice to the LORD. • Now get on with your work. You will not be given straw, but you must produce the full tally of bricks.' • When they were told that they must not let the daily number of bricks fall short, the Israelite foremen realised the

20 trouble they were in. • As they came from Pharaoh's presence they found Moses and Aaron waiting to meet them, • and said, 'May this bring the LORD's judgement down on you! You have made us stink in the nostrils of Pharaoh and his subjects; you have put a sword in their hands to slay us.'

• Moses went back to the LORD and said, 'Lord, why have you brought trouble on this people? And why did you ever send me? • Since I first went to Pharaoh to speak in your name he has treated your people cruelly, and you have done nothing

6. 1 at all to rescue them.' • The LORD answered, 'Now you will see what I shall do to Pharaoh: he will be compelled to let them go, he will be forced to drive them from his country.'

(REB)

Moses' First Approach to Pharaoh (cont.)

hood'. In fact the only phrase which is patently unhistorical is the *all over Egypt* in v.12, and even there the psychology is right: that is what it seemed like. Historical also is the organisation of the labour force, with Egyptian overseers and Hebrew *foremen*, and the foremen punished (14) for a shortfall in production by the workers. By a humane Egyptian regulation, direct access to the *Pharaoh* (15-19) could be granted even to slaves; but in this case the only result was a royal outburst.

Psychologically too the story has an uncanny resemblance to procedures in the Nazi concentration camps. Futile work like straw-gathering demoralised the workers, while the use of Hebrew foremen broke up national cohesion. Here the foremen round on Moses, who – this is the most astonishing feature of the whole tale – was *waiting* outside the audience-chamber (20). Moses in turn rounds on God, who promises to give such powerful help that in the end Pharaoh will not merely *let them go*, he will actually *drive them* out. Thus are introduced the ten plagues of Egypt, in which God and Moses work together without friction.

The Plagues of Egypt

All the 'signs and portents' which follow, up to but excluding the miracle at the Reed Sea, have two objects. First is that Pharaoh should *know that I am the LORD*: the theme is given in 7.17 and picked up often later. Second is that he should accept God's command given through Moses and so *let my people go*. Moses is represented as a prophet confronting a king, a common biblical theme, but he is also a skilled negotiator in the Wisdom tradition. Pharaoh too is shown, not entirely unsympathetically, as crafty diplomat as well as obstinate tyrant. At the theological level a number of problems arise (see below and on 10.20), but at the human level the progress of the negotiations is varied just enough to sustain interest.

Plague I: Blood

The LORD said to Moses, 'Pharaoh has been obdurate: he has refused to let the people go. • In the morning go to him on his way out to the river. Stand on the bank of the Nile to meet him, and take with you the staff that turned into a snake. • Say to him: "The LORD the God of the Hebrews sent me with this message for you: Let my people go in order to worship me in the wilderness. So far you have not listened. • Now the LORD says: By this you will know that I am the LORD. With this rod I hold in my hand, I shall strike the water of the Nile and it will be changed into blood. • The fish will die and the river will stink, and the Egyptians will be unable to drink water from the Nile." '

• Moses and Aaron did as the LORD had commanded. In the sight of Pharaoh and his courtiers Aaron lifted his staff and struck the water of the Nile, and all the water was changed to blood. • The fish died and the river stank, so that the Egyptians could not drink water from the Nile. There was blood everywhere in Egypt. • But the Egyptian magicians did the same thing by their spells. So Pharaoh still remained obstinate, as the LORD had foretold, and he did not listen to Moses and Aaron. • He turned and went into his palace, dismissing the matter from his mind.   (REB)

Plague I: Blood

The first plague is that of water turned to *blood*. Pharaoh is introduced on *the bank of the Nile*, perhaps taking a ritual bath in the sacred river like his daughter (2.5). He seems to have spent the day there, watching the spectacle. Like all the other plagues, the blood is best taken as arising from a natural phenomenon, in this case either a red water-weed or the red mud of the spring floods. Indeed it is possible to imagine a historical cp.stratum to the whole sequence. On this interpretation, excessive Nile flooding one summer could have led to a succession of natural disasters over a year, culminating in the death of Pharaoh's first-born and thus the exodus in the following spring (see further p.121f.). This would be perfectly compatible with the theological explanation of them outlined above.

But the whole sequence has an additional, magical, colouring. In plague I the Egyptian magicians compete successfully with Moses. This reassures Pharaoh, and so there are no negotiations. They do the same in plague II. In III however they fail, and are brought to recognise the 'hand of God' [8.19]: in VI they are a spent force [9.11], and thereafter they are not heard of. But the magic staff of Moses (7.15), with a similar one ascribed to Aaron, continues to be invoked up to IX. This magical colouring is generally alien to biblical narrative, and it may be the reason why there are so few references to plagues I-IX in the rest of the OT.

Plague IV: Flies

8.20 The LORD told Moses to rise early in the morning and stand in Pharaoh's path as he went out to the river, and to say to him, 'These are the words of the LORD: Let my people go in order to worship me. • If you refuse, I shall send swarms of flies on you, your courtiers, your people, and your houses; the houses of the Egyptians will be filled with the swarms and so will all the land they live in. • But on that day I shall make an exception of Goshen, the land where my people live: there will be no swarms there. Thus you will know that I, the LORD, am here in the land. • I shall make a distinction between my people and yours. Tomorrow this sign will appear.' • The LORD did this; dense swarms of flies infested Pharaoh's palace and the houses of his courtiers; throughout Egypt the land was threatened with ruin

25 by the swarms. • Pharaoh summoned Moses and Aaron and said to them, 'Go and sacrifice to your God, but in this country.' • 'That is impossible,' replied Moses, 'because the victim we are to sacrifice to the LORD our God is an abomination to the Egyptians. If the Egyptians see us offer such an animal, they will surely stone us to death. • We must go a three days' journey into the wilderness to sacrifice to the LORD our God, as he commands us.' • 'I shall let you go,' said Pharaoh, 'and you may sacrifice to your God in the wilderness; only do not go far. Now intercede for me.' • Moses answered, 'As soon as I leave you I shall intercede with the LORD. Tomorrow the swarms will depart from Pharaoh, his courtiers, and his people. Only your majesty must not trifle any more with the people by preventing them from going to sacrifice to the LORD.'

30 • Then Moses left Pharaoh and interceded with the LORD. • The LORD did as Moses had promised; he removed the swarms from Pharaoh, his courtiers, and his people; not one was left. • But once again Pharaoh became obdurate and would not let the people go.   (REB)

Plague IV: Flies

One new development in plague IV is the *distinction* made in its incidence as between Hebrews and Egyptians. This motif gradually grows in importance until it is central to plague X. Negotiations now proceed apace. Pharaoh clearly suspects the real intention of the Hebrews to escape, and tries to restrict them to Egypt.

Moses' reply (26) probably refers to an animal sacred to the Egyptians. Pharaoh makes a second concession in v.28, and then adds *intercede for me*, i.e. ask to have the plague removed. The request is abrupt (there is no *now* in the Hebrew) and perhaps shy: Pharaoh is beginning to 'know' the LORD.

Plague VIII: Locusts

10.3 Moses and Aaron went to Pharaoh and said to him, 'The LORD the God of the Hebrews has said: How long will you refuse to humble yourself before me? Let my people go in order to worship me. • If you refuse to let them go, tomorrow I

5 am going to bring locusts into your country. • They will cover the face of the land so that it cannot be seen. They will devour every tree that grows in your countryside. • Your houses and your courtiers' houses, every house in Egypt, will be full of them; your fathers never saw the like, nor their fathers before them; such a thing has not happened from their time until now.' With that he turned and left Pharaoh's presence.   ▸

Plague VIII: Locusts (cont.)

• Pharaoh's courtiers said to him, 'How long must we be caught in this man's toils? Let their menfolk go and worship the LORD their God. Do you not know by now that Egypt is ruined?' • So Moses and Aaron were brought back to Pharaoh, and he said to them, 'Go, worship the LORD your God; but who exactly is to go?' • 'Everyone,' said Moses, 'young and old, boys and girls, sheep and cattle; for we have to keep the LORD's pilgrim-feast.' • Pharaoh replied, 'The LORD be with you if I let you and your dependants go! You have some sinister purpose in mind. • No, your menfolk may go and worship the LORD, for that is what you were asking for.' And they were driven from Pharaoh's presence.

• The LORD said to Moses, 'Stretch out your hand over Egypt so that locusts may come and invade the land and devour all the vegetation in it, whatever the hail has left.' • When Moses stretched out his staff over the land of Egypt, the LORD sent a wind roaring in from the east all that day and all that night; and when morning came the east wind had brought the locusts. • They invaded the whole land of Egypt, and settled on all its territory in swarms so dense that the like of them had never been seen before, nor ever will be again. • They covered the surface of the whole land till it was black with them; they devoured all the vegetation and all the fruit of the trees that the hail had spared; there was no green left on tree or plant throughout all Egypt.

• Pharaoh hastily summoned Moses and Aaron. 'I have sinned against the LORD your God and against you,' he said. • 'Forgive my sin, I pray, just this once, and intercede with the LORD your God to remove this deadly plague from me.' • When Moses left Pharaoh and interceded with the LORD, • the wind was changed by the LORD into a westerly gale, which carried the locusts away and swept them into the Red Sea. Not one locust was left within the borders of Egypt. • But the LORD made Pharaoh obstinate, and he would not let the Israelites go.   (REB)

Plague VIII: Locusts

The story of the locusts follows a radically new pattern, in that the negotiations precede the plague itself. Moses and Aaron, having uttered their threat, make a dramatic exit (6). Pharaoh then, prompted for the first time by his courtiers, calls them back to talk. Moses, sensing a change, raises his demands (9), but only increases Pharaoh's (justified) suspicion and provokes his sarcasm. Negotiations break down, and the plague follows. The description of the swarms of *locusts*, though appropriately overwhelming, is not exaggerated: locusts can and periodically do devastate whole regions. Pharaoh is reduced to a much more abject contrition in 16f. (cp.8.28), but then again reneges. The author comments (20) that it was God who 'hardened Pharaoh's heart' (AV). This idea, which is common in Exodus, springs from the wish to ascribe all causality to God; but it creates more problems than it solves. Presumably Pharaoh's decision in v.20 cancels the permission he gave in v11 for the *menfolk* to go.

Plague IX, Darkness, and the Announcement of X

10.21 The LORD then said to Moses, 'Stretch out your hand towards heaven, and let darkness, darkness so thick that it can be felt, cover Egypt.' • So Moses stretched out his hand towards heaven, and for three days there was thick darkness over the whole of Egypt. • No one could see anyone else or move about for three days, but all the Israelites did have light where they were living.

• Pharaoh summoned Moses and said, 'Go and worship the LORD, but your flocks and herds are to stay here. Your wives and children can go with you too.'
25 • Moses said, 'But now you must give us sacrifices and burnt offerings to offer to the LORD our God. • And our livestock will go with us too; not a hoof will be left behind; for we may need animals from these to worship the LORD our God; for until we get there we ourselves cannot tell how we are to worship the LORD.'

• But the LORD made Pharaoh stubborn, and he refused to let them go.
• Pharaoh said to Moses, 'Out of my sight! Be sure you never see my face again, for the next time you see my face you die!'

11. 4 • Moses then said, 'The LORD says this, "At midnight I shall pass through Egypt, • and all the first-born in Egypt will die, from the first-born of Pharaoh, heir to his throne, to the first-born of the slave-girl at the mill, and all the first-born of the livestock. • And throughout Egypt there will be great wailing, such as never was before, nor will be again. • But against the Israelites, whether man or beast, never a dog shall bark, so that you may know that the LORD discriminates between Egypt and Israel. • Then all these officials of yours will come down to me and, bowing low before me, say: Go away, you and all the people who follow you! After which, I shall go."' And, hot with anger, he left Pharaoh's presence.

(NJB)

Plague IX, Darkness and the Announcement of X

If the text is accepted as it stands, 10.21-8 records plague IX, a sinister and palpable *darkness*, possibly modelled on the spring sand-storm or *hamsin*. Pharaoh is brought by it to make a further concession: the dependants may go, but the cattle must remain as a pledge of return. Moses then produces another of his clever arguments, which exasperates Pharaoh. Negotiations have now collapsed irrevocably, and Moses is dis-missed. Before departing, however, he announces the last plague of all, and thus heralds the epic story of the Passover and exodus.

But this sequence creaks somewhat, particularly in 10.23-4. If the darkness was still on, how could Pharaoh *summon* Moses; if it was ended, why should he make concessions? Possibly 10.24-8 once followed directly on to 10.15, thus eliminating the plague of darkness altogether.

The Passover and the Escape from Egypt

The LORD said to Moses and Aaron in Egypt: • 'This month is to be for you the first of the months; you are to make it the first month of the year. • Say to the whole community of Israel: On the tenth day of this month let each man procure a lamb or kid for his family, one for each household, • but if a household is too small for a lamb or kid, then, taking into account the number of persosn, the man and his nearest neighbour may take one between them. They are to share the cost according to the amount each person eats. • Your animal, taken either from the sheep or the goats, must be without blemish, a yearling male. • Have it in safe keeping until the fourteenth day of this month, and then all the assembled community of Israel must slaughter the victims between dusk and dark. • They must take some of the blood and smear it on the two doorposts and on the lintel of the houses in which they eat the victims. • On that night they must eat the flesh roasted on the fire; they must eat it with unleavened bread and bitter herbs. • You are not to eat any of it raw or even boiled in water, but roasted: head, shins, and entrails. • You are not to leave any of it till morning; anything left over until morning must be destroyed by fire.

• This is the way in which you are to eat it: have your belt fastened, sandals on your feet, and your staff in your hand, and you must eat in urgent haste. It is the LORD's Passover. • On that night I shall pass through the land of Egypt and kill every firstborn of man and beast. Thus I shall execute judgement, I the LORD, against all the gods of Egypt. • As for you, the blood will be a sign on the houses in which you are: when I see the blood I shall pass over you; when I strike Egypt, the mortal blow will not touch you.'   ◆

The Passover and the Escape from Egypt

After the mounting tension of thc ninc plagues we have come to the first dramatic peak of Exodus, namely the Passover, the tenth plague and the escape out of Egypt. The section is in two quite distinct parts, roughly:

1. the regular arrangements for (later) Passovers (1-20, P);
2. the story of the first Passover in its context (21-39, chiefly J).

Historical and literary considerations would have given us the second part first, and a modern reader might well start at v.21. But the final editor belonged to the P tradition and started with his own concerns, even though he then had to describe the first Passover in the future tense (12-13).

The English word *Passover* (11 and 21) was coined by Tyndale for his translation of this passage in 1530 in order to fit his use of *pass over* in 13 and 23. He did this in order to render a corresponding pun in Hebrew between *pesah* (the noun) and *pāsāh* (the verb, which in spite of appearances has no connection with English 'pass'). But the pun in Hebrew is the other way round, i.e. the story of the 'passing-over' is likely to have been fitted later to the more ancient ceremony of the *pesah* sacrifice.

The origin of the term *pesah* is unknown (its later history, through its Greek equivalent *pascha*, includes the English 'paschal' and the French 'Pâques', both referring to Easter). But many details of the ceremony, e.g. the roast lamb and the dress as for a journey, are most appropriate to a nomadic life. It is essentially a rite for the family or household (tent), including the sacrifice of a lamb or kid, a communal meal and the smearing of *the blood on the doorposts*. The last was crucial: its purpose was to protect the tent against a *destroyer* (23), i.e. a demon of the night,

The Passover and the Escape from Egypt (cont.)

12.21 • Moses summoned all the elders of Israel and said, 'Go at once, procure lambs for your families, and slaughter the Passover. • Then take a bunch of marjoram, dip it in the blood in the basin, and smear some blood from the basin on the lintel and the two doorposts. Nobody may go out through the door of his house till morning. • The LORD will go throughout Egypt and strike it, but when he sees the blood on the lintel and the two doorposts, he will pass over that door and not let the destroyer enter to strike you. • You are to observe this as a statute for you and

25 your children for all time; • when you enter the land which the LORD will give you as he promised, you are to observe this rite. • When your children ask you, "What is the meaning of this rite?" • you must say, "It is the LORD's Passover, for he passed over the houses of the Israelites in Egypt when he struck the Egyptians and spared our houses." ' The people bowed low in worship.

• The Israelites went and did exactly as the LORD had commanded Moses and Aaron; • and by midnight the LORD had struck down all the firstborn in Egypt, from the firstborn of Pharaoh on his throne to the firstborn of the prisoner in the

30 dungeon, besides the firstborn of cattle. • Before night was over Pharaoh rose, he and all his courtiers and all the Egyptians, and there was great wailing, for not a house in Egypt was without its dead.

• Pharaoh summoned Moses and Aaron while it was still night and said, 'Up with you! Be off, and leave my people, you and the Israelites. Go and worship the LORD, as you request; • take your sheep and cattle, and go; and ask God's blessing on me also.' • The Egyptians urged on the people and hurried them out of the country, 'or else', they said, 'we shall all be dead'.

37 • The Israelites set out from Rameses on the way to Succoth, about six hundred thousand men on foot, as well as women and children. • With them too went a large company of others, and animals in great numbers, both flocks and herds.   (REB)

The Passover and the Escape from Egypt (cont.)

for whose sake *nobody may go out till morning*. The original occasion for this ritual could have been the evening before the spring transhumance (cp. 11); that would have encouraged its subsequent association with the exodus. In later Judaism the ritual of the Passover changed in various respects (see p.171). But since then it has gradually reverted to its original status as a local family ritual, which is doubtless the secret of its lasting appeal.

After this priestly excursus J's narrative of the exodus is resumed in v.21, which follows on from 11.8. Here the description of the Passover is much better integrated into the context of the exodus. The instruction in vv.24-7 is obviously a later

addition (the *you* in v.24 is singular) but it has been incorporated into the traditional Jewish ritual. The death of *all the firstborn* is the last of the ten plagues, and J does not hesitate to ascribe it to God. If a historical kernel is to be sought here, it must be the death of Pharaoh's own firstborn child. Certainly it is upon Pharaoh that the story focuses. Verses 31-2 mark his total capitulation on all the points previously disputed, and a change not merely of policy but of heart. God's promise of 6.1 is made good.

The rest is postscript. *Succoth* (37) is east of Rameses. The number of *600,000* is greatly exaggerated, but the Israelites could indeed have been joined by *a large company of other* refugees (38).

The Miracle at the Reed Sea

0 They set out from Succoth and encamped at Etham on the edge of the wilderness. • And all the time the LORD went before them, by day a pillar of cloud to guide them on their journey, by night a pillar of fire to give them light; so they could travel both by day and by night. • The pillar of cloud never left its place in front of the people by day, nor did the pillar of fire by night.

1 • The LORD spoke to Moses. • 'Tell the Israelites', he said, 'they are to turn back and encamp before Pi-hahiroth, between Migdol and the sea to the east of Baal-zephon; your camp shall be opposite, by the sea. • Pharaoh will then think that the Israelites are finding themselves in difficult country, and are hemmed in by the wilderness. • I shall make Pharaoh obstinate, and he will pursue them, so that I may win glory for myself at the expense of Pharaoh and all his army; and the Egyptians will know that I am the LORD.' The Israelites did as they were ordered. ◢

The Miracle at the Reed Sea

In the mind of the biblical writers, the miraculous crossing of the Red Sea was the most momentous event in Hebrew history. It was *the* saving act par excellence, to which all others were referred, from the crossing of the Jordan to the return from exile, and indeed on into the NT. From it derived not only a wealth of imagery but also a way of looking at history, miracles and salvation. The dominant – though not the only – concept of a miracle in the OT is of a natural event, due to human or other agency, which occurs under the general providence of God and is used for his purposes. Only a narrow line divides this from a specific intervention by God, i.e. an event which is not contrary to the natural order but is caused by God for his purposes. But there is a big gap between that and the kind of events which in biblical terms may be called *super*natural i.e. either (i) an event caused by God which *is* contrary to the natural order (e.g. a floating axe-head) or (ii) an event caused by humans that is contrary to the natural order (i.e. magic), or (iii) an 'event' which is outside time, place and the natural order altogether (i.e. myth). In this sense there is plenty that is supernatural in the ten plagues, but scarcely anything in the miracle at the Reed Sea: only the magical use of Moses' staff in v.16 and the mythical division of the waters in vv.16 and 22.

There is therefore in the OT no necessary conflict between human free will or 'natural' causes and the purposes of God. We do not have to choose between natural and theological explanations of historical events, nor even to regard one as prior to the other. And that point is of especial relevance here.

For because of the importance of the story in question, scholars have made enormous efforts to locate it in history, i.e. to work out the precise where, when, what and why of it. In doing so they have recognised first of all that the chapter weaves together two accounts by J and P. The weaving is skilfully done, and there is only one major discrepancy between them, over the 'what'.

To start with the 'where', we cannot identify any of the places mentioned so conscientiously in v.2 by P. The phrase traditionally translated *Red Sea* [13.18] really means 'sea of reeds', i.e. papyrus swamp, and that could apply to any number of places on the 70-mile-long depression through which the Suez Canal now runs. Given however the proposed starting point of the Hebrews, it is likely to be near the northern end. It could indeed have been so near the Mediterranean as to be exposed to wind and tide, and that is how some have interpreted the fluctua-

The Miracle at the Reed Sea (cont.)

14. 5   • When it was reported to the Egyptian king that the Israelites had gone, he and his courtiers had a change of heart and said, 'What is this we have done? We have let our Israelite slaves go free!' • Pharaoh had his chariot yoked, and took his troops with him, • six hundred picked chariots and all the other chariots of Egypt, with a commander in each. • Then, made obstinate by the LORD, Pharaoh king of Egypt pursued the Israelites as they marched defiantly away. • The Egyptians, all Pharaoh's chariots and horses, cavalry and infantry, went in pursuit, and overtook them encamped beside the sea by Pi-hahiroth to the east of Baal-zephon.

10   • Pharaoh was almost upon them when the Israelites looked up and saw the Egyptians close behind, and in terror they clamoured to the LORD for help. • They said to Moses, 'Were there no graves in Egypt, that you have brought us here to perish in the wilderness? See what you have done to us by bringing us out of Egypt! • Is this not just what we meant when we said in Egypt, "Leave us alone; let us be slaves to the Egyptians"? Better for us to serve as slaves to the Egyptians than to perish in the wilderness.' • But Moses answered, 'Have no fear; stand firm and see the deliverance that the LORD will bring you this day; for as sure as you see the Egyptians now, you will never see them again. • The LORD will fight for you; so say no more.'

15   • The LORD said to Moses, 'What is the meaning of this clamour? Tell the Israelites to strike camp, • and you are to raise high your staff and hold your hand out over the sea to divide it asunder, so that the Israelites can pass through the sea on dry ground. • For my part I shall make the Egyptians obstinate and they will come after you; thus I shall win glory for myself at the expense of Pharaoh and his army, chariots and cavalry all together. • The Egyptians will know that I am the LORD when I win glory for myself at the expense of their Pharaoh, his chariots and horsemen.'

    • The pillar of cloud moved from the front and took up its position behind 20   them, • thus coming between the Egyptians and the Israelites. The cloud brought on darkness and early nightfall, so that contact was lost throughout the night.

    • Then Moses held out his hand over the sea, and the LORD drove the sea away with a strong east wind all night long, and turned the seabed into dry land. The waters were divided asunder, • and the Israelites went through the sea on the dry ground, while the waters formed a wall to right and left of them.   ▸

The Miracle at the Reed Sea (cont.)

tions of the waters. Somewhere along that line the Israelites had bivouacked when the Egyptians came up behind them unexpectedly, and they were caught between the Pharaoh and the reedy *sea* (9-10).

As to the 'when', the Egyptians seem to have arrived at dusk (the text of 14.20 is unfortunately corrupt). The Israelites made their crossing during the night, and the Egyptians followed them into the sea. Between 2 and 6 a.m. (24) the Egyptian

forces decided to withdraw, and it was then that disaster struck. Such is the time-table implied by the text. For a possible dating, see p.31.

We now come to the 'what'. It is here that J and P differ – though both agree in reporting no actual fighting. According to J, *a strong east wind* sent by God dried the sea enough for the Israelites to cross on foot, but not enough for the Egyptian cavalry and chariots. (Egyptian chariots

The Miracle at the Reed Sea (cont.)

• The Egyptians, all Pharaoh's horse, his chariots and cavalry, followed in pursuit into the sea. • In the morning watch the Lord looked down on the Egyptian army through the pillar of fire and cloud, and he threw them into a panic.

• He clogged their chariot wheels and made them drag along heavily, so that the Egyptians said, 'It is the Lord fighting for Israel against Egypt; let us flee.' • Then the Lord said to Moses, 'Hold your hand out over the sea, so that the water may flow back on the Egyptians, their chariots and horsemen.' • Moses held his hand out over the sea, and at daybreak the water returned to its usual place and the Egyptians fled before its advance, but the Lord swept them into the sea. • As the water came back it covered all Pharaoh's army, the chariots and cavalry, which had pressed the pursuit into the sea. Not one survived. • Meanwhile the Israelites had passed along the dry ground through the sea, with the water forming a wall for them to right and to left. • That day the Lord saved Israel from the power of Egypt. When the Israelites saw the Egyptians lying dead on the seashore, • and saw the great power which the Lord had put forth against Egypt, the people were in awe of the Lord and put their faith in him and in Moses his servant.   (REB)

The Miracle at the Reed Sea (cont.)

were built for two, a driver and a warrior, but on this occasion Pharaoh had adopted the Hittite custom of putting in a 'third man' – that is the literal translation of *commander* in 7 – so as to get more men there quickly.) The Egyptians, realising that they were getting bogged down, panicked and tried to go back (24-5) but at dawn they were caught by the water returning *to its usual place*, i.e. presumably rising.

According to P's version, Moses by raising his *staff* first cleaves the sea in two (16), so that the water piles up in *a wall* on either side (22, 29), thus allowing passage to the Israelites on dry ground; and then closes it again afterwards to drown the pursuing Egyptians (28). It is this more visually dramatic version which has struck the European imagination, but its origin clearly lies in the ANE creation myth, in which God cleaves the sea (representing primeval chaos) in two, cp. [Ps 74.13]: 'You cleft the sea-monster in two.'

So much (and no more) can safely be said about the 'where', 'when' and 'what'. There remains the 'why'. Here J and P speak with one voice in ascribing the causation to God. He was present, in one form or another, throughout their wanderings. J speaks of *a pillar of cloud by day* and *a pillar of fire by night* (13.21f.), and the pillar intervened twice in the actual event (19-20 and 24). But more than that, the whole operation was under his providence: in P the object was the same as in the ten plagues, viz. that the Egyptians shall *know that I am the Lord* (4); and in J the result is that Israel *were in awe of the Lord* (31).

There is indeed in J's lively narrative a curious similarity between the predicaments of Moses and Pharaoh. As the *courtiers* shilly-shally for the last time with Pharaoh (5), so do the Israelites for the first time with Moses (note the ironical *Were there no graves?* – in the land of the pyramids!). The parallel is pointed up by the repetition, which REB's translation obscures, of the same three words, *What is this we have done?* in v.5 and 'What is this you have done?' in v.11. Neither party really knew the Lord and his plans.

The Song of the Sea

15. 1 Then Moses and the Israelites sang this song to the LORD:

I will sing to the LORD,
for he has triumphed gloriously;
   horse and rider he has thrown into the sea.

2 The LORD is my strength and my might,
   and he has become my salvation;
this is my God, and I will praise him,
   my father's God, and I will exalt him.

3 The LORD is a warrior;
   the LORD is his name.

4 Pharaoh's chariots and his army he cast into the sea;
   his picked officers were sunk in the Red Sea.

5 The floods covered them;
   they went down into the depths like a stone.

6 Your right hand, O LORD,
   glorious in power –
your right hand, O LORD,
   shattered the enemy.

7 In the greatness of your majesty
   you overthrew your adversaries;
you sent out your fury,
   it consumed them like stubble.

8 At the blast of your nostrils the waters piled up,
   the floods stood up in a heap;
   the deeps congealed in the heart of the sea.

9 The enemy said, 'I will pursue, I will overtake,
   I will divide the spoil,
my desire shall have its fill of them.
   I will draw my sword,
   my hand shall destroy them.'

The Song of the Sea

This ancient hymn is in two parts, 1-12 (A) and 13-18 (B). It praises God for his saving acts: (A) in defeating the Egyptians at the Sea of Reeds and (B) in guiding the wanderings of the Israelites and establishing them in Canaan. In content it moves from war in Egypt to worship in Jerusalem (17); in form it opens with praise of the LORD and closes with an acclamation (18) typical of psalms. It was clearly used in, and presumably also composed for, Temple worship. There is an explicit refrain to v.1 in v.21.

But the two parts differ in important respects. Throughout part A YHWH (we are told in v.3 that *YHWH is his name*) is praised as *a warrior*. This is true of the general verses (2f., 6f., 11f.). It is even more true of the verses which illustrate the general point from the rout of the Egyptians (1, 4f., 9f.). All the emphasis here is upon the enemy forces; the Israelites are never mentioned. Strangely, the behaviour of the sea and the fate of the Egyptians are referred to in a haphazard sequence: the defeat of the Egyptians (1, 4), their

The Song of the Sea (cont.)

You blew with your wind, the sea covered them;
  they sank like lead in the mighty waters.
Who is like you, O LORD, among the gods?
  Who is like you, majestic in holiness,
    awesome in splendor, doing wonders?
You stretched out your right hand,
  the earth swallowed them.

In your steadfast love you led the people whom you redeemed;
  you guided them by your strength to your holy abode.
The peoples heard, they trembled;
  pangs seized the inhabitants of Philistia.
Then the chiefs of Edom were dismayed;
  trembling seized the leaders of Moab;
  all the inhabitants of Canaan melted away.
Terror and dread fell upon them;
  by the might of your arm, they became still as a stone
until your people, O LORD, passed by,
  until the people whom you acquired passed by.
You brought them in and planted them on the mountain of your own possession,
  the place, O LORD, that you made your abode,
  the sanctuary, O LORD, that your hands have established.
The LORD will reign forever and ever.

The Song of the Sea (cont.)

drowning (5), their boasts (9), their drowning (10) and death (12) – motifs which accord now with J's narrative in Ch. 14, now with P's, now with neither. This medley of images and incidents is quite unlike the sequential handling of the defeat of Sisera in the victory song of Deborah (Jg 5), and it is even more unlike part B.

For B is orderly and comparatively peaceful. At the beginning (13) and end (16-17) God brings his *people* out of Egypt (*redeemed** of v.13 is a technical term for the exodus) through to his *abode* on Mount Zion. In the middle (14-16b) various other *peoples* are introduced as *dismayed* by the passage of the Israelites. The list of them is reminiscent of the Merneptah stele, though the only one in common between the two is *Canaan*. But they are not defeated, nor is God any

longer the warrior. The rhythms in B are also smoother – more 3:3 and less 2:2 – and the language of the climax in v.17, especially *planted*, does everything to imply stability and permanence.

For these and other reasons it has been supposed that A (1-12, with the refrain in 21) is a much older poem to which B (13-18) was later added. If so, the addition is skilfully done, with v.12 as a link-verse. The Egyptians, having been *sunk* or *covered* by the sea three times (4, 5, 10), are finally *swallowed* by *earth*. The immediate reference must be to the grave or underworld, but the Hebrew word (*erets*) is that which regularly means the *land* of Israel, and so it leads the mind on to B. A and B are also linked by the echo of *like a stone* (5 and 16b); and the enemy's boasts in v.9 are balanced by the

The Song of the Sea (cont.)

15.20 • When the horses of Pharaoh with his chariots and his chariot drivers went into the sea, the LORD brought back the waters of the sea upon them; but the Israelites walked through the sea on dry ground. • Then the prophet Miriam, Aaron's sister, took a tambourine in her hand; and all the women went out after her with tambourines and with dancing. • And Miriam sang to them:

Sing to the LORD, for he has triumphed gloriously;
horse and rider he has thrown into the sea.   (NRSV)

The Song of the Sea (cont.)
silent stupefactions of 14-16.

The brief note at the end (20) provides the first mention of *Miriam* by name. She leads *all the women out*, with music and dance, to greet the victorious army on its return home, just as Saul was greeted by the women in 1 Sam 18.7. Her song is the first verse of the Song of the Sea, picked up and modified as a refrain. *Prophet* means no more than poet.

Quails and Manna

16. 2 The Israelites all complained to Moses and Aaron in the wilderness. • They said, 'If only we had died at the LORD's hand in Egypt, where we sat by the fleshpots and had plenty of bread! But you have brought us out into this wilderness to let

11 this whole assembly starve to death.' • The LORD spoke to Moses: • 'I have heard the complaints of the Israelites. Say to them: Between dusk and dark you will have flesh to eat and in the morning bread in plenty. You will know that I the LORD am your God.'

• That evening a flock of quails flew in and settled over the whole camp; in the morning a fall of dew lay all around it. • When the dew was gone, there over the surface of the wilderness fine flakes appeared, fine as hoar-frost on the ground.

15 • When the Israelites saw it, they said one to another, 'What is that?' because they did not know what it was. Moses said to them, 'That is the bread which the LORD has given you to eat. • Here is the command the LORD has given: Each ▶

Quails and Manna
No sooner had the Israelites set off after their escape from Pharaoh than they resumed their rhetorical *complaints* begun just before it (14.10-13). From now on these complaints play a surprisingly large part in their journey to the promised land. Usually (though not here) presented as obstacles to the advance, they take the place which in the epic journeys of other nations is filled by struggles against natural obstacles such as the weather, the terrain and wild beasts. Their prominence in the Pentateuch is probably due to the circumstances in which it reached its final form, i.e. the preference being expressed by some Jews in exile for the *fleshpots* of Babylon as against the uncertainties of a return.

On this second occasion God responded with unmerited generosity. Quails and manna are both natural phenomena, providentially supplied. *Quails* migrate in large numbers across the Sinai peninsula in spring and autumn. Exhausted by their flight, they are easy to catch and delicious to eat. *Manna* is found in the early summer under tamarisk trees in the same area. It is a yellowish-white sugary substance, excreted by certain insect larvae, which accumulates in the night but in the daytime, after the sun gets warm, is eaten by ants. Modern Bedouin still gather and boil it as a delicacy. Their name for it is *mann*; the etymology given in 15 (*man-hū* being

Quails and Manna (cont.)

of you is to gather as much as he can eat: let every man take an omer apiece for every person in his tent.' • The Israelites did this, and they gathered, some more, some less, • but when they measured it by the omer, those who had gathered more had not too much, and those who had gathered less had not too little. Each had just as much as he could eat. • Moses said, 'No one is to keep any of it till

20 morning.' • Some, however, did not listen to him; they kept part of it till morning, and it became full of maggots and stank, and Moses was angry with them.

• Each morning every man gathered as much as he needed; it melted away

31 when the sun grew hot. • Israel called the food manna; it was like coriander seed, but white, and it tasted like a wafer made with honey.   (REB)

Quails and Manna (cont.)

Hebrew for *What is that?*) is bogus.

The narrative is sober enough, except for the quantity gathered (an *omer* is two litres) and the suggestion in v.18 of some magical fit. There is a complementary story in Num 11 which says more about quails than manna and puts a different complexion on the whole incident.

Moses and Jethro

.5 Jethro, Moses' father-in-law, now came to him with his sons and his wife, to the

8 wilderness where he was encamped at the mountain of God. • Moses told him all that the LORD had done to Pharaoh and to Egypt for Israel's sake, and about all their hardships on the journey, and how the LORD had saved them. Jethro rejoiced at all the good the LORD had done for Israel in saving them from the power of Egypt.

Jethro said, 'Blessed be the LORD who has delivered you from the power of Egypt and of Pharaoh. Now I know that the LORD is the greatest of all gods, because he has delivered the people from the Egyptians who dealt so arrogantly

12 with them.' Jethro, Moses' father-in-law, brought a whole-offering and sacrifices for God; and Aaron and all the elders of Israel came and shared the meal with Jethro in the presence of God.   ▸

Moses and Jethro

This period of Moses' adult life ends, as it began, with a scene involving his father-in-law *Jethro* (cp. 3.1). The journey out of Egypt had brought the Israelites to Mt Sinai, the *mountain of God*, in territory then occupied by Midianites*. Jethro came to meet him, bringing the family whom Moses had sent back from Egypt, presumably when the troubles started.

Their first exchange is more important than it seems. Jethro is presented as being already a devotee of YHWH, probably indeed a priest of his (12). Taken together with the phrase 'the God of your father' in 3.6 (where see comment), it has suggested the theory that YHWH was originally a Midianite deity.

Jethro's advice *the next day*

Moses and Jethro (cont.)

18.13   • The next day Moses took his seat to settle disputes among the people, and he was surrounded from morning till evening. • At the sight of all that he was doing for the people, Jethro asked, 'What is this you are doing for the people? Why do you sit

15   alone with all of them standing round you from morning till evening?' • 'The people come to me to seek God's guidance,' Moses answered. • 'Whenever there is a dispute among them, they come to me, and I decide between one party and the other. I make known the statutes and laws of God.' • His father-in-law said to him, 'This is not the best way to do it. • You will only wear yourself out and wear out the people who are here. The task is too heavy for you; you cannot do it alone. • Now listen to me: take my advice, and God be with you. It is for you to be the people's

20   representative before God, and bring their disputes to him, • to instruct them in the statutes and laws, and teach them how they must behave and what they must do. • But you should search for capable, godfearing men among all the people, honest and incorruptible men, and appoint them over the people as officers over units of a thousand, of a hundred, of fifty, or of ten. • They can act as judges for the people at all times; difficult cases they should refer to you, but decide simple cases themselves. In this way your burden will be lightened, as they will be sharing it with you. • If you do this, then God will direct you and you will be able to go on. And, moreover, this whole people will arrive at its destination in harmony.'

25   • Moses heeded his father-in-law and did all he had suggested. • He chose capable men from all Israel and appointed them leaders of the people, officers over units of a thousand, of a hundred, of fifty, or of ten. • They sat as a permanent court, bringing the difficult cases to Moses but deciding simple cases themselves. • When his father-in-law went back to his own country, Moses set him on his way.   (REB)

Moses and Jethro (cont.)

envisages Moses in two conjoined roles. First, he is intermediary between the people and God and conveys *God's guidance* to them. Secondly, he resolves *disputes* between the people. The fact that these two roles are run together twice (16 and 19) tallies with the basic assumption, shortly to be made explicit on Mt Sinai, that God's law covers all aspects of life. But the remedy put into the mouth of Jethro is anachronistic. The division of the people into 10s, 100s and 1000s fits no circumstances before the monarchy, and even then is much better suited to military than legal purposes. Placed here, it looks forward to two themes: the giving of the law through Moses on Mt Sinai; and the sharing of the growing *burden* upon Moses (22, cp. Num 11.14).

Israel at Mount Sinai: Assembly and Theophany

19. 1   In the third month after Israel had left Egypt, they came to the wilderness of Sinai. • They encamped there, pitching their tents in front of the mountain. • Moses went up to God, and the LORD called to him from the mountain and said, 'This is what you are to say to the house of Jacob and tell the sons of Israel: • You yourselves have seen what I did to Egypt, and how I have carried you on eagles'

5   wings and brought you here to me. • If only you will now listen to me and keep my covenant, then out of all peoples you will become my special possession; for the whole earth is mine. • You will be to me a kingdom of priests, my holy nation. Those are the words you are to speak to the Israelites.'

> ## Israel at Mount Sinai: Assembly and Theophany (cont.)
>
> • Moses went down, and summoning the elders of the people he set before them all these commands which the LORD had laid on him. • As one the people answered, 'Whatever the LORD has said we shall do.' • When Moses reported to the LORD the pledge given by the people, • the LORD said to him, 'Go to the people and hallow them today and tomorrow and have them wash their clothes. • They must be ready by the third day, because on that day the LORD will descend on Mount Sinai in the sight of all the people.'
>
> • Moses came down from the mountain to the people. He hallowed them and they washed their clothes. • At dawn on the third day there were peals of thunder and flashes of lightning, dense cloud on the mountain, and a loud trumpet-blast; all the people in the camp trembled. • Moses brought the people out from the camp to meet God, and they took their stand at the foot of the mountain. • Mount Sinai was enveloped in smoke because the LORD had come down on it in fire; the smoke rose like the smoke from a kiln; all the mountain trembled violently, • and the sound of the trumpet grew ever louder.   (REB)

Israel at Mount Sinai: Assembly and Theophany

The Mt *Sinai* of the OT is traditionally identified with Jebel Musa (Mount Moses), an imposing 2,500 metre peak in the tip of the Sinai peninsula. The narrative in Chs 19-34 of what happened there is full of incoherences which cannot be resolved by separating it into its 'sources'. The text offered here is an abbreviation aimed to make sense without falsifying.

Verse 5 is the most succinct formulation in the OT of the *covenant** as a bilateral agreement. It now has to be (i) promulgated by God and (ii) ratified by both parties. For the promulgation Moses organises a most solemn assembly at the foot of the mountain.

The Ten Commandments

The special status of the ten commandments, already stressed by the solemn ritual, is further marked by a contrast. Alone of all the law codes in the OT, they are spoken by God direct to the people. The people are so overwhelmed by the experience that they ask Moses in future to act as their go-between: *do not let God speak to us or we shall die* (20.19).

The decalogue has always held great authority for Jews, both within the OT period and later, when it was recited regularly every morning in synagogue. But that custom died out, and paradoxically it was Christians who elevated the decalogue to the position it held for centuries in European thought. Full-scale commentaries on it were written by Augustine and Aquinas, Luther and Calvin, Lancelot Andrewes and even Goethe. In Protestant churches the text of it is often to be found prominently inscribed on the wall behind the altar, so it is not surprising that in such countries many people, when asked what Christianity stands for, mention first (sometimes only) the ten commandments.

Decalogue means 'ten words', which is the phrase used to describe it in Ex 34.28. There are quite a few such collections of ten 'words' in the Bible. The number was presumably chosen for easy memory, one for each finger. But there are two different ways of counting up the ten here. The Roman Catholic Church, following Augustine, differs from others in running together nos I and II (which is reasonable) and splitting no. X (which is less so). Of the other decalogues in the OT, the one in Dt [Ch.5] is almost identical to this one.

The Ten Commandments

20. 1 And God spake all these words, saying, • 'I am the LORD thy God, which have brought thee out of the land of Egypt, out of the house of bondage.

• THOU SHALT HAVE NO OTHER GODS BEFORE ME.

• THOU SHALT NOT MAKE UNTO THEE ANY GRAVEN IMAGE, or any likeness of any thing that is in heaven above, or that is in the earth beneath, or

5 that is in the water under the earth. • Thou shalt not bow down thyself to them, nor serve them: for I the LORD thy God am a jealous God, visiting the iniquity of the fathers upon the children unto the third and fourth generation of them that hate me; • And shewing mercy unto thousands of them that love me, and keep my commandments.

• THOU SHALT NOT TAKE THE NAME OF THE LORD THY GOD IN VAIN; for the LORD will not hold him guiltless that taketh his name in vain.

• REMEMBER THE SABBATH DAY, TO KEEP IT HOLY. • Six days shalt thou

10 labour, and do all thy work: • But the seventh day is the sabbath of the LORD thy God: in it thou shalt not do any work, thou, nor thy son, nor thy daughter, thy manservant, nor thy maidservant, nor thy cattle, nor thy stranger that is within thy gates: • For in six days the LORD made heaven and earth, the sea, and all that in them is, and rested the seventh day: wherefore the LORD blessed the sabbath day, and hallowed it.

• HONOUR THY FATHER AND THY MOTHER: that thy days may be long upon the land which the LORD thy God giveth thee.

• THOU SHALT NOT KILL.

• THOU SHALT NOT COMMIT ADULTERY .

15 • THOU SHALT NOT STEAL.

• THOU SHALT NOT BEAR FALSE WITNESS against thy neighbour.

• THOU SHALT NOT COVET thy neighbour's house, thou shalt not covet thy neighbour's wife, nor his manservant, nor his maidservant, nor his ox, nor his ass, nor any thing that is thy neighbour's.   (AV)

The Ten Commandments (cont.)

The 'words' of the decalogue may properly be called commandments. Addressed by God to Israel (treated as a single male person), they are all in the form of an unconditional command: there are no 'ifs' and 'buts' such as mark those in the following chapters. It is true that there are some amplifications (in nos II and X) and some reasons appended (to nos I and II, IV and V). But there are many grounds for regarding these as later additions, including the fact that in the version in Dt a *different* reason is given for no.IV. One can be fairly confident of recovering an original text, here printed in capitals.

But the ten commandments are not, in the strict sense, laws. No penalties are mentioned – though elsewhere in the OT nos I-IX are each severally accorded the death penalty – nor are any curses attached at the end, as in normal ANE and OT law codes. What they are is a list of the fundamental principles upon which the community rests i.e. those whose breach would most disrupt it. They are part social, part religious: loyalty to God is what keeps the community together. The social ones are not original: they go back to the beginnings of human society. At some time the rules governing relations between members of the community were grounded in the rules governing the relations between

The Ten Commandments (cont.)

8

• When all the people saw how it thundered and the lightning flashed, when they heard the trumpet sound and saw the mountain in smoke, they were afraid and trembled. They stood at a distance • and said to Moses, 'Speak to us yourself

20

and we will listen; but do not let God speak to us or we shall die.' • Moses answered, 'Do not be afraid. God has come only to test you, so that the fear of him may remain with you and preserve you from sinning.' • So the people kept their distance, while Moses approached the dark cloud where God was. (REB)

The Ten Commandments (cont.)

the community and its God, and bound together in a decalogue. In this form they have no known parallel in the ANE.

Finally there are some difficulties or traps of interpretation which require comment: it is given by commandment, not by verse.

I This is not yet monotheism: there is no suggestion that there *is* only one God.

II in its shortened form clearly refers to making a statue of YHWH, not one of other gods. The thinking behind this prohibition is uncertain. Probably it sprang originally from a fear that an image of YHWH, like his name (III), could be used for magical purposes. But very soon it came to be taken as an expression of his transcendence as compared to other gods (idols). *Jealous* in v.5 would be better rendered 'zealous'. The punishment is not meant as vindictive: it is quite common in early societies to punish the whole extended family (three or four generations living together) for the crime of its head.

III does not refer to frivolous use of God's *name* ('swearing') but to its abuse for malicious purposes, in cursing or spells. Pious Jews later took III to prohibit even the speaking or writing of the name of YHWH; which is the ultimate reason why AV and others use 'the LORD' in its place (see p.34).

IV The *sabbath* is in origin a day of rest from work. The prophets refer regularly to 'new moons and sabbaths', and it may be that the 28-day lunar cycle was divided into four, with a rest day for each phase

of the moon. The weekly observance of it became one of the key features of later Judaism. That is doubtless why two separate 'theologies' of it are given here and in Dt [5.15]: here the link is made with the creation, there with the exodus. But common to both is the point that it is a matter for every household in the community. The *stranger within thy gates* is the resident alien, not the passing visitor.

V with IV creates a gradual transition from the religious to the social regulations. It has in mind particularly the case of elderly parents within the extended family.

VI The word translated *kill* refers not to war or to legal execution but to the killing of a personal enemy.

VII *Adultery* in Jewish law is intercourse of a married or betrothed woman with another man.

VIII Probably this originally referred to kidnapping someone for purposes of slavery, cp. 21.16.

IX The Hebrew makes it clear that the reference is to *false witness* in a court of law.

X It is a surprise to find a mere feeling included in a list of actions. Probably the Hebrew word had more active connotations, viz. plotting to acquire. But plain covetousness had been heavily condemned in Egyptian Wisdom literature for 1,000 years before Moses. *House* here means household, and does not need the amplification. The classification of a *wife* as a chattel was standard in the patriarchal societies of the ANE.

'The Book of the Covenant'

20.22 The LORD said to Moses, 'Say this to the Israelites: "You know now that I have
21. 1 spoken from heaven to you." • These are the laws you are to set before them.'
(REB)

'The Book of the Covenant'

After the decalogue, the next three chapters continue with another, longer collection of regulations which is traditionally but misleadingly known as 'the book of the covenant'. The title is derived from 24.7.

The book of the covenant differs from the decalogue in two respects. First, it is a handbook of true laws, i.e. legal rulings collected for the benefit of village or tribal elders administering justice. Second, the form of the laws is predominantly conditional. Such laws typically begin with 'When . . .' and continue with a series of 'ifs'.

In these two respects the book of the covenant falls plumb into line with the common practice of ANE legal codes. We possess many of these codes, in part or whole, from Mesopotamian, Hittite etc. sources from 2000 BC onwards (see p.771+). In them we can find close parallels for almost every one of these regulations.

The collection is made up of two dissimilar parts. The main body (21.18-22.17, here printed in full) is more homogeneous and more 'secular': YHWH is mentioned only in 22.11, and there are no moral exhortations. It is also better ordered, in four sections:

1. 21.2-11   slave law
2. 21.12-17   capital offences
3. 21.18-36   bodily injuries
4. 22.1-17   damage to property

The comments which follow are based on those sections.

Slave Law

21. 2 'When you purchase a Hebrew as a slave, he will be your slave for six years; in the seventh year he is to go free without paying anything. • If he comes to you alone, he is to go away alone; but if he is already a married man, his wife is to go away with him. • If his master gives him a wife, and she bears him sons or daughters, the woman with her children belongs to her master, and the man must
5 go away alone. • But if the slave should say, 'I am devoted to my master and my wife and children; I do not wish to go free,' • then his master must bring him to God: he is to be brought to the door or the doorpost, and his master will pierce his ear with an awl; the man will then be his slave for life.   ▶

Slave Law

The section on slave law deals with two cases, that of a male *slave* and a female concubine. These are not war captives, who remain slaves all their lives, but *Hebrew* debt-slaves*. It is here laid down that after *six years* such a slave should be free to go. If he did so, he became a 'freedman', with a status somewhat below that of full citizen, like the Roman *libertus*. There was therefore no reason to suppose that he would find it any easier to make a living second time round. Since he would also have to leave behind him any family he had acquired during his service, he might well decide to stay with his master. For that event, a ceremony is provided. *His ear*, which is the symbol of obedience, is pierced as a sign of ownership; and the ceremony takes place in front of, i.e. in the witness of, the household gods on guard at *the door*. The case of the woman sold into concubinage is clearly

Slave Law (cont.)

7 • When a man sells his daughter into slavery, she is not to go free as male slaves may. • If she proves unpleasing to her master who had designated her for himself, he must let her be redeemed; he has treated her unfairly, and therefore he has no right to sell her to foreigners. • If he assigns her to his son, he must allow

0 her the rights of a daughter. • If he takes another woman, he must not deprive the first of meat, clothes, and conjugal rights; • if he does not provide her with these three things, she is to go free without payment.   (REB)

Slave Law (cont.)

different. If she pleases her husband, all is well. If she does not, he must let her father buy her back; he may not *sell her to foreigners*, which, to judge by ANE parallels, implies prostituting her.

It is surprising to find regulations about freeing slaves given pride of place in a collection of laws, even before capital offences. It may be due to the high importance given by the book of Exodus to the equivalence: exodus from Egypt = release from slavery. The deuteronomic code (15.12-18) does not give it the same prominence.

Capital Offences

12 Whoever strikes another man and kills him must be put to death. • But if he did not act with intent, but it came about by act of God, the slayer may flee to a place which I shall appoint for you. • But if a man wilfully kills another by treachery,

15 you are to take him even from my altar to be put to death. • Whoever strikes his father or mother must be put to death. • Whoever kidnaps an Israelite must be put to death, whether he has sold him, or the man is found in his possession. • Whoever reviles his father or mother must be put to death.   (REB)

Capital Offences

The next section consists of four prohibitions each incurring the death penalty. In form they belong with two others [22.19 and 20], as is shown by the English formula: *Whoever. . . must be put to death*. In Hebrew the similarity is even more striking and, if one pares them down to their minimum, they each consist of a five-word line, e.g. one-striking a-man and-he-dies shall-die the-death (12) This rhythmic form is reminiscent of the decalogue, and its uncompromising nature is typically Hebrew.

But a crucial distinction immediately follows, between murder and manslaughter: a man who did not intend to kill his victim may escape vengeance by taking asylum at a local sanctuary. When a son strikes his parent, the death penalty is prescribed, whether the blow is mortal or not; and the same applies (17) to a formal curse. The type of execution envisaged in most of these cases is public stoning, a method which distributes the blood-guilt evenly through the community.

Bodily Injuries

21. 18 When men quarrel and one hits another with a stone or with his fist, and the man is not killed but takes to his bed, • and if he recovers so as to walk about outside with his staff, then the one who struck him has no liability, except that he must pay compensation for the other's loss of time and see that his recovery is complete.

20 • When a man strikes his slave or his slave-girl with a stick and the slave dies on the spot, he must be punished. • But he is not to be punished if the slave survives for one day or two, because the slave is his property.

• When, in the course of a brawl, a man knocks against a pregnant woman so that she has a miscarriage but suffers no further injury, then the offender must pay whatever fine the woman's husband demands after assessment. • But where injury ensues, you are to give life for life, • eye for eye, tooth for tooth, hand for 25 hand, foot for foot, • burn for burn, bruise for bruise, wound for wound.

• When a man strikes his slave or slave-girl in the eye and destroys it, he must let the slave go free in compensation for the eye. • When he knocks out the tooth of a slave or a slave-girl, he must let the slave go free in compensation for the tooth.

• When an ox gores a man or a woman to death, the ox must be put to death by stoning, and its flesh is not to be eaten; the owner of the ox will be free from liability. • If, however, the ox has for some time past been a vicious animal, and the owner has been duly warned but has not kept it under control, and the ox kills a man or a woman, then the ox must be stoned to death, and the owner put to 30 death as well. • If, however, the penalty is commuted for a money payment, he must pay in redemption of his life whatever is imposed upon him. • If the ox gores a son or a daughter, the same ruling applies. • If the ox gores a slave or slave-girl, its owner must pay thirty shekels of silver to their master, and the ox must be stoned to death.   ▸

Bodily Injuries

Two principles underlie this section. The first is that of compensation payable by the offender to the victim. The second, which applies only in cases of unintentional injury, is the principle of equal damage, the *lex talionis* of vv.23-5. These two principles are in logical conflict with each other, yet ANE, no less than OT, law makes use of both and spends much time laying down which shall apply in which circumstances. It used to be thought that 'talion' was primitive, compensation more rational and civilised. But recent studies of ANE law have shown that talion was introduced relatively late, as a protection for the poor, who could otherwise be assaulted with relative impunity by the rich.

Unlike ANE law, Hebrew law in principle rejected compensation in cases of the murder of one free man by another. But this section considers three special cases. The first (20-1) is that where the victim is a slave. Normal cudgelling was part and parcel of a slave's life. If the beating is excessive, and the slave dies, it is *assumed* that it cannot be a case of murder, 'because he is worth money to his master'; so, although the master may have to be punished, he will not be put to death. Sadly, throughout the nineteenth century this verse was used in the USA to support the institution of slavery.

(The regulation of vv. 26-7 however shows a rare recognition that slaves are not mere chattels, as in vv.21 or 32, but have a human dignity of their own. It has no ANE parallel.)

Bodily Injuries (cont.)

• When a man removes the cover of a cistern or digs a cistern and leaves it uncovered, then if an ox or a donkey falls into it, • the owner of the cistern must make good the loss; he must pay the owner the price of the animal, and the dead beast will be his. • When one man's ox butts another's and kills it, they must sell the live ox, share the price, and also share the dead beast. • But if it is known that the ox has for some time past been vicious and the owner has not kept it under control, he must make good the loss, ox for ox, but the dead beast is his.(REB)

Bodily Injuries (cont.)

The second case (22) is that of a *miscarriage* caused by an assault. Here the victim is a foetus, and it is a case for compensation. ANE parallels show that the amount payable was 'assessed' on the age of the foetus at the time.

Thirdly, we have the special case of criminal negligence (29). This ranks as less heinous than murder, and so again *compensation* is allowed: for the death of a man the price is by negotiation, for a slave it is fixed. Fixed-price compensation is standard in ANE law, but in the OT this is the only instance of it.

Damage to Property

When a man steals an ox or a sheep and slaughters or sells it, he must repay five beasts for the ox and four sheep for the sheep. • He must pay in full; if he has no means, he is to be sold to pay for the theft. But if the animal is found alive in his possession, be it ox, donkey, or sheep, he must repay two for each one stolen.

• If a burglar is caught in the act and receives a fatal injury, it is not murder; but if he breaks in after sunrise and receives a fatal injury, then it is murder.

• When a man burns off a field or a vineyard and lets the fire spread so that it burns another man's field, he must make restitution from his own field according to the yield expected; and if the whole field is laid waste, he must make restitution from the best part of his own field or vineyard. • When a fire starts and spreads to a thorn hedge, so that sheaves, or standing grain, or a whole field is destroyed, whoever started the fire must make full restitution.

• When someone gives another silver or chattels for safe keeping, and they are stolen from that person's house, the thief, if apprehended, must restore twofold. • But if the thief is not apprehended, the owner of the house will have to appear before God for it to be ascertained whether or not he has laid hands on his neighbour's property.   ▸

Damage to Property

In the OT, unlike many ANE codes, damage to property is never punished by death. At the worst, compensation is payable, but that applies only in cases of (i) theft or seduction (16) and (ii) negligence (5, 6, 12, 14). The laws are for the most part clear and sensible, requiring comment only in the section 7-13.

This concerns any property that has been deposited with a friend e.g. during absence (7-8), together with animals entrusted e.g. to a herdsman (10-13), as opposed to being lent (14) or hired out (15). Deposition of property was a common practice before the invention of banks, and plays a part in the book of Tobit. Because the owner in this case took the initiative, he must then, if the property is stolen, accept the neighbour's declaration of innocence, provided that it is made at the local sanctuary (8). The same applies e.g. to a shepherd when a sheep in his care is injured.

Damage to Property (cont.)

22.9 • In every case of misappropriation involving an ox, a donkey, or a sheep, a cloak, or any lost property which may be claimed, each party must bring his case before God; the one whom God declares to be in the wrong will have to restore double to his neighbour.

10 • When someone gives a donkey, an ox, a sheep, or any beast into a neighbour's keeping, and it dies or is injured or is carried off, there being no witness, • then by swearing by the LORD it will have to be settled between them whether or not the neighbour has laid hands on the other's property. If not, no restitution is to be made and the owner must accept this. • If it has been stolen from the neighbour, he must make restitution to its owner. • If it has been mauled by a wild beast, he must bring it in as evidence; he will not have to make restitution for what has been mauled.

• When a man borrows a beast from his neighbour and it is injured or dies 15 while its owner is not present, the borrower must make full restitution; • but if the owner is with it, the borrower does not have to make restitution. If it was hired, only the hire is due.

• When a man seduces a virgin who is not yet betrothed, he must pay the bride-price for her to be his wife. • If her father refuses to give her to him, the seducer must pay in silver a sum equal to the bride-price for virgins.   (REB)

Damage to Property (cont.)

But v.9 introduces a variation, namely the case where a man claims as his own (literally, 'says "this is it" ') something in a neighbour's house. For this, the swearing of a mere oath is not enough: both parties submit the case to God, i.e. to the local priest for adjudication.

An Appendix

22.18 • You must not allow a witch to live.   1.

25 • If you advance money to any poor man amongst my people, you are not to act like a moneylender; you must not exact interest from him.   2.

• If you take your neighbour's cloak in pawn, return it to him by sunset, • because it is his only covering. It is the cloak in which he wraps his body; in what else can he sleep? If he appeals to me, I shall listen, for I am full of compassion.   3.

An Appendix

Appended to the Book of the Covenant is another collection of laws. Though of roughly equal antiquity, it is much more of a hodge-podge, both in content and in form. But some of its laws have had a great influence upon subsequent history, not only that of the Jews. Comments are made by numbers in the right-hand margin.

An Appendix (cont.)

• For six years you may sow your land and gather its produce; • but in the seventh year you must let it lie fallow and leave it alone. Let it provide food for the poor of your people, and what they leave the wild animals may eat. You are to do likewise with your vineyard and your olive grove.   **4.**

• Three times a year you are to keep a pilgrim-feast to me. • You are to celebrate the pilgrim-feast of Unleavened Bread: for seven days, as I have commanded you, you are to eat unleavened bread at the appointed time in the month of Abib, for in that month you came out of Egypt; and no one is to come into my presence without an offering. • You are to celebrate the pilgrim-feast of Harvest, with the firstfruits of your work in sowing the land, and the pilgrim-feast of Ingathering at the end of the year, when you gather the fruits of your work in from the land. • Those three times a year all your males are to come into the presence of the LORD God.   **5.**

• Do not boil a kid in its mother's milk.   (REB)   **6.**

An Appendix (cont.)

1. This law, to which there are many ANE parallels, was the authority for executing 'witches' in Europe and the USA as late as the eighteenth century. In ANE parallels the death penalty is not invariably imposed for sorcery; a Hittite law requires *a witch* to pay compensation to the victim for damage inflicted, and also to meet any consequential medical bills.

2. This is the basic prohibition of usury. It was extended later to all interest-bearing loans to *all* fellow-Israelites. The ANE parallels reveal regular interest rates between 20% and 50%, but the OT prohibition is not concerned with percentages. It is only recently that 'usury' has acquired a connotation of *excessive* interest.

4. The idea of the sabbath or sabbatical *year* has provided refreshment for agriculturists in times past and for academics more recently. It did not of course apply to the whole of a farmer's land in any one year, still less to the whole of Israel.

5. This is the oldest list of the three main *pilgrim-feasts* of the year, i.e. celebrations requiring a pilgrimage to the local sanctuary. They are obviously agricultural feasts in origin, but have been associated where possible with events from Israelite history. The *Unleavened Bread* was the feast of the new barley harvest in the spring, when for seven days bread was eaten without leaven, as a symbol of 'making new' the year's food supply. Next comes the *Harvest*, marking the end of the cereal crop. This took place after seven weeks or on the fiftieth day; hence its later titles of the feast of Weeks and (in Greek) Pentecost. Third was the *Ingathering* of the fruit harvest, especially grapes and olives, in the autumn. This was later known as Tabernacles, from the custom of moving out to live in makeshift huts during the harvest. The move enabled the owner to protect his ripe crops against predation, and is still practised in Mediterranean countries; the name Tabernacles also linked the feast to the wanderings in the Wilderness. Feasts added later to this calendar were Purim in March (see Esther 9.21+) and Hanukkah, Dedication or Lights in December (see 1 Macc 4.59).

6. This strange regulation forbids what was probably a Canaanite ritual. But it is the origin of a dietary rule still observed by strict Jews, not to mix meat and dairy products at the same meal.

The Covenant is Sealed

24. 3 Moses went and repeated to the people all the words of the LORD. With one voice the whole people answered, 'We will do everything the LORD has told us.' • Moses wrote down all the words of the LORD. Early in the morning he built an altar at the foot of the mountain, and erected twelve sacred pillars for the twelve 5 tribes of Israel. • He sent the young men of Israel and they sacrificed bulls to the LORD as whole-offerings and shared-offerings. • Moses took half the blood and put it in basins, and the other half he flung against the altar. • Moses then took the blood and flung it over the people, saying, 'This is the blood of the covenant which the LORD has made with you on the terms of this book.'

  • Moses went up with Aaron, Nadab, and Abihu, and seventy of the elders of 10 Israel, • and they saw the God of Israel. Under his feet there was, as it were, a pavement of sapphire, clear blue as the very heavens; • but the LORD did not stretch out his hand against the leaders of Israel. They saw God; they ate and they drank.

(REB)

The Covenant is Sealed

This passage is in two parts, 3-8 and 9-11: in the first the covenant is ratified by all the people at the foot of Mt Sinai, in the second by their representatives on the mountain. Both parts record events which are without parallel in the OT, but which have left their mark on the NT and so on the Christian Eucharist.

In the first, Moses read to the people the *words* of the decalogue and then *wrote* them *down* before the evening. An agreement was regularly sealed by *blood*: so boys will still cut their wrists to become blood-brothers. In this case, the blood was sprinkled equally on the high contracting parties: first on *the altar*, representing God, and then on *the people*.

In the second story a special privilege is granted to Moses and Aaron, with his two sons, and to 70 elders representing the people. The bald statement that *they saw the God of Israel* is breathtaking. Elsewhere in the OT the rule is: 'no mortal man may see me and live'. The author softens it by hinting that, although they saw the sky beneath him, shining bright as *sapphire*, they did not raise their eyes any higher (10). Even that might have been tempting providence (11). But God stayed his hand, while the final ritual was carried through to seal the covenant. Normally the contracting parties ate a meal together [Gen 31.54]; God could not partake, so *they ate* in his presence.

The Covenant Broken: the Golden Calf

2 • The LORD said to Moses, 'Come up to me on the mountain, stay there, and let me give you the stone tablets with the law and commandment I have written down for their instruction.' • Moses with Joshua his assistant set off up the
18 mountain of God; • Moses went up the mountain; there he stayed forty days and forty nights.

1 • When the people saw that Moses was so long in coming down from the mountain, they congregated before Aaron and said, 'Come, make us gods to go before us. As for this Moses, who brought us up from Egypt, we do not know what has become of him.' • Aaron answered, 'Take the gold rings from the ears of your wives and daughters, and bring them to me.' • So all the people stripped themselves of their gold ear-rings and brought them to Aaron. • He received them from their hands, cast the metal in a mould, and made it into the image of a bull-calf; then they said, 'Israel, these are your gods that brought you up from Egypt.'
5 • Seeing this, Aaron built an altar in front of it and announced, 'Tomorrow there is to be a feast to the LORD.' • Next day the people rose early, offered whole-offerings, and brought shared-offerings. After this they sat down to eat and drink and then gave themselves up to revelry.

• The LORD said to Moses, 'Go down at once, for your people, the people you brought up from Egypt, have committed a monstrous act. • They have lost no time in turning aside from the way which I commanded them to follow, and cast for themselves a metal image of a bull-calf; they have prostrated themselves before it, sacrificed to it, and said, "Israel, these are your gods that brought you up from Egypt." ' • The LORD said to Moses, 'I have considered this people, and
10 I see their stubbornness. • Now, let me alone to pour out my anger on them, so that I may put an end to them and make a great nation spring from you.'   ▸

The Covenant Broken: the Golden Calf

Almost as soon as the covenant was ratified, the people broke it. There are a number of contradictions in Chs 32-4. For example, whereas in the previous section *Moses* had written down the laws (24.4), now it is *the LORD* himself who does so (24.12; 32.15f.).

There is a running contrast throughout this story between the solemn pace of events on Mt Sinai and the seething activity in the Israelite camp below. Eventually *the people*'s anxiety came to a head (32.1). Rebellious to *Aaron*, sarcastic about Moses, they needed tangible reassurance for the journey ahead of them. From their *gold* jewellery Aaron makes the *bull-calf*, to represent their God. (REB's *gods* in 4 is

confusing: Heb *Elohim* is often used of a single god.) Aaron evidently intends that the calf should be worshipped as the LORD (5), i.e. the commandment which is being broken is not the first but the second (20.4). But the people made the occasion an excuse for a fertility rite. (The story is out of place in Sinai. It belongs in a context of Baal-worship, and may well be a retrojection of the story of Jeroboam's golden calf in 1 K 12.)

When the LORD hears of this the serenity of Sinai is broken: Moses must *go down at once*, and there is a touch of petulance in *your people* (32.7). Then we have various interludes to increase the suspense. First, God threatens to abandon

The Covenant Broken: the Golden Calf (cont.)

32.11   • Moses set himself to placate the LORD his God: 'LORD,' he said, 'why pour out your anger on your people, whom you brought out of Egypt with great power and a strong hand? • Why let the Egyptians say, "He meant evil when he took them out, to kill them in the mountains and wipe them off the face of the earth?" Turn from your anger, and think better of the evil you intend against your people. • Remember Abraham, Isaac, and Israel, your servants, to whom you swore by your own self: "I shall make your descendants countless as the stars in the heavens, and all this land, of which I have spoken, I shall give to them, and they will possess it for ever." ' • So the LORD thought better of the evil with which he had threatened his people.

15   • Moses went back down the mountain holding the two tablets of the Testimony, inscribed on both sides, on the front and on the back. • The tablets were the handiwork of God, and the writing was God's writing, engraved on the tablets. • Joshua, hearing the uproar the people were making, said to Moses, 'Listen! There is fighting in the camp.' • Moses replied,

> This is not the sound of warriors,
> nor the sound of a defeated people;
> it is the sound of singing that I hear.

• As he approached the camp, Moses saw the bull-calf and the dancing, and in a burst of anger he flung down the tablets and shattered them at the foot of the 20 mountain. • He took the calf they had made and burnt it; he ground it to powder, sprinkled it on water, and made the Israelites drink it.

   • He demanded of Aaron, 'What did this people do to you that you should have brought such great guilt upon them?' • Aaron replied, 'Please do not be angry, my lord. You know how wicked the people are. • They said to me, "Make us gods to go ahead of us, because, as for this Moses, who brought us up from 24 Egypt, we do not know what has become of him." • So I said to them, "Those of you who have any gold, take it off." They gave it to me, I threw it in the fire, and out came this bull-calf.'   ▸

The Covenant Broken: the Golden Calf (cont.)

the Israelites and *make a great nation spring from* Moses alone; Moses in reply tactfully says nothing of the reference to himself but intercedes, as usual, for the people. Next comes the pedantic description of *the tablets of the Testimony* (15-16), which is P's term for the decalogue. The exchange between Moses and his lieutenant *Joshua* is doubly ironical. It was not *fighting* in the literal sense, but it was a true conflict. It was *singing* in the literal sense, but underneath it lay tears. After the long slow introduction, Moses erupts into violent action. Symbolically, he smashes the *tablets* of the broken covenant and then he destroys the calf. The requirement to *drink it* is probably an ordeal to test their loyalty, as in Num 5.

Aaron's self-justification is deliciously inept. After the polite submission formula, he first blames the people and then feigns surprise: *out came this bull-calf.* Moses does not even deign to reply.

The Covenant Broken: the Golden Calf (cont.)

0 • The next day Moses said to the people, 'You have committed a great sin. Now I shall go up to the LORD; perhaps I may be able to secure pardon for your sin.' • When he went back to the LORD he said, 'Oh, what a great sin this people has committed: they have made themselves gods of gold. • Now if you will forgive them, forgive; but if not, blot out my name, I pray, from your book which you have written.' • The LORD answered Moses, 'Whoever has sinned against me, him I shall blot out from my book. • Now go, lead the people to the place of which I have told you. My angel will go ahead of you, but a day will come when I shall punish them for their sin.'   (REB)

The Covenant Broken: the Golden Calf (cont.)

But with *the people* next day he is the true leader. Whereas 'Aaron was too weak to restrain the people, Moses was strong enough to restrain even God' (Childs). In an astonishing inversion of God's offer in v.10, he offers himself in their place, and God relents. *Whoever has sinned* (note the different emphasis from the second commandment) will not escape punishment, but the people in general will be given another chance. First, however, the broken covenant must be restored.

The Tent of Meeting

3.7 Moses used to take the Tent and set it up outside the camp some distance away. He called it the Tent of Meeting, and everyone who sought the LORD would go outside the camp to the Tent of Meeting. • Whenever Moses went out to the Tent, all the people would rise and stand, each at the door of his tent, and follow Moses with their eyes until he had entered the Tent. • When Moses entered it, the pillar of cloud came down, and stayed at the entrance to the Tent while the LORD spoke
10 with Moses. • As soon as the people saw the pillar of cloud standing at the entrance to the Tent, they would all prostrate themselves, each at the door of his tent. • The LORD used to speak with Moses face to face, as one man speaks to another, and Moses then returned to the camp, but his attendant, Joshua son of Nun, never moved from inside the Tent.   (REB)

The Tent of Meeting

The theme of Moses' intercessions for the people is carried on in an ancient fragment which seems misplaced here. *The Tent of Meeting*, now mentioned for the first time, is much better suited to the wanderings in the desert than to the encampment in Sinai, where God was to be found on the mountain. The tent was set up by Moses at each halt as a holy place outside the camp, a kind of mobile Sinai to which anyone could resort who wished to consult God. God was not believed to dwell there permanently: it was only when Moses went in that He came down, at its entrance, in *the pillar of cloud*. Moses could then *speak with* him *face to face* – a phrase regularly used in the OT to distinguish Moses from all others.

The Covenant Restored

33.18 Moses prayed, 'Show me your glory.' • The LORD answered, 'I shall make all my goodness pass before you, and I shall pronounce in your hearing the name "LORD". I shall be gracious to whom I shall be gracious, and I shall have compassion on

20 whom I shall have compassion.' • But he added, 'My face you cannot see, for no mortal may see me and live.' • The LORD said, 'Here is a place beside me. Take your stand on the rock • and, when my glory passes by, I shall put you in a crevice of the rock and cover you with my hand until I have passed by. • Then I shall take away my hand, and you will see my back, but my face must not be seen.'

34. 1 • The LORD said to Moses, 'Cut for yourself two stone tablets like the former ones, and I shall write on them the words which were on the first tablets which you broke. • Be ready by morning, and then go up Mount Sinai, and present yourself to me there on the top. • No one is to go up with you, no one must even be seen anywhere on the mountain, nor must flocks or herds graze within sight of that mountain.' • So Moses cut two stone tablets like the first, and early in the morning he went up Mount Sinai as the LORD had commanded him, taking the two stone tablets in his hands.

5 • The LORD came down in the cloud, and, as Moses stood there in his presence, he pronounced the name 'LORD'. • He passed in front of Moses and proclaimed: 'The LORD, the LORD, a God compassionate and gracious, long-suffering, ever faithful and true, • remaining faithful to thousands, forgiving iniquity, rebellion, and sin but without acquitting the guilty, one who punishes children and grandchildren to the third and fourth generation for the iniquity of their fathers!' • At once Moses bowed to the ground in worship.

The Covenant Restored

The narrative as presented in the mss is still confused (e.g. the incident described at the end of Ch. 33 clearly belongs on Mt Sinai (v.22), yet Moses does not go up until 34.4), and even this abbreviated version has some loose ends.

There are two main elements in it: the final dramatic meeting between God and Moses on Mt Sinai, and the rather undramatic restoration of the broken covenant. In the former Moses is granted everything short of seeing God's face (for which his *glory* is here a reverential synonym), for *no mortal man may see me and live*. From that

ultimate experience he is gently protected (33.21-3). But God graciously reveals his *goodness* (33.19); and actually speaks his own holy name of YHWH, which REB as usual renders LORD (34.5; see p.34). These together constitute his nature, which is more fully described in 34.6-7.

That little hymn will echo down the pages of the OT (see e.g. Ps 103.8) and still be audible in the Muslim invocation 'In the name of Allah, the Compassionate, the Merciful' – another faith in which compassion sits side by side with severity (7b).

The Covenant Restored (cont.)

• The LORD said: 'Here and now I am making a covenant. In full view of all your people I shall do such miracles as have never been performed in all the world or in any nation. All the peoples among whom you live shall see the work of the LORD, for it is an awesome thing that I shall do for you.' • The LORD said to Moses, 'Write these words down, because the covenant I make with you and with Israel is on those terms.' • So Moses remained there with the LORD forty days and forty nights without food or drink. The LORD wrote down the words of the covenant, the Ten Commandments, on the tablets.　　　　　　　　　(REB)

The Covenant Restored (cont.)

Scholars generally suppose that the covenant narrative here was originally a second, shorter version of the *setting up* of the covenant, parallel to that in Chs 19-24. But the author has taken it and put it after the story of the golden calf to record the *restoration* of the covenant. Hence the motif of the breaking and recreation of the tablets (34.1, 4, 27-8), which does not cohere very well.

LEVITICUS

Introduction

The book Leviticus does not advance the narrative of the exodus from Egypt. Its title means literally 'the book of the Levites'. A more accurate title would be 'the book about priests and ritual', but even then 'ritual' must be understood to include all those aspects of everyday behaviour which were governed by the Torah as interpreted by the priests, cutting across our modern categories of religious and secular. The book is in fact a collection of regulations. All of them purport to have been given to Moses on Mount Sinai; but although some of them do go back to early times, most are later, and all have been edited after the exile, when the priesthood became more powerful.

The group of laws in Leviticus is one of at least three in the Pentateuch and, since it is neither so authoritative as those in Exodus nor so well ordered as those in Deuteronomy, the selection made here is illustrative rather than comprehensive.

It is not in principle surprising to find cultic and social regulations mixed (though it was not the practice in ANE law codes), since the gods were held to preside also over the ordering of society. But in Leviticus the connection between the two sometimes looks a little forced. There are stark juxtapositions like: 'you must not tattoo yourselves: I am the LORD' [19.28], and also explicit arguments of the form: the LORD brought you out of Egypt, *therefore* you must not exploit each other (see extracts from Chs 19 and 25 below). A similar argument is used in matters of holiness and cleanness, which are the characteristic topics of Leviticus. For example, 'I have made a clear separation between you and the nations, and you shall make a clear separation between clean and unclean beasts' [20.24f.].

Cleanness is treated in Chs 11-15. It is a purely ritual category, unconnected with either hygiene or morality. 'Unclean' in Leviticus does not imply 'dirty', 'offensive' or 'unhealthy'. The category is common to most religions, and indeed to secular societies like our own. It is probably a mistake to look for all-embracing rational explanations of it, beyond the gut feeling that in some sense the excluded animals are 'different'. The list of the different varies sharply from one society to another, cp. English queasiness about eating horse and dog, snail and frog. The avoidance of *pig*, which was shared by Israel's neighbours in antiquity and is still such a feature of Judaism and Islam, may go back to early nomadic days, when sheep and goats were the 'proper' meat. Pigs need too much water to be herded like them.

What the book of Leviticus does is to bring together a variety of customs and express them in formal and absolute terms. With its rules it also offers reasons. The reasons might be called proto-scientific, being based on observation (albeit not very close) of the natural world and classification of its phenomena. Their framework is ascribed, not unreasonably, to the creator of that world.

But God, though the creator of the world, is also set apart from it i.e. holy. Holiness is the fundamental concept in Leviticus. It dominates the regulations in Chs 17-26, which in consequence is known to scholars as 'the holiness code'; but its influence is felt throughout the book. The argument is summarized in 19.2 etc: 'you must be holy because I the LORD your God am holy.' Its fullest form is: just as God is set apart from the natural world, so within the natural world (i) Israel is set apart (for God) from the nations, (ii) certain (clean) objects are set apart from other (unclean) objects, and therefore (iii) Israel in general, and the priests in particular, must use only clean objects.

This argument presents problems.

First the status of Israel is ambiguous, being 'in the world but not of the world'. To put it differently, the word 'holy' cannot mean the same when used of God and of humans: God cannot be set apart *for God*. Secondly the distinction holy/profane is not at all the same as that of clean/unclean. On the contrary, objects which are holy are commonly 'unclean' in the sense of untouchable or unapproachable – see the story of Uzzah in [2 Sam 6.6+]. An object may thus be treated as unclean either because it is too holy or because it is too profane.

This is the anthropological concept of taboo. It is far from dead in our time, and our avoidance of certain words, e.g. 'cancer', can help us to view more sympathetically what in the priestly writings of the OT often seems a neurotic obsession with minutiae of behaviour. For at the bottom of the concept of taboo lies fear: that which is 'unclean', for whichever reason, brings danger.

Clean and Unclean Animals

.1 The LORD told Moses and Aaron • to say to the Israelites: These are the creatures you may eat: Of all the larger land animals • you may eat any hoofed animal which has cloven hoofs and also chews the cud; • those which only have cloven hoofs or only chew the cud you must not eat. These are: the camel, because though it

5 chews the cud it does not have cloven hoofs, and is unclean for you; • the rock-badger, because though it chews the cud it does not have cloven hoofs, and is unclean for you; • the hare, because though it chews the cud it does not have a parted foot; it is unclean for you; • the pig, because although it is a hoofed animal with cloven hoofs it does not chew the cud, and is unclean for you. • You are not to eat the flesh of these or even touch their dead carcasses; they are unclean for you.

• Of creatures that live in water these may be eaten: all, whether in salt water
10 or fresh, that have fins and scales; • but all, whether in salt or fresh water, that have neither fins nor scales, including both small creatures in shoals and larger creatures, you are to regard as prohibited. • They are prohibited to you; you must not eat their flesh, and their dead bodies you are to treat as prohibited. • Every creature in the water that has neither fins nor scales is prohibited to you.

• These are the birds you are to regard as prohibited, and for that reason they must not be eaten: the griffon-vulture, the black vulture, and the bearded vulture;
15 • the kite and every kind of falcon; • every kind of crow, • the desert-owl, the short-eared owl, the long-eared owl, and every kind of hawk; • the tawny owl, the fisher-owl, and the screech-owl; • the little owl, the horned owl, the osprey, • the stork, the various kinds of cormorant, the hoopoe, and the bat.   ▸

Clean and Unclean Animals

The last verse of Ch.11 sums up its purpose – *to make a distinction* – and this verb gives the clue to the procedure being followed. For it is a clear echo of the Priestly creation story in Genesis, where the same Hebrew verb is used repeatedly, though there translated 'to separate'. In the beginning God brought order out of chaos by a series of separations, particularly that between the earth, the seas and the vault of heaven. Those separations are here applied to animals, which are dealt with according to their habitat: land (1-8), sea (9-12) and sky (13-19). Each element has its proper kind of animals: those are the clean ones, others are anomalous and so unclean.

Clean and Unclean Animals (cont.)

11.20   • All winged creatures that swarm and go on all fours are prohibited to you,
• except those which have legs jointed above their feet for leaping on the ground.
• Of these you may eat every kind of great locust, every kind of long-headed
locust, every kind of green locust, and every kind of desert locust. • Every other
swarming winged creature that has four legs is prohibited to you.

29   • The following creatures that swarm on the ground are to be unclean to you:
the mole-rat, the jerboa, and every kind of thorn-tailed lizard; • the gecko, the
sand-gecko, the wall-gecko, the great lizard, and the chameleon. • Those among
swarming creatures are to be unclean to you; whoever touches them when they
are dead will be unclean till evening. • Anything on which any of them falls when
dead will be unclean, any article of wood, any garment or hide or sacking, any
article which may be put to use; it must be immersed in water and remain unclean
till evening, when it will be clean. • If any of the creatures falls into an earthenware
vessel, its contents will be unclean, and you must break the vessel. • Any food
which is fit for eating and then comes in contact with water from such a vessel

35   will be unclean, and any drink in such a vessel will be unclean. • Anything on
which the dead body of such a creature falls will be unclean; a clay oven or pot
must be broken, for they are unclean and you must treat them as such; • but a
spring or a cistern where water collects will remain clean, though whoever touches
the dead body will be unclean. • When any of their dead bodies falls on seed
intended for sowing, the seed remains clean; • but if the seed has been soaked in
water and any dead body falls on it, it will be unclean for you.

46   • Such, then, is the law concerning beast and bird, every living creature that
moves in the water, and all living creatures that swarm on the land, • the purpose
of the law being to make a distinction between the unclean and the clean, between
living creatures that may be eaten and those that may not be eaten.   (REB)

Clean and Unclean Animals (cont.)

On land the prototype is the domestic
animal – sheep, donkey, cattle, etc.
Anything which does not share all their
characteristics is unclean. (The *rock-badger*
and the *hare* do not actually chew the cud,
but they grind their teeth and so look as if
they do.) *In water* the proper characteristics
are both *fins and scales*; which rules out
e.g. crocodile and hippopotamus. Of *birds*,
most of the ones ruled out are birds of prey
which eat blood (see 17.10-14).

From these three categories we move to
the rest, described as *creatures that swarm*.
Those with wings and four legs (20) are
neither flesh nor fowl: creatures with four
legs (presumably insects were thought to
have four legs) should walk, not fly. The
exception is the *locust* with jointed legs
which equip it *for leaping on the ground*.

Others (29-30) *swarm on the ground*. Of
them the unclean are perhaps those which
seem to have hands but still go on all fours.

In the case of all these animals their
uncleanness is equated with their
inedibility. In v.31 we move to a different
but related theme, namely uncleanness
through contact with dead bodies of
animals. For example *lizards* etc. live on
the walls of houses and, when they die,
fall off *into* things. We also move here
into a different key: from absolute
prohibition to the consideration of special
cases. CommŸn sense now takes over. A
cooking *pot* (33) or an *oven* (35) made of
clay can be replaced with relative ease.
But a *cistern* full of *water* (36) or the *seed*
for next year's crop (37) are far too
valuable to be expended.

Childbirth

1 The LORD told Moses • to say to the Israelites: When a woman becomes pregnant and gives birth to a male child, she will be unclean for seven days, as in the period of her impurity through menstruation. • On the eighth day, the child is to have the flesh of his foreskin circumcised. • The woman must then wait for thirty-three days because her blood requires purification; she must touch nothing that is holy, and must not enter the sanctuary till her days of purification are completed. • If

5 she bears a female child, she will be unclean as in menstruation for fourteen days and must wait for sixty-six days because her blood requires purification.

(REB)

Childbirth

Childbirth is treated as analogous to menstruation (see below). No rational explanation is offered for doubling the *period of impurity* for *a female child*.

Skin Diseases

.1 When the LORD spoke to Moses he said: • This is the law concerning anyone suffering from a virulent skin disease. On the day when he is to be cleansed he is to be brought to the priest, • who will go outside the camp and examine him. If the person has recovered from his disease, • then the priest is to order two ritually clean small birds to be brought alive for the person who is to be cleansed,

5 together with cedar-wood, scarlet thread, and marjoram. • He must order one of the birds to be killed over an earthenware bowl containing fresh water. • He will then take the live bird together with the cedar-wood, scarlet thread, and marjoram and dip them all in the blood of the bird that has been killed over the fresh water. • He must sprinkle the blood seven times on the one who is to be cleansed from the skin disease and so cleanse him; the live bird he will release to fly away over the open country. • The person to be cleansed must wash his clothes, shave off all his hair, bathe in water, and so be ritually clean. He may then enter the camp, but must stay outside his tent for seven days. • On the seventh day he must shave off all the hair on his head, his beard, and his eyebrows, and then shave the rest of his hair, wash his clothes, and bathe in water; then he will be ritually clean.

(REB)

Skin Diseases

This *law* applies to someone who is already cured of *a virulent skin disease* – not leprosy, as the older translations have it, because leprosy was incurable in the ancient world. The procedure is designed therefore to keep away the evil spirits which had invaded the patient. For this purpose the ritual employs two kinds of magic. First are symbols of life: the *blood* of *one bird*, the *scarlet thread* (colour of blood) and *fresh* (literally 'living') *water*. Second are substances whose strong smell was believed to repel demons: *cedar-wood* and *marjoram*. The role of the *live bird* is to be understood on the analogy of the scapegoat, for which see 16.20-22. The phrase *stay outside his tent* in v.8 implies celibacy.

Body Fluids

15.16 When a man has emitted semen, he must bathe his whole body in water and be unclean till evening. • Every piece of clothing or leather on which there is any semen is to be washed and remain unclean till evening. • This applies also to the woman with whom a man has had intercourse; both must bathe in water and remain unclean till evening.

20 • When a woman has her discharge of blood, her impurity will last for seven days; anyone who touches her will be unclean till evening. • Everything on which she lies or sits during her impurity will be unclean, • and whoever touches her bedding must wash his clothes, bathe in water, and remain unclean till evening. • Whoever touches anything on which she sits must wash his clothes, bathe in water, and remain unclean till evening. • If it is the bed or seat where she is sitting, by touching it he will become unclean till evening. • If a man goes so far as to have intercourse with her and any of her discharge gets on to him, then he will be unclean for seven days, and any bedding on which he lies down will be unclean.   (REB)

Body Fluids

Quite a number of the regulations in the Torah govern sexual behaviour. This section concerns the normal physiological functions of men and women. Such taboos, which are extremely widespread, belong to an early stage of thinking when the *semen* and the menstrual *blood* were held to represent the mysterious life-force. The impurity is purely formal, and no ritual is prescribed for purification. Neither here nor anywhere else in the Bible is there any suggestion that 'sex is dirty'. *Intercourse* with a menstrual woman (24) is taboo almost everywhere.

The Day of Atonement

16.3-5 When Aaron enters the sanctuary, • he is to receive from the community of the Israelites two he-goats for a purification-offering. • Then he must take the two he-goats and set them before the LORD at the entrance to the Tent of Meeting. • He must cast lots over the two goats, one to be for the LORD and the other for Azazel. • He must present the goat on which the lot for the LORD has fallen and

10 deal with it as a purification-offering; • but the goat on which the lot for Azazel has fallen is to be made to stand alive before the LORD, for expiation to be made over it, before it is driven away into the wilderness to Azazel.   ▸

The Day of Atonement

This section contains three new concepts: expiation, atonement and the scapegoat. Of these three English words, the last two are special coinages made by Tyndale for his translation of the Bible – 'atonement' in 1513 for 2 Cor 5.18, 'scapegoat' for this passage in 1530. The third, *expiation*, which REB uses here to the exclusion of both the others, is a term borrowed from the Greco-Roman world: typically one expiated one's sins (and thereby placated a deity) by a sacrifice. The Priestly writer follows international usage in explaining (17.11) that 'it is the blood, that is the life, that makes expiation'. But he goes beyond it when he interprets sacrifice as a means of restoring a relationship between the people and God which had been broken by sin. It is this restoration or re-conciliation which Tyndale designated by his new term at-one-ment, and that is the word still used in English for the annual Jewish Day of Atonement (modern *Yom Kippur*).

The Day of Atonement (cont.)

• When Aaron has finished the purification, he is to bring forward the live goat. • Laying both his hands on its head he must confess over it all the iniquities of the Israelites and all their acts of rebellion, that is all their sins; he is to lay his hands on the head of the goat and send it away into the wilderness in the charge of a man who is waiting ready. • The goat will carry all their iniquities upon itself into some barren waste, where the man will release it, there in the wilderness.   (REB)

The Day of Atonement (cont.)

Ch. 16 describes the arrangements for the ancient Day of Atonement. The purpose of the ceremonies is to cover all the unexpiated transgressions, whether cultic or moral, of *the community* during the past year. Many of the details of the ritual are obscure, but what is said about the scapegoat is fairly clear. First, the casting of *lots* (8) was a common procedure designed to leave the choice to God. The two lots were *for the LORD and for Azazel*, the latter being a demon. On the second *goat* the priest laid *both hands* (in normal sacrifice one was enough) *on its head*, in order to transfer to it the extant *sins* of the people. He then sent it out into the land of demons, the *wilderness*, to die in *some barren waste*.

The Day of Atonement fell five days before the feast of Tabernacles or Booths [Ch. 23.33+]. Together they originally formed part of the great New Year Festival, which was celebrated by all Semitic peoples. Many features of the atonement ritual had their parallels in Babylon, including one whereby a condemned felon was paraded through the streets and expelled from the city. Such 'substitution' rituals are also attested from many other places and times.

Prohibition of Eating Blood

If any Israelite or alien settled in Israel consumes any blood, I shall set my face against him and cut him off from his people, • because the life of a creature is the blood, and I appoint it to make expiation on the altar for yourselves: it is the blood, which is the life, that makes expiation. • Therefore I have told you Israelites that neither you, nor any alien settled among you, is to consume blood.

• Any Israelite or alien settled in Israel who hunts beasts or birds that may lawfully be eaten must drain out the blood and cover it with earth, • because the life of every living creature is its blood, and I have forbidden the Israelites to consume the blood of any creature, because the life of every creature is its blood: whoever eats it is to be cut off.   (REB)

Prohibition of Eating Blood

These verses underlie the Jewish requirement of kosher food. The prohibition in itself is old, and is absolute. The idea behind it is probably that *the life* belongs to God.

A Summary of the Torah

19.1-2 The LORD told Moses • to say to the whole Israelite community: You must be holy, because I, the LORD your God, am holy. • Each one of you must revere his mother and father. You must keep my sabbaths. I am the LORD your God. • Do not resort to idols or make for yourselves gods of cast metal. I am the LORD your God.

9 • When you reap the harvest in your land, do not reap right up to the edges of
10 your field, or gather the gleanings of your crop. • Do not completely strip your vineyard, or pick up the fallen grapes; leave them for the poor and for the alien. I am the LORD your God.

• You must not steal; you must not cheat or deceive a fellow-countryman. • You must not swear in my name with intent to deceive and thus profane the name of your God. I am the LORD. • You are not to oppress your neighbour or rob him. Do not keep back a hired man's wages till next morning. • Do not treat the deaf with contempt, or put an obstacle in the way of the blind; you are to fear your God. I am the LORD.

• You are not to pervert justice, either by favouring the poor or by subservience to the great. You are to administer justice to your fellow-countryman with strict fairness. • Do not go about spreading slander among your father's kin; do not take sides against your neighbour on a capital charge. I am the LORD. • You are not to nurse hatred towards your brother. Reprove your fellow-countryman frankly, and so you will have no share in his guilt. • Never seek revenge or cherish a grudge towards your kinsfolk; you must love your neighbour as yourself. I am the LORD.
▸

A Summary of the Torah

Ch.19 is P's summary of the Torah. In it cultic and social regulations are found together, as is usual in the OT, in this case with no discernible sequence of thought.

In part the chapter may be seen in relation to the ten commandments of Exodus 20. Verses 3-4 give four of the first five in reverse order: V, IV, II, I. That reversal may account for the sequence *mother and father*, which (with [Lev 21.2]) is the only such instance in the OT. Verse 12 contains the misplaced III, vv.11 and 13 can be seen as an amplification of VIII, and v.16 of IX.

This selection includes other social provisions, mostly exemplifying that especial care for *the poor* and weak which runs like a golden thread through the Torah. The regulation about *gleaning* (10), so memorably treated in the book of Ruth, is a later adaptation of the primitive tradition of leaving part of the produce as a gift to the god e.g. of corn or wine, cp. the classical practice of pouring a libation. Verse 14 is usually translated 'you shall not curse' *the deaf*: a curse being an effective weapon, it was unfair to use it on a man who could not hear it. The sentiments are summed up in v,18, the best known verse of the book, where the term *your neighbour* should be taken to include the resident *alien* (34). But when it comes to the formality of the law, favour must not be shown to *the poor* any more than to *the great* (15).

A Summary of the Torah (cont.)

19 • You must observe my statutes. You may not allow two different kinds of animal to mate together. You are not to plant your field with two kinds of seed, nor to wear a garment woven with two kinds of yarn.

32 • Rise in the presence of grey hairs, give honour to the aged, and fear your God. I am the LORD.

• When an alien resides with you in your land, you must not oppress him. • He is to be treated as a native born among you. Love him as yourself, because you were aliens in Egypt. I am the LORD your God.   (REB)

A Summary of the Torah (cont.)

Finally v.19 is included as a splendid example of the dislike of confusing categories. It presumably dates from before mules were introduced, *c*.1000 BC.

The Protection of Family Land-holdings

.8 You are to count off seven sabbaths of years, that is seven times seven years, forty-nine years, • and in the seventh month on the tenth day of the month, on the Day of Atonement, you are to send the ram's horn throughout your land to sound a blast. • Hallow the fiftieth year and proclaim liberation in the land for all its inhabitants. It is to be a jubilee year for you: each of you is to return to his holding, everyone to his family.

23 • No land may be sold outright, because the land is mine, and you come to it as aliens and tenants of mine. • Throughout the whole land you hold, you must allow a right of redemption over land which has been sold.

• If one of you is reduced to poverty and sells part of his holding, his next-of-kin who has the duty of redemption may come and redeem what his kinsman has sold. • When a man has no such next-of-kin and himself becomes able to afford its redemption, • he must take into account the years since the sale and repay the purchaser the balance up to the jubilee. Then he may return to his holding. • But if the man cannot afford to buy back the property, it remains in the hands of the purchaser till the jubilee year. It then reverts to the original owner, and he can return to his holding.   (REB)

The Protection of Family Land-holdings

All ANE societies had the problem of protecting the small-holder against the danger of a gradual decline into debt-slavery*. Rulers from time to time pronounced a 'freeing from the burdens', which typically included a cancellation of debts and a restoration of mortgaged property. The *year* of the *jubilee* (a word which comes from the Heb. *yōbēl*, a *ram's horn*) was an attempt to regularize such a *liberation* (10) in Israel. The intention was humane, though no instance is recorded in the OT of its implementation.

There was however another partial safeguard for the poor man who had *to sell part of his holding*. That resided in the right of *redemption**, which was also imposed as a *duty* upon *his next-of-kin*. The duty of redemption plays an important part in the book of Ruth.

NUMBERS

Introduction

The framework of the Book of Numbers is the story of the travels of the Hebrews under Moses from Mount Sinai to the point where they were ready to cross the Jordan westwards into the promised land. The Hebrew title of the book, 'In the Desert', refers to that framework. Upon it is loosely strung a great miscellany of other material: lists (including censuses, from which derive the Greek title of the book, Numbers), laws, rituals, aetiologies*, folk-tales, fragments of old poetry etc. Numbers is in fact more 'bitty' than any other book of the Pentateuch. But this has its compensations: although the editing is finally due to the Priestly writer (P), much of the material comes from J, and some is of great antiquity.

The overarching theme of Numbers, as of the next two books, is the gradual realization of the third of God's promises to Abraham, that of the land. In literary terms we therefore have a continuation of the quest. But in this quest the chief obstacles arise from the various failings of the people and of Moses. Such an emphasis accorded with the priestly doctrine that the national calamities of the Jews, culminating in the exile, were due to their own disobedience.

The Paternity Ordeal

5. 11 The LORD told Moses • to say to the Israelites: 'When a married woman goes astray and is unfaithful to her husband • by having sexual intercourse with another man, and this happens without the husband's knowledge, and without the woman being detected because, though she has been defiled, there is no direct evidence against her and she was not caught in the act, • and when in such a case a fit of jealousy comes over the husband which makes him suspect his wife, whether 15 she is defiled or not; • then the husband must bring his wife to the priest.

• The priest must bring her forward and set her before the LORD. • He is to take holy water in an earthenware vessel, and take dust from the floor of the Tabernacle and add it to the water. • He must set the woman before the LORD and uncover her head. Holding in his own hand the ordeal-water which tests under pain of curse, • the priest must put the woman on oath and say to her, "If no man has had intercourse with you, if you have not gone astray and let yourself become defiled while owing obedience to your husband, then may your innocence be 20 established by the ordeal-water. • But if, while owing him obedience, you have gone astray and let yourself become defiled, if any man other than your husband has had intercourse with you," • (the priest shall here put the woman on oath with an adjuration, and shall continue) • "let this ordeal-water that tests under pain of curse enter your body, bringing upon you miscarriage and untimely birth." The woman must respond, "Amen, Amen." ▸

The Paternity Ordeal

The first ten chapters record preparations for the journey, especially items of a ritual and legal nature such as interested P. Particularly intriguing is the only explicit description in the Bible of the primitive practice of trial by *ordeal*, which is known all over the world and which survived in Europe until the middle ages. An ordeal is resorted to when human evidence is inadequate and the case is referred to divine judgement. In its basic form, the accused is required to administer a self-curse: 'If I am guilty of this offence, may I be punished in such and such a way.' But

The Paternity Ordeal (cont.)

3   • The priest is to write these curses on a scroll, wash them off into the ordeal-water, • and make the woman drink the ordeal-water; it will enter her body to test

7   her. • If she has let herself become defiled and has been unfaithful to her husband, then, when the priest makes her drink the ordeal-water and it enters her body to test her, she will suffer a miscarriage or untimely birth, and her name will be an example in adjuration among her kin. • But if the woman has not let herself become defiled and is pure, then her innocence is established and she will bear

31   her child. • No guilt will attach to the husband, but the woman must bear the penalty of her guilt.'   (REB)

The Paternity Ordeal (cont.)

for more serious accusations more is required: characteristically the accused submits to a *test*, with the implication that 'If you fail the test, you must be guilty of the offence'. The present case combines the two elements. The accused is a pregnant wife whose husband suspects that the child she is expecting is not his. The test is the drinking of *holy water* in which has been dissolved the text of her self-*curse*. If, after drinking the water, she suffers a *miscarriage* or a still *birth*, her guilt is regarded as established, and she and her lover are stoned to death [Lev 20.10]. There are parallels in other cultures to all the elements in this procedure, though not to the whole of it together. Here is an African husband of the Nyakusa tribe speaking c. 1950.

> If I eat food and start diarrhoea, they say: 'It is women, they have committed adultery'. My wives deny it. We go to divination and one is caught; if she agrees, that's that, but if she denies it, formerly we went to the poison ordeal. The woman drank alone, not I. If she vomited then I was defeated, the woman was good; but if it caught her then her father paid me one cow.   (quoted by Mary Douglas)

Neither modern Africa nor ancient Israel allows redress for a wrongly accused wife.

The Priestly Blessing

2,23 And the LORD spake unto Moses, saying, • Speak unto Aaron and unto his sons, saying, On this wise ye shall bless the children of Israel, saying unto them,

• The LORD bless thee, and keep thee:

25   • The LORD make his face shine upon thee, and be gracious unto thee:

• The LORD lift up his countenance upon thee, and give thee peace.

• And they shall put my name upon the children of Israel, and I will bless them.   (AV)

The Priestly Blessing

Another item of 'equipment' for the journey was a special blessing, given through Moses for use by the priests. It was indeed used in later Judaism at the end of services. But only in Temple services might the priest pronounce the Holy *Name*, i.e. YHWH, as bidden by v.27. In the synagogues the name was replaced by the title *the LORD* (so here in AV and REB). AV alone retains the singular *thee*, whose personal note is reinforced by the two references to the *face* of God. *Make to shine* is in the Hebrew more dynamic than it seems in English; *lift up* is the opposite of letting the face fall in anger (Gen 4.5). *Peace* as always is a thin translation of the Hebrew *shalom*, which means total well-being.

A shorter version of this blessing was found recently in Jerusalem and published in 1986. It is inscribed on a silver plate in Hebrew letters of the C7th BC, which

The Priestly Blessing (cont..)

makes it by far the oldest biblical ms we have. The text has just two verses:

> YHWH bless thee and keep thee
> YHWH make his face shine upon thee and give thee peace.

The three verses of the full text are also reminiscent of a Babylonian blessing. That blessing however invokes three separate deities, calling on the first to 'rejoice over you', the second to 'make his face shine upon you' and the third to 'lift up your head'. The Hebrew blessing gains immeasurably by its concentration of force.

The Departure from Sinai: Complaints on the Journey

10. 29 Moses said to Hobab his brother-in-law, the Midianite, 'We are setting out for the place which the LORD promised to give us. Come with us, and we shall deal generously with you, for the LORD has given an assurance of prosperity for Israel.' • But he replied, 'No, I would rather go to my own country and my own people.' • Moses said, 'Do not leave us, I beg you; for you know where we ought to camp in the wilderness, and you will be our guide. • If you will go with us, then all the prosperity with which the LORD favours us we shall share with you.' • Then they moved off from the mountain of the LORD and journeyed for three days.

11. 1 • The people began complaining loudly to the LORD about their hardships, and when he heard he became angry. Fire from the LORD broke out among them, and raged on the outskirts of the camp. • Moses, when appealed to by the people, interceded with the LORD, and the fire died down.

• A mixed company of strangers had joined the Israelites, and these people began to be greedy for better things. Even the Israelites themselves with renewed 5 weeping cried out, 'If only we had meat! • Remember how in Egypt we had fish for the asking, cucumbers and water-melons, leeks and onions and garlic. • Now our appetite is gone; wherever we look there is nothing except this manna.' • (The manna looked like coriander seed, the colour of bdellium. • The people went about collecting it to grind in handmills or pound in mortars; they cooked it in a pot and made it into cakes, which tasted like butter-cakes. When dew fell on the camp at night, the manna would fall with it.) ▸

The Departure from Sinai: Complaints on the Journey

On setting out (at last!) from Sinai Moses issued a warm invitation to his *brother-in-law* to join them. The Midianites* had been essential to his success so far, and as semi-nomads they would *know where to camp in the wilderness*.

The first incidents recorded from the march itself are complaints, made by some or all of the people to God, and therefore usually against Moses as the leader appointed by him. These repeated complaints are perhaps the outstanding feature in the narrative of the wanderings (see on Exod 16). The whole section comes from the J school. Even though it never received its final polish, it has the naturalism and the directness that mark the J tradition.

Chs 11-12 contain an account of three such episodes of complaint. The first (11.1-2) is brief and straightforward. Like an overture it introduces the general theme of hardships and resolves the problem easily through the intercession of Moses.

The second (11.4-34) is altogether more complex. It interweaves two themes which have already been met in Exodus: the sending of manna and quails to the people (Ch.16) and the spreading of the heavy burden of responsibility resting on Moses (Ch.18). But the themes, as well as being interwoven, are both given a new and ironical twist.

The Departure from Sinai: Complaints on the Journey (cont)

• Moses heard all the people lamenting in their families at the opening of their tents. The LORD became very angry, and Moses was troubled, • and said to the LORD, 'Why have you brought trouble on your servant? How have I displeased the LORD that I am burdened with all this people? • Am I their mother? Have I brought them into the world, and am I called on to carry them in my arms, like a nurse with a baby, to the land promised by you on oath to their fathers? • Where am I to find meat to give them all? They pester me with their wailing and their "Give us meat to eat." • This whole people is a burden too heavy for me; I cannot carry it alone. • If that is your purpose for me, then kill me outright: if I have found favour with you, spare me this trouble afflicting me.'

• The LORD answered Moses, 'Assemble for me seventy of Israel's elders, men known to you as elders and officers in the community; bring them to the Tent of Meeting, and there let them take their place with you. • I shall come down and speak with you there. I shall withdraw part of the spirit which is conferred on you and bestow it on them, and they will share with you the burden of the people; then you will not have to bear it alone. • And say to the people: Sanctify yourselves in readiness for tomorrow; you will have meat to eat. You wailed in the LORD's hearing; you said, "If only we had meat! In Egypt we lived well." The LORD will give you meat and you will eat it. • Not for one day only, nor for two days, nor five, nor ten, nor twenty, • but for a whole month you will eat it until it comes out at your nostrils and makes you sick; because you have rejected the LORD who is in your midst, wailing in his presence and saying, "Why did we ever come out of Egypt?" '

• Moses went out and told the people what the LORD had said. He assembled seventy men from the elders of the people and stationed them round the Tent. • Then the LORD descended in the cloud and spoke to him. He withdrew part of the spirit which had been conferred on Moses and bestowed it on the seventy elders; as the spirit alighted on them, they were seized by a prophetic ecstasy, for the first and only time.

The Departure from Sinai: Complaints on the Journey (cont.)

The story opens innocently enough, with the people hankering for the fleshpots of Egypt. But whereas in Exodus God answered their complaint by sending them *manna*, it turns out in Numbers that they have already had manna and don't like it – what they want is *meat*. This makes God *angry*. Moses, caught as usual in the middle, is *troubled*. He is cross with the people (13), but his chief resentment is directed at God (11-12). In short, the *burden* is *too heavy* for him (14).

God in reply goes first to the crux of the matter, the burden on Moses. He will arrange for *70 elders* to share it – but there is a strong hint that Moses will regret the change. Towards the people God is even more peremptory: they shall have their meat – enough to *make* them *sick*.

The two plans are then implemented in the order that God set them out. The 70 elders, instead of sharing Moses' judicial burden (as in Exod 18), are *seized by a prophetic ecstasy*. All but two of them are seized outside the camp, and *the spirit* left them again immediately (25). But two of them prophesied *there in the camp* and perhaps went on doing so. Now ecstatic prophecy is generally frowned upon in the OT, and the reaction of *Joshua* is typical.

The Departure from Sinai: Complaints on the Journey (cont.)

11.26   • Two men, one named Eldad and the other Medad, who had been enrolled with the seventy, were left behind in the camp. Though they had not gone out to the Tent, the spirit alighted on them none the less, and they were seized by prophetic ecstasy there in the camp. • A young man ran and told Moses that Eldad and Medad were in an ecstasy in the camp, • whereupon Joshua son of Nun, who had served since boyhood with Moses, broke in, 'Moses my lord, stop them!' • But Moses said to him, 'Are you jealous on my account? I wish that all the LORD's people were prophets and that the LORD would bestow his spirit on them all!'

30   • Moses then rejoined the camp with the elders of Israel.

• There sprang up a wind from the LORD, which drove quails in from the west, and they were flying all round the camp for the distance of a day's journey, three feet above the ground. • The people were busy gathering quails all that day and night, and all next day, and even those who got least gathered ten homers of them. They spread them out to dry all about the camp. • But the meat was scarcely between their teeth, and they had not so much as bitten it, when the LORD's anger flared up against the people and he struck them with a severe plague.   (REB)

The Departure from Sinai: Complaints on the Journey (cont.)

He also realised that Moses had lost face, and out of loyalty protested. Moses' reply in v.29 is remarkable. Whether it expresses a considered wish or a temporary bluster, it leaves Moses' own position ambiguous – to be clarified in the next chapter. But before then we have to learn the simpler outcome of God's other plan. *The meat* he sends the people turns out to be the *quails* of Exod 16, but this time they bring an epidemic which lasts until the camp moves on.

Personal Criticism of Moses

12.1   The Israelites went on to Hazeroth, and while they were there, • Miriam and Aaron began to find fault with Moses. They criticized him for his Cushite wife (for he had married a Cushite woman), • and they complained, 'Is Moses the only one by whom the LORD has spoken? Has he not spoken by us as well?' – though Moses was a man of great humility, the most humble man on earth. But the   ▶

Personal Criticism of Moses

The third episode (Ch.12) is obscure in some details but clear in its central thrust. The complaining is here personalised, though nothing is made of the private relations between the three main characters. Perhaps two narratives are interwoven: there are two distinct complaints, and two complainants whose names are inverted between vv.1 and 5. On that interpretation it was *Miriam* who complained about the *Cushite wife* (presumably an Ethiopian but not mentioned elsewhere), and who was punished by a mild skin-complaint not incurring uncleanness [Lev 13]. There may however be an extra element of irony here, if the complaint about a black woman was punished by a *white* affliction. It is then *Aaron* who complains that God has *spoken by us as well*, as indeed is recorded from time to time in Leviticus; having received God's reply in vv.6-8, he then repents and is not punished.

But the two narratives are now closely interwoven in such a way as to emphasize – and to resolve – the central issue of Moses' leadership. For in this third episode Moses reverts to the role he had

Personal Criticism of Moses (cont.)

LORD heard them • and at once said to Moses, Aaron, and Miriam, 'Go out all
5   three of you to the Tent of Meeting.' When they went out, • the LORD descended
in a pillar of cloud and, standing at the entrance to the tent, he summoned Aaron
6   and Miriam. The two of them came forward, • and the LORD said,

'Listen to my words.
If he were your prophet and nothing more,
I would make myself known to him in a vision,
I would speak with him in a dream.
7   But my servant Moses is not such a prophet;
of all my household he alone is faithful.
8   With him I speak face to face,
openly and not in riddles.
He sees the very form of the LORD.
How dare you speak against my servant Moses?'

10   • With his anger still hot against them, the LORD left them; • and as the cloud
moved from the tent, there was Miriam, her skin diseased and white as snow.
When Aaron, turning towards her, saw her skin diseased, • he said to Moses,
'My lord, do not make us pay the penalty of sin, foolish and wicked though we
have been. • Let her not be like something stillborn, whose flesh is half eaten
away when it comes from the womb.' • So Moses cried, 'LORD, not this! Heal
her, I pray.' • The LORD answered, 'Suppose her father had spat in her face,
would she not have to remain in disgrace for seven days? Let her be confined
15   outside the camp for seven days and then be brought back.' • So Miriam was
shut outside for seven days, and the people did not strike camp until she was
brought back. • After that they moved on from Hazeroth and pitched camp in the
wilderness of Paran.   (REB)

Personal Criticism of Moses (cont.)

in the first. He takes no part in the
complaining, and he is vindicated by God
in striking words which leave no doubt of
his unique position: prophets are spoken
to, Moses is listened to. He then resumes
his role as mediator: Aaron asks him to
intercede, and God reduces Miriam's
punishment to the bare minimum. But the
complaint, like the previous one, has
delayed the progress of the people. (For
Paran see map 1.) The other places
mentioned are unknown.

The Reconnaissance of Southern Israel

13.1   The LORD said to Moses, • 'Send men out to explore Canaan, the land which I am
going to give to the Israelites; from each ancestral tribe send one man, a man of
high rank.'

The Reconnaissance of Southern Israel

At the northern end of the wilderness of
Paran was the fertile oasis-complex of
Kadesh-barnea (13.26), the natural base
for an attempt to enter the promised land
from the west. But before any intrusion it
was only prudent to send forward scouts
to reconnoitre the *Negeb* (the southern
approaches). This reconnaissance was a
turning point in the journey, so it is not
surprising to find three different accounts
of it in the Pentateuch. Two of them are
amalgamated in Numbers, the third is in
[Dt Ch.1]. There are important differences
between the three accounts, but the first

The Reconnaissance of Southern Israel (cont.)

13.17   • When Moses sent them to explore Canaan, he said, 'Make your way up by the Negeb, up into the hill-country, • and see what the land is like, and whether the people who live there are strong or weak, few or many. • See whether the country in which they live is easy or difficult, and whether their towns are open or fortified. • Is the land fertile or barren, and is it wooded or not? Go boldly in and bring some of its fruit.' It was the season when the first grapes were ripe.

• Going up by the Negeb they came to Hebron, where the descendants of Anak were living. (Hebron was built seven years before Zoan in Egypt.) • They came to the wadi Eshcol, and there they cut a branch with a single bunch of grapes, which they carried on a pole between two of them; they also picked pomegranates and figs.

25   • After forty days they returned from exploring the country • and, coming back to Moses and Aaron and the whole community of Israelites at Kadesh in the wilderness of Paran, they made their report, and showed them the fruit of the country. • They gave Moses this account: 'We made our way into the land to which you sent us. It is flowing with milk and honey, and here is the fruit it grows; • but its inhabitants are formidable, and the towns are fortified and very large; indeed, we saw there the descendants of Anak. • We also saw the Amalekites who live in the Negeb, Hittites, Jebusites, and Amorites who live in the hill-country, and the Canaanites who live by the sea and along the Jordan.'

30   • Caleb silenced the people for Moses. 'Let us go up at once and occupy the country,' he said; 'we are well able to conquer it.' • But the men who had gone with him said, 'No, we cannot attack these people; they are too strong for us.' • Their report to the Israelites about the land which they had explored was discouraging: 'The country we explored', they said, 'will swallow up any who go to live in it. All the people we saw there are men of gigantic stature. • When we set eyes on the Nephilim (the sons of Anak belong to the Nephilim) we felt no bigger than grasshoppers; and that is how we must have been in their eyes.'

14. 1   • At this the whole Israelite community cried out in dismay and the people wept all night long. • Everyone complained against Moses and Aaron: 'If only we had died in Egypt or in the wilderness!' they said. • 'Why should the LORD bring us to this land, to die in battle and leave our wives and our dependants to become the spoils of war? It would be better for us to go back to Egypt.' • And they spoke of choosing someone to lead them back there.   ♦

The Reconnaissance of Southern Israel (cont.)

two are reasonably well harmonized and form the basis of this selection.

The scouts succeeded in penetrating some seventy miles from Kadesh to the important hill-town of Hebron. There they found everything larger than life. Reporting back, they gave first the good news and then the bad. On the one hand *a single bunch of* local *grapes* (Eshcol means 'cluster') took two men to carry. On the other *the inhabitants* were *men of*

giant stature. This intelligence evidently alarmed the people. *Caleb,* who was to prove one of the leaders of the next generation, had to *silence the people* before he could get a hearing for his confient speech. But most of his fellow-scouts shared – and fuelled – the people's pessimism: Far from their living off the fat of the land, the land of giants will devour them.

The scene changes in Ch.14, to take

The Reconnaissance of Southern Israel (cont.)

1   • The LORD said to Moses, 'How much longer will this people set me at naught?
How much longer will they refuse to trust me in spite of all the signs I have
shown among them? • Ten times they have challenged me and not obeyed my
25   voice. None of those who have set me at naught shall see this land. • But my
servant Caleb showed a different spirit and remained loyal to me. Because of this,
I shall bring him into the land in which he has already set foot, the territory of the
Amalekites and the Canaanites who dwell in the Vale, and I shall put his descendants
in possession of it. Tomorrow you must turn back and set out for the wilderness
by way of the Red Sea.'   (REB)

The Reconnaissance of Southern Israel (cont.)

the form of another complaint against
Moses and God. Once again, the people
would do better *to go back to Egypt*. God's
reply is decisive. They shall indeed *turn
back*, towards *the Red Sea* (specifically
to the Gulf of Aqaba). And because of
their lack of faith they will need to make a
circuitous approach to the promised land,
with the result that most of this generation
will not live to see it. Caleb is an exception
and, as a reward for his *different spirit*,
his tribe of Judah will be given the fertile
region of Hebron to occupy.

In other places Joshua is added to
Caleb as one who will see the promised
land, while Moses himself is explicitly
named among those who will not [Dt 1.37
etc.].

Venomous Snakes

1.4   From Mount Hor they left by way of the Red Sea to march round the flank of
5   Edom. But on the way the people grew impatient • and spoke against God and
Moses. 'Why have you brought us up from Egypt', they said, 'to die in the desert
where there is neither food nor water? We are heartily sick of this miserable
fare.' • Then the LORD sent venomous snakes among them, and they bit the
Israelites so that many of them died. • The people came to Moses and said, 'We
sinned when we spoke against the LORD and you. Plead with the LORD to rid us of
the snakes.' Moses interceded for the people, • and the LORD told him to make a
serpent and erect it as a standard, so that anyone who had been bitten could look at it
and recover. • So Moses made a bronze serpent and erected it as a standard, in order
that anyone bitten by a snake could look at the bronze serpent and recover.   (REB)

Venomous Snakes

Leaving *Mount Hor* (near Kadesh), the
Israelites skirted the Edomite territory at
the southern end of the Dead Sea. Here
they encountered an unpleasant kind of
desert *snake*. There is some implication
in the Hebrew that these snakes were
winged; and curiously Herodotus also
reported circumstantial travellers' tales of
winged snakes in that same general region.
The Hebrew writer ascribed them to what
is mercifully the last instance of complaining *against God and Moses*. Of more
interest is the notice that God *told* Moses
to make a bronze serpent as protection.
There has always been a general belief that
the hostility of a dangerous creature can
be averted by placating an image of it. Specifically also snakes are credited with powers of healing e.g. the snake was the symbol of the Greek god of healing, Asclepius.
This bronze snake of Moses, which strictly
was only for the people to *look at* here, is
said to have been preserved and later set
up in the Temple at Jerusalem, where sacrifices were still being offered to it in the
time of Hezekiah (2 K 18.4).

The Song of the Well

21.16 From there they went on to Be-er: this is the well where the LORD said to Moses, 'Gather the people together and I shall give them water.' • It was then that Israel sang this song:

> Spring up, O well! Greet it with song,
> the well dug by the princes,
> laid open by the leaders of the people
> with sceptre and staff,
> a gift from the wilderness.

(REB)

The Song of the Well

The next incident on the journey is also not precisely located. But room had to be found in the Pentateuch for this ancient 'song of the well', whose importance in later Judaism was such that it was sung in the synagogue every third sabbath, the other two being devoted to the two halves of the Song of the Sea (Ex 15). In the desert water is the staff of life, and great rituals still today surround its acquisition among Bedouin peoples. Such a well is a pit scraped out in the bed of a wadi, which fills up with water in the winter and has to be freshly dug and cleaned each spring. According to a modern traveller in the same region, 'each tent possesses its own *bir* . . . and though the chiefs seldom work with their own hands, it is always said "Sheik N dug this well".' This kind of song was originally addressed to the spirit of the well.

Balak Summons Balaam

22. 1 The Israelites moved on and encamped in the lowlands of Moab on the farther side of the Jordan opposite Jericho.

• Balak son of Zippor saw all that Israel had done to the Amorites, • and Moab was in terror of the people because there were so many of them. The Moabites were overcome with fear at the sight of them; • and they said to the elders of Midian, 'This horde will soon eat up everything round us as an ox eats up the new

5 grass in the field.' Balak son of Zippor, who was at that time king of Moab, • sent a deputation to summon Balaam son of Beor, who was at Pethor by the Euphrates in the land of the Amavites, with this message, 'A whole nation has just arrived from Egypt: they cover the face of the country and are settling at my very door. • Come at once and lay a curse on them, because they are too many for me. I may then be able to defeat them and drive them out of the country. I know that those whom you bless are blessed, and those whom you curse are cursed.'

• The elders of Moab and Midian took the fees for augury with them, and coming to Balaam they gave him Balak's message. • 'Spend this night here,' he replied, 'and I shall give you whatever answer the LORD gives me.' So the Moabite chiefs stayed with Balaam. • God came to Balaam and asked him, 'Who are these men with you?'   ♦

Balak Summons Balaam

The Israelites have now arrived at their last encampment before they cross the Jordan. It is in Moabite territory, where they are preserved by force of number. *Balak*, the Moabite king, of whom nothing else is known, sends for help to *Balaam*, a soothsayer of high status (he has *two servants*, 22) from the *Euphrates*. He wants two things from Balaam. The more important is a *curse* upon the Israelites. For the efficacy of a curse see p.79. Before a battle it was the ancient equivalent of a

Balak Summons Balaam (cont.)

• Balaam replied, 'Balak son of Zippor king of Moab has sent them to me and he says, • "A people which has just come out of Egypt is covering the face of the country. Come at once and put a curse on them for me; then I may be able to give battle and drive them away." ' • God said to Balaam, 'You are not to go with them or curse the people, because they are to be blessed.' • So when Balaam rose in the morning he said to Balak's chiefs, 'Go back to your own country; the LORD has refused to let me go with you.' • The Moabite chiefs took their leave and went back to Balak, and reported to him that Balaam had refused to come with them.

• Balak sent a second embassy, larger and more high-powered than the first. • When they came to Balaam they said, 'This is the message from Balak son of Zippor: "Let nothing stand in the way of your coming to me. • I shall confer great honour upon you and do whatever you ask me. But you must come and put a curse on this people for me." ' • Balaam gave this answer to Balak's messengers: 'Even if Balak were to give me all the silver and gold in his palace, I could not disobey the command of the LORD my God in anything, small or great. • But stay here for this night, as the others did, that I may learn what more the LORD may have to say to me.' • During the night God came to Balaam and said to him, 'If these men have come to summon you, then rise and go with them, but do only what I tell you.' • When morning came Balaam rose, saddled his donkey, and went with the Moabite chiefs.

• But God was angry because Balaam was going, and as he came riding on his donkey, accompanied by his two servants, the angel of the LORD took his stand in the road to bar his way. • When the donkey saw the angel standing in the road with his sword drawn, she turned off the road into the fields, and Balaam beat her to bring her back on to the road. • The angel of the LORD then stood where the road ran through a hollow, with enclosed vineyards on either side. • The donkey saw the angel and, squeezing herself against the wall, she crushed Balaam's foot against it, and again he beat her. • The angel of the LORD moved on farther and stood in a narrow place where there was no room to turn to either right or left. • When the donkey saw the angel, she lay down under Balaam. At that Balaam lost his temper and beat the donkey with his staff.

• The LORD then made the donkey speak, and she said to Balaam, 'What have I done? This is the third time you have beaten me.' • Balaam answered, 'You have been making a fool of me. If I had had a sword with me, I should have killed you on the spot.' • But the donkey answered, 'Am I not still the donkey which you have ridden all your life? Have I ever taken such a liberty with you before?' Balak He said, 'No.' • Then the LORD opened Balaam's eyes: he saw the angel of the LORD standing in the road with his sword drawn, and he bowed down and prostrated himself.   ♦

Balak Summons Balaam (cont.)

long-range bombardment. The less important is an *augury*, the taking of the omens e.g. about which is the best day for battle.

Balaam is represented in the story as one who believes not just in God but in *the* *LORD,* i.e. YHWH. Some scholars think that YHWH was originally worshipped by other peoples e.g. the Midianites (see on Exod 18). The story of *the donkey* does not fit well into the context (v.22 contradicts v.20), but it is told with skill and humour.

Balak Summons Balaam (cont.)

22.32 • The angel said to him, 'What do you mean by beating your donkey three times like this? I came out to bar your way, but you made straight for me, • and three times your donkey saw me and turned aside. If she had not turned aside, I should by now have killed you, while sparing her.' • 'I have done wrong,' Balaam replied to the angel of the LORD. 'I did not know that you stood confronting me

35 in the road. But now, if my journey displeases you, I shall turn back.' • The angel of the LORD said to Balaam, 'Go with the men; but say only what I tell you.' So Balaam went on with Balak's chiefs.   (REB)

Balak Summons Balaam (cont.)

It has many marks of folk-tale: the talking animal (the only one in the OT), the idea that an animal can see a spirit, the 'ascending' three-fold repetition. It is full also of homely touches, e.g. a donkey's way of protesting by knocking its rider's leg against a wall. *The angel* clearly represents God himself (cp. v.20).

Balaam Blesses Israel

22.36 When Balak heard that Balaam was coming, he went out to meet him as far as Ar of Moab by the Arnon on his frontier. • Balak said to Balaam, 'Did I not send time and again to summon you? Why did you not come? Did you think that I could not do you honour?' • Balaam replied, 'I have come, as you see. But now that I am here, what power have I of myself to say anything? It is only whatever word God puts into my mouth that I can speak.' • So Balaam went with Balak till they came to Kiriath-

40 huzoth, • and Balak slaughtered cattle and sheep and sent portions to Balaam and to the chiefs who were with him. • In the morning Balak took Balaam and led him up to Bamoth-baal, from where he could see the full extent of the Israelite host.

23.1 • Then Balaam said to Balak, 'Build me here seven altars and prepare for me seven bulls and seven rams.' • Balak followed Balaam's instructions; after offering a bull and a ram on each altar, • he said to him, 'I have prepared the seven altars, and I have offered the bull and the ram on each altar.' Balaam answered, 'You stand here beside your sacrifice, and let me go off by myself. It may be that the LORD will meet me. Whatever he reveals to me, I shall tell you.' He went off to a

5 height, where God met him. • The LORD put words into Balaam's mouth and said, 'Go back to Balak, and speak as I tell you.' • He went back, and found Balak standing by his sacrifice, and with him all the Moabite chiefs.   ▶

Balaam Blesses Israel

When Balaam approaches, *Balak* goes out to meet him on the frontier of his kingdom (36), and honours him further with gifts. Then he takes him to a place from which he can see the Israelites: this will make the curse (or, as the reader knows, the blessing) more efficacious. Finally Balak arranges a full-scale sacrifice of *seven bulls* and *seven rams* at seven altars. The lavish technology of paganism is contrasted with the word of the one God which cannot be bought for *silver and gold*. So Balaam pronounces his blessing and Balak reacts predictably.

The whole sequence is actually repeated three times (here reduced to one), echoing the three exchanges between Balaam and his donkey. But Balaam has a fourth oracle to deliver (24.15-18). This may be the nucleus round which the whole story was constructed. The *star* of v.17 is usually taken to refer to David, but REB's *comet*, together with *come forth* and *arise*, are all technical terms of astrology. *Seir* is a mountain of the *Moab* region.

Balaam is an imposing figure in the

Balaam Blesses Israel (cont.)

7 • Then Balaam uttered his oracle:

From Aram, from the mountains of the east,
   Balak king of Moab has brought me:
'Come, lay a curse on Jacob for me,' he said.
   'Come, denounce Israel.'

8 How can I curse someone God has not cursed,
   how denounce someone the LORD has not denounced?

9 From the rocky heights I see them,
   I watch them from the rounded hills.
I see a people that dwells apart,
   that has not made itself one with the nations.
Who can count the host of Jacob
   or number the myriads of Israel?

10 • At that Balak's anger was aroused against Balaam; beating his hands together, he cried, 'It was to curse my enemies that I summoned you, and three times you have persisted in blessing them. • Off with you at once to your own place! I promised to confer great honour upon you, but now the LORD has kept this honour from you.' • Balaam answered, 'But I said to your messengers: • "Were Balak to give me all the silver and gold in his palace, I could not disobey the command of the LORD by doing anything of my own will, good or bad. What the LORD says to me, that is what I must say." • Now I am going to my own people; but first, let me warn you what this people will do to yours in the days to come.'

15 • Then he uttered his oracle:

The word of Balaam son of Beor,
   the word of the man whose sight is clear,

16 the word of him who hears the words of God,
   who shares the knowledge of the Most High,
who with opened eyes sees in a trance
   the vision from the Almighty:

17 I see him, but not now;
   I behold him, but not near:
a star will come forth out of Jacob,
   a comet will arise from Israel.
He will smite the warriors of Moab,
   and beat down all the sons of Sheth.

18 Edom will be his by conquest
   and Seir, his enemy, will become his.

• Then Balaam arose and returned home, and Balak also went on his way.(REB)

Balaam Blesses Israel (cont.)

story, the ecstatic prophet whose *sight*, hearing and *knowledge* are all supernatural (24.16) – even though the ass saw more than the seer! And not just in the story: a recently discovered inscription (text on p.517f.) shows that Balaam was a notable figure outside the OT also. It is hard to know precisely what relation that inscription bears to this story. But it certainly establishes the *fame* of the gentile Balaam – which may explain why the Pentateuch gives to a foreign seer the honour of uttering its most far-reaching prophecy of Israel's future successes.

DEUTERONOMY

Introduction

Deuteronomy has a pivotal role in the Hebrew Bible. By claiming Moses for its author, it was accepted as the last book of the Torah or Pentateuch; but it was edited by the same hands as the next large group of the OT, viz. Joshua-2 Kings, and so can also be regarded as the first book in that group, which is known to scholars as the deuteronomic history.

The core of D (Chs 12-26) is generally identified with the 'book of the law', said to have been found by Hilkiah the high priest in Solomon's temple in 621 BC (see 2 K 22-23 with notes). That core contains some very early material, but was probably put together not long before it was 'found'. Many later additions were made, including passages which 'foretell' the return from exile (e.g. 30.1-7) and so can be no earlier than c.550 BC.

The title Deuteronomy, which comes from the Greek Bible, means 'second law'. Although this is strictly a mistranslation of the Hebrew, it makes good sense. For the core of the book is a collection of laws, which bears a close relationship to the earlier collection in Exodus 20-24 – indeed half of those in Exodus are also to be found here. Here, as there, the content is a mixture of cultic and social, and the form a mixture of absolute and conditional. In all respects save one, namely the OT's inclusion of cultic regulations, both collections closely resemble in turn such ANE codes as that of Hammurabi.

But an ANE law code is essentially a top-down document. The king – admittedly on behalf of the gods – is laying down what should happen. That form did not suit Deuteronomy's central doctrine, the covenant or agreement between YHWH and Israel. For a covenant document, the appropriate ANE model is a treaty, more particularly a treaty between a Great King and his vassals. Many of these vassal treaties survive, and

their standard form falls into sections which are roughly followed by the main body of the book of D, viz:

(i)   recollection of benefits   Chs 6-11
      conferred by overlord
      (in this case God)
(ii) detailed stipulations i.e.   Chs 12-26.15
      laws
(iii) acceptance of   Ch. 26.16-19
      obligation by vassals
      (Israel)
(iv) blessings and curses   Chs 27-28
(v)   recording and preser-   Ch. 31.7-13
      vation of treaty, with
      provision for public
      recital.

The doctrine of the covenant, i.e. that God too is under obligation, is the central contribution of Deuteronomy to Hebrew thought. Admittedly, it had been adumbrated by the great eighth-century prophets, especially Hosea. But D worked it out and established it. And it is that belief more than anything else which marked out the Jews in the ancient world, and has ever since given them the strength and cohesion needed to carry them through the appalling tribulations of their history.

Those tribulations had already begun with the collapse of Israel in 721 BC. The smaller kingdom of Judah was now directly exposed to the overwhelming might of Assyria, and even the acceptance of vassal status was no guarantee of survival. Hence the preaching tone which is so characteristic of D's style. The tone is insistent, with a tendency to overwhelm the reader with words, and earnest, as its subject warrants – though it is never shrill as the prophets can be. Above all it is rhetorical. The rhetoric is sometimes frigid, but at its best it is warm and humane e.g. 8.7-10. Altogether the style of D's sermons is that which corresponds most nearly to the expectations of a reader unfamiliar with the OT.

With the doctrine of the covenant go the related doctrines of the chosen people and the promised land. More loosely associated is D's fourth passionate concern, the centralization of worship in Jerusalem. The logic of that concern is not clear, but it seems to have been that a national identity depended upon the exclusive worship of YHWH and the rejection of 'other gods'. That term, as used by Dt, refers almost exclusively to Baal.

But it had long been the custom in both Israel and Judah for YHWH and Baal to be worshipped together in the same sanctuaries (see p.32). The prophets of Israel had protested against the custom, but to no avail. When Israel fell in 721,

the prophets of Judah, doubly convinced that its fall was due to this same syncretism, insisted that the worship of YHWH must be exclusive. That worship was the national cult, with the king at its head. What went on in the countryside could not be controlled. As in the early centuries of Christianity, the country was where the 'old religion' persisted, with its multiplicity of deities and cults – the very word 'pagan' originally meant merely 'villager'. It followed, in the eyes of Dt, that in order to ensure the integrity of the cult and thus the identity of the nation, it was necessary to centralize worship in the royal Temple in Jerusalem. Necessary it may have been; but, as later events were to show, it was not sufficient. Syncretism proved to be as prevalent in the Temple as in the provinces.

Moses' Last Plea

3.23 • It was then I made this plea to the LORD: • 'Lord GOD,' I said, 'you have begun to show to your servant your great power and your strong hand: what god is there in heaven or on earth who can match your works and mighty deeds?

25 • Let me cross over, I beg, and see that good land which lies on the other side of the Jordan, and the fine hill-country and the Lebanon.' • But because of you the LORD angrily brushed me aside and would not listen. 'Enough!' he answered. 'Say no more about this. • Go to the top of Pisgah and look west and north, south and east; look well at what you see, for you will not cross this river Jordan. • Give Joshua his commission, support and strengthen him, for he will lead this people across, and he will put them in possession of the land you see before you.' • So we remained in the glen opposite Beth-peor.   (REB)

Moses' Last Plea

In the first three chapters of D, the author presents Moses speaking to the people, giving them his summary of their journey through the wilderness* to the point now reached viz. in Transjordan below Mt Pisgah. He here concludes the summary on a poignant note about his own position.

During the wanderings in the wilderness, God had warned him more than once that he would not be allowed to enter the promised land. The reasons

given had varied but common to them all was *because of you*: i.e. Moses, as leader, must accept responsibility for the waywardness of the people. But having brought them to the end of their march, he had ventured to make this one last plea to YHWH, which was brusquely rejected. The rejection – and the manner of it – highlights the tragic loneliness of Moses' position. Immediately after this flashback the author inserts the laws, resuming the narrative of Moses' death in Ch. 31.

The Shema

6. 4 Hear, O Israel: The LORD is our God, the LORD alone. • You shall love the LORD your God with all your heart, and with all your soul, and with all your might. • Keep these words that I am commanding you today in your heart. • Recite them to your children and talk about them when you are at home and when you are away, when you lie down and when you rise. • Bind them as a sign on your hand,
9 fix them as an emblem on your forehead, • and write them on the doorposts of your house and on your gates.   (NRSV)

The Shema

These verses have played a central part in the development of Jewish piety throughout history. The first two are very old, but they are less simple than they look. Not too much should be read into *love*. It cannot imply any emotional feeling – that could never be commanded. It must mean rather 'be loyal to' as a vassal to a suzerain.

The Hebrew for *hear* is *shemā*, which has given its name to the section, and the Shema has long been recited twice a day by pious Jews. Since however *these*

words of v.6 is of uncertain reference, the Shema is sometimes taken to end at v.5, sometimes to go on to v.9 or indeed to include other passages. The same text, copied onto small scrolls, is bound (as a phylactery) onto the left arm and *forehead* during morning prayer, and is affixed (in a small box or *mezūzāh*) to the right-hand *door-post* of the faithful. Elsewhere in the ancient world amulets were worn and sayings of good omen inscribed over door-posts as protection against evil spirits.

A Sermon: God's Promises Fulfilled

8. 1 You must carefully observe every command I give you this day so that you may live and increase in numbers and enter and occupy the land which the LORD promised on oath to your forefathers. • Remember the whole way by which the LORD your God has led you these forty years in the wilderness to humble and test you, and to discover whether or not it was in your heart to keep his commandments. • So he afflicted you with hunger and then fed you on manna which neither you nor your fathers had known before, to teach you that people cannot live on bread alone, but that they live on every word that comes from the mouth of the LORD. • The clothes on your backs did not wear out, nor did your feet blister, all these
5 forty years. • Take to heart this lesson: that the LORD your God was disciplining you as a father disciplines his son. • Keep the commandments of the LORD your God, conforming to his ways and fearing him.   ▸

A Sermon: God's Promises Fulfilled

Ch.8.1-18 shows the author as teacher and preacher. He presents God *disciplining* Israel, explicitly *as a father* in v.5, but implicitly also as a teacher, with *lesson* (5) and *test* (2, 16). Meanwhile he himself is preaching the importance of the covenant – see the framing words *oath* and *your forefathers* in vv.1 and 18.

Within that frame are two themes. The outer one is the journey through the wild-

erness (2-6 and 14-16). From the *manna* incident (3 and 16) the author derives a novel lesson, but as often the best-known saying is the hardest to interpret. The *word that comes from the mouth of the LORD* (3) must refer to the manna – not, as it might elsewhere in D, the command-ments. Oblique light is thrown by a phrase from an Egyptian saying about the creator god Ptah, that 'man lives by what comes

A Sermon: God's Promises Fulfilled (cont.)

7   • The LORD your God is bringing you to a good land, a land with streams, springs, and underground waters gushing out in valley and hill, • a land with wheat and barley, vines, fig trees, and pomegranates, a land with olive oil and honey. • It is a land where you will never suffer any scarcity of food to eat, nor want for anything, a land whose stones are iron ore and from whose hills you will mine copper. • When you have plenty to eat, bless the LORD your God for the good land he has given you.

   • See that you do not forget the LORD your God by failing to keep his commandments, laws, and statutes which I give you this day. • When you have plenty to eat and live in fine houses of your own building, • when your herds and flocks, your silver and gold, and all your possessions increase, • do not become proud and forget the LORD your God who brought you out of Egypt, out of that land of slavery; • he led you through the vast and terrible wilderness infested with venomous snakes and scorpions, a thirsty, waterless land where he caused water to flow for you from the flinty rock; • he fed you in the wilderness with manna which your fathers had never known, to humble and test you, and in the end to make you prosper. • Nor must you say to yourselves, 'My own strength and energy have gained me this wealth.' • Remember the LORD your God; it is he who gives you strength to become prosperous, so fulfilling the covenant guaranteed by oath with your forefathers, as he does to this day.

   • The land which you are about to enter and occupy is not like the land of Egypt from which you have come, where, after sowing your seed, you regulated the water by means of your foot as in a vegetable garden. • But the land into which you are about to cross to occupy it is a land of mountains and valleys watered by the rain of heaven. • It is a land which the LORD your God tends and on which his eye rests from one year's end to the next. • If you pay heed to the commandments which I give you this day, to love the LORD your God and serve him with all your heart and soul, • then I shall send rain for your land in season, both autumn and spring rains, and you will gather your corn and new wine and oil, • and I shall provide pasture in the fields for your cattle: you will have all you want to eat.   (REB)

A Sermon: God's Promises Fulfilled (cont.)

forth from His mouth'. What is being contrasted, therefore, is not the material with the spiritual but people's self-sufficiency with their dependence upon God's creativity.

   The central – and so the most important – theme of the section is the promised land. The description of the land in vv.7-9 is lyrical in style and content; and the same is true of 11.11-12, which should be taken with it. Although the metre is not strict, the balance of the clauses and the strongly marked repetition of *a land (which)* . . .

give the impression of an older hymn of praise here incorporated. And the portrait it gives of the land is idealized. Contrary to 8.9, Palestine has no *iron* or *copper* west of the Jordan, and its water supply is far from being one of its assets. Moreover the lesson which the author seeks to draw in 11.10 is tendentious. It is true that Egypt was irrigated (by foot-pumps), and that ancient technology could not irrigate the *mountains and valleys* of Palestine; but Egypt also enjoyed the annual miracle of the Nile's overflowing.

The Deuteronomic Code

The centre of the book (Chs 12-26) is given to the laws themselves. They are roughly ordered according to the sequence of the decalogue in Ex 20 (of which D himself had included a version in [5.6-21]), moving gradually from what we might call the religious, i.e. duty to God, to the social, i.e. duty to neighbour. That general movement gives shape to the collection and will be followed here.

Many of the regulations in D are also found in Exodus and some in Leviticus. The selection here is made chiefly from those not in either, so it cannot be regarded as comprehensive. The three codes taken together show a mixture of the severe and the humane which is typical of ANE legislation. In D's case the severe category

includes 13.8-11, 20.16f. and 21.21, the humane 22.1-4 and much of Ch. 15.

But it should not be assumed without further evidence that any specific law was implemented. An ANE code was partly a public relations exercise, with some of its laws unrealistic. The punishments correspond in some degree to treaty curses or even to threats before a battle. They may indeed betray only the despair of the legislator, cp. the phrase *all Israel when they hear of it* which rounds off 13.11 and 21.21. Conversely there is no external evidence from OT times for a sabbath year (Ch. 15), any more than for the jubilee year of Lev 25. In short, it is safer to read the Dt code as a manifesto than as enacted legislation.

Centralization of Worship

12. 1 These are the statutes and laws which you must be careful to observe in the land which the LORD the God of your forefathers is giving you to occupy all your earthly life.
• You are to demolish completely all the sanctuaries where the nations whom you are dispossessing worship their gods, whether on high mountains or on hills or under every spreading tree. • Pull down their altars, break their sacred pillars, burn their sacred poles, and hack down the idols of their gods, and thus blot out the name of them from the place. • You must not adopt such practices in the
5 worship of the LORD your God; • instead you are to resort to the place which the LORD your God will choose out of all your tribes to receive his name that it may dwell there. Come there • and bring your whole-offerings and sacrifices, your tithes and contributions, your vows and freewill-offerings, and the firstborn of your herds and flocks. • You are to eat there before the LORD your God; so you will find joy in whatever you undertake, you and your families, because the LORD your God has blessed you.

16. 1 • Observe the month of Abib and celebrate the Passover to the LORD your God, for it was in that month that the LORD your God brought you out of Egypt by night. • Slaughter an animal from flock or herd as a Passover victim to the LORD your God in the place which he will choose as a dwelling for his name.
5 • You may not slaughter the Passover victim in any of the settlements which the LORD your God is giving you, • but only in the place which he will choose as a dwelling for his name; there you are to slaughter the Passover victim in the evening as the sun goes down, the time of your coming out of Egypt. • Cook it and eat it in the place which the LORD your God will choose, and then next morning set off back to your tents.   (REB)

Centralization of Worship

Pride of place in the covenant as set out by D is given to the centralization of worship. To maintain the fiction of Moses as author, *the place* cannot be named. For the thinking behind this requirement see p.167.

Among the feasts which are now to be celebrated in Jerusalem is the *Passover*. We know from Luke 2.41 that the pilgrimage was taken seriously in NT times. Eventually it became impracticable, but the toast 'Next year in Jerusalem' remains as a memorial and an aspiration.

Punishment for Apostasy

6 If your brother, your father's son or your mother's son, or your son or daughter, your beloved wife, or your dearest friend should entice you secretly to go and serve other gods – gods of whom neither you nor your fathers have had experience, • gods of the people round about you, near or far, at one end of the land or the other – • then you must not consent or listen. Show none of them mercy, neither spare nor shield them; • you are to put them to death, your own hand being the

10 first to be raised against them, and then all the people are to follow. • Stone them to death, because they tried to lead you astray from the Lord your God who brought you out of Egypt, out of that land where you were slaves. • All Israel when they hear of it will be afraid; never again will anything as wicked as this be done among you.   (REB)

Punishment for Apostasy

This regulation belongs with all those which put loyalty to party before ties of family and friendship. In one respect it is less savage than the Hebrew mss suggest. In place of *you are to put them to death* (8), the LXX* has 'you must report him'. This accords much better with the situation envisaged, namely a public trial before the people, *after* which the sentence of death is to be implemented. It was the witnesses who were required [D 17.7] to 'cast the first stone' (cp. the NT story of the woman taken in adultery). They were followed by *all the people*, so that the blood-guilt rested on no identifiable individual.

The Sabbath Year: the Law of Release

15. 1 At the end of every seventh year you must make a remission of debts. • This is how it is to be made: everyone who holds a pledge shall return the pledge of the person indebted to him. He must not press a fellow-countryman for repayment, for the Lord's year of remission has been declared. • You may press foreigners; but if it is a fellow-countryman that holds anything of yours, you must renounce all

4-5 claim on it. • There will never be any poor among you if only you obey the Lord your God by carefully keeping these commandments which I lay upon you this day; for the Lord your God will bless you with great prosperity in the land which he is giving you to occupy as your holding. • When the Lord your God blesses you, as he promised, you will lend to people of many nations, but you yourselves will borrow from none; you will rule many nations, but none will rule you.   ♦

The Sabbath Year: the Law of Release

The sabbath year is included in all the Israelite law codes. D's version begins with a law, in which *fellow-countryman* includes resident aliens, but soon turns into a sermon. Of the two encouraging promises in 4-6, the former (4) represents

The Sabbath Year: the Law of Release (cont.)

15. 7 • When in any of your settlements in the land which the LORD your God is giving you one of your fellow-countrymen becomes poor, do not be hard-hearted or close-fisted towards him in his need. • Be open-handed towards him and lend him on pledge as much as he needs. • See that you do not harbour the villainous thought that the seventh year, the year of remission, is near, and look askance at your needy countryman and give him nothing. If you do, he will appeal to the 10 LORD against you, and you will be found guilty of sin. • Give freely to him and do not begrudge him your bounty, because it is for this very bounty that the LORD your God will bless you in everything that you do or undertake. • The poor will always be with you in your land, and that is why I command you to be open-handed towards any of your countrymen there who are in poverty and need.

• Should a fellow-Hebrew, be it a man or a woman, sell himself to you as a slave, he is to serve you for six years. In the seventh year you must set him free, • and when you set him free, do not let him go empty-handed. • Give to him lavishly from your flock, from your threshing-floor and your winepress. Be generous to him, as the LORD your God has blessed you. • Do not resent it when you have to set him free, for his six years' service to you has been worth twice the wage of a hired man. Then the LORD your God will bless you in everything 15 you do. • Bear in mind that you were slaves in Egypt and the LORD your God redeemed you; that is why I am giving you this command today. • If, however, a slave is content to be with you and says, 'I shall not leave you; I love you and your family,' • then take an awl and pierce through his ear to the door, and he will be your slave for life. Treat a slave-girl in the same way.   (REB)

The Sabbath Year: the Law of Release (cont.)

an unfulfilled ideal and is overtaken by v.11, the latter (6a) was fulfilled after many centuries. The concern for the *thought* in v.9 and for feelings throughout is typical of D. The loan in v.8 would have to be without interest (Ex 22.25). Verses 12-17 deal with the even more tragic situation of the debt-slave*. D's procedure for his release after six years should be compared with the earlier one in Ex 21.2-6. Women are now included (12, 17) alongside men in the regulations. Similarly the slave's family are no longer regarded as chattels and held back when he goes free. And the provision of vv.13-14 would be vital in helping him to find his feet again. The whole section admirably shows the humanitarianism of D.

Murder and Homicide

19.15 A single witness will not suffice to convict anyone of a crime or offence of any kind; whatever the misdemeanour, the evidence of two witnesses or three is required to sustain the charge.   ▸

Murder and Homicide

The law about witnesses referred originally only to capital crimes, but is here extended to other charges. It is often mentioned in the Bible.

The regulations for a case of unsolved murder are very ancient. It was provided in Hammurabi's code that in such a case the responsibility lay upon the nearest town to compensate the victim's family. Here that town wishes also to purge itself

Murder and Homicide (cont.)

.1   • If, in the country which the LORD your God gives you as your possession, a victim of murder is found lying in the open country and it is not known who has killed that person, • your elders must measure the distance between the victim and the surrounding towns, • and establish which town is the nearest to the victim. The elders of that town must then take a heifer that has not yet been put to work or used as a draught animal under the yoke. • The elders of that town must bring the heifer down to a permanently flowing river, to a spot that has been neither 5 | ploughed nor sown, and there by the river they must break the heifer's neck. • All the elders of the town nearest to the victim of murder must then wash their hands in the stream, over the slaughtered heifer. • They must pronounce these words, 'Our hands have not shed this blood and our eyes have seen nothing.'   (NJB)

Murder and Homicide (cont.)

of any blood *guilt*. So its elders perform a ritual which is somewhat similar to that of the scapegoat. It is not a sacrifice: no blood is shed, and the place of killing is not an altar but a desert. When the elders *wash their hands* over the dead body, they purge their community and divert any divine retribution.

Regulations for War

.0.1 When you take the field against your enemies and are faced by horses and chariots, a force greater than yours, you need have no fear of them.

5   • The officers are to say to the army: 'Any man who has built a new house and has not dedicated it should go back to his house; otherwise he may die in battle and another man dedicate it. • Any man who has planted a vineyard and has not begun to use it should go back home; otherwise he may die in battle and another man get the use of it. • Any man who has pledged himself to take a woman in marriage and has not taken her should go back home; otherwise he may die in battle and another man take her.' • The officers must also say to the army: 'Let anyone who is afraid and has lost heart go back home; or his faint-heartedness may affect his comrades.' • When the officers have finished addressing the army, commanders will assume command.   ▶

Regulations for War

Ch.20 on war is inserted into the middle of the section just dealt with, on civil killing. Like many other OT 'laws', it needs to be treated with great reserve, as representing aspiration rather than reality.

For the regulation of vv.5-9 various reasons are offered. Most plausible is that of v.8, that a man with such matters on his mind would make a half-hearted soldier. (That seems to be the interpretation which Jesus gave when he used it in his parable, Lk 14.18+.) Less convincing is the reason given three times in vv.5-7, introduced by *otherwise*. In the case of v.7 yet another reason is offered by Dt [24.5], that a newly-wed man must stay at home for a year 'to make his new wife happy' (NJB).

Regulations for War (cont.)

20.10   • When you advance on a town to attack it, make an offer of peace. • If the offer is accepted and the town opens its gates to you, then all the people who live there are to be put to forced labour and work for you. • If the town does not make peace with you but gives battle, you are to lay siege to it • and, when the LORD your God delivers it into your hands, put every male in it to the sword; • but you may take the women, the dependants, and the livestock for yourselves, and plunder everything else in the town. You may enjoy the use of the spoil from your enemies which the LORD your God gives you.

15   • That is how you are to deal with towns at a great distance, as opposed to those which belong to nations near at hand. • In the towns of these nations whose land the LORD your God is giving you as your holding, you must not leave a soul alive. • As the LORD your God commanded you, you must destroy them under solemn ban – Hittites, Amorites, Canaanites, Perizzites, Hivites, Jebusites – • so that they may not teach you to imitate the abominable practices they have carried on for their gods, and so cause you to sin against the LORD your God.

• When in the course of war you lay siege to a town for a long time in order to take it, do not destroy its trees by taking an axe to them, for they provide you with food; you must not cut them down. The trees of the field are not people,
20   that you should besiege them. • But you may destroy or cut down any trees that you know do not yield food, and use them in siege-works against the town that is at war with you, until it falls.   (REB)

Regulations for War (cont.)

The section on sieges is clearly hypothetical, if only because the Israelites hardly ever laid siege to a town, at any rate after Dt was published. In any case the policy described in vv.11-14 was regular ANE practice. But that of vv.15-18, the *ban*, does need comment. It is repugnant enough as an aspiration, but it also plays a crucial part in the story of Saul (1 Sam 15), where we are told that God rejected him precisely because he did *not* enforce the ban.

Fortunately we have further light on it from a source outside the OT. In c.830 BC Mesha king of Moab had a stele* inscribed to record various events of his reign. Much of it concerns long-running hostilities between Moab and Israel, which are also expressed as a contest between Chemosh the God of Moab and YHWH the God of Israel. Of one enemy city Mesha says: 'I took it and killed its whole population, seven thousand male citizens and female citizens and servant girls, for I had put it under the ban for Chemosh. And I took the vessels of YHWH, and I hauled them before the face of Chemosh' (Smelik).

That kind of claim, which was common also in Assyrian royal inscriptions, is generally regarded by scholars as boastful propaganda rather than history. In that respect it is like some of the oracles pronounced by OT prophets against foreign nations. The best that can be said for D is that here the slaughter sometimes (14 but not 16) stops short of the women and children, unlike the Mesha stele and the command of Samuel to Saul in 1 S 15.3.

Regulations for War (cont.)

9
12 • When you are encamped against an enemy, you must be careful to avoid any foulness. • You must have a sign outside the camp showing where you can withdraw to relieve yourself. • As part of your equipment you are to have a trowel, and when you squat outside, you are to scrape a hole with it and then turn and cover your excrement. • For the LORD your God moves with your camp, to keep you safe and to hand over your enemies as you advance, and your camp must be kept holy for fear that he should see something offensive and go with you no farther.   (REB)

Regulations for War (cont.)

After this, the preservation order on *trees that yield fruit* is a breath of fresh air. Finally the regulation from Ch. 23, on cleanliness in camp, is centuries ahead of its time. The scrupulous observance of it, 2,000 years later, gave the Muslim armies of the Ottoman Turks a crucial advantage over their European opponents.

Regulations Concerning Life in the Family and Community

.18 When a man has a son who is rebellious and out of control, who does not obey his father and mother, or take heed when they punish him, • then his father and mother are to lay hold of him and bring him out to the elders of the town at the town gate, • and say, 'This son of ours is rebellious and out of control; he will not obey us, he is a wastrel and a drunkard.' • Then all the men of the town must stone him to death, and you will thereby rid yourselves of this wickedness. All Israel when they hear of it will be afraid.

1.

2. 1 • Should you see a fellow-countryman's ox or sheep straying, do not ignore it; you must take it back to him. • If the owner is not a near neighbour and you do not know who he is, bring the animal to your own house and keep it with you until he claims it; then give it back to him. • Do the same with his donkey or his cloak or anything else that your fellow-countryman loses. You may not ignore it. • Should you see your fellow-countryman's donkey or ox lying on the road, do
5 not ignore it; you must help him to raise it to its feet. • No woman may wear an article of man's clothing, nor may a man put on woman's dress; for those who do these things are abominable to the LORD your God. • When you come upon a bird's nest by the road, in a tree or on the ground, with fledgelings or eggs in it and the mother bird on the nest, do not take both mother and young. • Let the mother bird go free, and take only the young; then you will prosper and enjoy long life. • When you build a new house, put a parapet along the roof, or you will bring the guilt of bloodshed on your house if anyone should fall from it.   ▸

2.

Regulations Concerning Life in the Family and Community

The comments below refer to the numbers in the right-hand margin of the text.

1. The offence is serious, being a breach of the fifth commandment, and so involving the whole community. The severity of the penalty laid down may be for show: the aberrations of the young have always inspired a special anxiety in the old.

2. Transvestism (5) was a feature of the worship of Ishtar, the ANE goddess of sexual love. The word *abominable* shows that a cultic offence is being referred to. The protection of the *mother bird* (7) is prudential (cp. *prosper*) not humanitarian. The flat roofs of houses were much used, and to omit a *parapet* would be negligence on the part of the builder.

Regulations Concerning Life in the Family and Community (cont.)

23.15 • You must not surrender to his master a slave who has taken refuge with you. | 3.
• Let him stay with you anywhere he chooses in any one of your settlements, wherever suits him best; you must not force him.

24 • When you go into another man's vineyard, you may eat as many grapes | 4.
as you wish to satisfy your hunger, but you may not put any into your basket.
• When you go into another man's standing grain, you may pluck ears to rub in your hands, but you may not put a sickle to the standing crop.

24. 6 • No one may take millstones, or even the upper millstone alone, in pledge; | 5.
that would be taking a life in pledge.

10 • When you make any loan to anyone, do not enter his house to take a pledge | 6.
from him. • Wait outside, and the person whose creditor you are must bring the pledge out to you.

16 • Parents are not to be put to death for their children, nor children for their | 7.
parents; each one may be put to death only for his own sin.

25. 5 • When brothers live together and one of them dies without leaving a son, his | 8.
widow is not to marry outside the family. Her husband's brother is to have intercourse with her; he should take her in marriage and do his duty by her as her husband's brother. • The first son she bears will perpetuate the dead brother's name so that it may not be blotted out from Israel. • But if the man is unwilling to take his brother's wife, she must go to the elders at the town gate and say, 'My husband's brother refuses to perpetuate his brother's name in Israel; he will not do his duty by me.' • At this the elders of the town should summon him and reason with him. If he still stands his ground and says, 'I refuse to take her,' • his brother's widow must go up to him in the presence of the elders, pull his sandal off his foot, spit in his face, and declare: 'Thus we requite the man who will not build up his brother's family.'

10 • His family will be known in Israel as the house of the unsandalled man.

• When two men are fighting and the wife of one of them intervenes to drag her | 9.
husband clear of his opponent, if she puts out her hand and catches hold of the man by the genitals, • you must cut off her hand and show her no mercy.   (REB)

Regulations Concerning Life in the Family and Community (cont.)

3. The reference is to *a slave* from abroad. ANE treaties regularly provided for extradition of runaway slaves, but D rejects the practice.

4. This regulation, found only here, doubtless codifies a long-established custom.

5. This law is in unconditional form, and certainly old, though found only here. Women normally ground and baked daily.

6. Other ANE codes forbid entering a man's home for any reason whatsoever.

7. This is not so much a law as a general principle.

8. The custom described here is an ancient one, found also in Assyrian and Hittite legislation. Its objective is to *perpetuate the dead brother's name*, since it was only in his descendants that a man lived after death. If the brother-in-law refuses, he is brought into public humiliation by the *widow*. These customs form the background to the book of Ruth; see also Glossary s.v. Redeemer.

9. This is the only biblical instance of a procedure still common in Islamic law, punishment by mutilation. It is here applied because the woman's action might have damaged the man's prospects of paternity.

The Covenant Summarized

16 This day the LORD your God commands you to keep these statutes and laws: be careful to observe them with all your heart and soul. • You have recognized the LORD this day as your God; you are to conform to his ways, to keep his statutes, his commandments, and his laws, and to obey him. • The LORD has recognized you this day as his special possession, as he promised you, and you are to keep all his commandments; • high above all the nations which he has made he will raise you, to bring him praise and fame and glory, and to be a people holy to the LORD your God, according to his promise.   (REB)

The Covenant Summarized

Having transmitted to the people the laws themselves (Chs 12-26), Moses speaks for them in ratifying the covenant. He has been only the mediator: the high contracting parties are YHWH and Israel. Israel has *recognized* him as their God, and must keep these laws (17); he has *recognized* Israel as his *special possession* or *holy people*, and will fulfil his promises (18-19). Israel's obligations are absolute, YHWH's are conditional.

The Blessings and Curses

3. 1 If you faithfully obey the LORD your God by diligently observing all his commandments which I lay on you this day, then the LORD your God will raise you high above all nations of the earth, • and the following blessings will all come and light on you, because you obey the LORD your God. • A blessing on you in the town; a blessing on you in the country. • A blessing on the fruit of your body, the 5 fruit of your land and cattle, the offspring of your herds and lambing flocks. • A blessing on your basket and your kneading trough. • A blessing on you as you come in, and a blessing on you as you go out.

15   • But if you will not obey the LORD your God by diligently observing all his commandments and statutes which I lay upon you this day, then all the following curses will come and light upon you. • A curse on you in the town, a curse in the country. • A curse on your basket and your kneading trough. • A curse on the fruit of your body, the fruit of your land, the offspring of your herds and your lambing flocks. • A curse on you as you come in, and a curse on you as you go out.   (REB)

The Blessings and Curses

Blessings and curses were regularly added at the end of ANE laws and treaties. Those given here are the kernel on either side, later amplified. *Come in* (6) and *go out* (19) together by merismus* constitute all one's actions. Verses 2 and 15 show that the blessings and curses were personified.

Later Amplification of the Blessings and the Curses

28.27 May the LORD strike you with Egyptian boils and with tumours, scabs, and itch, for which you will find no cure. • May the LORD strike you with madness, blindness, and stupefaction; • so that you will grope about in broad daylight, just as a blind man gropes in darkness, and you will fail to find your way. You will be oppressed and robbed, day in, day out, with no one to save you. • A woman will be betrothed to you, but someone will ravish her; you will build a house but not live in it; you will plant a vineyard but not enjoy its fruit.

38   • You will carry plentiful seed to your fields, but you will harvest little, for locusts will devour it. • You will plant vineyards and cultivate them, but you will not drink the wine or gather the grapes, for the grub will eat them. • You will have olive trees everywhere in your territory, but you will not anoint yourselves with the oil, for your olives will drop off. • You will have sons and daughters, but they will not remain yours, for they will go into captivity. • All your trees and the fruit of the ground will be infested with the mole-cricket.

49   • May the LORD bring against you from afar, from the end of the earth, a nation which will swoop upon you like a vulture, a nation whose language you will not understand, • a nation of grim aspect with no regard for the old, no pity for the young. • Then, because of the dire straits to which you will be reduced when your enemy besieges you, you will eat your own children, the flesh of your sons and daughters whom the LORD your God has given you. • The most delicately bred and sensitive man will not share with his brother, or with the wife he 55 loves, or with his own remaining children • any of the meat which he is eating, the flesh of his own children. He is left with nothing else because of the dire straits to which you will be reduced within all your towns when the enemy besieges you. • The most delicately bred and sensitive woman, so delicate and sensitive that she would never venture to put a foot to the ground, will not share with her own husband or her son or her daughter • the afterbirth which she expels, or any boy or girl that she may bear. During the siege she herself will eat them secretly in her extreme want, in the dire straits to which the enemy will reduce you in your towns.   ▸

Later Amplification of the Blessings and the Curses

Later writers belonging to the same tradition could not forbear to amplify those relatively simple blessings and curses. Their additions fall into three sections.

The first section (further extracts from Ch. 28) carries on the catalogue of punishments for disloyalty until their climax in the fall of Jerusalem and the exile. It begins with set of curses (27-30) which is very close to those in an ANE treaty between Esarhaddon of Assyria 680-669 BC and his vassals, who then included Manasseh King of Judah. The treaty was found in 1955. The curses take up 250 of the 700 lines of the treaty, including the following:

> May Anu, king of the gods, rain upon all your houses exhaustion, sleeplessness, worries, ill health.
> May Shamash, the light of Heaven and earth, not give you a fair and equitable judgement, may he take away your eyesight.
> May Venus, the brightest among the stars, let your wives lie in the embrace of your enemy before your very eyes.
> (ANET 538)

Maybe the author of vv.27-30 had seen the text of this treaty, set up in Jerusalem.

Further curses include failures of crops, in the regular Ugaritic and Hebrew sequence: corn, wine and oil (38-41). Next come invaders (49-50), painted in

Later Amplification of the Blessings and the Curses (cont.)

4 • The LORD will disperse you among all peoples from one end of the earth to the other, and there you will serve other gods of whom neither you nor your forefathers have had experience, gods of wood and stone. • Among those nations you will find no peace, no resting-place for the sole of your foot. Then the LORD will give you an unquiet mind, dim eyes, and failing appetite. • Your life will hang continually in suspense, fear will beset you night and day, and you will find no security all your life long. • Every morning you will say, 'Would God it were evening!' and every evening, 'Would God it were morning!' because of the terror that fills your heart and because of the sights you see. • The LORD will bring you back sorrowing to Egypt by that very road of which I said to you, 'You shall not see that road again'; there you will offer yourselves for sale as slaves to your enemies, but there will be no buyer.

1 • When all these things have happened to you, the blessing and the curse of which I have offered you the choice, if you take them to heart there among all the nations to which the LORD your God has banished you, • if you and your children turn back to him and obey him heart and soul in all that I command you this day, • then the LORD your God will restore your fortunes. In compassion for you he will gather you again from all the peoples to which he has dispersed you. • Even though he has banished you to the ends of the earth, the LORD your God will

5 gather you from there, and from there he will fetch you home. • The LORD your God will bring you into the land which your forefathers occupied, and you will occupy it again; then he will bring you prosperity and make you more numerous than your forefathers were.

11 • This commandment that I lay on you today is not too difficult for you or beyond your reach. • It is not in the heavens, that you should say, 'Who will go up to the heavens for us to fetch it and tell it to us, so that we can keep it?' • Nor is it beyond the sea, that you should say, 'Who will cross the sea for us to ▶

Later Amplification of the Blessings and the Curses (cont.)

traditional colours, i.e. coming *from afar* and speaking an unintelligible *language*. Their siege (53-7) will bring horrors which, sick as they seem to us, were part of the regular ANE rhetoric of curses – and may well be realistic. After that will come dispersion abroad (64-7), the condition in which most Jews have lived for most of their history. Here the emphasis is on the *unquiet mind*, the daily terror all too familiar in Hitler's Germany. Finally the 'salvation history' of the Hebrews – exodus and wanderings – will be put into reverse, with an ironical anticlimax in v.68. All this leaves Ch.28 very heavily weighed down on the side of curses against blessings, but that too was part of the ANE tradition in such matters.

The second section (30.1-5) introduces a welcome change of tone. Its author, writing in exile, wishes to convey a message of hope. He does so by presenting the blessings and the curses not as alternative but as successive. If, after the disobediences and the punishments, Israel will *turn back to him*, God will implement the blessings.

The third section (30.11-20) betrays strong Wisdom influence. The idea of the Two Ways, one leading to evil and the other to good, was common in the ancient world. The general view was that the way to the good was, for one reason or another, *difficult* or remote. That view had been formulated as follows in a notable work, the *Babylonian Theodicy* (see p.408):

Later Amplification of the Blessings and the Curses (cont.)

30.14 fetch it and tell it to us, so that we can keep it?' • It is a thing very near to you, on your lips and in your heart ready to be kept.

15 • Today I offer you the choice of life and good, or death and evil. • If you obey the commandments of the LORD your God which I give you this day, by loving the LORD your God, conforming to his ways, and keeping his commandments, statutes, and laws, then you will live and increase, and the LORD your God will bless you in the land which you are about to enter to occupy. • But if in your heart you turn away and do not listen, and you are led astray to worship other gods and serve them, • I tell you here and now that you will perish, and not enjoy long life in the land which you will enter to occupy after crossing the Jordan. • I summon heaven and earth to witness against you this day: I offer you the choice of life or death, blessing or curse. Choose life and you and your descendants will live;

20 • love the LORD your God, obey him, and hold fast to him: that is life for you and length of days on the soil which the LORD swore to give to your forefathers, Abraham, Isaac, and Jacob. (REB)

Later Amplification of the Blessings and the Curses (cont.)

The divine mind, like the centre of the
    heavens, is remote.
Knowledge of it is difficult; the masses do
    not know it. (Lambert)

D here rejects that formulation, perhaps with democratic intent. In v.14 he echoes Jeremiah's famous words (31.33), that God will write his law *in their heart*. He can thus conclude his whole law with a powerful appeal. Reverting to the treaty form whereby the curses and the blessings are not successive but alternative, he proposes a stark and once-for-all choice, while at the same time implying that God's way is not only accessible but attractive. This little sermon is still in effective use.

Moses' Last Dispositions

31. 1 Moses, finishing this address to all Israel, • went on to say: At a hundred and twenty years old, I am no longer able to lead the campaign; and the LORD has told me that I shall not cross the Jordan.

7 • Moses summoned Joshua and in the sight of all Israel said to him: Be strong and resolute, for it is you who will lead this people into the land which the LORD swore to give their forefathers; you are to bring them into possession of it. • The LORD himself goes at your head; he will be with you; he will not let you down or forsake you. Do not be afraid or discouraged.

• Moses wrote down this law and gave it to the priests, the sons of Levi, who carried the Ark of the Covenant of the LORD, and to all the elders of Israel.

10 • Moses gave them this command: At the end of every seven years, at the appointed time for the year of remission, at the pilgrim-feast of Booths, • when all Israel comes to appear before the LORD your God in the place which he will choose, ▸

Moses' Last Dispositions

Moses has lived through three generations (3 x 40 = 120), and his own death approaches. It has long been known that *Joshua* will lead the Israelites across the Jordan; he must now be commissioned (7-8). Then Moses makes provision for the recording, safe-keeping and regular public recital of the covenant. All these

Moses' Last Dispositions (cont.)

12 this law is to be read in the hearing of all Israel. • Assemble the people, men, women, and dependants, together with the aliens residing in your settlements, so that they may listen, and learn to fear the LORD your God and observe all these laws with care. • Their children, too, who do not know the laws, will hear them, and learn to fear the LORD your God all their lives in the land which you will occupy after crossing the Jordan.   (REB)

Moses' Last Dispositions (cont.)

were standard requirements in ANE trea-   temple: in this case, the nearest equivalent
ties. The records were usually kept in a   is the *Ark of the Covenant*.

The Song of Moses

2. 8 When the Most High gave each nation its heritage,
        when he divided all mankind,
he laid down the boundaries for peoples
        according to the number of the sons of God;
9 but the LORD's share was his own people,
        Jacob was his allotted portion.

10 He found his people in a desert land,
        in a barren, howling waste.
He protected and trained them,
        he guarded them as the apple of his eye.
11 As an eagle watches over its nest,
        hovers above its young,
spreads its pinions and takes them up,
        and bears them on its wings,   ◆

The Song of Moses

The song of Moses is accorded the rare distinction in the MT* of being set out on the page line by line according to its 3+3 rhythm. But it is a late composition (c.550 BC) and for the most part derivative. It is not referred to in the body of Deuteronomy, but its theology certainly fits that of the book as a whole. This section of the song follows the same general argument as 8.1-18, but it has an originality of thought in vv.8-11, together with a tautness of expression, at least down to v.14, which mark it out from a typical deuteronomic sermon.

The idea in vv.8-9 is a clever way of reconciling Israel's unique relation to YHWH with that of the gentiles to their gods. In the beginning each of the nations was given one of the *sons of God* as a guardian angel, to whom therefore it was quite proper for them to pay honour; but YHWH claimed Israel for himself. The notion of the 'sons of God' is fairly common in the OT (esp. Ps 82.6), but it was too much here for the scribe of the medieval Hebrew text, who changed it to 'sons of Israel'. Fortunately the Greek text preserves the true reading, which has now been confirmed by one of the Dead Sea Scrolls.

The idea of vv.10-11 comes from Hosea, for whom (e.g. in 2.15) the *desert* wanderings were a kind of honeymoon period in the relations between YHWH and Israel. The *apple of the eye* is the pupil (Heb. 'little man'). *Eagles* do indeed show an especial care for their immature offspring in the various ways noted in this unusually extended simile.

The Song of Moses (cont.)

32.12   the LORD alone led his people,
        no alien god at his side.

13   He made them ride over the heights of the earth
        and fed them on the harvest of the fields;
    he satisfied them with honey from the crags
        and oil from the flinty rock,

14   curds from the cattle, milk from the herd,
        the fat of lambs' kidneys,
    of Bashan rams, and of goats,
        with the finest flour of wheat;
    and you, his people, drank red wine from the juice of the grape.

15   Jacob ate and was well fed,
        they grew fat and bloated and sleek.
    They forsook God their Maker
        and dishonoured the Rock of their salvation.

16   They roused his jealousy with alien gods
        and provoked him to anger with abominable practices.

18   You forsook the Creator who begot you
        and ceased to care for God who brought you to birth.   (REB)

The Song of Moses (cont.)

The next section (13-15) deals with the entry into the promised land. Israel was then 'riding high', provided with all the good things of the earth – even among the rocky outcrops olives grew and wild *honey* was to be found. But in prosperity they *grew bloated* and forgot YHWH who had (18) been to them both father and mother – the latter a rare idea in the OT (see comment on Is 66.13).

The Death of Moses

34. 1 Moses went up from the lowlands of Moab to Mount Nebo, to the top of Pisgah eastwards from Jericho, and the LORD showed him the whole land, from Gilead to Dan; • the whole of Naphtali; the territory of Ephraim and Manasseh, and all Judah as far as the western sea; • the Negeb and the plain; the valley of Jericho, city of palm trees, as far as Zoar. • The LORD said to him, 'This is the land which I swore to Abraham, Isaac, and Jacob that I would give to their descendants. I have let you see it with your own eyes, but you will not cross over into it.'

5   • There in the Moabite country Moses the servant of the LORD died, as the LORD had said. • He was buried in a valley in Moab opposite Beth-peor; but to this day no one knows his burial-place. • Moses was a hundred and twenty years old when he died, his sight undimmed, his vigour unimpaired. • The Israelites wept for Moses in the lowlands of Moab for thirty days.   ▼

The Death of Moses

The narrative is now resumed. From *Pisgah*, a peak in the *Nebo* hills, Moses saw far into the promised land, though it can only have been with the mind's eye that he saw north to Galilee, west to the Mediterranean (2) and south to the *Negeb*. The negative impression of v.4 is picked up by the notice about his burial-place in v.6, and is not eradicated by the unreserved praise of v.10. Moses remains

---

The Death of Moses (cont.)

10   • There has never yet risen in Israel a prophet like Moses, whom the LORD knew face to face: • remember all the signs and portents which the LORD sent him to show in Egypt to Pharaoh and all his servants and the whole land; • remember the strong hand of Moses and the awesome deeds which he did in the sight of all Israel. (REB)

The Death of Moses (cont.)

a great but shadowy figure, whose achievements and personality are elusive.

In assessing him we are thrown back entirely on the Pentateuch. There is no historical reference to him outside the OT, and surprisingly little mention of him within it, outside the Pentateuch. But if there is a historical kernel to the story of the exodus (see p.30f.), the Israelites must have had a leader.

And at first sight that leader's career is straightforward. As a young man he was diffident and clumsy, both in action (Ex 2.12-14) and in speech (4.10). Having matured, however, he became the architect of (i) the successful escape of the Israelites from their forced labour in Egypt and their somewhat less successful journey from there to the east bank of the Jordan, and (ii) their new-found cohesion in a loyalty to YHWH which had far-reaching implications for their social as well as their religious life.

But the Pentateuch supplies all too little by way of circumstantial detail. We see Moses negotiating with Pharaoh, but in a context which is so heightened by legend as to be unrealistic. At the 'Reed Sea' one cannot ascribe any specific move to him. At the important moment of the reconnaissance west of the Dead Sea, the various stories are too confused for us to disentangle his part. It is only when we find him worn out (Ex 18.18) or over-burdened (Num 11.11) by his responsibilities as leader that we begin to sense a three-dimensional figure.

The same goes for his religious experiences. Intimate moments like those of the theophanies on Mount Sinai are by definition not open to historical verification. But it is possible with editorial help to say something of Moses'

relationship with God – certainly with the God of the J tradition. Here we find God speaking to Aaron and Miriam in the highest possible terms of Moses (Num 12.6-8, a passage which lies behind the encomium of Dt 34.10). But privately, as one might say, relations between them were much less smooth. Even if we leave out of account the astonishing story of YHWH's attempt on Moses' life in Ex 4, there are still many tensions between them. What is interesting is that, whether it is Moses who is short-tempered with God (Num 11.11-13) or vice versa (Dt 3.26), the source of the friction is always Moses' 'prophetic' position as inter-mediary between God and the people. Time and again Moses intercedes on behalf of the people, often risking God's wrath in doing so (e.g. Ex 32.11). The most remarkable scene of all is that in which he rejects privileges offered him over against the people, and instead offers himself to be punished in their place (Ex 32.32).

It is in this sense that he is described editorially as 'the most humble man on earth' (Num 12.3). That is Moses' greatness – but also his tragedy, for in the last resort it was because of his identification with the people ('because of you', Dt 3.26) that he was denied the fulfilment of his career viz. entry to the promised land.

Moses is thus the leader caught between his superior and his subordinates, tenant of a symbolic wilderness between Egypt, where he was 'an alien in a foreign land', and the promised land which he never entered, starting life without a name and leaving it without a grave. Heroic as his achievements were, what remains in the mind is the tragedy of the lonely leader and the marginal man.

INTRODUCTION TO THE BOOKS JOSHUA–2 KINGS

Joshua is the first of a group of books known in the Hebrew Bible as 'former prophets'. These books carry on the national story down to the end of the monarchy and the start of the exile in Babylon. They have all been edited by the same hand, and are marked by a common style and theological colour. That colour is prophetic in a special sense.

The editor is known to scholars as 'the deuteronomic historian', DtH for short. He is deuteronomic, first, in his theology, which is dominated by the idea of the covenant. Essentially, kings and people prosper or fail in accordance with their loyalty or disloyalty to the covenant of D 12-26. Their past ups and downs can be seen as the fulfilment of the blessings and curses attached to it in D 27-8. And the analysis can be extrapolated, like that of Marx. Writing in the C 6th BC, the DtH wishes his warning to be taken to heart for the future. The lesson of the exile must be learned if there is to be a hope of a successful return. That is the sense in which his work is prophetic.

It is therefore surprising to find so little overlap between his work and that of the great 'writing prophets' of the C 8th – Isaiah, Amos and Hosea. True, the doctrine of the covenant can be traced back to Hosea, and Hosea and Isaiah disapprove, no less strongly than the DtH, of the worship of alien gods. But the DtH makes that almost his sole criterion. Only rarely does he cite the other great theme of the writing prophets, social injustice, even though it was prominent in the law as set out by D. The theology of the DtH is clear but narrow.

As a historian the DtH has one great merit: he preserves a considerable number of older records which are superior to his own work either as history or as literature or both. The finest poem in the OT, the Song of Deborah, he left untouched; the finest piece of sustained prose, the Court History of David, he touched, but in ways which are visible and therefore detachable.

In the DtH's presentation of events, the smaller ups and downs are overshadowed by one large one: the rise to a peak under David and the decline thereafter. The shape of his work is therefore not linear like the Pentateuch but pedimental* like so much of Hebrew prose and poetry. Very roughly, the themes of the six books can be summarised as follows:

Joshua: the acquisition of the land

Judges: disorder, with order gradually emerging

1 Samuel: Saul and the rise of the monarchy

2 Samuel: David and the height of the monarchy

1 Kings: Solomon and the decline of the monarchy

2 Kings: increasing disorder and the loss of the land.

The DtH then is the man who (i) collected and ordered the material, (ii) inserted pro-grammatic introductions and summaries between certain blocks of it and (iii) added short passages here and there within stories. His own contributions may read nowadays like adventitious moralising, but within the OT as a whole they are the cement that binds it together. They are recognisable not only by the theology but also by the style, which is like that of D (see Introd. to D) but without the warmth or other distinction.

JOSHUA

Programmatic Overture to the 'Conquest'

. 1 After the death of Moses the LORD's servant, the LORD said to Joshua son of Nun, Moses' assistant, • 'Now that my servant Moses is dead, get ready to cross the Jordan, you and all this people, to the land which I am giving to the Israelites. • Every place where you set foot is yours: I have given it to you, as I promised Moses. • From the desert and this Lebanon to the great river, the Euphrates, and across all the country westwards to the Great Sea, all of it is to be your territory. 5 • As long as you live no one will be able to stand against you: as I was with Moses, so shall I be with you; I shall not fail you or forsake you. • Be strong, be resolute; it is you who are to put this people in possession of the land which I swore to their forefathers I would give them. • Only be very strong and resolute. Observe diligently all the law which my servant Moses has given you; if you would succeed wherever you go, you must not swerve from it either to right or to left. • This book of the law must never be off your lips; you must keep it in mind day and night so that you may diligently observe everything that is written in it. Then you will prosper and be successful in everything you do. • This is my command: be strong, be resolute; do not be fearful or discouraged, for wherever you go the LORD your God is with you.'

10, 11 • Then Joshua instructed the officers • to pass through the camp and give this order to the people: 'Get food ready to take with you, for within three days you will be crossing this Jordan to occupy the country which the LORD your God is giving you to possess.'   (REB)

Programmatic Overture to the 'Conquest'

The book of Joshua, the first in this next group of books, cannot be treated as history, for the reasons set out on p.30+. It does however preserve some famous stories.

In Ch.1 the DtH shows Joshua as the successor to Moses and 'his' book as following Deuteronomy. The content and style are typical. Repetition emphasises the main points. We are assured eight times that God has given the land to the Israelites. The frontiers given are idealised: Israel never, even at the greatest extent claimed for David, reached so far. The four times repeated phrase *be strong and resolute* emphasises the high morale of those whom God supports, as against the frequent panic of their enemies.

Rahab and the Reconnaissance

2.1 Joshua son of Nun sent out two spies secretly from Shittim with orders to reconnoitre the land and especially Jericho. The two men set off and came to the house of a prostitute named Rahab to spend the night there. • When it was reported to the king of Jericho that some Israelites had arrived that night to explore the country, • he sent word to Rahab: 'Bring out the men who have come to you and are now in your house, for they have come to spy out the whole country.'   ▶

Rahab and the Reconnaissance

This famous story opens with some plausible circumstantial detail. *Shittim*, meaning 'Acacias', was a town on the east bank of Jordan opposite Jericho. *To reconnoitre* enemy territory was normal – Joshua himself had originally been sent in by Moses

Rahab and the Reconnaissance (cont.)

2. 5 • The woman, who had taken the two men and hidden them, replied, 'True, the men did come to me, but I did not know where they came from; • and at nightfall when it was time to shut the gate, they had gone. I do not know where they were going, but if you hurry after them you may overtake them.' • In fact, she had brought them up on to the roof and concealed them among the stalks of flax which she had laid out there in rows. • The messengers went in pursuit of them in the direction of the fords of the Jordan, and as soon as they had gone out the gate was closed.

9   • The men had not yet settled down, when Rahab came up to them on the
12   roof, • and said, 'I know that the LORD has given the land to you; terror of you has fallen upon us, and the whole country is panic-stricken. • Swear to me by the LORD that you will keep faith with my family, as I have kept faith with you. Give me a token of good faith; • promise that you will spare the lives of my father and mother, my brothers and sisters, and all who belong to them, and preserve us from death.' • The men replied, 'Our lives for yours, so long as you do not betray our business. When the LORD gives us the country, we shall deal loyally and faithfully by you.'

15   • She then let them down through a window by a rope; for the house where she lived was on an angle of the wall. • 'Make for the hills,' she said, 'or the pursuers will come upon you. Hide there for three days until they return; then go on your way.' • The men warned her that, unless she did what they told her, they would be free from the oath she had made them take. • 'When we invade the land,' they said, 'you must fasten this strand of scarlet cord in the window through which you have lowered us, and get everybody together here inside the house, your father and mother, your brothers, and all your family. • Should anybody go out of doors into the street, his blood will be on his own head; we shall be free of the oath. But if a hand is laid on anyone who stays indoors with you, his blood be on our heads! • Remember too that, if you betray our business, then
20   we shall be free of the oath you have made us take.' • 'It shall be as you say,' she replied, and sent them on their way. When they had gone, she fastened the strand of scarlet cord in the window.

• The men made their way into the hills and stayed there for three days until the pursuers returned. They had searched all along the road, but had not found them. • The two men then came down from the hills and crossed the river. When they joined up with Joshua son of Nun, they reported all that had happened to them.   (REB)

Rahab and the Reconnaissance (cont.)

as a spy (Num 13). A brothel is a good place for a foreigner to pick up information without attracting attention. *Flax* drying on a flat *roof* makes a good hiding place.

But there is a snag. The town of *Jericho,* having been destroyed in the C16th BC, was now unwalled and almost uninhabited, and remained so until it was rebuilt in the C9th. So the account of the reconnaissance and, more particularly, of *Rahab* and the *scarlet cord*, must have originated in some other context and been used here as too good to lose. Its theme is the favourite one of the quick-thinking woman who outsmarts all the men and so preserves her lineage.

The Crossing of the Jordan

Early in the morning Joshua and all the Israelites set out from Shittim and came to the Jordan, where they encamped before crossing. • At the end of three days the officers passed through the camp, • giving the people these instructions: 'When you see the Ark of the Covenant of the LORD your God being carried forward by the levitical priests, then you too must leave your positions and set out. Keep some distance behind, about two thousand cubits. It will show you the route you are to follow, for you have not travelled this way before.' • Joshua said to the people, 'Consecrate yourselves, for tomorrow the LORD will perform a great miracle among you.'

• Joshua said to the Israelites, 'Draw near and listen to the words of the LORD your God. • As soon as the priests carrying the Ark of the LORD, the LORD of all the earth, set foot in the waters of the Jordan, then the waters of the Jordan will be cut off; the water coming down from upstream will stand piled up like a bank.'

• The people set out from their encampment to cross the Jordan, with the priests in front carrying the Ark of the Covenant. • Now the Jordan is in full flood in all its reaches throughout the time of harvest, but as soon as the priests reached the Jordan and their feet touched the water at the edge, • the water flowing down from upstream was brought to a standstill; it piled up like a bank for a long way back, as far as Adam, a town near Zarethan. The water coming down to the sea of the Arabah, the Dead Sea, was completely cut off, and the people crossed over opposite Jericho.

The Crossing of the Jordan

The story of the miracle at the Jordan was designed as a close parallel to the miracle at the Reed Sea in Ex 13-14. Between them they frame the narrative of the wanderings, and mark the two momentous rites of passage. The parallel is made explicit in 4.23, as it is in Ps 114.3: 'The Sea saw that and fled; Jordan was driven back.'

There is however one big difference between the two stories. Nowhere at the Jordan is there any opposition: no enemy is in sight, none even expected. What we have in Jos 3-5 is ritual drama presented as history. The story is told by a priestly writer at great length (here drastically cut), and the liturgical nature of the proceedings is made clear at every turn. The central role is allotted to the *Ark of the Covenant*, carried by *priests*. The people *consecrate* them*selves* and follow behind (3.3-5). At the end the *Passover* is celebrated on the proper *day of the month* (5.10).

Ch.4 adds further liturgical information

The word *Gilgal* probably means stone circle (REB's footnote offers 'Rolling Stones'), and the sanctuary was an old one. Its cult legend linked the stones with the Jordan two miles away, and the number *twelve* suggested *one for each of the tribes*. Inside the circle at Gilgal a festival of the crossing was probably celebrated each year. We cannot recover all its details, but there was a procession, with priests carrying an object to represent the Ark, and a recital of the sacred story. (Such a ritual is echoed also in 2 Sam 15.23f.).

Now to the miracle. The Jordan, which at this point is flowing 350 metres below sea level, is quite easily fordable for most of the year. But in the spring, at the time of the Passover, when the snows on Mount Hermon are melting, it regularly becomes a flood. The very volume of the waters undermines the overhanging banks, which from time to time collapse, especially when (as fairly often) there is an earthquake. At a place called

The Crossing of the Jordan (cont.)

4. 1 • When the whole nation had completed the crossing of the Jordan, the LORD said to Joshua, • 'Choose twelve men from the people, one from each tribe, • and order them to take up twelve stones from this place in the middle of the Jordan, where the priests have taken their stand. They are to carry the stones across and place them in the camp where you spend the night.'

19 • On the tenth day of the first month the people went up from the Jordan and encamped in Gilgal in the district east of Jericho, • and there Joshua set up these twelve stones they had taken from the Jordan. • He said to the Israelites, 'In days to come, when your descendants ask their fathers what these stones mean, • you are to explain to them that Israel crossed this Jordan on dry land, • for the LORD your God dried up the waters of the Jordan in front of you until you had gone across, just as the LORD your God did at the Red Sea when he dried it up for us until we had crossed.'

5. 10 • While the Israelites were encamped in Gilgal, at sunset on the fourteenth day of the month they kept the Passover in the lowlands of Jericho.   (REB)

The Crossing of the Jordan (cont.)

Adam, some 15 miles north of Jericho, the river runs deep down between two walls of very soft limestone. There, in December 1267 and again in July 1927, the cliffs gave way, damming the stream and holding back the river for sixteen and twenty-one hours respectively. Admittedly that was not in flood time, but the mention of *Adam* in 3.16 suggests that some such memory lay behind the story of the miraculous crossing.

The Fall of Jericho

6. 1 Jericho was bolted and barred [against the Israelites]; no one could go out or in. • The LORD said to Joshua, 'See, I am delivering Jericho, its king, and his warriors into your hands. • You are to march round the city with all your fighting men [making the circuit of it once a day for six days. •Seven priests carrying seven trumpets made from rams' horns are to go ahead of the Ark. On the seventh day you are to march round the city seven times with the priests blowing their trumpets.] • At the blast of the rams' horns, [when you hear the trumpet sound] the whole army must raise a great shout; the city wall will collapse and the army will advance, every man straight ahead.'

• Joshua son of Nun summoned the priests and gave them instructions: 'Take up the Ark of the Covenant; let seven priests with seven trumpets of ram's horn go ahead of the Ark of the LORD. • Move on, march round the city, and let the men who have been drafted go in front of the Ark of the LORD.'   ▶

The Fall of Jericho

Since the site of Jericho was virtually unoccupied at the supposed time, the account of its 'fall' cannot be historical. Yet it is possible to see how its most famous feature arose. Walls of unbaked brick do indeed, when not repaired, gradually crumble, and that is how they were found when excavated in the C20th AD.

What the account in Ch.6 offers us, therefore, is the same as that in Chs 3-5 of crossing the Jordan: ritual drama dressed up as history. Common to both accounts is the procession of the *priests* with *the Ark of the Covenant*. Ch.6 however has also a military colouring, for on this occasion Joshua does have a putative enemy.

The Fall of Jericho (cont.)

• [After Joshua had issued this command to the army,] the seven priests carrying the seven trumpets of ram's horn before the LORD moved on and blew the trumpets; the Ark of the Covenant of the LORD followed them. • The drafted men marched in front of the priests who blew the trumpets, and the rearguard came behind the Ark, the trumpets sounding as they marched. • But Joshua commanded the army not to shout, or to raise their voices [or even utter a word], till the day when he would tell them to shout; then they were to give a mighty shout. • Thus he made the Ark of the LORD go round the city, [making the circuit of it once,] and then they returned to the camp and spent the night there. • Joshua rose early next morning, and the priests took up the Ark of the LORD. • The seven priests carrying the seven trumpets of ram's horn marched in front of the Ark of the LORD, blowing the trumpets as they went, with the drafted men in front of them and the rearguard following the Ark, the trumpets sounding as they marched.• They marched round the city once [on the second day] and returned to the camp; this they did for six days.

• On the seventh day they rose at dawn and marched seven times round the city [in the same way; that was the only day on which they marched round seven times]. • The seventh time, as the priests blew the trumpets, Joshua said to the army, 'Shout! The LORD has given you the city. • The city is to be under solemn ban: everything in it belongs to the LORD. No one is to be spared except the prostitute Rahab and everyone who is with her in the house, because she hid the men we sent. • And you must beware of coveting anything that is forbidden under the ban; you must take none of it for yourselves, or else you will put the Israelite camp itself under the ban and bring disaster on it. • All silver and gold, all the vessels of copper and iron, are to be holy; they belong to the LORD and must go into his treasury.'

• So [the people shouted and] the trumpets were blown, and when the army heard the trumpets sound, they raised a great shout, and the wall collapsed. The army advanced on the city, every man straight ahead, and they captured it. • Under the ban they destroyed everything there; they put everyone to the sword, men and women, young and old, as well as the cattle, the sheep, and the donkeys.

• The two men who had been sent out to reconnoitre the land were told by Joshua to go to the prostitute's house and bring out the woman and all who belonged to her, as they had sworn to do. • The young men went and brought out Rahab, her father and mother, her brothers, and all who belonged to her; they brought the whole family and placed them outside the Israelite camp. • The city and everything in it were then set on fire, except that the silver and gold and the vessels of copper and iron were deposited in the treasury of the LORD's house. • Thus Joshua spared the lives of Rahab the prostitute, her household, and all who belonged to her, because she had hidden the men whom Joshua had sent to reconnoitre Jericho; she and her family settled permanently among the Israelites.   (REB)

The Fall of Jericho (cont.)

He is therefore presented as following Torah regulations for the conduct of a war, especially *the ban*, for which see Dt 20.16.

The ritual of the 'capture' was presumably enacted at Gilgal, following that of the crossing, with the stone circle now representing the town of Jericho. The text of vv.1-21 has all P's liturgical fullness, even when the words in square brackets (absent from the LXX*) are omitted.

The final verses conclude the story of *Rahab* begun in Ch.2.

The Sun Stands Still

10.12 On that day when the LORD delivered up the Amorites into the hands of Israel, Joshua spoke with the LORD, and in the presence of Israel said:

> Stand still, you sun, at Gibeon;
> you moon, at the vale of Aijalon.

• The sun stood still and the moon halted until the nation had taken vengeance on its enemies, as indeed is written in the Book of Jashar. The sun stayed in mid-heaven and made no haste to set for almost a whole day. • Never before or since has there been such a day as that on which the LORD listened to the voice of a 15 mortal. Surely the LORD fought for Israel! • Then Joshua returned with all the Israelites to the camp at Gilgal. (REB)

The Sun Stands Still

Chs 7-12 describe the occupation of the promised land, first the south and then the north. These few verses are appended to a report of how Joshua at *Gibeon* defeated a coalition of five *Amorite* (i.e. Canaanite) kings. The report itself [10.5-11] says nothing of the sun standing still. The miracle was presumably suggested by the mention of Gibeon in the fragment of early poetry quoted here from the *Book of Jashar* (for which see 2 Sam 1.18). Prayers for the sun to stand still so as to prolong a day of battle (or the moon, to prolong a night of love) are common in the poetry of other peoples e.g. Homer *Iliad* 2.412+.

The Renewal of the Covenant

24. 1 Joshua assembled all the tribes of Israel at Shechem. He summoned the elders of Israel, the heads of families, the judges and officers. When they presented themselves before God, • Joshua said to all the people: 'This is the word of the LORD the God of Israel: Long ago your forefathers lived beyond the Euphrates and served other gods. • I took your ancestor Abraham from beside the Euphrates and led him through the length and breadth of Canaan. I gave him many 5 descendants. • Later I sent Moses and Aaron, and • I brought your forefathers out of Egypt. For a long time you lived in the wilderness, • and then I brought you 11 into the land of the Amorites who lived east of the Jordan. • Then you crossed the Jordan and came to Jericho. Its people fought against you, but I delivered them into your hands. ▸

The Renewal of the Covenant

After the 'conquest' of the land, Joshua at the end of his life presides over a formal renewal by the Israelites of their covenant with YHWH. The DtH presents it as an event of high import, suitably located at the important central town of *Shechem*.

But why should the covenant be renewed at this particular point of the narrative? Probably because, since it was originally established at Sinai, the Israelites had moved into new territory. It was the common belief of the ancient world that every land had its own gods. To enter a new land normally meant to respect the gods of that land in addition to any of one's own people.

The Renewal of the Covenant (cont.)

14 • Now hold the LORD in awe, and serve him in loyalty and truth. Put away the gods your fathers served beyond the Euphrates and in Egypt, and serve the LORD. • But if it does not please you to serve the LORD, choose here and now whom you will serve: the gods whom your forefathers served beyond the Euphrates, or the gods of the Amorites in whose land you are living. But I and my family, we shall serve the LORD.'

• The people answered, 'God forbid that we should forsake the LORD to serve other gods!' They declared: • The LORD drove out before us the Amorites and all the peoples who lived in that country. We too shall serve the LORD; he is our God.' • Joshua said to the people, 'You may not be able to serve the LORD. He is a holy God, a jealous God, and he will not forgive your rebellion and your sins.

20 • If you forsake the LORD and serve foreign deities, he will turn and bring disaster on you and make an end of you, even though he once brought you prosperity.' • The people answered, 'No; we shall serve the LORD.' • He said to them, 'You are witnesses against yourselves that you have chosen the LORD and will serve him.' 'Yes' they answered, 'we are witnesses.' • 'Then here and now banish the foreign gods that are among you,' he said to them, 'and turn your hearts to the LORD the God of Israel.' • The people replied, 'We shall serve the LORD our God and his voice we shall obey.'

25 • So Joshua made a covenant for the people that day; he drew up a statute and an ordinance for them in Shechem • and recorded its terms in the book of the law of God. He took a great stone and set it up there under the terebinth in the sanctuary of the LORD. • He said to all the people, 'You see this stone – it will be a witness against us; for it has heard all the words which the LORD has spoken to us. If you renounce your God, it will be a witness against you.' • Then Joshua dismissed the people, each man to his allotted holding.

29 • After these events, Joshua son of Nun, the servant of the LORD, died at the age of a hundred and ten. • Israel served the LORD throughout the lifetime of Joshua and of the elders who outlived him and who knew all that the LORD had done for Israel.   (REB)

The Renewal of the Covenant (cont.)

But this YHWH is *a jealous God* (19) who demands exclusive loyalty. It is impossible to worship both YHWH and *other gods* – indeed in the strictest sense you *may not be able to serve the LORD* at all (19), because he is too *holy*. (John Betjeman once began a sermon: 'It is a very *terrible* thing to be a Christian'.)

The book of Joshua is therefore rounded off with yet another liturgical narrative. And as with Gilgal, so with Shechem the narrative could be used – and was perhaps designed – as the basis for a regular liturgy of covenant renewal.

The Book of Judges at first sight belongs closely with that of Joshua. Its theme is the consolidation of the Israelite 'occupation'. As in Joshua, earlier stories have been collected and edited in such a way as to emphasise the overriding importance to Israel of loyalty to God. But within that broad similarity are two notable differences.

First, whereas there was only one Joshua – and will later be only one Saul – there are now many Judges. A 'judge' here is not just a legal figure but something more like a military governor of a province. Indeed the Hebrew *shōphēt*, translated 'judge', is the same word as the Phoenician *suffete*, the title of the chief magistrate at e.g. Tyre or Carthage. The typical judge was a charismatic leader of one Israelite tribe against its nearest gentile enemy. Other tribes sometimes co-operated, sometimes did not. Any claims that 'all Israel' is involved may safely be ascribed to the hand of the DtH.

Secondly, the 'history' has a different slant. No longer are the people represented as uniformly faithful to God, and thus continuously successful. On the contrary there are many records of the worship of other gods, all suitably punished by military failures. Events are therefore presented in a cyclical form: disloyalty → punishment → pleading → deliverance → 'peace' → renewed disloyalty. This cycle, which rarely includes any repentance, is announced in Ch.2 and repeated as a framework for the stories of many individual judges. In the last part of the book the emphasis is rather on *individual* lawlessness, from which in the concluding verse [21.25] is derived a kind of 'trailer' for the monarchy to come: 'In those days there was no king in Israel and every one did what was right in his own eyes.'

A Theological Introduction

2.10 When that whole generation was gathered to its forefathers, and was succeeded by another generation, who did not acknowledge the Lord and did not know what he had done for Israel, • then the Israelites did what was wrong in the eyes of the Lord by serving the baalim. • They forsook the Lord, their fathers' God who had brought them out of Egypt, and went after other gods, the gods of the peoples among whom they lived; by bowing down before them they provoked the Lord to anger; • they forsook the Lord and served the baalim and the ashtaroth. • In his anger the Lord made them the prey of bands of raiders and plunderers; he sold them into the power of their enemies around them, so that they could no longer stand against them. • Every time they went out to do battle the Lord brought disaster on them, as 15 he had said when he gave them his solemn warning; and they were in dire straits. • Then the Lord raised up judges to rescue them from the marauding bands, • yet even to their judges they did not listen. They prostituted themselves by worshipping other gods and bowed down before them; all too soon they abandoned the path of obedience to the Lord's commands which their forefathers had followed. They did not obey the Lord. • Whenever the Lord set up a judge over them, he was with that judge, and kept them safe from their enemies so long as the judge lived. The Lord would relent when he heard them groaning under oppression and tyranny. • But on the death of the judge they would relapse into corruption deeper than that of their predecessors and go after other gods; serving them and bowing before them, they would give up none of their evil practices and wilful ways. ▸

A Theological Introduction (cont.)

0 • So the LORD's anger was roused against Israel and he said, 'Because this nation has violated the covenant which I laid upon their forefathers, and has not obeyed me, • I for my part shall not drive out before them one individual of all the nations which Joshua left at his death. • Through them I shall test Israel, to see whether or not they will keep strictly to the way of the LORD as their forefathers did.' • So the LORD left those nations alone and made no haste to drive them out or give them into Joshua's hands.

1   • As a means of testing all the Israelites who had not taken part in the battles for Canaan, the LORD left these nations, • his purpose being to train succeeding generations of Israel in the art of warfare, or those at least who had not learnt it in former times.   (REB)

A Theological Introduction

The DtH's introduction sets out clearly if dully the theological message of the book as a whole, which also frames many individual episodes. Baal was the Canaanite god of rain and fertility, Astarte his consort, the same as Assyrian Ishtar. The plurals *baalim* and *ashtaroth* (13) are the various local manifestations of the two deities.

Chs.2.21-3.2 deal with a fact which evidently embarrassed the DtH, namely the continued existence of gentiles in the promised land. Not satisfied with the official explanation, that it was a punishment, he offers two others: it was a test of loyalty (2.22) and/or a training for war (3.2). All three are theological solutions to a purely theological problem.

Ehud

.12 Once again the Israelites did what was wrong in the eyes of the LORD, and because of this he roused King Eglon of Moab against Israel. • Eglon mustered the Ammonites and the Amalekites, attacked Israel, and took possession of the city of palm trees. • The Israelites were subject to King Eglon of Moab for eighteen years.

15   • Then they cried to the LORD for help, and to deliver them he raised up Ehud son of Gera the Benjamite; he was left-handed. The Israelites sent him to hand over their tribute to King Eglon. • Ehud had made himself a two-edged sword, about eighteen inches long, which he fastened on his right side under his clothes • when he brought the tribute to King Eglon. Eglon was a very fat man. • After Ehud had finished presenting the tribute, he sent on the men who had carried it, • while he himself turned back from the Carved Stones at Gilgal. 'My lord king,' he said, 'I have a message for you in private.' Eglon called for silence and dismissed

20 all his attendants. • Ehud then approached him as he sat in the roof-chamber of his summer palace. He said, 'Your majesty, I have a message from God for you.' As Eglon rose from his seat, • Ehud reached with his left hand, drew the sword from his right side, and drove it into Eglon's belly. • The hilt went in after the blade and the fat closed over the blade, for he did not draw the sword out but left it protruding behind. • Ehud then went out to the porch, where he shut the door on him and fastened it.   ▸

Ehud

The kernel of the story (14-26) relates the single-handed assassination of the Moabite king Eglon by the hero-deliverer Ehud. The narrative is remarkable in many ways.

First, it contains plenty of detail, a feature sometimes thought to mark Greek, as distinct from Hebrew, story-telling. We are given the specifications of the

Ehud (cont.)

• After he had gone, Eglon's servants came and, finding the doors fastened, they said, 'He must be relieving himself in the closet of his summer palace.'

3.25 • They waited until they became alarmed and, when he still did not open the door of the roof-chamber, they took the key and opened the door; and there was their master lying dead on the floor.

• While they had been waiting, Ehud had made good his escape; he passed the Carved Stones and escaped to Seirah. • Once there, he sounded the trumpet in the hill-country of Ephraim, and the Israelites went down from the hills with him at their head. • He said to them, 'Follow me, for the LORD has delivered your enemies, the Moabites, into your hands.' They went down after him, and held the fords of the Jordan against the Moabites, allowing no one to cross. • They killed at that time some ten thousand Moabites, all of them stalwart and valiant fighters;

30 not one escaped. • Moab became subject to Israel on that day, and the land was at peace for eighty years.   (REB)

Ehud (cont.)

weapon, the topography of the palace, and the physiology of the killing. AV and RSV go further in this last respect than the modern translations. In v.22 they convincingly render: 'the fat closed over the blade *so that he could* not draw the dagger out of his belly' – and they continue with the Vulgate's interpretation of an obscure Hebrew text, translating 'and the dirt came out' i.e. when the anal sphincter was relaxed.

Second, there is humour of all kinds, mostly rather crude. *Eglon* is *fat* by name (Eglon means 'fat calf') and by nature, i.e. slow of wit; and his fatness is given prominence in the telling (17). Ehud by contrast is quick-witted enough to afford the irony of v.20: the *message from God for you* is in fact the *sword*. The scatological humour of v.24 plays a double part in the story: it contributes to Ehud's getaway, and lends colour to the satirical portrait of the Moabite Eglon and his entourage.

But there is nothing crude in the dramatic presentation. The Hebrew text

draws immediate attention to Ehud's left-handedness. It does so by playing on the etymology of his tribal name Benjamin, which means 'son of the right hand', so that Ehud was the odd man out. But far from being a handicap, this enabled him to carry his weapon on the right and thus avoid suspicion. And it was (lit.) 'by his hand' that *the Israelites sent* their ironically named *tribute*.

As to Eglon, throughout the episode the only thing he says is *silence* (19), the only thing he does is to stand up (20). And when the servants eventually enter, the Hebrew text mirrors their successive focusing: *behold – their master – fallen to the floor – dead*. That was probably the end of the original story: the rest is anticlimax.

This exciting, if in some ways primitive, tale is set by the DtH in the framework which he uses for most of these episodes. *The city of palm trees* (13) is Jericho, which is presumably to be thought of as the site of Eglon's palace.

Deborah and Barak

Chs 4 and 5 present two versions of the same event, first in prose, then in poetry. The combination, which has parallels in the

ANE but is unique in the OT, testifies to the importance of the event, viz. an Israelite defeat of a joint force composed of

Deborah and Barak

After Ehud's death the Israelites once again did what was wrong in the eyes of the LORD, • and he sold them into the power of Jabin, the Canaanite king who ruled in Hazor. The commander of his forces was Sisera, who lived in Harosheth-of-the-Gentiles. • The Israelites cried to the LORD for help, because Sisera with his nine hundred iron-clad chariots had oppressed Israel harshly for twenty years.

• At that time Deborah wife of Lappidoth, a prophetess, was judge in Israel. • It was her custom to sit under the Palm Tree of Deborah between Ramah and Bethel in the hill-country of Ephraim, and Israelites seeking a judgement went up to her. • She sent for Barak son of Abinoam from Kedesh in Naphtali and said to him, 'This is the command of the LORD the God of Israel: Go and lead out ten thousand men from Naphtali and Zebulun and bring them with you to Mount Tabor. • I shall draw out to you at the wadi Kishon Jabin's commander Sisera, along with his chariots and troops, and deliver him into your power.' • Barak answered, 'If you go with me, I shall go, but if you will not go, neither shall I.' • 'Certainly I shall go with you,' she said, 'but this venture will bring you no glory, because the LORD will leave Sisera to fall into the hands of a woman.' Deborah set off with Barak and went to Kedesh. • Barak mustered Zebulun and Naphtali to Kedesh and marched up with ten thousand followers; Deborah went up with him. ◗

Deborah and Barak (cont.)

Canaanite infantry supported by Philistine chariots. But *iron-clad* (3) is an anachronism: the earliest use of iron in chariots is for Assyrian wheel-rims c.700 BC.

The victory song of Deborah is without question the earlier document. The prose version (Ch. 4) is later. At first sight it seems more 'historical', but the appearances are deceptive. Most of the proper names are obscure or unreliable, and it is impossible to reconstruct the campaign on a map. All we can reasonably be sure of is this. An Israelite force inspired by Deborah and commanded by Barak, having mustered on *Mount Tabor*, caught Sisera's army at a disadvantage in the valley of Jezreel and routed them. Sisera fled on foot to a nomad tent, where he was killed by Jael with a blow on the head. Ch.4 tells the story in three dramatic scenes: Deborah and Barak (4-10); the battle (12-16); Sisera and Jael (17-23).

Deborah (4) is presented as both judge and *prophetess*. Her name means 'bee', a common title of prophetesses in the ancient world. Her husband's name *Lappidoth* can mean 'lightning flash'.

Since Barak means 'lightning', it has been suggested that *Barak* was in fact her husband. That would surely be too cryptic for the audience, though it would add piquancy to the relations between the two. For whereas she has the confidence of prophetic certainty (7), he is a man of the world who weighs the odds and makes conditions. He needs her with him, as any army commander in the ancient world needed a prophet, to read the omens (LXX makes this explicit in v.8); which, when the time comes, she does (14). Meanwhile her reference to *a woman* (9) is doubly ironical: she rebukes his timidity and at the same time hints darkly at the future. He thinks she is referring to herself, the audience knows otherwise.

The battle itself is briefly told: the Hebrew story-tellers never mastered the art of battle narrative. Even the cause of Barak's victory is not made explicit, though it presumably has to do with the *wadi Kishon*. After a heavy rain-storm, such as is suggested by 5.21, the Kishon would overflow its banks and make the valley into a marsh. This would bog down the *chariots* of Sisera

Deborah and Barak (cont.)

4. 12 • When it was reported to Sisera that Barak son of Abinoam had gone up to Mount Tabor, • he mustered all nine hundred of his iron-clad chariots, along with all the troops he had, and marched from Harosheth-of-the-Gentiles to the wadi Kishon. • Deborah said to Barak, 'Up! This day the LORD is to give Sisera into your hands. See, the LORD has marched out at your head!' Barak came down 15 from Mount Tabor with ten thousand men at his back, • and the LORD threw Sisera and all his chariots and army into panic-stricken rout before Barak's onslaught; Sisera himself dismounted from his chariot and fled on foot. • Barak pursued the chariots and the troops as far as Harosheth, and the whole army was put to the sword; not a man was left alive.

• Meanwhile Sisera fled on foot to the tent of Jael wife of Heber the Kenite, because King Jabin of Hazor and the household of Heber the Kenite were on friendly terms. • Jael came out to greet Sisera and said, 'Come in, my lord, come in here; do not be afraid.' He went into the tent, and she covered him with a rug. • He said to her, 'Give me some water to drink, for I am thirsty.' She opened a 20 skin of milk, gave him a drink, and covered him again. • He said to her, 'Stand at the tent door, and if anyone comes and asks if there is a man here, say "No." ' • But as Sisera lay fast asleep through exhaustion Jael took a tent-peg, picked up a mallet, and, creeping up to him, drove the peg into his temple, so that it went down into the ground, and Sisera died. • When Barak came by in pursuit of Sisera, Jael went out to meet him. 'Come,' she said, 'I shall show you the man you are looking for.' He went in with her, and there was Sisera lying dead with the tent-peg in his temple. • That day God gave victory to the Israelites over King Jabin of Canaan, • and they pressed home their attacks upon him until he was destroyed.   (REB)

Deborah and Barak (cont.)

and he would have to *dismount* (15).

The climax which follows is told in the simple style, with much left to the imagination; dense, and therefore tense. *Sisera* runs for help to what he regards as a friendly Bedouin tent, and seeks the rights of a guest. Even if he had been unfavourably portrayed up to this point (which, unlike Eglon, he had not), his human need is bound now to excite sympathy. *Jael* in the absence of her husband invites him in. What is in her mind at this moment we are not told, but she gave him shelter and, in answer to his humble request ('please' in Hebrew, omitted by REB), the customary Bedouin yoghurt. For a moment he becomes the commander again (20): no 'please' this time, but *Stand* – and the imperative is in the masculine, as if he is addressing one of his own men! He then makes his last request: in answer to an en-

quiry she is to say 'nobody' – a crowning piece of irony. When he was fast asleep her eye fell on a *mallet* and a *tent-peg*. The tent-peg would be long and made of metal, as required in the dry soil of Palestine; the hammer too would be metal, as used by the men of her *Kenite* clan. Moreover as a Bedouin woman (whose role has always included the setting up of the tents) she would know the use of the tools. With them, in defiance of all the laws of hospitality, she murdered her guest.

The last verse rounds the tale off. In the final frame we see through the astonished eyes of Barak. The Heb.'behold' (preserved only in AV) marks the change in point of view: 'when he came into her tent behold Sisera lay dead'. And what Barak saw fulfilled Deborah's prophecy in v.9: *no glory* in it for him. As often in the OT, the women dominate.

The Song of Deborah

They sang a song that day, Deborah and Barak son of Abinoam, and the words were:

That the warriors in Israel unbound their hair,
that the people came forward with a will,
bless the LORD!

Listen, you kings! Give ear, you princes!
From me, from me comes a song for the LORD.
I shall glorify the LORD, the God of Israel.

LORD, when you set out from Seir,
when you marched from the field of Edom,
the earth shook, the heavens pelted,
the clouds pelted down water.
The mountains melted before the LORD of Sinai,
before the LORD, the God of Israel.

In the days of Shamgar son of Anath,
there were no more caravans;
those who went forth on their travels
took their way along by-paths.
The villages in Israel were no more,
they were no more until you arose, O Deborah,
until you arose, mother of Israel!
Was there one shield, one spear to be found
among the forty thousand men in Israel?

The Song of Deborah

The song of Deborah is by common consent one of the very oldest and finest poems in the OT. On grounds of vocabulary many regard it as having been composed soon after the event it celebrates (put at c. 1100 BC) and certainly before the time of Saul.

In the Hebrew Bible it has always been distinguished, together with the Song of the Sea (Ex 15), by being set out differently on the page: as the rabbis said, 'large brick over small brick and small brick over large brick'. The normal layout was 'small over small, large over large', which suited poetry like the psalms or Job, where most couplets contain two equal lines. But the parallelism in the Song of Deborah is much more complex. In particular it shares with Ugaritic narrative poetry a liking for the repetitive stairlike* parallelism (see p.22), which sweeps the audience along with the story.

Unfortunately the text of Judges 5 is particularly hard to interpret. As it stands, 22 of its 30 verses contain words of uncertain meaning, a greater concentration than anywhere else in the OT. The translation in such places is bound to be speculative, and some passages still defy interpretation, particularly in verses 8-11.

The opening section of the song (2-11) consists of four stanzas each ending in *Israel* (3, 5, 8, 11). In the first two the singer praises of YHWH who has *again* intervened to save his people. This is the oldest reference to YHWH – and by implication to the exodus – in the text of the OT. The second pair of stanzas turns to a more recent past, contrasting the situation before and after the rise of Deborah, in respect of both security and morale. *Shamgar* was a previous Judge. Danger on the roads (6) is often mentioned in ANE descriptions of anarchy. Now how-

The Song of Deborah (cont.)

5.9
My heart is with the leaders of Israel,
 with the people who came forward with a will!
Bless the LORD!

10
You who ride white donkeys
 and sit on saddle-blankets as you ride,
and you who go on foot,

11
 sing to the sound of the shepherds
 at the watering places!
There they extol the LORD's blessings,
 his saving acts for his villages in Israel!

12
Awake, awake, Deborah!
Awake, awake, declaim a song!
Up Barak! Take prisoners in plenty,
you son of Abinoam.

(NJB)

The Song of Deborah (cont)

ever travel is once again secure for the *caravans*, and the rich (with *saddle-blankets*) as well as the poor are called upon to celebrate God's victories. The Merneptah stele rejoices similarly:

One walks with unhindered stride
 on the way. . . .
One goes and comes with singing.

The poet then turns (12-18) to address the two heroes themselves, to praise the six tribes who rallied and to ridicule the absentees. Of the former, only *Zebulun* and *Napthali* were mentioned in Ch.4, but the others were the ones nearest to the battlefield and so most likely to have had some hand, perhaps small, in it. *With you, Benjamin* may be a war cry. *Machir* refers to the tribe of Manasseh. *Issachar* was presumably Deborah's own tribe.

Four tribes who stayed away were clearly expected to send some help. *Reuben* and *Gilead* lay east of the Jordan, where the grazing was particularly good for sheep. *Asher* lay in the north, near the coast; they and the men of *Dan* perhaps crewed for the Phoenicians. Max Weber noted that among modern Bedouin tribes 'participation in war expeditions is only indirectly compulsory, through ridicule and shame'.

The remaining two tribes, Judah and Simeon, were presumably too far south to deserve a shameful mention.

Another sudden transition takes us to the battle itself. The tempo accelerates again and the outcome is told in rapid repetitive hammer-blows. Much of the poetry, and therefore the drama, cannot be easily translated into English. Thus the order of words in v.19d is 'plunder of silver none they took', with a momentary pause after 'silver'. The effects of the original sometimes have to be transferred: so REB admirably introduces an alliteration in v.22a – though its *away*, which is not in the Hebrew, produces a rhythmic anticlimax. *Hammered* gives a foretaste of v.26, as *plunder* in v.19 anticipates v.30. The belief that the stars bring rain is found in Ugaritic epic too.

Unlike the prose version in ch.4, the Song of Deborah gives no details of the clash between the opposing armies. The credit goes to the *torrent Kishon* swollen with rain, i.e. to God who sent the rain (4d). *Meroz* is unknown. The curse upon it contrasts with the blessing on Jael, so perhaps it was a Canaanite village from which help could nevertheless be expected. Verses 24 and 25 continue the

The Song of Deborah (cont.)

Then down marched the column and its chieftains,
  the people of the LORD marching down like warriors.

The men of Ephraim rallied in the vale, crying,
  'We are with you, Benjamin! Your clansmen are here!'
Down came the marshals from Machir,
  from Zebulun the bearers of the musterer's staff.
The princes of Issachar were with Deborah,
  Issachar with Barak; down into the valley they rushed in pursuit.

Reuben however was split into factions;
  great were their heart-searchings.
Why did you linger by the sheepfolds
  to listen to the shrill calling of the shepherds?
Gilead stayed beyond Jordan;
  and Dan, why did he tarry by the ships?
Asher remained by the seashore,
  by its creeks he stayed.
The people of Zebulun risked their lives;
  so did Naphtali on the heights of the battlefield.

Kings came, they fought;
  then fought the kings of Canaan
at Taanach by the waters of Megiddo;
  no plunder of silver did they take.
The stars fought from heaven,
  the stars in their courses fought against Sisera.
The torrent of Kishon swept him away,
  the torrent barred his flight, the torrent of Kishon.
Then hammered the hoofs of his horses,
  his chargers galloped, galloped away.

A curse on Meroz, said the angel of the LORD;
  a curse, a curse on its inhabitants,
because they did not come to the help of the LORD,
  to the help of the LORD and the fighting men.
Blest above women be Jael
  wife of Heber the Kenite;
  blest above all women in the tents.
He asked for water: she gave him milk,
  she offered him curds in a bowl fit for a chieftain.
She reached out her hand for the tent-peg,
  her right hand for the workman's hammer.

The Song of Deborah (cont.)

5.26   With the hammer she struck Sisera, crushing his head;
            with a shattering blow she pierced his temple.

27   At her feet he sank, he fell, he lay prone;
            at her feet he sank down and fell.
        Where he sank down, there he fell, done to death.

28   The mother of Sisera peered through the lattice,
            through the window she peered and cried,
        'Why is his chariot so long in coming?
            Why is the clatter of his chariots so delayed?'

29   The wisest of her ladies answered her,
            yes, she found her own answer:

30   'They must be finding spoil, taking their shares,
            a damsel for each man, two damsels,
        booty of dyed stuffs for Sisera, booty of dyed stuffs,
            dyed stuff and brocade, two lengths of brocade to grace the victor's neck.'

31   So perish all your enemies, LORD;
            but let those who love you be like the sun rising in strength.

The land was at peace for forty years.   (REB)

The Song of Deborah (cont.)

slow approach (with Sisera's name long held up), v.26 accelerates and explodes, but v.27 slows right down to a single still frame. The actual mode of killing differs from that in Ch.4. Here Jael *struck* him with the *hammer*, while he was drinking, and he *fell*, as the vanquished are represented on ANE monuments, at the *feet* of his victor. Probably the *tent-peg* of v.26 was just part of a formulaic word-pair with the hammer, misunderstood by the later author of Ch.4.

For the final scene we have another abrupt transition, but this time the pace gradually slows, like the end of a Greek choral ode. ANE victory songs regularly contain a taunt-song, but this one is handled with such a rare delicacy as to hint rather at the common humanity of victor and vanquished. The scene is Sisera's palace, where the anxious queen mother (the direct opposite of the resolute tent-dweller Jael) presides as first lady over the harem. The first words in the

Hebrew text are *through the lattice*. The lattice is the normal window for a harem, so that the girls can see without being seen; but here it also brilliantly expresses the oblique view which the women have of events. Ironically, it is the *wisest of her ladies* who comes out with the (false) suggestion which the queen wishes to hear (this seems to be the meaning of v.29b). Israelite victors were allowed only one *damsel* each [Dt 21.11], and one was more than enough for Sisera. The body of this savage poem ends on the quietest of notes, with a girl's imagination playing on lengths of embroidered material. The concluding verse (31) harks back to the opening (3).

For intensity of 'fraught' dramatic poetry there is nothing in ancient literature to compare with the second half of the Song of Deborah, except the ode in Aeschylus' *Agamemnon* where the chorus tells of Agamemnon's sacrifice of Iphigeneia.

Gideon

1 The Israelites did what was wrong in the eyes of the LORD and he delivered them into the hands of Midian for seven years. • The Midianites were too strong for the Israelites, who were forced to find themselves hollow places in the mountains, in caves and fastnesses. • If the Israelites had sown seed, the Midianites and the Amalekites and other eastern tribes would come up and attack Israel, • pitching their camps in the country and destroying the crops as far as the outskirts of Gaza. They left nothing to support life in Israel, neither sheep nor ox nor donkey.
5 • They came up with their herds and their tents, swarming like locusts; they and their camels were past counting. They would come into the land and lay it waste. • The Israelites, brought to destitution by the Midianites, cried to the LORD for help.

7.1   • Gideon, with all his troops pitched camp at En-harod; the Midianite encampment was in the valley to the north of his by the hill at Moreh. • The LORD said to Gideon, 'Those with you are more than I need to deliver Midian into their hands: Israel might claim the glory for themselves and say that it is their own strength that has given them the victory. • Make a proclamation now to the army to say that anyone who is afraid or anxious is to leave Mount Galud at once and go home.' Twenty-two thousand of them went, and ten thousand remained.
     • 'There are still too many,' said the LORD to Gideon. 'Bring them down to the water, and I shall separate them for you there. If I say to you, "This man shall go
5 with you," he shall go; and if I say, "This man shall not go," he shall not go.' • When Gideon brought the men down to the water, the LORD said to him, 'Make every man who laps the water with his tongue like a dog stand on one side, and on the other every man who kneels down and drinks.' • The number of those who lapped, putting their hands to their mouths, was three hundred; all the rest had gone down on their knees to drink. • The LORD said, 'By means of the three hundred men who lapped I shall save you and give Midian into your power; the rest may go home.' • Gideon sent these Israelites home, but he kept the three hundred, and they took with them the jars and the trumpets which the people had.   ▶

Gideon

This time the conflict is between the tribe of Ephraim, settled on the uplands of central Palestine, and the *Midianites**. The introduction in Ch.6 paints a convincing scene.

But the famous story of Gideon's victory cannot be read as history. Indeed it should not really be called Gideon's victory at all, for the whole thrust of the narrative (summed up in 7.2) is to show it as God's victory achieved with the minimum of human help, and with no fight at all. The scene was only ten miles from Taanach (Ch.5): Gideon and his men are encamped

on *Mount Galud*, a spur of Mt Gilboa (see map 2), the Midianites in the fertile plain below. The narrative is in three parts: reduction, reconnaissance and ruse.

First, Gideon's forces are reduced, in two stages. The *proclamation* in 7.3 quotes Dt 20.8. Presumably that is also the explanation of the second reduction: those who went down on their knees are regarded as nervous. The final *300* is the only plausible number in the chapter: Mesha king of Moab boasted on his stele (c.830 BC) of using an army of '200 men, all first class warriors'.

Gideon (cont.)

The Midianite camp was below him in the valley, • and that night the LORD said to Gideon, 'Go down at once and attack the camp, for I have delivered it into your hands. • If you are afraid to do so, then go down first with your servant Purah, • and when you hear what they are saying, that will give you courage to attack the camp.' So he and his servant Purah went down to the outposts of the camp where the fighting men were stationed. • The Midianites, the Amalekites, and all the eastern tribes were so many that they lay there in the valley like a swarm of locusts; there was no counting their camels, which in number were like grains of sand on the seashore. • As Gideon came close, there was a man telling his comrades about a dream. He said, 'I dreamt that I saw a barley loaf rolling over and over through the Midianite camp; it came to a tent, struck it, and the tent collapsed and turned upside down.'• The other answered, 'This can be none other than the sword of Gideon son of Joash the Israelite. God has delivered Midian and the whole army into his hands.'

7.10

15   • When Gideon heard the account of the dream and its interpretation, he bowed down in worship. Then going back to the Israelite camp he said, 'Let us go! The LORD has delivered the camp of the Midianites into our hands.' • He divided the three hundred men into three companies, and furnished every man with a trumpet and an empty jar, with a torch inside each jar. • 'Watch me,' he said to them. 'When I come to the edge of the camp, do exactly as I do. • When I and those with me blow our trumpets, you too all round the camp blow your trumpets and shout, "For the LORD and for Gideon!" '

          • Gideon and the hundred men who were with him reached the outskirts of the camp at the beginning of the middle watch, just after the posting of the sentries. They blew the trumpets and smashed the jars they were holding. • All three companies blew their trumpets and smashed their jars; then, grasping the torches in their left hands and the trumpets in their right, they shouted, 'A sword for the LORD and for Gideon!' • Every man stood where he was, all round the camp, and the whole camp leapt up in a panic and took flight. • When the three hundred blew their trumpets, the LORD set all the men in the camp fighting against each other. They fled as far as Beth-shittah in the direction of Zererah.   (REB)

20

Gideon (cont.)

In line with the colouring of the whole narrative, the night reconnaissance is aimed solely at finding out about the enemy's morale. *Dreams* were regularly regarded in the ancient world as ominous, especially before a battle. The Torah disapproved of divination, so the dream is cleverly ascribed to a Midianite. In it, the *barley loaf* represents agriculture, the *tent* nomadism. As commonly in the OT, the small overthrows the large.

The psychological ruse of vv.16-22 was anticipated in v.8. The idea was to conceal the *torches* in the *jars* until the men were *all round the camp*, then to smash the jars on the ground and brandish the torches so that they burst into flames. The enemy would be thrown into confusion by the combination of fire and noise, the latter amplified by the *trumpets* and war cries.

Jotham's Fable

8
One day the trees went out
    to anoint a king to rule them.
They said to the olive tree, 'Be our king!'
9
The olive tree replied,
    'Must I forgo my oil
which gives honour to gods and men,
    to stand and sway over the trees?'

10
Then the trees said to the fig tree,
    'You come and be our king!'
11
The fig tree replied,
    'Must I forgo my sweetness,
forgo my excellent fruit,
    to go and sway over the trees?'

12
Then the trees said to the vine,
    'You come and be our king!'
13
The vine replied,
    'Must I forgo my wine
which cheers gods and men,
    to go and sway over the trees?'

14
Then the trees all said to the thorn bush,
    'You come and be our king!'
15
And the thorn bush replied to the trees,
    'If you are anointing me in good faith to be your king,
come and shelter in my shade.
    But, if not, fire will come out of the thorn bush
and devour the cedars of Lebanon.'   (NJB)

Jotham's Fable

This is the best example in the Bible of the kind of fable which we associate with Aesop. This one, the struggle of the trees for leadership, is found not only in Aesop but worldwide, and its gentile origin here is shown by the double mention of *gods and men*. The fable as a whole does not fit its immediate context in Judges, but it does fit the substratum of anti-royalist thinking which runs beneath the DtH and surfaces most notably in 1 Sam 8.

The pattern of 'three no's and a yes' is common in folk-tales (see Jg 16 etc.), but there are some typically Hebrew touches of irony. The three useful trees, which turned down the request, express their contempt for the monarchy by the verb whose overtones are well caught in NJB's *stand and sway*. The *thorn bush* which accepts the role has by contrast nothing to contribute. It produces no fruit, nor even effective *shade*. Its dry branches are the quickest to catch *fire* in summer, and then will burn down even the noblest of trees. The reference to *the cedars of Lebanon* suggests that the tendency here is not so much democratic as aristocratic; but either way it is anti-monarchical, 'the most powerful such composition in the history of the world' (Buber).

Jephthah's Daughter

11. 1 Jephthah the Gileadite was an intrepid warrior; he was the son of Gilead by a prostitute. • Gilead's wife also bore him sons, and when they grew up they drove Jephthah away, saying to him, •'You have no inheritance in our father's house; you are another woman's son.' • To escape his brothers, Jephthah fled and settled in the land of Tob, and a number of good-for-nothing fellows rallied to him and became his followers.

5 • The time came when the Ammonites launched an offensive against Israel • and, when the fighting began, the elders of Gilead went to fetch Jephthah from the land of Tob. • 'Come and be our commander so that we can fight the Ammonites,' they said to him. • But Jephthah answered, 'You drove me from my father's house in hatred. Why come to me now when you are in trouble?' • 'It is because of that', they replied, 'that we have turned to you now. Come with us, fight the Ammonites, and become head over all the inhabitants of Gilead.' • Jephthah said to them, 'If you ask me back to fight the Ammonites and if the LORD delivers 10 them into my hands, then I must become your head.' • The Gilead elders said to him, 'We swear by the LORD, who will be witness between us, that we will do what you say.' • Jephthah then went with the elders of Gilead, and the people made him their head and commander. And at Mizpah, in the presence of the LORD, Jephthah repeated the terms he had laid down.

29 • Then the spirit of the LORD came upon Jephthah, who passed through Gilead and Manasseh, over to the Ammonites. • Jephthah made this vow to the LORD: 'If you will deliver the Ammonites into my hands, • then the first creature that comes out of the door of my house to meet me when I return from them safely shall be the LORD's; I shall offer that as a whole-offering.' • So Jephthah crossed over to attack the Ammonites, and the LORD delivered them into his hands. When Jephthah arrived home in Mizpah, it was his daughter who came out to meet him with tambourines and dancing. She was his only child; apart from her he had neither 35 son nor daughter. • At the sight of her, he tore his clothes and said, 'Oh, my daughter, you have broken my*heart! Such calamity you have brought on me! I have made a vow to the LORD and I cannot go back on it.' • She replied,   ▶

Jephthah's Daughter

The scene now shifts to the east bank of Jordan, to the land of *Gilead* and to *Jephthah* the judge. Jephthah's name lives on in European literature for one grim story, the vow which led to his (literally) sacrificing his own daughter. The story is a well-known folk-tale, but it is made especially grim here by being presented (i) as historical fact and (ii) without any condemnation or apology. Human sacrifice in the OT was denounced in principle by both law and prophets. But here even the LORD's own position is equivocal: both when the *vow* is made (31) and when it is paid (35-36) he

maintains a diplomatic silence.

If the narrator on his part felt any disapproval, it is subtly registered. He (or she?) contrasts the victory welcome (34) with the anguish that followed (35), stressing the fact that the *daughter* was an *only child*. He increases our sympathy for her by contrasting the two reactions: Jephthah, in his distress, blames her, while she, with far more cause for blame, exonerates him. Her death is softened by euphemism; and, though she is allowed no name nor any children of her own, the story ends with her posthumous renown.

Jephthah's Daughter (cont.)

37 'Father, since you have made a vow to the LORD, do to me as your vow demands, now that the LORD has avenged you on the Ammonites, your enemies. • But, father, grant me this one favour: spare me for two months, that I may roam the hills with my companions and mourn that I must die a virgin.' • 'Go,' he said, and he let her depart for two months. She went with her companions and mourned her virginity on the hills.

• At the end of two months she came back to her father, and he fulfilled the vow he had made; she died a virgin. It became a tradition • that the daughters of Israel should go year by year and commemorate for four days the daughter of Jephthah the Gileadite.   (REB)

Jephthah's Daughter (cont.)

Conceivably also the narrator seeks to lessen our contempt for Jephthah by the account in 1-11 of his early life. Born an outsider, rejected by his countrymen save when a crisis looms, hungry for status (11), an *intrepid warrior* but an insecure man – was his vow perhaps an act of public bravado which recoiled most horribly upon his own head? Even if so, it was still his anonymous daughter who paid the price, and it would have been good to have the point made more clearly.

The Shibboleth

2. 4 Jephthah then mustered all the men of Gilead and fought Ephraim, and the Gileadites defeated them. • The Gileadites seized the fords of the Jordan and held them against Ephraim. When any Ephraimite who had escaped wished to cross, the men of Gilead would ask, 'Are you an Ephraimite?' and if he said, 'No,' • they would retort, 'Say "Shibboleth." ' He would say 'Sibboleth,' and because he could not pronounce the word properly, they seized him and killed him at the fords. At that time forty-two thousand men of Ephraim lost their lives.   (REB)

The Shibboleth

Jephthah figures in one other well-known incident. The *Ephraimites* resented Jephthah's victory over the *Ammonites*, and crossed the Jordan on a punitive raid into his territory. *Shibboleth* means 'ear of corn'. The different pronunciations in the two tribal dialects correspond to the later difference between the Hebrew and Arabic languages. So at the end of the second world war the Dutch Resistance used the pronunciation of 'Scheveningen' to identify fleeing Germans who were trying to pass themselves off as Dutchmen.

The SamsonCycle – Judges Chs 13-16

The story-cycle of Samson's exploits is less historical even than the others in the book of Judges. It is also more episodic, having no unifying theme more obvious, or more elevated, than the retaliatory sequence of Samson's various fights. Samson himself is not presented as a judge in anything but name, nor as admirable – still less heroic – in any serious sense, until the moment of his death. That last scene has influenced European art, literature and music, and gives his name a continuing resonance among those who have never heard of Joshua, Gideon or Samuel. For the sake of that renown, rather than its own merits, the cycle is here printed almost in full.

From Jg 13 right through to David's victories in 2 Sam 5 the chief threat to Israel came from the Philistines. Coming from the Aegean (see p.30), they had established themselves comparatively recently on the coastal strip south of Phoenicia. They and the Hebrews were now disputing the territory often known by their name as Palestine. (The equivalence is shown by the English translations of Ex 15.14, where AV gives 'Palestina', modern versions 'Philistia'.) The Philistines were technologically ahead of the Israelites (1 Sam 13.19+); Samson by contrast is represented as a child of nature, using his bare hands and no weapon more sophisticated than the jawbone of an ass.

Samson's Birth

13.1 Once more the Israelites did what was wrong in the eyes of the LORD, and he delivered them into the hands of the Philistines for forty years.

• There was a certain man from Zorah of the tribe of Dan whose name was Manoah and whose wife was barren; she had no child. • The angel of the LORD appeared to her and said, 'Though you are barren and have no child, you will conceive and give birth to a son. • Now be careful to drink no wine or strong drink, and

5 to eat no forbidden food. • You will conceive and give birth to a son, and no razor must touch his head, for the boy is to be a Nazirite, consecrated to God from birth. He will strike the first blow for Israel's freedom from the power of the Philistines.'

• The woman went and told her husband. 'A man of God came to me,' she said to him; 'his appearance was that of an angel of God, most terrible to see. I did not ask him where he came from, nor did he tell me his name, • but he said to me, "You are going to conceive and give birth to a son. From now on drink no wine or strong drink and eat no forbidden food, for the boy is to be a Nazirite, consecrated to God from his birth to the day of his death." '   ◆

Samson's Birth

The miraculous birth of the hero is a common theme in the Bible and outside it. Birth-stories regularly include (i) a revelation to (ii) a barren woman of (iii) a special destiny for her son – all features present here. To these and some other common motifs the author has added one distinctive feature, namely the *Nazirite* status of the son and also apparently (14) of his mother. A Nazirite was a man or woman consecrated to the LORD, who had vowed to abstain from the use of the razor, from contact with corpses and above all from

wine [Num 6.21+]. Now this is odd. In the rest of Samson's life the last two prohibitions play no part at all: there is no mention of his avoiding wine at his own wedding-party, and a man who killed as many men as he did can hardly have avoided touching a corpse. While the prohibition of a haircut is essential to the story in Ch.16, the idea that a warrior's strength depends on his long hair is a common one all over the world, cp. Jg 5.2, Achaeans in Homer, and Sikhs. Many scholars therefore suppose that the three references to the

Samson's Birth (cont.)

.8 • Manoah prayed to the LORD, 'If it is pleasing to you, Lord, let the man of God whom you sent come again to tell us what we are to do for the boy that is to be born.' • God heard Manoah's prayer, and the angel of God came again to the

10 woman, as she was sitting in the field. Her husband not being with her, • the woman ran quickly and said to him, 'The man who came to me the other day has appeared to me again.' • Manoah went with her at once and approached the man and said, 'Are you the man who talked with my wife?' 'Yes,' he replied, 'I am.' • 'Now when your words come true,' Manoah said, 'what kind of boy will he be and what will he do?' • The angel of the LORD answered, 'Your wife must be careful to do all that I told her: • she must not taste anything that comes from the vine; she must drink no wine or strong drink, and she must eat no forbidden food. She must do whatever I say.'

15 • Manoah said to the angel of the LORD, 'May we urge you to stay? Let us prepare a young goat for you.' • The angel replied, 'Though you urge me to stay, I shall not eat your food; but prepare a whole-offering if you will, and offer that to the LORD.' Manoah did not know that he was the angel of the LORD, • and said to him, 'What is your name? For we shall want to honour you when your words come true.' • The angel of the LORD said to him, 'How can you ask my name? It is a name of wonder.' • Manoah took a young goat with the proper grain-offering, and offered it on the rock to the LORD, to him whose works are full of

20 wonder. While Manoah and his wife were watching, • the flame went up from the altar towards heaven, and the angel of the LORD ascended in the flame. Seeing this, Manoah and his wife fell face downward to the ground.

• The angel of the LORD did not appear again to Manoah and his wife. When Manoah realised that it had been the angel of the LORD, • he said to his wife, 'We are doomed to die, for we have seen God.' • But she replied, 'If the LORD had wanted to kill us, he would not have accepted a whole-offering and a grain-

24-25 offering at our hands; he would not now have let us see and hear all this.' • The woman gave birth to a son and named him Samson. The LORD blessed him, and the spirit of the LORD began to move him.   (REB)

Samson's Birth (cont.)

Nazirite vow (13. 5,7; 16.17) – and perhaps the whole birth-story of Ch.13 – were added later to give the cycle a pious character otherwise notably lacking.

Be that as it may, the picture which Ch.13 offers of quiet and godly family life makes a welcome contrast to the noisy and reckless career of which it is the prelude. As usual in birth stories, the husband is portrayed less sympathetically than his wife. At first he feels left out; contrast his *tell us* in v.8 with her double *to me* in v.10. His attitude to the stranger swings from aggressive suspicion in v.11 to a gauche offer of *honour* in v.17. His wife is much quicker than he to recognise

the visitor as an *angel*, and has finally to correct him on a point of theology (22-23). But the subtlest touch is the variation between vv.5 and 7 in the announcement of the angel. As put into the mouth of the angel, the son will be *consecrated to God from birth*. When his wife reports it to Manoah, she adds the ominous words *to the day of his death*. That variation foreshadows the failure of his career.

It was a mother's role to name her son. *Samson* means 'sun-child', and that equivalence has prompted scholars to look in the story for traces of ANE sun myths (cp. Ps 19). But its general tone is much too earthy for mythology.

Samson's Wedding

14.1 Samson went down to Timnah, and at Timnah he noticed a woman, a Philistine girl. • He went home again and told his father and mother this. • 'At Timnah', he said, 'I noticed a woman, a Philistine girl. So now get her for me, to be my wife.' • His father and mother said to him, 'Is there no woman among your brothers' daughters or in our entire nation, for you to go and take a wife among these uncircumcised Philistines?' But Samson said to his father, 'Get that one for me; she is the one I am fond of.' • His father and mother did not know that all this came from the LORD, who was seeking grounds for a quarrel with the Philistines, since at this time the Philistines dominated Israel.

5   • Samson went down to Timnah and, as he reached the vineyards of Timnah, he saw a young lion coming roaring towards him. • The spirit of the LORD seized on him and he tore the lion to pieces with his bare hands as though it were a kid; but he did not tell his father or mother what he had done. • He went down and talked to the woman, and he became fond of her. • Not long after this, Samson went back to marry her. He went out of his way to look at the carcase of the lion, and there was a swarm of bees in the lion's body, and honey. • He took up some honey in his hand and ate it as he went along. On returning to his father and mother, he gave some to them, which they ate too, but he did not tell them that he had taken it from the lion's carcase. • His father then went down to the woman,
10 and Samson made a feast there, as is the custom for young men. • And when the Philistines saw him, they chose thirty companions to stay with him.

• Samson then said to them, 'Let me ask you a riddle. If you can give me the answer during the seven days of feasting, I shall give you thirty pieces of fine linen and thirty festal robes. • But if you cannot tell me the answer, then you in your turn must give me thirty pieces of fine linen and thirty festal robes.' 'Ask your riddle,' they replied, 'we are listening.' • So he said to them:

> Out of the eater came what is eaten,
> and out of the strong came what is sweet.   ◆

Samson's Wedding

Timnah, though only four miles away from Samson's home, was a foreign village. Philistine culture and religion were alien to the pious parents of Samson, but he did not share that piety.

The arrangements for the wedding are interrupted by the story of the lion and the swarm of bees. The killing of the lion is a typical heroic legend. Heracles did the same – and indeed there are other echoes of Heracles in the Samson cycle. This is not surprising since the Philistines had originally come from Crete. But the phrase *as a kid* (6) refers to the customary Bedouin way of distributing a roasted kid at a feast. The ancient world believed that

bees, like maggots, were spontaneously generated by the putrefaction of a carcass. The comings and goings of Samson and his parents in vv.5-9 are difficult to unravel, and it may be wiser to regard the whole lion-and-honey story as an insertion due to a misunderstanding of the exchange of riddles in vv.12-18.

Wedding celebrations traditionally included *seven days of feasting*, the marriage having been consummated on the first night (Gen 29.23-7). A standard feature of them everywhere in the ancient world was sexual jesting and riddling, the bawdy being part of the fertility ritual. The riddling was often competitive, with one

Samson's Wedding (cont.)

15   But three days went by and they could not solve the riddle. • On the fourth day they said to Samson's wife, 'Cajole your husband into explaining the riddle to us, or we shall burn you and your father's family to death. Did you invite us here to rob us?' • Samson's wife then went to him in tears and said, 'You only hate me, you do not love me. You have asked my fellow-countrymen a riddle and told not even me the answer.' He said to her, 'I have not told even my father or mother; why should I tell you?' • She wept on his neck for the seven days that their feasting lasted. She was so persistent that on the seventh day he told her the answer, and she told her fellow-countrymen.

    • So on the seventh day, before he went into the bedroom, the men of the town said to him:

> What is sweeter than honey,
> and what stronger than a lion?

He retorted:

> If you had not ploughed with my heifer,
> you would never have solved my riddle.

20 • Then the spirit of the LORD seized on him. He went down to Ashkelon, killed thirty men there, took what they wore and gave the festal robes to those who had answered the riddle, then burning with rage returned to his father's house. • Samson's wife was then given to the companion who had acted as his best man.   (NJB)

Samson's Wedding (cont.)

group capping another's offering. This is the explanation of the two *riddles* here. The second is the simpler. It is a true riddle, and (if it were not for vv.5-9) an easy one. The solution to it, in a wedding contest, is clearly (sexual) love. It is also the Philistines' answer to Samson's own riddle, and by giving it in the form of a second riddle they clearly win the contest. But how does Samson's first couplet come to refer to sexual love? The clue is provided by a proverb describing 'the way of an unfaithful wife: she eats, and then wipes her mouth, and says "I have done no harm"' [Prov 30.20].

Finally, Samson excuses his defeat with another proverb. Ploughing is a standard metaphor for sexual intercourse, so he managed to offend everyone. Then, in an access of temper, he rushed off on one of his killing sprees, leaving his wife in the *bridal chamber*.

Samson's Exploits

15.1 After a while, during the time of wheat harvest, Samson went to visit his wife, taking a young goat as a present for her. He said, 'I am going to my wife in our bridal chamber,' but her father would not let him in. • He said, 'I was sure that you were really hostile to her, so I gave her in marriage to your groomsman. Her young sister is better than she is – take her instead.' • Samson said, 'This time I shall settle my score with the Philistines; I shall do them some real harm.'   ▸

Samson's Exploits

This chapter records various feats of Samson, joined by the insistence on re-taliation (3, 7, 11). Verses 1-2 attempt a link with Ch.14.

Samson's Exploits (cont.)

15.5 • He went and caught three hundred jackals and got some torches; he tied the jackals tail to tail and fastened a torch between each pair of tails. • He then lit the torches and turned the jackals loose in the standing grain of the Philistines, setting fire to standing grain and sheaves, as well as to vineyards and olive groves.

  • 'Who has done this?' the Philistines demanded, and when they were told that it was Samson, because the Timnite, his father-in-law, had taken his wife and given her to his groomsman, they came and burnt her and her father to death. • Samson said to them, 'If you do things like that, I swear I will be revenged on you before I have done.' • He smote them hip and thigh, causing great slaughter; and after that he went down to live in a cave in the Rock of Etam.

9,10 • The Philistines came up and pitched camp in Judah, and overran Lehi. • The Judahites said, 'Why have you attacked us?' They answered, 'We have come to take Samson prisoner, and do to him as he did to us.' • Then three thousand men from Judah went down to the cave in the Rock of Etam, where they said to Samson, 'Surely you know that the Philistines are our masters? Now look what you have done to us.' He answered, 'I only did to them as they had done to me.' • They told him, 'We have come down to bind you and hand you over to the Philistines.' 'Swear to me that you will not set upon me yourselves,' he said. • 'No, we shall not kill you,' they answered; 'we shall only bind you and hand you over to them.' They bound him with two new ropes and brought him up from the cave in the Rock.

  • When Samson came to Lehi, the Philistines met him with shouts of triumph; but the spirit of the LORD suddenly seized him, the ropes on his arms became like

15 burnt tow, and his bonds melted away. • He came on the fresh jaw-bone of a donkey, and seizing it he slew a thousand men. • He made up this saying:

  'With the jaw-bone of a donkey I have flayed them like donkeys;
  with the jaw-bone of a donkey I have slain a thousand men.'
• Having said this he threw away the jaw-bone.   (REB)

Samson's Exploits (cont.)

The strange story of the *jackals* (4-5) is variously explained. Burning of crops is of course a regular guerrilla tactic; and since the *grain* was grown in the *olive groves*, the trees too would burn. In regular warfare both Hannibal and Tamburlaine used torches tied to animals as a means of causing panic. But we know also of two rituals practised at Rome in connection with the Feast of Ceres, goddess of corn, which seem relevant. In one, foxes with lighted torches attached to their tails were set loose and then chased; in the other, rust-coloured puppies were sacrificed. These rituals were designed to ensure that the crops would not be infected with a rust-coloured blight before the harvest. Both 'explanations' could have contributed to the story here. The burning in v.6 is Philistine retaliation for that of vv.4-5. Verse 8 is the origin of our phrase *hip and thigh*; it probably derives from wrestling.

The second exploit (9-17) contrasts the 3,000 *Judahite* collaborators with the single-handed Danite conqueror of a thousand Philistines. It includes another fragment of ancient poetry, this time a boast (16). The REB translation of the first line is an attempt to get round an untranslatable play on words in the Hebrew.

Delilah Betrays Samson

1 Samson then went to Gaza and, seeing a prostitute there, went in to her. • The men of Gaza being told, 'Samson has arrived,' surrounded the place and kept watch for him the whole night at the town gate. All that night they were going to make no move, thinking, 'Let us wait until daybreak, and then kill him.' • Till midnight, however, Samson stayed in bed, and then at midnight he got up, seized the doors of the town gate and the two posts as well; he tore them up, bar and all, hoisted them on to his shoulders and carried them to the top of the hill overlooking Hebron.

5 • After this, he fell in love with a woman in the Vale of Sorek; she was called Delilah. • The Philistine chiefs visited her and said, 'Cajole him and find out where his great strength comes from, and how we can master him, so that we can bind him and subdue him. In return we shall each give you eleven hundred silver shekels.'

• Delilah said to Samson, • 'Please tell me where your great strength comes from, and what would be needed to bind and subdue you.' • Samson replied, 'If I were bound with seven new bowstrings which had not yet been dried, I should lose my strength and become like any other man.' • The Philistine chiefs brought Delilah seven new bowstrings which had not yet been dried and she took them and bound him with them. • She had men concealed in her room, and she shouted, 'The Philistines are on you, Samson!' Then he snapped the bowstrings as a strand of tow snaps at a touch of the fire. So the secret of his strength remained unknown.

10 • Delilah then said to Samson, 'You have been laughing at me and telling me lies. But now please tell me what would be needed to bind you.' • He replied, 'If I were bound tightly with new ropes which have never been used, I should lose my strength and become like any other man.' • Delilah then took new ropes and bound him with them, and she shouted, 'The Philistines are on you, Samson!' She had men concealed in her room, but he snapped the ropes round his arms like thread. • Delilah then said to Samson, 'Up to now you have been laughing at me and telling me lies. Tell me what would be needed to bind you.' He replied, 'If you wove the seven locks of my hair into the warp of a cloth and beat them together tight with the reed, I should lose my strength and become like any other man.' • She lulled him to sleep, then wove the seven locks of his hair into the warp, beat them together tight with the reed and shouted, 'The Philistines are on you, Samson!' He woke from his sleep and pulled out both reed and warp. So the secret of his strength remained unknown.   ▸

Delilah Betrays Samson

The story in verses vv.1-3 is independent but it makes a good overture to what follows. It has the same location (Gaza) and the same protagonists (Samson and a Philistine woman), but a different outcome and a different tone. The comic hyperbole is continued from the previous chapter. The Philistines expect to have Samson at their mercy after an exhausting night, but are outwitted by his early departure.

Delilah is the last of the four women in Samson's life, and the only one to be named. She was a local girl from the *Sorek* valley. Her name is Hebrew, but she is presented as a tool of the Philistines. The famous story of her betrayal of Samson makes use of the magic number *seven* and the folk-tale pattern of 3+1. Samson's third answer puts Delilah surprisingly 'warm' – as if he had already lost his wits – but the whole 'tell me your secret' episode here is less convincing than the parallel

Delilah Betrays Samson (cont.)

16.15 • Delilah said to him, 'How can you say that you love me, when your heart is not with me? Three times now you have laughed at me and have not told me where your great strength comes from.' • And day after day she pestered him with her talk, nagging him till he grew sick to death of it. • At last he confided everything to her; he said to her, 'A razor has never touched my head, because I have been God's nazirite from my mother's womb. If my head were shorn, then my power would leave me and I should lose my strength and become like any other man.' • Delilah then realised that he had really confided in her; she sent for the Philistine princes with the message, 'Come just once more: he has confided everything to me.' And the Philistine chiefs came to her with the money in their hands. • She lulled Samson to sleep in her lap, summoned a man and had him shear off the seven locks from his head. Thus for the first time she got control over him, and 20 his strength left him. • She cried, 'The Philistines are on you, Samson!' He awoke from sleep, thinking, 'I shall break free as I have done time after time and shake myself clear.' But he did not know that the LORD had left him. • The Philistines seized him, put out his eyes and took him down to Gaza. They fettered him with a double chain of bronze and he spent his time turning the mill in the prison. • But his hair began to grow again when it had been cut off.   (NJB)

Delilah Betrays Samson (cont.)

one in Ch.14. In Samson's fourth answer the reference to the Nazirite vow is unnecessary, in the sense that the whole story-cycle would hang together perfectly well without it (see on Ch.13). We are in fact offered two other explanations of Samson's great strength: the length of his hair (cleverly exploited in v.22) and the spirit of the Lord (14.6, 19 etc.). But the three explanations are just compatible.

Samson's Revenge and Death

16. 23 The Philistine chiefs assembled to offer a great sacrifice to Dagon their god. And amid their festivities they said:

> Into our hands our god has delivered
> Samson our enemy.

• And as soon as the people saw their god, they acclaimed him, shouting his praises:

> Into our hands our god has delivered
> Samson our enemy,
> the man who laid our country waste
> and killed so many of us.

25 • And as their hearts were full of joy, they shouted, 'Summon Samson out to amuse us.' So Samson was summoned from prison, and he performed feats in front of them; then he was put to stand between the pillars. • Samson then ▸

Samson's Revenge and Death

'Eyeless in Gaza', Samson works like an animal, *turning* the great *mill*-stone of the *prison* (21) – a symbol of Israel's subjection (14.4). He is brought out for the enemy's celebrations. Their victory shout (24) is a rare example of rhyme in Hebrew poetry:

> *nāthan elōhēnū*
> *beyādēnū ōyevēnū*
> *mahrīv artsēnū*
> *hirbāh helālēnū*

Samson's Revenge and Death (cont.)

said to the boy who was leading him by the hand, 'Lead me where I can touch the pillars supporting the building, so that I can lean against them.' • Now the building was crowded with men and women. All the Philistine chiefs were there, while about three thousand men and women were watching Samson's feats from the terrace. • Samson called on the LORD and cried out, 'Lord GOD, I beg you, remember me; give me strength again this once, O God, and let me be revenged on the Philistines at one blow for my two eyes.' • And Samson took hold of the two central pillars supporting the building, and braced himself with his right arm round one and his left round the other; • and he shouted, 'Let me die with the Philistines!' He then heaved with all his might, and the building fell on the chiefs and on all the people there. Those whom he brought to their death by his death outnumbered those whom he had done to death during his life. • His brothers and the whole of his father's family came down and carried him away. They took him back and buried him between Zorah and Eshtaol in the tomb of Manoah his father. He had judged Israel for twenty years.   (NJB)

30

Samson's Revenge and Death (cont.)

Dagon was a West Semitic corn god, whom the Philistines had adopted on entry to the country. His *temple* had a *roof* supported on *two* main *pillars* which stood about 2 metres apart; archaeology confirms the picture given here. The narrative makes a fitting close to the cycle: after a seemingly endless see-saw of retaliation, equilibrium is at last restored in death.

In this final scene, Samson achieves a heroic status that had previously eluded him. He does it not so much by his death (unless kamikaze pilots and suicidal Muslim terrorists are all heroes) as by his blindness. So at least it seems to a modern reader who cannot put out of his mind the poignancy of Milton's words:

> Oh dark, dark, dark amid the blaze of
> noon,
> Irrecoverably dark!

But Milton's portrayal in *Samson Agonistes*, whether seen as poetry, drama or theology, goes so far beyond anything in Judges 13-16 as to be no guide to the original. In spite of his moving final prayer, which is the only evidence that he had learned anything from his mistakes, Samson was no more a tragic hero than he was a sun myth. As an anthropological type, he is closest to the Wild Man of medieval Europe. As a literary figure, he is a (typically Hebrew) down-market version of Enkidu or Heracles.

RUTH

Introduction

The Book of Ruth is to be found in the Hebrew Bible in a group of five 'scrolls', including Esther and the Song of Songs, which were read at each of the five major Jewish festivals. Ruth was read at the feast of Weeks, which marked the end of the harvest (cp. 2.23). The Greek translators (LXX) preferred to place it between Judges and Samuel, where it certainly fits well: its first verse links it to Judges and its last introduces the birth of David. Its portrayal of a peaceful and ordered, if strenuous, village life also contrasts happily with the anarchy of Judges and with the violence which surrounded David's rise to power. But it is not a work of history, rather a historical romance, to be read with a smile. Its heroine belongs with Tamar of Gen 38 (who is specifically named in 4.12) as a virtuous woman who will nevertheless go to unorthodox lengths in order to secure the continuation of the family name. As its position in the Hebrew Bible shows, Ruth is a late work, but the author tells her story in the very best tradition. It has a higher proportion (c.60%) of speech than any other OT book.

The Authorised Version has been kept for this book, partly for the sake of Ruth's famous speech in 1.16-17; but there are a number of places where it has to be corrected.

Naomi and Ruth in Trouble

1. 1 Now it came to pass in the days when the judges ruled, that there was a famine in the land. And a certain man of Bethlehemjudah went to sojourn in the country of Moab, he, and his wife, and his two sons. • And the name of the man was Elimelech, and the name of his wife Naomi, and the name of his two sons Mahlon and Chilion, Ephrathites of Bethlehemjudah. And they came into the country of Moab, and continued there. • And Elimelech Naomi's husband died; and she was left, and her two sons. • And they took them wives of the women of Moab; the name of the one was Orpah, and the name of the other Ruth: and they dwelled there about ten 5 years. • And Mahlon and Chilion died also both of them; and the woman was left of her two sons and her husband. • Then she arose with her daughters in law, that she might return from the country of Moab: for she had heard in the country of Moab how that the LORD had visited his people in giving them bread. • Wherefore she went forth out of the place where she was, and her two daughters in law with her; and they went on the way to return unto the land of Judah. ◆

Naomi and Ruth in Trouble

The opening verses (1-7) provide the background. *Famine* having struck the region of *Bethlehem*, a family of the *Ephrathite* clan decides to move to more fertile country which they can see from home across the Jordan valley. David similarly sent his parents to *Moab* for safety (1 Sam 22.3). The two sons married Moabite girls. No disapproval is expressed of this (contrast the case of Samson), but the names of the sons, which mean 'sickly' and 'weakling', fit their sterility and early deaths. The three women are thus left on their own, unprotected.

The central scene (8-18) introduces the pivot of the story, namely the custom whereby a widow is taken in marriage by her husband's next available kinsman. This custom, not confined to the Jews, was designed to ensure the preservation of the family, seen as descending through the male line. It had been invoked once

Naomi and Ruth in Trouble (cont.)

• And Naomi said unto her two daughters in law, Go, return each to her mother's house: the LORD deal kindly with you, as ye have dealt with the dead, and with me. • The LORD grant you that ye may find rest, each of you in the house of her husband. Then she kissed them; and they lifted up their voice, and wept. • And they said unto her, Surely we will return with thee unto thy people. • And Naomi said, Turn again, my daughters: why will ye go with me? are there yet any more sons in my womb, that they may be your husbands? • Turn again, my daughters, go your way; for I am too old to have an husband. If I should say, I have hope, if I should have an husband also to night, and should also bear sons; • would ye tarry for them till they were grown? would ye stay for them from having husbands? nay, my daughters; for it grieveth me much for your sakes that the hand of the LORD is gone out against me. • And they lifted up their voice, and wept again: and Orpah kissed her mother in law; but Ruth clave unto her.

• And she said, Behold, thy sister in law is gone back unto her people, and unto her gods: return thou after thy sister in law. • And Ruth said, Intreat me not to leave thee, or to return from following after thee: for whither thou goest, I will go; and where thou lodgest, I will lodge: thy people shall be my people, and thy God my God: • Where thou diest, will I die, and there will I be buried: the LORD do so to me, and more also, if ought but death part thee and me. • When she saw that she was stedfastly minded to go with her, then she left speaking unto her.

• So they two went until they came to Bethlehem. And it came to pass, when they were come to Bethlehem, that all the city was moved about them, and they said, Is this Naomi? • And she said unto them, Call me not Naomi, call me Mara: for the Almighty hath dealt very bitterly with me. • I went out full and the LORD hath brought me home again empty: why then call ye me Naomi, seeing the LORD hath testified against me, and the Almighty hath afflicted me?

• So Naomi returned, and Ruth the Moabitess, her daughter in law, with her, which returned out of the country of Moab: and they came to Bethlehem in the beginning of barley harvest.   (AV)

Naomi and Ruth in Trouble (cont.)

previously in the same family; see 4.12. Its importance in Ruth is underlined by *Naomi*'s lengthy explanation in 11-13, which includes an oblique reference (v.13 end) to the common ancient belief that one person's misfortune can rub off on another. Orpah then decides to leave, and incurs no disapproval; she is present in the story only as a foil for *Ruth*'s loyalty, so memorably expressed in 16-17. Family loyalty (or *kindness*, as AV here translates *hesedh*) is perhaps the central theme of the whole story, from its passing mention in 1.8 to the formal praise of 3.10.

In the third scene (19-22) we meet the women of Bethlehem, who come in here and at the end of the book (4.14-17) like a chorus in a Greek drama. In the Hebrew it is clear that they are women, and they (literally) buzz like bees at Naomi's return. She herself somewhat self-centredly laments her troubles with a typical word-play: *Naomi* can be translated 'my sweet', while *Mara* means 'bitter'. She then reveals a second axis of the story: from fulness to emptiness and back to fulness. The concept of emptiness includes not only famine but widowhood and barrenness, each of which will be rectified in turn. The last two words of the chapter give a skilful foretaste of what is to come.

Ruth Gleans in Boaz's Fields

2.1 And Naomi had a kinsman of her husband's, a mighty man of wealth, of the family of Elimelech; and his name was Boaz. • And Ruth the Moabitess said unto Naomi, Let me now go to the field, and glean ears of corn after him in whose sight I shall find grace. And she said unto her, Go, my daughter. • And she went, and came, and gleaned in the field after the reapers: and her hap was to light on a part of the field belonging unto Boaz, who was of the kindred of Elimelech. • And, behold, Boaz came from Bethlehem, and said unto the reapers, The LORD 5 be with you. And they answered him, The LORD bless thee. • Then said Boaz unto his servant that was set over the reapers, Whose damsel is this? • And the servant that was set over the reapers answered and said, It is the Moabitish damsel that came back with Naomi out of the country of Moab: • And she said, I pray you, let me glean and gather after the reapers among the sheaves: so she came, and hath continued even from the morning until now, that she tarried a little in the house.

• Then said Boaz unto Ruth, Hearest thou not, my daughter? Go not to glean in another field, neither go from hence, but abide here fast by my maidens: • Let thine eyes be on the field that they do reap, and go thou after them: have I not charged the young men that they shall not touch thee? and when thou art athirst, 10 go unto the vessels, and drink of that which the young men have drawn. • Then she fell on her face, and bowed herself to the ground, and said unto him, Why have I found grace in thine eyes, that thou shouldest take knowledge of me, seeing I am a stranger? • And Boaz answered and said unto her, It hath fully been shewed me, all that thou hast done unto thy mother in law since the death of thine husband: and how thou hast left thy father and thy mother, and the land of thy nativity, and art come unto a people which thou knewest not heretofore. • The LORD recompense thy work, and a full reward be given thee of the LORD God of Israel, under whose wings thou art come to trust. • Then she said, Let me find favour in thy sight, my lord; for that thou hast comforted me, and for that thou hast spoken friendly unto thine handmaid, though I be not like unto one of thine handmaidens. ▸

Ruth Gleans in Boaz's Fields

Ch.2 is also in three sections, of which the second is longest and most important. Verses 1-3 introduce first the hero, *Boaz*, rich but no longer young, then the context of gleaning, before bringing the two together by *hap*, and repeating the crucial fact that Boaz is a kinsman of Ruth's husband. The Hebrew law, like that of other ANE peoples, expressly encouraged the leaving of some part of the crop for 'the alien, the orphan and the widow' [Dt 24.19]. But it stopped short of a requirement, and permission had to be sought from the owner: hence the phrase in v.2 which is less misleadingly rendered in REB 'glean behind anyone who will allow me'. Gleaning was, for those in need, a matter of life and death, and we do wrong to treat this scene as a rural idyll.

The first exchanges between Boaz and Ruth are cleverly managed. He immediately asks about her, but in words which reveal his prime characteristic, a sense of responsibility. In such a society, a girl must belong to someone. When he learns who she is, he realises (though only in part) the irony of his question. He himself is, at least temporarily, responsible for her (hence *my daughter* in 8), and his first thought is to protect her from predators. The dangers to a young woman in the fields at harvest time were real enough (again, no idyll), and her safety was of concern both to him (8-9) and

Ruth Gleans in Boaz's Fields (cont.)

• And Boaz said unto her, 'At mealtime come thou hither, and eat of the bread, and dip thy morsel in the vinegar'. And she sat beside the reapers: and he reached her parched corn, and she did eat, and was sufficed, and left. • And when she was risen up to glean, Boaz commanded his young men, saying, Let her glean even among the sheaves, and reproach her not: • And let fall also some of the handfuls of purpose for her, and leave them, that she may glean them, and rebuke her not.

• So she gleaned in the field until even, and beat out that she had gleaned: and it was about an ephah of barley. • And she took it up, and went into the city: and her mother in law saw what she had gleaned: and she brought forth, and gave to her that she had reserved after she was sufficed. • And her mother in law said unto her, Where hast thou gleaned to day? and where wroughtest thou? blessed be he that did take knowledge of thee. And she shewed her mother in law with whom she had wrought, and said, The man's name with whom I wrought to day is Boaz. • And Naomi said unto her daughter in law, Blessed be he of the LORD, who hath not left off his kindness to the living and to the dead. And Naomi said unto her, The man is near of kin unto us, one of our next kinsmen. • And Ruth the Moabitess said, He said unto me also, Thou shalt keep fast by my young men, until they have ended all my harvest. • And Naomi said unto Ruth her daughter in law, It is good, my daughter, that thou go out with his maidens, that they meet thee not in any other field. • So she kept fast by the maidens of Boaz to glean unto the end of barley harvest and of wheat harvest; and dwelt with her mother in law.

(AV)

Ruth Gleans in Boaz's Fields (cont.)

subsequently to Naomi (v. 22, where the RSV is clearer: 'lest in another field you be molested').

Her surprised question in v.10 comes to the heart of the matter: she is only a foreigner, and he has 'taken notice' (REB) of her: why should he do so? In posing it she shows her own characteristic initiative. In this chapter, it was she who suggested the gleaning expedition, and her persistence in it surprised even the foreman (v.7, where RSV has the better text: ' . . . until now, without resting a moment'). Boaz's answer is intriguing, for he says not a word of their kinship. Instead he praises her (11) in terms which in part remind the audience of the famous call of Abraham (Gen 12.1) and then blesses her (12) in words which contain further irony. For it is he himself who will in the end *reward* her, and the word translated *wings* is also used for his 'skirt' in 3.9. In her brief speech of thanks (13)

the opening words are better rendered by RSV: 'You are most gracious to me, my lord'. Finally (14-16) Boaz goes well beyond the claims of anything but the kinship which he does not yet acknowledge. The niceties of gleaning conventions were important, and his generosity is well illustrated by a rabbinic ruling that gleaners were normally allowed only what fell by chance and not what the reaper dropped when his hand was pricked by a thorn or stung by a scorpion. The result was that Ruth went home laden. *An ephah* is 45 litres – a heavy load for a woman, but we knew Ruth was strong.

Naomi was immediately suspicious (19) – once again Ruth's sexuality comes to the surface. But as soon as Ruth mentioned the name *Boaz*, Naomi recognised and praised the *kindness* of *the LORD* towards *the living and the dead*. Ruth is mystified, so Naomi explains (*and Naomi said*): Boaz is *one of our next kinsmen*. The Hebrew word she uses there is usu-

Ruth Gleans in Boaz's Fields (cont.)

ally translated redeemer*. By Jewish custom, when a man died his next of kin had two duties. The first, which concerns Naomi here, was to take his widow and 'raise seed' to him posthumously by her. The second, which was also a right, was to buy back any property sold out of the family. These customs, designed to preserve the family and its inheritance, will prove crucial to the whole story of Ruth.

Meanwhile Boaz has invited her to go on gleaning for the remaining seven weeks between the beginning of the barley and the end of the wheat harvest. The change from *young men* in v.21 to *maidens* in vv.22-3 is probably not significant: the point is that she must stay with *his* people. But the hint in the last words of v.23 is not to be missed: we must wait a little longer for the other *harvest*.

The Threshing Floor at Night

3.1 Then Naomi her mother in law said unto her, My daughter, shall I not seek rest for thee, that it may be well with thee? • And now is not Boaz of our kindred, with whose maidens thou wast? Behold, he winnoweth barley to night in the threshingfloor. • Wash thyself therefore, and anoint thee, and put thy raiment upon thee, and get thee down to the floor: but make not thyself known unto the man, until he shall have done eating and drinking. • And it shall be, when he lieth down, that thou shalt mark the place where he shall lie, and thou shalt go in, and uncover his feet, and lay thee down; and he will tell thee what thou shalt do.
5 • And she said unto her, All that thou sayest unto me I will do.

• And she went down unto the floor, and did according to all that her mother in law bade her. • And when Boaz had eaten and drunk, and his heart was merry, he went to lie down at the end of the heap of corn: and she came softly, and uncovered his feet, and laid her down. • And it came to pass at midnight, that the man was afraid, and turned himself: and, behold, a woman lay at his feet. • And he said, Who art thou? And she answered, I am Ruth thine handmaid: spread
10 therefore thy skirt over thine handmaid; for thou art a near kinsman. • And he said, Blessed be thou of the LORD, my daughter: for thou hast shewed more kindness in the latter end than at the beginning, inasmuch as thou followedst not young men, whether poor or rich. • And now, my daughter, fear not; I will ◗

The Threshing Floor at Night

But Naomi could not wait. Desiring *rest,* i.e. serenity for Ruth (n.b. the word is picked up in the last verse of the chapter), she proposes a stratagem. The *threshingfloor* is a flat piece of beaten earth, usually circular (in Greece it was the home of drama, originally performed to celebrate the harvest). Situated on a slope below the hilltop village (*down, v.*3), it caught the steady evening breeze which was needed for winnowing. The threshed barley was thrown into the air, which blew away the chaff, leaving the grain to fall to the ground. And the master would sleep beside it until it was moved to his barns.

Naomi's scheme is reminiscent of Tamar's (4.12) in Gen 38. But where the earlier story is explicit, this is delicate and sensitive. *Feet* is a standard euphemism in Hebrew for sexual parts, and the use of *turned* in v.8 suggests that Ruth was in fact lying *beside* him. But the uncertainty is appropriate to the discretion of this story, and should not be violated. At first they are just *the man* and *a woman* (8). Then she identifies herself and invites him,

The Threshing Floor at Night (cont.)

do to thee all that thou requirest: for all the city of my people doth know that thou art a virtuous woman. • And now it is true that I am thy near kinsman: howbeit there is a kinsman nearer than I. • Tarry this night, and it shall be in the morning, that if he will perform unto thee the part of a kinsman, well; let him do the kinsman's part: but if he will not do the part of a kinsman to thee, then will I do the part of a kinsman to thee, as the LORD liveth: lie down until the morning. • And she lay at his feet until the morning: and she rose up before one could know another. And

5   he said, Let it not be known that a woman came into the floor. • Also he said, Bring the vail that thou hast upon thee, and hold it. And when she held it, he measured six measures of barley, and laid it on her: and she went into the city.

• And when she came to her mother in law, she said, Who art thou, my daughter? And she told her all that the man had done to her. • And she said, These six measures of barley gave he me; for he said to me, Go not empty unto thy mother in law. • Then said she, Sit still, my daughter, until thou know how the matter will fall: for the man will not be in rest, until he have finished the thing this day.   (AV)

The Threshing Floor at Night (cont.)

as her kinsman, to take her under his protection, quoting the very metaphor which he had used of God's protection in 2.12.

His reply begins, as in 2.11, with words of respectful praise: loyal to Naomi before, she has now shown even greater loyalty (*hesedh*) to Elimelech and Mahlon, by putting her duty to them before any natural inclination to seek a younger husband. And his praise in 3.11 actually puts her on an equality with himself: she is *a virtuous woman*, just as he in 2.1 was a *man of wealth*, the same Hebrew adjective being used in both cases. Now first he admits his kinship – and then springs a surprise on us all by revealing the exist-

ence of a *nearer kinsman* with prior claim. His own embarrassment is shown by his repetitiveness, but his care for Ruth continues. He is concerned for her protection (*tarry this night*) and for the reputations of both of them: she is to leave before there is enough light for her to be recognised (14). When she left he gave her more barley. In this respect at least she must not *go empty* (17) and the size of the gift suggests compensation. *Vail* in v.15 has nothing to do with avoiding recognition; REB translates 'cloak'. Naomi's question to Ruth on her return echoes that of Boaz in v.9, but in v.16 it carries the implication which is brought out by RSV's 'how did you fare?'

Boaz Marries Ruth

4.1 Then went Boaz up to the gate, and sat him down there: and, behold, the kinsman of whom Boaz spake came by; unto whom he said, Ho, such a one! turn aside, sit down here. And he turned aside, and sat down. • And he took ten men of the elders of the city, and said, Sit ye down here. And they sat down. • And he said unto the kinsman, Naomi, that is come again out of the country of Moab, selleth a parcel of land, which was our brother Elimelech's: • And I thought to advertise thee, saying, Buy it before the inhabitants, and before the elders of my people. If thou wilt redeem it, redeem it: but if thou wilt not redeem it, then tell me, that I may know: for there is none to redeem it beside thee; and I am after thee. And he 5 said, I will redeem it. • Then said Boaz, What day thou buyest the field of the hand of Naomi, thou must buy it also of Ruth the Moabitess, the wife of the dead, to raise up the name of the dead upon his inheritance. • And the kinsman said, I cannot redeem it for myself, lest I mar mine own inheritance: redeem thou my right to thyself; for I cannot redeem it.

• Now this was the manner in former time in Israel concerning redeeming and concerning changing, for to confirm all things; a man plucked off his shoe, and gave it to his neighbour: and this was a testimony in Israel. • Therefore the kinsman said unto Boaz, Buy it for thee. So he drew off his shoe. • And Boaz said unto the elders, and unto all the people, Ye are witnesses this day, that I have bought all that was Elimelech's, and all that was Chilion's and Mahlon's, of the 10 hand of Naomi. • Moreover Ruth the Moabitess, the wife of Mahlon, have I purchased to be my wife, to raise up the name of the dead upon his inheritance, that the name of the dead be not cut off from among his brethren, and from the gate of his place: ye are witnesses this day. • And all the people that were in the gate, and the elders, said, We are witnesses. The LORD make the woman that is come into thine house like Rachel and like Leah, which two did build the house of Israel: and do thou worthily in Ephratah, and be famous in Bethlehem: • And let thy house be like the house of Pharez, whom Tamar bare unto Judah, of the seed which the LORD shall give thee of this young woman. ▸

Boaz Marries Ruth

Ch.4, like all the others, is divided into three scenes, of which the first is set in the gate of Bethlehem. The open space just inside the gate was the place of business (v.2) and of judgement; it is also the place where Boaz could catch his *kinsman* going out to work in the fields. The phrase *such an one* (= modern 'so-and-so') is used by the narrator (who 'breaks frame' also in v.7), not by Boaz: REB correctly renders: 'Calling him by name . . .'. Boaz then springs another surprise on us, by asking him first about the *land* to which he also had right of redemption.

Formal procedures for the taking of the widow, as set out in Deut 25, differ somewhat from what we are led to understand here; so does the ritual of the *sandal*. But the legal details in Ruth are clear enough for the purposes of the story, except for one thing: the Hebrew text of v.5 cannot be construed. Most modern translations follow a footnote alternative to it, in which the kinsman is asked not to *buy it* (the field) *of* (from) *Ruth* but to buy Ruth herself. This was too much for him: he would have bought the field – and for a moment at the end of v.4 our hearts were in our mouths – but if he took her to wife, the field would pass to her children, not his. And so the way is clear for Boaz.

There remains the puzzle why he asked

Boaz Marries Ruth (cont.)

• So Boaz took Ruth, and she was his wife: and when he went in unto her, the LORD gave her conception, and she bare a son. • And the women said unto Naomi, Blessed be the LORD, which hath not left thee this day without a kinsman, that his name may be famous in Israel. • And he shall be unto thee a restorer of thy life, and a nourisher of thine old age: for thy daughter in law, which loveth thee, which is better to thee than seven sons, hath born him. • And Naomi took the child, and laid it in her bosom, and became nurse unto it. • And the women her neighbours gave it a name, saying, There is a son born to Naomi; and they called his name Obed: he is the father of Jesse, the father of David.   (AV)

5

Boaz Marries Ruth (cont.)

first about the land. Unless the incident is inserted solely to increase the dramatic tension, it is telling us something about Boaz. Perhaps he wanted to divert any possible gossip about Ruth and himself. Or can it be that, admirable and and even attractive as he found Ruth, he did not really want her to wife? If so – and the reticence of Hebrew story-telling leaves this possibility open – her exploit at the threshing floor did not merely *hasten* her ultimate success: it was indispensable.

The elders, having acted as witnesses to the transaction, go on to offer a blessing of fertility to Boaz and Ruth. Their words serve to link this village wedding to the great history of the nation: for *Rachel* and *Leah* between them were ancestresses of all the tribes of Israel, and Rachel's tomb was still pointed out in *Bethlehem*. The wedding itself is briefly told, and then to round off the story we revert to Naomi and her concerns: her 'chorus' of Bethlehemite women, her special friendship with Ruth, and (the final scene) her own emptiness (1.12) filled with the unexpected joy of nursing her grandson. All is now happily resolved, with everyone a winner – except for a final explosive surprise in the postscript. The eye of history now looks forward, and reveals that this boy's grandson is to be none other than king *David*. The reader finally sees the full import of God's concern for the workaday fortunes of two poor widows.

The prominence of Naomi at the be-

ginning and end of the book (Ruth's son is actually called Naomi's son in v.17), coupled with her important behind-the-scenes role all through, has led some to see her as the central figure of the book. But in fact the structure of it points clearly to Ruth and her relationship to Boaz. Each chapter falls into three sections, of which the middle is the longest and most important; and at the core of each chapter are the verses which mark the progress:

1.11-12 no hope of a kinsman-husband for Ruth

2.10 Boaz 'takes notice of' Ruth

3.9 Ruth offers herself to Boaz in the 'nuit blanche'

4.13 Boaz and Ruth consummate the marriage.

The reader's interest is held throughout by the reversal of the normal roles: here 'girl gets boy'. For this the custom of next-of-kin marriage provides the ideal setting, almost the excuse. If the author had any purposes beyond those of (i) telling a good story which (ii) commends family loyalty and (iii) illustrates God's care for his people, it may lie in (iv) the motif of a marriage to a Moabite woman. At various times in Jewish history such marriages were the subject of public disapproval (see esp. Ezra [9.12 and Ch.10]), and any story which had David descended from such a union would be bound to be used in the controversy. But that motif does not play a major part in our narrative.

THE FIRST BOOK OF SAMUEL

Introduction

The two books known to us as those of Samuel were originally one single book. The Jews themselves called it the Book of Samuel, even though Samuel himself scarcely appears outside the first quarter of the whole. The Septuagint kept the two books distinct but associated them with the two books of Kings as the four books of Reigns. This is a sensible classification, for the separation between 2 Samuel and 1 Kings is very arbitrary. But if one is going to be thorough, one ought to bring into the picture also the books of Joshua and Judges. These six books (known to scholars as the deuteronomic history or DtH) form part of a long continuous narrative which covers a period of about 600 years from the emergence of the Israelites in Palestine until the end of the monarchy.

The books of Samuel tell the story of the rise of a monarchy in Israel. First Saul becomes king of the northern tribes, then David of northern and southern together. That story accords with the evidence of Palestinian archaeology. The Israelites in the hill-country gradually developed as a nation, with villages growing and then coalescing into towns. Eventually the point was reached where population, wealth and organization were adequate to support a king and an army able to challenge the Philistines of the coastal strip. Saul may plausibly be dated c.1025 BC.

Ch.10 of 1 Samuel preserves a convincing account of Saul's election to office by the people. But that account is swamped by the religious concerns of the DtH, who introduces a whole set of theological cross-currents. The theology focuses on the person of Samuel, who thus becomes the central figure of the story. Not only is he the king-maker. He is also presented as the first of the great prophets, that long succession of men who so often stood out against the policy of the reigning king. There is thus an inherently ambivalent

attitude to the monarchy. This is visible at many places in the text, and scholars have in consequence been tempted to analyse the first half (Chs 1-15) of 1 Samuel into two main sources, one favourable and one hostile to the monarchy.

But the story is a good deal more complicated than that. Overlying the ambivalence towards the monarchy is a further tension in Samuel's personal relations with Saul. In the text as we have it Samuel was only gradually converted to the institution of the monarchy. His change of heart is quickened by the promise of the young Saul. But as time goes on he finds that he has to distinguish between Saul as friend and Saul as king. His duty finally requires him in spite of his friendship to act as God's agent in rejecting Saul as king. The resulting cross-currents of feeling and policy are handled with some skill by the final editor. Not that he succeeds in producing a smoothly running narrative where the signposts are clear. But up to a point the rough edges – the repetitions and contradictions – faithfully represent rough times, when the whole operation is still on a small enough scale for private feelings and public policy to influence one another.

The same kind of roughness and tension continues into the second half (Chs16-end) of 1 Samuel, which describes the public and private relations of Saul and David. Here again some of the stories have obvious pro-David colouring, while others are neutral or even pro-Saul. There may once have existed a fullish narrative of Saul's reign, which was gradually squeezed or modified by later tradition in favour of Samuel as the first prophet or of David as founder of the monarchy. But in the text as we have it all the traditions are present. They have been preserved in this selection and can easily be detected by the perceptive reader.

The whole book of 1 Samuel thus supplies the raw material both of 'the tragedy of King Saul' and of 'the rise of King David'. The rawness of this story, compared with that of David's reign and the succession (2 Sam 3-1 Kings 2), is like that of Michelangelo's giant Prisoners compared with the smooth finish of his David.

And strangely the text of the Hebrew mss (MT) is also much less polished here than usual. Scholars have long used some of the Greek mss (LXX) to supplement or correct it, and now some Hebrew fragments from Qumran* have come along to support them in doing so.

The Birth and Childhood of Samuel

.1 There was a certain man from Ramathaim, a Zuphite from the hill-country of Ephraim, named Elkanah son of Jeroham, son of Elihu, son of Tohu, son of Zuph an Ephraimite. • He had two wives, Hannah and Peninnah; Peninnah had children, but Hannah was childless. • Every year this man went up from his town to worship and offer sacrifice to the LORD of Hosts at Shiloh, where Eli's two sons, Hophni and Phinehas, were priests of the LORD.

5 • When Elkanah sacrificed, he gave several shares of the meat to his wife Peninnah with all her sons and daughters; • but to Hannah he gave only one share; the LORD had not granted her children, yet it was Hannah whom Elkanah loved. • Hannah's rival also used to torment and humiliate her because she had no children. • This happened year after year when they went up to the house of the LORD; her rival used to torment her, until she was in tears and would not eat. • Her husband Elkanah said to her, 'Hannah, why are you crying and eating nothing? Why are you so miserable? Am I not more to you than ten sons?'

9-10 • After they had finished eating and drinking at the sacrifice at Shiloh, Hannah rose in deep distress, and weeping bitterly stood before the LORD and prayed to him. Meanwhile Eli the priest was sitting on his seat beside the door of the temple of the LORD. • Hannah made this vow: 'LORD of Hosts, if you will only take notice of my trouble and remember me, if you will not forget me but grant me offspring, then I shall give the child to the LORD for the whole of his life, and no razor shall ever touch his head.'   ▸

The Birth and Childhood of Samuel

The book opens in the atmosphere of simple family piety which has always been the glory of Judaism. That bright mood is first highlighted by the contrasting wickedness of the sons of Eli, and then overshadowed by the loss of the Ark.

Shiloh, where the scene is set, was one of the most important shrines of Israel. At that time it housed the Ark, the oldest symbol of YHWH (for which see 1 K 8.7+). The Ark stood in the innermost room of the shrine, with a light burning before it. In front was the central room (*before the LORD*, v.9), into which a doorway (10) led from the courtyard. In the courtyard was the altar of sacrifice, and round it the

other rooms of the temple e.g. Eli's bedroom, public dining rooms etc.

To Shiloh the families of the region went at least once a year to celebrate the harvest festival. They brought with them an animal to *sacrifice*, after which the family partook of a common meal. To be *childless* was felt as a mark of God's disfavour. Hence Hannah's wretchedness, for which her husband offers impotent consolation; hence perhaps also the silence, contrary to usual Hebrew practice, of her prayer. The *vow* with which she accompanies it reminds the reader of Samson's mother's vow. By contrast with Hannah's innocence, Eli is first censorious (14), then pompously

The Birth and Childhood of Samuel (cont.)

1.13   • For a long time she went on praying before the LORD, while Eli watched her lips. • Hannah was praying silently; her lips were moving although her voice could not be heard, and Eli took her for a drunken woman. • 'Enough of this drunken behaviour!' 15 he said to her. 'Leave off until the effect of the wine has gone.' • 'Oh, sir!' she answered, 'I am a heart-broken woman; I have drunk neither wine nor strong drink, but I have been pouring out my feelings before the LORD. • Do not think me so devoid of shame, sir; all this time I have been speaking out of the depths of my grief and misery.' • Eli said, 'Go in peace, and may the God of Israel grant what you have asked of him.' • Hannah replied, 'May I be worthy of your kindness.' And no longer downcast she went away and had something to eat.

    • Next morning they were up early and, after prostrating themselves before the LORD, returned to their home at Ramah. Elkanah had intercourse with his wife 20 Hannah, and the LORD remembered her; • she conceived, and in due time bore a son, whom she named Samuel, 'because', she said, 'I asked the LORD for him'.

    • Elkanah with his whole household went up to make the annual sacrifice to the LORD and to keep his vow. • Hannah did not go; she said to her husband, 'After the child is weaned I shall come up with him to present him before the LORD; then he is to stay there always.' • Her husband Elkanah said to her, 'Do what you think best; stay at home until you have weaned him. Only, may the LORD indeed see your vow fulfilled.' So the woman stayed behind and nursed her son until she had weaned him.

    • When she had weaned him, she took him up with her. She took also a bull three years old, an ephah of flour, and a skin of wine, and she brought him, child as he was, 25 into the house of the LORD at Shiloh. • When the bull had been slaughtered, Hannah brought the boy to Eli • and said, 'Sir, as sure as you live, I am the woman who stood here beside you praying to the LORD. • It was this boy that I prayed for and the LORD has granted what I asked. • Now I make him over to the LORD; for his whole life he is lent to the LORD.' And they prostrated themselves there before the LORD.

2.11   Then Elkanah went home to Ramah, but the boy remained behind in the service 18 of the LORD under Eli the priest. • Samuel continued in the service of the LORD, a mere boy with a linen ephod fastened round him. • Every year his mother made him a little cloak and took it to him when she went up with her husband to offer the annual 20 sacrifice. • Eli would give his blessing to Elkanah and his wife and say, 'The LORD grant you children by this woman in place of the one whom you made over to the LORD.' Then they would return home. • The LORD showed his care for Hannah, and she conceived and gave birth to three sons and two daughters; meanwhile the boy Samuel grew up in the presence of the LORD.   (REB)

The Birth and Childhood of Samuel (cont.)

awards her success without even asking what she is praying for (17). As often, none of the men comes out of it well.

    The name given to the child (20) presents a puzzle. *Samuel* means not *I asked the LORD* but 'the name of the LORD'. The name most naturally suggested by the word *asked* (v.20, and twice in v.27) is not Samuel but Saul. But nobody knows

what inference to draw from this. The following year when the feast came round, *Elkanah went up* to Shiloh without Hannah and confirmed the vow on her behalf (21). She herself waited a few years till Samuel was *weaned*, and then took him up herself to do as she had vowed, i.e. to have him brought up *in the service of the LORD under Eli.*

The Call of Samuel

21 When Eli, now a very old man, heard a detailed account of how his sons were treating all the Israelites, and how they lay with the women who were serving at the entrance to the Tent of Meeting, • he said to them, 'Why do you do such things? I hear from every quarter how wickedly you behave. • Do stop it, my sons; for this is not a good report that I hear spreading among the Lord's people. • If someone sins against another, God will intervene; but if someone sins against the Lord, who can intercede for him?' They would not listen, however, to their father's rebuke, for the Lord meant to bring about their death. • The young Samuel, as he grew up, increasingly commended himself to the Lord and to the people.

3. 1   • The boy Samuel was in the Lord's service under Eli. In those days the word of the Lord was rarely heard, and there was no outpouring of vision. • One night Eli, whose eyes were dim and his sight failing, was lying down in his usual place, • while Samuel slept in the temple of the Lord where the Ark of God was. Before the lamp of God had gone out, • the Lord called him, and Samuel answered, 5 'Here I am!' • and ran to Eli saying, 'You called me: here I am.' 'No, I did not call you,' said Eli; 'lie down again.' So he went and lay down. • The Lord called Samuel again, and he got up and went to Eli. 'Here I am!' he said. 'Surely you called me.' 'I did not call, my son,' he answered; 'lie down again.' • Samuel had not yet come to know the Lord, and the word of the Lord had not been disclosed to him. • When the Lord called him for the third time, he again went to Eli and said, 'Here I am! You did call me.' Then Eli understood that it was the Lord calling the boy; • he told Samuel to go and lie down and said, 'If someone calls once more, say, "Speak, Lord; your servant is listening." ' So Samuel went and lay down in his place.

10   • Then the Lord came, and standing there called, 'Samuel, Samuel!' as before. Samuel answered, 'Speak, your servant is listening.' • The Lord said, 'Soon I shall do something in Israel which will ring in the ears of all who hear it. • When that day comes I shall make good every word from beginning to end that I have spoken against Eli and his family. • You are to tell him that my judgement on his house will stand for ever because he knew of his sons' blasphemies against God and did not restrain them.'

15   • Samuel lay down till morning, when he opened the doors of the house of the Lord; but he was afraid to tell Eli about the vision. • Eli called Samuel: 'Samuel, my son!' he said; and Samuel answered, 'Here I am!' • Eli asked, 'What did the Lord say to you? Do not hide it from me. God's curse upon you if you conceal from me one word of all that he said to you.' • Then Samuel told him everything, concealing nothing. Eli said, 'The Lord must do what is good in his eyes.'   ▶

The Call of Samuel

The innocence of young Samuel, already wearing the priestly garment, is now intercut for contrast with the corruption of Eli's sons; and Hannah's support to her son is similarly contrasted with Eli's feebleness as a father. The house of Eli is doomed: the future lies with Samuel.

The narrative of his call is masterly. The folk-tale motif of 'third time lucky' is coloured by vivid details of time and place, and also of character. The young Samuel humanly mistakes God's voice for Eli's. The scene is closed by Eli's words (18), which express the weariness

The Call of Samuel (cont.)

3.19 • As Samuel grew up, the LORD was with him, and none of his words went unfulfilled. • From Dan to Beersheba, all Israel recognised that Samuel was attested as a prophet of the LORD. • So the LORD continued to appear in Shiloh, because he had revealed himself there to Samuel.

4. 1 • Samuel's word had authority throughout Israel. (REB)

The Call of Samuel (cont.)

of the old man as well as the obedience of the priest.

With Samuel, a new kind of spiritual *authority* enters Israel. The story of his call is introduced with two technical terms of the prophetic tradition: *the word of the* LORD and *vision*. The implication, made explicit in 3.20, is that Samuel is the first to be called as *a prophet of the* LORD. Henceforward for many centuries the prophets will be the chief channels of God's word.

The People's Demand for a King

7.15 Samuel acted as judge in Israel as long as he lived, • and every year went on circuit to Bethel, Gilgal, and Mizpah; he dispensed justice at all these places. • But always he went back to Ramah; that was his home and the place from which he governed Israel, and there he built an altar to the LORD.

8. 1 • When Samuel grew old, he appointed his sons to be judges in Israel. • The eldest son was called Joel and the second Abiah; they acted as judges in Beersheba. • His sons did not follow their father's ways but were intent on their own profit, taking bribes and perverting the course of justice. • So all the elders of Israel met, 5 and came to Samuel at Ramah. • They said to him, 'You are now old and your sons do not follow your ways; appoint us a king to rule us, like all the other nations.' • But their request for a king displeased Samuel. He prayed to the LORD, • and the LORD told him, 'Listen to the people and all that they are saying; they have not rejected you, it is I whom they have rejected, I whom they will not have to be their king. • Hear what they have to say now, but give them a solemn warning and tell them what sort of king will rule them.' ▸

The People's Demand for a King

The next three chapters [4-6] contain the story of the capture of the Ark by the Philistines, which marked the lowest point in Israel's fortunes. Verses [2-14] of Ch.7 tell of Samuel's leadership against them. In that chapter he is treated as being judge over Israel in the extended sense familiar from the book of Judges, i.e. as being not only judicial but civil and even military leader of the community; and the same interpretation underlies the logic of 8.5.

The story of Ch.8 is interesting but difficult. It may well be that a prophet played a key role in establishing Saul as the first king of Israel, and that there was from the start some opposition in princi-

The People's Demand for a King (cont.)

• Samuel reported to the people who were asking him for a king all that the LORD had said to him. 'This will be the sort of king who will bear rule over you,' he said. 'He will take your sons and make them serve in his chariots and with his cavalry, and they will run before his chariot. • Some he will appoint officers over units of a thousand and units of fifty. Others will plough his fields and reap his harvest; others again will make weapons of war and equipment for the chariots. • He will take your daughters for perfumers, cooks, and bakers. • He will seize the best of your fields, vineyards, and olive groves, and give them to his courtiers. 5 • He will take a tenth of your grain and your vintage to give to his eunuchs and courtiers. • Your slaves, both men and women, and the best of your cattle and your donkeys he will take for his own use. • He will take a tenth of your flocks, and you yourselves will become his slaves. • There will come a day when you will cry out against the king whom you have chosen; but the LORD will not answer you on that day.'

• The people, however, refused to listen to Samuel. 'No,' they said, 'we must 20 have a king over us; • then we shall be like other nations, with a king to rule us, to lead us out to war and fight our battles.' • When Samuel heard what the people had decided, he told the LORD, • who said, 'Take them at their word and appoint them a king.' Samuel then dismissed all the Israelites to their homes.   (REB)

The People's Demand for a King (cont.)

ple to the monarchy. As presented here, Samuel himself first shared the reservations of principle, then overcame them, but finally came to be critical of Saul's actual conduct of affairs.

The principle at stake is crystallised in the words *like other nations* in vv.5 and 20. *The people* argue that the greater strength of Israel's neighbours lies in their possession of a hereditary monarchy: it is a matter not of prestige but of efficiency, especially in war (20). The objection is made at two levels. The first is theological (7). God was himself regarded as king over Israel: in Gideon's words 'I shall not rule over you, nor will my son; the LORD will rule over you' [Jg 8.23]. The second objection is pragmatic: a glance at foreign countries will show them how kings behave (11-17). The description of the behaviour is quite general and reads like part of a satire on monarchy from Egyptian Wisdom literature.

There remains a hint in vv.6-7 that Samuel has a third objection. One can read between the lines that he feels himself personally *rejected* by the people's request, but is overruled by the LORD. *Not you* in v.7 is to be taken, in accordance with standard Hebrew idiom, to mean 'not so much you'. Indeed by the end of the scene Samuel has managed to lose face both with the people and with God. But it is primarily God who has been rejected, and his tone in vv.7-9 and 22 bodes ill: in effect he says 'I'll show them!' (Gunn).

Samuel Anoints Saul

9. 1 There was a man from the territory of Benjamin, whose name was Kish. He was a man of substance, • and had a son named Saul, a young man in his prime; there was no better man among the Israelites than he. He stood a head taller than any of the people.

• One day some donkeys belonging to Saul's father Kish had strayed, so he said to his son Saul, 'Take one of the servants with you, and go and look for the donkeys.' • They crossed the hill-country of Ephraim and went through the district of Shalisha but did not find them; they passed through the district of Shaalim but they were not there; they passed through the district of Benjamin but again 5 did not find them. • When they reached the district of Zuph, Saul said to the servant who was with him, 'Come, we ought to turn back, or my father will stop thinking about the donkeys and begin to worry about us.' • The servant answered, 'There is a man of God in this town who has a great reputation, because everything he says comes true. Suppose we go there; he may tell us which way to take.' • Saul said, 'If we go, what shall we offer him? There is no food left in our packs and we have no present to give the man of God, nothing at all.' • The servant answered him again, 'Wait! I have here a quarter-shekel of silver. I can give that to the man, to tell us the way.' • Saul said, 'Good! Let us go to him.' So 10 they went to the town where the man of God lived. • (In Israel in days gone by, when someone wished to consult God, he would say, 'Let us go to the seer.' For what is nowadays called a prophet used to be called a seer.)

• As they were going up the ascent to the town they met some girls coming out to draw water and asked them, 'Shall we find the seer there?' • 'Yes,' they answered, 'he is ahead of you; hurry now, for he has just arrived in the town because there is a feast at the shrine today. • As you enter the town you will meet him before he goes up to the shrine to eat; the people will not start until he comes, for he has to bless the sacrifice before the invited company can eat. Go up now, and you will find him at once.' • So they went up to the town and, just as they were going in, there was Samuel coming towards them on his way up to the shrine.

15 • The day before Saul's arrival there, the LORD had disclosed his intention to Samuel: • 'At this time tomorrow', he said, 'I shall send you a man from the territory of Benjamin, and you are to anoint him prince over my people Israel. He will deliver my people from the Philistines; for I have seen the sufferings of my people, and their cry has reached my ears.' • The moment Saul appeared the LORD said to Samuel, 'Here is the man of whom I spoke to you. This man will govern my people.' • Saul came up to Samuel in the gateway and said, 'Tell me, please, where the seer lives.' • Samuel replied, 'I am the seer. Go on ahead of me to the shrine and eat with me today; in the morning I shall set you on your way, after telling you what you have 20 on your mind. • Trouble yourself no more about the donkeys lost three days ago; they have been found. To whom does the tribute of all Israel belong? It belongs to you and to your whole ancestral house.' • 'But I am a Benjamite,' said Saul, 'from the smallest of the tribes of Israel, and my family is the least important of all the families of the tribe of Benjamin. Why do you say this to me?'

• Samuel brought Saul and his servant into the dining-hall and gave them a place at the head of the invited company, about thirty in number. • He said to the cook, 'Bring the portion that I gave you and told you to put on one side.'

Samuel Anoints Saul (cont.)

4 • The cook took up the whole haunch and leg and put it before Saul; and Samuel said, 'Here is the portion of meat kept for you. Eat it: it has been reserved for you at this feast to which I have invited the people.'

5 Saul dined with Samuel that day, • and when they came down from the shrine to the town a bed was spread on the roof for Saul, and he stayed there that night. • At dawn Samuel called to Saul on the roof, 'Get up, and I shall set you on your way.' When Saul rose, he and Samuel went outside together, • and as they came to the edge of the town, Samuel said to Saul, 'Tell the boy to go on ahead.' He did so; then Samuel said, 'Stay here a moment, and I shall tell you what God has said.'

1 • Samuel took a flask of oil and poured it over Saul's head; he kissed him and said, 'The LORD anoints you prince over his people Israel. You are to rule the people of the LORD and deliver them from the enemies round about. You will receive a sign that the LORD has anointed you prince to govern his possession.'   (REB)

Samuel Anoints Saul

With Ch.9 the tone changes again to one of unproblematic success. Samuel, Saul and the LORD (17) are now advancing in friendly concert towards a providential goal. Nor can the lighter tone be ascribed simply to the fact that what Saul now becomes is not a king but a *prince* (9.16; 10.1).

The story of the lad who lost his donkeys but found a kingdom has all the appeal of a popular folk-tale. A series of surprises and coincidences lead to the quest achieved, fortune reversed and humility elevated (contrast what Saul says of his family in v.21 with what the narrator told us in v.2). One large coincidence – that Saul happens to consult Samuel, who is just at that moment expecting him on another matter – incorporates other smaller ones; see especially vv.12-14 and 18. The folk-tale origin of the story is also betrayed by the fact that the city is not named at all, nor is Samuel himself until v.14. By contrast the hero Saul is given an imposing introduction, complete with genealogy (1-2). The surprises include the fact that Saul found a specially invited company at the *feast* and a specially reserved *haunch* of meat.

The coincidences and surprises are of course presented by the narrator as part of God's providence, of which he gives some rather heavy hints (19b and 20b). Nevertheless the theology of the story, unlike that of Ch.8, is only a thin overlay. Samuel himself is initially portrayed as a local seer, a man whom one consults for a fee (8) about strayed animals. Hence the awkwardness of the transition in v.20 from the asses to the kingdom, i.e. from Samuel as seer to Samuel as prophet.

As to the topography, we must imagine a walled *town* on a hill-side. The merrily prattling girls are going down from it to the valley to *draw water*. Saul passes them on his way up; then, as he enters the gate (18), he meets Samuel coming out on his way to the *shrine* on the hill-top. Samuel tells Saul to *go on* up first (probably as a mark of honour), then joins him at the shrine and invites him to the room set aside for sacrificial feasts (22).

The legend of Saul's anointing is no more historical than the folk-tale of the lost asses into which it has been (in other respects skilfully) woven. When the monarchy finally came to be regarded as a divine institution, it became desirable to legitimise it by a symbolic story of how the first prophet anointed the first king – indeed the first two kings, for a similar story is told of Samuel and David in Ch.16.

Saul Acclaimed King

10.17 Samuel summoned the Israelites to the LORD at Mizpah • and said to them, 'This
is the word of the LORD the God of Israel: I brought Israel up from Egypt; I
delivered you from the Egyptians and from all the kingdoms that oppressed you.
• But today you have rejected your God who saved you from all your misery and
distress; you have said, "No, set a king over us." Therefore take up your positions now before the LORD tribe by tribe and clan by clan.'

20   • Samuel presented all the tribes of Israel, and Benjamin was picked by lot.
• Then he presented the tribe of Benjamin, family by family, and the family of Matri
was picked. He presented the family of Matri, man by man, and Saul son of Kish
was picked; but when search was made he was not to be found. • They went on
to ask the LORD, 'Will the man be coming?' The LORD answered, 'There he is,
hiding among the baggage.' • So some ran and fetched him out, and as he took
his stand among the people, he was a head taller than anyone else. • Samuel said
to the people, 'Look at the man whom the LORD has chosen; there is no one like
him in this whole nation.' They all acclaimed him, shouting, 'Long live the king!'

25   • Samuel explained to the people the nature of a king, and made a written
record of it on a scroll which he deposited before the LORD. He then dismissed
them to their homes. • Saul too went home to Gibeah, and with him went some
fighting men whose hearts God had moved. • But there were scoundrels who
said, 'How can this fellow deliver us?' They thought nothing of him and brought
him no gifts.   (REB)

Saul Acclaimed King

The latter part of Ch.10 contains a second, far more complex and ambiguous,
version of Saul's appointment as *king* (n.b.
not 'prince' here). Its anti-monarchical
tendency carries forward that of Ch.8.
Samuel is again hostile in principle yet
dominant in the proceedings. There are
strong signs of contempt for Saul (explicit
in v.27, implicit in v.22), which are not obliterated by v.23-26.

But the most interesting new twist lies
in what might be called the democratic
tendency, which from now on plays an
increasing part in the story. Two separate
democratic procedures are visible here:
the lot and the acclamation (24). The role
of *the people* is treated by the narrator as
merely confirmatory; but they will recur
as an important force at crucial moments
in Saul's career (14.45 and 15.24).

Saul's Wars against the Philistines

13.1 Saul was thirty years old when he became king, and he reigned over Israel for
twenty-two years.

19   • No blacksmith was to be found in the whole of Israel, for the Philistines
were determined to prevent the Hebrews from making swords and spears. • The
Israelites had all to go down to the Philistines for their ploughshares, mattocks,
axes, and sickles to be sharpened. • The charge was two thirds of a shekel for
ploughshares and mattocks, and one third of a shekel for sharpening the axes and
pointing the goads. • So when war broke out the followers of Saul and Jonathan
had neither sword nor spear; only Saul and Jonathan carried arms.

23   • The Philistines had posted a company of troops to hold the pass of Michmash,
14.1 • and one day Saul's son Jonathan said to his armour-bearer, 'Come, let us go
over to the Philistine outpost across there.' He did not tell his father, • who at ◆

Saul's Wars against the Philistines (cont.)

.6 the time had his tent under the pomegranate tree at Migron on the outskirts of Gibeah; with him were about six hundred men.

• Jonathan said to his armour-bearer, 'Let us go and pay a visit to the post of the uncircumcised yonder. Perhaps the LORD will do something for us. Nothing can stop him from winning a victory, by many or by few.' • The armour-bearer answered, 'Do what you will, go ahead; I am with you whatever you do.' • Jonathan said, 'We shall cross over and let the men see us. • If they say, "Stay there till we come to you," then we shall stay where we are and not go up to 10 them. • But if they say, "Come up to us," we shall go up; that will be the proof that the LORD has given them into our power.' • The two showed themselves to the Philistine outpost. 'Look!' said the Philistines. 'Hebrews coming out of the holes where they have been hiding!' • And they called across to Jonathan and his armour-bearer, 'Come up to us; we shall show you something.' Jonathan said to the armour-bearer, 'Come on, the LORD has put them into Israel's power.' • Jonathan climbed up on hands and feet, and the armour-bearer followed him. The Philistines fell before Jonathan, and the armour-bearer, coming behind, dispatched them. • In that first attack Jonathan and his armour-bearer killed about 15 twenty of them, like men cutting a furrow across a half-acre field. • Terror spread throughout the army in the camp and in the field; the men at the post and the raiding parties were terrified. The very ground quaked, and there was great panic.

16 • Saul's men on the watch in Gibeah of Benjamin saw the mob of Philistines 20 surging to and fro in confusion. • Then Saul and all his men made a concerted rush for the battlefield, where they found the enemy in complete disorder, every man's sword against his fellow. • Those Hebrews who up to now had been under the Philistines, and had been with them in camp, changed sides and joined the Israelites under Saul and Jonathan. • When all the Israelites in hiding in the hill-country of Ephraim heard that the Philistines were in flight, they also joined in and set off in close pursuit. • That day the LORD delivered Israel, and the fighting passed on beyond Beth-aven.

• The Israelites had been driven to exhaustion on that day. Saul had issued this warning to the troops: 'A curse on any man who takes food before ▶

Saul's Wars against the Philistines

Chs.11-14 of 1 Samuel are in a disordered state. What is clear is that Saul was the first Israelite leader to stand up to *the Philistines* successfully, though much of the credit for it is given by our present text first to Jonathan and then to David. (For the Philistines see p.206).

Ch.13.19-22 is a fascinating fragment of straight history, illustrating the background of warfare in the early Iron Age. Before Saul's campaigns, the Philistines had established something of a corner in metal technology.

Ch.14 tells a complex tale of a packed day's activities in the war against them. While Saul had stayed at his headquarters, *Jonathan* led a successful patrol which turned into a large-scale rout of the enemy (1-23). But the military events are of less significance than the subsequent contretemps between Saul and Jonathan on the evening of *that day* (24).

Saul had imposed a ban on any eating during the fighting. No reasons are offered in the text for the ban, and the LXX actually calls it 'a great blunder' (14.24).

Saul's Wars against the Philistines (cont.)

14.25 nightfall and before I have taken vengeance on my enemies.' So no one tasted any food. • There was honeycomb in the countryside; • but when his men came upon it, dripping with honey though it was, not one of them put his hand to his mouth for fear of the curse. • Jonathan, however, had not heard his father's interdict to the army, and he stretched out the stick that was in his hand, dipped the end of it in the honeycomb, put it to his mouth, and was refreshed. • One of the people said to him, 'Your father strictly forbade this, saying, "A curse on the man who eats food today!" ' • Jonathan said, 'My father has done the people 30 great harm; see how I am refreshed by this mere taste of honey. • How much better if the army had eaten today whatever they took from their enemies by way of spoil! Then there would indeed have been a great slaughter of Philistines.'

• Israel defeated the Philistines that day, and pursued them from Michmash to 36 Aijalon. • Saul said, 'Let us go down and make a night attack on the Philistines and harry them till daylight; we will not spare a single one of them.' His men answered, 'Do what you think best,' but the priest said, 'Let us first consult God.' • Saul enquired of God, 'Shall I pursue the Philistines? Will you put them into Israel's power?' But this time he received no answer. • So he said, 'Let all the leaders of the people come forward and let us find out where the sin lies this day. • As the Lord, the deliverer of Israel, lives, even if the sin lies in my son Jonathan, 40 he shall die.' Not a soul answered him. • Then he said to the Israelites, 'All of you stand on one side, and I and my son Jonathan will stand on the other.' His men answered, 'Do what you think best.' • Saul said to the Lord the God of Israel, 'Why have you not answered your servant today? Lord God of Israel, if this guilt lies in me or in my son Jonathan, let the lot be Urim; if it lies in your people Israel, let it be Thummim.' Jonathan and Saul were taken, and the people were cleared.

• Then Saul said, 'Cast lots between me and my son Jonathan'; and Jonathan was taken. • Saul said to Jonathan, 'Tell me what you have done.' Jonathan told him, 'True, I did taste a little honey on the tip of my stick. Here I am; I am ready to die.' • Then Saul swore a solemn oath that Jonathan should 45 die. • But his men said to Saul, 'Shall Jonathan die, Jonathan who has won this great victory in Israel? God forbid! As the Lord lives, not a hair of his head shall fall to the ground, for he has been at work with God today.' So the army delivered Jonathan and he did not die. • Saul broke off the pursuit of the Philistines, who then made their way home.   (REB)

Saul's Wars against the Philistines (cont.)

The breach of it by Jonathan, albeit unintentional, led to a crisis. When Saul at the end of the day sought guidance whether to continue the pursuit of the Philistines into the night, he could get *no answer* from God. Realising that an offence had been committed (38), the king had to discover who was responsible. The method chosen was that known as *Urim and Thummim*. This was a primitive means of deciding between two alternatives, so the procedure for reaching the answer could be lengthy. But in this case it did not take long to establish the guilt of Jonathan.

In this story all the narrator's sympathies are with Jonathan. He is represented as a brave and honourable fighter and guilty of only a technical offence. Moreover, although in the heat of battle he criticizes his father (29), he is later willing to face death without complaint. The people express a silent

Saul's Wars against the Philistines (cont.)

disapproval of Saul's action, which is more forceful even than their final support of Jonathan (39-45).

Saul by contrast is the less bold fighter and the less wise commander. More surprisingly, he is portrayed as over-pious. His original ban was inappropriate – Jonathan's criticism in 29-30 is not answered – and his obstinacy in adhering to it is contrasted unfavourably with the people's sensible search for a compromise. Saul's judgement of people and situations is already impaired before things come to a head between him and Samuel, and the reader wonders how long it can be before he is succeeded as king by Jonathan.

Summary of Saul's Reign

47 | When Saul had made his throne secure in Israel, he gave battle to his enemies on every side, the Moabites, the Ammonites, the Edomites, and the Philistines; and wherever he turned he met with victory. • He displayed his strength by defeating the Amalekites and freeing Israel from hostile raids.   (REB)

Summary of Saul's Reign

Saul is allowed the full formal assessment of his reign as he had been allowed the formal introduction in 13.1. And the assessment is an exceedingly favourable one. It ascribes victories to him over all the other traditional enemies of the Israelites as well as over the Philistines. But what is said is less telling than what is hinted by the placing of this summary. Saul's reign lasts in fact until Ch.31, but it is as good as ended now, because he is already a doomed man.

Saul's Final Rejection by God

5.1 | And Samuel said to Saul, 'The LORD sent me to anoint you king over his people Israel; now therefore hearken to the words of the LORD. • Thus says the LORD of hosts, "I will punish what Amalek did to Israel in opposing them on the way, when they came up out of Egypt. • Now go and smite Amalek, and utterly destroy all that they have; do not spare them, but kill both man and woman, infant and suckling, ox and sheep, camel and ass." '

7 | • And Saul defeated the Amalekites, from Havilah as far as Shur, which is east of Egypt. • And he took Agag the king of the Amalekites alive, and utterly destroyed all the people with the edge of the sword. • But Saul and the people spared Agag, and the best of the sheep and of the oxen and of the fatlings, and the lambs, and all that was good, and would not utterly destroy them; all that was despised and worthless they utterly destroyed.   ♦

Saul's Final Rejection by God

Ch.15 records the final rejection of Saul by Samuel as the mouthpiece of God. Formally, it is a complement to Ch.14: then Saul arraigned Jonathan, now he is himself arraigned, on what seem to us technical charges of impiety. In each case the accused attempts to justify himself but is found guilty. And in each case God, though he does not speak, is represented as pressing the charge. But for Saul, unlike Jonathan, there is no forgiveness.

Repugnant as this story is, at least there is no need to treat it as historical. It is clearly modelled on – and designed to support – the regulation of the ban in Dt 20, where see commentary. OT writers were implacably hostile to *the Amalekites**. According to [Ex 17.16], 'YHWH is at war with Amalek from generation to generation.' Samuel's command is therefore made quite explicit.

But so is the narrator's formal

Saul's Final Rejection by God (cont.)

15.10   • The word of the LORD came to Samuel: • 'I repent that I have made Saul king; for he has turned back from following me, and has not performed my commandments.' And Samuel was angry; and he cried to the LORD all night. • And Samuel rose early to meet Saul in the morning; and it was told Samuel, 'Saul came to Carmel, and behold, he set up a monument for himself and turned, and passed on, and went down to Gilgal.' • And Samuel came to Saul, and Saul said to him, 'Blessed be you to the LORD; I have performed the commandment of the LORD.' • And Samuel said, 'What then is this bleating of the sheep in my ears,

15   and the lowing of the oxen which I hear?' • Saul said, 'They have brought them from the Amalekites; for the people spared the best of the sheep and of the oxen, to sacrifice to the LORD your God; and the rest we have utterly destroyed.' • Then Samuel said to Saul, 'Stop! I will tell you what the LORD said to me this night.' And he said to him, 'Say on.'

   • And Samuel said, 'Though you are little in your own eyes, are you not the head of the tribes of Israel? The LORD anointed you king over Israel. • And the LORD sent you on a mission, and said, "Go, utterly destroy the sinners, the Amalekites, and fight against them until they are consumed." • Why then did you not obey the voice of the LORD? Why did you swoop on the spoil, and do what

20   was evil in the sight of the LORD?' • And Saul said to Samuel, 'I have obeyed the voice of the LORD, I have gone on the mission on which the LORD sent me, I have brought Agag the king of Amalek, and I have utterly destroyed the Amalekites. • But the people took of the spoil, sheep and oxen, the best of the things devoted to destruction, to sacrifice to the LORD your God in Gilgal.'   ▸

Saul's Final Rejection by God (cont.)

catalogue of the exceptions made by the disobedient Saul (9). Saul himself at first had no qualms: he went off to set up a *monument* to record his victory. When challenged by the rhetorical sarcasm of Samuel (14), he explained the exceptions: they were reserved as a special sacrifice to God. But his defence is weak. Not only does he omit mention of Agag. He also shifts his pronouns and attempts to shift the responsibility: *they spared* but *we destroyed*. Samuel brushes aside the attempt: it is *you* who *are the head of the tribes of Israel*. For the second time (19) he invites repentance, stressing the crucial issue of obedience, mentioned five times in vv.19-24. Saul still prevaricates.

Only at the third time of asking (24) does Saul honestly admit his sin, but he is still in the excuses business: he *feared the people*. This excuse carries no weight with Samuel. It confirms that Saul is not

just ungodly but unkingly, and Samuel dismisses his plea for forgiveness. Not until v.30 does Saul repent unreservedly.

The day's work is rounded off by Agag's death. In v.32 NRSV wisely prefers the LXX text, and translates: 'Agag came to him haltingly. Agag said, "Surely this is the bitterness of death".' With a grim quatrain, Samuel then ceremonially butchered the captive king *before the LORD*.

Throughout the chapter, Samuel is represented as the implacable agent of an implacable God. But the story allows him to retain a fraction of our sympathy by his continued affection for Saul, which is explicit in the framing verses (11, 35) and implicit in his change of heart in v.31.

As to Saul, we have to be content that he disobeyed specific instructions. Why he did so, we are not told, except for the fact that he deferred to the people. But in Ch.14 it was precisely the people whose

Saul's Final Rejection by God (cont.)

22 • And Samuel said,

Has the LORD as great delight in burnt offerings and sacrifices,
as in obeying the voice of the LORD?
Behold, to obey is better than sacrifice,
and to hearken than the fat of rams.

• And Saul said to Samuel, 'I have sinned; for I have transgressed the commandment of the LORD and your words, because I feared the people and obeyed their
25 voice. • Now therefore, I pray, pardon my sin, and return with me, that I may
worship the LORD.' • And Samuel said to Saul, 'I will not return with you; for you
have rejected the word of the LORD, and the LORD has rejected you from being king
over Israel.' • As Samuel turned to go away, Saul laid hold upon the skirt of his
robe, and it tore. • And Samuel said to him, 'The LORD has torn the kingdom of Israel
from you this day, and has given it to a neighbour of yours, who is better than
you. • And also the Glory of Israel will not lie or repent; for he is not a man, that he
30 should repent.' • Then he said, 'I have sinned; yet honour me now before the elders
of my people and before Israel, and return with me, that I may worship the LORD
your God.' • So Samuel turned back after Saul; and Saul worshiped the LORD.

• Then Samuel said, 'Bring here to me Agag the king of the Amalekites.' And
Agag came to him cheerfully. Agag said, 'Surely the bitterness of death is past.' • And
Samuel said, 'As your sword has made women childless, so shall your mother be
childless among women.' And Samuel hewed Agag in pieces before the LORD in
Gilgal. • Then Samuel went to Ramah; and Saul went up to his house in Gibeah of
35 Saul. • And Samuel did not see Saul again until the day of his death, but Samuel
grieved over Saul. And the LORD repented that he had made Saul king over Israel.

(RSV)

Saul's Final Rejection by God (cont.)

judgement was vindicated, while he himself was faulted for an excess of religios-
ity. The juxtaposition of the two chapters
suggests that Saul had no chance.

Saul is often described as closer to a
figure in Greek tragedy than any other in
the Old Testament. And of Greek tragedies the closest is Sophocles' *King Oedipus*. Both are 'tragedies of fate' in the
sense that, though the hero's character is
flawed, essentially it is fate against which
he is struggling, and the more he struggles the greater his ruin. But in the OT
fate is not the ultimate arbiter: behind fate
stands God. And so for a modern reader
the story inevitably raises a question
about the justice of God. It is the same
question as is raised by the book of Job
and by the story of the sacrifice of Isaac
in Gen 22. Now in Job certainly, and in

Genesis probably, the author himself was
troubled by that question; and so it appears here. For the chilling verse 29, in
which Samuel declares God's implacability,
is actually contradicted and overtrumped
in each of the framing verses (11, 35),
which record that God did *repent*, specifically of making Saul king. That contra-
diction, which is obscured by more recent
translations, shows that Samuel was
wrong, and thus allows Saul – and the
reader – to go on hoping.

Ch.15 ends the first half of I Samuel.
But it has links also with the second half.
The tearing of the cloak in v.28 foreshadows
a similar tearing in Ch.24. The ambiguous
reference in v.35 to *the day of his death*
inevitably hints at that last fateful meeting
of Saul with Samuel's ghost on the night
before the battle of Mount Gilboa (Ch. 28).

David is Chosen by God

16.1 The LORD said to Samuel, 'How long will you grieve because I have rejected Saul as king of Israel? Fill your horn with oil and take it with you; I am sending you to Jesse of Bethlehem; for I have chosen myself a king from among his sons.' • Samuel answered, 'How can I go? If Saul hears of it, he will kill me.' 'Take a heifer with you,' said the LORD; 'say you have come to offer a sacrifice to the LORD, • and invite Jesse to the sacrifice; then I shall show you what you must do. You are to anoint for me the man whom I indicate to you.' • Samuel did as the LORD had told him, and went to Bethlehem, where the elders came in haste to

5 meet him, saying, 'Why have you come? Is all well?' • 'All is well,' said Samuel; 'I have come to sacrifice to the LORD. Purify yourselves and come with me to the sacrifice.' He himself purified Jesse and his sons and invited them to the sacrifice.

• When they came, and Samuel saw Eliab, he thought, 'Surely here, before the LORD, is his anointed king.' • But the LORD said to him, 'Pay no attention to his outward appearance and stature, for I have rejected him. The LORD does not see as a mortal sees; mortals see only appearances but the LORD sees into the heart.' • Then Jesse called Abinadab and had him pass before Samuel, but he said, 'No, the LORD has not chosen this one.' • Next he presented Shammah, of whom

10 Samuel said, 'Nor has the LORD chosen him.' • Seven of his sons were presented to Samuel by Jesse, but he said, 'The LORD has not chosen any of these.'

• Samuel asked, 'Are these all the sons you have?' 'There is still the youngest,' replied Jesse, 'but he is looking after the sheep.' Samuel said to Jesse, 'Send and fetch him; we will not sit down until he comes.' • So he sent and fetched him. He was handsome, with ruddy cheeks and bright eyes. The LORD said, 'Rise and anoint him: this is the man.' • Samuel took the horn of oil and anointed him in the presence of his brothers, and the spirit of the LORD came upon David and was with him from that day onwards. Then Samuel set out on his way to Ramah.   ▸

David is Chosen by God

The LORD's rejection of Saul had evidently exhausted his resentment against the monarchy as such (8.7). At any rate, whereas in the case of Saul he had said to Samuel 'Appoint them [i.e. the people] a king', now for the succession he says *I have chosen myself a king*. The agent again is Samuel, whom the LORD may treat curtly (1-3), but who still puts the fear of god into *the elders* (4).

The story of the anointing has at its core a well known folk-tale scene, in which the more obvious elder sons are successively passed over in favour of the almost forgotten youngest. At one point the folk-tale clashes with the theology: good looks belong in the folk-tale (12) but do not suit OT theology (7). The reference to his *stature* in v.7 reminds us that Saul had been 'a head taller than anyone else'. The motif of *the sheep* hints at what is to become a dominant image of the Bible, that of king and God (and, later, of his Messiah) as shepherd. The Hebrew participle translated *he is looking after* here (11) is the very word translated 'is shepherd' in Ps 23.1, and the reader is encouraged to expect in David a different kind of kingship (contrast the fears of Ch.8).

David's name is dramatically held up

David is Chosen by God (cont.)

15 • The spirit of the LORD had forsaken Saul, and at times an evil spirit from the LORD would seize him suddenly. • His servants said to him, 'You see how an evil spirit from God seizes you; • sir, why do you not command your servants here to go and find someone who can play on the lyre? Then, when an evil spirit from God comes on you, he can play and you will recover.' • Saul said to his servants, 'Find me someone who can play well and bring him to me.' • One of his attendants said, 'I have seen a son of Jesse of Bethlehem who can play; he is a brave man and a good fighter, wise in speech and handsome, and the LORD is with him.' • Saul therefore dispatched messengers to ask Jesse to send him his son David, 20 who was with the sheep. • Jesse took a batch of bread, a skin of wine, and a kid, and sent them to Saul by his son David. • David came to Saul and entered his service; Saul loved him dearly, and David became his armour-bearer. • Saul sent word to Jesse: 'Allow David to stay in my service, for I am pleased with him.' • And whenever an evil spirit from God came upon Saul, David would take his lyre and play it, so that relief would come to Saul; he would recover and the evil spirit would leave him alone.   (REB)

David is Chosen by God (cont.)

until the anointing is completed (its completion is marked by the framing mention of the *horn of oil*), and he himself does not speak during it. This is no coincidence. For the anointing itself is never referred to, by David or by anyone else, on any subsequent occasion, even when he comes to be officially 'anointed' after the death of Saul. Clearly, therefore, it is an addition, intentionally placed here by the editor to set the tone for his story of David's rise to power. All, he is saying, is God's plan. His spirit now rests on David, and the phrase *the LORD is with him* is something of a refrain in these chapters, starting with v.18.

The focus then switches back to *Saul*, who by contrast has been deserted by *the spirit of the LORD* and is seized from time to time by *an evil spirit from the LORD* (14). But one should not press the OT for systematic terminology in such a field.

Here all we learn of Saul's fits of melancholia is that they are soothed by music. This, ironically, brings in David: for he who can now lull the evil spirit will soon become its chief stimulus and object. But for the present Saul's personal affection for David is unclouded.

David here, still silent, is presented chiefly as the minstrel-boy. That he was a gifted musician and poet need not be doubted. Even though we cannot identify any of the 'Psalms of David' as being incontrovertibly his, we can accept the authenticity of his laments for Saul and Jonathan (2 Sam 1) and for Abner (2 Sam 3). On the other hand his appointment as *armour-bearer* fits neither the preceding story, where he is too young to be at the family sacrifice (16.11), nor the next one, where he is *only a lad* (17.33). Indeed Ch.16 in general emphasises David's gentler qualities: he is here the handsome shepherd and the sensitive musician.

David and Goliath

17.1 The Philistines mustered their forces for war; they massed at Socoh in Judah and encamped between Socoh and Azekah at Ephes-dammim. • Saul and the Israelites also mustered, and they encamped in the valley of Elah. They drew up their lines of battle facing the Philistines, • the Philistines occupying a position on one hill and the Israelites on another, with a valley between them.

• A champion came out from the Philistine camp, a man named Goliath, from 5 Gath; he was over nine feet in height. • He had a bronze helmet on his head, and he wore plate armour of bronze, weighing five thousand shekels. • On his legs were bronze greaves, and one of his weapons was a bronze dagger. • The shaft of his spear was like a weaver's beam, and its head, which was of iron, weighed six hundred shekels. His shield-bearer marched ahead of him.

• The champion stood and shouted to the ranks of Israel, 'Why do you come out to do battle? I am the Philistine champion and you are Saul's men. Choose your man to meet me. • If he defeats and kills me in fair fight, we shall become your slaves; but 10 if I vanquish and kill him, you will be our slaves and serve us. • Here and now I challenge the ranks of Israel. Get me a man, and we will fight it out.' • When Saul and the Israelites heard what the Philistine said, they were all shaken and deeply afraid.

32 • David said to Saul, 'Let no one lose heart! I shall go and fight this Philistine.' • Saul answered, 'You are not able to fight this Philistine; you are only a lad, and he has been a fighting man all his life.' • David said to Saul, 'Sir, I am my father's shepherd; whenever a lion or bear comes and carries off a sheep from the flock, 35 • I go out after it and attack it and rescue the victim from its jaws. Then if it turns on me, I seize it by the beard and batter it to death. • I have killed lions and bears, and this uncircumcised Philistine will fare no better than they; he has defied the ranks of the living God. • The Lord who saved me from the lion and the bear will save me from this Philistine.' 'Go then,' said Saul; 'and the Lord be with you.'

David and Goliath

This chapter, famous as it is, contains two versions of events which are incompatible with each other and still more with Ch.16. One of the two, that contained in 12-31 and 55-8, is omitted in an important ms of the Septuagint; and that omission is followed here. The narrative that remains is relatively free of difficulties.

Goliath had armour like a medieval knight, of dimensions to match his size. His body armour weighed 56 kg, about a hundredweight; in addition, *his shield-bearer* went *ahead of him* carrying a shield which reached from the ground to eye-level. His weapons included an enormous *spear*, whose *iron head* weighed 7 kg, somewhat over a stone. The narrator presents him as 'an almost grotesquely quantita-tive embodiment of a hero' (Alter).

David is still portrayed as the shepherd-boy, deceptively handsome (v.42 picks up 16.12). But a shepherd's life in ancient Palestine was not idyllic. Over every hill lurked powerful predators from whom he must protect his flock. There follows a symbolic scene. Saul *put his own* armour *on David*; but it was too heavy for him – the LXX adds that he walked about in it once or twice and found himself exhausted – so he gave it back. That is to say: David *will* become king, but is not yet ready. Instead he goes out to fight with just his *sling*. We must not be too romantic about that: a contingent of slingers was a regular part of the most powerful ANE armies.

The engagement starts with threats

David and Goliath (cont.)

• He put his own tunic on David, placed a bronze helmet on his head, and gave him a coat of mail to wear; • he then fastened his sword on David over his tunic. But David held back, because he had not tried them, and said to Saul, 'I cannot
40 go with these, because I am not used to them.' David took them off, • then picked up his stick, chose five smooth stones from the wadi, and put them in a shepherd's bag which served as his pouch, and, sling in hand, went to meet the Philistine. • The Philistine, preceded by his shield-bearer, came on towards David. • He looked David up and down and had nothing but disdain for this lad with his ruddy cheeks and bright eyes. • He said to David, 'Am I a dog that you come out against me with sticks?' He cursed him in the name of his god, • and said, 'Come,
45 I shall give your flesh to the birds and the beasts.' • David answered, 'You have come against me with sword and spear and dagger, but I come against you in the name of the LORD of Hosts, the God of the ranks of Israel which you have defied. • The LORD will put you into my power this day; I shall strike you down and cut your head off and leave your carcass and the carcasses of the Philistines to the birds and the wild beasts; the whole world will know that there is a God in Israel. • All those who are gathered here will see that the LORD saves without sword or spear; the battle is the LORD's, and he will put you all into our power.'
• When the Philistine began moving closer to attack, David ran quickly to engage him. • Reaching into his bag, he took out a stone, which he slung and struck the Philistine on the forehead. The stone sank into his head, and he fell
50 prone on the ground. • So with sling and stone David proved the victor; though he had no sword, he struck down the Philistine and gave him a mortal wound. • He ran up to the Philistine and stood over him; then, grasping his sword, he drew it out of the scabbard, dispatched him, and cut off his head. When the Philistines saw the fate of their champion, they turned and fled.
• The men of Israel and Judah at once raised the war cry and closely pursued them all the way to Gath and up to the gates of Ekron. The road that runs to Shaaraim, Gath, and Ekron was strewn with their dead. • On their return from the pursuit of the Philistines, the Israelites plundered their camp.   (REB)

David and Goliath (cont.)

and curses, the psychological warfare which preceded the physical encounter. Each of them threatened to give the other's corpse to the wild beasts. Each of them also called upon his national god for support. The theological point of the story lies in verses 46b-7, which come just before the climax. The climax itself, suspensefully delayed by the verbal exchanges of verses 43-7 (and indeed 32-7) comes with swift surprise. The sling shot stuns Goliath, and David dispatches him with his own weapon – a favourite motif in the books of Samuel (1 S 26.8).

The story of David and Goliath is,

surprisingly, the only single combat in the OT. And the chapter as a whole is 'as close as the OT ever comes to an "epic" presentation of its materials' (Alter). The details of place (1-3, 52-3) and of the weaponry, the threats and the fight itself, the presence (albeit in the background) of the two gods – all these would fit the heroic world of the *Iliad*. Here it serves to emphasise the other side of David's character, the resourceful warrior and the man of action: in vv.48-53 he is the subject of eleven active verbs in quick succession. Together with Ch.16 it has laid the foundation for much that is to come.

David at Court

18. 1 That same day, when Saul had finished talking with David, he kept him and would not let him return any more to his father's house, for he saw that Jonathan had given his heart to David and had grown to love him as himself. • Jonathan and David made a solemn compact because each loved the other as dearly as himself. • Jonathan stripped off the cloak and tunic he was wearing, and gave them to David, together with his sword, his bow, and his belt.

5 • David succeeded so well in every venture on which Saul sent him that he was given command of the fighting forces, and his promotion pleased all ranks, even the officials round Saul.

• At the homecoming of the army and the return of David from slaying the Philistine, the women from all the cities and towns of Israel came out singing and dancing to meet King Saul, rejoicing with tambourines and three-stringed instruments • The women as they made merry sang to one another: 'Saul struck down thousands, but David tens of thousands.' • Saul was furious, and the words rankled. He said, 'They have ascribed to David tens of thousands and to me only

9 thousands. What more can they do but make him king?' • From that time forward Saul kept a jealous eye on David.

20 • But Michal, Saul's daughter, fell in love with David, and when Saul was told of this, he saw that it suited his plans. • He said to himself, 'I will give her to him; let her be the bait that lures him to his death at the hands of the Philistines.' So Saul proposed to make David his son-in-law, • and ordered his courtiers to say to David privately, 'The king is well disposed to you and you are dear to us all; now is the time for you to marry into the king's family.' • When they spoke in this way to David, he said to them, 'Do you think that marrying the king's daughter is a matter of so little consequence that a poor man of no account, like myself, can do it?'

David at Court

Ch.18 introduces an important new factor in the story, the proverbial friendship of David (now *kept* permanently at court) with Jonathan. The friendship was formally sealed by Jonathan's gift of his military equipment. But Jonathan was also the king's son, whom we last saw in Ch.14 already ripe for the succession. Now his gifts show his willingness to cede the throne to his friend.

David's successes in war against the Philistines, compressed here into a single verse (5), were by implication spread over a considerable time. They pleased all but one person. There was nothing unusual about the processional welcome given by

the women singing and dancing. Nor indeed was there any slight *intended* in the words of the victory song they sang: in parallel couplets 1,000 is regularly answered by 10,000 without invidious imputation (see e.g. Ps 91.7). Saul's jealous comment in v.8b contains his own first reference (ironical, here) to David's eventual succession.

The next thing we know is that *Saul's daughter Michal* has fallen *in love with David*. The mention of it – the only place in the OT where we are told that a woman loves a man – is to be seen not as a romantic note but as reinforcement of David's claim to the succession. Certainly David

David at Court (cont.)

4   • The courtiers reported what David had said, • and Saul replied, 'Tell David this: all the king wants as the bride-price is the foreskins of a hundred Philistines, by way of vengeance on his enemies.' Saul was counting on David's death at the hands of the Philistines. • The courtiers told David what Saul had said, and marriage with the king's daughter on these terms pleased him well. Before the appointed time, • David went out with his men and slew two hundred Philistines; he brought their foreskins and counted them out to the king in order to be accepted as his son-in-law. Saul then married his daughter Michal to David.

9   • An evil spirit from the LORD came on Saul as he was sitting in the house with a spear in his hand; and David was playing on the lyre. • Saul tried to pin David to the wall with the spear, but he dodged the king's thrust so that Saul drove the spear into the wall. David escaped and got safely away.

  That night • Saul sent servants to keep watch on David's house, intending to kill him in the morning. But David's wife Michal warned him to get away that night, 'or tomorrow', she said, 'you will be a dead man.' • She let David down through a window and he slipped away and escaped. • Michal then took their household god and put it on the bed; at its head she laid a goat's-hair rug and covered it all

15 with a cloak. • When the men arrived to arrest David she told them he was ill. • Saul, however, sent them back to see David for themselves. 'Bring him to me, bed and all,' he ordered, 'so that I may kill him.' • When they came, there was the household god on the bed and the goat's-hair rug at its head. • Saul said to Michal, 'Why have you played this trick on me and let my enemy get away?' Michal answered, 'He said to me, "Help me to escape or I shall kill you." '   (REB)

David at Court (cont.)

saw the marriage as a political move (26), and we are never told whether he loved her in return. The marriage negotiations incorporate traditional Near Eastern customs: Saul's use of intermediaries to arrange the marriage, David's polite disclaimers and the payment of a *bride-price*. The details of the latter, including David's cheerful overtrumping of Saul's grim demand, belong to folk-tale. But there is point in the *foreskins*: they showed that the dead were uncircumcised, and therefore Philistines.

The story of Saul's attempt to kill David with his *spear* does not fit well in the context, but it appears twice in 1 Sam ([18.10-11] and 19.9-10), so it is clearly part of the tradition. Saul's spear was always with him: it symbolises on one plane his military prowess and his royalty, on another his insecurity and uncertain temper.

The account of the night attack on David leaves many questions unanswered. How did Michal hear of the plot? How did David escape from a *house* under *watch*? – unless it was against the city wall, like Rahab's at Jericho. What precisely was Michal doing with the *household god*? And whose idea was it, David's or (in spite of her denial) Michal's? But even with these uncertainties, it is an exciting tale.

David Quits Jerusalem

20.1 David made his escape and came to Jonathan. 'What have I done?' he asked. 'What is my offence? What wrong does your father think I have done, that he seeks my life?' • Jonathan answered, 'God forbid! There is no thought of putting you to death. I am sure my father will not do anything whatever without telling me. Why should my father hide such a thing from me? I cannot believe it!' • David said, 'I am ready to swear to it: your father has said to himself, "Jonathan must not know this or he will resent it," because he knows that you have a high regard for me. As the LORD lives, your life upon it, I am only a step away from

4,5 death.' • Jonathan said to David, 'What do you want me to do for you?' • David answered, 'It is new moon tomorrow, and I am to dine with the king. But let me go and lie hidden in the fields until the third evening, • and if your father misses me, say, "David asked me for leave to hurry off on a visit to his home in Bethlehem, for it is the annual sacrifice there for the whole family." • If he says, "Good," it will be well for me; but if he flies into a rage, you will know that he is set on doing me harm. • My lord, keep faith with me; for you and I have entered into a solemn compact before the LORD. Kill me yourself if I am guilty, but do not let me fall into your father's hands.' • 'God forbid!' cried Jonathan.

10 'If I find my father set on doing you harm, I shall tell you.' • David answered Jonathan, 'How will you let me know if he answers harshly?'

19   • Jonathan said 'The day after tomorrow go down at nightfall to the place where you hid . . . ; stay by the mound there. • I shall shoot three arrows towards it as though aiming at a target. • Then I shall send my boy to find the arrows. If I say to him, "Look, the arrows are on this side of you; pick them up," then you can come out of hiding. You will be quite safe, I swear it, for there will be nothing amiss. • But if I say to him, "Look, the arrows are on the other side of you, farther on," then the LORD has said that you must go; • the LORD stands witness between us for ever to the pledges we have exchanged.'   ▸

David Quits Jerusalem

David, it seems, could scarcely believe that Saul meant to kill him, and wanted to make one last attempt to find out the truth before taking to the hills. The plan agreed between the two friends (4-23) is far from clear. No ancient ms. or modern translation provides a coherent sequence of events. Here the REB translation is followed except in v.19 where the mss are particularly obscure. The feast of the *new moon* was celebrated for two days (34) each month. David proposes to go into hiding and remain there for those two days. The absence will test Saul's good will to him (5-7). Jonathan then suggests a way in which he can, if the news is unfavourable, communicate it to David. The ruse of the *arrows* will allow him to do so without lending colour to Saul's suspicions – which may have envisaged a conspiracy of the two of them against him.

The scene at dinner however (24-34) contains plenty of vivid detail. Saul sits in *his customary seat*, back to *the wall*, with his *spear* to hand (33). *Beside* him sits his Commander in Chief, *Abner*; opposite him (LXX) is Jonathan, with *David's place empty*. On the first night Saul behaves rationally; on the second he asks an apparently straight question, which however reveals his hostility by the phrase *the son of Jesse*. Jonathan, alerted, gives an explanation that is a little too elaborate – and Saul explodes. His tirade

David Quits Jerusalem (cont.)

• David hid in the fields, and when the new moon came the king sat down to eat at mealtime. • Saul took his customary seat by the wall, and Abner sat beside him; Jonathan too was present, but David's place was empty. • That day Saul said nothing, for he thought that David was absent by some chance, perhaps because he was ritually unclean. • But on the second day, the day after the new moon, David's place was still empty, and Saul said to his son Jonathan, 'Why has the son of Jesse not come to the feast, either yesterday or today?' • Jonathan answered, 'David asked permission to go to Bethlehem. • He asked my leave and said, "Our family is holding a sacrifice in the town and my brother himself has told me to be there. Now, if you have any regard for me, let me slip away to see my brothers." That is why he has not come to the king's table.'

• Saul's anger blazed up against Jonathan and he said, 'You son of a crooked and rebellious mother! I know perfectly well you have made a friend of the son of Jesse only to bring shame on yourself and dishonour on your mother. • But as long as Jesse's son remains alive on the earth, neither you nor your kingdom will be established. Send at once and fetch him; he deserves to die.' • Jonathan answered his father, 'Deserves to die? Why? What has he done?' • At that, Saul picked up his spear and threatened to kill him; and Jonathan knew that his father was bent on David's death. • He left the table in a rage and ate nothing on the second day of the festival; for he was indignant on David's behalf and because his father had humiliated him.

• Next morning Jonathan, accompanied by a young boy, went out into the fields to keep the appointment with David. • He said to the boy, 'Run ahead and find the arrows I shoot.' As the boy ran on, he shot the arrows over his head. • When the boy reached the place where the arrows had fallen, Jonathan called out after him, 'Look, the arrows are beyond you. • Hurry! Go quickly! Do not delay.' The boy gathered up the arrows and brought them to his master; • but only Jonathan and David knew what this meant; the boy knew nothing. • David went off at once, while Jonathan returned to the town.   (REB)

David Quits Jerusalem (cont.)

starts with the traditional abuse of an enemy's *mother* (30). He then modulates into an argument designed to divide Jonathan from David. But the two friends are inseparable, as is shown dramatically in v.33 by Saul's action and Jonathan's reactions.

It has been said of the three characters in this story that 'Saul lowers dark and suspicious in the background, while the foreground is occupied by the two friends, young and brave, each unselfishly preferring the other' (Gressmann). It is true that Jonathan is portrayed as noble to the point of innocence (2). Even when the truth is out (31), he does his best to preserve his loyalty to his father as well as to his friend. But David, for once, shows little or no initiative; and the protestations of the two friends (in the full text) are somewhat repetitious. Consequently it is Saul who actually makes the strongest, though the least favourable, impression. Nevertheless the author has made his point. Saul's son and his daughter have now each helped David to escape from their murderous father. In the long run everything is working for David. In the short run he has many dangers and humiliations ahead of him.

David in the Wilderness

21.10 That day David went on his way, fleeing from Saul, and came to King Achish of Gath. • The servants of Achish said to him, 'Surely this is David, the king of his country, the man of whom they sang as they danced:

> Saul struck down thousands,
> but David tens of thousands.'

• These comments were not lost on David, and he became very much afraid of King Achish of Gath. • So he altered his behaviour in public and acted like a madman in front of them all, scrabbling on the double doors of the city gate and dribbling down his beard. • Achish said to his servants, 'The man is insane! Why 15 bring him to me? • Am I short of madmen that you bring this one to plague me? Must I have this fellow in my house?'

22. 1 • David stole away from there and went to the cave of Adullam, and, when his brothers and all the members of his family heard where he was, they went down and joined him there. • Everyone in any kind of distress or in debt or with a grievance gathered round him, about four hundred in number, and he became their chief.

• From there David went to Mizpeh in Moab and said to the king of Moab, 'Let my father and mother come and take shelter with you until I know what God will do for me.' • He left them at the court of the king of Moab, and they stayed there as long as David remained in his stronghold.

23.14 • David was living in the fastnesses of the wilderness of Ziph, in the hill-country, and though Saul went daily in search of him, God did not put him into his power. • David was at Horesh in the wilderness of Ziph when he learned that Saul had come out to seek his life. • Saul's son Jonathan came to David at Horesh and gave him fresh courage in God's name: • 'Do not be afraid!' he said, 'my father's hand will not touch you. You will become king of Israel and I shall rank after you. This my father knows.' • After the two of them had made a solemn compact before the LORD, David remained in Horesh and Jonathan went home.   (REB)

David in the Wilderness

Now an outlaw, David makes for Philistine territory, where he can be safe from Saul's pursuit. But his reputation – even the enemy recognizes him as *king of his country* (11) – creates other dangers, which David eludes astutely. The story of feigned madness suggests a folk-tale origin, and the anti-Philistine joke in v.15 belongs to the same tradition.

By contrast, the next two verses could be historical. *Adullam* is 15 miles east of Gath, on the edge of the hill-country of Judaea (see map 2). This was the region in which David spent most of his time as a fugitive from Saul. It was the natural home of all those at odds with society, and such people soon came to join his band of outlaws. There were many such bands operating in the late Bronze and early Iron Ages (see p.29).

The brief scene at *Horesh* marks Jonathan's final and formal 'abdication' in favour of David. His role thus fulfilled, Jonathan now disappears from the story.

David Spares Saul (1)

1 From there David went up and installed himself in the strongholds of En-gedi.
• Once Saul was back from pursuing the Philistines, he was told, 'David is now
in the desert of En-gedi.' • Saul thereupon took three thousand men selected from
all Israel and went in search of David and his men east of the Rocks of the
Mountain Goats. • He came to the sheepfolds along the route, where there was a
cave, and went in to cover his feet. Now David and his men were sitting in the
5 recesses of the cave; • David's men said to him, 'Today is the day of which the
LORD said to you, "I shall deliver your enemy into your power; do what you like
with him." ' David got up and, unobserved, cut off the border of Saul's cloak.
• Afterwards David reproached himself for having cut off the border of Saul's
cloak. • He said to his men, 'The LORD preserve me from doing such a thing to
my lord as to raise my hand against him, since he is the LORD's anointed.' • By
these words David restrained his men and would not let them attack Saul.

  • Saul then left the cave and went on his way. After this, David too left the
cave and called after Saul, 'My lord king!' Saul looked behind him and David,
bowing to the ground, prostrated himself. • David then said to Saul, 'Why do you
10 listen to people who say, "David intends your ruin"? • This very day you have
seen for yourself how the LORD put you in my power in the cave and how,
refusing to kill you, I spared you saying, "I will not raise my hand against my
lord, since he is the LORD's anointed." • Look, father, look at the border of your
cloak in my hand. Since, although I cut the border off your cloak, I did not kill
you, surely you realise that I intend neither mischief nor crime. I have not wronged
you, and yet you hunt me down to take my life. • May the LORD be judge between
me and you, and may the LORD avenge me on you; but I shall never lay a hand on
you! • (As the old proverb says: Wickedness comes out of wicked people, but ♦

David Spares Saul (1)

In Ch.23 Saul twice nearly caught David
as he moved from place to place in the
wilderness*. Ch.24 tells the first of two
stories – the other is in Ch.26 – of how
David caught Saul and could have killed
him but spared his life. There are many
similarities between the two stories, but
also important differences. It seems probable
that the two have a common origin, but
gradually diverged as they circulated and
then were brought together again by the
author. See also the note at end of Ch.26.

  The main features in both chapters are:
(i) Saul's position at David's mercy, (ii)
David's temptation by his men to kill Saul,
(iii) David's refusal to harm the LORD's
anointed, (iv) David's removal of a symbol
of Saul's royalty, (v) David's speech to Saul,
protesting his innocence, and (vi) Saul's
reply, admitting his mistake.

There are however two features which
are distinctive to Ch.24. The first is the
scene in the cave. The motif of Saul relieving himself has been seen as comic. This
it is not, though it cuts him down to the
level of common humanity, like the end of
Ch.28. In any case, the story requires that
he should be alone in the cave. David's
symbolic act in cutting off part of his
cloak recalls Samuel's comment in 15.28.
Strictly, it was an act of lèse-majesté,
which he immediately regretted (7b). But
he converts it into evidence of his good
faith (11); which moves Saul to a concession
– the second distinctive feature of Ch.24.
Already in v.12 David has called him father
and he has responded my son (17). Now in
v.20 Saul publicly acknowledges that David
will succeed him.

  On the surface therefore all seems set

David Spares Saul (1) (cont.)

24.15 I shall never lay a hand on you!) • On whose trail is the king of Israel campaigning? Whom are you pursuing? On the trail of a dead dog, of a flea! • May the LORD be the judge and decide between me and you; may he examine and defend my cause and give judgement for me by rescuing me from your clutches!'

• When David had finished saying this to Saul, Saul said, 'Is that your voice, my son David?' And Saul began to weep aloud. • 'You are upright and I am not,' he said to David, 'since you have behaved well to me, whereas I have behaved badly to you. • And today you have shown how well you have behaved to me,

20 since the LORD had put me in your power but you did not kill me. • When a man comes on his enemy, does he let him go unmolested? May the LORD reward you for the good you have done me today! • Now I know that you will indeed reign and that the sovereignty in Israel will pass into your hands. • Now swear to me by the LORD that you will not suppress my descendants once I am gone, or blot my name out of my family.'   (NJB)

David Spares Saul (1) (cont.)

fair. But the speeches of the protagonists (David ingratiatingly protesting his innocence and Saul sentimentally exaggerating his remorse) are too good to be true. David's oath to spare Saul's descendants serves only to prepare us for the worst.

David and Abigail

25.2 There was a man in Maon who had property at Carmel and owned three thousand sheep and a thousand goats; and he was shearing his flocks in Carmel. • His name was Nabal and his wife's name Abigail; she was a beautiful and intelligent woman, but her husband, a Calebite, was surly and mean. • David heard in the wilderness that Nabal was shearing his flocks, • and sent ten of his young men, saying to them, 'Go up to Carmel, find Nabal, and give him my greetings. • You are to say, "All good wishes for the year ahead! Prosperity to yourself, your household, and all that is yours! • I hear that you are shearing. Your shepherds have been with us lately and we did not molest them; nothing of theirs was missing all the time they were in Carmel. • Ask your own men and they will tell you. Receive my men kindly, for this is an auspicious day with us, and give what you can to David your son and your servant." '

• David's servants came and delivered this message to Nabal in David's name.
10 When they paused, • Nabal answered, 'Who is David? Who is this son of Jesse? In these days there are many slaves who break away from their masters. ◗

David and Abigail

Happily placed in the centre of the triptych, between the two parallel stories of Saul and David, is the romantic tale of David and Abigail. It is simply but subtly told, in a tone which recalls the story of Joseph in Genesis.

On the edge of the wilderness within range of David lived the wealthy farmer *Nabal*. The first we learn of him (2) is the size of his flock of *sheep*, and the last (37)

is the *seizure* he suffers on learning of the loss of five of them! David's men, like any outlaws, lived alternately by raids and by offering 'protection'. On this occasion David covered his blackmail with a polite formula to save face. It was the time of the annual *shearing*, the sheep-farmer's equivalent of the harvest – a time for celebration and, by Hebrew custom, for showing generosity to the poor (6-8).

David and Abigail (cont.)

11 • Am I to take my food and my wine and the meat I have provided for my shearers, and give it to men who come from I know not where?' • David's servants turned and made their way back to him and told him all this. • He said to his followers, 'Buckle on your swords, all of you.' So they buckled on their swords, as did David, and they followed him, four hundred of them, while two hundred stayed behind with the baggage.

• One of Nabal's servants said to Abigail, Nabal's wife, 'David sent messengers from the wilderness to ask our master politely for a present, and he flared up at

15 them. • The men have been very good to us and have not molested us, nor did we miss anything all the time we were going about with them in the open country. • They were as good as a wall round us, night and day, while we were minding the flocks. • Consider carefully what you had better do, for it is certain ruin for our master and his whole house; he is such a wretched fellow that it is no good talking to him.'

• Abigail hastily collected two hundred loaves and two skins of wine, five sheep ready dressed, five measures of roasted grain, a hundred bunches of raisins, and two hundred cakes of dried figs, and loaded them on donkeys, • but told her husband nothing about it. She said to her servants, 'Go on ahead, I shall

20 follow you.' • As she made her way on her donkey, hidden by the hill, there were David and his men coming down towards her, and she met them. • David had said, 'It was a waste of time to protect this fellow's property in the wilderness so well that nothing of his was missing. He has repaid me evil for good.' • David swore a solemn oath: 'God do the same to me and more if I leave him a single mother's son alive by morning!'

• When Abigail saw David she dismounted in haste and prostrated herself before him, bowing low to the ground • at his feet, and said, 'Let me take the blame, my lord, but allow your humble servant to speak out, and let my lord give

25 me a hearing. • How can you take any notice of this wretched fellow? He is just what his name Nabal means: "Churl" is his name, and churlish his behaviour. Sir, I did not myself see the men you sent. • And now, sir, the LORD has restrained you from starting a blood feud and from striking a blow for yourself. As the LORD lives, your life upon it, your enemies and all who want to see you ruined will be like Nabal. • Here is the present which I, your humble servant, have brought; give it to the young men under your command. • Forgive me, my lord, if I am   ◗

David and Abigail (cont.)

David's demand receives a characteristically *surly* reply from Nabal, presented as foil to his charming and intelligent wife *Abigail* – the chiastic* arrangement of v.3 highlights the contrast between them. David, when he hears the news, goes at once into action (13), though the implied threat is made explicit only when Abigail is on the point of meeting him (21-2). The presents she then brings him (18) ostentatiously overtrump Nabal's refusal.

David's phrase *he has repaid me evil for good* (21) is sheer effrontery, but it provides a link with the previous chapter (24.18). REB's *a single mother's son* (22) is more coy than AV's literal translation: 'him that pisseth against the wall'.

Her address to him is a masterpiece. From polite phrases of submission, appeasing his immediate wrath, she gradually moves through the offering of a *present* (tactfully – to his men, not to him),

David and Abigail (cont.)

presuming; for the LORD will establish your family for ever, because you have fought his battles. No calamity will overtake you as long as you live. • If anyone tries to pursue you and take your life, the LORD your God will wrap your life up and put it with his own treasure, but the lives of your enemies he will hurl away **25.**30 like stones from a sling. • When the LORD has made good all his promises to you, and has made you ruler of Israel, • there will be no reason why you should stumble or your courage should falter because you have shed innocent blood or struck a blow for yourself. Then when the LORD makes all you do prosper, remember me, your servant.'

• David said to Abigail, 'Blessed be the LORD the God of Israel who today has sent you to meet me. • A blessing on your good sense, a blessing on you because you have saved me today from the guilt of bloodshed and from striking a blow for myself. • For I swear by the life of the LORD the God of Israel who has kept me from doing you wrong: if you had not come at once to meet me, not a man of Nabal's household, not a single mother's son, would have been left alive by 35 morning.' • Then David accepted from her what she had brought him and said, 'Go home in peace; I have listened to you and I grant your request.'

• On her return she found Nabal holding a right royal banquet in his house. He grew merry and became very drunk, so drunk that his wife said nothing at all to him till daybreak. • In the morning, when the wine had worn off, she told him everything, and he had a seizure and lay there like a log. • Some ten days later the LORD struck him and he died.

• When David heard that Nabal was dead he said, 'Blessed be the LORD, who has himself punished Nabal for his insult, and has kept me his servant from doing wrong. The LORD has made Nabal's wrongdoing recoil on his own head.' David 40 then sent a message to Abigail proposing that she should become his wife. • His servants came to her at Carmel and said, 'David has sent us to fetch you to be his wife.' • She rose and prostrated herself with her face to the ground, and said, 'I am his slave to command; I would wash the feet of my lord's servants.' • Abigail made her preparations with all speed and, with her five maids in attendance and accompanied by David's messengers, she set out on a donkey; and she became David's wife.

• David had also married Ahinoam of Jezreel; both these women became his wives. • Saul meanwhile had given his daughter Michal, David's wife, to Palti son of Laish from Gallim.   (REB)

David and Abigail (cont.)

and a flattering reference to his defeat of Goliath (29), towards a longer and more glorious perspective. Like every important character in the book, she looks forward to David's succession to the throne, urging him to keep himself free of blood-guilt against that great destiny. (Verses 26-31 ostensibly refer to Nabal, but in the context of Chs 24 and 26 we inevitably think of Saul.) And all the time, as a beautiful woman, she hints at other developments: the death of her husband (*be like Nabal* v.26) and David's willingness to *remember* her when he comes into his kingdom. Similarly David's final phrase, which REB translates *I grant your request*, literally means 'I lift up your face'. Any experienced reader can anticipate the happy outcome.

David Spares Saul (2)

The Ziphites came to Saul at Gibeah with the news that David was in hiding on the hill of Hachilah overlooking Jeshimon. • Saul went down at once to the wilderness of Ziph, taking with him three thousand picked men, to search for David there. • He encamped beside the road on the hill of Hachilah overlooking Jeshimon, while David was still in the wilderness. As soon as David learnt that Saul had come to the wilderness in pursuit of him, • he sent out scouts and found that Saul had reached such and such a place. • He went at once to the place where Saul had pitched his camp, and observed where Saul and Abner son of Ner, the commander-in-chief, were lying. Saul lay within the lines with his troops encamped in a circle round him. • David turned to Ahimelech the Hittite and Abishai son of Zeruiah, Joab's brother, and said, 'Who will venture with me into the camp to Saul?' Abishai answered, 'I will.'

• David and Abishai entered the camp at night, and there was Saul lying asleep within the lines with his spear thrust into the ground beside his head. Abner and the army were asleep all around him. • Abishai said to David, 'God has put your enemy into your power today. Let me strike him and pin him to the ground with one thrust of the spear. I shall not have to strike twice.' • David said to him, 'Do him no harm. Who has ever lifted his hand against the LORD's anointed and gone unpunished? • As the LORD lives,' David went on, 'the LORD will strike him down; either his time will come and he will die, or he will go down to battle and meet his end. • God forbid that I should lift my hand against the LORD's anointed! But now let us take the spear which is by his head, and the water-jar, and go.' • So David took the spear and the water-jar from beside Saul's head, and they left. The whole camp was asleep; no one saw him, no one knew anything, no one woke. A deep sleep sent by the LORD had fallen on them.

• Then David crossed over to the other side and stood on the top of a hill at some distance; there was a wide stretch between them. • David shouted across to the army and hailed Abner son of Ner, 'Answer me, Abner!' He answered, 'Who are you to shout to the king?' • David said to Abner, 'Do you call yourself a man? Is there anyone like you in Israel? Why, then, did you not keep watch over your lord the king, when someone came to harm your lord the king? • This was not well done. As the LORD lives, you deserve to die, all of you, because ▶

David Spares Saul (2)

The second version of the story of David sparing Saul's life is more heroic and more specifically military than the first: doubtless it received its distinctive colouring round the camp fire. At the beginning David *sent out scouts* in the approved way, and his whole exploit required great daring in plan and execution. He treats *Abner* like an equal (v.19 exculpates Saul himself) but also with pride. Whereas in Ch.24 his conscience smote him, in Ch.26 he gives back *the spear* with no apology but with a reference (v.23) to the *reward* he expects for sparing the king's life. (The same variation may possibly be reflected in the respective images of a *dead dog* in 24.14 and a *partridge* in 26.20.) Consonant with the military colouring is the simple nationalistic theology of vv.19 and 20.

The narrative in Ch.26 is in general simpler than in Ch.24. Abner's silence after v.16 and David's curt reply in v.22 both

David Spares Saul (2) (cont.)

you have not kept watch over your master the LORD's anointed. Look! Where are the king's spear and the water-jar that were by his head?'

26.17 • Saul recognised David's voice and said, 'Is that you, David my son?' 'Yes, your majesty, it is,' said David. • 'Why must my lord pursue me? What have I done? What mischief am I plotting? • Listen, my lord king, to what I have to say. If it is the LORD who has set you against me, may an offering be acceptable to him; but if it is mortals, a curse on them in the LORD's name! For they have ousted me today from my share in the LORD's possession and have banished me 20 to serve other gods! • Do not let my blood be shed on foreign soil, far from the presence of the LORD, just because the king of Israel came out to look for a flea, as one might hunt a partridge over the hills.'

• Saul said, 'I have done wrong; come back, David my son. You have held my life precious this day, and I will never harm you again. I have been a fool, I have been sadly in the wrong.' • David answered, 'Here is the king's spear; let one of your men come across and fetch it. • The LORD who rewards uprightness and loyalty will reward the man into whose power he put you today, for I refused to lift my hand against the LORD's anointed. • As I held your life precious today, so 25 may the LORD hold mine precious and deliver me from every distress.' • Saul said to David, 'A blessing on you, David my son! You will do great things and be triumphant.' With that David went on his way and Saul returned home.

27.1 • David thought to himself, 'One of these days I shall be killed by Saul. The best thing for me to do will be to escape into Philistine territory; then Saul will give up all further hope of finding me anywhere in Israel, search as he may, and I shall escape his clutches.' • 'So David and his six hundred men set out and crossed the frontier to Achish son of Maoch, king of Gath. • David settled in Gath with Achish, taking with him his men and their families and his two wives, Ahinoam of Jezreel and Abigail of Carmel, Nabal's widow.   (REB)

David Spares Saul (2) (cont.)

belong to the older and more succinct tradition of Hebrew story-telling. But the phrase *lift my hand against the LORD's anointed* (three times in Ch.26, on top of two in Ch.24), while admittedly it has a pleasant irony when used by David, nevertheless becomes tedious by repetition; and Saul and David in their final exchange again protest rather too much. Verse 10 looks forward to Saul's death, and the phrase in v.16 *you deserve to die* (lit. 'you are sons of death') is the very one which leads to the climax in Nathan's denunciation of David (2 Sam 12.5). Such links serve two connected purposes: the

literary one of binding the story together and the theological one of suggesting that the sequence of events is 'meant', i.e. it all fits together as part of God's plan.

At the end of the incident we expect the reconciliation to lead to David's return to court. But, just as in Ch.24, war is resumed; and Saul and David never meet again. David spent over *a year in Philistine country*, where he seems to have become a vassal of king *Achish* and may even have been forced into apostasy (26.19). This part of the tradition evidently embarrassed the author, so the blame is laid heavily on others.

Saul and the Ghost of Samuel

.3 By this time Samuel was dead, and all Israel had mourned for him and buried him in Ramah, his own town; and Saul had banished from the land all who trafficked with ghosts and spirits. • The Philistines mustered and encamped at Shunem, and
5 Saul mustered all the Israelites and encamped at Gilboa. • At the sight of the Philistine forces, Saul was afraid, indeed struck to the heart by terror. • He enquired of the LORD, but the LORD did not answer him, neither by dreams, nor by Urim, nor by prophets. • So he said to his servants, 'Find a woman who has a familiar spirit, and I will go and enquire through her.' They told him that there was such a woman at En-dor.

• Saul put on different clothes and went in disguise with two of his men. He came to the woman by night and said, 'Tell me my fortune by consulting the dead, and call up the man I name to you.' • The woman answered, 'Surely you know what Saul has done, how he has made away with those who call up ghosts
10 and spirits; why do you press me to do what will lead to my death?' • Saul swore her an oath: 'As the LORD lives, no harm shall come to you for this.' • The woman asked whom she should call up, and Saul answered, 'Samuel.'

• When the woman saw Samuel appear, she shrieked and said to Saul, 'Why have you deceived me? You are Saul!' • The king said to her, 'Do not be afraid. What do you see?' The woman answered, 'I see a ghostly form coming up from the earth.' • 'What is it like?' he asked; she answered, 'Like an old man coming up, wrapped in a cloak.' Then Saul knew it was Samuel, and he bowed low with his face to the ground, and prostrated himself.

15 • Samuel said to Saul, 'Why have you disturbed me and raised me?' Saul answered, 'I am in great trouble; the Philistines are waging war against me, and God has turned away; he no longer answers me through prophets or through dreams, and I have summoned you to tell me what I should do.' • Samuel said, 'Why do you ask me, now that the LORD has turned from you and become your adversary? • He has done what he foretold through me. He has wrested the kingdom from your hand and given it to another, to David. • You have not obeyed the LORD, or executed the judgement of his fierce anger against the Amalekites; that is why he has done this to you today. • For the same reason the LORD will let your people Israel fall along with you into the hands of the Philistines. What is more, tomorrow you and your sons will be with me.'   •

Saul and the Ghost of Samuel

Saul's decline continues and his demoralization reaches its lowest ebb. Verse 3 sets the scene with utmost brevity. Saul had long ago lost God's favour (Ch.15); now he cannot even discover God's will (6). His last remaining contact, Samuel, has died, but like Oedipus and Macbeth he *had* to know at all costs. In desperation therefore he turned to necromancy – the very practice which he himself had forbidden.

The story is splendidly told. Suspense is achieved by a series of obstacles. Mystery is preserved by the omission of detail, e.g. we are not told the name of *the woman* nor how she called up the ghost. Excitement is increased by her sudden recognition first of Samuel, by his *cloak* (cp. Saul's spear), and then of Saul, perhaps because nobody else would have presumed to disturb Samuel. *Samuel*, cold and relentless as ever, begins ominously

Saul and the Ghost of Samuel (cont.)

28.20   • Saul was overcome, and terrified by Samuel's words he fell full length to the ground. He had no strength left, for he had eaten nothing all day and all night. • The woman went to Saul and, seeing how deeply shaken he was, she said, 'I listened to what you said and I risked my life to obey you. • Now listen to me: let me set before you a little food to give you strength for your journey.' • He refused to eat anything, but when his servants joined the woman in pressing him, he yielded, rose from the ground, and sat on the couch. • The woman had a fattened calf at home, which she quickly slaughtered; she also took some meal, kneaded 25 it, and baked unleavened loaves. • She set the food before Saul and his servants, and when they had eaten they set off that same night.   (REB)

Saul and the Ghost of Samuel (cont.)

without any greeting to Saul; and his second speech, though a little inflated, has a grim force, especially in the phrase *tomorrow you and your sons will be with me,* i.e. your family will be blotted out.

The tension is then finally relieved and the grimness softened by the woman's motherly care for the doomed king, the witch being so much more sympathetic than the prophet. This 'dying fall' not only rounds off the story but also wins back our sympathy for Saul, after many chapters, in time for the last scene.

Necromancy was universally practised in the ancient world, and it plays an important part in Greek and ANE literature. But it was clearly an infringement of God's sovereignty, and this is the only place in the Old Testament where it

(i) forms the centre of a story, and

(ii) escapes the disapproval of the narrator.

The fact that Saul banned it does not, of course, mean that he did not believe in it; and certainly in this story everyone believed that Samuel was really there. A typical feature of the practice, as of all magic, is that, if the right spells are pronounced, the ghost is compelled to rise, even against its will.

Saul's Defeat and Death

31.1 The Philistines engaged Israel in battle, and the Israelites were routed, leaving their dead on Mount Gilboa. • The Philistines closely pursued Saul and his sons, and Jonathan, Abinadab, and Malchishua, the sons of Saul, were killed. • The battle went hard for Saul, and when the archers caught up with him they wounded him severely. • He said to his armour-bearer, 'Draw your sword and run me through, so that these uncircumcised brutes may not come and taunt me and make sport of me.' But the armour-bearer refused; he dared not do it. Thereupon 5 Saul took his own sword and fell on it. • When the armour-bearer saw that Saul was dead, he too fell on his sword and died with him. • So they died together on that day, Saul, his three sons, and his armour-bearer, as well as all his men. • When the Israelites in the neighbourhood of the valley and of the Jordan saw that the other Israelites had fled and that Saul and his sons had perished, they fled likewise, abandoning their towns; and the Philistines moved in and occupied them.   •

Saul's Defeat and Death

The defeat on *Mt Gilboa* undid the one solid success of Saul's life, the liberation of the land from the Philistines. For the

rest he had failed all along the line – publicly as spiritual and civil leader (Chs 14-15), privately as father and friend (Chs

Saul's Defeat and Death (cont.)

.10

• Next day, when the Philistines came to strip the slain, they found Saul and his three sons lying dead on Mount Gilboa. • They cut off his head and stripped him of his armour; then they sent messengers through the length and breadth of their land to carry the good news to idols and people alike. • They deposited his armour in the temple of Ashtoreth and nailed his body on the wall of Bethshan.

• When the inhabitants of Jabesh-gilead heard what the Philistines had done to Saul, • all the warriors among them set out and journeyed through the night to recover the bodies of Saul and his sons from the wall of Bethshan. They brought them back to Jabesh and burned them; • they took the bones and buried them under the tamarisk tree in Jabesh, and for seven days they fasted.   (REB)

Saul's Defeat and Death (cont.)

19-22). There was nothing left to live for.

Suicide is not generally admired in the OT, but surely here the author is suggesting that this was a *fitting* end for the great warrior, just as Samson's was for the great strong man. That hint of sympathy is made explicit in the conclusion of the chapter, when *the inhabitants of Jabesh-gilead* came to recover his body. Their action recalls a time when Saul saved their city and was magnanimous in victory. Then when the people suggested to Samuel that Saul's detractors should be put to death, Saul had replied 'No man is to be put to death on a day when the LORD has won such a victory in Israel' [11.13]. Gressmann comments on the conclusion of Ch.31: 'Saul's sun sank blood-red over the very place from which he had set out as a young hero, to the cheers of his people, upon his promising career.'

What then had gone wrong? As a man, Saul was loved by people as unlike as the chilly Samuel and the hot-blooded David. But there was all too much on the other side. He could be mean as well as magnanimous. He was jealous and suspicious: paranoid we might say, if we could be sure that his suspicions were unfounded. In his black mood he was simply murderous – and we are told more

of Saul's moods than of any other character in OT narrative (18.8 etc.). His behaviour swung between the manic and the depressive, between 'the spirit of the LORD' and 'an evil spirit from the LORD'.

If one looks for a psychological link between those two poles, it seems to lie in a deep sense of inadequacy. Time and again the narrative brings it out (9.21; 10.22, 27; 15.17 etc.). Hence his concern for public recognition (15.12; 31.4); hence the desire for popularity (15.24) which led him to the sin that was never forgiven (28.18). And throughout his career that sense of inadequacy was fed by the man who should have supported him. Samuel was the black dog on his shoulder, hounding him even from beyond the grave.

And Samuel spoke for God. So Saul, the rejected, was totally alone. Even Samson found the LORD with him at the end, but Saul was irretrievably god-forsaken (28.15). Undermined on all sides, he could do nothing right; nevertheless as king he had to go on. Paradoxically, it is his very weakness that retains the sympathy of the reader. We cannot escape the feeling that his punishment far outweighs any guilt, and that is why 'Saul is the one great tragic hero of the bible' (Frye).

David's Lament for Saul and Jonathan

1.1 After Saul's death David returned from his victory over the Amalekites and spent two days in Ziklag. • On the third day a man came from Saul's camp; his clothes were torn and there was dust on his head. Coming into David's presence he fell to the ground and did obeisance. • David asked him where he had come from, and he replied, 'I have escaped from the Israelite camp.' • David said, 'What is the news? Tell me.' 'The army has been driven from the field,' he answered, 'many have fallen in battle, and Saul and Jonathan his son are dead.'

5 • David said to the young man who brought the news, 'How do you know that Saul and Jonathan are dead?' • He answered, 'It so happened that I was on Mount Gilboa and saw Saul leaning on his spear with the chariots and horsemen closing in on him. • He turned and, seeing me, called to me. I said, "What is it, sir?" • He asked me who I was, and I said, "An Amalekite." • He said to me, "Come and stand 10 over me and dispatch me. I still live, but the throes of death have seized me." • So I stood over him and dealt him the death blow, for I knew that, stricken as he was, he could not live. Then I took the crown from his head and the armlet from his arm, and I have brought them here to you, my lord.'

• At that David and all the men with him took hold of their clothes and tore them. • They mourned and wept, and they fasted till evening because Saul and Jonathan his son and the army of the LORD and the house of Israel had fallen in battle.

• David said to the young man who brought him the news, 'Where do you come from?' and he answered, 'I am the son of an alien, an Amalekite.' • 'How is it', said David, 'that you were not afraid to raise your hand to kill the LORD's 15 anointed?' • Summoning one of his own young men he ordered him to fall upon the Amalekite. The young man struck him down and he died. • David said, 'Your blood be on your own head; for out of your own mouth you condemned yourself by saying, "I killed the LORD's anointed." '   (REB)

David's Lament for Saul and Jonathan

The death of Saul concludes the story of David's rise to power. From Ch.16 on the narrative has been 'oriented towards the rising star of David' (Gordon). The tragedy of Saul has given place to the epic of David, though much of the material is common to both. Many features of these chapters are rare in the Bible but common in ANE and/ or Greek epic: the vow not to eat during a battle, the single combat, the necromancy and the noble suicide – all of which are pivotal incidents in the story of Saul. And, as far as *general* tendency goes, the C13th BC Hittite work known as the *Apology of King Hattusili* provides a close parallel. In it the king seeks to justify his usurpation of his nephew's throne. He claims that he was a favourite of his brother, the previous king, and insists that all along he has owed his success to the support of the goddess Ishtar (Kuhrt).

The description of Saul's death given by the *Amalekite* in vv.6-10 is not easy to reconcile with that in Ch.31. Some have therefore supposed it a fabrication: the man had come upon the royal insignia in the rout, and seen the chance to turn the find to his own advantage. But the narrator gives us no hint of such an interpretation. In any case David certainly accepted his story at face value and, as he said later [4.10], 'rewarded him for his news!'

Of recent translations of David's lament NRSV is most successful in combining dignity with intelligibility and faithfulness to the Hebrew text. Nevertheless

David's Lament for Saul and Jonathan (cont.)

17 • David intoned this lamentation over Saul and his son Jonathan. • (He ordered that The Song of the Bow be taught to the people of Judah; it is written in the Book of Jashar.) He said:

19 Your glory, O Israel, lies slain upon your high places!
    How the mighty have fallen!

20 Tell it not in Gath,
    proclaim it not in the streets of Ashkelon;
or the daughters of the Philistines will rejoice,
    the daughters of the uncircumcised will exult.

21 You mountains of Gilboa,
    let there be no dew or rain upon you,
    nor bounteous fields!
For there the shield of the mighty was defiled,
    the shield of Saul, anointed with oil no more.

22 From the blood of the slain,
    from the fat of the mighty,
the bow of Jonathan did not turn back,
    nor the sword of Saul return empty.

23 Saul and Jonathan, beloved and lovely!
    In life and in death they were not divided;
they were swifter than eagles,
    they were stronger than lions.

24 O daughters of Israel, weep over Saul,
    who clothed you with crimson, in luxury,
    who put ornaments of gold on your apparel.

25 How the mighty have fallen
    in the midst of the battle!

David's Lament for Saul and Jonathan (cont.)

there remain places where text and interpretation are extremely uncertain, notably in vv.21c and 25 *upon your high places*.

The thrice-repeated line *How the mighty have fallen!* provides the framework. The emphasis is not here, as is usual, thrown upon the centre, but upon the end. The movement is from the whole army (v.19) to Saul and Jonathan as a pair (22-3), then to Saul (24), and finally, with David's personal grief revealed, to Jonathan. The fact that the climax comes with Jonathan, not Saul, fits David as author.

The early part of the poem is national-military in tone. The first thought is of the enemy's exultation: David's hope that the Philistines will not hear of the victory is 'impossible but human' (Gressmann). David's bitterness then breaks out into a curse on the scene of the battle, vividly pictured as it is to remain for ever, its slopes fertile only in the crop of corroded (*perished*, v.27) weapons, once bright *with oil* and wielded by heroes whose exploits brought rich plunder to the women of Israel.

But gradually the more tender, personal note takes over. The weapons are themselves personified in v.22 and thus more

David's Lament for Saul and Jonathan (cont.)

Jonathan lies slain upon your high places.

1. 26   I am distressed for you, my brother Jonathan;
      greatly beloved were you to me;
  your love to me was wonderful,
    passing the love of women.

27   How the mighty have fallen,
      and the weapons of war perished!

(NRSV)

David's Lament for Saul and Jonathan (cont.)

easily symbolise their owners (which gives a double meaning to the final line of the poem). The *sword*, like the spear, recalls the aggressive, thrusting Saul, the *bow* the more gentle, even feminine, Jonathan (cp. 1 Sam 20 and the *honey* of 1 Sam 14). So sword and bow lead us to the love of Saul and Jonathan, and that gives place in turn to the greater love of Jonathan and David – the old friendship of Saul and David is passed over in silence. References to women likewise move from their public function as leaders of national rejoicing or lamentation (20 and 24) to the bold and intimate sentiment of v.26: *your love to me was wonderful, passing the love of women*. So Gilgamesh covered the dead body of his friend Enkidu 'like a bride'. The interweaving of the public and the personal continues to mark the tale of David's reign which follows, and it is precisely 'the love of women' from which we see his failures time and time again deriving.

David King in Hebron

2. 1 Afterwards David enquired of the LORD, 'Shall I go up into one of the towns of Judah?' The LORD answered, 'Go.' David asked, 'Where shall I go?' and the answer was, 'To Hebron.' • So David went up there with his two wives, Ahinoam of Jezreel and Abigail widow of Nabal of Carmel. • David also brought the men who had joined him, with their families, and they settled in Hebron and the neighbouring towns. • The men of Judah came, and there they anointed David king over the house of Judah.

8   • Meanwhile Saul's commander-in-chief, Abner son of Ner, had taken Saul's son Ishbosheth, brought him across to Mahanaim, • and made him king over Gilead, the Asherites, Jezreel, Ephraim, and Benjamin, and all Israel. • Ishbosheth was forty years old when he became king over Israel, and he reigned for two years. The tribe of Judah, however, followed David. • David's rule over Judah in Hebron lasted seven and a half years. ♦

David King in Hebron

The next section of the story (2 Sam Chs 2-5) tells how David's party gradually eliminated what remained of Saul's party, particularly Abner his Commander-in-Chief (Ch. 3) and Ishbosheth his surviving son [Ch. 4]. In each case the author makes extravagant efforts to convince us of David's personal innocence. The narrative is also rather scrappy. But it contains a number of incidents which set the scene for the more exciting story that follows.

The Israelite defeat on Mt Gilboa was so heavy that the Philistines could safely leave them alone for a while. This was David's opportunity, and he quickly exploited it. Judah, being his own tribe, was his natural power-base. He made for *Hebron*, its most important town, and was

David King in Hebron (cont.)

• Abner son of Ner, with the troops of Saul's son Ishbosheth, marched out from Mahanaim to Gibeon, • and Joab son of Zeruiah marched out with David's troops from Hebron. They met at the pool of Gibeon and took up their positions, one force on one side of the pool and the other on the opposite side. • Abner said to Joab, 'Let the young men come forward and join in single combat before us.'

15 Joab agreed. • So they came up, one by one, and took their places, twelve for Benjamin and Ishbosheth and twelve from David's men. • Each man seized his opponent by the head and thrust his sword into his opponent's side; and thus they fell together. That is why that place, which lies in Gibeon, was called the Field of Blades.

• There ensued a very hard-fought battle that day, and Abner and the men of Israel were defeated by David's troops. • All three sons of Zeruiah were there, Joab, Abishai, and Asahel. Asahel, who was swift as a gazelle of the plains,

20 • chased after Abner, swerving to neither right nor left in his pursuit. • Abner glanced back and said, 'Is it you, Asahel?' Asahel answered, 'It is.' • Abner said, 'Turn aside to right or left; tackle one of the young men and win his belt for yourself.' But Asahel would not abandon the pursuit. • Abner again urged him to give it up. 'Why should I kill you?' he said. 'How could I look Joab your brother in the face?' • When he still refused to turn away, Abner struck him in the belly with a back-thrust of his spear so that the spear came out through his back, and he fell dead in his tracks. All who came to the place where Asahel lay dead stopped there. • But Joab and Abishai kept up the pursuit of Abner, until, at sunset, they reached the hill of Ammah, opposite Giah on the road leading to the pastures of Gibeon.   ♦

David King in Hebron (cont.)

there *anointed king* (the text makes no reference to the anointing by Samuel in 1 Sam 15). Meanwhile *Abner* had taken *Ishbosheth* to safety east of Jordan. There he proclaimed him king of an optimistically wide area, described as *all Israel*.

The struggle between the two parties dragged on intermittently for some years. From it the author selects three incidents. The first (12-16) and the third (25-32) show the wish of both sides to keep down the *slaughter* of *kinsmen* (26). Initially the opponents tried to settle their differences by combat between representatives of the two tribes. The description of it in 16 is highly stylised, as if the writer is transferring to prose a visual representation he had seen (such a scene is depicted on a C9th BC relief from Mesopotamia). But the device failed, and battle began.

The most ominous incident is *Abner's* killing of *Asahel* (17-23). *Zeruiah*, a widow

of *Bethlehem* (32), had *three sons* of whom we have already met Joab and Abishai fighting with David in 1 Sam 26. When mentioned in the story, they are very often referred to as *sons of Zeruiah*. Such mention of a mother is rare in the OT.

The story of Asahel's death shares with folk-tale the pattern of 'third time (un)lucky'. But there are some subtle touches in the telling. The phrase to *turn aside to right or left* is commonly used in a metaphorical sense; here it is, as it were, translated back into 'a concrete image of the geometry of survival' (Alter). And Abner's reference in v.22 to Joab is loaded with tragic irony, in view of what is shortly to happen between them.

The battle narrative is schematic, as is usual in the OT, and the topography obscure. *The Arabah* here must mean the Jordan Valley. The casualty figures

David King in Hebron (cont.)

2.25 • The Benjamites rallied to Abner and, forming themselves into a single group, took their stand on the top of a hill. • Abner called to Joab, 'Must the slaughter go on for ever? Can you not see the bitterness that will result? How long before you recall the troops from the pursuit of their kinsmen?' • Joab answered, 'As God lives, if you had not spoken, they would not have given up the pursuit till morning.' • Then Joab sounded the trumpet, and the troops all halted; they abandoned the pursuit of the Israelites, and the fighting ceased.

30 • Abner and his men moved along the Arabah all that night, crossed the Jordan, and continued all morning till they reached Mahanaim. • After Joab returned from the pursuit of Abner, he mustered his troops and found that, besides Asahel, nineteen of David's men were missing. • David's forces had routed the Benjamites and the followers of Abner, killing three hundred and sixty of them. • They took up Asahel and buried him in his father's tomb at Bethlehem. Joab and his men marched all night, and as day broke they reached Hebron.   (REB)

David King in Hebron (cont.)

(30-31) indicate the small scale of the engagement, but they were large enough to incline both the commanders to a truce (25-28).

The Murder of Abner

3.1 There was a long war between the house of Saul and the house of David; David grew stronger and stronger, while the house of Saul became weaker and weaker.

6 • While there was war between the house of Saul and the house of David, Abner was making himself strong in the house of Saul. • Now Saul had a concubine whose name was Rizpah daughter of Aiah. And Ishbosheth said to Abner, 'Why have you gone in to my father's concubine?' • The words of Ishbosheth made Abner very angry; he said, 'Am I a dog's head for Judah? Today I keep showing loyalty to the house of your father Saul, to his brothers, and to his friends, and have not given you into the hand of David; and yet you charge me now with a crime concerning this woman. • So may God do to Abner and so may he add to it! For just what the LORD has sworn to David, that will I accomplish

10 for him, • to transfer the kingdom from the house of Saul, and set up the throne of David over Israel and over Judah, from Dan to Beer-sheba.' • And Ishbosheth could not answer Abner another word, because he feared him.   ▸

The Murder of Abner

Ch.3, after a quick summary of the fighting, switches to the two other main themes of 2 Sam, namely intrigue and sex. To take over a king's concubine was seen as a symbolic challenge, and the motif will recur at crucial points of the subsequent story. Ishbosheth's rash criticism of Abner (7) is the provocation (or the excuse?) for his change of allegiance. Verse 9 is an obvious piece of theological editing. Verse 11 is unusual in the OT in expressing

both the silence and its motive: normally the narrator leaves the reader to infer both.

David's demand in v.13 for the return of *Michal* (see 1 S 25.44) is clearly a political move, to strengthen the legitimacy of his claim to Saul's throne. By contrast, we have a poignant vignette of *Paltiel*: 'he appears from the darkness to weep for his wife' (Alter), and returns to it again, defeated by the men of power.

The power-game is now played out

The Murder of Abner (cont.)

• Abner sent messengers to David at Hebron, saying, 'To whom does the land belong? Make your covenant with me, and I will give you my support to bring all Israel over to you.' • He said, 'Good; I will make a covenant with you. But one thing I require of you: you shall never appear in my presence unless you bring Saul's daughter Michal when you come to see me.' • Then David sent messengers to Saul's son Ishbaal, saying, 'Give me my wife Michal, to whom I became engaged at the price of one hundred foreskins of the Philistines.' • Ishbaal sent and took her from her husband Paltiel the son of Laish. • But her husband went with her, weeping as he walked behind her all the way to Bahurim. Then Abner said to him, 'Go back home!' So he went back.

• When Abner came with twenty men to David at Hebron, David made a feast for Abner and the men who were with him. • Abner said to David, 'Let me go and rally all Israel to my lord the king, in order that they may make a covenant with you, and that you may reign over all that your heart desires.' So David dismissed Abner, and he went away in peace.

• Just then the servants of David arrived with Joab from a raid, bringing much spoil with them. But Abner was not with David at Hebron, for David had dismissed him, and he had gone away in peace. • When Joab and all the army that was with him came, it was told Joab, 'Abner son of Ner came to the king, and he has dismissed him, and he has gone away in peace.' • Then Joab went to the king and said, 'What have you done? Abner came to you; why did you dismiss him, so that he got away? • You know that Abner son of Ner came to deceive you, and to learn your comings and goings and to learn all that you are doing.'

• When Joab came out from David's presence, he sent messengers after Abner, and they brought him back from the cistern of Sirah; but David did not know about it. • When Abner returned to Hebron, Joab took him aside in the gateway to speak with him privately, and there he stabbed him in the stomach. So he died for shedding the blood of Asahel, Joab's brother. • Afterward, when David heard of it, he said, 'I and my kingdom are forever guiltless before the LORD for the blood of Abner son of Ner. • May the guilt fall on the head of Joab, and on all his father's house; and may the house of Joab never be without one who has a discharge, or who is leprous, or who holds a spindle, or who falls by the sword, or who lacks food!' • So Joab and his brother Abishai murdered Abner because he had killed their brother Asahel in the battle at Gibeon.

The Murder of Abner (cont.)

between David, *Joab* and *Abner*. Joab suspects Abner (and perhaps David too) of double-dealing. The contrast between David's and Joab's views of Abner is cleverly brought out in vv.21-4. Three successive verses end with the identical three Hebrew words: *he-dismissed-him and-he-went-away in-peace*. The fourth verse is Joab's, and it changes just the last word: *why did-you-dismiss-him* and-

he-has-gone for-good. Joab's motive for the murder is twice said to be the blood-feud, but he was glad to get rid of a possible rival. Though David would have found Abner useful, his immediate concern (backed by the narrator in vv.26 and 37) is to exculpate himself.

Verses 28-35 describe various public actions of David to this end. His curse on Joab's family echoes a Hittite punishment

The Murder of Abner (cont.)

3.31   • Then David said to Joab and to all the people who were with him, 'Tear your clothes, and put on sackcloth, and mourn over Abner.' And King David followed the bier. • They buried Abner at Hebron. The king lifted up his voice and wept at the grave of Abner, and all the people wept. • The king lamented for Abner, saying,

> 'Should Abner die as a fool dies?
34   Your hands were not bound,
>   your feet were not fettered;
>   as one falls before the wicked
>   you have fallen.'

35 And all the people wept over him again. • Then all the people came to persuade David to eat something while it was still day; but David swore, saying, 'So may God do to me, and more, if I taste bread or anything else before the sun goes down!' • All the people took notice of it, and it pleased them; just as everything the king did pleased all the people. • So all the people and all Israel understood that day that the king had no part in the killing of Abner son of Ner. • And the king said to his servants, 'Do you not know that a prince and a great man has fallen this day in Israel? • Today I am powerless, even though anointed king; these men, the sons of Zeruiah, are too violent for me. The LORD pay back the one who does wickedly in accordance with his wickedness!'   (NRSV)

The Murder of Abner (cont.)

for a man's disloyalty, that 'he be dressed in female clothes and handed a spindle'. David's lament for Abner, fragmentary but seemingly authentic, excuses his lack of resistance as due to treachery. The role of *the people* (32-6) in this is important, as it had often been in the case of Saul and Jonathan (1 S. 9, 14, 15), and the narrator breaks frame to underline it.

Finally, David had to explain why he had not punished Joab more severely. Here, in v.39, we come closer to the truth. It would be too easy to say that David was frightened of Joab and Abishai. Rather, they are represented, here and elsewhere, as espousing violent action which David thought either impolitic or distasteful. So in 1 S 26.6-8 'Abishai son of Zeruiah' had wanted to kill Saul, as he did Shimei twice

later (2 S 16.9; 19.21). The same divergence of attitude erupts in the argument between David and Joab after the death of Absalom (2 S 19.1-8). The *violent sons of Zeruiah* are thus simple dramatic foils to the much more complex David. For David could be violent too, but increasingly in 2 Sam he shows his softer side, which can be read as weakness, humanity or both. For the present, he leaves the punishment of Joab to the LORD; later he will bequeathe it to Solomon.

[Ch.4] records the murder of Ishbosheth by two Benjamites. When they report their deed to David, hoping for reward, he reminds them how he treated the Amalekite in Ch.1, and has them executed. The way is clear for him to succeed to Saul's throne.

David King in Jerusalem

5.1 All the tribes of Israel came to David at Hebron and said to him, 'We are your own flesh and blood. • In the past, while Saul was still king over us, it was you that led the forces of Israel on their campaigns. To you the LORD said, "You are to be shepherd of my people Israel; you are to be their prince." ' • The elders of Israel all came to the king at Hebron; there David made a covenant with them before the LORD, and they anointed David king over Israel.

4,5 • David came to the throne at the age of thirty and reigned for forty years. • In Hebron he had ruled over Judah for seven and a half years, and in Jerusalem he reigned over Israel and Judah combined for thirty-three years.

• The king and his men went to Jerusalem to attack the Jebusites, the inhabitants of that region. The Jebusites said to David, 'You will never come in here, not till you have disposed of the blind and the lame,' stressing that David would never come in. • None the less David did capture the stronghold of Zion, and it is now known as the City of David. • On that day David had said, 'Everyone who is eager to attack the Jebusites, let him get up the water-shaft to reach the lame and the blind.'

10 • David steadily grew more and more powerful, for the LORD the God of Hosts was with him. • King Hiram of Tyre sent envoys to David with cedar logs, and with them carpenters and stonemasons, who built David a house. • David knew by now that the LORD had confirmed him as king over Israel and had enhanced his royal power for the sake of his people Israel.   ▸

David King in Jerusalem

The next four chapters, like the last three, offer few literary excitements. But the history they record, if it can be relied upon, is of major importance.

First (5.2-5), the tribes loyal to Saul came over to David and anointed him *king over Israel* too. He now reigns over *Israel and Judah combined*, a phrase which shows that the country is not truly unified. In the following chapters 'Israel' is used sometimes of the north, sometimes of both together, and it is not always easy to be sure which is meant. Next we have the formal chronology of David's reign followed by the establishment of his new capital.

Jerusalem was the last of the independent Canaanite cities. Its position on a spur running south from the later Temple mount (see map 3) had been strengthened c.1800 BC by walls up to 8 metres thick, the source of the *Jebusites'* confidence that the city could be defended merely by *the blind and the lame*. They had the further advantage (confirmed by archaeo-

logy) of access to the spring Gihon in the Kidron valley via an underground *water-shaft* with an exit just outside the walls. But according to 2 Sam, this shaft also let in the enemy, and that is how David captured Jerusalem. [1 Chron 11.6] offers an alternative account which does not mention the shaft. 'David had said, "The first man to kill a Jebusite will become a commander", and the first man to go up [to the attack] was Joab son of Zeruiah, so he was given the command'.

For David the captured city was ideally situated near the tribal boundary between (his) Judah and (Saul's) Benjamin. Because *his men,* i.e. his private army, had taken it, it became his own royal possession and the site of his palace.

The peoples of the coast reacted variously. The Phoenicians, who never molested the Israelites, sent *cedars* of Lebanon for the palace. *The Philistines* had been prepared to tolerate David at Hebron, but saw his capture of Jerusalem

David King in Jerusalem (cont.)

5.17   • When the Philistines learnt that David had been anointed king over Israel, they came up in force to seek him out. David, getting wind of this, went down to the stronghold for refuge. • When the Philistines had come and overrun the valley of Rephaim, • David enquired of the LORD, 'If I attack the Philistines, will you deliver them into my hands?' The LORD answered, 'Go, I shall deliver the Philistines into your hands.' • He went and attacked and defeated them at Baal-perazim. • The Philistines abandoned their idols there, and David and his men carried them off.

6.1   • David again summoned the picked men of Israel, thirty thousand in all, • and went with the whole army that was then with him to Baalath-judah to fetch from 13 there the Ark of God. • When the bearers of the Ark of the LORD had gone six steps he sacrificed a bull and a buffalo. • He was wearing a linen ephod, and he danced with 15 abandon before the LORD, • as he and all the Israelites brought up the Ark of the LORD with acclamation and blowing of trumpets. • As the Ark of the LORD was entering the City of David, Saul's daughter Michal looked down from a window and saw King David leaping and whirling before the LORD, and she despised him in her heart.

• After they had brought the Ark of the LORD, they put it in its place inside the tent that David had set up for it, and David offered whole-offerings and shared-offerings before the LORD. • Having completed these sacrifices, David blessed the people in the name of the LORD of Hosts, • and distributed food to them all, a flat loaf of bread, a portion of meat, and a cake of raisins, to every man and woman in the whole gathering of the Israelites. Then all the people went home.   ◆

David King in Jerusalem (cont.)

as a threat. Their army came within a few miles. David's instinct was to seek cover. But a sally defeated the Philistines, and they never again seriously troubled Israel.

The end of the Philistine threat enabled David to take an important step, to bring back *the Ark* to Jerusalem. For the Hebrews the Ark was one of the oldest symbols of the presence of God with them. Latterly it had become especially associated with the Philistine war, and for a while before Saul's reign it had even been in Philistine hands. Under Saul surprisingly we hear nothing of it, but now David saw a new role for it. Its presence in *the City of David* would mark the end of the Philistine war, symbolise the LORD's approval of his own accession and establish Jerusalem as the capital. Later generations regarded the installation of the Ark as an event of great importance in their history. It may well have been celebrated annually, with Ps

24.7-10 [and Ps 132] used in the ritual.

David himself, as king and priest, played the central part in the ceremonial procession which brought it to Jerusalem. *Wearing* the *ephod*, a short priestly garment (14), he offered a sacrifice at the start of its journey and at the end, and *blessed* all *the people in the name of the LORD* (18). Formally, he was the patron and founder of the cult of YHWH in Jerusalem.

But he also, with customary lack of judgement, danced wildly in front of the Ark, *leaping and whirling before the LORD*. Such ritual dancing was the traditional way of greeting an army returning victorious from battle, and David was doubtless carried away also by his desire to please the people (see 3.36). But his behaviour drew bitter criticism from *Michal*. Her exchange with David displays a fascinating mixture of private and public motives on both their parts.

David King in Jerusalem (cont.)

20 • David returned to greet his household, and Michal, Saul's daughter, came out to meet him. She said, 'What a glorious day for the king of Israel, when he made an exhibition of himself in the sight of his servants' slave-girls, as any vulgar clown might do!' • David answered her, 'But it was done in the presence of the LORD, who chose me instead of your father and his family and appointed me prince over Israel, the people of the LORD. Before the LORD I shall dance for joy, yes, • and I shall earn yet more disgrace and demean myself still more in your eyes; but those slave-girls of whom you speak, they will hold me in honour for it.' • To her dying day Michal, Saul's daughter, was childless.   (REB)

David King in Jerusalem (cont.)

For *Saul's daughter*, as she is here pointedly called, love (1 Sam 18.20) had turned to hatred. She rebuked him publicly, sarcastically and in the third person. Her ostensible grounds are that he has not merely usurped but demeaned her father's throne; but what shows through is her sexual jealousy. David bites back on both counts: it is the LORD who has pre-ferred him to Saul, and he himself will prefer the judgement of the girls to hers. Then comes the splendidly ambiguous punchline (6.23). Michal's *childless*ness was a blow both to her and to Saul's dynasty; but was it chance or punishment; and, if the latter, was she punished by God or by David? This is story-telling as we shall meet it from Ch.9 onwards.

God's Promise to David

7.1 Once the king was established in his palace and the LORD had given him security from his enemies on all sides, • he said to Nathan the prophet, 'Here I am living in a house of cedar, while the Ark of God is housed in a tent.' • Nathan answered, 'Do whatever you have in mind, for the LORD is with you.' • But that same night

5 the word of the LORD came to Nathan: • 'Go and say to David my servant, This is the word of the LORD: Are you to build me a house to dwell in? • Down to this day I have never dwelt in a house since I brought Israel up from Egypt; I lived in a tent and a tabernacle. • Wherever I journeyed with Israel, did I ever ask any of the judges whom I appointed shepherds of my people Israel why they had not built me a cedar house?

• Then say this to my servant David: This is the word of the LORD of Hosts: I took you from the pastures and from following the sheep to be prince over my people Israel. • I have been with you wherever you have gone, and have destroyed all the enemies in your path. I shall bring you fame like the fame of the great ones of the

10 earth. • I shall assign a place for my people Israel; there I shall plant them to dwell in their own land. They will be disturbed no more; never again will the wicked oppress them as they did in the past, • from the day when I appointed judges over my people Israel; and I shall give you peace from all your enemies.   ◆

God's Promise to David

Ch.7, taken together with Ch.6, has the function of legitimising David's rule. It is not a straightforward chapter, but it contains some unequivocal words of great importance to the OT. God's promise to David in v.16 transfers to him the promise made to Abraham in Genesis 12 etc. It also underlies many of the psalms, and it will be confirmed by the survival of his dynasty down to the very end of the monarchy

God's Promise to David (cont.)

The LORD has told you that he would build up your royal house. • When your life ends and you rest with your forefathers, I shall set up one of your family, one of your own children, to succeed you, and I shall establish his kingdom. • It is he who is to build a house in honour of my name, and I shall establish his royal throne for all time. • I shall be a father to him, and he will be my son. When he does wrong, I shall punish him as any father might, and not spare the rod. • But my love will never be withdrawn from him as I withdrew it from Saul, whom I removed from your path. • Your family and your kingdom will be established for ever in my sight; your throne will endure for all time.   (REB)

7. 15

God's Promise to David (cont.)

in 2 Kings. Finally it will have a second and even longer life as the basis of the messianic hope which was adumbrated by Isaiah and carried on by other prophets right through to the New Testament.

The context of that promise in 2 Sam is an offer by David to *build a house* for the LORD, i.e. a temple for the Ark in place of the *tent* which he had just *set up* for it (6.17). The offer was made through *Nathan the prophet*, here first introduced, who also conveyed the reply. God's refusal seems to be grounded in the view

that the country is not yet sufficiently stable (*I shall give you peace* v.11). The reasoning is made quite explicit in 1 K 5.3; but the view has already been undermined by the narrator himself in v.1, so we are left with a puzzle. To temper the disappointment, God goes on to volunteer the reciprocal promise: he himself will *build* David's *house* (11) in the two senses of throne and dynasty. Moreover, to round it off neatly, David's son is to *build a house* (in the third sense of a temple) for the LORD.

David's Empire

8. 1

After this David attacked and subdued the Philistines, and took from them Metheg-ha-ammah. • He defeated the Moabites and made them lie along the ground, where he measured them off with a length of cord; for every two lengths that were to be put to death one full length was spared. The Moabites became subject to him and paid tribute.

• David also defeated Hadadezer the Rehobite, king of Zobah, who was on his way to restore his monument of victory by the river Euphrates. • From him David captured seventeen hundred horse and twenty thousand foot-soldiers; he

5

hamstrung all the chariot-horses, except a hundred which he retained. • When the Aramaeans of Damascus came to the aid of King Hadadezer of Zobah, David destroyed twenty-two thousand of them, • and stationed garrisons among these Aramaeans; they became subject to him and paid tribute.   ▸

David's Empire

Ch. 8 contains further scrappy material on David's victories. The defeated enemies, except the *Philistines*, are reduced to vassal status and pay *tribute*. Together with the Ammonites, whose similar subjection is rehearsed at greater length in Chs [10], 11 and 12, they constitute all the neighbouring peoples to north, east and south; the

implied claim in v.3 is that David's influence reached as far as the *Euphrates*.

For a century after Saul the Hebrew monarchy was, according to the OT, a force to be reckoned with in the Near East. There is no external corroboration of David's power, or even of his name, in contemporary sources, nor has archaeology

David's Empire (cont.)

13 • David made a great name for himself by the slaughter of eighteen thousand Edomites in the Valley of Salt. • He stationed garrisons throughout Edom, and all the Edomites became subject to him. The LORD gave David victory wherever he went.

• David ruled over the whole of Israel and maintained law and justice among all his people. • Joab son of Zeruiah was in command of the army; Jehoshaphat son of Ahilud was secretary of state; • Zadok and Abiathar son of Ahimelech, son of Ahitub, were priests; Seraiah was adjutant-general; • Benaiah son of Jehoiada commanded the Kerethite and Pelethite guards. David's sons were priests.   (REB)

David's Empire (cont.)

yet thrown up anything helpful, either in Jerusalem or outside. But his reign and Solomon's coincided with a temporary weakness on the part of the traditional powers of the ANE, especially Egypt and Assyria, so the timing is plausible.

Ch.8 ends with a list of David's leading men. He himself retained the role of Chief Justice. We see the beginnings of a civil service, due to be increased under Solomon. The royal bodyguard was, according to usual practice, made up of foreign mercenaries, in this case Philistines and their Cretan cousins. The fact that all *David's sons were priests* shows the royal hold on the cult too.

The Problem of Mephibosheth

9.1 David enquired, 'Is any member of Saul's family left, to whom I can show kindness for Jonathan's sake?' • A servant of Saul's family named Ziba was summoned to David, who asked, 'Are you Ziba?' He answered, 'Your servant, sir.' • The king asked, 'Is there any member of Saul's family still alive to whom I may show the kindness that God requires?' 'Yes,' said Ziba, 'there is still a son of Jonathan alive; he is a cripple, lame in both feet.' • 'Where is he?' said the king, and Ziba answered, 'He is staying with Machir son of Ammiel in Lo-debar.'

5 • The king had him fetched from Lo-debar, from the house of Machir son of Ammiel, • and when Mephibosheth, son of Jonathan and grandson of Saul, entered David's presence, he prostrated himself and did obeisance. David said to him, 'Mephibosheth!' and he answered, 'Your servant, sir.' • Then David said, 'Do not be afraid; I mean to show you kindness for your father Jonathan's sake; I shall restore to you the whole estate of your grandfather Saul and you will have a regular place at my table.' • Mephibosheth prostrated himself again and said, 'Who am I that you should spare a thought for a dead dog like me?'   ▸

The Problem of Mephibosheth

Suddenly with Ch.9 the orchestra stops tuning up and we hear the opening bars of the finest prose composition in the OT, often called the Court History of David, which occupies most of 2 S 9-20 with 1 K 1-2. Its largest section is the revolt of Absalom, but the same brilliant hand takes the story on to the David's death and Solomon's accession. Some comments upon it as a whole are made after 1 K 2.

David's enquiry through *Ziba* reveals the existence of *a son of Jonathan* living across the Jordan (cp. 2.8). *Mephibosheth* had been briefly introduced to the reader in an earlier verse [4.4]: 'He was five years old when word of the death of Saul and Jonathan came. His nurse had picked him up and fled, but as she hurried to get away he fell and was crippled.' Summoned now to David's presence, he twice *prostrated himself*, despite being both a cripple and *son of Jonathan and grandson of Saul* (6).

The Problem of Mephibosheth (cont.)

9.10 • David summoned Saul's servant Ziba and said, 'I assign to your master's grandson all the property that belonged to Saul and his family. • You, your sons and your slaves must cultivate the land and bring in the harvest to provide for your master's household, but Mephibosheth your master's grandson shall have a regular place at my table.'

Ziba, who had fifteen sons and twenty slaves, • answered: 'I shall do all that your majesty commands.' So Mephibosheth took his place in the royal household like one of the king's sons. • He had a young son, named Mica; and the members of Ziba's household were all Mephibosheth's servants, • while Mephibosheth lived in Jerusalem and had his regular place at the king's table, crippled as he was in both feet.   (REB)

The Problem of Mephibosheth (cont.)

Perhaps he had more to fear – and the invitation to eat at the court would hardly allay his fear. For David even a cripple posed some threat, and it was prudent to keep him close. But the restoration to him of Saul's *estate* at Gibea can have had no ulterior motive. We may therefore provisionally accept David's own thrice-repeated statement that he was prompted by loyalty (*hesedh*) to Jonathan. Indeed his phrase in v.3 echoes precisely Jonathan's words [1 S 20.14] 'I know that as long as I live you will show me faithful friendship as the LORD requires [lit. the *hesedh* of YHWH]; and if I should die you will continue loyal [lit. not shorten your *hesedh*] to my family forever.'

David Seduces Bathsheba and Murders Uriah

11.1 At the turn of the year, at the time when kings go campaigning, David sent Joab and with him his guards and all Israel. They massacred the Ammonites and laid siege to Rabbah-of-the-Ammonites. David, however, remained in Jerusalem. • It happened towards evening when David had got up from resting and was strolling on the palace roof, that from the roof he saw a woman bathing; the woman was very beautiful. • David made enquiries about this woman and was told, 'Why, that is Bathsheba daughter of Eliam and wife of Uriah the Hittite.' • David then sent messengers to fetch her. She came to him, and he lay with her, just after she 5 had purified herself from her period. She then went home again. • The woman conceived and sent word to David, 'I am pregnant.'   ▸

David Seduces Bathsheba and Murders Uriah

There now begins the exciting and closely woven narrative of the major crisis of David's reign – the rebellion of Absalom (11.1-20.22). It achieves psychological subtlety with great economy. To a modern reader perhaps its outstanding characteristic is the warts-and-all portrait it gives of the great national hero David. Ancient literature offers only one parallel: Achilles in the *Iliad*. And, like the *Iliad*, this narrative is better approached as drama than as history (see note at end of 1 K 2).

From the start public and private affairs, represented here by war and sex respectively, are interwoven. The two offer an ironical contrast, made explicit by Joab at the end of the story (12.28): while his men and other kings are at war, David rises lazily from his siesta (bed plays a large part in vv.2-13) and, from his *palace roof*, looks over the city for another kind of conquest. *Bathsheba* is ripe – surely she knew she would be seen? David enquires, summons and takes her. All is told briefly, even brutally, down to Bathsheba's two-word message *I am pregnant*; for she (unlike Abigail in 1 Sam 25) is at present far less important than her first husband.

David Seduces Bathsheba and Murders Uriah (cont.)

• David then sent word to Joab, 'Send me Uriah the Hittite,' whereupon Joab sent Uriah to David. • When Uriah reached him, David asked how Joab was and how the army was and how the war was going. • David then said to Uriah, 'Go down to your house and wash your feet.' Uriah left the palace and was followed by a present from the king's table. • Uriah, however, slept at the palace gate with all his master's bodyguard and did not go down to his house.

• This was reported to David; 'Uriah', they said 'has not gone down to his house.' So David asked Uriah, 'Haven't you just arrived from the journey? Why didn't you go down to your house?' • To which Uriah replied, 'The ark, Israel and Judah are lodged in huts; my master Joab and my lord's guards are camping in the open. Am I to go to my house, then, and eat and drink and sleep with my wife? As the LORD lives, and as you yourself live, I shall do no such thing!' • David then said to Uriah, 'Stay on here today; tomorrow I shall send you off.' So Uriah stayed that day in Jerusalem. • The next day, David invited him to eat and drink in his presence and made him drunk. In the evening, Uriah went out and bedded down with his master's bodyguard, but did not go down to his house.

• Next morning David wrote a letter to Joab and sent it by Uriah. • In the letter he wrote, 'Put Uriah out in front where the fighting is fiercest and then fall back, so that he gets wounded and killed.' • Joab, then besieging the city, stationed Uriah at a point where he knew that there would be tough fighters. • The people of the city sallied out and engaged Joab; there were casualties in the army, among David's guards, and Uriah the Hittite was killed as well. • Joab sent David a full account of the battle. • To the messenger he gave this order: 'When you have finished telling the king all about the battle, • if the king's anger is aroused and he says, "Why did you go near the town to give battle? • Why did you go near the ramparts?" you are to say, "Your servant Uriah the Hittite is dead too." '

• So the messenger set off and, on his arrival, told David everything that Joab had instructed him to say. David flew into a rage with Joab and said to the messenger, 'Why did you go near the ramparts? Who killed Abimelech son of Jerubbaal? Wasn't it a woman who dropped a millstone on him from the ramparts, causing his death at Thebez? Why did you go near the ramparts?'   ◆

David Seduces Bathsheba and Murders Uriah (cont.)

Uriah's piety provides a second contrast with David. Though of gentile descent, his name ('Yah is my light') is Hebrew, and he insists (even when drunk) on observing the rule of sexual abstinence during a campaign. Understanding the connotations of David's *wash your feet* (roughly equal to 'put your feet up'), he refused even to *go down to his house*, a key phrase repeated four times, three of them at the end of sentences (cp. comment on 3.21). Uriah's piety thus defeats David's plot and seals his own fate. For he will realise

that Bathsheba's child cannot be his, and sooner or later the truth will come out.

The scene changes to the siege of *Rabbah*, capital of *Ammon* (now Amman, capital of Jordan). *Joab*, unquestioningly, carries out David's instructions in spirit, if not to the letter: what matters is the word *dead*, which in Hebrew ends David's letter as it does the messenger's report (21, 24). But some of the royal guards are killed; Joab holds up news of Uriah's death. David's cynicism is exposed by his reply in v.25. Joab may relax – 'let not this thing be evil in

David Seduces Bathsheba and Murders Uriah (cont.)

• The messenger replied to David, 'Their men had won an initial advantage and then came out to engage us in the open. We then drove them back into the gateway, • but the archers shot at your retainers from the ramparts; some of the king's retainers lost their lives, and your servant Uriah the Hittite is dead too.'

11.25 • David then said to the messenger, 'Say this to Joab, "Do not take the matter to heart; the sword devours now one and now another. Attack the town in greater force and destroy it." That will encourage him.' • When Uriah's wife heard that her husband Uriah was dead, she mourned for her husband. • When the period of mourning was over, David sent to have her brought to his house; she became his wife and bore him a son. But what David had done displeased the LORD. (NJB)

David Seduces Bathsheba and Murders Uriah (cont.)

your eyes' – and prosecute the siege. David forgives himself. But 'the thing that David had done was evil in the eyes of the LORD' – an echo lost in modern translations.

David is Rebuked by Nathan and Repents

12. 1 The LORD sent the prophet Nathan to David. He came to him and said:

> In the same town were two men,
>> one rich, the other poor.

2 The rich man had flocks and herds
>> in great abundance;

3 the poor man had nothing but a ewe lamb,
>> only a single little one which he had bought.
> He fostered it and it grew up with him and his children,
>> eating his bread, drinking from his cup,
>> sleeping in his arms; it was like a daughter to him.

4 When a traveller came to stay, the rich man
>> would not take anything from his own flock or herd
>> to provide for the wayfarer who had come to him.
> Instead, he stole the poor man's lamb
>> and prepared that for his guest.   ♦

David is Rebuked by Nathan and Repents

Nathan's treatment of David here is a prototype of the way OT prophets were to handle kings. They could 'boldly rebuke vice'; often by parables which, like Jesus later, they might or might not explain. If the parable was sufficiently skilful, the recipient would himself draw the analogy.

Nathan's parable here is indeed skilful, both artistically and psychologically. The duty of hospitality was paramount, as it still is in many countries. A close parallel to the basic situation has been found in the customs of modern Palestinian Bedouin. If an unexpected guest arrives, a man may take a ewe from his neighbour's flock, provided that he himself is poor and the ewe is not marked, e.g. by a necklace, as being either a special favourite or reared in a tent. He must however tell the owner as soon as possible; if he fails to do so, he has to repay fourfold.

Nathan in his story sets up a contrast between two extreme types, a *rich man and a poor man*, who are allotted two and five lines respectively. The emotional centre of the parable is the description in v.3, where as it were the camera gradually homes in on the *lamb* nestling in his arms (*eat, drink* and *sleep* also provide an echo

David is Rebuked by Nathan and Repents (cont.)

.5 • David flew into a great rage with the man. 'As the LORD lives,' he said to Nathan 'the man who did this deserves to die. • For doing such a thing and for having shown no pity, he shall make fourfold restitution for the lamb.'

• Nathan then said to David, 'You are the man! The LORD God of Israel, says this, "I anointed you king of Israel, I saved you from Saul's clutches, • I gave you your master's household and your master's wives into your arms, I gave you the House of Israel and the House of Judah; and, if this is still too little, I shall give you other things as well. • Why did you show contempt for the LORD, by doing what displeases him? You put Uriah the Hittite to the sword, you took his wife to be your wife, causing his 10 death by the sword of the Ammonites. • For this, your household will never be free of the sword. Since you showed contempt for me and took the wife of Uriah the Hittite, to make her your wife, • the LORD says this, "Out of your own household I shall raise misfortune for you. Before your very eyes I shall take your wives and give them to your neighbour, who will lie with your wives in broad daylight. • You have worked in secret, but I shall work this for all Israel to see, in broad daylight." '

• David said to Nathan, 'I have sinned against the LORD.' Nathan then said to David, 'The LORD, for his part, forgives your sin; you are not to die. • But, since 15 you have outraged the LORD by doing this, the child born to you will die.' • And Nathan went home.

The LORD struck the child which Uriah's wife had borne to David and it fell gravely ill. • David pleaded with the LORD for the child; he kept a strict fast and went home and spent the night lying on the ground, covered with sacking.   ◆

David is Rebuked by Nathan and Repents (cont.)

of Uriah's words in 11.11). By contrast the rich man is lonely, mean and arrogant. In the analogy the lamb, which is both killed (like Uriah) and eaten (like Bathsheba, eating being a common metaphor for sex), stands for both of them. In each case the rich man had *shown no pity*, i.e. he had abused his strength. That is precisely the charge which Homer makes against Achilles in the *Iliad*.

And David in his comment not merely goes to the moral heart of the matter in his analysis: he also sees that two separate crimes are being exposed. For he proposes two separate punishments: death for the murder and *fourfold restitution* (the standard penalty, see Ex 22.1) for the theft. His quick understanding of the parable and his unequivocal repentance show that his conscience has not been asleep after all.

Nathan's homily (7-12) is by contrast heavy. It is not so much the imposition of

punishments (which hardly fit the crimes) as a demonstration that sins, even if repented and forgiven, have consequences. David's murder (9b-10a) and adultery (10b-11) lead to similar acts by and against his *household*, including his innocent *wives* – or, to put it in Greek terms, his hubris is a family curse. The reference to *the sword* in v.10a is general; the prediction of v.11 will be specifically fulfilled in 16.22.

David's repentance gains by its brevity. God accepts it, as he had not accepted Saul's in 1 S 15, and commutes the sentence of death which David had pronounced on himself (5). Not David but *the child*, the fruit of his sin, will die – an arrangement which, like the fate of David's wives, seems to raise no theological problems for the author.

The next section concerns the two sons born to David and Bathsheba. It is marked off by the contrast: *The LORD struck the* (unnamed) *child* of *Uriah's*

David is Rebuked by Nathan and Repents (cont.)

12.17 • The officials of his household stood round him, intending to get him off the ground, but he refused, nor would he take food with them. • On the seventh day the child died. David's retinue were afraid to tell him that the child was dead. 'Even when the child was alive', they thought, 'we reasoned with him and he would not listen to us. How can we tell him that the child is dead? He will do something desperate.' • David, however, noticed that his retinue were whispering among themselves, and realised that the child was dead. 'Is the child dead?' he asked the officers. They replied, 'He is dead.'

20 • David got off the ground, bathed and anointed himself and put on fresh clothes. Then he went into the LORD's sanctuary and prostrated himself. On returning to his house, he asked to be served with food and ate it. • His retinue said, 'Why are you acting like this? When the child was alive, you fasted and wept; now that the child is dead, you get up and take food!' • 'When the child was alive', he replied, 'I fasted and wept because I kept thinking, "Who knows? Perhaps the LORD will take pity on me and the child will live." • But now that he is dead, why should I fast? Can I bring him back again? I shall go to him but he cannot come back to me.' • David consoled his wife Bathsheba. He went to her and slept with her. She conceived and gave birth to a son, whom she called

25 Solomon. The LORD loved him • and made this known by means of the prophet Nathan, who named him Jedidiah, as the LORD had instructed.

• Joab assaulted Rabbah-of-the-Ammonites and captured the royal town. • He then sent messengers to tell David, 'I have assaulted Rabbah and captured the water supply. • So now muster the rest of the army, lay siege to the town and take it, or I will take it and the town will be called after me!' • So David mustered the whole army

30 and marched on Rabbah; he assaulted the town and captured it. • He took the crown off Milcom's head; it weighed one talent of gold, and in it was set a precious stone which went on David's head instead. He carried off great quantities of booty from the town.' • And he expelled its inhabitants, setting them to work with saws, iron picks and iron axes, employing them at brickmaking. He treated all the Ammonite towns in the same way. David and the whole army returned to Jerusalem.   (NJB)

David is Rebuked by Nathan and Repents (cont.)

(unnamed) *wife* (15) and: *The LORD loved the (twice-named) son* of David's *wife Bathsheba* (24). David's grief at the death of his first son is described in affecting detail through his actions and speeches, and also (a favourite trick of this author) through the eyes of his courtiers. It is somewhat inordinate (we are to understand the actions of v.18 as kept up for a whole week), especially by contrast with his reaction when the boy finally dies. His reply in vv.22-3 to the courtiers' question does not give the true reason for his behaviour – that it was his own sin for which the boy was suffering. But it shows his acceptance of the punishment, and also a more mature understanding (compared with his flippancy in 11.25) of death and therefore of life. So he deserves the forgiveness which YHWH shows in the special name ('beloved of Yah') given to his second son.

Finally we revert to the Ammonite war. NJB's *the royal town* (26) must refer to the citadel. Joab's message in v.28 recalls the implied criticism of 11.1-2. Victory over *Milcom* (30), god of *the Ammonites,* completes David's military supremacy.

The Rape of Tamar

3.1 After this, the following events took place. Absalom son of David had a beautiful sister whose name was Tamar; Amnon son of David fell in love with her. • Amnon was so obsessed with his sister Tamar that it made him ill, since she was a virgin and Amnon thought it impossible to do anything to her. • But Amnon had a friend called Jonadab son of Shimeah, David's brother, and Jonadab was a very shrewd man. • 'Son of the king,' he said, 'tell me why, morning after morning, you look so worn? Won't you tell me?' Amnon replied, 'I am in love 5 with Tamar, my brother Absalom's sister.' • Then Jonadab said, 'Take to your bed, pretend to be ill and, when your father comes to visit you, say, "Please let my sister Tamar come and give me something to eat; let her prepare the food where I can see. What she gives me I shall eat." ' • So Amnon lay down and pretended to be ill. The king then came to visit him and Amnon said to the king, 'Please let my sister Tamar come and make a cake or two where I can watch. What she gives me, I shall eat.' • David then sent word to Tamar at the palace, 'Go to your brother Amnon's house and prepare some food for him.' • Tamar went to the house of her brother Amnon who was lying there in bed. She took dough and kneaded it, and she made some cakes while he watched, and baked the cakes. • She then took the pan and dished them up in front of him, but he refused to eat. Amnon said, 'Let everyone leave me!' So everyone withdrew. 10 • Amnon then said to Tamar, 'Bring the food to the inner room, so that I can eat what you give me.' So Tamar took the cakes which she had made and brought them to her brother Amnon in the inner room. • And as she was offering the food to him, he caught hold of her and said, 'Come to bed with me, sister!' • She replied, 'No, brother! Do not force me! This is no way to behave in Israel. Do not do anything so disgraceful! • Wherever should I go? I should be marked with this shame, while you would become disgraced in Israel. Why not go and speak to the king? He will not refuse to give me to you.' • But he would not listen to her; he overpowered her and raped her.   ▸

The Rape of Tamar

David's sins came quickly home to roost. The next generation's violence was turned inwards upon the family. The first words of the next act show who are the real protagonists viz. *Absalom* and *David*. And of the two it is Absalom who counts: *Tamar* is introduced as *his sister* not as David's daughter, and in the sequel it is Absalom who acts, not David. Tamar and Amnon are subsidiary characters, although for the first scene they take centre stage.

Amnon's crime is not incest but rape. Verse 13 makes it clear that marriage to a half-sister was regarded as acceptable. But Amnon's thoughts were less honourable, and his problem was that he could not *do anything with her* (in his crude euphemism of v.2) because she was a virgin – and must remain so, as a princess, in order to be available for a dynastic marriage.

The lead up to the denouement is told with great skill. Two features stand out. First is the retardation. The repetitions (esp. 5-6), the exchange with David, the details of the baking, the refusal to eat until the room was cleared (9) and even Tamar's long desperate speech (12-13) – all these greatly increase the tension. Secondly, the fact that the reader, unlike Tamar, is privy to the plot gives the author scope for irony in the form of sexual innuendo. Amnon's address *my sister* (11) is a term of love-poetry common e.g. in the Song of Songs. More significant is

The Rape of Tamar (cont.)

13.15 • Amnon was then seized with extreme hatred for her; the hatred he now felt for her was greater than his earlier love. 'Get up and go!' he said. • She said, 'No, brother! To send me away would be worse than the other wrong you have done me!' But he would not listen to her. • He called his personal servant. 'Rid me of this woman!' he said. 'Throw her out and bolt the door behind her!' • (She was wearing a magnificent dress, for this was what the king's unmarried daughters wore in days gone by.) So the servant put her out and bolted the door behind her.

• Tamar put dust on her head, tore the magnificent dress which she was wearing, laid her hand on her head, and went away, crying aloud as she went.

20 • Her brother Absalom said to her, 'Has Amnon your brother been with you? Sister, be quiet; he is your brother; do not take the matter to heart!' Tamar, however, went back to her brother Absalom's house inconsolable.

• When King David heard the whole story, he was very angry; but he had no wish to harm his son Amnon, whom he loved because he was his first-born. • Absalom, however, would not so much as speak to Amnon, since he hated Amnon for having raped his sister Tamar.

(NJB)

The Rape of Tamar (cont.)

the way in which the verb 'to go to bed' changes key as the story goes on: in vv.5 and 6 it is neutral; in v.8 it has already a sexual overtone, which is made explicit in v.11; and in v.14 it is used transitively and violently 'he bedded her'. The long foreplay comes to a sudden climax.

Having had his way, Amnon wants only to get rid of her. To her he speaks just two words, omitting any address. When she demurs, he speaks past her to *his servant*. He even has *the door* bolted *behind her*, so that it looks as if she was making the advances. Her responses are described with extreme pathos. The beautiful *dress* that marked virgin princesses she tears to mark the loss of her virginity. The *dust* and *her hand on her head* are also gestures of mourning: the only future she could now expect is that described in 20.3. And the loud cry she gives is the cry for help and justice which a violated woman is expected to utter if she is innocent (see [Dt 22.27+], which also makes clear that the man must then marry her and may never divorce her).

In her distress she evidently runs to *Absalom*'s house. He comforts her but also urges her to *be quiet*, i.e. to take no (legal) action. He does so partly in order to keep the scandal within the family, but partly also, we may suppose, because he foresees that the king will do nothing. David's inability to discipline his son is ominous; so, more immediately, is Absalom's hatred of his half-brother.

The narrative of vv.1-22 is a work of great art, constructed in the favourite Hebrew pedimental* shape. Two patterns deserve notice. Simplest is the explicit framework of strong emotions: love at the start (1), love turning to hatred at the centre (15), hatred at the end (22). Secondly the centre is closely framed by words exchanged between Amnon and Tamar: vv.11-14 is echoed almost exactly by vv.15-16. In each case he speaks two words of command to her, she replies *No, brother* and gives her reasons, *but he would not listen to her*. And in the space between the two exchanges we have the loveless silence of the rape itself.

Absalom's Revenge

23 Two years later, when Absalom had the sheep-shearers at Baal-Hazor, which is near Ephraim, he invited all the king's sons. • Absalom went to the king and said, 'Now sir, your servant has the sheep-shearers. Will the king and his retinue be 25 pleased to come with your servant?' • 'No, my son,' the king replied, 'we must not all come and be a burden to you.' And though Absalom was insistent, he would not go but dismissed him. • Absalom persisted, 'Then at least let my brother Amnon come with us.' The king said, 'Why should he go with you?' • On Absalom's insistence, however, he let Amnon and all the king's sons to go with him. Absalom prepared a royal banquet • and then gave this order to the servants, 'Listen carefully; when Amnon's heart is merry with wine and I say, "Strike Amnon down", then kill him. Don't be afraid. Have I not myself given you the order? Use your strength and show your mettle!' • Absalom's servants treated Amnon as Absalom had ordered. The king's sons all leapt to their feet, mounted their mules and fled. 30 • While they were on the road, word reached David, 'Absalom has killed all the king's sons; not one of them is left.' • The king stood up, tore his clothes and threw himself on the ground. All his officers tore their clothes too. • Jonadab son of Shimeah, David's brother, then spoke up and said, 'Do not let my lord take to heart the report that all the young men, the king's sons, have been killed, since only Amnon is dead: for Absalom has been promising himself to do this since the day when Amnon raped his sister Tamar. • So my lord the king must not imagine that all the king's sons are dead; only Amnon is dead • and Absalom has fled.'

The man on sentry duty looked up and saw a large troop coming along the road from Bahurim. The sentry came to tell the king, 'I have seen some people coming 35 down the Bahurim road on the mountainside.' • Jonadab then said to the king, 'These are the king's sons arriving: what your servant said is exactly what happened.' • He had scarcely finished speaking when the king's sons arrived and wept aloud; the king and all his retinue wept aloud too. • Absalom had gone to Talmai son of Ammihud, king of Geshur. The king mourned for his son every day.   (NJB)

Absalom's Revenge

After the hypertension of that story even Absalom's revenge seems a little flat. The short-term interest lies in his skilful plotting to achieve his object, the long-term in the rift between him and David.

Absalom's plot via David against Amnon answers to Amnon's via David against Tamar. But this time David was on his guard (27). Cunningly, Absalom issues a formal invitation to the king and his court to join him for the great annual festival. David equally formally declines. Absalom then plays his bold card: let the king be represented by Amnon. In spite of his suspicions, David yields, and the rest of the family converges on Absalom's estate.

As soon as the deed is done they all disperse again, like a crowd of extras (but the *mules* are serious royal mounts: commoners rode, if at all, on donkeys). The scene changes to Jerusalem, where David anxiously awaits news. *Jonadab* comes in at the end of the story, shrewd again as at the beginning, and wishing everyone to know it (35). Meanwhile Absalom has taken refuge in the house of his maternal grandfather. Any blood feud which excused his killing of Amnon would also excuse retaliation against him; and there was no doubt where David's preference lay.

Attempts at Reconciliation between David and Absalom

13.38 When Absalom had gone to Geshur, he stayed there for three years. • Once the king was consoled over Amnon's death, his anger against Absalom subsided.

14. 1 • Now, Joab son of Zeruiah observed that the king was favourably inclined to Absalom. • Joab therefore sent to Tekoa for a wise woman. 'Pretend to be in mourning,' he said. 'Dress yourself in mourning, do not perfume yourself; act like a woman who has long been mourning for the dead. • Then go to the king and say this to him.' And Joab put the words into her mouth which she was to say. • So the woman of Tekoa went to the king and, falling on her face to the ground,

5 prostrated herself. 'Help, my lord king!' she said. • The king said, 'What is the matter?'

'As you see,' she replied, 'I am a widow; my husband is dead. • Your servant had two sons and out in the fields, where there was no one to intervene, they had a quarrel. And one of them struck the other one and killed him. • And now the whole clan has risen against your servant. "Give up the man who killed his brother," they say, "so that we can put him to death, to atone for the life of the brother whom he has murdered; and thus we shall destroy the heir as well." By this means, they will extinguish the ember still left to me, leaving my husband neither name nor survivor on the face of the earth.' • Then the king said to the woman, 'Go home; I myself shall give orders about your case.' • The woman of Tekoa said to the king, 'My lord king! May the guilt be on me and on my family; the

10 king and his throne are innocent of it.' • 'Bring me the man who threatened you,' the king replied, 'and he shall never hurt you again.' • She then said, 'Let the king be pleased to pronounce the name of the LORD your God, so that the avenger of blood may not do greater harm and destroy my son.' 'As the LORD lives,' he said, 'not one of your son's hairs shall fall to the ground!'   ▸

Attempts at Reconciliation between David and Absalom

Five years after Amnon's death David's grief began to be dulled. His thoughts turned increasingly to the exiled Absalom, now the next in line for the throne, but he procrastinated. *Joab*, ever the man of action, laid a plan to bring him to a decision. The plan was to entrap David by means of a fictitious parallel to his own situation. Structurally, the plan has much in common with that of Nathan in Ch.12, but there are plenty of differences too.

The *wise woman* lacks the authority of Nathan, and has to play her cards with greater care. Starting with an obeisance, she makes a formal appeal to David in his capacity as Chief Justice. Her case arises from the conflict between the claim of the blood-revenge and the need to preserve the male line of the family. Skilfully she

ends on the latter, which is the point of appeal to David. He gives a non-committal judgement and makes to dismiss her (8). When she persists, he promises her protection (10), but she is still not satisfied. She wants, and obtains, a guarantee on oath of immunity for her son.

Now at last she can come to the point, which she does boldly. Dropping the courtly speech in v.13 and addressing the king in the second person (NJB's translation is wrong in that respect), she stresses that the whole country is harmed by his leaving his (unnamed) son in exile. Verse 14a presumably refers to his mourning for Amnon (cp. 12.23). David, perceptive as ever, suspects the *hand* of *Joab*. The woman senses his change of tone and reverts to the courtly style. Frankly ad-

Attempts at Reconciliation between David and Absalom (cont.)

• Then the woman said, 'Permit your servant to say something else to my lord the king.' 'Go on,' he said. • The woman said, 'Why then has the king, who by giving this verdict has condemned himself, conceived the idea, against God's people's interests, of not bringing home the son whom he has banished? • We are all mortal; we are like water spilt on the ground, which cannot be gathered up again, nor does God raise up a corpse; let the king therefore make plans for his banished son not to remain far away from him in exile.'

.18   • Replying to the woman, the king said, 'Now do not evade the question which I am going to ask you.' The woman said, 'Let my lord the king ask his question.' • 'Is not Joab's hand behind you in all this?' the king asked. The woman replied, 'As you live, my lord king, I cannot escape what my lord the king says, either to right or to left. Yes, it was your servant Joab who gave me

20   my orders; he put all these words into your servant's mouth. • Your servant Joab did this to approach the matter indirectly, but my lord has the wisdom of the Angel of God; he knows everything that happens on earth!'

• The king then said to Joab, 'Very well, the suit is granted. Go and bring the young man Absalom back.' • Joab fell on his face to the ground, prostrated himself and blessed the king. 'My lord king,' Joab said, 'today your servant knows that he has won your favour, since the king has done what his servant asked.' • Joab then set off, went to Geshur, and brought Absalom back to Jerusalem. • The king, however, said, 'Let him retire to his own house; he is not to appear in my presence.' So Absalom retired to his own house and was not received by the king.

25   • In all Israel there was no one more praised for his beauty than Absalom; from the sole of his foot to the crown of his head, he could not be faulted. • When he cut his hair – he shaved it once a year because his hair got too heavy – he would weigh the hair: two hundred shekels, king's weight. • To Absalom were born three sons and one daughter called Tamar; she was a beautiful woman.

• Absalom lived in Jerusalem for two years without being received by the king. • Absalom then summoned Joab, intending to send him to the king, but Joab would not come to him. He sent for him a second time, but still he would not   ♦

Attempts at Reconciliation between David and Absalom (cont.)

mitting the plot, she covers her withdrawal by a trowelful of flattery: in the contest of *wisdom*, she (wisely) gives him best (20).

But who did win? At first, we think she did. But we soon find that the king is keeping his implied promise only to the letter, not in spirit (24). He refuses to receive Absalom – and sets no time limit. The pause is filled by the author with some fascinating information, whose relevance the reader must work out. Absalom's exaggeratedly luxuriant *hair* symbolises his attractiveness – the language here is that of love – but also a

fatal narcissism. A rabbinic comment notes: 'Absalom gloried in his hair – therefore he was hanged by his hair'. And the reference to his daughter *Tamar* (named, unlike his sons) shows that, if David remembered Amnon, Absalom had not forgotten his *beautiful* sister.

The final scene appears to advance the story and yet leaves even more doubt than before about the true feelings of David and Absalom. Joab withdraws into a strictly neutral position between them – though he could perhaps see positive gain in having Absalom under control but still

Attempts at Reconciliation between David and Absalom (cont.)

14.30 come. • At this, Absalom said to his retainers, 'Look, Joab's field is next to mine and he has barley in it; go and set it on fire.' Absalom's retainers set fire to the field. • Joab then stirred himself, went to Absalom in his house and asked, 'Why have your retainers set my field on fire?' • Absalom replied to Joab, 'Look, I sent word to you: Come here, so that I can send you to the king to say, 'Why come back from Geshur? Better for me to have been there still! 'Now I want to be received by the king, and if I am guilty, let him put me to death!' • Joab went to the king and told him this. He then summoned Absalom, who prostrated himself with his face to the ground before the king. And the king kissed Absalom. (NJB)

Attempts at Reconciliation between David and Absalom (cont.)

out of favour. Absalom, however, is frustrated by his position in limbo. He must have it resolved one way or the other, and is goaded into an action which could be seen as funny or irresponsible to taste. David again is forced to act, and we look – at last – to a resolution. Yet what hap-

pens is pure formality. *Absalom prostrated himself*, David *kissed* him, but no word of reconciliation was spoken on either side. As so often in this story, what purports to be a resolution is presented in such a way as to carry the tension forward to the next scene (cp. 6.23; 13.22, 37; 14.24).

Absalom's Rebellion

15. 1 After this, Absalom procured a chariot and horses, with fifty men to run ahead of him. • He would get up early and stand beside the road leading to the city gate; and whenever a man with some lawsuit had to come before the king's tribunal, Absalom would call out to him and ask, 'Which town are you from?' If he answered, 'Your servant is from one of the tribes of Israel,' • then Absalom would say, 'Look, your case is sound and just, but not one of the king's deputies will listen to you.' • Absalom would say, 'Oh, who will appoint me judge in the land? Then anyone
5 with a lawsuit or a plea could come to me and I should see he had justice!' • And whenever anyone came up to him to prostrate himself, he would stretch out his hand, draw him to him and kiss him. • Absalom acted like this with every Israelite who appealed to the king's tribunal, and so Absalom won the Israelites' hearts. ▸

Absalom's Rebellion

In the long and tense run-up (Chs 13 and 14 together span seven years) Absalom has on the whole been more sympathetically portrayed than David. But at 15.1 there is a clear change, and from now on Absalom progressively loses the support of the reader. Not that David necessarily gains what Absalom loses: he, as usual, is portrayed ambiguously, though the ambiguity here is not between good and evil but rather between activity and passivity.

For a while Absalom is content to challenge David's position. He does so in many ways: by outward show (1), by im-

pugning David's competence as Chief Justice (2-4) and by the old guile of the politician, pretending to a friendly interest in the individual (2,5) while all the time counting the votes. Gradually he '*stole* the hearts of the men of Israel' – so AV, which preserves the condemnation implied in the Hebrew verb. *Israel* here means the northern tribes, many of whom had never accepted David as Saul's heir.

Four further years elapse however (if the text is right) before Absalom is ready to strike. On the pseudo-pious pretext of paying a *vow* at his birthplace, he allays

Absalom's Rebellion (cont.)

• When four years had gone by, Absalom said to the king, 'Allow me to go to Hebron and fulfil the vow which I have made to the LORD; • for, when I was in Geshur, in Aram, your servant made this vow, "If the LORD brings me back to Jerusalem, I shall pay my devotions to the LORD in Hebron." ' • The king said to him, 'Go in peace.' So he set off and went to Hebron. • Absalom sent couriers throughout the tribes of Israel to say, 'When you hear the trumpet sound, you are to say, "Absalom is king at Hebron!" ' • With Absalom went two hundred men from Jerusalem; they had been invited and had gone in all innocence, unaware of what was going on. • Absalom sent for Ahithophel the Gilonite, David's counsellor, from Giloh his town, and had him with him while offering the sacrifices. The conspiracy grew in strength, since Absalom's supporters grew in number. (NJB)

.10

Absalom's Rebellion (cont.)

David's suspicions (as he had done in 13.27), and obtains leave to visit *Hebron*. David's words *go in peace*, the last that ever pass between father and son, lead straight into the war. Absalom raises the flag, and among those who join him is *Ahithophel*, David's own most trusted adviser (16.23), who will have a crucial role in the rebellion.

David's Flight from Jerusalem

A messenger came and told David, 'The men of Israel have shifted their allegiance to Absalom.' • David said to all his retinue then with him in Jerusalem, 'Up, let us flee, or we shall not escape from Absalom! Leave as quickly as you can, in case he mounts a sudden attack, overcomes us and puts the city to the sword.' • The king's retinue replied, 'Whatever my lord the king decides, we are at your service.' • The king set out on foot with his whole household, leaving ten concubines to look after the palace. • The king set out on foot with everyone following, and they halted at the last house. • All his officers stood at his side. All the Cherethites and all the Pelethites, with Ittai and all the six hundred Gittites who had come in his retinue from Gath, marched past the king. • The king said to Ittai the Gittite, 'You, why are you coming with us? Go back and stay with the king, for you are a foreigner, indeed an exile from your homeland. • You arrived only yesterday; should I take you wandering with us today, when I do not know myself where I am going? Go back, take your fellow countrymen with you, and may the LORD show you mercy and faithful love!' • Ittai replied to the king, 'As the LORD lives, and as my lord the king lives, wherever my lord the king may be, for death or ▶

5.15

20

David's Flight from Jerusalem

David's reaction to the news is astonishing. Nowhere in the whole story are we more in need of military and political information. True, Absalom had support now to the south as well as to the north; and his forces may have outnumbered David's. But why not defend the city, and why, after the decision to leave it had been taken, spend so much time on ceremonials? The section 13-31 certainly contains some puzzling features.

No problems are raised by the expressions of loyalty to David from his court and from his bodyguards, with whom we should evidently include *Ittai*. The exchange with Ittai is especially well handled. The virtue of the *foreigner* is a common biblical motif (cp. Uriah and the parable of the Good Samaritan). There are also echoes here of the famous scene between Naomi and Ruth: David's unselfishness evokes and strengthens Ittai's

David's Flight from Jerusalem (cont.)

life, your servant will be there too.' • David then said to Ittai, 'Go ahead, march past!' And Ittai of Gath marched past with all his men and with all his children too. • The entire population was weeping aloud as the king stood in the bed of the Kidron and everyone marched past him, making for the desert.

• Zadok was there too, and all the Levites with him, carrying the Ark of God. They set the Ark of God down beside Abiathar until everyone had finished marching out of the town. • The king then said to Zadok, 'Take the Ark of God back into the city. Should I win the LORD's favour, he will bring me back and allow me to see it and its tent once more. • But should he say, "You displease me," here I am: let him treat me as he sees fit.' • The king said to Zadok the priest, 'Look, you and Abiathar go back quietly into the city, with your two sons, your own son Ahimaaz and Jonathan son of Abiathar. • You see, I shall wait in the passes of the desert plain until word comes from you bringing me news.' • So Zadok and Abiathar took the Ark of God back to Jerusalem and stayed there.

• David then made his way up the Mount of Olives, weeping as he went, his head covered and his feet bare. And all the people with him had their heads covered and made their way up, weeping as they went. • David was then informed that Ahithophel was among the conspirators with Absalom. David said, 'I beg you, LORD, turn Ahithophel's advice to folly.'

• As David reached the summit, where God is worshipped, he saw Hushai the Archite, his friend, coming to meet him with his tunic torn and with earth on his head. • David said, 'If you go along with me, you will be a burden to me. • But if you go back to the city and say to Absalom, 'I am at your service, my lord king; once I was in your father's service, but now I shall serve you,' you will be able to thwart ▶

15.25

30

David's Flight from Jerusalem (cont.)

loyalty. Nor are there any problems in the leaving behind of the *concubines* (they are needed for 16.22) or in David's plans for spying on Absalom (27-8).

The puzzling features of the narrative are twofold. First are the ceremonials – not so much the march past but the procession of David and *all the people* (30, cp. 17 and 23). David led the way out of Jerusalem, where they halted at 'The House of the Distance' (so lit. the Hebrew) before descending into the *Kidron* valley. When they got to its (presumably dry) bed, David stood in the middle while the people went past him, just like the ritual crossing of the Jordan in Jos 3.17 (where see commentary). The people then went on *up the Mount of Olives*, and he followed (?), all of them making lamentation

together. For the first half of the procession *the Ark* and the priests came too, until David sent them *back to Jerusalem*.

His words in doing so (25-6) mark the second puzzling feature of the narrative, namely David's sudden but sincere and total submission to the will of God. What we seem to have is a psalm transposed into narrative form. When David brought the Ark to Jerusalem in Ch.6, he led the people in song and dance, procession and sacrifice – the ingredients of a psalm of thanksgiving. Now he moves the Ark (nearly) out of Jerusalem, and we are told of public procession and penance, and of the psalmist's own trust in God – the ingredients of a psalm of lament (see p.412f). In these two theological narratives we see some tension between David

---

David's Flight from Jerusalem (cont.)

35 Ahithophel's advice for me. • Surely the priests Zadok and Abiathar will be with you?
Anything you hear from the palace you must report to Zadok and Abiathar. • You see,
their two sons are there with them, Zadok's son Ahimaaz, and Abiathar's son Jonathan;
through these, you will send me word of everything you hear.' • Hushai, David's
friend, entered the city just as Absalom was reaching Jerusalem.   (NJB)

David's Flight from Jerusalem (cont.)

the psalmist and David the king.

And the theological thrust carries on
explicitly for a few more verses. Near the
top of the hill David learns of the defection
of *Ahithophel*, and turns to God with a
crucial petition for his defeat. Forthwith, at
the holy place itself, he sees *Hushai the*

Archite (from near Bethel) who will shortly
be instrumental in that defeat. David, who
at the bottom of the valley seemed
passive, now at the *summit* of the hill
begins to act, upheld by the favour of
God and the loyalty of his remaining
friends.

Encounters on Leaving Jerusalem

6.1 When David had moved on a little from the top of the ridge, he was met by Ziba
the servant of Mephibosheth, who had with him a pair of donkeys saddled and
loaded with two hundred loaves of bread, a hundred clusters of raisins, a hundred bunches of summer fruit, and a skin of wine. • The king asked, 'What are
you doing with these?' Ziba answered, 'The donkeys are for the king's family to
ride on, the bread and the summer fruit are for his servants to eat, and the wine for
anyone who becomes exhausted in the wilderness'. • The king asked, 'Where is your
master's grandson?' 'He is staying in Jerusalem,' said Ziba, 'for he thought that the
Israelites might now restore to him his grandfather's kingdom.' • The king said to
Ziba, 'You shall have everything that belongs to Mephibosheth.' Ziba said, 'I am
your humble servant, sir; may I always find favour with your majesty.'

5   • As King David approached Bahurim, a man of Saul's family, whose name
was Shimei son of Gera, came out, cursing all the while. • He showered stones
right and left on David and on all the king's servants and on everyone, soldiers
and people alike. • With curses Shimei shouted: 'Get out, get out, you murderous
scoundrel! • The LORD has taken vengeance on you for the blood of the house of
Saul whose throne you took, and he has given the kingdom to your son Absalom.
You murderer, see how your crimes have overtaken you!'

10   • Abishai son of Zeruiah said to the king, 'Why let this dead dog curse your
majesty? I will go across and strike off his head.' • But the king said, 'What has
this to do with us, you sons of Zeruiah? If he curses because the LORD has   ♦

Encounters on Leaving Jerusalem

The encounter with Hushai is the first of
three in succession. After Hushai the true
friend comes the false friend *Ziba* (16.1).
We last met him in Ch.9, when David
befriended him and *Mephibosheth*. Ziba
is hoping to turn the crisis to his own
advantage, which is exactly what he

accuses Mephibosheth of doing. David
now impetuously rewards him. Later
(Ch.19) his falsity will be revealed.

The third encounter is with a true
enemy (16.5). *Shimei's* violent *curses*
provoke an equally violent response from
Abishai (for the *sons of Zeruiah* see 3.39).

Encounters on Leaving Jerusalem (cont.)

16.11 told him to curse David, who can question it?' • David said to Abishai and to all his servants, 'If my very own son is out to kill me, who can wonder at this Benjamite? Let him be, let him curse; for the LORD has told him to. • Perhaps the LORD will mark my sufferings and bestow a blessing on me in place of the curse laid on me this day.' • David and his men continued on their way, and Shimei kept abreast along the ridge of the hill parallel to David's path, cursing as he went and hurling stones across the valley at him and covering him with dust. • When the king and all the people with him reached the Jordan, they rested there, for they were worn out.

(REB)

Encounters on Leaving Jerusalem (cont.)

Both of them are 'party men', representing opposite power-groups. David's (new?) confidence in God enables him to rise to an altogether higher level of insight and serenity. For the sake of argument he accepts Shimei's claim that Absalom's rebellion is a punishment for his treatment of Saul (not of Uriah, as Nathan implied in Ch.12). But he is content to leave his case in the hand of God, who perhaps will feel that David's *sufferings* (better: his humiliation) are already enough. By this one speech Abishai is silenced and Shimei brushed off. David resumes effective command of his troops and leads them on a twenty-mile march down to the *Jordan*. He got clear of Jerusalem only just in time.

Absalom in Pursuit of David

16.15 Absalom entered Jerusalem with all the men of Israel; with him was Ahithophel. • When Hushai the Archite, David's friend, reached Absalom, Hushai said to Absalom, 'Long live the king! Long live the king!' • Absalom said to Hushai, 'Is this your faithful love for your friend? Why didn't you go away with your friend?' • Hushai replied to Absalom, 'No, the man whom the LORD and this people and all the men of Israel have chosen, he is the man for me, and with him will I stay! • Besides, whom should I serve, if not his son? As I served your father, so shall I serve you.'

20 • Absalom said to Ahithophel, 'Think carefully. What shall we do?' • Ahithophel replied to Absalom, 'Go to your father's concubines whom he left to look after the palace; then all Israel will hear that you have thoroughly antagonised your father, and the resolution of all your supporters will be strengthened.' • So a tent was pitched for Absalom on the flat roof and, with all Israel watching, Absalom went to his father's concubines. • At the time, whatever advice Ahithophel gave was treated like a decision obtained from God; as by David, so by Absalom, was all Ahithophel's advice regarded.

Absalom in Pursuit of David

The narrative of Absalom's brief period in *Jerusalem* is built round a conflict of influence between *Ahithophel* and *Hushai*. Hushai has first to convince Absalom of his loyalty: but since we know that he is in fact loyal to David, the author can deploy his full resources of dramatic irony. In vv.16 and 18 it is simple: *the king* and *the man* both really mean David. In v.17 Absalom's sarcasm about his *faithful love* (*hesedh*) is ironically true. In v.19 he will (in reality) *serve* Absalom as (Absalom thinks) he *served* David. So Hushai is accepted, but Ahithophel's advice is sought first.

The first action he recommends is a

Absalom in Pursuit of David (cont.)

1 • Ahithophel said to Absalom, 'Let me choose twelve thousand men and set off this very night in pursuit of David. • I shall fall on him while he is tired and dispirited; I shall strike terror into him, and all the people who are with him will run away. I shall kill only the king, • and I shall then bring all the people back to you, like a bride returning to her husband. You seek the life of one individual only; the people as a whole will have peace.' • The suggestion seemed a good one to Absalom and all the elders of Israel.

5 • Then Absalom said, 'Now call Hushai the Archite, for us to hear what he too has to say.' • When Hushai had come to Absalom, Absalom said, 'This is what Ahithophel says. Are we to do as he suggests? If not, suggest something yourself.' • Hushai said to Absalom, 'On this occasion the advice given by Ahithophel is not good. • You know', Hushai went on, 'that your father and his men are great fighters and that they are now as angry as a wild bear robbed of her cubs. Your father is a man of war: he will not let the army rest during the night. • At this moment he is concealed in some hollow or other place. If at the outset there are casualties among our troops, word will go round that the army supporting Absalom has met

10 with disaster. • And then even the valiant, the truly lion-hearted, will be demoralised; for all Israel knows that your father is a champion and that the men with him are valiant. • For my part, I offer this advice: Summon all Israel, from Dan to Beersheba, to rally to you, as numerous as the sand on the seashore, and you take the field in person with them. • We shall reach him wherever he is to be found; we shall fall on him as the dew falls on the ground, and not leave him or any one of the men with him. • Should he retire into a town, all Israel will bring ropes to that town, and we shall drag it into the river-bed until not a pebble of it is to be found.' ❯

Absalom in Pursuit of David (cont.)

surprise. For a new king to take over his predecessor's harem was in one sense routine. But the public exhibition was at best unnecessary. The reason offered by Ahithophel is unconvincing and the historical probability, at a time of such urgency, nil. But the publicity fulfils the prophecy of Nathan in 12.11, and the *roof*, by a neat reversal, is the very one from which David had observed Bathsheba.

In the case of Ahithophel's second piece of advice the narrator's praise (16.23) was merited. Speed was imperative, and civil war to be avoided even at the cost of David's death. The simile in v.3 (preserved only in the LXX) must be a flattering reference to Absalom's personal attractiveness. The surprise here is not

that *the suggestion seemed a good one* but that Absalom asked for a second opinion.

Hushai starts well with *On this occasion*, and he scores a point later (11) by urging Absalom to take command *in person* instead of leaving it to Ahithophel. But for the rest it is a lame performance – or at least it would be if Hushai was not in fact seeking a respite for David. His criticism of Ahithophel's plan rests on David's well-known soldierly qualities, which frame that part of his speech (8, 10b); but the argument in v.9 is feeble. His own alternative plan veers between the the extremes of caution (11-12) and optimism (13). His rhetoric is also suspiciously florid. The three similes (8, 11, 12), none

Absalom in Pursuit of David (cont.)

• Then Absalom and all the people of Israel said, 'Hushai the Archite's advice is better than Ahithophel's,' the LORD having resolved to thwart Ahithophel's shrewd advice and so bring disaster on Absalom.

17.15 • Hushai then told the priests Zadok and Abiathar, 'Ahithophel gave such and such advice to Absalom and the elders of Israel, but I advised so and so. • Send with all speed to David and say, "Do not camp in the desert passes tonight, but get through them as fast as you can, or the king and his whole army may be annihilated."'

• Jonathan and Ahimaaz were posted at the Fuller's Spring; a servant-girl was to go and warn them and they in turn were to warn King David, since they could not give themselves away by coming into the city themselves. • A young man saw them nonetheless and told Absalom. The pair of them, however, made off quickly, reaching the house of a man in Bahurim. In his courtyard was a storage-well and they got down into it. • The woman took a piece of canvas and, spreading it over the mouth of the storage-well, scattered crushed grain on it so that nothing showed.

20 • When Absalom's servants reached the woman at the house, they said, 'Where are Ahimaaz and Jonathan?' The woman said, 'They have gone further on, towards the water.' They searched but, having found nothing, went back to Jerusalem.

• When they had gone, the men climbed out of the storage-well and went to warn King David. 'Set out!' they told David. 'Cross the water quickly, for Ahithophel has given such and such advice against you!' • So David and all the troops with him set off and crossed the Jordan. By dawn no one was left, all had crossed the Jordan.

• When Ahithophel saw that his advice had not been followed, he saddled his donkey and set off and went home to his own town. Then, having set his house in order, he hanged himself. He was buried in his father's tomb. (NJB)

Absalom in Pursuit of David (cont.)

of which is entirely apposite, read almost like parody. In spite of this, his advice carried the day; and we are told why.

Hushai then (15) reverts to his other role as the head of David's intelligence service in Jerusalem. We learn of the chain of information whereby the *priests* communicated with their sons through a *servant-girl*, whose visit to the *Fuller's Spring* (see map 3) would not attract attention. We learn of the narrow escape of the sons in a *storage-well*, hidden under some produce being dried in the sun. Such escapes, which are the stuff of folk-tale, help to keep up the tension, particularly now that the final outcome is not in doubt (17.14). We also learn

the content of the message sent by Hushai to David. It is that he must not lose a moment in his march, i.e. it is as if Hushai's advice had been rejected and Ahithophel's followed!

Ch.17.21-23 is a bridge passage. David and his men, after an all-night march, were safely across the Jordan by dawn – the timings are as much symbolic as literal. The wise Ahithophel could see that Absalom's cause was lost. The detail of v.23 shows the care with which he plans his suicide, an honourable death which enables his body to be buried in the family *tomb*. In spite of his change of sides, never explained by the author, Ahithophel wins and keeps our sympathy.

Absalom Defeated and Killed

24 By the time that Absalom had crossed the Jordan with the Israelites, David was already at Mahanaim. • Absalom had appointed Amasa as commander-in-chief in Joab's place; he was the son of a man named Ithra, an Ishmaelite, by Abigal daughter of Nahash and sister to Joab's mother Zeruiah. • The Israelites and Absalom camped in the district of Gilead.

• When David came to Mahanaim, he was met by Shobi son of Nahash from the Ammonite town Rabbah, Machir son of Ammiel from Lo-debar, and Barzillai the Gileadite from Rogelim, • bringing mattresses and blankets, bowls, and jugs. They brought also wheat and barley, flour and roasted grain, beans and lentils, • honey and curds, sheep and fat cattle, and offered them to David and his people to eat, knowing that the people must be hungry and thirsty and weary in the wilderness.

. 1 • David reviewed the troops who were with him, and appointed officers over units of a thousand and of a hundred. • He divided his army in three, one division under the command of Joab, one under Joab's brother Abishai son of Zeruiah, and the third under Ittai the Gittite. The king announced to the troops that he himself was coming out with them. • But they said, 'No, you must not; if we take to flight, no one will care, nor will they even if half of us are killed; but you are worth ten thousand of us, and it would be better now for you to remain in the town in support.' • The king answered, 'I shall do what you think best.' He stood beside the gate, while all the army marched past by hundreds and by thousands, 5 • and he gave this order to Joab, Abishai, and Ittai: 'Deal gently with the young man Absalom for my sake.' The whole army heard the king giving each of the officers the order about Absalom.

• The army took the field against the Israelites, and a battle was fought in the forest of Ephron. • There the Israelites were routed before the onslaught of David's men, and the loss of life was great, for twenty thousand fell. • The fighting spread over the whole countryside, and the forest took toll of more people that day than the sword.   ♦

Absalom Defeated and Killed

David, having crossed the Jordan, made for the walled town of *Mahanaim* in Gilead. We then learn some details of the opposing forces, though still not their relative strengths. On Absalom's side the command is given to *Amasa*, Joab's cousin. Absalom himself is mentioned in v.26 *after* his troops, a sign that his star is on the wane. David on the other hand receives support of two kinds. First his Ammonite and Gileadite friends bring him valuable supplies. *Machir* was clearly grateful for David's treatment of Mephibosheth (9.4); *Barzillai* appears here for the first time but not the last. Then his own troops show their devotion to

him in a remarkable tribute (18.3). David's concern however is not for his own safety but for that of *the young man Absalom* – his first loving reference to his son for years.

Battle was joined in an unidentified *forest*, or rather scrub land: rough terrain broken up by rocks and thickets, where professionals like David's bodyguard would have the advantage even over much greater numbers. The description of the fighting is formulaic, as usual in the OT. The repeated *that day* has an epic flavour, and the rhetorical flourish at the end (8b) is a battle topos* (cp. Jg 16.30).

Absalom Defeated and Killed (cont.)

18.10 • Some of David's men caught sight of Absalom; he was riding his mule and, as it passed beneath a large oak, his head was caught in its boughs; he was left in mid-air, while the mule went on from under him. • One of the men who saw this told Joab, 'I saw Absalom hanging from an oak.' • While the man was telling him, Joab broke in, 'You saw him? Why did you not strike him to the ground then and there? I would have given you ten pieces of silver and a belt.' • The man answered, 'If you were to put into my hands a thousand pieces of silver, I would not lift a finger against the king's son; we all heard the king giving orders to you and Abishai and Ittai to take care of the young man Absalom. • If I had dealt him a treacherous blow, the king would soon have known, and you would have kept well out of it.' • 'That is a lie!' said Joab. 'I will make a start and show you.' He picked up three javelins and drove them into Absalom's chest while he was held fast in the tree 15 and still alive. • Then ten young men who were Joab's armour-bearers closed in on Absalom, struck at him, and killed him. • Joab sounded the trumpet, and the army came back from the pursuit of Israel, because he had called on them to halt. • They took Absalom's body and flung it into a large pit in the forest, and raised over it a great cairn of stones. The Israelites all fled to their homes.   (REB)

Absalom Defeated and Killed (cont.)

But typically the author devotes less space to the rest of the battle than to the single episode of Absalom's death. There is much personal detail here, but little pathos: *Absalom* has by now forfeited all sympathy save that which derives from David. Ingloriously parted from his kingly mount – and thereby symbolically from his royalty – Absalom is at the mercy of the first comer. But that happens to be a private soldier who had taken to heart David's plea for gentleness. *Joab*, when informed, is angry and patronising, implying that a common soldier will readily forget his principles for a reward. In reply *the man* scorns the hypothetical reward and repeats what *we all heard the king* say: to kill Absalom after that would be plain treachery. He ends by returning Joab's contempt: officers are great ones for leaving their men to face the music. It is a remarkable speech, frank and effective. Joab covers his defeat by bluster – 'I cannot waste time arguing with you' (NJB) – and physical force, and then leaves his men to finish the job.

But just as we are about to condemn Joab, we are brought up short by the final statement that he *called* off *the pursuit*. He had done this once before, to save unnecessary bloodshed (2.27-8). Remembering Ahithophel's readiness to kill David on the same grounds (17.2-3), we can see overwhelming reasons of state for Joab's behaviour. The country will not have peace until Absalom is dead – and buried in an anonymous and ignominious grave.

David Mourns for Absalom

9 Then Ahimaaz son of Zadok said, 'Let me run, and carry tidings to the king that the LORD has delivered him from the power of his enemies.' • Joab said to him, 'You are not to carry tidings today; you may carry tidings another day, but today you shall not do so, because the king's son is dead.' • Then Joab said to a Cushite, 'Go, tell the king what you have seen.' The Cushite bowed before Joab, and ran. • Then Ahimaaz son of Zadok said again to Joab, 'Come what may, let me also run after the Cushite.' And Joab said, 'Why will you run, my son, seeing that you have no reward for the tidings?' • 'Come what may,' he said, 'I will run.' So he said to him, 'Run.' Then Ahimaaz ran by the way of the Plain, and outran the Cushite.

• Now David was sitting between the two gates. The sentinel went up to the roof of the gate by the wall, and when he looked up, he saw a man running alone. 25 • The sentinel shouted and told the king. The king said, 'If he is alone, there are tidings in his mouth.' He kept coming, and drew near. • Then the sentinel saw another man running; and the sentinel called to the gatekeeper and said, 'See, another man running alone!' The king said, 'He also is bringing tidings.' • The sentinel said, 'I think the running of the first one is like the running of Ahimaaz son of Zadok.' The king said, 'He is a good man, and comes with good tidings.'

• Then Ahimaaz cried out to the king, 'All is well!' He prostrated himself before the king with his face to the ground, and said, 'Blessed be the LORD your God, who has delivered up the men who raised their hand against my lord the king.' • The king said, 'Is it well with the young man Absalom?' Ahimaaz answered, 'When Joab sent your servant, I saw a great tumult, but I do not know 30 what it was.' • The king said, 'Turn aside, and stand here.' So he turned aside, and stood still. ◆

David Mourns for Absalom

Someone had to break the news to David in Mahanaim. *Ahimaaz*, appointed King's Messenger (15.36), volunteered. *Joab* remembered the fate of the Amalekite who reported Saul's death to David in Ch.1, and sent off an anonymous *Cushite* (Ethiopian) mercenary instead. But Ahimaaz gradually wore Joab down: their dialogue becomes progressively shorter until at the third time (lucky) he utters three words and Joab one. So the news is carried by two messengers, one white and the other black.

Recent excavations have shown that, at any rate from Jeroboam's time, many fortified towns in Israel had a double gateway. The inner gate was the normal one in the city wall. But from it projected two parallel walls which, after a dog-leg to the right, ran down to a second, outer gateway. David had posted a *sentinel* on *the roof of the gate by* (in) *the wall*, while he himself waited down in the small courtyard *between the two gates*, ready to question a messenger without delay.

The spotlight is thus turned full on David for what is the emotional climax of the story – not only of Absalom's revolt but of his whole reign. In it we see him still the victim of illusion. He has not yet faced the fact that he is bound to lose *either* his throne *or* his son. Whereas the *sentinel* reports the barest objective facts (on the second occasion he does not actually say *another man*, but again simply *a man*), David allows himself an optimistic interpretation. First and more plausibly, a single runner is at least not a rout; second and quite implausibly, *a good man* will be bringing *good* news. The first word

David Mourns for Absalom (cont.)

18.31   • Then the Cushite came; and the Cushite said, 'Good tidings for my lord the king! For the LORD has vindicated you this day, delivering you from the power of all who rose up against you.' The king said to the Cushite, 'Is it well with the young man Absalom?' The Cushite answered, 'May the enemies of my lord the king, and all who rise up to do you harm, be like that young man.'

• The king was deeply moved, and went up to the chamber over the gate, and wept; and as he went, he said, 'O my son Absalom, my son, my son Absalom! Would I had died instead of you, O Absalom, my son, my son!'

19. 1   • It was told Joab, 'The king is weeping and mourning for Absalom.' • So the victory that day was turned into mourning for all the troops; for the troops heard that day, 'The king is grieving for his son.' • The troops stole into the city that day as soldiers steal in who are ashamed when they flee in battle. • The king covered his face, and the king cried with a loud voice, 'O my son Absalom, O Absalom, my son, 5   my son!' • Then Joab came into the house to the king, and said, 'Today you have covered with shame the faces of all your officers who have saved your life today, and the lives of your sons and your daughters, and the lives of your wives and your concubines, • for love of those who hate you and for hatred of those who love you. You have made it clear today that commanders and officers are nothing to you; for I perceive that if Absalom were alive and all of us were dead today, then you would be pleased. • So go out at once and speak kindly to your servants; for I swear by the LORD, if you do not go, not a man will stay with you this night; and this will be worse for you than any disaster that has come upon you from your youth until now.' • Then the king got up and took his seat in the gate. The troops were all told, 'See, the king is sitting in the gate'; and all the troops came before the king. Meanwhile, all the Israelites had fled to their homes.   (NRSV)

David Mourns for Absalom (cont.)

of Ahimaaz, shouted according to the Hebrew from some way off, is '*Shalom!*'. David is deaf to the news of victory and echoes the word: '*Shalom* for young Absalom?' Ahimaaz evades the question, blaming Joab, and is stood down. The Cushite's answer, while still diplomatic, reveals the truth.

David withdraws, overwhelmed by grief. His sobs are audible in his repeated *my son* (and even more clearly in the Hebrew *benî*), which comes eight times in all, cp. Lear's 'Never, never, never, never, never' over Cordelia's body. But his pathetic wish to have *died instead of* Absalom shows him still unaware of the reality which, as king, he must be brought to face.

Once again action devolves upon *Joab*, whose crucial role is underlined by

his advance mention in 19.1. The effect of David's mourning upon the army is described in a brilliant simile drawn (rarely for the OT) from the concept of military honour. Their shamefaced bearing is answered by his withdrawal, with *face covered* – and a dramatic flashback (4) repeats his words of lamentation, as if for Joab to hear in person.

Joab's speech, his longest in the whole book, is blunt to the point of brutality. He dispenses with the usual courtly phrasing, and addresses David throughout in the second person. His urgent tone is shown by his fourfold *today*, with which belongs the variant *this night* of v.7. The accusations of vv.6-7 are almost too strong. The generalisation at the end of v.6 is rhetorically exaggerated; so is the whole

David Mourns for Absalom (cont.)

of v.7, which represents a bitter reversal of the people's loyalty in 18.3. Joab then barks out three sharp commands: get up, *go out and speak*, before ending with a dark forecast of what will otherwise happen.

Joab's violent words pierce the wall of David's private grief. He goes through the motions of coming out and of facing his troops. But it is noticeable that he *sits* (unlike the scene in 18.4 with which this one forms a frame); and his silence reveals

his continued grief and impotence.

The question arises, as at 14.21: did Joab win? Immediately, yes. He effectively forced David to act the king again. To do that, he certainly had to be blunt. But the 'overkill' of Joab's speech doubtless resulted from his consciousness of his own part in Absalom's death. Presumably David did not yet know of that; but when he came to know, the wound inflicted by Joab's speech will have rankled all the more.

David's Return to Jerusalem

9.9 Throughout all the tribes of Israel people were discussing it among themselves and saying, 'The king has saved us from our enemies and freed us from the power of the Philistines, and now he has fled the country because of Absalom. • But Absalom, whom we anointed king, has fallen in battle; so now why have we no plans for bringing the king back?'

• What all Israel was saying came to the king's ears, and he sent word to Zadok and Abiathar the priests: 'Ask the elders of Judah why they should be the last to bring the king back to his palace. • Tell them, "You are my brothers, my own flesh and blood; why are you last to bring me back?" • And say to Amasa, "You are my own flesh and blood. So help me God, you shall be my commander-in-chief for the rest of your life in place of Joab." ' • Thus David swayed the hearts of all in Judah, and one and all they sent to the king, urging him and his men to return. ▸

David's Return to Jerusalem

The next section has two functions. First, it rounds off the story of Absalom's revolt. The narrative of David's return to Jerusalem, like that of his departure from it in Chs 15-16, consists of a series of encounters. Secondly, it looks forward to later political events, indeed to the eventual separation of the two kingdoms of Israel and Judah. For in the power-vacuum left by the end of Absalom's revolt the old rivalries of north v. south and Saul v. David make an ominous reappearance.

That is the import of the opening scene. The first words resume from 18.17. *Israel* here must mean the ten northern

tribes. Their support of Absalom had gone so far that, as we learn here for the first time, they (though not God) had *anointed* him *king*; but now they are ready to return to their previous loyalty (5.3). David however is more concerned about his own tribe of *Judah*. Using the two priests again as his representatives (15.35), he rallies it to his side – to a man, unlike Israel (v. 40). And to his cousin *Amasa* he promises command of the army in place of Joab. Amasa's previous defection to Absalom (17.25) is in David's eyes almost a mark in his favour, as against Joab's brand of loyalty.

David's Return to Jerusalem (cont.)

19.15 • When on his way back the king reac2hed the Jordan, the men of Judah came to Gilgal to meet him and escort him across the river. • Shimei son of Gera the Benjamite from Bahurim hastened down among the men of Judah to meet King David • with a thousand men from Benjamin; Ziba was there too, the servant of Saul's family, with his fifteen sons and twenty servants. They rushed into the Jordan under the king's eyes • and crossed to and fro conveying his household in order to win his favour. Shimei son of Gera, when he had crossed the river, threw himself down before the king • and said, 'I beg your majesty not to remember how disgracefully your servant

20 behaved when your majesty left Jerusalem; do not hold it against me. • I humbly acknowledge that I did wrong, and today I am the first of all the house of Joseph to come down to meet your majesty.' • Abishai son of Zeruiah objected. 'Ought not Shimei to be put to death', he said, 'because he cursed the LORD's anointed prince?' • David answered, 'What right have you, you sons of Zeruiah, to oppose me today? Should anyone be put to death this day in Israel? I know now that I am king of Israel.' • The king said to Shimei, 'You shall not die,' and he confirmed it with an oath.

• Saul's grandson Mephibosheth also went down to meet the king. He had not bathed his feet, trimmed his beard, or washed his clothes, from the day the king

25 went away until he returned victorious. • When he came from Jerusalem to meet the king, David said to him, 'Why did you not go with me, Mephibosheth?' • He answered, 'Sir, my servant deceived me; I did intend to harness my donkey and ride with the king (for I am lame), • but his stories set your majesty against me. Your majesty is like the angel of God; you must do what you think right. • My father's whole family, one and all, deserved to die at your majesty's hands, but you gave me, your servant, my place at your table. What further favour can I expect of the king?' • The king answered, 'You have said enough. My decision is

30 that you and Ziba are to share the estate.' • Mephibosheth said, 'Let him have it all, now that your majesty has come home victorious.' ▸

David's Return to Jerusalem (cont.)

David's three encounters on his return mirror the three of his flight, typically in the reverse order: increasing hostility on the way down, increasing friendship on the way back. His return journey took him back across Jordan near Jericho. The text specifically mentions *Gilgal*, the shrine connected with Joshua's crossing, and a number of other touches suggest that the author saw a parallel between David and Joshua at this point. Gilgal lay in the territory of Saul's tribe Benjamin (unusually referred to as *the house of Joseph* in v.20),

which officially had the priority over Judah in escorting David (see v.43). So his first two encounters are with members of Saul's clan: Shimei and Mephibosheth.

The scene with *Shimei* follows very closely that of 16.5-13, including the intervention of Joab's brother *Abishai*. But David can afford to be magnanimous in victory. He kept his *oath* to Shimei in the letter but not in the spirit (1 K 2.8).

Next came the meeting with *Mephibosheth*, answering that in 16.1-4 with Ziba. Mephibosheth displays to David the

David's Return to Jerusalem (cont.)

31   • Barzillai the Gileadite too had come down from Rogelim, and he went as far as the Jordan with the king to escort him on his way. • Barzillai was very old, eighty years of age; it was he who had provided for the king while he was at Mahanaim, for he was a man of great wealth. • The king said to Barzillai, 'Cross over with me and I shall provide for you in my household in Jerusalem.' • Barzillai answered, 'Your servant is far too old to go up with your majesty to Jerusalem. 35 • I am now eighty years old. I cannot tell what is pleasant and what is not; I cannot taste what I eat or drink; I can no longer listen to the voices of men and women singing. Why should I be a further burden on your majesty? • Your servant will attend the king for a short way across the Jordan; and why should the king reward me so handsomely? • Let me go back and end my days in my own town near the grave of my father and mother. Here is my son Kimham; let him cross over with your majesty, and do for him what you think best.' • The king answered, 'Let Kimham cross with me, and I shall do for him whatever you think best; and I shall do for you whatever you ask.'

     • All the people crossed the Jordan while the king waited. The king then kissed 40 Barzillai and gave him his blessing. Barzillai returned home; • the king crossed to Gilgal, Kimham with him.

     The whole army of Judah had escorted the king over the river, as had also half the army of Israel. • But the Israelites all kept coming to the king and saying, 'Why should our brothers of Judah have got possession of the king's person by joining King David's own men and then escorting him and his household across the Jordan?' • The answer of all the men of Judah to the Israelites was, 'Because his majesty is our near kinsman. Why should you resent it? Have we eaten at the king's expense? Have we received any gifts?' • The men of Israel answered, 'We have ten times your interest in the king and, what is more, we are senior to you; why do you disparage us? Were we not the first to speak of bringing the king back?' The men of Judah used language even fiercer than the men of Israel.   (REB)

David's Return to Jerusalem (cont.)

evidence of his mourning and thus of his loyalty. His comparison of David to *the angel of God* was evidently formulaic (14.20). David does not know whether to believe him or *Ziba*, and gives a Solomonic judgement.

     Third comes the true friend *Barzillai*, who answers to Hushai on the outward journey. The exchange between David and the garrulous octogenarian shows reciprocal, even competitive, generosity. David's *provide* of v.33 picks up the *provided* of 32 (cp. also 17.28); and when

Barzillai says of his son (so LXX) *Kimham 'do for him what you think best'*, David corrects him: '*I shall do whatever you think best.*' The description of old age in v.35 will later be famously elaborated in Eccl 12.

     Finally the section ends as it began with *Israel* and *Judah* vying in comic possessiveness over David. The last sentence of it implies that Judah won the argument. But the whole story of Absalom's rebellion shows that, in spite of many references in 2 Sam to 'all Israel', David never effectively unified the country.

Sheba's Attempt at Secession

20. 1 A scoundrel named Sheba son of Bichri, a man of Benjamin, happened to be there. He sounded the trumpet and cried out:

> We have no share in David,
> no lot in the son of Jesse.
> Every man to his tent, O Israel!

• All the men of Israel deserted David to follow Sheba son of Bichri, but the men of Judah stood by their king and followed him from the Jordan to Jerusalem.

• When David went up to his palace in Jerusalem he took the ten concubines whom he had left in charge of the palace and put them in a house under guard; he maintained them but did not have intercourse with them. They were kept in seclusion, living as if they were widows until the day of their death.

• The king said to Amasa, 'Call up the men of Judah and appear before me 5 again in three days' time.' • Amasa went to call up the men of Judah, but he took longer than the time fixed by the king. • David said to Abishai, 'Sheba son of Bichri will give us more trouble than Absalom; take the royal bodyguard and follow him closely in case he occupies some fortified cities and escapes us.' • Joab, along with the Kerethite and Pelethite guards and all the fighting men, marched out behind Abishai, and left Jerusalem in pursuit of Sheba son of Bichri.

• When they reached the great stone in Gibeon, Amasa came to meet them. Joab was wearing his tunic and over it a belt supporting a sword in its scabbard. He came forward, concealing his treachery, • and said to Amasa, 'I hope you are well, my 10 brother,' and with his right hand he grasped Amasa's beard to kiss him. • Amasa was not on his guard against the sword in Joab's hand. Joab struck him with it in the belly and his entrails poured out to the ground; he did not have to strike a second blow, for Amasa was dead. Joab with his brother Abishai went on in pursuit of Sheba son of Bichri. • One of Joab's men stood over Amasa and called out, 'Follow Joab, all who are for Joab and for David!' • Amasa's body lay soaked in blood in the middle of the road, and when the man saw how all the people stopped, he rolled him off the road into the field and threw a cloak over him; for everyone who came by stopped at the sight of the body. • When it had been removed from the road, they all went on and followed Joab in pursuit of Sheba son of Bichri.   ▶

Sheba's Attempt at Secession

This curious chapter comes as an appendix to Absalom's rebellion, but also as an anticlimax. In place of the high drama of previous chapters the main incident (8-12) is crudely told, the main dialogue (16-21) flat. The style lacks subtlety, e.g. *Sheba son of Bichri* is referred to eight times in the identical phrase. The text and translation are also unreliable in a number of places, one of them important (6-7).

The first two verses link the chapter to what precedes. Sheba's words *We have no share* repudiate the *We have ten* shares (so the Hebrew) of 19.43. He is not advocating rebellion, only secession, i.e. a reversion to the situation of Saul's time. The idea appealed to the fickle northern tribes (2). The awkward v.3, recording the fate of the *concubines*, rounds off the story both of David's return (answering 15.16) and of the whole rebellion. Having been used by Absalom (16.22) they are placed by David in 'a macabre quarantine', *widows* for life.

Sheba's Attempt at Secession (cont.)

• Sheba passed through all the tribes of Israel until he came to Abel-beth-maacah,
15 and all the clan of Bichri rallied to him and followed him into the city. • Joab's forces
came up and besieged him in Abel-beth-maacah, raised a siege-ramp against it,
and began undermining the wall to bring it down. • Then a wise woman stood on
the rampart and called from the city, 'Listen, listen! Tell Joab to come here and
let me speak with him.' • When he came forward the woman said, 'Are you
Joab?' He answered, 'I am.' 'Listen to what I have to say, sir,' she said. 'I am
listening,' he replied. • 'In the old days', she went on, 'there was a saying, "Go
to Abel for the answer," and that settled the matter. • My town is known to be one
of the most peaceable and loyal in Israel; she is like a watchful mother in Israel,
and you are seeking to kill her. Would you destroy the LORD's own possession?'
20 • Joab answered, 'God forbid, far be it from me to ruin or destroy! • That is not
our aim; but a man from the hill-country of Ephraim named Sheba son of Bichri
has raised a revolt against King David. Surrender this one man, and I shall retire
from the city.' The woman said to Joab, 'His head will be thrown over the wall to
you.' • Then the woman went to the people, who, persuaded by her wisdom, cut
off Sheba's head and threw it to Joab. He then sounded the trumpet, and the
whole army withdrew from the town; they dispersed to their homes, while Joab
went back to the king in Jerusalem.   (REB)

Sheba's Attempt at Secession (cont.)

David took the threat of Sheba seriously (6) and his military response was rapid. In accordance with his promise, he gave *Amasa* the task of calling up the men of Judah. But he set him a time limit, and when it elapsed (we are not told why) he had to take alternative action. According to most mss he passed over Joab and turned next to *Abishai*. If the translation in v.8 is correct, *Joab* initially accepted the demotion. But he quickly asserted himself, killing the late-comer Amasa much as he had killed Abner in Ch.3. This time however he has no apparent grounds save personal rivalry. It is just possible that Amasa was plotting against David – that would fit vv.5 and 11 – but the details make clear the author's disapproval of the murder. For the first time in the whole long tale, Joab is clearly at fault. True, he reasserts his authority over the army (11), wins the campaign by a mixture of force (14-15) and diplomacy (16-21), and ends it in unchallenged command (22). But we never hear of him in action again until he comes to be murdered in his turn.

David's Last Days and Solomon's Accession

1.1 King David was now a very old man, and though wrapped in bedclothes he could not keep warm. • So his servants said to him, 'Let us find a young girl for my lord the king, to wait on the king and look after him; she will lie close beside you and this will keep my lord the king warm.' • Having searched for a beautiful girl throughout the territory of Israel, they found Abishag of Shunem and brought her to the king. • The girl was very beautiful. She looked after the king and waited on 5 him but the king did not have intercourse with her. • Now Adonijah son of Haggith was growing pretentious and saying, 'I shall be king!' Accordingly, he procured a chariot and team with fifty guards to run ahead of him. • Never once in his life had his father crossed him by saying, 'Why are you behaving like that?' He was very handsome too; his mother had given birth to him after Absalom. • He conferred with Joab son of Zeruiah and with the priest Abiathar, who both rallied to Adonijah's cause; • but neither Zadok the priest, nor Benaiah son of Jehoiada, nor the prophet Nathan, nor Shimei and Rei, nor David's champions, supported Adonijah.

• One day when Adonijah was sacrificing sheep, oxen and fattened calves at the Sliding Stone which is beside the Fuller's Spring, he invited all his brothers, 10 the royal princes, and all the men of Judah in the king's service; • but he did not invite the prophet Nathan, or Benaiah, or the champions, or his brother Solomon. • Nathan then said to Bathsheba, Solomon's mother, 'Have you not heard that, unknown to our lord David, Adonijah son of Haggith has become king? • Well, this is my advice to you if you want to save your own life and the life of your son Solomon. • Go straight in to King David and say, "My lord king, did you not make your servant this promise on oath: Your son Solomon is to be king after me; he is the one who is to sit on my throne? How is it, then, that Adonijah is king?" • And while you are still there talking to the king, I shall come in after you and confirm what you say.'

David's Last Days and Solomon's Accession

Our two books of Kings carry on without break the story begun in those of Samuel. In the LXX they are known as the four books of Reigns, of which the second is extended by some mss to 1 K 2.11 or 1 K 2.46. Such boundaries are arbitrary; better founded is the universal opinion of critics that the first two chapters of 2 K are by the same masterly pen which gave us most of 2 Sam 9-20. The narrative of Ch.1 in particular is technically the most complex description in the whole OT. It covers a double series of events in eleven different scenes (including two reported by a messenger) with eight main speakers, all so well interwoven that the reader is not lost for a moment.

The first scene portrays *David* as *old*, cold, bed-ridden (47) and impotent. Later events (2.21) make it clear that *Abishag* (from *Shunem* in Galilee) was meant for his harem. In countries where the king's potency was believed to influence the fertility of the soil, his failure as a man would cast doubt on his competence as king. So, in the Hebrew, David 'did not know' her, and equally he 'did not know' what Adonijah was up to (11 and 18).

David's Last Days and Solomon's Accession (cont.)

15 • So Bathsheba went to the king in his room (he was very old and Abishag of Shunem was in attendance on him). • She knelt, prostrated herself before the king, and the king said, 'What do you want?' • 'My lord,' she replied, 'you swore to your servant by the LORD your God, "Your son Solomon is to be king after me; he is the one who is to sit on my throne." • And now here is Adonijah king, and you, my lord king, knowing nothing about it! • He has sacrificed quantities of oxen, fattened calves and sheep, and invited all the royal princes, the priest Abiathar, and Joab the army commander; but he has not invited your servant
20 Solomon. • Yet you are the man, my lord king, to whom all Israel looks, to tell them who is to succeed my lord the king. • And when my lord the king falls asleep with his ancestors, Solomon and I shall be made to suffer for this.'

• She was still speaking to the king when the prophet Nathan came in. • The king was told, 'The prophet Nathan is here'; and he came into the king's presence and prostrated himself on his face before the king. • 'My lord king,' said Nathan, 'is this, then, your decree, "Adonijah is to be king after me; he is the one
25 who is to sit on my throne"? • For he has gone down today and sacrificed quantities of oxen, fattened calves and sheep, and invited all the royal princes,   ▸

David's Last Days and Solomon's Accession (cont.)

The portrait of *Adonijah* reminds us explicitly and implicitly that he is full brother to Absalom. *Handsome* is spoilt and ostentatious (cp. 2 Sam 14.25; 15.1), he was heir apparent but did not wish to wait. Again like Absalom he sent out invitations to a ceremonial banquet at a discreet distance from Jerusalem (see map 3 for the *Fuller's Spring*), which would seal the loyalties of his supporters. Those listed in vv.7 and 8 included the leading men of the state (see 2 Sam 8.15-18). When the list of those *not* included is repeated in v.10, the name of *Solomon* is added as a link to the next scene.

The rest of Ch.1 takes place within a single day. The planned banquet was tantamount to a bid for the throne and, since the animals had already been slaughtered (so the Hebrew of v.9), the other side had to act fast. *Nathan*, who knew of God's love for Solomon (2 Sam 12.24), decided to enlist *Bathsheba*'s aid. She took no persuading: the eventual fate of Adonijah shows how realistic was the danger referred to in v.12. (The Hebrew word used there for 'save yourself', *malleti*, is cognate with 'Malta', the name

which the Phoenician sailors gave to their port of refuge.) The *oath* ascribed to David in v.13 has not been previously mentioned, but this is no reason for supposing that Nathan invented it. His plan is ingeniously devised and cleverly executed. Particularly skilful are the variations that Bathsheba and Nathan play on the same story.

First, we are reminded of David's weak condition. Then Bathsheba boldly begins by quoting the oath – not '*did you not swear?*' but *you swore* – and strengthens it with the addition of *by the LORD your God*. With the promise she then contrasts the actuality; and the list of those *not* invited to the banquet is now reduced to the one. But David's past ignorance can still be redeemed by the decisive action expected of a king at the end of his reign. Otherwise, by contrast with his peaceful death, she and her son face assassination. Bathsheba plays the wife betrayed, beginning with a personal promise and ending with an appeal for protection.

Nathan, by contrast, is the statesman who has not been kept informed. His opening is even bolder than Bathsheba's

David's Last Days and Solomon's Accession (cont.)

1. 26 the army commanders, and the priest Abiathar; and they are there now, eating and drinking in his presence and shouting, "Long live King Adonijah!" • He has not, however, invited me your servant, Zadok the priest, Benaiah son of Jehoiada, or your servant Solomon. • Can it be that this is done with my lord the king's approval and that you have not told those loyal to you who is to succeed to the throne of my lord the king?'

• King David then spoke. 'Call Bathsheba to me,' he said. And she came into the king's presence and stood before him. • Then the king swore this oath, 'As 30 the LORD lives, who has delivered me from all adversity, • just as I swore to you by the LORD, God of Israel, that your son Solomon should be king after me and take my place on my throne, so I shall bring it about this very day.' • Bathsheba knelt down, prostrated herself on her face before the king and said, 'May my lord King David live for ever!' • Then King David said, 'Summon Zadok the priest, the prophet Nathan and Benaiah son of Jehoiada.' So they came into the king's presence. • 'Take the royal guard with you,' said the king, 'mount my son Solomon on my own mule and escort him down to Gihon. • There Zadok the priest and the prophet Nathan are to anoint him king of Israel; then sound the trumpet and 35 shout, "Long live King Solomon!" • Then you are to escort him back, and he is then to assume my throne and be king in place of me, for he is the man whom I have appointed as ruler of Israel and of Judah.' • Benaiah son of Jehoiada answered the king. 'Amen!' he said. 'And may the LORD, God of my lord the king, confirm it! • As the LORD has been with my lord the king, so may he be with Solomon and make his throne even greater than the throne of my lord King David!'

• Zadok the priest, the prophet Nathan, Benaiah son of Jehoiada, and the Cherethites and Pelethites then went down; they mounted Solomon on King David's mule and escorted him to Gihon. • Zadok the priest took the horn of oil from the Tent and anointed Solomon. They sounded the trumpet and all the people shouted, 40 'Long live King Solomon!' • The people all escorted him back, with pipes playing and loud rejoicing and shouts to split the earth.   ▸

David's Last Days and Solomon's Accession (cont.)

and, where she relied on the oath, he stresses the politics. He quotes (or invents) the *shout* of acclamation (25), and gives an encouragingly fuller list of loyalists (26). Having shocked the king into action, he ends with a more diplomatic version of his opening gambit.

David was thoroughly manipulated by the pair of them. Nathan of course had always known how to handle him, but for Bathsheba this last scene is a splendid ironic reversal of their first encounter so many years before. Then she was a mere pawn, now she is Queen. He, lusty then,

is now impotent. But he can still take command from his *bed* (47).

First, he repeats the oath, with the important variant *by the LORD God of Israel*: it is now a matter of national import. Then he gives orders for the anointing of *Solomon* as joint *king*. It is to take place at the nearer spring *Gihon* just outside the city wall (see map 3), perhaps in continuance of an ancient ritual requiring spring water. The procession has a military guard – and suddenly what had been a list of conspirators becomes a roll of honour (38). *The Tent* (39) was the

David's Last Days and Solomon's Accession (cont.)

• Adonijah and his guests, who had by then finished their meal, all heard the noise. Joab too heard the sound of the trumpet and said, 'What is that noise of uproar in the city?' • While he was still speaking, Jonathan son of Abiathar the priest arrived. 'Come in,' Adonijah said, 'you are an honest man, so you must be bringing good news.' • 'The truth is,' Jonathan answered, 'our lord King David has made Solomon king. • With him, the king sent Zadok the priest, the prophet Nathan, Benaiah son of Jehoiada and the Cherethites and Pelethites; they mounted

.45 him on the king's mule, • and Zadok the priest and the prophet Nathan have anointed him king at Gihon; and they have gone back again with shouts of joy and the city is now in an uproar; that was the noise you heard. • What is more, Solomon is seated on the royal throne. • And further, the king's officers have been to congratulate our lord King David with the words, "May your God make the name of Solomon more glorious than yours, and his throne more exalted than your own!" And the king bowed down on his bed, • and then said, "Blessed be the LORD, God of Israel, for setting one of my own sons on the throne while I am still alive to see it!" '

• At this, all Adonijah's guests, taking fright, got up and made off in their
50 several directions. • Adonijah, in terror of Solomon, got up and ran off to cling to the horns of the altar. • Solomon was told, 'You should know that Adonijah is terrified of King Solomon and is now clinging to the horns of the altar, saying, "Let King Solomon first swear to me that he will not have his servant executed." ' • 'Should he bear himself honourably,' Solomon answered, 'not one hair of his shall fall to the ground; but if he proves difficult, he shall die.' • King Solomon then sent for him to be brought down from the altar; he came and threw himself prostrate before King Solomon; Solomon said to him, 'Go to your house.' (NJB)

David's Last Days and Solomon's Accession (cont.)

housing for the Ark (2 Sam 6.17). The people's acclamation is still an important part of the ceremony, a survival from earlier practice, as is the title *ruler* (35) – where n.b. *of Israel and of Judah.*

The noise of *the trumpet*, echoing half a mile down the Kidron valley to the lower spring where Adonijah's friends are feasting, strikes the soldierly ear of Joab and suggests trouble. *While he was still speaking* (42) picks up the words of v.22 and underlines the extreme urgency of the day's events. Adonijah in vain optimism quotes the very proverb that David had used similarly in 2 Sam 18.27. Young *Jonathan* makes the longest speech of the chapter, naively emphasising both David's authority and Solomon's

legitimacy. By contrast the sudden panic of his audience is related in a sentence.

Adonijah, deserted, seeks asylum at the sanctuary. *The altar* was doubtless in front of the Tent; its *horns* were the projections at the four corners on which the blood of the sacrifice was smeared, and thus its most sacred part. From there he negotiates with Solomon – through a messenger, to underline the distance between them. *Solomon* has hitherto been in the background, acted upon rather than acting. Now his first words are decisive, but also evasive: a foretaste of his character. Adonijah is to go home, i.e. withdraw from public life; then he may live, provided that (in the words of an earlier English commentator) 'he behaves like a gentleman'.

David's Charge to Solomon

2. 1 As the time of David's death drew near, he gave this charge to his son Solomon:
• 'I am about to go the way of all the earth. Be strong and show yourself a man.
5 • You know how Joab son of Zeruiah treated me and what he did to two commanders-in-chief in Israel, Abner son of Ner and Amasa son of Jether. He killed them both, breaking the peace by bloody acts of war; and with that blood he stained the belt about his waist and the sandals on his feet. • Act as your wisdom prompts you, and do not let his grey hairs go down to the grave in peace. • Show constant friendship to the family of Barzillai of Gilead; let them have their place at your table; they rallied to me when I was a fugitive from your brother Absalom. • Do not forget Shimei son of Gera, the Benjamite from Bahurim, who cursed me bitterly the day I went to Mahanaim. True, he came down to meet me at the Jordan, and I swore by the LORD that I would not put him to death. • But you do not need to let him go unpunished now; you are a wise man and will know how to deal with him; bring down his grey hairs in blood to the grave.' ▸

David's Charge to Solomon

David's testament follows the accepted morality of the time: harm your enemies and benefit your friends. In the case of *Joab*, his two murders are singled out (2 Sam 3.27; 20.10) as the *public* offence he had given to David. *Barzillai* (cp. 2 Sam 17.27+; 19.32+) is placed in the middle for contrast. *Shimei* (cp. 2 Sam 16.5+; 19.19+) had no merits to offset his offence, and David's euphemism of v.6 is made explicit in v.9. The narrator presents David as leaving ultimate responsibility to Solomon's (worldly) wisdom, but the effect is to inculpate both of them.

The character of *David* in the OT is one of the most enigmatic in literature, certainly from the ancient world. That needs explanation. Some part of it may be due to the different sources which have clearly been used in the final work; but we should invoke that only as a last resort. We should, for example, allow for the possibility that David's character changed over time. Such changes are rare before the modern novel, though it can be said that Achilles *learned* humanity during the course of the *Iliad*; and David's career lasted for more than the ten years of the Trojan War. But what is unique about David is that (i) the basic tension in his character is present throughout his life, (ii) that ten-sion is not a simple one between good and evil, and so (iii) any change can be read either as improvement or as deterioration.

That basic tension is between tough and tender, connected with public/private and exemplified (later) by king/father. But it is present at the very start, in giant-killer/musician (1 Sam 16.18+), at the very end in his charges about Joab and Barzillai, and throughout his life. The tough-public David is seen particularly in the narrative of his rise to power and the extension of his empire, when his methods include every form of unscrupulous-ness. But against that must be set the David who loves Jonathan, inspires love in Michal, spares Saul when he has him at his mercy and weeps for his death; and who, as king, shows generosity to Mephi-bosheth and expresses a programmatic revulsion against the violence of his foil Joab (2 Sam 3.39). Throughout all the early period of his life God is with him, and he is uniformly successful and popular.

The first turning point comes with the murder of Uriah, the dirtiest act of David's life. True, he is genuinely penitent; but the consequences will out. Briefly, he loses his moral authority, both as king and as father. As king, he has to be goaded into action by Joab (12.28; 14.1+; 19.5+). As father, he

David's Charge to Solomon (cont.)

10 • So David rested with his forefathers and was buried in the city of David, • having reigned over Israel for forty years, seven in Hebron and thirty-three in Jerusalem. (REB)

David's Charge to Solomon (cont.)

totally fails to discipline his sons: Amnon (13.21), Adonijah (1 K 1.6) and above all Absalom. Having been frustratingly indecisive over Absalom's recall from exile, and blindly over-indulgent to his plotting, David is overwhelmed by grief at the death brought about by his own weakness. Yet the crisis of Chs 15-18 marked a second turning point. At the lowest ebb of his outward fortunes he responded, against all expectation, with humble piety, and rose again with his old resolution and a

new maturity. To the cursing Shimei he shows first tolerance (16.12) and then magnanimity (19.22). He is even ready to lose his throne if it is the will of God (15.26). Here at the public crisis of his life the 'tender' David stands out against the 'tough' policy of his advisers. Here – whatever came before or after – we can see king and psalmist as the same man. It is this unconventional mixture which, whether it be seen as strength or weakness, renders David so fascinating a character.

Solomon Disposes of his Enemies

13 Then Adonijah son of Haggith came to Bathsheba, Solomon's mother. 'Do you come as a friend?' she asked. 'As a friend,' he answered; • 'I have something to discuss with you.' 'Tell me,' she said. • 'You know', he went on, 'that the throne was mine and that all Israel was looking to me to be king; but I was passed over and the throne has gone to my brother; it was his by the will of the LORD. • Now I have one request to make of you; do not refuse me.' 'What is it?' she said. • He answered, 'Will you ask King Solomon (he will never refuse you) to give me Abishag the Shunammite in marriage?' • 'Very well,' said Bathsheba, 'I shall speak to the king on your behalf.'

20 • When Bathsheba went in to King Solomon to speak for Adonijah, the king rose to meet her and do obeisance to her. Then he seated himself on his throne, and a throne was set for the king's mother at his right hand. • She said, 'I have one small request to make of you; do not refuse me.' 'What is it, mother?' he replied. 'I will not refuse you.' • 'It is this,' she said, 'that Abishag the Shunammite be given in marriage to your brother Adonijah.' • At that King Solomon answered, 'Why do you ask that Abishag the Shunammite be given to Adonijah? You might as well ask the kingdom for him; he is my elder brother and has both Abiathar the priest and Joab son of Zeruiah on his side.' • Then he swore by the LORD: 'So help me God,   ▶

Solomon Disposes of his Enemies

Adonijah's action in asking for *Abishag* in marriage shows him naive in the extreme, and no match at all for Solomon. Not that it was foolish to approach the king through the queen mother, who controlled the harem *ex officio* and was accorded especial respect by the king (see v.19, where her title in Hebrew is literally 'the great lady'). His request to her is marred by self-pity (15), but she accepts the com-

mission and does her best for him. She presents his case exactly as he had presented it to her, except for two diplomatic additions, the epithet *small* and the words *your brother* (21). The result is an explosion. Solomon treats or pretends to treat the request as evidence of continuing conspiracy (see 2 Sam 16.21-2). Consciously or unconsciously, he had been looking for an excuse to get rid of Adonijah.

Solomon Disposes of his Enemies (cont.)

2.25 Adonijah must pay for this with his life. • As the LORD lives, who has established me and set me on the throne of David my father and has founded a house for me as he promised, this very day Adonijah must be put to death!' • King Solomon sent Benaiah son of Jehoiada with orders to strike him down; so Adonijah died.

• When news of all this reached Joab, he fled to the Tent of the LORD and laid hold of the horns of the altar; for he had sided with Adonijah, though not with Absalom. • When King Solomon was told that Joab had fled to the Tent of the LORD and was beside the altar, he sent Benaiah son of Jehoiada with orders to **30** strike him down. • Benaiah came to the Tent of the LORD and ordered Joab in the king's name to come away. But he said, 'No, I will die here.' Benaiah reported Joab's answer to the king, • and the king said, 'Let him have his way; strike him down and bury him, and so rid me and my father's house of the guilt for the blood that he wantonly shed. • The LORD will hold him responsible for his own death, because he struck down two innocent men who were better men than he, Abner son of Ner, commander of the army of Israel, and Amasa son of Jether, commander of the army of Judah, and ran them through with the sword, without my father David's knowledge. • Let the guilt of their blood recoil on Joab and his descendants for all time; but may David and his descendants, his house and his throne, enjoy perpetual prosperity from the LORD.' • Benaiah son of Jehoiada went up to the altar and struck Joab down and killed him, and he was buried at his house out in the **35** country. • The king appointed Benaiah to command the army in place of Joab. ▸

Solomon Disposes of his Enemies (cont.)

Joab saw the writing on the wall and sought asylum in his turn. The rule in Exod 21.14 was that, if a man kills another treacherously, he may be taken by force from the altar. That was indeed the formal charge against Joab, which Solomon repeats in v. 32 after David (2.5). But all parties knew that the real charge was personal. So *Benaiah* at first (30) holds back, and Solomon concedes the old warrior an honourable burial.

The fascination of Joab's portrait in 2 Sam-1 K lies in his relationship with David, of which there are three facets. First is his loyalty – but it is loyalty to David as king i.e. ultimately to the state. Reasons of state lead him in turn to risk the displeasure of the king in 2 Sam Ch.3, to goad him at the end of Ch.12, to circumvent him in Ch.14, to disobey his orders in Ch.18 – and finally to trample on his tenderest feelings in Ch.19. Second, he knows David's secret wishes (14.1) and can forecast his reactions (11.19+) – again,

until Ch.19. But third, he is always too violent for David: in deed, from 3.39 onwards; in word, in that same fateful Ch.19. The hurt he did to David in that speech, and the hurt David did him in return by the appointment of Amasa (19.13), destroyed their relationship, and left him a hollow man. All that remained to him was the selfish violence with which he struck at Amasa – and through him at David. But David had the last word.

There remains *Shimei*. His was a more straightforward case. Nevertheless his old curse (2 Sam 16.5+) still had force until Solomon nullified it by returning it *on* his *own head* and then, for extra assurance, invoking a blessing upon the royal house (44-5).

With the establishment of Solomon securely on the throne the Court History (CH) of David ends. The character of this masterpiece of Hebrew story-telling is best seen by comparing it with its nearest parallels inside and outside the OT. Outside the OT, it is not difficult to find

Solomon Disposes of his Enemies (cont.)

• Next the king sent for Shimei and said to him, 'Build yourself a house in Jerusalem and stay there; you are not to leave the city for any other place. • If ever you leave and cross the wadi Kidron, know for certain that you will die. Your blood will be on your own head.' • Shimei replied, 'I accept your sentence; I shall do as your majesty commands.'

For a long time Shimei remained in Jerusalem. • But when three years later two of his slaves ran away to Achish son of Maacah, king of Gath, and this was reported to Shimei, • he at once saddled his donkey and went to Achish in search of his slaves; he reached Gath and brought them back. • When King Solomon was informed that Shimei had gone from Jerusalem to Gath and back, • he sent for him and said, 'Did I not require you to swear by the LORD? Did I not give you this solemn warning: "If ever you leave this city for any other place, know for certain that you will die"? You said, "I accept your sentence; I shall obey" • Why then have you not kept the oath which you swore by the LORD, and the order which I gave you? • Shimei, you know in your heart what mischief you did to my father David; the LORD is now making that mischief recoil on your own head. • But King Solomon is blessed, and the throne of David will be secure before the LORD for all time.' • The king then gave orders to Benaiah son of Jehoiada, who went out and struck Shimei down, and he died. Thus Solomon's royal power was securely established.   (REB)

Solomon Disposes of his Enemies (cont.)

parallels, both in the ANE and in Homer, to structural incidents in the stories of Saul and David (see p.254); but if the author of the CH used them, he did so as Shakespeare used Holinshed. Inside the OT, the closest parallels are the stories of Joseph and Ruth, with which the CH shares many literary and theological characteristics. Like them, it delights in the interplay of character and event, which it conveys chiefly through dialogue. Like them, it makes only implicit moral judgements: 'sin' has its consequences rather than its punishment. God stands behind events as providence, rather than intervening as agent. Like them, the CH shows little interest in the cult – the Ark narratives in 2 Sam 6 and 15 are from a different source. But the CH surpasses them both in the scope and coherence of its structure: by contrast the book of Ruth is a miniature, while the Joseph story is repetitive and disjointed. Moreover the CH is more open in portraying the vices of its leading characters, and it also provides more in

the way of vivid detail – specifically more 'free motifs', i.e. detail unnecessary to the plot. In those senses it is a much more sophisticated production.

It is also more historical, i.e. it uses purportedly historical events as its raw material. Many have, therefore, claimed it as the first great work of Hebrew historiography. If that were taken to mean that every historical event described in it happened as described, it could not be substantiated: even a palace source could not know what passed e.g. between Amnon and Tamar. But its closest parallel outside the OT is indeed the histories of Herodotus. Herodotus is more sophisticated again, and more truly historical (see p.782); but he shares a penchant for palace intrigue, and he also shares an implicit theology, namely (in Greek terms) that *hubris* is overtaken by *nemesis*. The CH may indeed be roughly contemporary with Herodotus, for it is hardly conceivable that a work so critical of David could have seen the light of day before the end of the monarchy.

The Reign of Solomon

I Kings devotes nine chapters to Solomon's reign. Half the space (Chs 5-8) is given to his building of the Temple, a subject of great interest to the deuteronomic historian or DtH (see p.184) whose editorial hand from now on lies heavy on the narrative. We miss both the vivid detail and intricate texture of the CH. Fortunately the DtH preserves fairly accurately his widely varied sources, contenting himself for the most part with easily recognisable additions (e.g. 3.6, 14) and collocations. His initial approval of Solomon, stemming from the building of the Temple, shows itself in praise of his wisdom and wealth. The king is shown as a peace-loving consolidator of David's work, a shrewd, efficient organiser. But his character never comes alive.

Solomon's Wisdom

3.1 Solomon allied himself to Pharaoh king of Egypt by marrying his daughter. He brought her to the City of David, until he had finished building his palace and the house of the LORD and the wall round Jerusalem.

• The king went to Gibeon to offer a sacrifice, for that was the chief shrine,
5 where he used to offer a thousand whole-offerings on the altar. • That night the LORD appeared to Solomon there in a dream. God said, 'What shall I give you? Tell me.' • He answered, 'You have shown great and constant love to your servant David my father, because he walked before you in loyalty, righteousness, and integrity of heart; and you have maintained this great and constant love towards him and now you have given him a son to succeed him on the throne.

• 'Now, LORD my God, you have made your servant king in place of my father David, though I am a mere child, unskilled in leadership. • Here I am in the midst of your people, the people of your choice, too many to be numbered or counted. • Grant your servant, therefore, a heart with skill to listen, so that he may govern your people justly and distinguish good from evil. Otherwise who is equal to the task of governing this great people of yours?'   ▶

Solomon's Wisdom

Chs 3-4 contain stories of Solomon's wisdom. Wisdom in the ANE was a technical term (see p.364) with strong connotations of political skill. So we learn first of Solomon's dynastic alliance with *Egypt*. This suited Egypt too, it being weaker than usual: indeed Pharaohs succeeded one another so fast in C10th BC that we do not know which one was meant here. As dowry, his queen brought the important Philistine fortress of Gezer recently captured by Egypt (9.16).

Egypt provides also the background to the first story, that of Solomon's *dream* (3.4-15). Pharaohs regularly cast the stone-cut record of their reigns in the form of a dream which legitimated their accession and announced their policy. That form is closely followed here. In it the Pharaoh goes out to a shrine in the countryside to sleep the night, and offers *a sacrifice* to win the divine favour (cp. v.4). He then receives the dream in which God speaks of his election even in the womb (cp. *a child,* v.7) and of the special knowledge which has been given him to fulfil his role as king. The dream ends with a formula of recognition (cp.v.15a: if a dream, it must have come from God), after which the king returns to his capital, invites his court to a sacrificial *banquet* and reveals to them the content of his dream (15).

In Solomon's case however the content is not particularly Egyptian. It chiefly represents the Hebrew ideology of kingship. Where other OT texts (esp. 1 Sam 8) make the worst case against monarchy by referring to the bad habits of ANE kings, this makes the best case for it by repudiating those habits. Babylonian kings in particular

Solomon's Wisdom (cont.)

10 • The LORD was well pleased that this was what Solomon had asked for, • and God said, 'Because you have asked for this, and not for long life, or for wealth, or for the lives of your enemies, but have asked for discernment in administering justice, • I grant your request; I give you a heart so wise and so understanding that there has been none like you before your time, nor will there be after you. • What is more, I give you those things for which you did not ask, such wealth and glory as no king of your time can match. • If you conform to my ways and observe my ordinances and commandments, as your father David did, I will also
15 give you long life.' • Then Solomon awoke, and realised it was a dream. Solomon came to Jerusalem and gave a banquet for all his household.

• Two women who were prostitutes approached the king at that time, and as they stood before him • one said, 'My lord, this woman and I share a house, and I gave birth to a child when she was there with me. • On the third day after my baby was born she too gave birth to a child. We were alone; no one else was with us in the house; only the two of us were there. • During the night this woman's
20 child died because she lay on it, • and she got up in the middle of the night, took my baby from my side while I, your servant, was asleep, and laid it on her bosom, putting her dead child on mine. • When I got up in the morning to feed my baby, I found him dead; but when I looked at him closely, I found that it was not the child that I had borne.' • The other woman broke in, 'No, the living child is mine; yours is the dead one,' while the first insisted, 'No, the dead child is yours; mine is the living one.' So they went on arguing before the king.

• The king thought to himself, 'One of them says, "This is my child, the living one; yours is the dead one." The other says, "No, it is your child that is dead and mine that is alive." ' • Then he said, 'Fetch me a sword.' When a sword was
25 brought, • the king gave the order: 'Cut the living child in two and give half to one woman and half to the other.' • At this the woman who was the mother of the living child, moved with love for her child, said to the king, 'Oh, sir, let her have the baby! Whatever you do, do not kill it.' The other said, 'Let neither of us have it; cut it in two.' • The king then spoke up: 'Give the living baby to the first woman,' he said; 'do not kill it. She is its mother.' • When Israel heard the judgement which the king had given, they all stood in awe of him; for they saw that he possessed wisdom from God for administering justice.   (REB)

Solomon's Wisdom (cont.)

at the start of their reign prayed precisely for the objects listed in v.11 as not prayed for by Solomon. Solomon is portrayed as the ideal king by contrast. But the portrait fails to carry conviction. Ch.2 has just shown him lightly taking *the lives of* his *enemies*, and later chapters will boast of his *wealth*. Is the DtH being heavily ironical or merely failing to integrate his sources?

The story of the two mothers is the second illustration of Solomon's *wisdom*. It is an old ANE folk-tale, known in many forms from the C14th BC on. Behind this version lies an Indian one; the *two women* are not *prostitutes* but wives of the same man, giving added point to their rivalry: the mother of the first son achieves higher status. It also explains why they live in the same house and why the false mother wants the child killed (26). The contrast between her chilly words and the warm sentiments of the real mother is well done; so is the slanging match of v.22, where in each exchange the riposte is expressed in a neat chiasmus*.

Solomon's Wisdom (cont.)

4. 21   • Solomon ruled over all the kingdoms from the river Euphrates to Philistia and as far as the frontier of Egypt; they paid tribute and were subject to him all
25   his life. • All through his reign the people of Judah and Israel lived in peace,
29   everyone from Dan to Beersheba under his own vine and his own fig tree. • God gave Solomon deep wisdom and insight, and understanding as wide as the sand on the seashore, • so that Solomon's wisdom surpassed that of all the men of the east and of all Egypt. • He propounded three thousand proverbs, and his songs numbered
33   a thousand and five. • He discoursed of trees, from the cedar of Lebanon down to the marjoram that grows out of the wall, of beasts and birds, of reptiles and fish. • People of all races came to listen to the wisdom of Solomon, and he received gifts from all the kings in the world who had heard of his wisdom.   (REB)

Solomon's Wisdom (cont.)

The extent of empire claimed for Solomon (4.21) is the same as that for David, i.e. it stopped short of both *the Euphrates* and *Philistia*. But his reign is presented, unlike David's, as a time of peace for what are unusually called *Judah and Israel*. Peace and prosperity are regular motifs in the praise of ANE kings.

And the repute of Solomon's wisdom is finally said to have extended into the very countries of the ANE where there had for centuries been a famous tradition of Wisdom. In that tradition he himself is said to have composed *proverbs* (some of which would have used the nature lore of v.33) and *songs*. Much of Hebrew Wisdom literature, though written after his time, was traditionally ascribed to him, e.g. the first section of the book of Proverbs, with the whole of Ecclesiastes and the Song of Songs, and the Wisdom of Solomon from the Apocrypha.

Solomon's Buildings

5. 1   When Hiram king of Tyre heard that Solomon had been anointed king in his father's place, he sent envoys to him, because he had always been friendly with David. • Solomon sent this message to Hiram: • 'You know that my father David could not build a house for the name of the LORD his God, because of the armed nations surrounding him, until the LORD made them subject to him. • But now on every side the LORD my God has given me peace; there is no one to oppose me, I fear
5   no attack. • So I propose to build a house for the name of the LORD my God, following the promise given by the LORD to my father David: "Your son whom I shall set on the throne in your place will build the house for my name." • If therefore you will now give orders that cedars be felled and brought from Lebanon, my men will work with yours, and I shall pay you for your men whatever sum you fix; for, as you know, we have none so skilled at felling trees as your Sidonians.' • Hiram was greatly pleased to receive Solomon's message, and said, 'Blessed be the LORD today who has given David a wise son to rule over this great people.' ▶

Solomon's Buildings

Solomon's building programme follows immediately the section on his wisdom. The author makes an explicit link by inserting the epithet *wise* in the acces- sion-greeting formula of 5.7. Building programmes were part of what was expected of ANE kings, and the numerous inscriptions recording them

Solomon's Buildings (cont.)

.8 • He sent Solomon this reply: 'I have received your message. In this matter of timber, both cedar and pine, I shall do all you wish. • My men will bring down the logs from Lebanon to the sea and I shall make them up into rafts to be floated to the place you appoint; I shall have them broken up there and you can remove them. You, for your part, will meet my wishes if you provide the food for my

10 household.' • So Hiram kept Solomon supplied with all the cedar and pine that he wanted, • and Solomon supplied Hiram with twenty thousand kor of wheat as food for his household and twenty kor of oil of pounded olives; Solomon gave this yearly to Hiram. • The LORD bestowed wisdom on Solomon as he had promised him; there was peace between Hiram and Solomon and they concluded a treaty.

• King Solomon raised a forced levy from the whole of Israel amounting to thirty thousand men. • He sent them to Lebanon in monthly relays of ten thousand, so that the men spent one month in Lebanon and two at home; Adoniram

15 was superintendent of the levy. • Solomon had also seventy thousand hauliers and eighty thousand quarrymen, • apart from the three thousand three hundred foremen in charge of the work who superintended the labourers. • By the king's orders they quarried huge, costly blocks for laying the foundation of the LORD's house in hewn stone. • The builders supplied by Solomon and Hiram, together with the Gebalites, shaped the blocks and prepared both timber and stone for the building of the house.   ♦

Solomon's Buildings (cont.)

often ascribe them to the royal wisdom.

Israel has always been poor in timber, whereas the *cedars* of *Lebanon* had been renowned throughout the ANE for 1,000 years before Solomon. So when *Hiram* exchanged greetings with David's successor (cp. 2 Sam 5.11), Solomon lost no time in making a deal. Hiram was king of *Tyre* and *Sidon*, the two leading cities of Phoenicia; *Gebal* or Byblos (18) was a third. The Phoenician craftsmen were responsible for the skilled work of *felling* the timber, transporting it by sea and preparing it on site; also for the dressing of the *stone, quarried* in Jerusalem itself. The quarrying and the unskilled work was done by a *levy* of Israelites. *Forced* labour was common in the large ANE monarchies, but had not been used in Israel before; it proved most unpopular (12.4).

The outstanding feature of Solomon's building programme is the royal complex of palace and temple. Though something entirely new in Israel, this had long been

a regular feature, in concept and design, of ANE monarchies. Palace and temple were architecturally and functionally linked, with the former much larger than the latter. The linkage symbolised the royal status as representing the national god, divinely appointed as head of both state and cult. The architects of the new complex in Jerusalem were presumably Phoenician like the craftsmen [7.13+].

The *palace* (7.1-12) was much bigger than the Temple, so it is not surprising that it took twice as long to build; but it is given far less space by the author. The *House of the Forest of Lebanon* was perhaps used for ceremonial occasions; the *Hall of Justice* was for business, with the *Colonnade* serving as a waiting room. Verse 12 distinguishes the wall round the Temple from the one which enclosed the whole palace-temple complex. All the walls were built on the same principle: they rested on rough-hewn megaliths; then came *three courses of dressed*

Solomon's Buildings (cont.)

6.1 • It was in the four hundred and eightieth year after the Israelites had come out of Egypt, in the fourth year of Solomon's reign over Israel, in the second month of that year, the month of Ziv, that he began to build the house of the LORD. • The house which King Solomon built for the LORD was sixty cubits long by twenty cubits broad, and its height was thirty cubits. • The vestibule in front of the sanctuary was twenty cubits long, spanning the whole breadth of the

19 house, while it projected ten cubits in front of the house. • He prepared an inner shrine in the farthest recesses of the house to receive the Ark of the Covenant of the LORD. • This inner shrine was twenty cubits square and it stood twenty cubits

23 high; he overlaid it with red gold and made an altar of cedar. • In the inner shrine he carved two cherubim of wild olive wood, each ten cubits high. • Each wing of the cherubim was five cubits long, and from wingtip to wingtip was ten

27 cubits. • He put the cherubim within the inner shrine and their wings were spread, so that a wing of one cherub touched the wall on one side and a wing of the other touched the wall on the other side, and their other wings met in the middle; • he overlaid the cherubim with gold.

37 • In the fourth year of Solomon's reign, in the month of Ziv, the foundation of the house of the LORD was laid; • and in the eleventh year, in the month of Bul, which is the eighth month, the house was finished in all its details according to the specification. It had taken seven years to build.   (REB)

7.1 • As regards his palace, Solomon spent thirteen years on it before the building was completed. • He built the House of the Forest of Lebanon, a hundred cubits long, fifty cubits wide, and thirty cubits high, on four rows of cedar-wood pillars, • with lengths of cedar wood laid horizontally on the pillars. The upper part was panelled with cedar right down to the tie-beams on forty-five pillars, fifteen

7 in each row. • He also made the Hall of the Throne where he used to dispense justice, that is, the Hall of Justice; it was panelled in cedar from floor to beams. • His own living quarters, in the other court and inwards from the Hall, were of the same construction. And there was a house similar to this Hall for Pharaoh's daughter whom he had taken in marriage.

• All these buildings were of special stones cut to measure, trimmed on the

10 inner and outer sides with the saw, from the foundations to the coping – • the foundations were of special stones, huge stones, of ten and eight cubits, • and, above these, special stones, cut to measure, and cedar wood – • and, on the outside, the great court had three courses of dressed stone round it and one course of cedar beams; so also had the inner court of the Temple of the LORD and the vestibule of the Temple.   (NJB)

Solomon's Buildings (cont.)

masonry and *one of cedar*. When the buildings continued on up, the walls were probably topped with brick.

Unfortunately the long and detailed description of the Temple (Ch.6) and its furnishings [7.15-50] is not clear enough to enable a confident reconstruction. But its basic design conformed to a pattern which was common not only in the Levant but also in principle in Egypt and even Greece. It was a rectangular building consisting of three successive rooms,

Solomon's Buildings (cont.)

6   • The priests brought in the Ark of the Covenant of the LORD to its place in the inner shrine of the house, the Most Holy Place, beneath the wings of the cherubim. • The cherubim, whose wings were spread over the place of the Ark, formed a canopy above the Ark and its poles. • The poles projected, and their ends were visible from the Holy Place immediately in front of the inner shrine, but from nowhere else outside; they are there to this day. • There was nothing inside the Ark but the two stone tablets which Moses had deposited there at Horeb, when the LORD made the covenant with the Israelites after they left Egypt.

15   • This is the record of the forced labour which King Solomon conscripted to build the house of the LORD, his own palace, the wall of Jerusalem, and Hazor, Megiddo, and Gezer. • Gezer had been attacked and captured by Pharaoh king of Egypt, who had burnt it to the ground, put its Canaanite inhabitants to death, and given it as a marriage gift to his daughter, Solomon's wife. • Solomon rebuilt it. (REB)

Solomon's Buildings (cont.)

each extending across its whole width: first the *vestibule* (6.3) or portico, then the *sanctuary*, finally the *inner shrine* (6.19f, also called the most *the Most Holy Place* in 8.6). A *cubit* is just under half a metre. The whole temple was therefore small; but it has to be remembered that sacrifices and other rituals were conducted outside it. The cherubs (Hebrew plural *cherubim*) were winged creatures, used in Phoenicia as supporting decorations for a royal throne; here they are for the protection of the Ark (8.6).

Nothing has been rediscovered of Solomon's buildings on what is known today as the Temple Mount, but they are presented as overshadowing the City of David, in location, size and magnificence. The city walls now include both hills (see map 3). The fortifications of *Hazor, Megiddo and Gezer* are impressive, though some scholars date them later than Solomon. In any case, his reign was not a military success, as Ch.11 shows, nor could a small country, whose only natural resources were in agriculture, really afford such a lavish building programme. Solomon's 'glory' could not last.

Solomon's Wealth

9.26 King Solomon built a fleet of ships at Ezion-geber, near Elath on the shore of the Red Sea, in Edom. • Hiram sent men of his own to serve with the fleet, experienced seamen, to work with Solomon's men. • They went to Ophir and brought back four hundred and twenty talents of gold, which they delivered to King Solomon.

10. 1   • The queen of Sheba heard of Solomon's fame and came to test him with enigmatic questions. • She arrived in Jerusalem with a very large retinue, camels laden with spices, gold in vast quantity, and precious stones. When she came to Solomon, she talked to him about everything she had on her mind. • Solomon answered all her questions; not one of them was too hard for the king to answer. • When the queen of Sheba observed all the wisdom of Solomon, the palace he 5 had built, • the food on his table, the courtiers sitting around him, and his attendants standing behind in their livery, his cupbearers, and the whole-offerings which he used to offer in the house of the LORD, she was overcome with amazement. • She said to the king, 'The account which I heard in my own country about your achievements and your wisdom was true, • but I did not believe what they told me until I came and saw for myself. Indeed I was not told half of it; your wisdom and your prosperity far surpass all I had heard of them. • Happy are your wives, happy these courtiers of yours who are in attendance on you every day and hear your wisdom! • Blessed be the LORD your God who has delighted in you and has set you on the throne of Israel; because he loves Israel unendingly, he has made you king to 10 maintain law and justice.' • She presented the king with a hundred and twenty talents of gold, spices in great abundance, and precious stones. Never again did such a quantity of spices come as the queen of Sheba gave to King Solomon.   ⬦

Solomon's Wealth

To build a merchant *fleet* on the Gulf of Aqaba, 200 miles from Jerusalem, would indeed have been a notable feat. *Ezion-Geber* is now silted up half a mile inland of *Elath*, but excavation has found long nails, as used in ship-building, and lumps of pitch for caulking; there was also good timber growing nearby. As with the buildings in Jerusalem, Solomon used Phoenician experience. *Hiram*'s men probably built and crewed the ships, while Solomon's were the traders. *Ophir* is traditionally located in southern Arabia. Ch.10 contains two further references to the fleet (vv.11-12, 22), mentioning other precious cargoes (*almug-wood* is unidentified) and showing that the kings were jointly engaged in a profitable venture. In addition to sea-trading, Ezion-Geber also controlled the overland caravan routes from India and Arabia to Egypt.

Sheba was an independent kingdom in what is now Yemen, i.e. close to Ophir. The country produced its own spices and minerals, but it also enjoyed a fine commercial position, and presumably its ruler came to Jerusalem on a trade mission. The narrative displays another facet of Solomon's wisdom, namely his ability to *answer* riddles (3) or cap stories. Examples of such competitions are found in the OT in Jg 14 (Samson) and 1 Esdras 3-4; and the Jewish historian Josephus records a similar contest of words between Solomon and Hiram. The legendary colouring of the narrative is clearly designed to show how Solomon's combined wisdom and wealth impressed foreigners. But the romantic setting carries it all off. Even the pseudo-negative formula of admiration is fun when used by the Queen (*not half of it*, 7) or of her (*not one too hard*, 3; *never again*,

Solomon's Wealth (cont.)

• (Besides all this, Hiram's fleet of ships, which had brought gold from Ophir, brought also from Ophir huge cargoes of almug wood and precious stones. • The king used the wood to make stools for the house of the LORD and for the palace, as well as lyres and lutes for the singers. No such quantities of almug wood have ever been imported or even seen since that time.)

• King Solomon gave the queen of Sheba whatever she desired and asked for, in addition to all that he gave her of his royal bounty. Then she departed with her retinue and went back to her own land.

• The weight of gold which Solomon received in any one year was six hundred and sixty-six talents, • in addition to the tolls levied by the customs officers, the profits on foreign trade, and the tribute of the kings of Arabia and the regional governors. • King Solomon made two hundred shields of beaten gold, and six hundred shekels of gold went to the making of each one; • he also made three hundred bucklers of beaten gold, and three minas of gold went to the making of each buckler. The king put these into the House of the Forest of Lebanon.

• The king also made a great throne inlaid with ivory and overlaid with fine gold. • Six steps led up to the throne; at the back of the throne there was the head of a calf. There were armrests on each side of the seat, with a lion standing beside each of them, • while twelve lions stood on the six steps, one at either end of each step. Nothing like it had ever been made for any monarch. • All Solomon's drinking vessels were of gold, and all the plate in the House of the Forest of Lebanon was of red gold; no silver was used, for it was reckoned of no value in the days of Solomon. • The king had a fleet of merchantmen at sea with Hiram's fleet; once every three years this fleet of merchantmen came home, bringing gold and silver, ivory, apes, and monkeys.

• Thus King Solomon outdid all the kings of the earth in wealth and wisdom, • and the whole world courted him to hear the wisdom with which God had endowed his mind. • Each one brought his gift with him, vessels of silver and gold, garments, perfumes and spices, horses and mules in annual tribute.

• Solomon amassed chariots and horses; he had fourteen hundred chariots and twelve thousand horses; he stationed some in the chariot-towns, while others he kept at hand in Jerusalem. • He made silver as common in Jerusalem as stone, and cedar as plentiful as the sycomore-fig is in the Shephelah. • Horses were imported from Egypt and Kue for Solomon; the merchants of the king obtained them from Kue by purchase.   (REB)

Solomon's Wealth (cont.)

10), whereas it quickly becomes tedious when used in the author's catalogues (*no such . . . ever*, 12; *nothing like it . . . ever*, 20) – as indeed it would have done if Solomon had been entertaining a *king* of Sheba. It is not surprising that this tale has given birth to many legends among Jews, Muslims and Christians, including that of the origin of the Abyssinian royal house.

The second half of Ch.10 sounds impressive, but to a reader familiar with Deuteronomy it is ominous. Dt [17.16f.] imposes three prohibitions upon a king of Israel: he must not acquire (i) horses from Egypt or (ii) foreign wives or (iii) silver and gold in great quantities. The judgement of the DtH is implicit.

Solomon's Decline

11.1 King Solomon loved many foreign women; in addition to Pharaoh's daughter there were Moabite, Ammonite, Edomite, Sidonian, and Hittite women, • from the nations with whom the LORD had forbidden the Israelites to intermarry, 'because', he said, 'they will entice you to serve their gods'. But Solomon was devoted to them and loved them dearly. • He had seven hundred wives, all princesses, and three hundred concubines, and they influenced him, • for as he grew old, his wives turned his heart to follow other gods, and he did not remain wholly

5 loyal to the LORD his God as his father David had been. • He followed Ashtoreth, goddess of the Sidonians, and Milcom, the loathsome god of the Ammonites.

14 • The LORD raised up an adversary for Solomon, Hadad the Edomite, of the

23 royal house of Edom. • Another adversary God raised up against Solomon was Rezon son of Eliada, • He gathered men about him and became a captain of freebooters; he went to Damascus, occupied it, and became king there.

26 • Jeroboam son of Nebat, one of Solomon's courtiers, an Ephrathite from Zeredah, whose widowed mother was named Zeruah, rebelled against the

40 king. • Solomon sought to kill Jeroboam, but he fled to King Shishak in Egypt and remained there till Solomon's death.

• The other acts and events of Solomon's reign, and all his wisdom, are recorded in the annals of Solomon. • The reign of King Solomon in Jerusalem over the whole of Israel lasted forty years.   (REB)

Solomon's Decline

Ch.11 continues that judgement and makes it explicit.

Foreign wives, being permitted to retain their national worship, were a source of temptation; and Solomon fell, albeit in his *old* age. *Ashtoreth* is the name of a fertility goddess (= Babylonian Ishtar). *Milcom* is a title meaning 'king' (= Phoenician Moloch).

The author's standard theology dictates the punishment for Solomon's apostasy. It comes in three forms, together signifying the effective break-up of David's 'empire'.

Edom became restive and *Damascus* achieved independence. Both of these were soon to become thorns in the flesh of Israel. But the most immediate threat lay in the attempted rebellion of *Jeroboam*. His tribe Ephraim was the largest in the north, and from now on is often used to stand for the whole of it. For *Shishak* see below. The closing verses of Ch.11 are the normal formula used in the books of Kings. The period of *forty years* is formulaic too, being the conventional length of one generation.

The Kingdom Divided

12.1 Rehoboam went to Shechem, for all Israel had gone there to make him king. • When Jeroboam son of Nebat, who was still in Egypt, heard of it, he remained there, having taken refuge in Egypt to escape King Solomon. • The people now recalled him, and he and all the assembly of Israel came to Rehoboam and said, • 'Your father laid a harsh yoke upon us; but if you will now lighten the harsh

5 labour he imposed and the heavy yoke he laid on us, we shall serve you.' • 'Give me three days,' he said, 'and then come back.'

When the people had gone, • King Rehoboam consulted the elders who had been in attendance during the lifetime of his father Solomon: 'What answer do you advise me to give to this people?' • They said, 'If today you are willing to serve this people, show yourself their servant now and speak kindly to them, and they will be your ▸

The Kingdom Divided (cont.)

servants ever after.' • But he rejected the advice given him by the elders, and consulted the young men who had grown up with him, and were now in attendance; • he asked them, 'What answer do you advise me to give to this people's request that I should lighten the yoke which my father laid on them?' • The young men replied, 'Give this answer to the people who say that your father made their yoke heavy and ask you to lighten it; tell them: "My little finger is thicker than my father's loins. • My father laid a heavy yoke on you, but I shall make it heavier. My father whipped you, but I shall flay you." ' • Jeroboam and the people all came to Rehoboam on the third day, as the king had ordered. • The king gave them a harsh answer; he rejected the advice which the elders had given him • and spoke to the people as the young men had advised: 'My father made your yoke heavy, but I shall make it heavier. My father whipped you, but I shall flay you.'

• When all Israel saw that the king would not listen to them, they answered:

What share have we in David?

We have no lot in the son of Jesse.

Away to your tents, Israel!

Now see to your own house, David!

With that Israel went off to their homes. • Rehoboam ruled only over those Israelites who lived in the cities and towns of Judah. • King Rehoboam sent out Adoram, the commander of the forced levies, but when the Israelites stoned him to death, the king hastily mounted his chariot and fled to Jerusalem. • From that day to this Israel has been in rebellion against the house of David.

• When the men of Israel heard that Jeroboam had returned, they sent and called him to the assembly and made him king over the whole of Israel. The tribe of Judah alone stayed loyal to the house of David.   ♦

The Kingdom Divided

The split between north and south is laid at the door of Solomon's son and successor *Rehoboam*. In the south the monarchy was accepted by now as hereditary. In the north *the assembly of Israel*, which met at *Shechem*, retained some say in the matter. Having advance reservations about any son of Solomon, they decided to test the temper of Rehoboam. It was customary in the ANE for a king on his accession to announce some lightening of the burden: would he follow custom?

The language of Rehoboam's *young men* is extremely coarse, both in its obscene anatomical reference to Solomon (*loins* is clearly a euphemism) and in its relish for the infliction of pain. The former is too much even for the braggart Rehoboam, but he readily accepts the latter. REB's translation is a poor man's version of AV's 'my father chastised you

with whips, but I will chastise you with scorpions'; a 'scorpion' was a lash with metal insertions.

The response of the northern tribes was predictable. They quoted again the verse used by the dissident Shimei in 2 Sam 20.1, adding the fourth line which is necessary to round it off; and they suited the deed to the word. (Verse 17 illustrates the difficulty felt even by the ancient writers over the use of the term 'Israel'). Rehoboam, who had learned nothing, then attempted to impose the hated *levy* (1 K 5.13); and that settled the matter for good and all. The idea that *Judah alone stayed loyal to the house of David*, though central to the thinking of the DtH, is tendentious in the extreme. The OT itself concedes that the northern tribes had never wholeheartedly accepted David. The evidence of archaeology is even more

The Kingdom Divided (cont.)

12.25 • Jeroboam rebuilt Shechem in the hill-country of Ephraim and took up residence there. • 'As things now stand', he said to himself, 'the kingdom will revert to the house of David. • If these people go up to sacrifice in the house of the LORD in Jerusalem, it will revive their allegiance to their lord King Rehoboam of Judah, and they will kill me and return to King Rehoboam.' • After taking counsel about the matter he made two calves of gold and said to the people, 'You have gone up to Jerusalem long enough; here are your gods, Israel, that brought you up from Egypt.' • One he set up at Bethel and the other he put at Dan.

14.21 • In Judah Rehoboam son of Solomon had become king. He was forty-one years old when he came to the throne, and he reigned for seventeen years in Jerusalem, the city where the LORD had chosen, out of all the tribes of Israel, to set his name. • In the
25 fifth year of Rehoboam's reign King Shishak of Egypt attacked Jerusalem, • and carried away the treasures of the house of the LORD and of the king's palace; he seized everything, including all the gold shields made for Solomon. • King Rehoboam replaced them with bronze shields and entrusted them to the officers of the escort who guarded the entrance of the palace. • Whenever the king entered the house of the LORD, the escort carried them; afterwards they returned them to the guardroom. • The other acts and events of Rehoboam's reign are recorded in the annals of the kings of Judah. • There was continual fighting between him and Jeroboam.   (REB)

The Kingdom Divided (cont.)

challenging. It confirms the importance of Israel in C9th and C8th, but does not regard Judah as being of consequence until after the abolition of Israel in 721.

Jeroboam, who had been waiting in the wings, now accepted the throne of Israel, and we are immediately told of his building programme. As well as *Shechem*, he may have been responsible also for the imposing new fortifications which appear at this time at Hazor, Megiddo and Gezer.

He also tried, like any other monarch in the ANE (including Solomon), to establish the national cult independently of Jerusalem. The close link between kingship and cult is made clear by 12.27. *Dan*, the northernmost town of Israel, was a long-standing religious centre. Excavations there have revealed great new works from Jeroboam's time, including a magnificent stone platform 20 metres square, approached by a monumental flight of steps. Among the cult-objects found there were altars, model shrines and figurines of the bull-calf which probably represented Baal. The *golden calves* (12.28) would have been large-scale figures covered in gold leaf. As far as can

be seen, the cult at Dan was syncretistic i.e. the calves were meant to represent YHWH *as well as* Baal. But such syncretism was anathema to the DtH, and consequently Jeroboam (931-910) went down in history as the king who 'made Israel to sin'.

Meanwhile *Rehoboam* (931-913) was ruling Judah. He too incurred the disapproval of the DtH, and for similar reasons. His apostasy was 'punished' by an invasion from Egypt (926). It so happens that Pharaoh *Shishak* (c.945-924) left a skeletal record of this campaign in a temple at Karnak (*ANET* 263). That is the first external corroboration of a datable event in Hebrew history. In it Shishak gives the names of 156 'towns' which he claims to have taken in the Levant. Jerusalem is not listed among them, possibly because he was bought off by the *gold shields* – though to the DtH that incident represents not a salvation but a symbolic decline from gold to bronze. Shishak also claims that his four years' campaigning in the region yielded 400 tons of gold as booty, which (if true) helps put Solomon's annual income of 21 tons (10.14) in perspective .

Omri (885–874) and Ahab (874–853)

3 | In the thirty-first year of Asa king of Judah, Omri became king of Israel and reigned for twelve years. He reigned for six years at Tirzah. • Then for two talents of silver he bought the hill of Samaria from Shemer and on it built a town which he named Samaria after Shemer who had owned the hill. • Omri did what is displeasing to the LORD, and was worse than all his predecessors.

29 | • Ahab son of Omri became king of Israel in the thirty-eighth year of Asa king of Judah, and reigned over Israel for twenty-two years in Samaria. • Ahab son of Omri did what is displeasing to the LORD, and was worse than all his predecessors. • The least that he did was to follow the sinful example of Jeroboam son of Nebat: he married Jezebel daughter of Ethbaal, king of the Sidonians, and then proceeded to serve Baal and worship him. • He erected an altar to him in the temple of Baal which he built in Samaria. • Ahab also put up a sacred pole and committed other crimes as well, provoking the anger of the LORD, God of Israel, more than all the kings of Israel his predecessors.   (NJB)

Omri (885–874) and Ahab (874–853)

Of the divided kingdom, it soon proved that the north was not only larger but also richer and stronger than the south. *Omri* is the first person in Jewish history who is mentioned in any contemporary text outside the OT. Assyrian inscriptions record the tribute which he (wisely) paid, and regularly refer to Israel as 'the house of Omri' right down to the destruction of Samaria in 721. He is also referred to in the Mesha stele as having 'humbled Moab many years'. He must have been a considerable figure, but one would never guess that from the brief reference in the OT, which is concerned only with his religious policy.

Excavations of *Samaria* confirm a powerful walled city built on a greenfield site, with the royal palace superbly crafted by Phoenician masons. Moreover there is now for the first time archaeological evidence of trade as a source of Israelite prosperity. Copper, tin, iron, silver, gold, ivory and cedar are all found in C10th-9th strata. They could not have been paid for solely by agricultural surpluses. But Samaria could control, and so levy tolls from, the important E-W trade route up the Jordan and down the Jezreel valley.

Omri's successor *Ahab*, who had the royal palace fortified as an acropolis, is also spoken of wiis respect by Assyria. *ANET* 279 records the composition of a combined army which saw off an Assyrian invasion at the battle of Qarqar in 853. Ahab is said to have contributed 2,000 chariots and 10,000 men; and, though the actual figures are probably exaggerated to excuse a defeat, it may be significant that Ahab is credited with the largest contingent of chariots. But even this major event is passed over in silence by the DtH, who is much more interested in Ahab's marriage to *Jezebel* and its consequences.

Ethbaal was a priest of Ishtar who had usurped the throne of Tyre and *Sidon* at the same time as Omri of Israel, and the two kings made a prudent political alliance which they sealed in the usual way. Jezebel would of course expect to continue the worship of her country's gods. But Ahab *proceeded to serve Baal too. A sacred pole* (Heb. *ashērāh*) was a model of a tree with a goat rampant on either side; it represented Asherah the consort of El. The DtH presents Ahab as being, for the twenty years of his reign and the next seven chapters of Kings, the archopponent of the LORD.

Ahab and Elijah: the Great Drought

17.1 Elijah the Tishbite, of Tishbe in Gilead, said to Ahab, 'By the life of the LORD, God of Israel, whom I serve, there will be neither dew nor rain these coming years unless I give the word.'

• The word of the LORD came to him, • 'Go away from here, go east and hide by the torrent of Cherith, east of the Jordan. • You can drink from the stream,
5 and I have ordered the ravens to bring you food there.' • So he set out and did as the LORD had said; he went and stayed by the torrent of Cherith, east of the Jordan. • The ravens brought him bread in the morning and meat in the evening, and he quenched his thirst at the stream.

• But after a while the stream dried up, for the country had had no rain. • And then the word of the LORD came to him, • 'Up and go to Zarephath in Sidonia, and
10 stay there. I have ordered a widow there to give you food.' • So he went off to Sidon. And when he reached the city gate, there was a widow gathering sticks. Addressing her he said, 'Please bring a little water in a pitcher for me to drink.' • She was on her way to fetch it when he called after her. 'Please', he said, 'bring me a scrap of bread in your hand.' • 'As the LORD your God lives,' she replied, 'I have no baked bread, but only a handful of meal in a jar and a little oil in a jug; I am just ◗

Ahab and Elijah: the Great Drought

At this point *Elijah* comes in like a bolt from the blue, to fight for the LORD against Ahab and Baal. He is described as a *man* (or sometimes 'servant') *of God* rather than a prophet. Prophets at this stage of Hebrew history were bands of ecstatics who usually lived at sanctuaries (whether of God or Baal) and supported the authorities. A 'man of God' on the other hand was characteristically an outsider who challenged authority.

In this respect Elijah is a forerunner of the later 'writing prophets' from Hosea on (see p.318): like them, he publicly criticised the royal house for disloyalty to YHWH and for social crimes. But unlike them, Elijah and his successor Elisha are credited with a whole range of miracles. Most of them involve feeding or healing, but some are 'nature miracles' e.g. 2 K 2.8-14; 6.6. These include almost the only miracles ascribed to humans in the OT, for those of Exodus are explicitly ascribed to God. In this other respect, and in the kind of clairvoyance described in 2 K 5.26, Elijah and Elisha are presented as what anthropologists call shamans. But the OT terminology must not be pressed too far:

Elisha is referred to as both 'prophet' and 'man of God' within a single verse e.g. 2 K 5.8.

Elijah's first speech in 17.1 is a frontal challenge to Ahab. Baal, whom Ahab worshipped, claimed to control the *rain*; Elijah, on behalf of YHWH, made a counter-claim. Rainfall in Palestine has always been crucial but precarious; the heavy dew, especially in the uplands, is a welcome supplement or even substitute. A whole year's drought was a memorable disaster, and a Greek author writing many centuries later actually mentions one such as occurring in the reign of Ethbaal; a second year's would destroy almost all life.

Ahab's negative response to Elijah has to be inferred from Elijah's flight *east of Jordan*. Many ancient legends told of men being fed by birds – heroes usually by eagles, but Elijah by *ravens*, as creatures credited with foresight. Ahab however, as we learn later, pursued him even there (18.10) and so he moved to Baal's own territory, where two further 'miracles' are recorded of him. All three are explicitly credited to YHWH (4, 14, 22); together they add up to a demonstration that it is he, not Baal,

Ahab and Elijah: the Great Drought (cont.)

gathering a stick or two to go and prepare this for myself and my son to eat, and
.13 then we shall die.' • But Elijah said to her, 'Do not be afraid, go and do as you
have said; but first make a little scone of it for me and bring it to me, and then
make some for yourself and for your son. • For the LORD, God of Israel, says
this:

> Jar of meal shall not be spent,
>> jug of oil shall not be emptied,
> before the day when the LORD sends
>> rain on the face of the earth.'

15 • The woman went and did as Elijah told her and they ate the food, she, himself
and her son. • The jar of meal was not spent nor the jug of oil emptied, just as the
LORD had foretold through Elijah.

• It happened after this that the son of the mistress of the house fell sick; his illness
was so severe that in the end he expired. • And the woman said to Elijah, 'What
quarrel have you with me, man of God? Have you come here to bring my sins home
to me and to kill my son?' • 'Give me your son,' he said and, taking him from her lap,
20 he carried him to the upper room where he was staying and laid him on his bed. • He
cried out to the LORD, 'O LORD my God, by killing her son do you mean to bring grief
even to the widow who is looking after me?' • He stretched himself on the child three
times and cried out to the LORD, 'O LORD my God, may the soul of this child, I beg
you, come into him again!' • The LORD heard Elijah's prayer and the child's soul came
back into his body and he revived. • Elijah took the child, brought him down from the
upper room into the house, and gave him to his mother. 'Look,' Elijah said, 'your
son is alive.' • And the woman replied, 'Now I know you are a man of God and
the word of the LORD in your mouth is truth itself.'   (NJB)

Ahab and Elijah: the Great Drought (cont.)

who controls nature – the corn and the
oil, the life of animals and of men.

The last story (17-24) is particularly well
told. As to its content, we may contrast the
woman's reproach to Elijah, based on a
widespread belief that the presence of a holy
man threatens an ordinary sinful person,
with Elijah's reproach to God, which raises
the whole issue to a higher moral plane. His
resuscitation of the boy by bodily contact

again followed a common belief. In structure the story is pedimental*, e.g. the first
part of the widow's speech in v.18 is taken
back in v.24, her phrase *to kill my son* is
answered by *your son is alive* in v.23, and
the three actions he performs in v.19 are rehearsed in the opposite order in v.23. As
usual, the centre (20-22) is also the pivot.
For a variant of this story, told at much
greater length about Elisha, see 2 K 4.8-37.

The Contest on Mount Carmel

18.1 A long time went by, and the word of the LORD came to Elijah in the third year, 'Go, present yourself to Ahab, and I will send rain on the country.' So Elijah set off to present himself to Ahab.

As the famine was particularly severe in Samaria, • Ahab summoned Obadiah, the master of the palace – Obadiah held the LORD in great reverence: • when Jezebel was butchering the prophets of the LORD, Obadiah took a hundred of them and hid them, 5 fifty at a time, in a cave, and kept them provided with food and water – • and Ahab said to Obadiah, 'Come along, we must scour the country, all the springs and all the ravines in the hope of finding grass to keep horses and mules alive, or we shall have to slaughter some of our stock.'

• They divided the country for the purpose of their survey; Ahab went one way by himself and Obadiah went another way by himself. • While Obadiah was on his way, whom should he meet but Elijah. Recognising him he fell on his face and said, 'So it is you, my lord Elijah!' • 'Yes,' he replied, 'go and tell your master, "Elijah is here." ' • But Obadiah said, 'What sin I have committed, for 10 you to put your servant into Ahab's power and cause my death? • As the LORD your God lives, there is no nation or kingdom where my master has not sent in search of you; and when they said, "He is not there," he made the kingdom or nation swear an oath that they did not know where you were. • And now you say to me, "Go and tell your master: Elijah is here." • But as soon as I leave you, the spirit of the LORD will carry you away and I shall not know where; I shall go and tell Ahab; he will not be able to find you, and then he will kill me. Yet from his youth your servant has revered the LORD. • Has no one told my lord what I ➤

The Contest on Mountt Carmel

Ch.18 begins (1) with a reminder of the narrative frame, viz. the *rain*, which will be picked up again at the end (41-5). We are then introduced to *Obadiah* who, in a series of flashbacks, is shown as a foil to *Jezebel* (4) and as one who tries to be a loyal servant of both Ahab and the LORD (12). He had helped the king in his search for fodder for the *horses*, military purposes having priority. He had not helped the king in his other search. *Elijah* was presumably being sought as the only man who could undo the effects of his oath in 17.1, and his elusiveness is regarded by Obadiah as further evidence of his supernatural powers. This long rambling speech of Obadiah (9-14), which begins with the same startling accusation as that of the widow, reveals his anxiety and retards the action. By contrast, Elijah's brief and trenchant reply (15), reinforced by another oath, asserts his inner confidence and speeds the action to its first climax.

In their first confrontation since 17.1, Ahab too opens with a reproachful question. Elijah boldly returns the reproach upon him before announcing his own proposal. We have been told, and Ahab can easily guess, that his response to it will determine whether Elijah gives the word to end the drought. At first sight there is no connection between the two, but the king is in no position to demur. When all the cast is assembled, the curtain goes up for one of the greatest dramas of the OT, appropriately located on the dominant 500-metre peak of *Mount Carmel*. Elijah explains the connection: those who want rain will have to make a choice between *the LORD* and *Baal* (21). The verb translated *hobble* is found only here and in v.26, and seems to have been used for the sake of the rather forced play on words.

The contest itself (22-40) is treated in apparent independence from the drought. Ahab, sidelined, takes no further part until

The Contest on Mount Carmel (cont.)

did when Jezebel butchered the prophets of the LORD, how I hid a hundred of them in a cave, fifty at a time, and kept them provided with food and water? • Now you say
15 to me, "Go and tell your master: Elijah is here." Why, he will kill me!' • Elijah replied, 'As the LORD Sabaoth lives, whom I serve, I shall present myself to him today!'

• Obadiah went to find Ahab and tell him the news, and Ahab then went to find Elijah. • When he saw Elijah, Ahab said, 'So there you are, you scourge of Israel!' • 'Not I,' he replied, 'I am not the scourge of Israel, you and your family are; because you have deserted the LORD and followed Baal. • Now give orders for all Israel to gather round me on Mount Carmel, and also the four hundred prophets of Baal who eat at Jezebel's table.'
20 • Ahab called all Israel together and assembled the prophets on Mount Carmel. • Elijah stepped out in front of all the people. 'How long', he said, 'do you mean to hobble first on one leg then on the other? If the LORD is God, follow him; if Baal, follow him.' But the people had nothing to say. • Elijah then said to them, 'I, I alone, am left as a prophet of the LORD, while the prophets of Baal are four hundred and fifty. • Let two bulls be given us; let them choose one for themselves, dismember it but not set fire to it. I in my turn shall prepare the other bull, but not set fire to it. • You must call on the name of your god, and I shall call on the name of the LORD; the god who answers with fire, is God indeed.' The people
25 all answered, 'Agreed!' • Elijah then said to the prophets of Baal, 'Choose one ▶

The Contest on Mount Carmel (cont.)

the epilogue (41-6). It is *the people* who in his place will have to judge the contest. Some critics have tried to interpret it as a competition in rain-making rituals. But fire has never been a normal symbol of rain, whereas in the ancient world the spontaneous combustion of a sacrifice was taken as clear evidence of divine intervention. The contest is one simply of power.

The story of the contest is in three parts. Elijah, who is in control throughout, gives *the prophets of Baal* first innings and choice of new *bull*. Everything is done by the narrator to build up a picture of maximum activity and noise – 400 men dancing and shouting and gashing themselves for hours on end. All this is authentic enough: it is the tradition from which Muslim dervishes are descended, and still today the pilgrim to Mecca will perform a special hobble round the sacred black stone. The morning performance was repeated in the afternoon: in between, we have Elijah's delicious taunting. There is no knowing what Baal might be up to: he might be meditating, he might be

abroad (so Homer's godsiswhen absent from the action on Olympus, are said to have gone to visit the Ethiopians), or he might be *busy* (for the euphemism cp. Gen 24.63) – all these alternatives are listed under the heavily ironical rubric *for he is a god*, thus underscoring the difference between the two conceptions of deity. And throughout the long day the frenzy of his priests is met by Baal's total silence, repeated twice in the morning, thrice in the afternoon.

Then towards evening (36) it is Elijah's turn. The climax is near – but it is held up by seven verses of methodical preparation, all intently watched by the people. The symbolism of the *twelve stones* cp.explained, and the number of *jars* of water (4 x 3) is the same. The *water* is to make the miracle more impressive (38). Finally in response to Elijah's prayer the *fire* came, so fierce that it even (in the MT, omitted by NJB) consumed the stones and the earth. Action is now rapid. *The people* announce their verdict: *YHWH is God.* Elijah demands proof of their change of

The Contest on Mount Carmel (cont.)

18.25 bull and begin, for there are more of you. Call on the name of your god but light no fire.' • They took the bull and prepared it, and from morning to midday they called on the name of Baal. 'O Baal, answer us!' they cried, but there was no voice, no answer, as they performed their hobbling dance round the altar which they had made. • Midday came, and Elijah mocked them. 'Call louder,' he said, 'for he is a god: he is preoccupied or he is busy, or he has gone on a journey; perhaps he is asleep and needs to be woken up!' • So they shouted louder and gashed themselves, as their custom was, with swords and spears until the blood flowed down them. • Midday passed, and they ranted on until the time when the offering is presented; but there was no voice, no answer, no sign of attention.

30 • Then Elijah said to all the people, 'Come over to me,' and all the people came over to him. He repaired the LORD's altar which had been torn down. • Elijah took twelve stones, corresponding to the number of tribes of the sons of Jacob, to whom the word of the LORD had come, 'Israel is to be your name,' • and built an altar in the name of the LORD. Round the altar he dug a trench of a size to hold two measures of seed. • He then arranged the wood, dismembered the bull, and laid it on the wood. • Then he said, 'Fill four jars with water and pour it on the burnt offering and on the wood.' They did this. He said, 'Do it a second time;' they did it a second time. He said, 'Do it a third time;' they did it a third time.

35 • The water flowed round the altar until even the trench itself was full of water. • At the time when the offering is presented, Elijah the prophet stepped forward. 'LORD, God of Abraham, Isaac and Israel,' he said, 'let them know today that you are God in Israel, and that I am your servant, that I have done all these things at your command. • Answer me, LORD, answer me, so that this people may know that you, the LORD, are God and are winning back their hearts.'

• Then the LORD's fire fell and consumed the burnt offering and the wood and licked up the water in the trench. • When all the people saw this they fell on their

40 faces. 'The LORD is God,' they cried, 'The LORD is God!' • Elijah said, 'Seize the prophets of Baal: do not let one of them escape.' They seized them, and Elijah took them down to the Kishon, and there he slaughtered them.

• Elijah said to Ahab, 'Go back now, eat and drink; for I hear the approaching sound of rain.' • While Ahab went back to eat and drink, Elijah climbed to the top of Carmel and bowed down to the ground, putting his face between his knees. • 'Now go up', he told his servant, 'and look out to sea.' He went up and looked. 'There is nothing at all,' he said. Seven times Elijah told him to go back. • The seventh time, the servant said, 'Now there is a cloud, small as a man's hand, rising from the sea.' Elijah said, 'Go and say to Ahab, "Harness the chariot and go

45 down before the rain stops you." ' • And with that the sky grew dark with cloud and storm, and rain fell in torrents. Ahab mounted his chariot and made for Jezreel. • Hitching up his clothes, Elijah ran ahead of Ahab all the way to Jezreel.   (NJB)

The Contest on Mount Carmel (cont.)

heart. As in a holy war, the enemies of God must be offered as a sacrifice to him.

The way is now clear for the *rain* to come. The fast, observed in preparation for the sacrifice, may be ended. Elijah then with-

draws, as was his custom, for private prayer. Mt Carmel offers a superb view of rain coming from the west; but the magic number *seven* and Elijah's twenty-mile run *ahead of Ahab* restore the dominant genre of legend.

Elijah at Mount Horeb

.1 Ahab told Jezebel all that Elijah had done, and how he had slain all the prophets with the sword. • Then Jezebel sent a messenger to Elijah, saying, 'So may the gods do to me, and more also, if I do not make your life as the life of one of them by this time tomorrow.' • Then he was afraid, and he arose and went for his life, and came to Beersheba, which belongs to Judah, and left his servant there.

• But he himself went a day's journey into the wilderness, and came and sat down under a broom tree; and he asked that he might die, saying, 'It is enough; 5 now, O LORD, take away my life; for I am no better than my fathers.' • And he lay down and slept under a broom tree; and behold, an angel touched him, and said to him, 'Arise and eat.' • And he looked, and behold, there was at his head a cake baked on hot stones and a jar of water. And he ate and drank, and lay down again. • And the angel of the LORD came again a second time, and touched him, and said, 'Arise and eat, else the journey will be too great for you.' • And he arose, and ate and drank, and went in the strength of that food forty days and forty nights to Horeb the mount of God.

• And there he came to a cave, and lodged there; and behold, the word of the 10 LORD came to him, and he said to him, 'What are you doing here, Elijah?' • He said, 'I have been very jealous for the LORD, the God of hosts; for the people of Israel have forsaken thy covenant, thrown down thy altars, and slain thy prophets with the sword; and I, even I only, am left; and they seek my life, to take it away.' • And he said, 'Go forth, and stand upon the mount before the LORD.' ▸

Elijah at Mount Horeb

The first two and a half verses of Ch.19 conclude the narrative of Elijah's epic struggle against the worship of Baal. Once again, as in Ch.17, he is on the defensive, indeed initially on the run; for *Jezebel* was fiercer than Ahab. Her little speech opens with words of great spirit, preserved only in the LXX: 'If you are Elijah, then I am Jezebel.' And the antagonism was not just personal: her name ends in *Baal*, his in *Yah*. After that we must suppose some lapse of time before the central story of Ch.19. Indeed all the signs are that 19.4-18 was originally independent and belongs rather at the end of Elijah's life, i.e. *after* his confrontation with Ahab in Ch.21.

That story comes in two parts, separated from each other, as they are from what surrounds them, by a *journey*. Elijah was often in *the wilderness*, both literally and metaphorically. Now he was making a pilgrimage to Mt *Horeb*, alias Sinai. There he hoped like Moses to encounter God in all his glory, and to receive either an honourable discharge or a renewed commission with the strength to carry it out. For now he is near the end of his tether, both physically and spiritually. The first day of his journey (4-8) reveals his physical exhaustion. To meet it God twice sends him a dream-vision together with bodily nourishment; and he sets off revived.

At Horeb he took up his position in *a cave* as Moses did in Ex 33.22, when the glory of the LORD *passed by* – the same word as here in v.11. Corresponding to his repeated dream before, he now has a repeated conversation with God (10=14). The repetition is typical of Hebrew storytelling, and here as often serves to frame the central event, the theophany. Hitherto there have been many parallels with the Moses story, but now there is an important difference. Whereas in Exodus (19. 16+) the storm, the earthquake and the

Elijah at Mount Horeb (cont.)

And behold, the LORD passed by, and a great and strong wind rent the mountains, and broke in pieces the rocks before the LORD, but the LORD was not in the wind; **19.**12 and after the wind an earthquake, but the LORD was not in the earthquake; • and after the earthquake a fire, but the LORD was not in the fire; and after the fire a still small voice. • And when Elijah heard it, he wrapped his face in his mantle and went out and stood at the entrance of the cave. And behold, there came a voice to him, and said, 'What are you doing here, Elijah?' • He said, 'I have been very jealous for the LORD, the God of hosts; for the people of Israel have forsaken thy covenant, thrown down thy altars, and slain thy prophets with the sword; and I, 15 even I only, am left; and they seek my life, to take it away.' • And the LORD said to him, 'Go, return on your way to the wilderness of Damascus; and when you arrive, you shall anoint Hazael to be king over Syria; • and Jehu the son of Nimshi you shall anoint to be king over Israel; and Elisha the son of Shaphat of Abelmeholah you shall anoint to be prophet in your place. • And him who escapes from the sword of Hazael shall Jehu slay; and him who escapes from the sword of Jehu shall Elisha slay. • Yet I will leave seven thousand in Israel, all the knees that have not bowed to Baal, and every mouth that has not kissed him.'

• So he departed from there, and found Elisha the son of Shaphat, who was plowing, with twelve yoke of oxen before him, and he was with the twelfth. 20 Elijah passed by him and cast his mantle upon him. • And he left the oxen, and ran after Elijah, and said, 'Let me kiss my father and my mother, and then I will follow you.' And he said to him, 'Go back again; for what have I done to you?' • And he returned from following him, and took the yoke of oxen, and slew them, and boiled their flesh with the yokes of the oxen, and gave it to the people, and they ate. Then he arose and went after Elijah, and ministered to him. (RSV)

Elijah at Mount Horeb (cont.)

lightning symbolised God's presence, here they are distinguished from it. Ch.19 of 1 K is in this respect also the complement of Ch.18: '18 portrays the outer battle of faith, 19 deals with the inner struggle.' The translation *still small voice* preserves the numinous ambiguity of the Hebrew. The words imply a personal intimacy, but certainly no softness.

God's instructions in vv.15-18 look forward to final victory in the fight against Ahab. The three architects of his downfall are all mentioned, and Elijah is meta-phorically commissioned to *anoint* them. Two of them in fact he never meets in the text as we have it; but *Elisha* he finds immediately. Symbolically, he casts his prophetic mantle over him and calls him from the plough. With that, Elijah's work seems done. Some readers have seen in Elijah's complaint a streak of pride (*I only am left*, 10) and in God's reply something closer to dismissal than to early retirement. But that does not fit the *overall* presentation of the prophet in 1K-2 K (see on 2 K 2).

Naboth's Vineyard

.1 Some time later there occurred an incident involving Naboth of Jezreel, who had a vineyard in Jezreel adjoining the palace of King Ahab of Samaria. • Ahab made a proposal to Naboth: 'Your vineyard is close to my palace; let me have it for a garden, and I shall give you a better vineyard in exchange for it or, if you prefer, I shall give you its value in silver.' • But Naboth answered, 'The LORD forbid that I should surrender to you land which has always been in my family.' • Ahab went home sullen and angry because Naboth had refused to let him have his ancestral
5 holding. He took to his bed, covered his face, and refused to eat. • When his wife Jezebel came in to him and asked, 'Why this sullenness, and why do you refuse to eat?' • he replied, 'I proposed that Naboth of Jezreel should let me have his vineyard at its value or, if he liked, in exchange for another; but he refused to let me have it.' • 'Are you or are you not king in Israel?' retorted Jezebel. 'Come, eat and take heart; I shall make you a gift of the vineyard of Naboth of Jezreel.'
  • She wrote letters in Ahab's name, sealed them with his seal, and sent them to the elders and notables of Naboth's city, who sat in council with him. • She wrote: 'Proclaim a fast and give Naboth the seat of honour among the people.
10 • Opposite him seat two unprincipled rogues to charge him with cursing God and the king; then take him out and stone him to death.' • The elders and notables of Naboth's city carried out the instructions Jezebel had sent them in her letter: • they proclaimed a fast and gave Naboth the seat of honour. • The two unprincipled rogues came in, sat opposite him, and charged him publicly with cursing God and the king. He was then taken outside the city and stoned, • and word was sent to Jezebel that Naboth had been stoned to death.   ▶

Naboth's Vineyard

In this story the grounds for Elijah's criticism of Ahab are no longer cultic but ethical – a rare note in the DtH. Ch.19 was meant to recall not only God's appearance to Moses but also his giving of the ten commandments. In Ch.17 Ahab had broken nos I and II; in Ch.20 Elijah draws attention to his breach of VII and VIII – and he might have added X and (through Jezebel) IX. In view of that, there is irony in *Jezebel*'s care (10) to follow the letter of the law. In a capital offence two witnesses were needed, and stoning was the regular punishment; by ANE custom the property of the criminal was forfeit to the crown (15). But Jezebel's concept of kingship (7) was alien, and here we can see a connection between the cultic and the social. The worship of Baal was a threat to the national way of life.

The story of *Naboth's vineyard* has much in common with David's crime and Nathan's parable in 2 Sam 12. In both of them the king abuses his power over a subject and is arraigned by the prophet; he then repents, and the punishment is transferred from him to his son. But there are differences: Elijah is Ahab's *enemy* (20), not his ultimately loyal critic; and Ahab's dynasty, unlike David's, is doomed. The story itself is told with great skill. Everything underlines Ahab's weakness of character by comparison with Jezebel's villainous strength. He is explicitly shown as behaving like a spoilt child (4) and earning her contempt (7, 15). Less obvious is the contrast between his actual conversation with Naboth in the vineyard (2-3) and the report of it he gives Jezebel. In the report (6) he makes himself out more forceful than he was but omits Naboth's valid reason for refusal. It was fitting that, in reply to *letters in Ahab's*

Naboth's Vineyard (cont.)

21.15 • As soon as Jezebel heard of the death of Naboth, she said to Ahab, 'Get up and take possession of the vineyard which Naboth refused to sell you, for he is no longer alive; Naboth of Jezreel is dead.' • On hearing that Naboth was dead, Ahab got up and went to the vineyard to take possession.

• The word of the LORD came to Elijah the Tishbite: • 'Go down at once to King Ahab of Israel, who is in Samaria; you will find him in Naboth's vineyard, where he has gone to take possession. • Say to him, "This is the word of the 20 LORD: Have you murdered and seized property?" ' • Ahab said to Elijah, 'So you have found me, my enemy.' 'Yes,' he said. 'Because you have sold yourself to do what is wrong in the eyes of the LORD, • I shall bring disaster on you; I shall sweep you away and destroy every mother's son of the house of Ahab in Israel. • The LORD went on to say of Jezebel "Jezebel will be eaten by dogs near the rampart of Jezreel." '

27 • When Ahab heard Elijah's words, he tore his clothes, put on sackcloth, and fasted; he lay down in his sackcloth and went about moaning. • The word of the LORD came to Elijah the Tishbite: • 'Have you seen how Ahab has humbled himself before me? Because he has thus humbled himself, I shall not bring disaster on his house in his own lifetime, but in that of his son.'   (REB)

Naboth's Vineyard (cont.)

name (8), *word was sent to Jezebel* (14).

The dramatic climax comes in the confrontation between Ahab and Elijah, also appropriately in the vineyard. Elijah appears unannounced, as in 17.1, and Ahab's reaction (20) is cast in the same questioning form as in 18.17: 'Have you found me, O my enemy?' (RSV). Those two aggressive-defensive questions are the only sentences uttered by Ahab to Elijah in the long history of their conflict: on the first occasion aggression predominates, on the second defensiveness.

The Death of Ahab

22.1 There was a lull of three years, with no fighting between Aram and Israel. • Then, in the third year, Jehoshaphat king of Judah paid a visit to the king of Israel. • The king of Israel said to his officers, 'You are aware that Ramoth in Gilead belongs to us? And yet we do nothing to wrest it away from the king of Aram.' • He said to Jehoshaphat, 'Will you come with me to attack Ramoth in Gilead?' Jehoshaphat replied to the king of Israel, 'I will be as you, my men as yours, my horses as yours.'   ▸

The Death of Ahab

Ch.22 is not part of the Ahab-Elijah sequence. Elijah is not mentioned in it at all, and *Ahab* is named only once. The dating in v.1 is also dubious, but as usual the political context is only a wrapping for the religious message: that there is no escape from the word of God as transmitted through his prophet. The story itself however is both lively and deceptive; moreover it throws important light on the work of the great 'writing' prophets who are to come a century later.

Ahab and *Jehoshaphat* (870-848), kings of Israel and Judah respectively, are now united against a common enemy, and linked by a dynastic marriage [2 K 8.18], though Judah's position is inferior (4, 30). *Ramoth* was an important town *in Gilead*, which they properly wished to rescue from the control of *Aram* (Damascus).

The Death of Ahab (cont.)

2.5   • Jehoshaphat, however, said to the king of Israel, 'First, please enquire what the word of the LORD is.' • The king of Israel then called the prophets together, about four hundred of them. 'Should I go and attack Ramoth in Gilead,' he asked, 'or should I hold back?' 'Go ahead,' they replied, 'for the LORD has already given it to the king.' • Jehoshaphat, however, said, 'Is there no other prophet of the LORD here, so that we can enquire through him?' • The king of Israel said to Jehoshaphat, 'There is one more man through whom we can consult the LORD, but I hate him because he never has a favourable prophecy for me, only unfavourable ones; he is Micaiah son of Imlah.' 'I hope the king's words are unjustified,' said Jehoshaphat. • The king of Israel then summoned a court official and said, 'Bring Micaiah son of Imlah immediately.'

10   • The king of Israel and Jehoshaphat king of Judah were sitting each on his throne, wearing their robes, in an open space just outside the gate of Samaria, with all the prophets in a state of ecstasy before them. • Zedekiah son of Kenaanah, who had made himself some iron horns, said, 'The LORD says, "With horns like these you will gore the Aramaeans till you make an end of them." ' • And all the prophets cried ecstatically in the same vein, saying, 'March on Ramoth in Gilead! Success is sure, for the LORD has already given it to the king!'

   • The messenger who had gone to summon Micaiah said to him, 'Look here, what the prophets are saying is uniformly favourable to the king. I hope you will say the same as they do and speak favourably.' • Micaiah said, 'As the LORD lives, **15** I shall speak as the LORD tells me!' • When he came to the king, the king said, 'Micaiah, should we go and attack Ramoth in Gilead, or should we hold back?' He replied, 'Go ahead! Success is sure, for the LORD has already given it to the king!' • The king then said, 'How often must I put you on oath to tell me nothing but the truth in the name of the LORD?' • Then he spoke out:

> I saw all Israel scattered on the mountains
>   like sheep without a shepherd.
> And the LORD said, 'These have no master,
>   let them all go safely home!'

The Death of Ahab (cont.)

Jehoshaphat however, who is represented as prudent (5) and pious (7), urges that the will of God should first be known.

   Thus we are quickly led into the central scene of the chapter, the dispute between Micaiah and the official *prophets*. The latter (whose number is exaggerated, as with the 400 prophets of Baal in 18.19) were maintained at court to advise the king, like dream-interpreters in Egypt and astrologers in Babylon. By contrast *Micaiah*, though he is here also called a prophet rather than a 'man of God', is an outsider like Elijah. (He is to be distinguished from the later writing prophet Micah.) To fill the time while Micaiah is being fetched, we are given a brief demonstration of a 'symbolic action' (see p.519).

   Micaiah makes three speeches of increasing length. The first (15) is a big surprise to his audience – and also to the reader. But when we look closely at the words, we see they are ambiguous. They have their exact parallel in the response given by the Delphic oracle to a similar enquiry from Croesus 300 years later: 'If Croesus crosses the river Halys, he will destroy a great empire.' The king however still misunderstood the import, so

The Death of Ahab (cont.)

• At this the king of Israel said to Jehoshaphat, 'Did I not tell you that he never gives me favourable prophecies, but only unfavourable ones?' • Micaiah went on, 'Now listen to the word of the LORD. I saw the LORD seated on his throne with the whole array of heaven standing by him, on his right and on his left. • the LORD said, "Who will entice Ahab into marching to his death at Ramoth in Gilead?" At which some answered one way, and some another. • A spirit then came forward and stood before the LORD and said, "I will entice him." • "How?" the LORD asked. He replied, "I shall go and be a deceptive spirit in the mouths of all his prophets." The LORD said, "You will succeed in enticing him. Go and do it." • And now, you see, the LORD has put a deceptive spirit into the mouths of all your prophets here, for in fact the LORD has pronounced disaster on you.'

• Zedekiah son of Chenaanah then came up, struck Micaiah on the cheek and said, 'Which way did the LORD's spirit leave me, to speak to you?' • 'That is what you will find out,' Micaiah retorted, 'the day you go from room to room, trying to hide.' • The king of Israel said, 'Seize Micaiah and hand him over to Amon, governor of the city, and Joash, the king's son, • and say, "These are the king's orders: Put this man in prison and feed him on nothing but bread and water until I am safely home."' • Micaiah said, 'If you ever do get home safely, the LORD has not spoken through me.'

• The king of Israel and Jehoshaphat king of Judah marched on Ramoth in Gilead. • The king of Israel said to Jehoshaphat, 'I shall disguise myself to go into battle, but you put on your robes.' So the king of Israel disguised himself and went into battle. • Now, the king of Aram had given his chariot commanders the following order, 'Do not attack anyone of whatever rank, except the king of Israel.' • So, when the chariot commanders saw Jehoshaphat, they thought, 'That is obviously the king of Israel,' and surrounded him to attack. But when Jehoshaphat shouted his war cry • the chariot commanders, realising that he was not the king of Israel, broke off their pursuit.   ▸

22.20

25

30

The Death of Ahab (cont.)

Micaiah spoke again. This time (17) the message seems unmistakable – defeat for the army and death for the king.

Micaiah then *went on* (19-23) to offer an imaginative explanation of a problem which was to puzzle later generations greatly: how could prophets of the LORD come to make false prophesies? Drawing on accepted ideas of the heavenly council, he portrays God as himself uncertain how to bring about the already determined death of Ahab. A volunteer comes forward, *a deceptive spirit*, who is commissioned by God to operate *in the mouths of all his prophets* i.e. the official ones. That phrase confirms what the narrative

has already implied, that the deception of the prophecy lies as much in the hearer as in the speaker. When the words were uttered by the official prophets (6 and 12) the king was ready to believe them; when Micaiah, who had sworn to speak the truth, uttered the identical words (15), the king thought he was lying. The apparently naive 'vision' of Micaiah expresses an idea which applies to any text claiming inspiration, that its 'truth' depends as much upon the reader as upon the writer.

Zedekiah's interventions in vv.11 and 24 provide the frame for the central episode now concluded. Next comes the king, whose *Seize Micaiah* (26) picks up his

The Death of Ahab (cont.)

2.35 • Someone, however, drawing his bow without any special aim, shot the king of Israel between the joints of his armour. 'Turn about!' said the king to his charioteer. 'Get me out of the fighting; I am collapsing.' • But the battle grew fiercer as the day went on and the king had to be held upright in his chariot facing the Aramaeans, the blood from the wound running into the bottom of the chariot, until in the evening he died. • At sundown a shout ran through the ranks, 'Every man back to his town, every man back to his country! • The king is dead.' He was taken to Samaria and in Samaria the king was buried.   (NJB)

The Death of Ahab (cont.)

Bring Micaiah (9). His public rejection of the unwelcome prophecy is shown specifically by his words *until I am safely home*, which negate Micaiah's words in v.17. Privately however he is fearful enough to engage in a deception of his own in the battle. Initially it seems likely to succeed, but then comes the second surprise of the chapter. Three apparent coincidences – Jehoshaphat's *war-cry*, the 'bow at a venture' (34 AV), and the inability of his charioteer to turn round (35) – combine to show the hand of God in Ahab's death. But God had a helper in Ahab. By his blind persistence, first in summoning Micaiah and then in rejecting his prophecy, he brought about the fulfilment of God's word.

Elisha Succeeds Elijah

2. 1 This is what happened when the LORD took Elijah up to heaven in the whirlwind: 7 Elijah and Elisha set out from Gilgal . . . • As the two of them stood beside the Jordan, • Elijah took his cloak, rolled it up and struck the water; and the water divided to left and right, and the two of them crossed over dry-shod. • When they had crossed, Elijah said to Elisha, 'Make your request. What can I do for you before I am snatched away from you?' Elisha answered, 'Let me inherit a double share of your spirit.' 10 • 'Your request is difficult,' Elijah said. 'If you see me while I am being snatched away from you, it will be as you ask; if not, it will not be so.' • Now as they walked on, talking as they went, a chariot of fire appeared and horses of fire coming between the two of them; and Elijah went up to heaven in the whirlwind. • Elisha saw it, and shouted, 'My father! My father! Chariot of Israel and its chargers!' Then he lost sight of him, and taking hold of his own clothes he tore them in half. • He picked up Elijah's cloak which had fallen, and went back and stood on the bank of the Jordan. • He took Elijah's cloak and struck the water. 'Where is the LORD, the God of Elijah?' he cried. As he struck the water it divided to right and left, and Elisha crossed over.

(NJB)

Elisha Succeeds Elijah

Elisha, like Elijah, gathered round him a cycle of stories part historical and part legendary. The Elijah cycle had told briefly how the prophet's mantle had fallen on his successor; here we have the corresponding event from the beginning of the Elisha cycle, with the miraculous element typically more prominent.

The story of vv.8-14 is an imaginative fusion of legendary, mythical and historical elements. Elijah regularly wore 'a hair cloak and a leather loincloth' [2 K 1.8 NJB]. His *cloak* was symbolic (1 K 19.19) and also had magical powers. The crossing of the Jordan echoes two great moments in Jewish sacred history, the exodus and the entry into the holy land (*dry-shod* is the same word in all three narratives); but they are now going in the opposite direction, i.e. leaving the political land of Israel. Elisha's request follows the law whereby an eldest son inherits *a double share* of his father's property. But prophecy was a gift from God, and Elijah hesitates: let Elisha's worthiness be tested by his capacity as a 'seer'.

The ascension of Elijah combines two or three common mythical motifs: the sky-riders, the *chariot* of the sun and the taking up of a hero into *heaven*. But it is more than the sum of its parts, and Elisha's inspired exclamation (12) grounds it in the exodus story. Then it had been the chariots and *chargers* of Pharaoh which were involved, but these are the army *of Israel* and they represent God and Elijah. Elijah's assumption also bestows God's seal upon his life, and will permit later generations to hope for his return. Elisha's vision of it marks God's approval of him too, and entitles him to call Elijah *father*. He shows his new power by repeating Elijah's miracle with the river.

Elijah is a figure of enormous importance in the religious tradition of Israel, standing second only to Moses. He shared with Moses a fanatical devotion to YHWH – he may have been the first to discern in Baal-worship a threat to the national way of life – and also an attractive humanity. Himself the object of reproaches (Chs 17 and 18), he can reproach God on behalf of his people (17.20); he knows moments of deep despair (Ch.19); much of his life is spent in the wilderness, and he dies before the culmination of his work. In this he is unlike Elisha, who can be firm (Ch.2) and even wise (Ch.6), but has little compassion (5.27) and never seems to doubt.

Elisha and the Family of Shunem

8 It happened once that Elisha went over to Shunem. There was a well-to-do woman there who pressed him to accept hospitality, and afterwards whenever he came that way, he stopped there for a meal. • One day she said to her husband, 'I know
10 that this man who comes here regularly is a holy man of God. • Why not build up the wall to make him a small roof-chamber, and put in it a bed, a table, a seat, and a lamp, and let him stay there whenever he comes to us?'

• One time when he arrived there and went to this roof-chamber to lie down, • he said to Gehazi, his servant, 'Call this Shunammite woman.' When he called her and she appeared before the prophet, • Elisha said to his servant, 'Say to her, "You have taken all this trouble for us. What can I do for you? Shall I speak for you to the king or to the commander-in-chief?" ' But she replied, 'I am content where I am, among my own people.' • He said, 'Then what can be done for her?'
15 Gehazi said, 'There is only this: she has no child and her husband is old.' • 'Call her back,' Elisha said. When she was called and appeared in the doorway, • he said, 'In due season, this time next year, you will have a son in your arms.' But she said, 'No, no, my lord, you are a man of God and would not lie to your servant.' • Next year in due season the woman conceived and bore a son, as Elisha had foretold.

• When the child was old enough, he went out one day to his father among the reapers. • All of a sudden he cried out to his father, 'Oh, my head, my head!' His
20 father told a servant to carry the child to his mother, • and when he was brought to her, he sat on her lap till midday, and then he died. • She went up, laid him on the bed of the man of God, shut the door, and went out. • She called her ▶

Elisha and the Family of Shunem

The main part of this story is clearly a variant of the one told of Elijah in 1 K 17.17-24, though there is no reason to suppose that either is dependent on the other. Among a number of differences, this one incorporates (11-17) a version of the well-known folk-tale in which a heavenly visitor promises a gift to his hosts in reward for their hospitality. Sometimes, as with Abraham and Sarah in Gen 18, that gift is a son; in which case he normally (though not here) grows up to be a hero. The incorporation is skilfully managed, by the motif of the upper room and by v. 28. But a loose end shows in v.14: in the normal folk-tale it is the wife who is old whereas here it is the *husband* – yet he is still young enough to be in charge of the reaping in v.18!

The first section (8-17) establishes the relationship between the two protagonists. The *woman* is *well-to-do* and independ-ent (13), pious but not credulous. She addresses Elisha as *my lord* (16); she does not touch him except in her moment of greatest need (27, where note *Gehazi*'s reaction); and she makes lavish provision for his separate accommodation, which she does not enter without permission (contrast 15 and 37). He on the other hand sends *his servant* to summon her (12, 15, 36), and on the first occasion actually speaks to her through him. His manner towards her is solicitous, if a little patronising (13); Gehazi (14) is more practical.

The second section (18-30) contains reference to several ancient religious practices. When the boy died, his mother was so determined to get him brought back to life that she (i) gave no mourning cry, (ii) took him up to Elijah's *bed*, (iii) *shut the door* to keep his soul in and (iv) did not even tell her *husband* what had happened. He is in every

Elisha and the Family of Shunem (cont.)

husband and said, 'Send me one of the servants and a she-donkey; I must go to the man of God as fast as I can, and come straight back.' • 'Why go to him today?' he asked. 'It is neither new moon nor sabbath.' 'Never mind that,' she answered. • When the donkey was saddled, she said to her servant, 'Lead on and do not slacken pace unless I tell you.' • So she set out and came to the man of God on Mount Carmel.

4.25

The man of God spied her in the distance and said to Gehazi, his servant, 'That is the Shunammite woman coming. • Run and meet her, and ask, "Is all well with you? Is all well with your husband? Is all well with the boy?" ' She answered, 'All is well.' • When she reached the man of God on the hill, she clutched his feet. Gehazi came forward to push her away, but the man of God said, 'Let her alone; she is in great distress, and the LORD has concealed it from me and not told me.' • 'My lord,' she said, 'did I ask for a son? Did I not beg you not to raise my hopes and then dash them?' • Elisha turned to Gehazi: 'Hitch up your cloak; take my staff with you and run. If you meet anyone on the way, do not stop to greet him; if anyone greets you, do not answer. Lay my staff on the boy's face.' • But the mother cried, 'As the LORD lives, your life upon it, I shall not leave you.' So he got up and followed her.

30

• Gehazi went on ahead and laid the staff on the boy's face, but there was no sound or sign of life, so he went back to meet Elisha and told him that the boy had not stirred. • When Elisha entered the house, there was the dead boy, where he had been laid on the bed. • He went into the room, shut the door on the two of them, and prayed to the LORD. • Then, getting on to the bed, he lay upon the child, put his mouth to the child's mouth, his eyes to his eyes, and his hands to his hands; as he crouched upon him, the child's body grew warm. • Elisha got up and walked once up and down the room; getting on to the bed again, he crouched upon him, and the boy sneezed seven times and opened his eyes. • The prophet summoned Gehazi and said, 'Call the Shunammite woman.' She answered his call and the prophet said, 'Take up your child.' • She came in and prostrated herself before him. Then she took up her son and went out.   (REB)

35

Elisha and the Family of Shunem (cont.)

respect a foil to her, as in these stories husbands usually are cp. Samson's father and John Baptist's. Together with Elisha's foil Gehazi, he steps in to retard the narrative. His objection was that one waits for a holy day for a visit to *a man of God*. To him (23) as to Gehazi (26) she replies with the one word *shalom*; the translation *Never mind* in v.23 is fair enough, but the point is that at all costs she must avoid the ill-omened word 'dead'. That is also why her reproach in v.28 is muted (contrast 1 K 17.18). The mother throughout shows herself a woman of perception and dignity.

The final section opens with more re-

tardation. The notion of the magical *staff* recalls that of Moses in Ex 4.17 etc.; but whoever else believed in it, the mother did not (30). When Elisha himself arrived, events followed much the same pattern as in the case of Elijah in 1 K 17. The author tells us less about his prayer and more about his 'medical' measures. His *walk* in 35 restored his strength so that he could master the evil spirit in the child's body. The *sneeze* (35) is the sign that the breath has re-entered it. The story is rounded off by his mother carrying him out, just as he had been carried in at the start (19); the same Hebrew word is used each time.

Elisha and Naaman

1 Naaman, commander of the army of the king of Aram, was a great man and in high favor with his master, because by him the LORD had given victory to Aram. The man, though a mighty warrior, suffered from leprosy. • Now the Arameans on one of their raids had taken a young girl captive from the land of Israel, and she served Naaman's wife. • She said to her mistress, 'If only my lord were with the prophet who is in Samaria! He would cure him of his leprosy.' • So Naaman went in 5 and told his lord just what the girl from the land of Israel had said. • And the king of Aram said, 'Go then, and I will send along a letter to the king of Israel.'

He went, taking with him ten talents of silver, six thousand shekels of gold, and ten sets of garments. • He brought the letter to the king of Israel, which read, 'When this letter reaches you, know that I have sent to you my servant Naaman, that you may cure him of his leprosy.' • When the king of Israel read the letter, he tore his clothes and said, 'Am I God, to give death or life, that this man sends word to me to cure a man of his leprosy? Just look and see how he is trying to pick a quarrel with me.'

• But when Elisha the man of God heard that the king of Israel had torn his clothes, he sent a message to the king, 'Why have you torn your clothes? Let him come to me, that he may learn that there is a prophet in Israel.' • So Naaman came with his horses and chariots, and halted at the entrance of 10 Elisha's house. • Elisha sent a messenger to him, saying, 'Go, wash in the Jordan seven times, and your flesh shall be restored and you shall be clean.' • But Naaman became angry and went away, saying, 'I thought that for me he would surely come out, and stand and call on the name of the LORD his God, and would wave his hand over the spot, and cure the leprosy! • Are not Abana and Pharpar, the rivers of Damascus, better than all the waters of Israel? Could I not wash in them, and be clean?' He turned and went away in a rage. ▶

Elisha and Naaman

Ch.5 has two parts: the healing of *Naaman* (1-14) and its aftermath. Both parts celebrate the powers of Elisha, but whereas in the second the interest is ultimately theological, the first is closer to social satire.

Verse 1 introduces Field-Marshal Lord Naaman GCB etc., and poses the problem – though his *leprosy* was a mild kind, which did not inhibit social contact. Verse 2 hints at the solution: in his own household was an anonymous foreign *girl*, abducted in a border raid and sold into slavery, literally 'a little girl' by contrast to the 'great man'. She not only knew the answer, but could present it tactfully, in the form of a wish (3). Then the two kings, also anonymous, are wheeled on. Their relationship is uneasy and status-conscious: *Aram* is peremptory (6), *Israel* paranoid (7). When the true *man of God* (contrast *Am I God?* in 7) comes into the action, he is unimpressed by rank. Far from being a royal functionary, as Aram thought, he puts his king down; and then when Naaman appears he sends out instructions to him through *a messenger*.

The climax of the first part is masterly. Naaman explodes, just as the king of Israel had in v.7. The Hebrew word-order reveals the emphasis of his expectations: 'To (a man like) me he will most certainly come out . . .'. But no protocol, no prayer (n.b.), no ritual, not even a *river of Damascus* – what an accumulation of insults! The situation is only saved now, as at the

Elisha and Naaman (cont.)

5.13 • But his servants approached and said to him, 'Father, if the prophet had commanded you to do something difficult, would you not have done it? How much more, when all he said to you was, "Wash, and be clean"?' • So he went down and immersed himself seven times in the Jordan, according to the word of the man of God; his flesh was restored like the flesh of a young boy, and he was clean.

15 • Then he returned to the man of God, he and all his company; he came and stood before him and said, 'Now I know that there is no God in all the earth except in Israel; please accept a present from your servant.' • But he said, 'As the LORD lives, whom I serve, I will accept nothing!' He urged him to accept, but he refused. • Then Naaman said, 'If not, please let two mule-loads of earth be given to your servant; for your servant will no longer offer burnt offering or sacrifice to any god except the LORD. • But may the LORD pardon your servant on one count: when my master goes into the house of Rimmon to worship there, leaning on my arm, and I bow down in the house of Rimmon, when I do bow down in the house of Rimmon, may the LORD pardon your servant on this one count.' • He said to him, 'Go in peace.'

Elisha and Naaman (cont.)

start, by the *servants*. They see right through him – what the *great man* wanted was to be told to do 'some great thing' (so the Hebrew, lost in NRSV) – but their respectful address and their argument persuade him: both literally and metaphorically, he *went down*. The end is quick. Stripped of his clothes and his pretensions, he bathes in Jordan. The last three words of v.14 answer those of v.1: the mighty man has become like a *young boy*, but the leper is *clean*.

The rest of the chapter records the varied reactions of three people to these events. The biggest surprise is provided by Naaman. Cured now of his pomposity, he is courteous to Elisha, genial to Gehazi and generous to both. His religious 'conversion', as the first proselyte in the OT, is of particular interest to the author. His new monotheism is remarkable but limited: the God of Israel has control over all the earth, but he resides *in Israel* and his worship can only be carried out on Israelite *earth* – this last a common enough belief in the ANE.

Naaman also asks for permission to join in the public worship of his national god. The wordy embarrassment of his request is couched in perfect pedimental* form, which AV, being more literal, preserves better than any of the modern translations. 'In this [one] thing / the LORD pardon thy servant / that when my master goeth into the house of Rimmon . . . / and he leaneth on my hand . . . / when I bow myself in the house of Rimmon / the LORD pardon thy servant / in this [one] thing.' *Rimmon* was a title of Hadad, the Aramaean equivalent of Baal. The site of Hadad's temple in Damascus has been successively occupied by a temple of Zeus/Jupiter, a church of St John, and lastly by the great Ummayid mosque.

Then while Naaman continues in his new-found humility (contrast *jumped down* in v.21 with his 'jumped up' behaviour in v.9), *Gehazi* the trusty servant is revealed as liar and cheat. His echo of Elisha's oath *As the LORD lives* points up his disloyalty to God as well as to his master.

Elisha and Naaman (cont.)

20   But when Naaman had gone from him a short distance, • Gehazi, the servant of Elisha the man of God, thought, 'My master has let that Aramean Naaman off too lightly by not accepting from him what he offered. As the LORD lives, I will run after him and get something out of him.' • So Gehazi went after Naaman. When Naaman saw someone running after him, he jumped down from the chariot to meet him and said, 'Is everything all right?' • He replied, 'Yes, but my master has sent me to say, "Two members of a company of prophets have just come to me from the hill country of Ephraim; please give them a talent of silver and two changes of clothing." ' • Naaman said, 'Please accept two talents.' He urged him, and tied up two talents of silver in two bags, with two changes of clothing, and gave them to two of his servants, who carried them in front of Gehazi. • When he came to the citadel, he took the bags from them, and stored them inside; he dismissed the men, and they left.

25   • He went in and stood before his master; and Elisha said to him, 'Where have you been, Gehazi?' He answered, 'Your servant has not gone anywhere at all.' • But he said to him, 'Did I not go with you in spirit when someone left his chariot to meet you? Is this a time to accept money and to accept clothing, olive orchards and vineyards, sheep and oxen, and male and female slaves? • Therefore the leprosy of Naaman shall cling to you, and to your descendants forever.' So he left his presence leprous, as white as snow.   (NRSV)

Elisha and Naaman (cont.)

Elisha, having been remote in the first part, comes forward in v.16. He refuses *a present* from Naaman but grants him the dispensation. He is equally fair to the dishonest Gehazi. That he who took Naaman's property should also catch his *leprosy* provides poetic justice for Gehazi and a fitting frame* for the chapter.

The Miracle of the Axe Head

6.1   The company of prophets who were with Elisha said to him, 'As you see, this place where we live with you is too cramped for us. • Let us go to the Jordan and each fetch a log, and make ourselves a place to live in.' The prophet said, 'Yes, go.' • One of them said, 'Please, sir, come with us.' 'I shall come,' he said, • and he went with them. When they reached the Jordan and began cutting down trees 5 • it chanced that, as one of them was felling a trunk, the head of his axe flew off into the water. 'Oh, master!' he exclaimed. 'It was borrowed.' • 'Where did it fall?' asked the man of God. When shown the place, he cut off a piece of wood and threw it into the water and made the iron float. • Elisha said, 'Lift it out.' So he reached down and picked it up.   (REB)

The Miracle of the Axe Head

Ch.5, though officially located in Samaria, really belongs with the 'Jordan' narrative of Ch.2; and 6.1-7 is another Jordan miracle. *Iron* was still a precious metal at this time.

Jehu's Coup d'Etat

9.1 Elisha the prophet summoned one of the company of prophets and said to him, 'Get ready for the road; take this flask of oil with you and go to Ramoth-gilead. • When you arrive, look there for Jehu son of Jehoshaphat, son of Nimshi; go in and call him aside from his fellow-officers, and lead him through to an inner room. • Take the flask and pour the oil on his head and say, "This is the word of the LORD: I anoint you king over Israel." After that open the door and flee for your life.'

4,5 • The young prophet went to Ramoth-gilead, • and when he arrived, he found the officers sitting together. He said, 'Sir, I have a word for you.' 'For which of us?' asked Jehu. 'For you, sir,' he said. • Jehu rose and went into the house, where the prophet poured the oil on his head, saying, 'This is the word of the LORD the God of Israel: I anoint you king over Israel, the people of the LORD.'

11 • When Jehu rejoined the king's officers, they said to him, 'Is all well? What did this crazy fellow want with you?' 'You know him and his ideas,' he said. • 'That is no answer!' they replied. 'Tell us what happened.' 'I shall tell you exactly what he said: "This is the word of the LORD: I anoint you king over Israel." ' • They snatched up their cloaks and spread them under him at the top of the steps, and they sounded the trumpet and shouted, 'Jehu is king.'

• Jehu son of Jehoshaphat, son of Nimshi, organized a conspiracy against Jehoram, while Jehoram and all the Israelites were defending Ramoth-gilead against 15 King Hazael of Aram. • King Jehoram had returned to Jezreel to recover from the wounds inflicted on him by the Aramaeans in his battle against Hazael. Jehu said to his colleagues, 'If you are on my side, see that no one escapes from the city to carry the news to Jezreel.' • He mounted his chariot and drove to Jezreel, for Jehoram was laid up there and King Ahaziah of Judah had gone down to visit him. ▸

Jehu's Coup d'Etat

We are now in 841, with Ahab's son Jehoram on the throne of Israel. Jehu's *coup d'état* against him had been fore-shadowed in 1 K 19.15-17, where Elisha and *Hazael* were also mentioned as playing a part in the overthrow of Ahab's line. Hazael's part (15) was indirect and purely military. His attack had had the effect of separating Jehoram, now *laid up* wounded in *Jezreel*, from his army in *Ramoth-gilead*, and thus offering Jehu his chance (14-16). Elisha's part was also somewhat indirect: he must have been old or ill – at any rate we do not hear of him again in 2 K until the deathbed scene [13.14-19]. In his place he sent one of the band of prophets with whom he was living, an ecstatic (hence *crazy* in 11), for the important purpose of anointing *Jehu*, cp. Samuel's anointing of Saul and David. But equally important was acclamation by the army, together with the

ritual *trumpet*-blast (13).

For this was essentially a military coup, and the historical Jehu need have had no religious objectives. It is true that, as presented here, the end of Jehoram is linked with the misdeeds of Ahab. The location of his death *by the plot of Naboth* (21) is pointed. Jehu's reference to *Jezebel*'s idolatry (22b) is clearly a later, pious addition: apart from its improbable content, it entirely spoils the splendidly taut dialogue of the dramatic scene 17-24.

That scene has much in common with the announcement of Absalom's death in 2 Sam 18. Those watching from the walls interpret the successive signs: is it *shalom* i.e. is the intent friendly and the news good? The tension mounts as we learn that it is a *troop*, not a messenger, then that two successive horsemen do not return, finally that *Jehu*, identified by his

Jehu's Coup d'Etat (cont.)

17   • The watchman standing on the watch-tower in Jezreel saw Jehu's troops approaching and called out, 'I see a troop of men.' Jehoram said, 'Fetch a horseman and send to meet them and ask if they come peaceably.' • The horseman went to meet him and said, 'The king asks, "Is it peace?" ' Jehu said, 'Peace? What is that to do with you? Fall in behind me.' The watchman reported, 'The messenger has met them but is not coming back.' • A second horseman was sent; when he met them, he also said, 'The king asks, "Is it peace?" ' 'Peace?'

20   said Jehu. 'What is that to do with you? Fall in behind me.' • The watchman reported, 'He has met them but is not coming back. The driving is like the driving of Jehu son of Nimshi, for he drives furiously.'

• 'Harness my chariot,' said Jehoram. When it was ready King Jehoram of Israel and King Ahaziah of Judah went out each in his own chariot to meet Jehu, and they met him by the plot of Naboth of Jezreel. • When Jehoram saw Jehu, he said, 'Is it peace, Jehu?' He replied, 'Do you call it peace while your mother Jezebel keeps up her obscene idol-worship and monstrous sorceries?' • Jehoram wheeled about and fled, crying out, 'Treachery, Ahaziah!' • Jehu drew his bow and shot Jehoram between the shoulders; the arrow pierced his heart and he slumped down in his chariot.   (REB)

Jehu's Coup d'Etat (cont.)

characteristically *furious driving* as Ahimaaz was by his running in 2 Sam 18.27, has come himself. If it is Jehu, then either Ramoth-Gilead is lost or there is treachery. *Jehoram* overestimates his popularity and underestimates Jehu's boldness. When Jehoram was killed, Jehu pursued and killed *Ahaziah* too, before returning for a more formidable foe.

The events narrated here may be the subject of an inscription in Old Aramaic

discovered at Dan in 1993. The interpretation of the (damaged) inscription is disputed, but it can be read as a victory stele* with restored text as follows: 'I . . . ed [Jeho]ram king of Israel and killed [Ahaz]iah son of . . . of the house of David'. If the restoration is accepted, the inscription contains by far the earliest mention of David outside the OT. The writing fits the date c.840 BC, and the stele was presumably set up by Hazael.

The End of Ahab's Dynasty: Jehu's Reign (841-814)

9.30   Then Jehu came to Jezreel. When Jezebel heard what had happened she painted her eyes and adorned her hair, and she stood looking down from a window. • As Jehu entered the gate, she said, 'Is it peace, you Zimri, you murderer of your master?' • He looked up at the window and said, 'Who is on my side? Who?' Two or three eunuchs looked out to him, • and he said, 'Throw her down.' They threw her down, and some of her blood splashed on to the wall and the   ▶

The End of Ahab's Dynasty: Jehu's Reign (841-814)

Jezebel is now queen mother, with all that that implies of power (see 1 K 2.13). Defiantly, she puts on her warpaint and taunts *Jehu* with a reference to another usurper *Zimri*, who reigned only seven days [1 K 16.15]. Jehu does not address her while alive, and waits till after his meal to give instructions for her corpse. The lapse of time is

enough for the *dogs* foretold by Elijah.

Jehu had the rest of Ahab's family killed, in *Jezreel* and in *Samaria*, then he dealt with the Baal-worship she had introduced. The narrator makes no adverse comment on Jehu's treachery but lets slip a point of historical interest, that Ahab was never a whole-hearted worshipper of

The End of Ahab's Dynasty: Jehu's Reign (841-814) (cont.)

9.35 horses, which trampled her underfoot. • Jehu went in and ate and drank. 'See to this accursed woman,' he said, 'and bury her; for she is a king's daughter.' • But when they went to bury her they found nothing of her but the skull, the feet, and the palms of her hands. • When they went back and told him, Jehu said, 'It is the word of the LORD which his servant Elijah the Tishbite spoke, when he said, "In the plot of ground at Jezreel the dogs will devour the flesh of Jezebel" '.

10.11 • Jehu put to death all who were left of the house of Ahab in Jezreel, as well as all
17 Ahab's nobles, his close friends, and priests, until he had left not one survivor. • When he came to Samaria, he put to death all of Ahab's house who were left there and so blotted it out, in fulfilment of the word which the LORD had spoken to Elijah.

  • Jehu called all the people together and said to them, 'Ahab served the Baal a little; Jehu will serve him much. • Now summon all the prophets of Baal, all his ministers and priests; not one must be missing. For I am holding a great sacrifice to Baal, and no one who is missing from it shall live.' In this way Jehu outwitted the
20 ministers of Baal in order to destroy them. • Jehu gave the order, 'Proclaim a sacred ceremony for Baal.' This was done, • and Jehu himself sent word throughout Israel. All the ministers of Baal came; there was not a man left who did not come, and when they went into the temple of Baal, it was filled from end to end. • Jehu said to the person who had charge of the wardrobe, 'Bring out robes for all the ministers of Baal'; and he brought them out. • Then Jehu and Jehonadab son of Rechab went into the temple of Baal and said to the ministers, 'Look carefully and make sure that there are no servants of the LORD here with you, but only the ministers of Baal.' • Then they went in to offer sacrifices and whole-offerings.

  Jehu had stationed eighty of his men outside and warned them, 'I shall hold you responsible for these men, and if anyone of you lets one of them escape he
25 will pay for it with his own life.' • When he had finished offering the whole-offering, Jehu ordered the guards and officers to go in and cut them all down, and let not one of them escape. They were slain without quarter, and the guard and the officers threw them out. Then going into the keep of the temple of Baal, • they brought out the sacred pole from the temple and burnt it; • they overthrew the sacred pillar of the Baal and pulled down the temple itself and made a privy of it – as it is today. • Thus Jehu stamped out the worship of Baal in Israel. (REB)

The End of Ahab's Dynasty: Jehu's Reign (841-814) (cont.)

Baal (10.18). The *robes* of v.22 are vestments worn for worship; perhaps here they also helped to identify the victims.

Jehu's reign marked the peak of Israelite prosperity. Archaeology shows no later monumental building and the pattern of house-building changed. Whereas in the C9th all town houses were similar, the C8th began to see a polarization. The houses of the rich remained fine – in the capital they became even finer (Amos 5.11). But in the poorer quarter many were very primitive, and in one excavated town,

Tell el Fara, the two quarters were actually separated by a wall. The change in urban housing is exactly paralleled by that concentration of land-ownership which so angered the great C8th prophets (e.g. Isaiah 5.8+). One factor at work was undoubtedly the heavy burden of tribute to Assyria, payable from 841 onwards. The tribute had to be paid in silver and gold, acquired partly by the sale of agricultural surpluses. The need for higher production was met in the classic way, by the expropriation of small-holders.

The End of the Northern Kingdom (721 BC)

1 In the twelfth year of King Ahaz of Judah, Hoshea son of Elah became king over Israel and he reigned in Samaria for nine years. • King Shalmaneser of Assyria marched up against Hoshea, who had been tributary to him, • but when the king of Assyria discovered that Hoshea was being disloyal to him, sending envoys to the king of Egypt at So, and withholding the annual tribute which he had been 5 paying, the king of Assyria seized and imprisoned him. • He overran the whole country and, reaching Samaria, besieged it for three years. • In the ninth year of Hoshea he captured Samaria and deported its people to Assyria, and settled them 24 in Halah and on the Habor, the river of Gozan, and in the towns of Media. • Then the king of Assyria brought people from Babylon, Cuthah, Avva, Hamath, and Sepharvaim, and settled them in the towns of Samaria in place of the Israelites; so they occupied Samaria and lived in its towns.   (REB)

The End of the Northern Kingdom (721 BC)

After Jehu the northern kingdom lasted another century in steady decline. Politically it was a time of turmoil for all the small states of the ANE. As the great Assyrian empire inexorably grew, they oscillated between crippling vassalage and ineffective intrigue. Coalitions of small states had no chance: only Egypt was big enough to provide substantial backing, but its policy had always tended to be defensive. In the end Israel, like its old enemy Aram a few years before, was incorporated into the Assyrian empire. The siege was begun, according to 2 K, by *Shalmaneser* V in 724, but it was his successor Sargon II who claimed to have completed the work *three years* later:

> At the beginning of my royal rule . . . I besieged and conquered Samaria, led away as booty 27,290 inhabitants of it. I formed from among them a contingent of 50 chariots. . . . The town I rebuilt better than it was

before and settled therein people from countries which I myself had conquered. I placed an officer of mine as governor over them and imposed upon them tribute as is customary for Assyrian citizens. (*ANET* 284-5)

Deportation was a standard instrument of Assyrian policy. The '50 chariots' show how Israel had declined since Ahab's reputed 2,000 (p.311).

The spare record of these events in 2 K is embellished by the DtH with a full theological commentary [7-17] along his usual lines. All the misfortunes that befell Israel are ascribed to disloyalty to YHWH. Every instance given of such disloyalty is religious in the narrow sense of cultic. Yet at this very same period there were living and writing three of the greatest prophets, Hosea, Amos and Isaiah, whose analysis of official policy, though equally hostile, was altogether more profound.

Hezekiah's Jerusalem (716-687)

18.1 In the third year of Hoshea son of Elah, king of Israel, Hezekiah son of King Ahaz of Judah became king. • He was twenty-five years old when he came to the throne, and he reigned in Jerusalem for twenty-nine years; his mother was Abi daughter of Zechariah. • He did what was right in the eyes of the LORD, as his ancestor David had done. • It was he who suppressed the shrines, smashed the sacred pillars, cut down every sacred pole, and broke up the bronze serpent that Moses had made, for up to that time the Israelites had been in the habit of burning sacrifices to it; they called it Nehushtan. • He put his trust in the LORD the God of

5 Israel; there was nobody like him among all the kings of Judah who succeeded him or among those who had gone before him. • He remained loyal to the LORD and did not fail in his allegiance to him, and he kept the commandments which the LORD had given to Moses. • The LORD was with him and he prospered in all that he undertook.

(REB)

Hezekiah's Jerusalem (716-687)

Israel having lost its independence, the spotlight is on Judah. This tiny country, smaller and less ambitious than Israel, was now sandwiched between Assyria and Egypt, looking to the latter for some support in maintaining a precarious independence, but wisely paying tribute to the former. The Assyrian record of tribute paid by king Ahaz c. 735 BC (*ANET* 282) contains the first mention of Judah in any source outside the OT.

Ahaz was succeeded by his son Hezekiah, whom the DtH rightly judges to be outstanding *among all the kings of Judah* in the 350 years of the state's independent existence. That judgement rests initially on his religious policy, summarized in 2 K 18.4. But (except for the reference to *the bronze serpent*, for which see Num 21.8) everything in Ch.18 about Hezekiah is said again in Chs 22-23 about his great-grandson Josiah, and in much greater detail; so comment is reserved till then on the religious policy itself and the political purpose it certainly had.

For, as the DtH makes clear, Hezekiah had political ambitions. And here the extensive evidence of archaeology comes in to support and amplify the text of the OT. Recent excavations in Jerusalem have shown that he extended the city walls, knocking down houses so as to build new sections up to 7 metres thick, and thus quad-rupled the area enclosed. The population increased proportionately, no doubt in part because of the influx of refugees from Israel, to a figure which may be as high as 25,000. That has to be compared with about 5,000 in the time of Solomon c.950, and the same again under Nehemiah c.450 BC.

And the increased population needed an improved water supply. Citadels depended crucially on their access to water. The fortunate ones, like Mycenae, were able to tunnel down to a spring within the walls. Jerusalem depended on the spring Gihon, which gushed irregularly in a cave above the Kidron valley, just outside the walls but close enough to deter enemy access. Hitherto it had been reached via a tunnel, 70 metres long, which sloped down from inside the walls (2 S 5.8). Hezekiah now had a new tunnel cut, sloping in the other direction, along a natural fault in the limestone (see Map 3). This carried the water by gravity for 533 metres under the city of David until it emerged into an underground cistern, inside the newly extended walls. The cistern was known in NT times as the Pool of Siloam; and the tunnel likewise is now called the Tunnel of Siloam. Archaeologists in the last 100 years have not only opened up the tunnel but have also found an inscription cut in the rock by the workmen. A gang had been working

Hezekiah's Jerusalem (716-687) (cont.)

from each end, and the inscription records the triumphant moment when they met:

> While there were still three cubits to be cut through, there was heard the voice of a man calling to his fellow. . . . And when the tunnel was driven through, the quarrymen hewed, each man towards his fellow, axe against axe; and the water flowed from the spring toward the reservoir for 1200 cubits. (*ANET* 321)

This notable achievement is mentioned casually by the DtH in his final summary of Hezekiah's reign (20.20). [Is 22.9-11]

gives more detail but is hard to interpret.

Hezekiah tightened his economic grip on the countryside of Judah. The evidence comes from jar-handles of his time, inscribed LMLK i.e. 'for [or belonging to] the king'. Hundreds of handles have been found all over the country, including 250 from Jerusalem alone. It is uncertain if the wine and oil in the jars was for export or for stock-piling against a siege, but with the other evidence they show a new scale of organization in the state of Judah. Now for the first time, it seems, Jerusalem was a city to reckon with.

Hezekiah's Rebellion Crushed by Assyria (701 BC)

8. 7 Hezekiah rebelled against the king of Assyria and was no longer subject to him; • he conquered the Philistine country as far as Gaza and its boundaries, from watch-tower to fortified city.

13   • In the fourteenth year of King Hezekiah's reign, King Sennacherib of Assyria attacked and captured all the fortified towns of Judah. • Hezekiah sent a message to the king of Assyria at Lachish: 'I have done wrong; withdraw from me, and I shall pay any penalty you impose upon me.'   ▸

Hezekiah's Rebellion Crushed by Assyria (701 BC)

Nor was Hezekiah's policy purely defensive. With tacit Egyptian support, he took advantage of a temporary decline in Assyrian power after 705 BC, refusing to pay tribute. More rashly, he *conquered the Philistine country*. The notice in v.8 is corroborated by an Assyrian royal inscription, which adds that Hezekiah had imprisoned the pro-Assyrian king of Ekron.

So in 701 BC King Sennacherib 'came down like a wolf on the fold', and wrought widespread vengeance, which he recorded:

> As to Hezekiah the Jew, he did not submit to my yoke, I laid siege to 46 of his strong cities, walled forts and the countless small villages in their vicinity, and conquered them by means of well-stamped earth ramps, battering-rams brought near etc.

Strongest of these cities – stronger in-

deed than Jerusalem before Hezekiah – was *Lachish*. Of its siege Sennacherib had a magnificent sculpture made in low relief to adorn his palace at Nineveh; it is now in the British Museum, and photographs of it can be found in most illustrated bibles. From these places, he goes on,

> I drove out 200,150 people, young and old, male and female [with their livestock], and considered them booty. . . . His towns which I had plundered I took away from his country and gave them to [various Philistine kings]. Thus I reduced his country, but I still increased the tribute due to me as his overlord, to be delivered annually. [And the record concludes] Hezekiah himself . . . did send me later to Nineveh, my lordly city, 30 talents of gold, 800 talents of silver, precious stones . . . his own daughters, concubines, male and female musicians. (*ANET* 288)

Hezekiah's Rebellion Crushed by Assyria (701 BC) (cont.)

18.14   The king of Assyria laid on Hezekiah king of Judah a penalty of three hundred talents of silver and thirty talents of gold; • and Hezekiah gave him all the silver found in the house of the LORD and in the treasuries of the palace. • At that time Hezekiah stripped of their gold the doors of the temple of the LORD and the door-frames which he himself had plated, and gave it to the king of Assyria.   (REB)

Hezekiah's Rebellion Crushed by Assyria (701 BC) (cont.)

In view of the tendency of one side to maximise such matters (the figure of 200,150 looks highly exaggerated), and of the other to minimise them, agreement over the *30 talents of gold* is remarkable.

A connoisseur of historical documents will also note the tacit agreement over the fate of Jerusalem itself. Sennacherib says: 'Hezekiah I made a prisoner in Jerusalem, his royal residence, like a bird in a cage. I surrounded him with earthworks in order to molest those who were leaving his city's gate', and adds only that 'his irregular and elite troops which he had brought into Jerusalem, his royal residence, in order to strengthen it, deserted him.' The corresponding story in 2 K Chs 18-19 contains as much huffing and puffing as the Assyrian inscription, but through it all there emerges the clear historical fact that Hezekiah bought off the Assyrians, who did withdraw from Jerusalem without instituting a siege. To find out what happened in the interim, we can make cautious use of the vivid, if embellished, narrative of the DtH.

The Assyrians at the Walls of Jerusalem

18.17   From Lachish the king of Assyria sent the commander-in-chief, the chief eunuch, and the chief officer with a strong force to King Hezekiah at Jerusalem. They marched up and when they reached Jerusalem they halted by the conduit of the Upper Pool on the causeway leading to the Fuller's Field. • When they called for the king, the comptroller of the household, Eliakim son of Hilkiah, came out to them with Shebna, the adjutant-general, and Joah son of Asaph, the secretary of state.

• The chief officer said to them, 'Tell Hezekiah that this is the message of the Great King, the king of Assyria: "What ground have you for this confidence of

20   yours? • Do you think words can take the place of skill and military strength? On whom then do you rely for support in your rebellion against me? • On Egypt? Egypt is a splintered cane that will run into a man's hand and pierce it if he leans on it. That is what Pharaoh king of Egypt proves to all who rely on him. • And if you tell me that you are relying on the LORD your God, is he not the god whose shrines and altars Hezekiah has suppressed, telling Judah and Jerusalem they must worship at this altar in Jerusalem?" '

• 'Now, make a deal with my master the king of Assyria: I shall give you two thousand horses if you can find riders for them. • How then can you reject the authority of even the least of my master's servants and rely on Egypt for chariots

25   and horsemen? • Do you think that I have come to attack this place and destroy it without the consent of the LORD? No; the LORD himself said to me, "Go up and destroy this land." '   ◆

The Assyrians at the Walls of Jerusalem (cont.)

• Eliakim son of Hilkiah, Shebna, and Joah said to the chief officer, 'Please speak to us in Aramaic, for we understand it; do not speak Hebrew to us within earshot of the people on the city wall.' • The chief officer answered, 'Is it to your master and to you that my master has sent me to say this? Is it not to the people sitting on the wall who, like you, will have to eat their own dung and drink their own urine?'

‣30 • Then he stood and shouted in Hebrew, 'Hear the message of the Great King, the king of Assyria! • These are the king's words: "Do not be taken in by Hezekiah. He is powerless to save you from me. • Do not let him persuade you to rely on the LORD, and tell you that the LORD will surely save you and that this city will never be surrendered to the king of Assyria." • Do not listen to Hezekiah, for this is what the king of Assyria says: "Make your peace with me, and surrender. Then every one of you will eat the fruit of his own vine and of his own fig tree, and drink the water of his own cistern, • until I come and take you to a land like your own, a land of grain and new wine, of bread and vineyards, of olives, fine oil, and honey – life for you all, instead of death. Do not listen to Hezekiah; he will only mislead you by telling you ‣

The Assyrians at the Walls of Jerusalem

Sennacherib himself, being busy at *Lachish*, did not come up to Jerusalem but sent his *chief officer* with a detachment. They encamped on a *causeway* or spur to the north of the city (see Map 3). Their camp was outside the newly enclosed higher quarter, for whose benefit *the Upper Pool* (to be distinguished from the Pool of Siloam) had been dug. To them Hezekiah, though *called for* himself, sent out a delegation of appropriate status.

The Assyrian *chief officer* at Jerusalem was a diplomat with a knowledge of the Hebrew language and religion. His two speeches were designed to divide the people of Jerusalem from their king, and so to secure a negotiated surrender. The first was neatly constructed; see the table below. The effectiveness of this speech is shown by the reaction of the Jewish leaders, who feared further desertions.

Aramaic (26) was now the diplomatic language of the ANE.

The second speech of the chief officer (vv.29-35) was varied, so as to appeal directly to *the people sitting on the wall*. Its structure is the more familiar biblical structure, and each point is introduced by a scornful naming of *Hezekiah* (REB loses the force of this in v.30 by substituting a weak *him* for the name).

Emphasised at the centre (31-32) is a new argument, clever but suspiciously deuteronomic: nothing about military or diplomatic strength, as in the first speech, but a soothing *ad hominem* appeal. To *surrender* will guarantee life and food *until I come and take* (i.e. deport) *you to a land like your own*: the alternative is starvation (27) and/or death.

On either side of that argument is a reprise of the religious point already

Introduction: *what ground have you for confidence?*			19
A	1	you have no power of your own	20
	2	*Egypt* will let you down	21
	3	*YHWH your God* will not support you	22
B	1	Sennacherib has power of his own	23
	2	his *servants* have more *authority* than *Egypt*	24
	3	he is supported by *YHWH himself*	25

The Assyrians at the Walls of Jerusalem (cont.)

18.33 that the LORD will save you. • Did any god of the nations save his land from the king of Assyria's power? • Where are the gods of Hamath and Arpad? Where are the gods of Sepharvaim, Hena, and Ivvah? Where are the gods of Samaria? Did they save Samaria from me? • Among all the gods of the nations is there one who saved his land from me? So how is the LORD to save Jerusalem?" '

• The people remained silent and said not a word in reply, for the king had given orders that no one was to answer him. (REB)

The Assyrians at the Walls of Jerusalem (cont.)

made in the first speech. *YHWH* will not *save* you (30, picked up at the very end in 35), any more than other gods have saved their peoples from Assyria. We need not be surprised at the use of this theological argument: Assyrian royal inscriptions contain many mentions of the gods who have yielded the victories listed.

There is a close parallel to this story in an Assyrian document of some thirty years earlier. The situation then was this.

The city of Babylon had taken sides with a rebel and closed its gates to the king of Assyria. He sent an officer to persuade the Babylonians to return to their loyalty. The officer reported back to the king by letter:

> We came to Babylon. We took our stand before the Marduk gate and argued with the Man of Babylon. We said, 'Why do you act hostilely against us for the sake of them?' We used many arguments. . . . They would not agree to come out. (Saggs)

Isaiah and the Assyrian Withdrawal

18.37 • Eliakim son of Hilkiah, comptroller of the household, Shebna the adjutant-general, and Joah son of Asaph, secretary of state, came to Hezekiah with their clothes torn and

19. 1 reported the words of the chief officer. • When King Hezekiah heard their report, he tore his clothes, put on sackcloth, and went into the house of the LORD. • He sent Eliakim comptroller of the household, Shebna the adjutant-general, and the senior

20 priests, all wearing sackcloth, to the prophet Isaiah son of Amoz. • Isaiah son of Amoz sent Hezekiah the following message: 'This is the word of the LORD the God of Israel: I have heard your prayer to me concerning King Sennacherib of Assyria, • and this is the word that the LORD has spoken against him:

32   He will not enter this city
      or shoot an arrow there,
   he will not advance against it with shield
      or cast up a siege-ramp against it.

33   By the way he came he will go back;
      he will not enter this city.
   This is the word of the LORD.'   ◆

Isaiah and the Assyrian Withdrawal

The speeches of the Assyrian chief officer at Jerusalem were a skilful mixture of the mailed fist and the kid glove, and *Hezekiah* was justifiably alarmed. In his indecision he followed the usual practice of seeking an oracle (19.1). But the chief temple prophet at this time was none other than the great *Isaiah*. Born c.765, he had been playing an important part in national politics for some thirty years, and had often had to give unpopular advice. This time the word of the LORD was more welcome; and Sennacherib did indeed withdraw from Judah.

Isaiah and the Assyrian Withdrawal (cont.)

35   • That night the angel of the LORD went out and struck down a hundred and eighty-five thousand in the Assyrian camp; when morning dawned, there they all lay dead. • King Sennacherib of Assyria broke camp and marched away; he went back to Nineveh and remained there.

20   • The other events of Hezekiah's reign, his exploits, and how he made the pool and the conduit and brought water into the city, are recorded in the annals of the kings of Judah.   (REB)

Isaiah and the Assyrian Withdrawal (cont.)

As to what made him do so, the 'miraculous' explanation (35) recalls a passage in Herodotus. He records that, when Sennacherib invaded Egypt a few years later, the Pharaoh marched out to meet him at the frontier. 'During the night thousands of field mice swarmed over the Assyrians and ate their quivers, their bowstrings and the leather handles of their shields, so that on the following day, having no arms to fight with, they had to withdraw.' Rationalists have pointed to the connection of mice with disease, and suggested that a plague may have struck Sennacherib's army on both occasions – unless indeed one is a doublet of the other.

The close connection between Hezekiah and Isaiah – the greatest of the kings and the greatest of the prophets – was important to later Jewish tradition, and played its part in structuring the biblical book of Isaiah (see p.522). Hezekiah's name is also to be found in the Book of Proverbs. An editorial note at the head of Chs 25-29 records that they were 'transcribed by the men of Hezekiah'.

Josiah (640-609) and Religious Reform

2. 1   Josiah was eight years old when he came to the throne, and he reigned for thirty-one years in Jerusalem. • He did what the LORD regards as right, and in every respect followed the example of his ancestor David, not deviating from it to right or left.

10   • In the eighteenth year of King Josiah, the king sent the secretary Shaphan son of Azaliah, son of Meshullam to the Temple of the LORD. • Then Shaphan the secretary informed the king, 'The priest Hilkiah has given me a book'; and Shaphan

3. 1   read it aloud in the king's presence. • The king then had all the elders of Judah and of Jerusalem summoned to him, • and the king went up to the Temple of the LORD with all the people of Judah and all the inhabitants of Jerusalem, priests, prophets and the whole populace, high and low. In their hearing he read out the entire contents of the Book of the Covenant discovered in the Temple of the LORD. ▶

Josiah (640-609) and Religious Reform

Half a century elapsed between the death of Hezekiah and the accession of his great-grandson *Josiah* in 640. During that period the balance of power began to change in the ANE. Gradually Assyria was overtaken by the rising power of Babylon, 300 miles further down the valley. Eventually Nineveh itself was captured in 612, and the neo-Babylonian or Chaldaean empire took over from Assyria. While conflict lasted in Mesopotamia the iron grip was relaxed, and even the kings of Judah were able to raise their heads in a way that had not been possible for a long time.

However the main event of Josiah's reign, in the eyes of the DtH, was something quite different. In 622 BC there was discovered in the Temple a document called *the Book of the Covenant*. Josiah

Josiah (640-609) and Religious Reform (cont.)

23. 3 • The king then, standing on the dais, bound himself by the covenant before the LORD, to follow the LORD, to keep his commandments, decrees and laws with all his heart and soul, and to carry out the terms of the covenant as written in this book. All the people pledged their allegiance to the covenant.

• The king ordered Hilkiah to remove all the cult objects which had been made for Baal, Asherah and the whole array of heaven; he burnt them outside Jerusalem in the fields of the Kidron and had the ashes taken to Bethel. • And from the Temple of the LORD he took the sacred pole outside Jerusalem to the Kidron valley and in the Kidron valley he burnt it, reducing it to ashes and throwing its

11 ashes on the common burial-ground. • He destroyed the horses which the kings of Judah had dedicated to the sun at the entrance to the Temple of the LORD, near the apartment of Nathan-Melech the official, in the precincts, and he burned the

13 solar chariot. • The king rendered unsanctified the high places facing Jerusalem, to the south of the Mount of Olives, which Solomon king of Israel had built for Astarte the Sidonian abomination, for Chemosh the Moabite abomination, and for Milcom the Ammonite abomination. • He also smashed the sacred pillars, cut down the sacred poles, and covered with human bones the places where they had stood.

• As for the altar which was at Bethel, the high place built by Jeroboam son of Nebat who had led Israel into sin, he demolished this altar and this high place as well, in the same way, breaking up its stones and reducing them to powder. The

19 sacred pole he burned. • Josiah also destroyed all the shrines on the high ▸

Josiah (640-609) and Religious Reform (cont.)

immediately recognised its importance. At a public ceremony he pledged himself to follow it, and *all the people* did likewise. He then set about implementing its provisions in the religious sphere.

The DtH describes that implementation, generally known as 'Josiah's reforms', in great detail. And both the content and the wording of the account turn out to bear a close resemblance to the religious provisions of Deuteronomy, especially Chs 12-26. Some scholars have therefore suspected that the DtH invented the story of finding the Book of the Covenant in the Temple so as to enhance the authority of a book he held dear and the reforms it recommended. There are indeed ANE parallels to the basic situation here, where a king 'finds' in a temple a 'lost' document which supports an unpopular policy. But even if that suspicion is correct, nothing follows about the historicity of Josiah's reform

programme or about the date of Dt.

That programme had two aspects, one negative and one positive. Negatively he is said to have eradicated all pagan places and objects of worship. The list of them contains some very surprising features. It starts with Solomon's *Temple* itself, which had contained *cult objects made for Baal* and *Asherah*, and for *the whole array of heaven*. (For *Solomon's* own deities see 1 K 11.7.) Outside Jerusalem Josiah's chief focus is on the *high places*, i.e. rock-*altars* on hill-tops, with their *sacred poles*.

Modern archaeology fully confirms the wide spread of these other cults. Excavations at Dan and elsewhere have revealed the nature of a high place and its cult-objects, including the *pillars* sacred to El and the *poles* (stylized trees) of his consort Asherah. Some of these cults were of foreign deities worshipped separately, but many were

Josiah (640-609) and Religious Reform (cont.)

places which were in the towns of Samaria and which the kings of Israel had built to provoke the LORD's anger; he treated these places exactly as he had treated the one at Bethel.

21 • The king gave this order to the whole people: 'Celebrate a Passover to the LORD your God, as prescribed in this Book of the Covenant.' • No Passover like this had ever been celebrated since the days when the judges ruled Israel, nor

25 throughout the entire period of the kings of Israel and the kings of Judah. • No king before him turned to the LORD as he did, with all his heart, all his soul, all his strength, in perfect loyalty to the Law of Moses; nor did any king like him arise again.

29 • In his times, Pharaoh Necho king of Egypt was advancing to meet the king of Assyria at the River Euphrates, and King Josiah went to intercept him; but Necho killed him at Megiddo in the first encounter. • His retainers carried his body from Megiddo by chariot; they brought him to Jerusalem and buried him in his own tomb.   (NJB)

Josiah (640-609) and Religious Reform (cont.)

syncretistic, i.e. in them other deities were worshipped *as* YHWH. For this syncretism, and for the intense hostility to it on the part of the DtH and the prophets, see p.33.

So much for the negative side of Josiah's reforms. The positive side was the institution of a grand *Passover* celebration *in Jerusalem*, also *as prescribed in the Book of the Covenant.* Certainly Dt did so prescribe, and the prescription fits what we can piece together of Josiah's general policy.

For it is clear that for Josiah, as for Hezekiah and Jeroboam (1 K 12.27), and indeed for most monarchs of the ANE, religion and what we would call politics went hand in hand. In a period of Assyrian weakness, he managed to assert his authority over at least some of *the towns*

of what was now the Assyrian province of *Samaria*, including *Bethel* if not the northernmost Dan. And archaeology has made the surprising discovery of a fortress, built by Josiah and manned by Greek mercenaries, in the coastal plain due west of Samaria.

In that context Josiah's religious reform is best seen as a cultural revolution with nationalistic overtones, aimed at raising the morale of the people and securing their loyalty to the throne. True, he overreached himself at the end, attempting to intervene between *Pharaoh Necho* and *the king of Assyria.* But until that misjudgement his reign had been long, prosperous and successful. His influence on the text of the OT, and thus on later Judaism, is probably greater than that of any king of Israel or Judah.

The End of the Southern Kingdom (609-587 BC)

23.34 | Pharaoh Necho then made Eliakim son of Josiah king and changed his name to Jehoiakim. • Jehoiakim was twenty-five years old when he came to the throne, and he reigned for eleven years in Jerusalem.

24. 1 | • In his times, Nebuchadnezzar king of Babylon invaded, and Jehoiakim became his vassal for three years, but then rebelled against him. • So he sent armed bands of Chaldaeans, Aramaeans, Moabites and Ammonites against him. • Then

6 | Jehoiakim fell asleep with his ancestors; his son Jehoiachin succeeded him. • Jehoiachin was eighteen years old when he came to the throne, and he reigned for three months in Jerusalem.

10 | • At that time the troops of Nebuchadnezzar king of Babylon advanced on Jerusalem, and the city was besieged. • Nebuchadnezzar king of Babylon advanced on the city and his generals laid siege to it. • Jehoiachin king of Judah – he, his mother, his retinue, his nobles and his officials – then surrendered to the king of Babylon, and the king of Babylon took them prisoner in the eighth year of

14 | his reign. • He carried all Jerusalem off into exile, all the nobles and all the notables, ten thousand of these were exiled, with all the blacksmiths and metalworkers; only the poorest people in the country were left behind.

17 | • The king of Babylon deposed Jehoiachin in favour of his paternal uncle Mattaniah, whose name he changed to Zedekiah. • Zedekiah was twenty-one years old when he came to the throne, and he reigned for eleven years in Jerusalem.

20 | • Zedekiah rebelled against the king of Babylon.   ▸

The End of the Southern Kingdom (609-587 BC)

Five years after Josiah's death both Necho and the king of Assyria were defeated at Carchemish (see Map 1) by Nebuchadnezzar king of Babylon (605-562). To the subject peoples the change made no long-term difference. The kings of Judah after Josiah still had to tread a tightrope between Babylon, strong but far away, and Egypt, weak but near. The prophet Jeremiah, active at this time (and whose book contains vital background information), always advised against provocation of Babylon; but successive kings were swayed in the other direction.

First of them was *Jehoiakim* (609-598), whose policy was opposed by Jeremiah (Chs 7, 26, 36) and paid for by his son *Jehoiachin*. Jehoiachin's inevitable *surrender* was followed by the first deportation to Babylon. Jeremiah gives the figure of deportees more plausibly as 3,023, among whom was probably the prophet Ezekiel. From Babylonian records we learn the date of the surrender, 16 March 597 by our reckoning.

Jehoiachin's uncle and successor *Zedekiah* (597-587) also made the mistake of trying to organize a coalition against Babylon. The result was disaster. The *siege* lasted 18 months (Dec 589-midsummer 587), except for a temporary lifting in the middle when an Egyptian army approached (Jer 37-38). A month after the surrender there followed the sacking of the city, including the *Temple*, and a further deportation of 832 citizens.

The End of the Southern Kingdom (609-587 BC) (cont.)

1 • In the ninth year of his reign, in the tenth month, on the tenth day of the month, Nebuchadnezzar king of Babylon advanced on Jerusalem with his entire army; he pitched camp in front of the city and threw up earthworks round it. • The city lay under siege till the eleventh year of King Zedekiah. • In the fourth month, on the ninth day of the month, when famine was raging in the city and there was no food for the populace, • a breach was made in the city wall. The king then made his escape under cover of dark, with all the fighting men, by way of the gate between the two walls, which is near the king's garden – the Chaldaeans had surrounded the city – and made his way towards the Arabah.

5 • The Chaldaean troops pursued the king and caught up with him in the Plains of Jericho, where all his troops deserted. • The Chaldaeans captured the king and took him to the king of Babylon at Riblah, who passed sentence on him. • He had Zedekiah's sons slaughtered before his eyes, then put out Zedekiah's eyes and, loading him with chains, carried him off to Babylon. • In the fifth month, on the seventh day of the month – it was in the nineteenth year of Nebuchadnezzar king of Babylon – Nebuzaradan commander of the guard, a member of the king of 10 Babylon's staff, entered Jerusalem. • He burned down the Temple of the LORD, the royal palace and all the houses in Jerusalem. • The Chaldaean troops who accompanied the commander of the guard demolished the walls surrounding Jerusalem. • Nebuzaradan commander of the guard deported the remainder of the population left in the city, the deserters who had gone over to the king of Babylon, 27 and the rest of the common people. • But the commander of the guard left some of the poor country people behind as vineyard workers and ploughmen.

• In the thirty-seventh year of the exile of Jehoiachin king of Judah, in the twelfth month, on the twenty-seventh day of the month, Evil-Merodach king of Babylon, in the year he came to the throne, pardoned Jehoiachin king of Judah 30 and released him from prison. • He treated him with kindness and allotted him a seat above those of the other kings who were with him in Babylon. • So Jehoiachin laid aside his prisoner's garb, and for the rest of his life always ate at the king's table. • And his upkeep was permanently ensured by the king, day after day, for the rest of his life.   (NJB)

The End of the Southern Kingdom (609-587 BC) (cont.)

But the Babylonians did not introduce foreign settlers into the country of Judah, as the Assyrians had done when they deported the people of Israel (2 K 17.24). For the history of what followed we have to turn again to Jeremiah (Chs 39-40).

The last four verses of 2 K are a postscript, added in exile to give a glimmer of hope. In 562 Nebuchadnezzar's son declared an amnesty on his accession. *Jehoiachin*, the last king of David's line, was released from house-arrest, though he was still detained in Babylon 'at His Majesty's pleasure'. A Babylonian text (*ANET* 308) records the issue of his regular ration of oil.

EXILE AND RETURN

In the perspective of history it can be seen that the Babylonian exile in C6th BC was only a part of the larger and longer movement known as the dispersion of the Jews or (in the Greek word) the diaspora. That movement had begun long before the exile, with Egypt as the favoured destination. From about C4th BC it accelerated until it had spread to all the large areas of population in the ANE as well as Greece and Italy, and the Jews of the dispersion outnumbered those of the homeland. But Jerusalem was always the focus of the national consciousness – for none more than those who had been deported to Babylon.

It was in fact only twenty-three years after the 'release' of Jehoiachin that the Babylonian empire itself was overthrown in turn by Cyrus the Great, king of the Persians. In 539 BC the Persians, an Indo-European people, became masters of the ANE, and remained so for two centuries until Alexander the Great.

The history of the Jews during and after the Babylonian exile is much less well known than during the preceding period. The OT contains no continuous narrative which has either the reliability or the literary skill of the books of Samuel and Kings. The main sources are the prophetic books, which contain biography as well as what might be called commentary on current affairs. The chief of them are: Jeremiah, which is especially valuable for conditions in Judaea after 587; Ezekiel and Second Isaiah for conditions in Babylon during the exile; and [Haggai] and [Zechariah] for the return.

The OT also contains one ostensibly historical work relating to the period. It consists of the four books: [1 and 2 Chronicles], Ezra and Nehemiah; and it is generally known as the work of the Chronicler. The two books of [Chronicles] cover the period from David down to the exile; they add nothing to the two books of Kings that is of interest to the general reader, and so are omitted from this selection. Ezra and Nehemiah cover the return, and a brief extract from each is included, telling of the rebuilding of (i) the Temple and (ii) the walls of Jerusalem. Like all the work of the Chronicler, they are as close to theology as to history, i.e. the events are chosen, ordered and narrated in such a way as to put across a message. The relevant part of that message, under the overarching belief in God's special providence for the Jews, is as follows: that the 'true' Israel consisted of the families who were deported from Jerusalem to Babylon; that they all took the first available opportunity to return; that their chief concern was to rebuild the Temple; and that worship in it, after a break of 50 years, was then resumed in continuity with the best traditions of Moses, David and Solomon.

That message is more or less tendentious in all respects. First, the deportees were but a small proportion of the population. According to the MT* of Jeremiah [52.30], they totalled only 4,600. Nor were they the 'best' in anything but social class. Next, they varied greatly in their enthusiasm for returning. True, there were some who could not wait to get back, like the author of Ps 137. At the other extreme were some who did so well there that they never returned; we know for example of a Jewish family which prospered in banking in Babylon. In between were those who needed – but perhaps also heeded – Jeremiah's advice (Ch.29) to make the best of it. We can imagine a succession of such people drifting back over many years: among them were Ezra and Nehemiah, who returned, independently of each other, about a century after permission was first given.

Ezra Describes the Rebuilding of the Temple

1.1 In the first year of Cyrus king of Persia – to fulfil the word of the LORD spoken through Jeremiah – the LORD roused the spirit of Cyrus king of Persia to issue a proclamation and to have it publicly displayed throughout his kingdom:

• Cyrus king of Persia says this, The LORD, the God of heaven, has given me all the kingdoms of the earth and has appointed me to build him a Temple in Jerusalem, in Judah. • Whoever among you belongs to the full tally of his people, may his God be with him! Let him go up to Jerusalem, in Judah, and build the Temple of the LORD, God of Israel, who is the God in Jerusalem.

5 • Then the heads of families of Judah and of Benjamin, the priests and the Levites, in fact all whose spirit had been roused by God, prepared to go and rebuild the Temple of the LORD in Jerusalem; • and all their neighbours gave them every kind of help: silver, gold, equipment, riding beasts and valuable presents, in addition to their voluntary offerings.

• Furthermore, King Cyrus handed over the articles belonging to the Temple of the LORD which Nebuchadnezzar had carried away from Jerusalem and put in the temple of his god.

3. 1 • When the seventh month came after the Israelites had been resettled in their towns, the people gathered as one person in Jerusalem. • Then Jeshua son of Jozadak, with his brother priests, and Zerubbabel son of Shealtiel, with his brothers, set about rebuilding the altar of the God of Israel, to offer burnt offerings on it as prescribed in the Law of Moses man of God. • They erected the altar on its old site, despite their fear of the people of the country. • They also contributed **7** money for the masons and carpenters, and food, drink and oil for the Sidonians and Tyrians for bringing cedar wood from Lebanon by sea to Jaffa, for which Cyrus king of Persia had given permission. ◆

Ezra Describes the Rebuilding of the Temple

The Book of Ezra begins with the accession of *Cyrus* and his decree authorizing the initial return of the Jews and the rebuilding of the Temple. There is no reason to doubt the general sense of this decree. In addition to other evidence of Persian tolerance in religious matters, we possess an actual inscription of Cyrus which records what might be called the metropolitan version of the Ezra decree. Known as the Cyrus cylinder, it has two parts. The first records his past exploits (for the text see p.558). In the second part Cyrus himself speaks (by ANE convention) in the first person. He describes how he treated the inhabitants of Babylon and the vassal states, and adds:

[As for] the sacred cities on the far side of the Tigris, whose sites have long been in ruins: the gods who lived in them I brought back to their place and established a permanent dwelling for them; all their people I gathered and brought back to their homes.

The decree in the book of Ezra is an ethnic version of the same policy, addressed to Jews throughout the empire. Cyrus therefore refers not to Marduk but to YHWH, whom in typical gentile fashion he describes as *the god in Jerusalem*.

To restart the sacrificial worship, the first thing to tackle was the altar outside the Temple. The *people of the country* (3.3) are those from neighbouring territories who, according to the books of Chronicles, had occupied the estates of the deportees and resented their return. The hiring of the Phoenician craftsmen and the transport of *cedar from Lebanon* (7) is an echo of the building of Solomon's

Ezra Describes the Rebuilding of the Temple (cont.)

3.8   • It was in the second month of the second year after their arrival at the Temple of God in Jerusalem that Zerubbabel son of Shealtiel and Jeshua son of Jozadak, with the rest of their brothers, the priests, the Levites and all the people
10   who had returned to Jerusalem from captivity, began the work. • When the builders had laid the foundations of the Temple of the LORD, all the people raised a mighty shout of praise to the LORD, since the foundations of the Temple of the LORD had now been laid. • Many of the older priests, Levites and heads of families, who had seen the first temple, wept very loudly when the foundations of this one were laid before their eyes, but many others shouted aloud for joy, • so that nobody could distinguish the noise of the joyful shout from the noise of the people's weeping; for the people shouted so loudly that the noise could be heard far away.

(NJB)

Ezra Describes the Rebuilding of the Temple (cont.)

Temple (1 K 5); this underlines the continuity – even though the old men *wept* for the come-down. The indistinguishability of the cries is a topos*.

But the actual building of the Temple hung fire for one reason and another, and it was not until the reign of Darius I some twenty years later that real progress was made. That we know from the prophet [Haggai], who also confirms that the impetus was due to two people mentioned here: *Jeshua* the High Priest and *Zerubbabel* the civil governor. Zerubbabel

is an important figure in the later books of the OT, partly because he was of David's line: his father Shealtiel was a son of the last king Jehoiachin, and they appear in the genealogy of Jesus in Matt 1.12.

Another sixty-odd years elapse before Ezra himself enters the story [in Ch. 7]. In the pages of the Chronicler he never comes to life as a person, unlike his contemporary Nehemiah, but as time went on he came more and more to be seen as the ideal scribe and thus as the archetypal figure of post-exilic Judaism.

Nehemiah on the Rebuilding of the Walls

2.11   When I arrived in Jerusalem, I waited three days. • Then I set out by night, taking a few men with me, but without telling anyone what my God was prompting me to do for Jerusalem. Taking no beast with me except the one on which I myself rode, • I went out by night through the Valley Gate towards the Dragon Spring and the Dung Gate; and I inspected the places where the walls of Jerusalem had been broken down, and its gates, which had been destroyed by fire. • Then I passed on to the Fountain Gate and the King's Pool; but there was no room for
15   me to ride through. • I went up the valley by night and inspected the city wall; then I re-entered the city through the Valley Gate. So I arrived back • without the magistrates knowing where I had been or what I was doing, for I had not yet told the ◗

Nehemiah on the Rebuilding of the Walls

Nehemiah tells his story in the first person, the first author to do so in the 'historical' books. He was a cupbearer (a high official) of the Persian king Artaxerxes c. 445 BC, who secured appointment as governor of Judaea together with authority to

rebuild the walls of Jerusalem. His first act on arrival was a nocturnal reconnaissance. Archaeology confirms the wide spread of the ruins (2.14), but does not enable us to locate all the gates etc.; *the valley* is the valley of Kidron and *the King's Pool* must

Nehemiah on the Rebuilding of the Walls (cont.)

Jews, neither the priests, the nobles, the magistrates, nor any of those who would be responsible for the work.

.17   • Then I said to them, 'You see what trouble we are in: Jerusalem lies in ruins, its gates destroyed by fire. Come, let us rebuild the wall of Jerusalem and suffer derision no more.' • I told them also how the gracious hand of my God had been upon me and also what the king had said to me. They replied, 'Let us start the rebuilding,' and they set about the work vigorously and to good purpose.

4.6   • We built up the wall until it was continuous all round up to half its height; and the people worked with a will. • But when Sanballat and Tobiah, and the Arabs and Ammonites and Ashdodites, heard that the new work on the walls of Jerusalem had made progress and that the closing up of the breaches had gone ahead, they were furious, • and all banded together to launch an attack on Jerusalem and create confusion. • So we prayed to our God, and posted a guard against them
10   day and night. • In Judah it was said:

> The labourers' strength has failed,
>   and there is too much rubble;
> by ourselves we shall never be able
>   to rebuild the wall.

• Our adversaries said, 'Before they know it or see anything, we shall be upon them, killing them and putting an end to the work.' • When the Jews living nearby came into the city, they warned us a dozen times that our adversaries would gather from every place where they lived to attack us. • Accordingly I posted my people by families, armed with swords, spears, and bows.
16   • From that day forward half the men under me were engaged in the actual building, while the other half stood by holding their spears, shields, and bows, and wearing coats of mail; and officers supervised all the people of Judah • who were engaged on the wall. The porters carrying the loads held their load with one hand and a weapon with the other. • The builders had their swords attached to their belts as they built. The trumpeter stayed beside me, • and I said to the nobles, the magistrates, and all the people: 'The work is great and extends over much ground, and we are
20   widely separated on the wall, each man at some distance from his neighbour. • Wherever you hear the trumpet sound, rally to us there, and our God will fight for us.'
       • So with half the men holding spears we continued the work from daybreak until the stars came out. • At the same time I had said to the people, 'Let every man ▸

Nehemiah on the Rebuilding of the Walls (cont.)

have been Hezekiah's Siloam Pool (see map 3). The reason for Nehemiah's initial secrecy emerges quickly.

Sanballat was governor of Samaria, which was the name of the Persian district covering the old northern kingdom, and he regarded himself as superior in rank to Nehemiah. *Tobiah* was governor of Ammon, and *Arab* tribes now occu-

pied the southern border of Judaea; which meant that all her neighbours were united in hostility.

Nehemiah's reaction shows his usual positive and persuasive leadership (e.g. the *we* of 2.17). His attitude in 4.9 anticipates Cromwell's 'Trust in God and keep your powder dry.' The working day was extended (21) by an hour beyond the

Nehemiah on the Rebuilding of the Walls (cont.)

and his servant remain all night inside Jerusalem, to act as a guard for us by night and a working party by day.' • Neither I nor my kinsmen nor the men under me nor my bodyguard ever took off our clothes; each one kept his right hand on his spear.

5.1 • There came a time when the common people, both men and women, raised a great outcry against their fellow-Jews. • Some complained that they had to give their sons and daughters as pledges for food to eat to keep themselves alive; • others that they were mortgaging their fields, vineyards, and homes to buy grain during the famine; • still others that they were borrowing money on their fields and vineyards to

5 pay the king's tax. • 'But', they said, 'our bodily needs are the same as other people's, our children are as good as theirs; yet here we are, forcing our sons and daughters into slavery. Some of our daughters are already enslaved, and there is nothing we can do, because our fields and vineyards now belong to others.'

• When I heard their outcry and the story they told, I was greatly incensed, • but I controlled my feelings and reasoned with the nobles and the magistrates. I said to them, 'You are holding your fellow-Jews as pledges for debt.' I rebuked them severely • and said, 'As far as we have been able, we have bought back our fellow-Jews who had been sold to foreigners; but you are now selling your own fellow-countrymen, and they will have to be bought back by us!' They were silent and had not a word to say.

• I went on, 'What you are doing is wrong. You ought to live so much in the fear of our God that you are above reproach in the eyes of the nations who are

10 our enemies. • Speaking for myself, I and my kinsmen and the men under me are advancing them money and grain. Let us give up this taking of pledges for debt. • This very day give them back their fields and vineyards, their olive groves and houses, as well as the income in money, in grain, new wine, and oil.' 'We shall give them back', they promised, 'and exact nothing more. We shall do as you say.' Then after summoning the priests I put the offenders on oath to do as they had promised. • Also I shook out the fold of my robe and said, 'So may God shake out from house and property every man who fails to keep this promise. May he be shaken out like this and emptied!' All the assembled people said 'Amen' and praised the LORD; and they did as they had promised.   (REB)

Nehemiah on the Rebuilding of the Walls (cont.)

normal time of sunset. The plan of v.22 was necessary to prevent infiltration. By dint of all these measures, 'the wall was finished' in 52 days [6.15].

From the building of the wall we switch suddenly to an unrelated problem, the decline of *the common people* into debt-slavery* (5.1-5). That foreigners should take advantage of Jews was bad enough; that Jews should exploit other Jews in this

way had always called forth the strongest criticism, especially from the prophets. The books of Leviticus and Deuteronomy (15.12-17) made provision against it, and here Nehemiah is repre-sented as implementing that ideal legisla-tion. As before, he is both firm and diplo-matic (v. 10). His symbolic action (v.12) had the effect of a curse upon those who refused to comply.

INTRODUCTION TO THE HISTORICAL ROMANCES

Esther, Daniel 1-6, Tobit, Judith etc.

With the Book of Esther we finally leave behind the great tradition of powerful Hebrew prose which runs from Genesis through to 2 Kings. That tradition was based on short taut units of story, about the length of one chapter, woven together into longer sequences. Apart from some legendary material, especially miracles ascribed to the heroes, the general tone was sober and even humanistic. Obviously it was 'religious' writing, but it was not pious – except, admittedly, for some parts of the Priestly and deuteronomic works, which are not heavily represented in this selection. God's presence was sometimes felt at work behind the scenes, e.g. in the tale of Joseph or in the book of Ruth. More often he is present in the stories, but the very fact of being one of the *dramatis personae* renders him responsive to men's acts and words. One way or another therefore the human actors retained – though they often abused – their initiative. The earlier writings could also be called historical, in the sense that their authors sought to place their stories in a wider context, both nationally and internationally. But not until the books of Kings did we find what a modern historian expects as a minimal framework, the rulers set in a wider context.

From the Book of Esther onwards Hebrew narrative prose changes. Except for the books of the Maccabees, it all falls under the heading of romance. In a romance the basic ingredients of the plot, mixed in varying proportions, are the following: (i) love, or at least sex; (ii) either a journey (quest) or a conflict (military, political or religious); and (iii) at least one reversal of fortune (peripeteia*, in the technical term). Finally, the story leads to (iv) a 'happy' ending, usually with the weak prevailing over the strong. As far as that goes, the tale of Joseph and the Book of Ruth rank as romances.

But the later biblical romances differ in a number of respects. To start with religion, men no longer wrestle with God: they are more concerned with maintaining their own pieties in the face of their enemies and persecutors, and the romances record their success in doing so. Some of them rely on miracles of the older style (e.g. Daniel 1-6) but the dominant tone is a kind of realism which was popular in Persian and Greek literature of the period.

Historical realism is sought by detailed references to famous kings and their regnal years and by the citation of 'official' documents. Scenic realism is sought by detailed descriptions of the 'props' – buildings, furnishings, clothes, jewellery – and by dramatic gestures with them. Psychological realism is sought not only through speeches and 'prayers' but by authorial comment. Yet the characters hardly ever come to life, and the language used suffers from the associated weaknesses of rhetorical inflation and prosaic flabbiness. In modern terms, the whole effect is closest to the historical novel, or costume drama, with touches of opera and of genre-painting. In spite of – or perhaps because of – all that, these stories achieved a wide popular appeal among the Jews, and have sustained it into the Christian tradition: indeed their influence on European art and music has been greater than upon European literature.

The Bible contains two other kinds of writing which belong to the same period (roughly the last 500 years BC). The first is apocalyptic*, which stands in the same relation to earlier prophecy as the prose romances to earlier narrative. The second is Wisdom writing, and it is there above all (especially in Job and Ecclesiastes) that we can recognise and salute the continuing genius of Hebrew literature.

ESTHER

Introduction

The Book of Esther has two themes. The main one is an escape of the Jews from a pogrom under the Persian empire. The other is the institution of the popular festival of Purim. According to the book, the festival was established in order to celebrate the escape, and Esther is still the prescribed synagogue reading for Purim.

Purim is, and has always been, as near to a 'secular' feast as one can get, with wine flowing freely; indeed it may originally have sprung from a Persian New Year festival. Accordingly, it is not surprising to find a markedly secular tone in the Hebrew text of Esther (for the Greek additions see below). The name of God is never mentioned explicitly, nor is providence referred to except allusively in 4.14. No religious belief or pious practice is mentioned at any point. Feasting however is a feature of the story: five banquets are described, and a great deal of other drinking alluded to. Moreover the morality of the book is crude: the treatment of many characters is unfeelingly, even gratuitously, cruel, and the author shows no qualms. Some of the cruelties are inflicted upon Jews, some by them. In conse-

quence, the rabbis hesitated long before admitting Esther to the canon* (it is the only book in the Hebrew Bible of which no fragments have been found at Qumran*), and many devout Christians, notably Luther, have regretted that they did so.

When all that is said, the story is well constructed. Events follow clearly and quite plausibly to their climax, and the reversals of fortune are neatly enough contrived. The author's interest in event rather than character has given a free hand to later writers, especially dramatists. More than 150 plays have been written on the Esther theme by authors as distinguished as Lope de Vega, Racine, Goethe, Grillparzer and Max Brod. Racine, writing a tragedy, had to make Haman rather than Esther the central character; Goethe's handling is nearer to comic opera.

The Greek (LXX) manuscripts of Esther contain chunks of additional material which make the book about half as long again. Christians award this material only secondary status, and from a literary point of view even that is rather high. The full LXX text is printed in NJB, and in REB under Apocrypha.

The Fall of Queen Vashti

1.1 The events here related happened in the days of Ahasuerus, that Ahasuerus who ruled from India to Ethiopia, a hundred and twenty-seven provinces, • at the time when he was settled on the royal throne in Susa, the capital city. • In the third year of his reign he gave a banquet for all his officers and his courtiers; the Persians and Medes in full force, along with his nobles and provincial rulers, were in attendance. • He put on display for many days, a hundred and eighty in all, the dazzling wealth of his kingdom and the pomp and splendour of his realm. 5 • At the end of that time the king gave a banquet for all the people present in Susa the capital city, both high and low; it lasted for seven days and was held in the garden court of the royal pavilion. • There were white curtains and violet hangings fastened to silver rings by cords of fine linen with purple thread; the pillars were of marble, and gold and silver couches were placed on a mosaic pavement of malachite, marble, mother-of-pearl, and turquoise. • Wine was served in golden goblets, each of a different design: the king's wine flowed in royal style, • and the drinking was according to no fixed rule, for the king had laid down that all the palace stewards should respect the wishes of each guest. • Queen Vashti too gave a banquet for the women inside the royal palace of King Ahasuerus.

The Fall of Queen Vashti (cont.)

10 • On the seventh day, when he was merry with wine, the king ordered Mehuman, Biztha, Harbona, Bigtha, Abagtha, Zethar, and Carcas, the seven eunuchs who were in attendance on the king's person, • to bring Queen Vashti into his presence wearing her royal diadem, in order to display her beauty to the people and to the officers; for she was indeed a beautiful woman. • But when the royal command was conveyed to her by the eunuchs, Queen Vashti refused to come. This greatly incensed the king, and his wrath flared up. • He conferred with wise men versed in precedents, for it was his custom to consult all who were expert in law and usage. • Those closest to the king were Carshena, Shethar, Admatha, Tarshish, Meres, Marsena, and Memucan, the seven vicegerents of Persia and Media; they had access to the king and occupied the premier positions in the kingdom. •

15 'What', he asked, 'does the law require to be done with Queen Vashti for disobeying my royal command conveyed to her by the eunuchs?'

• In the presence of the king and the vicegerents, Memucan declared: 'Queen Vashti has done wrong, not to the king alone, but also to all the officers and to all the peoples in every province of King Ahasuerus. • The queen's conduct will come to the ears of all women and embolden them to treat their husbands with disrespect; they will say, "King Ahasuerus ordered Queen Vashti to be brought before him, but she would not come!" • The great ladies of Persia and Media, who have heard what the queen has said, will quote this day to all the king's officers, and there will be no end to the disrespect and discord!   ▸

The Fall of Queen Vashti

The first chapter breathes power (1) and wealth (3, 6), wielded by an absolute monarch (19-22). The name *Ahasuerus* is the Hebrew equivalent of Xerxes, the Persian king who unsuccessfully invaded Greece in 480 BC. He is portrayed as quick to anger but also ready to seek advice – two characteristics required for the development of the story. *Vashti* is unknown to history, but she also is necessary to the story, so as to make room for the improbable rise of Esther. Many features of the chapter are entirely convincing: the great public *banquet* in the winter residence of *Susa*, the private party *for the women* of the court, the consultation with the *wise men*, the importance of the *eunuchs*, and the promulgation of the *edict* in every *language* and *script*. These are all attested elsewhere of the Persian court. To back them up, the author also uses a number of Persian words, including *datam*, an *edict* (19, 20 etc.). Old Persian being an Indo-european language, that is the same word as Latin *datum* i.e. something given or laid down. Plausible also is the argument in v. 16 that the queen's offence, having been committed in public (hence the importance of *all the people* in v. 5), must rank as an affair of state. Other details are less convincing, e.g. the banquet lasting half a year (4).

The chapter makes play with two sexual motifs familiar in romance. First is the king's desire, as the climax of the seven days, to show off his wife's beauty (11). The mention of *wearing her royal diadem* suggested to the rabbis that she was otherwise naked – probably wrongly, though Herodotus does have a famous story of an eastern king wanting to show his wife naked to his most trusted courtier. Vashti's dignified refusal is contrasted with the bluster of the men. Those who command a great empire are satirised as fearing the loss of domestic authority.

The Fall of Queen Vashti (cont.)

1.20 • 'If it please your majesty, let a royal decree be issued by you, and let it be inscribed among the laws of the Persians and Medes, never to be revoked, that Vashti shall not again appear before King Ahasuerus; and let your majesty give her place as queen to another who is more worthy of it than she. • When the edict made by the king is proclaimed throughout the length and breadth of the kingdom, all women, high and low alike, will give honour to their husbands.'

• The advice pleased the king and the vicegerents, and the king did as Memucan had proposed. • Dispatches were sent to all the king's provinces, to every province in its own script and to every people in their own language, in order that each man, whatever language he spoke, should be master in his own house. (REB)

The Fall of Queen Vashti (cont.)

This second motif, the question 'who wears the trousers?' (17-22), has always been a theme of popular (until recently, comic) literature. It is ironically appropriate here, since the king will soon find himself completely dominated by his new queen.

Ch. 1 also illustrates the author's verbal repetitiveness. In v.4 we find two word-pairs and two parallel phrases, which together add up to very little; also one of his pedantic additions 'a long time, 180 days'. The speed and tension of the narrative is further slackened by lists (6, 10, 14), flashbacks (8b) and informative asides (13).

Esther Becomes Queen

2.1 Some time later, when the anger of King Ahasuerus had died down, he called Vashti to mind, remembering what she had done and what had been decreed against her. • The king's attendants said: 'Let there be sought out for your majesty beautiful young virgins; • let your majesty appoint commissioners in every province of your kingdom to assemble all these beautiful young virgins and bring them to the women's quarters in the capital Susa. Have them placed under the care of Hegai, the king's eunuch who has charge of the women, and let him provide the cosmetics they need. • The girl who is most acceptable to the king shall become queen in place of Vashti.' The advice pleased the king, and he acted on it.

5 • In Susa the capital there lived a Jew named Mordecai son of Jair, son of Shimei, son of Kish, a Benjamite; • he had been taken into exile from Jerusalem among those whom King Nebuchadnezzar of Babylon had carried away with King Jehoiachin of Judah. • He had a foster-child Hadassah, that is, Esther, his uncle's daughter, who had neither father nor mother. She was a beautiful and charming girl, and after the death of her parents, Mordecai had adopted her as his own daughter.

• When the king's order and decree were proclaimed and many girls were brought to Susa the capital to be committed to the care of Hegai, who had charge of the women, Esther too was taken to the palace to be entrusted to him. • He found her pleasing, and she received his special favour: he promptly supplied her with her cosmetics and her allowance of food, and also with seven specially chosen maids from the king's palace. She and her maids were marked out for favourable treatment in the women's quarters. ▸

Esther Becomes Queen (cont.)

10 • Esther had not disclosed her race or family, because Mordecai had forbidden her to do so. • Every day Mordecai would walk past the forecourt of the women's quarters to learn how Esther fared and what was happening to her.

• The full period of preparation before a girl went to King Ahasuerus was twelve months: six months' treatment with oil of myrrh, and six months' with perfumes and cosmetics. At the end of this each girl's turn came, • and, when she went from the women's quarters to the king's palace, she was allowed to take with her whatever she asked. • She would enter the palace in the evening and return in the morning to another part of the women's quarters, to be under the care of Shaashgaz, the king's eunuch in charge of the concubines. She would not go again to the king unless he expressed a wish for her and she was summoned by name.

15 • When the turn came for Esther, the girl Mordecai had adopted, the daughter of his uncle Abihail, to go in to the king, she asked for nothing to take with her except what was advised by Hegai, the king's eunuch in charge of the women. Esther charmed all who saw her, • and when she was brought to King Ahasuerus in the royal palace, in the tenth month, the month of Tebeth, in the seventh year of his reign, • the king loved her more than any of his other women. He treated her with greater favour and kindness than all the rest of the virgins, and placed a royal diadem on her head, making her queen in place of Vashti. • Then in Esther's honour the king gave a great banquet, to which were invited all his officers and courtiers. He also proclaimed a holiday throughout his provinces and distributed gifts worthy of a king.

21 • One day when Mordecai was at court, two of the king's eunuchs, Bigthan and Teresh, keepers of the threshold who were disaffected, were plotting to assassinate King Ahasuerus. • This became known to Mordecai, who told Queen Esther; and she, on behalf of Mordecai, informed the king. • The matter was investigated and, the report being confirmed, the two men were hanged on the gallows. All this was recorded in the court chronicle in the king's presence.   (REB)

Esther Becomes Queen

Ch. 2 introduces two more of the main characters, Mordecai and Esther, and also gives important hints of future developments. Mordecai is introduced as belonging to the family of King Saul. If the chronology of v.6 were accepted, he would now be about 120, but these telescopings are common in the historical romances. His name *Mordecai* is Persian-Babylonian, derived from the god Marduk. In the case of Esther we are given both her names: *Hadassah* is Hebrew for myrtle, *Esther* its Persian alternative, perhaps the same as the goddess Ishtar.

The two Jewish characters fill complementary roles. Esther must have the ear of the king, and therefore cannot take risks. To become queen, she must conceal her nationality (10). And when she succeeds, she must conform to Persian customs: she cannot afford the adherence to strict Judaism which is claimed for Tobit, Judith and Daniel. But while Esther is with the king, Mordecai is working off stage (10, 22), and can afford a risk (11).

The competition for the role of queen is a favourite theme of romance, best known in the story of Scheherazade from the *1,001 Nights*. Esther succeeded not by telling stories but, apart from her beauty, by her modesty and compliance (15) – quite a change from Vashti! The contrast is underlined by the special *banquet* given for her by the king (18). The excursus on harem life in vv.12-14 has little

Esther Becomes Queen (cont.)

relevance to the story, but it adds 'realism', and popular curiosity about such matters is perennial.

The incident of vv.21-23 is a crucial link in the story, as will appear in Ch. 6. The author often handles events like this by flashbacks (see vv.5-7 and 10; the latter has two, one within another). Here however he needs the incident to sustain the narrative: without it, we might think the whole tale was over with v.18. Historically it is entirely plausible: Xerxes did

have his scribes record meritorious deeds at the battle of Salamis, and he was in fact assassinated in just such a palace intrigue. The fact that two *eunuchs* are bodyguards shows that 'eunuch' has come to mean no more than 'court official'.

The flabbiness of the author's descriptions is seen e.g. in v.15 (which repeats information from vv.3 and 7) and v.17, where REB's *virgins* is very coy. By contrast his silence about motives in vv.10 and 15 is quite in the old tradition.

Haman's Plot against the Jews

3. 1 It was after those events that King Ahasuerus promoted Haman son of Hammedatha the Agagite, advancing him and giving him precedence above all his fellow-officers. • Everyone in attendance on the king at court bowed down and did obeisance to Haman, for so the king had commanded; but Mordecai would not bow or do obeisance. • The courtiers said to him, 'Why do you flout his majesty's command?' • They challenged him day after day, and when he refused to listen they informed Haman, in order to discover if Mordecai's con-
5 duct would be tolerated, for he had told them that he was a Jew. • Haman was furious when he saw that Mordecai was not bowing down or doing obeisance to him; • but having learnt who Mordecai's people were, he scorned to lay hands on him alone; he looked for a way to exterminate not only Mordecai but all the Jews throughout the whole kingdom.

• Haman said to King Ahasuerus: 'Dispersed in scattered groups among the peoples throughout the provinces of your realm, there is a certain people whose laws are different from those of every other people. They do not observe the king's laws, and it does not befit your majesty to tolerate them. • If it please your majesty, let an order be drawn up for their destruction; and I shall hand over to your majesty's officials the sum of ten thousand talents of silver, to be deposited
10 in the royal treasury.' • The king drew off the signet ring from his finger and gave it to Haman son of Hammedatha the Agagite, the enemy of the Jews. • 'Keep the money,' he said, 'and deal with the people as you think best.'   ▸

Haman's Plot against the Jews

Ch. 3 introduces the last of the four main characters, and the action quickens. The hostility between Haman and Mordecai is racial, alike in its cause and in its consequence. *Haman* is presented as a descendant of Saul's enemy Agag, king of the Amalekites, who were hereditary enemies of the Jews. It was therefore a matter of national pride that Mordecai refused obeisance to Haman – and he tactlessly let

the reason be known (v.4, an awkward flashback, but essential to the story). Haman's reactions of anger (5) and contempt (6) combine the two chief emotions in the author's repertoire (cp. 1.12, 18 and 2.1).

Haman's presentation of his case to the king is dramatically skilful: he conceals both the name of the *certain people* and his own motivation. It also contains material of the direst historical import. For

Haman's Plot against the Jews (cont.)

• On the thirteenth day of the first month the king's secretaries were summoned and, in accordance with Haman's instructions, a writ was issued to the king's satraps and the governors of every province, and to the rulers over each separate people. It was drawn up in the name of King Ahasuerus and sealed with the king's signet, and transcribed for each province in its own script and for each people in their own language. • Dispatches were sent by courier to all the king's provinces with orders to destroy, slay, and exterminate all Jews, young and old, women and children, in one day, the thirteenth day of the twelfth month, the month of Adar; their goods were to be treated as spoil. • A copy of the writ was to be issued as a decree in every province and to be publicly displayed to all the peoples, so that they might be ready for that day. • At the king's command the couriers set off post-haste, and the decree was issued in Susa the capital city. The king and Haman sat down to carouse, but in the city of Susa confusion reigned.   (REB)

15

Haman's Plot against the Jews (cont.)

this is the very charge which has been made throughout history against the Jews of the dispersion. From the time of the Babylonian exile onwards, the Jews have sought to preserve their national identity by adherence to those parts of the Torah which Catholicished them from their gentProtestantours. And all the efforts which the Jews made to safeguard their own way of life were turned into grounds of hatred, fear and contempt by those who outnumbered them. Jewish literature is full of defences of their position, Greek and Latin of attacks upon it. The charge is summed up in the Greek addition to this chapter [v.13d, NJB], that the Jews are 'in opposition to all humanity'. It was later extended to the Christians, of whom Tacitus says that after the fire of Rome in 64 AD they were cruelly punished 'not so much for causing the fire as for their hatred of the human race'. It is not a long step from there to the Holocaust.

Haman's approach to the king included a fantastic bribe, equal to two-thirds of the annual revenue of the empire. This offer proved superfluous; but the advice, once again, was accepted. The gift of *the signet-ring* symbolised the highest trust: there is an echo here of the same trust shown by Pharaoh to Joseph in Gen 41.42. Historically, the imperial postal service (12) was a vaunted invention of the Persians. The *writ* is summarized with a verbosity which for once is effective, as representing legal diction (13). The Greek additions include what purports to be its actual text, but it is a poor imitation. For ancient history does record an actual such document. In 88 BC Mithradates the (Persian) king of Pontus organised a massacre of all the Romans within his sphere of influence. According to the Greek historian Appian,

he wrote secretly to all satraps and city governors that on the 30th day thereafter they should set upon all Romans and Italians in their towns and upon their wives and children and freedmen of Italian birth, and having killed them throw their bodies out unburied, and share their goods with King Mithradates. . . . These secret orders he sent to all the cities at the same time. When the appointed day came atrocities of the most varied kinds were perpetrated throughout Asia [i.e. what is now Western Turkey].

Ancient authors give figures of the deaths in that massacre ranging from 80,000 to 150,000.

Mordecai Persuades Esther to Intercede

4.1   When Mordecai learnt of all that had been done, he tore his clothes and put on sackcloth and ashes. He went out through the city, lamenting loudly and bitterly, • until he came right in front of the palace gate; no one wearing sackcloth was allowed to pass through that gate. • In every province reached by the royal command and decree there was great mourning among the Jews, with fasting and weeping and beating of the breast; most of them lay down on beds of sackcloth and ashes. • When Queen Esther's maids and eunuchs came in and told her, she was greatly distraught. She sent clothes for Mordecai to wear instead of his sackcloth; but he would not accept them.

5   • Esther then summoned Hathach, one of the king's eunuchs appointed to wait on her, and ordered him to find out from Mordecai what was the trouble and the reason for it. • Hathach went out to Mordecai in the city square opposite the palace, • and Mordecai told him all that had happened to him and how much money Haman had offered to pay into the royal treasury for the destruction of the Jews. • He also gave him a copy of the writ for their extermination, which had been issued in Susa, so that he might show it to Esther and tell her about it, directing her to go to the king to implore his favour and intercede for her people.

9,10   • When Hathach came in and informed Esther of what Mordecai had said, • she told him to take back this message: • 'All the courtiers and the people in the king's provinces know that if any person, man or woman, enters the royal presence in the inner court without being summoned, there is but one law: that person shall be put to death, unless the king extends to him the gold sceptre; only then may he live. What is more, I have not been summoned to the king for the last thirty days.' ▶

Mordecai Persuades Esther to Intercede

Ch. 4 marks two important transitions. The lead is transferred from Mordecai to Esther, and the focus from the city to the palace and finally (5.1) to its inner court. The first section 1-7 moves slowly. The main points are these. Mordecai and all the Jews (though not yet Esther) adopted the mourning rituals commonly used to avert a catastrophe. Mordecai's own *bitter* cry (1) was however something different viz. a protest against injustice (the same word is used of the deceived Esau's cry in Gen 27.34). He would indeed have made his protest to the king were it not for the Persian custom whereby people of ill omen might not come into the royal presence. Verse 4 then introduces what is to be dramatically the most interesting sequence of the chapter (and psychologically, of the book), namely a developing tension and even a role-reversal (17) between Esther and Mordecai – conducted through messengers.

First she would help him gain access to the king, but he refuses – for she, not he, must be the intercessor. Then with v.9 the tension rises. For we now learn that Esther has lost her own easy access to the king. For the first time in five years a whole month has passed *without* her *being summoned* to the king. To approach him uninvited would be to risk her life. Mordecai does not deny the risk (which indeed Herodotus confirms as true of the Persian court), but presses her to accept it. His speech is the nearest the book gets to a theological reference. The words *from another quarter* (14) imply a divine intervention, in which case Esther must expect to be called to account for her failure to help her people.

Mordecai's arguments steel Esther's resolve. What will be will be – she uses the same idiom as Jacob in Gen 43.14 – and she prepares herself for the ordeal.

Mordecai Persuades Esther to Intercede (cont.)

16
• When Mordecai was told what Esther had said, • he sent this reply, 'Do not imagine, Esther, that, because you are in the royal palace, you alone of all the Jews will escape. • If you remain silent at such a time as this, relief and deliverance for the Jews will appear from another quarter; but you and your father's family will perish. And who knows whether it is not for a time like this that you have become queen?' • Esther sent this answer back to Mordecai: • 'Go and assemble all the Jews that are in Susa, and fast on my behalf; for three days, night and day, take neither food nor drink, and I also will fast with my maids. After that, in defiance of the law, I shall go to the king; if I perish, I perish.' • Mordecai then went away and did exactly as Esther had bidden him.   (REB)

Mordecai Persuades Esther to Intercede (cont.)

Fasting was another ritual of mourning, so it serves with v.3 to frame the chapter. It also reasserts her identification with her own people by contrast with all that Persian feasting. Yet strangely what is not said here is almost more striking than what is. Commonly fasting is associated with prayer: so for example in the parallel scene in the book of Judith. It is as if the (Hebrew) author is wilfully omitting all reference to prayer. The author of the Greek additions however inserts two prayers here, a long one for Mordecai and an even longer one for Esther.

Plotting by Both Sides

5.1
On the third day Esther arrayed herself in her royal robes and stood in the inner court, facing the palace itself; the king was seated on his royal throne in the palace, opposite the entrance. • When he caught sight of Queen Esther standing in the court, he extended to her the gold sceptre he held, for she had obtained his favour. Esther approached and touched the tip of the sceptre. • The king said to her, 'What is it, Queen Esther? Whatever you request, up to half my kingdom, it shall be granted you.' • 'If it please your majesty,' she answered, 'will you come today, my LORD, and Haman with you, to a banquet I have prepared for you?'
5
• The king gave orders for Haman to be brought with all speed to meet Esther's wishes; and the king and Haman went to the banquet she had prepared.

• Over the wine the king said to Esther, 'Whatever you ask will be given you; whatever you request, up to half my kingdom, will be granted.' • Esther replied, 'What I ask and request is this: • If I have found favour with your majesty, and if it please you, my LORD, to give me what I ask and to grant my request, will ▶

Plotting by Both Sides

Ch. 5 builds up the tension on both sides. On Esther's side, the Hebrew of the first two verses moves matters on with speed. By contrast the Greek text adds various colourful details: Esther's 'face radiated joy and love, but her heart shrank with fear'. On her entry, the king 'looked up afire with majesty and blazing with anger'. The queen sank to the floor in a faint, 'but God changed the king's heart, inducing a milder spirit. He sprang from his throne in alarm, and took her in his arms etc. etc.'.

The offer of a free wish, *up to half* the *kingdom*, is a common feature of folk-tales. Esther's reply in v.4 is a surprise, but must not be misunderstood. The dinner-party is not itself her wish; it is to be the occasion for revealing her wish. This is made clear by the last words of v.8. But when it comes to it she coquettishly makes them wait yet

Plotting by Both Sides (cont.)

5.10

your majesty and Haman come again tomorrow to the banquet that I shall prepare for you both? Tomorrow I shall do as your majesty says.'

• Haman left the royal presence that day overjoyed and in the best of spirits, but as soon as he saw Mordecai in the king's court and observed that he did not rise or defer to him, he was furious; • yet he kept control of himself. When he arrived home, he sent for his friends and for Zeresh his wife • and held forth to them about the splendour of his wealth and his many sons, and how the king had promoted him and advanced him above the other officers and courtiers. • 'Nor is that all,' Haman went on; 'Queen Esther had no one but myself come with the king to the banquet which she had prepared; and I am invited by her again tomorrow with the king. • Yet all this gives me no satisfaction so long as I see that Jew Mordecai in attendance at the king's court.' • His wife Zeresh and all his friends said to him, 'Have a gallows set up, seventy-five feet high, and in the morning propose to the king that Mordecai be hanged on it. Then you can go with the king to the banquet and enjoy yourself.' This advice seemed good to Haman, and he set up the gallows.   (REB)

Plotting by Both Sides (cont.)

another day, thus increasing the dramatic tension – the standard 'third time lucky'.

The next scene (9-14) echoes the tone of Ch. 1. 'Farcical but black, it depicts the sinister in a domestic setting' (Clines). Like the king, the eminently hissable villain fears loss of face: indeed his outstanding characteristic is his pride, i.e. love of position (9, 13) and boastfullness (10-12). His self-*control* in v.10 is out of character but necessary to avoid a premature climax

to the story. His reference to his *many sons* (11) accords with the values of the Persian nobility as described by Herodotus: 'They attest their manliness first by valour in battle, second by siring many sons: the king sends presents each year to the man who has most.' By the same token Haman wishes to expose Mordecai to maximum ridicule: hence the height of the *gallows*. All this prepares splendidly for the reversal which will come within 24 hours.

The Humiliation of Haman

6.1

That night sleep eluded the king, so he ordered the chronicle of memorable events to be brought, and it was read to him. • There it was found recorded how Mordecai had furnished information about Bigthana and Teresh, the two royal eunuchs among the keepers of the threshold who had plotted to assassinate King Ahasuerus. • When the king asked what honour or dignity had been conferred on Mordecai for this, his attendants said, 'Nothing has been done for him.' • 'Who is in the court?' said the king. As Haman had just then entered the outer court of the palace to propose to the king that Mordecai should be hanged on the gallows he

5

had prepared for him, • the king's attendants replied, 'Haman is standing there in the court.' 'Let him enter!' commanded the king. • When he came in, the king ▶

The Humiliation of Haman

Ch. 6 records the first step in Haman's downfall: his pride is humbled to the point where, instead of Mordecai honouring

him, he must honour Mordecai. The sequence of events is linked by coincidences, in which the eye of faith

The Humiliation of Haman (cont.)

asked him, 'What should be done for the man whom the king wishes to honour?' Haman thought to himself, 'Whom, other than myself, would the king wish to honour?' • So he answered, 'For the man whom the king wishes to honour, • let there be brought a royal robe which the king himself has worn, and a horse on which the king rides, with a royal diadem on its head. • Let the robe and the horse be handed over to one of the king's noble officers, and let him invest the man whom the king wishes to honour and lead him mounted on the horse through the city square, proclaiming as he goes: "This is what is done for the man whom the king wishes to honour." ' • The king said to Haman, 'Take the robe and the horse at once, as you have said, and do this for Mordecai the Jew who is present at court. Let nothing be omitted of all you have proposed.' • Haman took the robe and the horse, invested Mordecai, and led him on horseback through the city square, proclaiming before him: 'This is what is done for the man whom the king wishes to honour.'

• Mordecai then returned to court, while Haman in grief hurried off home with his head veiled. • When he told his wife Zeresh and all his friends everything that had happened to him, the response he got from his advisers and Zeresh was: 'If you have begun to fall before Mordecai, and he is a Jew, you cannot get the better of him; your downfall before him is certain.'   (REB)

The Humiliation of Haman (cont.)

discerns the action of providence; but they are not obtrusive. The royal insomnia, which is the setting of the *Arabian Nights*, is also a common theme in Persian contexts in the Bible e.g. Dan 6.18. Herodotus confirms that Persian kings not only recorded details of meritorious deeds but made it a point of honour to reward them. Haman's appearance at dawn follows his plan of 5.14, but he was never given the chance to make his petition.

Instead there follows a magnificent scene of comic irony, with Haman combining the roles of the fool in ANE Wisdom literature and the *alazon*, or vainglorious man, of Greek comedy. In line with his own proposals, which mirror but exceed what Pharaoh did for Joseph in Gen 41.42-3, extravagant honours are heaped upon his enemy, while he himself is reduced to the humble role of groom – all in full public view. The *diadem* worn by the *horse* in v.8 is a misinterpretation of the ceremonial top-knot such as is represented in the wall-reliefs of Persepolis. The only puzzle here is the king's use of the phrase *Mordecai the Jew* (10). Mordecai had neither concealed nor paraded his nationality (3.4), but we do not expect such a casual reference here while the royal decree of extermination is still in force. Evidently the king still did not know the identity of the nation he had condemned.

When the investiture is over, Mordecai returns modestly to his post, while Haman hurries home. His friends observe him in mourning and console him with the prospect of worse to come, a warning which is reinforced by the sinister tone of v.14. The motif of a gentile forecast of Jewish victory is common in the OT from Rahab the harlot onwards (Jos 2); to a Jewish reader it was an acknowledgement of providence.

Haman Hanged

6.14 While they were still talking with him, the king's eunuchs arrived and Haman was hurried off to the banquet Esther had prepared.

7. 1 • So the king and Haman went to Queen Esther's banquet, • and again on that second day over the wine the king said, 'Whatever you ask will be given you, Queen Esther. Whatever you request, up to half my kingdom, it will be granted.' • She answered, 'If I have found favour with your majesty, and if it please you, my Lord, what I ask is that my own life and the lives of my people be spared. • For we have been sold, I and my people, to be destroyed, slain, and exterminated. If it had been a matter of selling us, men and women alike, into slavery, I should have kept silence; for then our plight would not have been such as to 5 injure the king's interests.' • King Ahasuerus demanded, 'Who is he, and where is he, who has dared to do such a thing?' • 'A ruthless enemy,' she answered, 'this wicked Haman!' Haman stood aghast before the king and queen. • In a rage the king rose from the banquet and went into the garden of the pavilion, while Haman remained where he was to plead for his life with Queen Esther; for he saw that in the king's mind his fate was determined.

• When the king returned from the pavilion garden to the banqueting hall, Haman had flung himself on the couch where Esther was reclining. The king exclaimed, 'Will he even assault the queen in the palace before my very eyes?' The words had no sooner left the king's lips than Haman's face was covered. • Harbona, one of the eunuchs in attendance on the king, said, 'There is a gallows seventy-five feet high standing at Haman's house; he had it erected for Mordecai, whose evidence once saved your majesty.' 'Let Haman be hanged on it!' said the 10 king. • So they hanged Haman on the gallows he had prepared for Mordecai. Then the king's anger subsided.   (REB)

Haman Hanged

The denouement comes at yet another *banquet*. Esther now, on the third occasion, comes out with her request. The exchange is marked by parallelism on both sides, of which the last instance is lost by REB; AV follows the Hebrew by rendering: 'let my life be given me at my petition, and my people at my request.' The last part of v.4 is obscure, but probably means '... *such as to* justify troubling the king'. In v.6 Esther answers the king's two questions in turn: (i) an *enemy* (ii) here before you. The king, in his usual *rage*, then goes out into the garden – for purposes of narrative.

The scene between Haman and Esther, melodramatic in itself, is necessary to the story in two respects. First it provides another reversal of fortune, with the perse-cutor imploring the help of his intended victim. Second, it provides what was previously lacking, a capital offence, since the king himself has authorized the edict of extermination. Caught in a compromising position, perhaps clasping the knees of the queen, Haman knows the game is up, and covers his *face* in anticipation of death. But in Persia 'it was not the custom for anyone to be put to death for a single offence, even by the king: his bad deeds had first to be weighed against the good' – so (again) Herodotus reports approvingly. At this point a crucial revelation is made by the otherwise insignificant *Harbona* (9). The *gallows*, of which he informs the king, is both the climax of Haman's misdeeds, being intended for a benefactor of the king, and the instrument of his downfall.

The Jews Saved

1 That same day King Ahasuerus gave Queen Esther the property of Haman, the enemy of the Jews, and Mordecai came into the king's presence, for Esther had revealed his relationship to her. • The king drew off his signet ring, which he had taken back from Haman, and gave it to Mordecai. Esther put Mordecai in charge of Haman's property.

• Once again Esther addressed the king, falling at his feet and imploring him with tears to thwart the wickedness of Haman the Agagite and frustrate his plot against the Jews. • The king extended his gold sceptre towards her, and she rose 5 and stood before him. • 'May it please your majesty,' Esther said; 'if I have found favour with you, and if what I propose seems right to your majesty and I have won your approval, let a writ be issued to recall the dispatches which Haman son of Hammedatha the Agagite wrote in pursuance of his plan to destroy the Jews in all the royal provinces. • For how can I bear to witness the disaster which threatens my people? How can I bear to witness the destruction of my kindred?' • King Ahasuerus said to Queen Esther and to Mordecai the Jew, 'I have given Haman's property to Esther, and he has been hanged on the gallows because he threatened the lives of the Jews. • Now you may issue a writ in my name concerning the Jews, in whatever terms you think fit, and seal it with the royal signet; no order written in the name of the king and sealed with the royal signet can be rescinded.'   ▸

The Jews Saved

By Persian custom, the estate of a traitor was forfeit to the king, who passed it to Esther in compensation. The position of vizier, symbolized by the *signet-ring* (3.10), is given to Mordecai. With that the story of Haman is over, and also the tighter narrative style we have enjoyed since Ch. 3. But the danger to the Jews remains. And here the puzzle returns, for the Jews were not mentioned once in Ch. 7, and even by the end of it the king did not know Esther's nationality. Though everybody knew Mordecai was a Jew (6.10), only Mordecai knew that Esther was the same. Haman obviously guessed it in 7.6, but he died before revealing it. The king is supposed to have learned it first when Esther told him of her relationship to Mordecai in 8.1. On learning it, he shows no more interest than he had shown in the original edict of persecution. But it is that edict which poses the continuing threat; and Esther's task now is to get it neutralized – as far as possible. For it cannot simply be revoked, as is explained in v.8 (and repeated in Dan 6.8).

Esther therefore makes an immediate plea to the king, falling at *his feet* in supplication. His use of the *sceptre* has nothing to do with access: the Persepolis relief shows that he kept it with him throughout an audience. Her speech begins with no fewer than four formulae of deprecation (5). The last of these is personal, and is picked up by her main argument, which is also based on her own suffering.

The king cannot grant her specific request for a revocation of the edict. That apart, he will allow her a free hand, with the *signet* ring to authorize it. As in Ch. 3 (of which the narrative here has many

The Jews Saved (cont.)

8. 10 • On the twenty-third day of the third month, the month of Sivan, the king's secretaries were summoned, and a writ exactly as Mordecai directed was issued to the Jews, and to the satraps, the governors, and the rulers of the hundred and twenty provinces from India to Ethiopia; it was issued for each province in its own script and for each people in their own language, and also for the Jews in their script and language. • The writ was drawn up in the name of King Ahasuerus and sealed with the royal signet, and dispatches were sent by couriers mounted on horses from the royal stables. • By these dispatches the king granted permission to the Jews in each and every city to assemble in self-defence, and to destroy, slay, and exterminate every man, woman, and child, of any people or province which might attack them, and to treat their goods as spoil, • throughout all the provinces of King Ahasuerus, in one day, the thirteenth day of Adar, the twelfth month. • A copy of the writ was to be issued as a decree in every province and published to all peoples, and the Jews were to be ready for that day, the day of vengeance on their enemies. • Couriers, mounted on horses from the royal stables, set off post-haste at the king's urgent command; and the decree was proclaimed also in Susa the capital.

15 • When Mordecai left the king's presence in a royal robe of violet and white, wearing an imposing gold crown and a cloak of fine linen with purple thread, the city of Susa shouted for joy. • All was light and joy, gladness and honour for the Jews; • in every province and city reached by the royal command and decree there was joy and gladness for the Jews, feasting and holiday. And many of the peoples of the world professed Judaism, because fear of the Jews had fallen on them.   (REB)

The Jews Saved (cont.)

echoes) he effectively washes his hands of the affair, leaving others to solve it. The solution is to issue a second edict, a *writ* allowing the Jews to defend themselves against the attacks encouraged by the first. The dating of it leaves nine months still to go before the day, which allows the Jews time to organize concerted action in *self-defence*.

The final three verses of Ch. 8 effectively conclude the main theme of the book, viz. the escape of the Jews from a threatened pogrom. Mordecai is clothed in Persian royal colours of *violet* edged with *white*, which picks up the curtaining in 1.6. His own finery and the *joy* in *Susa* answer to the 'confusion' in Susa and his own 'sackcloth and ashes' in 3.15-4.1: the reversed order typically underscores the reversal of fortunes. The extremely full diction of vv.16-17 makes for a rallentando at the close of the narrative. The claim that *many* gentiles *professed Judaism* need not be taken seriously.

The Feast of Purim

1 On the thirteenth day of Adar, the twelfth month, the time came for the king's command and decree to be carried out. That very day on which the enemies of the Jews had hoped to triumph over them was to become the day when the Jews should triumph over those who hated them. • Throughout all the provinces of King Ahasuerus, the Jews assembled in their cities to attack those who had sought to bring disaster on them. None could offer resistance, because fear of them had 5 fallen on all the peoples. • The Jews put all their enemies to the sword. There was great slaughter and destruction, and they worked their will on those who hated 16 them. • In Susa the capital the Jews slaughtered five hundred men. • The rest of the Jews throughout the king's provinces rallied in self-defence and so had respite from their enemies; they slaughtered seventy-five thousand of those who hated them, but they took no plunder.

20   • Mordecai put these things on record, and he sent letters to all the Jews throughout the provinces of King Ahasuerus, both near and far, • requiring them to observe annually the fourteenth and fifteenth days of the month of Adar • as the days on which the Jews had respite from their enemies; that was the month which was changed for them from sorrow into joy, from a time of mourning to a holiday. They were to observe them as days of feasting and joy, days for sending presents of food to one another and gifts to the poor.   (REB)

The Feast of Purim

Ch. 9 seems rather tacked on to the main story. It records (i) not a defence but a pre-emptive *slaughter* by the Jews of their *enemies*, and (ii) the institution of the feast of Purim to celebrate the event. The slaughter has been the subject of much moralizing. But once it is seen that the book of Esther is 'popular' melodrama, there is no reason to be surprised if the morality is popular morality: in a just cause retaliation is permitted and a pre-emptive strike (v.2) excused. As to the feast of *Purim*, omitted verses give unconvincing accounts both of its duration and of the meaning of the name. Perhaps the simplest explanation is that Purim means 'portions' and refers to the *presents* of food (AV 'portions') which were given: it is thus not only a celebration of a famous national escape but also an expression of that solidarity which has been one of the strengths of Judaism down the ages.

For Esther is the original diaspora novel. The gentile state is not here seen as systematically hostile. But, like Ahasuerus himself, it is capricious. At any time, on the least provocation, it may turn on the Jews, whose life in consequence is permanently precarious. Their best policy in normal times is to keep their heads down. In times of crisis they must deploy their prime weapon, the ability to outwit and outmanoeuvre their enemies. But they have two other weapons of defence as well. One is the solidarity referred to. The other is humour – including, in the case of Esther, 'almost literally gallows humour' (Fox). This policy has served them well, except where (as classically described in Dt 28.65+) the gentile state *has* been systematically hostile.

INTRODUCTION TO THE WISDOM LITERATURE

'Wisdom literature' is a modern term coined to denote an extensive class of writing shared by the OT with the whole ANE. In form it included proverbs and riddles, fable and allegory, instruction and argument, hymns and prayers, biography and autobiography. Certain whole books of the OT and Apocrypha are classed as Wisdom books: Proverbs, Job, Ecclesiastes (Eccl), Ecclesiasticus (Ecclus) and Wisdom of Solomon. But many other books contain Wisdom sections or passages, most notably the stories of Joseph (Gen 37+) and Daniel (Dan 1-6), certain psalms, e.g. 73, and the late work 2 Esdras.

At the core of Wisdom literature is writing which does one of three things. It may describe a personified Wisdom, e.g. the hymn praising her in Job 28 and her self-praise in Prov 9 or Ecclus 24. It may tell of a man consciously seeking Wisdom, like Solomon in Eccl Chs 1-2, or exemplifying it like Daniel. Or it may give explicit advice about practical wisdom, i.e. wise conduct. But round that core there gathered a penumbra of writing which shared the same subject matter viz. the human condition in the world. The authors of all these works are presumably to be found among the 'wise men' who were recognised as a third group in Israelite society alongside the priests and the prophets [Jer 18.18].

This subject matter may seem to be the same as that of the rest of the OT. But the Wisdom writers (except Ecclus) interpreted the key terms differently. 'Human' for them was generalised: not the members of the chosen race but Everyman – and as often living in Egypt (Joseph), Babylon (Daniel) or Arabia (Job) as in Israel (Solomon). The concept of 'world' was similarly wider than elsewhere in the OT. It included natural phenomena as objects of study, and in that sense the regularities observed in nature by the Wisdom writers may be regarded as the first steps in ANE science (Job Chs 28, 39-41; Wisd Sol

Ch. 7). And when the Wisdom writers speak of God they mostly speak of him as revealed in the world. God is to them much more the principle of order in nature than he is the God of Israel's covenant and the Temple worship (Ecclus again is an exception, with Wisd Sol). As such, he is less often known by his personal name of YHWH (the LORD) than by his impersonal and more international titles (see p.34f.).

As the principle of order, God was also to be seen in the ordering of society. Here too the Wisdom writers were interested in the observed regularities of cause and effect – the first steps in *social* science. And the ordering was essentially a moral one, designed so that the wise and the good should prosper while the unrighteous suffer. But that innocent belief appeared to have a less innocent corollary: that all those who prosper deserve their fortune – and so do all those who suffer. Consequently there can be no thought of social reform. The most that can be expected is charity for the poor and strict justice for the weak. Wisdom knows little of that compassion which marks the law and the prophets (Job Chs 24 and 31 is here the exception).

Women on the other hand play an important but ambivalent role in society. The seductress is purely disruptive (see Prov 7 and its Egyptian original), but the virtuous housewife of Prov 31 holds more than the family together. In fact female figures embody most strikingly that opposition between wisdom and folly which lies at the heart of the Wisdom literature.

So the Wisdom concept of order included the social structure as it existed. Even Job complains that deference is dead: 'My retainers have forgotten me' (19.13+). Ecclus (Ch. 39) smugly contrasts his own leisure as a scribe with the disabling toil of the working classes. The many Wisdom recommendations about the conduct of life seem to be aimed at two quite different audiences. To the young of their own class the Wisdom teachers offer tips for the top: how to get on in the world and 'stand before kings'. To the general run of humanity their commonest advice is 'be content with little'.

In any traditional society wisdom tends to be conservative. It is the old who are most prone to make generalisations about life, and their advice normally errs on the side of caution. Egyptian Wisdom was particularly fond of the contrast between the 'heated', i.e. impetuous, and the 'tranquil' man; see also p.478. Other ANE Wisdom, including that of the OT, went further, being written largely by and for the rich and educated.

Education, however, is two-edged. It can, as in Proverbs and Ecclus, mean just the passing on of traditional beliefs and values. But it can also entail questioning and challenging them. People who reflect with an open mind on their experience will sooner or later come to doubt the easy equation of virtue with prosperity and of wickedness with suffering. And when they do so they will ask awkward ques-

tions about God's justice. Such questions animate the second and more remarkable sequence of Jewish Wisdom writings: Job, Eccl, Ps 73, Wisd Sol Chs 2-5 and 2 Esdras.

Everything that has been said hitherto about the Wisdom writings of the OT applies equally to the rest of the ANE. Egypt in general stands closer to the Bible, with its praise of *Ma'at*, the divine principle of order (see on Prov 8), its multiplicity of *Instructions* and its occasional satire and pessimism. But the problem of theodicy could be side-stepped in Egypt by the belief in an after-life, so it is in Babylon that we find the closer parallels to Job (see p.407f.). Greece too had its Wisdom writers: not only the earlier traditionalists like Hesiod and Solon, but those later sceptics, the sophists. The sophists throw light from another culture on the ambivalent role of education. In their case advice on how to get on in the world went hand in hand with a scepticism even more radical than that of their great contemporary, the author of Job.

JOB

Introduction

The Book of Job is universally acknowledged as one of the world's masterpieces. It has two outstanding merits, though each is flawed. First, its poetry (almost all in 3:3 rhythm) is superb. For sustained intensity of feeling, elevation of language and vividness of imagery it has few rivals. But it has the defect of much Hebrew poetry, at least to western ears. There is too much of the 'rushing mighty wind' and not enough of the 'still small voice'. That fault, however, if it lies in the poet and not in the reader, is one which can be met by selection, and for this reason some even of the most high-flown poetry is omitted here.

Secondly, its theme is as noble and tragic as can be, the wrestling of a man with god, specifically of a righteous man

with an apparently unjust god. In the technical language of theology, the book of Job is a theodicy*, an attempt, like Milton's, 'to justify the ways of God to man'. Its historical achievement is to have put to silence the traditional doctrine that a man's suffering is all a punishment for sin. But such a cold analysis is almost a caricature of the book. Its impact derives from the passionate personal relationships between Job and God and, to a lesser extent, between Job and his friends. Here lies what seems to many readers (again, perhaps, to those in the western tradition) the second weakness, in the structure of the book.

Job has three parts. First is a prose folk-tale with a common enough theme. It tells of (i) a challenge to the hero and his apparent fall; and (ii) his ultimate triumph and restoration. This folk-tale supplies the frame of the book, i.e. (i) the prologue in Chs 1-2 and (ii) the epilogue in Ch. 42. Into the frame have been fitted the two longer poetical parts: Job's debates with the friends (Chs 3-32) and with God (Chs 38-42.6). The joints between prose and poetry have been quite skilfully smoothed over (2.11-13 and 42.7-10). The story-line of the poetical parts also has some superficial folk-tale features. Job has *three* friends and *three* cycles of debate with them. These debates, and that with God which follows, are a little like the tests undergone by a folk-tale hero. But the tone, both literary and theological, of the poetry is far removed from that of the prologue and epilogue.

In the first and longer set of debates, the friends, commonly but incorrectly known as 'Job's comforters', propound the traditional theodicy while Job, maintaining his innocence, rejects it. Their dialogue does not show any progressive development of thought and argument. Each speaker repeats his piece without much reference to the last one. The development lies rather in an increasing intensity of feeling, of mutual hostility between Job and the friends, and of bitter criticism by the 'innocent' Job of the 'unjust' God. After that dialogue is concluded, a fourth friend is introduced who harangues Job from Chs 33 to 37. Almost all critics regard him as an intrusion who spoils the climax of the drama. For in the third part (Chs 38-42) God himself comes to confront Job in a scene of tremendous power. Yet even here there is some doubt whether God succeeds in answering Job's criticism. A discussion of that and some related issues is left to the end (see p.405).

And even that doubt is part of a wider uncertainty about how to read the book. For Job goes far beyond others in the OT who challenged God – Abraham, Moses and Jeremiah to his face, and the Preacher (Ecclesiastes) behind his back. Job's challenge is not only more sustained but far more hostile. His strategy is varied: praise, complaint, cross-questioning, even in the end submission – all are in his repertoire. But so are irony and even parody, with the result that it is often hard to tell how far his tongue is in his cheek. We can enjoy his parodies of his friends' pious arguments, or of psalms of praise and trust in God. But when it comes to the final confrontation, he leaves us with a lingering doubt whether his submission (40.5) and his repentance (42.6) might not be ironical too. Worse still, God seems to catch the style, and we cannot be certain what is the tone, and hence the interpretation, of the answer he gives.

One possibility of course is that Job's criticism is unanswered because it is unanswerable. Certainly it has continued to torment the religious mind and to inspire the literary imagination. *King Lear*, *Paradise Lost* and Goethe's *Faust* all deal with aspects of Job's conflict. More recently James Macleish's *J.B.* (1958), a play directly based on the biblical book, proved a commercial success.

One other difficulty faces readers of Job. The Hebrew text is among the most difficult in the OT. This is due not so much to errors of transmission as to the extremely wide vocabulary of the author. There are more words in Job than in any other OT book which are not found elsewhere in ancient Hebrew. Their meaning has to be inferred from the context and from cognate Semitic languages, ancient and modern. The inferences are often so precarious that modern translations diverge widely one from another.

The language gives no clue to the date of the book's composition. Nor are there any historical or literary allusions that could help. Only the individualistic tone may perhaps provide an indication that Job is post-exilic, say c.400 BC.

Prologue in Heaven

1 There was a man in the land of Uz, whose name was Job; and that man was perfect and upright, and one that feared God, and eschewed evil. • And there were born unto him seven sons and three daughters. • His substance also was seven thousand sheep, and three thousand camels, and five hundred yoke of oxen, and five hundred she asses, and a very great household; so that this man was the greatest of all the men of the east. • And his sons went and feasted in their houses, every one his 5 day; and sent and called for their three sisters to eat and to drink with them. • And it was so, when the days of their feasting were gone about, that Job sent and sanctified them, and rose up early in the morning, and offered burnt offerings according to the number of them all: for Job said, It may be that my sons have sinned, and cursed God in their hearts. Thus did Job continually.

• Now there was a day when the sons of God came to present themselves before the LORD, and Satan came also among them. • And the LORD said unto Satan, Whence comest thou? Then Satan answered the LORD, and said, From going to and fro in the earth, and from walking up and down in it. • And the LORD said unto Satan, Hast thou considered my servant Job, that there is none like him in the earth, a perfect and an upright man, one that feareth God, and escheweth evil? • Then Satan answered the LORD, and said, Doth Job fear God for nought? 10 • Hast not thou made an hedge about him, and about his house, and about all that he hath on every side? thou hast blessed the work of his hands, and his substance is increased in the land. • But put forth thine hand now, and touch all that he hath, and he will curse thee to thy face. • And the LORD said unto Satan, ♦

Prologue in Heaven

The prologue proper (1.1-2.10) consists of five scenes, set alternately on earth and in heaven. It is simply but skilfully told, in the best spare style of Genesis. The colouring also is patriarchal. Job is portrayed as like Abraham but richer: a semi-nomadic sheikh living on the fringes of the desert east of the Jordan. But his wealth is less notable than his virtue and piety. He is *perfect* as the circle and *upright* as the straight line. His possessions likewise, the reward of his virtue, show an arithmetical perfection. *Seven sons* was the ideal blessing (Ruth 4.15). Seven and *three* add up to ten (the fingers of both hands) – all of them regarded in the ANE as perfect numbers. Two whole verses (4-5) are given to showing his scrupulousness in the case of offences which (i) *it may be* had been committed (ii) by his *sons* (iii) *in their hearts*. Family wealth and solidarity can bring their own risks, which he does his best to cover retrospectively. The fact that the girls are unmarried shows that Job is still quite a young man.

The second scene is set in the heavenly council. There are many such scenes in the OT, of which that in 1 K. 22.19-23 is the closest. Mentions of *Satan* however are rarer. Strictly he is '*the* Satan', i.e. the Adversary (so REB translates), opponent directly of man, indirectly of God. He is evasive in his replies (1.7 and 2.2) and known in advance to be cynical about human goodness (1.9). His role as the cunning tempter and sower of distrust is like that of the serpent in the Garden of Eden, except that (astonishingly) it is here God whom he successfully tempts, though it is still man who suffers. The construction in 1.11 and 2.5 is a Hebrew idiom. Literally translated, it is 'if *he will* not *curse* you', with a suppressed main clause along the lines of the English idiom 'I'll be damned if etc.'. It is therefore not strictly accurate to call it a bet, even though Goethe made it into

Prologue in Heaven (cont.)

Behold, all that he hath is in thy power; only upon himself put not forth thine hand. So Satan went forth from the presence of the LORD.

1.15 • And there was a day when his sons and his daughters were eating and drinking wine in their eldest brother's house: • And there came a messenger unto Job, and said, The oxen were plowing, and the asses feeding beside them: • And the Sabaeans fell upon them, and took them away; yea, they have slain the servants with the edge of the sword; and I only am escaped alone to tell thee. • While he was yet speaking, there came also another, and said, The fire of God is fallen from heaven, and hath burned up the sheep, and the servants, and consumed them; and I only am escaped alone to tell thee. • While he was yet speaking, there came also another, and said, The Chaldaeans made out three bands, and fell upon the camels, and have carried them away, yea, and slain the servants with the edge of the sword; and I only am escaped alone to tell thee. • While he was yet speaking, there came also another, and said, Thy sons and thy daughters were eating and drinking wine in their eldest brother's house: • And, behold, there came a great wind from the wilderness, and smote the four corners of the house, and it fell upon the young men, and they are dead; and I only am escaped alone to tell thee.

20 • Then Job arose, and rent his mantle, and shaved his head, and fell down upon the ground, and worshipped, • And said,

> Naked came I out of my mother's womb,
> and naked shall I return thither:
> the LORD gave, and the LORD hath taken away;
> blessed be the name of the LORD.

• In all this Job sinned not, nor charged God foolishly.   ▸

Prologue in Heaven (cont.)

one in the prologue to *Faust* which he modelled on this passage. A self-curse of that kind brings pressure on the person to whom it is uttered, and Job uses the same technique in Ch. 31 to press God to confront him. God's behaviour in the prologue is of course utterly inexcusable, Satan or no Satan; but it is not presented as history and so is not disturbing like the story of Abraham and Isaac in Gen 22.

The fourfold report of the disasters is in the best folk-tale tradition. *Sabaeans* and *Chaldaeans* are here marauding no-mads. *The fire of God* is lightning. Job's re-actions include regular mourning rituals. Prostration shows resignation to the will of God. Generations of Christian mourners who have heard the quatrain of v.21 recited at the graveside must have wondered how to interpret the second line. Ch. 3 shows that *mother's womb* must be taken literally,

in which case *return thither* is used figura-tively, on the grounds that life after death is as shadowy as it is before birth. The third line, according to a modern traveller, is still used by some Bedouin Arabs: after a death the next of kin recites: 'His Lord gave him, his Lord has taken him away.' In the last line Job's blessing is the exact opposite of the predicted curse.

Back in heaven for scene 4, *the LORD* cannot contain his glee. *Without a cause* (2.3) picks up *for nought* (1.9) – they are the same in Hebrew. *Integrity* is the abstract noun of *perfect*. There is in fact something of the perfectionist (in our sense) about Job. *Skin for skin* is clearly a proverb, though not one found elsewhere. Presum-ably it means that *a man* will always give someone else's skin to save his own. It is necessary to *save his life*, i.e. to spare it, so that the story can continue.

Prologue in Heaven (cont.)

1 • Again there was a day when the sons of God came to present themselves before the LORD, and Satan came also among them to present himself before the LORD. • And the LORD said unto Satan, From whence comest thou? And Satan answered the LORD, and said, From going to and fro in the earth, and from walking up and down in it. • And the LORD said unto Satan, Hast thou considered my servant Job, that there is none like him in the earth, a perfect and an upright man, one that feareth God, and escheweth evil? and still he holdeth fast his integrity, although thou movedst me against him, to destroy him without cause. • And Satan answered the LORD, and

5 said, Skin for skin, yea, all that a man hath will he give for his life. • But put forth thine hand now, and touch his bone and his flesh, and he will curse thee to thy face. • And the LORD said unto Satan, Behold, he is in thine hand; but save his life.

• So went Satan forth from the presence of the LORD, and smote Job with sore boils from the sole of his foot unto his crown. • And he took him a potsherd to scrape himself withal; and he sat down among the ashes. • Then said his wife unto him, Dost

10 thou still retain thine integrity? curse God, and die. • But he said unto her, Thou speakest as one of the foolish women speaketh. What? shall we receive good at the hand of God, and shall we not receive evil? In all this did not Job sin with his lips.

• Now when Job's three friends heard of all this evil that was come upon him, they came every one from his own place; Eliphaz the Temanite, and Bildad the Shuhite, and Zophar the Naamathite: for they had made an appointment together to come to mourn with him and to comfort him. • And when they lifted up their eyes afar off, and knew him not, they lifted up their voice, and wept; and they rent every one his mantle, and sprinkled dust upon their heads toward heaven. • So they sat down with him upon the ground seven days and seven nights, and none spake a word unto him: for they saw that his grief was very great.   (AV)

Prologue in Heaven (cont.)

Job's illness is not diagnosed, but it is clearly meant to be intolerable both to himself (hence the scratching, which is a metaphor of Job's behaviour in Chs 3-31) and to his friends. Being ritually unclean, he had to 'stay outside the settlement' [Lev 13.46]. LXX makes clear that he sat on the refuse dump where the dung was burnt. A Church father wrote in the C4th AD that pilgrims came to Arabia from the ends of the earth to visit what was called 'Job's dunghill'.

Job's *wife* makes a brief but dramatic appearance. Rather like Tobit's wife Anna (Tob 2.14), she urges him to give up the hopeless struggle. To *curse God* would bring death and thus release. In fact she sees the problem before he does, which is why he is cross with her. But her words have their effect. Previously (1.21) he had spoken of God as YHWH, positively, and blessed him. Now he speaks of him as Elohim, questioningly, without the blessing. The author's final comment in 2.10 is correctly interpreted by the Talmud as a gloss designed to reconcile the folk-tale to the poem which follows: '*Job did not sin with his lips*, but in his heart he did.'

The last three verses of Ch. 2 are the poet's own bridge-passage, bringing the *three friends* abruptly on stage so that the poem can begin. We have to suppose a long interval for the news to travel to other places in Arabia. *Teman* had a reputation for wisdom. On arrival they mourned with him in the customary way and also, by throwing *dust towards heaven*, sought to avert the evil from themselves. A later Jewish mourning custom, whereby visitors keep silence until the bereaved speaks, was modelled upon this initial tactfulness of Job's friends.

Job Curses the Day of his Birth

3.1-2   After this Job broke his silence
and cursed the day of his birth:

3   Perish the day when I was born,
       and the night which said, 'A boy is conceived!'

4   May that day turn to darkness;
       may God above not look for it,

6   May it not be counted among the days of the year
       or reckoned in the cycle of the months.

7   May that night be barren for ever,
       may no cry of joy be heard in it.

9   May no star shine out in its twilight;
       may it wait for a dawn that never breaks,
       and never see the eyelids of the morning,

10   because it did not shut the doors of the womb that bore me
       and keep trouble away from my sight.

                                                         (REB)

11   Why was I not stillborn,
       why did I not perish when I came from the womb?

12   Why was I ever laid on my mother's knees
       or put to suck at her breasts?

13   For now I should be lying in the quiet grave,
       asleep in death, at rest.

17   There the wicked cease from troubling,
       and there the weary are at rest.

18   There the prisoners are at ease together;
       they do not hear the voice of the taskmaster.

19   The small and the great are there,
       and the slaves are free from their masters.

Job Curses the Day of his Birth

Job opens with a lament in Ch. 3 more poignant than any in the psalms, to be compared only with its briefer model, Jer 20.14-18. In cursing *the day of his birth*, Job was cursing his life and thus cursing God indirectly, though not 'to his face'. However he is not at this stage much taken up with the problem of God's justice (only v.23) and his repeated *Why?* in v.11f. is more of a complaint than a question.

Verse 3 is in the logical, not the chronological order: Job wishes he had never been born – no, never even conceived! The curse on *that day* has two parts: that it be dark as night and that it be struck off the list, presumably that of 'lucky' days (6). The curses on *that night* are: that it see no love-making or conception (7, picked up by 10a); and that daylight never come to end it. The evocative phrase *see the eyelids of the morning* is owed to the NEB. From conception we move forward again to pregnancy and birth.

By contrast the poet turns in v.13 to paint an almost idyllic picture of *death*. Sheol (17-19) is viewed above all as a place of *rest* and *ease*. The commonality of death puts an end to the suffering

Job Curses the Day of his Birth (cont.)

20 Why is light given to one in misery,
and life to the bitter in soul,

21 who long for death, but it does not come,
and dig for it more than for hidden treasures;

22 who rejoice exceedingly,
and are glad when they find the grave?

23 Why is light given to one who cannot see the way,
whom God has fenced in?

24 For my sighing comes like my bread,
and my groanings are poured out like water.

25 Truly the thing that I fear comes upon me,
and what I dread befalls me.

26 I am not at ease, nor am I quiet;
I have no rest; but trouble comes. (NRSV)

Job Curses the Day of his Birth (cont.)

inflicted by man on man. Likewise *the bitter in soul* will *long for death* (20-21). This view of death is more Egyptian than Hebraic. The second half of the poem is framed by the contrasted keywords *trouble* and *rest*, inverted between vv.17 and 26.

Eliphaz urges Job to Repent

4.1 Then Eliphaz the Temanite answered:

2 If one ventures a word with you, will you be offended?
But who can keep from speaking?

3 See, you have instructed many;
you have strengthened the weak hands.

4 Your words have supported those who were stumbling,
and you have made firm the feeble knees.

5 But now it has come to you, and you are impatient;
it touches you, and you are dismayed.

6 Is not your fear of God your confidence,
and the integrity of your ways your hope?

7 Think now, who that was innocent ever perished?
Or where were the upright cut off?

Eliphaz urges Job to Repent

In the first cycle of speeches (Chs 4 -14) Eliphaz opens for the friends, and immediately shows himself the opposite of Job. Respectable and restrained, he only wants to help. His measured couplets are a fitting expression of the orthodox view that in God's world the good are always rewarded and the wicked always punished, at any rate in the end. Fully accepting Job's *integrity* (there is no irony in 4.6), he urges him to take the long view. *You are impatient*, he says, revealing his own impatience with Job: God will not let the *innocent perish* (7).

Eliphaz urges Job to Repent (cont.)

4. 8 As I have seen, those who plow iniquity
and sow trouble reap the same.

9 By the breath of God they perish,
and by the blast of his anger they are consumed.

12 Now a word came stealing to me,
my ear received the whisper of it.

13 Amid thoughts from visions of the night,
when deep sleep falls on mortals,

14 dread came upon me, and trembling,
which made all my bones shake.

15 A spirit glided past my face;
the hair of my flesh bristled.

16 It stood still,
but I could not discern its appearance.
A form was before my eyes;
there was silence, then I heard a voice:

17 'Can mortals be righteous before God?
Can human beings be pure before their Maker?

18 Even in his servants he puts no trust,
and his angels he charges with error;

19 how much more those who live in houses of clay,
whose foundation is in the dust,
who are crushed like a moth.

20 Between morning and evening they are destroyed;
they perish forever without any regarding it.

21 Their tent-cord is plucked up within them,
and they die devoid of wisdom.'

5. 6 For misery does not come from the earth,
nor does trouble sprout from the ground;

7 but human beings are born to trouble
just as sparks fly upward.

Eliphaz urges Job to Repent (cont.)

But the orthodox theodicy* had a couple of other cards up its sleeve, and Eliphaz proceeds to play them now, showing the whole strength of his hand at the start. First, it is not credible that there should be an *entirely* innocent person. Human righteousness is relative, it can never be absolute *before God* (17). Logically this is a fair point, but it is no help to Job. That may be why Eliphaz wraps it up as he does. Wisdom teachers usually spoke from their own experience (4.8). But in this case he claims the authority of a dream, described in nervously baroque detail. He backs it up with a frigid argument about *angels*. Even they can fall into *error*, how much more *human beings* who *are born to* create *trouble* – such must be the original meaning of 5.7a.

Eliphaz urges Job to Repent (cont.)

8 As for me, I would seek God,
      and to God I would commit my cause.
9 He does great things and unsearchable,
      marvelous things without number.

17 How happy is the one whom God reproves;
      therefore do not despise the discipline of the Almighty.
18 For he wounds, but he binds up;
      he strikes, but his hands heal.
19 He will deliver you from six troubles;
      in seven no harm shall touch you.
22 At destruction and famine you shall laugh,
      and shall not fear the wild animals of the earth.
23 For you shall be in league with the stones of the field,
      and the wild animals shall be at peace with you.
25 You shall know that your descendants will be many,
      and your offspring like the grass of the earth.
26 You shall come to your grave in ripe old age,
      as a shock of grain comes up to the threshing floor in its season.
27 See, we have searched this out; it is true.
      Hear, and know it for yourself.   (NRSV)

Eliphaz urges Job to Repent (cont.)

That being so, says the prudent Eliphaz, he would *commit* his *cause to God*. And in support of that advice, he plays his remaining card. Suffering, he says, is not always retributive; it can also be educative (17). As such it should be welcomed and (the hint is delicate) made the occasion for a change of life. The sufferer will then find himself restored and protected (for the numerical formulation of v.19 see on Prov Ch. 30), and an idyllic future will await him. The idea of *peace* with *the wild animals* is a topos* familiar from the description of the messianic kingdom in Is.11.6-8. The reference to *the stones of the field* which must be cleared before the crops of v.26 can be sown has no parallel in the OT, but fits the general Wisdom notion of the correspondence between human life and the world of nature.

This speech of Eliphaz is programmatic in two respects. First, it sets out the whole of the traditional theodicy. Neither he nor his colleagues have any important argument to add in the exchanges which follow. Secondly it foreshadows the climax of the action. For in the end Job does *commit his cause to God* and does accept that *human beings* cannot *be pure before their Maker*.

Job Accuses his Friends of Treachery. . .

6. 1   Then Job answered:

8   O that I might have my request,
            and that God would grant my desire;

9   that it would please God to crush me,
            that he would let loose his hand and cut me off!

14   Those who withhold kindness from a friend
            forsake the fear of the Almighty.

15   My companions are treacherous like a torrent-bed,
            like freshets that pass away,

16   that run dark with ice,
            turbid with melting snow.

17   In time of heat they disappear;
            when it is hot, they vanish from their place.

18   The caravans turn aside from their course;
            they go up into the waste, and perish.

19   The caravans of Tema look,
            the travelers of Sheba hope.

20   They are disappointed because they were confident;
            they come there and are confounded.

21   Such you have now become to me;
            you see my calamity, and are afraid.   (NRSV)

Job Accuses his Friends of Treachery . . .

Job in reply continues his complaint from Ch. 3 as if Eliphaz had never spoken. Verse 8 might come from any of the complaint psalms, but it is less a quotation than a parody, as 9 shows: Job's *request* is not for health but death. When he does turn to Eliphaz (14) he deals only indirectly with his arguments. His point is that they have shown Eliphaz to be a *treacherous* *companion*. The image is one which Jeremiah had used (15.18), but Job characteristically elaborates it. In the summer a wadi is dry, and in the winter (so v.16 seems to say, though the translation is uncertain) it is nothing but *snow* and *ice*. Verse 21 contains a pun: the Hebrew words for *you see* and you *are afraid* are virtually identical.

. . . and God of Spying on him

7. 1   Does not every mortal have hard service on earth,
            and are not his days like those of a hired labourer,

2   like those of a slave longing for the shade
            or a servant kept waiting for his wages?

3   So months of futility are my portion,
            troubled nights are my lot.   ▸

. . . and God of Spying on him

Ch. 7 again begins with complaint. Human life is nothing but *hard service*, like the conscript labour which ANE kings always enforced, or like work on the land where relief comes only at the end of the day (2a). For Job himself, as for all invalids, *the night* is the worst time.

... and God of Spying on him (cont.)

4
When I lie down, I think,
   When will it be day, that I may rise?
But the night drags on,
   and I do nothing but toss till dawn.

5
My body is infested with worms,
   and scabs cover my skin;
   it is cracked and discharging.

11
But I cannot hold my peace;
   I shall speak out in my anguish of spirit
   and complain in my bitterness of soul.

12
Am I the monster of the deep, am I the sea serpent,
   that you set a watch over me?

13
When I think that my bed will comfort me,
   that sleep will relieve my complaint,

14
you terrify me with dreams
   and affright me through visions.

17
What is man, that you make much of him
   and turn your thoughts towards him,

18
only to punish him morning after morning
   or to test him every hour of the day?

19
Will you not look away from me for an instant,
   leave me long enough to swallow my spittle?

20
If I have sinned, what harm can I do you,
   you watcher of the human heart?
Why have you made me your target?
   Why have I become a burden to you?

21
Why do you not pardon my offence
   and take away my guilt?
For soon I shall lie in the dust of the grave;
   you may seek me, but I shall be no more.   (REB)

... and God of Spying on him (cont.)

So in 7.12 for the first time he addresses God directly. He might as well be one of the old enemies, *the sea serpent* who opposed God at the creation. (This old ANE myth, for which see p.27, plays a frequent part in the book of Job, and forms the climax of God's reply in Ch. 41). Even when Job does get to *sleep*, God sends him nightmares. *Death would be* preferable; failing that, will God not *let him alone*? Brilliantly he parodies in v.17 the words of the great hymn of praise Psalm 8.5: '*What is man that* thou shouldest remember him?' He seems also to have in mind the more ambiguous Psalm 139 (on which see commentary). The vivid image of v.19 lives on in Arabic, where 'Let me *swallow my spittle*' means 'Wait a moment'. The argument of v.20 is clever – human sin cannot harm God – but the rest of the book shows that, here and in v.21, Job is not admitting the possibility of anything more than an inadvertent *offence*.

Bildad: God's Justice is Sure

8. 1 Then Bildad the Shuhite spoke up:

2   How long will you go on saying such things,
        those long-winded ramblings of an old man?
3   Does God pervert justice?
        Does the Almighty pervert what is right?
4   If your sons sinned against him,
        he has left them to be victims of their own iniquity.

8   Enquire now of older generations
        and consider the experience of their forefathers;
9   for we are but of yesterday and know nothing;
        our days on earth are but a passing shadow.
10   Will they not teach you and tell you
        and pour out the wisdom of their minds?
11   Can rushes thrive where there is no marsh?
        Can reeds flourish without water?
12   While still in flower and not ready for cutting,
        they would wither before any green plant.
13   Such is the fate of all who forget God;
        the life-thread of the godless breaks off;
14   his confidence is gossamer,
        and the basis of his trust a spider's web.
15   He leans against his house, but it does not stand;
        he clutches at it, but it does not hold firm.

(REB)

Bildad: God's Justice is Sure

Bildad has nothing to say that has not already been said by Eliphaz, but he is blunter in expression. He too cites external authority for his views. In his case it is the tradition of society, for one generation is too short to see the working out of God's system of rewards and punishments. The downfall of the wicked he illustrates with three images. First (11-13) they are like Nile plants (both the botanical names in v.11 are Egyptian loan-words) which *wither without water*. The second is suggested by an ambiguity in v.13b. Heb. *tiqwah*, which REB translates *thread*, can also mean 'hope', which other translators prefer here. In fact the poet must have intended both meanings, since both are picked up in v.14, and *spider's web* in turn suggests the third image of a mud-brick *house* collapsing.

Job has no Hope of a Fair Trial . . .

1   Then Job answered:

2   Indeed I know that this is so;
            but how can a mortal be just before God?
3   If one wished to contend with him,
            one could not answer him once in a thousand.
4   He is wise in heart, and mighty in strength
            – who has resisted him, and succeeded? –
5   he who removes mountains, and they do not know it,
            when he overturns them in his anger;
6   who shakes the earth out of its place,
            and its pillars tremble;
7   who commands the sun, and it does not rise;
            who seals up the stars;
8   who alone stretched out the heavens
            and trampled the back of the sea dragon;
9   who made the Bear and Orion,
            the Pleiades and the chambers of the south;
10   who does great things beyond understanding,
            and marvelous things without number.
11   Look, he passes by me, and I do not see him;
            he moves on, but I do not perceive him.
12   He snatches away; who can stop him?
            Who will say to him, 'What are you doing?'

14   How then can I answer him,
            choosing my words with him?
15   Though I am innocent, I cannot answer him;
            I must appeal for mercy to my accuser.
16   If I summoned him and he answered me,
            I do not believe that he would listen to my voice.
20   Though I am innocent, my own mouth would condemn me;
            though I am blameless, he would prove me perverse.   ◆

Job has no Hope of a Fair Trial . . .

Job in his third speech disregards Bildad and goes back to Eliphaz. He first expresses ironical agreement with the view that 'mortals cannot be righteous before God' (4.17), but gives it a different meaning, namely that human beings cannot win a case against God, because God is too powerful. Eliphaz too had spoken of God's power, and Job quotes his words back at him (9.10 = 5.9) to round off his own sardonic version of the theme. For to Job that power is destructive as well as beneficent. He who (in the myth) *trampled the back of the sea dragon* and set the stars in place (8-9) is also responsible for earthquakes (6) and eclipses (7). To human beings he is elusive (11) and arbitrary (12).

But the thought of a man bringing a case against God (*If I summoned him*, 16) is one of supreme audacity. It is a parody of that standard prophetic scenario, God's lawsuit against men. And even to envisage it is to see its absurdity.

Job has no Hope of a Fair Trial . . . (cont.)

9. 22   It is all one; therefore I say,
                he destroys both the blameless and the wicked.

23   When disaster brings sudden death,
                he mocks at the calamity of the innocent.

24   The earth is given into the hand of the wicked;
                he covers the eyes of its judges
                – if it is not he, who then is it?

25   My days are swifter than a runner;
                they flee away, they see no good.

26   They go by like skiffs of reed,
                like an eagle swooping on the prey.

27   If I say, 'I will forget my complaint;
                I will put off my sad countenance and be of good cheer,'

28   I become afraid of all my suffering,
                for I know you will not hold me innocent.

29   I shall be condemned;
                why then do I labor in vain?

30   If I wash myself with soap
                and cleanse my hands with lye,

31   yet you will plunge me into filth,
                and my own clothes will abhor me.

32   For he is not a mortal, as I am, that I might answer him,
                that we should come to trial together.

33   There is no umpire between us,
                who might lay his hand on us both.

34   If he would take his rod away from me,
                and not let dread of him terrify me,

35   then I would speak without fear of him,
                for I know I am not what I am thought to be.   (NRSV)

Job has no Hope of a Fair Trial . . . (cont.)

With his accuser as judge, Job has no hope of a fair trial. Indeed in God's eyes *it is all one* (22) whether a man is *blameless* or *wicked*. The text hereabouts is uncertain, but there is no doubt of the general line of argument, which represents the bitterest indictment of God in the whole book.

In the next section (25-35) Job takes up his theme of the brief span of life remaining to him. The three images of vv.25-6 all express speed of movement, but there are overtones of fragility in the papyrus boat and of violence in the *eagle*. It would be a waste of that brief time now to adopt a pretence either of happiness (27) or of penitence (30). For God, now addressed in person, is his enemy (28b, 31) and will not relent. Nor is there, alas, any *umpire*, i.e. arbiter (REB), to whom he can appeal over God's head – that is the price of monotheism for both God and human beings; cp. also v.24c.

... and is Reduced to Despair

1   I am sickened of life;
        I shall give free rein to my complaints,
        speaking out in the bitterness of my soul.

8   Your hands shaped and fashioned me;
        and will you at once turn and destroy me?

9   Recall that you moulded me like clay;
        and would you reduce me to dust again?

10   Did you not pour me out like milk
        and curdle me like cheese,

11   clothe me with skin and flesh
        and knit me together with bones and sinews?

12   You granted me life and continuing favour,
        and your providence watched over my spirit.

13   Yet this was the secret purpose of your heart,
        and I know what was your intent:

14   that, if I sinned, you would be watching me
        and would not absolve me of my guilt.

20   Is not my life short and fleeting?
        Let me be, that I may be happy for a moment,

21   before I depart to a land of gloom,
        a land of deepest darkness, never to return,

22   a land of dense darkness and disorder,
        increasing darkness lit by no ray of light.   **(REB)**

... and is Reduced to Despair

The strain is telling on Job, and he swings back and forth between defiance and despair. In 10.8-14 he uses his favourite device of quoting pious doctrine and adding a subversive comment. This time the comments are interwoven (8b, 9b and 13-14). In summary they point to the paradox that God is both his creator and his persecutor. Verse 9 uses the Genesis myth (2.7) that humans were created from the *dust* of the earth, v.10 a pre-scientific belief that on conception the *milk* (semen) is *curdled* into *cheese* (embryo) in the mother's womb. That meticulous process is to be taken as evidence not of God's *providence* but of his relentless spying, for it is now clear that God always meant to destroy him. There is another clear echo here of Ps 139, perhaps as a parody (but see commentary there).

Zophar: Job should Admit his Ignorance

11. 1 Then Zophar the Naamathite spoke up:

4   You claim that your opinions are sound;
        you say to God, I am spotless in your sight.

5   But if only God would speak
        and open his lips to reply,

6   to expound to you the secrets of wisdom,
        for wonderful are its achievements!
     Know then that God exacts from you
        less than your sin deserves.

7   Can you fathom the mystery of God,
        or attain to the limits of the Almighty?

8   They are higher than the heavens. What can you do?
        They are deeper than Sheol. What can you know?

11   He surely knows who are false,
        and when he sees iniquity, does he not take note of it?

12   A fool will attain to understanding
        when a wild ass's foal is born a human being!

13   If only you had directed your heart rightly
        and spread out your hands in prayer to him!

15   Then you could hold up your head without fault;
        you would be steadfast and fearless.   (REB)

Zophar: Job should Admit his Ignorance

Zophar's speech, though not important in content, plays a part in the book because it anticipates the climax of Chs 38-42. God will indeed then *speak* to Job, and these two verses (7-8) summarise what he will say. Meanwhile he knows *who are false* (11). The friends are no longer accepting Job's protestations of innocence: his sufferings are now said to be *less than* his *sin deserves* (6). *If only* he had made a genuine repentance, he might by now have been restored. But that was too much to ask: for a *fool* to grow wise is like an *ass* giving birth to *a human* (12). The proverb has the same form as those in Prov 26.

> # God's Wisdom and Power are Known to All . . .
>
> 1 Then Job answered:
>
> 2 No doubt you are the people,
>   and wisdom will die with you.
>
> 3 But I have understanding as well as you;
>   I am not inferior to you.
>   Who does not know such things as these?
>
> 7 Ask the animals, and they will teach you;
>   the birds of the air, and they will tell you;
>
> 8 ask the plants of the earth, and they will teach you;
>   and the fish of the sea will declare to you.
>
> 9 Who among all these does not know
>   that the hand of the LORD has done this?
>
> 13 With God are wisdom and strength;
>   he has counsel and understanding.
>
> 14 If he tears down, no one can rebuild;
>   if he shuts someone in, no one can open up.
>
> 15 If he withholds the waters, they dry up;
>   if he sends them out, they overwhelm the land.
>
> 16 With him are strength and wisdom;
>   the deceived and the deceiver are his.
>
> 17 He leads counselors away stripped,
>   and makes fools of judges.
>
> 20 He deprives of speech those who are trusted,
>   and takes away the discernment of the elders.
>
> 23 He makes nations great, then destroys them;
>   he enlarges nations, then leads them away.
>
> 24 He strips understanding from the leaders of the earth,
>   and makes them wander in a pathless waste.
>
> (NRSV)

God's Wisdom and Power are Known to All . . .

Job is given three chapters in which to round off the first cycle of speeches. He opens with the usual personalities. The sarcasm of v.2 is underlined by the presence of eight m's in six Hebrew words, parodying the pomposity of the friends. Then like any Wisdom teacher he looks for lessons in nature, beginning with the animal world – another trailer for God's speeches at the end of the book. But Job the ironist will stand the usual argument on its head. As before (Ch. 9) with God's *strength*, so here also with God's *wisdom* (13), he can echo the pious hymn. But in Job's formulation God is revealed as the author of destruction (14), of social and political disorder (17-24), and even of the very chaos which creation was supposed to have tamed, e.g. there is always either drought or flood (15). And v.16b shows that his cynicism is not confined to God: humans are either cheats (the successful) or their dupes, and this is God's plan.

... but Job will Challenge him even at the Cost of his Life ...

13.

8
> Must you take God's part,
>   putting his case for him?

9
> Will all go well when he examines you?
>   Can you deceive him as you could a human being?

10
> He will most surely expose you
>   if you take his part by falsely accusing me.

13
> Be silent, leave me to speak my mind,
>   and let what may come upon me!

15
> If he wishes to slay me, I have nothing to lose;
>   I shall still defend my conduct to his face.

20
> God, grant me these two conditions only,
>   and then I shall not hide out of your sight:

21
> remove your hand from upon me
>   and let not fear of you strike me with dismay.

22
> Then summon me, and I shall respond;
>   or let me speak first, and you answer me.

23
> How many crimes and sins are laid to my charge?
>   Let me know my offence and my sin.

24
> Why do you hide your face
>   and treat me as your enemy?

25
> Will you harass a wind-driven leaf
>   and pursue dry chaff,

26
> that you draw up bitter charges against me,
>   making me heir to the iniquities of my youth,

27
> putting my feet in the stocks,
>   keeping a close watch on all I do,
>   and setting a slave-mark on my instep?   (REB)

... but Job will Challenge him even at the Cost of his Life ...

Job next turns to dismiss the arguments of the friends. They may think they are taking *God's part*, but in fact *he will expose* them – which is what he does at the end of the book (42.7). Meanwhile let them just *be silent* (13). For Job is determined to challenge God, whatever the consequences. His reference to death is literal: he has in mind an ordeal by oath, such as he finally undergoes in Ch. 31, where his assertions are equivalent to 'may I die if . . .'.

In v.15 the Hebrew text offers two readings. One is followed by AV: 'Yea, though he slay me, yet will I trust in him.' But those words express a deeper faith than Job shows in the rest of the book, and most moderns follow the alternative text which inserts a negative: 'I will *not* hope'.

At 13.20 he turns to address God directly, as he is doing increasingly. This time he badly overplays his hand. by making *two conditions*. Not surprisingly God says nothing (we must suppose a pause after v.23); and later, when he does respond, he disregards them.

At 13.25 Job reverts to another theme of his, that he is too frail to be worth God's attention. True, he made mistakes when young, but that does not justify his being branded like a *slave*.

... or is there a Possibility of Mercy?

1 Man that is born of a woman
   is of few days, and full of trouble.

2 He comes forth like a flower, and withers;
   he flees like a shadow, and continues not.

7 For there is hope for a tree,
   if it be cut down, that it will sprout again,
   and that its shoots will not cease.

8 Though its root grow old in the earth,
   and its stump die in the ground,

9 yet at the scent of water it will bud
   and put forth branches like a young plant.

10 But man dies, and is laid low;
   man breathes his last, and where is he?

11 As waters fail from a lake,
   and a river wastes away and dries up,

12 so man lies down and rises not again;
   till the heavens are no more he will not awake,
   or be roused out of his sleep.

13 Oh that thou wouldest hide me in Sheol,
   that thou wouldest conceal me until thy wrath be past,
   that thou wouldest appoint me a set time, and remember me!

14 All the days of my service I would wait,
   till my release should come.

15 Thou wouldest call, and I would answer thee;
   thou wouldest long for the work of thy hands.

18 But the mountain falls and crumbles away,
   and the rock is removed from its place;

19 the waters wear away the stones;
   the torrents wash away the soil of the earth;
   so thou destroyest the hope of man.

20 Thou prevailest for ever against him, and he passes;
   thou changest his countenance, and sendest him away.

21 His sons come to honor, and he does not know it;
   they are brought low, and he perceives it not.   (RSV)

... or is there a Possibility of Mercy?

In Ch.14 Job develops further the linked themes of the brevity of life and the finality of death, each of which might be grounds for God's mercy. In vv.7-9 he skilfully reverses the conventional image which likens a human death to *a tree cut down*. In vv.13-15 he explores, even while denying, a new possibility. What if *Sheol* were only a temporary refuge, from which God might recall him out of love *for the work of* his *hands*? Wistfully he plays with that idea – but then returns to harsh reality. The sequence of decay is clearly marked by the successive stages in the image of vv.18-19: *mountain→rock→stones→soil*. Old age and death *change* a man's *countenance*, and he dies without knowing what will happen to his children.

Job Reaffirms his Innocence

15. 1 Eliphaz of Teman spoke next. He said:

12 How passion carries you away!
   And how you roll your eyes,

13 when you vent your anger on God
   and speeches come tripping off your tongue!

14 How can anyone be pure,
   anyone born of woman be upright?

15 God cannot rely even on his holy ones,
   to him, even the heavens seem impure.

16 How much more, this hateful, corrupt thing, humanity,
   which soaks up wickedness like water!   (NJB)

16. 1 Job answered:

2 I have heard such things so often before!
   You are trouble-makers one and all!

3 You say, 'Will this windbag never have done?'
   or 'What makes him so stubborn in argument?'

11 God has left me at the mercy of malefactors,
   he has cast me into the power of the wicked.

12 I was at ease, but he savaged me,
   seized me by the neck, and worried me.
   He set me up as his target;

13 his arrows rained on me from every side.

14 He made breach after breach in my defences;
   like a warrior he rushed on me.   ▶

Job Reaffirms his Innocence

In the second cycle of speeches (Chs 15-21) the friends largely repeat arguments already used, though with greater vehemence and even venom. For example 15.14-16 are a reprise of 4.17-21, but here *humanity* is denigrated wholesale, in a way quite untypical of the OT, as not merely ephemeral but *hateful* and *corrupt*. Eliphaz also makes a good debating point: whatever Job did before he was stricken, his words since provide all the proof needed of his impiety.

Job's reply in Ch.16 opens with an exchange of pleasantries, one of the rare occasions when one party takes notice of what another has said. He then repeats, with three variations of image, his charge that God has savagely attacked him (12-14).

Job Reaffirms his Innocence (cont.)

5   I stitched sackcloth together to cover my body
    and laid my forehead in the dust;
6   my cheeks were inflamed with weeping
    and dark shadows were round my eyes.
7   Yet my hands were free from violence
    and my prayer was sincere.

8   Let not the earth cover my blood,
    and let my cry for justice find no rest!
9   For now my witness is in heaven;
    there is One on high ready to answer for me.
21   If only there were one to arbitrate between man and God,
    as between a man and his neighbour!
22   For there are but few years to come
    before I take the road from which there is no return.

1   My mind is distraught, my days are numbered,
    and the grave awaits me.
2   Wherever I turn, I am taunted,
    and my eye meets nothing but sneers.
3   Be my surety with yourself,
    for who else will pledge himself for me?   (REB)

Job Reaffirms his Innocence (cont.)

As a result of the attacks, he is mourning as for his own death. *Forehead* in v.15b (literally, 'horn' AV) is a symbol for dignity, *dust* represents both humiliation and burial. Yet he can claim for himself the innocence which Isaiah (53.9) had ascribed to the suffering servant. Like a victim of murder, his *blood* will *cry* for vengeance and must not be silenced (see Gen 4.10).

In the next few verses we run into one of the major problems in understanding Job's idea of God. In v.21 he again toys with the notion of an arbitrator, but rejects it as before (9.33). In truth there is no third party – a fact which has all along made nonsense of Job's favourite courtroom analogy. Consequently he must ask God to be his *witness*, his advocate (19) and even his *surety*, i.e. to go bail for him (17.3). The prosaic westerner stumbles at the logical inconsistencies in Job's position, and looks for an explanation in his emotional state. But that is to misunderstand the mind of the Hebrew poet. The three images of vv.19-21 may be logically incompatible but psychologically they reinforce each other. God at the Great Assize thus not only judges but represents both sides. Nor are these alternative or successive roles which he plays. In strict monotheism there can be only one God, of mercy and of wrath. But the two separable qualities make it possible in religious discourse to speak of appealing from the god of wrath to the god of mercy. Such at least is the traditional Jewish interpretation of Job, and modern Christian theology can speak of 'the God above God'. But the Koran, being stricter, insists that 'there is no refuge from God but unto him.'

Job Confident of Ultimate Vindication

19. 23 Oh that my words were written!
    Oh that they were inscribed in a book!

24 Oh that with an iron pen and lead
    they were graven in the rock for ever!

25 For I know that my Redeemer lives,
    and at last he will stand upon the earth;

26 and after my skin has been thus destroyed,
    then from my flesh I shall see God,

27 whom I shall see on my side,
    and my eyes shall behold, and not another.   (RSV)

Job Confident of Ultimate Vindication

Bildad's speech in [Ch.18] offers nothing new, and Job pursues the train of thought which he began in Ch.16. He first wishes his cry for justice and vengeance to be recorded – even to be carved on a *rock*-face, like ANE inscriptions – so that it would survive the death which he regards as imminent. But that unrealistic wish is replaced by a certainty of a different kind. Though he himself may die, he has a champion who will live – see *Redeemer* in Glossary.

This is the best known and most dis-puted passage in Job. The text of v.25b and (even more) v.26 is uncertain, and the difficulties are compounded by the familiarity of the AV wording used by Handel: 'yet in my flesh shall I see God.' But the Hebrew certainly makes no reference to any resurrection of the body. The central point of dispute is whether the redeemer is God himself or another heavenly being. Tempting as the latter may be to Christians, Jewish monotheism clearly demands the former (see on Ch. 16).

Job Notes the Prosperity of the Wicked

21. 7 Why do the wicked live on,
    hale in old age, and great and powerful?

8 They see their children settled around them,
    their descendants flourishing.

10 Their bull breeds without fail;
    their cow calves and does not cast her calf.

11 Like flocks they produce babes in droves,
    and their little ones skip and dance;

12 they rejoice with tambourine and lyre
    and make merry to the sound of the flute.

13 They live out their days in prosperity,
    and they go down to Sheol in peace.

14 They say to God, 'Leave us alone;
    we do not want to know your ways!'   ▸

Job Notes the Prosperity of the Wicked

In [Ch.20] Zophar again insisted that the wicked always come to grief, implying that Job is suffering for his own sins. Job in reply claims for *the wicked* all the *prosperity* that, in the orthodox scenario, was reserved for the righteous. His parody this time is more charming than bitter. The picture is rounded off (14) by an attributed speech which exposes the theology of the wicked. The treatment is exactly like the passage in Ps 73.3-12, which makes a close parallel to this section of Job's speech. The psalmist's approach is however more detached because he is

Job Notes the Prosperity of the Wicked (cont.)

29 Have you never questioned travellers?
Do you not accept the evidence they bring:

30 that a wicked person is spared when disaster comes
and conveyed to safety before the day of wrath?

33 When he is borne to the grave,
all the world escorts him, before and behind;
the dust of earth is sweet to him,
and thousands keep watch at his tomb. (REB)

Job Notes the the Prosperity of the Wicked (cont.)

not, like Job, engaged in self-defence.

The fate of the wicked man is taken up again in vv.29-33, with emphasis on his funeral. The translation of v.29 is uncertain in detail, and REB rearranges vv.32-3. But the telling touches are secure: the long funeral procession and the *tomb* guarded against robbers. We have however parted company with Job's own predicament. In Zophar's speech the subject has become the wicked ruler (cp. *powerful* in 7b) as in Plato's *Republic*.

Eliphaz: Job should Seek Reconciliation with God

1 Then Eliphaz the Temanite answered:

2 Can a mortal be of use to God?
Can even the wisest be of service to him?

3 Is it any pleasure to the Almighty if you are righteous,
or is it gain to him if you make your ways blameless?

4 Is it for your piety that he reproves you,
and enters into judgement with you?

5 Is not your wickedness great?
There is no end to your iniquities.

21 Agree with God, and be at peace;
in this way good will come to you.

27 You will pray to him, and he will hear you,
and you will pay your vows.

28 You will decide on a matter, and it will be established for you,
and light will shine on your ways.

30 He will deliver even those who are guilty;
they will escape because of the cleanness of your hands. (NRSV)

Eliphaz: Job should Seek Reconciliation with God

Eliphaz begins the third cycle of speeches (Chs 22-24) with a curious argument. Since Job cannot *be of use to God*, God can have no ulterior motive in his treatment of Job, and therefore Job's sufferings can only be put down to his own *wickedness*. The utterance of that word seems to release Eliphaz. Hitherto he has at least provisionally accepted Job's innocence. Now he rounds on him: *there is no end to your iniquities*.

However he ends on a friendlier note, and adds a new point (30). A penitent Job, restored to righteousness, will be in a position to help *deliver* other offenders. As often, one of the friends here gives a foretaste of the denouement: at the very end of the poem Job is told by God to intercede – for the friends! (42.8).

Job still Uncertain what to Expect of God

23. 1 Then Job answered:

2   Today also my complaint is bitter;
        his hand is heavy despite my groaning.

3   Oh, that I knew where I might find him,
        that I might come even to his dwelling!

5   I would learn what he would answer me,
        and understand what he would say to me.

6   Would he contend with me in the greatness of his power?
        No; but he would give heed to me.

7   There an upright person could reason with him,
        and I should be acquitted forever by my judge.

13   But he stands alone and who can dissuade him?
        What he desires, that he does.

15   Therefore I am terrified at his presence;
        when I consider, I am in dread of him.   (NRSV)

24. 2   The wicked move boundary stones,
        and pasture flocks they have stolen.

3   They drive off the donkey belonging to the fatherless,
        and lead away the widow's ox with a rope.

4   They jostle the poor out of the way;
        the destitute in the land are forced into hiding together.

5   The poor rise early like the wild ass,
        when it scours the wilderness for food;
        but though they work till nightfall, their children go hungry.

7   Without clothing, they pass the night naked
        and with no cover against the cold.

10   Naked and bare they go about their work;
        those who carry the sheaves go hungry;

11   they press the oil in the shade where two walls meet,
        they tread the winepress but themselves go thirsty.

12   Far from the city, they groan as if dying,
        and like those mortally wounded they cry out;
        but God remains deaf to their prayer.   (REB)

Job still Uncertain what to Expect of God

In Ch.23 the distraught Job veers from one extreme mood to another. First he drops ideas of a third party and wants only to *find* God. If he can achieve that, he is now confident of receiving a courteous hearing and an unreserved acquittal. But then he swings back to terror at the prospect of *his presence*.

In Ch.24 he starts more objectively. Taking up a theme of the prophets, the oppression of the poor by the rich, he develops a passionate description of the miseries of poverty (5-12). First, it reduces men to animals in the search for *food* (5) and *shelter* (7). Secondly (the repeated *naked* makes the link), if they can get work they benefit only their employer (10-11). The final phrase shows why Job feels so passionately: *God* is as *deaf to* them as to himself.

Where is Wisdom to be Found?

1 Silver has its mines,
  and gold a place for refining.

2 Iron is extracted from the earth,
  the smelted rocks yield copper.

3 Man makes an end of darkness,
  to the utmost limit he digs
  the black rock in shadow dark as death.

4 Foreigners bore into ravines
  in unfrequented places,
  swinging suspended far from human beings.

5 That earth from which bread comes
  is ravaged underground by fire.

6 There, the rocks have veins of sapphire
  and their dust contains gold.

7 That is a path unknown to birds of prey,
  unseen by the eye of any vulture;

8 a path not trodden by the lordly beasts,
  where no lion ever walked.

9 Man attacks the flint,
  upturning mountains by their roots.

10 He cuts canals through the rock,
  on the watch for anything precious.

11 He explores the sources of rivers,
  bringing hidden things to light.

12 But where does Wisdom come from?
  Where is Intelligence to be found?

Where is Wisdom to be Found?

Ch. 28 does not fit in Job's mouth, and NJB rightly treats it as an independent hymn. In it the quest for Wisdom is compared in two respects to the quest for precious stones. Explicitly, Wisdom is even more inaccessible; implicitly, it is even more valuable. This fine poem has three clear sections: (i) the quest for precious stones (1-12); (ii) the quest for Wisdom (13-20, with 20 repeating 12 and marking off the first two sections); and (iii) God's revelation of Wisdom (21-28). It has much in common with various praises of Wisdom in Proverbs, especially 3.13-18 for section (ii) and 8.12-31 for (iii). In the book of Job it forms a kind of inter-mezzo, 'tuning up' (Alter) for God's great speech to come in Ch. 38.

The translation of the first section is made more uncertain by our ignorance of ancient mining. The geology of course is unchanged. *Iron* and *copper* (2) are found just east of the Jordan. Other precious metals, however, have to be mined in remote areas (4), usually desert (7-8). The lode-bearing rocks were not *flint* (9) but granite, and *sapphire* (6) should be 'lapis lazuli' (as REB in both instances). Mining was done by labour-gangs of prisoners of war (4) and criminals, who worked in the most inhuman conditions. Miners were let down in baskets by ropes (4), and wore lamps on their heads for working in the *darkness* (3a). *Fire* (5) probably refers to volcanic action. There is thus a contrast between the peaceful activities on *the earth* and the violence underneath it. Subterranean disturbances were the

Where is Wisdom to be Found? (cont.)

28. 13   No human being knows the way to her,
          she is not to be found on earth where they live.

14   'She is not in me,' says the Abyss;
          'Nor here,' replies the Sea.

15   She cannot be bought with solid gold,
          nor paid for with any weight of silver,

16   nor valued against gold of Ophir,
          precious agate or sapphire.

17   Neither gold nor glass compares with her,
          for her, a vase of fine gold would be no exchange,

18   let alone coral or crystal:
          better go fishing for Wisdom than for pearls!

19   Topaz from Cush is worthless in comparison,
          and gold, even refined, is valueless.

20   But where does Wisdom come from?
          Where is Intelligence to be found?

21   She cannot be seen by any living creature,
          she is hidden from the birds of the sky.

22   Perdition and Death both say,
          'We have heard only rumours of her.'

23   God alone understands her path
          and knows where she is to be found.

25   When he willed to give weight to the wind
          and measured out the waters with a gauge,

26   when he imposed a law on the rain
          and mapped a route for thunderclaps to follow,

27   then he saw and evaluated her,
          looked her through and through, assessing her.

28   Then he said to human beings,
          'Wisdom? – that is fear of the LORD;
          Intelligence? – avoidance of evil.'

(NJB)

Where is Wisdom to be Found? (cont.)

source of many ancient myths, of which the best known is that of the Greek Titans. There is thus already in the first section an overtone of *hubris* in the activities of man the technologist. The corresponding ANE myth was that of the *Abyss* or *Sea* (14), which was conquered by God at creation; and the sea again is contrasted with the earth.

The second section argues that economic man is no more successful than technological man in the search for wisdom. This section is somewhat repetitive, but biblical authors found it hard to resist catalogues of precious stones (Is 54.11+; Rev 21.18+). *Glass* (17) was a rare and precious commodity before Roman times. *Ophir* was the usual source of gold; *Cush* is Ethiopia.

The third section contrasts the earth with what is above and what is below it, and again draws on mythical ideas. This time the myth is the Ugaritic 'Struggle of Baal with Mot', where we find not only

Where is Wisdom to be Found? (cont.)

personified *Death* (= *Mot* in Ugaritic and Hebrew) but also the motif of searching for someone both in the world and in the underworld. NJB's use of initial capitals brings out the mythical colouring of the two parallel verses 22 and 14.

The third figure on the cosmic stage is the personified Wisdom herself. Her home is *hidden* from human eyes but she was with God at the time of creation (the hints of 25-7 are more fully worked out in Prov Ch. 8) when he *imposed law* and order on nature. That same order has been revealed by him to *human beings*: as applied to their affairs it is (i) *the fear of the LORD,* i.e. religion, and (ii) *the avoidance of evil,* i.e. morality. The final thrust of Ch.28 could thus be regarded as a poetical equivalent of the sermon in Dt 30.11-14.

Job's Former Happiness

1   Job again took up his discourse and said:

2   Oh, that I were as in the months of old,
        as in the days when God watched over me;

4   when I was in my prime,
        when the friendship of God was upon my tent;

5   when the Almighty was still with me,
        when my children were around me;

6   when my steps were washed with milk,
        and the rock poured out for me streams of oil!

7   When I went out to the gate of the city,
        when I took my seat in the square,

8   the young men saw me and withdrew,
        and the aged rose up and stood;

9   the nobles refrained from talking,
        and laid their hands on their mouths;

21   They listened to me, and waited,
        and kept silence for my counsel.

22   After I spoke they did not speak again,
        and my word dropped upon them like dew.

23   They waited for me as for the rain;
        they opened their mouths as for the spring rain.

25   I chose their way, and sat as chief,
        and I lived like a king among his troops.

11   When the ear heard, it commended me,
        and when the eye saw, it approved;   ▶

Job's Former Happiness

The next three chapters belong together. Ch. 29 describes the estate Job formerly enjoyed, favoured by God and respected by men. Ch. 30 contrasts his past with his present in both respects. In Ch. 31 he protests his innocence, insisting in particular upon his lifelong concern for his neighbour – the very grounds for the respect in which he was formerly held (29.11+).

Job's Former Happiness (cont.)

29. 12 because I delivered the poor who cried,
    and the orphan who had no helper.

13 The blessing of the wretched came upon me,
    and I caused the widow's heart to sing for joy.

14 I put on righteousness, and it clothed me;
    my justice was like a robe and a turban.

15 I was eyes to the blind,
    and feet to the lame.

16 I was a father to the needy,
    and I championed the cause of the stranger.

17 I broke the fangs of the unrighteous,
    and made them drop their prey from their teeth.

18 Then I thought, 'I shall die in my nest,
    and I shall multiply my days like the phoenix;

19 my roots spread out to the waters,
    with the dew all night on my branches;

20 my glory was fresh with me,
    and my bow ever new in my hand.'   (NRSV)

Job's Former Happiness (cont.)

Ch.29 paints an idealised picture of a patriarchal society. Verses 21-5 have here been transposed as in REB and NJB, but the language of NRSV is more appropriate. *Bow* (20) is a symbol of manly vigour. The last verses show Job still accepting the orthodox correlation between virtue and happiness.

His Present Misery

30. 1 But now I am laughed to scorn
        by men of a younger generation,
    men whose fathers I would have disdained
        to put with the dogs guarding my flock.

2 What use to me was the strength of their arms,
        since their vigour had wasted away?

3 Gaunt with want and hunger,
        they gnawed roots in the desert.

5 Driven out from human society,
        pursued like thieves with hue and cry,

6 they made their homes in gullies and ravines,
        in holes in the ground and rocky clefts;

7 they howled like beasts among the bushes,
        huddled together beneath the scrub,

8 vile, disreputable wretches,
        outcasts from the haunts of men.   ▸

His Present Misery

The contrasting lament of Ch.30 is structured round a threefold *But now* in vv.1, 9 and 16 (obscured by REB in 9 and 16). Typically an ANE lament painted the speaker's misery in the strongest colours possible, so as to arouse the sympathy of the god. But here Job's language goes to the extreme,

His Present Misery (cont.)

9   Now I have become the target of their taunts;
      my name is a byword among them.

0   They abhor me, they shun me,
      they dare to spit in my face.

1   They run wild and savage me;
      at sight of me they throw off all restraint.

12   On my right flank they attack in a mob;
      they raise their siege-ramps against me;

13   to destroy me they tear down my crumbling defences,
      and scramble up against me unhindered;

14   they burst in as through a gaping breach;
      at the moment of the crash they come in waves.

15   Terror after terror overwhelms me;
      my noble designs are swept away as by the wind,
      and my hope of deliverance vanishes like a cloud.

16   So now my life ebbs away;
      misery has me daily in its grip.

17   By night pain pierces my very bones,
      and there is ceaseless throbbing in my veins.

19   God himself has flung me down in the mud;
      I have become no better than dust or ashes.

20   I call out to you, God, but you do not answer,
      I stand up to plead, but you keep aloof.

21   You have turned cruelly against me;
      with your strong hand you persecute me.

22   You snatch me up and mount me on the wind;
      the tempest tosses me about.

23   I know that you will hand me over to death,
      to the place appointed for all mortals.

His Present Misery (cont.)

with a sustained violence of imagery that equals and perhaps exceeds anything in the OT.

The greatest hyperbole comes in the first part (1-8), where he launches into a bitter denunciation of the *younger generation*. Astonishingly their only crime is the poverty to which at other times he shows himself so sympathetic (Chs. 24, 29, 31, not to mention 30.24-25). Scholars who have read these verses literally have been driven to extremities of interpretation: either the passage is interpolated or it reveals Job as deeply hypo-critical. But a literal reading suits neither the general flamboyance of the chapter nor the rhetoric of these actual verses, where Job's young enemies are *driven out from human society* etc., and yet a few lines later *dare to spit in* his *face*. Job is not a hypocrite, but he is easily carried away by the exuberance of his own rhetoric.

The second section (9-15) depicts the attacks on him by his fellows. In the third his own pain (16-17) and misery (27-31) frame God's persecution of him (19-23). The themes are old ones of his, the imagery more extravagant than ever.

His Present Misery (cont.)

30.24 Yet no beggar held out his hand to me in vain
    for relief in his distress.

25 Did I not weep for the unfortunate?
    Did not my heart grieve for the destitute?

26 Yet evil has come though I expected good,
    and when I looked for light, darkness came.

27 My bowels are in ferment and know no peace;
    days of misery stretch out in front of me.

28 I go about dejected and comfortless;
    I rise in the assembly, only to appeal for help.

29 The wolf is now my brother,
    the desert-owls have become my companions.

30 My blackened skin peels off,
    and my body is scorched by the heat.

31 My lyre has been tuned for a dirge,
    my flute to the sound of weeping.

(REB)

Job's Oath of Clearance

31.9 If my heart has been seduced by a woman,
    or if I have lurked at my neighbour's door,

10 let my wife go and grind for someone else,
    let others have intercourse with her!

13 If I have ever infringed the rights of slave
    or slave-girl in legal actions against me –

14 what shall I do, when God stands up?
    What shall I say, when he holds his assize?

15 Did he not create them in the womb like me,
    the same God forming us in the womb?

16 Have I been insensible to the needs of the poor,
    or let a widow's eyes grow dim?

17 Have I eaten my bit of bread on my own
    without sharing it with the orphan?

Job's Oath of Clearance

Ch.31 is crucial in the drama of Job. In it he not merely protests his innocence – he has done that often enough before – but backs his protest with a series of oaths which take the form of a self-curse. The self-curse was a kind of ordeal, such as was commonly employed in the ANE, including Israel, when legal disputes could not otherwise be resolved (see on Num 5). Characteristically the accused would deny the charge with a formula: 'If I have done A or B, may I suffer X or Y'. In the extreme case the curse was 'may I die'. If the curse was fulfilled, the accused was regarded as guilty; if it was not, the accusation was shown up as false. This is the formula which Job now uses, with the aim of settling the issue once and for

Job's Oath of Clearance (cont.)

9
Have I ever seen a wretch in need of clothing,
or the poor with nothing to wear,

0
without his having cause to bless me from his heart,
as he felt the warmth of the fleece from my lambs?

1
Have I raised my hand against an orphan,
presuming on my credit at the gate?

2
If so, let my shoulder fall from its socket,
let my arm break off at the elbow!

4
Have I put my faith in gold,
saying to fine gold, 'Ah, my security'?

5
Have I ever gloated over my great wealth,
or the riches that my hands have won?

26
Or has the sight of the sun in its glory,
or the glow of the moon as it walked the sky,

27
secretly stolen my heart,
so that I blew them a kiss?

28
That too would be a criminal offence,
to have denied the supreme God.

29
Have I rejoiced at my enemy's misfortune,
or exulted when disaster overtook him?

Job's Oath of Clearance (cont.)

all. In that sense he is bringing pressure to bear on God.

This ANE 'oath of clearance' was used either in a law court to deny a specific charge or in a religious context to claim a general purity or innocence. Its use here by Job falls between the two. On the one hand it is general, as the context demands. On the other hand, none of the offences is strictly cultic and only one could be called religious. Some, indeed, are social offences. But none is the kind of specific offence which forms the bulk of ANE legal codes, whether inside or outside the OT. On the contrary what distinguishes this list is that it mostly refers not to actions but to thoughts and feelings. The chapter has therefore been seen as the acme of OT morality.

Adultery (i.e. a man with a married woman) was a common theme of Wisdom literature, and its treatment here is typical. The curse itself has an awful appropriateness (note the *double entendre* of *grind* in

v.10) but it falls upon the wrong person viz. the already injured wife. The punishment accords with ancient ideas of solidarity, but the modern reader can only feel revulsion.

Job next refers to his treatment of people lacking privilege or protection. ANE law and custom (and OT prophets) constantly express concern for all of them. But v.15 goes futher than any other OT passage (Prov 22.2 is the nearest) in inferring the brotherhood of man from the fatherhood of God. In v.21 the *orphan* stands for all the defenceless, and Job denies *presuming on* his own influence. The curse in v.22 applies directly to v.21 but indirectly to the whole section.

Thirdly Job repudiates (perhaps a little wistfully) two offences which fall under the general heading of idolatry. As a rich man, he (i.e. the character Job) was tempted to be a miser, as a sage and lover of nature to adore *the sun* and *moon*.

Then comes perhaps the most remarkable verse of all (29). Many pages of the

Job's Oath of Clearance (cont.)

31.32 No stranger ever had to sleep outside,
  my door was always open to the traveller.

33 Have I ever concealed my transgression from others
  or kept my fault a secret in my breast?

34 Have I ever stood in fear of common gossip,
  or dreaded any family's contempt,
  and so kept quiet, not venturing out of doors?

35 Will no one give me a hearing?
  I have said my last word; now let Shaddai reply!
  When my adversary has drafted his writ against me

36 I shall wear it on my shoulder,
  and bind it round my head like a royal turban.

37 I shall give him an account of my every step
  and go as boldly as a prince to meet him.

40b End of the words of Job.

                  (NJB)

Job's Oath of Clearance (cont.)

OT are disfigured by gloating over an *enemy's misfortune*, whether in prospect or in retrospect. No other passage so clearly repudiates that attitude. Prov 24.17f. and 25.21f. counsel against it, but undermine the morality by adding a cynical motive. Finally (in this selection) Job refers to his hospitality to *strangers* (32) and to his openness about his own mistakes, as a result of which he has been impervious to *common gossip* (34).

Backed by this oath of clearance, Job can repeat his demand that God appear to answer him. The various translations of 35-7 differ in detail, but the burden is clear. He has made this demand often before, but its final formulation is more solemn – and confident to the point of bravado.

God Reveals the Order of Creation

The next three and a half chapters mark the climax of the book. After a prolonged dramatic pause, God finally appears. And it is not now the remote Shaddai but YHWH the 'personal' God of the Hebrews. YHWH, who is here mentioned for the first time in the dialogue, is seen in a storm, the usual OT context of his appearance.

He makes two long speeches and Job gives two short answers. It is clear that Job submits, but it is not clear why, i.e. what he is repenting of, and what God has said to make him change his mind so totally. Some scholars hold that God does not actually *say* anything: he merely is seen. That view can claim some support from Job's second answer (42.5). Against it is the intrinsic improbability of such a very long 'non-speech' from God, especially since what Job has asked for throughout the book is precisely an answer. But if God does give an answer, it is certainly a dusty one, indirect at best, and open to a wide range of interpretations.

At one extreme is the view that God just bullies Job, whose submission is tongue-in-cheek. At the other is that God's speech displays to Job his grand design (38.2). Its central feature is order – a marvellous, beautiful and therefore implicitly moral order in which he cares equally for all his creatures. The position followed here is nearer to the latter than to the former.

God Reveals the Order of Creation

1 Then the LORD answered Job out of the tempest:

2   Who is this who darkens counsel
        with words devoid of knowledge?

3   Brace yourself and stand up like a man;
        I shall put questions to you, and you must answer.

4   Where were you when I laid the earth's foundations?
        Tell me, if you know and understand.

5   Who fixed its dimensions? Surely you know!
        Who stretched a measuring line over it?

6   On what do its supporting pillars rest?
        Who set its corner-stone in place,

7   while the morning stars sang in chorus
        and the sons of God all shouted for joy?

God Reveals the Order of Creation (cont.)

What then is the tone of God's speeches? Given Job's heated challenge, it would be surprising if God were not heated too. Formally, he uses the same sequence of questions, mostly rhetorical-indignant, as Job and the friends do – now it is *his* turn (38.3b). This is the style of the author, and indeed of much Hebrew poetry. God also prefaces each of his speeches with personal remarks, just like Job and the friends (38.2; 40.6-8). And if at times he is ironical and even sarcastic (e.g. 38.5a; 40.10-14), that too is part of the Hebrew tradition of disputation. The irony of 38.3, repeated at 40.7, sets the tone for the whole encounter. God pretends to be challenging Job as an equal. Behind the pretence lies not so much the anger of an overlord as the teasing of a father, who does not take Job quite as seriously as Job takes himself.

At any rate God never answers Job's basic question. As he shows in 40.8 (one of the two places where he criticises Job), he rejects the proposed dilemma. He is therefore not concerned to *put* Job *in the wrong so as* to prove himself right. Indeed Job may be presumed innocent of the charges he denied in Ch.31, since his self-curses have not been fulfilled. Of Job's suffering God says nothing, of jus-tice itself next to nothing – only the oblique reference in 40.9-14. So much is obvious to any reader. Less obvious is that he says very little about human beings at all. The rare mentions of them are all negative (e.g. 38.26) or dismissive (39.7, 18, 25). Whereas in Genesis man was the climax of creation, God here stops short of that climax. Instead he sings a paean to the wonders of what 38.33 (REB) calls *nature*, thus exemplifying that design of his which Job had obscured (38.2, his only other criticism of Job).

God begins, as in Genesis, with the inanimate cosmos (38.4+). In describing this part of creation, the poet follows traditional accounts, drawing heavily on the mythology shared by the OT with the rest of the ANE. The *earth* was regarded as a building supported on *pillars*. As such, the laying of its foundation-stone is delightfully celebrated by the whole 'host of heaven', including the *sons of God* (whom we met in 1.15) and the *stars* (who in the ANE ranked as deities). Much of God's first speech in Ch.38 is an indirect answer to Job's first speech in Ch.3, an answer not in argument but in imagery. Ch.3 was dominated by images of darkness and death, Ch.38 by those of light and life. So the music of the spheres in v.7

God Reveals the Order of Creation (cont.)

38. 8   Who supported the sea at its birth,
     when it burst in flood from the womb –

9   when I wrapped it in a blanket of cloud
     and swaddled it in dense fog,

10   when I established its bounds,
     set its barred doors in place,

11   and said, 'Thus far may you come but no farther;
     here your surging waves must halt'?

17   Have the portals of death been revealed to you?
     Have you seen the door-keepers of the place of darkness?

22   Have you visited the storehouses of the snow
     or seen the arsenal where hail is stored,

23   which I have kept ready for the day of calamity,
     for war and for the hour of battle?

25   Who has cut channels for the downpour
     and cleared a path for the thunderbolt,

26   for rain to fall on land devoid of people,
     on the uninhabited wilderness,

27   clothing waste and derelict lands with green
     and making grass spring up on thirsty ground?

31   Can you bind the cluster of the Pleiades
     or loose Orion's belt?

33   Did you proclaim the rules that govern the heavens
     or determine the laws of nature on the earth?

God Reveals the Order of Creation (cont.)

drowns Job's curses in 3.7-9: 'may no cry of joy be heard' and 'no star shine out'.

The sea (8-11) as always represents the chaos upon which God imposed order when he *established its bounds*. After eight lines each on earth and sea, we have a brief reference to the underworld, which in ANE and Greek myth (but not in the OT) could be *visited* by heroes. *Snow* and *hail*, like death, are portrayed as enemies of human beings, and *rain* (26) falls without reference to them. Verse 31 is a splendid example of Hebrew parallelism, built upon the antithesis between binding the loose *cluster* of the seven *Pleiades* and loosening the tight *belt* of the constellation *Orion*. The reference to the stars recalls Psalm 8 which Job had previously parodied: 'When I consider your heavens, the works of your fingers . . . what is man that you should be mindful of him?' The cosmos is ordered and beautiful, but it operates without reference to man who cannot understand, still less control it.

God Reveals the Order of Creation (cont.)

39 Can you hunt prey for the lioness
    and satisfy the appetite of young lions,

40 as they crouch in the lair
    or lie in wait in the covert?

41 Who provides the raven with its quarry
    when its fledgelings cry aloud,
    croaking for lack of food?

.1 Do you know when the mountain goats give birth?
    Do you attend the wild doe when she is calving?

2   Can you count the months that they carry their young
    or know the time of their delivery,

4   when the fawns growing and thriving in the open country
    leave and do not return?

5   Who has let the Syrian wild ass range at will
    and given the Arabian wild ass its freedom?

6   I have made its haunts in the wilderness
    and its home in the saltings;

7   it disdains the noise of the city
    and does not obey a driver's shout;

8   it roams the hills as its pasture
    in search of a morsel of green.

9   Is the wild ox willing to serve you
    or spend the night in your stall?

10 Can you harness its strength with ropes;
    will it harrow the furrows after you?

12 Can you rely on it to come,
    bringing your grain to the threshing-floor?

13 The wings of the ostrich are stunted;
    her pinions and plumage being so scanty

14 she leaves her eggs on the ground
    and lets them be kept warm by the sand. ▸

God Reveals the Order of Creation (cont.)

The same tone continues in the second part of the hymn, the 'carnival of the animals' (38.39+). The ten animals, all then to be seen in the deserts and mountains round the Jordan valley, have in common that they are not domesticated: the war-horse may be technically tame, but is portrayed as still half-wild. For the first four the emphasis is on God's care: he is concerned for the food of the *lioness* and the *raven* and for the family life of *the mountain goat* and *the wild doe*. The next pair (39.5-12) are the wild cousins of humanity's chief beasts of burden – if only they also would *obey* and *serve*! *The wild ass* is linked to the previous pair by the theme of God's care (6), the *wild ox* to the next by his indifference to humans.

The ostrich, a symbol of the bizarre in nature, scorns both humans (18) and human feelings (16). The ostrich has always been maligned by folk-lore. As

God Reveals the Order of Creation (cont.)

39.15 She is unmindful that a foot may crush them,
or a wild animal trample on them;

16 she treats her chicks heartlessly
as if they were not her own,
not caring if her labour is wasted.

17 For God has denied her wisdom
and left her without sense,

18 while like a cock she struts over the uplands,
scorning both horse and rider.

19 Do you give the horse his strength?
Have you clothed his neck with a mane?

20 Do you make him quiver like a locust's wings,
when his shrill neighing strikes terror?

21 He shows his mettle as he paws and prances;
in his might he charges the armoured line.

22 He scorns alarms and knows no dismay;
he does not shy away before the sword.

23 The quiver rattles at his side,
the spear and sabre flash.

24 Trembling with eagerness, he devours the ground
and when the trumpet sounds there is no holding him;

25 at the trumpet-call he cries 'Aha!'
and from afar he scents the battle,
the shouting of the captains, and the war cries.

26 Does your skill teach the hawk to use its pinions
and spread its wings towards the south?

27 Do you instruct the eagle to soar aloft
and build its nest high up?

28 It dwells among the rocks and there it has its nest,
secure on a rocky crag;

29 from there it searches for food,
keenly scanning the distance,

30 that its brood may be gorged with blood;
wherever the slain are, it is there.

(REB)

God Reveals the Order of Creation (cont.)

well as hiding her head in the sand (17), she was erroneously believed to *abandon* both *eggs* and *chicks*. The mention of *the horse* in v.18 leads to the most splendid description of all. In the ancient world the horse was used for war and hunting, never for husbandry. Here more than anywhere the exuberance of the language reflects the exuberance of creation. The sequence of pairs ends with two birds of prey. God's plan is shown in the migration of *the hawk* and the *secure nest* and *keen* sight *of the eagle*. This whole second part (38.39 - 39.30) continues the downgrading of human beings and goes further in the upgrading of the animals, most of whose actions are expressed in verbs which belong primarily in human contexts.

Interlude: Exchange between God and Job

1 And the LORD said to Job:
2   Shall a faultfinder contend with the Almighty?
          Anyone who argues with God must respond.

3 Then Job answered the LORD:
4   See, I am of small account; what shall I answer you?
          I lay my hand on my mouth.
5   I have spoken once, and I will not answer;
          twice, but will proceed no further.

6 Then the LORD answered Job out of the whirlwind:
7   Gird up your loins like a man;
          I will question you, and you declare to me.
8   Will you even put me in the wrong?
          Will you condemn me that you may be justified?
9   Have you an arm like God,
          and can you thunder with a voice like his?
10   Deck yourself with majesty and dignity;
          clothe yourself with glory and splendor.
11   Pour out the overflowings of your anger,
          and look on all who are proud, and abase them.
12   Look on all who are proud, and bring them low;
          tread down the wicked where they stand.
13   Hide them all in the dust together;
          bind their faces in the world below.
14   Then I will also acknowledge to you
          that your own right hand can give you victory.   (NRSV)

Interlude: Exchange between God and Job

God's first speech overwhelms Job. He has said too much already (the idiom of *once . . . twice* cleverly suggests that) and he will say no more. But God will not let him off so easily: having demanded an argument, Job cannot now withdraw. And here (40.10-14) God does respond, if obliquely, to Job's criticism of his justice. It is a remarkable response. On the surface God challenges Job to do better: if he can destroy *all* (repeated three times) the evil in the world God will salute him – as God! The implication can only be that God's power is not unlimited: he can confine the enemy but not eliminate it altogether. But for God to admit that is not to accept Job's accusation of wholesale injustice.

God's Speech Concluded

God therefore continues to illustrate his management of the universe by a baroque description of a sixth pair of animals. But they are not just more of the same, as is shown by their Hebrew names, Behemoth and Leviathan. *Behemoth* means literally 'beasts', but the plural is used, like the royal 'we' in English, to signify power; so we might translate it 'The Beast'. *Leviathan* was originally the dragon associated in Ugaritic myth with the sea of chaos defeated by God at the creation (see p.27). Later it came to be used more widely of any monstrous beast. Here it clearly corresponds in many respects to the crocodile.

God's Speech Concluded

40.15   Look at Behemoth,
      which I made just as I made you;
      it eats grass like an ox.

16   Its strength is in its loins,
      and its power in the muscles of its belly.

17   It makes its tail stiff like a cedar;
      the sinews of its thighs are knit together.

18   Its bones are tubes of bronze,
      its limbs like bars of iron.

21   Under the lotus plants it lies,
      in the covert of the reeds and in the marsh.

23   Even if the river is turbulent, it is not frightened;
      it is confident though Jordan rushes against its mouth.

41.1   Can you draw out Leviathan with a fishhook,
      or press down its tongue with a cord?

3   Will it make many supplications to you?
      Will it speak soft words to you?

4   Will it make a covenant with you
      to be taken as your servant forever?

5   Will you play with it as with a bird,
      or will you put it on leash for your girls?

6   Will traders bargain over it?
      Will they divide it up among the merchants?

13   Who can strip off its outer garment?
      Who can penetrate its double coat of mail?

14   Who can open the doors of its face?
      There is terror all around its teeth.

15   Its back is made of shields in rows,
      shut up closely as with a seal.
    One is so near to another
      that no air can come between them.

God's Speech Concluded

Similarly Behemoth has much in common with the hippopotamus, its regular pair in ancient art and literature. In Egyptian myth the conquest of the hippopotamus was the task of the god Horus. Unlike the animals of Ch.39, these two are therefore enemies not only of men but of *the gods* (see 41.25). They symbolise the hostile powers of chaos and pride. Each is typically at home in the *turbulent* waters of chaos (40.23 and 41.31), and the whole description ends suitably on the note of pride (41.34; cp. 40.12).

Of the two beasts Behemoth is marginally the less threatening, having been created by God as a herbivore (40.15). He is remarkable for his size, strength and sexual vigour – *tail* in v.17a is a euphemism. The *lotus* here is not a lily but a thorny bush. *Jordan* (23) is surprising, though the crocodile was found in ancient times in some rivers of Palestine.

The description of Leviathan starts with a gentle irony (41.3.6), but high drama soon takes over. Verses 18 and 21 spring straight from dragon-mythology. The Hebrew for *sneezes* is *atīshōth*. In Egyptian hieroglyphs the eye of the crocodile is the

God's Speech Concluded (cont.)

6   Its sneezes flash forth light,
8   and its eyes are like the eyelids of the dawn.
      Its breath kindles coals,
21   and a flame comes out of its mouth.
      When it raises itself up the gods are afraid;
25   at the crashing they are beside themselves.
      Though the sword reaches it, it does not avail,
26   nor does the spear, the dart, or the javelin.
      Its underparts are like sharp potsherds;
30   it spreads itself like a threshing sledge on the mire.
      It makes the deep boil like a pot;
31   it makes the sea like a pot of ointment.
      On earth it has no equal,
33   a creature without fear.
      It surveys everything that is lofty;
34   it is king over all that are proud.   (NRSV)

God's Speech Concluded (cont.)

symbol of *dawn* (18b). For *threshing sledge* (30) see Amos 1.3. The *ointment* of 31b is also to be taken as boiling. *Surveys* in 34 means 'looks in the eye' (so NJB).

Job's Submission

1   Then Job answered the LORD:
2   I know that you can do all things,
            and that no purpose of yours can be thwarted.
3   Therefore I have uttered what I did not understand,
            things too wonderful for me, which I did not know.
5   I had heard of you by the hearing of the ear,
            but now my eye sees you;
6   therefore I despise myself,
            and repent in dust and ashes.   (NRSV)

Job's Submission

God's second speech brings Job not merely to silence but to repentance. Two things have happened to cause this change of heart. First, he has in some sense *seen* God. The vision has by itself met one of his charges, namely that God is indifferent. It has also overwhelmed him, rendering trivial his own attempts to solve theological problems. Similarly Thomas Aquinas in old age had a vision which, he said, 'made all that I have written seem like straw' – and laid down his pen for good. He has also seen as God sees. What God has said to him about 'nature' has forced him to abandon his obsessive egocentricity and look outside himself. And to see as God sees is humbling, not because God is all-powerful but paradoxically because he admits the limitations of his own power. By shifting the ground of debate, God has made it possible for Job also to admit, not to the sins he denied to the friends, but to the *hubris* of challenging God. The two admissions enable a reconciliation. And although Job has received strictly no answer to the question about his own suffering, he has been shown enough to help him to live with it in a world where order in general predominates.

The Epilogue

42.7 When the LORD had finished speaking to Job, he said to Eliphaz the Temanite, 'My anger is aroused against you and your two friends, because, unlike my servant Job, you have not spoken as you ought about me. • Now take seven bulls and seven rams, go to my servant Job and offer a whole-offering for yourselves, and he will intercede for you. I shall surely show him favour by not being harsh with you because you have not spoken as you ought about me as he has done.' • Then Eliphaz the Temanite and Bildad the Shuhite and Zophar the Naamathite went and carried out the LORD's command, and the LORD showed favour to Job 10 • when he had interceded for his friends.

The LORD restored Job's fortunes, and gave him twice the possessions he had before. • All Job's brothers and sisters and his acquaintance of former days came and feasted with him in his home. They consoled and comforted him for all the misfortunes which the LORD had inflicted on him, and each of them gave him a sheep and a gold ring. • Thus the LORD blessed the end of Job's life more than the beginning: he had fourteen thousand sheep and six thousand camels, a thousand yoke of oxen, and as many she-donkeys. • He also had seven sons and three daughters; • he named his eldest daughter Jemimah, the second Keziah, and the 15 third Keren-happuch. • There were no women in all the world so beautiful as Job's daughters; and their father gave them an inheritance with their brothers.

• Thereafter Job lived another hundred and forty years; he saw his sons and his grandsons to four generations, • and he died at a very great age.   (REB)

The Epilogue

Verses 7-9 are the poet's jointure, seeing the three friends off before we get back to the folk-tale. The LORD addresses Eliphaz as (presumably) the senior of them, and what he says is the greatest of the many surprises in the book. True, Job had himself predicted that God would rebuke them for falsely accusing him (13.10). But since then we have had Job himself reduced to silence and repentance. Perhaps God finds the honest challenger more acceptable than the people whom Coleridge called 'orthodox liars'. But there may also be a more personal side to it. Job having recognised God, God now recognises Job. Remarkably, God then goes further, suggesting that Job will *intercede* for the friends – a delightfully ironic twist to Eliphaz's patronising promise to Job (22.30). And God's recognition enables Job to do precisely that. The new Job can look beyond himself,

and he starts by putting thirty chapters of hostility behind him. This mutual reconciliation of all parties to the dialogue marks the conclusion of the poem, whose fundamental theme was that of relationships.

The way is now clear for the conclusion also of the folk-tale, which is more concerned with externals. The outcast is welcomed back into society and the bankrupt given the wherewithal to start again in business. By the end of his life he had doubled his possessions – perhaps a reference to the provision in the Torah for double restitution in case of theft (Ex 22.7+). Only in the matter of *daughters* is the number of three maintained, for a larger number would have been an embarrassment. But his special affection for them is shown by the names which they alone are given: dove, cassia (a perfume; cp. Prov 7.17) and a horn of kohl (eye-shadow). He also broke with older tradition by giving them *an inherit-ance* even though they had brothers. Finally his own life was twice the allotted span (Ps 90.10), and so he saw twice the usual number of generations (Ps 128.6) before dying like the patriarchs. His wife, however, is not even mentioned in the epilogue.

The folk-tale as preserved in the book of Job has six scenes, of which the last two are set on earth. Originally there must have been a seventh scene set in heaven, between the present nos.5 and 6, telling of Satan's humiliation at the failure of his experiment. When the poet took over the folk-tale, that scene had to go. Before the poem, it would spoil the suspense; after-wards, it would be an anti-climax and an irrelevance – for once God and Job have met we are no longer interested in Satan. Into the gap, the poet inserted his poem with its two jointures.

Afterword to Job

Any careful reading of Job raises a number of issues in the reader's mind. First of these is its integrity in the literary sense of the word.

The position adopted in the comment-ary is that the author took an old prose folk-tale and modified it somewhat so as to serve as a framework for a poem which he himself composed in dialogue form. Of the present poem (3.2-42.6), Ch.28 is a separate composition, perhaps by the same author, while [Chs 32-37] are a later addition from a different and feebler pen. The grounds for regarding the folk-tale as separate from the poem are many. Chief is the difference in seriousness between the two parts. Though ostensibly about the same characters in the same predica-ment of innocent suffering, the folk-tale functions at a very superficial level compared with the depth and power of the poetry. The epilogue in particular is an anti-climax. The prologue is necessary to guarantee Job's innocence, yet the role of the Satan is never referred to by any of the participants in the poem. In the folk-tale God is pliant, Job pious (at least out-wardly) and submissive; in the poem Job is bitter to the point of blasphemy, whereas God, whether speaking or silent, maintains his sovereign dignity. The friends who create most of the poetic dialogue are absent from the prose, though introduced and later dismissed in the author's jointures between the prose and the poetry.

Chs 38-42 raise other issues of literary integrity. Many readers have asked questions: (i) what light do God's speeches throw on the problem which obsesses Job, namely why an innocent man suffers? (ii) what does God say that causes Job to repent? (iii) why does God then say that Job has spoken the truth about him? To these questions the commentary has suggested answers, some more confidently than others. Most important of them is the first, especially if (as is commonly supposed) the main purpose of the whole book is to deal with the theological 'problem of suffering'.

That problem arises from the fact that the distribution of suffering in the world is not what would be expected in advance from the governance of a single benevo-lent deity. No such problem arises if there is no god, or many gods, or even a single malevolent or indifferent god. On the other hand a devil (e.g. the Satan in the book of Job) provides no solution: unless such a being is equivalent to a second god, his existence only pushes the problem one stage further back.

Before the book of Job was written the accepted explanation in Israel was that all suffering is a punishment for sin, whether intentional or inadvertent. Down to the exile this explanation had taken a collective form: people suffered for the sins of their society, or of their parents.

Gradually however such collective interpretations lost sway. Ezekiel 18 is the classic exposition of the revised version: that people suffer only for their own sins. This is the view espoused in the Book of Job not only by the friends but also, at least unconsciously, by himself: it is what fuels his desperate anxiety to establish his innocence. It was the achievement of the author to ensure that it was never taken seriously again. Nor was that merely a theological point: subsequent sufferers no longer had to cope with guilt on top of their pain.

But they were still left with the problem of faith: where suffering is *not* due to sin, how can a good God allow it? One 'solution' which is never entertained for a moment in Job is that there is no God. Two other kinds of solution are adumbrated, though neither is followed through. The first kind is the partial solution offered e.g. by Eliphaz in 5.17+, that suffering is (sometimes) corrective. Similarly Elihu in [Chs 32-7] suggests that suffering (sometimes) tests character, sifting the good from the bad. More interestingly, 22.28-30 hints at the view developed in Isaiah 53, that innocent suffering can be vicariously redemptive, i.e. the suffering of the innocent A can redeem the guilty B. These and other similar views (e.g. the non-biblical view that suffering sometimes ennobles) are partial in the sense that they can at most be valid in some cases though not in others.

Of course it may be more sensible to follow this kind of approach, i.e. to treat each case separately. But for those who still seek a general explanation which will cover all (or all other) cases, the best on offer is still that suggested by God's speech in 40.10-14, that there are forms of suffering which God *cannot* prevent. Philosophers of religion will want to argue further about possible meanings of the word 'cannot'. The ordinary 'believer'

may be content with the trusting words which Job uttered in innocence at the beginning and could have repeated with insight at the end: 'The LORD gave, and the LORD has taken away; blessed be the name of the LORD.' That is as far as the book of Job takes it, though Jeremiah may have gone one step further, in suggesting that God himself suffers too (see Jer 9.18).

Another way of coming at the meaning of Job is to ask what kind of a book it is. Put most simply, it is a story within a story. Each story contains a build-up of tension which leads to a resolution. The folk-tale is chiefly a story of events, the embedded poem a story of arguments. But there are arguments among the events and events among the arguments. Put like that, it invites comparison with two kinds of Greek literature, dialogue and drama. Plato's *Republic*, for example, is a dialogue about the nature of justice. The arguments develop to the point where they can go no further. In the end Socrates introduces a 'myth' which sets human justice in the context of a divine order of things. That seems very like the Book of Job. But there are two main differences. First, there is no real development of the arguments in Job: the participants repeat themselves, with increasing vehemence and decreasing reference to each other. Second, the myth in the *Republic* brings in the theory of the transmigration of souls. By that theory the imbalance between sin and suffering in this life is redressed in the next life – though unlike any biblical doctrine of heaven and hell, Plato's 'next life' is a reincarnation in *this* world.

Closer than Plato to the OT is Greek tragic drama, with its fundamental theme of *hubris* and *nemesis*: if men overstep the limits of humanity the gods will strike them down. And of Greek tragedies the closest is the *Prometheus Bound* of Aeschylus. Prometheus is a Titan or giant who had disobeyed Zeus by stealing fire to give to men. As punishment he is chained to a rock while vultures gnaw his perpetually renewed liver. Prometheus admits he did wrong, but insists that his punishment is altogether excessive. His opening and closing words invoke heaven and earth to witness the injustice he is suffering. In between there is no action: he just converses with the chorus and with three visitors in succession. They agree with him that he does not deserve the punishment which a tyrannical Zeus has inflicted upon him. But like Job's friends they advise him in his own interest to seek pardon and mercy. Prometheus himself says much that is reminiscent of Job. As well as lamenting his pains, he wishes Zeus had hurled him into Hades, where he would have been safe from the mockery of gods and men. For himself he absolutely refuses to yield. 'I know,' he says, 'that Zeus is hard and that he keeps justice in his own pocket. But the time will come when he will soften and approach me in mutual friendship.'

In the *Prometheus Bound* Zeus does not appear, and the two antagonists remain implacable. But the last play of the trilogy is entitled *Prometheus Unbound* and, though the play is lost, we know that they were finally reconciled. There are thus many similarities between Job and Prometheus.

D.H. Lawrence said provocatively that in the Book of Job 'we have preserved, of a trilogy that is really *Prometheus Unbound*, only the *Prometheus Bound* and terribly suffering on the rock of his own egoism.' But the differences are also great, especially the fact that in Aeschylus' play Zeus *is* in the wrong and has as much to learn as Prometheus.

It seems therefore that such resemblances as there are between Job and works of Greek literature derive not from any familiarity of the one with the other but from the independent pursuit of the same quest, 'to justify the ways of God to men'. The case may well be different with certain works belonging to the Wisdom tradition of the ANE. With them it may be presumed on the contrary that the author of Job *was* familiar. Extracts from three of these works, all Babylonian, follow.

In *A Lamentation to a Man's God* (*ANET* 589-591, c.2000 BC) a prologue introduces 'a young man who uses not his strength for evil', but who nevertheless is sent 'bitter suffering'. Like Job, he laments his condition:

> My god, the day shines bright over the land, [but] for me the day is black.

(His god is his personal god who represents him among the high gods.) Unlike Job, he makes prompt confession of his sins, for

> They say – the sages – a word righteous and straightforward:
> Never has a sinless child been born to its mother.

Finally an epilogue tells how

> His bitter weeping was heard by his god.
> He turned the young man's suffering into joy.

Next comes a poem known by its opening words *I Will Praise the Lord of Wisdom* (*ANET* 596-600, c.1500 BC). Here the sufferer speaks throughout, appealing over the head of his personal god to the supreme god, Marduk.

> My god has forsaken me, my goddess has cut me off . . .
> All day long the tormentor torments me, and at night he does not let me breathe easily for a minute [cp. Job Ch.7] . . .
> My proud head is bowed to the ground; even a youngster has turned back my broad chest [cp. Job 30.1] . . .
> I had my land keep the god's rites and brought my people to value the goddess's name [cp. Job 1.5] . . .
> Who can know the will of the gods in heaven?
> I am perplexed at these things . . .

He then tells of three dreams (cp. Job 4.12+) informing him that Marduk has heard his prayer. The end echoes the beginning:

> The Lord set me on my feet, the Lord restored me to health.

The third poem (*ANET* 601-4, c.1000 BC) is known to scholars as *The Babylonian Theodicy*. It consists entirely of a dialogue between a sufferer and his friend. They address each other with great politeness throughout, e.g.:

> Where is the wise man of your calibre?
> Where is the scholar who can rival you?,

which is very close to e.g. Job 12.2 except that it is not sarcastic. The sufferer complains:

> In the world things are turned round
>   a father tows a boat along the canal
>   while his son lies in bed ...
> What has it profited me that I have bowed down to my god?
> I must bow even to a person who is lower than I. [cp. Job 30.1]

The friend replies:

> The mind of the god, like the centre of the heavens, is remote ...
> [The gods] gave twisted speech to men;
> With lies, not truth, they endowed them for ever.

At the end of our text the sufferer prays:

> May the god who has abandoned me give me help,

and presumably his prayer is answered.

In these three works there are notable similarities of form with Job, but also crucial differences of theology. In Babylonian religion all suffering was sent by a god as a punishment for sin. Since the gods had also put sin into the world in the first place, the problem facing the sufferer reduced itself to finding which deity he had offended (cp. Jonah 1) and then how to win him or her round. For the latter purpose the recognised methods were (i) to bemoan one's wretchedness as piteously as possible, (ii) to confess one's sins and (iii) to praise the deity in question. That is why none of the Babylonian works exhibits the spiritual agony which gives the Book of Job its peculiar power.

There remains the question: what is the resolution of Job's agony? Certainly the book provides no solution to the theological problem discussed above. Yet by the end (42.6) Job has come to terms with his predicament. D.H. Lawrence hinted at the key. Up to Ch.38 Job was 'suffering on the rock of his own egoism', obsessed with his own 'integrity' and unable to tolerate uncertainty. In the course of Chs 38-42 he underwent a painful reorientation, seeing the world – and his own place in it – in a new light. He then recognised God, and God in turn (42.7) recognised him. Thus changed and strengthened, he could intercede for his friends. The conflicts are thus resolved in a general reconciliation. Some critics have wished for that reason to treat the book as some sort of comedy; but the intensity of the previous conflicts leave it far closer to tragedy.

INTRODUCTION TO THE PSALMS

1. David and the Canon

The words psalm and psalter (a collection of psalms) come from an onomatopoeic Greek word 'psallo' meaning 'I pluck the strings'. A psalm is thus a song sung to a plucked instrument, e.g. a lyre or harp. Hebrew tradition ascribed to David, that skilled harpist, dancer and 'singer of the songs of Israel' (2 Sam 23.1 AV), the inspiration behind the psalter. In fact a few of our psalms may have been composed before his time (29, [68]), and most were certainly later; but he may well have written most of 18, the text of which is also found ascribed to him in 2 Sam 22, and some others.

David, however, contributed much more to the psalter than his own composition and performance. It was he who brought the Ark to Jerusalem and so formally established the cult of YHWH there, even though the building of the Temple was left to his son Solomon. He may also have established the guilds of singers who played such an important part in the cult, and whose names are recorded above the Hebrew text of some psalms, e.g. the sons of Asaph and Korahites. (Those superscriptions were added later to the Hebrew text and are generally disregarded in this book.) Whatever use was made of the psalter, the congregation was not invited to sing, except for acclamations like *Hallelujah*, and perhaps sometimes a refrain as in Psalms 8 and 46. The more 'private' psalms were intoned by cantors, the more 'public' ones sung by cantor and/or choir, often antiphonally. The music was difficult and had to be learned, like the words, by heart. It seems likely therefore that some of the temple singers composed psalms of their own. Later they seem to have been thought of as scribes (45.1) or learned men; but in either case they are to be distinguished from the priests, whose function was to preside over the sacrifices.

From such origins the psalms grew gradually over about 600 years. First, small collections were put together: some known by David's name, some by their guild (Asaph or the Korahites), some by their context in worship, e.g. songs of ascent, sung by pilgrims approaching the Temple, and *Hallel* psalms sung at the Passover.

Later, the collections were re-grouped in five 'books'. The principles of grouping are not obvious, except that in Pss 42-83 (book 2 and part of book 3) the word used for God is chiefly Elohim, whereas in the rest of the psalter it is almost always YHWH. Eventually Ps 1 was added as an introduction and Ps 150 as a doxology, to round off the collection. But that process took a long time. For the 40 psalm-scrolls found at Qumran contain fifteen psalms absent from the MT, which shows that the canon of the psalter was still fluid in the mid-C1st BC.

The Bible also contains many psalms which are not in the psalter. They range in time from the earliest of all Hebrew poems (the song of Deborah in Judges 5) which may go back to the C12th BC, through such psalms as that of King Hezekiah [Is 38], right down to the *Magnificat* and other New Testament psalms. And the tradition has continued into Christianity, whether in the composition of psalms in the Hebrew style, such as the *Te Deum*, or in the translation of Hebrew psalms into the European style of strict rhythm and rhyme.

2. Temple Rituals

But to revert to the psalter and to Solomon's Temple, its original setting. It is surprising how little the OT has to say about what went on in the Temple itself, apart from the sacrifices. We do know of regular pilgrimages to Jerusalem for the great feasts. They are represented by a number of psalms (121, 122), and we can follow the pilgrims as they approach across country, enter the city and cross from the outer to the inner court of the Temple (84.7). We also have 'entrance liturgies', preserved most dramatically in Ps 24 (see commentary). And we know that at one of the festivals a procession went around the city on a kind of beating of the bounds (48.12), led by singers, musicians and dancers, with the king present. The people meanwhile stood in the Temple court eagerly awaiting their arrival to begin the songs of praise [68.24-26].

But as to the ritual actually followed at these great festivals, we have to rely on hints. Psalm 48.8 gives a first clue. It was evidently not just a case of hearing a recital of the saving deeds of God, though that certainly played an important part in Temple worship, but 'what we had heard we saw for ourselves'. What was this ritual drama? This is where scholars draw upon the substantial evidence from the myth and ritual of other Semitic peoples.

There are many passing references in the OT to the ANE creation myth, whereby God in the beginning established his orderly rule by defeating the sea monster of chaos. The monster was known variously as Tiamat in Babylon and Yam or Lotan in Ugarit*, and many OT passages contain the related Hebrew words tehōm, yām and Leviāthān (see e.g. Pss [74.13f.] and 104.7). In Babylon that victory was celebrated in an annual cultic drama at the New Year Festival. At the climax of the drama the god Marduk (i.e.

his statue) took his throne in his temple, amid general acclamation, upon an object described as 'the sea'.

There are hints in the OT of a ritual in Jerusalem like that of Babylon. Some scholars suppose that a similar ceremony took place each year at the feast of Tabernacles, which marked the New Year. At its climax the Ark, representing YHWH, was enthroned in the Holy of Holies. The proper psalms for the occasion included 24, 29 and 93, together with others which begin with the acclamation 'YHWH is king' (translated by REB 'has become king').

Most psalms however were composed not for the great annual feasts, but for the various occasions which occurred unpredictably in the course of a year, when an individual or a family or even the representatives of the nation went up to the Temple to pray (or to give thanks) for help of one kind or another. Prayer would naturally be made e.g. when ill, when confessing sin or when protesting innocence. Thanksgiving would naturally be made e.g. on recovery from illness, in fulfilment of a vow or with an offering of first-fruits. There must have been services for such occasions. Again, the OT nowhere tells us explicitly what form they took. To find out, we have to piece together the internal evidence of the psalms with the external evidence that we have from other countries of the ANE.

Now one of the most striking features of the psalms is the way in which many of them change during their course from one mood and content to another. Students and practitioners of religion are familiar with the various ingredients of prayers (and indeed hymns), especially: praise, contrition, thanksgiving, supplication and intercession. Many psalms contain a mixture of these moods, with a change from one to another marked in printing by a gap between sections.

How should we regard these mixtures? It may be said that in times of distress one's various emotions are not so clearly distinguished: one *feels* them all at once, and may not disentangle them in mind. But there is more to it than that. Many psalms seem to have represented the text for a whole liturgy, with different sections being sung, perhaps by different people, in the various parts of the service. Reference has already been made to Psalm 24 as a 'liturgy', and something similar is likely to have happened also in the case of the many prayers which move from lament through petition to thanksgiving. But does the thanksgiving in such cases anticipate a subsequent granting of the petition? Or has something already happened during the 'service' to justify it – just as in the Christian Eucharist, after receiving communion, the congregation may resume the liturgy with the words 'We thank thee. . . .'

There are in fact good grounds for supposing that something did happen. Some psalms refer to a response from God, e.g. [35.3]: 'Let me hear you declare "I am your salvation" '. Some actually include one, e.g. 46.10. In others again the text includes words which, whoever they were spoken by, fulfil that function (85.9-13; 91.14-16). And in the Hebrew text of Ps 22 there is the interesting insertion between vv.21 and 22: 'Thou hast answered me'. The same liturgical sequence was regular in the ANE, e.g. 'The goddess Ishtar heard my anxious sighs, and "Fear not" she said and filled my heart with confidence' (*ANET* 451); also in Greece (*Herondas* VI). Probably some similar divine response, spoken by a priest or Temple prophet and known to scholars as a 'salvation oracle', has fallen out of other Hebrew psalms, e.g. in Ps 13 between vv.4 and 5. But at the very least there is a sharp change of key in the middle of such psalms, strongly marked in the Hebrew by an adversative: 'But I . . .' or 'But thou . . .'.

3. Kinds of Psalms

The 150 psalms in the psalter cover the whole gamut of man's addresses to God, springing from many different situations and expressing many different moods. But they are not grouped in the psalter according to either situation or mood, which makes it hard to find one's way about. In this selection the traditional sequence is kept, but for the reader coming new to them there is much to said for reading them in groups according to their literary kind. Two kinds can be roughly distinguished, together with certain sub-kinds; and the basic distinction is that between hymn and prayer.

A : Hymns

This group of psalms, the largest in this selection, needs some explanation. The term 'hymn' is being used, as in Christian worship, to designate public songs in which the dominant mood is one of praise, thanksgiving and trust. Scholars make a distinction between praise and thanksgiving: one praises God for what he is in himself and for what he has done in creation; one thanks him for what he does in nature and in history. But this distinction is modern and a little arbitrary. In Hebrew, as in Greek, there is one word for both praise and thanks. And the OT regularly expresses myth in terms of history and vice versa (e.g. Pss 46, 114).

The basic structure of hymns is simple. In full, it begins with a call to praise; the main body celebrates God's qualities or deeds; and it concludes in various ways with e.g. a blessing, an expression of trust or another public call to praise. Psalms of this kind in this selection include:

Praise: 8, 19, 29, 65, 104, 113, 114
Thanksgiving: 103, 124
Trust: 23, 46, 91, 131

The category of hymns also includes three other clear sub-groups. The first celebrates YHWH as king (93, 98) or judge

(82). With this group we may place 48, which celebrates YHWH in Zion, and thus links Temple with palace, since Zion was the location of both.

The second sub-group focuses explicitly upon the Temple and its worship. It consists of: pilgrim songs, sung by pilgrims on their way to the Temple for the great feasts (121 and 122, with the closely associated 84); entrance liturgies, sung on entry to the Temple (15, 24); and one might also include here the 'musicians' psalm' 150. The third sub-group is of hymns for royal occasions: a coronation (2) or a marriage (45). If their presence seems anomalous, it has to be remembered that the king was head of the national cult, just as the monarch is titular head of the Church of England.

B : Prayers

The term 'prayer' is used, as in Christian practice, to denote a private or public address to God, whose characteristic tone is that of a plaint or petition, but which may also contain substantial elements of praise, repentance or indeed thanksgiving. It has been said that 'the cry to God in the psalms is always somewhere in the middle between petition and praise, i.e. it is never mere lament or petition, but it can be mere praise' (Weiser). Indeed in this respect the tone of the psalms seems to contrast sharply with that of the prophets. Whereas a prophetic oracle often ends on a note of doom, a psalm rarely does so. This, however, is a difference not of theology but of context. The prophets foretell misfortune for the faithless, but the psalms are for the worshipper who has already shown his faith by coming to the Temple: in principle he has kept the covenant, and God will surely respond. Nevertheless there are times when the 'happy ending' of a lament psalm seems a little unconvincing.

Since prayers cover a wider range of situations and emotions than hymns, their possible components are more numerous. At most they may contain:
1. invocation
2. lament, i.e. account of trouble
3. petition (or more rarely thanks) for help
4. argument, i.e. reason why God should act: e.g. conformity to his reputation or past action, guilt or innocence of speaker, helplessness or confidence of speaker
5. vow or pledge
6. praises and blessings

But this analysis must not be taken too strictly. Components may vary greatly in length, or indeed be missing altogether, according to the context. Moreover the order is not fixed.

Psalms of this kind in this selection include:

Individual lament: 13, 22, 42-3, 55.7-15, 102

Communal lament: 90, 137

Repentance: 51, 130

Entreaty: 85, 123, 126

Thanksgiving: 18, 30

But it will be seen that this classification is a little arbitrary, especially where psalms of thanksgiving are concerned.

One final group of psalms is perhaps best treated also as prayers. These are reflective or meditative psalms, which show some affinities with Wisdom literature, and indeed are sometimes known as Wisdom psalms. They are, in this selection, 73, 127, 128, 133, 139.

Conversely there is one type of prayer which is not found in the psalms, namely intercession. This is odd, considering the number of references to intercession in the OT (e.g. Is 53.12; Job 40), and also examples of it (e.g. Abraham in Gen 18, Moses in Ex 32). But there seems to have been no recognised form for it in Israel or in the rest of the ANE.

4. Social Context of Psalms

Scholars have also attempted to classify psalms according to social context. They have asked, for example, whether a given psalm was composed for use by an individual or by a group, even by the whole people. Was it for use in the privacy of a man's room or in the Temple? If the latter, was it for one of the great public liturgies (days of rejoicing or repentance) or for private or family occasions, e.g. thanksgiving after illness? But such distinctions of social context are not easy to sustain. For example, it might at first sight appear that 'I-psalms' belong in an individual, if not necessarily a domestic, context. But the 'I' may well be an individual who represents the congregation or the people as a whole, whether the speaker is the king (e.g. 2.6) or some Temple official. Also in any case the Israelite who prayed prayed as a member of God's people. So we find in many of the psalms an oscillation between individual and nation, e.g. in 22.2-6 we have: 'I . . . Israel . . . I', and in 121.3-5 'he that keepeth thee . . . he that keepeth Israel . . . thy keeper'. That oscillation meant that a psalm originally composed for public use could be used privately, and vice versa. During the course of centuries, a psalm could change its context more than once.

But when the 'I' is *not* a representative person, whose piety is the psalm expressing? One can distinguish three individuals involved in the use of psalms in the Temple: the poet, the singer and the worshipper. Normally the poet would be connected with the Temple, perhaps as a singer, perhaps in some other capacity. The poem then expresses *his* piety, just like the poems of George Herbert or Gerard Manley Hopkins. When subsequently the worshipper came to the Temple, he chose from the collection a psalm which suited his situation, thus making it his own – indeed in some Babylonian psalms there is space for the insertion of his own name. Finally, the singer sang it for him.

For that purpose the psalter had to contain psalms expressed in language that was general enough to apply to a variety of situations. Even what look like specific references are often, by the conventions of psalm-writing, intended generally or metaphorically. Thus the poet will frequently refer to himself as poor. But so does Jeremiah in his own, very personal, poems [20.13], when we know that in the literal sense he was not poor at all [32.9]. Again the poet will describe himself as near to death, or even as having descended to Sheol; but this was a common usage in Egyptian psalms where the context shows clearly that it was not meant to be taken literally. The same may go for references to illness or to false accusations. It was the convention that the poet should stress his misery in order to elicit God's support, and no great attention need be paid to the details of the plaint.

Robert Alter has brilliantly drawn attention to a cognate feature of the psalms, namely the conventional nature of the imagery as compared with the fireworks of Job or the prophets.

This is a kind of poetry in which the strength and beauty of the individual poem are usually realised through a deft restatement or refashioning of the expected. Thus the speakers represent the state of protection they seek from God or for which they thank him as a shield or buckler, a tower or fortress, a sheltering wing, a canopy or booth, cooling shade; the dangers that beset them are ravening beasts, serpents, arrows, burning coals, pestilence. The poets seem perfectly comfortable with this set repertoire of images. Indeed, the familiarity of the metaphors is precisely their chief advantage. The counters of poetic idiom have been worn to a lovely smoothness by long usage, and that is why they sit so comfortably in the hand of the poet, or – perhaps more relevantly – in the hand of the ordinary worshipper for whom these poems were made.

5. Some Difficulties with Psalms

To Christians the psalms are the most familiar part of the Hebrew Bible, partly because of their deep influence upon Christian hymns and prayers. But they contain some puzzling and even alien features which deserve a special mention.

One such is the prevalence of the lament or complaint. This is an element present in most of the prayer-psalms, and which so dominates the psalter that nearly half the psalms in it are commonly classified by scholars as public or private laments. In this selection, the proportion of them has been cut, because in our ears they quickly become tedious. That judgement is partly aesthetic – there *is* a great deal of repetitiveness in these laments – but it does go deeper. It is no coincidence that, though complaint psalms were common throughout the ANE (see below), there are few examples of them in Greco-Roman religion. This is one of those cases where, in the Christian tradition, Greece has prevailed over Israel. The place of lament has perhaps been taken by the confession of sin, which in ANE psalms was normally associated with it, and which has tended to dominate Protestant prayer, both private and public. Not that confession is absent from the psalter or from the ancient world as a whole, whether the sin is ethical, as in Ps 15, or cultic, as probably in 24.4 ('clean hands') and in most of the ANE. There is also in the psalter and in ANE psalms a feature absent from Christian, as from Greco-Roman, worship – a 'negative confession' or protestation of innocence e.g. in Ps 18.21-3 or (more fully and typically) Job 31.

Another feature of the psalter which puzzles some Christians is the vow, i.e. a promise of an offering which the suppliant will make if his petition is granted. There are many references to vows in the psalter, e.g. [56.12] 'I have bound myself with vows to thee, O God, and will redeem them with due thank offerings.' The vow might be one of sacrifice, as in that case, or of public praise (13.6) or of both (22.25-6; see comment). Such vows were a practice universal in ANE as well as in Greco-Roman religion, and they have been retained in Catholic Christianity; it is the Protestants here who are the odd ones out.

A final element which many find uncomfortable in the psalter is less common but more offensive: the cursing. The Hebrews, like all other peoples in the ancient world, regularly asked God to destroy their enemies and felt no compunction in doing so. If we have advanced, it is in the compunction. Especially jarring is the dissonance shown in the outburst of vindictiveness at the end of the musical Psalm 137. But the dissonance is there; it is part of human nature. The modern parallel is close: the guards at Belsen, dividing their time between Mozart quartets and massacres of Jewish prisoners.

6. Hymns & Prayers in ANE Literature

It is unnerving that the psalms, often regarded as the heart of the Hebrew religion, seem so similar to the many hymns and prayers that have come down to us from Babylon and Egypt. In genre and themes, in images and phrases, in metre and syntax, scarcely a verse in the psalter cannot be parallelled from one or both of those quarters. Individually, the parallels are often helpful, in elucidating obscurities in the Hebrew; but cumulatively they pose a question which it is hard to answer but impossible to evade.

It is hard to answer for technical reasons. The languages are obscure, the chronology uncertain, the texts fragmentary. Any generalisation one makes may be refuted by a new discovery. Yet the question of ANE influence on the psalter is too important to ignore. What can be said about it?

Historically, any influence that Babylonian psalms exerted on Israel must have been exercised in one of two ways: either early but indirectly, through Ugarit and

Canaan, or late and directly, during the exile. Egypt is a different matter: contacts were continuous, and there is evidence of direct Egyptian influence on the court in Jerusalem from Solomon's time on.

The position of the psalter as far as Babylonian influences go is rather like the creation myth: in spite of the similarities in literary form, there are important differences of theology, i.e. beliefs about relations between God and human beings. Note the following main features of Babylonian 'psalms', whether of praise or of lamentation. The god is addressed at length, with cult-titles enumerated so as to compel him, and praise extended to flattery. The speaker is usually the king. His enemies are regarded as sorcerers and demons, and indeed magic is never far away. In Israel the 'I' is only rarely the king, and many psalms use 'we', which is not found in Babylon. When it comes to penitence, the sins of the Israelites are usually ethical; in Babylon they are chiefly cultic. When it comes to praise, the Hebrew alone offers thanks for a specific saving act. In short 'the Israelite stands more upright before his God.' And if a man can converse with God, like Adam, or argue with him, like Job, and expect an answer, that has a profound effect on the tone and register of his prayers and hymns. Some of that difference of tone can be seen in the comparison of Psalm 127 with its Babylonian precursor.

The Egyptian psalms have a different tone again from the Babylonian. Where the latter show anxiety or self-abasement, the former show joy and self-assurance. To this the Egyptians could add, as their paintings show, a love of beauty in the created world. Psalm 104, heavily influenced by Pharaoh Akhnaten's *Hymn to the Sun*, shows this delightfully.

There remains Ugarit* as a representative of Canaanite religion. Here we can speak confidently of a deep and wide influence on the content and forms of Hebrew worship. The OT itself constantly criticises the continuance of Canaanite religion. Now the text of the OT has been amply confirmed by archaeological evidence (see p.32). Although the literature we have from Ugarit is almost entirely poetic myth – there are at most two fragments of prayers – the myths shed light on the content and ritual context of certain psalms. This, taken together with other features, such as the cult-titles and a certain type of parallelism (see p.21+), show Canaanite influence in a number of psalms (e.g. 93) and make it likely that Ps 29 has in fact been taken over more or less direct from Canaanite worship.

In sum then, we have three cases of something like borrowing, one each from Babylonian (127), Egyptian (104) and Ugaritic originals. But it is better to think not so much of individual borrowing as a sharing in a common ANE stock and style, inherited for the most part through Ugarit. This stock in turn was not self-contained. Ugarit was in close touch with (Mycenaean) Greece, and so we are not surprised to find some features of ANE psalms also present in Homer. More surprising is the close resemblance between Ps 139 and an Indian prayer; in this case the link is presumably Iran.

7. English Translations of Psalms
Finally a brief word needs to be said on the choice between the translations. For singing, nothing yet beats Miles Coverdale's version for the *Great Bible* (1539). This had established itself by 1662, so the compilers of the Book of Common Prayer used it instead of the AV (1611) as being 'smoother and more easy to sing'. But Coverdale has many mistakes and obscurities, and this selection is designed for private reading, not public singing. The choice has therefore often fallen upon REB. But for those who have grown up with Coverdale, *The Psalms: a New Translation for Worship* (1976), combines his rhythms with modern scholarship.

Psalm 2

1 Why are the nations in turmoil?
　　Why do the peoples hatch their futile plots?
2 Kings of the earth stand ready,
　　and princes conspire together
　　against the LORD and his anointed king.
3 'Let us break their fetters,' they cry,
　　'let us throw off their chains!'

4 He who sits enthroned in the heavens laughs,
　　the LORD derides them;
5 then angrily he rebukes them,
　　threatening them in his wrath.
6 'I myself have enthroned my king', he says,
　　'on Zion, my holy mountain.'

7 I shall announce the decree of the LORD:
　　'You are my son,' he said to me;
　　'this day I become your father.
8 Ask of me what you will:
　　I shall give you nations as your domain,
　　the earth to its farthest ends as your possession.
9 You will break them with a rod of iron,
　　shatter them like an earthen pot.'

10 Be mindful, then, you kings;
　　take warning, you earthly rulers:
11-12 worship the LORD with reverence;
　　tremble, and pay glad homage to the king,
　　for fear the LORD may become angry
　　and you may be struck down in mid-course;
　　for his anger flares up in a moment.
Happy are all who find refuge in him!

(REB)

Psalm 2

This is a royal hymn celebrating the enthronement of a king in Jerusalem. The king himself recited (or sang) vv.7-9, and possibly the rest as well.

The idea that a king at his accession was adopted as God's *son* (7) was widespread in the ANE (though the actual words 'son of God' are never used of a king in the OT). The closest parallel comes from Egypt. In the ritual for the accession of a Pharaoh the god Amon-Re said to him, 'I am your father, I have begotten you. . . . I give into your command the lands that I have created.' At the same time the new Pharaoh was given a set of potsherds, each bearing the name of a foreign nation, which he ceremonially smashed (cp. v.9).

This psalm however fits not the accession of the king but its subsequent, perhaps annual, celebration. The ANE tone of boastful nationalism, which was politically inappropriate to ancient Jerusalem, is here transposed to the religious sphere. Behind and above the king it is *the LORD* who *sits enthroned* (4), and it is he whom the *earthly rulers* are to *worship* (10f.).

Psalm 2 (cont.)

The structure of the psalm is straight-forward. Of the four roughly equal stanzas, the first and the last are concerned with the *kings of the earth*. Together they frame the central pair, which concern *the Lord and his anointed*; and within that pair the vv.6 and 7 form the keystone of the whole arch. But there is another movement in the psalm. It opens in *turmoil* (the tone of the question in v.1 is one of amazement at their *futile* buzzing), but closes on the quiet note of *refuge in* the Lord.

Psalm 8

1 O Lord our Governor,
    how glorious is your name in all the earth!

2 Your majesty above the heavens is yet recounted
    by the mouths of babes and sucklings.
3 You have founded a strong defence against your adversaries,
    to quell the enemy and the avenger.

4 When I consider your heavens. the work of your fingers,
    the moon and the stars which you have set in order,
5 what is man, that you should be mindful of him,
    or the son of man, that you should care for him?
6 Yet you have made him little less than a god
    and have crowned him with glory and honour.
7 You have made him the master of your handiwork,
    and have put all things in subjection beneath his feet:
8 all sheep and oxen,
    and all the creatures of the field,
9 the birds of the air and the fish of the sea,
    and everything that moves in the pathways of the great waters.

10 O Lord our Governor,
    how glorious is your name in all the earth!   (PNTW)

Psalm 8

A hymn to the majesty of the creator and the dignity of man. This magnificent psalm is not without difficulties (in partic-ular, the text of v.2 and the relevance of v.3 are both uncertain), but they do not obscure the main point. Structurally, it begins and ends with praise of God, in choric refrain (1ab=10ab) marked off from the rest of the psalm by the plural *our* in contrast to the singular of v.4a.

As is common with such a structure, the climax comes in the middle, in the strik-ing vv.5 and 6. At the beginning the praise is objective, but v.4 introduces the per-sonal note. The poet, like Pascal and oth-ers, is overwhelmed by the immensity and the orderliness which is shown especially in the *night* sky. His meditation leads to the dramatic question of v.5 and the as-tonished exclamation of v.6. Then the tempo is slowed again by the longish list in vv.8 and 9 before the solo voice is fi-nally taken up in the choric refrain.

This hymn shows Hebrew thought set midway between ANE and Greek. In the rest of ANE literature the king is elevated, even deified, and ordinary humans corre-spondingly lowered in the scale. In Greek thought human power is often wrested from the gods (Prometheus) or exercised apart from them (the famous Sophoclean chorus, which begins 'many are the mar-vels of the world and none more marvel-lous than man', does not mention any god

Psalm 8 (cont.)

until the very end). But in biblical humanism the god-king is eliminated: *man is little less than a god* and *crowned* like a king. He has dominion on the LORD's behalf over everything: the Hebrew word-order in v.7b is *all things you have put* etc., and the *all* is expanded in v.8. Man's

glory (6) echoes and enhances that of *the* LORD in the refrain. Psalm 8 is far from anything outside the OT but very close to Genesis 1 both in content and in sequence (heavens, stars, man's likeness to God, his mastery over the beasts), though more personal in tone.

Psalm 13

1   How long, LORD, will you leave me forgotten,
        how long hide your face from me?
2   How long must I suffer anguish in my soul,
        grief in my heart day after day?
    How long will my enemy lord it over me?

3   Look now, LORD my God, and answer me.
        Give light to my eyes lest I sleep the sleep of death,
4   lest my enemy say, 'I have overthrown him,'
        and my adversaries rejoice at my downfall.

5   As for me, I trust in your unfailing love;
        my heart will rejoice when I am brought to safety.
6   I shall sing to the LORD, for he has granted all my desire.   (REB)

Psalm 13

A particularly compact and well articulated example of the individual lament. At the beginning the psalmist is in deep despair. To *hide your face from me* (1) is to abandon me; contrast *look* (3). This sense of abandonment by God is the source of his own *anguish*, described as *death* (3), and of his *enemy*'s gloating. The psalm moves steadily from despairing questions (1,2) through hopeful requests (3,4) to statements of *trust* (5,6). By the end the psalmist can even use the perfect tense: *he has granted* etc.

A Babylonian lament to Ishtar follows the same movement and also contains a number of detailed similarities:

> How long wilt thou be angered so
>   that thy face is turned away....
> How long shall my adversaries plan
>   evil against me....
> Death and trouble are bringing me to
>   an end....
> Look at me, O my lady, accept my
>   prayer....
> As for me, let me glorify thy divinity
>   and thy might:
> 'Ishtar indeed is exalted, Ishtar indeed
>   is queen.'
>   (*ANET* 384-5, rearranged)

But there are important differences. The Babylonian poet laments primarily his loss of prosperity, the psalmist his loss of contact with God. More significantly, there is nothing in the former corresponding to the psalm's sharp change of mood at the start of v.5, marked by a 'But' in Hebrew. Hence the thought that a 'salvation oracle' may have been spoken after v.4 (see p.411).

Psalm 15

1 LORD, who may lodge in your tent?
  Who may dwell on your holy mountain?
2 One of blameless life, who does what is right
  and speaks the truth from his heart;
3 who has no malice on his tongue,
  who never wrongs his fellow,
  and tells no tales against his neighbour;
4 who shows his scorn for those the LORD rejects,
  but honours those who fear the LORD;
  who holds to his oath even to his own hurt,
5 who does not put his money out to usury,
  and never accepts a bribe against the innocent.
  He who behaves in this way will remain unshaken.   (REB)

Psalm 15

All ancient religions required certain conditions to be fulfilled before an adherent might approach the god or consult a priest. Most of these conditions were cultic but some, as here, were ethical. The ten conditions specified here omit all the big sins, e.g. the contents of the ten commandments, which presumably could be taken for granted; they represent the quieter virtues and vices, mostly those of the heart and the tongue. In form, v.1 is a question put by the visitor, vv.2-5 the answer by a Temple official. At first sight the question and answer do not fit too well together – compare v.5c with v.1 – but exactly the same form is found in 24.3-6. It seems that the form is artificial here, being adopted as a means of conveying moral teaching.

Psalm 18

1 I love you, LORD, my strength.
2 The LORD is my lofty crag, my fortress, my champion,
  my God, my rock in whom I find shelter,
  my shield and sure defender, my strong tower.
3 I shall call to the LORD to whom all praise is due;
  then I shall be made safe from my enemies.

4 The bonds of death encompassed me
  and destructive torrents overtook me,
5 the bonds of Sheol tightened about me,
  the snares of death were set to catch me.

Psalm 18

This is in two main parts. Part I (4-29) is a hymn of thanksgiving for deliverance, part II (30-46) is a song of victory. The whole psalm is found with minor variations in 2 Sam 22, where the Hebrew superscription says it was sung by David 'when the LORD delivered him from the power of his enemies and from Saul'. Various features of the psalm fit David's position well, at any rate if we take the superscription in the reverse order. In part I the author is passive, still innocent and not yet a king; in part II he is an active, victorious monarch. Other features argue for a later origin. Whatever its date, it is an imposing piece, though perhaps more grandiose than grand.

The introduction vv.1-3 is commensurate with the length of the whole psalm, containing seven images for the protec-

Psalm 18 (cont.)

6   When in anguish of heart I cried to the LORD
        and called for help to my God,
     he heard me from his temple,
        and my cry reached his ears.

7   The earth shook and quaked,
        the foundations of the mountains trembled,
        shaking because of his anger.

8   Smoke went up from his nostrils,
        devouring fire from his mouth,
        glowing coals and searing heat.

9   He parted the heavens and came down;
        thick darkness lay under his feet.

10   He flew on the back of a cherub;
        he swooped on the wings of the wind.

11   He made darkness around him his covering,
        dense vapour his canopy.

12   Thick clouds came from the radiance before him,
        hail and glowing coals.

13   The LORD thundered from the heavens;
        the Most High raised his voice
        amid hail and glowing coals.

14   He loosed arrows, he sped them far and wide,
        he hurled forth lightning shafts and sent them echoing.

15   The channels of the waters were exposed,
        earth's foundations laid bare
     at the LORD's rebuke,
        at the blast of breath from his nostrils.

Psalm 18 (cont.)

tion given by God, like the roll of drums at the start of a royal review. Three of them are picked up in the middle (30-32), and *rock* also at the end (46). Part I consists of two sections: 4-19 God's rescue of him from his enemies; 20-9 his reflection upon it. The rescue operation is described with the full panoply of Ugaritic myth. In that tradition the mythical enemy is variously Mot (the god of *death* 4-5) or Yam (the *mighty waters* 15-6), both of whom appear in the MT* here. Between them (7-14) is a picture of a theophany, drawn also from ANE tradition. The picture recalls the theophany on Mt Sinai in Ex 19, with volcanic features added (8,12). It also has an unexpected 'cousin' in Homer (*Il*.1.43+), where the god Apollo *heard* the prayer of his priest who *called for help*, *came down* from Olympus and *loosed* his *arrows* at the priests' *enemies*.

With v.19 the heavenly drama is over and the focus is again on the psalmist himself. He has been *brought into* an open space, a description which would certainly fit David's position after the death of Saul. But when he goes on, in a more prosaic passage, to raise the question *why* God saves, we can no longer think of David. The protestation of innocence in vv.20-4 would be intolerable if uttered by the notorious sinner and penitent familiar to us from 2 Sam. Moreover the concepts are those of Deuteronomy at the earliest; *righteousness*, clean hands, *his decrees*, etc.

Psalm 18 (cont.)

16   He reached down from on high and took me,
       he drew me out of mighty waters,

17   he delivered me from my enemies, strong as they were,
       from my foes when they grew too powerful for me.

18   They confronted me in my hour of peril,
       but the LORD was my buttress.

19   He brought me into untrammelled liberty;
       he rescued me because he delighted in me.

20   The LORD repaid me as my righteousness deserved;
       because my conduct was spotless he rewarded me,

21   for I have kept to the ways of the LORD
       and have not turned from my God to wickedness.

22   All his laws I keep before me,
       and have never failed to follow his decrees.

23   In his sight I was blameless
       and kept myself from wrongdoing;

24   because my conduct was spotless in his eyes,
       the LORD rewarded me as my righteousness deserved.

25   To the loyal you show yourself loyal
       and blameless to the blameless.

26   To the pure you show yourself pure,
       but skilful in your dealings with the perverse.

27   You bring humble folk to safety,
       but humiliate those who look so high and mighty.

28   LORD, you make my lamp burn bright;
       my God will lighten my darkness.

29   With your help I storm a rampart,
       and by my God's aid I leap over a wall.

32   It is God who girds me with strength
       and makes my way free from blame,

33   who makes me swift as a hind
       and sets me secure on the heights,

34   who trains my hands for battle
       so that my arms can aim a bronze-tipped bow.

35   You have given me the shield of your salvation;
       your right hand sustains me;
       you stoop down to make me great.

Psalm 18 (cont.)

David's authorship of the rest can only be saved by treating these eight verses as a later addition. But by vv.28-9 we are back again with strong simple images ready for part II.

In part II the author opens by praising God for equipping him for *battle* (32-5), for victory (36-42) and for empire (43-6). The general description here is reminiscent of portrayals of the king in ANE literature and art, where the king himself takes centre stage and his army is

Psalm 18 (cont.)

36 You made room for my steps;
    my feet have not slipped.
 I pursue and overtake my enemies;
37   until I have made an end of them I do not turn back.
 I strike them down and they can rise no more;
38   they fall prostrate at my feet.
 You gird me with strength for the battle
39   and subdue my assailants beneath me.
 You set my foot on my enemies' necks,
40   and I wipe out those who hate me.
 They cry, but there is no one to save them;
41   they cry to the LORD, but he does not answer.
 I shall beat them as fine as dust before the wind,
42   like mud in the streets I shall trample them.
 You set me free from the people who challenge me,
43   and make me master of nations.
    A people I never knew will be my subjects.
 Foreigners will come fawning to me;
44   as soon as they hear tell of me they will submit.
 Foreigners will be disheartened
45   and come trembling from their strongholds.
 The LORD lives! Blessed is my rock!
46   High above all is God, my safe refuge.

 You grant me vengeance, God,
47   laying nations prostrate at my feet;
 you free me from my enemies,
48   setting me over my assailants;
    you are my deliverer from violent men.
 Therefore, LORD, I shall praise you among the nations
49   and sing psalms to your name,
 to one who gives his king great victories
50   and keeps faith with his anointed,
    with David and his descendants for ever.   (REB)

Psalm 18 (cont.)

small or non-existent. In detail, for v.39 cp. a Pharaoh's boast 'They fall one upon another and I kill whom I will; whoever falls rises no more', and for v.40 the many reliefs of victorious kings with their foot on the necks of their defeated foes. Verse 41 is of more interest. If it is taken literally, *cry to the LORD* must imply victory over fellow-Israelites, preceding mastery of the *nations* in v.43b. This would suit David.

But it may be just a contrast to v.6, as *set me free* (43, 48) picks up the central theme of part I.

The final section of the psalm lays its emphasis upon the king's own achievements. As is common to the ANE genre, the author refers to himself in the third person (50) as *his anointed* – less probably *David* than one of *his descendants*.

Psalm 19

1   The heavens declare the glory of God,
         and the firmament proclaims his handiwork;
2   one day tells it to another,
         and night to night communicates knowledge.
3   There is no speech or language
         nor are their voices heard;
4   yet their sound has gone out through all the world,
         and their words to the ends of the earth.
5   There he has pitched a tent for the sun,
         which comes out as a bridegroom from his chamber
         and rejoices like a strong man to run his course.
6   Its rising is at one end of the heavens,
         and its circuit to their farthest bound,
         and nothing is hidden from its heat.

7   The law of the LORD is perfect, reviving the soul,
         the command of the LORD is true and makes wise the simple.
8   The precepts of the LORD are right and rejoice the heart;
         the commandment of the LORD is pure, and gives light to the eyes.
9   The fear of the LORD is clean and endures for ever;
         the judgements of the LORD are unchanging and righteous every one,
10   More to be desired are they than gold, even much fine gold;
         sweeter also than honey, than the honey that drips from the comb. ♦

Psalm 19

At first sight Psalm 19 consists of two unconnected halves: the praise of *God* (El) in the *heavens* (1-6) and the praise of *the LORD* (YHWH) in *the law* or Torah (7-end). In fact there are important links of thought between the two, though the differences of tone and rhythm make it unlikely that they were composed by the same hand.

The first half is a powerful fragment of a hymn – fragment, because it has no conclusion. In it, the psalmist praises the creator through the creation. Specifically it is the heavenly bodies who *declare* his *glory*, 'forever singing as they shine "the hand that made us is divine"' (Addison). Verse 4 refers especially to the stars, which were sometimes thought of by the Babylonians as the silent 'writing of the heavens'. What is said of *the sun* in v.5 is even more clearly grounded in mythology. In various ANE myths he is known as the *bridegroom* and the *strong man*. He sets off each day from his *tent* to *run his course*; and at night, in a Greek myth, he sleeps in the arms of his beloved. The psalmist has ranged widely for his imagery, unless he is drawing directly from a lost Babylonian hymn to the sun-god, Shamash. But if he is, he has made it clear in 5a that the sun, for him, is no god but at most an agent of the creator.

The connection of thought between the two halves of the psalm derives from the universal belief of the ancient world that the sun god had an especial care for justice. As the sun dominates the order of the cosmos, so the law upholds the order of society. Ancient hymns to the sun god regularly refer to that all-seeing eye from which *nothing is hidden*. So the way was open for the addition of the somewhat pedestrian second half of the psalm.

Psalm 19 (cont.)

11   Moreover by them is your servant taught,
        and in keeping them there is great reward.

12   Who can know his own unwitting sins?
        O cleanse me from my secret faults.

13   Keep your servant also from presumptuous sins,
        lest they get the mastery over me;
        so I shall be clean, and innocent of great offence.

14   May the words of my mouth
        and the meditation of my heart
    be acceptable in your sight,
        O LORD, my strength and my redeemer.   (PNTW)

Psalm 19 (cont.)

But within the second half there is a lesser break. Down to v.10 the praises of God have been sung impersonally. At v.11 the psalmist enters in person, and brings the two halves together by applying them to himself. *Unwitting* (12) translates the same Hebrew word as the *hidden* of (6), and *heart* in v.14 echoes that of v.8.

Psalm 22

1   My God, my God, why have you forsaken me?
        Why are you so far from saving me,
        so far from heeding my groans?

2   My God, by day I cry to you,
        but there is no answer;
        in the night I cry with no respite.

3   You, the praise of Israel,
        are enthroned in the sanctuary.

4   In you our fathers put their trust;
        they trusted, and you rescued them.

5   To you they cried and were delivered;
        in you they trusted and were not discomfited.   ▶

Psalm 22

An individual lament (1-21) culminating, as is customary, in praise to God (22-31) for answering it. The lament is divided into two well-constructed sections, linked by the two concepts *far from me* (1, 11, 19) and *deliver* (5, 8, 20). The general ground for complaint is that *you have forsaken me*. Many of the themes are conventional e.g. the mockery (6-8) and other assaults of his enemies (12f., 16) and his own lack of any *helper* (11). The same applies even to the poignant verses 14-15. In western literature it is (since Sappho) in love poetry that we expect to find such a detailed physical description of the poet's anguish and *death*, but the ANE convention seems to have kept it for religious use. Interest therefore centres on the construction, which is clear and subtle. For Christians there is a further interest, that Jesus was impressed by this portrayal of an innocent man and, according to Matthew (27.46), quoted v.1 on the cross. Matthew indeed seems to have modified his account of the Passion in other respects to fit Psalm 22 (verses 35 and 43 of Mt 27 take up vv.18 and 8 respectively of Ps 22; see also Wisd Sol 2.18-20).

The first section (1-11) falls into five layered groups of two or three verses each,

Psalm 22 (cont.)

6   But I am a worm, not a man,
        abused by everyone, scorned by the people.

7   All who see me jeer at me,
        grimace at me, and wag their heads:

8   'He threw himself on the LORD for rescue;
        let the LORD deliver him, for he holds him dear!'

9   But you are he who brought me from the womb,
        who laid me at my mother's breast.

10   To your care I was entrusted at birth;
        from my mother's womb you have been my God.

11   Do not remain far from me,
        for trouble is near and I have no helper.

12   A herd of bulls surrounds me,
        great bulls of Bashan beset me.

13   Lions ravening and roaring
        open their mouths wide against me.

14   My strength drains away like water
        and all my bones are racked.
    My heart has turned to wax
        and melts within me.

15   My mouth is dry as a potsherd,
        and my tongue sticks to my gums;
        I am laid low in the dust of death.

16   Hounds are all about me;
        a band of ruffians rings me round,
        and they have bound me hand and foot.

17   I tell my tale of misery,
        while they look on gloating.

18   They share out my clothes among them
        and cast lots for my garments.

19   But do not remain far away, LORD;
        you are my help, come quickly to my aid.

20   Deliver me from the sword,
        my precious life from the axe.

21   Save me from the lion's mouth,
        this poor body from the horns of the wild ox.

Psalm 22 (cont.)

which oscillate between despair and cheer. The first answers the fifth – *Why are you so far from me?* (1) and *Do not remain far from me* (11). The second and the fourth give grounds for cheer: God delivered *our fathers* (4) and *he laid me at my mother's breast* (9). But in the middle (6-8) the psalmist thinks of the scorn of *the people*: here with great skill he puts into their mouths words calculated to provoke God to action lest he too incur scorn.

In the second section (12-21) the poet speaks in more detail of his enemies and the effect they have on him. In 12-15 they are pictured as wild animals, and his reaction is intense physical fear. In 16-18 they are *ruffians* who maltreat him in various ways. Again the poet calls on God – *do*

Psalm 22 (cont.)

22 I shall declare your fame to my associates,
    praising you in the midst of the assembly.

23 You that fear the LORD, praise him;
    hold him in honour, all you descendants of Jacob,
    revere him, you descendants of Israel.

24 For he has not scorned him who is downtrodden,
    nor shrunk in loathing from his plight,
  nor hidden his face from him,
    but he has listened to his cry for help.

25 You inspire my praise in the great assembly;
    I shall fulfil my vows in the sight of those who fear you.

26 Let the humble eat and be satisfied.
    Let those who seek the LORD praise him.
    May you always be in good heart!

27 Let all the ends of the earth remember
    and turn again to the LORD;
    let all the families of the nations bow before him.

28 For kingly power belongs to the LORD;
    dominion over the nations is his.

29 How can those who sleep in the earth do him homage,
    how can those who go down to the grave do obeisance?
  But I shall live for his sake;

30   my descendants will serve him.
The coming generation will be told of the LORD;

31   they will make known his righteous deeds,
  declaring to a people yet unborn:
    'The LORD has acted.'   (REB)

Psalm 22 (cont.)

not remain far away (19) – to deliver him from his enemies, whether seen as human (20) or animal (21).

Then at v.22 there is a sudden change of key – into the major, as it were. The change is explicitly marked in the Hebrew text, where the last word of v.21 means 'thou hast answered me'. Both REB and NJB reject that MT reading in favour of the LXX's *this poor body*. But the Hebrew is entirely in line with the normal movement of lament psalms; see p.411f. There could in fact easily have been room between vv.21 and 22 for a 'salvation oracle'.

At any rate the psalmist's anxiety is now allayed (v.24 answers vv.1-2), and he proceeds to *fulfil* his *vows* (25). Vows normally included both *praise* and

sacrifice. The sacrifice would provide a meal for the faithful (26a). The praise must of course be public, hence the many references to *the assembly*. From there by ANE psalm-convention it must spread outwards in space and time, to include *all the nations* (27f.) and future generations (30f.), stopping short only of the dead (29).

As often in the longer psalms, the grip seems to slacken towards the end. Compared with the lament, the praise lacks fire and pace. But it comes good at the very end, in the single strong word *rāsāh*, 'he has done it'. That word perhaps inspired the other single word which, according to John's gospel, ended Jesus' life: *tetelestai*, 'it has been accomplished'.

Psalm 23

1   The LORD is my shepherd,
     therefore can I lack nothing.
2   He will make me lie down in green pastures
     and lead me beside still waters.
3   He will refresh my soul,
     and guide me in right pathways for his name's sake.
4   Though I walk through the valley of the shadow of death,
     I will fear no evil;
  for you are with me,
     your rod and your staff comfort me.

5   You spread a table before me
     in the face of those who trouble me;
  you have anointed my head with oil,
     and my cup will be full.
6   Surely your goodness and loving-kindness
     will follow me all the days of my life,
     and I shall dwell in the house of the LORD for ever.   (PNTW)

Psalm 23

A psalm of trust in God's loving care. The care is expressed in two images. God is to the psalmist as a *shepherd* to sheep (1-4) and as host to guests (5-6). With the LORD as shepherd, the sheep feel secure enough to browse. Palestine is full of valleys which are deep and narrow and dark, the haunt of wolves and robbers. Shepherds then as now carried both a *rod*, i.e. a club for defence, and a *staff*, i.e. a crook for guidance. The notion of the good ruler as shepherd is common in ANE literature and in the OT, but its use here is uniquely personal – literally 'YHWH pasturing *me*'.

The image of the shepherd has earned Ps 23 a special popularity. The detail in which it is worked out, rare in Hebrew poetry, is much more appealing to the western ear than the usual piling up of separate images as in Ps 18.2. Two of its phrases have passed into almost proverbial use in English: 'green pastures' and 'the valley of the shadow of death'. The latter is now regarded by scholars as a mistranslation, and the newer versions have replaced it by something like 'a valley of deepest darkness' (REB). But Coverdale's mistake (*o felix culpa*), like many of Tyndale's coinages, stands in the language in its own right.

The second image, that of the host, is surprisingly rare in the OT. The relationship of guest and host was deeply important in the ancient world, and remains so wherever travel is hazardous. Both to pour *oil* over the guest's *head* and to feed him 'in presence of his foes' (which is what the Hebrew means) were signs of especial welcome and honour.

Both these images illustrate how God 'feeds' his faithful servant. The first is more ample, but the second adds the festive touch. It also puts God and man on a more equal footing. Indeed the psalmist becomes closer to God as the psalm proceeds; in vv.4 and 5 he switches to address him as second person, and at the end he vows never to leave his presence. *The house of the LORD* is ostensibly the Temple, as in Ps 84.4 etc., but it keeps a hint of hospitality from v.5.

Psalm 24

1 The earth is the LORD's and all that is in it,
    the compass of the world and those who dwell therein.
2 For he has founded it upon the seas
    and established it upon the waters.

3 Who shall ascend the hill of the LORD
    or who shall stand in his holy place?
4 He that has clean hands and a pure heart,
    who has not set his soul upon idols,
    nor sworn his oath to a lie.
5 He shall receive blessing from the LORD
    and recompense from the God of his salvation.
6 Of such a kind as this are those who seek him,
    those who seek your face, O God of Jacob.

7 Lift up your heads, O you gates,
    and be lifted up, you everlasting doors,
    and the King of glory shall come in.
8 'Who is the King of glory?'
    The LORD strong and mighty,
    the LORD mighty in battle.
9 Lift up your heads, O you gates,
    and be lifted up, you everlasting doors,
    and the King of glory shall come in.
10 'Who is the King of glory?'
    The LORD of hosts,
    he is the King of glory.   (PNTW)

Psalm 24

This psalm has at least two parts, vv.3-6 and 7-10; the preface (1-2) belongs with 7-10 if with either.

Verses 3-6 are a so-called 'Torah liturgy', which closely resembles Ps 15. It is followed in vv.7-10 by a more genuinely dramatic 'entrance liturgy'. Here it is not a worshipper but God who is to enter his Temple, and the *dramatis personae* are different. The leader of the procession calls upon the *doors* of the Temple to open. The mechanism implied in *lift up your heads* is unknown, but the phrase had also a metaphorical meaning like English 'hold your heads high'. There was a widespread ancient belief that to the right person a door will open of its own accord. The Temple official asks which God is to enter, and is given an answer. But the answer is not precise enough, and the address and the question have to be repeated, with great dramatic effect. This time the correct cult-title viz. *the LORD of hosts* is given (10). The psalm ends as the gates open and the LORD enters his Temple.

The title LORD of hosts is used of YHWH as warrior king and is especially linked in Hebrew tradition with the Ark of the Covenant. Clearly this psalm belongs to a ceremony in which the Ark was installed in the Temple. Some scholars think of the original occasion under Solomon (1 K 8.6+). But if the general practice of the ANE was followed, that installation would have been celebrated annually in Jerusalem, and this psalm would have formed an impressive part of the liturgy (see p.410).

Psalm 29

1 Ascribe to the LORD, you angelic powers,
      ascribe to the LORD glory and might.

2 Ascribe to the LORD the glory due to his name;
      in holy attire worship the LORD.

3 The voice of the LORD echoes over the waters;
      the God of glory thunders;
      the LORD thunders over the mighty waters,

4 the voice of the LORD in power,
      the voice of the LORD in majesty.

5 The voice of the LORD breaks the cedar trees,
      the LORD shatters the cedars of Lebanon.

6 He makes Lebanon skip like a calf,
      Sirion like a young wild ox.

7 The voice of the LORD makes flames of fire burst forth;

8 the voice of the LORD makes the wilderness writhe in travail,
      the LORD makes the wilderness of Kadesh writhe.

9 The voice of the LORD makes the hinds calve;
      he strips the forest bare,
      and in his temple all cry, 'Glory!'

10 The LORD is king above the flood,
      the LORD has taken his royal seat as king for ever.

11 The LORD will give strength to his people;
      the LORD will bless his people with peace.   (REB)

Psalm 29

This hymn to YHWH as lord of the Storm is one of the oldest psalms in the Psalter, with so many Ugaritic* features that many scholars believe it to be adapted from a Ugaritic hymn to Baal as storm god. The hymn celebrates *the voice of the LORD*, the thunder, repeated seven times; *the LORD* alone is mentioned another eleven times. These are but the most obvious of the many repetitions – one source of the poem's power. At the beginning is the typical Ugaritic stairlike parallelism (see p.22) in its full three-line form, and there are weaker versions of it in vv.3, 5, 8. These repetitions not only have incantatory effect but are especially appropriate to a prolonged thunderstorm with its *echoes* (3a). Moreover, the resonances of myth and imagery are used to heighten the majesty of the hymn. Thunder, lightning (7) and earthquake (8) are so powerful that

they can disturb the course of nature (6, 9). Even more powerful are the *mighty waters* (3, 10) which recall the ANE myth – in the Ugaritic version it was the thunder of Baal himself who subdued them. And the whole ANE background of the OT is present in v.1 when, instead of the usual call to *men* to praise God, here the summons is to the other gods (Hebrew 'sons of gods', translated by REB *angelic powers*) to praise the *king* of gods (10).

Some scholars have seen in vv.3-8 a description of a storm which comes in over the Mediterranean, then centres over *Lebanon* and Anti-Lebanon (*Sirion*) in the north and finally goes round to the south (*Kadesh*). But that would be out of place in Hebrew poetry. Even if the poets had the geographical knowledge, a sequential description of this kind was alien to them. Hebrew images achieve their effect by cu-

Psalm 29 (cont.)

mulation, not by logical structure.

The text of Psalm 29 is not in good shape. Verse 7 looks as if it has lost its other half. The same seems to have happened to v.9c, unless perhaps it is misplaced. Verse 11 strikes many as an anticlimax. Perhaps it was added to ease the adoption of this magnificent pagan hymn.

Psalm 30

1   I will extol you, O LORD, for you have drawn me up,
   and did not let my foes rejoice over me.
2   O LORD my God, I cried to you for help,
   and you have healed me.
3   O LORD, you brought up my soul from Sheol,
   restored me to life that I should not go down to the Pit.

4   Sing praises to the LORD, O you his faithful ones,
   and give thanks to his holy name.
5   For his anger is but for a moment;
   his favor is for a lifetime.
  Weeping may linger for the night,
   but joy comes with the morning.

6   As for me, I said in my prosperity,
   'I shall never be moved.'
7   By your favor, O LORD,
   you had established me as a strong mountain;
  you hid your face;
   I was dismayed.

8   To you, O LORD, I cried,
   and to the LORD I made supplication:
9   'What profit is there in my death,
   if I go down to the Pit?
  Will the dust praise you?
   Will it tell of your faithfulness?
10   Hear, O LORD, and be gracious to me!
   O LORD, be my helper!'
11   You have turned my mourning into dancing;
   you have taken off my sackcloth
   and clothed me with joy,
12   so that my soul may praise you and not be silent.
   O LORD my God, I will give thanks to you forever.   (NRSV)

Psalm 30

This psalm of thanksgiving for personal deliverance contains all the usual parts, though in a slightly odd order. Verses 1-3 provide an introductory summary, including even the *foes*. If v.3 is taken literally, the psalmist has been saved from mortal illness. Then, in the only two verses *not* addressed to God, he invites his fellow-worshippers to join his *praises* (4), and offers them the fruits of his own thinking. Verse 5 has a close parallel in an ancient Egyptian hymn: 'when he is angry, it is only for a moment'. It also sets out the programme for the rest of the psalm:

Psalm 30 (cont.)

weeping is taken up in 7b-10, *joy* in 11-12 – the whole story presented as a flashback. It starts with the complacency (6-7a) out of which he was shaken by misfortune (7b). His brief lament (9-10) uses an argument common in Psalms. Finally we come back to the song (and dance!) of praise which is the burden of the psalm.

According to the Mishnah, when worshippers came to the Temple bringing their first fruits they were met in the outer court by the Levites who sang this psalm on their behalf. It thus appropriately reviews the ups and downs, often sudden, of life over a year in which the good nevertheless outweighs the bad.

Psalm 42-43

.1 As a deer longs for the running brooks,
        so longs my soul for you, O God.

2 My soul is thirsty for God, thirsty for the living God;
        when shall I come and see his face?

3 My tears have been my food day and night,
        while they ask me all day long 'Where now is your God?'

4 As I pour out my soul by myself, I remember this:
        how I went to the house of the Mighty One, into the temple of God,

5 to the shouts and songs of thanksgiving,
        a multitude keeping high festival.

6 Why are you so full of heaviness, my soul,
        and why so unquiet within me?

7 O put your trust in God,
        for I will praise him yet, who is my deliverer and my God.

8 My soul is heavy within me; therefore I will remember you
        from the land of Jordan,
        from Mizar among the hills of Hermon.

9 Deep calls to deep in the roar of your waters,
        all your waves and breakers have gone over me.

Psalm 42-43

The most obvious feature of this lament psalm is the refrain which guarantees the unity of Psalms 42 and 43 and divides the whole into three stanzas. The poem is bound together also by other repetitions (42.3b = 42.12b; 42.11b = 43.2b), as well as by more subtle echoes e.g. *remember* (42.4, 8) and *forgotten* (42.11).

As in the best laments, the poet uses many conventional motifs but combines them in a fresh and moving way. For example, *my tears* are *my food* (3) is an ANE topos* (see on Psalm 102 for a Babylonian parallel) but it is given new life by its metaphorical context of *thirst* (1-2). More importantly, the simple question *When shall I come and see his face?* grows to form the central theme running through the psalm. For we learn from 42.8 that the poet has to live outside Judaea and far from the Temple, in which he had perhaps been a singer (43.4). As with Psalm 137, the distant memory of its *festival* worship brings mixed feelings. In the first stanza (42.4f) it exacerbates his present distress (*nessun maggior dolore*).

Psalm 42-43 (cont.)

42.10   Surely the LORD will grant his loving mercy in the day-time,
      and in the night his song will be with me,
      a prayer to the God of my life.

11   I will say to God, my rock, Why have you forgotten me,
      why must I go like a mourner, because the enemy oppresses me?

12   Like a sword through my bones my enemies have mocked me,
      while they ask me all day long 'Where now is your God?'

13   Why are you so full of heaviness, my soul
      and why so unquiet within me?

14   O put your trust in God,
      for I will praise him yet, who is my deliverer and my God.

43.1   Give judgement for me, O God,
      take up my cause against an ungodly people,
      deliver me from deceitful and wicked men.

2   For you are God my refuge – why have you turned me away?
      why must I go like a mourner because the enemy oppresses me?

3   O send out your light and your truth and let them lead me,
      let them guide me to your holy hill and to your dwelling.

4   Then I shall go to the altar of God, to God my joy and my delight,
      and to the harp I shall sing your praises, O God, my God.

5   Why are you so full of heaviness, my soul
      and why so unquiet within me?
   O put your trust in God,
      for I will praise him yet, who is my deliverer and my God. (PNTW)

Psalm 42-43 (cont.)

In the second it offers a ray of hope when all around (42.8-12) is black – and the references to *day and night* (42.10) bravely cancel those of 42.3. In the third stanza i.e. in Ps 43 the psalmist exultantly anticipates a renewal of pilgrimage (43.3) and sacrifice (4). This will directly answer his own initial question (*go* of 4 should be translated 'come' to pick up 42.2) and indirectly silence the question of his *enemies* in 42.3 and 12.

This gradual movement of the three stanzas, from misery through hope-against-hope to total confidence, is common in lament psalms. But here it is given added resonance by the four-line refrain which provides the formal structure of the poem. On the first occasion the emphasis within the refrain is strongly on the first two lines, which are underscored by the opening words of the second stanza *my soul is heavy within me*. But by the third occasion the emphasis is entirely reversed and the whole psalm ends on its note of trust.

This truly charming poem, with no vindictiveness and scarcely any self-pity, is quite unsentimental, even towards God. On the one hand the poet remembers (42.8f.) that it was God who overwhelmed him in *waves* of misery. It was as if *deep calls to deep*, i.e. the waters of death under the earth were acting in concert with the waters above the earth, as they had done once upon a time to cause the Flood (Gen 7.11). But at the same time the poet still *longs for* him (the water image modulates) as for *running brooks*. His piety is a remarkable combination of personal warmth and Temple devotion.

Psalm 45

1   My heart is stirred by a noble theme,
        I address my poem to the king,
        my tongue the pen of an expert scribe.

2   Of all men you are the most handsome,
        gracefulness is a dew upon your lips,
        for God has blessed you for ever.

3   Warrior, strap your sword at your side,
        in your majesty and splendour advance,

4   ride on in the cause of truth, gentleness and uprightness.
        Stretch the bowstring tight, lending terror to your right hand.

5   Your arrows are sharp, nations lie at your mercy,
        the king's enemies lose heart.

6   Your throne is from God, for ever and ever,
        the sceptre of your kingship a sceptre of justice,

7   you love uprightness and detest evil.
      This is why God, your God, has anointed you
        with oil of gladness, as none of your rivals,

8   your robes all myrrh and aloes.
      From palaces of ivory, harps bring you joy,

9   in your retinue are daughters of kings,
        the consort at your right hand in gold of Ophir.

10   Listen, my daughter, attend to my words and hear;
        forget your own nation and your ancestral home,

11   then the king will fall in love with your beauty;
        he is your lord, bow down before him.

12   The daughter of Tyre will court your favour with gifts,

13   and the richest of peoples with jewels set in gold.

Psalm 45

A royal wedding psalm, this superb hymn is unique in the OT. Written in the best courtly style, both formal and delicate, it draws heavily on ANE conventions. The poet is conscious also of his *own* dignity as *an expert scribe* – see the framing verses 1, 17.

He first addresses the king (2-9), idealising him in ANE terms. He has defeated his *enemies* (3-5) apparently unaided, as in many a triumphal relief, and the marks of his reign are peace, *justice* and prosperity. And now this *handsome* and *graceful* man (a rare note for the OT) is to be married.

The mention of *oil* (7) and music (8) recalls the ceremony of his accession and also leads into that of the wedding. With the court assembled in the throne-room, the bride is brought in, to take her place at the king's *right hand* (9). There she is offered some frank advice, not just as a woman (11) but as a foreign princess. The advice comes apparently from the poet, though by ANE convention it would have come rather from the Queen Mother. (The translation of 12-13 is uncertain.) From the public ceremony she passes with her *retinue* into the interior of the *palace* (14-15), while the poet addresses a final word to the king, tactfully referring to his hopes of *sons* (16).

The psalmist here uses all his impressionistic skill to evoke the glory of

Psalm 45 (cont.)

14   Clothed in brocade, the king's daughter is led within
          to the king with the maidens of her retinue;
      her companions are brought to her,
15   they enter the king's palace with joy and rejoicing.
16   Instead of your ancestors you will have sons;
          you will make them rulers over the whole world.
17   I will make your name endure from generation to generation,
          so nations will sing your praise for ever and ever.   (NJB)

Psalm 45 (cont.)

the occasion. Whether he is ostensibly describing past, present or future – and Hebrew verbs are elusive in their time-reference – he assails all the senses. There is the scent of *myrrh and aloes*, the sound of *harps* and *rejoicing*, the sight of robes of *brocade* and *jewels set in gold*, and the feel of furniture inlaid with *ivory*, a specialist product of *Tyre*. The most natural interpretation of this psalm is that it was originally composed for a historical dynastic wedding in Jerusalem.

Psalm 46

1   God is our refuge and strength,
          a very present help in trouble.
2   Therefore we will not fear, though the earth be moved
          and though the mountains are shaken in the midst of the sea;
3   though the waters rage and foam
          and though the mountains quake at the rising of the sea.

4   There is a river whose streams make glad the city of God,
          the holy dwelling-place of the Most High.
5   God is in the midst of her, therefore she shall not be moved.
          God will help her, and at break of day.
6   The nations make uproar, and the kingdoms are shaken;
          but God has lifted his voice, and the earth shall tremble.

7   The LORD of hosts is with us,
          the God of Jacob is our stronghold.   ▶

Psalm 46

A hymn of trust in God-in-Zion, composed in high poetry, using the stately 4:4 metre. It is an enormously exciting psalm, yet its meaning is hard to pin down. Essentially it contrasts the impotent fury of God's en-emies with the security and serenity of his friends. It has therefore been able to inspire both the warrior (5) and the mystic (10a).

To Europeans it is Luther's psalm. Luther wrote his metrical version of it, *Ein Feste Burg*, to celebrate the withdrawal of the Turkish armies from the siege of Vienna in 1529. If his hymn seems triumphalist, his commentary is not. A city's impregnability (if any) is due, he says, entirely to the presence of God in it. That interpretation is faithful to the psalm. For it could well have been written to celebrate the withdrawal of the Assyrian army from the siege of Jerusalem in 701 BC – *break of day* (5) would then refer to the incident of 2 K 19.35 (see also Is 17.14 'before morning').

But the rest of the psalm transcends history. The first section is pure myth. In ANE mythology the primeval chaos is represented by the 'mighty *waters*' (3),

Psalm 46 (cont.)

8   Come then and see what the LORD has done,
         what destruction he has brought upon the earth.
9   He makes wars to cease in all the world,
         he breaks the bow and shatters the spear,
         and burns the chariots in the fire.
10   'Be still, and know that 1 am God:
         I will be exalted among the nations,
         I will be exalted upon the earth.'

11   The LORD of hosts is with us,
         the God of Jacob is our stronghold.   (PNTW)

Psalm 46 (cont.)

often accompanied by an earthquake (2b, 3b), which God had to tame before creation could begin. Here they are contrasted with an equally mythical *river*, located in the actually riverless Jerusalem. (For the title *the Most High* see p.35). But history has intruded even here. In 1948 the new Israeli settlers quoted this verse when they diverted the dangerous torrent of the Yarmuk to irrigate and *make glad* many square miles of wilderness.

The final section again is beyond history. *The nations* are invited by the poet to *see what the LORD has done* – the ironical *destruction* (8) is explained in v.9 – and are then dramatically addressed by God himself. *Be still* (plural) literally means 'stop fighting', but the mystical interpretation is not illegitimate.

The structure of the psalm is made obvious by the refrain of vv. 7 and 11, which, as a marginal note in the MT shows, was certainly repeated also after v.3. Less obviously, certain repeated keywords show the parallel between the mythical and the historical battles. Especially *the earth* is *moved* (2) and *the kingdoms are* moved (6a Hebrew), but Zion *shall not be moved* (5).

Psalm 48

1   Great is the LORD and most worthy of praise
         in the city of our God,
2   the holy mountain, towering in beauty,
         the joy of the whole world:
     Mount Zion in the heart of the north,
         the settlement of the great king;
3   God himself among its palaces
         has proved himself its bulwark.   ▸

Psalm 48

A song of Zion, praising God on *the holy mountain*. Zion was the hill in Jerusalem on which Solomon built his Temple and royal palace. The phrase *in the heart of the north* is obviously not to be taken literally. Like the 'river' of Ps 46.4 it is a survival from an earlier cult in Jerusalem, 'the north' being the location of El's holy mountain in Canaanite myth. The idea of an assault by the *kings*, who however *fled* at the sight of God (4-7), is also not historical but mythical.

Psalm 48 (cont.)

4   For look, kings made alliance,
         together they advanced;

5   without a second glance, when they saw,
         they panicked and fled away.

6   Trembling seized them on the spot,
         pains like those of a woman in labour;

7   it was the east wind,
         that wrecker of ships from Tarshish.

8   What we had heard we saw for ourselves
         in the city of our God,
     in the city of the LORD of Hosts,
         which God has established for ever.

9   We reflect on your faithful love, God,
         in your temple!

10   Both your name and your praise, God,
         are over the whole wide world.

11   Your right hand is full of saving justice,
         Mount Zion rejoices,
     the daughters of Judah delight
         because of your saving justice.

12   Go round Zion, walk right through her,
         count her bastions,

13   admire her walls,
         examine her palaces,
     to tell future generations

14   that such is God;
     our God for ever and ever,
         he is our guide!

(NJB)

Psalm 48 (cont.)

Peculiar to Psalm 48 is the tantalising hint of a cultic dramatisation of this victory which *we saw for ourselves*. The ritual seems to have started in the Temple and continued outside by a procession like a beating of the bounds (12), whose purpose was presumably to reinforce the impregnability of the holy mountain (*walls* and *palaces* in 13 echo 3). The command to *tell future generations* in v.13c completes the cycle of myth and ritual – we tell *what we ourselves had heard* (8).

Psalm 51

1   Have mercy on me, O God, in your enduring goodness;
         according to the fulness of your compassion blot out my offences.
2   Wash me thoroughly from my wickedness
         and cleanse me from my sin.
3   For I acknowledge my rebellion
         and my sin is ever before me.
4   Against you only have I sinned and done what is evil in your eyes,
         so you will be just in your sentence and blameless in your judging.
5   Surely in wickedness I was brought to birth:
         and in sin my mother conceived me.
7   Purge me with hyssop, and I shall be clean;
         wash me, and I shall be whiter than snow.
8   Make me hear of joy and gladness,
         let the bones which you have broken rejoice.
9   Hide your face from my sins
         and blot out all my iniquities.

10   Create in me a clean heart, O God,
         and renew a right spirit within me.
11   Do not cast me out from your presence,
         do not take your holy spirit from me.
12   O give me the gladness of your help again
         and support me with a willing spirit.
14   O Lord God of my salvation, deliver me from bloodshed;
         and my tongue shall sing of your righteousness.   ▶

Psalm 51

This penitential prayer has the superscription in the MT: 'A psalm of David, when the prophet Nathan came to him because he had been with Bathsheba' (see 2 Sam 12). But the text itself mentions no specific sin. Typically, the psalm will fit any situation of repentance.

After a brief introduction it falls into two main parts. The first part looks to the past, being (i) the confession (3-5) and (ii) the prayer for forgiveness (7-9). The second part looks to the future, being (iii) a prayer for renewal (10-12) and finally (iv) a promise of response (14-17). The two parts are introduced by the contrasting words *rebellion* (3) and *a clean heart* (10), and the four elements are arranged in a typical chiastic* order.

The theology is of great interest also, though made more difficult by uncertainties of text and interpretation. 4a echoes David's first words after hearing Nathan's rebuke: 'I have sinned against the Lord' (2 Sam 12.13), i.e. all sin is in the last resort against God. Verse 5 should not be taken to imply any idea of 'original sin', which is absent from the Hebrew Bible. Verse 7 refers to purification rituals which take place after the psalm is sung.

Create in v.10a is the special Hebrew word reserved for *God*'s creation. It marks a sharp break between the two parts of the psalm. The general emphasis in vv.10-12 and 17 on a new *heart and spirit*, though typical of Jeremiah, is unique in the psalms, where such a prayer is normally for deliverance or salvation. Verse 11b is unique in the OT in suggesting that

Psalm 51 (cont.)

15   O LORD, open my lips,
        and my mouth shall proclaim your praise.

16   You take no pleasure in sacrifice, or I would give it;
        burnt-offerings you do not want.

17   The sacrifice of God is a broken spirit:
        a broken and contrite heart, O God, you will not despise.

18   In your graciousness do good to Zion,
        rebuild the walls of Jerusalem

19   Then will you delight in right sacrifices, in burnt-offerings and oblations,
        then will they offer young bulls upon your altar.   (PNTW)

Psalm 51 (cont.)

God's *holy spirit* can dwell permanently in people to produce a steady inclination to good: elsewhere the spirit takes temporary possession of them. Verses 14-15 are tantamount to a vow: if God forgives him, etc., then he will *proclaim* God's *praise*. *Bloodshed* means blood guilt. Strictures on *sacrifice* are common in both psalms and prophets e.g. Is 1.13+; but here alone the contrast is with a truly *contrite heart*.

The whole tone is nicely caught by Traherne in his *Meditation* (3.83) on it:

What can more melt and dissolve a Lover than the tears of an offending and returning Friend? The falling out of Lovers is the beginning of Love: the renewing, the repairing and the strengthening of it.

Psalm 55

7   O for the wings of a dove,
        that I might fly away and find rest

8   Then I would flee far off
        and make my lodging in the wilderness.

9   I would hasten to find me a refuge
        out of the blast of slander,

10   out of the tempest of their calumny, O LORD,
        and far from their double tongues.

11   For I have seen violence and strife in the city;
        day and night they go round it upon its walls.

12   Evil and wickedness are within it,
        oppression and fraud do not depart from its streets.

13   It was not an enemy that reviled me
        or I might have borne it;
    it was not my foe that dealt so insolently with me,
        or I might have hidden myself from him;

14   but it was you, a man like myself,
        my companion and my familiar friend.

Psalm 55

In the middle of a conventional psalm of lament, there suddenly comes a passage wrung from the heart. The *violence* and corruption of *city* life (11) are such that the poet longs to escape into *the wilderness*.

The *dove* is a fast but supposedly gentle bird, and the wilderness* is seen as a place of refuge from so-called civilisation. For all the glories of city life have been corrupted. Where *walls* should *go round* to protect

Psalm 55 (cont.)

5
Together we enjoyed sweet fellowship
in the house of our God.

18
But I will call to God,
and the LORD my God will save me.   (PNTW)

Psalm 55 (cont.)

the city, *violence* stalks *day and night*. Its *streets,* which should be the scene of honest business, are filled with *fraud*. Above all, the pleasures of *fellowship* – even of shared worship – with a friend have turned sour through treachery. The final complaint of betrayal recalls the Book of Jeremiah (indeed the whole passage is close to Jer 9.2+), but even Jeremiah has nothing to equal the poignancy of the psalmist's direct address to his *familiar friend*.

The text of Ps 55 is in poor condition, but v.18 is included here so that the excerpt ends on the customary note of confidence.

Psalm 65

1
You are to be praised, O God, in Zion;
to you shall vows be paid, you that answer prayer.

2
To you shall all flesh come to confess their sins.
When our misdeeds prevail against us you will purge them away.

3
Blessed is the man whom you choose and take to yourself
to dwell within your courts.
We shall be filled with the good things of your house,
of your holy temple.

4
You will answer us in your righteousness
with terrible deeds, O God our saviour,
you that are the hope of all the ends of the earth
and of the distant seas;

5
who by your strength made fast the mountains,
you that are girded with power;

6
who stilled the raging of the seas,
the roaring of the waves and the tumult of the peoples.

7
Those who dwell at the ends of the earth are afraid at your wonders,
the dawn and the evening sing your praises.

8
You tend the earth and water it,
you make it rich and fertile.

9
The river of God is full of water,
and so providing for the earth, you provide grain for men.

10
You drench its furrows, you level the ridges between,
you soften it with showers and bless its early growth.

11
You crown the year with your goodness,
and the tracks where you have passed drip with fatness.

Psalm 65

Praise of *God in Zion* for the autumn rains. The introduction (1-3) somewhat surprisingly lists *the good things of* worship in the *temple*: praise, *prayer* and *vows*, confession and forgiveness. The next section (4-7) praises God for his *terrible deeds* in creation, which are the admiration of *the ends of the earth*, east and west. Those deeds include his defeat of the *seas* of chaos. Only since then has the way been

Psalm 65 (cont.)

12   The pastures of the wilderness run over
          and the hills are girded with joy.

13   The meadows are clothed with sheep;
          and the valleys stand so thick with corn,
          they shout for joy and sing.   (PNTW)

Psalm 65 (cont.)

open for *the river of God*, the mythical source of the sweet rains of autumn. This delightful psalm ends on a sustained note of exultation from here and now which echoes and intensifies that of there and then (v.7).

Psalm 73

1   Assuredly God is good to the upright,
          to those who are pure in heart!

2   My feet had almost slipped,
          my foothold had all but given way,

3   because boasters roused my envy
          when I saw how the wicked prosper.

4   No painful suffering for them!
          They are sleek and sound in body;

5   they are not in trouble like ordinary mortals,
          nor are they afflicted like other folk.

6   Therefore they wear pride like a necklace
          and violence like a robe that wraps them round.

7   Their eyes gleam through folds of fat,
          while vain fancies flit through their minds.

8   Their talk is all mockery and malice;
          high-handedly they threaten oppression.

9   Their slanders reach up to heaven,
          while their tongues are never still on earth.

11   They say, 'How does God know?
          Does the Most High know or care?'

12   Such are the wicked;
          unshakeably secure, they pile up wealth.

Psalm 73

A psalm of reflection on Job's problem (and in Job's 3:3 metre) namely *how the wicked prosper* (3). This is the only theological problem known to the OT: not 'does God exist?' but '*does* he *know*?' (11). It is tackled autobiographically, as often in Wisdom writings. In neither drama, poetry nor theology does it reach the heights of Job or of Psalm 90, but it is still a fine psalm. Text and interpretation are doubtful in various places, some of which matter.

There are three main sections, each introduced by Heb. *āk*, which REB translates *assuredly* in v.1 and *indeed* in vv.13 and 18. The first section sets the problem, the second marks the turning point, the third gives the answer. The introductory verse anticipates the conclusion: this, together with the *almost* of v.2, removes any suspense from the narrative, but suspense is not important in a psalm. The first verse also introduces one of the key-words of the psalm, *heart*; it comes again in vv.7 (where REB translates it *mind*), 13 and 26.

The first section is dominated by *the wicked*. They are described objectively, as in Job, not as personal enemies, which is

Psalm 73 (cont.)

13   Indeed it was all for nothing I kept my heart pure
         and washed my hands free from guilt!
14   For all day long I suffer affliction
         and every morning brings new punishment.
15   Had I thought to speak as they do,
         I should have been false to your people.
16   I set my mind to understand this
         but I found it too hard for me,
17   until I went into God's sanctuary,
         where I saw clearly what their destiny would be.

18   Indeed you place them on slippery ground
         and drive them headlong into utter ruin!
19   In a moment they are destroyed,
         disasters making an end of them,
20   like a dream when one awakes, Lord,
         like images dismissed when one rouses from sleep!

23   Yet I am always with you;
         you hold my right hand.
24   You guide me by your counsel
         and afterwards you will receive me with glory.
25   Whom have I in heaven but you?
         And having you, I desire nothing else on earth.
26   Though heart and body fail,
         yet God is the rock of my heart, my portion for ever.
27   Those who are far from you will perish;
         you will destroy all who are unfaithful to you.
28   But my chief good is to be near you, God;
         I have chosen you, LORD God, to be my refuge,
         and I shall recount all your works.   (REB)

Psalm 73 (cont.)

usual in psalms. At v. 13 we turn to the author's own reflections. His first thought is that his own loyalty had been *for nothing*. But in v.15b he addresses God, the first step on the way leading through his intellectual wrestlings (16) to his enlightenment in the Temple.

When it comes, the theoretical solution of vv.18-20 is an anticlimax. It is that the wicked are *on slippery ground* (picking up the image of 2) and will come to a bad end, an argument advanced by Job's friends but dismissed by him. The *destiny* (literally the 'afterwards') of the wicked in v.17b is contrasted with the honourable end God

has in store for the godly. The same contrast is in Isaiah 14.18+, making it clear that *afterwards* (24) refers to the end of this life, not to a subsequent one. But the psalmist has more to say. By v.20 he has *dismissed* the wicked and reverted to his relationship with God. In v.23 he strikingly inverts the usual formula of the salvation oracle in which it is God who says to the worshipper *I am with you* (e.g. Is 41.10). For what matters in the last resort is not prosperity or suffering but being *near* to God (23-26). The last verse picks up *good* and *God* from v.1, so that the note of confidence frames the psalm.

Psalm 82

1   God takes his place in the court of heaven
          to pronounce judgement among the gods:

2   'How much longer will you judge unjustly
          and favour the wicked?
3   Uphold the cause of the weak and the fatherless,
          and see right done to the afflicted and destitute.
4   Rescue the weak and the needy,
          and save them from the clutches of the wicked.'
5   But these gods know nothing and understand nothing,
          they walk about in darkness;
              meanwhile earth's foundations are all giving way.
6   'This is my sentence:
          Though you are gods, all sons of the Most High,
7   yet you shall die as mortals die,
          and fall as any prince does.'

8   God, arise and judge the earth,
          for all the nations are yours.   (REB)

Psalm 82

The theme of this old and powerful psalm is *God* as *judge* – the two words which frame it in vv.1 and 8. Its background is ANE polytheism. In the ANE, as in Homer, many of the lesser gods are sons of the supreme god, and relations between him and them are often strained. There are a number of references to this scheme in the OT, most of them elusive and none as explicit as this. Even here these '*sons* of god' are not named, let alone worshipped, though we do know the title of their father. *The most High* (6) translates *El Elyon*.

From time to time God would call these 'sons' into council and sit in *judgement* *among* them (1). The preposition 'among' is ambiguous: it could mean 'with them', as in the prologue to Job, or it could mean 'upon them', as here. For what happens in vv.2-4 is that they are arraigned for their failure to ensure social justice. With great theological economy the author combines the two objects of prophetic criticism, polytheism and social injustice – and his reference to *earth's foundations* (5) is also in true prophetic style. As a result of their failure they receive God's *sentence*, to be reduced to the ranks and *die as mortals die* (7). When they *fall*, God himself will *arise* to judge not only heaven (1) but *all the nations* (8).

Psalm 84

1   LORD of Hosts,
          how dearly loved is your dwelling-place!
2   I pine and faint with longing
          for the courts of the LORD's temple;
              my whole being cries out with joy to the living God.
3   Even the sparrow finds a home,
          and the swallow has her nest
      where she rears her brood beside your altars,
          LORD of Hosts, my King and God.   ▸

Psalm 84 (cont.)

4   Happy are those who dwell in your house;
           they never cease to praise you!
5   Happy those whose refuge is in you,
           whose hearts are set on the pilgrim ways!
6   As they pass through the waterless valley
           the LORD fills it with springs,
           and the early rain covers it with pools.
7   So they pass on from outer wall to inner,
           and the God of gods shows himself in Zion

8   LORD God of Hosts, hear my prayer;
           God of Jacob, listen.
10   Better one day in your courts
           than a thousand days in my home;
       better to linger by the threshold of God's house
           than to live in the dwellings of the wicked.
11   The LORD God is a sun and shield;
           grace and honour are his to bestow.
       The LORD withholds no good thing
           from those whose life is blameless.
12   O LORD of Hosts,
           happy are they who trust in you!   (REB)

Psalm 84

A song in praise of the Temple at Jerusalem, not in itself but as the house where *the living God* (2) *shows himself* (7). The psalmist, filled with *longing* for it (2), blesses (4) all who come there. He starts, delightfully, with the birds who nest there (3) – God's loving care extends even to them. After mentioning the Temple officials and the singers (4), he speaks at greater length of the pilgrims – perhaps he was one himself – who finally arrive after an arduous journey (5-7). Even a single day's visit to the outer court is deeply precious (10). All this is open to those *who trust in* the LORD *of Hosts*, the title which recurs as a refrain throughout the psalm (1, 3, 8, 12).

Psalm 85

1   O LORD you were gracious to your land,
           you restored the fortunes of Jacob.
2   You forgave the iniquity of your people,
           and covered all their sin.
3   You put aside all your wrath
           and turned away from your fierce indignation.   ▸

Psalm 85

Psalm 85 is not easy to interpret, partly because of the common difficulty of telling what period of time the Hebrew verbs refer to; but it seems to be a more complex version of Psalm 126. Seen in this light, it is in three parts, referring in turn to past, present and future. Its structure is that of a communal lament, but the weighting of the parts – and in particular of the images – leaves an overwhelming impression of hope and confidence.

Psalm 85 (cont.)

4   Return to us again, O God our saviour,
          and let your anger cease from us.

5   Will you be displeased with us for ever,
          will you stretch out your wrath, from one generation to another?

6   Will you not give us life again,
          that your people may rejoice in you?

7   Show us your mercy, O LORD,
          and grant us your salvation.

8   I will hear what the LORD God will speak,
          for he will speak peace to his people,
          to his faithful ones whose hearts are turned to him.

9   Truly his salvation is near to those that fear him
          and his glory shall dwell in our land.

10   Mercy and truth are met together,
          righteousness and peace have kissed each other;

11   truth shall flourish out of the earth
          righteousness shall look down from heaven.

12   The LORD will also give us all that is good,
          and our land shall yield its plenty.

13   For righteousness shall go before him
          and tread the path before his feet.   (PNTW)

Psalm 85 (cont.)

The first section (1-3) refers to God's past help – presumably the return from exile (1) – interpreted as evidence of his forgiveness (2). But the early hopes of the people after the return were disappointed, and now they need help again (4-7). The third section opens with one speaker asking to *hear what God will speak* (8) and another responding for God (9-13). (Perhaps indeed the whole psalm is a liturgy – see p.411).

The message of comfort is conveyed in high poetry. The chain of abstract nouns is unusually long for the OT, but the treatment is typically Hebrew. The abstractions themselves are not personifications but permanent attributes of God, which he may send as blessings upon men. When he does, their dealings with one another are coloured to match. *Mercy* (Heb. *hesedh*) *and truth* are better rendered 'love and faithfulness' (REB). *Peace* (*shalom*) has its usual connotation of prosperity.

The total picture is built up layer upon layer, not articulated into a single design. But the layers are intricately paired off. Thus in v.11 *righteousness shall look down* like the sun, while *truth* springs up like a plant. The same vertical movement is seen in v.12 but the arrangement in the two verses is chiastic*: up-down-down-up. In the flanking verses 10 and 13, however, the movement is horizontal – a further chiasmus. The last line of all is plausibly emended by REB, in conformity with an ANE topos*, to read 'and peace on the path he treads', i.e. *righteousness* is his vanguard, peace his rearguard.

But this final section, like the psalm as a whole, was composed as a hymn to be sung, not a treatise to be analysed.

Psalm 90

1 Lord, you have been our refuge
in all generations.

2 Before the mountains were brought forth,
or ever you had formed the earth and the world,
from everlasting to everlasting you are God.

3 You turn us back to dust,
and say, 'Turn back, you mortals.'

4 For a thousand years in your sight
are like yesterday when it is past,
or like a watch in the night.

5 You sweep them away; they are like a dream,
like grass that is renewed in the morning;

6 in the morning it flourishes and is renewed;
in the evening it fades and withers.

7 For we are consumed by your anger;
by your wrath we are overwhelmed.

8 You have set our iniquities before you,
our secret sins in the light of your countenance.

9 For all our days pass away under your wrath;
our years come to an end like a sigh.

10 The days of our life are seventy years,
or perhaps eighty, if we are strong;
even then their span is only toil and trouble;
they are soon gone, and we fly away.

11 Who considers the power of your anger?
Your wrath is as great as the fear that is due you.

Psalm 90

A magnificent psalm of communal lament, whose main theme is the brevity of human life. In the first part (1-6) man's transience is contrasted with God's permanence, in language of lapidary and uncomplaining directness. The second part (7-17) is more complicated and its sequence of thought more obscure.

The psalm begins with an expression of trust in God who is *everlasting* down the *generations* and indeed ever since the beginning of creation. By contrast, human beings are bidden to *turn back* to the *dust* from which they were created (Gen 3.19). Even time itself is as nothing in God's *sight*: in 4-5 the poet gradually contracts his vision from *1,000 years* to a *day* to *a watch in the night* (three hours) to *a dream*. The last image of transience is *grass* (5), which leads into the second part (*withers . . . consumed*).

In the next section (7-11) the theme of God's permanence is dropped, while that of man's transience is interwoven with two new ideas. On man's side are *sins* (8) and unhappiness (10), on God's side *wrath* and *anger*, words which frame the section.

Psalm 90 (cont.)

12 So teach us to count our days
    that we may gain a wise heart.
13 Turn, O Lord! How long?
    Have compassion on your servants!
14 Satisfy us in the morning with your steadfast love,
    so that we may rejoice and be glad all our days.
15 Make us glad as many days as you have afflicted us,
    and as many years as we have seen evil.
16 Let your work be manifest to your servants,
    and your glorious power to their children.
17 Let the favor of the Lord our God be upon us,
    and prosper for us the work of our hands –
    O prosper the work of our hands!

(NRSV)

Psalm 90 (cont.)

The resolution comes in the final section (12-17), which is one long prayer. Instead of our transience being the result of our sins, it could become a source of wisdom (12). We could then (13, echoing 3) pray God himself to *turn* back, replacing his anger by *love* (14), and instead of being *afflicted* we should *rejoice*. Even the time-scale would be – or at least seem to be – extended: the contraction of vv.4-5 is reversed by the expansion *morning – days – years* in 14-15. The reason is that with our new-found wisdom we think not just of ourselves as individuals but of our *children*, who correspond to the *generations* of v.1 In such a perspective we can even ask God to *prosper the work of our hands*, and with that hope we have (almost) recovered the confidence with which the psalm began.

Psalm 91

1 You who live in the shelter of the Most High,
    who abide in the shadow of the Almighty,
2 will say to the Lord, 'My refuge and my fortress;
    my God, in whom I trust.'
3 For he will deliver you from the snare of the fowler
    and from the deadly pestilence;
4 he will cover you with his pinions,
    and under his wings you will find refuge;
    his faithfulness is a shield and buckler.
5 You will not fear the terror of the night,
    or the arrow that flies by day,
6 or the pestilence that stalks in darkness,
    or the destruction that wastes at noonday.

Psalm 91

A psalm of confidence, whose theme is God's protection of the faithful against the dangers which threaten them. The treatment is typically Hebraic. Protection and dangers are each expressed in a piled-up series of heterogeneous images. The images are mostly grouped in pairs, but it is hard to discern any larger structure in the psalm, at any rate in its earlier verses. Perhaps however the gradual emergence of structure represents the gradual increase in the psalmist's confidence.

Psalm 91 (cont.)

7   A thousand may fall at your side,
         ten thousand at your right hand,
         but it will not come near you.

8   You will only look with your eyes
         and see the punishment of the wicked.

9   Because you have made the LORD your refuge,
         the Most High your dwelling place,

10   no evil shall befall you,
         no scourge come near your tent.

11   For he will command his angels concerning you
         to guard you in all your ways.

12   On their hands they will bear you up,
         so that you will not dash your foot against a stone.

13   You will tread on the lion and the adder,
         the young lion and the serpent you will trample under foot.

14   Those who love me, I will deliver;
         I will protect those who know my name.

15   When they call to me, I will answer them;
         I will be with them in trouble,
         I will rescue them and honor them.

16   With long life I will satisfy them,
         and show them my salvation.   (NRSV)

Psalm 91 (cont.)

Most of the images are conventional, and thus sit easily together, though it is odd to find birds on both sides of the equation in vv.3-4. In vv.5-6 the dangers probably derive from demons, whether of *the night* or the *noonday*. The latter would include sunstroke, perhaps while out in the fields like 2 K 4.19-20 – there are plenty of ANE references to demons abroad at high noon. The military metaphors underlying vv.2-4 erupt into a battle (7-8) in which *you* can actually *see* *the wicked* fall at your side. Finally comes the best developed picture of all: a journey on which *his angels* will *guard you* from every conceivable peril (11-13).

All this (1-13) is addressed to *you*. It thus has the form of an oracle of reassurance spoken by the priest on God's behalf. But in v.14 God himself takes over to give authoritative confirmation. He says nothing of the dangers and little of the protection, but speaks of the relationship of *love* (cp. *trust* of v.2) on which it is all based. NRSV's translation of 14-16 pluralises the believer so as to avoid the Hebrew 'he/him', and so loses the intimacy of the relationship.

Psalm 93

1   The LORD is king, robed in majesty,
        robed is the LORD and girded with power.

2   The world is indeed set firm, it can never be shaken;
        your throne is set firm from of old,
        from all eternity you exist.

3   The rivers lift up, O LORD,
        the rivers lift up their voices,
        the rivers lift up their thunder.

4   Greater than the voice of many waters,
        more majestic than the breakers of the sea,
        the LORD is majestic in the heights.

5   Your decrees stand firm, unshakeable,
        holiness is the beauty of your house,
        O LORD, for all time to come.   (NJB)

Psalm 93

This whole psalm orchestrates the acclamation *The LORD is king*. God's majesty is shown chiefly by his establishing the earth firm in spite of the challenge of the *many waters*. The poet is here clearly drawing on ANE myth; and the triple stairlike* parallelism of vv.3 and 4 suggests an Ugaritic origin. But myth, being timeless, can look forward as well as back: as God's *throne is set firm from of old* (2), so his *decrees stand firm for all time to come*, and his victory over the powers of chaos is present and future as well as past.

Psalm 98

1   Sing a new song to the LORD,
        for he has done marvellous deeds;
        his right hand and his holy arm have won him victory.

2   The LORD has made his victory known;
        he has displayed his saving righteousness to all the nations.

3   He has remembered his love for Jacob,
        his faithfulness towards the house of Israel.
    All the ends of the earth have seen
        the victory of our God.

4   Acclaim the LORD, all the earth;
        break into songs of joy, sing psalms.

5   Sing psalms in the LORD's honour with the lyre,
        with the lyre and with resounding music,

6   with trumpet and echoing horn
        acclaim the presence of the LORD our King.

Psalm 98

This splendid psalm belongs with the YHWH king group (see p.411). But the enthronement motif in vv.4-8 (*acclaim* in 4 and 6, *clap hands* in 8) is less emphasised here than the preceding *victory* in vv.1-3 and the future judgement in v.9. Nu-merous echoes in Second Isaiah make it likely that the victory of vv.1-3 is the rescue of the Jews from exile in Babylon, which demonstrated *his faithfulness* to a sceptical world. It is that which gives confidence in his future coming *to judge the earth*.

Psalm 98 (cont.)

7   Let the sea resound and everything in it,
         the world and those who dwell there.
8   Let the rivers clap their hands,
         let the mountains sing aloud together
9   before the LORD; for he comes
         to judge the earth.
     He will judge the world with justice
         and the peoples with equity.

(REB)

Psalm 102

1   LORD, hear my prayer
         and let my cry come to you.
2   Do not hide your face from me in the day of my trouble;
         turn your ear to me and, when I call, be swift to answer.
3   For my days pass away like smoke,
         and my bones burn as in a furnace.
4   My heart is scorched and withered like grass,
         and I forget to eat my bread.
5   I am weary with the sound of my groaning,
         my bones stick fast to my skin.
6   I have become like an owl in the wilderness,
         like a screech-owl among the ruins.
7   I keep watch and flit to and fro,
         like a sparrow upon a housetop,

8   My enemies taunt me all day long
         and those who rave at me make oaths against me.
9   Surely I have eaten ashes for bread
         and mingled my drink with tears,
10   because of your wrath and indignation,
         for you have taken me up and tossed me aside.
11   My days decline like a shadow
         and I wither away like grass.

Psalm 102

The beginning and end of an individual lament, into which the hymn of [12-22] fits badly. The nature of a lament is well caught by the superscription in the MT: 'A prayer of someone afflicted, who in misfortune pours out sorrows before the LORD'. As with all such, it is hard to be sure how to interpret the details. The *owl* and the *sparrow* are generally taken to be symbols of loneliness, with translation to suit, e.g. REB's 'solitary on a roof top'. But *flit* goes nicely with the theme of the psalm. For the rest, the images are conventional, with parallels elsewhere in the OT or ANE. For example, compare v.9 with this from a Babylonian psalm:

I ate no food, weeping was my bread;
I drank no water, tears were my drink.

Psalm 102 (cont.)

24   Do not take me away, O God, in the midst of my life:
        you, whose years extend through all generations.

25   In the beginning you laid the foundations of the earth,
        and the heavens are the work of your hands.

26   They shall perish, but you will endure.
        They shall all grow old like a garment;
        like clothes you will change them, and they shall pass away.

27   But you are the same for ever,
        and your years will never fail.

28   The children of your servants shall rest secure,
        and their seed shall be established in your sight.   (PNTW)

Psalm 102 (cont.)

We should therefore not try e.g. to calculate the poet's age, like Dante's, from *in the midst of my life* (24). He is just comparing the brevity of human life, like the perishability of the cosmos (25-6), with God's existence beyond time. Symbolically, *my days* (3, 11, 24 Heb) are contrasted with *your years* (24, 27).

This theme is at first sight the same as that of Psalm 90, but the tone is different: bitterness like that of v.10 is more reminiscent of Job 30.21+. Nevertheless by the end the psalmist has been able, here as in Psalm 90, to derive some consolation from God's permanence, if not for himself, at least for the *children* of the faithful.

Psalm 103

1   Praise the LORD, O my soul,
        and all that is within me, praise his holy name.

2   Praise the LORD, O my soul,
        and forget not all his benefits;

3   who forgives all your sin
        and heals all your infirmities,

4   who redeems your life from the Pit
        and crowns you with mercy and compassion;

5   who satisfies your being with good things,
        so that your youth is renewed like an eagle's.

6   The LORD works righteousness
        and justice for all who are opressed.

7   He made known his ways to Moses
        and his works to the children of Israel.

8   The LORD is full of compassion and mercy,
        slow to anger and of great goodness.   ▸

Psalm 103

A psalm of praise which makes something of a pair with Ps 104. In content they are complementary, in form they each begin and end with the address by the poet to his own *soul*. Ps 103 is in four sections. In the first (1-5) the poet speaks of his own personal experience of God's active love (note the transitive verbs of 3-5). The second (6-14) tells of God's mercy to his people as a whole, but the treatment is still personal. In v.8 the poet quotes God's description of himself to Moses in Exodus

Psalm 103 (cont.)

9   He will not always be chiding
        nor will he keep his anger for ever.
10 He has not dealt with us according to our sins,
        nor rewarded us according to our wickedness.
11 For as the heavens are high above the earth,
        so great is his mercy over those that fear him;
12 as far as the east is from the west,
        so far has he set our sins from us.
13 As a father is tender towards his children,
        so is the LORD tender to those that fear him.
14 For he knows of what we are made,
        he remembers that we are but dust.

15 The days of man are but as grass,
        he flourishes like a flower of the field;
16 when the wind goes over it, it is gone,
        and its place will know it no more.
17 But the merciful goodness of the LORD
        endures for ever and ever toward those that fear him,
        and his righteousness upon their children's children;
18 upon those who keep his covenant
        and remember his commandments to do them

19 The LORD has established his throne in heaven,
        and his kingdom rules over all.
20 Praise the LORD, all you his angels, you that excel in strength,
        you that fulfil his word and obey the voice of his commandment.
21 Praise the LORD, all you his hosts,
        his servants who do his will.
22 Praise the LORD, all his works, in all places of his dominion;
        praise the LORD, O my soul!   (PNTW)

Psalm 103 (cont.)

34.6, but softens it considerably. In v.10 he defines God's *mercy*, in vv.11-12 he illustrates it, using the two familiar spatial dimensions (cp. Ps 113.3+, 139.8+). Then, seeming to find them too remote, he switches to the close, personal image of the loving *father*.

In v.14, which links the second and third sections, the transience of human life is given as a reason for God's tenderness; the same argument is used elsewhere in the OT, but more plaintively and therefore less effectively. And God offers not merely forgiveness but comfort: brief our own lives may be, but his love extends to our *children's children* (15-18). The fourth and last section extends the 'call to praise' into the realm of *heaven* (19-22), but after those great chords the concerto ends as it began with the solo instrument.

This fine song, one of the finest in the psalter, is all of a piece. God is transcendent yet infinitely loving. And the high concepts are brought down to the human scale by references to daily life – fathers, children and *youth*; the *eagle* and the *flower of the field*. The dark side of experience (suffering, sin, death) is not glossed over – there is no sentimentality here – but God's fatherly love can always raise us above it.

Psalm 104

1   Bless the LORD, O my soul,
        O LORD my God, how great you are!
2   Clothed with majesty and honour,
        wrapped in light as in a garment.

3   You have stretched out the heavens like a tent-cloth,
        and laid the beams of your dwelling upon their waters;
4   you make the clouds your chariot.
        and ride upon the wings of the wind;
5   you make the winds your messengers
        and flames of fire your ministers;
6   you have set the earth on its foundations
        so that it shall never be moved.
7   The deep covered it as with a mantle,
        the waters stood above the hills.
8   At your rebuke they fled,
        at the voice of your thunder they hurried away;
9   they went up to the mountains, they went down by the valleys,
        to the place which you had appointed for them.
10   You fixed a limit which they may not pass;
        they shall not return again to cover the earth.

11   You send springs into the gullies,
        which run between the hills;
12   they give drink to every beast of the field
        and the wild asses quench their thirst.
13   Beside them the birds of the air build their nests
        and sing among the branches.

14   You water the mountains from your dwelling on high,
        and the earth is filled by the fruits of your work.   ▶

Psalm 104

A hymn of praise to God as creator. Between the opening (1-2) and closing (33-7) verses of praise, the body of the psalm consists of two unequal parts. The first (3-10) describes God's original work of creation, the second (11-32) his permanent work in sustaining the created order.

Like God's speeches in Job 38-41, this psalm is often classed as 'nature poetry'. This it is not, if only because 'Israel did not know the concept of nature' apart from God (von Rad). And the images of God here are not static but dynamic: builder, farmer, father, and above all creator of order.

In the beginning, when *the deep* (as in the ANE creation myth) threatened chaos (7), he established order by dividing it in two (8-10). In the *wide sea* he tamed even the grim monster *Leviathan, to sport* like a dolphin (28). On land there is the ground water (11) and the rain (14), which together support the flora (15-18) and the fauna: birds (13, 19), cattle (15), wild animals (12, 20, 23-24) and mankind (15-17, 25) – all bound together in one interlocking whole.

In that last section certain features call for comment. First, humans are given no separate space. They may by implication have a privileged position in relation to the vegetable kingdom (15-17), but they are at most first among equals in the animal kingdom. God's care for *all* his *creatures* is

Psalm 104 (cont.)

5   You cause the grass to grow for the cattle
           and all green things for the servants of mankind.
6   You bring food out of the earth
           and wine that makes glad the heart of man,
7   oil to give him a shining countenance
           and bread to strengthen his heart.
8   The trees of the LORD are well-watered.
           the cedars of Lebanon that he has planted,
9   where the birds build their nests,
           and the stork makes her home in the pine-tops.
10   The high hills are a refuge for the wild goats,
           and the crags a cover for the conies.

21   You created the moon to mark the seasons,
           and the sun knows the hour of its setting.
22   You make darkness, and it is night
           in which all the beasts of the forest move by stealth.
23   The lions roar for their prey,
           seeking their food from God.
24   When the sun rises, they retire
           and lay themselves down in their dens.
25   Man goes out to his work,
           and to his labour until the evening.   ▶

Psalm 104 (cont.)

emphasised (26, 29), even if they are, from the human point of view, unproductive (12, 20) or dangerous (22). It is all much closer to Job 38-41 than to Ps 8 or Gen 1-2.

In vv.21-5 the ecology of the animal kingdom is described in relation not to the rain (as in 12-18) but to the 24-hour cycle. The two verses 27-8 about the sea and its creatures seem out of place. They isolate the verse of general praise (26) which would more happily lead straight into the subsection 29-32: God's *wisdom* would then be exemplified in another cycle of the animate creation, that of life and death. These somewhat puzzling features can all be illuminated from an unexpected direction.

For the whole psalm is much influenced by ANE poetry, but the section 15-32 is especially close to the great *Hymn to the Sun* of Akhnaten, the pharaoh who tried to introduce a more specific sun-worship to the Egyptians c.1370 BC. Here are some extracts from that hymn, with its line-numbers on the left and corresponding verse-numbers of Psalm 104 on the right:

3. When you set on the western horizon   21
    the earth lies in darkness as in death. 22
4. Every lion has come forth from his den
    and all the snakes bite. . . .   23
    At daybreak, when you have arisen
    on the horizon   24
5. the whole land goes to work.   25
    All beasts are satisfied with their pasture,
    the trees and plants become green.   15
    The birds flutter in their nests, raising
    their wings in worship before your spirit. 19
6. The ships sail upstream and down,   28
    every way is open because you
    appear, the fish in the river dart   (28)
    before your face. . . .
7. How manifold are your works! . . .   26
12. When you have risen they live,   32
    and when you set they die.   31

(*NERT* 18)

Akhnaten's hymn explains the emphasis in Psalm 104.21-5 on the 24-hour cycle and shows that the mention of the sea-

Psalm 104 (cont.)

26   LORD how various are your works:
       in wisdom you have made them all, and the earth is full of your creatures.

27   There is the wide, immeasurable sea,
       there move living things without number, great and small;

28   there go the ships, to and fro,
       and there is that Leviathan, whom you formed to sport in the deep.

29   These all look to you
       to give them their food in due season.

30   When you give it to them, they gather it;
       when you open your hand they are satisfied with good things.

31   When you hide your face, they are troubled;
       when you take away their breath, they die and return to their dust.

32   When you send forth your spirit they are created;
       and you renew the face of the earth.

33   May the glory of the LORD endure for ever,
       may the LORD rejoice in his works.

34   If he look upon the earth, it shall tremble;
       if he but touch the mountains, they shall smoke.

35   I will sing to the LORD as long as I live
       I will praise my God while I have any being.

36   May my meditation be pleasing to him,
       for my joy shall be in the LORD.

37   Bless the LORD, O my soul; O praise the LORD.   (PNTW)

Psalm 104 (cont.)

creatures in vv.27-8 (a natural transposition from the Nile) should follow immediately, with the summary v.26 postponed. The relative downgrading of human beings is also typical of Egyptian compared with Hebrew thought.

But at the same time some crucial theological changes are visible. Akhnaten ascribes all to the sun, the psalmist all, including the sun, to YHWH. The role of the sun is limited in the psalm to providing sleep for *lions* and *work* for *man*. The demarcation of the *seasons* is ascribed to the *moon* (21) and the growth of the *grass* etc. to the rain (15).

The final verses of 104 are scrappy. Verses 35-7 answer 1a; *my meditation* (36) means 'my poem' (cp. Ps 45.1).

Psalm 113

1   Praise the LORD, O sing praises, you that are his servants,
       O praise the name of the LORD.

2   Let the name of the LORD be blessed
       from this time forward and for ever.

3   From the rising of the sun to its going down
       let the name of the LORD be praised.

Psalm 113

The first of the Hallel psalms, a group (Pss 113-8) marked by the opening summons *praise the LORD* (Heb *Hallelu-YAH*). They were used on festival occasions in the Temple and also at the family Passover, Pss 113 and 114 before the meal itself.

Psalm 113 (cont.)

4   The LORD is exalted over all the nations
        and his glory is above the heavens.
5   Who can be likened to the LORD our God
        in heaven or upon the earth,
6   who has his dwelling so high
        yet condescends to look on things beneath?
7   He raises the lowly from the dust
        and lifts the poor from out of the dungheap;
8   he gives them a place among the princes
        even among the princes of his people.
9   He causes the barren woman to keep house
        and makes her a joyful mother of children.
        Praise the LORD.   (PNTW)

Psalm 113 (cont.)

Pss 113 is a particularly neat little psalm, both in detail and as a whole. For detail, see the many polarities and e.g. the way *nations* and *heavens* of v.4 are picked up chiastically by *heaven* and *earth* in the next verse. As to the whole, its two halves are linked and summarised in the central v.6 The extent of a king's majesty was regularly expressed in ANE poetry by references to east and west. That is followed here by reference to the other axis, *high* and *low*, which had favourite theological overtones: God the transcendent nevertheless *condescends* to care for *the lowly* and *raises* them to the heights. The *dungheap* (7) was outside the city and therefore implied a man's loss of civic status. The pregnancy of the *barren woman* is a theme especially suited to the conclusion of a psalm of praise: it is *joyful* in itself, and it carries the imagination over the bounds of the psalm into the future, cp. Ps 127 etc.

Psalm 114

1   When Israel came out of Egypt,
2   the house of Jacob from a barbaric people,
     Judah became God's sanctuary,
3   Israel his domain.

     The sea fled at the sight;
4   Jordan turned back.
     The mountains skipped like rams,
        the hills like lambs of the flock.

Psalm 114

A highly imaginative treatment of the saving acts that accompanied the great period from the exodus to the entry into the promised land.

The two chief miracles, the crossing of the Red *Sea* and of the *Jordan*, had already been assimilated in the tradition (Joshua 4.23) and probably also in the cult.

Psalm 114 (cont.)

5   What made you, the sea, flee away?
    Jordan, what made you turn back?

6   Why did you skip like rams, you mountains,
    and like lambs, you hills?

7   Earth, dance at the presence of the LORD,
    at the presence of the God of Jacob,

8   who turned the rock into a pool of water,
    the flinty cliff into a welling spring.   (REB)

Psalm 114 (cont.)

Now the poet adds the earthquake on Mount Sinai (4-6) and also (8) the creation of the spring at Kadesh [Num 20]. Moreover the descriptions are given extra flourishes, e.g. in Joshua the Jordan merely stops, while here it flows backwards. The whole treatment of history is typically Hebrew and typically poetic. But of course it is not just history. The old ANE creation myth once again peeps through: God's mastery over sea and river repeated the original victory over the mighty waters. However the relation between God and the elements is here treated lightly, even humorously: they are not compelled but respond of their own free will. The questions put to them in vv.5 and 6 reinforce this impression. Then instead of waiting for their answer the poet switches at the climax of the psalm into a dramatic imperative, admirably rendered *dance* by REB. The vividness of the treatment and the number of verbs of movement suggests a possible setting in cultic drama.

Psalm 121

1   I will lift up mine eyes unto the hills:
    from whence cometh my help?

2   My help cometh even from the LORD,
    who hath made heaven and earth.

3   He will not suffer thy foot to be moved,
    and he that keepeth thee will not sleep.

4   Behold, he that keepeth Israel
    shall neither slumber nor sleep.

5   The LORD himself is thy keeper;
    the LORD is thy defence upon thy right hand,

6   so that the sun shall not burn thee by day,
    neither the moon by night.

7   The LORD shall preserve thee from all evil,
    yea, it is even he that shall keep thy soul.

8   The LORD shall preserve thy going out and thy coming in
    from this time forth for evermore.   (Coverdale)

Psalm 121

This psalm is one of a group (120-34) known to Jews as 'songs of ascents' i.e. psalms associated with the pilgrimages to Jerusalem required of all loyal Jews (122.4). Notionally, the pilgrims are now approaching the *hills* of Jerusalem. The first two verses are illuminated by a graffito scratched c.500 BC in a chamber tomb 20 miles SW of Jerusalem (*NERT* 251):

    YHWH is God of the whole earth,
    The mountains of Judah belong to the
      god of Jerusalem.

Psalm 121 (cont.)

Interpreted in that light, the pilgrim asks the question in v.1b (it has to be a question; the Hebrew cannot be translated as a relative clause), and then answers it himself in v.2, thus declaring his trust in YHWH.

The rest of the psalm (3-8) is spoken not by him but to him by a third party, presumably a priest. It sounds like a blessing pronounced upon the pilgrim as he sets out for Jerusalem. The blessing then refers to dangers from the track-surface (3a), footpads (5b), sunstroke (6) and all the perils of the night (3, 4, 6). It was a common belief in the ancient world that moonlight was dangerous cp. our word 'lunatic'. The all-encompassing nature of God's protection is brought out by two devices. One is the use of merismus* to denote totality: *heaven/earth, sun/moon, day/night, going out/coming in*. The other is repetition: *the LORD* five times and *keep* six. The soothing assonance of *keep* and *sleep* is Coverdale's.

Psalm 122

1   I was glad when they said unto me,
      We will go into the house of the LORD.

2   Our feet shall stand
      in thy gates, O Jerusalem.

3   Jerusalem is built as a city
      that is at unity in itself.

4   For thither the tribes go up, even the tribes of the LORD,
      to testify unto Israel, to give thanks unto the name of the LORD.

5   For there is the seat of judgement,
      even the seat of the house of David.

6   O pray for the peace of Jerusalem:
      they shall prosper that love thee.

7   Peace be within thy walls
      and plenteousness within thy palaces.

8   For my brethren and companions' sakes
      I will wish thee prosperity.

9   Yea, because of the house of the LORD our God
      I will seek to do thee good.

Psalm 122

Another 'song of ascents'. This time the perils of the journey are forgotten, and the pilgrims recall the exciting moment weeks ago when the pilgrimage was first mooted (1). Having done so, they turn to admiration: '*Jerusalem, built as a city!*' (the *is* of 3a is not in the Hebrew). It was the *unity* of the buildings that took their breath away: the *gates* (2), the *walls* (7) and the *palaces* (5, 7), but above all the Temple, *the house of the LORD*, which frames the psalm (1, 9). From admiration they turn to blessings, in which they address the city itself (6-9). In this context the repeated *peace* is doubly significant. First it is a word-play, since the name *Jerusalem* was popularly connected with *shalom*. Second, *shalom* was (then as now) used as a greeting, and so was particularly suited to the context of a pilgrim visit.

Psalm 123

1 I lift my eyes to you
   whose throne is in heaven.
2 As the eyes of slaves follow their master's hand
   or the eyes of a slave-girl the hand of her mistress,
   so our eyes are turned to the LORD our God,
   awaiting his favour.
3 Show us your favour, LORD, show us favour,
   for we have suffered insult enough.
4 Too long have we had to suffer
   the insults of the arrogant,
   the contempt of the proud.   (REB)

Psalm 123

A simple prayer of entreaty, centred on a single unifying image: the *eyes* of the inferior focused expectantly on the *hand* of the superior (cp. 104.29f.). The repetitive parallelism of v.2ab expresses the impatience which is explicit in the *too long* of v.4a. The image also enables the transition from individual (1) to nation (3-4).

Psalm 124

1 If the LORD had not been on our side –
   let Israel now say –
2 if the LORD had not been on our side
   when our foes attacked,
3 then they would have swallowed us alive
   in the heat of their anger against us.
4 Then the waters would have carried us away
   and the torrent swept over us;
   then over us would have swept
   the raging waters.
5 Blessed be the LORD, who did not leave us
   a prey for their teeth.
6 We have escaped like a bird from the fowler's trap;
   the trap is broken, and we have escaped.
7 Our help is in the name of the LORD,
   maker of heaven and earth.   (REB)

Psalm 124

A collective psalm of thanksgiving for deliverance. The repetition at the beginning is cultic: perhaps a cantor sang v.1a, then added 1b parenthetically ('say after me'), with the congregation picking it up at 2a. Babylonian thanksgiving psalms often begin with the words 'If such and such a god had not been on our side. . .'. The actual *foes* are unspecified – perhaps so that the psalm could be used on different occasions – but typically referred to by a series of images. Verses 3-5 say what would have happened, 6-7 what did. *Teeth* (5) picks up *swallowed* (3), but otherwise there is no correspondence between the two pictures, of the danger and the escape. The images are conventional, the psalm simple and direct.

Psalm 126

1 When the LORD turned again the captivity of Sion,
      then were we like unto them that dream.

2 Then was our mouth filled with laughter
      and our tongue with joy.

3 Then said they among the heathen,
      'The LORD hath done great things for them.'

4 Yea, the LORD hath done great things for us already,
      whereof we rejoice.

5 Turn our captivity, O LORD,
      as the rivers in the south.

6 They that sow in tears
      shall reap in joy.

7 He that now goeth on his way weeping and beareth forth good seed
      shall doubtless come again with joy and bring his sheaves with him.

(Coverdale)

Psalm 126

Psalm 126 is a more personal version of Psalm 85 and makes a more immediate appeal. Both psalms move from past help via present appeal to future hope, but the tone of Ps 126 is even more confident.

The return from exile (1) was a surprise (Second Isaiah testifies to that) and a delight. It also had the merit of silencing the gibes of *the heathen*. Now we need help again – this time *captivity* (5) is clearly metaphorical. The image of restoration in v.5b, namely the arrival of the autumn rains in the *south* (Heb. *negeb*), leads easily to that of the final section. The message of comfort is here conveyed in a proverb (6) which is elaborated (7). Ancient sowing rituals often included *weeping* because (so classical authors tell us) the *good seed* is symbolically being interred. So the *tears* are less real than the *joy*, and the happiness of the ending echoes that of the opening.

Psalm 127

1 Unless the LORD builds the house,
      those who build it labour in vain.
   Unless the LORD guards the city,
      the guard keeps watch in vain.

2 It is in vain that you rise up early
      and go late to rest,
   eating the bread of anxious toil;
      for he provides for his beloved during sleep.   ♦

Psalm 127

A psalm of trust. This psalm is a warning. At first sight there is no connection between the first two verses and the last two, and some older commentators printed them as separate. But then a close parallel was discovered in a Sumerian hymn to the goddess Nisaba, from which this is an extract:

Nisaba, where you do not found it
Man builds no house, builds no city,
Builds no palace, sets up no king,
Establishes no cult for the gods.

You are the mistress who gives happiness.
You lay good seed in the womb,
You cause the fruit of the womb to grow,
You cause the mother to love her child.

(von Soden)

Psalm 127 (cont.)

3   Sons are indeed a heritage from the LORD,
          the fruit of the womb a reward.
4   Like arrows in the hand of a warrior
          are the sons of one's youth.
5   Happy is the man who has
          his quiver full of them.
      He shall not be put to shame
          when he speaks with his enemies in the gate.   (NRSV)

Psalm 127 (cont.)

It is hard not to think of some direct influence here. The differences are easily accountable: e.g. the goddess's care for the mother becomes the LORD's care for the father. The psalmist has also added various humanising touches: the contrast between trusting God and 'sweating to make a living' (so NJB translates 2c), and the vignette in v.5cd of the man appearing in court surrounded by his burly *sons*, which is itself a peace-time application of the proverb in v.4. Above all he has created an imaginative link between the two parts of the psalm. *Sleep* in v.2d is both the opposite of *anxious toil* and the context of conception.

Psalms 128

1   Blessed is everyone who fears the LORD
          and walks in the confine of his ways.
2   You will eat the fruit of your labours:
          happy shall you be and all shall go well with you.
3   Your wife within your house
          shall be as a fruitful vine,
4   your children around your table
          like the fresh shoots of the olive.
5   Behold, thus shall the man be blessed,
          who lives in the fear of the LORD.

6   May the LORD so bless you from Zion
          that you see Jerusalem in prosperity all the days of your life.
7   May you see your children's children,
          and in Israel let there be peace.   (PNTW)

Psalm 128

A delightful little Wisdom psalm of blessing upon the faithful Jew. He is typically a father of a family, working his own land and producing enough for them to live on (contrast the curse of Amos 5.11). The scene of vv.3-4 is indoors but the imagery is still that of successful farming, well above the subsistence level. The first five verses, framed by the words *blessed* and *fear the LORD*, concern only the family unit. The last two characteristically extend the horizon in space and time, but the tone remains that of an almost idyllic quietism, typical of a later period.

Psalm 130

1 Out of the depths have I called to you, O LORD;
   LORD, hear my voice.
2 O let your ears consider well
   the voice of my supplication.
3 If you, LORD, should note what we do wrong,
   who then, O LORD, could stand?
4 But there is forgiveness with you,
   so that you shall be feared.
5 I wait for the LORD, my soul waits for him,
   and in his word is my hope.
6 My soul looks for the LORD,
   more than watchmen for the morning,
   more, I say, than watchmen for the morning.
7 for with the LORD there is mercy,
   and with him is ample redemption.

(PNTW)

Psalm 130

A plea for *forgiveness* which moves, as often, from lament to confidence. The thought is clear and coherent. God does not tot up sins (3a). He forgives both individual and nation: *with you* in v.4 is picked up by *with him* in v.7. Verse 4b is open to misunderstanding: *fear* is not the opposite of *hope* (5), merely the technical term for a good relationship with God. The emphasis throughout is on God's grace.

Psalm 131

1 LORD, my heart is not haughty,
   I do not set my sights too high.
   I have taken no part in great affairs,
   in wonders beyond my scope.
2 No, I hold myself in quiet and silence,
   like a little child in its mother's arms,
   like a little child, so I keep myself.

3 Let Israel hope in the LORD
   henceforth and for ever.

(NJB)

Psalm 131

A psalm of humble trust, whose meaning is conveyed in one simple image. The humility, which is nevertheless far from servile, is typical of Jewish piety at its best. The switch to *Israel* is less appropriate than usual and suggests that v.3 was added later for liturgical purposes.

Psalm 133

1 Behold how good and how lovely it is
   when brothers live together in unity
2 It is fragrant as oil upon the head,
   that runs down over the beard.
3 It is like a dew of Hermon,
   like the dew that falls upon the hill of Zion.
4 For there the LORD has commanded his blessing,
   which is life for evermore.   (PNTW)

Psalm 133

A quintessentially Jewish psalm of praise. Officially it is *Zion* (4) which is being praised, but the emphasis is all on fellowship (the fellowship of the pilgrimage?), exemplified by that *unity* between *brothers* which came so hard to the patriarchs in Genesis. *Oil upon the head* is a symbol of wealth and happiness running over, *dew* of abundance and prosperity – the fruits of such fellowship. Both images have the unexpectedness of many in the Song of Songs (see p.502), with which this psalm shares an unabashed joy of living.

Psalm 137

1 By the rivers of Babylon we sat down and wept
   as we remembered Zion.
2 On the willow trees there
   we hung up our lyres,
3 for there those who had carried us captive
   asked us to sing them a song,
   our captors called on us to be joyful:
   'Sing us one of the songs of Zion.'
4 How could we sing the LORD's song
   in a foreign land?
5 If I forget you, Jerusalem,
   may my right hand wither away;
6 let my tongue cling to the roof of my mouth
   if I do not remember you,
   if I do not set Jerusalem
   above my chief joy.   ▶

Psalm 137

The mood of this deeply felt psalm swings from lament through anger and pride to hatred, becoming more and more violent as it goes on. The exile in Babylon is past, but the memory of it is as bitter as if it was yesterday.

The first four verses convey the sense of exile perfectly. Every touch counts. The canals of *Babylon* are the sharpest contrast to the wadis of Judaea. At the same time they fit weeping, for which in the ANE one *sat down*. *Lyres* are instruments of happiness, out of place *there*. It was common in antiquity for captors to get prisoners to sing their native songs. Here the insult was the greater in that it was *a song of Zion* called for, i.e. a *joyful* pilgrim-song like Psalm 122. To a pious Jew such an act would indeed be *to forget,* i.e. to dishonour, *Jerusalem*. That

Psalm 137 (cont.)

7   Remember, LORD, against the Edomites
        the day when Jerusalem fell,
    how they shouted, 'Down with it, down with it,
        down to its very foundations!'
8   Babylon, Babylon the destroyer,
        happy is he who repays you
        for what you did to us!
9   Happy is he who seizes your babes
        and dashes them against a rock.   (REB)

Psalm 137 (cont.)

thought he abjures with a double self-curse, for which he changes from *we* to *I*: if I were to play and sing there, let me never play (5b) or sing (6a) again. Only in Jerusalem is true *joy*.

Thus fuelled, the poet's patriotic anger finally bursts out. It is directed specifically against *the Edomites*, who had earned the lasting hatred of the Jews for joining in the final assault against Jerusalem in 587 BC. In v.8 the mss begin 'daughter of Babylon', which most translations retain.

The mention of *Babylon* is required as a frame with v.1, but Babylon itself had now fallen, and 'daughter' is best taken to refer to Edom as her vassal. The use of *remember* in v.7a is ironical, as is the use of the blessing formula (8b, 9a) for what are plain curses; and the reference to *babes* parodies the conventional reference at the end of psalms (e.g. 113, 127) to blessings on generations still to come. Such treatment of children was common in antiquity after the siege of a revolted vassal-city.

Psalm 139

1   O LORD, you have searched me out and known me:
        you know when I sit or when I stand,
        you comprehend my thoughts long before.
2   You discern my path and the places where I rest;
        you are acquainted with all my ways.
3   For there is not a word on my tongue
        but you, LORD, know it altogether;
4   You have encompassed me behind and before
        and have laid your hand upon me.
5   Such knowledge is too wonderful for me,
        so high that I cannot endure it.   ▸

Psalm 139

This remarkable psalm deals with ideas which are more familiar outside the OT than inside it, and so it is not easy to be sure of the tone which the author intends. In structure it falls clearly into four stanzas:

1-5   God, you know me through and
        through
6-11 I cannot escape you anywhere
12-18 You made me and know all about
        me
19-24 God, slay the wicked and test my
        innocence

Psalm 139 (cont.)

6 Where shall I go from your spirit
     or where shall I flee from your presence?

7 If I ascend into heaven you are there.
     if I make my bed in the grave you are there also.

8 If I spread out my wings towards the morning
     or dwell in the uttermost parts of the sea,

9 even there your hand shall lead me,
     and your right hand shall hold me.

10 If I say 'Surely the darkness will cover me,
     and the night will enclose me',

11 the darkness is no darkness with you,
     but the night is as clear as the day;
     the darkness and the light are both alike.

12 For you have created my inward parts,
     you knit me together in my mother's womb.

13 I will praise you, for you are to be feared:
     fearful are your acts, and wonderful your works.

14 You knew my soul, and my bones were not hidden from you,
     when I was formed in secret, and woven in the depths of the earth.

15 Your eyes saw my limbs when they were yet imperfect
     and in your book were all my members written;

16 day by day they were fashioned,
     and not one was late in growing.

17 How deep are your thoughts to me, O God,
     and how great is the sum of them!

18 Were I to count them, they are more in number than the sand;
     were I to come to the end, I would still be with you.

Psalm 139 (cont.)

The best starting point for interpretation is an Indian hymn to Varuna, god of night, from the *Atharvaveda* (before 1000 BC).

1. The Great Guardian among the Gods
    Sees as if from near.
    He that thinks he is moving stealthily –
    All this the God knows.

2. If a man stands, walks or sneaks about,
    If he slinks away, goes into hiding;
    If two persons sit together and scheme,
    King Varuna is there as a third and knows it.

4. He that should flee beyond the heaven far away
    Would not be far from King Varuna.
    His spies come hither from heaven,
    With a thousand eyes do they watch over the earth.

7. With a hundred snares, O Varuna,
    Surround him that speaks falsehoods.
    Let the liar not go free from thee,
    O thou that observest men.

(In v.4 the 'spies' are the stars, the eyes of night.)

Psalm 139 (cont.)

19   If only you would slay the wicked, O God;
          if only the men of blood would depart from me!
20   For they affront you by their evil,
          and your enemies exalt themselves against you.
21   Do I not hate them, O LORD, that hate you,
          do I not loathe those who rebel against you?
22   I hate them with a perfect hatred;
          they have become my enemies.
23   Search me out, O God, and know my heart;
          put me to the proof and know my thoughts.
24   Look well lest there be any way of wickedness in me,
          and lead me in the way that is everlasting.   (PNTW)

Psalm 139 (cont.)

The parallels between this Indian hymn and Psalm 139 are too striking to be coincidental, although it does not follow that there is any direct borrowing. There are of course numerous differences, notably that, whereas the hymn to Varuna is general, the poet of Psalm 139 is concerned solely with *his* personal relationship to God. In that sense, the tone of the psalmist is much more like that of Job. And Job's speech in 7.11-21 suggests that the psalmist's speech in 139.1-6 is not, as appears at first sight, pure praise, but contains if not a tinge of resentment against God for spying on him, or at least some reluctant admiration.

The second section of the psalm moves gradually from God's own omniscience to his omnipresence (the transition is eased by 6b). Here too, there is some latent irony, even in the fine passage in vv.6-9: this is clearly based on Amos 9.2-4, which describes the situation of the *wicked*. 'The poet's realisation that he cannot escape God has a paralysing rather than a liberating effect' (Weiser). Verses 7 and 8 make the lightest of references to mythical heroes who climbed to heaven or descended to hell (the *bed* of v.7b has its own irony) as does v.8 to the idea of the 'magic journey'. But myth or magic, God defeats them.

The third section is more straightforward. The poet's attitude here is one of pure praise and trust (13). God's knowledge and power are exemplified by the mystery, *not hidden from* him, of the child's growth in the womb or, as v.14b has it, *in the depths of the earth*. The thought here is closest to Eccl 11.5. The *book* of life is mentioned quite often in the OT e.g. Ex 32.32. Verse 17 answers v.2: God knows all my *thoughts*, but I can never fathom his.

Had the poem been a hymn, that echo would have rounded it off in best Hebrew style. But in the fourth section the poet adds petitions of a kind that belong rather with prayers. The *hatred* of vv.19-22 is a standard ingredient of treaties in the ancient world, where partners swore to 'hold the same people as friends and enemies'. Finally, the protestation on behalf of himself (23f.) brings back that ambivalent note which runs through this powerful but mysterious psalm.

Psalm 150

1   Praise the LORD, O praise God in his sanctuary,
         praise him in the firmament of his power.
2   Praise him for his mighty acts,
         praise him according to his abundant goodness.
3   Praise him in the blast of the ram's horn,
         praise him upon the lute and harp.
4   Praise him with the timbrel and dances,
         praise him upon the strings and pipe.
5   Praise him on the high-sounding cymbals;
         praise him upon the loud cymbals.
6   Let everything that has breath praise the LORD:
         O praise the LORD!   (PNTW)

Psalm 150

The musicians' psalm, specially placed as a kind of doxology to the psalter. All other sounds are taken up into a sustained crescendo of orchestral praise.

PROVERBS

Introduction

Until recent times proverbs have played an important part in the life of all peoples, to guide conduct or clinch argument. All literatures contain collections of proverbs. Yet each collection contains much common material, whether borrowed or independently arrived at. The Hebrew collections, like the rest of Hebrew Wisdom literature, are inseparable from the wider ANE tradition from which they sprang (see p.364).

The chief such collection in the OT is the Book of Proverbs. The title verse ascribes the whole book to Solomon, and the same claim is made more modestly for the two largest sub-collections in it. By Jewish tradition Solomon himself composed 3,000 proverbs (1 K 5.12). He was also known for cultivating contacts with foreign nations. It is therefore not surprising to find two of the smaller sub-collections in Proverbs attributed to foreign sages, with a third (22.17-24.22) clearly though anonymously modelled on an Egyptian work, the *Wisdom of Amenemope* of c.700 BC (*ANET* 421).

Taken in sequence, the book of Proverbs is made up as follows:

Chs 1-9: Introduction
Chs 10-24: 'Proverbs of Solomon'
Chs 25-29: 'Further proverbs of Solomon, transcribed at the court of Hezekiah King of Judah' c.700
Chs 30-31: An appendix: sayings of other sages, some named, some not.

It is thought that the two sub-collections ascribed specifically to Solomon are the oldest parts of the book, and the introduction the latest. The latter is probably post-exilic, say 500 BC, the former of almost any antiquity.

The Hebrew word *māshāl*, commonly translated 'proverb', actually has a wider meaning. This includes any pointed and memorable saying, i.e. the whole range of material included in the OT book. Most of that material does indeed consist of proverbs expressed in the ANE's traditional two-line parallelism. To modern ears the addition of a second line tends to weaken the effect of the whole, and it is noticeable that those which have passed into English have all been reduced to a single line, usually the first (see pp.479-81, nos 14, 20, 28, 29). But there is another type of two-liner which, by virtue of its form, achieves the pungency and the open texture which are the hall-marks of the best proverbs (see 25.11+). Attractive also are some of the rather longer 'numerical sayings' (see 30.18+). Longer still are some set-piece dramatic poems which offer either a warning against temptation or a praise of Wisdom. These longer poems are mostly to be found in Chs 1-9. Outstanding among them is the self-praise of Wisdom in Ch. 8.

All proverbs encapsulate group wisdom. Sometimes the group is an elite. This is the case with many Egyptian collections which were put together by and for civil servants. Some of the Hebrew proverbs come from that kind of milieu, as do also the rather self-conscious praises of wisdom. Most Hebrew Wisdom belongs in the more humdrum context of family and business affairs. Yet the scale of values is much the same in both cases. The prevailing mood is one of bourgeois moderation, which leaves no room for heroism or deep piety. Its overarching principle is the maintenance of order: in society, in the home, within the individual and (though the concept was not known to the ANE) in nature.

In Egypt the concept of order (*ma'at*) was highly developed, as one would expect from a sophisticated but hierarchical society (cp. that of Confucius). *Ma'at* was not only personified but treated as a goddess. The Hebrews had a close equivalent to the concept of *ma'at* in *tsedāqāh*, the word we usually translate 'justice'. But for the maintenance of this order only YHWH could in Hebrew eyes be responsible: justice could at the most be an attribute of his. They were however willing to admit a personified (though not deified) Wisdom, and she plays a part in Hebrew Wisdom literature which is close to that of *Ma'at* in Egyptian.

Since God upheld the social order, the requirements of religion and of what we would call 'wordly wisdom' were identical (see p.478 nos. 5 and 8-10). One way or another, those who met those requirements would be rewarded, their transgressors punished. Of the religion of Abraham and the prophets, Proverbs knows little. God himself is inscrutable and his behaviour arbitrary (see e.g. p.482 no.39). Though sometimes referred to by his personal name of YHWH, he is hard to distinguish from the supreme deity of the ANE pantheon.

The Editor's Introduction

1. 1 The proverbs of Solomon son of David, king of Israel,

2   by which mankind will come to wisdom and instruction,
         will understand words that bring understanding,

3   and will attain to a well-instructed intelligence,
         righteousness, justice, and probity.

4   The simple will be endowed with shrewdness
         and the young with knowledge and discretion.

5   By listening to them the wise will increase their learning,
         those with understanding will acquire skill

6   to understand proverbs and parables,
         the sayings and riddles of the wise.

7   The fear of the LORD is the foundation of knowledge;
         it is fools who scorn wisdom and instruction.   (REB)

The Editor's Introduction

The book opens with its title, appended to which is a wordy statement of its purpose. The latter is a common feature of Egyptian Instructions. *Amenemope* starts similarly: 'The beginning of the teaching of life, the testimony for prosperity, all precepts for intercourse with elders . . . to make him prosper upon earth . . . to steer him away from evil . . .' (*ANET* 421). In the flood of near-synonyms one may distinguish between the benefits which the course of study is to confer at the elementary (4) and the advanced (5-6) levels. The apparent emphasis is upon the practical application of Wisdom, but at the highest level the study is to be an end in itself. Such has always been the twofold claim for an education in the humanities.

Before proceeding like *Amenemope* to the instructions proper, our book pauses to insert a motto verse in order to give the collection a slant of its own. Verse 7a, in which *the LORD* is, as always, YHWH the God of the Hebrews, is found in almost identical form twice more in strategic places in Proverbs [9.10 and 15.33]. The case is stated here with moderation – it is only the *foundation,* i.e. it is necessary rather than sufficient – but the editor has put down his marker.

Wisdom's own Warning

20   Wisdom cries aloud in the open air,
         and raises her voice in public places.

21   She calls at the top of the bustling streets;
         at the approaches to the city gates she says:

22   'How long will you simple fools
         be content with your simplicity?

23   If only you would respond to my reproof,
         I would fill you with my spirit
         and make my precepts known to you.

24   But because you refused to listen to my call,
         because no one heeded when I stretched out my hand,

25   because you rejected all my advice
         and would have none of my reproof,

26   I in turn shall laugh at your doom
         and deride you when terror comes,

27   The insolent delight in their insolence;
         the stupid hate knowledge.

28   When they call to me, I shall not answer;
         when they seek, they will not find me.

32   For simpletons who turn a deaf ear come to grief,
         and the stupid are ruined by their own complacency.

33   But whoever listens to me will live without a care,
         undisturbed by fear of misfortune.'　　　　　　　(REB)

Wisdom's own Warning

Chs 1-9, like Chs 30-1, consist for the most part not of discrete and specific instructions but of more extended pieces, anything from five verses to a chapter in length. Some of these amount to little: they can be summarised as saying 'listen to my advice, because it will profit you'. But among them are some more interesting pieces, of two main kinds. In one a personified Wisdom speaks of herself and invites the attention of men. In the other advice is given to a young man about women: how to avoid the temptations of the wicked and (much more briefly) how to appreciate the virtues of the good. The two themes are related, in that Wisdom too is personified as an attractive woman, and her relationship – indeed rivalry – with the temptress is brought out in Chs 7 and 9.

    The first speech by personified Wisdom (1.20-33), like the second (8.1-36), opens with Wisdom taking up a position, like any public teacher or preacher, at a busy place in the city and calling upon the people to listen. But after that common opening they diverge. In the first the audience fails to respond and is berated. The terms used have much in common with the discourse of prophets, both in form ('because ... therefore ...') and in content. For example, many prophets were exercised about the failure of their message to get through. There is however an important difference. The prophets castigate sin, threaten intervention by God, and summon to repentance. Wisdom writers castigate folly, point out its natural consequences (so here v.32) and invite a choice. Wisdom herself does not intervene: the most she will do is to withdraw (28) and *laugh* (26). For the question of 'who' this Wisdom is, see Ch. 8.

The Benefits of Wisdom

3.13   Happy are those who find wisdom,
  and those who get understanding,

14   for her income is better than silver,
  and her revenue better than gold.

15   She is more precious than jewels,
  and nothing you desire can compare with her.

16   Long life is in her right hand;
  in her left hand are riches and honor.

17   Her ways are ways of pleasantness,
  and all her paths are peace.

18   She is a tree of life to those who lay hold of her;
  those who hold her fast are called happy.   (NRSV)

The Benefits of Wisdom

The next praise of Wisdom, this time in the third person, anticipates the themes of her great poem of self-praise in Ch. 8. The section is expressed as a beatitude, a form common to ANE and Greek wisdom; the *happy* here also serves as a frame. Verse 14 treats Wisdom as an investment.

The imagery of v.16 comes ultimately from Egypt, where the goddess *Ma'at* was often shown holding a symbol of *life* in one hand and of *riches* in the other. The *tree of life* had likewise played an important part in Mesopotamian myth. But both references seem here to be purely literary.

Praise of Married Love

5.15   Drink waters out of thine own cistern,
  and running waters out of thine own well.

18   Let thy fountain be blessed,
  and rejoice with the wife of thy youth.

19   Let her be as the loving hind and pleasant roe;
  let her breasts satisfy thee at all times;
  and be thou ravished always with her love.

20   And why wilt thou, my son, be ravished with a strange woman,
  and embrace the bosom of a stranger?   (AV)

Praise of Married Love

Chs 1-9 contain no fewer than five extended warnings against loose women – a standard theme of ANE wisdom – but only here is anything said in contrasting praise of married love. The move from *fountain* to *breasts* is typically Hebrew.

Against Adultery: (i) Fatherly Advice

20 My son, observe your father's commands
        and do not abandon the teaching of your mother.
23 For a commandment is a lamp, and teaching a light,
        reproof and correction point the way to life,
24 to keep you from the wife of another man,
        from the seductive tongue of the loose woman.
25 Do not be infatuated by her beauty
        or let her glance captivate you;
26 for a prostitute can be had for the price of a loaf,
        but a married woman is after the prize of a life.
27 Can a man kindle a fire in his bosom
        without setting his clothes alight?
28 If a man walks on live coals,
        will his feet not be scorched?
29 So is he who commits adultery with his neighbour's wife;
        no one can touch such a woman and go free.
30 Is not a thief contemptible if he steals,
        even to satisfy his appetite when he is hungry?
31 And, if he is caught, must he not pay seven times over
        and surrender all that his house contains?
32 So one who commits adultery is a senseless fool:
        he dishonours the woman and ruins himself;
33 he will get nothing but blows and contumely
        and can never live down the disgrace;
34 for a husband's anger is rooted in jealousy
        and he will show no mercy when he takes revenge;
35 compensation will not buy his forgiveness,
        nor will a present, however large, purchase his connivance.   (REB)

Against Adultery: (i) Fatherly Advice

This passage, a warning against an adulterous liaison, is complementary to the next on the same theme (7.6-23). The latter, which deals with the initial seduction, should logically be read before this, which describes rather the consequences of discovery. The opening (20) suggests a family setting for the advice, but Egyptian instructions regularly use *my son* as a conventional address. Here as elsewhere the initiative and thus the blame is laid on the woman, so as to make the advice more palatable to the young man. The argument advanced in v.26 is different from that in vv.32-5 but not incompatible. REB's *price of a loaf . . . prize of a life* (26) is clever, and entirely in the spirit of the pun-loving book of Proverbs, though closer to LXX than to MT. To risk this kind of entanglement is to play with *fire*: it is as stupid as trying to *kindle* a flame in the shelter of one's *clothes*. The *thief* (30) provides an *a fortiori* argument: he loses men's respect and is heavily fined into the bargain. But a *jealous husband* will *show no mercy*. He will never accept the *compensation* which ANE law allowed, and the adulterer must expect a broken head and a ruined career. The punishments here show how far removed we are from the world of the Torah, which was much less severe on the thief (Exod 22) but prescribed the death penalty for both a married woman and her lover [Dt 22.22].

Against Adultery: (ii) What Wisdom Saw

7. 1 My son, keep my words;
    store up my commands in your mind.

2 Keep my commands if you would live,
    and treasure my teaching as the apple of your eye.

3 Wear them like a ring on your finger;
    inscribe them on the tablet of your memory.

4 Call Wisdom your sister,
    greet understanding as a familiar friend;

5 then they will save you from the adulteress,
    from the loose woman with her seductive words.

6 I glanced out of the window of my house,
    I looked down through the lattice;

7 among the young men there I noticed
    a lad devoid of all sense.

8 He was passing along the street at her corner,
    stepping out in the direction of her house

9 at twilight, as the day faded,
    at dusk as the night grew dark,

10 and there a woman came to meet him.
    She was dressed like a prostitute, full of wiles,

11 flighty and inconstant,
    a woman never content to stay at home,

12 lying in wait by every corner,
    now in the street, now in the public squares.

13 She caught hold of him and kissed him;
    brazenly she accosted him and said,

14 'I had a sacrifice, an offering, to make
    and I have paid my vows today;

15 so I came out to meet you,
    to look for you, and now I have found you.

16 I have spread coverings on my couch,
    coloured linen from Egypt.

17 I have perfumed my bed
    with myrrh, aloes, and cassia.

Against Adultery: (ii) What Wisdom Saw

The version of this theme provided by Ch. 7 is the most polished in plan and the most lively in execution. Its introduction and conclusion contain typical instructional material, but the main section is cast in autobiographical form. This form (which is a favourite of Ecclesiastes, see p.490), allows a freer and more imaginative treatment, as here in the central speech of the adulteress herself (14-20). As before, the *loose woman* is married, but this time she is promiscuous (26). The whole reads like a dramatisation of a paragraph from the Egyptian *Instruction of Ani* c.1500 BC (*ANET* 420, slightly altered):

Against Adultery: (ii) What Wisdom Saw (cont.)

18 Come! Let us drown ourselves in pleasure,
    let us abandon ourselves to a night of love;
19 for my husband is not at home.
    He has gone away on a long journey,
20 taking a bag of silver with him;
    he will not be home until full moon.'
21 Persuasively she cajoled him,
    coaxing him with seductive words.
22 He followed her, the simple fool,
    like an ox on its way to be slaughtered,
    like an antelope bounding into the noose,
23 like a bird hurrying into the trap;
    he did not know he was risking his life
    until the arrow pierced his vitals.
24 But now, my sons, listen to me,
    and attend to what I say.
25 Do not let desire entice you into her ways,
    do not stray down her paths;
26 many has she wounded and laid low,
    and her victims are without number.
27 Her house is the entrance to Sheol,
    leading down to the halls of death.

(REB)

Against Adultery: (ii) What Wisdom Saw (cont.)

Be on your guard against a woman from abroad,
who is not known in her own town. . . .
a woman who is far away from her husband.
'I am sleek', she says to you every day. . . .
It is a great crime, worthy of death.

The introduction (1-5) has two points of interest. First, the sage wishes his teaching to be taken to heart. *The apple of your eye*, i.e. the pupil, is much more personal than *a light* in 6.23, and a man's signet-ring was like an identity card. Secondly, to *call Wisdom your sister*, within a literary tradition where 'sister' also means 'wife', is to hint at a rivalry between her and the adulteress.

This rivalry gives added piquancy to the narrative, which is spoken by Wisdom herself. She is here represented as observing the whole scene from the *lattice window* of her *house*, exactly as many a queen in the OT *looked down* from the women's quarters of the palace (e.g. Jezebel in 2 K 9.30). In the street below she saw a group of immature *young men*, target of her normal teachings. One of them was walking towards the loose woman's *house* when she came out to meet him, *dressed* for the kill. Having first *kissed him*, she invites him in. A sumptuous dinner awaits him, the meat from a *sacrifice* she has just offered. The *couch* for the banquet is *spread* with imported *linen*, and her *bed* is richly scented. All is done to impress the green youth, and to allay any anxieties he may have about her *husband*, who is presumably a rich merchant. The victim puts up no fight, as the piled-up similes show. The mention of the *ox* provides an ironical echo of her invitation in v.14. One can picture him running up the stairs two at a time (22c) – but from that moment onwards the slope leads inexorably *down* to ruin.

Wisdom and her Role in Creation

8. 1
Hear how Wisdom calls
   and understanding lifts her voice.

2
She takes her stand at the crossroads,
   by the wayside, at the top of the hill;

3
beside the gate, at the entrance to the city,
   at the approach by the portals she cries aloud:

4
'It is to you I call,
   to all mankind I appeal:

5
understand, you simpletons, what it is to be shrewd;
   you stupid people, understand what it is to have sense.

6
Listen! For I shall speak clearly,
   you will have plain speech from me.

12
I am Wisdom, I bestow shrewdness
   and show the way to knowledge and discretion.

14
From me come advice and ability;
   understanding and power are mine.

15
Through me kings hold sway
   and governors enact just laws.

17
Those who love me I love,
   and those who search for me will find me.

18
In my hands are riches and honour,
   boundless wealth and prosperity.

21
I endow with riches those who love me;
   I shall fill their treasuries.

22
The LORD created me the first of his works
   long ago, before all else that he made.

23
I was formed in earliest times,
   at the beginning, before earth itself.

Wisdom and her Role in Creation

This chapter is one of the high spots of OT Wisdom literature, particularly but not only for the third section (22-31) on Wisdom's role at the creation of the world. That is led up to by two earlier sections and rounded off by a shorter conclusion. Almost all of it is in the form of a speech by Wisdom commending herself. In this it is like the briefer passage 1.20-33, which complements and illuminates it.

As before, Wisdom takes her stand in the most public of places (the details of 2-3 succeed only in confusing), and addresses everybody – no elite, coterie or sect, but rather for preference the untutored. To them she will offer her instruction, not in codes or hints but in *plain* language (6).

The second section (12-21) is introduced by the self-predication (*I am Wisdom*) which always steps up the dramatic tension. From Wisdom come the gifts of the civil servant (12, 14), of royalty (15) and of the business man (18, 21, an unexpected climax). The surprising verse in this section is v.17. There are no exact OT parallels to it, but many Egyptian scarabs of C10th-7th BC bear inscriptions like 'Isis [etc.] loves him who loves her'.

Between the second and third sections LXX inserts what is clearly designed as a link-verse:

If I declare to you the things which happen everyday,
I shall not forget to recount the things of old.

Wisdom and her Role in Creation (cont.)

24   I was born when there was yet no ocean,
    when there were no springs brimming with water.

25   Before the mountains were settled in their place,
    before the hills I was born,

26   when as yet he had made neither land nor streams
    nor the mass of the earth's soil.

27   When he set the heavens in place I was there,
    when he girdled the ocean with the horizon,

28   when he fixed the canopy of clouds overhead
    and confined the springs of the deep,

29   when he prescribed limits for the sea
    so that the waters do not transgress his command,
    when he made earth's foundations firm.

30   Then I was at his side each day,
    his darling and delight,
    playing in his presence continually,

31   playing over his whole world,
    while my delight was in mankind.

Wisdom and her Role in Creation (cont.)

In truth the change *is* somewhat abrupt, and it has been thought that the third section was originally an independent poem. In its present context it represents a further heightening of the claims of Wisdom, by moving from politics and economics to philosophy and theology. The content of the new claim is clear enough. Wisdom was *created* (22) by YHWH *before* all his other *works*, before the *earth*, the *ocean* and the *heavens* . She was indeed present *at his side* (30) throughout the process of creation, *playing* like a child with a new toy. And just as he delighted in her, so her *delight was in* newly-created *mankind*. The details of creation need not delay us. Unlike the first chapter of Genesis, the author is not concerned with the articulation of the parts but with the simple before (23-6) and after (27-30). For this he uses the resonant ANE formula: *When there was yet no. . .* (24, 26).

After the climax the poem is swiftly brought to a close. *Mankind* of v.31 (lit. 'sons of men') echoes v.4 and leads naturally to *sons* in v.32. The concluding

verses are in the conventional style of an instruction, unless the imagery of v.34bc implies waiting not for school to open but for the beloved to emerge.

Which raises the question, what did the author mean his readers to understand by this personified Wisdom? If we look for light in the rest of the OT, we shall find plenty of personifications of abstract qualities. In particular Ps 85.10-13 has a personified righteousness 'looking down from heaven' and 'going in front of YHWH'. Righteousness here is clearly a personified attribute of God himself. Add to that Ps 104.24: 'in wisdom you have made them all', and we may seem to be nearly there. But perhaps not quite. In the Egyptian religion from which Ps 104 springs, Wisdom is the goddess *Ma'at*, whose figure lies behind so much Egyptian Wisdom literature. In that literature she is also referred to as beloved daughter of the creator god, who was with him before the creation of the world. The author of these poems in Proverbs managed to enrich his description with those ideas without compromising his

Wisdom and her Role in Creation (cont.)

8. 32   Now, sons, listen to me;
        happy are those who keep to my ways.

33   Listen to instruction and grow wise;
        do not ignore it.

34   Happy the one who listens to me,
        watching daily at my threshold
        with his eyes on the doorway!

35   For whoever finds me finds life
        and wins favour with the LORD,

36   but whoever fails to find me deprives himself,
        and all who hate me are in love with death.'
        (REB)

Wisdom and her Role in Creation (cont.)

monotheism – hence the emphasis on *the LORD created me* in 8.22 – and so to present a figure unparalleled in the OT.

But there is more still. The Hebrew word in v.30 which REB translates *darling* is of disputed meaning. AV took it the same way: 'one brought up' is a (darling) child. But if the Hebrew consonants are given different vowels, a different meaning emerges, viz. the 'master-craftsman' of NRSV and NJB. And the latter was the reading preferred by the LXX and clearly dominant in Judaism from c.250 BC onwards. For the idea was much developed in the later Wisdom literature (Wisd Sol 7.22a), and was very influential in early Christianity as helping to explain the nature of Jesus. That is why Paul calls Jesus 'the Wisdom of God' (1 Cor 1.24) and the prologue to John's gospel says of him that he 'was in the beginning with God: all things were made through him'. So much (and more) has hung upon the LXX translator's reading of a single word!

Wisdom and Stupidity Contrasted

9. 1   Wisdom has built her house;
        she has hewn her seven pillars.

2   Now, having slaughtered a beast, spiced her wine,
        and spread her table,

3   she has sent her maidens to proclaim
        from the highest point of the town:

4   'Let the simple turn in here.'
        She says to him who lacks sense,

5   'Come, eat the food I have prepared
        and taste the wine that I have spiced.

6   Abandon the company of simpletons and you will live,
        you will advance in understanding.'

Wisdom and Stupidity Contrasted

The introductory chapters end with yet another description of the loose woman, but this time she is contrasted, not (as in Ch. 5) with the good wife, but (following the hint of 7.4-5) with the lady Wisdom herself. The contrast is based on two par-allel narratives of an invitation to dinner. Together they represent dramatically the choice that lies before the young.

Wisdom lives in a grand *house* with a portico: *seven* is a 'perfect' number. Just like the loose woman of 7.14, she has

Wisdom and Stupidity Contrasted (cont.)

13   The Lady Stupidity is a flighty creature;
         a fool, she cares for nothing.
14   She sits at the door of her house,
         on a seat in the highest part of the town,
15   to invite the passers-by indoors
         as they hurry on their way:
16   'Turn in here, simpleton,' she says,
         and to him who lacks sense she says,
17   'Stolen water is sweet
         and bread eaten in secret tastes good.'
18   Little does he know that the dead are there,
         that her guests are in the depths of Sheol.   (REB)

Wisdom and Stupidity Contrasted (cont.)

sacrificed an animal and so can offer the best in meat and drink. It would not become her to *sit at the door of her house* (14), so she sends out her servants (3) to approach particularly the untutored (as in 8.5) and invite them to dinner.

The contrasting narrative about *The Lady Stupidity* is sadly inferior. The reference to *the highest part of the town* belongs rather to the picture of Wisdom herself (9.3 etc.). Verse 16 is too similar to v.4, though the proverb in v.17 makes it spicier than its parallel v.5. The chapter ends with the stock contrast between life (6) and death (18) i.e. success and ruin.

Proverbs Chs 10-22 etc.

The main body of the Book of Proverbs (10.1-22.10, probably its oldest part), consists of sayings which scarcely ever extend beyond two lines. No logical principle is detectable in the ordering. So those printed here have been shuffled and dealt again in five categories according to content (or in a few cases their form). This is partly a subjective procedure, for there is no generally agreed scheme of classification.

Formally the sayings can be divided into instructions and 'sentences' i.e. aphorisms; the former have the verb in the imperative, the latter in the indicative. But that distinction is largely irrelevant to content, since most 'sentences' also *imply* a recommendation about conduct. A modern reader might be more interested to see them arranged on a scale cynical→ prudential→ moral→ religious→ pious. But such a scale would simply not have been recognised by the author or his readers. If in ancient Egypt 'the purely secular was the purely trivial' (Frankfort), how much more so in ancient Israel!

Into the same five categories have been inserted a few sayings from the other parts of the book which deal, sometimes more fully, with the same topics. They are all numbered sequentially here for ease of cross-reference, and tabulated with their chapter and verse references on p.486.

A. Business, Wealth and Poverty

1. Accuracy of scales and balances is the LORD's concern;
     all the weights in the bag are his business.

2. 'A bad bargain!' says the buyer to the seller,
     but off he goes to brag about it.

3. Anger is mollified by a covert gift,
     raging fury by a present under cover of the cloak.

4. Better is little with the fear of the LORD
     than great treasure and trouble therewith.
   Better is a dinner of herbs where love is,
     than a stalled ox and hatred therewith.

5. Bread got by fraud may taste good,
     but afterwards it turns to grit in the mouth.

6. The poor is hated even of his own neighbour:
     but the rich hath many friends.

7. Those who oppress the poor insult their Maker,
     but those who are kind to the needy honor him.

8. He who is generous to the poor lends to the LORD,
     who will recompense him for his deed.

9. Whoever stops his ears at the cry of the helpless
     will himself cry for help and not be answered.

A. Business, Wealth and Poverty

1. A matter of concern both to ANE Wisdom and to the Hebrew prophets.
3. Not infallible advice – see 6.35.
4. cp. *Amenemope*: 'Better is bread when the heart is happy than riches with sorrow.' Many ANE proverbs use this 'better A than B' form. *Trouble* in the first verse is not the same as *hatred* in the second: it refers to the anxiety inseparable from wealth, or at any rate from ambition. As the similarity of form between the two verses shows, *the fear of the LORD* liberates from that sort of ambition.

5. Can be read as an answer to 9.17.
7. *their Maker* means 'him who made *the poor*'.
9. Nos 6-9 illustrate the convergence in the ANE mind of prudential, moral and religious considerations.

B. Speech and Silence

10. Experience uses few words;
      discernment keeps a cool head.
    Even a fool, if he keeps his mouth shut, will seem wise;
      if he holds his tongue, he will seem intelligent.

11. He that answereth a matter before he heareth it,
      it is folly and shame unto him.

12. In a lawsuit the first speaker seems right,
      until another comes forward to cross examine him.

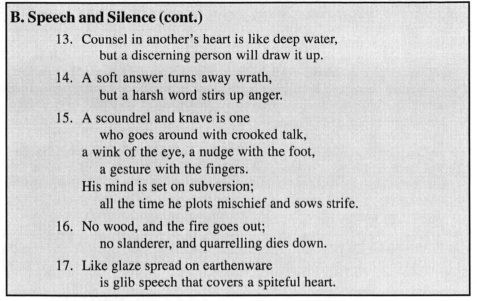

B. Speech and Silence (cont.)

13. Counsel in another's heart is like deep water,
    but a discerning person will draw it up.

14. A soft answer turns away wrath,
    but a harsh word stirs up anger.

15. A scoundrel and knave is one
    who goes around with crooked talk,
    a wink of the eye, a nudge with the foot,
    a gesture with the fingers.
    His mind is set on subversion;
    all the time he plots mischief and sows strife.

16. No wood, and the fire goes out;
    no slanderer, and quarrelling dies down.

17. Like glaze spread on earthenware
    is glib speech that covers a spiteful heart.

B. Speech and Silence

12. The specific reference to a lawsuit has a general implication: viz. don't jump to conclusions.

14. *soft* i.e. conciliatory, *harsh* i.e. cutting.

15. The word translated *scoundrel* is in Hebrew 'Belial', which in later Judaism (and thence in the NT and Milton) came to be used as a proper name for an arch-devil. Curiously, our word 'devil', from Greek *diabolos*, properly means 'he who sets one person against another' – exactly the point being made here.

16. Much of ANE Wisdom literature is devoted to the subject of speech – its power and its pitfalls; see also 25.11-14. The commendation of silence is part of a more general approach to life which is illustrated in the next section.

C. Cautiousness

18. It is dangerous to dedicate a gift rashly,
    to make a vow and then have second thoughts.

19. Do not congratulate yourself about tomorrow,
    since you do not know what today will bring forth.

20. Pride goes before destruction,
    and a haughty spirit before a fall.

21. Do not push yourself forward at court
    or take your stand where the great assemble;
    for it is better to be told, 'Come up here',
    than to be moved down to make room for a nobleman.

22. A king's rage is like a lion's roar,
    but his favour is like dew on the grass.

C. Cautiousness

18. The situation envisaged is that of someone who, in a moment of need, makes a rash vow which he later regrets (like Jephthah in Jg 11). But the principle of thinking before acting is of general relevance.

C. Cautiousness (cont.)

19. One reason for caution is the unpredictability of the future. The point is made much more vividly by the proverb quoted in 1 K 20.11: 'Let not him that girds on his armour boast himself as he that puts it off'. It is given theological support in nos 32 and 33.

20. The English proverb is rightly compressed into a single line. *Pride* means failure to recognise one's limitations, like the Greek *hubris*.

21. Not only *at court*!

22. Shows the ambiguity even of an apparently simple proverb. The commentators take the *dew* as fructifying; but dew is also a symbol of evanescence (Hos 6.4), which gives an ironical twist here.

Other proverbs which reinforce the generally cautious approach of Wisdom literature are nos 10, 11, 32, 33; cp. also the warnings against bad women in Chs 1-9 and against drunkenness in 23.29-35.

D. Family Affairs etc.

23. Do not withhold discipline from a boy;
     take the stick to him, and save him from death.

24. Like a gold ring in a pig's snout
     is a beautiful woman without good sense.

25. The way of an unfaithful wife is this:
     she eats, then wipes her mouth
     and says, 'I have done nothing wrong.'

26. The sluggard protests, 'There is a lion in the road,
     a lion at large on the street.'
     A door turns on its hinges,
     a sluggard on his bed.
     A sluggard dips his hand into the dish
     but is too lazy to lift it to his mouth.

27. Go to the ant, thou sluggard;
     consider her ways, and be wise:
     which having no guide,
     overseer, or ruler,
     provideth her meat in the summer,
     and gathereth her food in the harvest.
     How long wilt thou sleep, O sluggard?
     When wilt thou arise out of thy sleep?
     Yet a little sleep, a little slumber,
     a little folding of the hands to sleep:
     So shall thy poverty come as one that travelleth
     and thy want as an armed man.

D. Family Affairs etc.

23. A fragment from the Wisdom of *Ahikar* is very close: 'If I smite thee, my son, thou wilt not die, but if I leave thee to thine own heart [thou wilt not live].' (*ANET* 428). For a theological parallel see no. 36.

25. Eating is often a symbol of sexual intercourse. Women get a poor press

D. Family Affairs etc. (cont.)

28. A merry heart maketh a cheerful countenance,
        but by sorrow of the heart the spirit is broken.

29. Hope deferred makes the heart sick,
        but a desire fulfilled is a tree of life.

30. Anyone narrowing his eyes intends dishonesty,
        and one who pinches his lips is bent on mischief.

31. By wisdom a house is built,
        by understanding it is made strong;
    by knowledge its storerooms are filled
        with riches of every kind, rare and desirable.

D. Family Affairs etc. (cont.)

in ANE Wisdom; but there is still Ch. 31 to come.

26. Three separate jokes against a frequent butt of Wisdom literature. The first means 'any excuse to avoid going to work', the second that he is permanently hinged to his *bed* and can turn only from one side to the other.

27. The *ant* is an admirable symbol of industry, but LXX replaces it with the 'bee', which has its own attractions. *One that travelleth* means a vagabond.

28. 'Inner happiness is reflected in the lines of the face'(McKane).

29. Repeated disappointment breaks the spirit.

30. Folk wisdom has always believed in a correspondence between traits of countenance and of character.

31. How to acquire a desirable residence.

E. Theological Reflections

32. The horse is made ready for the day of battle,
        but the victory belongs to the LORD.

33. Do not think to repay evil for evil;
        wait for the LORD to deliver you.

34. If thine enemy be hungry, give him bread to eat;
        And if he be thirsty, give him water to drink:
    For thou shalt heap coals of fire upon his head,
        And the LORD shall reward thee.

E. Theological Reflections

32. Many ANE proverbs are variations on the theme that 'man proposes, God disposes', e.g. 'One thing are the words which men say; another is that which the god does' (*Amenemope*, *ANET* 423). Only the context can show whether such a proverb is being used to express caution or piety; and, if piety, whether the mood is one of fear, confidence or resignation.

33. This too could be pious or cautious.

34. The reference here is probably to an Egyptian rite in which a penitent carried a basin of glowing embers on his head. The advice is thus not, as it appears, cynical. It means that by showing him forgiveness you will bring him to repentance, which is how Paul took it (Rom 12.20). Even so, the tone is not as attractive as this much

E. Theological Reflections (cont.)

35. Do not rejoice at the fall of your enemy;
       do not gloat when he is brought down,
    or the LORD will be displeased at the sight,
       and will cease to be angry with him.

36. My son, despise not the chastening of the LORD;
       neither be weary of his correction.
    For whom the LORD loveth he correcteth,
       even as a father the son in whom he delighteth.

37. Sacrifice from a wicked person is an abomination to the LORD,
       the more so when it is offered from impure motives.

38. The poor and the oppressors have this in common:
       it is the LORD who gives light to the eyes of both.

39. The glory of God is to keep things hidden,
       but the glory of kings is to fathom them.

E. Theological Reflections (cont.)

earlier Babylonian precept (*ANET* 595):

> Do not return evil to your adversary,
> requite with kindness the one who
> does evil to you. . . .
> At this one's god takes pleasure.

35. Here however the moral tone plummets.

36. A rudimentary treatment of the theological problem of suffering.

37. Strong words (by Wisdom standards) are here used in support of the prophetic condemnation of hypocritical worship.

38. Here on the other hand are acquiescent and non-prophetic words on social injustice.

39. 'Mystery is integral to the idea of God, wisdom to that of a king' (Scott).

The Ill Effects of Wine

23.29   Whose is the misery? Whose the remorse?
             Whose are the quarrels and the anxiety?
          Who gets the bruises without knowing why?
             Whose eyes are bloodshot?

30   Those who linger late over their wine,
         those always sampling some new spiced liquor.

31   Do not gulp down the wine, the strong red wine,
         when the droplets form on the side of the cup.

32   It may flow smoothly
         but in the end it will bite like a snake
         and poison like a cobra.   ♦

The Ill Effects of Wine

This is a curious little poem, without close parallel either in the OT or outside it. Unfortunately nobody has succeeded in translating it convincingly, which is not entirely due to the presence in it of words whose meaning is uncertain. The first part is a series of questions amounting almost to a riddle, which is then answered. The second part (31-5) consists of an exhortation supported by

The Ill Effects of Wine (cont.)

33   Then your eyes will see strange sights,
          your wits and your speech will be confused;
34   you become like a man tossing out at sea,
          like one who clings to the top of the rigging;
35   you say, 'If I am struck down, what do I care?
          If I am overcome, what of it?
      As soon as I wake up,
          I shall turn to the wine again.'

                                                                    (REB)

The Ill Effects of Wine (cont.)

a description of the effects of drink. These are shown to be the exact opposite of all that Wisdom stands for: confusion of *wits and speech*, loss of physical control, and a devil-may-care irresponsibility. This part is neatly rounded off so as to suggest an unending cycle of drinking.

Proverbs Collected under Hezekiah

11   Like apples of gold set in silver filigree
          is a word spoken in season.
12   Like a golden ear-ring or a necklace of Nubian gold
          is a wise person's reproof in an attentive ear.
13   Like the coolness of snow in harvest time
          is a trusty messenger to those who send him;
          he brings new life to his masters.
14   Like clouds and wind that bring no rain
          is he who boasts of gifts he never gives.
18   Like a club, a sword, or a sharp arrow
          is a false witness who denounces his friend.
19   Like a decaying tooth or a sprained ankle
          is a perfidious person relied on in the day of trouble.
26. 7 A proverb in the mouth of fools
          dangles helpless as the legs of the lame.
11   A fool who repeats his folly
          is like a dog returning to its vomit.

                                                                    (REB)

Proverbs Collected under Hezekiah

Ch. 25 is introduced by an editorial subheading: 'More proverbs of Solomon transcribed by the men of Hezekiah king of Judah'. The small collection, which seems to include Ch. 26 as well, makes much use of a kind of simile where the two lines are simply juxtaposed without even the 'like . . . is . . . ' of most English translations. This form allows much greater play to the imagination than the more elementary types of parallelism. The collector has also shown more interest in grouping his proverbs, by content as well as image.

The selection here consists of four pairs. The first and second pairs are both about speech, and they use images of *gold* and of weather respectively. *Snow*, or at any rate ice, might still come from Mt Lebanon in April. The third pair concerns *false friend*ship, the fourth is taken from a longer passage characterising the *fool*.

Numerical Sayings

30.18   Three things are too wonderful for me;
              four I do not understand:

19   the way of an eagle in the sky,
              the way of a snake on a rock,
        the way of a ship on the high seas,
              and the way of a man with a girl.

21   Under three things the earth trembles;
              under four it cannot bear up:

22   a slave when he becomes king,
              and a fool when glutted with food;

23   an unloved woman when she gets a husband,
              and a maid when she succeeds her mistress.

24   Four things on earth are small,
              yet they are exceedingly wise:

25   the ants are a people without strength,
              yet they provide their food in the summer;

26   the badgers are a people without power,
              yet they make their homes in the rocks;

27   the locusts have no king,
              yet all of them march in rank;

28   the lizard can be grasped in the hand,
              yet it is found in kings' palaces.   (NRSV)

Numerical Sayings

The second half of Ch. 30 constitutes another separate collection. It has two distinctive features. First, it is made up chiefly of numerical sayings of the so-called X / X + 1 type. This type was common across the ANE, partly no doubt because it fits parallelism so well. Secondly, many of the sayings in this collection draw upon the world of nature, particularly animals. The Wisdom schools were interested in nature chiefly for the light it threw on human beings. There are thus elements here both of the riddle and of the fable, and what links the two is a delight in wonders.

In the first saying (18-19) there is a progression from animal up to human and from the least to the most mysterious, viz. the attraction and love between the sexes.

The second saying is more of a miscellany. The statement that *the earth trembles* might be true literally of the first 'intolerable', but is comic exaggeration in the case of the other three: the unpleasant woman who unexpectedly *gets a husband*; the *fool* who eats (and drinks) too much; and the *maid* who supplants *her mistress* in her husband's affections, probably by bearing him a son (see the story of Hagar in Gen 16). This is the stuff of satire, not serious criticism. But it is skilfully put together: a and b are men, c and d are women, but a and d are parallel in meaning.

The third saying, confined to the number four, has more point. Here are four parables of the sage who may lack other advantages but succeeds through his wisdom. *Ants* plan for the future (as in 6.8). Rock-*badgers* are protected by *the rocks* in which they live. The third example is the weakest: the lack of a *king* is irrelevant and, though the 'military' organisation of *locusts* is remarkable (see Joel 2), it has no analogue among the wise. But the gecko or house-*lizard* makes the point excellently: harmless it may be, but it lives in the place of power.

Praise of a Capable Wife

10 A capable wife who can find?
She is far more precious than jewels.

11 The heart of her husband trusts in her,
and he will have no lack of gain.

12 She does him good, and not harm,
all the days of her life.

13 She seeks wool and flax,
and works with willing hands.

14 She is like the ships of the merchant,
she brings her food from far away.

15 She rises while it is still night
and provides food for her household
and tasks for her servant girls.

16 She considers a field and buys it;
with the fruit of her hands she plants a vineyard.

17 She girds herself with strength,
and makes her arms strong.

18 She perceives that her merchandise is profitable.
Her lamp does not go out at night.

19 She puts her hands to the distaff,
and her hands hold the spindle.

20 She opens her hand to the poor,
and reaches out her hands to the needy.

21 She is not afraid for her household when it snows,
for all her household are clothed in crimson.

Praise of a Capable Wife

The book of Proverbs is concluded by a delightful poem in praise of 'the perfect housewife' (NJB). We have no close parallel to it in ANE wisdom literature, though the subject has naturally attracted writers of all ages and cultures. The poem is an acrostic: each of its 21 couplets begins with the succeeding letter of the Hebrew alphabet. The exigencies of the form have meant that, though each verse stands happily on its own, the sequence of thought which runs through the whole is not direct. For example her husband is mentioned in vv.11, 23 and 28 (23 is particularly out of place), and weaving etc. in vv.13, 19 and 24. Yet the typical Hebrew technique of circular repetition has a cumulative effect, so the whole is more than the sum of its parts.

The portrait thus painted is recognisable and credible, if limited. Love is nowhere mentioned (contrast 5.19). The emphasis is on her management of her household and business. In a sense she is the female counterpart of that anonymous hero of the wisdom literature, the wise man. The portrait also provides a quiet echo of the dramatic self-praise by a personified Wisdom in earlier chapters.

The opening question (10a) implies that such perfection is rare. We can picture her muscular arms and her dress tucked up for housework (17). She can make and wear *fine clothing* too (22), but she does not forget her charitable duty to *the poor* (20). Most of the poem is straightforward but there are some difficulties. *Crimson* in v.21 makes poor sense, and most modern translations follow the LXX, e.g. 'double cloaks' (REB).

Praise of a Capable Wife (cont.)

31.22 She makes herself coverings;
    her clothing is fine linen and purple.

23 Her husband is known in the city gates,
    taking his seat among the elders of the land.

24 She makes linen garments and sells them;
    she supplies the merchant with sashes.

25 Strength and dignity are her clothing,
    and she laughs at the time to come.

26 She opens her mouth with wisdom,
    and the teaching of kindness is on her tongue.

27 She looks well to the ways of her household,
    and does not eat the bread of idleness.

28 Her children rise up and call her happy;
    her husband too, and he praises her:

29 'Many women have done excellently,
    but you surpass them all.'

30 Charm is deceitful, and beauty is vain,
    but a woman who fears the LORD is to be praised.

31 Give her a share in the fruit of her hands,
    and let her works praise her in the city gates.   (NRSV)

Praise of a Capable Wife (cont.)

Who fears the LORD in v.30 is surprising in a poem with no other pious reference. The verse was perhaps added to echo 1.7 and frame the whole book. *Give her a share in the fruit of her hands* (31) means 'give her credit for her achievements'. The final reference to *the city gates* picks up v.23 and puts her at least on a par with her husband.

Table of shorter extracts from Proverbs Chs 10-22

A.	1.	16.11	REB		21.	25.6-7	REB
	2.	20.14	REB	D.	22.	19.12	REB
	3.	21.14	NJB		23.	23.13	REB
	4.	15.16-17	AV		24.	11.22	REB
	5.	20.17	REB		25.	30.20	REB
	6.	14.20	AV		26.	26.13-15	REB
	7.	14.31	NRSV		27.	6.6-11	AV
	8.	19.17	REB		28.	15.13	AV
	9.	21.13	REB		29.	13.12	RSV
B.	10.	17.27-8	REB		30.	16.30	REB
	11.	18.13	AV		31.	24.3-4	NJB
	12.	18.17	REB	E.	32.	21.31	RSV
	13.	20.5	REB		33.	20.22	REB
	14.	15.1	NRSV		34.	25.21-2	AV
	15.	6.12-14	REB		35.	24.17-18	REB
	16.	26.20	NJB		36.	3.11-12	AV
	17.	26.23	REB		37.	21.27	REB
C.	18.	20.25	REB		38.	29.13	REB
	19.	27.1	NJB		39.	25.2	REB
	20.	16.18	NRSV				

ECCLESIASTES

Introduction

The anonymous author of this book is known to posterity by his nickname or title – in English traditionally 'The Preacher' (more recently 'The Teacher' NRSV or 'The Speaker' REB), in Hebrew *Qoheleth*, in Greek *Ecclesiastes* (E). English bibles have mostly retained the Greek title alongside the English. But modern translations, e.g. NJB, are increasingly preferring the Hebrew *Qoheleth*. This has the advantage of avoiding confusion with the apocryphal book Ecclesiasticus.

'The Preacher' was a sage, i.e. teacher of wisdom, living in Jerusalem c.300-250 BC. The book is a distillation of his lifetime's thinking – and remarkable thinking it is. Jerusalem in his time was under the control of the Greek rulers of Egypt, and educated Jews were being irresistibly drawn into the cosmopolitan culture of the hellenistic world. E's book is the first fruit of the meeting between these two cultures, Greek and Hebrew.

True to its message, the Book of Ecclesiastes lacks any clearly visible plan. An outer framework is provided by two famous passages. The 'autobiographical' narrative of a working life in the first two chapters is answered by a description of old age and death at the end. There may also be an inner frame in two poetic passages on the subject of time and chance (3.1-8 and 9.11-12). For the rest there is no logical progression, though the book is a clear unity, bound together by its tone and by certain other features. Structurally, E favours a sequence which at its fullest has the following ingredients: (i) his own experience or observation; (ii) his reflection upon it; (iii) his theoretical conclusion; (iv) his practical advice. (This sequence has been perceived by some as applying also to the book as a whole. Certainly E's experiences are mostly to be found in Chs 1-6, while 7-12 concentrate upon his conclusions.)

In the exposition of this sequence the author also uses a repeated set of key words, phrases and themes. Thus in (i) we find 'I have seen', 'under the sun'; in (ii) 'I applied my mind', 'I said to myself'; in (iii) 'all is vanity', 'wise men and fools die the same death'; in (iv) 'there is nothing better for a man than to enjoy himself'. His key-words include not only the traditional concepts of wisdom and folly but profit, work, business and pleasure – a surprisingly modern list. The whole book consists of variations on these and a few cognate themes; see e.g. the different orchestrations of the *carpe diem* or 'gather ye rosebuds' theme in 2.24; 3.13; 9.7-9.

Even those brief quotations show that E's comments on human life are untypical of the OT. His picture of God is equally unusual. God in E is tantamount to fate. He distributes his favours capriciously, certainly not according to merit (9.2), nor indeed according to any other discoverable plan (9.11). Anyone who thinks he has discovered God's plan is mistaken: if God has a plan at all, he has purposely concealed it from men, to keep them in their place (3.11; 8.17). This is certainly not the God of the OT. There is no covenant, no revelation, not even any word from God to man. Indeed if 'all is vanity' and there is no purpose in life, there is no place for that trust which is basic to all religion.

Inevitably one asks how such a book came to be included in the Bible. The quick answer is: only by the skin of its teeth. A rabbinic commentary says that 'the Sages intended to store away the book because they found in it ideas that leaned towards heresy'. They also stumbled at the contradictions within it. Its enemies quoted one verse, its friends countered with another. In the end, says Jerome, it was the last two verses of the book that tipped the scales in its favour.

But the contradictions remain, and it is now the 'orthodox' verses which pose the problem to any critical reader. Some of them, notably the crucial gloss 12.13, and perhaps also 11.9b, can safely be ascribed to pious editors who wished to preserve young minds from danger. But most are now seen as examples of a standard Wisdom technique, quoting one view before rejecting it in favour of another, a technique recognised by NJB in 2.13f. and by REB in 9.16.

Read with the rest of the OT, E seems negative, even cynical. But when his work is compared with its closer parallels in ANE and Greek literature, the picture is more complex. Take for example the theme of *carpe diem*, which is found all over the ancient world. The earliest example known to us comes from *Gilgamesh*, and is quoted on E 9.8-11 below.

Other close parallels are to be found in the Egyptian *Songs of the Harpist*, sung at funeral feasts from c. 1300 BC onwards. Neatest of them is this:

Rivers flow to the north,
winds blow to the south.
Man goes to his hour:
enjoy the day you have.

Greek versions of the theme commonly use the same tripartite formula as E: '(Let us) eat, drink and X', where X is sometimes 'make love', sometimes 'be active'. E uses only the latter, and what he has to say about activity is positive. Work should be a source of enjoyment for its own sake (2.10; 3.22), not pursued grimly or obsessively to amass a fortune or defeat a rival.

He is no less critical of the obsessional pursuit of things good in themselves, viz. wisdom (1.18) and virtue (7.16 – perhaps the most surprising sentence in the whole OT). The doctrine of 'moderation in all things' has various psychological roots. E advocates it to avoid disappointment after pitching one's hopes too high.

Perhaps indeed a disappointed idealism is the key to much of E's work, including the inconsistencies. Unless the 'auto-biography' in Chs1-2 is *entirely* fictional, he had in his time hoped too much in turn both from wisdom and from wealth. His disapproval of injustice (3.16) is based on the belief that things *ought to* be different, though God will not intervene to redress the balance. Even the little phrase which introduces his version of *carpe diem*, 'there is nothing better than . . .', suggests that he still believes there ought to be something better.

E was contemporary with the great hellenistic* schools of philosophy, including Sceptics, Cynics and hedonistic Cyrenaics. He himself had his moments of scepticism (3.21) and cynicism (3.18), and more than moments of hedonism. But he was not a thoroughgoing adherent of any of these schools any more than of orthodox Judaism. Curiously, the system of thought closest to E's is modern existentialism, which grew out of a similar context, viz. a technically efficient and highly organised international society in which the individual felt rootless and powerless.

What E lacks in philosophical rigour, social conscience and religious depth, he makes up for in literary charm. Much of his attractiveness lies in a reluctance to dogmatise. Instead of shouting at you, he plucks a little apologetically at your sleeve and, if you are willing to listen, shares his thoughts with you as one man of the world to another. Also, in the words of his pupil (12.10 NJB) he 'took pains to write in an attractive style'. His writing lacks the passion of Job, but has a cool, elegiac dignity exactly suited to its content. Much of his book is in rhythmic form, but the parallelism is rarely flat, as in Proverbs, and often – more often than NRSV and REB show – rises to poetic heights. Finally he could deploy all the resources of the Wisdom teacher – riddle and paradox, pathos and (his forte) irony – which he used to explore every human pretension, including (final irony) wisdom itself.

Vanity of Vanities

2 Vanity of vanities, says the Teacher,
    vanity of vanities! All is vanity.
3 What do people gain from all the toil
    at which they toil under the sun?
4 A generation goes, and a generation comes,
    but the earth remains forever.
5 The sun rises and the sun goes down,
    and hurries to the place where it rises.
6 The wind blows to the south,
    and goes around to the north;
round and round goes the wind,
    and on its circuits the wind returns.
7 All streams run to the sea,
    but the sea is not full;
to the place where the streams flow,
    there they continue to flow.
8 All things are wearisome;
    more than one can express;
the eye is not satisfied with seeing,
    or the ear filled with hearing.
9 What has been is what will be,
    and what has been done is what will be done;
    there is nothing new under the sun.
10 Is there a thing of which it is said, 'See, this is new'?
    It has already been, in the ages before us.
11 The people of long ago are not remembered,
    nor will there be any remembrance
    of people yet to come
    by those who come after them.   (NRSV)

Vanity of Vanities

E's book opens, as it closes (12.8), with a programmatic statement of his main theme. *Vanity* is used in its older sense of futility or pointlessness. The primary meaning of the Heb. *hebel*, which it translates, is 'mist' or 'breath'. Here again the image is as old as *Gilgamesh*:

> As for mankind, numbered are their days,
> whatever they achieve is but the wind.
> (*ANET* 79)

The 'of' in *vanity of vanities* means 'greatest of', as in 'Song of Songs'. *Under the sun*, which occurs 29 times in the book, is not found elsewhere in the OT. It defines E's field of enquiry as the everyday experience of everybody, irrespective of race and creed. Here it has the further overtone of 'the burden and the heat of the day'.

The poem of vv.4-11 is framed by mentions of the succession of the generations. The contrast between the transience of man and the permanence of the cosmos – elsewhere in the Bible a source of awe – here leads only to world-weariness. The ceaseless movements *of the sun* (E-W), *the wind* (N-S) and *the streams* all do nothing but mark time. Civilisation makes no real progress (9-10): if it seems to do so, that is only because human memory is defective (11). And if there is no progress, there is no meaning. In all this the author includes the reader in the club (see the *us* at the end of 10) – the first such occasion in the OT.

A Career: the Pursuit of Wisdom and Pleasure

1.12 I, the Preacher, have reigned over Israel in Jerusalem. • Wisely I have applied myself to investigation and exploration of everything that happens under heaven. What a wearisome task God has given humanity to keep us busy! • I have seen everything that is done under the sun: how futile it all is, mere chasing after the wind!

15   What is twisted cannot be straightened,
        what is not there cannot be counted.

• I thought to myself: I have acquired a greater stock of wisdom than anyone before me in Jerusalem. I myself have mastered every kind of wisdom and science. • I have applied myself to understanding philosophy and science, stupidity and folly, and I now realise that all this too is chasing after the wind.

        Much wisdom, much grief;
        the more knowledge, the more sorrow.

2. 1 • I thought to myself, 'Very well, I will try pleasure and see what enjoyment has to offer.' And this was futile too. • This laughter, I reflected, is a madness, this pleasure no use at all. • I decided to hand my body over to drinking wine, my mind still guiding me in wisdom; I resolved to embrace folly, to discover the best way for people to spend their days under the sun. • I worked on a grand scale:

5 built myself palaces, planted vineyards; • made myself gardens and orchards, planting every kind of fruit tree in them; • had pools made for watering the young trees of my plantations. • I bought slaves, male and female, had home-born slaves as well; herds and flocks I had too, more than anyone in Jerusalem before me. • I amassed silver and gold, the treasures of kings and provinces; acquired singers, men and women, and every human luxury, chest upon chest of it.

• So I grew great, greater than anyone in Jerusalem before me; nor did my

10 wisdom leave me. • I denied my eyes nothing that they desired, refused my heart no pleasure, for I found all my hard work a pleasure, such was the return for all my efforts. • I then reflected on all that my hands had achieved and all the effort I had put into its achieving. What futility it all was, what chasing after the wind! There is nothing to be gained under the sun.

• My reflections then turned to wisdom, stupidity and folly. • More is to be   ▶

A Career: the Pursuit of Wisdom and Pleasure

The passage 1.12-2.26 is the longest unified composition in the book. In it E makes skilful use of a literary convention found alike in ANE Wisdom and in Greek popular philosophy. All preachers know that their message will appeal more if presented as autobiography. E uses a form of it known as a 'royal fiction'. In Egypt a Pharaoh's name lent extra weight to advice, so the reference to Solomon (1.12), legendary embodiment of wealth and wisdom, lends piquancy to a Jewish sage's verdict that all achievement – however great – is vanity.

The 'autobiography' has four sections. In the first (1.12-18) the author pursues and achieves wisdom, not just the traditional lore of the ANE but (in NJB's translation) the new *philosophy* and *science* brought by the Greeks. But it all proves *futile*. Next (2.1-11) he tries the life of *pleasure*. The joint reference in 2.3 to *wisdom* and *folly* together implies a systematic pursuit of pleasure. *Orchards* in 2.5 translates the Persian word from which we derive 'paradise', and the long description of vv.4-8 is like the picture of paradise in the Koran. But all the *pleasure* and *all the effort* proved to be *futility*, NJB's translation of *hebel*. The verdict of v.11 is typically anticipated in v.1.

The third part (2.12-23) opens by

A Career: the Pursuit of Wisdom and Pleasure (cont.)

gained from wisdom than from folly, just as one gains more from light than from darkness; this, of course, I see:

14
>   The wise have their eyes open,
>   the fool walks in the dark.

No doubt! But I know, too, that one fate awaits them both. • 'Since the fool's fate', I thought to myself, 'will be my fate too, what is the point of my having been wise?' I realised that this too is futile. • For there is no lasting memory for the wise or the fool, and in the days to come both will be forgotten; the wise, no less than the fool, must die. • Life I have come to hate, for what is done under the sun disgusts me; all is futility and chasing after the wind. • All I have toiled for under the sun and now bequeath to my successor I have come to hate; • who knows whether he will be wise or a fool? Yet he will be master of all the work into which I have put my efforts and

20 wisdom under the sun. That is futile too. • I have come to despair of all the efforts I have expended under the sun. • For here is one who has laboured wisely, skilfully and successfully and must leave what is his own to someone who has not toiled for it at all. This is futile too, and grossly unjust; • for what does he gain for all the toil and strain that he has undergone under the sun • since his days are full of sorrow, his work is full of stress and even at night he has no peace of mind? This is futile too.

(NJB)

25 • There is nothing better for a man than that he should eat and drink, and find enjoyment in his toil. This also, I saw, is from the hand of God; • for apart from him who can eat or who can have enjoyment? • For to the man who pleases him God gives wisdom and knowledge and joy; but to the sinner he gives the work of gathering and heaping, only to give to one who pleases God. This also is vanity and a striving after wind.   (RSV)

A Career: the Pursuit of Wisdom and Pleasure (cont.)

comparing *wisdom* and *folly*. For a moment, when E quotes the orthodox view (14), we stumble. But then he undermines it: any superiority of wisdom is cancelled by the fact that *one fate awaits them both.* Even the consolation of a good name after death is rejected: *both will be forgotten.* In the face of death all human ambition is futile.

The final part (2.24-6) begins with the first statement of E's minimalist creed. Pleasure in moderation has, like wisdom, a relative if not an absolute worth. When he goes on to say that it *is from the hand of God*, he seems once again to be lapsing into orthodoxy. But though God is the source of all good things, his distribution of them is arbitrary. The man who in v.21 came into wealth without having *toiled for it at all* now turns out to be *one who pleases God.* Any (orthodox) attempt to

correlate virtue with its rewards is yet another *vanity*. There is a remarkable parallel to this last point in an Egyptian epitaph c. 300 BC: 'God it is who puts . . . into the heart of the man he hates, in order to give his goods to another man whom he loves'.

The composition of 1.12-2.26 is intricate. The content is held together not by a clear demarcation of its four sections but rather by a criss-crossing between them of its themes and phrases, which creates a typically Hebrew density of texture. The 'royal fiction' is gradually forgotten, never to reappear in the book. But beneath it emerges another pattern of greater significance, the sequence: experience-reflection-conclusion (see p.487). Early in the passage that pattern is repeated rapidly: it is used three times in the first part. Gradually however the cycle lengthens, and the emphasis is thrown increasingly upon the conclusions.

Human Knowledge and Freedom Illusory

3.1 For everything there is a season, and a time for every matter under heaven:

2 a time to be born, and a time to die;
   a time to plant, and a time to pluck up what is planted;

3 a time to kill, and a time to heal;
   a time to break down, and a time to build up;

4 a time to weep, and a time to laugh;
   a time to mourn, and a time to dance;

5 a time to throw away stones, and a time to gather stones together;
   a time to embrace, and a time to refrain from embracing;

6 a time to seek, and a time to lose;
   a time to keep, and a time to throw away;

7 a time to tear, and a time to sew;
   a time to keep silence, and a time to speak;

8 a time to love, and a time to hate;
   a time for war, and a time for peace.   ♦

Human Knowledge and Freedom Illusory

In Chs 1-2 E had much to say about the futility of men's actions as seen from the human angle. Now (3.1-15) he turns to look at them from God's point of view. The conclusion he comes to is the same.

The famous poem which opens Ch. 3 has more in it than meets the eye. Each line contains a pair of opposed actions, one desirable or 'white' (W), the other undesirable or 'black' (B). Each couplet or verse contains two such pairs, with the same meaning and in the same order, either BW or WB. (Each pair of verses however contains one each of BW and WB, in an intricate pattern.) We owe our understanding of some actions to the rabbis. Thus it was the custom to *tear* one's clothes at the start of a period of mourning and to *keep silence* during it, but to *sew* up the rents and to resume conversation at the end of it (7). *To throw away stones* (5) was a euphemism for sexual intercourse, to *gather* them for abstention, such as was also practised during mourning. Since vv. 4, 5 and 7 refer to mourning, while 2, 3 and 8 concern death, v.6 is probably about bereavement. Now the notion of 'black' and 'white' days suggests astrology and that suggestion is strengthened by the numbers involved: the poem has seven verses (the number of the planets) and 28 actions (the number of days in the lunar month).

But if the poem is astrological in origin, E has adapted it for his own purposes. He

Human Knowledge and Freedom Illusory (cont.)

10 • What gain have the workers from their toil? • I have seen the business that God has given to everyone to be busy with. • He has made everything suitable for its time; moreover he has put a sense of past and future into their minds, yet they cannot find out what God has done from the beginning to the end. • I know that there is nothing better for them than to be happy and enjoy themselves as long as they live; • moreover, it is God's gift that all should eat and drink and take pleasure in all their toil. • I know that whatever God does endures forever; nothing can be added to it, nor anything taken from it; God has done this, so that all should

15 stand in awe before him. • That which is, already has been; that which is to be, already is; and God seeks out what has gone by. (NRSV)

Human Knowledge and Freedom Illusory (cont.)

rounds it off typically with a rhetorical question (9) which draws out the meaning he is giving it. People's actions are effective only if they happen to have been done at a time which was predetermined without regard for them. For E it is of course not the stars who fixed the times but God. Yet God turns out to be not so different from fate after all. True, he provides all the context of life, including such happiness as is available to human beings (12-13). But they can neither comprehend his work (11) nor amend or affect it in any way (14).

At one stroke, the whole OT tradition of prophecy and prayer is dismissed. There is even a hint, sharpened up later (7.14 and 8.17 REB), that God purposely keeps human beings in ignorance and so *in awe*. Finally, E reverts in v.15 to the cyclical theory of history he expounded in Ch. 1.

The Failings of Society

16 • Moreover I saw under the sun that in the place of justice, wickedness was there, and in the place of righteousness, wickedness was there as well. • he has appointed a time for every matter, and for every work. • I said in my heart with regard to human beings that God is testing them to show that they are but animals. • For the fate of humans and the fate of animals is the same; as one dies, so dies the other. They all have the same breath, and humans have no advantage

20 over the animals; for all is vanity. • All go to one place; all are from the dust, and all turn to dust again. • Who knows whether the human spirit goes upward and the spirit of animals goes downward to the earth? • So I saw that there is nothing better than that all should enjoy their work, for that is their lot; who can bring them to see what will be after them? ▸

The Failings of Society

In the next section E turns his attention to society, following his usual pattern of observation-reflection-conclusion. First (3.16-22) he observes the kind of injustice which moved the prophets to passionate indignation. To him it poses only an intellectual problem. Human society, he concludes, is designed to encourage the law of the jungle (18). It thus punctures any human claims to a higher status and fate than the animals (19-21). Some Jews were evidently toying with the idea (found in Euripides) that *the human spirit goes upward*; E dismisses it here as unsupported by evidence (but see 12.7). When he turns to the related theme of the

The Failings of Society (cont.)

4.1 • Again I saw all the oppressions that are practiced under the sun. Look, the tears of the oppressed – with no one to comfort them! On the side of their oppressors there was power – with no one to comfort them. • And I thought the dead, who have already died, more fortunate than the living, who are still alive; • but better than both is the one who has not yet been, and has not seen the evil deeds that are done under the sun.   (NRSV)

• I considered all toil and all achievement and saw that it springs from rivalry between one person and another. This too is futility and a chasing of the wind.

5,6 • The fool folds his arms and wastes away. • Better one hand full, along with peace of mind, than two full, along with toil; that is a chasing of the wind.

• Here again I saw futility under the sun: • someone without a friend, without son or brother, toiling endlessly yet never satisfied with his wealth – 'For whom', he asks, 'am I toiling and denying myself the good things of life?' This too is futile, a worthless task. • Two are better than one, for their partnership yields this

10 advantage: • if one falls, the other can help his companion up again; but woe betide the solitary person who when down has no partner to help him up. • And if two lie side by side they keep each other warm; but how can one keep warm by himself? • If anyone is alone, an assailant may overpower him, but two can resist; and a cord of three strands is not quickly snapped.   (REB)

The Failings of Society (cont.)

oppression of the weak by the strong, he shows a rare emotion: the repetition of *no one to comfort them* has been found especially poignant. But his conclusion (4.2f.) is typically stark. For its utter pessimism the nearest parallel is found in a chorus of Sophocles: 'Not to be born is best of all; second best is to go as quickly as possible to the place from which one has come.'

E then considers attitudes to hard work. All too often it is inspired solely by envy. Admittedly total idleness is destructive in a different way (5). But E recommends a more relaxed middle position (6). From this he moves to praise co-operation – on prudential rather than moral grounds. Verse 12 is another which has a close parallel in *Gilgamesh*: 'Two men will not die . . . a towrope of three strands cannot be cut.' For once there is no cynical comment to end the passage.

The Golden Mean

13 Consider God's handiwork; who can straighten what he has made crooked? •When things go well, be glad; but when they go ill, consider this: God has set the one alongside the other in such a way that no one can find out what is to happen 15 afterwards. • In my futile existence I have seen it all, from the righteous perishing in their righteousness to the wicked growing old in wickedness. • Do not be over-righteous and do not be over-wise. Why should you destroy yourself? • Do not be over-wicked and do not be a fool. Why die before your time? • It is good to hold on to the one thing and not lose hold of the other; for someone who fears God will succeed both ways.   (REB)

The Golden Mean

Once again E stresses the unpredictability of events, this time as an argument for taking life as it comes (13-14). He repudiates the orthodox view that *righteousness* is rewarded with long life (15) and then goes much further in counselling moderation in the pursuit both of righteousness and of wisdom, so as not to *destroy your-self* by perfectionism. The doctrine of the golden mean is found in folk wisdom everywhere. Here however it strikes at the heart of Hebrew orthodoxy as expressed both in the Torah and in Wisdom teaching. Verse 18 is obscure, but E seems to be recommending a compromise position as most pleasing to God.

Only Death is Certain

16 I applied my mind to acquire wisdom and to observe the tasks undertaken on earth, when mortal eyes are never closed in sleep day or night; • and always I perceived that God has so ordered it that no human being should be able to discover what is happening here under the sun. However hard he may try, he will not find out; the wise may think they know, but they cannot find the truth of it.

1   • To all this I applied my mind, and I understood – that the righteous and the wise and whatever they do are under God's control; but whether they will earn love or hatred they have no way of knowing. Everything that confronts them, everything is futile, • since one and the same fate comes to all, just and unjust alike, good and bad, ritually clean and unclean, to the one who offers sacrifice and to the one who does not. The good and the sinner fare alike, he who can take an oath and he who dares not. • This is what is wrong in all that is done here under the sun: that one and the same fate befalls everyone. The minds of mortals are full of evil; there is madness in their minds throughout their lives, and afterwards they go down to join the dead.   (REB)

Only Death is Certain

In the next section E restates his main themes with greater force and feeling. All events are unpredictable, except death which awaits everyone. Therefore enjoy life while you may: everything else is governed by chance.

REB goes further than other translations of 8.17 in making God positively seek to keep men in ignorance. They do not even know which of their doings will win his *love* and which his *hatred* (9.1). Their only certainty is death the leveller. The abruptness of death is well got by the Hebrew of 9.3 which breaks off with two words 'and-then to-the-dead!'.

The contrast between the *dead* and

Only Death is Certain (cont.)

9.5 • But whoever is joined with all the living has hope, for a living dog is better than a dead lion. • The living know that they will die, but the dead know nothing; they have no more reward, and even the memory of them is lost. • Their love and their hate and their envy have already perished; never again will they have any share in all that happens under the sun.

• Go, eat your bread with enjoyment, and drink your wine with a merry heart; for God has long ago approved what you do. • Let your garments always be white; do not let oil be lacking on your head. • Enjoy life with the wife whom you love, all the days of your vain life that are given you under the sun, because that

10 is your portion in life and in your toil at which you toil under the sun. • Whatever your hand finds to do, do with your might; for there is no work or thought or knowledge or wisdom in Sheol, to which you are going.

• Again I saw that under the sun the race is not to the swift, nor the battle to the strong, nor bread to the wise, nor riches to the intelligent, nor favor to the skillful; but time and chance happen to them all. • For no one can anticipate the time of disaster. Like fish taken in a cruel net, and like birds caught in a snare, so mortals are snared at a time of calamity, when it suddenly falls upon them.   (NRSV)

Only Death is Certain (cont.)

the *living* is summarised in a typical Eastern proverb: the king compared with the scavenger (4). The dead have not even the *reward* of posthumous *memory*. In 6 the tone becomes more elevated. It starts with a rhyming triple knell for the three nouns: *gam ahavātām gam sinātām gam qinātām*. This verse is the strongest expression in the OT of the finality of death.

But from it there follows the most passionate (and poetical) of E's many exhortations to enjoy life while it lasts. This theme and even this treatment of it were common both in ANE and Greek literature. Closest to E is this passage from the Old Babylonian version of *Gilgamesh,* whose author shares the ability to paint a sombre theme in bright colours.

> When the gods created mankind,
> death they dispensed to mankind,
> life they kept for themselves.
> But you, Gilgamesh, let your belly be full,
> enjoy yourself always by day and by night!
> Make merry each day,
> dance and play day and night!
> Let your clothes be clean,
> let your head be washed!
> Gaze on the child who holds your hand,

> let your wife enjoy your repeated embrace!
> For such is the destiny [of mortal men].
>   (George 123)

(For parallels outside the OT see p.488).

Elsewhere in the OT the *carpe diem* theme it is cited only with disapproval, but E almost succeeds here by sleight of mind in reconciling it with OT thought. He argues that 'he who has enjoyed the delights of life has thereby (long ago) won God's favour' (Gordis). This neatly inverts the orthodox position that those who win God's favour will (subsequently) be rewarded. *White garments* and *oil* for the *head* are signs of more than everyday festivity. NRSV's *the wife* narrows the Hebrew, which only says 'a woman' (so REB). Human *love* is commended only this once by E, and even here the woman is little more than an extension of the man, while the child, such a charming feature of *Gilgamesh*, is missing altogether. The words *all the days of your vain life* are repeated in the MT at the end of the verse (cp. 4.4 for the trick) lest the note of joy should seem unconfined. Similarly the uncharacteristic enthusiasm of *with* all

Only Death is Certain (cont.)

15 • This too is an example of wisdom as I have observed it here under the sun, and I find it of great significance. • There was once a small town with few inhabitants, which a great king came to attack; he surrounded it and constructed huge siege-works against it. • There was in it a poor wise man, and he saved the town by his wisdom. But no one remembered that poor man. • I thought, 'Surely wisdom is better than strength'; but a poor man's wisdom is despised, and his words go unheeded.   (REB)

Only Death is Certain (cont.)

your might (10) is tempered by another list of the activities unavailable in *Sheol*.

The famous verse 11 takes the various careers open to ambitious young men in the hellenistic world. It is surprising to find sport mentioned first until one remembers the enthusiasm of some Jews a little later for the establishment of a gymnasium in Jerusalem (2 Macc 4.12). Other careers mentioned are soldiering, philosophy, business and politics – in all cases E, like any teacher, laments and excuses the failure of his most able pupils to get to the top of their professions. That failure is ascribed to *time and chance*. The reference to time takes us back to the poem of 3.2-8 and sharpens it up. Time can be propitious, but it can also be *evil*, lying in wait like a *snare*. Either way human freedom is minimal.

Finally a short parable on the limitations of *wisdom*. As often, E quotes the orthodox view (16a), but then counters it with his own. This is that wisdom without wealth is ineffective – the typical predicament of the intellectual in the vast hellenistic world.

Prudent Planning

1 Send your grain across the seas, and in time you will get a return. • Divide your merchandise among seven or perhaps eight ventures, since you do not know what disasters are in store for the world. • He who keeps watching the wind will

5 never sow, and he who keeps his eye on the clouds will never reap. • As you do not know how a pregnant woman comes to have a body and a living spirit in her womb, so you do not know the work of God, the maker of all things. • In the morning sow your seed in good time, and do not let your hands slack off until evening, for you do not know whether this or that sowing will be successful, or whether both alike will do well.   (REB)

Prudent Planning

After a chapter [10] of fairly traditional Wisdom precepts, E offers some advice of his own on the conduct of business. The unifying image is that of the seed as a symbol of the future, whether the sowing and reaping of it by the farmer (4, 6) or the handling of it by the merchant (1, 2) or the growth of it in the womb of the *pregnant woman* (5). These processes cannot be understood by human beings, still less predicted (2, 6). But that is no reason for timidity and procrastination – rather for spreading one's risks by cautious diversification. The positive tone of this advice amplifies that of 9.10, and this time there is no pessimistic rider. AV's translation of v.1, 'Cast your bread upon the waters' etc., follows an old interpretation that E is recommending charitable giving; but that fits the context poorly.

Youth, Old Age and Death

11.7   The light of day is sweet, and pleasant to the eye is the sight of the sun. • However many years a person may live, he should rejoice in all of them. But let him remember the days of darkness, for they will be many. Everything that is to come will be futility.

• Delight in your youth, young man, make the most of your early days; let your heart and your eyes show you the way; but remember that for all these

10   things God will call you to account. • Banish vexation from your mind, and shake off the troubles of the body, for youth and the prime of life are mere futility. (REB)

Youth, Old Age and Death

E ends his book with a virtuoso description of old age and death, which answers to his 'autobiographical' narrative of an active career in the first two chapters. He opens (11.7-8) with a reprise of his favourite contrast between life and death (*the days of darkness*) but quickly modulates to a related contrast between youth and old age, the apogee and the nadir of life. As with life, so with *youth*, his advice is to *make the most of* it (9) because it is so fleeting (10). In giving this advice he switches from the third person of v.8 to the second person to address his pupil. One senses a note of regret here for his own missed opportunities. Certainly the aptest comment on the last clause of v.9 is that of a rabbi of the C3rd AD: 'Every man must render an account before God of all the good things he beheld in life and did not enjoy'. If that is the right interpretation, the *but* of REB should be translated 'and', as it equally well can be.

But many scholars bracket that clause like 12.14 (see below).

The first seven verses of Ch. 12 consist of one remarkable long sentence, which has the same *shape* as Jer 13.16 (NRSV):

> Give glory to the LORD your God,
> before he brings darkness,
> before your feet stumble
> on the mountains at twilight . . .

But E's *Remember your creator* is only a nod to God. As the parallel with 11.8 shows, it means no more than 'make the most of' *your youth*. To that brief injunction is appended with apparent casualness a subordinate clause, introduced by *before*, about old age. That clause then rumbles on and on like thunder. The 'before' is picked up in two later verses (2 and 6), between which is inserted a long *when* clause. And the longer the sentence goes on, the more youth is forgotten and old age and death dominate.

Youth, Old Age and Death (cont.)

1 • Remember your creator in the days of your youth, before the days of trouble come, and the years draw near when you will say, 'I have no pleasure in them'; • before the sun and the light and the moon and the stars are darkened and the clouds return with the rain; • in the day when the guards of the house tremble, and the strong men are bent, and the women who grind cease working because they are few, and those who look through the windows see dimly; • when the doors on the street are shut, and the sound of the grinding is low, and

5 one rises up at the sound of a bird, and all the daughters of song are brought low; • when one is afraid of heights, and terrors are in the road; the almond tree blossoms, the grasshopper drags itself along and desire fails; because all must go to their eternal home, and the mourners will go about the streets; • before the silver cord is snapped, and the golden bowl is broken, and the pitcher is broken at the fountain, and the wheel broken at the cistern, • and the dust returns to the earth as it was, and the breath returns to God who gave it.

• Vanity of vanities, says the Teacher; all is vanity.   (NRSV)

Youth, Old Age and Death (cont.)

The description of them is one of the most famous things in the whole OT. It is typically Hebrew, exuberant to the point of incoherence. Not only do the images tumble over each other. More than that: metaphor is apparently mixed on the one hand with factual reporting and on the other with riddling symbolism. The mixture is alien to western taste, but there is a surprising parallel to it in a Sumerian poem about old age:

My grain-roasting fails,
My youthful vigour and strength have left
    my loins,
My black mountain has produced white
    gypsum,
My mongoose, which used to eat strong-
    smelling things, does not stretch its neck
    towards beer and butter. (Alster)

In any case, the exuberance of E carries it off. What could have been a grey catalogue takes on the colours of a kaleidoscope.

The first set of images (2) is straightforward, answering those of 11.7. Next (3) the human body is presented in the allegory of a great man's house looked after by four groups of servants. Two groups are male, representing arms and legs, two are female, representing teeth and eyes. In vv. 4 and 5 much is uncertain, but *the doors on the street* and *the sound of the grinding* perhaps stand for ears and voice. Then come factual references to the light sleep of the old (*one rises up . . .*) and to their fear of heights and of travel. The *almond blossom* is white hair cp. the 'white gypsum' of the Sumerian poem. *Desire* of course is sexual, more delicate than the Sumerian 'mongoose'. Eventually death itself supervenes. The (literal) funeral procession (5) is followed by a pair of images (6). First is an ornamental lamp, suspended from the ceiling by its *silver cord* (i.e. chain), with its *golden bowl* containing the oil. Second are two ways of getting water. Water, like light, is a symbol of life, but the *cistern* or pit is also a common synonym for Sheol, and leads easily to mention of *the earth* in 7.

The long sentence ends, as it began (12.1a), with a reference to the creative activity of God. The two references reinforce each other and round off the poem neatly. But 12.7b is hard to reconcile with the scepticism of 3.21, and some regard both references as part of the pious editing.

Two Epilogues

12.10 Besides being wise, the Preacher also taught the people knowledge, weighing and studying and arranging proverbs with great care. • The Preacher sought to find pleasing words, and uprightly he wrote words of truth. • The sayings of the wise are like goads, and like nails firmly fixed are the collected sayings which are given by one Shepherd. • My son, beware of anything beyond these. Of making many books there is no end, and much study is a weariness of the flesh.

• The end of the matter; all has been heard. Fear God, and keep his commandments; for this is the whole duty of man. • For God will bring every deed into judgement, with every secret thing, whether good or evil. (RSV)

Two Epilogues

E's own book ends in 12.8 with his signature tune, echoing 1.2. There follow two epilogues by other hands. In the first (9-12) a pupil gives a valuable description of his master's object and method. Here, for the first time in the OT, literature is explicitly self-conscious. The *Shepherd* of v.11 is presumably *the Preacher* him-self. Verse 12 shows that his pupil had learned the style.

The second epilogue (13-14) is from a different stable. What purports to be a summary of the book is in fact a travesty. These two verses can be confidently ascribed to a pious editor, on whom see p.487f.

THE SONG OF SONGS

Introduction

The Song of Songs, i.e. the Song *par excellence,* is a collection of dramatised poems which express the feelings and celebrate the passion of two young lovers in certain phases of their love. All the poems are suffused by a playful romantic atmosphere which is unique in the OT. They are also linked by many repetitions, not only of motifs and phrases but of whole verses. For example 'I charge you, daughters of Jerusalem, that you do not disturb love' is found three times; and so, with variations, is 'I am my beloved's and he is mine'. This pervasive homogeneity makes it unusually difficult to be sure where one poem ends and the next begins, or even where one speaker takes over from another. But there is a corresponding gain: the poems in the Song have been left relatively untouched, without the heavy editing which often obscures the oracles of the prophets.

By the same token, no sequence is detectable in the arrangement of the poems: no progression of thought or action. True, the book is framed by a pair of poems which compare the beloved to a vineyard (1.5-6 and 8.11-12), and in places two or three shorter units have apparently been fitted together to make a longer one. But if the book has an overall structure it has not yet been discovered. In all these respects the Song is in the same case as the book which immediately precedes it in English Bibles, Ecclesiastes – though the Preacher would have smiled at the illusions of the lovers.

The Song occupies a unique place in the history of literature. On the one hand its influence on European love poetry has been enormous. On the other hand it was itself heavily influenced by Egyptian love poetry (ELP). It so happens that we possess about as much of the latter as there is of the Song. Most of the ELP texts were written c.1300 BC, and the points of resemblance between the two collections

are so many that it would be tedious to list them. Simpler is to pick out the salient features of the Song, all of which unless otherwise stated are found also in the ELP. But it should also be said here that 'the Song far surpasses them, in the sensuousness of its language, the richness of its imagery and the ardour of the love it depicts' (Fox).

Like all Hebrew poetry the Song consists entirely of speech, without any narrative *mise-en-scène.* Most of it is spoken by one or other of the lovers. There is also what in Greek drama would be a chorus, addressed as 'daughters of Jerusalem', who listen and occasionally speak (ELP has various other interlocutors in the place of the chorus). Unfortunately the MT contains no attribution to speakers, but the best mss of the LXX come to our partial rescue. They mark the changes of speaker, and ascribe sections to 'bridegroom', 'bride' and to a variety of companions of one or the other. Those ascriptions are followed by REB, except that it does not distinguish between the different groups of 'companions'.

But in fact the poems themselves cannot have been composed for recital at a wedding. Nowhere do they mention that key topic of wedding songs, the hope of children. Only one poem in the Song even refers to a wedding (3.6-11). In the next poem the lover calls his girl 'my bride' among other terms of endearment. But two others have her living with her mother (3.4; 8.2), so it is not surprising that there are many partings and other obstacles to their passion (3.1+; 5.2+).

Nevertheless whatever their external circumstances, subjectively their love is in two respects like married love. First, it is erotic in the best and broadest sense. They delight in each other's bodies, and there is no doubt that they are already lovers. But the language of the poems, though frank, is delicate. Apart from breasts, sexual anatomy is not explicit but symbolic or euphemistic. And there is no sniggering: where there is a *double entendre,* as in all love poetry (e.g. 5.4), it is left as a hint between adults. Nor is there any voyeurism: the camera stops at the bedroom door. As with death in Greek tragedy, the consummation takes place off stage.

Secondly, the love is reciprocal, and evenly balanced between the pair. It is also faithful, exclusive and assumed to be lifelong (8.6). The status which in ancient society fitted most of these poems is that of a betrothed couple, who might be termed 'non-live-in lovers'. All in all, the Song idealises love. Unlike the ELP, it makes no serious mention of infidelity – at most there are lovers' teases (1.7f.; 3.1f.) – nor does drunkenness play a part in the love-making. If the Hebrew poet wrote of such matters, they were not included in the canonical text (see below).

But although the lovers display a certain charming *naiveté,* there is nothing naive about the Song itself. The discovery of the ELP has confirmed that the poems in the Song too are literary compositions through and through. This is immediately evident in some of the forms that it uses, especially the 'masques'. The book contains two masques. In one the lovers play the part of king and queen, in the other of shepherds. The former, which we met as the 'royal fiction' in Eccl Chs 1-2, is found in 3.6+, the latter in 1.7+. Both derive from ancient Egypt, but their subsequent histories diverge. The royal masque lives on in Arabian and Orthodox Christian wedding rites. The shepherd masque entered the European tradition of love poetry through hellenistic Alexandria (Theocritus and Vergil) and died only recently. Each makes a deep appeal to lovers. The former expresses their sense of exaltation, the latter of escape. But only sophisticated city-dwellers play at being shepherds.

The Song contains one other form of urban love poetry which started life in Egypt and became very popular in Greece and Rome. That is the 'door-song', which was typically a complaint spoken by a lover shut out at his beloved's door. The same setting is used for two subtle and elusive poems (2.8+ and 5.2+) in the Song; but there is no complaining here, because the love is mutual.

There remains the most remarkable of all the forms used in the Song, commonly known by the name of its Arabic descendant, the *wasf.* A *wasf* is a song in praise of the physical charms of the beloved. It typically begins and ends in general terms, but the core of it consists of a series of similitudes praising separate features in turn, usually from the head downwards. There are three *wasf*s in the Song: 4.1+; 5.10+; 7.1+. In the second it is she who praises him, in the other two he praises her.

The similes in the *wasf*s (and indeed, though less strikingly, outside them) are remarkably mixed. Some do not go beyond a conventional and vague romanticism. Others are, at least to us, so unconventional as to present a critical puzzle, seeming to range from the brilliant to the grotesque. These are dealt with as they occur in the commentary, but three general remarks may be made here. First, although most of them are visual, they are not realistic: we learn not what the beloved looked like but what kinds of looks were admired. Second, in any one *wasf* the similes are apt to be randomly mixed, both in the senses to which they appeal – usually sight, but often smell – and in the source of the comparison: animals, flowers, places, buildings and works of art, all jumbled together. These two points are illustrated by a *wasf* from the ELP:

> Long of neck, white of breast,
> her hair true lapis lazuli.
> Her arms surpass gold,
> her fingers are like lotuses.

Third, the basic simile is often embellished by further clauses which, like similes in Homer, take on a life of their own e.g. 4.14; 5.12; 7.7+. And perhaps some sidelight is thrown on the *wasf* from a conversation in modern Egypt. 'I asked Omar if his betrothed was beautiful. He answered with decorous vagueness that she was "a moon", but declined mentioning her hair, eyes, etc. It is a liberty to describe a woman minutely' (Lucie Duff-Gordon).

But over and above many of these similes is one great architectonic image, that of love's garden. The city and the wild countryside each play their part in the Song, but the central role is occupied by what lies between them, the cultivated land. This is not just the context but the symbol of their love. The beloved *is* the vineyard (1.6; 8.12), the orchard (4.13) and above all the garden.

The fullest treatment of 'love's garden' is in 4.12-5.1, where see commentary for details. A close parallel to it is provided by this poem from Egypt (Fox, p. 26):

I am your favourite sister,
I am yours like the field
planted with flowers
and with all sorts of fragrant plants.
Pleasant is the canal within it,
which your own hand scooped out . . .
To hear your voice is pomegranate wine to me;
I draw life from hearing it.
Could I see you with every glance,
it would be better for me
than to eat or to drink.

In each poem the detail has the same function. It is not descriptive, still less allegorical, but purely evocative. The beauty of nature supports and echoes the beauty which the lovers see in each other. To a Hebrew reader love's garden would also recall the Garden of Eden, another symbol of innocent love. But in this love's garden there is no serpent.

Such are the main components of the Song. Taken as a whole, it seems that, although it has some features of drama, it is actually closer to ballet. Its emotions and incidents are passionate in feeling but formally expressed in a limited number of set steps and stylised scenes. The 'speeches' of the lovers are not so much dialogues (1.7f. and 4.16f. are the nearest

to dialogue) as parallel displays, sometimes solo, sometimes *à deux*, sometimes in front of the *corps de ballet*.

Be that as it may, there is no doubt of its subject – the love of a man and a woman. That love is portrayed without mention of God or reference to the religion of Israel. Even the place-names have been privatised. The question was therefore inevitably raised, as with Ecclesiastes, whether it should be accepted into the canon of the Hebrew Bible. In its favour was that it too was ascribed to Solomon. But the Mishnah records a sharp division of opinion among the rabbis. The day was carried by the advocacy of the great Rabbi Aqiba (c.100 AD). 'All the Writings are holy,' he said, 'but the Song of Songs is the Holy of Holies.'

Aqiba however was not defending it as a straight love-song. On the contrary, 'he who trills his voice in chanting the Song of Songs in the banquet-house and treats it as a secular song has no part in the life to come.' His own interpretation was that the lover represents God and the beloved Israel. That kind of interpretation prevailed for centuries among both Jews and Christians. Nowadays the Song is almost universally recognised as concerned solely with human love. Yet its portrayal of that love is such that a modern reader can share Aqiba's contempt for any vulgarisation of it.

Being the nearest thing to lyric poetry in the OT, the Song is also the hardest book to render into English prose. At every turn the translator is betrayed by the overtones of English words. Take for instance the various translations of 1.13:

'A bundle of myrrh is my wellbeloved unto me; he shall lie all night betwixt my breasts' (AV)
'My beloved is to me a bag of myrrh, that lies between my breasts' (NRSV)
'My love is a sachet of myrrh lying between my breasts' (NJB)

AV is the only one to keep the word-order in the first line, and the only one to make explicit the 'all night' implied by the Hebrew. NJB, like REB, rightly preserves the ambiguous reference in 'lying'. But the associations of 'sachet' are scarcely happier than those of 'bag'. Similar difficulties arise with the terms used to describe the lovers in the headings. NRSV and REB use 'bride' and 'bridegroom' throughout, which in the view of this commentary is wrong. NJB's 'lover' (m.) and 'beloved' (f.) are better, provided they are not taken to imply that the initiative is always his.

For the last and, from one point of view, the most important feature of the Song is the leading role of 'the beloved'. There is no scene from which she is absent; she speaks more lines than he does and reveals her feelings more fully. He by contrast is seen almost entirely through her eyes. In a word, 'the Song is *her* song' (Fox). And that is unique in the OT: hers is the only female voice in it to speak directly, not through a narrator. Is the author a woman, then? 'Yes, surely, at least in part' (Murphy).

Lovers' Fancies

The Song of Songs, which is Solomon's.

1.5 | **She:** | I am black and beautiful,
| | | O daughters of Jerusalem,
| | | like the tents of Kedar,
| | | like the curtains of Solomon.

6 | | Do not gaze at me because I am dark,
| | | because the sun has gazed on me.
| | | My mother's sons were angry with me;
| | | they made me keeper of the vineyards,
| | | but my own vineyard I have not kept!

7 | **She:** | Tell me, you whom my soul loves,
| | | where you pasture your flock,
| | | where you make it lie down at noon;
| | | for why should I be like one who is veiled
| | | beside the flocks of your companions?

8 | **He:** | If you do not know, O fairest among women,
| | | follow the tracks of the flock,
| | | and pasture your kids
| | | beside the shepherds' tents.

Lovers' Fancies

The title verse, added later, claims *Solomon* for author, just as the book of Psalms claimed David. The book opens with a set of poems in playful dialogue. In them the lovers adopt various roles, rustic in the first two, royal in the next three.

In 1.5-6 she presents herself as a sunburnt country girl whom the 'fair' *daughters of Jerusalem* would look down on. *Kedar* is a nomadic tribe whose *tents* were woven from black goat-hair. Her tan is due to a family dispute: in looking after the family's *vineyards* she has failed to protect her *own* (i.e. her body) from the sun.

In vv.7-8 he is tending his sheep, she her goats. She wants to know where she can find him at siesta time. If he will not tell her, i.e. invite her, she may have to seek other company. It seems that he calls her bluff. *If* she really does *not know*, i.e. if she is waiting for him to make the first move, she is welcome to the others!

Lovers' Fancies (cont.)

9	He:	I compare you, my love,
		to a mare among Pharaoh's chariots.
10		Your cheeks are comely with ornaments,
		your neck with strings of jewels.
11		We will make you ornaments of gold,
		studded with silver.
12	She:	While the king was on his couch,
		my nard gave forth its fragrance.
13		My beloved is to me a bag of myrrh
		that lies between my breasts.
14		My beloved is to me a cluster of henna blossoms
		in the vineyards of En-gedi.
15	He:	Ah, you are beautiful, my love;
		ah, you are beautiful; your eyes are doves.
16	She:	Ah, you are beautiful, my beloved,
		truly lovely.
17		Our couch is green;
		the beams of our house are cedar,
		our rafters are pine.
2, 1	She:	I am a rose of Sharon,
		a lily of the valleys.
2	He:	As a lily among brambles,
		so is my love among maidens.
3	She:	As an apple tree among the trees of the wood,
		so is my beloved among young men.
		With great delight I sat in his shadow,
		and his fruit was sweet to my taste.

(NRSV)

Lovers' Fancies (cont.)

The next three poems use the setting of the 'royal masque'. First (9-11), he pays her a high compliment. In the ancient world horses were reserved for the royal pursuits of war and hunting. This particular *mare* is not only beautiful but richly caparisoned, and soon to be more so. Her reply (12-14) switches from the sense of sight to that of smell. When the royal couple lie together, all the perfumes of the Orient yield their *fragrance*. For the translation of v.13 see above. *Henna* is a sweet-smelling flower growing in fertile *Engedi* (see Map 2 B3). In the third poem (15-17) he praises her and looks at her *eyes*: *doves* belong to love-goddesses, and so come to be messengers of love. She then praises him and looks at their *couch*. Finally they join in a make-believe. The trees above them are their *house* – no, not a mere house but a palace, with a *cedar* roof.

In the last poem (2.1-3) the compliments become competitive, as often in ancient love-poetry. Each speaker, whether one of the lovers or a group of supporters, picks up and caps the previous remark. Here she starts coquettishly, as in 1.5: the implication is that she is a commonplace flower. He corrects her at the level of the hedgerow (2), whereupon she moves to the higher level of the forest and 'wins' by having the last word and a double ration of lines.

A Confidence

2.4 **She:** He has taken me to his cellar,
and his banner over me is love.
Feed me with raisin cakes,

5 restore me with apples,
for I am sick with love. (NJB)

6 O that his left hand were under my head,
and that his right hand embraced me!

7 I adjure you, O daughters of Jerusalem,
by the gazelles or the wild does:
do not stir up or awaken love
until it is ready! (NRSV)

A Confidence

Apples, emblems of love, link this poem to the previous one. The interpretation is uncertain, but she seems to be using the chorus as a device for revealing her own emotions. He has invited her to a 'house of wine' (so the Hebrew behind NJB's *cellar*), promising love. She is weak with longing (lovesickness is a topos* in the ELP also) and unable to take anything but the food of love. In anticipation she charges the chorus not to interrupt their love prematurely.

A Tryst in Springtime

2.8 **She:** The voice of my beloved!
Look, he comes,
leaping upon the mountains,
bounding over the hills.

9 My beloved is like a gazelle
or a young stag.
Look, there he stands
behind our wall,
gazing in at the windows,
looking through the lattice.

10 My beloved speaks and says to me:
'Arise, my love, my fair one,
and come away;

11 for now the winter is past,
the rain is over and gone.' ♦

A Tryst in Springtime

She is here a city girl, living with her parents but expecting a clandestine visit from him. The breathless excitement with which each of them awaits their tryst is expressed by her in words (8ab), by him in movement (8c-9b). He then stands outside her *lattice window* to speak to her. His speech is a variation of the door-song, a standard form of ancient love-poetry (see p.502). Here he invites her to escape with him into the country. The double invitation (10, 13) frames a lyrical description of spring which is closer to nature poetry than anything else in the OT, or indeed from Egypt. Yet nature is not here being described for its own sake. Each separate item in 12-13 was an accepted emblem of love, spring has always been the lovers' season, and the countryside itself,

A Tryst in Springtime (cont.)

12 **She:**   The flowers appear on the earth;
        the time of singing has come,
    and the voice of the turtledove
        is heard in our land.

13   The fig tree puts forth its figs,
        and the vines are in blossom;
        they give forth fragrance.
    Arise, my love, my fair one,
        and come away.

(NRSV)

A Tryst in Springtime (cont.)

especially to urban sophisticates, is a symbol of love's freedom. Verse 12 contains an instance of a rare subtlety in Hebrew poetry. The word translated 'singing' also means 'pruning', and so the middle line of the three can do double duty, creating a pair both with the first and with the third. This subtlety is known as 'Janus parallelism'. AV's 'turtle' in v.12 actually meant *turtledove* but provided Lewis Carroll with innocent merriment.

The whole speech of the lover, in stricter parallelism than is usual in the Song, is as near perfection as can be. Yet *she* speaks it for him – why? Is it perhaps her fantasy, like the next poem?

Lost and Found

3. 1 **She:**   Night after night on my bed
        I have sought my true love;
        I have sought him, but I have not found him.

2   I said, 'I will rise and go the rounds of the city
        through streets and squares,
    seeking my true love.'
        I sought him, but could not find him.

3   The watchmen came upon me,
        as they made their rounds of the city.
        'Have you seen my true love?' I asked them.

4   Scarcely had I left them behind
        when I met my true love.
    I held him and would not let him go
        till I had brought him to my mother's house,
        to the room of her who conceived me.

(REB)

5   I adjure you, O daughters of Jerusalem,
        by the gazelles or the wild does:
    do not stir up or awaken love
        until it is ready!

(NRSV)

Lost and Found

This poem, a companion piece to 5.2-8, is generally taken as a lover's fantasy or dream. The girl is again lying alone in bed at night, another type-scene of ancient love-poetry. She desperately misses her lover – note the repeated motif of *sought but not found* – and wonders if he still loves her. In her imagination she boldly roams the *streets* looking for him. Meeting the night-*watchmen* on patrol (stock characters in such poetry), she puts to them a distraught and unanswerable question. Then suddenly she finds him and drags him off home. She ends as before by adjuring the chorus not to interrupt their amours (3.5 = 2.7 = 8.4).

A Wedding Procession

3. 6 Poet: What is this coming up from the desert
    like a column of smoke,
breathing of myrrh and frankincense
    and every exotic perfume?

7   Here comes Solomon's litter.
    Around it are sixty champions,
the flower of the warriors of Israel;
    all of them skilled swordsmen,
    expert in war.

8   Each man has his sword at his side,
    against alarms by night.

9   King Solomon
    has had a palanquin made
    of wood from Lebanon.

10   He has had the posts made of silver,
    the canopy of gold,
the seat of purple;
    the centre is inlaid with ebony.

11   Daughters of Zion,
    come and see King Solomon,
wearing the diadem with which his mother crowned him
    on his wedding day,
    on the day of his heart's joy.

(NJB)

A Wedding Procession

This is the only poem in the Song which is clearly a wedding-song. The poet is here speaking on behalf of the lovers. Their wedding procession will be the most glorious imaginable. They will be – or rather, they actually are for the day – Solomon and his queen, with all the accoutrements of royalty. The Preacher likewise imagined himself Solomon, if in more prosaic fashion (Eccl 1.12+).

The wedding procession escorted the bride from her house to the groom's. As often in classical Arabic love-poetry, the scene is set by an enquiry about a woman riding into view on the horizon. (The opening of Is Ch 63 belongs in the same tradition). Is it a camel train raising the dust as it brings spices across the desert? No, it is *Solomon's* own *litter*, which he has sent to fetch the bride. He has also sent a guard of honour to protect her on the journey. (An attack on such a procession is vividly described in 1 Macc [9.37+] c.160 BC.) The litter itself – let us call it by the grander term of *palanquin* – has all the latest embellishments. And here finally comes Solomon himself, wearing the wedding crown, to greet her. It was the custom in ancient Israel, as it still is at a Greek Orthodox wedding, for the bride and groom both to be *crowned* as part of the *wedding* ceremony, so the royal fiction lay close to hand.

Praise of a Bride

1 He: How beautiful you are, my love,
                   how very beautiful!
              Your eyes are doves
                   behind your veil.
              Your hair is like a flock of goats,
                   moving down the slopes of Gilead.

2   Your teeth are like a flock of shorn ewes
                   that have come up from the washing,
              all of which bear twins,
                   and not one among them is bereaved.

3   Your lips are like a crimson thread,
                   and your mouth is lovely.
              Your cheeks are like halves of a pomegranate
                   behind your veil.

4   Your neck is like the tower of David,
                   built in courses;
              on it hang a thousand bucklers,
                   all of them shields of warriors.

5   Your two breasts are like two fawns,
                   twins of a gazelle,
                   that feed among the lilies.

7   You are altogether beautiful, my love;
                   there is no flaw in you.

9   You have ravished my heart,
                   my sister, my bride,
              you have ravished my heart with a glance of your eyes,
                   with one jewel of your necklace.

Praise of a Bride

Perhaps we should regard the poem in Ch. 4 as following on directly from the wedding context of Ch. 3. Not that the mention of her *veil* in 4.1 and 3, or his address to her as *my bride* in 4.11 and 5.1 are either of them conclusive. But whoever put Ch. 4 here probably thought of the lovers as now man and wife.

At any rate it seems to be a single poem in three parts. The first (4.1-7) is a *wasf*, i.e. a series of similes applied to the physical features of the beloved (see p.502). Some of these similes are conventional enough, e.g. those for *eyes*, *lips* and *breasts*. Others are striking. Glossy black hair, dressed in the ancient Egyptian style, does indeed ripple down over the head and shoulders *like a flock of goats* running down a hillside. Goats in Semitic parallelism bring sheep in their train. Here the comparison of *teeth* with *shorn ewes* brings out their symmetry and their whiteness by contrast with her black hair. The simile chosen for her *neck* probably refers to an ornamental collar of a kind still worn in some African countries, where long necks are admired. This consisted of layers of gold rings, up to ten in all, lying on top of one another like the stone *courses* of a round *tower*. It was an ancient custom to hang *shields* on towers, like coats of arms on medieval castles. But in v.4cd, as in 5c, the simile takes on a life of its own. The *tower of David*, which is not men-

Praise of a Bride (cont.)

4.10 **He:** How sweet is your love, my sister, my bride!
how much better is your love than wine,
and the fragrance of your oils than any spice!

11 Your lips distill nectar, my bride;
honey and milk are under your tongue;
the scent of your garments is like the scent of Lebanon.

12 A garden locked is my sister, my bride,
a garden locked, a fountain sealed.

13 Your channel is an orchard of pomegranates
with all choicest fruits,
henna with nard,

14 nard and saffron, calamus and cinnamon,
with all trees of frankincense,
myrrh and aloes,
with all chief spices –

15 a garden fountain, a well of living water,
and flowing streams from Lebanon.

16 **She:** Awake, O north wind,
and come, O south wind!
Blow upon my garden
that its fragrance may be wafted abroad.
Let my beloved come to his garden,
and eat its choicest fruits.

5.1 **He:** I come to my garden, my sister, my bride;
I gather my myrrh with my spice,
I eat my honeycomb with my honey,
I drink my wine with my milk.

Chorus: Eat, friends, drink,
and be drunk with love. (NRSV)

Praise of a Bride (cont.)

tioned elsewhere in the OT, seems to be no particular tower: rather it functions like *Gilead* in v.1 to lend grandeur to the praise.

The second section (9-15) continues the praises of the beloved, no longer *seriatim*. As usual in the Song, the images are fused with the objects to which they refer. Thus in v.9 the *necklace* is also her *eyes*, and in v.10 the *oils* are also her *love*. In a similar ambiguity, her *lips* (11) give both kisses and love-talk. From v.12 on we move to a sustained double image in which the beloved is both a *garden* and the *fountain* which waters it. The plants in the garden are chosen for their variety – many of them never grew in Israel

– and for their fragrance: in this part of the poem smell is the dominant sense. The garden is walled, and the wall is *locked*. So too within it the fresh-water spring is *sealed* i.e. locked, a practice still found e.g. in the Greek countryside. Clearly the lover is claiming her for his own.

She too has in mind an exclusive love. The *fragrance* is to *be wafted* only to her *beloved*, so that he comes to take *my garden* as *his garden*. And *come* he does, claiming the garden and all that is in it with an eight-fold *my*. As their love is then consummated in silence, it is left to the chorus to urge them to *drink* deeply of *love*.

Deserted and Reunited

2 He: I sleep, but my heart is awake.
   I hear my love knocking.
Open to me, my sister, my beloved,
   my dove, my perfect one,
for my head is wet with dew,
   my hair with the drops of night.

3 She: I have taken off my tunic,
   am I to put it on again?
I have washed my feet,
   am I to dirty them again?

4 My love thrust his hand
   through the hole in the door;
   I trembled to the core of my being.

5 Then I got up
   to open to my love,
myrrh ran off my hands,
   pure myrrh off my fingers,
   on to the handle of the bolt.

6 I opened to my love,
   but he had turned and gone.
My soul failed at his flight,
   I sought but could not find him,
   I called, but he did not answer.

7 The watchmen met me,
   those who go on their rounds in the city.
They beat me, they wounded me,
   they took my cloak away from me:
   those guardians of the ramparts!

8 She: I charge you, daughters of Jerusalem,
   if you should find my love,
what are you to tell him?
   – That I am sick with love!

Deserted and Reunited

Another longish sequence which can be read as a single poem in three sections. The first (5.2-8) is a companion piece to 3.1-4. The beloved is again lying in bed at night in her mother's house, already prepared for a night of love (v.5; cf. Prov 7.17). He knocks, asking her to *open*, a verb which is used three times with no specific object. He can put his hand through the keyhole but cannot enter until she brings the key. At first she teasingly makes excuses (3), but then when she gets up she finds him *gone*. As before she pursues him through *the city* and runs into *the watchmen*. This time the story ends differently. The watchmen, judging from her behaviour that she is a loose woman (cp. Prov 7.12), *beat* her and take her *cloak away*. They represent the disapproval of society, perhaps also of her subconscious. Over against them are the chorus, whose help she enlists in finding him.

Deserted and Reunited (cont.)

5.9 | **Chorus:** What makes your lover better than other lovers,
O loveliest of women?
What makes your lover better than other lovers,
to put us under such an oath?

10 | **She:** My love is fresh and ruddy,
to be known among ten thousand.

11 | His head is golden, purest gold,
his locks are palm fronds
and black as the raven.

12 | His eyes are like doves
beside the water-courses,
bathing themselves in milk,
perching on a fountain-rim.

13 | His cheeks are beds of spices,
banks sweetly scented.
His lips are lilies,
distilling pure myrrh.

14 | His hands are golden, rounded,
set with jewels of Tarshish.
His belly a block of ivory
covered with sapphires.

15 | His legs are alabaster columns
set in sockets of pure gold.
His appearance is that of Lebanon,
unrivalled as the cedars.

16 | His conversation is sweetness itself,
he is altogether lovable.
Such is my love, such is my friend,
O daughters of Jerusalem.

6.1 | **Chorus:** Where did your lover go,
O loveliest of women?
Which way did your lover turn
so that we can help you seek him?   ▸

Deserted and Reunited (cont.)

Their question in v.9 makes a transition to the second section (5.10-16): another *wasf*, but this time in the mouth of the beloved. Her general picture portrays him as tall (15), dark and handsome (10a) as well as charming (16a) – the type may be conventional but the chorus will recognise him as an outstanding member of it (10b, cp.15). Many of his specific features she then compares to items of statuary, which even by Egyptian standards must surely be meant as a parody of the genre. The most intriguing simile is that of v.12, where the regulation *doves* are given three alternative locations. The *milk* may refer to the white of the *eyes* by contrast with his black hair. All the similes of v.13 speak of his fragrance, a favourite theme of the Song.

> ## Deserted and Reunited (cont.)
>
> 2 **She:**   My love went down to his garden,
>   to the beds of spices,
>   to pasture his flock on the grass
>   and gather lilies.
>
> 3   I belong to my love, and my love to me.
>   He pastures his flock among the lilies.
>
> (NJB)

Deserted and Reunited (cont.)

The third section (6.1-3) is a surprise. Even if the chorus can still ask her, so long after 5.8, *which way* he went, we do not expect her to say that he has after all come *to his garden* i.e. to her. If the passage 5.2-6.3 really makes one poem, she seems at this point to be trying to reassure herself that he still loves her; in which case the whole thing is perhaps a fantasy or dream like 3.1-4. The reciprocity of 6.3a is neatly expressed in Hebrew by (i) a chiasmus*, which the English can render, and (ii) an assonance which it cannot: *anī ledōdī wedōdī lī.*

> ## Royal Praises
>
> 6.4 **He:**   You are beautiful as Tirzah, my love,
>   comely as Jerusalem,
>   terrible as an army with banners.
>
> 5   Turn away your eyes from me,
>   for they overwhelm me!
>
> 8   There are sixty queens and eighty concubines,
>   and maidens without number.
>
> 9   My dove, my perfect one,
>   is the only one,
>   the darling of her mother,
>   flawless to her that bore her.
>   The maidens saw her and called her happy;
>   the queens and concubines also,
>   and they praised her.
>
> 10   Who is this that looks forth like the dawn,
>   fair as the moon,
>   bright as the sun,
>   terrible as an army with banners?
>
> ♦

Royal Praises

Like 3.6-11, this two-part poem makes use of the 'royal masque'. In the first part (Ch.6), he compares her favourably to all the ladies of the harem, who themselves sing her praises (6.8-10). The warm uniqueness of *the only one* is contrasted with the chilly arithmetic of v.8. In the second part she is *queenly* (7.1) and has ensnared *a king* (i.e. him) *in* her (regally purple) *tresses* (7.5). Many of the similes in both parts are grander than usual, especially the framing place-names. *Tirzah* was an early capital of Israel, as *Jerusalem* of Judah.

Ch. 6 also introduces a new note into the love-poetry. There is something *terrible* about her beauty. Specifically her *eyes*, which as in 4.1 focus her beauty,

Royal Praises (cont.)

7.1 **He:** How graceful are your feet in sandals,
O queenly maiden!
Your rounded thighs are like jewels,
the work of a master hand.

2 Your navel is a rounded bowl
that never lacks mixed wine.
Your belly is a heap of wheat,
encircled with lilies.

3 Your two breasts are like two fawns,
twins of a gazelle.

4 Your neck is like an ivory tower.
Your eyes are pools in Heshbon,
by the gate of Bath-rabbim.
Your nose is like a tower of Lebanon,
overlooking Damascus.

5 Your head crowns you like Carmel,
and your flowing locks are like purple;
a king is held captive in the tresses. (NRSV)

Royal Praises (cont.)

overwhelm her lover. The note is picked up in 6.10c as a frame.

The second part of the poem (7.1-5) is another *wasf*. It differs from the earlier ones in working upwards from her *feet* and in referring to parts of her body usually clothed (7.1-3). The restraint shown here is in sharp contrast to the anatomical explicitness of certain Babylonian poetry, quite sharp enough to demolish the old theory that the Song too derived from ANE fertility rituals. The motif of the love-trap (7.5) is found also in the ELP: 'with her hair she has thrown nets over me'.

Mutual Love

7.6 **He:** How beautiful, how entrancing you are,
my loved one, daughter of delights!

7 You are stately as a palm tree,
and your breasts are like clusters of fruit.

8 I said, 'Let me climb up into the palm
to grasp its fronds.'
May I find your breasts like clusters of grapes on the vine,
your breath sweet-scented like apples,

9 Your mouth like fragrant wine
flowing smoothly to meet my caresses,
gliding over my lips and teeth. (REB)

Mutual Love

Once again a chain of love-poems can be read as a sequence. His song (7.6-9), involving all five senses, is more frankly physical even than before. The initial comparison of her stature to a *palm-tree* was conventional enough, but from there the imagery and the action of the poem grows in a way that is natural yet miraculous. Typically, her *breasts* are *clusters* of both dates and *grapes*. *Breath* in v.8 translates

Mutual Love (cont.)

10 **She:**   I am my beloved's,
                   and his desire is for me.
11   Come, my beloved,
                   let us go forth into the fields,
                   and lodge in the villages;
12   let us go out early to the vineyards,
                   and see whether the vines have budded,
               whether the grape blossoms have opened
                   and the pomegranates are in bloom.
               There I will give you my love.
13   The mandrakes give forth fragrance,
                   and over our doors are all choice fruits,
               new as well as old,
                   which I have laid up for you, O my beloved.

8.1   O that you were like a brother to me,
                   who nursed at my mother's breast!
               If I met you outside, I would kiss you,
                   and no one would despise me.
2   I would lead you and bring you
                   into the house of my mother,
                   and into the chamber of the one who bore me.
               I would give you spiced wine to drink,
                   the juice of my pomegranates.
3   O that his left hand were under my head,
                   and that his right hand embraced me!
4   I adjure you, O daughters of Jerusalem,
                   do not stir up or awaken love
                   until it is ready!   (NRSV)

Mutual Love (cont.)

Hebrew 'nose': the reference is to the widespread custom of nose-kissing. *Mouth* means saliva. A classical Arabic poem has an exact parallel: 'My beloved's saliva is like a draft of perfumed wine.'

The response (7.10-13) opens with a variation on the formula of mutual love (6.3a). Subtly she corrects that unequal relationship between the sexes which had been part of Eve's punishment in Gen 3.16: 'Your desire shall be for your husband, and he shall rule over you.' Here *his desire is for* her, i.e. (as far as this half of it goes) she rules him. And so she takes the initiative. Switching from the third to the second person (a feature also of the ELP), she invites him to the country, just as he invited her in

2.10. Once again nature is in harmony with love, and she *will give* him the fruits of both, which she has *laid up for* him. *Mandrakes* were a well-known aphrodisiac.

Ch. 8 begins with her wishing she could acknowledge him openly as her lover. Verse 1 has a close parallel in an ELP:

If only mother knew my heart . . .
Then I could hurry to my brother
And kiss him before his company
And not be ashamed for anyone.

But gradually in vv.2-4 fantasy takes over from logic. Having invited him home *like a brother*, she *would give* him the same fruits as in 7.13. They would make love, and the scene would end with her customary charge to her companions not to disturb them.

Love Strong as Death

8. 6   **He:**   Wear me as a seal over your heart,
         as a seal upon your arm;
     for love is strong as death,
         passion cruel as the grave;
     it blazes up like a blazing fire,
         fiercer than any flame.

7   Many waters cannot quench love,
         no flood can sweep it away;
     if someone were to offer for love
         all the wealth in his house,
         it would be laughed to scorn.   (REB)

Love Strong as Death

Signet-seals in the ancient world were worn either on a cord round the neck, i.e. *over* the *heart,* or in a ring on the finger or *arm.* As an image the *seal* expressed identity, intimacy, ownership and permanence. Not surprisingly we find the same motif in the ELP:

> If only I were her little seal-ring,
> the keeper of her finger.

But where the Egyptian lover continues in personal vein, saying that he would then 'see her each and every day', the Hebrew gives a different motivation. A seal was also worn as an amulet, to protect against danger and *death* – hence the *for* in v.6c.

The praise of love in vv.6c-7b is unlike anything else in the Song. *Cruel* is better translated 'fierce' i.e. elemental. *Love* is here a deceptively modern-looking abstraction. But behind it can be heard rumbles of ancient myth – a ruthless goddess of Love in combat with a god of Death, and the victory of the skygod, who is armed with the lightning, over the primeval chaos for which *many waters* is almost a technical term in the OT. After that the commercial note of v.7c-e falls rather flat, but it does show that we are not here talking of marriage: a bride *can* be bought, love cannot.

Love's Vineyard

8. 11   **He:**   Solomon had a vineyard at Baal-hamon;
     he entrusted the vineyard to keepers;
     each one was to bring for its fruit a thousand pieces of silver.

12   My vineyard, my very own, is for myself;
     you, O Solomon, may have the thousand,
     and the keepers of the fruit two hundred!   (NRSV)

Love's Vineyard

The last complete unit in the Song provides a frame with Ch.1 and also picks up motifs from Chs 3 and 6. In 6.9 the lover praised his beloved above all the royal harem: the name of *Solomon* was not mentioned then but it was not far to seek. Now he similarly praises his own vineyard above that of Solomon. Solomon's may yield a fortune, but he has to let it out to *keepers* and pay them a fifth of the profit. This the lover contrasts with *my vineyard, my very own.* That was the

unusual phrase which the beloved had coined of herself in 1.6 (though NRSV did not bring it out there). Now at the end of the book her vineyard has become his, just as 'her garden' of 4.16 became his in 5.1. *For myself* is not a sudden flash of chauvinism: the Hebrew implies not that he owns it but that he will look after it himself, which neither she in 1.6 nor Solomon here had been able to do. The mutuality of their love is maintained to the end.

INTRODUCTION TO THE PROPHETS

1. The Nature of Prophecy

One way and another, prophets loom large in the OT – indeed ancient Judaism may be called above all a prophetic religion. In the Hebrew Bible the books Joshua-2 Kings are entitled 'the former prophets', and those from Isaiah onwards (less Daniel) 'the latter prophets'. Moreover the latter are placed immediately after the former, with 'the writings', viz. the rest of it, relegated to third place. The Greek translators of the LXX, however, put the writings before the prophets, perhaps because they had one eye on the wider world and thought the prophets less reader-friendly. The Christian Church has in this respect followed the LXX rather than the MT.

Quite apart from many references to prophets in the 'historical' books, some three-quarters of the other books in the OT are ascribed to named prophets. In Christian tradition, the four whose books are longest are known as 'major', the remaining twelve as 'minor'. (The MT knows the latter more neutrally as 'the twelve'). Of these sixteen, five are of outstanding merit as thinkers and writers. In chronological order they are Amos and Hosea; Isaiah of Jerusalem; Jeremiah; and Second Isaiah (Chs 40-55). Between them they cover a span of c.250 years.

The word 'prophet' has a wide range of meanings. Its Greek original means basically a 'spokesman', someone who 'speaks for' a god or even another person. But *pro* in Greek means not only 'for' but 'fore', and from earliest times those who spoke *for* God were also expected to *fore-*tell the future. Every ancient society had its seers (often ecstatics) and diviners, whether attached to a sanctuary or free-lance, and all those meanings were encompassed in the Semitic word *nābī*, for which the LXX translators chose 'prophet' as the equivalent.

The word *nābī* is first found in some C18th BC texts from Mari on the Middle Euphrates. These texts reveal a type and range of prophetic activity that is already quite close to what we see in the OT. The Mari prophet typically claimed to be sent by a god with a message for a king (or in one case for the inhabitants of a city). The message, which often began 'The god so-and-so sent me', might enjoin religious acts, e.g. the offering of a sacrifice; or it might give advice on political and military matters, e.g. a warning of an impending revolt or a recommendation not to go on a campaign. The most striking resemblance to the OT lay in the prophet's sense of being a divine messenger. Formulae like those of Mari are found throughout the OT, from the prophet's own claim that 'the Lord sent me' to the many, many oracles which begin 'Thus says the Lord'.

But a much closer parallel to the OT, in time and place, is provided by an Aramaic inscription found in 1975 at Deir Alla in Jordan. The inscription was painted c.800 BC on a plastered wall which later collapsed in an earthquake, possibly that of c.760 mentioned in Amos 1.1. The restored text, though incomplete, is of great interest. The heading offers an immediate surprise: 'Warnings from the Book of Balaam son of Beor'. For that is the very name of the prophet featured at length in Numbers 22-24 (where see commentary). The text continues as follows:

> He was a seer of the gods. The gods came to him one night in a vision, according to the command of El, and they spoke to him. Balaam got up in the morning and behold [it was] a vision. . . . He fasted and kept weeping. His kinsfolk came to him and said 'O Balaam son of Beor, why are you fasting and why are you weeping?'
>> [Balaam replied:]
> 'Sit down and let me tell you the [words of] the Shaddayin;
> come and see the work of the gods.
> When the gods met together

and the Shaddayin arranged a meeting,
they said to Shagar:
"Do not open the latches of heaven.
In your clouds darkness reigns with no
   glimmer,
pitch darkness with no clear night.
Do not growl for ever . . ." . . .
You people, whether you hate it or [   ],
you will need an ash-heap under your head,
you will lie in your eternal resting-place to
   decay.'
                      [translation after Dijkstra]

The deities mentioned here (who include
Baal in another fragment) are all members
of the Canaanite pantheon, though El and
Shaddai both appear in the OT also as
titles of YHWH (p.34f.). Shagar seems to
be threatening a catastrophe and the other
gods trying to stop her. Balaam himself
expects the catastrophe to come – the first
instance outside the Bible of a prophet
foretelling doom to his own people. The
embedding of an oracle in a narrative is of
course common in the OT.

When we move to the OT itself, we
find within it a steady differentiation of
types of prophet – even though *nābī*
continues to be used of all of them. The
'canonical' prophets, i.e. those whose
books we have, gradually distanced
themselves from the ecstatic prophets.
Ecstasy was a feature especially of
Canaanite religion: see the description in
1 K 18 of the self-mutilating priests of
Baal. Within Israel we hear of bands of
ecstatic prophets stimulated by music or
by wine. The great prophets of the OT
were certainly inspired by religious and
poetic enthusiasm, but they are never
found employing artificial stimuli: if theirs
was ecstasy, it was of a quieter kind.

There was also a general distinction
to be made between institutional and unattached prophets. Institutional prophets
were typically on the staff of a temple or
of the royal house (like Amos's opponent
Amaziah), and their messages were
normally of comfort to those whose bread
they ate. To the unattached prophets a

temple – even the Temple in Jerusalem –
may have been a source of deep personal
inspiration, but neither its buildings (Jer
7.4) nor its cult (Mic 6.6-8) were of ultimate value. Moreover their message was
rarely one of comfort and peace, either to
king or to people. On the contrary they
tended to be regarded as 'troublers of
Israel' in the tradition of Elijah in 1 K 21.
The distinction between the institutional
and the unattached prophet is stressed
many times in the OT, notably in the case
of Moses in Num 12.10, of Micaiah in 1 K
22, and of Jeremiah in Jer 27-28. But in the
important case of Isaiah it is invalid.

There is another distinction which
must not be pushed too far. Some modern
scholars have set up the prophets as the
true voice of Israel as against the law on
the one hand and the Temple worship on
the other. But the text of the OT lends no
support to this sharp contrast. The
prophets share much of the theology and
many of the literary forms and images of
the Temple psalmists. Likewise the books
of the law, especially Deuteronomy, reflect
the concern of the great prophets for social
justice and for the moral motive. The
editors of the OT have ensured that it is
all of a piece.

It is in this last point that we must look
for what distinguishes the great prophets, not so much from the rest of the OT
as from other prophets of Israel and the
ANE. To them the religious and the moral
were inseparable. God was not only holy,
i.e. transcendent but righteous, i.e. moral.

And they made his concerns their
own. Not that there is any sign of their
being swept up into a mystical union with
God: indeed, when addressed by him they
regularly argue and answer back on behalf either of themselves or, more often,
of the people. For the biblical prophets
were intermediaries, and had responsibilities in both directions. From Abraham
(Gen 18) and Moses (Ex 32) onwards they
are presented as interceding bravely on

behalf of the people. It is in Jeremiah that this tradition comes to its climax. Caught between God and the people, he expresses and shares the feelings of both.

But the main task of all the prophets was to convey God's word to the people, in season and out of season, at whatever cost in anguish and unpopularity. The force that held them to the task is most vividly expressed in the narratives of their call. But the call was a life sentence. Their conscience, once aroused, remained the source of their authority and of their inspiration – though if 'ecstasy' is too strong a word, 'inspiration' is perhaps too weak.

Both at the moment of call and later, the hearing of the word was often accompanied by the seeing of a vision. The vision might be of God, or it might be of something quite mundane, e.g. an almond tree, a plumb-line, a potter at his wheel. Poets often trace the genesis of a poem to an image, whether figurative or literal. The image sets off a train of thought, which in turn is gradually crystallised into a communicable shape. So it was with the prophets, and their message too was always expressed with the verbal concentration and the emotional tension of poetry.

But in transmitting their message the prophets did not restrict themselves to the spoken word. They also used another medium, corresponding to the visions that had accompanied their own inspiration, viz. the so-called 'symbolic actions'. To a modern reader this is the strangest element in the prophetic books, and even now it is not fully explained. We must recognise that such actions were common enough in the life of ancient Israel: for example a man's clothes often represented his person, like the cloak of Saul (1 Sam 15.27f.; 24.5f.) or the sandal of Elimelech (Ruth 4.7f.). So it was no surprise when Isaiah wore mourning garb, albeit for three years [20.3], as a sign of misfortune to come. Likewise Hosea (Ch.1) and Isaiah [Ch.8] were by no means the only fathers in the ancient world to choose a name for their child which signified their own aspirations. Indeed actions of this kind were much more than teaching aids: like the pronouncement of a curse, the performance of a symbolic action was widely believed to help in bringing about the event symbolised. This is the explanation not only of the oracles uttered against foreign nations by the prophets but also of symbolic acts of aggression as e.g. in 1 K 22.11. But other symbolic actions by the great prophets are much harder to explain. For example, when Hosea reports that God told him to marry a temple prostitute in order to draw attention to his countrymen's religious infidelity, and that he did so (1.2f.), it is hard to take it either as a literal record or as some kind of literary convention.

Psychologically parallel to the symbolic actions are two features of the prophets' use of language. First is what is called 'the prophetic perfect', whereby the prophet is so transported in imagination that he describes the event he foresees as having already happened. Many languages use this construction in contexts of personal ruin e.g. 'I am undone' (Is 6.5), but Hebrew uses it much more widely e.g. in the famous messianic prophecy of Is 9.2-7. Secondly, the prophets do not always distinguish sharply between a final and a consecutive clause, i.e. between an intended and an unintended consequence. Both those usages rest upon an idea of historical cause and effect which is alien to us, and sometimes unnerving, especially in the older translations.

2. The Prophetic Oracles

At the core of the prophetic books is that which gives them their name and their reputation – the oracles themselves. The term 'oracle', which is derived from the Greco-Roman world, is not altogether happy but has become standard. It means a discrete utterance, which was sometimes as short as a single verse and usually in poetical form. The nearest equivalent in the OT to the prophetic oracles are the psalms. But the prophets went further than the psalmists in the dramatic fervour, indeed the violence, of their utterance. They pulled out all the emotional stops to stir their hearers, and they used every rhetorical device – command and question, contrast and repetition, satire and irony – to shame them into repentance or rouse them to action.

The action required of them was in principle to change their ways and return to their loyalty to God. But the appeal took a very wide variety of forms, corresponding to four main methods of inducing people to change their ways. First is the threat of judgement and of punishment. The basic shape of such an oracle is clear and simple: 'Because you . . . therefore thus says the LORD: "I will . . ." '. The judgement oracle is sometimes dressed in the imagery of a courtroom: there are charges, witnesses, speeches for prosecution and defence, verdict and sentence. God is presented as judge, stern but just. This is the formidable tone which is characteristic of Amos, who more than any other prophet writes as if it is already too late for a change of heart.

Somewhat similar is the tone of Amos's contemporary Isaiah. If Amos sees God as judge, Isaiah sees him rather as king, transcendent in majesty. Inasmuch as a king is responsible for all his people, not just the malefactors, the tone of Isaiah is more majestic, less strident; but still the main emphasis is on God's righteous anger.

The second mode of appeal is the re-proach. A reproach is effective in proportion as it is made not in hurt pride but in hurt love. The latter is the tone especially of Hosea and Jeremiah. Hosea presents God as parent; Jeremiah goes further in hinting at God's suffering *with* his people.

Thirdly, an appeal may be reinforced by an argument. 'Come, let us reason together', says God in Isaiah. But these are no Platonic dialogues, and the argument usually consists of two parts: (i) an objection raised or attributed and (ii) a forceful counter by the prophet, relying more on emotion than on logic.

It was left to Second Isaiah to develop a fourth distinctive mode of appeal. With him God is still king – that is one reason why his works are properly bound in with 'First' Isaiah – but, marvellously, he is both king and redeemer of his people. God's majesty is so unchallengeable that he can confine his appeal to a promise – the unconditional promise of salvation.

On the whole the sterner tones predominate in the pre-exilic prophets (Hosea is the exception), when Israel was still independent and could hope, if she changed her ways, to remain so. With the exile the situation changed radically: the punishment threatened by the earlier prophets was now being inflicted – 'she has received of the LORD's hand double for all her sins' – and the tone of the exilic prophets was more comforting (particularly Second Isaiah, but also in places Jeremiah and Ezekiel).

It would be a mistake, however, to classify the great prophets too sharply by the tone of their message. Except for Second Isaiah, each of the books ascribed to them contains a wide range of prophecies: both of 'weal' and of 'woe', both conditional and unconditional. Scholars have tended, on finding prophecies of 'weal' in pre-exilic books, to regard them as later additions, especially as they often come at the end of the collection (Hos 14, Am 9, Is 35, Jer

30-31). But there is no logical reason why a prophet who is critical of the present may not look to a more hopeful future, even if disaster may need to come first; and an editor would naturally place such hopes at the end of his collection. There is good parallel in many individual psalms beginning in lamentation and ending in confidence.

The nature of the original oracles – short, sharp and poetical – guaranteed not only their immediate impact but also their survival in memory, both during the prophet's lifetime and after it. Gradually they came to be written down (Jer 36 is the *locus classicus* for this development) and collections were made of them. Sometimes these collections were made by the prophet himself, sometimes by his disciples, who may even have constitued a 'school'.

From most points of view it does not matter who was the author of a given oracle: it is the text itself which matters. But there precisely is the rub. For the mss of the prophetic books, unlike those of the psalms, contain little to tell the reader where one oracle ends and another begins. Sometimes of course there are good clues, the introduction of a new speaker or a new addressee, or the favourite frame-structure of a Hebrew poem where the end echoes the beginning. But often the reader is left to make the judgement for himself on criteria which are bound to be subjective. This poses an acute problem of interpretation, since the meaning of any verse depends to a large extent upon the whole poem of which it is a part.

Some scholars hold that similarly any given oracle needs to be read in the light of those on either side of it. But the view taken here, which is the general critical view today, is that the arrangement of the oracles in the prophetic books as we have them is the work not of the author but of a later editor. Most of the prophets, on this view, composed relatively short oracles, less than a single chapter in length; and the editors in arranging them followed principles of their own which have no particular authority. If this were not so, a selection could be seriously misleading.

In addition to oracles addressed to Israel, the prophetic books as we have them contain two other main kinds of material. First are oracles against foreign nations. These form a surprisingly large part of the text, being placed typically after the oracles which criticise Israel and before those which comfort her. The attacks on foreign nations are made sometimes on moral grounds, sometimes on grounds of idolatry, sometimes in support of the prophet's insistence that a foreign alliance is no substitute for a return to God. Often introduced by the phrase 'Woe to . . .', these oracles are not far removed from the curses which would precede an engagement in ancient warfare. Just as the soldiers' curses were designed in part to raise the morale of the home side, so the prophets' oracles against foreign nations may have had the subsidiary function of sweetening the criticisms made of Israel herself. To a modern reader this invective, though often technically brilliant (e.g. Is 14), can soon become tedious. We tend to welcome the rarer note of favour to a foreign nation: not so much when Isaiah calls Assyria 'the rod of mine anger' as when Second Isaiah says of the Persian Cyrus 'I have called you, though you have not known me' – a development which culminates in the book of Jonah.

Secondly the prophetic books contain a good deal of prose narrative of the prophet's life, whether in the first or third person. In most cases this includes the story of the prophet's call, which will establish his claim to authority and may also set out his programme. The most extensive such narrative is that in Jeremiah, where the prose background adds even greater depth and poignancy to the anguished personal poems.

ISAIAH

The Isaiah Scroll

More obviously than any other book of the OT, the Isaiah scroll grew over time – perhaps over as much as 300 years. It contains the work of *at least* four different writers woven together to form a whole:

- (a) the oracles of Isaiah of Jerusalem in the late C8th, viz. most of Chs1-23 and 28-31 (First Isaiah, I[1] for short)
- (b) the writings of an unnamed prophet in mid-C6th Babylon, viz. the whole of Chs 40-55, together perhaps with Ch.35 (Second Isaiah, I[2] for short)
- (c) later writings in the same tradition, chiefly Chs 56-66 (sometimes referred to as Third Isaiah), but also Chs 24-7 and perhaps others
- (d) a chunk of narrative taken almost word for word from 2 K 18-20 and inserted into the Isaiah scroll as Chs [36-9].

Between I[1] and I[2] there was an interval of 150 years. In that interval occurred the great historical watershed of the OT: the fall of Jerusalem and the deportation to Babylon. As the scroll grew, the interval had to be bridged. One pillar of the bridge is provided by [Ch.39], which contains a prophecy, improbably ascribed to I[1], of the exile in Babylon. Another is Ch.35, on which see commentary.

But why should anyone have wanted to join I[1] and I[2] in the same scroll? Perhaps there was a 'school' which continued I[1]'s work after his death, and to which I[2] belonged – indeed I[2] may even have had, or taken, the name Isaiah. Such people would have been able, with the hindsight of the exile, to discern, behind the events of recent centuries, 'a plan prepared for the whole world' (Is 14.26).

In the implementation of that plan, YHWH was seen to have two agents. One was gentile. For I[1] Assyria was 'the rod of my anger'. For I[2] Cyrus, the Persian deliverer from exile, became 'my shepherd' and even 'my anointed'. The other agent was a figure representing Israel. For I[1] that was king Hezekiah, whose loyalty to YHWH had, if not averted, at least postponed the punishment due for her sins. For I[2], writing when she had already 'paid double' for them (40.2), it is a mysterious figure called 'the servant of YHWH' who will bring salvation. By these two strong threads the main components of the Isaiah scroll were bound together, perhaps by I[2] himself. There are also many smaller links and echoes, e.g. the phrase 'high and lofty' used in 2.12, 6.1 and 52.13. For Chs 56-66 see on Ch.57.

The Hebrew text of the Isaiah scroll is particularly well preserved. This judgement was confirmed by the discovery at Qumran of a text of the complete book, copied in C1st BC. Here and there it supports a reading of the LXX, or even a modern conjecture, against MT, but mostly it agrees with MT 'more closely than one would have imagined possible'. It follows not that the MT is faultless but that its faults antedate even the LXX translation.

Isaiah 1–39

Isaiah ben Amoz is the first biblical author who also plays an important part in his country's affairs as recorded in the historical books (2 K 19-20). The two sources together yield the following outline of his life.

He was born c.765 BC into a Judaean family of some position, with easy access to the centres of power i.e. the Temple and the royal house. He was perhaps already a Temple prophet when he saw his famous vision in c.740 BC (6.1). Certainly by 701 BC he had become *the* official prophet to the king (2 K 19.2). But his thinking remained entirely independent – indeed critical – of the establishment. His earliest oracles had two main themes. First, he criticised the moral corruption of the national life, particularly the oppression of the rich by the poor. Second, he criticised the king's foreign policy. Isaiah insisted that 'in quietness and in trust' sc. in the LORD 'shall be your strength'. But king Ahaz (736-716) became involved in the intrigues of Israel and Damascus against Assyria, of whose empire all three states were vassals. Failing to persuade the king, Isaiah seems to have withdrawn for some years from public life [8.16-18].

In 716 Ahaz was succeeded by his son Hezekiah, whose foreign policy was based on similar attempts at intrigue against Assyria, this time in concert with Egypt. Isaiah's renewed warnings (e.g. 19.5-10), were again ineffective. But when in 701 BC the Assyrian king Sennacherib invaded Judaea and invested Jerusalem, the king repented and sought guidance. Isaiah now comforted him and correctly forecast the enemy's withdrawal (2 K 19). Beyond that he looked forward to the ultimate downfall of the Assyrian empire (Ch. 10), and (if passages like 9.6-7 are by him and not by a later writer) to the establishment of a righteous kingdom in Judah.

Isaiah's two main concerns – his country's foreign policy and its social behaviour – were linked by his conception of YHWH as LORD of all human affairs. His favourite title 'the Holy One of Israel' gave a new emphasis to an old idea. In all religions, God is 'holy' in the sense of 'set apart' from men. Isaiah added the moral dimension: God is righteous in his dealings with people, and he demands righteousness from them in their dealings with one another. His sway also extends also over foreign nations. Consequently no foreign alliance could be a substitute for fidelity and righteousness at home.

The style of I[1] is appropriate to his themes. Though no less forceful than Amos and Hosea, he is more majestic, fuller and less abrupt in expression, and more flowing in composition. His imagery is exuberant, and often includes features drawn from myth (e.g. Chs 14, 17) which add a cosmic dimension. Other hallmarks of his style are his fondness for repetitions of words (e.g. 24.1-4), for lists (e.g. 2.12-16; 3.2-3) and for triplets (e.g. 6.10). He also inclines to a diminuendo at the conclusion of his oracles (e.g. 10.14), a characteristic which, like many others, he shares with Second Isaiah (e.g. 40.31).

God's Lawsuit against Judah

1 The vision of Isaiah son of Amoz, which he saw concerning Judah and Jerusalem in the days of Uzziah, Jotham, Ahaz, and Hezekiah, kings of Judah.

2   Hear, O heavens, and listen, O earth;
      for the LORD has spoken:
    I reared children and brought them up,
      but they have rebelled against me.

3   The ox knows its owner,
      and the donkey its master's crib;
    but Israel does not know,
      my people do not understand.

God's Lawsuit against Judah

Ch. 1 introduces Isaiah himself (n.b. *Amoz* has no connection with the prophet Amos) and some of his main themes. The framework is that of the lawsuit of God v. Israel (see p.520), which has certain traditional ingredients.

The first section (2-3) is prefaced by a summons to *earth* and *heavens* to act as witnesses. That was a regular feature of ANE vassal-treaties, the context from which *rebelled* also comes. But the LORD's reproach here relies upon an image more appropriate to the relation with Israel, namely sonship: the complaint is of unfilial behaviour. The contrast of the son with the domestic animals looks like folk-wisdom, but it is cleverly used. Knowledge and understanding are what usually

God's Lawsuit against Judah (cont.)

1.10
Hear the word of the LORD,
    you rulers of Sodom!
Listen to the teaching of our God,
    you people of Gomorrah!

11
What to me is the multitude of your sacrifices?
    says the LORD;
I have had enough of burnt offerings of rams
    and the fat of fed beasts;
I do not delight in the blood of bulls,
    or of lambs, or of goats.

15
When you stretch out your hands,
    I will hide my eyes from you;
even though you make many prayers,
    I will not listen;
    your hands are full of blood.

16
Wash yourselves; make yourselves clean;
    remove the evil of your doings
    from before my eyes;
cease to do evil,

17
    learn to do good;
seek justice,
    rescue the oppressed,
defend the orphan,
    plead for the widow.

18
Come now, let us argue it out,
    says the LORD:
though your sins are like scarlet,
    they shall be like snow;
though they are red like crimson,
    they shall become like wool.

19
If you are willing and obedient,
    you shall eat the good of the land;

20
but if you refuse and rebel,
    you shall be devoured by the sword;
    for the mouth of the LORD has spoken.

(NRSV)

God's Lawsuit against Judah (cont.)

The second section (10-17) is also a common ingredient in the lawsuit form as used by the prophets: see e.g. Micah Ch.6. It is a preemptive rejection of an excuse put up by the defendant, that he has fulfilled all his religious obligations. The rejection is always expressed by a contrast between formal worship and social justice. To interpret the contrast correctly it is necessary to know something of ancient religion. Nobody in the ANE or the Greco-Roman world ever presumed that the god would automatically accept his offering. To secure acceptance, there were

God's Lawsuit against Judah (cont.)

certain prerequisites. Many of these were ritual, but some also were moral, see e.g. Pss 15 and 24. So here the sense of the oracle taken as a whole is that God is rejecting their offerings because of their injustices. Moreover in rejecting their *sacrifices* (11) he rejected also the *prayers* (15) that always accompanied them. There is no contrast here between sacrifice (bad) and prayer (good).

Now for some detailed points. The opening words arraign all classes: both *rulers – of Sodom*! and *people – of Gomorrah*! The object of I's violent criticism is the perversion of justice. *Rulers* means magistrates, and *the orphan* and *the widow* of v.17 typify the weak, whose claims played an important part in all ANE law codes. The normal posture for prayer

in antiquity had the arms raised with open palms to heaven; but God will neither hear the prayer nor see the *hands*, stained as they are with the *blood* of human victims. At v.16 there is a change of tone and metre: time is up, the commands are urgent, the lines are shortened to 2:2.

The third section (18-20) continues the forensic setting, as *argue it out* shows. We come now to the verdict, expressed not as final but as conditional. There is still a last chance of avoiding sentence, but the choice is theirs. *Scarlet* and *crimson* are a regular word-pair in the OT; *snow* and *wool* are not elsewhere found paired, but the poet doubtless chose *semer* (wool) for its assonance with *sheleg* (snow). The contrast between *eat* (19) and *be devoured* (20) is typically prophetic.

Punishment for Pride

12   For the LORD of hosts has a day
          against all that is proud and lofty,
          against all that is lifted up and high;
13   against all the cedars of Lebanon,
          lofty and lifted up;
          and against all the oaks of Bashan;
14   against all the high mountains,
          and against all the lofty hills;
15   against every high tower,
          and against every fortified wall;
16   against all the ships of Tarshish,
          and against all the beautiful craft.
17   The haughtiness of people shall be humbled,
          and the pride of everyone shall be brought low;
          and the LORD alone will be exalted on that day.   (NRSV)

Punishment for Pride

This oracle warns of the judgement to come upon *all that is lofty* in Judah. There are two movements in vv.13-16. First we move from natural (13-14) to man-made (15-16) objects. Second, God passes through the land from north to south like a storm, as in Ps 19. *Ships of Tarshish* means simply large ocean-going merchant

ships. The theme of *hubris* and *nemesis* is common to Greek and Hebrew thought, but the oracle also uses two typically Hebrew ideas as a frame: that of the coming *day* of the LORD, which is found in most of the prophets, and that of God *alone* being *exalted*, which is an especial theme of Isaiah.

Threat of Social Breakdown

3.1
The LORD, the LORD of Hosts,
is about to strip Jerusalem and Judah
of every prop and stay,

2
warriors and soldiers,
judges, prophets, diviners, and elders,

3
captains of companies and men of good standing,
counsellors, skilled magicians, and expert enchanters.

4
I shall appoint youths to positions of authority,
and they will govern as the whim takes them.

5
The people will deal oppressively with one another,
everyone oppressing his neighbour;
the young will be arrogant towards their elders,
mere nobodies towards men of rank.

6
A man will take hold of his brother in his father's house,
saying, 'You have a cloak, you shall be our chief;
our stricken family shall be in your charge.'

7
But the brother will at once reply,
'I cannot heal society's wounds
when in my house there is neither bread nor cloak.
You shall not put me in authority over the people.'   (REB)

Threat of Social Breakdown

Isaiah warns his countrymen that God will reduce Judah to a state of anarchy as a result of revolution or of defeat and deportation. Verses 2 and 3 list all those who might have given leadership or counsel, whether official or unofficial. As in the previous oracle, the long list emphasises the thoroughness of God's work, though here there are two notable omissions: the king and the priest. The role of leaders will be taken over by the young and inexperienced, and in this and other ways the natural order of society will be turned upside down. This is a common ANE topos*, cp. the Egyptian *Prophecy of Neferti* (*ANET* 445): 'I show thee the land topsy turvy. Men salute respectfully him who formerly saluted'. A German scholar has written of these verses (4-5): 'anyone who remembers the months that followed May 1945 in Germany will have the sensation, on reading this passage, of being carried right back to those days'. Verses 6-7 provide an illustrative instance of the breakdown of morale: even within the clan, the responsibility of leadership will be shunned. The *cloak* here is presumably evidence of previous status.

'Grinding the faces of the poor'

3.13
The LORD standeth up to plead,
and standeth to judge the people.

14
The LORD will enter into judgement with the ancients of his people,
and the princes thereof:
for ye have eaten up the vineyard;
the spoil of the poor is in your houses.

15
What mean ye that ye beat my people to pieces,
and grind the faces of the poor? saith the LORD God of hosts.   (AV)

'Grinding the faces of the poor'

In this 'lawsuit' the defendants are the rich and powerful, the very people who had the responsibility of protecting the poor against their oppressors. All the English translations retain the famous image, *grind the faces of the poor*, but in its AV setting it still seems new-minted.

Punishment for the Pride of Judah's Women

The LORD said:

16
>   Because the daughters of Zion are haughty
>   and walk with outstretched necks,
>   glancing wantonly with their eyes,
>   mincing along as they go,
>   tinkling with their feet;

17
>   the LORD will afflict with scabs
>   the heads of the daughters of Zion,
>   and the LORD will lay bare their secret parts.

18
• In that day the LORD will take away the finery of the anklets, the headbands, and the crescents; • the pendants, the bracelets, and the scarfs; • the headdresses, the armlets, the sashes, the perfume boxes, and the amulets; • the signet rings and nose rings; • the festal robes, the mantles, the cloaks, and the handbags; • the garments of gauze, the linen garments, the turbans, and the veils.

24
>   Instead of perfume there will be a stench;
>   and instead of a sash, a rope;
>   and instead of well-set hair, baldness;
>   and instead of a rich robe, a binding of sackcloth;
>   instead of beauty, shame.

(NRSV)

Punishment for the Pride of Judah's Women

This oracle is a counterpart to 2.12-17. Both threaten punishment for pride, the former for the display of (chiefly male) power, the latter for the display of female luxury. Some details of text and translation are uncertain, but the main thrust is clear. Isaiah's original oracle is in vv.16, 17 and 24. The threat here is of defeat, capture (the *rope* and the shaven head) and slavery (the *sackcloth* and the *shame* i.e. branding) – all typically expressed as a series of reversals. Into the middle has been skilfully inserted a prose catalogue of 21 articles of female finery. Logically it does not fit – the removals of vv.18-23 interrupt the reversals of 17 and 24 – but its effect is powerful. The list itself is quite in keeping with Isaiah's style, though its function here is to demonstrate not God's thoroughness, as in 2.12+ and 3.1+, but the women's extravagance. The NRSV translation, unlike REB and NJB, retains the 'ands' and 'thes' of the Hebrew. It thus preserves not only the rhythm for reading aloud but the full meaning: *the* means 'their notorious'. Historically the list can be taken as evidence of the wealth of Judah in the later days of the monarchy; but such conspicuous expenditure by the rich does not make for social cohesion.

The Song of the Vineyard

5.1 Let me sing for my beloved
     my love-song concerning his vineyard:
My beloved had a vineyard
2   on a very fertile hill.
He dug it and cleared it of stones,
     and planted it with choice vines;
he built a watchtower in the midst of it,
     and hewed out a wine vat in it;
he expected it to yield grapes,
     but it yielded wild grapes.

3 And now, inhabitants of Jerusalem
     and people of Judah,
judge between me
     and my vineyard.
4 What more was there to do for my vineyard
     that I have not done in it?
When I expected it to yield grapes,
     why did it yield wild grapes?

5 And now I will tell you
     what I will do to my vineyard.
I will remove its hedge,
     and it shall be devoured;
I will break down its wall,
     and it shall be trampled down.
6 I will make it a waste;
     it shall not be pruned or hoed,
     and it shall be overgrown with briers and thorns;
I will also command the clouds
     that they rain no rain upon it.

The Song of the Vineyard

In this short parable Isaiah uses his full resources to bring about a gradual change of mood in his hearers, from gentle amusement to righteous indignation. He starts by claiming to address a *beloved* friend who owns a *vineyard*. The friend loves his vineyard and has lavished every care on it. He has planted the best (purple) *vines*, built a *watchtower* for protection against thieves, and hewn a winepress out of the solid rock. But the grapes it has produced are blighted and bitter.

The tone then changes (the *and now* marks the point where the first skin comes off the onion) to a mock lawsuit: Isaiah, now purporting to represent his friend, asks his fellow-countrymen to *judge between* him and his vineyard. Since a vineyard was also a common ANE metaphor for a wife (Song 8.11), the song is easily interpreted as a complaint against a faithless wife. So the singer has the audience with him while he goes on to say what his friend will do to 'punish' his vineyard. He will leave it derelict and open to intrusion.

But then comes the surprise: only one speaker can *command the clouds* to *rain no rain* on it. Suddenly the second skin comes off the onion and the truth dawns. Isaiah's light-hearted song (like Nathan's

The Song of the Vineyard (cont.)

7   For the vineyard of the LORD of hosts
        is the house of Israel,
    and the people of Judah
        are his pleasant planting;
    he expected justice,
        but saw bloodshed;
    righteousness,
        but heard a cry!   (NRSV)

The Song of the Vineyard (cont.)

parable in 2 Sam 12) has turned into a deadly serious indictment by God – of the audience itself. The final verse rams its point home by the two plays on words which alas cannot be rendered in English. God *expected* (the key-word of v.7 picks up vv.2 and 4) justice (*mishpāt*) and found bloodshed (*mispāh*); expecting *tsedāqāh* (righteousness), he found *tse'āqāh*, which is the technical term in Jewish law for the victim's *cry* of protest against injustice.

Greedy Landowners

8   Woe to those who add house to house
        and join field to field
    until there is nowhere left
        and they are the sole inhabitants of the country.
9   The LORD of hosts has sworn this in my hearing,
    'Many houses will be brought to ruin,
        great and fine ones left untenanted;
10   for ten acres of vineyard will yield only one barrel,
        and ten bushel of seed will yield only one bushel.'   (NJB)

Greedy Landowners

In theory, the promised land was to be regarded as God's property, lent to the Hebrews as a group, or at the smallest to the clan, and not to be sold outright by one individual to another (Lev 25). In practice, national prosperity had undermined the old attitudes, and the rich in Israel, as elsewhere in the ANE, had in course of time extended their own estates. The poor were gradually reduced to the status of debt-slaves*, and the gulf between the classes left the country prey to invasion. As a result the large estates, which formerly had many tenants but now have one, will end by having none at all, and the land will revert to nature. The mention of the *vineyard* in v.10 makes a link with the preceding oracle, and the theme of v.9 with the next but one (6.11).

Invasion by the Assyrian Army

26   He hoists a signal for a distant nation,
        he whistles them up from the ends of the earth;
        and see how swift, how fleet they come!   ▶

Invasion by the Assyrian Army

Sooner or later God will summon the Assyrian army to invade. Neither he nor they need to be named, and the picture can be painted with a few powerful strokes. The opening is conventional. God's summons is regularly effected by combined sight and sound – the standard raised aloft and the trumpet or the *whistle* blown. Regularly also the avenging troops come from far, the unfamiliar being all the more frightening.

Invasion by the Assyrian Army (cont.)

5. 27   None of them tired, none of them stumbling,
            none of them asleep or drowsy,
        none of them with belt unfastened,
            none of them with broken sandal-strap.
28   Their arrows are sharpened,
            their bows all strung,
        their horses' hoofs you would think were flint
            and their wheels, a whirlwind!
29   Their roar is like that of a lioness,
            like fierce young lions they roar,
        growling they seize their prey
            and carry it off, with no one to prevent it.   (NJB)

Invasion by the Assyrian Army (cont.)

Assyrian kings themselves boasted of their army's speed on the march, but for the rest its advance is seen through the eyes of its petrified victims. Its fitness and its discipline are faultless. The archers, its striking force, keep their *bows* perma-nently *strung*. Their battle cry is like the *roar* of a *lion*, the most terrifying beast known in Israel. The end too can be left to the imagination. The final phrase is a formula often used to round off oracles of doom (Is 47.15 etc.).

Isaiah's Vision in the Temple

6. 1   In the year that King Uzziah died, I saw the LORD sitting on a throne, high and lofty; and the hem of his robe filled the temple. • Seraphs were in attendance above him; each had six wings: with two they covered their faces, and with two they covered their feet, and with two they flew. • And one called to another and said:

'Holy, holy, holy is the LORD of hosts;
    the whole earth is full of his glory.'

• The pivots on the thresholds shook at the voices of those who called, and the
5   house filled with smoke. • And I said: 'Woe is me! I am lost, for I am a man of unclean lips, and I live among a people of unclean lips; yet my eyes have seen the King, the LORD of hosts!'   ▸

Isaiah's Vision in the Temple

The justly famous narrative of Ch.6 is not without its problems, but it is best to start by taking it at its face value. Taken so, it records, from a standpoint of some years later, the crucial event in Isaiah's life. It is in two parts: (i) the vision (1-7) and (ii) the mission (8-11).

One day in about 740 BC Isaiah went into Solomon's Temple. The occasion was probably the New Year feast of the Taber-nacles, when the kingship of God was celebrated (see p.410). As a prophet he had a privileged position in the ceremonies, and at the moment of his vision was standing outside the sanctuary which led into the inner shrine, the Holy of Holies. In the latter was the Ark on a stepped platform, representing the LORD enthroned, protected by two seraphs or winged creatures (desribed in 1 K 6). The ceremonies included the antiphonal singing of psalms and the offering of incense, burnt on a special altar. Transported by the worship, Isaiah *saw the LORD* – a claim

Isaiah's Vision in the Temple (cont.)

6   • Then one of the seraphs flew to me, holding a live coal that had been taken from the altar with a pair of tongs. • The seraph touched my mouth with it and said: 'Now that this has touched your lips, your guilt has departed and your sin is blotted out.' • Then I heard the voice of the LORD saying, 'Whom shall I send, and who will go for us?' And I said, 'Here am I; send me!' • And he said, 'Go and say to this people:

> "Keep listening, but do not comprehend;
> keep looking, but do not understand."
10   Make the mind of this people dull,
> and stop their ears,
> and shut their eyes,
> so that they may not look with their eyes,
> and listen with their ears,
> and comprehend with their minds,
> and turn and be healed.'

Isaiah's Vision in the Temple (cont.)

which in itself was so daring as to be near blasphemy – and did so not in imagination but with his own *eyes* (5).

The focus of the whole narrative is upon the utter transcendence of God. There is no attempt to describe his appearance – that was left to Ezekiel 1 – but every circumstantial detail reinforces the picture. The *hem of his robe* extended from the inner shrine out into the sanctuary. He is surrounded by his council (8, *for us*) and guarded by winged creatures in human form (here called *seraphs* but hardly to be distinguished from the cherubim of 1 K 6). Heavenly beings though they are, they 'veil their faces from the presence'. With two other wings they cover their private parts, for which the Hebrew euphemism is *feet*. The psalm they sing is like many of the so-called enthronement psalms, especially Ps 47.6-8. For the meaning of *holy* see p146f.; the threefold repetition of it (the *trisagion* of the Orthodox Church) provides the emphasis not otherwise achievable in a language that lacks superlatives. God is LORD *of* (the heavenly) *hosts* as well as of *the whole earth*; *his glory* is the outward manifestation of his holiness. The shaking of the doorposts (4) may be due ei-

ther to the music or to the kind of earth-tremor which often figured in ancient reports of a theophany.

Isaiah's response is one of dread. Not only had God said: 'No human being can see me and survive' (Ex 33.20), but he himself also felt ritually and morally *unclean*, a partner in the solidarity of human *guilt*. God however knew his fear and sent a seraph to purify his *lips* with a *coal from the* incense *altar*.

The mention of the *people* and the *lips* (5) prepares the transition to the second part of the chapter, the mission. It is noticeable that Isaiah volunteers for service, unlike e.g. Moses and Jeremiah. God then gives him the message to deliver – and it is here that the difficulties start. First, the public message itself (9cd) has no content: it is not threat, nor promise, nor appeal; at best it is a gloss on some other absent message. Secondly, the private commentary which, carefully constructed as it is (note the triple chiasmus*), follows in v.10 is at first sight extremely harsh. One may seek to ease it in various ways. Linguistically, it may be said that 'the imperatives' (*make* etc.) 'have the force of the indicative' (NJB). Psychologically it may be pointed out that

Isaiah's Vision in the Temple (cont.)

6. 11   Then I said, 'How long, O LORD?' And he said:

'Until cities lie waste
    without inhabitant,
and houses without people,
    and the land is utterly desolate.'

(NRSV)

Isaiah's Vision in the Temple (cont.)

a call to repentance can in the case of a hardened sinner be actually counterproductive. But we must not smooth it out too much, because Isaiah's next question (11) shows that he too felt the harshness. God's reply to it, taken with v.10, means that Judah is now so far gone along the road to perdition that nothing can save her until after she has paid the full penalty of invasion and deportation.

The nature of vv.9-10 suggests that the chapter as a whole is not a straightforward narrative of Isaiah's call. The vision of vv.1-7 is authentic enough – too vivid not to be remembered all his life – but the record of the commissioning reflects his frustration many years at the rejection of his preaching. Convinced as always of God's majesty, he is driven to conclude that the rejection itself had been part of the divine purpose all along. (The story in 1 K 22.19-22 is also suggestive.)

First Messianic Prophecy

9. 2   The people who walked in darkness
         have seen a great light;
      those who lived in a land of deep darkness –
         on them light has shined.

3   You have multiplied the nation,
         you have increased its joy;
      they rejoice before you
         as with joy at the harvest,
         as people exult when dividing plunder.

4   For the yoke of their burden,
         and the bar across their shoulders,
      the rod of their oppressor,
         you have broken as on the day of Midian.

5   For all the boots of the tramping warriors
         and all the garments rolled in blood
         shall be burned as fuel for the fire.   ▸

First Messianic Prophecy

The following five chapters (7-12) contain two (perhaps three) famous 'messianic' prophecies. The word Messiah, which is not found in any of them, needs explanation. It is a Hebrew word meaning 'anointed', and in the OT it had three meanings in succession. First (i) it was used of David and his royal descendants, with reference to David's original anointing as king by Samuel in 1 S 16. Then (ii) it came to be used of an expected king of David's line who should achieve one or both of two things: (a) restore the political independence and military power which Israel enjoyed under David, and (b) inaugurate a reign of justice and peace. The former (a) is clearly a Jewish concept, but the latter (b) was an aspiration widely shared both in the ANE and in the Greco-Roman world.

First Messianic Prophecy (cont.)

6   For a child has been born for us,
        a son given to us;
    authority rests upon his shoulders;
        and he is named
    Wonderful Counselor, Mighty God,
        Everlasting Father, Prince of Peace.
7   His authority shall grow continually,
        and there shall be endless peace
    for the throne of David and his kingdom.
        He will establish and uphold it
    with justice and with righteousness
        from this time onward and forevermore.
    The zeal of the LORD of hosts will do this.   (NRSV)

First Messianic Prophecy (cont.)

Finally (iii), as time went by and there seemed less and less prospect of this hope being fulfilled, many Jews postponed its realisation from history into eschatology* i.e. the events at and after the end of history. In the time of Jesus, both the second and third meanings were alive. Jesus himself claimed to be the Messiah, particularly in sense ii(b). This claim was and is rejected by believing Jews, who continue to expect the coming of the Messiah. Christians however accepted it: indeed the title 'Christ' is only the Greek for 'Messiah'. They believe not that the prophets foresaw the life of Jesus but that the life of Jesus fulfils these and other messianic prophecies (see p.549) and thus that the prophecies illuminate the life.

The messianic prophecy of Ch.9 takes the general form of a hymn, with particular echoes of the royal Ps 2 esp. vv.7-9. It has three parts. The first (2-3) announces a theme of joy, since God has delivered his people. The imagery of v.3e hints at what is then made explicit in the second part (4-5): the deliverance is from foreign invasion (for *Midian* see Jg 6-7). The invaders are presumably the Assyrians, since the word for *boots* is Assyrian. The third part (6-7) gives a third reason for rejoicing, which is developed so much more fully than the other two that it is clearly the climax of the poem.

Evidently a crown prince *has been born*, and the succession to the throne of David guaranteed. Isaiah has the highest expectations of his reign, but they are moral rather than military: indeed *peace* is a strong motif, picking up the theme of v.5, the decommissioning of the weapons. An unusual feature is the giving of the titles in v.6. This is modelled on the Egyptian custom, not otherwise attested in Israel, of giving honorific 'throne names' to a new king at his accession. The title *Mighty God* in particular is strong meat for the OT but common enough in the royal ideology of the ANE.

The hymn was thus composed by Isaiah, as 'prophet laureate', for a royal occasion. If the occasion was a birth, it is the only such poem extant from Israel. But the strong similarities to Hebrew enthronement psalms, coupled with the Egyptian parallel, suggest that it may have been composed rather for an accession: Ps 2.7 shows how the new king could be regarded as God's son. Either way the hymn is truly messianic. Jewish tradition attaches it firmly to Hezekiah son of Ahaz, upon whom great hopes were rested, not least by Isaiah (2 K 19).

As well as the two messianic prophecies of Chs 9 and 11, there is a third which is often taken to belong with them. It con-

First Messianic Prophecy (cont.)

sists of a single verse [7.14] which in the AV was translated as follows. 'The LORD himself shall give you a sign: Behold a virgin shall conceive and bear a son, and shall call his name Immanuel.' Since Matthew's gospel (1.23) quotes this verse as foretelling the 'virgin birth' of Jesus, it has inevitably been much debated – more ink is said to have been spilt over it than over any OT other verse. But both the Greek (LXX) translation, which Matthew used, and the AV misrepresented the Hebrew, which refers not to *a virgin* but to 'a young woman'. The verse therefore cannot conceivably foretell the 'virgin birth' of Jesus. But what it does mean is far from clear. Since the person who is to be given the sign is king Ahaz (grandson of king Uzziah of Ch.6), the young woman may be a wife of his. The *name* she is to give him, 'God with us', could well then have a messianic significance.

Ruin for the King of Assyria

10. 5   The Assyrian! He is the rod I wield in my anger,
            the staff in the hand of my wrath.

6   I send him against a godless nation,
            I bid him march against a people who rouse my fury,
    to pillage and plunder at will,
            to trample them down like mud in the street.

7   But this man's purpose is lawless,
            and lawless are the plans in his mind;
    for his thought is only to destroy
            and to wipe out nation after nation.

8   'Are not my commanders all kings?' he boasts.   ▸

Ruin for the King of Assyria

Isaiah now turns from the hubris of his own countrymen to that of *The Assyrian*. This time he introduces his utterance with the word *hoy*, sometimes translated 'woe' but here represented by REB's exclamation mark!

The Assyrians are indicted for the ruthlessness of their armies and the boastfulness of their kings. To make his point, Isaiah uses a dramatic device much favoured by OT prophets, the attribution of thoughts to the object of his criticism. The king of Assyria *boasts* that he has client *kings* to command his contingents (8a). Like any ANE monarch, he claims both power and *wisdom*, and goes on to show his contempt for the conventions of war. Finally (14) he expresses his scorn for his opponents in one of Isaiah's most brilliant conclusions: a vivid image, a triad to round off all the preceding pairs, and a diminuendo in which the crash of arms declines to total, deathly silence. The last two sentences are also highly onomatopoeic in the Hebrew (cp. AV 'peeped'): *pōtseh peh umetsaptsēp*.

The fascinating thing about this attributed interior monologue is the extent to which it is mirrored in the public records of the Assyrian kings themselves. For those of Sargon and Sennacherib, contemporaries of Isaiah, see notes on 2 K 17-18. The annals of Tiglath Pileser, Sargon's predecessor (744-727), say of Damascus: '592 towns (=villages) of the country of Damascus I destroyed, making them look like hills of ruined cities over which the floods had swept', and of Menahem king of Samaria [2 K 15.19]: 'I overwhelmed him like a snowstorm and he fled like a bird, alone' (*ANET* 283). An earlier Assyrian king Shalmaneser I began his 'throne inscription': 'I am Shalmaneser, who has smashed all his enemies like

Ruin for the King of Assyria (cont.)

13
    'By my own might I have done it,
        and in my own far-seeing wisdom
    I have swept aside the frontiers of nations
        and plundered their treasures;
        like a bull I have trampled on their inhabitants.

14
    My hand has come on the wealth of nations as on a nest,
        and, as one gathers eggs that have been abandoned,
        so have I taken every land;
    not a wing fluttered,
        not a beak gaped, no cheep was heard.'

15
    Will the axe set itself up against the hewer,
        or the saw claim mastery over the sawyer?

24
    The LORD of Hosts has sworn this oath:
    'As I purposed, so most surely it will be;
        as I planned, so it will take place:

25
    I shall break the Assyrian in my own land
        and trample him down on my mountains;
    his yoke will be lifted from my people,
        his burden taken from their shoulders.'

26
    This is the plan prepared for the whole world,
        this the hand stretched out over all the nations.

27
    For the LORD of Hosts has prepared his plan:
        who can frustrate it?
    His is the hand that is stretched out,
        and who can turn it back?   (REB)

Ruin for the King of Assyria (cont.)

earthenware, the strong man, unsparing, who shows no mercy in battle', and included in his annals the boast: 'With their corpses I spanned the Orontes before there was a bridge' (*ANET* 276, 279). Never was the device of attribution more fairly used.

But the LORD reminds him of the distinction between instrument and agent (v.15 picking up v.5) and goes on to overtrump him in every respect. The speech of the king of Assyria is answered by the speech of the king of kings. It is his plan, not that of the Assyrians, which will be realised, and it is a *plan* for *the whole world* (14.26 answers 10.7 and 13). The correspondences show that this is the missing conclusion to 10.5-15.

Second Messianic Prophecy

11. 1   A shoot shall come out from the stump of Jesse,
    and a branch shall grow out of his roots.

2   The spirit of the LORD shall rest on him,
    the spirit of wisdom and understanding,
the spirit of counsel and might,
    the spirit of knowledge and the fear of the LORD.

3   He shall not judge by what his eyes see,
    or decide by what his ears hear;

4   but with righteousness he shall judge the poor,
    and decide with equity for the meek of the earth;
he shall strike the earth with the rod of his mouth,
    and with the breath of his lips he shall kill the wicked.

5   Righteousness shall be the belt around his waist,
    and faithfulness the belt around his loins.

6   The wolf shall live with the lamb,
    the leopard shall lie down with the kid,
the calf and the lion and the fatling together,
    and a little child shall lead them.

7   The cow and the bear shall graze,
    their young shall lie down together;
and the lion shall eat straw like the ox.

8   The nursing child shall play over the hole of the asp,
    and the weaned child shall put its hand on the adder's den.

9   They will not hurt or destroy
    on all my holy mountain;
for the earth will be full of the knowledge of the LORD
    as the waters cover the sea.   (NRSV)

Second Messianic Prophecy

The finest of Isaiah's full messianic prophecies foretells the coming of a prince of David's house who will inaugurate a reign of justice and peace. It may be seen as an amplification of 9.7, and thus refer to a specific prince, born or enthroned as king. But the picture is so idealised that its affinities seem to lie rather with general ANE and Greco-Roman millenarian literature (see below). Be that as it may, it is superbly crafted and perennially inspiring.

From the family tree of *Jesse*, father of David, will spring a new scion. Upon him will *rest the spirit of the LORD*, as upon David after his anointing, a threefold spirit which will combine all the virtues claimed for ANE kings with *the fear of the LORD*.

The coming prince is depicted primarily as judge. He will not be impressed by appearances nor take note of hearsay (3). His verdicts, influenced by *equity* rather than by legal niceties, will tend to favour the weak as against the strong (in v.4c translate '*strike* the ruthless' with REB) – a motif which the royal ideology of Israel shared with that of the ANE.

In vv.6-7 we move to a new theme, the coming harmony of the animal world. Carnivore and herbivore will live together among animals as among humans – indeed the king of the carnivores will actually *become* a herbivore! The young herdsman of v.6d leads into the theme of v.8, which links those of vv.4-5 and 6-7,

Second Messianic Prophecy (cont.)

viz. the relation of humans and animals. Finally the harmony is generalised throughout the *holy* land (9a) and the poem comes back to its beginning by reference to *the* Lord as the inspiration of all.

The stately poetry suits the theme beautifully. Order and peace are suggested by long lines (all 3s and 4s) and by the parallelism, which is formal yet varied. (In v.6c LXX gives a preferable text, followed by REB: 'the calf and the lion *will feed* together'.) The brief violence of the imagery in v.4cd and the pyrotechnics of the illustrations in vv.6-8 contrast with the dignified simplicity of the abstract nouns which dominate the beginning (2-4b), middle (5) and end (9) of the poem. And the final cadence of v.9c is even finer in the Hebrew, which has the identical rhythm combined with assonance: *kammayīm layyām mekammīm.*

ANE parallels include the following. From a Sumerian paradise myth: 'the lion kills not, the wolf snatches not the lamb' (*ANET* 38). From a Sumerian epic: 'on this day there is no snake, no scorpion, no hyena, no lion . . . no anxiety, no fear, and men will have no more enemies' (*NERT* 86). From an Egyptian prophecy: 'Then it is that a king will come . . . the son of a woman in the land of Nubia . . . and justice will come into its place, while wrongdoing is driven out' (*ANET* 445-6). All these are centuries before Isaiah. And centuries *after* him was written the most famous Greco-Roman work in the same tradition, Vergil's Fourth Eclogue. This foretells the birth of a boy who in a republic like Rome could not be a king but is a son of Jupiter. He will inaugurate a period of worldwide peace in which, among other paradisal features, 'the cattle will have no fear of huge lions'. The enormous time-span of this kind of writing shows what a hold the millenarian idea has had upon the human imagination.

A Dirge for an Enemy King

4 See how still the oppressor has become,
how still his raging arrogance!
5 The Lord has broken the rod of the wicked,
the sceptre of rulers
6 who in anger struck down peoples
with unerring blows,
who in fury trod nations underfoot
with relentless persecution.

7 The whole world rests undisturbed;
it breaks into cries of joy.
8 The very pines and the cedars of Lebanon exult:
'Since you have been laid low,' they say,
'no woodman comes to cut us down.' ◆

A Dirge for an Enemy King

This 'song of derision' is one of the finest poems in the OT. It takes its rhythm (3:2) and much of its form from a funeral lament. But since it is a hated enemy who has died, the customary features of a lament are used for exultant parody. In content it is highly dramatic. There are five successive scenes, set with the usual symmetry in the following order: (i) earth, 4-8; (ii) Sheol i.e. the underworld, 9-11; (iii) heaven, 12-14; (iv) Sheol, 15-17; (v) earth, 18-21. The implied theme throughout is: 'the higher the pride, the further the fall'. That theme is common to all peo-

A Dirge for an Enemy King (cont.)

14. 9   Sheol below was all astir
        to greet you at your coming;
     she roused for you the ancient dead,
        all that were leaders on earth;
     she had all who had been kings of the nations
        get up from their thrones.

10   All greet you with these words:
     'So you too are impotent as we are,
        and have become like one of us!'

11   Your pride has been brought down to Sheol,
        to the throng of your victims;
     maggots are the mattress beneath you,
        and worms your coverlet.

12   Bright morning star,
        how you have fallen from heaven,
        thrown to earth, prostrate among the nations!

13   You thought to yourself:
     'I shall scale the heavens
        to set my throne high above the mighty stars;
     I shall take my seat on the mountain
        where the gods assemble
        in the far recesses of the north.

14   I shall ascend beyond the towering clouds
        and make myself like the Most High!'

A Dirge for an Enemy King (cont.)

ples, but nothing like this song survives from the ancient world outside the OT. In Hebrew literature there is a plethora of exultations over fallen enemies – political weakness left invective as the only available form of counter-attack – but all of them are more or less crude by comparison with this. It is notable that there is no specifically Hebrew reference in this poem after the initial mention of *the Lord*, and that looks like a later addition, since it throws out the strict metre.

(i) In the first section the irony is intense. In v.7 the phrase *the whole world rests* is a parody of the boast regularly used by kings sated with conquests. Verse 8 parodies two standard features of the dirge: the words of the bereaved family ('since you are dead, there is no one to protect us'); and the topos* of nature lamenting the departed. The *cedars* are here used as symbols of height – note the up-and-down counterpoint in v.8bc – and of royalty, since they were regularly used in the building of ANE palaces. There is also an implication of sacrilege, which is corroborated by an inscription of Nebuchadnezzar (*ANET* 306). He there describes Lebanon as 'the luxurious forest of [the God] Marduk, the high cedars of which no other king had felled' (a lie), and boasts of the 'mighty cedars, high and strong, of precious beauty and of excellent dark quality', which he carried off 'like reed-stalks'.

(ii) Conversations in the abode of the dead between those who have been leaders on earth are a feature of Greek literature too, from the *Odyssey* onwards, and rarely fail of their effect. The burden here lies on the words *you too* which stress his common humanity and underline the

A Dirge for an Enemy King (cont.)

15	Instead you are brought down to Sheol,
	into the depths of the abyss.
16	Those who see you stare at you,
	reflecting as they gaze:
	'Is this the man who shook the earth,
	who made kingdoms quake,
17	who turned the world into a desert
	and laid its cities in ruins,
	who never set his prisoners free?'
18	All the kings of every nation lie in honour,
	each in his last resting-place.
19	But you have been flung out without burial
	like some loathsome carrion,
	a carcass trampled underfoot,
	a companion to the slain pierced by the sword
	who have gone down to the stony abyss.
20	You will not be joined in burial with those kings,
	for you have ruined your land,
	brought death to your people.
	That wicked dynasty will never again be mentioned! (REB)

A Dirge for an Enemy King (cont.)

fall of his pride. The Hebrew concept of Sheol is very like that of the Greek Hades, and unlike the Christian Hell, but inevitably it is sometimes confused with the grave, as in v.11cd.

(iii) 'He himself is at length brought upon the stage' (Lowth). We move at this point into a famous theme of Ugaritic* and other myths. The way in which the morning star rises first but fades quickly after dawn led naturally to the myth that it had attempted to set itself up in opposition to the sun as supreme but had been cast down. REB's *bright morning star* represents Hebrew *Hebel* (bright one) son of *Shahar* (morning). The latter is a known divinity in the Ugaritic pantheon, and the former will doubtless prove to be another.

(iv) The formula *Is this the man who . . . ?* (16) is used to point the contrast between past renown and present ignominy; cp. [23.7] of the city of Tyre.

(v) The final section reverts to the parody of the funeral dirge, but text and translation are uncertain. REB's transla-

tion of v.19 envisages the tyrant slain in battle, his corpse lying unburied among those of his own troops. This is by contrast with the standard consolation of a funeral dirge, that the dead man has been properly buried *in his last resting place*. It is hard for a modern reader to imagine the horror which was felt throughout the ancient world at the thought of one's corpse being exposed to birds and beasts of prey, but the whole plot of Sophocles' *Antigone* hangs upon it. Verse 20d preempts another standard consolation, that the dead man's name lives on in his descendants. In the Hebrew both these verses are introduced by a strong negative: '*Not* share will you . . . ' and '*Not* be named will they'. But the final irony of the whole poem is precisely that it nowhere gives the name or even the country of the tyrant whose death it celebrates. In 1944, when the news of Hitler's suicide reached units of the German army, a pastor read parts of this dirge to the assembled troops. It was received in an awed silence.

An Enemy Assault Defeated

17. 12
Ah, the thunder of many peoples,
  they thunder like the thundering of the sea!
Ah, the roar of nations,
  they roar like the roaring of mighty waters!

13
The nations roar like the roaring of many waters,
  but he will rebuke them, and they will flee far away,
chased like chaff on the mountains before the wind
  and whirling dust before the storm.

14
At evening time, lo, terror!
  Before morning, they are no more.   (NRSV)

An Enemy Assault Defeated

Isaiah here draws on another ANE myth, God's defeat of the *Sea* or *mighty waters* (see p.27). Repetitions of *thunder* and *roar* (verbs and nouns), representing the assault of the sea, parallel exactly some lines of a Ugaritic poem about Baal, which run

Surges, surges the surge of the Sea,
the surge of the Sea against his throne.

Isaiah adds the effect of assonance: of v.13 Hebrew words in v.12, six end in -*īm* and five in -*ōn* or -*ūn*. The myth is here applied to an attack by a foreign army. Verse 14 could well refer to the disappearance of Sennacherib's troops in 701 BC (see 2 K 19.35, with Ps 46.5 'at break of day').

The Decline of Egypt

19. 5
The waters of the Nile will disappear,
  the river bed will be parched and dry,
  and its channels will give off a stench.

6
Egypt's canals will fail altogether;
  reeds and rushes will wither away.

7
The lotus beside the Nile
  and everything sown along the river will dry up;
  they will blow away and vanish.

8
The fishermen will groan and lament;
  all who cast their hooks into the Nile
  and those who spread nets on the water will lose heart.

9
The flax-dressers will be dejected,
  the women carding and the men weaving grow pale.

10
Egypt's spinners will be downcast,
  and all her artisans sick at heart.   (REB)

The Decline of Egypt

King Hezekiah, like his father Ahaz, thought he could protect his country against Assyria by political intrigue, this time with Egypt. Isaiah rejected all such manoeuvres: loyalty to the LORD was both necessary and sufficient for the salvation of Israel. Among his methods of discouragement was a series of oracles 'against' Egypt. This one is a dramatic precursor of a modern newspaper leader pointing out the weakness of a potential ally whose economy depends on a single source. Without *the Nile* and its annual flooding the fishing and textile industries would collapse, as would the export of papyrus. We have a remarkable parallel to this oracle in the Egyptian *Prophecy of Neferti* (*ANET* 445) c.1000 years earlier:

The Decline of Egypt (cont.)

'The rivers of Egypt are empty, so that the water is crossed on foot. . . . Damaged are those good things, those fish ponds overflowing with fish and fowl. . . . Everything good is disappeared'.

Fishing and weaving were favourite subjects in ancient Egyptian literature and art, as were the flora and fauna of the Nile.

International Harmony

23 • When that day comes there will be a highway between Egypt and Assyria. The Assyrians will link up with Egypt and the Egyptians with Assyria, and Egyptians will worship with Assyrians. • When that day comes Israel will rank as a third with Egypt and Assyria and be a blessing in the world. • This is the blessing the LORD of Hosts will give: 'Blessed be Egypt my people, Assyria my handiwork, and Israel my possession.'   (REB)

International Harmony

A later writer, in a moment of rare vision, suggests a different effect that the day of the LORD (*that day*) will have on international relations. The phrases *my people* and *my handiwork* are normally in the OT reserved for Israel; their use here to express the new generous spirit abroad is intentionally shocking. The shock was too much for the LXX translators, who renationalised the text to read: 'Blessed be my people who are in Egypt and in Assyria, and Israel my possession'.

Downfall of an Upstart

15 These were the words of the LORD, the LORD of Hosts:

    Go to the steward, this Shebna,
        comptroller of the household, and say:

16   What have you here, or whom have you here,
        that you have hewn out a tomb here for yourself?
    Why should he hew his tomb in an eminent place,
        and carve for himself a resting-place in the rock?

17   The LORD is about to shake you out,
        as a garment is shaken to rid it of lice;

18   he will roll you up tightly
        and throw you like a ball
    into a land of vast expanses.
        There you will die,
    and there your chariot of honour will remain,
        bringing disgrace on your master's household.   (REB)

Downfall of an Upstart

This is Isaiah's only oracle against a named individual. *Shebna* was an official at the court of king Hezekiah (2 K 18.18 'adjutant-general' REB). From small beginnings, he had risen to power in the state and was planning a suitably grandiose *rock-tomb* for himself just outside Jerusalem. Presumably his offence lay not only in this but in the part he had played in the king's equally grandiose policy of military alliance against Assyria. When the policy has proved unsuccessful, he will be deported into that *land of vast expanses*. The double *there* of v.18 answers and supersedes the treble *here* of v.16 as *disgrace* follows hard on the heels of *honour*.

The Day of the Lord (i): the Punishment

24. 1   See how the LORD lays the earth waste,
        makes it a desert, buckles its surface,
        scatters its inhabitants,

2   priest and people alike, master and slave,
        mistress and maid, seller and buyer,
        lender and borrower, creditor and debtor.

3   Ravaged, ravaged the earth will be,
        despoiled, despoiled,
    for the LORD has uttered this word.

4   The earth is mourning, pining away,
        the pick of earth's people are withering away.

5   The earth is defiled
        by the feet of its inhabitants,
    for they have transgressed the laws,
        violated the decree, broken the everlasting covenant.

6   That is why the curse has consumed the earth
        and its inhabitants pay the penalty,
    That is why the inhabitants of the earth have been burnt up
        and few people are left.

18   Yes, the sluice-gates above are open,
        the foundations of the earth are quaking.

19   A cracking, the earth cracks open,
        a jolting, the earth gives a jolt,
        a lurching, the earth lurches backwards and forwards.

20   The earth will reel to and fro like a drunkard,
        it will be shaken like a shanty;
    so heavy will be its sin on it,
        it will fall, never to rise again.   (NJB)

The Day of the Lord (i): the Punishment

Chs 24-27 are among the latest parts of Isaiah. They are concerned with the coming of God in judgement upon the whole earth and what happens thereafter. Many of their ideas were more fully developed in apocalyptic* books like Daniel.

In Ch. 24 the order of creation is being reversed; God himself is bringing chaos back, because men have *broken the covenant*, specifically that with Noah (Gen 9); its breach will be punished by a second Flood (v.18 echoes the wording of Gen 7.11). Other features of the visitation are earthquake (1,19) and depopulation (6).

The poet takes various stylistic features from Isaiah (the list of v.2, the verbal repetitions of 3 and 19, and the triplets of 5 and 19); but he adds an intensity, almost a frenzy, of his own, both of content (20d) and of language. NJB reproduces the repetitions, but no translation can convey the assonances of the Hebrew, which add their incantation to the general impression of a dirge, e.g. in vv.3 and 4a.

    hibbōq tibbōq hāārets
    wehibbōts tibbōts . . .
    āvlāh nāvlāh hāārets.

Bright in *Peake's Commentary* rendered it:
    Shattered-shivered is the earth,
    rent-riven,
    shaken-staggered is the earth.

The language may seem artificial – but at least nobody living in a nuclear age can say that it is too *strong* for the subject.

The Day of the Lord (ii): the Rewards

6   On this mountain the LORD of Hosts will prepare
    a banquet of rich fare for all the peoples,
a banquet of wines well matured,
    richest fare and well-matured wines strained clear.

7   On this mountain the LORD will destroy
    that veil shrouding all the peoples,
the pall thrown over all the nations.

8   He will destroy death for ever.
Then the LORD God will wipe away the tears
    from every face,
and throughout the world
    remove the indignities from his people.
The LORD has spoken.

19 Your dead will live,
    their bodies will rise again.
Those who sleep in the earth
    will awake and shout for joy;
for your dew is a dew of sparkling light,
    and the earth will bring those long dead to birth again.

. 1 On that day the LORD with his cruel sword,
    his mighty and powerful sword, will punish
Leviathan that twisting sea serpent,
    that writhing serpent Leviathan;
he will slay the monster of the deep.   (REB)

The Day of the Lord (ii): the Rewards

Apocalypses spoke not only of punishment but of rewards. One of the rewards is the final *banquet* spread by God on Mount Zion. Adjectives are rare in Hebrew, so the string of them describing the *wines* in v.6 has all the more force. Surprisingly, the banquet will be for *all peoples* – note the repeated *all* and *every*. There will follow a new era for mankind, including the abolition of *tears* and *death*.

Like many apocalyptic themes, this has close parallels in Ugaritic myth. The Baal epic (for which see p.772) tells of Baal's victory over Mot (Death), followed by a victory feast, at which his consort Anath says:

I will take war away from the earth,
banish all strife from the soil. (*ANET* 137)

Another reward in apocalyptic writing is some form of resurrection. Here in 26.19 it is evidently restricted to Jews, since the words *your* (sing.) *dead will rise again* come at the end of a hymn to YHWH. If the poet intended a literal resurrection, as in Dan 12.1f., he was probably the earliest OT writer to do so. But it may be only a metaphor for the ending of the dispersion (cp. the *indignities* of 25.8e).

Thirdly (27.1), God will once again *slay* the mythical sea-dragon of chaos, thus repeating his original act of creation. This time the Baal epic is so close that it is hard not to think of a direct influence from it. Some 25 lines before the couplet just quoted, Anath says:

The Day of the Lord (ii): the Rewards (cont)

I fought *the deep*, the beloved of El,
I bound *the monster* and slew him,
I fought the *writing serpent*.

The italicised words are identical between the two passages, and the serpent's name in Ugaritic is Lotan, the
same word as Heb. *Leviathan*. There is
a very similar passage in [Ps 74.13f.].

God the Farmer

28. 23   Listen and hear what I say,
                attend and hear my words.

24   Will the ploughman spend his whole time ploughing,
                breaking up his ground and harrowing it?

25   Does he not, once he has levelled it,
                broadcast the dill and scatter the cummin?
        Does he not put in the wheat and barley in rows,
                and vetches along the edge?

26   Does not his God instruct him
                and train him aright?

27   Dill must not be threshed with a threshing-sledge,
                nor the cartwheel rolled over cummin;
        but dill is beaten out with a rod,
                and cummin with a flail.

28   Grain is crushed, but not too long or too finely;
                cartwheels runble over it and thresh it,
                but they do not grind it fine.

29   Even this knowledge comes from the LORD of Hosts,
                whose counsel is wonderful
                and whose wisdom is great.   (REB)

God the Farmer

This little poem has a more classical *shape* than almost any in the OT. Its two stanzas are of equal length; each deals eith a separate aspect of an arable farmer's life; and each ends by ascribing the relevant wisdom to God. Most of it is typical of ANE Wisdom: the opening couplet, the phrase *his God* (26) and the doctrine of the 'proper time' (24, 28).

Any wise farmer knows that not all cereal crops are sown alike. *Dill* and *cummin*, being cheap, are scattered *broadcast*; *wheat*, being valuable, needs care; *vetches* will grow in the poor ground at the *edge* of the field. Similarly, not all crops are threshed alike. Heavy instruments are too rough for cereals whose seeds are easily lost. Wheat may be threshed, but *not too long*; after that, it must be winnowed.

In the last two lines Isaiah claims the parable for Israel by identifying the *God* of v.26 with *the LORD of Hosts*. As the source of the farmer's *wisdom*, he too knows what he is doing and when. So by implication, Isaiah's hearers must be patient.

The Cracked Wall

12 | These are the words of the Holy One of Israel:
> You have rejected this warning
> > and put your trust in devious and dishonest practices
> > on which you lean for support,

13 | > therefore you shall find this iniquity
> > like a crack running down
> a high wall, which bulges out
> > and suddenly, all in an instant,
> > comes crashing down.

14 | > It crashes and breaks like an earthen jar
> > shattered beyond repair,
> so that among the fragments not a shard is found
> > to take an ember from the hearth,
> > or to scoop water from a pool.   (REB)

The Cracked Wall

This brief oracle has lost its head, so we have to infer that the *rejected warning* was against social injustice. It is a fine example of Isaiah's imagery: indeed the composition clearly began with the poet's seeing the image itself. The *practices* to which certain people looked for *support* will come *crashing down* (a typical reversal) as *a wall* crashes: we imagine the destruction of the walls of Jerusalem and perhaps also the crack in the fabric of society which will precede it. The wall in turn is compared to a broken *jar*. This was a regular comparison in ANE royal rhetoric (Ps 2.9n.) and it is here further personalised by the addition of *beyond repair* (NRSV 'ruthlessly', Heb. 'he will not spare'). It conjures up the vision of survivors scraping together the means of subsistence (fire and *water*) among the ruins. The diminuendo at the close is characteristic of Isaiah.

Destruction and Desolation for Edom

4. 1 | Come near and listen, you nations,
> pay attention, you peoples.

2 | For the LORD is angry with all the nations,
> enraged with all their hordes.

4 | The heavens will be rolled up like a scroll
> and all their array will fade away,
> as fade the leaves falling from the vine,
> > as fade those falling from the fig tree.

5 | For my sword has drunk deep in the heavens:
> see how it now falls on Edom,
> on the people vowed to destruction,
> > to punish them.   ♦

Destruction and Desolation for Edom

With Chs 34 and 35 we move closer to the apocalyptic tone of Chs 24-7. They are juxtaposed to form a pair on the 'weal and woe' principle. The images of 34.4 are not biblical, probably coming from Babylonian star-myths. The *sword* of v.5 skilfully brings the scene down to earth, where God's judgement *falls* on Israel's hostile neighbour *Edom*, whose fate will be that of nearby Sodom and Gomorrah (9).

Destruction and Desolation for Edom (cont.)

34. 9
> Its streams will turn into pitch,
>> its dust into brimstone,
> its country will turn into blazing pitch.
>> no one will travel through it for ever and ever.

13
> Brambles will grow in its bastions,
>> nettles and thorn-bushes in its fortresses,
> it will be the lair of jackals,
>> an enclosure for ostriches.

14
> Wild cats will meet hyenas there,
>> satyr will call to satyr,
> there Lilith too will lurk
>> and find somewhere to rest.

15
> The snake will nest and lay eggs there,
>> will hatch and gather its young into the shade;
> and there the vultures will assemble,
>> each one with its mate.   (NJB)

Destruction and Desolation for Edom (cont.)

There follows a long description of the desolation of the wretched country. By contrast to the violent activity of verses 2-5, there is now no sound to be heard or movement to be seen but that of wild and unclean animals. The picture here is presented in terms which occur also in the curses attached to ANE vassal-treaties. For example an inscription of c.750 BC contains the following curse upon the city of Arpad in case of a breach: 'The sound of the lyre shall not be heard, only lamentation. . . . Its vegetation will not ripen. Arpad will be a desolated mound for gazelles, foxes, hares, wild-cats, owls and magpies' (*ANET* 660). A mythological note is added by the reference in v.14 the *satyr* and the night-hag (Heb. *Lilith*, a Babylonian demon). All these creatures have ousted human beings.

Streams in the Desert

35. 1
> The wilderness and the dry land shall be glad,
>> the desert shall rejoice and blossom;

2
> like the crocus it shall blossom abundantly,
>> and rejoice with joy and singing.
> The glory of Lebanon shall be given to it,
>> the majesty of Carmel and Sharon.
> They shall see the glory of the LORD,
>> the majesty of our God.   ♦

Streams in the Desert

Ch.35, it has been said, follows Ch.34 as Dante's *Paradiso* follows his *Inferno*. But it is not simply a case of joy replacing sadness and 'white' images replacing 'black'. To some extent, the process that occurred in the second half of 34 is reversed in the first half of 35. There a *wilderness* was created, here it is abolished. Some of the actual words are picked up: *streams* i.e. wadis in 34.9 and 35.6, the *lair/haunt of jackals* in 34.13 and 35.7. The depopulation of 34 is answered by the stress in 35 upon the presence of *God's people*; and even *the desert* will *rejoice* and sing.

Streams in the Desert (cont.)

3   Strengthen the weak hands,
       and make firm the feeble knees.
4   Say to those who are of a fearful heart,
       'Be strong, do not fear!
    Here is your God.
       He will come with vengeance,
    with terrible recompense.
       He will come and save you.'
5   Then the eyes of the blind shall be opened,
       and the ears of the deaf unstopped;
6   then the lame shall leap like a deer,
       and the tongue of the speechless sing for joy.
    For waters shall break forth in the wilderness,
       and streams in the desert;
7   the burning sand shall become a pool,
       and the thirsty ground springs of water;
    the haunt of jackals shall become a swamp,
       the grass shall become reeds and rushes.
8   A highway shall be there,
       and it shall be called the Holy Way;
    the unclean shall not travel on it,
       but it shall be for God's people;
       no traveler, not even fools, shall go astray.
9   No lion shall be there,
       nor shall any ravenous beast come up on it;
    they shall not be found there,
       but the redeemed shall walk there.
10   And the ransomed of the LORD shall return,
       and come to Zion with singing;
    everlasting joy shall be upon their heads;
       they shall obtain joy and gladness,
       and sorrow and sighing shall flee away.   **(NRSV)**

Streams in the Desert (cont.)

Nevertheless the two poems were clearly not designed as a diptych. Edom plays no part in 35, nor are there enough correspondences between the two chapters in the descriptive imagery, which is dominated in 34 by animals, in 35 by water and plants, focused upon the flowering of the desert. Moreover in 35 this miraculous flowering accompanies and symbolises other mighty works. The infirm will be healed (5-6), a Sacred Way opened, and the LORD's *redeemed* will return home along it. The whole picture contains many details found in 'messianic' literature both in the OT and outside it (see commentary on 9.2-7). But the closest resemblance is to Is 40.1-11 and 41.18-20. Indeed there are many signs here of the pen of Second Isaiah. As well as ideas like those of the *ransom*, the *highway* and *streams in the desert*, the exhortation *do not fear* is a favourite of his, as is the 3:3:4 rhythm of vv.3-4b (cp. 40.21 etc.).

Isaiah 40–66

With Ch.40 of the Book of Isaiah we move into a new world, that of exile in Babylon. We know that for some of the deportees life was quite pleasant. But the despairing cry of Ps 137 catches the deepest feelings of the time and expresses the lasting scar upon the national consciousness. On the one hand they saw themselves as being the 'true' Jerusalem; on the other they hoped against hope for a return from the waters of Babylon to their own rocky citadel. For such men the author of Chs 40-55, known to us as Second Isaiah (I²), wrote his message of comfort.

It was not long after the death of Nebuchadnezzar in 562 BC that the Babylonian empire began to crumble. Among its tributaries had always been two related Indo-European tribes, the Medes and Persians, of whom the Medes were the senior partner. But in 559 BC Cyrus II, king of Persia, took the internal leadership from the Medes, and then in 546 he startled the world by attacking and defeating Croesus, king of Lydia. That victory took him to the shores of the Aegean and provided him with legendary wealth. But almost more striking was the clemency he showed to his defeated enemies, famously narrated by Herodotus. A new and doubly bright star had risen in the ANE. In 539 his troops occupied Babylon itself, and he gave the Jewish exiles permission to return home (see p.344). During those seven years after 546 I² was able to foresee both the fall of the city and the return of the exiles.

His message therefore is entirely different in tone from that of the pre-exilic prophets. The sins which they castigated had met the punishment which they foretold. Threats and warnings are now no longer in place; nor are reproaches or even arguments, except against two linked failings: apostasy and timidity. The success of Babylonian arms had, in the eyes of some Jews, been reinforced by the pomp of Babylonian myth and ritual; the LORD on the other hand seemed to have deserted them. Against this defeatism, I² insists with all the force at his command that the LORD is transcendent, master both of creation and of history, the 'Holy One of Israel' and the only ruler of princes. It is in this respect that his message, and even his terminology, is most clearly akin to that of Isaiah[1], though the tone is gentler: the LORD is 'Holy One' *and* 'Redeemer' (54.5 etc.). Heathen gods by contrast are things of nothing, objects of ridicule like their worshippers. But the main thrust of I²'s mind is not on the past nor even on the present but on the future, on what the LORD *will do*. He will intervene to save and restore his people, and he will do so freely and unconditionally (55.1). He will also (in some sense and at some ultimate time) incorporate the gentiles into his kingdom.

The oracles of I² have a new historical context, a new message – and also new forms. Of the old forms (see p.520), only the reproach and the argument survive, both somewhat attenuated. Centre stage is held by two forms which derive rather from psalms – and here one must remember how much there is in common between Hebrew and Babylonian psalms. First is the hymn of praise to God and of confidence in him. Second is what is known technically as the 'salvation oracle', the moment (relatively rare in the Hebrew psalms we have – see p.411) when the priest or the temple prophet replies on behalf of God to the worshipper with the assurance that God has heard him and will save him. The latter is characteristic of I², especially when the words are spoken by God himself in the first person. These two forms are clearly cognate in tone, and so we commonly find them combined, with a brief hymn typically concluding the salvation oracle.

Second Isaiah's work is also much more unified than any other prophet's.

Some scholars suppose both that his oracles were circulated in written form, to escape the attention of the Babylonian authorities, and that he himself edited them i.e. put them together in their present shape. At any rate the same feeling-tone prevails almost throughout Chs 40-55. Not that there is much in the way of logical or chronological sequence or even dramatic shape visible. For the most part the same themes are repeated, developed, transposed, interwoven, as in a symphonic poem.

The same goes for most of the images. There are three great unifying images in Second Isaiah. The most comprehensive is water, the multifarious symbol – physically of creation and life, spiritually of recreation or redemption, geographically of the return home across the desert. Water is the centre of a cluster of interrelated images which recur in rotation throughout the book. The other two images are personal figures and therefore capable of some dramatic development. The better known is the servant of the LORD, of whom more is revealed on four successive occasions in Chs 42-53 (see further below). The more complex is a female figure, that of Zion (i.e. Jerusalem) as God's wife: first beloved, then childless and/or rejected, but finally restored to love and motherhood, she binds together Chs 49-55.

Chs 40-55 have been similarly 'smoothed' into the scroll of Isaiah – indeed they may never have been published separately, any more than Chs 1-39. There is no obvious new beginning at 40.1 or end at 55.13. True, Ch.40 is seen, on closer inspection, to record an inaugural vision, but it reads almost as an echo of Ch.6, with nothing to signal a new author or a new date. Within Chs 1-39 there are also various forward links, some of which may be from the pen of I[2] himself (see commentary on Ch. 35, and also The Isaiah Scroll p.522).

The so-called 'servant songs' of I[2] are an exception to what was said above about structural sequence. Here we seem to have four poems which gradually build up a biographical portrait of an ideal servant of the LORD – his call, his mission, his suffering, death and vindication. Though they are so firmly embedded into their context that it is often hard to tell where each individual poem begins and ends (in this selection they are taken to be 42.1-7; 49.1-6; 50.4-7; 52.13 - 53.12), scholarly opinion is united in seeing them as a group. It is far from united, however, in answering the question: in writing of the servant, whom did the author have in mind?

To this question – one of the most interesting and disputed in the whole OT – there are two main kinds of answer. First, the traditional Jewish answer is clear: the prophet meant the nation of Israel, as he says in e.g. 49.3. On this view, which is shared by an increasing number of Christian scholars, the portrait of the servant as an individual is only the imaginative extension of such common OT phrases as 'Israel, my son'. Other interpreters take the personal details as evidence that an individual was intended – though that individual might himself be in some sense a representative Israelite. The NT authors certainly interpreted the life of Jesus in the light of the servant songs, especially the fourth; and that interpretation probably went back to Jesus himself. That would not of course imply that I[2] 'foresaw' the coming of Jesus of Nazareth; rather that I[2] was thought to be writing about a coming Messiah, and Jesus applied the prophecy to himself i.e. he saw his own life as fulfilling it.

Alternatively the servant may be a representative prophet. It is indeed striking how far the especial characteristics of the suffering servant correspond to those of Jeremiah, 'despised and rejected of men', 'a man of sorrows', who could 'offer his back to the smiters' and also 'set his face like a flint', and whose sufferings were certainly in some sense *on behalf of* his people (cp.

Mt 16.15, where some thought Jesus to be 'Jeremiah or one of the prophets' returned). Others have even seen in the suffering servant a self-portrait by I², an identification which would profoundly affect our reading of Chs 40-55.

There are in fact some good arguments for and against all these alternatives. On balance it is the traditional Jewish interpretation that seems the most convincing i.e. I² had primarily in mind the Jewish nation. But once he had decided to personify the nation in this way, it was natural both that he should incorporate into his portrait some elements drawn from representative individuals, and that some subsequent readers should apply that portrait to a later individual.

The Prophet's Call and Message

40. 1 Comfort, O comfort my people,
  says your God.

2 Speak tenderly to Jerusalem,
  and cry to her
 that she has served her term,
  that her penalty is paid,
 that she has received from the LORD's hand
  double for all her sins.

3 A voice cries out:
 'In the wilderness prepare the way of the LORD,
  make straight in the desert a highway for our God.

4 Every valley shall be lifted up,
  and every mountain and hill be made low;
 the uneven ground shall become level,
  and the rough places a plain.

5 Then the glory of the LORD shall be revealed,
  and all people shall see it together,
  for the mouth of the LORD has spoken.'

The Prophet's Call and Message

The 'book' of Second Isaiah opens with a carefully constructed poem which both summarises his message and claims God's authority for it. In function and form the poem is comparable to the narrative of his predecessor's inaugural vision in Ch.6, though there are many points of difference, as would be expected after a lapse of 150 years and a move from Jerusalem to Babylon.

The first difference is of setting. The prophet receives his commission from God not in his Temple but in his heavenly council. The council is referred to often enough in the OT (e.g. Gen 1.26 'in our image'; Ps 82.1), and it was accepted that prophets were admitted to it (e.g. Is 6.8 'for us'). Here it is the members of the council, including the prophet, who are commanded (in the plural) to *comfort my people*. Those same members are the singers in this 'cantata for many voices' (NJB). But they are not named or identified, nor is it easy to allocate the speeches between them and the poet himself. There is thus an air of mystery here which serves, like the vision of Ch.6, to emphasise the transcendence of God.

The whole poem (1-11) is spoken or sung by the prophet himself, addressing the people in exile (*your God* of 1). It is he who introduces the other speakers: first

The Prophet's Call and Message (cont.)

6 A voice says, 'Cry out!'
  And I said, 'What shall I cry?'
  All people are grass,
      their constancy is like the flower of the field.
7 The grass withers, the flower fades,
      when the breath of the LORD blows upon it;
      surely the people are grass.
8 The grass withers, the flower fades;
      but the word of our God will stand forever.

9 Get you up to a high mountain,
      O herald of good tidings to Zion;
  lift up your voice with strength,
      O herald of good tidings to Jerusalem,
      lift it up, do not fear;
  say to the cities of Judah,
      'Here is your God!'   ▸

The Prophet's Call and Message (cont.)

God himself (1-2); then an angel (3-5); then a second angel (6), from whom after an exchange (6-8) he takes over in his own voice (9-11). The dramatic structure thus provides a movement from God via the angels to the poet i.e. from heaven to earth. In content there is likewise a movement, from the punishment of the exile through the journey across the desert to the arrival back in the holy land.

The poem falls into four corresponding sections. The first opens with the new note of *comfort*. Israel has *paid her penalty* (*double* in v.2 is of course not literal), and she is free to look forward.

The second section (3-5), which envisages the return across *the desert*, combines two associations. In the foreground is the notion with which the exiles were familiar from Babylonian festivals, of the processional route along which the god's statue was carried, cp. a hymn to Nebo:

Make his way good, renew his road,
Make straight the path, hew out for him
  a track.

But behind it lies the national appeal of the original exodus from Egypt.

The dramatic entry of the prophet himself in v.6 is owed to the Dead Sea Scroll of Isaiah. Other Hebrew mss give 'he said', but modern translations have gratefully followed the reading of the scroll. That however still leaves a problem. The beautiful verses 6-8, which are clearly adapted from Ps 103. 15-17, seem to have little relevance in their new context. An attractive suggestion is to punctuate the exchange differently as follows:

Angel: Cry!
Prophet: What shall I cry?
      All people are grass . . .
      The grass withers, the flower fades.
      Surely the people are grass?
Angel: 'The grass withers, the flower fades.'
      But the word of our God will stand
      for ever.

The prophet is then demurring at his 'call', as many other prophets demurred. His ground is that the people are too weak to respond to his message. But the angel sets the strength of God's word against the weakness of the people – a major theme of the rest of the book.

In the fourth section the prophet instructs a herald to proclaim the good news

The Prophet's Call and Message (cont.)

40.10
See, the Lord GOD comes with might,
  and his arm rules for him;
his reward is with him,
  and his recompense before him.

11
He will feed his flock like a shepherd;
  he will gather the lambs in his arms,
and carry them in his bosom,
  and gently lead the mother sheep.

(NRSV)

The Prophet's Call and Message (cont.)

to the homeland. God himself is portrayed first as a victorious commander, distributing the spoils; but the picture modulates to that of *shepherd*, to recapture the softer tone of the opening. The bathos of *the mother sheep* at the end is a sad come-down from the lovely clausula of AV 'and shall gently lead those that are with young'.

The Power of the Lord

40.18
To whom then will you liken God,
  or what likeness compare with him?

21
Have you not known? Have you not heard?
  Has it not been told you from the beginning?
  Have you not understood from the foundations of the earth?

22
It is he who sits above the circle of the earth,
  and its inhabitants are like grasshoppers;
who stretches out the heavens like a curtain,
  and spreads them like a tent to live in;

23
who brings princes to naught,
  and makes the rulers of the earth as nothing.

24
Scarcely are they planted, scarcely sown,
  scarcely has their stem taken root in the earth,
when he blows upon them, and they wither,
  and the tempest carries them off like stubble.

25
To whom then will you compare me,
  or who is my equal? says the Holy One.

26
Lift up your eyes on high and see:
  Who created these?
He who brings out their host and numbers them,
  calling them all by name;
because he is great in strength,
  mighty in power,
  not one is missing.

The Power of the Lord

The last part of Ch.40 consists of two linked poems. In each of them the prophet rebuts an objection from his countrymen. The first objection (v.18) is implied: that the LORD cannot save them, because he is weaker than the Babylonian gods.

The second is explicit (27): that he has lost interest in them. The two rebuttals,

---

The Power of the Lord (cont.)

27   Why do you say, O Jacob,
          and speak, O Israel,
      'My way is hidden from the LORD,
          and my right is disregarded by my God'?
28   Have you not known? Have you not heard?
      The LORD is the everlasting God,
          the Creator of the ends of the earth.
      He does not faint or grow weary;
          his understanding is unsearchable.
29   He gives power to the faint,
          and strengthens the powerless.
30   Even youths will faint and be weary,
          and the young will fall exhausted;
31   but those who wait for the LORD shall renew their strength,
          they shall mount up with wings like eagles,
      they shall run and not be weary,
          they shall walk and not faint.   (NRSV)

The Power of the Lord (cont.)

introduced by parallel challenges (21 and 28) are typically Hebrew i.e. not so much arguments as counter-assertions, based on a recall to their ancestral faith. The first is direct, that the LORD is the creator of everything; the second indirect, that he is constant and, if they are constant too, he can impart to them his *strength*.

The style in each case draws upon the hymnic tradition, common to Babylon and the Hebrew psalter. This is seen in the use of participles of praise – the verbs of vv.22, 26cd and 29, all rendered as main verbs, are in fact participles. The incomparability topos* of vv.18 and 25 is frequent in Babylonian hymns e.g. of Ishtar 'To her greatness who can be equal?'

As to content, the cosmography of v.22 is also common to both traditions. The Babylonian creation myth was publicly recited as part of the annual New Year Festival, and Isaiah is here explicitly claiming for YHWH the honours ascribed in it to Marduk as Lord of creation (22) and of history (23-4). In v.26 he goes further, insisting that *the Holy One* actually *created* the other gods. That too is a regular feature of ANE hymns, but in this case it is the more plausible in that the Babylonian gods were all identified with the stars, the greater with the planets, the lesser with the fixed stars. The Babylonian myth ascribes great importance to the *calling them by name* (26): it lists 50 titles for Marduk with their meanings. But YHWH uses the names of the gods to summon them on parade in demonstration of his superior power.

The motif of the *power* of the LORD is carried over into the second poem (27-31). But as in v.11 it modulates to a note of tenderness as the poet encourages the faint-hearted in a beautifully constructed passage. The paired adjectives *faint* and *weary* provide a chiastic* frame (28d and 31cd), and the threefold decrescendo of 31b-d makes a marvellous conclusion. I² makes even more use than I¹ of the triplet. Perhaps his favourite form of it is one which may be expressed as 1+1+2, as in 40.24ab, 41.10cd, 42.2 etc. But there are many other varieties of triplet which he uses with great skill to avoid any monotony in the typical binary parallelism.

Promises of Salvation

41. 8   But you, Israel, my servant,
             Jacob, whom I have chosen,
             the offspring of Abraham, my friend;

9   you whom I took from the ends of the earth,
             and called from its farthest corners,
             saying to you, 'You are my servant,
             I have chosen you and not cast you off';

10   do not fear, for I am with you,
             do not be afraid, for I am your God;
             I will strengthen you, I will help you,
             I will uphold you with my victorious right hand.

14   Do not fear, you worm Jacob,
             you insect Israel!
             I will help you, says the LORD;
             your Redeemer is the Holy One of Israel.

15   Now, I will make of you a threshing sledge,
             sharp, new, and having teeth;
             you shall thresh the mountains and crush them,
             and you shall make the hills like chaff.

16   You shall winnow them and the wind shall carry them away,
             and the tempest shall scatter them.
             Then you shall rejoice in the LORD;
             in the Holy One of Israel you shall glory.   ▸

Promises of Salvation

From Ch.41 come three poems of encouragement to the exiles. Each adapts the form of a well known type of psalm, where a plea to God is answered by a so-called salvation oracle (see p.411). In the psalms most of the space and emphasis is given to the complaint, with the appellant stressing his present misfortune. Here however the emphasis falls increasingly upon the promises: the *servant* will be strong (10), the *worm* will overcome all obstacles (15), the *poor and needy* (17) and the thirsty ones will be given *water* in *the wilderness* as they return to the holy land.

Behind the psalms lie ANE formulae. A series of oracles given on behalf of Ishtar to Esarhaddon king of Assyria c.760 BC (*ANET* 449f.) contain the following close parallels to the language of I²:

> Esarhaddon, fear not. . . . I am the great divine lady, I am Ishtar of Arbela. . . . I will go before you and behind you. . . .

> When you were small I sustained you. . . . 'Fear not, O King', I said to you, 'I have not abandoned you'. . . . I love you greatly.

We see there the basic ingredients of such salvation oracles. The deity (i) identifies herself and (ii) addresses the suppliant with (iii) a formula of encouragement, most commonly 'Fear not'; she reminds him (iv) of past support ('I have . . .') and promises (v) the same for the future ('I will . . .'). All those ingredients are found in 41.8-10.

But, as usual with I², the ANE formulae are used in the service of a deeper theology. The concept of 'servant', here first mentioned (8), he will develop along entirely new lines. As titles of God he uses his predecessor's favourite *the Holy One of Israel*, and adds his own *Redeemer**.

Typical of Hebrew poetry is also the violent and at first sight incongruous imagery of 14-16. First, the *worm* of 14, trodden under foot, is transformed into

Promises of Salvation (cont.)

17   When the poor and needy seek water,
      and there is none,
      and their tongue is parched with thirst,
    I the LORD will answer them,
      I the God of Israel will not forsake them.

18   I will open rivers on the bare heights,
      and fountains in the midst of the valleys;
    I will make the wilderness a pool of water,
      and the dry land springs of water.

19   I will put in the wilderness the cedar,
      the acacia, the myrtle, and the olive;
    I will set in the desert the cypress,
      the plane and the pine together,

20   so that all may see and know,
      all may consider and understand,
    that the hand of the LORD has done this,
      the Holy One of Israel has created it.   (NRSV)

Promises of Salvation (cont.)

an instrument which does the treading. The *sledge* is a board studded with nails used for separating the grain from the chaff. The *mountains* and *hills* are the obstacles both literal and metaphorical to the return of the exiles, as in 40.4. Similarly the imagery of 17-19 is neither narrowly factual nor vaguely romantic. It would make factual sense: for example, an inscription of Pharaoh Seti I c.1300 BC records the setting up of a watering place in the desert; and the trees of 19 do give shade. But as always with I² the imagery has one foot in the world of space and time and one in the world of God's purpose for his people. Every word of v.18 has both a literal and a metaphorical meaning, and no one can say which has priority.

First Servant Song: God's Commission

2.1   Here is my servant, whom I uphold,
      my chosen, in whom my soul delights;
    I have put my spirit upon him;
      he will bring forth justice to the nations.

2   He will not cry or lift up his voice,
      or make it heard in the street;

3   a bruised reed he will not break,
      and a dimly burning wick he will not quench;
      he will faithfully bring forth justice.

4   He will not grow faint or be crushed
      until he has established justice in the earth;
      and the coastlands wait for his teaching.

First Servant Song: God's Commission

In the first of the four servant songs (see p.549) God tells how he commissioned the servant for his task: to *establish justice* in the earth. The phrase is repeated with variations three times (1, 3, 4). The English word *justice* represents a Hebrew word which has a far wider meaning. When God turns to address the servant directly (6-7), the emphasis upon illumination implies a prophetic mission *to the*

First Servant Song: God's Commission (cont.)

42. 5   Thus says God, the LORD,
      who created the heavens and stretched them out,
         who spread out the earth and what comes from it,
      who gives breath to the people upon it
         and spirit to those who walk in it:

6   I am the LORD, I have called you in righteousness,
      I have taken you by the hand and kept you;
   I have given you as a covenant to the people,
      a light to the nations,

7   to open the eyes that are blind,
      to bring out the prisoners from the dungeon,
      from the prison those who sit in darkness.

8   I am the LORD, that is my name;
      my glory I give to no other,
      nor my praise to idols.

9   See, the former things have come to pass,
      and new things I now declare;
   before they spring forth,
      I tell you of them.   (NRSV)

First Servant Song: God's Commission (cont.)

nations; so presumably does the obscure *covenant*.

As to the conduct of the mission, the negative images of vv.2 and 3 seem to say that he will not shout people down or be overbearing in the kind of way the world expects of a charismatic figure. But neither (4) will he himself be overborne or discouraged. The verbs in v.4a are the same as those just used in v.3ab, and a literal translation of v.4a would run 'he will not *burn dimly* or be *bruised*'. The description so far could fit either the Jewish nation or an individual.

Verse 9 is taken by some to refer to the structure of the Isaiah scroll. *The former things* are then the oracles of I[1], the *new things* those of I[2].

A Satire on Idolatry

44. 14 A man plants a cedar and the rain makes it grow, so that later on he will have a tree to cut down; or he picks out in the forest an ilex or an oak which he will raise 16 into a stout tree for himself. • One half of the wood he burns in the fire and on this he roasts meat, so that he may eat this and be satisfied; he also warms himself and he says, 'Good! I can feel the heat as I watch the flames.' • Then what is left of the wood he makes into a god, an image to which he bows down and prostrates himself; he prays to it and says, 'Save me; for you are my god.'   (REB)

A Satire on Idolatry

The OT contains many satires on idolatry. Most of them are rather ponderous; this, though not by I[2], has a certain lightness of touch. Not that it is serious theology, for there is plenty of evidence that educated worshippers of pagan gods did not confuse the idol with the deity; but it may have been effective if directed to Jews inclined to apostasy. There is no ANE parallel to it, but a satire of Horace (1.8) makes the same point in the same shape, so it was probably something of a topos*. Horace's craftsman, having a log of fig-wood, wonders whether to make a bench or a statue of Priapus, and 'preferred it to be a god'.

Cyrus as God's Agent

24 Thus says the LORD, your Redeemer,
who formed you from birth:
I am the LORD who made all things,
by myself I stretched out the heavens,
alone I fashioned the earth.

25 I frustrate false prophets and their omens,
and make fools of diviners;
I reverse what wise men say
and make nonsense of their wisdom.

26 I confirm my servants' prophecies
and bring about my messengers' plans.
Of Jerusalem I say, 'She will be inhabited once more,'
and of the towns of Judah, 'They will be rebuilt;
I shall restore their ruins.'

27 I say to the deep waters, 'Be dried up;
I shall make your streams run dry.'

28 I say to Cyrus, 'You will be my shepherd
to fulfil all my purpose,
so that Jerusalem may be rebuilt
and the foundations of the temple be laid.'   ▸

Cyrus as God's Agent

We now come to the dramatic climax of I²'s message. The high generalities give place to a specific prediction, the most remarkable one in the whole of OT prophecy. It is that the Persian king Cyrus is God's own appointed agent for the overthrow of the Babylonian empire and the release of the Jews. The prediction is preceded by an argument designed to make it nevertheless credible.

The argument (44.24-8) is in essence the LORD's claim to sole control of cosmic and human affairs. In form it again uses the Babylonian hymn-style. The participles used for this in Hebrew, as in Babylonian, are best rendered in English as timeless nouns, e.g. *your redeemer,* rather than by verbs in the past (*who formed* etc.) or the present tense (*I frustrate* etc.). The line of argument is that God alone created the world (24), and he alone plans and knows the course of history (25). (As a matter of fact, whereas a number of Hebrew prophets warned of the fall of Jerusalem, the fall of Babylon was not, as far as we know, foretold by any of the Babylonian *diviners*.) God's plans include the future of his chosen people (26) and the overthrow of Babylon (hinted at in 27). Then comes a shock for Jewish ears. The utterances put into YHWH's mouth in 26-28 are all quotations from familiar psalms. But suddenly they are told that the man he has chosen as his *shepherd* is not, as they would expect in a psalm, David, but the Persian *Cyrus*.

Finally in 45.1 comes what is little short of an affront: Cyrus is actually *his anointed*! Isaiah of Jerusalem had called the Assyrian king 'the rod of my anger', but never before (or indeed after) in the OT is a gentile said to be anointed. However what is given with one hand is taken away with the other. Tremendous emphasis is laid upon the fact that all his victories and honours are a gift from the LORD. God's immediate motive is the rescue of Israel his *servant* (a title denied to Cyrus);

Cyrus as God's Agent (cont.)

45. 1 Thus says the LORD to Cyrus his anointed,
    whom he has taken by the right hand,
subduing nations before him
    and stripping kings of their strength;
before whom doors will be opened
    and no gates barred:

2 I myself shall go before you
    and level the swelling hills;
I shall break down bronze gates
    and cut through iron bars.

3 I shall give you treasures from dark vaults,
    and hoards from secret places,
so that you may know that I am the LORD,
    Israel's God, who calls you by name.

4 For the sake of Jacob my servant
    and Israel my chosen one
I have called you by name
    and given you a title, though you have not known me.

5 I am the LORD, and there is none other;
    apart from me there is no god.
Though you have not known me I shall strengthen you,

6 so that from east to west
    all may know there is none besides me:
I am the LORD, and there is none other;

7 I make the light, I create the darkness;
    author alike of wellbeing and woe,
    I, the LORD, do all these things.

8 Rain righteousness, you heavens,
    let the skies above pour it down,
let the earth open for it
    that salvation may flourish
with righteousness growing beside it.
    I, the LORD, have created this.   (REB)

Cyrus as God's Agent (cont.)

but his ultimate scope is much wider (6). In form, vv.1-7 are an enthronement oracle of a kind common in the ANE and exemplified in the OT by Ps 2.7-9. Cyrus's own inscription recording his conquest of Babylon and enthronement as its king is astonishingly similar (*ANET* 315). It is in two parts. The first speaks of him in the third person and records how Marduk

scanned and looked through all the countries, searching for a righteous ruler willing to lead him [i.e. Marduk] in the annual procession.

Then he pronounced the name of Cyrus to become ruler of all the world. . . . Marduk ordered him to march against his city Babylon, going at his side like a real friend. . . . Without any battle, he made him enter his town Babylon, sparing any calamity.

In the second part Cyrus himself speaks, recording his decision to restore to their own countries the various deportees with the images of their gods (quoted on p.345). And that decision about the Jews has indeed proved to be the most enduring

Cyrus as God's Agent (cont.)
achievement of Cyrus.

The formulaic nature of texts like these shows that we must not look for close historical parallels to I²'s words in 45.2c-3b. But evidently he was expecting an assault on Babylon instead of the peaceful entry which in fact occurred. That is to say that Isaiah was writing prophecy before the event, while Cyrus was writing 'history' after it, and the two accounts are independent of each other.

The oracle itself is rounded off in v.8 with a hymn, a favourite device of I². The hymn develops further the water imagery of 41.17-20, and celebrates God's *righteousness* and *salvation*, which in this context are tantamount to his triumph.

A Theological Contrast

6.1
Bel bows down, Nebo stoops,
  their idols are on beasts and cattle;
these things you carry are loaded
  as burdens on weary animals.

2
They stoop, they bow down together;
  they cannot save the burden,
  but themselves go into captivity.

3
Listen to me, O house of Jacob,
  all the remnant of the house of Israel,
who have been borne by me from your birth,
  carried from the womb;

4
even to your old age I am he,
  even when you turn gray I will carry you.
I have made, and I will bear;
  I will carry and will save.   (NRSV)

A Theological Contrast

This is a neat little satire on the gods of Babylon, portrayed as caught up in the ruin of their city. The basic contrast, between the gods who are carried by their worshippers and the god who carries his people, contains a serious theological point, though it still rests upon the assumption that no Babylonian distinguished between Bel and his statues.

The irony begins with the heathen gods themselves bowing low in defeat. So, in the Ugaritic epic about Baal, we have (in the same victory metre) 'Yamm collapses, he falls to the ground', and elsewhere 'The gods drop their heads down upon their knees' (*ANET* 130-1). But the full contrast comes with the picture, common in antiquity, of the gods' statues being carried to safety before the advance of a victorious army. So an earlier king of Babylon, fearing attack by the king of Assyria c.710 BC, 'gathered the gods in their shrines, shipped them on vessels and took himself off'.

Isaiah now foresees something similar happening at the approach of Cyrus. *Bel* (= Baal) was a title of Marduk, the tutelary deity of Babylon, *Nebo* the god among other things of prophecy: the current rulers of Babylon, Nabonidus and his co-regent Belshazzar, were named each after one of them. But in the event Cyrus actually restored the worship of Marduk after its interruption by Nabonidus (see on Dan 4); which again shows that I² was prophesying *before* Cyrus's arrival. The power of this satire is increased by its short sentences and its strong repeated verbs – five of them in v.4. The same verse has a five-fold *ani*, the Hebrew word for 'I', which in an inflected language has much more emphasis than in English.

Lament for Babylon

47. 1
Come down and sit in the dust,
  virgin daughter of Babylon.
Descend from your throne and sit on the ground,
  daughter of the Chaldaeans;
never again will you be called
  tender and delicate.

2
Take the handmill, grind meal, remove your veil;
  strip off your skirt, bare your thighs, wade through rivers,

3
so that your nakedness may be seen,
  your shame exposed.

5
Go into the darkness and sit in silence,
  daughter of the Chaldaeans;
for never again will you be called
  queen of many kingdoms.

6
I was angry with my people;
  I dishonoured my own possession
  and surrendered them into your power.
You showed them no mercy;
  even on the aged you laid a very heavy yoke.

7
You said, 'I shall reign a queen for ever';
  you gave no thought to your actions,
  nor did you consider their outcome.

8
Now listen to this,
  you lover of luxury, carefree on your throne,
saying to yourself,
  'I am, and there is none other.
I shall never sit in widow's mourning,
  never know the loss of children.'

Lament for Babylon

Ch.47 celebrates the divine punishment (in secular terms poetic justice) about to befall *Babylon*. It is typical of Hebrew poetry: dramatic in expression, with much alliteration and repetition, but lacking the sequential development usual in western poetry. This is the only oracle against a foreign nation in I², and is typically less vindictive than the many such oracles by other prophets. The prevailing metre is the *qīnāh* 3:2, characteristic of laments.

The poem has three sections. The opening (1-5) portrays a simple reversal and expresses it in two images. The first (1-3) is particularly vivid – a movement from *throne* to *ground* and from pampering to slavery. The virgin princess is put with the slaves to the mill. Her menial garb (hair let down, *skirt* hitched up) exposes her to sexual abuse. In the second image (v.5 closely follows v.1) the movement is from centre-stage to the obscurity of prison. But the *daughter* is now a *queen*, ruler of a wide empire – and that sets off a different train of thought, followed rather windingly in the central section (6-10).

That empire had included the Jews, but Babylon failed to realise that their presence in captivity was evidence not of *her* power but of the LORD's. So she had felt free to treat them badly, wrongly supposing (i) that she would *reign a queen forever*, (ii) that *no one can see* her and so (iii) that she could inflict *widowhood* etc. on others while remaining secure herself. Her arrogance and complacency are

Lament for Babylon (cont.)

9 Yet suddenly, in a single day,
    both these things will come upon you;
they will both come upon you in full measure:
    loss of children and widowhood,
    despite your many sorceries, all your countless spells.

10 Secure in your wicked ways
    you thought, 'No one can see me.'
It was your wisdom and knowledge
    that led you astray.
You said to yourself,
    'I am, and there is none other.'

11 Therefore evil will overtake you,
    and you will not know how to conjure it away;
disaster will befall you,
    and you will not be able to avert it;
ruin all unforeseen
    will suddenly come upon you.

12 Persist in your spells and your many sorceries,
    in which you have trafficked all your life.
Maybe you can get help from them!
    Maybe you will yet inspire terror!

13 In spite of your many wiles you are powerless.
    Let your astrologers, your star-gazers
who foretell your future month by month,
    persist, and save you!

14 But they are like stubble
    and fire burns them up;
    they cannot snatch themselves from the flame.
It is not a glowing coal to warm them,
    not a fire for them to sit by!

15 So much for your magicians
    with whom you have trafficked all your life:
they have wandered off, each his own way,
    and there is not one to save you.

(REB)

Lament for Babylon (cont.)

summed up in her repeated claim: *I am, and there is none other*. And her miscalculations (10b) lead into the third section.

Here the attack is upon two aspects of Babylonian religion: astrology and magic. It has been said that in Babylon 'nothing was too great or too small to become the subject of an astrological forecast', and almanacs of lucky and unlucky days were compiled *month by month* (13). Magic's job was to *conjure away* the unlucky (11). Astrology had at least some connection with true knowledge, and the use of *wisdom* in 10 may not be entirely ironical. But there is no doubt of the sarcasm in vv.12-13, and the final scene of this powerful poem presents the *astrologers* and *magicians*, having failed respectively to predict or to avert calamity, deserting their city and scurrying off to safety. The formula *and there is not one to save* is a favourite ending to prophetic oracles of doom.

Second Servant Song: the Mission Begun

49. 1 Listen to me, O coastlands,
    pay attention, you peoples from far away!
The LORD called me before I was born,
    while I was in my mother's womb he named me.

2 He made my mouth like a sharp sword,
    in the shadow of his hand he hid me;
he made me a polished arrow,
    in his quiver he hid me away.

3 And he said to me, 'You are my servant,
    Israel, in whom I will be glorified.'

4 But I said, 'I have labored in vain,
    I have spent my strength for nothing and vanity;
yet surely my cause is with the LORD,
    and my reward with my God.'

5 And now the LORD says,
    who formed me in the womb to be his servant,
to bring Jacob back to him,
    and that Israel might be gathered to him,
for I am honored in the sight of the LORD,
    and my God has become my strength –

6 he says,
'It is too light a thing that you should be my servant
    to raise up the tribes of Jacob
    and to restore the survivors of Israel;
I will give you as a light to the nations,
    that my salvation may reach to the end of the earth.'

7 Thus says the LORD,
    the Redeemer of Israel and his Holy One,
to one deeply despised, abhorred by the nations,
    the slave of rulers,
'Kings shall see and stand up,
    princes, and they shall prostrate themselves,
because of the LORD, who is faithful,
    the Holy One of Israel, who has chosen you.'

(NRSV)

Second Servant Song: the Mission Begun

The second of the servant songs carries on the story from 42.7. The continuation is spoken by the servant himself addressing the nations. First we learn how he himself saw his original commission, and we meet a new emphasis upon the *sword* i.e. the cutting edge of his preaching (2): it is a kind of secret weapon of God, kept in reserve (cp.42.2) until the moment of truth comes. We also learn that, in spite of v.42.4, he did become discouraged and needed reassurance from God (4). When this came, it was paradoxical: God showed confidence in him by extending his mission (6). It is here that a notorious problem arises over the identification of the servant. If he is Israel (3), how can he *restore the survivors of Israel* ?

Verse 7, though not strictly part of the servant song, adds a new theme which will become very important later viz. the contempt of *the nations* for the servant.

Zion's Children Restored to Her

8 Thus says the LORD:
 In a time of favor I have answered you,
  on a day of salvation I have helped you;
 I have kept you and given you
  as a covenant to the people,
 to establish the land,
  to apportion the desolate heritages;
9 saying to the prisoners, 'Come out,'
  to those who are in darkness, 'Show yourselves.'
 They shall feed along the ways,
  on all the bare heights shall be their pasture;
10 they shall not hunger or thirst,
  neither scorching wind nor sun shall strike them down,
 for he who has pity on them will lead them,
  and by springs of water will guide them.
11 And I will turn all my mountains into a road,
  and my highways shall be raised up.
12 Lo, these shall come from far away,
  and lo, these from the north and from the west,
  and these from the land of Syene.
13 Sing for joy, O heavens, and exult, O earth;
  break forth, O mountains, into singing!
 For the LORD has comforted his people,
  and will have compassion on his suffering ones.

14 But Zion said, 'The LORD has forsaken me,
  my lord has forgotten me.'
15 Can a woman forget her nursing child,
  or show no compassion for the child of her womb?
 Even these may forget,
  yet I will not forget you.

Zion's Children Restored to Her

Verses 8-13 are a link. Addressed to a single male, it picks up the theme of the second servant song. It then amplifies what was said in 40.3-4 about the journey home across the desert, adding a picture of the return of the dispersion from the ends of the earth. *Syene* (12) was the southernmost Jewish colony of the time, at the modern Aswan in upper Egypt. The oracle proper is rounded off by a triplet in v.12, followed by a hymn in v.13.

 The poem in vv.14-23 has the same form – an oracle of salvation in answer to a brief complaint (14) – and carries the same message about the return of the dispersion. It introduces an important new image that will play a fruitful part in the remaining chapters of I[2]: that of *Zion* (the city of Jerusalem) personified as a deserted wife. It is God her *lord,* i.e. husband (14b), who has deserted her, leaving her walls to be destroyed and her children to be torn from her. He promises to have both conditions reversed. The nations will hurry to rebuild her walls (17) and to restore her lost children (18, 20-3). The picture of the latter is highly dramatic. God himself will *raise* his *signal* to *the nations* – I[2] quotes the phrase verbatim from I[1] (5.26), but reverses the tenor of the prophecy from one of doom to exultation. Gentile *queens* will nurse the Jewish children and *kings*

Zion's Children Restored to Her (cont.)

49.16   See, I have inscribed you on the palms of my hands;
        your walls are continually before me.

17   Your builders outdo your destroyers,
        and those who laid you waste go away from you.

18   Lift up your eyes all around and see;
        they all gather, they come to you.
    As I live, says the LORD,
    you shall put all of them on like an ornament,
        and like a bride you shall bind them on.

19   Surely your waste and your desolate places
        and your devastated land –
    surely now you will be too crowded for your inhabitants,
        and those who swallowed you up will be far away.

20   The children born in the time of your bereavement
        will yet say in your hearing:
    'The place is too crowded for me;
        make room for me to settle.'

21   Then you will say in your heart,
        'Who has borne me these?
    I was bereaved and barren,
        exiled and put away –
        so who has reared these?
    I was left all alone –
        where then have these come from?'

22   Thus says the LORD God:
    I will soon lift up my hand to the nations,
        and raise my signal to the peoples;
    and they shall bring your sons in their bosom,
        and your daughters shall be carried on their shoulders.
    Kings shall be your foster fathers,

23   and their queens your nursing mothers.
    With their faces to the ground they shall bow down to you,
        and lick the dust of your feet.
    Then you will know that I am the LORD;
        those who wait for me shall not be put to shame.   **(NRSV)**

Zion's Children Restored to Her (cont.)

will humbly carry them back to their mother – look, she can *see* the procession coming even now (18 picks up 12). Their return will entitle her to come out of mourning and wear her finery – indeed they *are* her wedding jewels (18). The vivid images tumble over themselves in typically Hebrew fashion, but the most potent is reserved for YHWH himself. His concern for her is more constant even than the tenderest human love, her own love for her children. The depth of feeling throughout is shown by the repeated mention of parts of the body: particularly between her and her children (15, 18, 20) but also between both of them and the nations (22-3). More touching than any, however, is the restraint of v.16a: do we picture God drawing an outline of the *walls* of Jerusalem *on the palms of* his *hands*?

Third Servant Song: his Suffering

4   The Lord GOD has given me a disciple's tongue,
       for me to know how to give a word of comfort to the weary.
    Morning by morning he makes my ear alert
       to listen like a disciple.
5   The Lord GOD has opened my ear
       and I have not resisted,
    I have not turned away.
6   I have offered my back to those who struck me,
       my cheeks to those who plucked my beard;
    I have not turned my face away
       from insult and spitting.
7   The Lord GOD comes to my help,
       this is why insult has not touched me,
    this is why I have set my face like flint
       and know that I shall not be put to shame.   (NJB)

Third Servant Song: his Suffering

The third servant song amplifies one verse from the second (49.4) and adds an important new note: the suffering of the servant. The emphasis is now on his obedience and discipleship. The phrase *comfort to the weary* picks up I²'s own message as set out at the beginning and end of Ch.40. What is said of his suffering is particularly reminiscent of Jeremiah's 'confessions' (see Jer 15.18; 20.10). But there is a vital difference. In rising above the insults – pulling out the hairs of the *beard* was one of the gravest known – the servant is challenging the concept of personal honour which dominated the ancient world, both ANE and Greco-Roman. It is not that he is insensitive: note again the physicality of the description, with six parts of his body mentioned. But he is confident of the LORD's *help*, and in that knowledge can endure the sufferings. Of all the four songs this is the one where it is most tempting to see the servant as an individual.

News of God's Victory

2. 7   How beautiful upon the mountains
           are the feet of the messenger
        who announces peace,
           who brings good news,
        who announces salvation,
           who says to Zion, 'Your God reigns.'
8   Listen! Your sentinels lift up their voices,
           together they sing for joy;
        for in plain sight they see
           the return of the LORD to Zion.
9   Break forth together into singing,
           you ruins of Jerusalem;
        for the LORD has comforted his people,
           he has redeemed Jerusalem.

News of God's Victory (cont.)

52.10
The LORD has bared his holy arm
   before the eyes of all the nations;
and all the ends of the earth shall see
   the salvation of our God.

(NRSV)

News of God's Victory

This is the most purely exultant of all I²'s poems of the return. It echoes 40.9: the command given there is now fulfilled. The *messenger* brings the thrilling news expressed in the acclamation familiar from the psalms: 'the LORD is king'. The *news* is picked up by the *sentinels* standing upon the city walls, and in the hymn which follows (9-10) the *ruins* themselves are invited to celebrate the victory. A warrior bares an *arm* by taking it out of the folds of his tunic so that he can wield his sword.

Fourth Servant Song: his Rejection, Death and Vindication

52.13
See, my servant shall prosper;
   he shall be exalted and lifted up,
   and shall be very high.

14
Just as there were many who were astonished at him
   – so marred was his appearance, beyond human semblance,
   and his form beyond that of mortals –

15
so he shall startle many nations;
   kings shall shut their mouths because of him;
for that which had not been told them they shall see,
   and that which they had not heard they shall contemplate.

53. 1
Who has believed what we have heard?
   And to whom has the arm of the LORD been revealed?

2
For he grew up before him like a young plant,
   and like a root out of dry ground;
he had no form or majesty that we should look at him,
   nothing in his appearance that we should desire him.

3
He was despised and rejected by others;
   a man of suffering and acquainted with infirmity;
and as one from whom others hide their faces
   he was despised, and we held him of no account.   ▶

Fourth Servant Song: his Rejection, Death and Vindication

The fourth servant song is the most exciting and yet difficult passage in the whole OT. First, the Hebrew text contains a large number of words of uncertain meaning, including 46 not found elsewhere in I². There are problems of translation in every verse, many of them severe. Secondly, I²'s style is always allusive (e.g. he does not identify the 'we' who speak the greater part of it) and his descriptions poetical (e.g. it is not clear how literally he intends the servant's disfigurement in 52.14 or even his death in 53.9). But there is an extra difficulty here, deriving from the central position the passage has always held in Christian thinking. The messianic interpretation dominated not only the NT but (until recently) all the English translations, and even now it is not easy for any English-speaking Christian to approach the text dispassionately.

Its structure however is clear enough. There are five sections, arranged in the typical pedimental* shape. The first

Fourth Servant Song: his Rejection, Death and Vindication (cont.)

4
Surely he has borne our infirmities
and carried our diseases;
yet we accounted him stricken,
struck down by God, and afflicted.

5
But he was wounded for our transgressions,
crushed for our iniquities;
upon him was the punishment that made us whole,
and by his bruises we are healed.

6
All we like sheep have gone astray;
we have all turned to our own way,
and the LORD has laid on him
the iniquity of us all.

7
He was oppressed, and he was afflicted,
yet he did not open his mouth;
like a lamb that is led to the slaughter,
and like a sheep that before its shearers is silent,
so he did not open his mouth.

Fourth Servant Song: his Rejection, Death and Vindication (cont.)

(52.13-15) and last (53.10-12) tell of the servant's ultimate exaltation, with God himself speaking each time to guarantee it. The second and fourth sections, which cover respectively his youth and his death, describe his sufferings. The structure typically throws weight on the central section (53.4-6), in which those who had humiliated the servant say how they came to change their minds about him and by the same token about themselves: they came to see that *his* innocent sufferings (and death?) were in some sense a punishment for *their* sins. In the conclusion (53.10-12) God promises to vindicate his servant and restore him to honour, precisely because, like the scapegoat in Lev 16.22, he *bore the sin of many*. The events are presented as a succession of reversals, with humble and proud, guilty and innocent changing places; but the whole is held together formally by the repeated contrast between the one and the many, and emotionally by the trajectory from humiliation to triumph.

Now to some detailed points. Verses 52.14 and 15 compare the amazement of the many before and after the great reversal. Verse 52.14 anticipates 53.2-3. The past sufferings of the servant are described in both social and physical terms. Socially he was an outcast, like a leper – 52.14 does not mean that he *was* a leper. But now (15) the *kings* of the nations are going to be struck dumb by something even more remarkable, indeed unheard of.

In Ch.53 the kings speak for themselves. What they have just heard is indeed incredible. For this person (the anonymous *he* is typical of I[2]) was indeed weak and unimpressive (2). His misfortunes were such that men avoided his gaze for fear of contamination (3). Indeed they shared the common ANE view – the view of Job's comforters – that his sufferings must be a punishment for his sins: he must in fact be *struck down by God*.

But with v.4 the kings reveal the light that has dawned upon them – *surely* should be translated 'yet', and the emphasis in 4 and 5 is on *our*. They now see that the sins for which he was suffering were their own. This realisation leads them to a verse (6) of collective penitence, which begins and ends with the same Hebrew word. They then go on to describe the servant's ultimate suffering and death: uncomplaining and unresisting, he was

> **Fourth Servant Song: his Rejection, Death and Vindication (cont.)**
>
> **53.** 8   By a perversion of justice he was taken away.
>   Who could have imagined his future?
>   For he was cut off from the land of the living,
>   stricken for the transgression of my people.
>
> 9   They made his grave with the wicked
>   and his tomb with the rich,
>   although he had done no violence,
>   and there was no deceit in his mouth.
>
> 10   Yet it was the will of the LORD to crush him with pain.
>   When you make his life an offering for sin,
>   he shall see his offspring, and shall prolong his days;
>   through him the will of the LORD shall prosper.
>
> 11   Out of his anguish he shall see light;
>   he shall find satisfaction through his knowledge.
>   The righteous one, my servant, shall make many righteous,
>   and he shall bear their iniquities.
>
> 12   Therefore I will allot him a portion with the great,
>   and he shall divide the spoil with the strong;
>   because he poured out himself to death,
>   and was numbered with the transgressors;
>   yet he bore the sin of many,
>   and made intercession for the transgressors.   (NRSV)

Fourth Servant Song: his Rejection, Death and Vindication (cont.)

unjustly condemned and buried with the *wicked* and the *rich* – a traditional OT equivalence – in spite of his innocence.

But the last word is with the LORD. The servant's career is all his own will – both the past sufferings and the future reward. He then takes up the story, announcing the final reversal. The interpretation of vv.10-12 is obscure in detail, but two points are certain. First, the kings were right: the servant's sufferings (and death) were sacrificial. Therefore, secondly, he will *prolong his days* and *see his offspring*; and from disesteem (the nadir of 53.3) he will be exalted among *the great*.

Who, then, did I[2] have in mind in writing like this of the servant? Only one answer fits his situation and message. It is Israel, despised by the nations (42.7 etc.), who had 'died' in deportation and exile (cp. Ez 37), Israel who in the return from exile will live again and see her children (49.22f.), to the amazement of the nations (52.10 etc). Remarkably as some of the details fit the gospel narrative of Jesus's passion, the idea of an *individual* resurrection had no currency in Israel until some centuries after the time of I[2].

But on any interpretation there is one startling new theological concept to be found in this fourth servant song. It is technically known as 'vicarious suffering', and its effect has been expressed as follows in relation to this passage.

> They [the 'we' of the text] found themselves compelled to reflect upon the contrast between what the servant was and what he had suffered, and what they themselves were and deserved to suffer, until they were moved to repentance and confession. The servant had wrought in them a change of mind. . . . This meant, for them, that 'the LORD laid on him the iniquity of us all'. (North)

That is the effect the life and death of Jesus has had upon Christians. It is also the effect the sufferings and deaths of the Jews in the Holocaust has had upon Jews, Christians and thousands of others.

Zion Restored to God's Love

1   Sing, O barren one who did not bear;
         burst into song and shout,
         you who have not been in labor!
     For the children of the desolate woman will be more
         than the children of her that is married, says the LORD.

2   Enlarge the site of your tent,
         and let the curtains of your habitations be stretched out;
     do not hold back; lengthen your cords
         and strengthen your stakes.

3   For you will spread out to the right and to the left,
         and your descendants will possess the nations
         and will settle the desolate towns.

4   Do not fear, for you will not be ashamed;
         do not be discouraged, for you will not suffer disgrace;
     for you will forget the shame of your youth,
         and the disgrace of your widowhood you will remember no more.

5   For your Maker is your husband,
         the LORD of hosts is his name;
     the Holy One of Israel is your Redeemer,
         the God of the whole earth he is called.

6   For the LORD has called you
         like a wife forsaken and grieved in spirit,
     like the wife of a man's youth when she is cast off,
         says your God.

7   For a brief moment I abandoned you,
         but with great compassion I will gather you.

8   In overflowing wrath for a moment
         I hid my face from you,
     but with everlasting love I will have compassion on you,
         says the LORD, your Redeemer.

Zion Restored to God's Love

This poem forms a pair with 49.14-23. I² here resumes the image of Zion as a deserted wife, but with some changes. The first is no more than a variation: it is not that she lost her children but that she never had any – which allows the poet to open with the shock command to a barren woman to sing. He then tells her to *enlarge* her *tent* – extend the partition-*curtains*, 'let out its ropes and drive the pegs home' (REB). It has always been women's work among nomadic peoples to look after the tent. Not that the Jews of I²'s time lived any longer in tents, but he is consciously harking back to the time of the patriarchs, to whom the promises of v.3 were originally made.

But with vv.5-8 he takes up and develops Hosea's great metaphor, in which God is the husband of Zion/Israel. She was originally *a wife of youth* (6), a term used in a polygamous society to mean the first and favourite wife. In a flash of anger he had repudiated her – and in the ancient world a deserted wife was more scorned than pitied (4). Now however he will take her back and love her everlastingly. As often in Hebrew, the intensity of an emotion is expressed by its duration in time; cp. Ps 30.5.

Zion Restored to God's Love (cont.)

54. 9 This is like the days of Noah to me:
Just as I swore that the waters of Noah
would never again go over the earth,
so I have sworn that I will not be angry with you
and will not rebuke you.

10 For the mountains may depart
and the hills be removed,
but my steadfast love shall not depart from you,
and my covenant of peace shall not be removed,
says the LORD, who has compassion on you.

11 O afflicted one, storm-tossed, and not comforted,
I am about to set your stones in antimony,
and lay your foundations with lapis lazuli.

12 I will make your pinnacles of rubies,
your gates of jewels,
and all your wall of precious stones.

(NRSV)

Zion Restored to God's Love (cont.)

God then as it were reminds himself of the Flood and of the *promise* he made after it of 'never again' (Gen 8.21). The term *covenant* (10) combines that promise to Noah with Hosea's notion of the marriage-contract. Throughout this passage God's 'humanity', if it may be so put, is reminiscent of J, the great writer of the Pentateuch. In the fine concluding verse (10) I² uses his favourite trope to illustrate the LORD's unchanging qualities: A and B, being other proverbial symbols of the quality in question, may change or fail, but he will not (cp. 40.30+; 49.15).

In v.11 he moves to a different theme, namely the jewelled splendour of the new Jerusalem. In the old city the use of precious stones was approved only for the Temple. Here there is no mention of a temple, perhaps because the whole city could be regarded as the dwelling place of God. The motif of the jewelled city probably comes from the use in Assyrian buildings of bricks faced with blue glass, which kings in their boastful inscriptions described as being built with *lapis lazuli*. *Antimony* seems to have been used as a mortar for setting coloured stones in early floor-mosaics. The motif was a great favourite with later apocalyptic writers – the version in Rev 21 has no fewer than twelve jewels in all.

Concluding Words of Encouragement

1   Ho, everyone who thirsts, come to the waters;
        and you that have no money, come, buy and eat!
    Come, buy wine and milk
        without money and without price.
2   Why do you spend your money for that which is not bread,
        and your labor for that which does not satisfy?
    Listen carefully to me, and eat what is good,
        and delight yourselves in rich food.

6   Seek the LORD while he may be found,
        call upon him while he is near;
7   let the wicked forsake their way,
        and the unrighteous their thoughts;
    let them return to the LORD, that he may have mercy on them,
        and to our God, for he will abundantly pardon.
8   For my thoughts are not your thoughts,
        nor are your ways my ways, says the LORD.
9   For as the heavens are higher than the earth,
        so are my ways higher than your ways
        and my thoughts than your thoughts.

10   For as the rain and the snow come down from heaven,
        and do not return there until they have watered the earth,
    making it bring forth and sprout,
        giving seed to the sower and bread to the eater,
11   so shall my word be that goes out from my mouth;
        it shall not return to me empty,
    but it shall accomplish that which I purpose,
        and succeed in the thing for which I sent it.

Concluding Words of Encouragement

Three short poems conclude the work of Second Isaiah. In the first (1-2) a special note of urgency is heard, expressed by eight imperatives. They begin with, and take their form from, the cry of the water-seller which has always been familiar in the cities of the east. But what is on offer – free – is not just the bare necessities but the good things of life: *wine*, *milk* and *rich food*. The exiles must now choose whether they will accept this offer or prefer *that which does not satisfy*. The contrast is not between material and spiritual goods, which would be alien to the OT, but between the allurements of life in Babylon and the promise of the return home.

Second (6-11) comes a more reflective poem in slower tempo. The exiles must prepare for the return by prayer and repentance, confident of *pardon*. If they say they can see no signs of a return being permitted, the prophet answers that God's purposes are different from those of men and women (8) and above their comprehension (9). The *heaven/earth* metaphor in v.9 suggests a further point, a final application of the poet's favourite water-imagery. God's *word* is like the *rain from heaven*: when it comes down it does not *return empty* as an ineffective word of a man does (Luke 10.6); it always achieves its purpose, which is to give life (10-11).

Concluding Words of Encouragement (cont.)

55.12   For you shall go out in joy,
       and be led back in peace;
   the mountains and the hills before you
       shall burst into song,
       and all the trees of the field shall clap their hands.

13   Instead of the thorn shall come up the cypress;
       instead of the brier shall come up the myrtle;
   and it shall be to the LORD for a memorial,
       for an everlasting sign that shall not be cut off.   (NRSV)

Concluding Words of Encouragement (cont.)

The last two verses rightly abandon argument. Instead they echo the comforting message and the exultant imagery of 40.1-5, and thus round off the book of I².

God's Unconditional Mercy

57.15   For thus says the high and lofty one
       who inhabits eternity, whose name is Holy:
   I dwell in the high and holy place,
       and also with those who are contrite and humble in spirit,
   to revive the spirit of the humble,
       and to revive the heart of the contrite.

16   For I will not continually accuse,
       nor will I always be angry;
   for then the spirits would grow faint before me,
       even the souls that I have made.

17   Because of their wicked covetousness I was angry;
       I struck them, I hid and was angry;
   but they kept turning back to their own ways.

18   I have seen their ways, but I will heal them;
       I will lead them and repay them with comfort,
       creating for their mourners the fruit of the lips.

19   Peace, peace, to the far and the near, says the LORD;
       and I will heal them.   (NRSV)

God's Unconditional Mercy

The remaining chapters of the Isaiah scroll may be seen as a kind of appendix. The oracles in it contain important echoes both of I¹ and of I², together with some apocalyptic* features which will be developed by subsequent writers in that tradition (see p.646).

For example this first brief oracle of comfort begins with a title *the high and lofty one* which comes from Is 6.1. But its main message in 16-19 is typical of I² (e.g. 54.7-9): God tempers his anger out of unconditional mercy, otherwise it would be more than men could bear (16). The *fruit of the lips,* i.e. word of God, was of *peace* to both *far* and *near,* which by Hebrew idiom (merismus*) meant 'all'.

The New Jerusalem

1   Arise, shine; for thy light is come,
        and the glory of the LORD is risen upon thee.
2   For, behold, the darkness shall cover the earth,
        and gross darkness the people:
        but the LORD shall arise upon thee,
        and his glory shall be seen upon thee.
3   And the Gentiles shall come to thy light,
        and kings to the brightness of thy rising.

19   The sun shall be no more thy light by day;
        neither for brightness shall the moon give light unto thee:
        but the LORD shall be unto thee an everlasting light,
        and thy God thy glory.
20   Thy sun shall no more go down;
        neither shall thy moon withdraw itself:
        for the LORD shall be thine everlasting light,
        and the days of thy mourning shall be ended.   (AV)

The New Jerusalem

Ch.60 is a glowing description of the New Jerusalem – something between the earthly city pictured by I² as repeopled by the Jews returning from exile, and the heavenly city imagined by later apocalyptic writers as awaiting the faithful at the end of time.

The poet addresses the city as a wife and mother (cp. 49.14-21). Prostrate now, she is to *arise* and *shine*. Light is the dominant image of the poem, especially of its beginning and end, being the glory of God, the illumination of men and also the embellishment of the city. Rudyard Kipling wrote a short story in which it was Shakespeare who suggested to the translators of the AV various phrases here, including the words *to the brightness of thy rising*, which, he says, echo the 'trumpet' of *Arise, shine, for thy light* . . . ; Handel too emphasised the *thy*.

Verses 1-3 also contain a good example of Hebrew pedimental* composition. It is most striking in the central section which can be set out as follows:

        for thy-light is-come
        and-the-glory
            of-the-LORD
                upon-thee is-risen.
                (For behold)
                    darkness shall-cover the-earth
                    and-gross-darkness the people
                but-upon-thee will-arise
                the-LORD
                and-his-glory shall-be-seen upon-thee
                and-the-Gentiles shall-come to-thy-light.

This setting out also shows the movement from light to dark and back again.

Verses 19-20 are the first appearance of what will become an apocalyptic topos*. In the beginning, light was the first thing to be created (Gen 1.3). Now at the end it is again no longer needed, because God himself has taken up his abode in the city and he will be *thy sun* and *thy moon*.

The Prophet's Good News

61. 1 The spirit of the LORD God is upon me,
  because the LORD has anointed me;
he has sent me to bring good news to the oppressed,
  to bind up the brokenhearted,
to proclaim liberty to the captives,
  and release to the prisoners;

2 to proclaim the year of the LORD's favor,
  and the day of vengeance of our God;
to comfort all who mourn;

3   to give them a garland instead of ashes,
the oil of gladness instead of mourning,
  the mantle of praise instead of a faint spirit.
They will be called oaks of righteousness,
  the planting of the LORD, to display his glory. (NRSV)

The Prophet's Good News

Here too the poet is much influenced by I², this time by the servant songs (see especially 42.1 and 7). He sees himself as fulfilling the prophetic role of the servant, particularly in comforting his people. What in earlier days had been specific technical terms have now become part of conventional language: *spirit* and *anointed* of himself, and *oppressed*, *captives* etc. of his audience. Similarly *vengeance* here means no more than the kind of restoration exemplified in v.3. The list of reversals there echoes that of Isaiah 3.24 and typically includes a play on words which might be rendered 'sashes *instead of ashes*'.

This is the passage of scripture which (down to v.2a) Jesus read in the synagogue at the beginning of his ministry. Having done so, he began to expound it with the words 'Today this scripture has been fulfilled in your ears' (Luke 4.16+).

The Grapes of Wrath

63. 1 'Who is this that comes from Edom,
  from Bozrah in garments stained crimson?
Who is this so splendidly robed,
  marching in his great might?'

'It is I, announcing vindication,
  mighty to save.'

2 'Why are your robes red,
  and your garments like theirs who tread the winepress?'

3 'I have trodden the winepress alone,
  and from the peoples no one was with me;   ▶

The Grapes of Wrath

This brief dialogue, which would make a Scottish ballad, shows the dark obverse of the bright New Jerusalem. *Edom* was the most hated of Israel's neighbours, especially since the fall of Jerusalem (Ps 137.7; Is 34.5); *Bozrah* was its capital. The two proper names are similar to the Hebrew words for 'red' and 'vintager' respectively, which may be more than coincidence, since Edom was famous for its wine. All this would be picked up by a Jewish reader of v.1, just as he would immediately know who is the mysterious saviour of v.1. The watchman's second

The Grapes of Wrath (cont.)

I trod them in my anger
   and trampled them in my wrath;
their juice spattered on my garments,
   and stained all my robes.

4   For the day of vengeance was in my heart,
   and the year for my redeeming work had come.

5   I looked, but there was no helper;
   I stared, but there was no one to sustain me;
so my own arm brought me victory,
   and my wrath sustained me.

6   I trampled down peoples in my anger,
   I crushed them in my wrath,
   and I poured out their lifeblood on the earth.'   (NRSV)

The Grapes of Wrath (cont.)

question suggests a simile to which the LORD then gives a grim twist: yes, he has *trodden the winepress*, and his clothes are *stained* with the *juice*. The grapes which he *trampled* in his *wrath* are his and Israel's enemies, finally destroyed on 'the day of the LORD'. The theology is crude, but the image of the winepress, here first used, will prove perennially powerful in apocalyptic writing.

Jerusalem as a Joy

17   For I am about to create new heavens
   and a new earth;
the former things shall not be remembered
   or come to mind.

18   But be glad and rejoice forever
   in what I am creating;
for I am about to create Jerusalem as a joy,
   and its people as a delight.

19   I will rejoice in Jerusalem,
   and delight in my people;
no more shall the sound of weeping be heard in it,
   or the cry of distress.

21   They shall build houses and inhabit them;
   they shall plant vineyards and eat their fruit.

22   They shall not build and another inhabit.
   they shall not plant and another eat;
for like the days of a tree shall the days of my people be,
   and my chosen shall long enjoy the works of their hands.

Jerusalem as a Joy

This picture of the New Jerusalem is a mixture of the apocalyptic and the realistic. The sentence *I create new heavens and a new earth* (with the special word for 'create' used in Gen 1) is the basic apocalyptic* idea. But the focus narrows rapidly to *Jerusalem*, whose new estate is to be a source of *rejoicing* (six times altogether in 18-19). Many of its features are derived by reversing the warnings of earlier prophets, which in the meantime had been fulfilled, e.g. vv.21-22b reverses Am 5.11. More boldly, vv.22d-23a modify the

Jerusalem as a Joy (cont.)

65.23
They shall not labor in vain,
    or bear children for calamity;
for they shall be offspring blessed by the LORD –
    and their descendants as well.

24
Before they call I will answer,
    while they are yet speaking I will hear.

25
The wolf and the lamb shall feed together,
    the lion shall eat straw like the ox;
    but the serpent – its food shall be dust!
They shall not hurt or destroy
    on all my holy mountain, says the LORD.   (NRSV)

Jerusalem as a Joy (cont.)

punishments of 'our first parents' in Gen 3.16+, while that of *the serpent* (25c, cp.Gen 3.14) is confirmed. The other animal references of v.25 echo Is 11.9, thus bringing back the apocalyptic tone of v.17 and rounding off the poem.

Comfort in Jerusalem

66.10
Rejoice with Jerusalem, and be glad for her,
    all you who love her;
rejoice with her in joy,
    all you who mourn over her –

11
that you may drink deeply with delight
    from her glorious bosom.

12
For thus says the LORD:
I will extend prosperity to her like a river,
    and the wealth of the nations like an overflowing stream;
and you shall nurse and be carried on her arm,
    and dandled on her knees.

13
As a mother comforts her child,
    so I will comfort you;
    you shall be comforted in Jerusalem.

14
You shall see, and your heart shall rejoice;
    your bodies shall flourish like the grass;
and it shall be known that the hand of the LORD is with his servants,
    and his indignation is against his enemies.   (NRSV)

Comfort in Jerusalem

This final song about the New Jerusalem shares the joyous emphasis of the previous poem, with three different Hebrew words for 'rejoice' in v.10. Many of the ideas and phrases in it come from I², particularly Ch.40. The triple *comfort* here echoes the double in 40.1, and *flourish like the grass* annuls the negative of 40.6+. That Jerusalem should suckle her children is not surprising after Ch.49. But there is one important new development: since Jerusalem is the earthly counterpart of God, the poet can here (13) go further and compare him to *a mother* more explicitly than in 46.3 and 49.15. Indeed what might be called feminine imagery is more pervasive in these chapters than anywhere else in the OT outside the Song of Songs (Dt 32.18 is a rare exception) – perhaps evidence of a female author?

JEREMIAH

Introduction

The Book of Jeremiah is one of the most dramatic, but also one of the most complicated, in the OT – just like the period of history in which he lived. It was a time when empires were rising and falling right across the Near East. Jerusalem was caught up in these events, the city besieged and conquered, her walls pulled down and her people deported. The turmoil of the times is reflected in Jeremiah's book and in his personality.

Jeremiah's preaching began effectively under King Jehoiakim 609-598 BC. At that time the power of Assyria was in terminal decline, and Jehoiakim opted for vassalage to Egypt instead (2 K 23). But he entirely failed to discern the rising power of Babylon in succession to Assyria. Jeremiah, who saw it clearly, insisted that the real threat was 'the foe from the north'. His chief message, however, ran much deeper than that. Like earlier prophets, he denounced the rottenness of Judahite society and foretold the certain vengeance of God. His criticisms led him into conflict with king, court and people. But he was vindicated when Nebuchadnezzar sent troops in 598 to besiege Jerusalem and call the city to order (2 K 24). At the crucial moment Jehoiakim died. His young son Jehoiachin forthwith surrendered; he, his court and some others were deported to Babylon (597).

But his uncle Zedekiah, who then became king, was foolish enough to resume the anti-Babylonian policy. Jeremiah now came out even more strongly than before. He saw no future whatever in revolt against or even provocation of Babylon. To the deportees he wrote a letter (Ch.29) advising them to make the best of their exile. And when Nebuchadnezzar sent a stronger force in 589 to reduce Jerusalem, Jeremiah advised the king officially and the people individually to surrender (Chs 37-38).

Against him were ranged other prophets urging resistance. The king vacillated, but in the end yielded to the war party and had Jeremiah arrested (Ch.38). He was not released until the city finally fell in 587 (Ch.39). The outline of these events is given in 2 K 25; it is the book of Jeremiah which brings them alive.

The king and most of the rest of the landowners were now taken off in the second deportation to Babylon. Judah became a province of the Babylonian empire, with Gedaliah as governor (Ch.40). Jeremiah stayed behind in Jerusalem until Gedaliah was murdered [Ch.41]. He then moved to Egypt – the perennial refuge for Jews in biblical times – and is last heard of at work there [Chs 42-4].

The Book of Jeremiah is unlike any other prophetic book in being roughly half poetry and half prose; most of the poetry is in the first half, most of the prose in the second. The poetry is (or purports to be) *by him*, the prose narrative *about him*. But there is an intermediate category. Embedded in the narrative are many sermons etc. in a rhythmic prose, which also purport to be by him. In the mss of the book of Jeremiah the arrangement of that material, both between and within the three categories, is extremely confusing, being neither in chronological nor in any other consistent sequence.

A further complication is provided by the wide discrepancies – wider than in any other OT book – between the Hebrew (MT) and the Greek (LXX) manuscripts. Most notably the LXX text is about 12% shorter, and among the material missing from it are some 50 occurrences of the phrase translated 'this is the word of the LORD'. There are also significant differences of order. For example, the collection of oracles against foreign nations, which in MT (and all English translations) forms Chs[46-51], is found in LXX after 25.13. And this difference is not just one between the two languages i.e. between a Palestinian and an Alexandrian text in the C3rd BC. For among the four fragments of the Hebrew text of Jeremiah found at Qumran is one which is closer to the LXX than to the MT. That is to say that even in first-century BC Judaea the text of Jeremiah was still in a fluid state. Of the two main traditions, many scholars regard LXX as the better, i.e. closer to the original.

Those who wish to establish the chronological sequence of events in Jeremiah's life, and as far as possible to fit his poetry into that sequence, will turn first to the biographical passages in prose, many of which have specific dates prefixed to them. Unfortunately the fit between prose and poetry is not as close as we should wish. Even the 'dated' chapters are out of sequence: chronologically they should run 26, 36, [45], 29, 34, 37-44. In this edition Chs 26 and 36 have been moved to their chronological position.

The plain narrative (here Chs 26 and 34-40) is written in a fine mature style, whose features are summarised on p.595. It is generally taken to be the work of Jeremiah's friend Baruch. The rhythmic prose (here chiefly in Chs 1, 7, 29 and 31) has a core of Jeremiah's thoughts and phrases, but much of it is a rhetorical paraphrase by later hands. Stylistically, both the sermons and the narratives are much influenced by Deuteronomy.

For the relation between the narrative prose and the poetry the key text is Ch.36. There we learn how in 605 BC Jeremiah dictated to Baruch *all the words* that God had spoken to him to date *about Jerusalem and Judah*. Some months later, when the king had burned that scroll, Jeremiah repeated the process, adding *much else to the same effect*. Whatever the first scroll contained, the second probably contained most of the poems now in the first twenty or so chapters. The critical tone of those poems is enough to explain the violent reaction of the king.

In respect of content, Jeremiah's poems (oracles) fall squarely in the tradition of earlier prophets. The main targets of his criticism are social corruption, religious apostasy and political entanglements. But he adds one new one; the complacent assumption in Jerusalem that the presence of the Temple will guarantee the inviolabilty of the city. He thus offended almost everybody.

Fortunately, he also had a small but important group of friends and supporters. As well as Baruch, it included Gedaliah, Gemariah and others whose names we know. These people shared an attachment to Deuteronomy, so they are known to scholars as 'deuteronomists'. The group survived the destruction of Jerusalem and continued their work in exile. It was they who put together the so-called deuteronomic history (DtH), i.e. the books Joshua-2 Kings, and it was they who took on from Baruch the editing of Jeremiah's oracles.

In his choice of forms for those oracles, Jeremiah differed somewhat from his predecessors. Where they *threatened* the punishment to come, and so favoured a lawsuit or judgement form, he tends rather to describe or lament. His descriptions are full of vivid detail, and the more frightening for being largely objective. For his lamentations he adapts the form, familiar from the psalms, of the so-called 'communal lament' (see p.412). The significance of this form is that in it the poet identifies himself with, those who do (or in this case will) suffer.

Jeremiah also uses the 'individual lament' form for the most striking of all his poems. In these poems, sometimes unhelpfully called his 'confessions' (here Chs 15 and 20), he pours out his feelings more revealingly than any other writer in the OT. He speaks of the public hostility which his message has aroused and of his own inner conflicts and doubts about his role as a prophet. He begs for the release which he knows cannot be granted and – most remarkable of all – blames God for his predicament. Poignant as these 'confessions' are, it is a mistake to call them 'lyric poetry' or to suppose that they were intended for private circulation. They are as much part of his proclamation as are the call-narratives of other prophets. Both help to deperson- alise the criticism and thus to defuse the conflict. They also authenticate the prophet's claim that his word comes from God. This last point is of particular importance in the light of Jeremiah's many conflicts with other prophets whose message fed the national mood of complacency.

In our interpretation of Jeremiah's poetry we have the usual handicap of not knowing where each poem begins and ends. Moreover many of them use a dramatic dialogue form which includes God, Jeremiah, the people – and even others. This form allows him to explore a situation and to express the emotions involved to a greater depth than his pre- decessors. But it leaves us often unable to tell who is speaking – the more so since we cannot trust the mss for the formula 'thus saith the LORD' (see above). Scholars argue endlessly about the attributions. But perhaps we should read the poem-sequences more as we do choric odes in Greek tragedy, where various members of the chorus express views from different angles which together build up a multi-dimensional picture.

Such an analogy implies a fundamental unity between the various speakers involved. And that may indeed be the case with Jeremiah. At one level his poetry reveals the conflicts between the three parties: God, the people, and himself caught in the middle. But many interpreters have seen a deeper level where all three are caught in shared suffering. All suffer, but Jeremiah – and even perhaps God himself (see note on 9.17-

22) – suffers with and for the people. If this interpretation is correct, Jeremiah's thinking and the sufferings of his life put him in a biblical tradition which began with Hosea and leads on through Isaiah 53 to the passion story in the gospels.

In the European tradition the name of Jeremiah is commonly associated with lamentation. The association derived partly from the fact that the Book of [Lamentations] in the OT bears his name and is placed immediately after his in the canon. That book contains five laments over the fall of Jerusalem. They are good examples of their genre, but they are omitted from this selection in favour of other laments from the psalms and indeed from the Book of Jeremiah. For Jeremiah *did* utter laments, both anticipatory dirges for his country and expressions of frustration and suffering on his own behalf. But in both cases there were good objective grounds for the lament, and the note of self-pity which is heard e.g. in some of the psalms is mostly absent in Jeremiah. In that sense his reputation is unfair.

It is also unfair in another sense. If one reads the book of Jeremiah as a whole, the predominant impression is not of lament, if that implies the wringing of the hands. It is of a man of sensitivity but also of great courage, living in constant turmoil and conflict in turbulent and threatening times, battling to keep his head above water but never submerged. Nor must we forget the great message which he offered in Ch.31, in which he was able to look ahead in hope, beyond the fall of Jerusalem, beyond even the collapse of the old covenant, to a new and more personal relationship between God and his people.

A historian of Israel makes the following judgement on Jeremiah. In the short term he was a heroic failure. But, by detaching the national religion from the Temple, he enabled it – and thereby his people – to survive what in advance had seemed the unthinkable disaster (Bright).

Jeremiah's Call and Message

1. 1 The words of Jeremiah son of Hilkiah, one of the priests at Anathoth in Benjamin.
• The word of the LORD came to him in the thirteenth year of the reign of Josiah son of Amon, king of Judah. • It came also during the reign of Jehoiakim son of Josiah, king of Judah, until the end of the eleventh year of Zedekiah son of Josiah, king of Judah. In the fifth month the inhabitants of Jerusalem were carried off into exile.

5 • This word of the LORD came to me: • 'Before I formed you in the womb I chose you, and before you were born I consecrated you; I appointed you a prophet to the nations.' • 'Ah! Lord GOD,' I answered, 'I am not skilled in speaking; I am too young.' • But the LORD said, 'Do not plead that you are too young; for you are to go to whatever people I send you, and say whatever I tell you to say. • Fear none of them, for I shall be with you to keep you safe.' This was the word of the LORD.• Then the LORD stretched out his hand, and touching my mouth said 10 to me, 'See, I put my words into your mouth. • This day I give you authority over nations and kingdoms to uproot and to pull down, to destroy and to demolish, to build and to plant.'

• The word of the LORD came to me: 'What is it that you see, Jeremiah?' 'A branch of an almond tree,' I answered. • 'You are right,' said the LORD to me, 'for I am on the watch to carry out my threat.'

• The word of the LORD came to me a second time: 'What is it that you see?' 'A cauldron on a fire,' I said; 'it is fanned by the wind and tilted away from the north.'

14 • The LORD said:
> From the north disaster will be let loose
>> against all who live in the land.

17 > Brace yourself, Jeremiah;
>> stand up and speak to them.
> Tell them everything I bid you;
>> when you confront them
> do not let your spirit break,
>> or I shall break you before their eyes.
18 > This day I make you a fortified city,
>> an iron pillar, a bronze wall,
> to withstand the whole land,
>> the kings and princes of Judah,
>> its priests, and its people.
19 > Though they attack you, they will not prevail,
>> for I shall be with you to keep you safe.
> This is the word of the LORD.   (REB)

Jeremiah's Call and Message

The various sections of Ch.1 are mostly written in a rhythmic prose, which some modern translations print as verse.

The first section (1-3) is an editor's title page. It gives Jeremiah's family, and home (3 miles north of Jerusalem), and also a dating of his prophetic activity. Probably he was first called when *young* (6), like Samuel, in 627 BC, but did not begin his public ministry until *the reign of Jehoiakim* (609-598). For the historical context here referred to see p.577.

Jeremiah's Call and Message (cont.)

The narrative of his call is fairly conventional. Heroic figures in the ancient world were commonly identified before birth, and Hebrew prophets often protested their unsuitability for the task; cp. especially the story of Moses' call. The list of six verbs in v.10 (of which the centre pair adds nothing and spoils the assonance of the other four) summarises the effect of Jeremiah's preaching.

There follow two typical prophetic 'visions': everyday objects in which the seer saw a message to transmit. The first works by means of a pun: the Hebrew for almond tree (*shāqēd*) suggested that for *on the watch* (*shōqēd*). But that message needed the clarification of the second. A pot-au-feu *tilted away from the north* suggested a meal suddenly interrupted by raiders from the north, the quarter from which all enemies came but Egypt.

The last section (17-19) harks back to vv.7-8. But in spite of repeating the words of the salvation oracle (8a=19b; cp. Is 41.10 with note), its effect is rather to alert the reader to the dangers Jeremiah will have to face. The simile of the *fortified city* is, in the context, rather ambivalent.

Apostasy Condemned

10 Cross to the coasts and islands of Kittim and see,
　　　　send to Kedar and observe closely,
　　　　see whether there has been anything like this:
11 has a nation ever exchanged its gods,
　　　　and these no gods at all?
　　Yet my people have exchanged their glory ᾿
　　　　for a god altogether powerless.
12 Be aghast at this, you heavens,
　　　　shudder in utter horror,
　　　　says the LORD.
13 My people have committed two sins:
　　　　they have rejected me,
　　　　a source of living water,
　　and they have hewn out for themselves cisterns,
　　　　cracked cisterns which hold no water.   (REB)

Apostasy Condemned

This powerful little poem is directed against the nation's apostasy in deserting the LORD for Baal. It is in two parts. First (10-11) the claim is made that nowhere on earth, west or east, has *a nation* changed *its gods*. In fact it was common enough in the ancient world for a defeated nation to accept the gods of its conquerors and (more to the point here) for syncretism to grow up between neighbouring peoples. But the satire is effective, especially the verb *exchanged*, which properly belongs in the world of barter.

The rhetoric is reinforced in 12 by raising the appeal from earth to *heaven*, and in 13 by a superb double image. The contrast between a never-failing spring of *living* (i.e. running) *water* and a *cracked cistern* is telling. Cisterns were hollowed out of the rock to hold the produce of the short rainy season against the dry one. Since Palestinian rock is porous limestone they have to be plastered, and when the plaster cracks the water seeps out. Both halves of this image reappear later: the first perhaps unconsciously, where Jeremiah is put into a cistern with no water in it (38.6), the second consciously and bitterly, when he complains that God is to him like 'a brook which fails' (15.18).

Invasion Foretold

4. 5   Declare this in Judah,
        proclaim it in Jerusalem.
    Blow the trumpet throughout the land.
        Shout aloud the command: 'Assemble!
        Let us move back to the fortified towns.'

6   Raise the signal – to Zion!
        Make for safety without delay,
    for I am about to bring disaster out of the north
        and dire destruction.

7   A lion has risen from his lair,
        the destroyer of nations;
    he has broken camp and marched out
        to devastate your land
        and make your cities waste and empty.

8   Therefore put on sackcloth,
        beat the breast and wail,
    for the fierce anger of the LORD
        is not averted from us.   (REB)

11   A scorching wind from the desert heights
        sweeps down on my people;
        it is no breeze for winnowing or for cleansing.

12   A wind too strong for these
        will come at my bidding.

19   My anguish, my anguish! I writhe in pain!
        Oh, the walls of my heart!
    My heart is beating wildly;
        I cannot keep silent;
    for I hear the sound of the trumpet,
        the alarm of war.

20   Disaster overtakes disaster,
        the whole land is laid waste.
    Suddenly my tents are destroyed,
        my curtains in a moment.

21   How long must I see the standard,
        and hear the sound of the trumpet?

23   I looked on the earth, and lo, it was waste and void;
        and to the heavens, and they had no light.

24   I looked on the mountains, and lo, they were quaking,
        and all the hills moved to and fro.

25   I looked, and lo, there was no one at all,
        and all the birds of the air had fled.

26   I looked, and lo, the fruitful land was a desert,
        and all its cities were laid in ruins
        before the LORD, before his fierce anger.   (NRSV)

Invasion Foretold

Chs 4 and 6 contain a collection of poems which depict the imminent coming of an enemy from the north bringing disaster upon the land. The impressionistic detail lends vividness, and the short lines urgency. The force of the message is further heightened by the dramatic presentation; but this creates a difficulty of interpretation, since the text gives few reliable indications of changes of speaker, and modern scholars differ in their attributions. The original poems were filled out with subsequent reflections, most of which have been omitted in this selection.

In the first poem God speaks to the people (5-7). Then in v.8 Jeremiah takes over with a call to a public lament.

The second poem (11-12), in which God is speaking again, brings a new image. The sirocco *from the desert* can blow in Palestine for as long as two weeks, with temperatures over 100⁰ F (35⁰ C). It is a wind with no redeeming features: it cannot even be used *for*

winnowing, because it blows away the wheat and the chaff indiscriminately (cp. the theme of 5.1-6).

In vv.19-21 Jeremiah speaks in his own person, as in v.8. But here in a passionate outburst he identifies himself completely with the people. The violent language portrays in v.19 his internal *anguish,* in v.20 the ruin of *the whole land.* The *trumpet* motif picks up v.5.

For vv.23-6 we change key and also metre (4+3). The vision here is not prophetic but apocalyptic*, the disaster not in time but at the end of it. In such writing the end-time corresponds to the beginning, so the creation as told in Genesis 1-2 is undone. The inanimate world reverts to chaos (*waste and void*) and darkness. Animal life is extinguished both in *the earth* and *the heavens* (25 picks up 23); inmates of Auschwitz and Birkenau recall that no *birds* sang there. Cultivation ceases (26 picks up 23) and with it civilisation. The bleak landscape is all too close to that of a nuclear winter.

A Corrupt Society

5. 1
Go up and down the streets of Jerusalem,
see, take note;
search through her wide squares:
can you find anyone who acts justly,
anyone who seeks the truth,
that I may forgive that city?

2
People may swear by the life of the LORD,
but in fact they perjure themselves. ♦

A Corrupt Society

Ch.5 is a diatribe against the sins of Judah, with special emphasis on the ruling classes. The first section (1-6) opens with a challenge from God to find a single just person in *Jerusalem.* There is an obvious echo here of the famous

dialogue between God and Abraham in Gen 18. To *swear by* God's name while disobeying his commands (2) is to take his name in vain.

Jeremiah replies in vv.4-5. He purports to have carried out the search enjoined,

A Corrupt Society (cont.)

5. 4 I said, 'After all, these are the poor,
   these are folk without understanding,
  who do not know the way of the LORD,
   the ordinances of their God.

5 I shall go to the great ones
   and speak with them;
  for they will know the way of the LORD,
   the ordinances of their God.'
  But they too have broken the yoke
   and snapped their traces.

6 So a lion out of the scrub will strike them down,
   a wolf from the plains will savage them;
  a leopard will prowl about their towns
   and maul any who venture out,
  for their rebellious deeds are many,
   their apostasies past counting.

26 For among my people there are scoundrels
   who, like fowlers, lay snares and set deadly traps;
   they prey on their fellows.

27 Their houses are full of fraud,
   as a cage is full of birds.
  They grow great and rich,

28   sleek and bloated;
  they turn a blind eye to wickedness
   and refuse to do justice;
  the claims of the fatherless they do not uphold,
   nor do they defend the poor at law.

30 An appalling thing, an outrage,
   has appeared in this land:

31 prophets prophesy lies
   and priests are in league with them,
   and my people love to have it so!   (REB)

A Corrupt Society (cont.)

and reports back in two ironical stages. His first attempt had been unsuccesful – but what would you expect among *the poor* and uneducated? Now he will try *the great* and learned – but lo and behold they are no better. So destruction is certain.

In the second section God speaks throughout, not to but of *my people* (note the frame in vv.26 and 31). Here the attack is clearly upon the rich and their exploitation of the poor. They *set traps* for *their fellows* in the sense of reducing them to serfdom. The metaphor is carried forward in the *cage full of* (netted) *birds*, where NJB translates more concretely: 'their houses are full of loot.' From the rich we turn to the religious leadership of *priests* and Temple *prophets*, as in Ch.26 below. But *a people* gets the leaders it deserves – the indictment of Ch.5 is comprehensive.

Corruption and Invasion

9 Thus says the LORD of hosts:

> Glean thoroughly as a vine
>> the remnant of Israel;
> like a grape-gatherer, pass your hand again
>> over its branches.

10 'To whom shall I speak and give warning,
>> that they may hear?
> See, their ears are closed,
>> they cannot listen.
> The word of the LORD is to them an object of scorn;
>> they take no pleasure in it.

11 But I am full of the wrath of the LORD;
>> I am weary of holding it in.'

> Pour it out on the children in the street,
>> and on the gatherings of young men as well;
> both husband and wife shall be taken,
>> the old folk and the very aged.

12 Their houses shall be turned over to others,
>> their fields and wives together;
> for I will stretch out my hand
>> against the inhabitants of the land, says the LORD.

13 For from the least to the greatest of them,
>> everyone is greedy for unjust gain;
> and from prophet to priest,
>> everyone deals falsely.

14 They have treated the wound of my people carelessly,
>> saying, 'Peace, peace,'
> when there is no peace.   (NRSV)

Corruption and Invasion

Ch.6 contains another dramatic exchange. The idea in v.9, like that in 5.1-6, is of looking for anything worth saving in a corrupt society. Verses 10-11b are spoken by Jeremiah, 11c-14 by God. The corruption of society is thoroughgoing, but again a major responsibility lies with the religious leaders. *Peace*, as always in Hebrew, includes all forms of well-being; never-theless an older English reader will recall Churchill's vain warnings against the Nazi threat in the 1930s.

Much of Jeremiah's output was directed against 'false prophets' (14). It makes tedious reading now, and none of it is included in this selection. But it was very important at the time, in two ways. Politically, the conflicting views concerned the weightiest public issue of the day. Psychologically, the existence of this well-entrenched opposition meant that Jeremiah needed constant reassurance. For the only convincing test of 'falsity' lay in the outcome of events.

Jeremiah's Temple Sermon

7. 1 This word came from the LORD to Jeremiah. • Stand at the gate of the LORD's house and there make this proclamation: Hear the word of the LORD, all you of Judah who come in through these gates to worship him. • These are the words of the LORD of Hosts the God of Israel: Amend your ways and your deeds, that I may let you live in this place. • You keep saying, 'This place is the temple of the LORD, the temple of the LORD, the temple of the LORD!' This slogan of yours is a

5 lie; put no trust in it. • If you amend your ways and your deeds, deal fairly with one another, • cease to oppress the alien, the fatherless, and the widow, if you shed no innocent blood in this place and do not run after other gods to your own ruin, • then I shall let you live in this place, in the land which long ago I gave to your forefathers for all time.

• You gain nothing by putting your trust in this lie. • You steal, you murder, you commit adultery and perjury, you burn sacrifices to Baal, and you run after

10 other gods whom you have not known; • will you then come and stand before me in this house which bears my name, and say, 'We are safe'? Safe, you think, to indulge in all these abominations! • Do you regard this house which bears my name as a bandits' cave? I warn you, I myself have seen all this, says the LORD.

• Go to my shrine at Shiloh, which once I made a dwelling for my name, and see what I did to it because of the wickedness of my people Israel. • Now you have done all these things, says the LORD; though I spoke to you again and again, you did not listen, and though I called, you did not respond. • Therefore what I did to Shiloh I shall do to this house which bears my name, the house in which

15 you put your trust, the place I gave to you and your forefathers; • I shall fling you away out of my presence, as I did with all your kinsfolk, all Ephraim's offspring.   ▶

Jeremiah's Temple Sermon

The famous Temple sermon is recorded twice in our Book of Jeremiah. Ch.7 gives a fuller version of the sermon itself; Ch.26 gives a shorter version, prefaced by a date 'in the first year of king Jehoiakim' (= 609 BC) and followed by a narrative of its aftermath. Both chapters are written in the deuteronomic style, but there is no reason to doubt that our text gives the sense of of Jer's sermon and some of his actual words (esp. in 7.4 and 11), with a generally reliable report of its aftermath.

This brave, powerful and provocative utterance by the prophet was a direct challenge to the ideology of the political and religious establishment in Jerusalem. Over the centuries there had grown up a belief that the city's inviolability was guaranteed by that of the Temple, and the Temple in turn by YHWH whose house it was. That belief had been reinforced a century earlier (701) when Isaiah had correctly foretold the withdrawal of Sennacherib's besieging army (2 K 19). But Jeremiah saw it quite differently. Like Deuteronomy, he was convinced that the covenant with YHWH was conditional, and the condition was not being met.

Jeremiah's Temple Sermon (cont)

7 • The priests, the prophets, and all the people heard Jeremiah say this in the Lord's house • and, when he came to the end of what the Lord had charged him to say to them, the priests and prophets and all the people seized him and threatened him with death. • 'Why', they demanded, 'do you prophesy in the Lord's name that this house will become like Shiloh and this city an uninhabited ruin?' The 10 people all crowded round Jeremiah in the Lord's house. • When the chief officers of Judah heard what was happening, they went up from the royal palace to the Lord's house and took their places there at the entrance of the New Gate.

• The priests and the prophets said to the officers and all the people, 'This man deserves to be condemned to death, because he has prophesied against this city, as you yourselves have heard.' • Then Jeremiah said to all the officers and people, 'The Lord it was who sent me to prophesy against this house and this city all the things you have heard. • Now, if you mend your ways and your actions and obey the Lord your God, he may relent and revoke the disaster which he has pronounced against you. • But here I am in your hands; do with me 15 whatever you think right and proper. • Only you may be certain that, if you put me to death, you and this city and those who live in it will be guilty of murdering an innocent man; for truly it was the Lord who sent me to you to say all this to you.'

• The officers and all the people then said to the priests and the prophets, 'This man ought not to be condemned to death, for he has spoken to us in the name of the Lord our God.'   (REB)

Jeremiah's Temple Sermon (cont.)

He took his stand in the *gate* between the outer and the inner courts of the Temple on a feast day when all the tribes were represented there. The main thrust of his argument is one familiar from Isaiah 1.11+, that God wants 'mercy, not sacrifice'. As it is, the people are using the Temple as *bandits* use their *cave,* i.e. as a refuge for their crimes. Remember *Shiloh,* says Jeremiah, the shrine of Eli and Samuel, which God had allowed the Philistines to destroy in punishment for the crimes of Eli's sons (1 Sam 1-4). Now God will abandon Judah as he has already abandoned the northern kingdom (called *Ephraim* in 7.15).

Not surprisingly the religious establishment reacted, and Jeremiah's life was in jeopardy. But the commotion was audible in the *palace* next door. Officials hurried across to restore order, and set up a formal court (*took their places*) to try the offender. The demand for the death penalty (26.11) rested upon Dt [18.20]: 'the prophet who presumes to utter in my name what I have not commanded him . . . shall die', for it seemed self-evident that God *could* not have commanded Jeremiah to speak so. His defence rested therefore upon his insistence that *the Lord* had indeed *sent* him (12 and 15). And that insistence carried the day – note how *all the people* swung at the last to the side of political authority.

The People's Folly and Fate

8. 4   When people fall, do they not get up again?
            If they go astray, do they not turn back?

5   Why then has this people turned away
            in perpetual backsliding?
      They have held fast to deceit,
            they have refused to return.

6   All of them turn to their own course,
            like a horse plunging headlong into battle.

7   Even the stork in the heavens
            knows its times;
      and the turtledove, swallow, and crane
            observe the time of their coming;
      but my people do not
            know the ordinance of the LORD.

18   My joy is gone, grief is upon me,
            my heart is sick.

19   Hark, the cry of my poor people
            from far and wide in the land:
      'Is the LORD not in Zion?
            Is her King not in her?

20   The harvest is past, the summer is ended,
            and we are not saved.'

21   For the hurt of my poor people I am hurt,
            I mourn, and dismay has taken hold of me.

22   Is there no balm in Gilead?
            Is there no physician there?
      Why then has the health of my poor people
            not been restored?

9. 1   O that my head were a spring of water,
            and my eyes a fountain of tears,
      so that I might weep day and night
            for the slain of my poor people!

(NRSV)

The People's Folly and Fate

Ch.8.4-7 castigates the unnaturalness of the people's behaviour. In 4-6 J contrasts it with that of normal people, using two of his favourite turns of style. One is the triple question (4-5), also used in v.22. All three questions are rhetorical: the first two expect the answer 'of course', and they set things up for the indignation of the third. The other is the play upon the meanings of the Hebrew verb *sūv*, which can mean both *turn away* and *return*. Normal people vary their direction, whereas the *backsliding* of *this people* is *perpetual*. In v.7 the people are contrasted with migratory birds, whose annual movements follow what we might call natural law. The gentleness of the birds balances the violence of the *plunging horse*.

Ch.8 ends with a sustained elegy, in which Jeremiah shares in advance the grief which will fall upon his *poor people*. They feel abandoned by God (19), deprived of food (20) and incurably wounded (21-22); *Gilead* was known for its balsam trees.

A Dirge for Zion

2
    O that I had in the desert
        a traveler's lodging place,
    that I might leave my people
        and go away from them!
    For they are all adulterers,
        a band of traitors.

3
    They bend their tongues like bows;
        they have grown strong in the land for falsehood, and not for truth.

17
    Thus says the LORD of hosts:
    'Consider, and call for the mourning women to come;
        send for the skilled women to come;

18
    let them quickly raise a dirge over us,
        so that our eyes may run down with tears,
        and our eyelids flow with water.'

20
    Hear, O women, the word of the LORD,
        and let your ears receive the word of his mouth;
    teach to your daughters a dirge,
        and each to her neighbor a lament.

21
    'Death has come up into our windows,
        it has entered our palaces,
    to cut off the children from the streets
        and the young men from the squares.'

22
    Human corpses shall fall
        like dung upon the open field,
    like sheaves behind the reaper,
        and no one shall gather them.

(NRSV)

A Dirge for Zion

A new poem (and in MT and LXX a new chapter) begins in 9.2. The metre changes and so, briefly, does Jeremiah's mood, to one of disgust at the people's actions. If he could escape from his involvement with them he would, but it is too close. The idea here is very like that of Ps 55, and indeed some have thought Jeremiah to be the author of that psalm. The society in which he lives is built upon dishonesty: in AV's words, from which Bunyan derived the name of a character in *Pilgrim's Progress*, 'they are not valiant for the truth'.

In 9.17-22 the poet, speaking for God, calls upon the professional *mourning women* who still today in the East lead and stimulate the bereaved in funeral ceremonies. The metre in the *dirge* proper(21-22) is the *qīnāh* (3+2). The images are splendid. That of v.21 recalls the scene in the Ugaritic myth where Baal is reluctant to have *windows* put in his *palace* lest Mot, the *death* god, should enter through them and carry off his wives – and his fear is realised. Verse 22 contains the first known use of the image of death *the reaper*. When corpses lie unburied, civilisation has finally broken down.

A careful attention to the text in this poem (especially the *us . . . our . . . our* in v.18) shows that Jeremiah is hinting at something beyond that identification, to which we are now used, between himself and the suffering people. The suggestion is that God also suffers with his people. The same idea is implicit in [2.7], where God says, 'I have given the beloved of my heart into the hands of her enemies'.

True Wisdom

9. 23 These are the words of the LORD:

> Let not the wise boast of their wisdom,
>   nor the valiant of their valour;
>   let not the wealthy boast of their wealth;

24 but if anyone must boast, let him boast of this:
>   that he understands and acknowledges me.
> For I am the LORD, I show unfailing love,
>   I do justice and right on the earth;
>   for in these I take pleasure.   (REB)

True Wisdom

This brief sermon sets the knowledge of the LORD over against worldly criteria: *wisdom* in v.23 is clearly *worldly* wisdom. The contrast of values is summarised in a pair of triplets, but the key word is *boast*. The first triplet is of the kind of thing the worldly – particularly males – do boast of. The second triplet is of the LORD's actions (*love, justice, right*), which are expected also of those who *acknowledge* him. These attributes are not analysed further; but they are given point by the gentle irony of *boast*, for they are the very qualities which people do *not* boast of.

The Prophet Intercedes

10. 17 Gather up your goods and flee the country,
>   for you are living under siege.

18 These are the words of the LORD:
> This time I shall throw out
>   the whole population of the land,
>   and I shall press them and squeeze them dry.

19 Oh, the pain of my wounds!
>   The injuries I suffer are cruel.
> 'I am laid low,' I said, 'and must endure it.

20 My tent is wrecked, my tent-ropes all severed,
>   my children have left me and are gone,
> there is no one left to pitch my tent again,
>   no one to put up its curtains.'

23 I am aware, LORD,
>   that no one's ways are of his own choosing;
> nor is it within his power
>   to determine his course in life.

24 Correct me, LORD, but with justice, not in anger,
>   or you will bring me almost to nothing.   (REB)

The Prophet Intercedes

After two verses spoken for God (17-18), Jer replies on behalf of Jerusalem. The form is that of a communal lament, the speaker being identified with the community. A plea (23-4) follows the complaint (19-20). The image of v.20 was later reversed by I^2 (54.2). The terms of v.24 are surprising: Jer's contrast between *justice* and *anger* is tougher than the one we expect, between 'mercy' and 'justice'.

Too Late for Repentance?

15 Hear and give ear; do not be haughty,
    for the LORD has spoken.
16 Give glory to the LORD your God
    before he brings darkness,
and before your feet stumble
    on the mountains at twilight;
while you look for light,
    he turns it into gloom
    and makes it deep darkness.
17 But if you will not listen,
    my soul will weep in secret for your pride;
my eyes will weep bitterly and run down with tears,
    because the LORD's flock has been taken captive.

20 Lift up your eyes and see
    those who come from the north.
Where is the flock that was given you,
    your beautiful flock?
22 And if you say in your heart,
    'Why have these things come upon me?'
it is for the greatness of your iniquity
    that your skirts are lifted up,
    and you are violated.
23 Can Ethiopians change their skin
    or leopards their spots?
Then also you can do good
    who are accustomed to do evil.
25 This is your lot,
    the portion I have measured out to you, says the LORD,
because you have forgotten me
    and trusted in lies.
26 I myself will lift up your skirts over your face,
    and your shame will be seen.   (NRSV)

Too Late for Repentance?

In answer to the question whether it is too late for repentance, most OT prophets vacillated, as Jer does here. At the start of v.16 there is nominally still time, but doubts are raised by the image of shepherds in the hills who wait for the dawn – only to find it is an even blacker night. Verse 20 is addressed to a personified Jerusalem, who has failed to look after the *flock that was given* her.

By v.23 pessimism has taken over, though the famous analogy of the *leopard* is strictly inappropriate, since what Jer is really talking about is *custom*. The poem in vv.22-6, framed by the reference to *skirts*, develops an image associated especially with Hosea. Judah's worship of other gods is treated as infidelity, and will meet a fit punishment in public exposure.

A Prayer in Time of Drought

14. 1 The word of the LORD that came to Jeremiah concerning the drought:

2   Judah mourns
        and her gates languish;
    they lie in gloom on the ground,
        and the cry of Jerusalem goes up.

3   Her nobles send their servants for water;
        they come to the cisterns,
    they find no water,
        they return with their vessels empty.
    They are ashamed and dismayed
        and cover their heads,

4   because the ground is cracked.
        Because there has been no rain on the land
    the farmers are dismayed;
        they cover their heads.

5   Even the doe in the field forsakes her newborn fawn
        because there is no grass.

6   The wild asses stand on the bare heights,
        they pant for air like jackals;
    their eyes fail
        because there is no herbage.

7   Although our iniquities testify against us,
        act, O LORD, for your name's sake;
    our apostasies indeed are many,
        and we have sinned against you.

8   O hope of Israel,
        its savior in time of trouble,
    why should you be like a stranger in the land,
        like a traveler turning aside for the night?

9   Why should you be like someone confused,
        like a mighty warrior who cannot give help?
    Yet you, O LORD, are in the midst of us,
        and we are called by your name;
        do not forsake us!

10   Thus says the LORD concerning this people:
    Truly they have loved to wander,
        they have not restrained their feet;
    therefore the LORD does not accept them,
        now he will remember their iniquity
        and punish their sins.

(NRSV)

A Prayer in Time of Drought

As often in communal laments, description of the calamity (2-6) is followed by confession of sins and appeal for help. *Drought*, like invasion, was a constant threat in the ANE. It led to total devastation – note the sequence *no water, no rain, no grass, no herbage*. The sufferings of the animals are the more poignant for their innocence. A modern commentator kindly points out that carotene in grass produces Vitamin A, lack of which causes blindness (6). *Pant for air* is better rendered by REB's 'snuff the wind'.

The people's confession (7) is perfunctory, and their appeal (8-9) a personal reproach. God is behaving like a *traveller* who looks in just *for the night*, whereas he should belong intimately among them: the word translated *midst* means also 'womb', and to be *called by* someone's *name* implies paternity. So the petition receives a dusty answer. Instead of the 'salvation oracle' which often ends a lament psalm, *the* Lord *does not accept them*. (Alternatively, if REB is right to detach v.10 from the lament, he is silent).

Jehoiakim Burns Jeremiah's Scroll

1 In the fourth year of Jehoiakim son of Josiah, king of Judah, this word came to Jeremiah from the Lord: • Take a scroll and write on it all the words I have spoken to you about Jerusalem, Judah, and all the nations, from the day that I first spoke to you during the reign of Josiah down to the present day.

• Jeremiah summoned Baruch son of Neriah, and Baruch wrote on the scroll

5 at Jeremiah's dictation everything the Lord had said to him. • He gave Baruch this instruction: 'As I am debarred from going to the Lord's house, • you must go there and on a fast-day read aloud to the people the words of the Lord from the scroll you wrote at my dictation. You are to read them in the hearing of all those who come in from the towns of Judah.' • Baruch son of Neriah did all that the prophet Jeremiah had told him, about reading from the scroll the words of the Lord in the Lord's house.   ▸

Jehoiakim Burns Jeremiah's Scroll

Ch.36, brought forward here because of the light it throws on Chs 15-20, contains one of the most vivid historical narratives in the OT. It is about Jeremiah, not by him: the presumption is that it is by his friend and scribe Baruch. Ostensibly it records the moment when king Jehoiakim finally rejected the warnings of Jeremiah and thereby condemned his country to ruin. In a longer perspective it is also the first glowing instance in history of the failure of book-burning. As George Steiner wrote about this chapter: 'The Temple may be destroyed; the texts which it housed sing in the winds that scatter them'. Indeed the hero of the whole narrative is not Jeremiah or Baruch but *the scroll*, whose

whereabouts are noted at every turn (esp. v.20).

The story opens in the year 604 BC. It was only a few months since the Assyrian empire had been overthrown by the new power of Babylon under king Nebuchadnezzar. A critical moment had come for Jehoiakim, offering one last chance of survival for his little kingdom. In that situation Jeremiah would lay the Lord's challenge formally and finally before the nation.

For this purpose he needed the widest audience possible, such as gathered at the Temple on national feast or fast days. He could not go there himself after his previous narrow escape (Ch.7). In his

Jehoiakim Burns Jeremiah's Scroll (cont.)

36. 9   • In the ninth month of the fifth year of the reign of Jehoiakim son of Josiah, king of Judah, all the people in Jerusalem and all who came there from the towns

10   of Judah proclaimed a fast before the LORD. • Then in the LORD's house Baruch read aloud Jeremiah's words from the scroll to all the people; he read them from the room of Gemariah son of the adjutant-general Shaphan, which was in the upper court at the entrance to the New Gate of the LORD's house.

• When Micaiah son of Gemariah, son of Shaphan, heard all the LORD's words from the scroll • he went down to the palace, to the chief adviser's room, where he found the officers all in session: Elishama the chief adviser, Delaiah son of Shemaiah, Elnathan son of Akbor, Gemariah son of Shaphan, Zedekiah son of Hananiah, and all the other officers. • Micaiah reported to them everything he had heard Baruch read from the scroll in the hearing of the people. • Then the officers sent Jehudi son of Nethaniah, son of Shelemiah, son of Cushi, to Baruch with this order: 'Come here and bring the scroll from which you read to the people.'

15   When Baruch son of Neriah appeared before them with the scroll, • they said to him, 'Sit down and read it to us,' and he did so. • When they had listened to it, they turned to each other in alarm and said, 'We must certainly report this to the king.' • They asked Baruch to explain to them how he had come to write all this. • He answered, 'Jeremiah dictated every word of it to me, and I wrote it down with ink on the scroll.' • The officers said to him, 'You and Jeremiah must go

20   into hiding so that no one may know where you are.' • When they had deposited the scroll in the room of Elishama the chief adviser, they went to the court and reported the whole affair to the king.

• The king sent Jehudi for the scroll and, when he had fetched it from the room of Elishama the chief adviser, Jehudi read it out to the king and to all the officers in attendance on him. • Since it was the ninth month of the year, the king was sitting in his winter apartments with a fire burning in a brazier in front of him. • Every time Jehudi read three or four columns of the scroll, the king cut them off with a penknife and threw them into the fire in the brazier. He went on doing so until the entire scroll had been destroyed on the fire. • Neither the king nor any of his courtiers showed any alarm or tore their clothes as they listened to

25   these words; • and though Elnathan, Delaiah, and Gemariah begged the king not to burn the scroll, he refused to listen, • but ordered Jerahmeel, a royal prince, Seraiah son of Azriel, and Shelemiah son of Abdeel to arrest Baruch the scribe and the prophet Jeremiah. But the LORD had hidden them.

28   • After the king had burnt the scroll with all that Baruch had written on it at Jeremiah's dictation, the word of the LORD came to Jeremiah: • Take another scroll and write on it everything that was on the first scroll which King Jehoiakim of Judah burnt.

32   • Then Jeremiah took another scroll and gave it to the scribe Baruch son of Neriah, who wrote on it at Jeremiah's dictation all the words of the book which Jehoiakim king of Judah had burnt in the fire; and much else was added to the same effect.   (REB)

Jehoiakim Burns Jeremiah's Scroll (cont.)

place Baruch, who had taken down the text from Jeremiah's dictation (a quasi-legal point repeated four times in the chapter), would read it to the people.

The day chosen for the reading was in the *ninth month* (Nisan = Nov/Dec) of 604. According to later rabbinic sources, it was the custom to call a three-day *fast* each year if no autumn rain had fallen by 1 Nisan. We are not here, unlike Ch.7, told of the people's reaction, because the story moves quickly up the social scale. We are introduced to a number of high court officials who play an interesting role in the story. Most important for it is *Gemariah*. As a cabinet minister he had an apartment in the palace complex next to the Temple, and he now lent a balcony of it, in his own absence, for the reading.

Gemariah's importance lies not in himself but in his father and his son. His father *Shaphan* had been *adjutant-general* seventeen years before when 'the book of the Covenant' was found in the Temple (2 K 22): indeed Shaphan had on that occasion played the part now played by Baruch – of which more below. His son *Micaiah*, who *heard* Baruch's reading, felt the matter should be reported to the cabinet. The cabinet sent for Baruch with the scroll and asked him courteously ('*sit down*, please' in Hebrew) to read it. Their verdict was immediate: the king must be told, and Jeremiah and Baruch must go into hiding.

The narrator's slow progression up the social ranks (there is one more delay to come in 20-21) serves two purposes. It heightens the tension of the events (cp. the *alarm* of 16 and the *hiding* in 19) and it distances the king, to whom all eyes ultimately turn. In this and in other respects the narrative is a fine example of the fuller style in Hebrew story-telling. And for the denouement the scene is set with consummate skill. The circumstantial detail, which has been a feature of the narrative throughout, is increased, with the actors and the props all identified for the camera. The king's responsibility for the burning of the roll is doubly underscored. First, it was no sudden impulse: on the contrary he burned *every three or four columns* of a papyrus roll which contained say 50 columns. Second, at least three of the cabinet tried to dissuade him. And for good measure v. 24 hints at a third, editorial point. When Gemariah's father Shaphan had read the 'book of the Covenant' to the king's father Josiah, 2 K 22.11 tells us explicitly that the pious king responded by tearing his clothes. The contrast between the 'good' and the 'bad' kings is exactly in line with the theology of the DtH.

Jehoiakim's action in burning the scroll was highly symbolic. But by ancient thinking it was more: words had power, and the king wished to destroy them. By the same token a rewriting would resurrect the power. The rewritten scroll (28) probably contained most of the poems in the first twenty chapters or so of our present book.

The story of Ch.36 has much in common with that of Ch.7. But in 7 the king is absent, in 36 Jeremiah, so that the two men do not confront each other in either chapter. Whichever version one follows, it records the last occasion on which the prophet tries (and fails) to dissuade the king from his futile provocation of Babylon. In 598 Jehoiakim died, and was succeeded by his young son, confusingly named Jehoiachin. When Nebuchadnezzar made a show of force outside Jerusalem, Jehoiachin promptly surrendered and was deported to Babylon along with 'all the people of substance'. The national story is told in 2 K 24.8-16. But before we continue it, we must go back to Jer Chs 15-20, which record the prophet's private agonies during those years.

Jeremiah's Complaint Rejected

15.15 LORD, you know;
remember me, and vindicate me,
  avenge me on my persecutors.
Be patient with me and do not put me off,
  see what reproaches I endure for your sake.

16 When I came on your words I devoured them;
  they were joy and happiness to me,
  for you, LORD God of Hosts, have named me yours.

17 I have never kept company with revellers,
  never made merry with them;
because I felt your hand upon me I have sat alone,
  for you have filled me with indignation.

18 Why then is my pain unending,
  and my wound desperate, past all healing?
You are to me like a brook that fails,
  whose waters are not to be relied on.

Jeremiah's Complaint Rejected

This remarkable section consists of a complaint by Jeremiah (15-18), with a response by God (19-20). Individual laments are familiar from the psalter, and many of the features present here can be found there also. In this context it is worth looking at Ps 22.1, 7. Psalm 22 may well have illuminated Jeremiah's self-understanding, as it later did that of Jesus (Mark 15.34). Among other features, it was common for the individual in a complaint to protest his innocence (e.g. Ps 18.20). But Jeremiah's portrayal of his plight fits his life too closely for us to read his complaints as conventional. The prose sections of the book give external support to his protestation that he has *sat alone*, and his own poems illustrate the *indignation* which provoked the hostility of his countrymen.

But behind Jeremiah's countrymen stands YHWH. The complaint is addressed directly to him and, as it goes on, is more and more outspoken in its reproach of him. Elijah had in his time been driven to reproach God (1 K 17.20; 19.4, 10, 14), but Jeremiah goes even further. In the end he implicitly takes back one of his finest images of God, 'a spring of living water' (2.13) and compares him rather to a wadi, *not to be relied on* because in summer its bed is dry.

Jeremiah's Complaint Rejected (cont.)

19
This was the LORD's answer:
If you turn back to me, I shall take you back
    and you will stand before me.
If you can separate the precious from the base,
    you will be my spokesman.
This people may turn again to you,
    but you are not to turn to them.

20
To withstand them I shall make you strong,
    an unscaled wall of bronze.
Though they attack you, they will not prevail,
    for I am with you to save
    and deliver you, says the LORD;

(REB)

Jeremiah's Complaint Rejected (cont.)

In reply God addresses the man, as in the book of Job, rather than answering his complaint. He begins with a rebuke – all the more surprising to a reader who at this point in a psalm would have been expecting a salvation oracle (see p.411). He uses Jeremiah's favourite pun on 'return' (e.g. 8.4) to recall him to loyalty. As God's *spokesman* he must be tough, supporting him against *the people*. In return God will *make* him *strong to withstand them*: *a wall of bronze* repeats the promise made at his call (1.18). The honesty of these verses is astonishing. The Book of Job makes similar charges against God; but here it is the man who made the charge who first recorded it and then accepted the rebuke for having made it.

At the Potter's House

1
These are the words which came to Jeremiah from the LORD: • Go down now to the potter's house, and there I shall tell you what I have to say. • I went down to the potter's house, where I found him working at the wheel. • Now and then a vessel he was making from the clay would be spoilt in his hands, and he would remould it into another vessel to his liking.

5
    • Then the word of the LORD came to me: • Israel, can I not deal with you as this potter deals with his clay? says the LORD. House of Israel, you are clay in my hands like the clay in his.

(REB)

At the Potter's House

This famous vignette has close links to Ch.1, and its gentle tone suggests a much earlier period in Jer's life. The circumstantial detail makes it clear that Jer was not seeing a vision. The image of *potter* and *clay* was a standard illustration of God's control over human affairs, but Jer has used it along the lines of 1.10, and the *spoilt* clay will be remoulded.

Jeremiah's Agony

20. 7 O LORD, you have enticed me,
and I was enticed;
you have overpowered me,
and you have prevailed.
I have become a laughingstock all day long;
everyone mocks me.

8 For whenever I speak, I must cry out,
I must shout, 'Violence and destruction!'
For the word of the LORD has become for me
a reproach and derision all day long.

9 If I say, 'I will not mention him,
or speak any more in his name,'
then within me there is something like a burning fire
shut up in my bones;
I am weary with holding it in,
and I cannot.

10 For I hear many whispering:
'Denounce him! Let us denounce him!'
All my close friends
are watching for me to stumble.
'Perhaps he can be enticed,
and we can prevail against him,
and take our revenge on him.'

11 But the LORD is with me like a dread warrior;
therefore my persecutors will stumble,
and they will not prevail.
They will be greatly shamed,
for they will not succeed.
Their eternal dishonor
will never be forgotten.

Jeremiah's Agony

This is the most agonised of all Jer's 'confessions'. He opens even more bitterly than in 15.18 with an accusation that God has placed him in an intolerable dilemma. If he speaks God's word, he is derided; if he tries to suppress it, he is torn in two: 'what had been an outward reproach now becomes an inward torture.' He has *many* enemies, and even his *close friends* have turned against him. The motif of false friends is common enough in the complaint psalms (most movingly Ps 55.12+). But Jer gives it an extra twist. By picking up in v.10fg the same two verbs (*entice* and *prevail*) which he had used in v.7ad, he is implicitly accusing YHWH of being another treacherous friend.

Jeremiah's Agony (cont.)

12 O LORD of hosts, you test the righteous,
>   you see the heart and the mind;
> let me see your retribution upon them,
>   for to you I have committed my cause.

14 Cursed be the day
>   on which I was born!
> The day when my mother bore me,
>   let it not be blessed!

15 Cursed be the man
>   who brought the news to my father,
> saying, 'A child is born to you, a son,'
>   making him very glad.

16 Let that man be like the cities
>   that the LORD overthrew without pity;

17 because he did not kill me in the womb;
>   so my mother would have been my grave,
>   and her womb forever great.

18 Why did I come forth from the womb
>   to see toil and sorrow,
>   and spend my days in shame?   (NRSV)

Jeremiah's Agony (cont.)

Then suddenly in v.11 he changes his tone, from despair to confidence. He is sure that it is his enemies who will stumble and not prevail, and he prays for revenge – in all three cases his words in the Hebrew of 11-12 pick up theirs of 10, though NRSV changes the last to *retribution*. All that is a standard feature of lament psalms.

But it is succeeded in v.14 by a poem expressive of the uttermost misery. In his despair he wishes he had never been born. Being forbidden to curse his mother and father, he curses the *day* his *mother bore* him and the messenger who *brought the news to* his *father* – not just a *child*, but a *son*! The final question (18), with its echo of God's words at his call (1.5), is clearly addressed to God. The accusation implied in it, together with that expressed in v.7, is as near as any OT writer can get to cursing God. It has indeed a very close parallel in Job who,

being tempted by Satan to curse God, cursed instead the day of his birth (Ch.3). And this time Jeremiah receives no answer from God at all – not even the rebuke of Ch.15.

Some light is also thrown on J's 'confessions' by a figure from another masterpiece of ancient literature, Aeschylus' *Agamemnon*. Cassandra was a prophetess of Apollo who had refused his advances and in punishment been fated to foretell the truth but never be believed. At the climax of the play, she foresees in prophetic frenzy the ruin of the city and her own as well as Agamemnon's death. The frenzy wracks her body: it 'comes over me like a fire'. In her agony she rounds on Apollo for bringing her to this. In a play upon his name, she accuses him of now being her 'destroyer for the second time'. The poetry of the *Agamemnon* is more dramatic, that of Job more sustained; but Jeremiah was writing no play.

Jeremiah's Letter to the First Deportees

29. 1 This is the text of the letter that the prophet Jeremiah sent from Jerusalem to those who were left of the elders in exile, to the priests, the prophets and all the people whom Nebuchadnezzar had deported from Jerusalem to Babylon.

3 • The letter was entrusted to Elasah son of Shaphan and to Gemariah son of Hilkiah, whom Zedekiah king of Judah had sent to Babylon, to Nebuchadnezzar king of Babylon. The letter said:

5 • The LORD of Hosts, the God of Israel, says this to all the exiles deported from Jerusalem to Babylon: • 'Build houses, settle down; plant gardens and eat what they produce; • marry and have sons and daughters; choose wives for your sons, find husbands for your daughters so that these can bear sons and daughters in their turn; you must increase there and not decrease. • Work for the good of the city to which I have exiled you; pray to the LORD on its behalf, since on its welfare yours depends.'   (NJB)

Jeremiah's Letter to the First Deportees

After the more private chapters, the Book of Jeremiah resumes the national story, though still through the prophet's eyes. It is now fifteen years after the events of Ch.36. The deportation of 597 is a fait accompli. Ex-king Jehoiachin is in exile in Babylon with many of his people, and has been succeeded on the throne by his uncle Zedekiah (2 K 24.17+). Zedekiah however has resumed the anti-Babylonian policy, and so provoked a formal siege of Jerusalem. Jeremiah, who has consistently opposed that policy, is now under arrest *in the court of the guardhouse* (the story of how he got there is not told till Chs 37-8), but he still finds ways of making his point.

His letter to the first deportees shows his positive attitude to the exile. He took advantage of his friendship with some of the court circle (two brothers of *Elasah* have figured earlier as protectors of Jeremiah) to send a letter by some representatives of *Zedekiah* to them in *Babylon*. The advice he gave was notable. That they should make the best of their situation (5-6) is merely the sensible course which Jews of the dispersion have followed throughout history, usually with great success. But that they should actually *pray to the LORD on its behalf* (7) goes a good deal further. True, the reason given is prudential. But there are not many instances in the OT of intercession for gentiles: Job's final prayer for his friends is perhaps the nearest parallel.

Jeremiah Buys a Field

32. 8 Just as the LORD had foretold, my cousin Hanamel came to me in the court of the guardhouse and said, 'Buy my field at Anathoth in Benjamin. You have the right of redemption and possession as next-of-kin, so buy it for yourself.'

I recognised that this instruction came from the LORD, • so I bought the field at Anathoth from my cousin Hanamel and weighed out the price for him, seventeen 10 shekels of silver. • I signed and sealed the deed, had it witnessed, and then weighed the money on the scales. • I took my copies of the deed of purchase, both the sealed and the unsealed copies, • and handed them over to Baruch son of Neriah, son of Mahseiah, in the presence of Hanamel my cousin and the witnesses whose names were subscribed on the deed of purchase, and of the Judaeans sitting in the court of the guardhouse. • In their presence I gave my instructions to Baruch: ◗

Jeremiah Buys a Field (cont.)

• These are the words of the LORD of Hosts the God of Israel: Take these copies of the deed of purchase, both the sealed and the unsealed copies, and deposit them in an earthenware jar so that they may be preserved for a long time to come.

•15 • For these are the words of the LORD of Hosts the God of Israel: Houses, fields, and vineyards will again be bought and sold in this land.   (REB)

Jeremiah Buys a Field

While still under arrest Jeremiah finds another way of demonstrating his political views. The *field* in his home village of *Anathoth* was offered to him as next-of-kin for redemption*. The price was paid in *silver*: coinage had not yet come into use, so the amount is expressed by weight, one *shekel* being c.11.5*g*. The *deed* was executed on papyrus in *two copies*, one *sealed* for security, the other left open for consultation. Recent excavations in Jerusalem have unearthed many sealings (i.e. imprints of seals) which had been affixed to papyrus documents. Two of these, found together, bear the names respectively of *Baruch* and of Jerahmeel who in 36.26 was sent to arrest him! Alas, the documents themselves had been burned, presumably in the sack of 587 BC (2 K 25.9).

Jeremiah's action was designed to show that after the fall of Jerusalem life would go on again. He had no illusions about the horrors of a sack or a conquest, but here as in Ch.29 he shows a remarkably sober appraisal of their aftermath.

Slaves Briefly Freed

. 8 The word that came to Jeremiah from the LORD after King Zedekiah had entered into an agreement with all the people in Jerusalem to proclaim freedom for their slaves: • everyone who had Hebrew slaves, male or female, was to set them free;

10 no one was to keep a fellow-Jew in servitude. • All the officers and people, having entered this agreement to set free their slaves, both male and female, and not to keep them in servitude any longer, fulfilled its terms and let them go. • Afterwards, however, they changed their minds and forced back again into slavery the men and women whom they had freed.

   • Then this word came from the LORD to Jeremiah: . . .

21 • I shall deliver King Zedekiah of Judah and his officers to their enemies who seek their lives and to the army of the king of Babylon, which is now raising the siege. • I shall give the command, says the LORD, and bring them back to this city. They will attack it, capture it, and burn it to the ground. I shall make the towns and cities of Judah desolate and unpeopled.   (REB)

Slaves Briefly Freed

This is a fascinating historical vignette, very Jewish yet without parallel in the Bible. It was not unknown in the ancient world for slaves to be freed in a national crisis e.g. during a siege, either so that they could join in the defence or so that their owners would not have to feed them. So it happened in Jerusalem – though many of the *slaves* in this case were not foreign war-captives but Jewish debt-slaves*. These were now *freed* in the sense that their debts were remitted. But then the Babylonians, in the summer of 588, lifted the siege (21), and the owners cancelled the remission. This may well have been fairly normal behaviour. But a later deuteronomic editor brought it under the regulations for the sabbath year (Dt 15.12-18) and made it the occasion for a lengthy sermon.

Jeremiah's Arrest and Imprisonment – First Version

37. 11 After the Chaldaean army raised the siege of Jerusalem in the face of the advance of Pharaoh's army, • Jeremiah was on the way out from Jerusalem to go into Benjamite territory to take possession of his holding among the people there. • Irijah son of Shelemiah, son of Hananiah, the officer of the guard, was at the Benjamin Gate when Jeremiah reached it, and he arrested the prophet, accusing him of defecting to the Chaldaeans. • 'That is not true!' said Jeremiah. 'I am not going over to the Chaldaeans.' Irijah refused to listen but brought him under arrest before the officers. • The officers, furious with Jeremiah, had him flogged and imprisoned in the house of Jonathan the scribe, which had been converted **15** into a jail. • Jeremiah was put into a vaulted pit beneath the house, and he remained there many days.

• King Zedekiah had Jeremiah brought to him and questioned him privately in the palace, asking if there was a word from the LORD. 'There is,' said Jeremiah; 'you will fall into the hands of the king of Babylon.' • Jeremiah went on, 'What wrong have I done to you or your courtiers or this people, that you have thrown me into prison? • I pray you now, my lord king, give me a hearing and let my petition be accepted: do not send me back to the house of Jonathan the scribe, or **20** I shall die there.' • Then King Zedekiah gave the order for Jeremiah to be committed to the court of the guardhouse, and as long as there was bread in the city he was granted a daily ration of one loaf from the Street of the Bakers. So Jeremiah remained in the court of the guardhouse.   (REB)

Jeremiah's Arrest and Imprisonment – First Version

Chs 37-38 flash back to the story of Jeremiah's actual arrest and imprisonment, events which precede those of Chs 29 and 32. To confuse matters further, the text offers us two alternative accounts of this important episode, either of which could be historical, but not both. The second, in Ch.38, is the fuller and more vivid. But the version in Ch.37 has its points too, and is retained here for purposes of comparison.

The date in 37.11 is again the summer of 588, when the siege has been lifted, and Jeremiah could hope to slip out of Jerusalem on a visit to his family home just to the north. (The *holding* in question cannot be the field he bought from his cousin in Ch.32, because that transaction took place later, while he was in prison.) At the gate of the city he was arrested by the guard-commander on the suspicion – not unnatural in view of his repeated advice to surrender – that he was going over to the enemy. His denials were rejected by the *officers* i.e. leading men, who (unlike Ch.38) had him flogged and put in an underground cistern being used as *a jail*. At this time of year a cistern would contain no water, only a deep sediment of mud on the floor (38.6). Since Jonathan was a palace official, his house was inside the palace complex.

While Jeremiah was there, the king consulted him. *Zedekiah* is quite

Jeremiah's Arrest and Imprisonment – First Version (cont.)

sympathetically presented in these chapters. He is personally well disposed to Jeremiah, but afraid of his courtiers and even of the people. What he wants is reassurance, preferably of the kind Isaiah was able to give king Hezekiah. This Jeremiah rather curtly refuses. The king by contrast generously agrees to improve the prophet's conditions. Though still under house-arrest, he is free to receive visitors (Ch.32), and also guaranteed a *bread ration* as long as the city could hold out. The traders congregated in particular streets as they still do today in Jerusalem and generally in the Near East. This section of the story, like the last (37.16) and the next two (38.6, 13), ends on the matter-of-fact note that is typical of the author – presumably Baruch.

Jeremiah's Arrest and Imprisonment – Second Version

1 Shephatiah son of Mattan, Gedaliah son of Pashhur, Jucal son of Shelemiah, and Pashhur son of Malchiah heard how Jeremiah was addressing all the people; he was saying: • These are the words of the LORD: Whoever remains in this city will die by sword, famine, or pestilence, but whoever surrenders to the Chaldaeans will survive; he will escape with his life. • These are the words of the LORD: This city will assuredly be delivered into the power of the king of Babylon's army, and be captured.

• The officers said to the king, 'This man ought to be put to death. By talking in this way he is demoralising the soldiers left in the city and indeed the rest of the 5 people. It is not the people's welfare he seeks but their ruin.' • King Zedekiah said, 'He is in your hands; the king is powerless against you.' • So they took Jeremiah and put him into the cistern in the court of the guardhouse, letting him down with ropes. There was no water in the cistern, only mud, and Jeremiah sank in the mud.   ▸

Jeremiah's Arrest and Imprisonment – Second Version

Ch.38 begins with the alternative version of Jeremiah's arrest. Again the story is plausible and the action of the officials reasonable. Jeremiah did indeed give this advice often enough. 38.2 is repeated from [21.9], and ends with the same idiom: 'his life shall be his loot' – a soldier's quip made on his return from a campaign empty-handed but alive. The REB translation of v.4 conceals another military idiom which AV preserves: 'he weakeneth the hands of the men of war'.

Interestingly, this idiom is used in one of the very few Hebrew documents we have from this period, the Lachish letters. When the Babylonians marched against Jerusalem in 588, they began by reducing the country towns. Of these, the one which held out longest was Lachish [34.7], now reoccupied on a smaller scale after its destruction by Sennacherib. A captain of an outpost there scratched a note on a potsherd to his garrison commander in which he actually complains of 'the letter of the king and the letters of the princes' in Jerusalem, which 'are not good, but weaken our hands. As YHWH thy god liveth, truly since thy servant read the letters there hath been no peace for thy servant.' (*ANET* 322). This remarkable document substantiates what Jeremiah records of the king's hesitations about war policy.

The officials demanded the death

Jeremiah's Arrest and Imprisonment – Second Version (cont.)

• Ebed-melech the Cushite, a eunuch, who was in the palace, heard that they had put Jeremiah into a cistern and he went to tell the king, who was seated at the Benjamin Gate. • 'Your majesty,' he said, 'these men have acted viciously in their treatment of the prophet Jeremiah. They have thrown him into a cistern, and he **38.**10 will die of hunger where he is, for there is no more bread in the city.' • The king instructed Ebed-melech the Cushite to take three men with him and hoist Jeremiah out of the cistern before he perished. • Ebed-melech went to the palace with the men and took some tattered, cast-off clothes from a storeroom and lowered them with ropes to Jeremiah in the cistern. • He called to Jeremiah, 'Put these old clothes under your armpits to pad the ropes.' Jeremiah did so, • and they pulled him up out of the cistern with the ropes. Jeremiah remained in the court of the guardhouse.

• King Zedekiah sent for the prophet Jeremiah and had him brought to the third entrance of the LORD's house. 'I want to ask you something,' he said to 15 him; 'hide nothing from me.' • Jeremiah answered, 'If I speak out, you will certainly put me to death; if I offer advice, you will disregard it.' • King Zedekiah secretly made this promise on oath to Jeremiah: 'By the life of the LORD who gave us our lives, I shall not put you to death, nor shall I hand you over to these men who are seeking your life.' • Jeremiah said to Zedekiah, 'These are the words of the LORD the God of Hosts, the God of Israel: If you go out and surrender to the officers of the king of Babylon, you will live and this city will not be burnt down; you and your family will survive.• If, however, you do not surrender to the officers of the king of Babylon, this city will fall into the hands of the Chaldaeans, who will burn it down; you yourself will not escape them.' • The king said to Jeremiah, 'I am afraid of the Judaeans who have gone over to the enemy. The Chaldaeans may give me up to them, and their treatment of me will be ruthless.' 20 • Jeremiah answered, 'You will not be given up. If you obey the LORD in everything I tell you, all will be well with you and your life will be spared. • But if you refuse to surrender, this is what the LORD has shown me: • all the women left in the king of Judah's palace will be led out to the officers of the king of Babylon. Those women will say to you:

"Your own friends have misled you
    and proved too strong for you;
when your feet sank in the mud
    they turned and left you."

• All your women and children will be led out to the Chaldaeans and you yourself will not escape; you will be seized by the king of Babylon, and this city will be burnt down.'

Jeremiah's Arrest and Imprisonment – Second Version (cont.)

penalty for Jeremiah, presumably on the grounds of treason. The king washed his hands of the matter, whereupon they threw him into the *cistern in the court of the guardhouse*. The text then adds an astonishing note: those who had wanted his head and been given a free hand by the king now *let him down* into the cistern *with ropes*! Clearly the king must have added, as God added to Satan about Job, a stipulation that they spare Jeremiah's life.

Jeremiah's Arrest and Imprisonment – Second Version (cont.)

25

• Zedekiah said to Jeremiah, 'On pain of death let no one know about this conversation. • If the officers hear that I have been speaking with you and they come and say to you, "Tell us what you said to the king and what he said to you; hide nothing from us, and we shall not put you to death," • you must reply, "I was petitioning the king not to send me back to the house of Jonathan to die there." ' •The officers did all come and question Jeremiah, and he said to them just what the king had told him to say; so they left off questioning him and were none the wiser. • Jeremiah remained in the court of the guardhouse till the day Jerusalem fell. (REB)

Jeremiah's Arrest and Imprisonment – Second Version (cont.)

Enter then (7) a character who had no role in the first version of the story but now intercedes with the king to save Jeremiah. It is common in the OT for such roles to be given to foreigners whose goodness shows up the behaviour of the Jewish officials. An Ethiopian *eunuch* (a term meaning no more than junior official) would have to wait until he could catch the king alone. Zedekiah then acted quickly and, as in Ch.37, had Jeremiah transferred from the cistern to *the court of the guardhouse*.

Again in this version he consults Jeremiah privately, this time by the gate leading from the palace into the Temple grounds (14). At the interview he is, as before, sympathetically portrayed. The implication of v.19 is that he himself would like to abandon the resistance. But he is weak, frightened of his officials (25) but also of the people *who have already gone over to the* invaders (19). The quatrain of 22 (perhaps from a popular song) put in the mouths of the women contains an ironical play on the idea of sinking *in the mud* (cp. v.6). This points up the fact that the roles of king and prophet have been reversed. Jeremiah is now secure, and with a white lie (27) he actually protects the king from his own officials.

The mention of *the house of Jonathan* (26) represents an attempt to harmonise the two versions. The existence of the two is so strange to us that we look for two different authors. But the similarities of the events is paralleled by the similarity of treatment. It is not just a matter of the formula which closes the paragraphs in both, nor of the portrayal of the king in his role-reversal with Jeremiah. It is the portrayal of Jeremiah himself. Baruch allows no admiration or even sympathy to peep through his narrative. Here, as in Ch.36 etc, Jeremiah is not the living person we know from his poems. He is only a vehicle for the word of the LORD, which Zedekiah in the end rejects – and is doomed. For the Hebrew liking for two parallel versions of events see p.18.

The Fall of Jerusalem 587 BC

39. 1 In the tenth month of the ninth year of the reign of King Zedekiah of Judah, King Nebuchadnezzar of Babylon advanced with his whole army against Jerusalem, and they laid siege to it. • In the fourth month of the eleventh year of Zedekiah, on the ninth day of the month, the city capitulated.

11 • King Nebuchadnezzar of Babylon sent orders about Jeremiah to Nebuzaradan captain of the guard. • 'Hold him,' he said, 'and take good care of him; let him come to no harm, but do for him whatever he asks.' • So Nebuzaradan captain of the guard sent Nebushazban the chief eunuch, Nergalsarezer the commander of the frontier troops, and all the chief officers of the king of Babylon, • and they fetched Jeremiah from the court of the guardhouse and handed him over to Gedaliah son of Ahikam, son of Shaphan, to take him out to his residence. So he stayed with his own people.

15 • While Jeremiah was imprisoned the word of the LORD had come to him in the court of the guardhouse: • Go and say to Ebed-melech the Cushite: These are the words of the LORD of Hosts the God of Israel: I shall make good the words I have spoken against this city, foretelling ruin and not wellbeing, and when that day comes you will recall them. • But I shall preserve you on that day, says the LORD, and you will not be handed over to the men you fear. • I shall keep you safe, and you will not fall a victim to the sword; because you trusted in me you will escape with your life. This is the word of the LORD.   (REB)

The Fall of Jerusalem 587 BC

For the general history of the next year or two – the fall of Jerusalem in 587 BC and its immediate aftermath – the editor of the Book of Jeremiah relies heavily on 2 Kings 25. From that source derive 39.1-2, and 40.7-9. But there are other matters as well. One is the promise to *Ebed-melech* who had saved Jeremiah from the cistern. This black African receives the only unconditional 'salvation oracle' of the whole sad period (39.16+); and its position as a flashback is an editorial confirmation that it was fulfilled.

Chs 39 and 40 also contain two accounts of the release of Jeremiah by the Babylonians and of his joining *Gedaliah*, whom the Babylonians had *appointed* to be the new *governor*. Again the two accounts are virtually irreconcilable. By the first (39.11+), Jeremiah was set free straight from *the court of the guardhouse*. By the second (40.1+) he was discovered among a group of prisoners at *Ramah* on the northern frontier of Judah awaiting deportation, and released there.

The Fall of Jerusalem 587 BC (cont.)

1 • The word that came to Jeremiah from the LORD after Nebuzaradan the captain of the guard had let him go from Ramah, when he took him bound in fetters along with all the captives of Jerusalem and Judah who were being exiled to Babylon. • The captain of the guard took Jeremiah and said to him, • 'Now look, I have just released you today from the fetters on your hands. If you wish to come with me to Babylon, come, and I will take good care of you; but if you do not wish to come with me to Babylon, you need not come. See, the whole land is before you;

5 go wherever you think it good and right to go.' • So the captain of the guard gave him an allowance of food and a present, and let him go. • Then Jeremiah went to Gedaliah son of Ahikam at Mizpah, and stayed with him among the people who were left in the land.

• When all the leaders of the forces in the open country and their troops heard that the king of Babylon had appointed Gedaliah son of Ahikam governor in the land, and had committed to him men, women, and children, those of the poorest of the land who had not been taken into exile to Babylon, • they went to Gedaliah at Mizpah – Ishmael son of Nethaniah, Johanan son of Kareah, Seraiah son of Tanhumeth, the sons of Ephai the Netophathite, Jezaniah son of the Maacathite, they and their troops. • Gedaliah son of Ahikam son of Shaphan swore to them and their troops, saying, 'Do not be afraid to serve the Chaldeans. Stay in the

10 land and serve the king of Babylon, and it shall go well with you. • As for me, I am staying at Mizpah to represent you before the Chaldeans who come to us; but as for you, gather wine and summer fruits and oil, and store them in your vessels, and live in the towns that you have taken over.'   (NRSV)

The Fall of Jerusalem 587 BC (cont.)

As in Chs 37 and 38, certain features are common to the two versions. First the Babylonians treated him with special consideration. He had been a known opponent of Zedekiah's rebellion, and also a protégé of Gedaliah's family [26.24]. Secondly, Jeremiah was determined to stay with his own people – see the typical Baruch-style end of both stories (39.14; 40.6). The advice of Gedaliah in 40.9-10 fits Jeremiah's symbolic purchase of the field at Anathoth (Ch.32).

The list of the resistance leaders in 40.8 contains three names of interest. *Jezaniah* must surely be the same person as the Jaazaniah who owned a seal of c.600 BC found at *Mizpah*. The other two names dominate the story of the next three chapters. First, *Ishmael* murdered Gedaliah. Then *Johanan* rallied the remnant of the people and decided – as Jews often did when there was trouble at home – to emigrate to Egypt. Before leaving, he asked Jeremiah 'to pray that the LORD may tell us which way we ought to go and what we ought to do'. The word he received in reply was that they should stay in Judaea. Johanan refused to accept the oracle, and took Jeremiah and Baruch with him to Egypt. The Book of Jeremiah continues in a desultory way for a further nine chapters, but the story of the prophet ends effectively in Ch.38.

The New Covenant

31. 31 The days are surely coming, says the LORD, when I will make a new covenant with the house of Israel and the house of Judah. • It will not be like the covenant that I made with their ancestors when I took them by the hand to bring them out of the land of Egypt – a covenant that they broke, though I was their husband, says the LORD. • But this is the covenant that I will make with the house of Israel after those days, says the LORD: I will put my law within them, and I will write it on their hearts; and I will be their God, and they shall be my people. • No longer shall they teach one another, or say to each other, 'Know the LORD,' for they shall all know me, from the least of them to the greatest, says the LORD; for I will forgive their iniquity, and remember their sin no more.   (NRSV)

The New Covenant

Those who arranged the prophetic books commonly placed a collection of oracles of hope after those of warning, just as lament psalms often end on a note of confidence. In the book of Jeremiah that collection consists of Chs 30 and 31. Many of the poems in it are later additions predicting a glorious return from exile in terms which do not fit Jeremiah's expressed views about the length of the exile (29.1-8), and in language which is closely reminiscent of Second Isaiah. But among them is one important passage. Though composed in rhythmic prose, it fits the ideas and language of Jeremiah's poetry well enough to be confidently regarded as his.

In it he sees that, at some future date after the people have borne their punishment for breaking the covenant made with Moses on Sinai (*husband* is a term from Hosea Chs 1-2), God will forgive them and replace it with *a new covenant*. It is hard to be sure exactly what is new here. It is not the terms of the covenant; there is no suggestion of any change in them. Nor is it simply the emphasis on the (individual) *heart*, which is already found in the famous words of Dt 6.6 (n.b. heart is singular, both there and, despite most English translations, here). But Jeremiah does seem to be going beyond Dt on two points. First the covenant will be *written* on the heart, not on stone tablets, as in Exodus, nor even on phylacteries, as in Dt. That may be a rhetorical point; the second is not. It is, explicitly, that nobody will any longer need, as in Dt, to *teach* his children the covenant, because everyone will *know the LORD*. The implication seems to be that the traditional channels of communication between God and the individual will be rendered superfluous: neither prophet nor priest nor parent – nor indeed the written word – will be needed, because the human heart will be, so to speak, directly attuned to God. That is not, as it may seem, a sentimental doctrine, for the heart in Hebrew is the seat not of the emotions but of the mind and will.

Surprisingly, this idea is not found in any later passage of the OT. But it was taken up by the Qumran sect, who called themselves 'members of the new covenant'. Jesus applied it to himself at the Last Supper in speaking of 'the new covenant in my blood' (1 Cor 11.25); and when the canon of Christian literature came to be set up, the Church gave it the title of the New Covenant or Testament. But Christians have found it no easier than Jews to live up to the high spirituality so attractively adumbrated by Jeremiah.

EZEKIEL

Introduction

The compilers of the OT put the Book of Ezekiel next after those of Isaiah and Jeremiah. It is the next longest after theirs and it follows chronologically, since Ezekiel wrote from exile in Babylon c. 593-571 BC.

At first sight he also carries on the autobiographical tradition of Jeremiah. He gives us detailed information not only of the time and place of his visions, but also about his wife and children, his house and its furniture, his life with his family and disciples. But appearances are deceptive: in spite of all the information, we end by knowing Ezekiel far less well than e.g. Hosea or even Amos. He is in fact one of the most difficult of OT writers, and perhaps the most alien.

Some of the difficulties may not be his fault. For, first, the text in the Hebrew mss is full of amplifications and repetitions. Some of them are obviously due to a later hand: those have been cut, with the result that this selection looks unusually bitty. Others however may be original. For the priest Ezekiel certainly shares much with the Priestly writers of the Pentateuch: a theology which stresses God's holiness, and a style of liturgical fullness. In some contexts (notably the visions of God in Chs 1 and 2) this style adds an appropriate colour.

Second, although the text makes it clear on many occasions that Ezekiel was writing in exile in Babylon, almost all his prophecies concern Jerusalem, and his visions often give a strong impression that he was actually present there. It is tempting to alter the text, by cutting and transposing, so as to create two ministries for Ezekiel: the first in Jerusalem, from 593 to its fall in 587, the second in exile till the last recorded date of 571. But the case for surgery is inconclusive, and the traditional sequence is retained here. We must then suppose that, although Ezekiel talks *about* Jerusalem (as he does about Tyre, Egypt etc.), he is talking *to* exiles in Babylon. Many of them of course had their hopes and fears still centred on Jerusalem, as Ps 137 (which is worth re-reading here) shows.

A third specific source of puzzlement is the 'symbolic actions' ascribed to him in the text. Other prophets had performed such actions, but they loom much larger in Ezekiel. Here again the difficulties may be partly due to the addition of later material to the original narratives. One narrative in particular seems to defy explanation (see 4.4-8).

But even if all those difficulties were resolved, we should still be left with an alien author. His theology of sin and punishment is harsh, lacking the compassion which one welcomes in e.g. Jeremiah. In one place he suggests that God had a malign purpose in giving the Torah:

> I gave them statutes that were not good and ordinances by which they could not live . . . so that they might learn that I am the LORD.   [20.25-6 NRSV]

He also revels in the details of punishment [Ch.9] and of sexual misdemeanours [Chs 16, 23]. In both respects his tone resembles that of the Roman satirist Juvenal, suggesting a man who represses his own fantasies and covers a deep insecurity with an outer dogmatism.

His style is of a piece. His images, though apparently 'poetical', are often taken from the common stock and cerebrally worked out [Chs 17, 19]. The detail is frequently pedantic, the general impression baroque. If one reads the whole, one seems to be looking at a medieval scene of the Last Judgement, but with hell much more vividly represented than heaven. In this selection the balance is reversed.

In spite of these strictures, Ezekiel is an important figure in post-exilic Judaism – he has indeed been called its father. In doctrine his insistence on individual responsibility (Ch. 18), in practice his emphasis on ritual purity [Chs 4, 44], and in style his foreshadowing of later apocalyptic* – all these were to prove influential in the tradition.

His book is carefully planned in four main sections:
1. Chs 4-24: reproaches addressed to Jews before the siege of Jerusalem
2. Chs 25-32: oracles against the nations
3. Chs 33-39: comfort to Jews during and after the siege
4. Chs 40-48: constitution of the future restored community in Jerusalem.

Ezekiel's Vision of the Glory of the Lord

1. 1 Now it came to pass in the thirtieth year, in the fourth month, in the fifth day of the month, as I was among the captives by the river of Chebar, that the heavens were opened, and I saw visions of God. • In the fifth day of the month, which was the fifth year of king Jehoiachin's captivity, • the word of the LORD came expressly unto Ezekiel the priest, the son of Buzi, in the land of the Chaldeans by the river Chebar; and the hand of the LORD was there upon him.

• And I looked, and, behold, a whirlwind came out of the north, a great cloud, and a fire infolding itself, and a brightness was about it, and out of the midst 5 thereof as the colour of amber, out of the midst of the fire. • Also out of the midst thereof came the likeness of four living creatures. And this was their appearance; they had the likeness of a man. • And every one had four faces, and every one had four wings. • And their feet were straight feet; and the sole of their feet was like the sole of a calf's foot: and they sparkled like the colour of burnished brass. • And they had the hands of a man under their wings on their four sides; and they four had their faces and their wings. • Their wings were joined one to another; 10 they turned not when they went; they went every one straight forward. • As for the likeness of their faces, they four had the face of a man, and the face of a lion, on the right side: and they four had the face of an ox on the left side; they four also had the face of an eagle. • Thus were their faces: and their wings were stretched upward; two wings of every one were joined one to another, and two covered their bodies. • And they went every one straight forward: whither the spirit was to go, they went; and they turned not when they went. • As for the likeness of the living creatures, their appearance was like burning coals of fire, and like the appearance of lamps: it went up and down among the living creatures; and the fire was bright, and out of the fire went forth lightning. • And the living creatures ran and returned as the appearance of a flash of lightning.   ▶

Ezekiel's Vision of the Glory of the Lord

The first two verses represent two alternative introductions. If we take them together, we get this information. Ezekiel was a *priest* who was in exile in Babylon near the river (really a canal) *Chebar*. In the *fifth year* of exile, 593 BC, *in* (his?) *thirtieth year*, he saw *visions of God*, in which he was called to be a prophet.

Ezekiel's description of the glory of God has been criticized as opaque. But that is no weakness. A 'photographic' representation would have suited neither the nature of the vision nor its content. As it is, the very vagueness of the detail, mythical rather than mechanical, and the mesmeric fulness of diction, both help to convey the transcendence of the vision. Language may well be a less suitable medium than music or painting for representing the glory of God; but what language can do is done here –

Ezekiel's Vision of the Glory of the Lord (cont.)

5 • Now as I beheld the living creatures, behold one wheel upon the earth by the living creatures, with his four faces. • The appearance of the wheels and their work was like unto the colour of a beryl: and they four had one likeness: and their appearance and their work was as it were a wheel in the middle of a wheel. • When they went, they went upon their four sides: and they turned not when they went. • As for their rings, they were so high that they were dreadful; and their rings were full of eyes round about them four. • And when the living creatures went, the wheels went by them: and when the living creatures were lifted 20 up from the earth, the wheels were lifted up. • Whithersoever the spirit was to go, they went, thither was their spirit to go; and the wheels were lifted up over against them: for the spirit of the living creature was in the wheels. • When those went, these went; and when those stood, these stood; and when those were lifted up from the earth, the wheels were lifted up over against them: for the spirit of the living creature was in the wheels.

• And the likeness of the firmament upon the heads of the living creature was as the colour of the terrible crystal, stretched forth over their heads above. • And under the firmament were their wings straight, the one toward the other: every one had two, which covered on this side, and every one had two, which covered on that side, their bodies. • And when they went, I heard the noise of their wings, like the noise of great waters, as the voice of the Almighty, the voice of speech, 25 as the noise of an host: when they stood, they let down their wings. • And there was a voice from the firmament that was over their heads, when they stood, and had let down their wings.

• And above the firmament that was over their heads was the likeness of a throne, as the appearance of a sapphire stone: and upon the likeness of the throne was the likeness as the appearance of a man above upon it. • And I saw as the colour of amber, as the appearance of fire round about within it, from the appearance of his loins even upward, and from the appearance of his loins even downward, I saw as it were the appearance of fire, and it had brightness round about. • As the appearance of the bow that is in the cloud in the day of rain, so was the appearance of the brightness round about. This was the appearance of the likeness of the glory of the LORD. And when I saw it, I fell upon my face, and I heard a voice of one that spake.   (AV)

Ezekiel's Vision of the Glory of the Lord (cont.)

Ezekiel's word-painting with the added music of the Authorised Version.

To make some prosaic points, the *creatures* are later identified [10.18] as the cherubs whose wings protected the Ark in the Temple (1 K 8.7). Beside the creatures were *wheels* (15-21) upon which rested a *firmament* i.e. platform (22-25); together they made a chariot, the proper vehicle for a king. The phrase *a wheel in the middle of a wheel* (16), more familiar as 'wheels within wheels', perhaps describes pairs of wheels set at right angles to each other and thus not needing to turn. God can move in all directions: he is not confined to Jerusalem but is with the exiles in Babylon too. As the vision approaches its climax, the reverential circumlocutions increase. The word *likeness* comes six times in all, and when we finally learn, only in the last verse, what the vision was of, we are told, not that 'this was the LORD' but that *this was the appearance of the likeness of the glory of the LORD* (28).

Ezekiel's Call

2.1 He said, Son of man, get to your feet; I will speak to you. • As he said these words the spirit came into me and put me on my feet, and I heard him speaking to me. • He said, Son of man, I am sending you to the Israelites, to the rebels who have rebelled against me. They and their ancestors have been in revolt against me up to the present day. • Because they are stubborn and obstinate children, I am 5 sending you to them, to say, 'The LORD says this.' • Whether they listen or not, this tribe of rebels will know there is a prophet among them. • And you, son of man, do not be afraid of them or of what they say, though you find yourself surrounded with brambles and sitting on scorpions. Do not be afraid of their words or alarmed by their looks, for they are a tribe of rebels. • You are to deliver my words to them whether they listen or not, for they are a tribe of rebels. • But you, son of man, are to listen to what I say to you; do not be a rebel like that rebellious tribe. Open your mouth and eat what I am about to give you.

10   • When I looked, there was a hand stretching out to me, holding a scroll. • He unrolled it in front of me; it was written on, front and back; on it was written **3.**1 'Lamentations, dirges and cries of grief '. • He then said, Son of man, eat what you see; eat this scroll, then go and speak to the House of Israel. • I opened my mouth; he gave me the scroll to eat • and then said, Son of man, feed on this scroll which I am giving you and eat your fill. So I ate it, and it tasted sweet as honey.

        • He then said, Son of man, go to the House of Israel and tell them what I have 5 said. • You are not being sent to a nation that speaks a difficult foreign language; you are being sent to the House of Israel. • Not to big nations that speak difficult foreign languages, and whose words you would not understand – if I sent you to them, they would listen to you; • but the House of Israel will not listen to you because it will not listen to me. The whole House of Israel is defiant and obsti-nate. • But now, I am making you as defiant as they are, and as obstinate as they are; • I am making your resolution as hard as a diamond, harder than flint. So do not be afraid of them, do not be overawed by them, for they are a tribe of rebels.

10   • Then he said, Son of man, take to heart everything I say to you, listen carefully, • then go to your exiled countrymen and talk to them. Say to them, 'The Lord GOD says this,' whether they listen or not.

        • The spirit lifted me up, and behind me I heard a great vibrating sound, Blessed be the glory of the LORD in his dwelling-place! • This was the sound of the living creatures' wings beating against each other, and the sound of the wheels beside them: a great vibrating sound. • The spirit lifted me up and took me, and I 15 went, bitter and angry, and the hand of the LORD lay heavy on me. • I came to Tel Abib, to the exiles beside the River Chebar where they were living, and there I stayed with them in a stupor for seven days.   (NJB)

Ezekiel's Call

The term *son of man* is used throughout the book as the form of address by God to Ezekiel, contrasting Ezekiel's mortality with God's transcendence; REB translates it simply 'man', NRSV 'mortal'. The components of Ezekiel's call correspond to those of Isaiah and Jeremiah. In 3.1-3 Ezekiel takes up God's statement to Jeremiah (1.9) 'I am putting my words into your mouth', and elaborates it with characteristic realism. The comment in 3.3 *it tasted sweet as honey* is striking so soon after 2.10; with Ezekiel one cannot rule out the possibility of intentional 'hardness' (cp.3.9).

In 3.12-15 the vision of the glory of God, which had been interrupted, is brought to its conclusion.

Symbolic Actions about the Coming Siege of Jerusalem

22 While I was there the hand of the LORD came on me; he said, Get up, go out into the valley, and there I shall speak to you. • I got up and went out into the valley; the glory of the LORD was resting there, like the glory I had seen by the River Chebar, and I fell to the ground. • The spirit of the LORD then entered me and put me on my feet and spoke to me.

25 • He said, Go and shut yourself in your house. • Son of man, you are about to be tied and bound, and unable to mix with other people. • I am going to make your tongue stick to the roof of your mouth; you will be dumb, and no longer able to reprove them, for they are a tribe of rebels. • When I speak to you, however, I shall open your mouth and then you will say to them, 'The Lord GOD says this: Let anyone prepared to listen, listen; let anyone who refuses, refuse!' – for they are a tribe of rebels.

4.1 • For your part, son of man, take a brick and lay it in front of you; on it scratch a city, Jerusalem. • You are then to besiege it, trench round it, build earthworks, pitch camps and bring up battering-rams all round. • Then take an iron pan and place it as though it were an iron wall between you and the city. Then fix your gaze on it; it is being besieged and you are besieging it. This is a sign for the House of Israel.   ▸

Symbolic Actions about the Coming Siege of Jerusalem

There are considerable difficulties here, but a shortened text gives some coherence. Ezekiel's experience left him not merely dumb but more generally paralysed. Being unable to speak, he mimed his message about the forthcoming siege of Jerusalem in four parts. Three of them are fairly clear, and there is no reason to doubt that Ezekiel literally performed the symbolic actions as recorded.

First is the *brick* besieged (4.1-3). Mud bricks were used in Babylonia for cuneiform writing, and sieges were a favourite subject of ANE reliefs (see on 2 K 18). *Iron pan* perhaps represents God's iron determination set between Ezekiel and the city. Second is the food rationed (4.9-12). The ration amounts to 200g of food and just over one litre of water a day. But almost worse to a devout Jew was the ritual uncleanness – a constant problem during a siege. Thirdly, the cut hair (5.1-2) represents various fates of the besieged.

The action of 4.4-8, however, is

Symbolic Actions about the Coming Siege of Jerusalem (cont.)

4. 5 • Lie down on your left side and take the guilt of the House of Israel on yourself. You will bear their guilt for as many days as you lie on that side. • Allowing one day for every year of their guilt, I ordain that you bear it for three hundred and ninety days; this is how you will bear the House of Israel's guilt. • And when you have finished doing this, you are to lie down again, on your right side, and bear the guilt of the House of Judah for forty days. I have set the length for you as one day for one year. • Then fix your gaze on the siege of Jerusalem, raise your bared arm and prophesy against her. • Look, I am going to tie you up and you will not be able to turn over from one side to the other until the period of your seclusion is over.

10 • Now take wheat, barley, beans, lentils, millet and spelt; put them all in the same pot and make them into bread for yourself. You are to eat it for as many days as you are lying on your side – three hundred and ninety days. • Of this food, you are to weigh out a daily portion of twenty shekels and eat it a little piece at a time. • And you are to ration the water you drink – a sixth of a hin – drinking that a little at a time. • You are to eat this in the form of a barley cake baked where they can see you, on human dung.

5. 1 • Son of man, take a sharp sword, use it like a barber's razor and run it over your head and beard. Then take scales and divide the hair you have cut off. • Burn one-third inside the city, while the days of the siege are working themselves out. Then take another third and chop it up with the sword all round the city. The last third you are to scatter to the wind, while I unsheathe the sword behind them.

12. 3 • So, son of man, pack an exile's bundle and set off for exile by daylight while they watch. You will leave your home and go somewhere else while they watch. Then perhaps they will see that they are a tribe of rebels. • You will pack your baggage like an exile's bundle, by daylight, while they watch, and leave like an 5 exile in the evening, while they watch. • While they watch, make a hole in the wall, and go out through it. While they watch, you will shoulder your pack and go out into the dark; you will cover your face so that you cannot see the ground, since I have made you an omen for the House of Israel.

• I did as I had been told. I packed my baggage like an exile's bundle, by daylight; and in the evening I made a hole through the wall with my hands; then I went out into the dark and shouldered my pack while they watched.

• Next morning the word of the LORD was addressed to me as follows, • Son of man, did not the House of Israel, did not that tribe of rebels, ask you, 'What 10 are you doing?' • Say, 'The LORD says this: This prophecy concerns Jerusalem and the whole House of Israel who live there.' • Say, 'I am an omen for you; as I have done, so will be done to them; they will be deported into exile.'   (NJB)

Symbolic Actions about the Coming Siege of Jerusalem (cont.)

much more obscure, partly because of the lengths of time referred to. The difficulty is not removed by taking the *tie you up* of v.8 as referring metaphorically to a paralysis.

With these may be taken a fifth symbolic action from a later chapter (12.3-11) representing the emigration of those whom in 5.2 he had *to scatter to the wind.*

Individual Responsibility

1 The word of the LORD was addressed to me as follows, • Why do you keep
repeating this proverb in the land of Israel:

> The parents have eaten unripe grapes;
> and the children's teeth are set on edge?

• As I live – declares the Lord GOD – you will have no further cause to repeat
this proverb in Israel. • Look, all life belongs to me; the father's life and the son's
life, both alike belong to me. The one who has sinned is the one to die.

5 • But if a man is upright, his actions law-abiding and upright, • and he does not
eat on the mountains or raise his eyes to the foul idols of the House of Israel,
does not defile his neighbour's wife or touch a woman during her periods, •
oppresses no one, returns the pledge on a debt, does not rob, gives his own food
to the hungry, his clothes to those who lack clothing, • does not lend for profit,
does not charge interest, abstains from evil, gives honest judgement between one
person and another, • keeps my laws and sincerely respects my judgements –
someone like this is truly upright and will live – declares the Lord GOD.

10 • But if he has a son prone to violence and bloodshed, who commits one of
these misdeeds – • even though the father never has – . . . • such a person will by
14 no means live; he will die, and his blood be on his own head. • But if he in turn has
a son who, in spite of seeing all the sins that his father has committed, does not
imitate him, . . . • he will not die for his father's sins: he will most certainly live.

• Now, you say, 'Why doesn't the son bear his father's guilt?' If the son has
been law-abiding and upright, has kept all my laws and followed them, most
20 certainly he will live. • The one who has sinned is the one who must die; a son is
not to bear his father's guilt, nor a father his son's guilt. The upright will be
credited with his uprightness, and the wicked with his wickedness.

• If the wicked, however, renounces all the sins he has committed, respects
my laws and is law-abiding and upright, he will most certainly live; he will not
die. • None of the crimes he committed will be remembered against him from
then on; he will most certainly live because of his upright actions. • Would I take
pleasure in the death of the wicked – declares the Lord GOD – and not prefer to
see him renounce his wickedness and live?   ▸

Individual Responsibility

An interesting chapter, both in content
and in form. As to content, what E does
here is to work out the implications of a
teaching formulated briefly in a verse of
Deuteronomy (24.16), namely that,
contrary to some words appended to the
first commandment, God does *not* 'visit
the sins of the fathers upon the children'
(Ex 20.5). This is not necessarily a
consoling doctrine: its corollary is that, if
the Jews in exile are being punished, it is
for their own sins and not for those of
their fathers.

The argument is tight, more like that
of the later rabbis than of the earlier
prophets. Technically it is a disputation.
E starts by quoting and rejecting a well-
known proverb (AV's translation 'sour
grapes' has passed into English usage
with quite a different meaning). Next he
follows the consequences of his rejection,
considering three generations in turn: the
upright man (5-9), his wicked *son* (10+ +)
and his *upright* grandson (14+). Then in

Individual Responsibility (cont.)

• But if the upright abandons uprightness and does wrong by copying all the loathsome practices of the wicked, is he to live? All his upright actions will be forgotten from then on; for the infidelity of which he is guilty and the sin which he has committed, he will most certainly die.

18.25
30

• Now, you say, 'What the Lord does is unjust.' Now listen, House of Israel: is what I do unjust? Is it not what you do that is unjust? • So in future, House of Israel, I shall judge each of you by what that person does – declares the Lord GOD. Repent, renounce all your crimes, avoid all occasions for guilt. • Shake off all the crimes you have committed, and make yourselves a new heart and a new spirit! Why die, House of Israel? • I take no pleasure in the death of anyone – declares the Lord GOD – so repent and live!   (NJB)

Individual Responsibility (cont.)

answer to an objection (19) he states two principles. First (20), each man is independent of his parents. Second, each man is independent of his own past: allowance is made for a change of heart – in either direction! (21-23 and 24). The second principle is challenged by the *House of Israel*, but God stands firm. The exposition is rounded off (30-32) with words which show Ez at his most humane.

The Siege of Jerusalem Begins

24. 1
In the ninth year, on the tenth day of the tenth month, the word of the LORD was addressed to me as follows, • Son of man, write down today's date, yes, today's, for this very day the king of Babylon began his attack on Jerusalem. • So pronounce a parable for this tribe of rebels. Say, 'The Lord GOD says this:

> Put the pot on the fire;
>   put it on; pour the water in!
> Now put the cuts of meat all in together,
>   all the best cuts, leg and shoulder.
> Fill it with the best bones.

5

> Take the best of the flock,
>   then heap wood underneath;
> boil it thoroughly
>   until even the bones are cooked.

> Disaster is in store for the bloody city!
> I too plan to build a great fire.

10

>   Heap on the wood, light it,
> cook the meat, prepare the seasoning
>   let the bones burn!'

(NJB)

The Siege of Jerusalem Begins

The prophet's message is again conveyed in this chapter by a symbolic action. It is preceded by a date, around the turn of the year 589/588: Ezekiel in Babylon writes the date down so that its accuracy can be checked later. He quotes a cooking song, an ancient 'Polly, put the kettle on', perhaps miming the actions at the same time (3b-5), and then gives the interpretation (9-10). The little scene is all the grimmer for its domesticity.

A Dirge for Tyre: the Wreck of the Galleon

1 The word of the LORD came to me: • Now you, mortal, raise a lamentation over Tyre, • and say to Tyre, which sits at the entrance to the sea, merchant of the peoples on many coastlands, Thus says the Lord GOD:

> O Tyre, you have said,
>   'I am perfect in beauty.'
4 Your borders are in the heart of the seas;
>   your builders made perfect your beauty.
5 They made all your planks
>   of fir trees from Senir;
> they took a cedar from Lebanon
>   to make a mast for you.
6 From oaks of Bashan
>   they made your oars;
> they made your deck of pines
>   from the coasts of Cyprus,
>   inlaid with ivory.
7 Of fine embroidered linen from Egypt
>   was your sail,
>   serving as your ensign;
> blue and purple from the coasts of Elishah
>   was your awning.
8 The inhabitants of Sidon and Arvad
>   were your rowers;
> skilled men of Zemer were within you,
>   they were your pilots.
9 The elders of Gebal and its artisans were within you,
>   caulking your seams.
25 So you were filled and heavily laden
>   in the heart of the seas.

A Dirge for Tyre: the Wreck of the Galleon

No prophet has more to say against Tyre than Ez. Having been a great commercial city for centuries, the island of Tyre played a leading part in the anti-Babylonian conspiracy down to 587, but then deserted Jerusalem and gloated over her fate. As soon as Jerusalem fell, Nebuchadnezzar began a siege of Tyre, but contrary to Ez's forecast he abandoned it after 13 years. Tyre did not fall until 332 BC when Alexander built a causeway out from the mainland.

The dirge form was often used for a prophecy of doom, most notably in Isaiah Ch.14. Ez's comparison of Tyre to a galleon is felicitous: it fits her wealth and beauty (*perfect in beauty* is a favourite phrase of his), her role in trade and her position as an island. The details are well chosen to lend colour to the descriptions. *Senir* (5) and *Bashan* (6) are near Mount Hermon; *Sidon, Arvad* (8) and *Gebal* (9) are other Phoenician ports; the remaining places are unidentified.

The first part of the poem, picturing the glory of Tyre, is framed by the words *in the heart of the seas* (4, 25). The identical framing words are used, with

A Dirge for Tyre: the Wreck of the Galleon (cont.)

27.26   Your rowers have brought you
                into the high seas.
            The east wind has wrecked you
                in the heart of the seas.

27   Your riches, your wares, your merchandise,
                your mariners and your pilots,
            your caulkers, your dealers in merchandise,
                and all your warriors within you,
            sink into the heart of the seas
                on the day of your ruin.

28   At the sound of the cry of your pilots
                the countryside shakes,

29   The mariners and all the pilots of the sea
                stand on the shore.

32   In their wailing they raise a lamentation for you,
                and lament over you:

            'Who was ever like Tyre
                in the midst of the sea?

33   When your wares came from the seas,
                you satisfied many peoples;
            with your abundant wealth and merchandise
                you enriched the kings of the earth.

34   Now you are wrecked by the seas,
                in the depths of the waters;
            your merchandise and all your crew
                have sunk with you.

35   All the inhabitants of the coastlands
                are appalled at you;
            and their kings are horribly afraid,
                their faces are convulsed.

36   The merchants among the peoples hiss at you;
                you have come to a dreadful end
                and shall be no more forever.'   (NRSV)

A Dirge for Tyre: the Wreck of the Galleon (cont.)

ironical intent, for the briefer second part (26d, 27). This records her ruin, sunk by *the east wind*, the great enemy of ships in those waters. The reader would have in mind Ps 48.7: 'thou didst break the ships of the sea through the east wind'; but there is no reference here to God as the agent of Tyre's downfall, nor indeed to Baal as her champion. The only theology is that of 'pride before a fall', and even that is not stressed.

The third part consists of the actual dirge sung over her by the *inhabitants of the coastlands* (35). It is noticeable that there is no gloating on their part. The formula *Who is/was like* (32) implied admiration, and to *hiss* (36) was to show astonishment, not disapproval. There is in fact a genuine note of sadness audible in the dirge, as when the Roman conqueror Marcellus wept over the fall of Syracuse.

Two Oracles against Egypt

1 In the tenth year, on the twelfth day of the tenth month, the word of the LORD
was addressed to me as follows, • Son of man, turn towards Pharaoh king of
Egypt and prophesy against him and against the whole of Egypt. • Speak and say,
'The Lord GOD says this:

> Look, I am against you, Pharaoh king of Egypt –
> > the great crocodile wallowing in his Niles
> > who thought: My Nile is mine, I made it.

4 I shall put hooks through your jaws,
> make your Nile fish stick to your scales,
and pull you out of your Niles
> with all your Nile fish sticking to your scales.

5 I shall drop you in the desert, with all your Nile fish.
> You will fall in the wilds
> and not be taken up or buried.
I shall give you as food
> to the wild animals and the birds of heaven.'

.1 • In the eleventh year, on the first day of the third month, the word of the
LORD was addressed to me as follows, • Son of man, say to Pharaoh king of
Egypt and his throng of subjects:

> 'What can compare with you for greatness?
> > I know: a cedar tree in the Lebanon
> with noble branches, dense foliage, lofty height.
> > Its top pierces the clouds.

4 The waters have made it grow, the deep has made it tall,
> pouring its rivers round the place where it is planted,
> sending rivulets to all the wild trees.

5 This is why its height was greater than that of other wild trees,
> its branches increased in number, its boughs stretched wide,
> because of the plentiful waters making it grow.

6 All the birds of heaven nested in its branches;
> under its boughs all wild animals dropped their young;
> in its shade sat many, many people.   ▸

Two Oracles against Egypt

The *crocodile* image for *Pharaoh* in Ch.29
is in western eyes a good deal less
sympathetic than the ship image for Tyre.
But in Egyptian religion the crocodile was
the sacred animal of the Nile (the plural
Niles refers to its many mouths), just as
the Pharaoh was regarded as responsible
(*I made it*) for its flooding. Upon that
flooding depended the prosperity of the
country; consequently the transfer from
river to *desert* in v.5 is a symbol of death

not just for the crocodile but for the
people. The repeated references to the
Nile fish add a detail that is too grotesque
even for Ezekiel, and should be regarded
as a later addition designed to include *the
whole of Egypt* (2) with its *Pharaoh*.

The comparison of Pharaoh to a *cedar*
in Ch.31 seems much more straightforward. The idea of a cosmic tree, with
its branches reaching up to *the clouds*
and its roots down to *the deep* i.e. to

Two Oracles against Egypt (cont.)

31.7 It was beautiful in its size, in the span of its boughs;
for its roots were in plentiful waters.

8 There was no cedar like it in the garden of God,
no cypress had branches such as these,
no plane tree could match its boughs,
no tree in the garden of God could rival its beauty.

9 I had made it so lovely with its many branches
that it was the envy of every tree in Eden, in the garden of God.'

10 • Very well, the Lord GOD says this:
'Since it has raised itself to its full height, has lifted its top into the clouds, and has grown arrogant about its height, • I have handed it over to the prince of the nations, for him to treat as its wickedness deserves; I have rejected it. • Foreigners, the most barbarous of nations, have cut it down and deserted it. On the mountains, in all the valleys, lie its branches; its broken boughs are in every ravine throughout the country; everybody in the country has fled its shade and deserted it. • On its wreckage perch all the birds of heaven; all the wild animals have advanced on its branches.'   (NJB)

Two Oracles against Egypt (cont.)

'the waters beneath', was widespread in the ancient world. There are parallels not only in the ANE but also in Indian, Latin and Germanic literature. The poem itself (3-9) may well have existed before Ez: nothing in it seems to justify the appended oracle (10-13) with its epithets *arrogant* and *wicked*. Daniel Ch. 4 uses the same sequence of tree-image plus prophecy.

The Good Shepherd

33. 30 As for you, mortal, your people who talk together about you by the walls, and at the doors of the houses, say to one another, each to a neighbor, 'Come and hear what the word is that comes from the LORD.' • They come to you as people come, and they sit before you as my people, and they hear your words, but they will not obey them. For flattery is on their lips, but their heart is set on their gain. • To them you are like a singer of love songs, one who has a beautiful voice and plays well on an instrument; they hear what you say, but they will not do it. • When this comes – and come it will! – then they shall know that a prophet has been among them.   ▸

The Good Shepherd

The concluding verses of Ch.33 make a distinction that is relevant to much of the OT. In the priestly and prophetic traditions, to both of which Ez belonged, the object of writing was not to charm but to convert. Fortunately for readers outside those traditions, the OT contains plenty of writing which ignores the distinction, and some which is almost pure charm. Paradoxically, this little story paints an unusually charming picture of Ezekiel.

The Good Shepherd (cont.)

1 • The word of the LORD came to me: • Mortal, prophesy against the shepherds of Israel: prophesy, and say to them – to the shepherds: Thus says the LORD GOD: Ah, you shepherds of Israel who have been feeding yourselves! Should not shepherds feed the sheep? • You eat the fat, you clothe yourselves with the wool, you slaughter the fatlings; but you do not feed the sheep. • You have not strengthened the weak, you have not healed the sick, you have not bound up the injured, you have not brought back the strayed, you have not sought the lost, but with force 5 and harshness you have ruled them. • So they were scattered, because there was no shepherd; and scattered, they became food for all the wild animals. • My sheep were scattered, they wandered over all the mountains and on every high hill; my sheep were scattered over all the face of the earth, with no one to search or seek for them.

10 • Therefore, you shepherds, hear the word of the LORD: • I am against the shepherds; and I will demand my sheep at their hand, and put a stop to their feeding the sheep; no longer shall the shepherds feed themselves. I will rescue my sheep from their mouths, so that they may not be food for them.

• For thus says the Lord GOD: I myself will search for my sheep, and will seek them out. • As shepherds seek out their flocks when they are among their scattered sheep, so I will seek out my sheep. I will rescue them from all the places to which they have been scattered on a day of clouds and thick darkness. • I will bring them out from the peoples and gather them from the countries, and will bring them into their own land; and I will feed them on the mountains of Israel, by the watercourses, and in all the inhabited parts of the land. • I will feed them with good pasture, and the mountain heights of Israel shall be their pasture; there they shall lie down in good grazing land, and they shall feed on rich pasture on the 15 mountains of Israel. • I myself will be the shepherd of my sheep, and I will make them lie down, says the Lord GOD. • I will seek the lost, and I will bring back the strayed, and I will bind up the injured, and I will strengthen the weak, but the fat and the strong I will destroy. I will feed them with justice.

23 • I will set up over them one shepherd, my servant David, and he shall feed them: he shall feed them and be their shepherd. • And I the LORD will be their God, and my servant David a prince among them; I the LORD have spoken.

(NRSV)

The Good Shepherd (cont.)

Ch. 34 similarly shows him gentler than usual. The image of the king as the shepherd of his people was widespread in the ANE. Here, in a sustained treatment of the theme, God announces that, since the rulers of Israel have proved false *shepherds* (1-7), he will take over the role himself (11-16) and *bring them into their own land*. But then a variation is introduced: under himself God will set *David*, the shepherd-king, over his flock (23 f.). The picture gradually merges into that of the messianic kingdom (see commentary on Isaiah 9 and 11).

The Valley of Dry Bones

37. 1 The hand of the LORD was upon me, and carried me out in the spirit of the LORD, and set me down in the midst of the valley which was full of bones, • And caused me to pass by them round about: and, behold, there were very many in the open valley; and, lo, they were very dry. • And he said unto me, Son of man, can these bones live? and I answered, O Lord GOD, thou knowest. • Again he said unto me, Prophesy upon these bones, and say unto them, O ye dry bones, hear the word

5 of the LORD. • Thus saith the Lord GOD unto these bones; Behold, I will cause breath to enter into you, and ye shall live: • And I will lay sinews upon you, and will bring up flesh upon you, and cover you with skin, and put breath in you, and ye shall live; and ye shall know that I am the LORD.

• So I prophesied as I was commanded: and as I prophesied, there was a noise, and behold a shaking, and the bones came together, bone to his bone. • And when I beheld, lo, the sinews and the flesh came up upon them, and the skin covered them above: but there was no breath in them. • Then said he unto me, Prophesy unto the wind, prophesy, son of man, and say to the wind, Thus saith the Lord GOD; Come from the four winds, O breath, and breathe upon these

10 slain, that they may live. • So I prophesied as he commanded me, and the breath came into them, and they lived, and stood up upon their feet, an exceeding great army.

• Then he said unto me, Son of man, these bones are the whole house of Israel: behold, they say, Our bones are dried, and our hope is lost: we are cut off for our parts. • Therefore prophesy and say unto them, Thus saith the LORD God; Behold, O my people, I will open your graves, and cause you to come up out of your graves, and bring you into the land of Israel. • And ye shall know that I am the LORD, when I have opened your graves, O my people, and brought you up out of your graves, • And shall put my spirit in you, and ye shall live, and I shall place you in your own land: then shall ye know that I the LORD have spoken it, and performed it, saith the LORD.   (AV)

The Valley of Dry Bones

This is deservedly the best known passage in Ezekiel and a favourite of artists from the C4th AD synagogue at Dura onwards. The vision is strong and simple, and it fits the oracle perfectly. Even today bones can be seen lying scattered on the dry ground in the Middle East, picked clean by the vultures and whitened by the sun, as dead as dead can be. To restore life, the bones must be reassembled and the bodies reanimated.

Somewhat surprisingly, this is done in two stages (7-9), perhaps on the analogy of the two-stage creation of man in Gen 2.7. *Breath, spirit* and *wind* are all expressed by the same word *rūach* in Hebrew. The 'death' of the exiles is a loss above all of *hope* (11); hence to raise them from their *graves* is the same as to *bring* them home *into the land of Israel* (12 f.). This is a prophecy not of individual resurrection but of national restoration.

A Vision of the Restored Jerusalem

1   In the twenty-fifth year of our exile, at the beginning of the year, on the tenth day of the month, in the fourteenth year after the city was struck down, on that very day, the hand of the LORD was upon me, and he brought me there. • He brought me, in visions of God, to the land of Israel, and set me down upon a very high mountain, on which was a structure like a city to the south. • When he brought me there, a man was there, whose appearance shone like bronze, with a linen cord and a measuring reed in his hand; and he was standing in the gateway. • The man said to me, 'Mortal, look closely and listen attentively, and set your mind upon all that I shall show you, for you were brought here in order that I might show it to you; declare all that you see to the house of Israel.'

1   • Then he brought me to the gate, the gate facing east. • And there, the glory of the God of Israel was coming from the east; the sound was like the sound of mighty waters; and the earth shone with his glory. • The vision I saw was like the vision that I had seen when he came to destroy the city, and like the vision that I had seen by the river Chebar; and I fell upon my face. • As the glory of the LORD

5   entered the temple by the gate facing east, • the spirit lifted me up, and brought me into the inner court; and the glory of the LORD filled the temple.

1   • Then he brought me back to the entrance of the temple; there, water was flowing from below the threshold of the temple toward the east (for the temple faced east); and the water was flowing down from below the south end of the threshold of the temple, south of the altar. • Then he brought me out by way of the north gate, and led me around on the outside to the outer gate that faces toward the east; and the water was coming out on the south side.

         • Going on eastward with a cord in his hand, the man measured one thousand cubits, and then led me through the water; and it was ankle-deep. • Again he measured one thousand, and led me through the water; and it was knee-deep. Again he measured one thousand, and led me through the water; and it was up to

5   the waist. • Again he measured one thousand, and it was a river that I could not cross, for the water had risen; it was deep enough to swim in, a river that could not be crossed. • He said to me, 'Mortal, have you seen this?'   ▸

A Vision of the Restored Jerusalem

The long and elaborate vision which concludes the Book of Ezekiel is introduced, in a way that was to become typical in later apocalyptic*, by an angel (40.3). The *cord* and the *measuring reed* are important to what follows: the description of the new Jerusalem is meticulous in its detail, again a characteristic of post-exilic Judaism. 43.3 carefully ties this vision in with the two earlier ones of Chs 1 and [11].

The most striking feature of the vision

A Vision of the Restored Jerusalem (cont.)

Then he led me back along the bank of the river. • As I came back, I saw on the bank of the river a great many trees on the one side and on the other. • He said to me, 'This water flows toward the eastern region and goes down into the Arabah; and when it enters the sea, the sea of stagnant waters, the water will become fresh. • Wherever the river goes, every living creature that swarms will **47.10** live, and there will be very many fish, once these waters reach there. It will become fresh; and everything will live where the river goes. • People will stand fishing beside the sea from En-gedi to En-eglaim; it will be a place for the spreading of nets; its fish will be of a great many kinds, like the fish of the Great Sea. • But its swamps and marshes will not become fresh; they are to be left for salt. • On the banks, on both sides of the river, there will grow all kinds of trees for food. Their leaves will not wither nor their fruit fail, but they will bear fresh fruit every month, because the water for them flows from the sanctuary. Their fruit will be for food, and their leaves for healing.'   (NRSV)

A Vision of the Restored Jerusalem (cont.)

is the description in Ch.47 of the spring issuing from below the Temple to fertilize and sweeten the heart of the country. A lack of sweet water has always been the greatest obstacle to the prosperity of Palestine in general and Jerusalem in particular. The prophet dreams of a river whose streams will not only 'gladden the city of God' (Ps 46.4) but actually sweeten the sulphurous waters of the Dead Sea. The *Arabah* (8) is the rift valley in which lies the sea i.e. the Dead Sea; *En-gedi* and *En-eglaim* are villages on either side of it. *The Great Sea* of 10 is the Mediterranean. The OT's favourite water symbolism is particularly potent here.

DANIEL

Introduction

It has long been recognised that Daniel is two books in one. Sir Isaac Newton put it that 'the last six chapters contain prophecies written by Daniel himself', whereas the first six are 'a collection of historical papers written by other authors'. We prefer now to call the first half (A) a collection of historical romances, or more specifically court tales, the second (B) not prophecy but its romantic equivalent, apocalyptic* (for which see p.646). But the distinction between the two parts remains obvious and all-pervading. In A the hero Daniel is presented as living in exile in C6th BC Babylon, where among other adventures he interprets their dreams for kings. In B he is relating his own visions, which have to be interpreted for him and which purport to predict events in Judaea over the next four centuries. To complicate matters further, the book is written in two different languages: from 2.4b to the end of Ch.7 in Aramaic, the rest in Hebrew.

Daniel is the name of a hero in ANE legend. In Ugaritic epic he is a good king; in the Book of Ezekiel [28.3] he is proverbial for righteousness and wisdom. His portrayal here (and in the story of Susanna) fits traditional ANE portraits of the wise man, particularly that of Joseph in Genesis 37+. Nowhere however is he presented as a prophet, and the Hebrew Bible (unlike the OT) rightly classes the book of Daniel not with the prophets but with the Writings.

Chs 1-6 (A) consist of a series of stories loosely strung together round the name of Daniel. He is here an exiled Jew successfully established at the court in Babylon. The stories are of two types. In Chs 2, 4 and 5 the king has a dream or vision which Daniel interprets as forecasting the fate of the monarch himself. Ch.2 speaks also of remoter kingdoms, and does so in an apocalyptic tone which looks forward to B. In Chs 3 and 6 however the Jewish hero Daniel (for whom in Ch.3 his three companions act as a surrogate) has to endure attempts, by king or courtiers, to make him abandon certain features of his religion. In each case Daniel is providentially saved – there are strong legendary features here – and the king is brought to acknowledge the sovereignty of the hero's god. But as in the court tales of Joseph and Esther, authority is portrayed as usually benevolent: there is no persecution, and so no need for revolution.

All five chapters display one of the central characteristics of romance: the hero, who represents the weak, succeeds without difficulty in defeating his rich and powerful enemies. These stories seem to have originated at various periods ranging from Babylonian through Persian down to Greek (e.g. three of the seven musical instruments in Ch.3 have Greek names), and to have circulated independently for some time. When eventually they were brought together here, they were given an unreliable historical setting (see on Ch. 2), But individually they are among the best known of the stories in the OT, and they are told – and indeed woven together – with considerable artistry.

The core of B (Chs 7-12) is a survey, disguised as prophecy, of Jewish history, during the period from the end of the Babylonian exile down to the present (c.170 BC). The present is dominated by the persecution of the Jews under Antiochus Epiphanes, which is chronicled in the books of Maccabees. As the period unfolds and the final years approach, so the history becomes increasingly detailed and (though expressed in code) accurate, until suddenly it parts company with historical facts in describing the death of the persecutor himself. Scholars infer that these 'prophecies' were written during the persecution (but before the death of

Antiochus) with the aim of lending credibility both to the conclusion, that it will soon be over, and to the corollary, that steadfast resistance will be rewarded. Such a mixture, i.e. pseudo-prophecy followed by genuine prediction, was common in the ancient world, both ANE and Greco-Roman. It is also the principle upon which Marx based his own apocalypse: the more plausible the historical retrospect, the more convincing the forecast of salvation.

Section B has more appeal to the specialist historian or theologian than to the general reader, and must have been less effective in encouraging the resistance movement. But some of its phrases, e.g. 'the ancient of days' and 'the son of man' in Ch.7, have echoed in the consciousness of Christian Europe, as has the vision of the resurrection in 12.2.

The author of B gave his 'prophecies' additional weight by ascribing them to a famous figure: Daniel. Such use of a pseudonym was common both within Judaism (e.g. Jonah) and without (e.g. Homer or Orpheus in Greek literature). He further buttressed them by prefacing them with the collection of stories about Daniel which make up A. These stories are presented in such a way as to reinforce the messages that (i) earthly tyrants, however strong and hostile, still fall under the dominion of God and (ii) those who resist to the end will overcome. We may see the hand of the author both in the weaving together of the stories in A and in their linking to his own 'prophecies' in B. In this larger plan, [Ch.1] forms an introduction and Chs 2 and 7 act as a link between the two parts.

The problem of the two languages remains unsolved. Probably the whole was originally written in Aramaic, a language cognate to Hebrew but with a much wider currency, and then gradually translated into a late and rather halting Hebrew. Interestingly, the Qumran sect had many copies of Daniel, one written before 100 BC, but none of them shows a different linguistic distribution of the text. The Greek versions of Daniel, as of Esther, contain a good deal of additional material, relegated in Protestant bibles to the Apocrypha. Of that material only the story of Daniel and Susanna is retained here (p.752++).

Nebuchadnezzar's First Dream : the Succession of Kingdoms

1   In the second year of his reign, Nebuchadnezzar had a series of dreams; he was
perturbed by this and sleep deserted him. • The king then had magicians and
soothsayers, sorcerers and Chaldaeans summoned to tell him what his dreams
meant. They arrived and stood in the king's presence. • The king said to them, 'I
have had a dream, and my mind is troubled by a wish to understand it.' • The
Chaldaeans answered the king: 'May your majesty live for ever! Tell your servants the dream, and we shall reveal its meaning for you.'

5   • The king answered the Chaldaeans, 'This is my firm resolve: if you cannot
tell me what I dreamt and what it means, I shall have you torn limb from limb and
your houses turned into dunghills. • If, on the other hand, you can tell me what I
dreamt and what it means, I shall give you presents, rewards and high honour. So
tell me what I dreamt and what it means.' • A second time they said, 'Let the king
tell his dream to his servants, and we shall reveal its meaning.' • But the king
retorted, 'It is plain to me that you are trying to gain time, knowing my proclaimed resolve. • If you do not interpret my dream for me, there will be but one
sentence passed on you all; you have agreed among yourselves to make me
misleading and tortuous speeches while the time goes by. So tell me what my
10 dream was, and then I shall know whether you can interpret it.' • The Chaldaeans
answered the king, 'Nobody in the world could explain the king's problem; what
is more, no other king, governor or chief would think of putting such a question
to any magician, soothsayer or Chaldaean. • The question the king asks is difficult, and no one can find the king an answer to it, except the gods, whose
dwelling is not with mortals.' • At this the king flew into a rage and ordered all the
Babylonian sages to be put to death.   ▸

Nebuchadnezzar's First Dream : the Succession of Kingdoms

[Ch.1] had told how Nebuchadnezzar king
of Babylon overthrew Jerusalem and deported many Jews, including Daniel and
three companions. In fact Jerusalem did
not fall until long after the king's *second
year* (2.1). This is the first of many mistakes in Chs 2-6 which arise from trying
too hard to clothe a romance in historical
plausibility.

The first of Daniel's adventures differs from the others in that, at least in its
present form, it contains (39-45) one of
those schematic 'forecasts' of history
which are so important in Chs 7-12. There
are signs in the text that the author added
this part precisely in order to bind the two
sections of his book together. The rest of

the chapter is straightforward enough.

The idea that a king's dream had political implications was widespread in the
ANE. Daniel's own role and achievements
here follow those of Joseph's
interpretation of Pharaoh's dream in Gen
41, both in general and in certain details.
For example the gentile wise men
(*Chaldaeans* here means no more than
'astrologers') are shown up by their own
king as incompetent and even ridiculous
(v.8). The threefold exchange between
them (3-4, 5-7, 8-11), increasing in length
each time, serves both to portray their
wordy desperation and to heighten the
dramatic tension as we wait for Daniel's
entry. The hero by contrast is not only

Nebuchadnezzar's First Dream : the Succession of Kingdoms (cont.)

2.24 • So Daniel went to see Arioch, whom the king had made responsible for putting the Babylonian sages to death. Going in, he said, 'Do not put the Babylonian sages to death. Take me into the king's presence and I will reveal the meaning to 25 the king.' • Arioch lost no time in bringing Daniel to the king. 'Among the exiles from Judah,' he said, 'I have discovered a man who can reveal the meaning to the king.' • The king said to Daniel (who had been given the name Belteshazzar), 'Can you tell me what I dreamt and what it means?' • Facing the king, Daniel replied, 'None of the sages, soothsayers, magicians or exorcists has been able to tell the king the truth of the mystery which the king has propounded; • but there is a God in heaven who reveals mysteries and who has shown King Nebuchadnezzar what is to take place in the final days. These, then, are the dream and the visions that passed through your head as you lay in bed.

31 • 'You have had a vision, Your Majesty; this is what you saw: a statue, a great statue of extreme brightness, stood before you, terrible to see. • The head of this statue was of fine gold, its chest and arms were of silver, its belly and thighs of bronze, • its legs of iron, its feet part iron, part clay. • While you were gazing, a 35 stone broke away, untouched by any hand, and struck the statue, struck its feet of iron and clay and shattered them. • Then, iron and clay, bronze, silver and gold, all broke into pieces as fine as chaff on the threshing-floor in summer. The wind blew them away, leaving not a trace behind. And the stone that had struck the statue grew into a great mountain, filling the whole world. • This was the dream; we shall now explain to the king what it means.

• 'You, Your Majesty, king of kings, to whom the God of heaven has given sovereignty, power, strength and honour – • human beings, wild animals, birds of the air, wherever they live, he has entrusted to your rule, making you king of them all – you are the golden head. • And, after you, another kingdom will rise, not as great as yours, and then a third, of bronze, which will rule the whole 40 world. • There will be a fourth kingdom, hard as iron, as iron that pulverises and crushes all. Like iron that breaks everything to pieces, it will crush and break all the earlier kingdoms.

• In the days of those kings, the God of heaven will set up a kingdom which will never be destroyed, and this kingdom will not pass into the hands of another race: it will shatter and absorb all the previous kingdoms and itself last for ever – 45 • just as you saw a stone, untouched by hand, break away from the mountain and reduce iron, bronze, earthenware, silver and gold to powder. The Great God has shown the king what is to take place. The dream is true, the interpretation exact.'

• At this, King Nebuchadnezzar fell prostrate before Daniel; he gave orders for Daniel to be offered an oblation and a fragrant sacrifice. • The king said to Daniel, 'Your god is indeed the God of gods, the Master of kings, and the Revealer of Mysteries, since you have been able to reveal this mystery.' • The king then conferred high rank on Daniel and gave him many handsome presents. He also made him governor of the whole province of Babylon and head of all the sages of Babylon. • At Daniel's request, the king entrusted the affairs of the province of Babylon to Shadrach, Meshach and Abed-Nego; Daniel himself remained in attendance on the king.   (NJB)

Nebuchadnezzar's First Dream : the Succession of Kingdoms (cont.)

competent but unselfish. He is concerned for his gentile competitors (24) and he ascribes his own success to God (28). The king accepts the ascription (47, cp.11) and rewards him handsomely (48). The chief innovation here, as far as the story-line goes, is the absurd requirement that the wise men shall reveal the dream itself as well as its interpretation; that is unparalleled in ancient literature.

As to the content of Nebuchadnezzar's dream, much of it unites two long-standing traditions. The idea of four successive ages symbolised by gold, silver, bronze and iron goes back at least to the Greek poet Hesiod of the C8th BC. In Hesiod, as with us, the Golden Age represents a glorious mythical past, while Bronze and Iron belong to mundane history. At the same time as Hesiod, writers of many ANE countries were developing an analogous idea for the historical succession of empires. Like him they were drawn to the number four, but whereas Hesiod had seen a steady decline (in virtue) they saw rather a steady increase (in power). They differed among themselves both in the identification of the four empires and in what they saw as the end of the process. Members of the currently ruling nation regarded their own dominance as the climax; their subjects however looked beyond it to a further stage when they or their friends would seize power – and of course keep it for ever.

These two traditional ideas were put together (perhaps first) by the author of Daniel. To them he added a third: that the final kingdom will belong not to another world-ruler but to God himself. He also introduced two powerful, if confusing, new images.

First, the kingdoms of this world, whatever their component metal, are collectively symbolised by an idol with *feet . . . of clay* (34), the phrase which Marx took with glee and applied to the ruling class. The motif derives from a problem in ancient technology. A bronze statue, if solid, was too heavy and too expensive; if hollow, it was apt to collapse under its own weight. One solution was to fill the hollow with clay which when baked with the metal became terracotta; and some surviving ancient statues do indeed have legs partly of clay.

By contrast with the fragility of the idol, God's coming kingdom is symbolised by a stone *untouched by hand* (an epithet of great weight in an aniconic* religion) derived from the holy mountain. It will come *in the final days* (28) and will *last for ever* (44, an ironical contrast to the *live for ever* of 4). But really it belongs in a different time-scale, which is why it can destroy all the previous four empires at once.

This strongly apocalyptic* element skilfully anticipates much of Chs 7-12, especially Ch.7. It is true that, except for the flattering verses 37-38, it does not sit very well in the traditional narrative framework of Ch.2. But for most readers the resonance of its mysterious images is such as to silence the demand for a prosaic verisimilitude.

At the very end of the chapter the author's stitching is visible. Verse 49 corrects v.48 in order to introduce the next adventure. Daniel's three companions are referred to by the Babylonian names which they had been given just as he had (v.26).

The Burning Fiery Furnace

3. 1 King Nebuchadnezzar made an image of gold, whose height was sixty cubits and its breadth six cubits. He set it up on the plain of Dura, in the province of Babylon. • Then King Nebuchadnezzar sent to assemble the satraps, the prefects, and the governors, the counselors, the treasurers, the justices, the magistrates, and all the officials of the provinces to come to the dedication of the image which King Nebuchadnezzar had set up. • Then the satraps, the prefects, and the governors, the counselors, the treasurers, the justices, the magistrates, and all the officials of the provinces, were assembled for the dedication of the image that King Nebuchadnezzar had set up; and they stood before the image that Nebuchadnezzar had set up. • And the herald proclaimed aloud, 'You are commanded, O peoples,

5 nations, and languages, • that when you hear the sound of the horn, pipe, lyre, trigon, harp, bagpipe, and every kind of music, you are to fall down and worship the golden image that King Nebuchadnezzar has set up; • and whoever does not fall down and worship shall immediately be cast into a burning fiery furnace.' • Therefore, as soon as all the peoples heard the sound of the horn, pipe, lyre, trigon, harp, bagpipe, and every kind of music, all the peoples, nations, and languages fell down and worshiped the golden image which King Nebuchadnezzar had set up.

• Therefore at that time certain Chaldaeans came forward and maliciously accused the Jews. • They said to King Nebuchadnezzar, 'O king, live for ever!

10 • You, O king, have made a decree, that every man who hears the sound of the horn, pipe, lyre, trigon, harp, bagpipe, and every kind of music, shall fall down and worship the golden image; • and whoever does not fall down and worship shall be cast into a burning fiery furnace. • There are certain Jews whom you have appointed over the affairs of the province of Babylon: Shadrach, Meshach, and Abednego. These men, O king, pay no heed to you; they do not serve your gods or worship the golden image which you have set up.'   ♦

The Burning Fiery Furnace

The next adventure belongs to Daniel's three companions. It corresponds in the collection to his own ordeal in the den of lions in Ch.6. Both follow the same pattern. First, the hero is required by royal edict to break the first commandment but refuses to do so. Secondly, information is laid by his enemies, as a result of which the king has him arrested and subjected to a terrifying ordeal. Thirdly, God intervenes through an angel to save him; and the king is so impressed that he withdraws his edict and rewards the hero. Some features of this pattern are also found in the dream-interpretation stories of Chs 2, 4 and 5; but the violence of Chs 3 and 6 lends a different overall colour, closer in some ways to that of the martyr stories of e.g. 2 Macc 7.

In the first part of Ch.3 however the violence is muted and the tone is almost ceremonial. We knew from Ch.2 that the author had a relish for lists, though that was a mere four (2, 27); here the eight officials (2, 3) and six musical instruments (5, 7, 10, 15!) ostensibly emphasise the power of the king and the solemnity of the undertaking, yet leave an aftertaste of satire. Similarly the phrase *the image that King Nebuchadnezzar had set up* appears in one form or another eight times in vv.1-18.

The *image of gold*, whose dimensions are expressed in terms of the Babylonian

The Burning Fiery Furnace (cont.)

• Then Nebuchadnezzar in furious rage commanded that Shadrach, Meshach, and Abednego be brought. Then they brought these men before the king. • Nebuchadnezzar said to them, 'Is it true, O Shadrach, Meshach, and Abednego, that you do not serve my gods or worship the golden image which I have set up?

15 • Now if you are ready when you hear the sound of the horn, pipe, lyre, trigon, harp, bagpipe, and every kind of music, to fall down and worship the image which I have made, well and good; but if you do not worship, you shall immediately be cast into a burning fiery furnace; and who is the god that will deliver you out of my hands?'

• Shadrach, Meshach, and Abednego answered the king, 'O Nebuchadnezzar, we have no need to answer you in this matter. • If it be so, our God whom we serve is able to deliver us from the burning fiery furnace; and he will deliver us out of your hand, O king. • But if not, be it known to you, O king, that we will not serve your gods or worship the golden image which you have set up.'

• Then Nebuchadnezzar was full of fury, and the expression of his face was changed against Shadrach, Meshach, and Abednego. He ordered the furnace

20 heated seven times more than it was wont to be heated. • And he ordered certain mighty men of his army to bind Shadrach, Meshach, and Abednego, and to cast them into the burning fiery furnace. • Then these men were bound in their mantles, their tunics, their hats, and their other garments, and they were cast into the burning fiery furnace. • Because the king's order was strict and the furnace very hot, the flame of the fire slew those men who took up Shadrach, Meshach, and Abednego. • And these three men, Shadrach, Meshach, and Abednego, fell bound into the burning fiery furnace.

• Then King Nebuchadnezzar was astonished and rose up in haste. He said to his counselors, 'Did we not cast three men bound into the fire?' They answered

25 the king, 'True, O king.' • He answered, 'But I see four men loose, walking in the midst of the fire, and they are not hurt; and the appearance of the fourth is like a son of the gods.'   ▶

The Burning Fiery Furnace (cont.)

base six, makes a link with the vision of Ch.2. Whether it represents the king or a god, to worship it was blasphemy to a Jew. The king himself is once again a cardboard figure whose chief emotion is anger (v.13, cp. 2.12), symbolised by the flames of the furnace (19). But stage tyrants are also fickle: watching the scene of the rescue through his eyes (24-9), we observe him switch, through amazement, to redirect his wrath against the enemies of the Jewish God.

As to the three young men, their expression of faith in verses 16-18 seems all the nobler for being reserved. But later writers wished to counteract the reservation, and so we find in the LXX two long insertions at this point: the Prayer of Azariah and the Song of the Three Holy Children. Catholic bibles print them in the text of Ch.3, Protestant ones place them in the Apocrypha. The second of them, under its Latin title of the *Benedicite*, is also to be found in the Anglican *Book of Common Prayer* and is sometimes sung at evensong.

The Burning Fiery Furnace (cont.)

3.26 • Then Nebuchadnezzar came near to the door of the burning fiery furnace and said, 'Shadrach, Meshach, and Abednego, servants of the Most High God, come forth, and come here!' Then Shadrach, Meshach, and Abednego came out from the fire. • And the satraps, the prefects, the governors, and the king's counselors gathered together and saw that the fire had not had any power over the bodies of those men; the hair of their heads was not singed, their mantles were not harmed, and no smell of fire had come upon them. • Nebuchadnezzar said, 'Blessed be the God of Shadrach, Meshach, and Abednego, who has sent his angel and delivered his servants, who trusted in him, and set at nought the king's command, and yielded up their bodies rather than serve and worship any god except their own God. • Therefore I make a decree: Any people, nation, or language that speaks anything against the God of Shadrach, Meshach, and Abednego shall be torn limb from limb, and their houses laid in ruins; for there is

30 no other god who is able to deliver in this way.' • Then the king promoted Shadrach, Meshach, and Abednego in the province of Babylon.   (RSV)

The Burning Fiery Furnace (cont.)

To seek the exact nature of the *burning fiery furnace* is a mistake. Ordeal by fire was widespread before history began; Jeremiah [29.22] spoke of being 'roasted alive by the king of Babylon' as a punishment for exiles; since the Holocaust the concept of a crematory oven has become even more horrible. Similarly the author knew what he was doing in his mysterious description of *the fourth* man in v. 25.

Nebuchadnezzar's Second Dream and Madness

4.1 King Nebuchadnezzar to all peoples, nations, and languages that live throughout the earth: May you have abundant prosperity! • The signs and wonders that the Most High God has worked for me I am pleased to recount.

3   How great are his signs,
         how mighty his wonders!
     His kingdom is an everlasting kingdom,
         and his sovereignty is from generation to generation.

• I, Nebuchadnezzar, was living at ease in my home and prospering in my palace.

5 • I saw a dream that frightened me; my fantasies in bed and the visions of my head terrified me. • So I made a decree that all the wise men of Babylon should be brought before me, in order that they might tell me the interpretation of the dream. • Then the magicians, the enchanters, the Chaldeans, and the diviners came in, and I told them the dream, but they could not tell me its interpretation. • At last Daniel came in before me – he who was named Belteshazzar after the name of my god, and who is endowed with a spirit of the holy gods – and I told him the dream: ▸

Nebuchadnezzar's Second Dream and Madness

This chapter begins rather like Ch.2. The king has an alarming dream which, unlike his other wise men, Daniel is able to interpret. But there are big differences. Formally, most of the story is told through a letter, written *by* the king, which records the foreboding dream and his ultimate cure from the madness. But the rest of the story – the interpretation of the dream and the incidence of the madness – is told *about* Daniel and the king in the third person, presumably for the sake of variation.

Nebuchadnezzar's Second Dream and Madness (cont.)

• 'O Belteshazzar, chief of the magicians, I know that you are endowed with a spirit of the holy gods and that no mystery is too difficult for you. Hear the dream that I saw; tell me its interpretation.

10   Upon my bed this is what I saw;
          there was a tree at the center of the earth,
          and its height was great.

11   The tree grew great and strong,
          its top reached to heaven,
          and it was visible to the ends of the whole earth.

12   Its foliage was beautiful,
          its fruit abundant,
          and it provided food for all.
      The animals of the field found shade under it,
          the birds of the air nested in its branches,
          and from it all living beings were fed.

• I continued looking, in the visions of my head as I lay in bed, and there was
14 a holy watcher, coming down from heaven. • He cried aloud and said:
      "Cut down the tree and chop off its branches,
          strip off its foliage and scatter its fruit.
      Let the animals flee from beneath it
          and the birds from its branches.

15   But leave its stump and roots in the ground,
          with a band of iron and bronze,
          in the tender grass of the field.
      Let him be bathed with the dew of heaven.
          and let his lot be with the animals of the field
          in the grass of the earth.

16   Let his mind be changed from that of a human,
          and let the mind of an animal be given to him.
      And let seven times pass over him."

Nebuchadnezzar's Second Dream and Madness (cont.)

A second difference is that in Ch.4 Nebuchadnezzar's actions are represented as much more overtly theological than in Ch.2. Retrospectively he recognises the hand of *the Most High God* (2 etc.) or the *King of heaven* (37). He describes Daniel as inspired by *the holy gods* (8, 18) and his own vision as sent by *a holy watcher from heaven* i.e. an angel (13). Yet though he is ready to worship Daniel's god, he continues to refer to Bel i.e. Marduk as *my god* (8).

But it is the nature of the dream which gives the story its imaginative force. The image of the *tree* was not uncommon in the ANE to express the power – and indeed the fall – of a great king. Ezekiel 31 contains what might be regarded as an earlier version of this passage viz. an admiring description of the great tree followed by a forecast of its fall. A remoter ancestor of Daniel's tree, as of Ezekiel's, is the one in the garden of Eden, whose fruit was also beautiful, edible and indirectly beneficial. And the 'punishment' of Genesis 3 may have suggested the sudden and awkward modulation in the middle of v.15 from the tree itself to the person

Nebuchadnezzar's Second Dream and Madness (cont.)

4.18 • This is the dream that I, King Nebuchadnezzar, saw. Now you, Belteshazzar, declare the interpretation, since all the wise men of my kingdom are unable to tell me the interpretation. You are able, however, for you are endowed with a spirit of the holy gods.'

• Then Daniel, who was called Belteshazzar, was severely distressed for a while. His thoughts terrified him. The king said, 'Belteshazzar, do not let the dream or the interpretation terrify you.' Belteshazzar answered, 'My lord, may the dream be for those who hate you, and its interpretation for your enemies!

20 • The tree that you saw, which grew great and strong, so that its top reached to heaven and was visible to the end of the whole earth, • whose foliage was beautiful and its fruit abundant, and which provided food for all, under which animals of the field lived, and in whose branches the birds of the air had nests – • it is you, O king! You have grown great and strong. Your greatness has increased and reaches to heaven, and your sovereignty to the ends of the earth. • And whereas the king saw a holy watcher coming down from heaven and saying, "Cut down the tree and destroy it, but leave its stump and roots in the ground, with a band of iron and bronze, in the grass of the field; and let him be bathed with the dew of heaven, and let his lot be with the animals of the field, until seven times pass over him" – • this is the interpretation, O king, and it is a decree of the Most High that

25 has come upon my lord the king: • You shall be driven away from human society, and your dwelling shall be with the wild animals. You shall be made to eat grass like oxen, you shall be bathed with the dew of heaven, and seven times shall pass over you, until you have learned that the Most High has sovereignty over the kingdom of mortals, and gives it to whom he will. • As it was commanded to leave the stump and roots of the tree, your kingdom shall be reestablished for you from the time that you learn that Heaven is sovereign. • Therefore, O king, may my counsel be acceptable to you: atone for your sins with righteousness, and your iniquities with mercy to the oppressed, so that your prosperity may be prolonged.'

• All this came upon King Nebuchadnezzar. • At the end of twelve months he

30 was walking on the roof of the royal palace of Babylon, • and the king said, 'Is this not magnificent Babylon, which I have built as a royal capital by my mighty power and for my glorious majesty?' • While the words were still in the king's mouth, a voice came from heaven: 'O King Nebuchadnezzar, to you it is declared: The kingdom has departed from you! • You shall be driven away from human society, and your dwelling shall be with the animals of the field. You shall be made to eat grass like oxen, and seven times shall pass over you, until ▶

Nebuchadnezzar's Second Dream and Madness (cont.)

whom it represents. Just as the tree was cut down to a stump, so he who had aspired to superhuman status is now reduced to the subhuman, and banished from *human society* (25).

The meaning of this vision was so horrific that both Daniel and the king shrank from the obvious interpretation.

Daniel (in the polite formula used for bad news in 2 Sam 18.32) would have liked to redirect it to the king's enemies (19); failing that, he offered the chance of avoiding it by an active repentance (26-27). But the king's pride was too ingrained, like that of earlier builders of *magnificent Babylon* (30, cp. Gen 11).

Nebuchadnezzar's Second Dream and Madness (cont.)

33 you have learned that the Most High has sovereignty over the kingdom of mortals and gives it to whom he will.' • Immediately the sentence was fulfilled against Nebuchadnezzar. He was driven away from human society, ate grass like oxen, and his body was bathed with the dew of heaven, until his hair grew as long as eagles' feathers and his nails became like birds' claws.

• When that period was over, I, Nebuchadnezzar, lifted my eyes to heaven, • and my majesty and splendor were restored to me for the glory of my kingdom. My counselors and my lords sought me out, I was reestablished over my kingdom, and still more greatness was added to me. • Now I, Nebuchadnezzar, praise and extol and honor the King of heaven,

for all his works are truth,
and his ways are justice;
and he is able to bring low
those who walk in pride.   (NRSV)

Nebuchadnezzar's Second Dream and Madness (cont.)

So *the sentence was fulfilled against him* (33) for seven years (*times*, 16 etc.). In his banishment he came to repent, as 5.21 says more clearly than Ch.4. Eventually both his reason and his *majesty* were restored to him.

Yet there is nothing vindictive in this portrait of Nebuchadnezzar – rather regret at his overthrow and pleasure at his restoration. Such a tone was the likely consequence of putting most of the story into the mouth of the king. It is reinforced by the poetical quality of the writing, not only in the dream report, rightly printed as poetry in NRSV, but also in parts of the prose narrative.

Finally, we can in the case of this chapter go beyond the usual guesswork about the origins of the story. They are to be found in the closing years of the Babylonian empire, in the reign of Nebuchadnezzar's fourth and last successor Nabonidus (556-539). First we have a chronicle of Nabonidus' reign recording that for several years of it he withdrew from Babylon to Tema, an oasis town in Arabia (*ANET* 306). Second, we have a hostile account of the final years of it by the priests of Babylon, accusing him of madness and asserting that his

failure to carry out his cultic duties in the capital was punished by the loss of empire to the Persian conqueror Cyrus (*ANET* 311+). Third, and closest to Dan 4, we now have a Jewish document from Qumran entitled *The Prayer of Nabonidus*, of which the following is a restored extract:

The words of the prayer that Nabonidus the Great King prayed when he was smitten by decree of the Most High God in Tema: 'I was smitten by a malignant inflammation for seven years and I was banished far from men, until I prayed to the Most High God and a soothsayer forgave my sin. This was a Jewish man of the exiles, [and he said]: "Recount this in writing to glorify and exalt the name of the [Most High God]". And I wrote this: "I was afflicted with a malignant inflammation in Tema. For seven years I prayed to the gods of silver and gold, bronze, iron, wood, stone and clay, because I believed that they were gods".'

The most striking resemblance here is the fact that in both texts the story is partly conveyed by the king himself in writing. But there are also some equally striking differences, and the combination of the two suggests that Dan 4 and the *Prayer of Nabonidus* have a common ancestor in a Babylonian-Persian propaganda story against Nabonidus.

The Writing on the Wall

5.1 King Belshazzar gave a grand banquet for a thousand of his nobles and he was drinking wine in their presence. • Under the influence of the wine, Belshazzar gave orders for the vessels of gold and silver which his father Nebuchadnezzar had taken from the temple at Jerusalem to be fetched, so that he and his nobles, along with his concubines and courtesans, might drink from them. • So those vessels belonging to the house of God, the temple at Jerusalem, were brought, and the king, the nobles, and the concubines and courtesans drank from them. • They drank their wine and they praised their gods of gold, silver, bronze, iron, wood, and stone.

5 • Suddenly there appeared the fingers of a human hand writing on the plaster of the palace wall opposite the lamp, and the king saw the palm of the hand as it wrote. • At this the king turned pale; dismay filled his mind, the strength went from his legs, and his knees knocked together. • He called in a loud voice for the exorcists, Chaldaeans, and diviners to be brought in; then, addressing Babylon's wise men, he said, 'Whoever reads this writing and tells me its interpretation shall be robed in purple and have a gold chain hung round his neck, and he shall rank third in the kingdom.' • All the king's wise men came, but they could neither read the writing nor make known to the king its interpretation. • Then his deep dismay drove all colour from King Belshazzar's cheeks, and his nobles were in a state of confusion.

10 • Drawn by what the king and his nobles were saying, the queen entered the banqueting hall: 'Long live the king!' she said. 'Why this dismay, and why do you look so pale? • There is a man in your kingdom who has the spirit of the holy gods in him; he was known in your father's time to possess clear insight and godlike wisdom, so that King Nebuchadnezzar, your father, appointed him chief of the magicians, exorcists, Chaldaeans, and diviners. • This Daniel, whom the king named Belteshazzar, is known to have exceptional ability, with knowledge and insight, and the gift of interpreting dreams, explaining riddles, and unravelling problems; let him be summoned now and he will give the interpretation.' ▸

The Writing on the Wall

Ch.5 is presented as a continuation of Ch.4. Once again Daniel interprets a vision, this time for *Belshazzar* who is called son of Nebuchadnezzar; and in so doing he refers explicitly (18-21) to his previous interpretation. The fact that we now have a new king gives the author two advantages. First, he can once again tell the favourite story of an unknown Jew's *rise* to position at court (10-13). Second, he can contrast the father's repentance with the wilful blasphemy of the son (21-22), whose punishment is therefore to be unconditional.

The fall of Babylon is much better attested than the madness of Nabonidus, whom Ch.5 continues to miscall Nebuchadnezzar. Babylonian sources tell us that, while Nabonidus was in Tema, his eldest son Belshazzar acted as regent in the capital, and indeed was there on 16 Tishri 529 BC, when it fell without a fight to the army of Cyrus. Herodotus adds that the Persians took the city by night when the Babylonians were heedlessly celebrating a public festival. What a setting for another story about our hero!

The Writing on the Wall (cont.)

• Daniel was then brought into the royal presence, and the king addressed him: 'So you are Daniel, one of the Jewish exiles whom my royal father brought from Judah. • I am informed that the spirit of the gods resides in you and that you are known as a man of clear insight and exceptional wisdom. • The wise men, the exorcists, have just been brought before me to read this writing and make known its interpretation to me, but they have been unable to give its meaning. • I am told that you are able to furnish interpretations and unravel problems. Now, if you can read the writing and make known the interpretation, you shall be robed in purple and have a gold chain hung round your neck, and you shall rank third in the kingdom.' • Daniel replied, 'Your majesty, I do not look for gifts from you; give your rewards to another. Nevertheless I shall read your majesty the writing and make known to you its interpretation.

• 'My lord king, the Most High God gave a kingdom with power, glory, and majesty to your father Nebuchadnezzar. • But, when he became haughty and stubborn and presumptuous, he was deposed from his royal throne and stripped of his glory. • He was banished from human society, and his mind became like that of an animal; he had to live with the wild asses and to feed on grass like oxen, and his body was drenched with the dew of heaven, until he came to acknowledge that the Most High God is sovereign over the realm of humanity and appoints over it whom he will. • But although you knew all this, you, his son Belshazzar, did not humble your heart. • You have set yourself up against the LORD of heaven; his temple vessels have been fetched for you and your nobles, your concubines and courtesans to drink from them. You have praised gods fashioned from silver, gold, bronze, iron, wood, and stone, which cannot see or hear or know, and you have not given glory to God, from whom comes your every breath, and in whose charge are all your ways. • That is why he sent the hand and why it wrote this inscription.

• 'The words inscribed were: "Mene mene tekel upharsin." • Their interpretation is this: mene, God has numbered the days of your kingdom and brought it to an end; • tekel, you have been weighed in the balance and found wanting; •upharsin, your kingdom has been divided and given to the Medes and Persians.'   ▶

The Writing on the Wall (cont.)

And it is told with all the accoutrements of romance. The great royal banquet, the golden goblets, the presence of the queen and the wise men – all these recall the 'Persian' Ch.1 of Esther. The sudden contrast when the hand appears and the exaggerated description of the king's reaction (6, 9) are typical of hellenistic story-telling. And the author has given full rein to his own love of lists from v.2 onwards.

After the excitement of v.5, the tension is allowed to drop. There is a moment of surprise when Daniel ungraciously refuses the king's offer of *gifts*. But Daniel's long 'sermon' in 18-24, recapitulating much of Ch.4, allows the tension to build up again for the denouement.

The message turns out to be a set of clever puns like a clue in a crossword puzzle. The words written on the wall are ostensibly those of Babylonian weights, widely used in the ANE and normally expressed in English as mina, shekel and paratz, in which 1 mina = 60 shekels and

The Writing on the Wall (cont.)

• Then at Belshazzar's command Daniel was robed in purple and a gold chain was hung round his neck, and proclamation was made that he should rank third in the kingdom.

5.30 • That very night Belshazzar king of the Chaldaeans was slain, • and Darius the Mede took the kingdom, being then about sixty-two years old.   (REB)

The Writing on the Wall (cont.)

1 paratz = half a mina. But the words used for the weights are derived from verbs of measurement, and can also be rendered *numbered*, *weighed* and *divided* respectively. As a flourish, 'paratz' is also punningly interpreted as *to the Persians*. Verse 29 is surprising – the king's reward does not fit such a forecast of doom, and Daniel's acceptance does not fit v.17 – but it was part of the traditional tale (see 2.46-8 and Gen 41.42). Another element of the tradition is missing, namely the king's acknowledgement of Daniel's god. Before he could conform to it, Belshazzar was overtaken by fate – the only king in all these stories to die.

The end of the story introduces a non-person, *Darius the Mede*. The Medes were indeed cousins to the Persians, but their brief period of rule was past: they had already been defeated some years earlier by the Persian Cyrus, who thereupon styled himself 'King of the Medes and Persians'. This is perhaps the source of the persistent but mistaken Jewish belief in a Median empire between the Babylonian and the Persian. Cyrus himself *was* aged about 62 when he conquered Babylon. He was succeeded by Darius the Great seven years later.

Daniel in the Lions' Den

6.1 It pleased Darius to set over the kingdom one hundred twenty satraps, stationed throughout the whole kingdom, • and over them three presidents, including Daniel; to these the satraps gave account, so that the king might suffer no loss. • Soon Daniel distinguished himself above all the other presidents and satraps because an excellent spirit was in him, and the king planned to appoint him over the whole kingdom. • So the presidents and the satraps tried to find grounds for complaint against Daniel in connection with the kingdom. But they could find no grounds for complaint or any corruption, because he was faithful, and no negli-
5 gence or corruption could be found in him. • The men said, 'We shall not find any ground for complaint against this Daniel unless we find it in connection with the law of his God.'   ▸

Daniel in the Lions' Den

Ch.6 is closely parallel to Ch.3, but it also has important differences. Chief of these is the sympathetic portrayal of *Darius*. He is introduced as a great organiser of empire, which indeed the historical Darius was. By contrast, the decree requiring that *for thirty days* (7) he should himself, as a god, be the exclusive recipient of prayers – that was alien to all ancient religion and particularly to the Persians. Indeed the author seems to have sensed this, because he makes every effort to present it as an error committed in a moment of weakness and repented at leisure. Far more clearly than in Ch.3, the real villains are Daniel's enemies at court.

Daniel himself is not fully realised as a character: as elsewhere, he is more of a type than an individual. But there is a pleasant contrast between the frenzied

Daniel in the Lions' Den (cont.)

• So the presidents and satraps conspired and came to the king and said to him, 'O King Darius, live forever! • All the presidents of the kingdom, the prefects and the satraps, the counselors and the governors are agreed that the king should establish an ordinance and enforce an interdict, that whoever prays to anyone, divine or human, for thirty days, except to you, O king, shall be thrown into a den of lions. • Now, O king, establish the interdict and sign the document, so that it cannot be changed, according to the law of the Medes and the Persians, which cannot be revoked.' • Therefore King Darius signed the document and
10   interdict.

• Although Daniel knew that the document had been signed, he continued to go to his house, which had windows in its upper room open toward Jerusalem, and to get down on his knees three times a day to pray to his God and praise him, just as he had done previously. • The conspirators came and found Daniel praying and seeking mercy before his God. • Then they approached the king and said concerning the interdict, 'O king! Did you not sign an interdict, that anyone who prays to anyone, divine or human, within thirty days except to you, O king, shall be thrown into a den of lions?' The king answered, 'The thing stands fast, according to the law of the Medes and Persians, which cannot be revoked.' • Then they responded to the king, 'Daniel, one of the exiles from Judah, pays no attention to you, O king, or to the interdict you have signed, but he is saying his prayers three times a day.'

• When the king heard the charge, he was very much distressed. He was
15   determined to save Daniel, and until the sun went down he made every effort to rescue him. • Then the conspirators came to the king and said to him, 'Know, O king, that it is a law of the Medes and Persians that no interdict or ordinance that the king establishes can be changed.'   ▸

Daniel in the Lions' Den (cont.)

activity of king and courtiers in vv.1-9 and Daniel's reaction in 10. Thrice-daily prayer *toward Jerusalem* was a custom that had grown up in the exile (cp. Muslims today, facing Mecca). The upper room guaranteed peace; the open window, though making him visible, symbolises his freedom – soon to be exchanged for the lions' den, sealed by the authorities. The den itself doubtless also symbolises hell/sheol/'the pit', which is some justification for modern translations which call it 'the lions' pit'. His deliverance from it, as from the burning fiery furnace, prefigures the resurrection of which we shall hear more in Ch.12.

Darius is not only weak but paradoxically less free than the man he has incarcerated. (The immutability of Persian royal decrees, which is an important motif in Esther 8.8, is attested also by a Greek historian.) But of his good will to Daniel there is ample evidence (14, 18-20). And already in v.20 he falls over himself to speak well of Daniel's god: note the significant phrase *the living god*, with Daniel's ironical reply *O king, live for ever* – and NRSV's happy use of *deliver* between them. It is only the logical conclusion that he should finally punish his officials, reward Daniel and issue a new *decree*.

Daniel in the Lions' Den (cont.)

6. 16   • Then the king gave the command, and Daniel was brought and thrown into the den of lions. The king said to Daniel, 'May your God, whom you faithfully serve, deliver you!' • A stone was brought and laid on the mouth of the den, and the king sealed it with his own signet and with the signet of his lords, so that nothing might be changed concerning Daniel. • Then the king went to his palace and spent the night fasting; no food was brought to him, and sleep fled from him.

20   • Then, at break of day, the king got up and hurried to the den of lions. • When he came near the den where Daniel was, he cried out anxiously to Daniel, 'O Daniel, servant of the living God, has your God whom you faithfully serve been able to deliver you from the lions?' • Daniel then said to the king, 'O king, live forever! • My God sent his angel and shut the lions' mouths so that they would not hurt me, because I was found blameless before him; and also before you, O king, I have done no wrong.' • Then the king was exceedingly glad and commanded that Daniel be taken up out of the den. So Daniel was taken up out of the den, and no kind of harm was found on him, because he had trusted in his God. • The king gave a command, and those who had accused Daniel were brought and thrown into the den of lions – they, their children, and their wives. Before they reached the bottom of the den the lions overpowered them and broke all their bones in pieces.

25   • Then King Darius wrote to all peoples and nations of every language throughout the whole world: 'May you have abundant prosperity! • I make a decree, that in all my royal dominion people should tremble and fear before the God of Daniel'.

(NRSV)

Daniel in the Lions' Den (cont.)

There is plenty of historical evidence that Persian kings, and many of their hellenistic successors except Antiochus IV, did allow the Jews to worship in freedom (while not, of course, requiring other nations to join them). This favourable portrait of Darius throws into relief the burning hatred of Antiochus which motivates the second half of the book.

The Kingdoms are Judged

7. 1   In the first year of Belshazzar king of Babylon, Daniel had a dream and visions of his head as he lay in his bed. Then he wrote down the dream, and told the sum of the matter. • Daniel said, I saw in my vision by night, and behold, the four winds of heaven were stirring up the great sea. • And four great beasts came up out of the sea, different from one another. • The first was like a lion and had eagles' wings. Then as I looked its wings were plucked off, and it was lifted up from the ground and made to stand upon two feet like a man; and the mind of a

The Kingdoms are Judged

Ch.7 faces both ways in the book of Daniel. It is the first of the more detailed apocalypses* of section B, but it also looks back to Ch.2. Daniel's vision here carries on from that of Nebuchadnezzar there: the new material was too important to be revealed to a pagan king, and even the clever Daniel had to have it interpreted for him.

The vision begins (vv.1-7) with *four beasts* rising up out of the primeval *sea* of chaos. Like the four metals in Ch.2, they

The Kingdoms are Judged (cont.)

7.5 man was given to it. • And behold, another beast, a second one, like a bear. It was raised up on one side; it had three ribs in its mouth between its teeth; and it was told, 'Arise, devour much flesh.' • After this I looked, and lo, another, like a leopard, with four wings of a bird on its back; and the beast had four heads; and dominion was given to it. • After this I saw in the night visions, and behold, a fourth beast, terrible and dreadful and exceedingly strong; and it had great iron teeth; it devoured and broke in pieces, and stamped the residue with its feet. It was different from all the beasts that were before it; and it had ten horns. • I considered the horns, and behold, there came up among them another horn, a little one, before which three of the first horns were plucked up by the roots; and behold, in this horn were eyes like the eyes of a man, and a mouth speaking great

9 things. • As I looked,
> thrones were placed
> and one that was ancient of days took his seat;
> his raiment was white as snow,
> and the hair of his head like pure wool;
> his throne was fiery flames,
> its wheels were burning fire.

10
> A stream of fire issued
> and came forth from before him;
> a thousand thousands served him,
> and ten thousand times ten thousand stood before him;
> the court sat in judgement,
> and the books were opened.

11 • And as I looked, the beast was slain, and its body destroyed and given over to be burned with fire.

13 • I saw in the night visions,
> and behold, with the clouds of heaven
> there came one like a son of man,
> and he came to the Ancient of Days
> and was presented before him.

The Kingdoms are Judged (cont.)

represent the four successive empires which in Jewish tradition dominated the ANE between the exile and the present time viz. the persecution by Antiochus IV. The *fourth beast* is the Greeks, and its *ten horns* are the hellenistic* kings who succeeded Alexander (see p.756f.).

It we omit v.8 for the moment, the vision goes on to describe the heavenly *judgement* (9-10) which is to bring the Greek empire to an end (11) and establish instead the kingdom of *one like a son of man* (13-14). This passage has made an indelible impression both on later Judaism

and upon Christianity from the gospels onwards. The judgement scene draws on established OT traditions, except that nowhere else is God portrayed as *ancient*. *Thrones* (9) are seats for the heavenly council, presided over by God (cp. Ps 82.1). The whiteness of his *raiment* denotes purity, that of his *hair* age and wisdom. The *fire* is for refining, and the *wheels* of God's *throne* are from Ezekiel 1. *The books* (10) are those where God records good and bad deeds: in the case of the fourth *beast* they only needed to be *opened* for the verdict to be obvious (11).

The Kingdoms are Judged (cont.)

7. 14
And to him was given dominion
    and glory and kingdom,
that all peoples, nations, and languages
    should serve him;
his dominion is an everlasting dominion,
    which shall not pass away,
and his kingdom one
    that shall not be destroyed.

15 • As for me, Daniel, my spirit within me was anxious and the visions of my head alarmed me. • I approached one of those who stood there and asked him the truth concerning all this. So he told me, and made known to me the interpretation of the things. • 'These four great beasts are four kings who shall arise out of the earth. • But the saints of the Most High shall receive the kingdom, and possess the kingdom for ever, for ever and ever.'

• Then I desired to know the truth concerning the fourth beast, which was different from all the rest, exceedingly terrible, with its teeth of iron and claws of bronze; and which devoured and broke in pieces, and stamped the residue with

20 its feet; • and concerning the ten horns that were on its head, and the other horn which came up and before which three of them fell, the horn which had eyes and a mouth that spoke great things, and which seemed greater than its fellows.

23
Thus he said: 'As for the fourth beast,
there shall be a fourth kingdom on earth,
    which shall be different from all the kingdoms,
and it shall devour the whole earth,
    and trample it down, and break it to pieces.

24
As for the ten horns,
out of this kingdom
    ten kings shall arise,
    and another shall arise after them;
he shall be different from the former ones,
    and shall put down three kings.

The Kingdoms are Judged (cont.)

Daniel is overwhelmed by the experience, and seeks guidance from *one of those who stood there* i.e. an angel. The angel makes it clear (18) that the one like a son of man is more than an individual: he represents *the saints of the Most High* i.e. the loyal people of God. It is easy to see how the phrase 'son of man' later developed the messianic sense it bears in the gospels (Mark 9.31 etc.).

Daniel then asks for more detail about *the fourth beast*, with its 10 + 1 horns. A careful study of the text, especially v.24, shows that the references to the eleventh horn are a later addition, made in the time of Antiochus IV himself; but once inserted he becomes the main focus of interest. We hear of his blasphemy – *speaking great things* (8) *against the Most High* (25) – and of his interference in the Jewish worship and observance of *the law*, of which more detail is given in 1 Macc 1. But we are assured that his overthrow is certain and that the period (half a sabbath year 25e) is already determined, after which the rule of the saints will begin.

The Kingdoms are Judged (cont.)

25 He shall speak words against the Most High,
　　　　and shall wear out the saints of the Most High,
　　　　and shall think to change the times and the law;
　　and they shall be given into his hand
　　　　for a time, two times, and half a time.

26 But the court shall sit in judgement,
　　　　and his dominion shall be taken away,
　　　　to be consumed and destroyed to the end.

27 And the kingdom and the dominion
　　　　and the greatness of the kingdoms under the whole heaven
　　　　shall be given to the people of the saints of the Most High;
　　their kingdom shall be an everlasting kingdom,
　　　　and all dominions shall serve and obey them.'

• Here is the end of the matter. As for me, Daniel, my thoughts greatly alarmed me, and my color changed; but I kept the matter in my mind.　　　　(RSV)

The Kingdoms are Judged (cont.)

Many features help to give this chapter its power. First are the mysterious descriptions of the protagonists: the Ancient of Days, the son of man, the saints of the Most High. Second is the incantatory language, nearly but not quite overdone – the multiplication of synonyms and the repetitions of words and clauses. Third and most important is the confident promise of final victory for those suffering oppression i.e. for most of humanity most of the time.

The Consummation

21 In his place shall arise a contemptible person on whom royal majesty had not been conferred; he shall come in without warning and obtain the kingdom through intrigue. • Armies shall be utterly swept away and broken before him, and the

25 prince of the covenant as well. • He shall stir up his power and determination against the king of the south with a great army, and the king of the south shall wage war with a much greater and stronger army. But he shall not succeed, for plots shall be devised against him • by those who eat of the royal rations. They shall break him, his army shall be swept away, and many shall fall slain. • The two kings, their minds bent on evil, shall sit at one table and exchange lies. But it ▶

The Consummation

For Chs 10-12, the final section of the book, there is a change of machinery. We still have Daniel and the angel, but there are no more symbolic visions: instead the angel *tells* Daniel what is going to happen. The language of the angel is still the same mixture of clarity and obscurity which is found in all prophecies everywhere, whether genuine or not, from the Delphic oracle to 'The Stars Foretell'. But since these in Daniel are largely pseudo-prophecies (see Introd. to Daniel), we find the detail increasing as the *time* of the utterance approaches. This selection picks it up at the accession of Antiochus IV to the Seleucid throne.

The first part (21-36) tells of his usurpation of the throne in 175 BC and his sacking of the anointed high priest (22). Then comes his first campaign against Egypt in 170. Verse 27 implies that *lies* are all you can expect from kings, and

The Consummation (cont.)

shall not succeed, for there remains an end at the time appointed. • He shall return to his land with great wealth, but his heart shall be set against the holy covenant. He shall work his will, and return to his own land.

11. 30 • 'At the time appointed he shall return and come into the south, but this time it shall not be as it was before. • For ships of Kittim shall come against him, and he shall lose heart and withdraw. He shall be enraged and take action against the holy covenant. He shall turn back and pay heed to those who forsake the holy covenant. • Forces sent by him shall occupy and profane the temple and fortress. They shall abolish the regular burnt offering and set up the abomination that makes desolate. • He shall seduce with intrigue those who violate the covenant; but the people who are loyal to their God shall stand firm and take action. • The wise among the people shall give understanding to many; for some days, however, they shall fall by sword and flame, and suffer captivity and plunder. • When they fall victim, they shall receive a little help, and many shall join them insin-

35 cerely. • Some of the wise shall fall, so that they may be refined, purified, and cleansed, until the time of the end, for there is still an interval until the time appointed.

• 'The king shall act as he pleases. He shall exalt himself and consider himself greater than any god, and shall speak horrendous things against the God of gods. He shall prosper until the period of wrath is completed, for what is determined shall be done.   ▸

The Consummation (cont.)

ends with the main theme of this whole section, namely that all events are predetermined by God. Antiochus' second campaign against Egypt in 168 (v. 29) did indeed end in humiliation. Just when victory seemed in sight, a Roman envoy appeared on the scene and told him to withdraw his army; for Rome (= *Kittim* in v.30) was now interested in maintaining the balance of power in the Near East. When Antiochus temporised, the Roman drew a circle around him in the sand and demanded an answer before he stepped outside it. Antiochus agreed to *withdraw* (30), but it was now all the more necessary for him to stamp out any dissidence in Judaea. That meant intervening in support of the hellenising party among the Jews (referred to in 30 and 32), forbidding the practice of the Torah (30-31) and instituting the persecution (33). All this is recounted in uncoded language in 1 Macc 1 and 2

Macc 5 (see p.757+, where the *abomination* is explained).

The books of Maccabees celebrate the eventual victory of the Jewish resistance. At the time 'Daniel' was writing, however, in 166 BC, only *a little help* (34) was to be expected from that quarter. Antiochus would continue to *act as he pleases* (36) for a period of time which Daniel is confident will be short.

To demonstrate his confidence he proceeds in 40-45 to describe it in detail. Antiochus will invade and plunder Egypt and neighbouring territories. He will then be recalled by news of trouble in the East, but will die, with poetic justice, between Jerusalem and the Mediterranean. None of that happened: instead of mounting a third campaign against Egypt, he went east and there met his end in November 164. A few weeks later Judas Maccabaeus recovered and purified the Temple, well within the 3½-year period foretold in 7.25.

The Consummation (cont.)

.40   '• At the time of the end the king of the south shall attack him. But the king of the north shall rush upon him like a whirlwind, with chariots and horsemen, and with many ships. He shall advance against countries and pass through like a flood. • He shall come into the beautiful land, and tens of thousands shall fall victim, but Edom and Moab and the main part of the Ammonites shall escape from his power. • He shall stretch out his hand against the countries, and the land of Egypt shall not escape. • He shall become ruler of the treasures of gold and of silver, and all the riches of Egypt; and the Libyans and the Ethiopians shall follow in his train. • But reports from the east and the north shall alarm him, and he shall

45   go out with great fury to bring ruin and complete destruction to many. • He shall pitch his palatial tents between the sea and the beautiful holy mountain. Yet he shall come to his end, with no one to help him.

2. 1   '• At that time Michael, the great prince, the protector of your people, shall arise. There shall be a time of anguish, such as has never occurred since nations first came into existence. But at that time your people shall be delivered, everyone who is found written in the book. • Many of those who sleep in the dust of the earth shall awake, some to everlasting life, and some to shame and everlasting contempt. • Those who are wise shall shine like the brightness of the sky, and those who lead many to righteousness, like the stars forever and ever. • But you, Daniel, keep the words secret and the book sealed until the time of the end.'   (NRSV)

The Consummation (cont.)

When the book was written, those rewarding events were still in the future, and the persecution was still at its height. The author's aim throughout was to strengthen the will of the people to resist to the death. Already in Chs 2 and 7 he had made two points. First, God had determined that gentile domination would end soon. Second, it would be replaced by the kingdom of God and his people. But what of those who had given their lives for their faith? How could they share in the coming kingdom? Wrestling with this problem, the author breaks through in 12.1-3 to belief in the resurrection of the righteous. These verses are indeed the clearest statement of that belief in the Hebrew Bible, but the oracular-poetic language still leaves some difficulties of interpretation.

Michael (12.1) is the guardian angel of Israel, who intervenes on behalf of his people as army commander and judge. *The book* (singular) is God's 'book of life',

often referred to in the Bible (Exod 32.33 etc.). The Hebrew of v.2 is a little unclear about the categories of people intended, but almost certainly it is only Jews who will be raised, and not necessarily even all of them. The two sentences are in parallel, and so the *wise* are to be identified with *those who lead many to righteousness*. They do this 'leading' by their teaching: as 11.33 put it, the wise *give understanding*. But 11.35 hints that they also do so by their suffering, like the servant of the LORD in Second Isaiah. The two terms, 'the wise' and 'the many', were adopted not long afterwards by the Qumran community, as technical terms for the Master and the rank and file respectively.

The angel's final command to Daniel to *keep the words secret until the time of the end* is a necessary part of the literary scaffolding. It preempts the sceptical question: why were these 'prophecies' by the famous Daniel not published long before now?

Postscript: the Book of Daniel and Later Apocalyptic Writings.

The noun 'apocalypse' is the Greek equivalent of 'revelation'. The NT book Revelation is entitled in Greek the Apocalypse of John, and the Book of Daniel is sometimes called the Old Testament Apocalypse. The adjective 'apocalyptic' is used technically to designate parts of other biblical books which are like Daniel and Revelation, e.g. Is 24-27 and Mk 13, together with a considerable body of late Jewish literature not in the Bible. It is also used more loosely to refer to one feature of those books, namely their eschatology i.e. description of what will happen at the end of the world.

The general term 'revelation' and the particular 'eschatology' both fall within the definition of classical Hebrew prophecy. Apocalyptic is in fact a specialised development of prophetic writing. Like prophecy, it assumes that the seer is in touch with a heavenly world which controls the nature and the events of this world, whether past, present or future. But later apocalyptic has also three special features, all of which can be seen clearly in Daniel.

First, the simple 'vision' of the prophet has been elaborated. Instead of the word or vision of the LORD coming directly, there is now an angel to mediate *both* the message *and* its interpretation. Next, there is a strong element of mystery in the process. The word of the LORD is no longer proclaimed openly; it is wrapped in esoteric symbolism (Dan 7.19-24); it is to be concealed until a given moment (Dan 12.4) and then revealed only to 'the wise' (11.33; 12.3); and it is further guarded by the author's use of a pseudonym. Third, whereas the prophetic message led characteristically to a summons 'Repent ye', now *what is determined shall be done* right up until *the time appointed* (11.35-6). There is thus no room for either historical contingency or individual morality. That is why apocalyptic writing, though often powerful in its imagery, can seem frighteningly impersonal.

These characteristics of apocalyptic literature suited the circumstances of the vast hellenistic world, where neither the individual nor even a small country like Judaea counted for much, and where the only hope of better times lay in a supernatural intervention. But if such an intervention was to succeed, the *revelation* of it must be directed – almost restricted – to a few. That restriction could be achieved in three ways. One was the traditional folk way of the parable, such as is used in Dan 2-6. The second was that of the poetic image, whose very imprecision added to its power; so Dan 7.9-14 and 12.1-3. The third was by arcane allusion to detail, as in Ch.11 and the rest of Ch.7. This last is the way of all coterie literature, including that of contemporary Alexandrian poetry. It easily lapses into frigidity, which is why little of it is retained here. The other two ways are those of the prophets. In that sense it can be said that apocalyptic represents, on literary as well as theological criteria, a degeneration from prophetic writing.

HOSEA

Introduction

With the Book of Hosea we jump back 600 years from the latest book in the Hebrew Bible to one of the earliest. Hosea was a contemporary of Amos and Micah, the first of the so-called 'writing prophets' c.750 BC. Archaeology confirms that until then literacy had not been widespread in Israel. And not only is Hosea one of the earliest identifiable OT writers, he is also one of the very finest: original in thought and passionate in expression. Unfortunately he is not easy for us to read.

Unlike Amos and Micah and the slightly younger Isaiah, Hosea lived in the northern kingdom, Israel, whose history during that period is summarised in 2 K Chs 14-16. It was a period of apparently settled prosperity in both kingdoms, with two long-lived kings: Jeroboam II (783-743) in Israel and Uzziah (781-740) in Judah. But dark clouds were visible to some, including the prophets. They did not know that Tiglath-Pileser III, who ascended the thone of Assyria in 745, would prove a great and ruthless conqueror, but there were other signs to be read by the discerning eye.

Compared with those other prophets, Hosea does not go into detail about either social injustice or political misjudgment, both of which weakened the two kingdoms. The main thrust of his indig-nation is directed against Baal-worship, which undermined the social and cultural unity of the nation. Out of this concern he derived with great boldness an insight into God's love for Israel.

The combination of these two themes, God's love for his people and his anger at their disloyalty, proved enormously influential, not only upon later prophets but upon the authors of Deuteronomy and the so-called deuteronomic history. But where the deuteronomists wrote sermons, Hosea was a poet who thought first in images. Many of his images have passed into the currency of the English language, e.g. 'they have sown the wind and shall reap the whirlwind' [8.7 AV], which may indeed have been a proverb already in his day. More significantly, there are no fewer than 32 images for God in his book, two of which can accommodate the polar perspectives of anger and love. Of these the more immediately appealing is that of God as parent (not necessarily father), elaborated in Ch.11. The second, of God as husband to Israel (expounded in Chs 1-3) is more striking: more moving and yet more elusive.

Hosea was led to propose it by the circumstances of his own tempestuous marriage. His wife Gomer before her marriage had been a temple prostitute in a sanctuary of Baal, and now after it she left him to resume her profession.

Temples in the ANE regularly provided a range of services. Traders known as temple servants sold their goods in the precincts and doubtless paid a commission to the priests. Among them were prostitutes of both sexes. This prostitution is sometimes referred to as 'ritual', as if it was in some sense a religious act; but the evidence for that theory is slender and it is coming to be discarded. Nevertheless even if not ritual, it was a practice abhorred by strict worshippers of YHWH as being associated with sanctuaries of Baal. When king Josiah purged the Jerusalem Temple of baalist syncretism* a century after Hosea, he 'broke down the houses of the male temple prostitutes that were in the house of the LORD' [2 K 23.7].

So when Gomer left Hosea, she was doubly unfaithful, to her husband and to YHWH. From this Hosea derived the figurative contrast between Baalism and Yahwism as between casual sex and married love. To put it simply, a marriage has the following ingredients: contract or covenant, faithful love, and procreation.

In that threefold sense YHWH is 'husband' of his people – or sometimes (for none of Hosea's images is exclusive) of the land. By contrast, for the people to worship Baal is infidelity: either adultery or prostitution.

And this was no mere formal analysis on Hosea's part. What is moving in his work is the extension of this analogy into the subjective realm. In himself he was torn apart by two conflicting emotions: passionate anger at his wife's behaviour, and an equally passionate love and desire for her return. God, he saw, must suffer the same conflict about Israel. But (here he uses his model for predictive purposes) in the very last resort love will prevail over anger, and he will take her back even if she does not repent.

This insight, once gained, was not lost. Jeremiah was deeply influenced by it. Second Isaiah elaborated it in the exile. In the NT Paul adapted it in his doctrine of the marriage of Christ and the Church. But never again does it throb as in the pages of Hosea.

For Hosea, as befits one whose main themes are love and anger, writes with barely controlled passion. Partly in consequence, the Hebrew text is often extremely difficult to understand – hence wide discrepancies between the various English translations. Earlier scholars ascribed this difficulty to corruption in the MT. Nowadays it is more often put down to our ignorance of the Hebrew language in the C 8th BC, and Hosea's own bold and original use of it.

Hosea's Marriage: Infidelity, Punishment and Forgiveness

1.1 The word of the LORD that came to Hosea son of Beeri, in the days of Kings Uzziah, Jotham, Ahaz, and Hezekiah of Judah, and in the days of King Jeroboam son of Joash of Israel.

• When the LORD first spoke through Hosea, the LORD said to Hosea, 'Go, take for yourself a wife of whoredom and have children of whoredom, for the land commits great whoredom by forsaking the LORD.' • So he went and took Gomer daughter of Diblaim, and she conceived and bore him a son.

2.2
    Plead with your mother, plead –
        for she is not my wife,
        and I am not her husband –
    that she put away her whoring from her face,
        and her adultery from between her breasts,

3
    or I will strip her naked
        and expose her as in the day she was born,
    and make her like a wilderness,
        and turn her into a parched land,
        and kill her with thirst.

Hosea's Marriage: Infidelity, Punishment and Forgiveness

After an editorial verse which makes Hosea a rough contemporary of Isaiah, we jump straight in with a telescoped summary of his marriage and its meaning. The interpretation of 1.2 is disputed, like much in the first two chapters, but the following seems the most probable sequence of events. The LORD's original command (which does duty here for the longer call-narratives found in most prophetic books) was to get married and have children. But when Gomer later proved unfaithful, the analogy with Israel's unfaithfulness struck him so forcibly that he saw his marriage to *a wife of whoredom* as 'meant' from the start. Seen retrospectively, it had been a symbolic action.

Hosea's Marriage: Infidelity, Punishment and Forgiveness (cont.)

4 Upon her children also I will have no pity,
  because they are children of whoredom.
5 For their mother has played the whore;
  she who conceived them has acted shamefully.
 For she said, 'I will go after my lovers;
  they give me my bread and my water,
  my wool and my flax, my oil and my drink.'
8 She did not know
  that it was I who gave her
  the grain, the wine, and the oil,
 and who lavished upon her silver
  and gold that they used for Baal.
9 Therefore I will take back
  my grain in its time,
  and my wine in its season;
 and I will take away my wool and my flax,
  which were to cover her nakedness.
10 Now I will uncover her shame
  in the sight of her lovers,
  and no one shall rescue her out of my hand.
13 I will punish her for the festival days of the Baals,
  when she offered incense to them
 and decked herself with her ring and jewelry,
  and went after her lovers,
  and forgot me, says the LORD.   (NRSV)

Hosea's Marriage: Infidelity, Punishment and Forgiveness (cont.)

Where Ch.1 sets the scene with third-person narrative, Ch.2 describes the upshot in the form of a first-person meditation. Ostensibly it is spoken by God of the unfaithful Israel, but most of it could equally well be spoken by Hosea of Gomer, so deeply fused are the two relationships in the poet's mind. It clearly falls into two sections: (i) threats of punishment (2-13) and (ii) an offer of reconciliation (14-20). Beyond that however its structure is complex, with ideas and images intricately woven together.

In the first section, where the prophet's marriage predominates. Gomer has apparently left home. Approaching her through their children, Hosea demands that she give up her trade and return to him. But the thought of her body inflames him: if she will not return, he will punish her appropriately in accordance with ANE custom. Violent as his treatment seems to us, it falls a long way short of the death penalty enjoined by Jewish law for the adultery of a married woman. Verse 3c introduces the important but ambiguous motif of the *wilderness*, here used negatively to represent *thirst* and lack of fertility. The idea of fertility is taken further in v.5. Gomer-Israel looks to her *lovers*, i.e. to the Baals, to provide her with food, clothing and luxuries, not realising that these things come rather from her husband. The remaining verses of the first section echo the images already introduced: her nakedness (10 from 3), her adornments (13 from 2), the fruits of the earth (9 from 5) and finally her pursuit of her lovers (13 from 5). The last concludes the section except for two poignant Hebrew words: 'but-me she-forgot'.

Hosea's Marriage: Infidelity, Punishment and Forgiveness (cont.)

2. 14   But now I shall woo her,
              lead her into the wilderness,
              and speak words of encouragement to her.

15   There shall she respond as in her youth,
              as when she came up from Egypt.

19   • I shall betroth you to myself for ever, bestowing righteousness and justice,
        loyalty and love; • I shall betroth you to myself, making you faithful, and you
        will know the LORD.

                                                                                            (REB)

Hosea's Marriage: Infidelity, Punishment and Forgiveness (cont.)

The second section provides a startling reversal of the first. Verse 14 actually begins in Hebrew with the same word 'therefore' as in v.9; REB's *But* is more logical but far less dramatic. Out of pure love God announces a change of heart: he will actually go out and *woo her*. With it goes a typically Hebrew reversal of image – the *wilderness* (14) now symbolises the 'honeymoon' period of the relationship. He will once again 'speak to her heart' (so literally the Hebrew of v.14c), and she will *respond* – another word with sexual overtones.

Then he turns to address her even more intimately. Theirs will be a new marriage, based on *hesedh* i.e. *loyalty*. He will *betroth* her as if she were once again a virgin, and the marriage will be consummated anew (*know*, 20).

The Indictment

4. 1   Hear the word of the LORD, O people of Israel;
              for the LORD has an indictment against the inhabitants of the land.
        There is no faithfulness or loyalty,
              and no knowledge of God in the land.

2   Swearing, lying, and murder,
              and stealing and adultery break out;
              bloodshed follows bloodshed.

3   Therefore the land mourns,
              and all who live in it languish;
              together with the wild animals
              and the birds of the air,
              even the fish of the sea are perishing.

                                                                                           (NRSV)

The Indictment

The central chapters of Hosea (4-11), which drop the marriage metaphor, open with the common lawsuit form. The charge in 4.2 is literal: breach of the social commandments. But the underlying principle remains the same: what is missing in Israel is *loyalty* and *knowledge of God*, two sides of the same coin.

An Exchange between God and the People

12
Therefore I am like maggots to Ephraim,
    and like rottenness to the house of Judah.

13
When Ephraim saw his sickness,
    and Judah his wound,
then Ephraim went to Assyria,
    and sent to the great king.
But he is not able to cure you
    or heal your wound.

14
For I will be like a lion to Ephraim,
    and like a young lion to the house of Judah.
I myself will tear and go away;
    I will carry off, and no one shall rescue.

15
I will return again to my place
    until they acknowledge their guilt and seek my face.
In their distress they will beg my favor:

6.1
'Come, let us return to the LORD;
    for it is he who has torn, and he will heal us;
    he has struck down, and he will bind us up.

2
After two days he will revive us;
    on the third day he will raise us up,
    that we may live before him.

3
Let us know, let us press on to know the LORD;
    his appearing is as sure as the dawn;
he will come to us like the showers,
    like the spring rains that water the earth.'

An Exchange between God and the People

The exchange between God and the people consists of three 'speeches' which, as usual in Hosea, are intricately linked by their images. First the LORD speaks in two chilling similes of his relationship to them, making no distinction between the two kingdoms of *Ephraim* (= Israel) and *Judah*. In 12 he is a 'festering sore' to them (REB). Ephraim wrongly supposed that the *great king* of *Assyria* would *cure* him, for kings were thought to have such powers. In v.14 the LORD is a *lion*, which will carry off its prey to its lair. But his savagery has a paradoxical purpose, to bring about a change of heart in the people (5.15).

So they sing a psalm of penitence, whose liturgical intention is shown by the assonance of four future verbs in 1-2 ending in -ēnū. Ch. 6.1 echoes the LORD's two similes. The references to death and resurrection in 6.2 belong to the language of lament psalms (see p.412), and like *the third day* are not to be taken literally. The psalm ends, as is customary, with an expression of confidence that the LORD will hear them. Mention of *the spring rains* show that the idea of fertility is still present.

An Exchange between God and the People (cont.)

6. 4   What shall I do with you, O Ephraim?
        What shall I do with you, O Judah?
    Your love is like a morning cloud,
        like the dew that goes away early.

5   Therefore I have hewn them by the prophets,
        I have killed them by the words of my mouth,

6   For I desire steadfast love and not sacrifice,
        the knowledge of God rather than burnt offerings.   (NRSV)

An Exchange between God and the People (cont.)

But is the psalm just a little too smooth, the repentance too pat? At any rate the LORD's response (4-6) is reserved. He is undecided whether to destroy or to save. Their *love* (*hesedh*) is never more than short-lived. Insubstantial as *dew* (an image that picks up *dawn* in 3b), it vanishes as the day wears on, unlike proper rain. That is why he has attacked them – again the verbs are violent – through *the prophets*. The phrase *knowledge of God* picks up the people's words *to know the LORD* (3). It suggests that God recognises their good intentions, but is for the moment undecided *what* to *do with* them – just like Hosea with Gomer.

The form in which Hosea here expresses God's demands is one which other prophets also favoured. It needs careful attention if it is not to be misunderstood. The formulation can be either absolute, as here in v.6a (I *desire* A, *not* B), or relative, as here in v.6b (A *rather than* B). And the parallelism shows that the two formulations are equivalent i.e. God is not rejecting *sacrifice* as such.

God's Parental Love is Inexhaustible

11. 1   When Israel was a child, I loved him,
        and out of Egypt I called my son.

2   The more I called them,
        the more they went from me;
    they kept sacrificing to the Baals,
        and offering incense to idols.

God's Parental Love is Inexhaustible

This is the finest passage in Hosea and perhaps the tenderest of the whole OT. It develops the image of God as parent, an image which is complementary to that of God as husband (Chs 1-2) and more immediately accessible.

God's Parental Love is Inexhaustible (cont.)

3
Yet it was I who taught Ephraim to walk,
    I took them up in my arms;
      but they did not know that I healed them.

4
I led them with cords of human kindness,
    with bands of love.
I was to them like those
    who lift infants to their cheeks.
    I bent down to them and fed them.

5
They shall return to the land of Egypt,
    and Assyria shall be their king,
    because they have refused to return to me.

6
The sword rages in their cities,
    it consumes their oracle-priests,
    and devours because of their schemes.

8
How can I give you up, Ephraim?
    How can I hand you over, O Israel?
My heart recoils within me;
    my compassion grows warm and tender.

9
I will not execute my fierce anger;
    I will not again destroy Ephraim;
for I am God and no mortal,
    the Holy One in your midst,
    and I will not come in wrath.

(NRSV)

God's Parental Love is Inexhaustible (cont.)

The image is stated in v.1 and elaborated in vv.3-4. The details are touching, though the text is in places uncertain. In v.4d many translate 'I lifted them like a little child to my cheek'. The story begins with the exodus. Again *Israel/Ephraim* has betrayed God's love (2) and so will be severely punished (5-6). This time however the sequence continues further. In God's mind anger *cannot* in the last resort prevail over love. The Mosaic law, recorded in Dt 21.18-21, would sanction the death penalty for a delinquent son as for an unfaithful wife; but the LORD will rise above such laws. And he will do so precisely because he is *God and no mortal*, the *Holy One*, the Other. Passages like [Num 23.19] and 1 Sam 15.29 show how paradoxical Hosea's use of this topos* must have seemed to his countrymen.

God's Love is Free

13. 4   I have been the LORD your God
        ever since the land of Egypt;
    you know no God but me,
        and besides me there is no savior.

5   It was I who fed you in the wilderness,
        in the land of drought.

6   When I fed them, they were satisfied;
        they were satisfied, and their heart was proud;
        therefore they forgot me.

7   So I will become like a lion to them,
        like a leopard I will lurk beside the way.

8   I will fall upon them like a bear robbed of her cubs,
        and will tear open the covering of their heart;
    there I will devour them like a lion,
        as a wild animal would mangle them.

14. 4   I will heal their disloyalty;
        I will love them freely,
        for my anger has turned from them.

5   I will be like the dew to Israel;
        he shall blossom like the lily,
        he shall strike root like the forests of Lebanon.

6   His shoots shall spread out;
        his beauty shall be like the olive tree,
        and his fragrance like that of Lebanon.

7   They shall again live beneath my shadow,
        they shall flourish as a garden;
    they shall blossom like the vine,
        their fragrance shall be like the wine of Lebanon.

8   What more has Ephraim to do with idols?
        It is I who answer and look after you.
    I am like an evergreen cypress;
        your fruit comes from me.   (NRSV)

God's Love is Free

These last two poems of Hosea maintain the balance between the fierceness and the tenderness of God. The first is as savage as any prophetic oracle. The mutual knowledge of the *wilderness* days did not survive the corruption of prosperity in the promised land. So the shepherd will turn *leopard. I will lurk* (Heb. *yāshūr*) suggests the threat of Assyria (*asshūr*), but in v.8 he *will devour them* himself. The switch from *you* in vv.4-5 to *them* in vv.6-8 is perhaps significant – though Hosea (or his mss) does often switch person for no apparent reason.

But in the end God's anger is overtaken by love. The theology of 14.4 is important. It is not that Israel will escape the punishment which in any case can be seen as the inevitable consequence of her actions. Rather God will afterwards offer her reconciliation *freely* i.e. she will not have to buy his favour either with special

God's Love is Free (cont.)

rituals or even, it seems, by repentance. In the very last resort he will take her back as she is.

Then in a final riot of images (all of them related, which is rare in Hebrew poetry) Hosea portrays the restoration of the people. God is first and last. In 14.5 he is like *the dew*, the heavy dew which is all the moisture available during the long hot summer of Palestine. In 8 he is the *evergreen* tree which gives shelter from the sun. So protected, Israel will *blossom* like all the flowers and trees. The imagery has two overtones. First, it is the language of love in Israel, as is shown by the many comparisons of the beloved to flowers etc. in the Song of Songs. Specifically, Song 2.2-3 contains Hosea's *lily* (5), *shadow* (7) and *fruit* (8) in the same sequence. And the language of love is also the language of peace.

But there is a second, polemical intent. Corn, *wine* and oil are all mentioned in the Hebrew of vv.6-7, and v.8 is explicit: the fruits of the earth come not from *idols* but from God. In both these respects the last chapter of Hosea's book echoes the story of his marriage in Chs 1-2.

JOEL

The Day of the Lord

1. 1   The word of the LORD which came to Joel son of Pethuel.

2   Hear this, you elders;
         listen to me, all you inhabitants of the land!
      Has the like of this happened in your days
         or in the days of your forefathers?

3   Tell it to your children and let them tell it to theirs;
         let one generation pass it on to another.

4   What the locust has left,
         the swarmer devours;
      what the swarmer has left,
         the hopper devours;
      and what the hopper has left,
         the grub devours.

5   Wake up, you drunkards, and weep!
         Mourn for the new wine,
      all you wine-drinkers,
         for it is denied to you.

6   A horde, vast and past counting,
         has invaded my land;
      they have teeth like a lion's teeth;
         they have the fangs of a lioness.

7   They have laid waste my vines
         and left my fig trees broken;
      they have plucked them bare
         and stripped them of their bark,
         leaving the branches white.

The Day of the Lord

Neither the title verse nor the rest of his short book tells us anything significant about Joel. Scholarly opinion inclines to date him c.400 BC. This is partly because an unusually large number of 'his' verses are found also in other prophets, including post-exilic works like Jonah; and the more economical hypothesis is that *he* was quoting *them*.

The first two chapters cover much the same ground as each other; a plague of locusts has invaded and devastated Israel, and the prophet calls the people to a national day of repentance. Ch.1 gives a rhetorical but relatively straightforward account of the plague and its effects. Verse 4 is a version of the inescapability topos* (cp. Amos 5.19), in which the various insects are not certainly identifiable. *Vines* and *fig trees* (7) are standard symbols of prosperity. Here the vines are so ruined that even the normally stupefied *drunkards* can see and *mourn for* the Beaujolais nouveau. In 1915 a plague of locusts in Palestine doubled the price of wine.

The Day of the Lord (cont.)

‑2
> Blow the trumpet in Zion,
>> sound the alarm on my holy mountain!
> Let all the inhabitants of the land tremble,
>> for the day of the LORD is coming,
> a day of darkness and gloom is at hand,
>> a day of cloud and dense fog.
> Like blackness spread over the mountains
>> a vast and countless host appears;
> their like has never been known,
>> nor will be in all the ages to come.

3
> Their vanguard is a devouring fire,
>> their rearguard a leaping flame;
> before them the land is a garden of Eden,
>> but behind them it is a desolate waste;
>> nothing survives their passing.

The Day of the Lord (cont.)

In Ch.2 Joel takes the facts of Ch.1 and adds his own highly charged and highly wrought interpretation. He now sees the locusts as God's army come to punish his unfaithful people. The language of Ch.2, especially in the first section, vv.1-11, is such that the reader cannot be sure what is literal and what is figurative. But perhaps we may do the prophet the honour of regarding his ambiguities as intentional. They certainly help to create a nightmarish atmosphere as a basis for his summons to repentance in the second section, 2.12-17.

These first two sections of Ch.2 are linked by the call *Blow the trumpet in Zion* (1,15). The ram's horn trumpet could call to war or to liturgy. The military sense predominates in v.1 but the religious implications are brought out by *my holy mountain* (the prophet speaks for God here but soon switches back), and made explicit by the announcement of the mighty theme, *the day of the LORD*. Typically, the conclusion is announced at the beginning and then repeated at the end to form a frame; and the pedimental* structure of the first section vv.1-11 is further shown e.g. by the references to *darkness* in vv. 2 and 10. Darkness is a regular feature of the day of the LORD, but in v.2 it is also literal: many observers have spoken of a swarm of locusts 'darkening the sun'. The incomparability topos* at the end of vv. 1-2 is found also in the description of the Egyptian plague of locusts in [Ex 10.14]. The comparison with *horses* (4) is pointed up by the fact that a locust's head looks like a horse's, a fact which is reflected in the German and Italian words for locust. *Chariots* are even more terrible, in sound as well as sight.

The Day of the Lord (cont.)

2. 4 In appearance like horses,
      like cavalry they charge;

5 they bound over the peaks
      with a din like chariots,
   like crackling flames burning up stubble,
      like a vast host in battle array.

6 Nations tremble at their onset,
      every face is drained of colour.

7 Like warriors they charge,
      like soldiers they scale the walls;
   each keeps in line
      with no confusion in the ranks,

8 none jostling his neighbour;
      each keeps to his course.
      Weapons cannot halt their attack;

9 they burst into the city,
      race along the wall,
   climb into the houses,
      entering like thieves through the windows.

10 At their onset the earth shakes,
      the heavens shudder,
   sun and moon are darkened,
      and the stars withhold their light.

11 The LORD thunders as he leads his host;
      his is a mighty army,
      countless are those who do his bidding.
   Great is the day of the LORD and most terrible;
      who can endure it?

The Day of the Lord (cont.)

The reference to *burning stubble* is also a sound effect: the noise of locusts eating has been likened to the crackling of a bush on fire. Finally they are upon us, invading the city itself (7-9).

The comparison of locusts to an army is admirably handled. The tempo is kept fast by the short two-stress lines, but the regular parallelism brings out the tight discipline of the relentless advance. It is all so vivid that some interpreters (in spite of the *like* in v.7) have supposed the passage to be comparing an army to locusts instead of vice versa. But the military comparison is regularly found in descriptions of locust plagues e.g. this from Palestine in 1845: 'Wave after wave poured down upon us, those behind bridging over those already killed.'

With v.10 Joel moves beyond any distinction between literal and metaphorical, into the realm of apocalyptic*. *The earth shakes* and *the heavens shudder* have nothing to do with locusts, but belong with descriptions of theophanies. Looking back, we can see other traces of the same language e.g. *nations tremble* in v.6 and the emphasis on *fire* in v.3. *Terrible* indeed is *the day of the LORD* (11).

The first section of Ch.2 ends in v.11 with an apparently rhetorical question, which however leads skilfully into the second section. For Joel answers it by

The Day of the Lord (cont.)

2   Yet even now, says the LORD,
     turn back to me wholeheartedly
          with fasting, weeping, and mourning.
3   Rend your hearts and not your garments,
          and turn back to the LORD your God,
     for he is gracious and compassionate,
          long-suffering and ever constant,
          ready always to relent when he threatens disaster.
14   It may be he will turn back and relent
          and leave a blessing behind him,
     blessing enough for grain-offerings and drink-offerings
          to be presented to the LORD your God.
15   Blow the trumpet in Zion,
          appoint a solemn fast,
          proclaim a day of abstinence.
16   Gather the people together,
          appoint a solemn assembly;
     summon the elders,
          gather the children,
          even babes at the breast;
     bid the bridegroom leave his wedding-chamber
          and the bride her bower.
17   Let the priests, the ministers of the LORD,
          stand weeping between the porch and the altar
     and say, 'Spare your people, LORD;
          do not expose your own people to insult,
     to be made a byword by other nations.
          Why should the peoples say, 'Where is their God?'   (REB)

The Day of the Lord (cont.)

quoting *the LORD* himself. The *heart*, as always in Hebrew, is the seat not of the emotions but of the will. The rituals of repentance, including the tearing of clothes, are of no avail without a change of will. The much-quoted *rend your hearts and not your garments* should not be misinterpreted. The whole section shows that Joel is deprecating not ritual expression as such, only the idea that it can replace true conversion. For the Hebrew idiom see note on Hos 6.6. The command *turn back* is left without explanation: nowhere do we learn the nature of the people's sin. But the language is that of the covenant. The description of God's character in v.13 derives from the narrative of Exodus 34.6, which runs like the refrain of a hymn throughout the OT.

Joel then (15-16) prescribes the ritual for the day of repentance, reverting to the rapid two-stress lines to express urgency. This ritual requires the participation of the whole people. Even those who are exempt from military service (including the newly-wed – see Dt 20.7) must play their part. Finally (17) he gives an outline of a standard communal lament, familiar from the psalms and elsewhere. These last three verses contain few surprises or fireworks: the poet sees no problems in traditional practices, if only the people would be warned and turn back.

Israel Restored

2. 18   Then the LORD became jealous for his land,
    and had pity on his people.

19   In response to his people the LORD said:
I am sending you
    grain, wine, and oil,
    and you will be satisfied;
and I will no more make you
    a mockery among the nations.

25   I will repay you for the years
    that the swarming locust has eaten,
the hopper, the destroyer, and the cutter,
    my great army, which I sent against you.

26   You shall eat in plenty and be satisfied,
    and praise the name of the LORD your God,
    who has dealt wondrously with you.
And my people shall never again be put to shame.

27   You shall know that I am in the midst of Israel,
    and that I, the LORD, am your God and there is no other.
And my people shall never again be put to shame.

28   Then afterward
    I will pour out my spirit on all flesh;
your sons and your daughters shall prophesy,
    your old men shall dream dreams,
    and your young men shall see visions.

29   Even on the male and female slaves,
    in those days, I will pour out my spirit.

Israel Restored

Surprises start again in the third section of Ch.2 with v.18. The rhetorical question at the end of v.17 again acts as a link, and then *the LORD* himself responds to the appeal of *his people*. Such responses, both in the psalms and in prophecy, commonly include promises to end, to reverse or to divert the misfortunes complained of. So here vv.19ef and 27c end the process of v.17de, while v.25 reverses that of 1.4.

But the highlight of this third section is the glorious oracle of vv.28-29. It is marked out as originally independent by the framing words *I will pour out my spirit*. This oracle represents the fulfilment of Moses' wish in Num 11.29: 'I wish that all the LORD's people were prophets and that the LORD would confer his spirit upon them all.' Prophetesses were common enough in Israel (e.g. Jg 4.4), though no book of OT prophecy is ascribed to a woman. What is remarkable here is the inclusion of the *slaves* i.e. foreign slaves of the Jews, who were nevertheless regarded as part of the community of Israel.

Israel Restored (cont.)

30 • I will show portents in the heavens and on the earth, blood and fire and columns of smoke. • The sun shall be turned to darkness, and the moon to blood, before the great and terrible day of the LORD comes. • Then everyone who calls on the name of the LORD shall be saved; for in Mount Zion and in Jerusalem there shall be those who escape, as the LORD has said, and among the survivors shall be those whom the LORD calls.

1 • For then, in those days and at that time, when I restore the fortunes of Judah and Jerusalem, • I will gather all the nations and bring them down to the valley of Jehoshaphat, and I will enter into judgment with them there, on account of my people and my heritage Israel, because they have scattered them among the nations. They have divided my land, • and cast lots for my people, and traded boys for prostitutes, and sold girls for wine, and drunk it down.   (NRSV)

Israel Restored (cont.)

The description in vv.30-31 of the cosmic signs of the end seems at first merely to repeat the themes of vv.1-2 and 10. But as one reads on into Ch.3 it becomes clear that here is the greatest reversal of all. The Jews have already suffered enough and, if loyal to the covenant, *shall be saved. The day of the LORD*, which in this sense is still to come, will after all be a day of his *judgment* on *all the nations*. *Jehoshaphat* (literally, 'YHWH judges') is a symbolic name for the place of that judgement.

AMOS

Introduction

Amos was roughly contemporary with Isaiah and Hosea, among the first of the 'writing' prophets. He was a solid peasant farmer from Judah, but his preaching was directed entirely against Israel, in particular against its capital, Samaria, and its chief cult-centre, Bethel. His ministry was probably short, and his message is correspondingly sharp. He has virtually nothing to say on either of the themes that were occupying Hosea: the purity of the cult and the 'personal' relations between Israel and God. His concern is public morality, especially social justice, and his criticism is directed mainly at the upper classes. True, he sometimes speaks as if the whole people is under condemnation. But since his theme is the oppression of the poor by the rich, such language must point not backward to a common guilt but forward to a common national punishment.

Amos's concern for the weaker members of society was not peculiar to him. It is found in all the legal codes, and to a lesser extent in the Wisdom literature, of the OT and the whole ANE. But nowhere previously had it been expressed with such vehemence, even ferocity. The intensity of his language derives from the intensity of his inner conviction that what is being flouted is not the mere edict of an earthly monarch but the will of God. And that is why, in a favourite motif of his, punishment is inescapable. The full Book of Amos does contain a suggestion in one place that God may relent, and it ends (as do many prophetic books) with a forecast of ultimate restoration. But those passages are omitted from this selection, in the belief (subjective, but shared by many scholars) that they are later additions which weaken the uncompromising force of the rest of the book.

Like other prophets, Amos uses an abundance of images, almost all drawn from the ordinary circumstances of life. But his writing has two features of its own. First, he is not restricted to the short punchy oracle, but uses also a longer serial form. Such is the 'sermon' in Chs 1-2 and the set of vision narratives in Chs 7-8. The second feature is more important, being a matter not just of form but also of substance. Amos loves to turn against his audience their own religious assumptions both of belief and of worship. Their hope for 'the day of the LORD' (5.18), their sacred ceremonies (5.21), even the presence of God in their sanctuary (9.1) – all these will turn to their ruin. The argument is summed up with crushing brevity in 3.2: precisely *because* they have had these special privileges their punishment for disloyalty will be the more dire.

A Circuit of Judgements

1.1 Words of Amos one of the shepherds of Tekoa. The visions he had about Israel, in the time of Uzziah king of Judah and Jeroboam son of Joash, king of Israel, two years before the earthquake. ▸

A Circuit of Judgements

Three points are worth noting in the editorial title-verse. First Tekoa, where Amos was a sheep-farmer, lay on the ridge of Judaea some 15 miles south of Jerusalem. At 800 metres above sea level, he could look down from his home: east across the desert and over the Dead Sea to the hills of Moab and Ammon; and west over the Philistine towns to the Mediterranean. He was literally a man of wide horizons. Secondly, he was a visionary. His *visions* are recorded later,

A Circuit of Judgements (cont.)

3   The LORD says this:

> For the three crimes, the four crimes of Damascus,
>> I have made my decree and will not relent:
> because they have threshed Gilead
>> with iron threshing-sledges,

4
> I shall send fire down on the House of Hazael
>> to devour the palaces of Ben-Hadad;

5
> I shall break the gate-bar of Damascus,
>> I shall destroy the inhabitant of Bikath-Aven,
> the holder of the sceptre in Beth-Eden,
>> and the people of Aram will be deported to Kir,
> the LORD says.

A Circuit of Judgements (cont.)

though they came first; his book opens with the first of the *words*. Thirdly, archaeological evidence suggests a rough date of 760 BC for *the earthquake*, which accords well with the chronology of the two kings. *Two years* cleverly conveys the hint of imminent disaster.

His 'sermon' in 1.3-2.16 is one of the most remarkable utterances in the whole OT. It is probably the oldest oracle by any of the 'writing' prophets, yet in content it is one of the boldest, especially considering that it was delivered by a southerner in the northern kingdom. In form it is among the longest and the most clearly structured, with four exactly parallel stanzas leading to a totally unexpected climax in the fifth. (The full text of Amos presents seven stanzas followed by the climactic eighth. But the extra three only weaken the force of the rest.)

These first four stanzas each contain an oracle of the Lord's judgement against one of Israel's neighbours. Each is of ten lines, plus an opening and closing formula referring to him. The indictment is introduced in each case by an ascending numerical formula common in ANE folk wisdom, like the 'third and fourth generation' of the second commandment.

Then, surprisingly, only one crime is mentioned, as if that one is the last straw which exhausts the Lord's patience. In each case, it is what we should call a war-crime, and it is followed by the appropriate punishment viz. a crushing military defeat. As recorded in many ANE inscriptions, the victors burn the royal palace, and the king and his chiefs suffer most. But what is not found in ANE inscriptions is the insistence that all this is the doing of a god whose own people – certainly in one case (2.1) and probably in all four – have *not* been victims of the crimes he is punishing.

Each of the four oracles needs its own brief comment. *Damascus* (3) was capital of *Aram,* i.e. Syria, whose ruling house was founded by *Hazael* and contained many kings called *Ben-Hadad.* Their crime was a particularly brutal attack on *Gilead.* For *threshing-sledges* see p.555. The *gate bar* was the enormous iron bar which held the city gates shut. *Bikath Eden* means 'valley of luxury', *Beth Aven* 'house of pleasure' i.e. brothel; both are rude names for Damascus. *Kir* is where the Aramaeans are supposed to have come from; the Lord will simply put history into reverse.

A Circuit of Judgements (cont.)

1. 6 The LORD says this:

For the three crimes, the four crimes of Gaza,
  I have made my decree and will not relent:
because they have deported entire nations
  as slaves to Edom,
7 I shall send fire down on the walls of Gaza
  to devour its palaces;
8 I shall destroy the inhabitant of Ashdod,
  the holder of the sceptre in Ashkelon;
I shall turn my hand against Ekron
  and the remnant of the Philistines will perish,
  says the Lord GOD.

13 The LORD says this:

For the three crimes, the four crimes of the Ammonites,
  I have made my decree and will not relent:
because they have disembowelled
  the pregnant women of Gilead
  in order to extend their own frontiers,
14 I shall light a fire against the walls of Rabbah
  to devour its palaces
amid war cries on the day of battle,
  in a whirlwind on the day of storm,
15 and their king shall go into captivity,
  he and his chief men with him,
  says the LORD.

2. 1 The LORD says this:

For the three crimes, the four crimes of Moab,
  I have made my decree and will not relent:
because they have burnt the bones
  of the king of Edom to ash,
2 I shall send fire down into Moab
  to devour the palaces of Kerioth,
and Moab will die in the tumult,
  amid war cries and the blare of trumpets;
3 I shall destroy the ruler there
  and slaughter all the chief men there with him,
  says the LORD.

A Circuit of Judgements (cont.)

Gaza (6) was the chief town of the *Philistine* confederacy; others are named in v.8. Their crime was to capture whole (village) populations and sell them *as slaves* to the Edomites. *The Ammonites* (13), whose capital was *Rabbah*, had also behaved savagely against *Gilead*. In ancient border wars it was quite common to destroy the unborn children of the defeated enemy so as to depopulate his land. Agamemmon threatened it in the *Iliad*, and Menahem king of Israel carried

A Circuit of Judgements (cont.)

6   The LORD says this:

> For the three crimes, the four crimes of Israel,
>   I have made my decree and will not relent:
> because they have sold the upright for silver
>   and the poor for a pair of sandals,

7   because they have crushed the heads of the weak into the dust
>   and thrust the rights of the oppressed to one side,
> father and son sleeping with the same girl
>   and thus profaning my holy name,

8   lying down beside every altar
>   on clothes acquired as pledges,
> and drinking the wine of the people they have fined
>   in the house of their god.   ▸

A Circuit of Judgements (cont.)

it out soon after Amos's time [2 K 15.16].

Finally Ammon's neighbour *Moab* (2.1) committed a crime universally execrated in antiquity by maltreating the corpse of a defeated enemy and denying it proper burial. Each of these three last crimes is an example of the abuse by the strong of the weak and defenceless – prisoners of war, pregnant women and the dead. Though there was no *law* against such actions, Amos could count on public opinion to support his condemnation of them, especially when they were committed by neighbours – and therefore enemies – of Israel.

So far so good. Official prophets in the ANE were expected on certain formal occasions, e.g. before a battle, to utter curses on the enemy and blessings on the home side. So on this occasion his audience had enjoyed the former and were looking forward to the latter. In its place comes Amos's master-stroke: the same basic formula, and the same inexorable condemnation – but this time of Israel herself. The indictment in Israel's case consisted of peace-time equivalents of the war-crimes, various cases where the rich have oppressed *the poor* and *the weak*, who from the start are identified with *the upright*. First comes the reduction of the poor to debt-slaves*, who can then

be sold by one rich man to another, whether for money or for land. By Hebrew law land sold was symbolised by *a pair of sandals* (6d; cp. Ruth 4.7). Next we have a general reference (7ab) to the corruption of justice, a favourite theme of Amos. This is followed by two breaches of specific laws designed to protect the weak. By the first, the head of a family might take a slave-girl either as his own or as his son's concubine, but not both (Ex 21.8f). By the second, if a rich man takes a poor man's clothes as a pledge for a loan, he must return them by nightfall (Ex 22.26f.). Finally the magistrates are accused of appropriating to their own use the goods confiscated in lieu of fines.

All this a modern reader can readily understand and admire. That Amos should treat social injustice as no less vicious than war-crimes shocked his contemporaries but not us. But the fact that we can nod is due primarily to Amos himself and the other OT prophets – mediated in part by Marx. And it may be Marx who is responsible for the fact that what shocks *us* is rather the fact that here too Amos drags God in. The injustices he castigates are, he says, an affront to God who forbade them in the first place and is now expected to tolerate their being flaunted in his very presence (8d).

A Circuit of Judgements (cont.)

2.13   Very well! Like a cart overloaded with sheaves
            I will crush you where you stand;
14   flight will be cut off for the swift,
            the strong will have no chance to exert his strength
      nor the warrior be able to save his life;
15   the archer will not stand his ground,
      the swift of foot will not escape,
            nor will the horseman save his life;
16   even the bravest of warriors
            will jettison his arms and run away, that day! –
      declares the LORD!   (NJB)

A Circuit of Judgements (cont.)

So now he will punish the strong who are oppressing the weak within Israel. The image of 13 is peaceful, though it suggests an unwelcome form of reaping. That of 14 reverts to war. Three carefully balanced couplets build up to an ironical climax: only *the bravest of warriors* will save his life, and that by running away without his arms. The orchestral crescendo ends with two staccato words: *that day*!

Amos Speaks with Authority

3.1   Hear this word that the LORD has spoken against you, O people of Israel, against the whole family that I brought up out of the land of Egypt:

2   You only have I known
                of all the families of the earth;
           therefore I will punish you
                for all your iniquities.

3   Do two walk together
                unless they have made an appointment?
4   Does a lion roar in the forest,
                when it has no prey?
5   Does a young lion cry out from its den,
                if it has caught nothing?
           Does a bird fall into a snare on the earth,
                when there is no trap for it?
6   Does a snare spring up from the ground,
                when it has taken nothing?   ♦

Amos Speaks with Authority

The first two verses of Ch.3 show once again Amos's love of the shocking paradox, concentrated here in the *therefore* of v.2. The one-verse oracle is preemptive. If any of his hearers wishes to claim special privileges for Israel, his answer is: for 'privileges' read 'responsibilities'. God has *known* (i.e. had a special relationship with) Israel *only*, therefore he will punish her all the more thoroughly. Logically this oracle belongs at the start of Amos's preaching, before the detailed indictment of Ch.2.

His audience seems to have reacted by challenging his authority to speak in this way. In vv.3-8 he answers such a challenge: he speaks on the authority, and at the irresistible command, of the LORD.

Amos Speaks with Authority (Cont.)

7   Is a trumpet blown in a city,
     and the people are not afraid?
8   Does disaster befall a city,
     unless the LORD has done it?
The lion has roared;
     who will not fear?
The Lord GOD has spoken;
     who can but prophesy?   (NRSV)

Amos Speaks with Authority (Cont.)

He makes his point in the style of folk wisdom: a series of parallels (3-6) leading to a conclusion (8b), all expressed in rhetorical questions. The shape of the argument, which owes its force to rhetoric rather than logic, is that every event we experience is linked with another event in a nexus of cause and effect. If *two* people are walking *together* in open country, they must be friends – otherwise it would be too much of a risk. If *a lion* roars, it must have made a kill – to roar earlier would frighten the prey. If *a bird* falls to *earth*, it must have been hit by a projectile; if a bird *trap* is sprung, there must be a bird in it. In all these cases the argument is from effect to cause. As we get nearer the climax, the direction oscillates, but all the examples (except the opening v.3) are of sinister and threatening events. *In a city*, the blowing of the war-*trumpet* causes fear, but a natural calamity e.g. a famine is caused by God. Finally the *roar* of the *lion* causes *fear* (8cd unites 4a and 5a), but prophecy is caused by God. The punch-line in v.8f. is typically unexpected. By it Amos skilfully claims the authority, while disclaiming the office, of a prophet.

The 'Cows of Bashan'

1   Listen to this saying, you cows of Bashan
     living on the hill of Samaria,
exploiting the weak and ill-treating the poor,
     saying to your husbands, 'Bring us something to drink!'
2   The Lord GOD has sworn by his holiness:
     Look, the days will soon be on you
when he will use hooks to drag you away
     and fish-hooks for the very last of you;
3   through the breaches in the wall you will leave,
     each one straight ahead,
and be herded away towards Hermon –
     declares the LORD.   (NJB)

The 'Cows of Bashan'

Amos here attacks the rich *husbands* of Israel through the wives whom they indulge. It can only have been the men who were directly *exploiting the poor*, but his savage metaphor fits the women. *Bashan* was a fertile pasture-land whose *cows* were among the fattest. The description of their punishment mixes two images. As cattle are *herded*, by a ring through the nose or a *hook* in the forehead, in single file through a gate, so Israelite prisoners will be roped together, by a ring through the nose or lip (an Assyrian custom), and led away *through the breaches in the* city *wall* towards *Hermon* en route for Assyria.

Social Injustice and Religious Formalism

5. 11   Therefore because you trample on the poor
              and take from them levies of grain,
           you have built houses of hewn stone,
              but you shall not live in them;
           you have planted pleasant vineyards,
              but you shall not drink their wine.

12   For I know how many are your transgressions,
        and how great are your sins —
     you who afflict the righteous, who take a bribe,
        and push aside the needy in the gate.

13   Therefore the prudent will keep silent in such a time;
        for it is an evil time.

18   Alas for you who desire the day of the LORD!
        Why do you want the day of the LORD?
        It is darkness, not light;

19   as if someone fled from a lion,
        and was met by a bear;
     or went into the house and rested a hand against the wall,
        and was bitten by a snake.

20   Is not the day of the LORD darkness, not light,
        and gloom with no brightness in it?

Social Injustice and Religious Formalism

The rich are here indicted for reducing *the poor* to debt-slavery* (cp.2.6), while they themselves live in luxury. *Houses* were normally built of mud bricks, *hewn stone* being reserved for palaces and temples; but modern excavation of C8th Samaria has found an unusual number of stone-built private houses. A country with such extremes of wealth was a natural prey to an invader, and Samaria fell to Assyria a generation after Amos. Even in the local law-courts (held *in the* city *gate*) the rich can *bribe* their way at the expense of *the needy*, here typically identified with *the righteous*. The oracle ends on a sinister note which we shall hear again from Amos (6.10; 8.3).

Then once again Amos upsets the people's complacency by turning a belief (18-20) and a practice (21-4) of theirs on its head. *The day of the LORD*, of which this is perhaps the first mention in the OT, meant the day of God's intervention. It will bring inescapable disaster — for themselves. The simile describes the fate of a single man (*or* in v.19c should be translated 'and'). Having escaped from the *bear* into his *house*, he *rested a hand against the wall*, from relief as well as exhaustion, and was fatally bitten by a snake. For the topos* compare Joel 1.4.

Social Injustice and Religious Formalism (cont.)

1   I hate, I despise your festivals,
        and I take no delight in your solemn assemblies.
22   Even though you offer me your burnt offerings and grain offerings,
        I will not accept them;
     and the offerings of well-being of your fatted animals
        I will not look upon.
23   Take away from me the noise of your songs;
        I will not listen to the melody of your harps.
24   But let justice roll down like waters,
        and righteousness like an everflowing stream.   (NRSV)

Social Injustice and Religious Formalism (cont.)

Amos's denunciation of the cult is equally shocking. The cult was designed to win God's favour: its effect is clearly the opposite. *Festivals* (21), sacrifices (22) and hymns (23) – these he not merely *will not accept* but actually hates. Being accompanied by injustice, they actually worsen the relations between him and Israel. His demands are expressed in a powerful word-pair. The Hebrew *tsedāqāh*, translated *righteousness* by NRSV and 'uprightness' by NJB, is broader and less smug than either: it combines our notions of integrity and neighbourliness. The *everflowing stream* is contrasted with a wadi which dries up in summer. The whole splendid section 21-24 is closely parallel to Is 1.10-17 and Mic 6.6-8.

Extravagance and its Punishment

5.1 Disaster for those so comfortable in Zion
        and for those so confident on the hill of Samaria,
     the notables of this first of nations,
        those to whom the House of Israel has recourse!

4   Lying on ivory beds
        and sprawling on their divans,
     they dine on lambs from the flock,
        and stall-fattened veal;
5   they bawl to the sound of the lyre
        and, like David, they invent musical instruments;
6   they drink wine by the bowlful,
        and lard themselves with the finest oils,
        but for the ruin of Joseph they care nothing.   ♦

Extravagance and its Punishment

Amos here attacks the rich not only of *Israel* but also of *Zion* i.e. Judah. They are charged with complacency (1), self-indulgence (4) and lack of *care* for *Joseph* i.e. their fellow-countrymen. The indictment of their luxury has many heads, each illustrated by a telling detail. Archaeology has confirmed the fine *ivory* inlay of the furniture. The practice of reclining at banquets, later common, here seems to be a recent introduction, perhaps from abroad. Most people in antiquity ate meat only on special – often religious – occasions. Their banquets included musical entertainment of which Amos, like many puritans, disapproved (*bawl* v.5).

> ## Extravagance and its Punishment (cont.)
>
> **6.** 7 That is why they will now go into captivity,
> heading the column of captives.
> The sprawlers' revelry is over.
>
> 9 If ten people are left in a single house,
> they will die
> 10 and a few will be left to carry
> the bones from the house,
> and they will say to anyone deep inside the house,
> 'Any more there?' and he will answer, 'No.'
> Then he will say, 'Hush! –
> The LORD's name must not be mentioned.'
>
> 12 Can horses gallop over rocks?
> Can the sea be ploughed with oxen?
> Yet you have changed justice into poison,
> and the fruit of uprightness into wormwood,   (NJB)

Extravagance and its Punishment (cont.)

Their punishment will fit their position as leaders: they will *head the column* of deportees. The drunken *sprawl* of v.7c picks up that of v.4b as a frame.

And with the siege will come, it seems, the plague. Amos is here at his most sinister. Those who are still alive will recognise the hand of the LORD but, from a superstitious fear of provoking him further, will not dare to *mention* his *name*.

Verse 12 is a typical prophetic argument: to *pervert* justice is contrary to natural law. The translation of v.12b provides a unique instance of a successful emendation of the MT. The Hebrew *babbeqārîm* means, if anything, 'in the morning'. Emended in 1772 to *bebāqār yām*, it yields *the sea . . . with oxen*. This reading, though lacking any ancient authority, is certainly correct.

> ## Amos's Visions and the Challenge from Amaziah
>
> **7.** 1 This was what the Lord GOD showed me: it was a swarm of locusts hatching when the later corn, which comes after the king's early crop, was beginning to sprout. • As they devoured every trace of vegetation in the land, I said, 'Lord GOD, forgive, I pray you. How can Jacob survive? He is so small.' • The LORD relented. 'This will not happen,' he said.
>
> • This was what the Lord GOD showed me: the Lord GOD was summoning a flame of fire to devour the great abyss, and to devour the land. • I said, 'Lord
> 5 GOD, cease, I pray you. How can Jacob survive? He is so small.' • The LORD relented. 'This also will not happen,' he said.

Amos's Visions and the Challenge from Amaziah

The next major section of Amos is made up of five short narratives. Four of them record visions of his, the fifth his confrontation with the official prophet Amaziah. The last has been inserted by an editor between visions 3 and 4, and is transposed here to follow the latter.

For the four vision narratives were obviously composed as a sequence of two pairs. That can be seen, first and most clearly, from the stylised forms of each of the pairs; secondly, from certain cross-

Amos's Visions and the Challenge from Amaziah (cont.)

7 • This was what the LORD showed me: there he was standing by a wall built with the aid of a plumb-line, and he had a plumb-line in his hand. • The LORD asked me, 'What do you see, Amos?' 'A plumb-line', I answered. Then the LORD said, 'I am setting a plumb-line in the midst of my people Israel; never again shall I pardon them. • The shrines of Isaac will be desolated and the sanctuaries of Israel laid waste; and sword in hand I shall rise against the house of Jeroboam.'

1 • This was what the Lord GOD showed me: it was a basket of summer fruit. • 'What is that you are looking at, Amos?' he said. I answered, 'A basket of ripe summer fruit.' Then the LORD said to me, 'The time is ripe for my people Israel. Never again shall I pardon them. • On that day, says the Lord GOD, the palace songs will give way to lamentation: "So many corpses, flung out everywhere! Silence!" '   (REB)

Amos's Visions and the Challenge from Amaziah (cont.)

references between them, e.g. *also* in 7.6 and *Never again* in 7.8 and 8.2; thirdly from a progression in the content.

The form of the first two is almost identical. In each case God *showed* Amos a tableau of a disaster. The first was an assault by *locusts* upon the second crop of hay (so NJB in place of REB's *corn*). The first crop had gone to *the king*; the second was for local use, and on it depended the feed for the livestock during the long dry summer. The meaning of the vision is all too clear, and Amos intercedes on behalf of the people (here called *Jacob*), as prophets had done from Abraham (Gen 18) and Moses (Num 14) onwards. His ground is skilfully chosen to appeal to God's well-known penchant for the weak. The exchange between him and God is as terse as anything in the great compressed narratives of Genesis. He asks *'forgive'*, even though the people had not repented; God says nothing about forgiveness, merely that the disaster *will not happen*.

In the second vision (4) the disaster is of a more cosmic nature. *The great abyss* refers to the waters under the earth,

believed in ANE cosmology to be the source of wells and springs: if it dried up, *the land* would die. Amos again intercedes in one word, but this time asks God not to forgive but only to *cease*.

For the second pair of visions the form changes somewhat. Amos is now shown not a tableau but an object from everyday life. The object is a symbol with potentially sinister implications. God calls Amos (by name) to focus upon it. He then applies it to the historical situation, and preempts any intercession. The *plumb-line* implies a threat to pull down the *wall* if it is not upright. Accordingly the *shrines* of the countryside *and the sanctuaries* of the cult-centres will be *laid waste*. As usual in Amos, social morality is linked with religion: there is no reference here to idolatry.

In the fourth vision (8.2) the sinister potentiality of the object is brought out by the word-play between the Hebrew words *qaits* (summer) and *qēts* (end), rendered by REB's double *ripe*. Women singers were an adornment of ancient monarchies: here they will be called on to lead the dirge, which ends like 6.10 with a menacing command of *silence*.

Amos's Visions and the Challenge from Amaziah (cont.)

7. 10   • Amaziah, the priest of Bethel, reported to King Jeroboam of Israel: 'Amos has conspired against you here in the heart of Israel; the country cannot tolerate all his words. • This is what he is saying: "Jeroboam will die by the sword, and the Israelites will assuredly be deported from their native land." ' • To Amos himself Amaziah said, 'Seer, go away! Off with you to Judah! Earn your living and do your prophesying there. • But never prophesy again at Bethel, for this is the king's sanctuary, a royal shrine.' • 'I was no prophet,' Amos replied to Amaziah,

15   'nor was I a prophet's son; I was a herdsman and fig-grower. • But the Lord took me as I followed the flock and it was the Lord who said to me, "Go and prophesy to my people Israel." • So now listen to the word of the Lord. You tell me I am not to prophesy against Israel or speak out against the people of Isaac. • Now these are the words of the Lord: Your wife will become a prostitute in the city, and your sons and daughters will fall by the sword. Your land will be parcelled out with a measuring line, you yourself will die in a heathen country, and Israel will be deported from their native land.'   (REB)

Amos's Visions and the Challenge from Amaziah (cont.)

The psychology of the visions seems to vary between the two pairs. The second pair, like those of Jeremiah's call, were triggered by Amos's concentration on an object which he actually saw. The first pair however must have been in the mind's eye, perhaps during a trance. They may well have been seen over quite a span of time, though one should not make too much of the gap between the spring of the first and the autumn of the fourth. But they were composed and published together. Collectively they function as a call-narrative – here only in the book does God address the prophet by name – and that constitutes another link with the inserted story of 7.10-17.

This intriguing story, told not by Amos but about him, is the only time in his book that we know the context of an oracle of his. *Bethel* was *the king's sanctuary* in the most literal sense. It had been founded by Jeroboam I (1 K 12.29) when the northern kingdom split off, precisely as a rival to Jerusalem. Both *the priest Amaziah* and the current *king Jeroboam* II suspected Amos of having *conspired against* the king – not surprisingly after the examples of Elijah

(1 K 18) and Elisha (2 K 9). Amaziah recognised Amos as a *seer* – a title which is clearly equivalent to prophet – and thereby conceded some efficacy to his words. Amaziah is not so much contemptuous as anxious. Hence the compromise he offers: let Amos go back and prophesy at home.

Amos in reply is concerned to justify not the content of his oracles but their authority. He is not a professional or hereditary prophet, on the staff of a palace or temple. He is a man of independent means, a sheep-farmer and market-gardener. *But the Lord took* him. He himself therefore has no choice but to prophesy; Amaziah, by trying to prevent him, only brings down the anger of the Lord upon himself and (in accordance with ancient thought) his family. This is not mere spite on Amos's part, nor bluster to cover his withdrawal. The two men are divided on a deep point of principle, which is brought out by the structure of the story. The Amaziah narrative (10-13) mentions the king three times, God not at all; Amos in his reply does the exact opposite. He, like the God for whom he speaks, is not open to compromise.

A Fifth Vision

1 I saw the LORD standing beside the altar, and he said:
Strike the capitals until the thresholds shake,
and shatter them on the heads of all the people;
and those who are left I will kill with the sword;
not one of them shall flee away,
not one of them shall escape.

2 Though they dig into Sheol,
from there shall my hand take them;
though they climb up to heaven,
from there I will bring them down.

3 Though they hide themselves on the top of Carmel,
from there I will search out and take them;
and though they hide from my sight at the bottom of the sea,
there I will command the sea-serpent, and it shall bite them.

4 And though they go into captivity in front of their enemies,
there I will command the sword, and it shall kill them;
and I will fix my eyes on them
for harm and not for good.

(NRSV)

A Fifth Vision

Amos's fifth vision, here recorded, was different in form from the other four. In his mind's eye God was *beside the altar*, presumably of Bethel, *standing* i.e. ready to deliver judgement. The divine command, addressed perhaps to an angel, was to *strike* the sanctuary from *capitals* down to *thresholds*. The image is that of an earthquake, and some scholars connect it with the one mentioned in 1.1. But there is a secondary implication underlying the obscure Hebrew, that Israel will be shattered from the *heads* down to *all the people*.

What follows is a theological version of the inescapability topos*, very like that of Ps 139.7-12. Hell and *heaven*, the highest mountain of Israel and *the bottom of the sea* – none of these places will offer refuge. There are mythical overtones to all of them, most clearly in the reference to *the sea-serpent*; but the sequence ends on a note of stark realism (4). Even in the sanctuary, if God's *eyes* are *on them*, it will be *for harm and not for good*.

JONAH

Introduction

The Book of Jonah is a surprise – indeed a series of surprises from beginning to end. To start with, it contains no oracles *by* a prophet: instead it is a story *about* a prophet. But unlike the many other OT stories about prophets, it makes no serious claim to be historical. Rather it is a story with a moral. In that sense, its nearest OT equivalent is the Book of Ruth. But in content and tone it is quite different. The story-line has been described as 'a series of practical jokes played by God on his prophet' (NJB). Of the four main characters in the book, Jonah hardly puts a foot right, while the sailors and the Ninevites hardly put one wrong. The LORD himself initiates more and more of the action as the story proceeds, but in accordance with the older tradition of Hebrew story-telling his intentions have to be divined from his actions – until he reveals all in his final speech.

The dominant tone of the book is one of deadpan irony which enables the author to weave together a variety of ingredients. On the one hand are extravagant numbers and miraculous happenings, on the other a penetrating psychology of resentment. Stylistically too he is master both of simple rapid narrative and of sophisticated parody, including mock-heroic (4.3). Given also his propensity for holding up vital clues till later in the story (notably 1.10, 4.2 and probably 4.5), it is hard at times to resist the conclusion that the author too is playing practical jokes on the reader.

All this helps to explain why so many different views have been put forward about the moral of the story. In fact it can only be what is expressed in the last two verses: YHWH's loving and forgiving care for all his creatures, including repentant sinners, infants and even (final joke) farm animals. The racial issue is secondary. The fact that both the sailors and the Ninevites are gentiles is nowhere made explicit, nor are the Ninevites said to have been 'converted'. The same emphasis is apparent in the portrayal of Jonah. He is ridiculed not for chauvinism but for being self-righteous and unforgiving, the very antithesis of that quality of mercy which characterises YHWH.

It remains an unsolved question why the author chose to make his anti-hero a prophet. Perhaps he represents a strand of exilic or post-exilic Judaism which criticised some of the canonical prophets for their emphasis on punishment rather than on repentance and forgiveness. If so, it is the final irony that the book was later classified among those of the prophets themselves.

Structurally the book falls into two parallel halves, one on sea, one on land. Each of them could have made a story on its own, but they gain greatly from the conjunction, which has been skilfully managed so as to show up the similarities and yet contrasts between them. Most obviously, the sailors in Ch.1 correspond to the Ninevites in Ch.3. The opening three verses of each half correspond to the other, with the phrase 'great city of Nineveh' picked up again at the end (4.11) to round off the whole. Other echoes are audible in the prayers of 1.6 and 3.9 and in the unusual verb 'ordained' repeated four times when God brings in an instrument from nature to educate Jonah: the great fish of 1.17 and three times in 4.6-8. In between the two halves the mss carry a psalm of thanksgiving [2.1-9] which is inappropriate in both content and location.

Jonah Tries to Escape God's Charge

1 The word of the LORD came to Jonah son of Amittai: • 'Go to the great city of Nineveh; go and denounce it, for I am confronted by its wickedness.' • But to escape from the LORD Jonah set out for Tarshish. He went down to Joppa, where he found a ship bound for Tarshish. He paid the fare and went on board to travel with it to Tarshish out of the reach of the LORD.

• The LORD let loose a hurricane on the sea, which rose so high that the ship 5 threatened to break up in the storm. • The sailors were terror-stricken; everyone cried out to his own god for help, and they threw things overboard to lighten the ship. Meanwhile Jonah, who had gone below deck, was lying there fast asleep. • When the captain came upon him he said, 'What, fast asleep? Get up and call to your god! Perhaps he will spare a thought for us, and we shall not perish.'

• The sailors said among themselves, 'Let us cast lots to find who is to blame for our misfortune.' They cast lots, and when Jonah was singled out • They questioned him: 'What is your business? Where do you come from? Which is your country? What is your nationality?' • 'I am a Hebrew,' he answered, 'and I worship the LORD the God of heaven, who made both sea and dry land.' ▶

Jonah Tries to Escape God's Charge

The first two verses read like the opening of almost any prophetic book. *Jonah* ben *Amittai* is known from 2 K [14.25] as a prophet in the northern kingdom in the time of Jeroboam II c.750 BC. *Nineveh* was notorious as the capital of the Assyrian empire during its years of greatest success, and is here a symbol of size, power and wickedness. What is unusual is that Jonah was told to get up and *go* there to *denounce* it, for most OT denunciations were made from a safe distance. And what is unparalleled in the OT is that he should indeed 'get up' – but only to run away to the opposite edge of the known world, viz. to Tartessus in Spain.

The ship was hardly out of port when *the LORD* showed his anger by sending a severe *storm*, and the rest of Ch.1 describes the various reactions of *the sailors* and Jonah to it. The sailors try everything, starting with prayer. By the universal belief of the ancient world, when a natural disaster has struck a group of people, it is because one or more of the gods is angry with one or more of the group. If *all* the group pray, each to his own god, there is a chance of appeasing

him quickly. When prayer failed, they turned to practicality. In the course of their activity *the captain* came across Jonah, *fast asleep* below deck. Whatever Jonah's reasons – as often, we are left to guess them – he was rebuked by the captain who unconsciously echoed God's command to *get up* and pray. Jonah evidently ignored the request.

The sailors now tried another approach. The name of the offended deity could be found by identifying the offending mortal, and the regular way to identify him was by *lot*, which the deity himself would validate.

When the lot fell on Jonah there was a moment of confusion. The sailors all asked him questions at once. Strangely they omitted the crucial one, but he answered it none the less: as *a Hebrew* he fears *the LORD* i.e. YHWH. In addition to the name he mentioned a title more familiar to gentiles, *the god of Heaven*, and then gave a brief descriptive formula (9). His quotation of the formula is a delightful piece of irony. Jonah knows the words but fails to apply them to himself, inasmuch as he was still *trying to escape from the LORD* (indeed, if the

Jonah Tries to Escape God's Charge (cont.)

1.10 • At this the sailors were even more afraid. 'What is this you have done?' they said, because they knew he was trying to escape from the LORD, for he had told them. • 'What must we do with you to make the sea calm for us?' they asked; for it was getting worse. • 'Pick me up and throw me overboard,' he replied; 'then the sea will go down. I know it is my fault that this great storm has struck you.' • Though the crew rowed hard to put back to land it was no use, for the sea was running higher and higher. • At last they called to the LORD, 'Do not let us perish, LORD, for this man's life; do not hold us responsible for the death of an innocent man, for all this, LORD, is what you yourself have brought 15 about.' • Then they took Jonah and threw him overboard, and the raging of the sea subsided. •Seized by a great fear of the LORD, the men offered a sacrifice and made vows to him.

• The LORD ordained that a great fish should swallow Jonah, and he remained in its belly for three days and three nights.   (REB)

Jonah Tries to Escape God's Charge (cont.)

text of v.10 is correct, *he had told them* already). To expiate his offence, they must *throw* him *overboard*. Again we are not told why he suggested the idea himself. Was it altruism or a death wish? The latter would be more typical of him (see Ch.4) but perhaps we may allow him a moment of unselfishness.

The sailors responded by trying to return him directly to his own land and god, but the sea was too big. They are now revealed as men of perception, scruple and generosity. Addressing YHWH as the deity responsible, they ask forgiveness for sacrificing *an innocent*

man. When they had done the deed, *the sea subsided*. Fully persuaded now of the power of YHWH, they make all the proper offerings and *exeunt* loaded with approval.

Meanwhile Jonah, the reluctantly successful missionary, is still in the sea. His rescue from there belongs to the realm of fairy story, though there have been many attempts by scholars to identify a *great fish* capable of providing such hospitality. There are numerous parallels in legend to the saving of a man by a marine creature (e.g. Arion and the dolphin).

Jonah's Preaching and Nineveh's Repentance

2.10 • The LORD commanded the fish, and it spewed Jonah out on the dry land.
3. 1 • A second time the word of the LORD came to Jonah: • 'Go to the great city of Nineveh; go and denounce it in the words I give you.' • Jonah obeyed and went at once to Nineveh. It was a vast city, three days' journey across, • and Jonah began by going a day's journey into it. Then he proclaimed: 'In forty days Nineveh will be overthrown!'   ▸

Jonah's Preaching and Nineveh's Repentance

With Jonah's return to *dry land* the cycle begins again. The commands of 1.2 are repeated in 3.2, and this time there is no awkward hesitation. The size of Nineveh was proverbial, but the

figures in v.4 are not to be taken literally. Excavation has shown that at its widest it was three miles across, a size which however accords with a citizen body of *120,000* (4.11).

Jonah's Preaching and Nineveh's Repentance (cont.)

5 • The people of Nineveh took to heart this warning from God; they declared a public fast, and high and low alike put on sackcloth. • When the news reached the king of Nineveh he rose from his throne, laid aside his robes of state, covered himself with sackcloth, and sat in ashes. • He had this proclamation made in Nineveh: 'By decree of the king and his nobles, neither man nor beast is to touch any food; neither herd nor flock may eat or drink. • Every person and every animal is to be covered with sackcloth. Let all pray with fervour to God, and let them abandon their wicked ways and the injustice they practise. • It may be that 10 God will relent and turn from his fierce anger: and so we shall not perish.' • When God saw what they did and how they gave up their wicked ways, he relented and did not inflict on them the punishment he had threatened.   (REB)

Jonah's Preaching and Nineveh's Repentance (cont.)

The repentance of the Ninevites is described with almost excessive fullness, to show that it was no mere formality. Verse 5 is a summary, which is then expanded in 6-9. The *king*'s change of heart is typically shown by the chiastic order of the verbs: *rose ... laid aside ... covered himself ... sat.* (*Sackcloth* is Heb. *saq*, a rare instance of a Hebrew word that has come down into English, via Greek and Latin.) Ostensibly humbled, he is the greater for it. From *the king and his nobles* (a Persian formula, which may give a clue to the dating of the book) goes out what purports to be a *decree*. The rituals of repentance enjoined were those common everywhere in the ANE, including Israel. It was important that the whole community should take part. But the inclusion of the animals is another piece of fantasy. The closest historical parallel is a custom attested in Persia whereby the horses of nobles had their manes clipped and were caparisoned in

black to pull their master's funeral cortège (cp. our use of black cars).

In much of this the Ninevites correspond to the sailors in Ch.1. But unlike the sailors they had something to repent of. The Assyrians were the most brutal of the successive imperial powers of the ANE, and nobody needed to hear the detailed indictment lying behind the word *injustice* in v.8. The author's interest is focused on the theology of their repentance. His treatment of it makes play with two Hebrew words: *sūv*, meaning turn, which is used six times in 8b-10, and *rā'ā*, which (surprisingly to our thinking) means 'evil' in the two senses of (i) wickedness and (ii) disaster. So the Ninevites 'turn' from the 'evil' they have done, and God reciprocates by turning from the evil which he said he would do. But 'God' throughout Ch.3 is not YHWH, of whom they had not heard, but *Elohim*: there is no question of the Ninevites being converted to Judaism.

God Teaches Jonah a Lesson

4.1 This greatly displeased Jonah. In anger • he prayed to the LORD: 'It is just as I feared, LORD, when I was still in my own country, and it was to forestall this that I tried to escape to Tarshish. I knew that you are a gracious and compassionate God, long-suffering, ever constant, always ready to relent and not inflict punishment. • Now take away my life, LORD: I should be better dead than alive.' • 'Are you right to be angry?' said the LORD.

5 • Jonah went out and sat down to the east of Nineveh, where he made himself a shelter and sat in its shade, waiting to see what would happen in the city. • The LORD God ordained that a climbing gourd should grow up above Jonah's head to throw its shade over him and relieve his discomfort, and he was very glad of it. • But at dawn the next day God ordained that a worm should attack the gourd, and it withered; • and when the sun came up God ordained that a scorching wind should blow from the east. The sun beat down on Jonah's head till he grew faint, and he prayed for death; 'I should be better dead than alive,' he said. • At this God asked, 'Are you right to be angry over the gourd?' 'Yes,' Jonah replied, 10 'mortally angry!' • But the LORD said, 'You are sorry about the gourd, though you did not have the trouble of growing it, a plant which came up one night and died the next. • And should not I be sorry about the great city of Nineveh, with its hundred and twenty thousand people who cannot tell their right hand from their left, as well as cattle without number?'

(REB)

God Teaches Jonah a Lesson

In Ch.4 the tone of irony returns with a vengeance. Verse 1 continues the play on *rā'ā*, and says literally that this (i.e. their good) 'was evil to Jonah, a great evil'. He then reveals the extent to which his own theology is topsy-turvy. As in 1.9 he *knew* the formulae of his religion but did not understand them. Astonishingly he makes YHWH's *compassion* into grounds for complaint (2). That, he now tells us, was why in the first place he *tried to escape*, presumably because his forecast of destruction stood to be falsified; and now that it has happened, he has lost so much face that he wants to die. In the last sentence (3) he is quoting Elijah, whose sense of failure in 1 K 19.4 finally exploded into the same despairing words. But in Jonah's mouth the noble pose serves only to point up the childish self-centredness of his whole attitude.

YHWH's rebuke is initially gentle. To it Jonah does not reply (cp.1.10). Obstinately he still hopes against hope to see Nineveh punished. In most translations he *now* goes to build a shelter outside the city; but the Hebrew could mean that he had built it *previously* and now went back to it, which gives a smoother sequence. The *shelter* would consist of a few cut branches leant together (the same 'tabernacles' as were used at the great feast), and would provide inadequate shade. God therefore played a trick on Jonah. First, he *ordained* a fast-growing creeper to thicken the shade. A *gourd* can grow a foot in a month, but this 'beanstalk' is magic, like the great fish. Jonah forthwith switched from his 'great anger' of 4.1 to 'great joy' (the word 'great' occurs 14 times in the book); but the intervention of the *worm* and the *wind*, also *ordained* by God, sent him back to the sulks again.

God Teaches Jonah a Lesson (cont.)

Thereupon God (who again in vv.7-9 is given the more distant and impersonal title of *Elohim*) repeats his earlier question, with a little sting in the tail which draws attention to Jonah's childishness. This time Jonah is provoked to answer, and thus lays himself open to the final rebuke. Now at last YHWH declares his hand – but he does so in the ironical style that is characteristic of the book. The 'argument' of v.10 is just a tease, for the only thing Jonah has ever been *sorry about* is himself. And the great declaration of v.11 is expressed as a rhetorical question and said with a smile. The people of Nineveh are referred to indulgently as children, and even the *cattle* who had fasted with them (3.7) are included in the LORD's loving care. On that marvellous throwaway phrase the book ends – without our ever learning whether Jonah also repented and was forgiven.

The end of the book of Jonah is a little reminiscent of the end of Job. Jonah too has been concerned with the ultimate theological question, the relation under God between sin and suffering. Jonah too has stood up to God, albeit in a less heroic way, and at the end is teased out of his self-centredness. The theology of Jonah is of course more straightforward, because it is easier to account for the sparing of sinners than for the suffering of the righteous. But seen as literature, the tragedy of Job strikes a much deeper chord than the comedy of Jonah.

MICAH

Social Injustice and its Punishment

1.1 The word of the LORD that came to Micah of Moresheth in the days of Kings Jotham, Ahaz, and Hezekiah of Judah, which he saw concerning Samaria and Jerusalem.

2.1
> Alas for those who devise wickedness
>   and evil deeds on their beds!
> When the morning dawns, they perform it,
>   because it is in their power.

2
> They covet fields, and seize them;
>   houses, and take them away;
> they oppress householder and house,
>   people and their inheritance.

3
> Therefore thus says the LORD:
> Now, I am devising against this family an evil
>   from which you cannot remove your necks;
> and you shall not walk haughtily,
>   for it will be an evil time.

3.1
> Listen, you heads of Jacob
>   and rulers of the house of Israel!
> Should you not know justice? –

2
>   you who hate the good and love the evil,
> who tear the skin off my people,
>   and the flesh off their bones;

3
> who eat the flesh of my people,
>   flay their skin off them,
> break their bones in pieces,
>   and chop them up like meat in a kettle,
>   like flesh in a caldron.

4
> Then they will cry to the LORD,
>   but he will not answer them;
> he will hide his face from them at that time,
>   because they have acted wickedly.

(NRSV)

Social Injustice and its Punishment

The title verse tells us all that is known about Micah. He was a contemporary of Isaiah who came from a village 25 miles SW of Jerusalem in the low hill-country, but addressed his preaching to the northern as well as the southern kingdom. His chief concern was social justice, which is the subject of the first two oracles here.

Ch.2.1-3 is a model crime-and-punishment oracle. The crime was that of the rich in, first, depriving the poor of their property, and then reducing them to debt-slavery*. Micah emphasises the element of criminal planning, giving a lively description of its psychology (1).

Social Injustice and its Punishment (cont.)

The punishment, as usual, will fit the crime. God too *is devising evil* – the same two words, with *evil* repeated to round off v.3. NRSV's *family* means the 'gang', who are now addressed directly. *Necks* are the symbols both of walking *haughtily* and of submitting to a conqueror's yoke.

In the second oracle (3.1-4) Micah turns his attention to the corruption of *justice* – of what should have been the ultimate protection of the poor. Justice was administered by the elders i.e. *heads* of families, who turn out to be either the same people as the rich of the last oracle or in their power. The indictment of v.2a is general (one misses the kind of specification given by Isaiah 1.16 in a parallel passage) and does little to prepare for the violence of the rest of vv. 2-3. Admittedly the basic metaphor was fairly conventional cp. e.g. [Ps 14.4] 'evildoers who eat up my people as they eat bread'. But Micah takes it further than any other OT author. His picture is more vivid, and also more insistent: the image is not developed but repeated – *ad nauseam*, some may feel. The violence of his language may be explained by his sense of being powerless to help those to whom he feels closest, *my people* of vv.2 and 3. The description of punishment in v.4 is something of an anticlimax after vv.1-3.

Universal Peace to Come

1 It shall come to pass in the latter days
　　　　that the mountain of the house of the LORD
　　shall be established as the highest of the mountains,
　　　　and shall be raised up above the hills;
　　and peoples shall flow to it,
2　　　　and many nations shall come, and say:
　　'Come, let us go up to the mountain of the LORD,
　　　　to the house of the God of Jacob;
　　that he may teach us his ways
　　　　and we may walk in his paths.'
　　For out of Zion shall go forth the law,
　　　　and the word of the LORD from Jerusalem.　　　　▶

Universal Peace to Come

This justly famous prophecy describes an ideal future by contrast with the sordid present which has been the burden of Chs 1-3. Like all descriptions of golden ages, whether set in the past or in the future, it must be read as poetry, not prose. Its time is *in the latter days*, corresponding to 'once upon a time'. Its place is a transfigured *Jerusalem*. In height above sea level, Jerusalem is overtopped by the Mount of Olives next door to it. But seen as the *mountain of the house of the LORD*, it will be *raised up* above the seats of all other deities. To it therefore will come *many nations* seeking instruction. There is no suggestion that the nations are making a political submission, nor that they have been converted to Judaism. Rather, as his use of the technical term *go up* shows, Micah is envisaging the regular pilgrimage to Jerusalem enjoined upon faithful Jews, and extending it to the nations. There will be two complementary movements: they will come up to Jerusalem, while God's *word* will *go forth* from it and so reach *nations afar off*.

Universal Peace to Come (cont.)

4. 3   He shall judge between many peoples,
              and shall decide for strong nations afar off;
          and they shall beat their swords into plowshares,
              and their spears into pruning hooks;
          nation shall not lift up sword against nation,
              neither shall they learn war any more;
4   but they shall sit every man under his vine and under his fig tree,
              and none shall make them afraid;
          for the mouth of the LORD of hosts has spoken.   (RSV)

Universal Peace to Come (cont.)

The idea of universal peace, common to all millennial aspirations, has never been expressed more memorably. The high generalisations are brought down to concrete images of *swords* and *plowshares*, and the huge canvas of *many nations* is reduced to the human scale of a single small-holder sitting peaceably *under his vine*. The picture of v.4 was used proverbially in Israel to describe the reign of Solomon (1 K 4.25; also usurped by a foreigner for rhetorical purposes in 2 K 18.31). No picture of peace could be more telling.

The first three verses of this oracle (4.1-3) are found also in the book of Isaiah [2.2-4], where they are introduced by an editorial verse which explicitly claims their authorship for him. If that is the case, we may still congratulate Micah on adding the fourth and final verse.

A King of David's Line

5. 2   But from you, Bethlehem in Ephrathah,
              small as you are among Judah's clans,
          from you will come a king for me over Israel,
              one whose origins are far back in the past, in ancient times.
4   He will rise up to lead them
              in the strength of the LORD,
              in the majesty of the name of the LORD his God.
          They will enjoy security, for then his greatness will reach
              to the ends of the earth.
5   And he shall be a man of peace.   (REB)

A King of David's Line

This oracle is messianic in the sense of looking to the coming of a descendant of David who will restore his kingdom. It is intentionally veiled and capable of more than one interpretation, but it must have been written after the end of David's line. *Ephrathah* is the region in which *Bethlehem* lay. The theme of a great man's rise from small beginnings is a favourite one of the OT. The word translated *lead* in 4 belongs properly to shepherds, which also points to David.

True Religion

6   Wherewith shall I come before the LORD,
        and bow myself before the high God?
     shall I come before him with burnt offerings,
        with calves of a year old?
7   Will the LORD be pleased with thousands of rams,
        or with ten thousands of rivers of oil?
     shall I give my firstborn for my transgression,
        the fruit of my body for the sin of my soul?

8   He hath shewed thee, O man, what is good;
        and what doth the LORD require of thee,
     but to do justly, and to love mercy,
        and to walk humbly with thy God?   (AV)

True Religion

All ancient peoples believed that their deities had to be approached in the right way if their favour was to be secured. Requirements fell into two main categories: (i) a specific ritual, of gift or words, and (ii) a moral way of life. The OT contains a number of comments on the absolute and relative importance of these two requirements. This passage seems very like Is 1.10-17 and Am 5.21-4, but the treatment here is more sophisticated. Micah uses the form of the 'entrance liturgy', as in Pss 15 and 24, where the worshipper explicitly asks the question, what he must do to be admitted to the temple, and is given an answer by a priest. Micah adapts the form ironically to show up the folly of supposing that any cultic sacrifice can be adequate by itself. The list of offerings suggested increases steadily in value. *Calves* could be offered from a week old, so a yearling is already well above the minimum. The *thousands of rams* and the *10,000 rivers of oil* are obviously rhetorical exaggerations (for the numerical progression cp.1 Sam. 18.7). The climax comes with the awful sacrifice of the *first-born*. Child sacrifice *was* sometimes practised in the ANE, including Israel. But it is always condemned in the OT, and here the horror of the mere thought is used to clinch the argument. If God rejects a greater sacrifice, why should he accept a lesser?

Instead, as in the parallel passages of both prophets and psalms, the requirements of the LORD are summarised in the simplest of non-rhetorical and non-technical terms. As with all such summaries, however, the simplicity is deceptive. *Man* in Hebrew is as much collective as individual: the form of address is used to emphasise the distance between him and God. *Mercy* translates Hebrew *hesedh* which REB and NJB render 'loyalty'. The last clause shows that what is being summarised here is not morality but religion.

NAHUM

The Final Assault

1. 1 Prophecy about Nineveh. Book of the vision of Nahum of Elkosh.

2. 2
> The destroyer has advanced on you,
>> guarding the siege-works, watching the road,
>> bracing himself, mustering great strength!

4
> The shields of his fighting men show red,
>> his warriors are dressed in scarlet;
> the metal of the chariots sparkles
>> as he prepares for battle;
> the horsemen are impatient for action;

5
>> the chariots storm through the streets,
>> jostling one another in the squares;
> they look like blazing flames,
>> like lightning they dash to and fro.

6
> His captains are called out;
>> stumbling as they go,
> they speed towards the wall,
>> and the mantelet is put in position.

7
> The sluices of the River are opened,
>> and the palace melts in terror.

The Final Assault

The Book of Nahum (who is not mentioned elsewhere in the OT) consists of a single oracle, more powerful than edifying. It celebrates and perhaps even predicts the downfall of *Nineveh*. Nineveh was the capital of the Assyrian empire during its last and in some ways greatest period, from c.730 BC until it fell to the Babylonians in 612 BC. That downfall had been predictable for some years. But a prophecy was no mere prediction: it was also seen as a word of power capable of helping to bring about the events it foretold (cp. Marx's prophecy of the collapse of capitalism).

Ch. 2 pictures the final assault on the city. The first section (2-6), which deals with the siege itself, is framed by the references to *siege-works* (2) and *mantelet* (6). The latter is a wall of shields, like the Roman *testudo*, and is often portrayed in Assyrian victory-reliefs. The intervening verses portray the *mustering* of the enemy troops. Some details of translation are not certain, but there is no doubt of the emphasis on (i) colour and light and (ii) thrusting movement. The leather of *shields* was sometimes painted *red* as a protection; *scarlet* uniforms were worn by the Babylonian army.

In v.7 we jump to the actual fall of the city. Nineveh lay on the Tigris, whose powerful waters were controlled by a series of dams. But should a dam break, as happened from time to time, she was at the mercy of floods which could literally *melt* her mud-brick buildings. To Nahum and his audience, with Noah's flood in mind, no punishment could be more fitting. In his mind he saw the statue of her protectress Ishtar *carried away*. Ishtar was goddess of sex and war.

The Final Assault (cont.)

8   Beauty is taken captive, carried away,
          her slave-girls moaning like doves
9   and beating their breasts.
      Nineveh is like a lake,
          whose waters are draining away.
      'Stop! Stop!' But no one turns back.
10   'Plunder the silver! Plunder the gold!'
      There is no end to the treasure,
          a mass of everything you could desire!
11   Ravaged, wrecked, ruined!
          Heart fails and knees give way,
      anguish is in the loins of all,
          and every face grows pale!

12   Where is the lions' den now,
          the cave of the lion's whelps,
      where the lion and lioness walked with their cubs
          and no one molested them,
13   where the lion would tear up food for his whelps
          and strangle the kill for his mates,
      where he filled his caverns with prey
          and his lairs with spoil?
14   Look, I am against you! – declares the LORD of Hosts –
          I shall send your chariots up in smoke,
          and the sword will devour your whelps;
      I shall cut short your depredations on earth,
          and the voices of your envoys will be heard no more.   (NJB)

The Final Assault (cont.)

Her *slave-girls* were temple prostitutes, and v.8 is replete with sexual innuendo. The section ends as it began with the theme of the *waters*, now *draining away* like her power, or perhaps like her soldiers (9cd).

In the next section (10-14) we move to the sack of Nineveh. The accumulated *plunder* of her conquests is now looted from her in turn. The powerful v.11 begins with three verbs of similar meaning and sound but increasing length, in Hebrew: *būqāh, mebūqāh, mebullāqāh*. It then uses four parts of the body to depict human collapse: the *heart* is the seat of courage, the *knees* of strength, the *loins* of sexual vigour – and the whole tale can be read in *every pale face*. Since Ishtar was often depicted as mounted on a lion, or even herself as a lioness, it was natural for her city to be imagined as a lions' den, and the loot as the prey brought back for the *cubs*. Verse 14 rounds off the whole chapter. In it the *LORD of Hosts* himself addresses Nineveh, announcing its punishment. Typically, the *whelps* are now themselves devoured. The *envoys* had been the agents of Assyrian military diplomacy, like the one in 2 K 18.

The Fall of Nineveh

3. 1   Disaster to the city of blood,
        packed throughout with lies,
    stuffed with booty,
        where plundering has no end!

2   The crack of the whip!
        The rumble of wheels!
    Galloping horse,
        jolting chariot,

3   charging cavalry,
        flashing swords,
        gleaming spears,
    a mass of wounded,
        hosts of dead,
    countless corpses;
        they stumble over corpses –

4   because of the countless whorings of the harlot,
        the graceful beauty, the cunning witch,
    who enslaved nations by her harlotries
        and tribes by her spells.

5   Look, I am against you! – declares the LORD of Hosts –
        I shall lift your skirts as high as your face
    and show your nakedness to the nations,
        your shame to the kingdoms.

6   I shall pelt you with filth,
        I shall shame you and put you in the pillory.

7   Then all who look at you
        will shrink from you and say,
    'Nineveh has been ruined!'
        Who will mourn for her?
        Where would I find people to comfort you?

The Fall of Nineveh

Ch.3 opens with a complex section (1-6). The curse of v.1 leads into a second and even more impressionistic picture of the assault. The eleven lines, of two stresses each, hammer home the sounds and sights of a massacre. In vv.4-6 we move to a new metaphor, that of Ishtar's city as the great whore. Prostitution and sorcery commonly went together in the ancient world (e.g. 2 K 9.22). Verse 5 repeats the form of 2.14, and the punishment this time is the standard punishment of the prostitute throughout history.

Verse 7 forms a frame with the last verse of the book. Both verses give the comments of foreigners. *All who look at you* (7) is picked up by *all who hear of you* (19), and each verse ends with a rhetorical question. In between come three sections in no particular sequence, which read like

The Fall of Nineveh (cont.)

8   Are you better off than No-Amon
        situated among rivers,
    her defences the seas,
        her rampart the waters?

9   In Ethiopia and Egypt
        lay her strength, and it was boundless;
    Put and the Libyans served in her army.

10   But she too went into exile,
        into captivity;
    her little ones too were dashed to pieces
        at every crossroad;
    lots were drawn for her nobles,
        all her great men were put in chains.

11   You too will become drunk,
        you will go into hiding;
    you too will have to search
        for a refuge from the enemy.

12   Your fortifications are all fig trees,
        with early ripening figs:
    as soon as they are shaken,
        they fall into the mouth of the eater.

13   Look at your people:
        you are a nation of women!
    The gates of your country
        gape open to your enemies;
        fire has devoured their bars!

14   Draw yourselves water for the siege,
        strengthen your fortifications!
    Into the mud with you, puddle the clay,
        repair the brick-kiln!

15   There the fire will burn you up,
        the sword will cut you down.

The Fall of Nineveh (cont.)

left-overs from the previous chapter. First (8-11) comes the comparison with Egyptian Thebes, the city of the god *Amon*, which the Assyrians had sacked in 663. Her god, her river, her allies (*Put* is not certainly identified) – all proved unable to save her. Her fate was that which regularly befell defeated cities in the ANE, and v.11, though its text is quite uncertain, clearly foretold equal misery for Nineveh.

The next section (12-15b) takes us back to the siege itself. The satirical similes (*figs* and *women*) are tantamount to a curse on all her defences. The dramatic series of commands in v.14 portray the frantic last-minute efforts of the besieged – all doomed to fail.

The Fall of Nineveh (cont.)

Make yourselves as numerous as locusts,
   make yourselves as numerous as the hoppers,

3. 16   let your commercial agents
   outnumber the stars of heaven,
your garrisons, like locusts,
   and your marshals, like swarms of hoppers!
They settle on the walls
   when the day is cold.
The sun appears,
   the locusts spread their wings, they fly away,
   away they fly, no one knows where.

18   Alas, your shepherds are asleep,
   king of Assyria,
   your bravest men slumber;
your people are scattered on the mountains
   with no one to gather them.

19   There is no remedy for your wound,
   your injury is past healing.
All who hear the news of you
   clap their hands at your downfall.
For who has not felt
   your unrelenting cruelty?   (NJB)

The Fall of Nineveh (cont.)

The text of the third section (15c-17) is again uncertain, but it appears to be saying that, despite the size of its army and the extent of its bureaucracy, the empire will suddenly disappear into thin air (17). By way of a comparison with Nahum, it is interesting to read Assurbanipal's own typically boastful account (*ANET* 295) of his conquest of Egyptian Thebes (*No-Amon* of 3.8) in 633 BC. and the much more prosaic record in the *Babylonian Chronicle* of the fall of Nineveh in 612 (*ANET* 305). One is also reminded of the final collapse of Nazi Germany, the twentieth-century equivalent of all that Nineveh meant to Nahum: not just another military power but the very incarnation of evil.

ZECHARIAH

The Reign of the Coming King

9
Daughter of Zion, rejoice with all your heart;
  shout in triumph, daughter of Jerusalem!
See, your king is coming to you,
  his cause won, his victory gained,
humble and mounted on a donkey,
  on a colt, the foal of a donkey.

10
He will banish the chariot from Ephraim,
  the war-horse from Jerusalem;
the warrior's bow will be banished,
  and he will proclaim peace to the nations.
His rule will extend from sea to sea,
  from the River to the ends of the earth.

(REB)

The Reign of the Coming King

This famous messianic oracle belongs in spirit with those of Isaiah 9 and 11 and the servant songs of Second Isaiah. Its theme is expressed by a contrast between the coming king and the great conquerors of the ANE. They rode in a *chariot* or (later) on a *war-horse*, and some Hebrew prophecies expected the Messiah, when he came, to do likewise [Jer 22.4]. But historical kings of Israel and Judah never possessed either: their usual mount was a mule (I K 1.38), though princes might have to be content with a donkey [2 Sam 19.26]. Here the choice of a *donkey* symbolises the contrast: the coming king will be victorious but *humble*. That combination, which also underpins the fourth servant song (Is 53), must have been well-known in later Judaism. Jesus applied it to himself when he rode a donkey at his last entry into Jerusalem, and the crowds readily understood his meaning, even if Matthew's gospel (21.2-7) notoriously misread the word-pair in v.9ef as implying *two* donkeys!

Zechariah then develops the theme of peace further. The new king will *banish* weapons of war from the reunited kingdoms of Israel (*Ephraim*) and Judah. Nor will he need them in order to *extend his rule* grandly in all directions. It will stretch from the Mediterranean to the Euphrates: the other two boundaries are left purposely vague. This combination of empire with peace later became part of the ideology of the Roman empire (Vergil, *Aeneid* 6.851+).

Zechariah 9.9-10 from Codex Sinaiticus on page 690: The Greek Codex Sinaiticus was copied in Alexandria in the mid-fourth century AD, some 600 years earlier than the Leningrad Codex (see page 36) of the Hebrew Bible (MT*). It has lost the greater part of Genesis but contains most of the rest of the OT, including the Apocrypha, and the whole NT. Its calligraphy is a joy, and its text is among the best witnesses we have to the Greek translation of the OT (LXX*).

The discovery in the nineteenth century of Sinaiticus (in St. Catherine's Monastery on Mount Sinai, whence its name), led to the first revision of AV/KJV, known as the Revised Version. The Codex is now on permament display at the British Library.

THE OLD TESTAMENT APOCRYPHA

Text of Zechariah 9.9-10
from Codex Sinaiticus

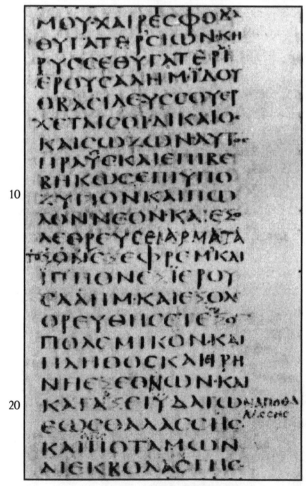

This extract shows clearly the two distinct hands of calligrapher and corrector. The corrector's work is significant in two places. In line 12 (v.10a) he has rightly changed the termination of the verb so as to read '*He will banish*'. Presumably the calligrapher had written 'I will banish', a less satisfactory reading which survives in the MT*. In line 20 (v.10e) the corrector has rightly added '*from sea*' omitted by the calligrapher.

THE FIRST BOOK OF ESDRAS

A Competition at Court

1 King Darius gave a great banquet for all his retainers, for all the members of his household, all the chief men of Media and Persia, • along with the whole body of satraps, commanders, and governors of his empire in the hundred and twenty-seven satrapies from India to Ethiopia. • After eating and drinking as much as they wanted, they withdrew. King Darius retired to his bedchamber, where he lay down and fell fast asleep.

• Then the three young men of the king's personal bodyguard said among 5 themselves: • 'Let each of us name the thing he judges to be strongest, and to the one whose opinion appears wisest let King Darius give rich gifts and prizes: • he shall be robed in purple, drink from gold cups, and sleep on a golden bed; he shall have a chariot with gold-studded bridles, and a turban of fine linen, and a chain around his neck. • His wisdom shall give him the right to sit next to the king and to bear the title Kinsman of Darius.' • Each then put his opinion in writing, affixed his seal, and placed it under the king's pillow. • 'When the king wakes,' they said, 'the writing will be given him, and the king and the three chief men of Persia shall judge whose opinion is wisest; the award will be made to that man on the evidence of what he has written.' ♦

A Competition at Court

The apocryphal book known in English as 1 Esdras, and elsewhere usually as 3 Ezra, is not really a distinct book at all. Most of it merely reproduces the Book of Ezra, together with sections of the books of Chronicles and Nehemiah dealing with the return of the Jews from exile. But inserted into 1 Esdras is this delightful and intriguing story which is not preserved elsewhere in the biblical writings.

The general form of the story is widespread. After a banquet a competition is held in which participants must answer a question of the form 'What is the most ... thing in the world?' Each in turn seeks to outdo his predecessor, and the last to speak usually wins. The OT contains traces of such a competition in Samson's riddles (Jg 14.18); and a highly sophisticated version of one is to be found in Plato's *Symposium*. But the story seems to have been particularly at home in the ANE, and the Persian setting here may well be original. A number of motifs from 3.1-6 are also found in the Book of Esther: the Persian king's feast for his nobles, his sleeplessness and the prizes that he offers (see Est 1.1-3; 6.1; 6.8). More significantly, the tone of Esther – secular and even frivolous – is to be found in the first three of the four answers in Esdras.

The scene in 1 Esdras is well set except for one improbability. It could only have been the king who offered such *prizes*, and only at his suggestion could the answers have been *placed under* his *pillow*; it must therefore also have been he who proposed the competition. And that is how the story was told by the Jewish historian Josephus c.100 AD.

A Competition at Court (cont.)

3.10   • One wrote, 'Wine is strongest.' • The second wrote, 'The king is strongest.' • The third wrote, 'Women are strongest, but truth conquers all.' • When the king awoke, he was handed what they had written. Having read it • he summoned all the chief men of Persia and Media, satraps, commanders, governors, and chief

15   officers, • and took his seat in the council-chamber. What each of the three had written was then read out before them. • 'Call the young men,' said the king, 'and let them explain their opinions.' They were summoned and, on coming in, • were asked to clarify what they had written.

     The first, who spoke about the strength of wine, began: • 'Sirs, how true it is that wine is strongest! It bemuses the wits of all who drink it: • king and orphan,

20   slave and free, poor and rich, on them all it has the same effect. • It turns all thoughts to revelry and mirth; it brings forgetfulness of grief and debt. • It makes everyone feel rich; it cares nothing for king or satrap, but sets all men talking in millions. • When they are in their cups, they forget to be friendly to friends and relations, and before long are drawing their swords; • and when they awake after their wine, they cannot remember what they have done. • Sirs, is not wine the strongest, seeing that it makes men behave in this way?' With that he ended his speech.

4. 1   • Then the second, he who spoke of the strength of the king, began: • 'Sirs, is not man the strongest, man who subdues land and sea and everything in them? • But the strongest of men is the king; he is their lord and master, and they obey whatever command he gives them. • If he bids them make war on one another, they do so; if he dispatches them against his enemies, they march off and make

5   their way over mountains and walls and towers. • They kill and are killed, but they never disobey the king's command. If they are victorious they bring everything, spoil and all else, to the king. • Again, take those who do not serve as soldiers or go to war, but work the land: they sow and reap, and lay the harvest before the king. They compel each other to pay him their tribute. • Though he is no more than one man, if he orders them to kill, they kill; if he orders them to release, they release. He orders them • to smite and they beat, to demolish and they demolish, to build and they build, • to cut down and they cut down, to plant

10   and they plant. • People and troops all obey him. Further, while he himself is at table, whether he eats, drinks, or goes to sleep, • they stand in attendance round him and none can leave and see to his own affairs; in nothing whatever do they disobey. • Sirs, surely the king must be the strongest, when he commands such obedience!' With that he ended.   ▸

A Competition at Court (cont.)

The first three answers – *wine, king, women* – appear straightforward. They are given in ascending length, with the third longer than the other two put together. The first two are brief and to the point; the third, though rambling, is far the wittiest and best fitted to the courtly setting. But there are clues to show that the first two are now in the wrong order. The page who praised wine twice claimed it to be stronger than the king (3.19, 21), while the one who praised the king made no reference to wine. It is indeed likely that in such a context the king would have to come first, and the likelihood is confirmed by 4.14.

A Competition at Court (cont.)

    • The third, he who spoke about women and truth, was Zerubbabel; he began:
• 'Sirs, it is true that the king is great, that men are many, and that wine is strong,
but who rules over them? Who is the master? Women, surely! • The king and all
his people, lords over land and sea, were born of women, • and from them they
came. Women brought up the men who planted the vineyards which yield the
wine. • They make the clothes men wear and they bring honour to men; without
women men could not exist.

    • 'If men have amassed gold and silver and all manner of beautiful things, and
then see a woman with a lovely face and figure, • they leave it all to gape and
stare at her with open mouth, and every one of them will prefer her above gold
and silver or any thing of beauty. • A man will abandon his father who brought
him up, abandon even his country, and become one with his wife. • To the end of
his days he stays with her, forgetful of father, mother, and country. • Here is the
proof that women are your masters: do you not toil and sweat and then bring all
you earn and give it to your wives? • A man will take his sword and sally forth to
plunder and steal, to sail on sea and river; • he confronts lions, he goes about in
the dark; and when he has stolen and robbed and looted, he brings the spoil home
to his beloved.

    • 'A man loves his wife above father or mother. • For women's sakes many
men have been driven out of their minds, many have become slaves, • many have
perished or come to grief or taken to evil ways. • Now do you believe me?
Certainly the king wields great authority; no country dare lift a finger against him.
• Yet I watched him with Apame, his favourite concubine, daughter of the
celebrated Bartacus. She was sitting on the king's right, • and she took the diadem
off his head and put it on her own. She was slapping his face with her left hand,
• and all the king did was gape at her open-mouthed. When she laughed at him he
laughed; when she was cross with him he coaxed her to make it up with him.
• Sirs, if women do as well as this, how can their strength be denied?' • The king
and the chief men looked at one another.   ▶

15

20

25

30

A Competition at Court (cont.)

A more obvious suture in the story is
the addition of the fourth answer, *truth.*
When the three set out on their competition they agreed: '*Let each of us name
one thing he judges to be strongest*' –
REB's translation of 3.5 is misleading.

A Competition at Court (cont.)

Zerubbabel then went on to speak about truth: • 'Sirs, we have seen that women are strong. The earth is vast, the sky is lofty, yet the sun, swift in its course, **4.** 35 moves through the circle of the sky and speeds home in a single day. • How great is the sun which can do this! But truth too is great; it is stronger than all else. • The whole earth calls on truth, and the sky praises her; all created things shake and tremble. With her there is no injustice. • There is injustice in wine, and in kings, and in women, injustice in all men and in all their works, whatever they may be. There is no truth in them, and in their injustice they shall perish. • But truth abides and remains strong for ever; she lives and is sovereign for ever and ever.

• 'There is no favouritism with her, no partiality; rather she exacts justice 40 from everyone who is wicked or unjust. All approve what she does; • in her judgements there is no injustice. Hers are strength and royalty, the authority and majesty of all ages. Praise be to the God of truth!'

• As Zerubbabel finished speaking, all the people shouted, 'Great is truth: truth is strongest!' • Then the king said to him, 'Ask what you will, even beyond what is laid down in the terms, and we shall grant it you. You have been proved to be the wisest, and you shall sit next to me and be called my Kinsman.'   (REB)

A Competition at Court (cont.)

And the praise of truth is clearly an insertion (4.34-41). It differs totally from the other three in being not a courtly speech but a lofty hymn. The concept of truth, as here portrayed, was common throughout the ANE. In particular, Egyptian *Ma'at* and Persian *Arsha* were deities of order, representing both truth and (as here) justice. The hymn is unlikely to be Jewish in origin, otherwise the praise would have been of Wisdom, but its elevated tone clearly appealed to the Jewish editor.

For there is another layer to this story in its present form, namely its weaving into the book of 1 Esdras. The weaver's hand is visible in his identification of the third page with *Zerubbabel* (for whom see Ezra 3.1) in 4.13 and in the title *God of truth* in 4.40.

Having adapted the story thus, he fitted it into 1 Esdras to provide the occasion for the Persian king's release of the Jews from exile in Babylon [4.43-5.3].

And the history of the story does not end there. On the one hand it contains traces of an even remoter past. References in 4.2, 14f., and 34 suggest that there was once a fuller version of it containing other candidates e.g. man, earth, sea, sky, sun. As it happens, all of these do occur in an Ethiopian version, which has a list of ten candidates in all (including wine but excluding truth) and brings out women as the winner. But on the other hand it is truth that has won in the long run. For the Latin version of v.41, though itself a mistranslation, has had a European currency in its own right: 'magna est veritas et praevalebit.'

THE SECOND BOOK OF ESDRAS

Introduction

The central chapters (3-14) of 2 Esdras were written about 100 AD by a thoughtful Jew who was still in deep distress of spirit as a result of the destruction of Jerusalem by Roman troops under Titus in 70 AD. For good reason, he used the cover of the earlier destruction of Jerusalem by the Babylonians. He also took for himself from that earlier period the pen-name of Ezra (3.1) or Esdras. Ezra had led one of the groups returning from the Babylonian exile (see p.345f.), and was a much respected figure in later Judaism.

The author's distress was caused not so much by the wound inflicted in 70 AD on Jewish national pride – deep and lasting though that was – but rather by the seismic shock to his faith in God. The question with which he wrestled is fundamentally that of Job, expressed in national terms: how can the world as he has experienced it be part of God's plan? But his method of handling it owes more to the later Book of Daniel and the apocalyptic tradition, on which see Postscript to Daniel (p.646).

2 Esdras also has many affinities with the NT Book of Revelation, which is its near contemporary. (This and other NT echoes are evidence not of Christian influence but of the common circulation of many apocalyptic ideas and images.) Like Revelation, it is structured into a series of seven visionary dialogues, in all of which 'Ezra' is guided by the angel Uriel. But whereas in the first three of them the emphasis is on the dialogue, in the last four it is on the vision. The tone changes markedly in the middle – so much so that some critics have supposed two different authors.

The first part of the book (down to 9.22) is a mixture of apocalyptic with Wisdom literature. It is here that Ezra presses the questions 'Why?' and 'How long?' Inevitably these questions carry an overtone of plaint. Seen as a whole, the book moves, like many single psalms and whole prophetic books, from distress to consolation. But there is no self-pity and no vindictiveness. On the contrary, all men have sinned, whether Jews or gentiles, and all men are under judgement, the author himself included.

The outstanding feature of 2 Esdras, from a literary as well as a theological point of view, is the author's refusal in the first part to be satisfied with the traditional pieties. Like Job, he keeps insisting that his questions have not been satisfactorily answered. But the angel, unlike Job's friends, does make some show of engaging with those questions, and in that respect this book contains the nearest to a true dialogue that we have – or perhaps could have – in the Bible.

So by the end of the first part, Ezra is still not convinced: an impasse has been reached, as in Job and as in many Platonic dialogues. The author therefore moves, as in those other cases, from argument into myth. As a classical scholar says of the *Republic*, Plato makes that move 'when he wishes to convey religious or moral truths for which plain prose is inadequate' (Lee). But the move inevitably lessens the dramatic tension, and it takes great skill to carry it off. That skill is lacking in 2 Esdras, and so Ezra's 'conversion' from challenger to supporter is unconvincing.

The book is written mainly in prose, but parallelism is frequent and many passages could be printed as verse. The prose is generally straightforward. Sometimes it lapses into late Jewish prolixity, where a point is protracted to many parallel lines – the record is eighteen in [10.21-22]. But the author had also a gift for short sentences. Some of these are in the Hebrew tradition, while others are more redolent of high-flown Greek pessimism e.g. 'The world has lost its youth and time is growing old' [14.10].

Alone of books in the Apocrypha, 2 Esdras is not extant either in its original Hebrew/Aramaic or in a Greek translation: only in Latin, Syriac and some other versions. It is not included in the Apocrypha as printed in many countries e.g. Germany and USA. It is also known to different Christian denominations under different titles, of which the commonest is IV Ezra.

The passages chosen from the first part (3.1-9.22) show the sequence of argument as we would analyse it, not as the author developed it. In the full text each of the first three dialogues covers the same ground, and the argument tends to go round and around, like music, before moving on to the next point. The extracts from the first dialogue give the basic complaint uttered by Ezra in prayer to God (Ch.3) followed by the angel's first two answers: (i) that a man with his 'limited mind' [4.11] cannot expect to understand such things and (ii) that the present evil age is due to pass away (4.22-end).

Ezra Questions God's Plan

3. 1 In the thirtieth year after the fall of Jerusalem, I Ezra was in Babylon. Lying on my bed I was troubled and my mind filled with perplexity as I reflected on the desolation of Zion and the prosperity of those who lived in Babylon. • I was deeply disturbed in spirit, and full of fear I addressed the Most High. • 'My Master and Lord,' I said, 'was it not you alone who in the beginning spoke the
5 word that formed the world? At your command the dust • brought forth Adam. His body was lifeless; yours were the hands that had moulded it, and you breathed the breath of life into it and he became a living person. • You led him into paradise, which you yourself had planted before the earth came into being. • You gave him your one commandment to obéy; and when he disobeyed it, you made both him and his descendants subject to death.

'From him there sprang nations and tribes, peoples and families, too numer-
12 ous to count. • The population of the earth expanded; families and peoples increased, nation upon nation. But once again they began to sin, more wickedly than those before them. • When they sinned, you chose for yourself one of them; Abraham was his name. • Him you loved, and to him alone, secretly at dead of night, you disclosed how the world would end. • You made an everlasting cov-
20 enant with him and promised never to abandon his descendants. • But you did not take away their evil heart and thus enable your law to bear fruit in them; • for the first man, Adam, burdened as he was with an evil heart, sinned and was overcome, and not only he but all who were descended from him. • So the weakness became inveterate, and although your law was in your people's hearts, a rooted wickedness was there too; thus the good came to nothing, and what was evil
27 persisted. • And so you handed over your city into the power of your enemies. ▶

Ezra Questions God's Plan

Ezra or Esdras expresses his complaint in historical form. He rehearses at some length what he has been brought up to believe is the history of God's saving acts towards his people. But the rehearsal is ironical: if that was God's plan, he says, it has not worked. True, men have sinned. But their sin is due to their *evil heart*, which God has failed to *take away* (20-22). The doctrine of the 'evil heart' is rare in the OT (Gen 6.5; 8.21), but it is common

---

Ezra Questions God's Plan (cont.)

28 • 'I had thought that perhaps those in Babylon lead better lives, and that is why Zion is in subjection. • But when I arrived here, I saw wickedness beyond reckoning, and with my own eyes I have seen evildoers in great numbers these thirty years. My

30 heart sank • because I observed how you tolerate sinners and spare the godless, how you have destroyed your own people but preserved your enemies. You have given no indication • to anyone how your ways are to be understood. • Is Babylon more virtuous than Zion?'   (REB)

Ezra Questions God's Plan (cont.)

enough in later Judaism. It came into Christianity through Paul (Rom 5.12f.), as the doctrine of 'original sin'. The typi- cal apocalyptic tradition that God taught *Abraham secretly* (14) is also absent from, and alien to, the Hebrew Bible.

The Angel's Reply: Look to the Future

4.1 Uriel, the angel who was sent to me, replied: • 'You are completely at a loss to understand this world; can you then expect to understand the way of the Most

22 High?'
• 'But, my lord, please tell me,' I asked, 'why have I been given the faculty of understanding? • My question is not about the distant heavens, but about what happens every day before our eyes. Why has Israel been made a byword among the Gentiles? Why has the people you loved been put at the mercy of godless nations? Why has the law of our fathers been brought to nothing, and the written covenants made a dead letter? • We pass from the world like a flight of locusts,

25 our life is but a vapour, and we are not worth the Lord's pity. • What then will he do for us who bear his name? Those are my questions.'
• He answered: 'If you survive, you will see; if you live long enough, you will marvel. For this present age is passing away; • it is full of sorrow and weakness, too full to grasp what is promised in due time for the godly. • The evil about which you ask me has been sown, but the time for reaping is not yet. • Until the crop of evil has been reaped as well as sown, until the ground where it was sown has vanished, there will be no room for the field where the good is sown.'

33 • I asked, 'But when? How long have we to wait? Why are our lives short and miserable?'   (REB)

The Angel's Reply: Look to the Future

The angel's first answer is one of the standard moves in a traditional theodicy*, but Ezra brushes it aside with a further, clearly rhetorical, question (22). He then reverts to his original question but, seeing that he is getting nowhere in asking about the past and the present, he asks also about the future (25). This enables the angel to draw upon familiar ideas and images. At the end of *this present age* (26) will come *the time for reaping* (28) and then for *what is promised in due time for the godly*.

Ezra is Not Satisfied

7. 3 He said: 'Imagine a sea set in a vast open space and spreading far and wide, • but the entrance to it narrow like the gorge of a river. • If anyone wishes to reach this sea, whether to set eyes on it or to gain control of it, how can he arrive at its broad, open waters without passing through the narrow gorge? • Or again, imagine a city built in a plain, a city full of every good thing, • but the entrance to it narrow and steep, with fire to the right and deep water to the left. • Between the fire and the water there is only one path, and that wide enough for but one 9 person at a time. • If someone has been given this city as a legacy, how can he take possession of his inheritance except by passing through this dangerous approach?' • I agreed: 'That is the only way, my lord.'

The angel said: 'Such is the lot of Israel. • It was for Israel that I made the world, and when Adam transgressed my decrees the creation came under judge14 ment. • Everyone must therefore enter this narrow and futile existence; otherwise they can never attain the blessings in store. • Then why are you so disquieted and perturbed, Ezra, at the thought that you are mortal and must die? • Why have you not turned your mind from the present to the future?'

• 'My master and lord,' I replied, 'in your law you have laid it down that the just shall inherit these blessings, but the ungodly shall perish. • The just, therefore, can endure this narrow life and look for the spacious life hereafter; but those who have lived a wicked life will have gone through the narrows without ever reaching the open spaces.'

19 • He said: 'You are not a better judge than God, nor wiser than the Most High. • Better that many now living should perish, than that the law which God has set before them should be despised! • God has given clear instructions to all when they come into this world, telling them how to attain life and how to avoid punishment.'

62 • I said: 'Mother Earth, if the human mind, like the rest of creation, is but a product of the dust, why did you bring it forth? • It would have been better if the very dust had never come into being, for then the mind would never have been produced. • But, as it is, our mind grows up with us and we are tortured by it, for we realise we are doomed to die. • What sorrow for mankind; what happiness for the wild beasts! What sorrow for every mother's son; what joy for the cattle and flocks! ▶

Ezra is Not Satisfied

In the next dialogue the angel comes up with a more plausible image. Life is a quest, either on *sea* (3-5) or on land (6-9), in which the only approach to the desired goal is through a *narrow entrance*. By using the quest image, Uriel hopes to keep Ezra focused on *the future* (16) and the *blessings in store*.

But Ezra will not be diverted from his original question about the justice of God's plan for the world. Much to his credit, he now shifts his concern from the faithful few to the many sinners (18) – and it is possible that he has in mind gentiles as well as Jews. The angel's uncompromising reply (note *all* in 21) provokes him to a powerful protest. In the rest of Chs 7-9 he deploys a two-pronged argument: that (i) the original plan of creation was harsh on the majority, but that (ii) scripture itself, recognising this, provides for a mitigation of the

Ezra is Not Satisfied (cont.)

• How much better their lot than ours! They have no judgement to expect, no knowledge of torment, no knowledge of salvation promised them after death.'

70 • The angel replied: 'When the Most High was making the world and Adam and his descendants, he first of all planned the judgement and what goes with it. • Your own words, when you said that man's mind grows up with him, will give you the answer. • It was in spite of having a mind that the people of this world sinned, and that is why torment awaits them: they received the commandments, but did not keep them; they accepted the law, then violated it. • What defence will they be able to make at the judgement, what answer at the last day?'

02 • 'If I have found favour with you, my lord,' I said, 'tell me one thing more: on the day of judgement will the just be able to plead for the wicked, or by prayer win pardon for them from the Most High? • Can fathers do so for their sons, or sons for their parents? Can brothers pray for brothers, relatives and friends for their nearest and dearest?'

• 'Since you have found favour with me', the angel replied, 'this too I will tell you. The day of judgement is decisive and sets its seal on the truth for all to see. In the present age a father cannot send his son in his place, nor a son his father,

05 nor a master his slave, nor a man his best friend, to be ill for him, or sleep, or eat, or be cured for him. • In like manner no one shall ever ask pardon for another; every individual will be held responsible for his own wickedness or goodness when that day comes.'

• To this I replied: 'But how is it, then, that we read of intercessions in scripture? First, there is Abraham, who prayed for the people of Sodom; then Moses,

11 who prayed for our ancestors when they sinned in the wilderness. • If, then, in an age when corruption had spread and wickedness increased, the just made entreaty for the wicked, why cannot it be the same on the day of judgement?'

• The answer he gave me was: 'The present world is not the end, and the glory of God does not stay in it continually. That is why the strong have prayed for the weak. • But the day of judgement will be the end of the present world and the beginning of the eternal world to come, a world in which corruption will have

15 disappeared. • On the day of judgement, therefore, there can be no mercy for those who have lost their case, no reversal for those who have won.'   ▸

Ezra is Not Satisfied (cont.)

harshness. And this argument is strong enough to be used twice, first in 7.62-111, secondly in 7.116-139.

For the first prong of it, he develops his previous rhetorical question (4.22) into a deep pessimism about the whole creation, but especially *the human mind* (62). His criticism has the intellectual passion of Job's, but he is too respectful to address God directly. Instead he complains first to the lay figure of *Mother*

Earth, and then, when the angel remains obdurate, to *Adam* (118). The basic point, that the creation has been mismanaged, is seen in the repeated formula *it would have been better if* . . . At v.116 he harks back to his strange idea (3.20) that Adam ought somehow to have *been restrained*, and goes on to identify himself more clearly with *the wicked* (119). For the second prong of his argument he quotes scripture in two respects. It approves *intercession* (106)

Ezra is Not Satisfied (cont.)

7.116   • I replied, 'But this is my point, my first point and my last: how much better it would have been if the earth had never produced Adam at all, or, once it had done so, if he had been restrained from sinning! • O Adam, what have you done? Though the sin was yours, the fall was not yours alone; it was ours also, the fall of all your descendants. • What good is the promise of immortality to us, when

123 we have committed mortal sins? • What good is the revelation to us of paradise and its imperishable fruit, the source of perfect satisfaction and healing? For we shall never enter it.'

127   • The angel replied, 'This is the thought for every man on earth to keep in mind during the battle of life: • if he is defeated, he must accept the sufferings you have mentioned, but if he is victorious, the rewards I have been describing will be his.'

132   • 'My lord,' I said, 'I know that the Most High is now called compassionate, because he has compassion on those yet unborn; • and merciful, because he shows mercy to those who repent and live by his law; • and rich in forgiveness, because again and again he forgives sinners, past, present, and to come. • And he is also called Judge, for unless he grants pardon to those who have been created by his word, and blots out their countless offences, only a very few of the entire human race would, I suppose, be spared.'

8.41   In reply to me the angel said: • 'The farmer sows many seeds in the ground and plants many plants, but not all the seeds come up safely in due season, nor do all the plants strike root. It is the same in the world of men: not all who are sown will be saved.'

   • To that I replied: 'If I have found favour with you, let me speak. • The farmer's seed may not come up, because you did not give it rain at the right time, or it may rot because of too much rain; • but man, who was fashioned by your hands and called your image because he is made like you, and for whose sake you formed everything, will you really compare him with seed sown by a farmer?'

46   • He answered: 'The present is for those now alive, the future for those yet to come. • It is not possible for you to love my creation with a love greater than mine – far from it! But never again rank yourself among the unjust, as so often you have done. • Yet the Most High approves • of the proper modesty you have shown; you have not sought great glory by including yourself among the godly.'

9.14   • I answered, • 'I repeat what I have said again and again: the lost outnumber the saved • as a wave exceeds a drop of water.'   (REB)

Ezra is Not Satisfied (cont.)

by the *just* for *the wicked*; and it insists that God himself is *rich in forgiveness* (132+). But nothing Ezra can say makes any impact upon the implacable angel, and it is clear that the dialogue is running into the sands. When the angel tries to revive a discredited metaphor (8.41), Ezra rightly dismisses it. And when the angel finally retreats behind an ironical compliment upon his modesty, Ezra remains heroically unselfish and undeflected.

The Vision of the Man from the Sea

.2 In my dream, a wind arose from the sea and set all its waves in turmoil. • As I watched, the wind brought a figure like that of a man out of the depths, and he flew with the clouds of heaven. Wherever he turned his face, everything he looked at trembled, • and wherever the sound of his voice reached, everyone who heard it melted as wax at the touch of fire.

5   • Next I saw a countless host of men gathering from the four winds of heaven to vanquish the man who had come up out of the sea. • I saw that the man hewed

9   out for himself a great mountain, and flew on to it. • When he saw the hordes advancing to the attack, he did not so much as lift a finger against them. He had no spear in his hand, no weapon at all; • only, as I watched, he poured out what appeared to be a stream of fire from his mouth, a breath of flame from his lips with a storm of sparks from his tongue. • These, the stream of fire, the breath of flame, and the great storm, combined into one mass which fell on the host prepared for battle, and burnt them all up. I was astounded at the sight.

       • After that, I saw the man come down from the mountain and summon to himself a different, a peaceful company. • He was joined by great numbers of men, some with joy on their faces, others with sorrow, some coming from captivity, and some bringing others to him as an offering. I woke up overcome by terror, and I prayed to the Most High: • 'O Lord, from first to last you have revealed those wonders to me, and judged me worthy to have my prayers an

15   swered. • Now show me the meaning of this dream also.'

21   • 'Yes,' he replied, 'I shall disclose the meaning of the vision, and tell you

25   what you ask. • The man you saw coming up from the heart of the sea • is he whom the Most High has held in readiness during many ages; through him he will deliver the world he has made, and he will determine the destiny of those who survive. • As for the breath of flame, the fire, and the storm you saw issuing from the mouth of the man, • so that without spear or any other weapon in his hand he crushed the onslaught of the hordes advancing to fight against him, the meaning is this: • the day is near when the Most High will start bringing deliverance to

30   those on earth. • Its panic-stricken inhabitants • will plot hostilities against one another, city against city, region against region, nation against nation, kingdom against kingdom.'   ▸

The Vision of the Man from the Sea

Up to Ch.9 the book has presented a genuine argument, with neither side yielding. We are probably meant to read it as an interior dialogue, i.e. the author himself swung between the two views which he was striving unsuccessfully to reconcile. But at this point Ezra suddenly switches to take his theology, and even his tone, from the angel. From [9.23] onwards, i.e. for the last four visions, the dialogue *form* is maintained, but Ezra asks questions only for information and accepts the answers he is given. We have perforce to regard his doubts as assuaged. But since the author gives no grounds for his 'conversion', the rest of the book inevitably falls flat.

The vision of the *man from the sea* is in the central apocalyptic* tradition. Like its NT contemporary, Revelation, it draws much from Daniel. Certainly the messianic figure in v.3 of a man who *flew with the clouds of heaven* comes

The Vision of the Man from the Sea (cont.)

13.32   • 'When that happens, and all the signs that I have shown you take place, then my son will be revealed, he whom you saw as a man coming up out of the sea. • At the sound of his voice all nations will leave their own territories and their separate wars, • and unite as you saw in your vision in one large host past counting, all intent on overpowering him. • When he takes his stand on the summit of Mount Zion, • my son will convict of their godless deeds the nations that confront him; this is symbolised by the flame. • And he will destroy them without effort by means of the law – and that is like the fire.

40   • You saw him assemble a company which was different and peaceful. • They are the ten tribes that were taken into exile in the days of King Hoshea, whom King Shalmaneser of Assyria made captive. • But then they resolved to leave behind the gentile population and go to a more distant region never yet inhabited, and there at least to be obedient to their laws, which in their own country they had failed to keep. • Their long journey through that region called Arzareth took a year and a half. • They have lived there ever since, until this final age. Now they are on their way back.'   (REB)

The Vision of the Man from the Sea (cont.)

from Dan 7.13. The further description of him in vv.32 and 37 as *my son* is probably a mistranslation for 'my servant' – the same word in Greek means both.

Standard apocalyptic features in the vision include: *Mount Zion* (35) as the home of the Messiah; the 'time of troubles' (31) culminating in the final battle (34) against the godless; the last judgement, leading to destruction for those convicted (37-8); and the welcome home for the Jews, including those from the dispersion.

More unusual is the reference in 40-47 to the ten tribes of Israel. These tribes were supposed to have been lost when the northern kingdom of Israel was carried off into exile. Later Judaism developed many legends about the ten tribes. Here we see a relatively simple development, where speculation can still be traced to its source. The name *Arzareth* (45) is an invented Hebrew word meaning 'other land'. It is derived from Dt [29.28], where God is said to have uprooted the idolatrous Jews and 'banished them to another land, where they are until this day'. The idea that they have been living in *a distant region never yet inhabited* (41) explains why nothing has been heard of them in the interim. This tradition has lasted for a long time among the Jews. It is also still occasionally met in Britain as a component, together with Egyptian pyramid lore, of the beliefs of the British Israelites.

TOBIT

Introduction

The Book of Tobit is a story about two related Jewish families living in the dispersion in what are now Iraq and Iran. Each family falls, through illness, into misfortune. Tobit, head of one family, loses his job and goes blind. Sarah, daughter of the other family, is possessed by a demon who prevents her successive attempts at marriage. Both call upon God, who intervenes through his angel Raphael, 'the healer'. Raphael guides Tobit's son Tobias on a quest which leads to his marriage with his kinswoman Sarah. In the end the health and fortunes of both families are restored.

The basic story of the book comes from a combination of two common folk-tales, known as 'The Grateful Dead' and 'The Dangerous Bride'. The combination itself is found in twenty-four different versions, which come from most parts of Europe, with one also from Armenia. The last, which is the most relevant to Tobit, runs briefly as follows.

A rich merchant on his travels saw some foreigners maltreating the corpse of a man who had died owing them money. Being a pious man, he paid the debt and gave the corpse honourable burial. Later, having fallen into poverty and other misfortunes, he followed the advice of a mysterious slave and married a rich man's daughter. She had had five previous husbands, but on each occasion they had been killed on their wedding night by a serpent coming out of her mouth. This time however as the serpent came out in search of its victim it was killed by the slave, who thereupon revealed that he was the spirit of the dead man.

To bring that folk-tale into line with basic Jewish thinking, certain changes had to be made. In particular, the Jews could never have a dead man coming back to life and showing gratitude. It follows that the slave-companion of the folk-tale

can no longer be identical with the dead man. It was a master-stroke – though one natural to the Bible – to make him into an angel. This means that God can guide the action without dominating it. But the presence of the angel in the foreground and of God in the background leaves a much humbler role for the hero: the only 'heroic' deeds in Tobit are done by the angel. In fact the character who was the hero in the folk-tale is here split into two, father and son; but their original identity may account for their having the same name, which means 'YHWH is my good'. Tobias, being only a boy, does not need to be a hero yet; Tobit, being old and blind, need no longer be. But being each of them weak in different ways, they are more realistic representatives of the Jewish people; for the true heroism of the book of Tobit is the heroism not of action (as in Judith) but of suffering.

From this and other sources the author constructed a story which is coherent and well-rounded. It has its prologue and epilogue like Job; moving inwards towards the centre, one next finds two sections (Chs 3 and 10-11) where the fortunes of the two families are interwoven; finally there is the core (Chs 4-9) where the interest follows Tobias as he moves on his quest from one family to the other and then, after the climax of the wedding, back again.

The story as developed by the author conveys a wide range of religious messages. First, God's providence is always present – this time explicitly in the form of Raphael. Angels played an essential part in Old Persian religion (known as Zoroastrianism), bridging the gap between the holiness of God and the impurity of man. The idea fitted Hebrew theology well enough, and so from the exile onwards we find an increasingly developed doctrine of angels in Judaism. Raphael, here first mentioned in the Bible, was later to be ranked as one of the three archangels.

God's protection is earned by the performance of pious duties. The author of Tobit lays great emphasis on prayer and almsgiving. But he has an especial concern for marriage, incorporating traditional Jewish values: that sex is good but married love is better; and that youth is good but married old age is also among God's blessings (8.17). The author can smile at the strains of married life, but he admires its strength too.

The original Aramaic text of Tobit is now lost. But we have Aramaic as well as Hebrew fragments from Qumran. As complete texts we have two different Greek versions, one fuller than the other. The fuller is known as S, from the ms. *Sinaiticus* in which it is preserved. The shorter text, B, seems to have been pruned for stylistic reasons. The Qumran fragments generally support S, and sometimes preserve readings which are not in either Greek text e.g. 'he salted' in 6.5. These major variations between the mss suggest that the book is a late work, perhaps as late as the first century BC. That would account for the fact that it is not in the canon, unlike the much less edifying book of Esther.

The translators of the Authorized Version (who did their work before S was discovered) used the text of B, and those of RSV followed suit. Newer versions (REB, NJB) have preferred S. For an example of both see p.713. The fullness of S can be tedious, but is has a chatty charm that is appropriate to what Luther rightly called a comedy of bourgeois married life.

The book has been quite a popular subject for European drama, but more so for cantatas and oratorios (Haydn and Gounod) and for painting – Botticelli, Raphael and especially Rembrandt, who often painted the blind Tobit.

The Troubles of Tobit

1. 1 This is the story of Tobit son of Tobiel, of the tribe of Naphtali. • In the time of King Shalmaneser of Assyria he was taken captive from Thisbe which is south of Kedesh-naphtali in Upper Galilee.

9 • When I grew up, I took a wife from our kindred and had by her a son whom
10 I called Tobias. • After the deportation to Assyria in which I was taken captive and came to Nineveh, everyone of my family and nation ate gentile food; • but I myself scrupulously avoided doing so. • And since I was wholeheartedly mindful of my God, • the Most High endowed me with a presence which won me the favour of Shalmaneser, and I became his buyer of supplies. • During his lifetime I used to travel to Media and buy for him there, and I deposited bags of money to the value of ten talents of silver with my kinsman Gabael son of Gabri in Media.
15 • When Shalmaneser died and was succeeded by his son Sennacherib, the roads to Media passed out of Assyrian control and I could no longer make the journey.

The Troubles of Tobit

The introductory verses (1-2), in the third person, provide the usual detailed pseudo-historical setting. For the Assyrian conquest of Samaria in 721 BC see 2 K 17.6, which mentions *Media* (14) among the countries to which Jews were then deported. The stress on marriage within the kinship group (9) is one which will link the two families whose fortunes make up the book. A second link is the (somewhat contrived) deposit of the *ten talents*, a large sum of money (14).

The Troubles of Tobit (cont.)

16 • In the days of Shalmaneser, I had done many acts of charity to my fellow-countrymen: I would share my food with the hungry • and provide clothing for those who had none, and if I saw the dead body of anyone of my people thrown outside the wall of Nineveh, I gave it burial. • One of the Ninevites disclosed to the king that it was I who had been giving burial to his victims and that I had gone into hiding. When I learnt that the king knew about me and was seeking my life,

20 I was alarmed and made my escape. • All that I possessed was seized and confiscated for the royal treasury; I was left with nothing but Anna my wife and my son Tobias.

2.1 • During the reign of Esarhaddon, I returned to my house, and my wife Anna and my son Tobias were restored to me. At our festival of Pentecost, that is the feast of Weeks, a fine meal was prepared for me and I took my place. • The table being laid and food in plenty put before me, I said to Tobias: 'My son, go out and, if you find among our people captive here in Nineveh some poor man who is wholeheartedly mindful of God, bring him back to share my meal. I shall wait for you, son, till you return.' • Tobias went to look for a poor man of our people, but came straight back and cried, 'Father!' 'Yes, my son?' I replied. 'Father,' he answered, 'one of our nation has been murdered! His body is lying in the market-place; he has just been strangled.' • I jumped up and left my meal untasted. I took the body from the square and put it in one of the outbuildings until sunset when I

5 could bury it; • then I went indoors, duly bathed myself, and ate my food in sorrow. • I recalled the words of the prophet Amos in the passage about Bethel:

> Your festivals shall be turned into mourning,
>   and all your songs into lamentation,

and I wept. • When the sun had gone down, I went and dug a grave and buried the body. • My neighbours jeered. 'Is he no longer afraid?' they said. 'He ran away last time, when they were hunting for him to put him to death for this very offence; and here he is again burying the dead!'   ▸

The Troubles of Tobit (cont.)

Tobit's rise and fall are part of the stock-in-trade of these romances, but the reason for the fall is unusual in the OT. The proper burial of the dead was a sacred duty enjoined by many religions, which is no doubt why the tale of 'The Grateful Dead' is so widespread. In this case however the bodies were those of offenders against the king, executed and thrown *outside the wall* (17) onto the city rubbish-dump.

But Tobit's concern for burying the dead was to cost him not merely his job (1.20) but also (indirectly) his sight. The scene in 2.1+ should have been a happy one. The family was gathered to celebrate the *feast of Weeks*. In Israel a Jewish family would invite the aliens among them; in exile they invite a fellow-deportee. But the feast was spoiled (6) by the need to rescue a corpse and then (after sunset, for concealment) to bury it. The contact caused ritual impurity: Tobit must not only *bathe* twice (5, 9) but also *sleep* outside the house. And that is how he got the blindness which, for the sake of the story, has to be curable in the end.

The Troubles of Tobit (cont.)

2. 10 • That night, after bathing myself, I went into my courtyard and lay down to sleep by the courtyard wall, leaving my face uncovered because of the heat. • I did not know that there were sparrows in the wall above me, and their droppings fell, still warm, right into my eyes and produced white patches. I went to the doctors to be cured, but the more they treated me with their ointments, the more my eyes became blinded by the white patches, until I lost my sight.

• At that time Anna my wife used to earn money by women's work, spinning and weaving, • and her employers would pay her when she took them what she had done. One day, the seventh of Dystrus, after she had cut off the piece she had woven and delivered it, they not only paid her wages in full, but also gave her a kid from their herd of goats to take home. • When my wife came into the house to me, the kid began to bleat, and I called out to her: 'Where does that kid come from? I hope it was not stolen? Return it to its owners; we have no right to eat anything stolen.' • But she assured me: 'It was given me as a present, over and above my wages.' I did not believe her and insisted that she return it, and I blushed with shame for what she had done. Her rejoinder was: 'So much for all your acts of charity and all your good works! Everyone can now see what you are really like.'   (REB)

The Troubles of Tobit (cont.)

We are then shown, in a sad but convincing little scene (2.11+), how their misfortunes put the marriage under strain. *Dystrus* is the Greek name for the month Adar, which we learn from Esther 9.22 was the time for giving presents to the poor. But Tobit is suspicious of his wife's independence: ostensibly he accuses *Anna* of theft, but he surely implies infidelity. She is stung into a retort of which the last five words mean 'how much good they have done you!'

The Troubles of Sarah

3. 7 On the same day it happened that Sarah, the daughter of Raguel who lived at Ecbatana in Media, also had to listen to taunts, from one of her father's servant-girls. • Sarah had been given in marriage to seven husbands and, before the marriages could be duly consummated, each one of them had been killed by the evil demon Asmodaeus. The servant said to her: 'It is you who kill your husbands! You have already been given in marriage to seven, and you have not borne the name of any one of them. • Why punish us because they are dead? Go and join your husbands. I hope we never see son or daughter of yours!'   ◆

The Troubles of Sarah

We switch now to the troubles of the other family. The parallel is underlined in a number of ways: *Sarah*, like her second cousin Tobias, is an only child, and the more precious for that; Sarah and Tobit both pray in their distress (the prayers are omitted here); and the section about Sarah opens and closes with a formal synchronism. Sarah's misfortunes are a version of the folk-tale of 'The Dangerous Bride' (see p.703); there is a hint of it also in Gen 38.11). The demon *Asmodaeus* (8) appears here for the first time in Jewish literature. In a later work of c.300 AD he introduces himself as follows: 'My role is to conspire against the newly wed and to prevent

The Troubles of Sarah (cont.)

10   • Deeply distressed at that, she went in tears to the roof-chamber of her father's house, meaning to hang herself. But she had second thoughts and said to herself: 'Perhaps they will taunt my father and say, "You had one dear daughter and she hanged herself because of her troubles," and so I shall bring my aged father in sorrow to his grave. No, I will not hang myself; it would be better to beg the Lord to let me die and not live on to hear such reproaches.'

16   • At that very moment the prayers of both were heard in the glorious presence of God, • and Raphael was sent to cure the two of them: Tobit by removing the white patches from his eyes so that he might see God's light again, and Sarah daughter of Raguel by giving her in marriage to Tobias son of Tobit and by setting her free from the evil demon Asmodaeus, for it was the destiny of Tobias and of no other suitor to possess her. At the moment when Tobit went back into his house from the courtyard, Sarah came down from her father's roof-chamber.

                                                       (REB)

The Troubles of Sarah (cont.)

them from consummating the marriage.' His name probably means 'the destroyer', which is answered by that of *Raphael* 'the healer'.

     The detail of v.17 theoretically removes what we would call the suspense from the story. But in fact any reader of romances knows that the problems will be solved eventually, and is concerned as much with the means as with the end. The early identification of Raphael also allows for some amusing dramatic irony in Ch.5.

The Quest of Tobias

4. 1   That same day Tobit remembered the money he had deposited with Gabael at Rages in Media, • and he said to himself, 'I have asked for death; before I die I ought to send for my son Tobias and explain to him about this money.' • So he sent for Tobias and, when he came, said to him: 'When I die, give me decent burial. Honour your mother, and do not abandon her as long as she lives; do what will please her, and never grieve her heart in any way. • Remember, my son, all the hazards she faced for your sake while you were in her womb. When she dies, bury her beside me in the same grave.

12   • 'Be on your guard, my son, against fornication; and above all choose your wife from the race of your ancestors. Do not take a foreign wife, one not of your father's tribe, for we are descendants of the prophets. My son, remember that back to the earliest days our ancestors, Noah, Abraham, Isaac, Jacob, all chose wives from their kindred. They were blessed in their children, and their descendants will possess the land.   ♦

The Quest of Tobias

The concluding verses of Ch.3 slip back into speaking of Tobit in the third person – necessarily so, since the reader now has privileged information. It is odd that Tobit did not *remember the money* (4.1) before, when Anna first went out to work; and even now he brings in a reference to it rather inconsequentially at the end of a longish speech of parting advice. Indeed the motif of the money, which was not

The Quest of Tobias (cont.)

4. 20   • 'And now, my son, I should tell you that I have ten talents of silver on deposit with Gabael son of Gabri at Rages in Media. • Do not be anxious because we have become poor; there is great wealth awaiting you, if only you fear God and avoid all wickedness and do what is good in the sight of the Lord your God.'

(REB)

The Quest of Tobias (cont.)

strictly necessary in the first place (Tobias could perfectly well have been sent to find Sarah) is only half-heartedly worked into the story. It looks like an alternative version of the motif of the treasure to be won by the hero in the traditional folk-tale of the quest, played down by the author as being of lesser interest. Of much greater interest to him was family life and love, and it is not surprising that Tobit's advice should begin with that. The recommendation here to marry within the *tribe* (12) should not be taken too literally, or it would be more stringent than anything recorded of the patriarchs (here called *prophets*).

Raphael

5. 1   Tobias then replied to his father Tobit, 'Father, I shall do everything you have told me. • But how am I to recover the silver from him? He does not know me, nor I him. What token am I to give him for him to believe me and hand the silver over to me? And besides, I do not know what roads to take for this journey into Media.' • Then Tobit answered his son Tobias, 'Each of us set his signature to a note which I cut in two, so that each could keep half of it. I took one piece, and put the other with the silver. To think it was twenty years ago I left this silver in his keeping! And now, my child, find a trustworthy travelling companion – we shall pay him for his time until you arrive back – and then go and collect the silver from Gabael.'

    • Tobias went out to look for a man who knew the way to go with him to Media. Outside he found Raphael the angel standing facing him, though he did 5   not guess he was an angel of God. • He said, 'Where do you come from, friend?' The angel replied, 'I am one of your brother Israelites; I have come to these parts to look for work.' Tobias asked, 'Do you know the road to Media?' • The other replied, 'Certainly I do, I have been there many times;' • Tobias said, 'Wait for me, friend, while I go and tell my father; I need you to come with me; I shall pay you for your time.' • The other replied, 'Good, I shall wait; but do not be long.'

▸

Raphael

In the ancient world it was common to leave money in the safe keeping of a friend: the parties would then cut an object into two, taking half each, in such a way that the genuineness of any claim- ant could be easily established. Here the object is a clay tablet or a piece of papyrus, on which, to make assurance doubly sure, each party had written *his signature*.

Raphael (cont.)

• Tobias went in and told his father that he had found one of their brother Israelites. And the father said, 'Fetch him in; I want to find out about his family and tribe. I must see if he is going to be a reliable companion for you, my child.' So Tobias went out and called him, 'Friend,' he said, 'my father wants you.'

10 • The angel came into the house. • Tobit said, 'Brother, what family and what tribe do you belong to? Will you tell me, brother?' • 'What does my tribe matter to you?' the angel said. Tobit said, 'I want to be quite sure whose son you are and what your name is.' • The angel said, 'I am Azarias, son of the great Ananias, one of your kinsmen.' • 'Welcome and greetings, brother! Do not be offended at my wanting to know the name of your family; I find you are my kinsman of a good and honourable line.'

15 • He went on, 'I engage you at a drachma a day, with the same expenses as my own son's. Complete the journey with my son • and I shall go beyond the agreed

17 wage.' • Then he turned to his son. 'My child', he said, 'prepare what you need for the journey, and set off with your brother. May God in heaven protect you abroad and bring you both back to me safe and sound! May his angel go with you and protect you, my child!'

Tobias left the house to set out and kissed his father and mother. Tobit said, 'A happy journey!' • His mother burst into tears and said to Tobit, 'Why must you send my child away? Is he not the staff of our hands, as he goes about before us? • Surely money is not the only thing that matters? Surely it is not as precious

20 as our child? • The way of life God had already given us was good enough.' • He said, 'Do not think such thoughts. Going away and coming back, all will be well with our child. You will see for yourself when he comes back safe and sound! Do not think such thoughts; do not worry on their account, my sister. • A good angel will go with him; he will have a good journey and come back to us well and happy.'

6.1 • And she dried her tears.   (NJB)

Raphael (cont.)

In the exchanges which follow, the longer text of S brings out the fussiness of Tobit and the fearfulness of Anna, both of them delightfully unheroic. Tobit believes in proper agreements (3, 15): *a drachma* is a regular wage for *a day*. He is also concerned to establish the genealogy – of an angel! Anna is anxious for her son's safety on the long journey, and would gladly write off the money for his sake. Tobit's faith is contrasted with her timidity. His assurance that *you will see for yourself* (21) is a nice touch from the blind husband. His calling her *sister*

has no especial significance: the Greek words for 'brother' and 'sister' are used loosely throughout the book for any relationship down to and including membership of the same tribe.

Raphael on the other hand can be pleasantly sharp, as is shown by v.8 and by the B text of v.12 (here the longer one), where he says: 'Is it a tribe and family you want or a hired man to go with your son?' He also offers many chances of dramatic irony, most obviously in Tobit's references to an *angel* in vv.17 and 22.

The Journey

6. 1 The youth and the angel left the house together; the dog followed Tobias out and accompanied them. They travelled until night overtook them, and then camped by the river Tigris. • Tobias went down to bathe his feet in the river, and a huge fish leapt out of the water and tried to swallow his foot. He cried out, • and the angel said to him, 'Seize the fish and hold it fast.' So Tobias caught hold of it and dragged it up on the bank. • The angel said: 'Split open the fish and take out its gall, heart, and liver; keep them by you, but throw the guts away; the gall, heart,

5 and liver can be used as remedies.' • Tobias split the fish open, and put its gall, heart, and liver on one side. He broiled and ate part of the fish; the rest he salted and kept.

They continued the journey together, and when they came near to Media • the youth asked the angel: 'Azarias, my friend, what remedy is there in the fish's heart and liver and in its gall?' • He replied: 'You can use the heart and liver as a fumigation for any man or woman attacked by a demon or evil spirit; the attack will cease, and it will give no further trouble. • The gall is for anointing a person's eyes when white patches have spread over them; after one has blown on the patches, the eyes will recover.'

10 • When he had entered Media and was already approaching Ecbatana, • Raphael said to the youth, 'Tobias, my friend.' 'Yes?' he replied. Raphael said: 'We must stay tonight with Raguel, who is a relative of yours. He has a daughter named Sarah, but no other children, neither sons nor daughters. • You as her next of kin have the right to marry her and inherit her father's property. • The girl is sensible, brave, and very beautiful indeed, and her father is an honourable man.'

• At this Tobias protested: 'Azarias, my friend, I have heard she has already been given to seven husbands who died in the bridal chamber; the very night they went into the bridal chamber to her they died. • A demon kills them, I have been told. And now it is my turn to be afraid; he does her no harm, because he loves her, but he kills any man who tries to come near her. I am my father's only child, and I fear that, were I to die, grief for me would bring my father and mother to their grave; and they have no other son to bury them.'   ◆

The Journey

The dog is a surprise. Although dogs were familiar household animals in Mesopotamia and Greece (cp. Odysseus' homecoming), in the OT they were only scavengers or at best watchdogs. Moreover this one plays a negligible part in the rest of the story (see p.715). Doubtless it had a more important role in the old folk-tale e.g. helping the hero to overcome the dragon.

The use of (i) fumigation for driving away demons and (ii) fishes' *gall* for curing leucoma is common in ANE magical and medical texts respectively. The mixture of magic and medicine may seem odd, but much magic is only primitive medicine.

The marriage now takes precedence in the story over the recovery of the money. As Sarah's next of kin, Tobias has the right to marry her: it was indeed his duty, according to the custom of the book of Ruth. Raphael's praise of Sarah includes the rare adjective *sensible*, and for a moment a modern reader's hope is raised: perhaps she is not going to be pre-

The Journey (cont.)

5   • Raphael said: 'But have you forgotten your father's instructions? He told you to take a wife from your father's kindred. Now be guided by me, my friend: marry Sarah, and do not worry about the demon. I am sure that this night she will be given to you as your wife. • When you enter the bridal chamber, take some of the fish's liver and its heart, and put them on the burning incense. The smell will spread, • and when it reaches the demon he will make off, never to be seen near her any more. When you are about to go to bed with her, both of you must first stand up and pray, beseeching the Lord of heaven to grant you mercy and protection. Have no fear; she was destined for you before the world was made. You will rescue her and she will go with you. I have no doubt you will have children by her and they will be very dear to you. Now do not worry!' When Tobias heard what Raphael said, and learnt that Sarah was his kinswoman and of his father's house, he was filled with love for her and set his heart on her.

(REB)

The Journey (cont.)

sented as a mere chattel. But as the story unfolds the hope is dashed, and the only word she utters in the rest of the book is 'Amen' (8.8). The mention of Sarah also reminds Tobias of what he had heard about her: to be her next of kin was a doubtful privilege! Reassured by Raphael, he *fell deeply in love with her* – for this is a story not about romantic love but about (arranged) marriage.

Tobias's Arrival and Wedding

7.1   As they entered Ecbatana Tobias said, 'Azarias, my friend, take me straight to our kinsman Raguel.' So he took him to Raguel's house, where they found him sitting by the courtyard gate. They greeted him first, and he replied, 'Greetings to you, my friends. You are indeed welcome.' When he brought them into his house, • he said to Edna his wife, 'Is not this young man like my kinsman Tobit?' • Edna questioned them, 'Friends, where do you come from?' 'We belong to the tribe of Naphtali, now in captivity at Nineveh,' they answered. • 'Do you know our kinsman Tobit?' she asked, and they replied, 'Yes, we do.' 'Is he well?' she said.
5   • 'He is alive and well,' they answered, and Tobias added, 'He is my father.' • Raguel jumped up and, with tears in his eyes, he kissed him. • 'God bless you, my boy,' he said, 'son of a good and upright father. But what a calamity that so just and charitable a man has lost his sight!' He embraced Tobias his kinsman and wept; • Edna his wife and their daughter Sarah also wept for Tobit.
    Raguel slaughtered a ram from the flock and entertained them royally. They bathed and then, after washing their hands, took their places for the meal. Tobias said to Raphael, 'Azarias, my friend, ask Raguel to give me Sarah my kinswoman.' ◆

Tobias's Arrival and Wedding

The S text of Ch.7 moves slowly. But in a traditional society the rituals of greeting after a journey (1-8) are prolonged and emotional. Over dinner, at which only the men are present, Tobias eventually becomes impatient

Tobias's Arrival and Wedding (cont.)

7. **10** • Raguel overheard this and said to the young man: 'Eat and drink tonight, and enjoy yourself. • There is no one but yourself who should have my daughter Sarah; indeed I ought not to give her to anyone else, since you are my nearest kinsman. However, I must reveal the truth to you, my son: • I have given her in marriage to seven of our kinsmen, and they all died on their wedding night. My son, eat and drink now, and may the Lord deal kindly with you both.' Tobias answered, 'I shall not eat again or drink until you have disposed of this business of mine.' • Raguel said to him, 'I shall do so: I give her to you in accordance with the decree in the book of Moses, and Heaven itself has decreed that she shall be yours. Take your kinswoman; from now on you belong to her and she to you, from today she is yours for ever. May all go well with you both this night, my son; may the Lord of heaven grant you mercy and peace.'

• Raguel called for Sarah and, when she came, he took her by the hand and gave her to Tobias with these words: 'Receive my daughter as your wedded wife in accordance with the law, the decree written in the book of Moses; keep her and take her safely home to your father. And may the God of heaven grant you prosperity and peace.' • Then he sent for her mother and told her to fetch a roll of papyrus, and he wrote out and put his seal on a marriage contract giving Sarah to
15 Tobias as his wife according to this decree. • After that they began to eat and drink.

• Raguel called his wife and said, 'My dear, get the other bedroom ready and take her in there.' • Edna went and prepared the room as he had told her, and brought Sarah into it. She wept over her, and then drying her tears said: • 'Take heart, dear daughter; the Lord of heaven give you gladness instead of sorrow. Take heart, daughter!' Then she went out.   (REB)

Tobias's Arrival and Wedding (cont.)

(11), like Isaac in his wooing of Rebecca (Gen 24.33) – and indeed like the reader. But we must observe the full ceremony of the marriage, including the drawing-up of the *contract* (14), before we can get to the climax.

The Wedding Night

8. **1** When they had finished eating and drinking and were ready for bed, the young man was escorted to the bedroom. • Tobias recalled what Raphael told him; he removed the fish's liver and heart from the bag in which he had them, and put them on the burning incense. • The smell from the fish kept the demon away, and he made off into Upper Egypt. Raphael followed him there and promptly bound him hand and foot.

• After they were left alone and the door was shut, Tobias got up from the bed, saying to Sarah, 'Rise, my love; let us pray and beseech our Lord to show us
5 mercy and keep us in safety.' • She got up, and they began to pray that they might be kept safe. Tobias said: 'We praise you, God of our fathers, we praise your name for ever and ever. Let the heavens and all your creation praise you for ever. ◆

The Wedding Night

The story of the climax itself, by contrast, is so condensed that we cannot be quite sure what is supposed to have happened. Medieval Hebrew versions of the story have the demon actually inhabiting Sarah's body, which fits the folk-tale well.

The Wedding Night (cont.)

• You made Adam and also Eve his wife, who was to be his partner and support; and those two were the parents of the human race. This was your word: "It is not good for the man to be alone; let us provide a partner suited to him." • So now I take this my beloved to wife, not out of lust but in true marriage. Grant that she and I may find mercy and grow old together.' • They both said 'Amen, Amen,' • and they slept through the night.

10   Raguel rose and summoned his servants, and they went out and dug a grave, • for he thought, 'Tobias may be dead, and then we shall have to face scorn and taunts.' • When they had finished digging the grave, Raguel went into the house and called his wife: • 'Send one of the servant-girls', he said, 'to go in and see whether he is alive; for if he is dead, let us bury him so that no one may know.' • They lit a lamp, opened the door, and sent a servant in; and she found them sound asleep together. • She came out and told them, 'He is alive and has come to no harm.' • Then Raguel ordered his servants to fill in the grave before dawn came.

19   • Telling his wife to bake a great batch of bread, he went to the herd and brought two oxen and four rams and ordered his servants to get them ready; so they set about the preparations. • Then calling Tobias he said: 'You shall not stir from here for two weeks. Stay; eat and drink with us, and cheer my daughter's heart after all her suffering. • Here and now take half of all I possess, and may you have a safe journey back to your father; the other half will come to you both when I and my wife die. Be reassured, my son, I am your father and Edna is your mother; now and always we are as close to you as we are to your wife. You have nothing to fear, my son.'   (REB)

The Wedding Night (cont.)

When driven off by the fumigation, it characteristically made for a waterless place at the edge of the known world, where it was *bound* by Raphael like the demon in Matthew 12.29.

When the escort party had left Tobias alone with Sarah, he got into bed but then *got up* again (4), remembering the need first to commend their marriage to God. In his prayer *true marriage* (7) means marriage undertaken with a vow of life-long fidelity (cp. the happy phrase *grow old together*). *Slept through the night* (9) does not imply that the marriage was not consummated; in fact it certainly was, or the wedding celebrations would not have been held. The obscurities of this part of the story may be due to the author's reticence.

Meanwhile Raguel does not know whether the fumigation has been successful. So he goes through a macabre procedure: first, so as not to lose face with the neighbours, he *dug a grave* ready; then, so as not to lose face with Tobias, he filled it in. The account of the wedding generally follows the patriarchal stories in Genesis, except for financial matters. Whereas the patriarchs paid a bride-price for their wives, Raguel followed the Assyrian custom and himself provided the dowry. The motif of *half* his wealth however (21) belongs to the old folk-tale tradition, whereby the hero wins the princess and half the kingdom.

To illustrate the difference between the S and the B texts, here is the equivalent in B of 8.19-21: 'He made a wedding feast for them for a fortnight. Before the period was up, he forbade Tobias on oath to leave until the fortnight's celebrations were completed: then he should take half his property and go home with his blessing: the rest when I and my wife die'.

The End of the Story

9. 1 Tobias sent for Raphael and said: • 'Azarias, my friend, take four servants and two camels with you, and go to Rages. Make your way to Gabael's house, give him the note of hand and collect the money; then bring him with you to the
5 wedding feast'. • So Raphael went with the four servants and two camels to Rages in Media and stayed the night with Gabael. He delivered the note of hand and informed him that Tobit's son Tobias had taken a wife and was inviting him to the wedding feast. At once Gabael counted out to him the bags with their seals intact, and they put them together. • They all made an early start and came to the wedding.

10. 1 • Day by day Tobit was keeping count of the time Tobias would take for his journey there and for his journey back. When the time was up and his son had not made his appearance, • Tobit said: 'Perhaps he has been detained there? Or perhaps Gabael is dead and there is no one to give him the money?' • And he grew anxious. • Anna his wife said: 'My child has perished. He is no longer in the land
5 of the living.' She began to weep, lamenting for her son: • 'O my child, the light of my eyes, why did I let you go?' • Tobit said to her: 'Hush! Do not worry, my dear; he is all right. Something has happened there to distract them. The man who went with him is one of our kinsmen and can be trusted. My dear, do not grieve for him; he will soon be back.' • 'Hush yourself!' she retorted. 'Do not try to deceive me. My child has perished.' Each day she would rush out to keep watch on the road her son had taken, and would listen to no one; and when she came indoors at sunset she was unable to sleep, but lamented and wept the whole night long.

11. 1 • Tobias parted from Raguel in good health and spirits . . . • When they reached Caserin close to Nineveh, Raphael said: 'You know how your father was when we left him. • Let us hurry on ahead of your wife and see that the house is ready before the others arrive'; • and as the two of them went on together he added, 'Bring the fish-gall in your hand.' The dog went with the angel and Tobias, following at their heels.

5 • Anna sat watching the road by which her son would return. • She caught sight of him coming and exclaimed to his father, 'Here he comes – your son and the man who went with him!' • Before Tobias reached his father's house Raphael said: 'I know for certain that his eyes will be opened'.

10 • As Tobit rose to his feet and came stumbling out through the courtyard gate, • Tobias went up to him with the fish-gall in his hand. He blew into his father's eyes and then, taking him by the arm and saying, 'Do not be alarmed, father,' • he applied the remedy carefully • and with both hands peeled off the patches from the corners of Tobit's eyes. Tobit threw his arms round him • and burst into
15 tears. • Tobias went inside, rejoicing and praising God with all his might. He told his father about the success of his journey and the recovery of the money, and how he had married Raguel's daughter Sarah.   ▸

The End of the Story (cont.)

1 • After the wedding celebrations were over, Tobit sent for Tobias. 'My son,' he said, 'when you pay the man who went with you, see that you give him something extra, over and above his wages.' • Tobias asked: 'How much shall I pay him, father? It would not hurt to give him half the money he and I brought back. • He has kept me safe, cured my wife, helped me bring the money, and healed you. How much extra shall I pay him?' • Tobit replied, 'It would be right,

5 my son, for him to be given half of all that he has brought with him.' • So Tobias called him and said, 'Half of all that you have brought with you is to be yours for your wages; take it, and may you fare well.'

11 • Then Raphael called them both aside and said to them: • 'I will tell you the whole truth, hiding nothing from you. • Now Tobit, when you and Sarah prayed, it was I who brought your prayers to be remembered in the glorious presence of the Lord. • So too when you buried the dead: that day when without hesitation you got up from your meal to go and bury the dead man, I was sent to test you.

15 • At the same time God sent me to cure both you and Sarah your daughter-in-law. • I am Raphael, one of the seven angels who stand in attendance on the Lord and enter his glorious presence.'

20 • Both of them were deeply shaken and prostrated themselves in fear. • But he said to them: 'Do not be afraid, peace be with you; praise God for ever. • And now praise the Lord, give thanks to God here on earth; I am about to ascend to him who sent me. Write down everything that has happened to you.' • He then ascended and, when they rose to their feet, was no longer to be seen.   (REB)

The End of the Story

The climax of the story is now over, but a number of loose ends remain to be tidied up. First (Ch.9) there is *the money* to be fetched from *Rages*. This is arranged by Tobias, who has become a man and takes the initiative for the first time, with six imperative verbs running. Raphael returns with it in time to join the end of *the wedding feast*.

We then switch (Ch.10) to Tobit and Anna back in Nineveh. Again the contrast between Tobit and Anna is well depicted. He is anxious about the arrangements and the money, she simply about the danger to her son. As mother, she both supposes him dead and goes out to look for his return. As husband, he is first *anxious* himself (3), but then when she worries turns round to reassure her.

After prolonged leave-taking in Ecbatana, the party left for home (Ch.11). In a few mss *the dog* (4) ran on ahead and is the first thing to be seen by Anna; but in most it still plays no part in the action. The word translated *patches* (13) is the same as is used in the story of Paul's cure from blindness in Acts 9.18: 'it seemed that *scales* fell from his eyes'.

It remains only (Ch.12) for Raphael, generously rewarded, to disclose himself and explain what he had been doing. The idea of angels as intercessors has been influential in Catholicism, and vv.20-21 have a number of echoes in the Ascension narratives of the NT.

JUDITH

Introduction

The Book of Judith has proved as popular in the European tradition as that of Esther, but in art rather than drama. Its plot is too simple to hold a theatre audience, but it rises to a single climactic incident of great visual power and possibilities. The list of artists who have tackled it includes Donatello, Michelangelo, Mantegna and Botticelli.

The two heroines, Esther and Judith, have much in common. Each of them was a beautiful woman who used her charms to outwit the enemy of her people and save them from destruction. There is however one obvious difference, that Judith, though unscrupulous in some ways, is a model of personal and formal piety. In the light of that, it is remarkable that the rabbis admitted Esther to the canon but excluded Judith. The simplest explanation of that exclusion is that Judith was written too late for serious consideration. No doubt there was once a Hebrew text of it (all that survives is the LXX translation), but it is unlikely to have been written much before 100 BC.

The book falls naturally into two parts. The first part [Chs 1-7] is introductory – Judith does not appear until Ch.8. The introduction ostensibly provides a historical and geographical background to the main story, but this cannot be taken seriously. What it supplies is rather a dramatic contrast to the main story: in the first part the action is dominated by the gentile warrior and the fear inspired by his violence, in the second by the Jewish widow and the admiration evoked by her beauty. The introduction may be summarised as follows. Holophernes, as commander-in-chief of the imperial forces (variously referred to in the book as Assyrians, Babylonians and Persians), is conducting a large-scale punitive operation against the peoples of the west. He is successful everywhere, until he comes to Judaea. The Jews have recently returned from exile, and the high priest is their political and military ruler. He decides that the defence of the country is to rest upon the (otherwise unknown) town of Bethulia, which lies on a 'high mountain' and controls the approach route from the north. Holophernes decides not to attack Bethulia but to besiege it, and in particular to seize the spring in the valley below it which provided its water. After 34 days of siege the people of the town are at the end of their tether. They blame Ozias the chief magistrate for not coming to terms with the enemy; he asks for five days' grace, after which he will surrender if no help comes.

Judith Enters the Action

1 News of what was happening reached Judith, daughter of Merari. • Her husband Manasses, who belonged to the same tribe and clan as she did, had died during the barley harvest. • While he was out in the fields supervising the binding of the sheaves, he suffered sunstroke; he took to his bed and died in Bethulia his native town and was buried beside his ancestors in the field between Dothan and Balamon.

5 • For three years and four months Judith had lived in her house as a widow; • she had a shelter erected on the roof, and she put on sackcloth and always wore mourning. • She was beautiful and very attractive. Manasses had left her gold and silver, slaves and slave-girls, livestock and land, and she lived on her property. • No one had a word to say against her, for she was a deeply religious woman.

• When Judith heard how the people, demoralised by the shortage of water, had made shameful demands on Ozias the magistrate, and how he had given

10 them his oath to surrender the town to the Assyrians at the end of five days, • she sent her maid who had charge of everything she owned to ask Ozias, Chabris, and Charmis, the elders of the town, to come and see her.

• On their arrival she said: 'Listen to me, magistrates of Bethulia. It was wrong of you to speak as you did to the people today, binding yourselves and God in a solemn contract to surrender the town to our enemies unless the Lord sends relief within so many days. Who are you to put God to the test at a time like this,

15 and to usurp his role in human affairs? • For even if he does not choose to help us within the five days, he has the power to shield us at any time he pleases, or equally he can let us be destroyed by our enemies. • It is not for you to impose conditions on the Lord our God, because God will neither yield to threats nor be bargained with like a mere mortal. • So while we wait for the deliverance which is his to give, let us appeal to him for help. If he sees fit, he will hear us.'

28 • Ozias replied, 'You have spoken from the wisdom of your heart, and what you say no one can deny. • This is not the first time you have given proof of your wisdom; throughout your life we have all recognised your good sense and sound judgement. • But the people were desperate with thirst, and drove us to make this promise and bind ourselves by an oath we may not break. • You are a devout woman; pray for us now and ask the Lord to send the rain to fill our cisterns, and then we shall be faint no more.'   ▸

Judith Enters the Action

Judith is introduced quickly. Her name means 'Jewess', with the overtone of 'par excellence'. We learn that she is a *widow*, pious and *beautiful* – and already a picture begins to form in our minds. But then we are told that since her husband's death she has managed a substantial estate (7) without even a male steward (10); and for the present it is her 'masculine' spirit that predominates. Sending (by means of another woman) for the magistrates, who are the more comic for being three to her one, she berates them for timidity before giving them a (rather impressive) lecture on theology. In reply (28+) their spokesman offers the same weak excuse that Saul offered in 1 Sam 14, and then makes the mistake of patronising her: let her do her womanly bit, by praying, and no doubt God will *send rain* – a true miracle in a Palestinian August!

Judith Enters the Action (cont.)

8. 32 • 'Listen to me,' said Judith. 'I am going to do something which will be remembered among our countrymen for all generations. • Be at the gate tonight; I shall go out with my maid and, before the day on which you have promised to surrender the town to our enemies, the Lord will deliver Israel by my hand. • But do not question me about my plan; I shall tell you nothing until I have accomplished what I mean to do.' • Ozias and the magistrates said to her, 'Go with our blessing, and may you have the guidance of the Lord God as you take vengeance on our
36 enemies.' • They then left her roof-shelter and returned to their posts.   (REB)

Judith Enters the Action (cont.)

Well, Judith *will* pray [Ch.9], but she has had enough of talk. She and her *maid* will go out among the enemy by night: the men are allowed to watch but not to ask questions. Dismissed, they *return to* the *posts* for which they are so ill-fitted.

Judith Goes to the Enemy Camp

10. 1 When Judith had ended this prayer to the God of Israel, • she rose from where she had been lying prostrate, called her maid, and went down into the house in which she spent her sabbaths and days of festival. • She removed the sackcloth she was wearing and laid aside her widow's dress. After bathing, she anointed herself with rich perfume. She arranged her hair elaborately, tied it with a ribbon, and arrayed herself in her gayest clothes, those she used to wear while her husband Manasses was still alive. • She put sandals on her feet and adorned herself with anklets, bracelets and rings, her earrings, and all her ornaments, and made herself very attractive, to catch the eye of any man who saw her. • She gave her maid a
5 skin of wine and a flask of oil; she filled a bag with roasted grain, cakes of dried figs, and loaves of fine bread, packed up her utensils, and gave it all to her maid to carry.

• From the house they made their way to the town gate of Bethulia, where they found Ozias standing with Chabris and Charmis, the elders of the town. • When they beheld Judith transformed in appearance and quite differently dressed, they marvelled at her beauty and said to her, • 'The God of our fathers grant that you meet with favour and accomplish what you are undertaking, so that Israel may triumph and Jerusalem be exalted!' Judith bowed in worship to God • and then said, 'Give the order for the gate to be opened for me, and I shall go and carry out all we have spoken of.' They ordered the young men to do as she
10 asked, • and when the gate was opened Judith went out, accompanied by her maid. The men of the town gazed after her until she had gone down the hillside and along the valley, where they lost sight of her.   ▶

Judith Goes to the Enemy Camp

Judith's preparations for her adventures are pure romance. Her change of clothes (3) has not only its obvious purpose – she is dressed to kill – but also a symbolic meaning: just as mourning expresses national defeat, so fine clothes presage national victory. The list of ornaments in v.4 recalls a famous list in Isaiah 3.18-23, but here the tone is one of unreserved relish. Her departure from Bethulia and

Judith Goes to the Enemy Camp (cont.)

1 • As the two women were making their way straight down the valley, they were confronted by an Assyrian outpost • who stopped Judith and questioned her: 'What is your nationality? Where have you come from, and where are you going?' 'I am a Hebrew,' she replied; 'but I am running away from my people, because they are about to fall into your hands and become your prey. • I am on my way to Holophernes, your commander-in-chief, with accurate information for him: I shall show him a route by which he can gain control of the entire hill-country without one of you suffering injury or worse.'

• The men listened to her story, looking at her face and marvelling at her 15 beauty. • 'By coming down at once to see our master you have saved your life,' they said. 'You must go to his tent straight away; some of us will escort you and hand you over. • When you are in his presence, do not be afraid; just tell him what you have told us, and he will treat you well.' • They detailed a hundred of their number to accompany her and her maid, and the two women were conducted to Holophernes' tent.

• As the news of her coming spread from tent to tent, men ran from all parts of the camp and gathered in a circle round her as she stood outside Holophernes' tent waiting for him to be told about her. • Admiration for her beauty led them to feel admiration for all Israelites; they said to each other, 'Who could despise a nation whose women are like these? We had better not leave a man of them alive, for if they get away they will be able to outwit the whole world.'

20 • Holophernes' bodyguard and all his attendants came out and escorted her into the tent, • where he was resting on his bed under a mosquito-net of purple interwoven with gold, emeralds, and precious stones. • When Judith was announced he came out to the front part of the tent, with silver lamps carried before him. • She entered his presence, and he and his attendants all marvelled at the beauty of her face. She prostrated herself and did obeisance to him, but his slaves raised her up.   (REB)

Judith Goes to the Enemy Camp (cont.)

approach to the enemy camp (10-11) is, as it were, followed by the camera. This, like much else in the chapter, is in the best tradition of OT narrative, where journeys are passed rapidly but much space is devoted to preparations and to dialogue. Traditional also is the motif of gentile susceptibility to the beauty of Jewish women (see Gen 12.11), which in v.19 is given a humorous twist. Romantic however is the repeated mention (7, 14, 19, 23 – in identical words in the Greek, though varied in English translation) of admiration felt by four successive groups of men.

Holophernes Befriends Judith

11. 1 Do not be alarmed, madam,' said Holophernes; 'there is no cause for fear. I have never injured anyone who chose to serve Nebuchadnezzar, king of all the earth. • I should never have raised my spear against your people in the hill-country had they not insulted me; they have brought it on themselves. • Now tell me why you have run away from them and joined us. You have saved your life by coming. Be reassured! You are in no danger, this night or at any time; • no one will harm you. On the contrary, you will enjoy the benefits that are accorded to the subjects of my master, King Nebuchadnezzar.'

5 • Judith replied, 'My lord, grant your slave a hearing and listen to what I have to say to you. The information I am giving you tonight is the truth. • If you follow my advice, through you God will accomplish a great thing, and my lord will not fail to attain his ends.

10 • No punishment ever befalls our race nor does the sword subdue them, except when they sin against their God. • And yet, my lord, you are not to be thwarted and cheated of success; they are doomed to die, and sin has them in its power, for whenever they do wrong they arouse their God's anger. • Since they have run out of food and their water supply is desperately low, they have decided to lay hands on their cattle, proposing to eat all the things that God by his laws has strictly prohibited. • They have sent to Jerusalem for permission from the

15 senate, because even the people there have done this. • As soon as ever the word comes and they act on it, that same day they will be given up to you to be destroyed.   ▶

Holophernes Befriends Judith

Holophernes is immediately captivated by his captive. His first speech (1-4) exudes protectiveness – when in fact he is the one who needs protection. The mention of *Nebuchadnezzar* is another of the anachronisms which just have to be overlooked in a romance. Assyrians, Babylonians and Persians were *successive* masters of Mesopotamia and Palestine, so it is historically impossible to combine even two of the three, viz. Assyrian troops, a Babylonian king and Persian general.

Judith's speech is a tissue of lies, prefaced by a bare-faced claim to veracity. Critics ancient and modern have tied themselves in knots arguing about the morality of it. But the whole moral argument is misconceived: if it is legitimate to kill your enemy in war, it can hardly be wrong to lie to him. The purpose of the speech is to lay the essential traps. For her plan to succeed, she must (i) win the confidence of Holophernes and (ii) guarantee him *delayed* victory, the delay (of four days at most) being designed to lull his suspicion and excite his desire so that she can (iii) contrive a situation where she can kill him. For total success, she must finally (iv) escape herself, and tell the Jews about his death before his own troops hear of it.

Aim (i) is achieved by her beauty and her knowledge (5). Aim (ii) is pursued in 10-15 which gives a (purely fictitious) reason both for the delay and for the ultimate victory: fictitious, because people under siege cannot afford to be nice in diet, avoiding e.g. rats, lizards, locusts

	Holophernes Befriends Judith (cont.)
16	• 'When I learnt all this, my lord, I left them and made my escape; the things that God has sent me to do with you will be the wonder of the whole world, wherever men hear about them. • For I, your servant, am a godfearing woman: day and night I worship the God of heaven. I shall stay with you now, my lord, and each night I shall go out into the valley and pray to God, and when they have committed their sins he will tell me. • Immediately I bring you word, you may go out at the head of your army; you will meet with no resistance.'
20	• Judith's words delighted Holophernes and all those in attendance on him and, amazed at her wisdom, • they declared, 'From one end of the earth to the other there is not a woman to compare with her for beauty of face or shrewdness of speech.' • Holophernes assured her, 'Your God has done well in sending you out from your people, to bring strength to us and destruction to those who have insulted my lord! • Your looks are striking and your words are wise. Do as you have promised, and your God shall be my god, and you shall live in King Nebuchadnezzar's palace and be renowned throughout the whole world.'
.1	• Holophernes then told them to bring her in where his silver was set out, and gave orders for a meal to be served to her from his own food and wine. • But Judith said, 'I must not eat of it for fear I should be breaking our law. What I have brought will be sufficient for my needs.' • 'But', asked Holophernes, 'where can we get you a fresh supply of the same kind if you use up all you have with you? There is no one from your people here among us.' • Judith replied, 'As sure as you live, my lord, I shall not finish what I have with me before God accomplishes by my hand what he has purposed.' ▸

Holophernes Befriends Judith (cont.)

(Lev 11). Aim (iv) is to be achieved by establishing her regular exit from the camp. In vv.17-18 she cleverly links (iv) and (ii) by suggesting that only so can she find out when the moment for the assault has come.

A feature of Judith's speech is dramatic irony. This is particularly noticeable in v.6 (where *my lord* is ambiguous, cp. 1 K 22.6 with note); in v.16, which is echoed by a credulous Holophernes at the end

(23); and in 12.4 especially *by my hand*.

Holophernes' phrase *your God shall be my god* (23) is a clear reminiscence of Ruth's protestation (Ruth 1.16); but here there is no implication of a conversion, since a gentile would regard all religions as equally valid. The final scene of the day (12.1-4) stresses Judith's strict adherence to dietary regulations (contrast 11.12), and her simple food by comparison with his extravagance.

Holophernes Befriends Judith (cont.)

12.5   • Holophernes' attendants conducted her to a tent, and she slept until midnight. Shortly before the dawn watch she rose • and sent this request to Holophernes: 'May it please my lord to give orders for me to be allowed to go out and pray.' • Holophernes ordered his bodyguard not to prevent her. She stayed in the camp for three days, going out each night into the valley of Bethulia and bathing in the spring at the camp. • When she came up out of the water she would pray the Lord, the God of Israel, to prosper her undertaking to restore his people. • Then she returned to the camp purified, and remained in the tent until she took her evening meal.   (REB)

Holophernes Befriends Judith (cont.)

The next section (12.5-9) contains one surprise. Her bathing, which was not mentioned previously, has now become a main feature, and the reader wonders what its purpose was. Ostensibly it followed a Pharisaic ritual of washing before prayer. But a later Jewish version of the story suggests a different explanation. In this, Judith resists the advances of Holophernes on the grounds that she is having her period: until it is over, she must go and purify herself every night. This ruse gives her a perfect excuse for the delay she needs, and may well represent the original folk-tale version of the story.

Judith Kills Holophernes

12.10   On the fourth day Holophernes gave a banquet, inviting only his own staff and none of the other officers. • He said to Bagoas, the officer in charge of his personal affairs, 'Go and persuade that Hebrew woman you are looking after to come and join us and eat and drink in our company. • We shall be disgraced if we let a woman like this go without seducing her. If we do not seduce her, everyone will laugh at us!' • Bagoas then left Holophernes and went to see Judith. 'Would this young and lovely woman condescend to come to my lord?' he asked. 'She will occupy the seat of honour opposite him, drink the joyful wine with us and be treated today like one of the Assyrian ladies who stand in the palace of Nebuchadnezzar.' • 'Who am I', Judith replied, 'to resist my lord? I shall not hesitate to do whatever he wishes, and doing this will be my joy to my dying day.'

15   • So she got up and put on her dress and all her feminine adornments. Her maid preceded her, and on the floor in front of Holophernes spread the fleece which Bagoas had given Judith for her daily use to lie on as she ate.   ▶

Judith Kills Holophernes

The climax of the story is powerful, and the occasional extravagance not inappropriate; for example, the four separate uses of *day* in 14, 16, 18, 20 express hyperbole. The lecherousness of Holophernes and his men is tellingly revealed by v.12 (where the Greek has two *different* verbs for NJB's *seduce*, the second much blunter): they would all lose face if Judith remained in her own separate tent (12.5). The courage of Judith is impressive, as is the sheer physical strength for which she understandably prays in 13.7.

Judith Kills Holophernes (cont.)

16 • Judith came in and took her place. The heart of Holophernes was ravished at the sight; his very soul was stirred. He was seized with a violent desire to sleep with her; and indeed since the first day he saw her, he had been waiting for an opportunity to seduce her. • 'Drink then!' Holophernes said. 'Enjoy yourself with us!' • 'I am delighted to do so, my lord, for since my birth I have never felt my life more worthwhile than today.' • She took what her maid had prepared, and ate and drank facing him. • Holophernes was so enchanted with her that he drank far more wine than he had drunk on any other day in his life.

. 1 • It grew late and his staff hurried away. Bagoas closed the tent from the outside, having shown out those who still lingered in his lord's presence. They went to their beds wearied with too much drinking, • and Judith was left alone in the tent with Holophernes who had collapsed wine-sodden on his bed. • Judith then told her maid to stay just outside the bedroom and wait for her to come out, as she did every morning. She had let it be understood she would be going out to her prayers and had also spoken of her intention to Bagoas.

6 • By now everyone had left Holophernes. • With that she went up to the bedpost by Holophernes' head and took down his scimitar; • coming closer to the bed she caught him by the hair and said, 'Make me strong today, Lord God of Israel!' • Twice she struck at his neck with all her might, and cut off his head. • She then rolled his body off the bed and pulled down the canopy from the bedposts. After which, she went out and gave the head of Holophernes to her 10 maid • who put it in her food bag. The two then left the camp together, as they always did when they went to pray. Once they were out of the camp, they skirted the ravine, climbed the slope to Bethulia and made for the gates.

(NJB)

Judith Kills Holophernes (cont.)

The irony continues, both of speech (12.14, 18) and of situation. Holophernes' plan to be left alone with Judith (13.1) recoils on his own head. She, being unarmed, must kill him with his own sword, for which the author cleverly uses a Persian word. The sword in question was actually straight, but the use of *scimitar* in most English translations has influenced many paintings etc. *Canopy* however is a Greek word meaning 'mosquito-net' (so REB translates): Greek *cōnōpion* is derived from *cōnōps* (=cone-faced), a mosquito.

Victory Celebrations

13.11 From a distance Judith called to the guards: 'Open up! Open the gate! God, our God, is with us, still showing his strength in Israel and his might against our enemies. Today he has shown it!' • When the townspeople heard her voice, they hurried down to the gate and summoned the elders of the town. • Everyone, high and low, came running, hardly able to believe that Judith had returned. They opened the gate, and welcomed in the two women. Then, kindling a fire to give light, they gathered round them. • Judith raised her voice: 'Praise God! O praise him!' she cried. 'Give praise to God who has not withdrawn his mercy from the house of Israel, but has crushed our enemies by my hand this very night!'

15 • She took the head from the bag and showed it to them. 'Look!' she said. 'The head of Holophernes, the Assyrian commander-in-chief! And here is the net under which he lay drunk! The Lord has struck him down by a woman's hand! • And I swear by the Lord who has brought me safely along the way I have travelled, that, though my face lured him to his destruction, he committed no sin with me, and my honour is unblemished.'

• The people were all astounded at what she had done; and bowing in worship to God, they spoke with one voice: 'Praise be to you, our God, who has this day humiliated the enemies of your people!'

14. 1 • Judith said to them: 'Listen to me, my friends; take this head and hang it out on the battlements. • Then at daybreak, as soon as the sun rises, let every able-bodied man among you arm himself; march out of the town with a leader before you, as if you were going down to the plain to attack the Assyrian outpost, but do not go down.'

11 • At dawn they hung Holophernes' head on the wall; then every man took up his weapons, and they marched out in companies towards the approaches to the town. • The moment the Assyrians set eyes on them, they passed word to their leaders, who went to the commanders, captains, and all the other officers. • They presented themselves at Holophernes' tent and said to his steward: 'Wake our master! These slaves have had the audacity to come down and offer battle. They are asking to be utterly wiped out.' • Bagoas went in and knocked at the screen of the inner tent,

15 supposing that Holophernes was sleeping with Judith. • When there was no reply, he drew aside the screen, entered the sleeping apartment, and found the dead body sprawled over a footstool, with the head gone. • He gave a great cry, wailing and groaning aloud, and tearing his clothes. • He went into the tent which Judith had occupied, and not finding her there he burst out, shouting to the troops, • 'The slaves have fooled us. One Hebrew woman has brought shame on King Nebuchadnezzar's

19 house. Look! Holophernes is lying on the ground, headless!' • At his words the officers of the Assyrian army were appalled and tore their clothes, and the camp rang with their shouting and wild cries. ▸

Victory Celebrations

After the denouement the narrative inevitably slackens, and only the highlights are retained here. The excitement of Judith's return is expressed in the doubled *open* and *God* of 13.11 and the triple *praise* of v.14. The display of the defeated enemy's *head* was common enough: a historical example near at hand is the Greek general Nicanor in c.160 BC [1 M 7.47]. The victory celebrations of

Victory Celebrations (cont.)

.1 • When news of those events spread to the men in the camp, they were thrown into confusion. • Terrified and panic-stricken and making no attempt to keep together, they streamed out as if by a common impulse, seeking to escape by any and every path across the plain and the hill-country.

6 • The inhabitants of Bethulia fell on the Assyrian camp and made themselves
11 rich with the spoils. • The looting of the camp went on for thirty days. Judith was given Holophernes' tent, with all his silver, and his couches, bowls, and furniture. She loaded her mule, then got her wagons ready and piled the goods on them.

• The Israelite women all came flocking to see her; they sang her praises, and some performed a dance in her honour. She took garlanded wands and distributed them among the women who accompanied her, • and she and those who were with her crowned themselves with olive leaves. Then, at the head of the people, she led the women in the dance; the men of Israel, in full armour, followed, all wearing garlands on their heads and singing hymns.

.1 • In the presence of all Israel, Judith began this hymn of praise and thanksgiving, which was echoed by the people:

4
The Assyrian came from the mountains of the north;
    his armies came in such myriads
that his troops choked the valleys,
    the cavalry covered the hills.

5
He threatened to set my whole land on fire,
    to put my young men to the sword
and dash my infants to the ground,
    to take my children as booty,
    my maidens as spoil.

6
7
The Lord Almighty has thwarted them by a woman's hand.
    It was no young man that brought their champion low;
no Titan struck him down,
    no tall giant set upon him;
but Judith, Merari's daughter,
    disarmed him by her beauty.

Victory Celebrations (cont.)

15.12-13 were traditional in form (e.g. 1 Sam 18.6), except for the *olive* crowns which are a Greek feature. The song of Judith in Ch.16 is modelled after those of Miriam (Ex 15) and Deborah (Jg 5). Part of it (here vv.4-5) is to be spoken by Judith, part (6-12) about her, perhaps by the people. The extended parallelism (with three limbs in v.11, four in 8 and five in 5) is typical of late psalm-writing, but the central section vv.7-9 has the compression and the irony we meet in the prose

Victory Celebrations (cont.)

16.8   To raise up the afflicted in Israel
        she laid aside her widow's dress;
    she anointed her face with perfume,
        bound her hair with a ribbon,
    and chose a linen gown to beguile him.
9   Her sandal entranced his eye,
    her beauty took his heart captive –
        and the sword cut through his neck!

10   The Persians shuddered at her daring,
        the Medes were daunted by her boldness.
11   Then my lowly ones shouted in triumph
        and the enemy were dismayed;
    my weak ones shouted
        and the enemy cowered in fear;
    they raised their voices
        and the enemy took to flight.
12   The sons of maidservants ran them through,
        wounding them like runaway slaves;
        they were destroyed by the army of my Lord.

21 • Judith went back to Bethulia, where she lived on her estate, and throughout her lifetime was renowned in the whole country. • Though she had many suitors, she remained a widow all her days after her husband Manasses died and was gathered to his fathers. • Her fame continued to increase, and she lived on in her husband's house until she was a hundred and five years old. She gave her maid her liberty. She died in Bethulia and was laid in the burial cave beside her husband Manasses.

25 • No one dared to threaten the Israelites again in Judith's lifetime, or indeed for a long time after her death.

                                                (REB)

Victory Celebrations (cont.)

narrative: indeed the slow detail of her dressing is especially effective as a prelude to the trenchant climax *the sword cut through his neck*. The anachronism of *Assyrian* in v.4 with *Persians* in v.10 need not disturb us.

The conclusion of the book rounds off the portrayal of a pious life. For a widow to remain unmarried was regarded by Jews (Anna in Luke's gospel 2.36f.) and gentiles (Dido in *Aeneid* IV) as showing especial fidelity. The mention of the *maid*, as of *Manasseh*, makes a frame with Ch.8. Her very long life recalls the patriarchs, and the final words class her implicitly among the Judges of Israel. She is thus a truly national heroine, who combines the older martial with the newer pious traditions. It is no surprise that the French use the book as a source of readings in honour of Joan of Arc.

THE WISDOM OF SOLOMON

Introduction

The book called the Wisdom of Solomon, written in Greek, is a typical product of Alexandrian Jewry c.50 BC. The anonymous author and his readers had for generations now spoken Greek and grown up no less familiar with Greek culture than with their own. His book goes further than its predecessors (Eccl and Ecclus) in attempting to show that the two traditions, far from being incompatible, can illuminate each other. Though he is addressing a Jewish audience first, he has one eye also on gentiles. For that reason he avoids all proper names which might be alien to them (Adam, Solomon, etc.) as well as any explicit quotations from the Bible.

In form the book shows many features of the hellenistic* diatribe, especially in the first nine chapters. The diatribe was a kind of lay sermon, which sprang from Greek philosophy crossed with ANE Wisdom. As Greek philosophy gradually became less academic and more popular, so its typical form changed. Logical argument tended to give way to assertion, strengthened and enlivened by all possible devices of rhetoric. In Wisd Sol many such devices are visible. Ideas are presented in autobiographical form (Ch. 8) and arguments dressed up in dramatic confrontation (Chs 2-5). The vocabulary is rich and recondite. The whole book contains 315 Greek words not found elsewhere in the LXX, many of them compounds. Of twenty adjectives in the list of 7.22-3, thirteen are compounds, one of them found here alone in surviving Greek literature, another here first.

Much of this vocabulary is consciously poetic, as are many of the images. The author has also a special penchant for lists, not only of epithets and similes (e.g. 5.10-14) but of noun-phrases e.g. the branches of science in 7.17-20. Likewise he regularly extends his parallelism into four and five limbs.

In content also the book belongs firmly in its hellenistic milieu. To us it is chiefly notable for some interesting and potentially important thoughts about death and immortality. They have no parallel in the OT but they have influenced later Jewish and Christian thinking considerably. Since however the author was neither philosopher nor theologian, his use of those two key terms – and of the related term 'soul' – is hard to pin down precisely.

'Death' with him is sometimes literal and physical e.g. 2.20. In this sense it clearly comes to all. Sometimes however it is spiritual: in that sense, the ungodly or unrighteous can be said to be 'dead' while still physically alive (1.12, picking up Prov 8.36). Similarly the 'immortality' of the righteous begins in this life but continues after their (physical) death. This is roughly the sense in which we might say – and could have said even before his death – that 'Shakespeare is immortal'. That general idea was quite common in the hellenistic world, but Wisd Sol seems to have given it an impetus within Judaism.

More controversial is his use of the term 'soul'. The thinking of Plato and of many later Greek philosophers tended to a sharp distinction between soul and body: the soul existed before the body, was now 'entombed' in it, but would survive it, migrating to another body. Wisd Sol often uses this kind of language e.g. 'A perishable body weighs down the soul' [9.15 REB]. He seems to accept the pre-existence of the soul (8.20), though not its transmigration. And when he speaks of immortality he commonly ascribes it specifically to the soul (3.1-3), though unlike Plato he does not hold *all* souls to be immortal. It is therefore not surprising that he nowhere mentions the idea of the resurrection of the body, which was gradually developed as a kind of Hebrew parallel to the more Greek idea of the immortality of the soul.

If the author's concept of immortality is vague but grand (3.1-9), and that of the soul hesitant and confused, he is at his best in his hymn to Wisdom (Chs. 8-9). Here he successfully combines the two traditions into something new. The theological setting is Hebrew, the intellectual passion is Plato's, but the mystical fervour is the author's own.

The first five chapters of Wisd Sol treat a theme which is fundamental to the OT, viz. the contrast between the good and the bad man. They are opposed in respect of their aims in life, their conduct, and their status or reward – 'immortality' and 'death' respectively. The core of the treatment here is a narrative in which an unnamed 'upright' man is persecuted by a band of the 'godless' but is saved by God and finally sees his enemies humbled.

In telling this story the author draws upon a wide range of traditions. First in time and importance is Second Isaiah's portrait of the servant of the LORD, especially the fourth servant song in Chs 52-53. Some of the detailed echoes are pointed out below, but the whole song is well worth reading again here. Next come the Wisdom tales, especially Chs 3

and 6 of Daniel. But in those tales the good man is typically saved *before* death. When therefore the author of Wisd Sol is referring to rewards *after* death, he takes his colouring from apocalyptic* writings such as Dan 12.

He does however also use quite a different tradition. Plato's dialogues contain a number of passages where the fate of the just man is compared with that of the unjust. His picture of the just man is based upon the fate of his beloved teacher Socrates, unjustly put to death by the Athenians in 399 BC. There is therefore much irony when Plato in the *Republic* has one of Socrates' enemies address him with the following prediction:

> The just man will be scourged and racked and finally after suffering every lesser torture will be crucified, only to recognise that one ought to aim in one's life not to *be* just but to *seem* so.

Elsewhere in the *Republic* Socrates gives his reasons why any short-term victory of the unjust will be reversed in the long run. They are based on a theory of the soul for which see on 8.19f.

And the fascinating literary history of these passages does not stop there. For they came in their turn to influence the account in Matthew's gospel of the crucifixion of Jesus (see on 2.18).

Persecution of the Just by the Unjust

12 Do not court death by the errors of your ways,
        nor invite destruction through the work of your hands.
13 For God did not make Death,
        he takes no pleasure in destroying the living,
14 and Hades has no power over the world:
15   for uprightness is immortal.

16 But the godless call for Death with deed and word,
        counting him friend, they wear themselves out for him;
    with him they make a pact,
        worthy as they are to belong to him.

.1 And this is the false argument they use.
        'Our life is short and dreary,
    there is no remedy when our end comes,
        no one is known to have come back from Hades.
2   We came into being by chance
        and afterwards shall be as though we had never been.
4   In time, our name will be forgotten,
        nobody will remember what we have done;
    our life will pass away like wisps of cloud,
        dissolving like the mist
    that the sun's rays drive away
        and that its heat dispels.

6   Come then, let us enjoy the good things of today,
        let us use created things with the zest of youth:
7   take our fill of the dearest wines and perfumes,
        on no account forgo the flowers of spring,
8   but crown ourselves with rosebuds before they wither,
9   let us leave the signs of our revelry everywhere,
        since this is our portion, this our lot!   ▶

Persecution of the Just by the Unjust

The first section of the narrative is given a theological framework, of which the beginning (1.12-15) is picked up more systematically in the conclusion (2.21-4). Those here called *the godless* (1.16) must originally have been apostate Jews (2.12cd), but the category has been extended to include others. They are here brought on stage, as by both Isaiah and Plato, to say how they see things. They begin with a relatively innocent scepticism (2.1-4) and hedonism (2.6-9) which do not go far beyond the conclusions of the Preacher (e.g. Eccl 2.16, 24).

Persecution of the Just by the Unjust (cont.)

2. 10   As for the upright man who is poor, let us oppress him;
        let us not spare the widow,
        nor respect old age, white-haired with many years.

11   Let our might be the yardstick of right,
        since weakness argues its own futility.

12   Let us lay traps for the upright man, since he annoys us
        and opposes our way of life,
    reproaches us for our sins against the Law,
        and accuses us of sins against our upbringing.

13   He claims to have knowledge of God,
        and calls himself a child of the Lord.

14   We see him as a reproof to our way of thinking,
        the very sight of him weighs our spirits down;

15   for his kind of life is not like other people's,
        and his ways are quite different.

16   He proclaims the final end of the upright as blessed
        and boasts of having God for his father.

17   Let us see if what he says is true,
        and test him to see what sort of end he will have.

18   For if the upright man is God's son, God will help him
        and rescue him from the clutches of his enemies.

19   Let us test him with cruelty and with torture,
        and thus explore this gentleness of his
        and put his patience to the test.

20   Let us condemn him to a shameful death
        since God will rescue him—or so he claims.'

21   This is the way they reason, but they are misled,
        since their malice makes them blind.

22   They do not know the hidden things of God,
        they do not hope for the reward of holiness.

23   For God created human beings to be immortal,
        he made them as an image of his own nature.

24   Death came into the world only through the Devil's envy,
        as those who belong to him find to their cost.

        (NJB)

Persecution of the Just by the Unjust (cont.)

Then however (2.10) they begin to reveal their hand. The logical conclusion of hedonism, so the author implies, is behaviour which flouts all moral standards. Contrary to the Torah, they oppress *the poor* and *the widow* and the *old*. Contrary to the teaching of Socrates, they treat *might* as *right*. Their especial animosity is reserved for *the upright man*. He has not merely criticised them personally but challenged the values of the world (15) and claimed divine authority for doing so (16). (The Greek word translated *son* in 18 can also mean 'servant', but the translation 'son' here is guaranteed by v.16.) And so the ungodly decide to *test* his two claims: one about *the final end of the upright* in general, the other about his own status. This is the passage which (together with

Persecution of the Just by the Unjust (cont.)

Ps 22.8) was echoed by the priests in Matt 27.43: 'for he said, "I am God's son".'

The author then (2.21) resumes his framing theological commentary. What he has to say about death and immortality is based on a misinterpretation of Gen 1-3. The phrase 'Let us make man in our own image' (Gen 1.26) he takes to imply that *God created human beings to be immortal.* If this is then taken with *uprightness is immortal* (1.15), he is saying that immortality is offered to all but the offer is accepted only by some, i.e. those who choose uprightness. If others can *court death* (1.12), they do so because of the serpent, here identified as *the Devil.* He out of spite (so REB, better than NJB's *envy*) introduced everything bad into a world which before then was all good. The author leaves it uncertain whether we should here regard death and immortality as literal or metaphorical.

The Reward of the Righteous

3. 1 But the souls of the righteous are in the hand of God, and there shall no torment touch them. • In the sight of the unwise they seemed to die: and their departure is taken for misery, • and their going from us to be utter destruction: but they are in peace. • For though they be punished in the sight of men, yet is their hope full of **5** immortality. • And having been a little chastised, they shall be greatly rewarded: for God proved them, and found them worthy for himself. • As gold in the furnace hath he tried them, and received them as a burnt offering. • And in the time of their visitation they shall shine, and run to and fro like sparks among the stubble. • They shall judge the nations, and have dominion over the people, and **9** their Lord shall reign for ever. • They that put their trust in him shall understand the truth: and such as be faithful in love shall abide with him: for grace and mercy is to his saints, and he hath care for his elect.   (AV)

The Reward of the Righteous

This famous description of the salvation of the righteous is something of a surprise after what has preceded it. In turning from the godless to *the righteous* (= upright) the author switches from singular to plural and from present to future tense. Moreover the godless have become *the unwise* (2) and they include *us* (3). But the underlying sequence of thought continues. The contrast between appearance and reality, implicit in Ch. 2, is now made explicit. *Hope* in 3.4 echoes 2.22, and *the truth* of 3.9 refers to *the hidden things* of 2.22.

But the weight of the passage falls upon the idea of *immortality,* which is here further developed in a more personal way. Much hangs upon the phrase *seemed to die* (2). Presumably the ungodly carried out their test of 2.20, and the righteous man was actually put to *a shameful death.* Then 3.2 does not so much deny death as assert immortality.

Proved in v.5 means 'tested'; *received* (6) is 'accepted', a technical term of ancient sacrifice. *The time of their visitation* (7) is when God intervenes on their behalf. *The stubble* (7) probably refers to the uselessness of the ungodly whom the righteous burn up, thus reversing the fire image of v.6. But the details should not be pressed. As with Dan 12.2-3, the power of the passage rests partly upon the generality of its images. It is not for nothing that it is often read at Christian funeral services.

Judgement upon the Godless

5. 1   Then the upright will stand up boldly
        to face those who had oppressed him.

2   And, seeing him, they will be seized with terrible fear,
        amazed that he should have been so unexpectedly saved.

3   Stricken with remorse, they will say to one another
        with groans and labouring breath,

4   'This is the one whom we used to mock,
        making him the butt of our insults, fools that we were!
    His life we regarded as madness,
        his ending as without honour.

5   How has he come to be counted as one of the children of God
        and to have his lot among the holy ones?

6   Clearly we have strayed from the way of truth;
        the light of justice has not shone for us,
        the sun has not risen for us.

8   What good has arrogance been to us?
        What has been the purpose of our riches and boastfullness?

9   All those things have passed like a shadow,
        passed like a fleeting rumour.

10   Like a ship that cuts through heaving waves –
        leaving no trace to show where it has passed,
        no wake from its keel in the waves.

11   Or like a bird flying through the air –
        leaving no proof of its passing.

12   Or like an arrow shot at a mark,
        the pierced air closing so quickly on itself,
        there is no knowing which way the arrow has passed.

13   So with us: scarcely born, we disappear;
        of virtue not a trace have we to show,
        we have spent ourselves in our own wickedness!'

Judgement upon the Godless

Finally we come to a second dramatic confrontation, still in the future tense carried on from Ch.3. The scenario is this. When the ungodly eventually die too and come to judgement, they are astonished to find their victim *the upright man* already vindicated and present *among the holy ones* (5.5). But again the scenic details should not be pressed. The author's interest is above all in the psychology of the godless. Their new insight (concentrated in the word translated *clearly* in 5.6) is tantamount to a self-condemnation.

Formally, verses 5.4-13 are a counterpart of 2.1-20. In 5.5 the ungodly concede to the righteous what they had denied him in 2.13. In 5.9-14 they see that the criticisms they had previously made of life in general (2.1-4) apply only to their own behaviour. These two reversals are typically presented in reverse order.

Judgement upon the Godless (cont.)

14 For the hope of the godless is like chaff carried on the wind,
        like fine spray driven by the storm;
    it disperses like smoke before the wind,
        goes away like the memory of a one-day guest.
15 But the upright live for ever,
        their recompense is with the Lord,
        and the Most High takes care of them.   (NJB)

Judgement upon the Godless (cont.)

Much of this scene derives from Is Chs .52-3. In particular the sequence of thought in 5.2-6 and many of its details reflect Is 52.14-53.6. Peculiar to Wisd Sol is the accumulation of similes in 5.10-14, where the effect is undermined by the repetitions which continue even into the author's comments in v.14. After the pile-up of 'poetic' diction, it is a relief to end on the more homely metaphor of v.14d, which comes from Jeremiah 14.8.

A King's Search for Wisdom

22 What Wisdom is, and how she came into being, I shall tell you; I shall not conceal her mysteries from you. • Wise men in plenty are the world's salvation, and a prudent king is the sheet-anchor of his people. • Therefore learn what I have to teach you, and it will be for your good.

7.1 • I too am a mortal like everyone else, descended from the first man, who was made of dust, • and in my mother's womb I was wrought into flesh during a ten-month space, compacted in blood from the seed of her husband and the pleasure that accompanies sleep. • When I was born, I breathed the common air and was laid on the earth that all mortals tread; and the first sound I uttered, as all do, was a cry; • they wrapped me up and nursed me and cared for me. • No king begins life in any other way; • for all come into life by a single path, and by a single path they go out again.   ◂

A King's Search for Wisdom

In Chs 6-9, which form the second major section of the book, the author sings the praise of Wisdom. To give shape to his praise he adopts the fiction, common in the Wisdom literature, of a royal auto-biography. He does not name the king, but it is clear from many echoes of 1 Kings that, like the Preacher before him, he has Solomon in mind – hence the name which posterity has given to his book. He fills out his 'narrative' with various insertions derived more from Greek philosophy than from the OT. Yet the whole is still composed in Hebraic parallelism, though REB (unlike NJB) prints it as prose.

Ch. 6 is introductory. In its last few verses the author denies keeping any esoteric or *hidden* (7.21) knowledge up his sleeve. *Mysteries* in 6.22 is a Greek technical term. The hellenistic world, like our own world, was full of 'mystery' religions, cults and sects.

The beginning of Ch. 7 takes up a parallel theme. Though a king, the author is a *mortal*. Unlike many hellenistic monarchs, he claims no divine status. Verse 2 follows a contemporary scientific theory of conception. It was supposed that the *seed*, on meeting the (menstrual) *blood*, became *compacted* into the embryo, and moreover that the *pleasure* was essential to the efficacy of the act.

A King's Search for Wisdom (cont.)

7. 7   • Therefore I prayed, and prudence was given me; I called for help, and there came to me a spirit of Wisdom. • I valued her above sceptre and throne, and reckoned riches as nothing beside her; • I counted no precious stone her equal, because compared with her all the gold in the world is but a handful of sand, and

10   silver worth no more than clay. • I loved her more than health and beauty; I preferred her to the light of day, for her radiance is unsleeping. • So all good things together came to me with her, and in her hands was wealth past counting. • Everything was mine to enjoy, for all follow where Wisdom leads; yet I was in ignorance that she is the source of them all. • What I learnt with pure intention I now share ungrudgingly, nor do I hoard for myself the wealth that comes from her. • She is an inexhaustible treasure for mortals, and those who profit by it become God's friends, commended to him by the gifts they derive from her instruction.

15   • God grant that I may speak according to his will, and that my own thoughts may be worthy of his gifts, for even Wisdom is under God's direction and he corrects the wise; • we and our words, prudence and knowledge and craftsmanship, all are in his hand. • He it was who gave me true understanding of things as they are: a knowledge of the structure of the world and the operation of the elements; • the beginning and end of epochs and their middle course; the alternating solstices and changing seasons; • the cycles of the years and the

20   constellations; • the nature of living creatures and behaviour of wild beasts; the violent force of winds and human thought; the varieties of plants and the virtues of roots. • I learnt it all, hidden or manifest, • for I was taught by Wisdom, by her whose skill made all things.   (REB)

A King's Search for Wisdom (cont.)

The prayer of 7.15 echoes one in Plato's dialogue *Timaeus*:

> Before discoursing on such an important matter as the whole of reality, we ought to pray to the gods that we may speak according to their will and in conformity with our own premises.

God's *gifts* (15) are itemised in 17+. They constitute nothing less than the whole corpus of scientific knowledge. The list follows the kind of classification accepted since Aristotle. The technical terms are avoided, as unsuited to the high style, but the references are to: metaphysics and physics (17), history, astronomy and meteorology (18-19), zoology, psychology, botany and pharmacy (20) – all of them Greek words which we still use. The *winds* in v.20 should be translated 'spirits' with NJB (i.e. psychic influences on *human thought*, including the occult), even though the concept seems to us out of place. For the rest, this is by far the fullest and most favourable reference to science in the whole Bible.

Hymn to Wisdom

22 In Wisdom there is a spirit intelligent and holy, unique in its kind yet made up of many parts, subtle, free-moving, lucid, spotless, clear, neither harmed nor harming, loving what is good, eager, unhampered, beneficent, • kindly towards mortals, steadfast, unerring, untouched by care, all-powerful, all-surveying, and permeating every intelligent, pure, and most subtle spirit. • For Wisdom moves more easily than motion itself; she is so pure she pervades and permeates all things. • Like a

25 fine mist she rises from the power of God, a clear effluence from the glory of the Almighty; so nothing defiled can enter into her by stealth. • She is the radiance that streams from everlasting light, the flawless mirror of the active power of God, and the image of his goodness. • She is but one, yet can do all things; herself unchanging, she makes all things new; age after age she enters into holy souls, and makes them friends of God and prophets.   ▶

Hymn to Wisdom

The author now turns to address Wisdom herself. His virtuoso hymn treats of her *spirit* (22-3), her activity (23-4 and 27) and her relation to God (25-7). The Greek of vv.22-3 gives her twenty-one epithets strung together. The first twenty of these consist of one word each, often a compound word for which there is no English equivalent, e.g. *made up of many parts*. The last one is much longer (*permeating . . . spirit*). Such lists of epithets or titles were frequently used for calling upon ancient deities, and twenty-one was a common total, being the product of two 'perfect' numbers 3 x 7.

There is no clear pattern in the list here, nor should too much be made of any one item. But through it runs a strong current of Plato's thought, especially his dualistic preference for the immaterial over the material. Thus the spirit of Wisdom is *subtle* i.e. tenuous, *free-moving, unhampered, unchanging* (27); she is so fine that she can permeate *every* (other)

pure spirit. The same idea is present in the five successive images of vv.25-6, *fine mist, clear effluence*, etc. By the same token Wisdom is a spirit free from the contagion of the world: *spotless* and *untouched by care*. From Greek philosophy stems also the contrast between the *one* and the *many* which features in vv.22 and 27. The whole hymn is highly abstract, even mystical.

Yet it is part of mystical belief that the mortal may nevertheless enjoy communion with the divine. The OT spoke often of the spirit of God resting upon his *friends and prophets* (7.27). Plato, perhaps more surprisingly, would talk of a love-affair between the soul and wisdom, e.g. in the *Republic*:

The true lover of knowledge pursues his passion until he has grasped real Being and entered into union with it; and the offspring of this union is truth. Not until he has found this knowledge and true life does he rest from travail.

Hymn to Wisdom (cont.)

8. 2   • Wisdom I loved; I sought her out when I was young and longed to win her
4 for my bride; I was in love with her beauty. • She is initiated into the knowledge
that belongs to God, and she chooses what his works are to be.

9   • So I determined to take her home to live with me, knowing that she would be
my counsellor in prosperity and my comfort in anxiety and grief. • Through her,
I thought, I shall win fame in the eyes of the people and honour among older
men, young though I am. • When I sit in judgement, I shall prove myself acute,
and the great will admire me. • Through her I shall have immortality and leave an
15 undying memory to those who come after me. • I shall show myself a good king,
and on the battlefield a brave one. • When I come home, I shall find rest with her.

  • I turned this over in my mind, and I perceived that there is immortality in
kinship with Wisdom. • So I went about in search of some way to win her for
my own. • As a child I was born to excellence, and a noble soul fell to my lot;
20 • or rather, I myself was noble, and I entered into an undefiled body; • but I saw
that there was no way to gain possession of her except by gift of God – and it was
itself a mark of understanding to know from whom that gift must come. So I
pleaded with the Lord, and from the depths of my heart I prayed to him.

(REB)

Hymn to Wisdom (cont.)

It is the Platonic image which the author of Wisd Sol develops so enthusiastically in Ch. 8. His confident hope of ultimate bliss (including Plato's *rest* in v.16) contrasts sharply with the disillusion the Preacher felt with his acquisition of Wisdom (Eccl 1.18). And the enthusiasm spills over into his treatment of another of his source-passages. The statement that Wisdom actually *chooses* God's *works* for him (v.4) goes far beyond the original in Prov 8.27, 30. The author's only remaining problem is *how* to get hold of Wisdom. Here he decides, after a self-congratulatory comment (21), to follow the example of Solomon's prayer in 1 K 8; which he proceeds to do in [Ch. 9].

But before that we are given the two tantalising verses 19-20. Together with 7.2-3 they illustrate the difficulty of pinning down this writer's ideas. In 7.2-3 a young person is a body. In 8.19 that body received a *soul*, presumably at birth – so far this is orthodox Hebrew belief. But that is then corrected in v.20 and replaced by a more Platonic formulation. By this, *I myself* i.e. the pre-existent soul *entered into* the *body*; and whereas the soul was *noble*, the best that can be said for the body is that it is *undefiled*.

ECCLESIASTICUS

Introduction

The book traditionally known to Christians as Ecclesiasticus was written in Hebrew c.190 BC by Jesus, son of Sira. That title (Greek for 'the churchy book') was given it by the early Church, which held it in higher esteem than the rabbis did. The rabbis knew it as 'The Wisdom of Jesus ben Sira', and increasingly today it is referred to by its author's name as 'ben Sira'. This avoids confusion with the very dissimilar book Ecclesiastes.

For long ben Sira's book was known to us only in the Greek translation made by his grandson (see the Translator's Preface). But in 1896 an exciting discovery was made in the storeroom of a synagogue in Cairo – medieval mss containing some two thirds of the original Hebrew text. More recently other Hebrew fragments, copied in the first century AD, have been found at Qumran* and Masada. There are important divergences between the Greek and Hebrew mss and between one Hebrew ms and another, which suggest that there probably never was an accepted text of the book.

Ben Sira was a man of his time – and a fascinating time it was. Alone in the ancient world, the temple state of Jerusalem was resisting the encroachment of hellenistic* culture. Politically and economically, of course, Judaea was part of the Seleucid empire (see on 1 Macc 1). Moreover many Jews were attracted by Greek culture – literature and art, science and technology, philosophy and even religion. In the words of 2 Macc 4.14, 'they cared above everything for hellenic honours'. But there were many shades of opinion among the Jews. The educated classes, for example, tended to look for an accommodation between hellenism and Judaism, with the two traditions mixed in varying proportions to taste. Among them ben Sira was very much at the conservative end of the spectrum, though even he was influenced more than he realised by hellenism. He however was a moderate compared with those who were to take the centre of the stage soon after him. Within two or three decades of his book's appearance, the peaceful competition between the two cultures was to erupt into the fierce conflict recorded in the books of the Maccabees. Those violent events – and even the violent emotions that fuelled them – seem remote from the cool pages of ben Sira the teacher of wisdom.

The author's conservatism shows itself across the whole range of his teaching. The key passage is Ch.24, where he boldly takes the ANE Wisdom tradition to which he was heir and identifies it with the law of Moses. As part of a theology of culture this is impressive. But his application of it was less so. Generally he took the less admirable aspects of each tradition, viz. the selfishness of Wisdom in preference to the altruism of the Torah, and the dogmatism of the Torah against the open-mindedness of Wisdom.

Of all OT books, Ecclesiasticus is closest in spirit and in content to Proverbs. Like Proverbs, it contains (i) a large number of miscellaneous maxims and (ii) a smaller number of more extended – and more challenging – pieces. It differs from Proverbs in beginning with (i), mostly in Chs 3-23, and keeping (ii) for the second half of the book, from Ch. 24 on. The editorial principle followed here for the maxims is the same as for Proverbs, viz. to group the more interesting ones by themes, irrespective of their place in the book (see table on p.739).

Ben Sira's social advice, not only about etiquette but about morality, reveals the limitations of his knowledge and sympathies (see nos 3-8 and 10). Only on the subject of forgiveness (no. 12) does he rise to a higher level. Intellectually he is ambivalent. The section on doctors in

Ch. 38 shows that, where applied science trenches on religion, he is a 'belt and braces' man. On more speculative issues he may be capable of applying his own mind to problems (no. 13), but he certainly does not encourage his pupils to do the same (no. 8).

In this general temper of mind ben Sira represents one main stream of post-exilic Judaism. To express it in New Testament terms, he is a scribe and proud of it. He can reconcile the pursuit of worldly success with a delight in religious observance, but we miss in him the warmth of personal piety which marks e.g. the book of Tobit and will later characterise the Pharisees.

The same coolness is a feature of ben Sira's style. Perhaps it takes a writer of genius, like the Preacher, to use parallelism* as a clothing for sage reflections. Certainly in ben Sira's case there is not enough intellectual or emotional charge in the first line of each couplet to carry the second. When he essays poetical flights, as in a number of learned hymns omitted from this selection, he falls to the ground after a few wing-beats. In general, he has lost the vigour of Hebrew writing without acquiring the rigour of Greek.

Yet his book is essentially a literary work. He is explicit about the tradition in which he writes: 'I was like a gleaner following the grape-pickers' [33.16]. He is also the first OT author to name himself: 'I, Jesus ben Sira, of Jerusalem have provided in this book instruction in good sense and understanding' [50.27 REB]. Moreover the book as a whole does have a shape – much more so than Proverbs. It is this conscious literary quality which shows hellenistic influence most clearly. But the basis of its thought remains as Jewish as anything in the OT. Ben Sira has a distinctive, if minor, voice.

The Translator's Preface

A legacy of great value has come down to us through the law, the prophets, and the writers who followed in their steps, and Israel deserves recognition for its traditions of learning and wisdom. It is the duty of those who study the scriptures not only to become expert themselves, but also to use their scholarship for the benefit of the world outside through both the spoken and the written word. For that reason my grandfather Jesus, who had applied himself diligently to the study of the law, the prophets, and the other writings of our ancestors, and had gained a considerable proficiency in them, was moved to compile a book of his own on the themes of learning and wisdom, in order that, with this further help, scholars might make greater progress in their studies by living as the law directs.   ▸

The Translator's Preface

The preface by the author's grandson is a document of great historical interest. In it he says why he has translated his grandfather's work from Hebrew into Greek. When he emigrated from Jerusalem to Alexandria in 132 BC he found a substantial colony of his fellow-countrymen already there. Some families had become so hellenised that they had forgotten their Hebrew and were sitting light to the Torah. Already a century earlier the Hebrew Bible had been translated into Greek for their benefit, the translation we know as the Septuagint. That Bible consisted of three sections: *the law* (Torah), *the prophets* and *the writings*. But the canon* of the last section was still fluid, with a number of books having uncertain status. Among them was the one now being translated into Greek.

The translator had two aims. First, he wanted to recall his compatriots to *live according to the law*: his first and last paragraphs end with that point. In this

The Translator's Preface (cont.)

You are asked, then, to read with sympathetic attention, and to make allowances wherever you think that, in spite of all the devoted work that has been put into the translation, some of the expressions I have used are inadequate. For what is said in Hebrew does not have the same force when translated into another tongue. Not only the present work, but even the law itself, as well as the prophets and the other writings, are not a little different when spoken in the original.

When I came to Egypt and settled there in the thirty-eighth year of the reign of King Euergetes, I found much scope for giving instruction; and I thought it very necessary to spend some energy and labour on the translation of this book. Ever since then I have applied my skill night and day to complete it, and to publish it for the use of those who have made their home in a foreign land, and wish to study and so train themselves to live according to the law.   (REB)

The Translator's Preface (cont.)

he had one eye on the orthodox Jews in Jerusalem, to whom he apologises for his inevitably *inadequate translation*. But his opening sentence shows that he is also aiming at an international readership. His translation is part of the long campaign by educated Jews to establish their claim that Israel's *traditions of learning and wisdom deserve recognition* right across the hellenistic world. Both these aims had been in the mind of his *grandfather* too.

Ecclesiasticus: Assorted Maxims

As with the book of Proverbs, some of the shorter pieces are here grouped by themes. (Of the five themes distinguished on pp.477+ +, the first three are run together here under the general heading of Prudence.) Their references are as follows, those from NJB in italics, the rest from REB:

A. Prudence	C. Morality, Religion, Philosophy
1. *8.1-14 excerpted*, 16	8. *3.21-23*
2. 12.1-2, 5; *29.20*	9. *10.4-8*
3. *13.1 , 2, 9-10*	10. 11.21, 26, 28
4. 31.12-31 excerpted;	11. 14.11-14
32.1-2, *3-4, 7-8, 13*	12. 28.2-4
	13. 33.10-15
B. Family Affairs	
5. 30.1, 7-10	
6. 42.9-10, 14	
7. 7.20-21; 33.24-26, 30-31	

A. Prudence

1. Do not try conclusions with anyone influential,
       in case you later fall into his clutches.
   Do not quarrel with anyone rich,
       in case he puts his weight against you.
   Do not argue with anyone argumentative,
       do not pile wood on that fire.
   Do not joke with anyone uncouth,
       for fear of hearing your ancestors insulted.

   Do not revile a repentant sinner;
       remember that we all are guilty.
   Do not despise anyone in old age,
       after all, some of us too are growing old.
   Do not gloat over anyone's death,
       remember that we all have to die.

   Do not lend to anyone who is stronger than you are –
       if you do lend, resign yourself to loss.
   Do not go to law with a judge,
       since judgement will be given in his favour. (NJB)
   Do not fall out with a hot-tempered man
       or travel with him across the desert. (REB)

2. If you do a good turn, make sure to whom you are doing it;
       then you will have credit for your kindness.
   A good turn done to a godfearing person will be repaid,
       if not by him, then by the Most High.

   Do good to the humble,
       give nothing to the godless.
   Refuse him bread, do not give him any,
       it might make him stronger than you are. (REB)

   Come to your neighbour's help as far as you can,
       but take care not to fall into the same plight. (NJB)

A. Prudence

1. Much ANE Wisdom is cast in the form of negative instructions, but this group of aphorisms is linked by content as well as form.

   In line 7 REB's 'never make fun of' is better than NJB's *joke with*. The second paragraph rises above the level of mere prudence.

2. Here, as often in OT Wisdom, considerations of prudence, morality and religion are juxtaposed. The last verse refers to giving surety to a *neighbour* in financial trouble.

A. Prudence (cont.)

3. Whoever touches pitch will be defiled,
    and anyone who associates with the proud will come to be like
        them.
    Do not try to carry a burden too heavy for you,
        do not associate with someone more powerful and wealthy than
            yourself.

    When an influential person invites you, show reluctance,
        and he will press his invitation all the more.
    Do not thrust yourself forward, in case you are pushed aside,
        but do not stand aloof, or you will be overlooked.   (NJB)

4. When seated at a grand table
    do not smack your lips and exclaim, 'What a feast!'

    Do not reach for everything within sight,
        or jostle your fellow-guest at the dish;
    Eat what is set before you, but not like a beast;
        do not munch your food and make yourself objectionable.
    Be the first to stop for good manners' sake
        and do not be a glutton, or you will give offence.

    Do not use wine to prove your manhood,
        for wine has been the ruin of many.
    Wine brings gaiety and high spirits
        if people know when to drink and when to stop;
    but wine in excess makes for bitter feelings
        and leads to offence and retaliation.
    At a banquet do not rebuke your fellow-guest
        or make him feel small while he is enjoying himself.

    Are you chosen to preside at a feast? Do not put on airs;
        mix with the others as one of them.
    Look after them and only then sit down yourself;
        discharge your duties before you take your place.
    Let the enjoyment of others be your pleasure,
        and you will win a garland for good manners.   (REB)

A. Prudence (cont.)

3. The risks of mixing out of one's own class are a common theme of ANE Wisdom.

4. The section on behaviour at dinner parties is of some social interest. The first part of it has close parallels in Egyptian Wisdom. The relevant paragraph of the *Instructions of Ptahhotep* (*ANET* 412) opens: 'If thou art sitting at the table of one greater than thyself . . . ', which shows the social context to be typically ANE.

A. Prudence (cont.)

Speak, old man – it is proper that you should –
  but with discretion: do not spoil the music.
If someone is singing, do not ramble on
  and do not play the sage at the wrong moment.

Speak, young man, when you must,
  but twice at most, and then only if questioned.
Keep to the point, say much in few words;
  give the impression of knowing but not wanting to speak.

And for all this bless your Creator,
  who intoxicates you with his favours.   (NJB)

A. Prudence (cont.)

But the affinity of the second part is rather with Greek advice on moderation in drinking, and the context is now one of social equality, albeit among the better off. Hellenistic also are the election of a president for a banquet, the wearing of a *garland*, the musical entertainment and the concept of the good speaker. But the concluding note is one of Jewish piety, expressed with humour. The whole passage witnesses to a meeting of three cultures.

B. Family Affairs

5. A man who loves his son will not spare the rod,
      and then in his old age he may have joy of him.
   A man who coddles his son will bandage every scratch
      and be on tenterhooks at every cry.
   An unbroken horse turns out stubborn,
      and an unchecked son turns out headstrong.
   Pamper a boy and he will shock you;
      join in his games and he will grieve you.
   Do not share his laughter, or you will share his pain
      and end by grinding your teeth.   (REB)

6. A daughter is a secret anxiety to her father,
      and worry about her keeps him awake at night:
   when she is young, for fear she may grow too old to marry,
      and when she is married, for fear her husband may divorce her;
   when she is a virgin, for fear she may be seduced
      and become pregnant in her father's house;
   when she has a husband, for fear she may prove unfaithful,
      and after marriage, for fear she may be barren.
   Better a man's wickedness than a woman's goodness;
      it is woman who brings shame and disgrace.   ♦

B. Family Affairs

5. This stern advice is typical of the ancient world. In most ancient languages a single word covered the whole range of activities running from 'punishment' through 'instruction' to 'education'.

6. This kind of satire on women has its parallels in Greek and Egyptian literature, but is alien to the general spirit of the OT.

B. Family Affairs (cont.)

7. Do not ill-treat a servant who works honestly
   or a hireling whose heart is in his work.
   Regard a good servant with deep affection
   and do not withhold his freedom from him.

   Fodder, the stick, and burdens for a donkey;
   for a servant – bread, discipline, and work!
   Keep your slave at work, if you want rest for yourself;
   if you let him slack, he will be looking for his liberty.
   The ox is tamed by yoke and harness,
   the bad servant by rack and torture.
   If you have only one servant, treat him as you do yourself,
   because you bought him at a high price.
   If you have only one servant, treat him like a brother;
   you will need him as much as you need yourself.　　　　　　(REB)

B. Family Affairs (cont.)

7. Ben Sira's advice on the treatment of slaves is deeply confused, doubtless because of the gap between the ideal and the actual. His *freedom* is that which the Torah required to be offered to a Jewish slave after six years (Dt 15.12).

C. Morality, Religion, Philosophy

8. Do not try to understand things that are too difficult for you,
   or try to discover what is beyond your powers.
   Concentrate on what has been assigned you,
   you have no need to worry over mysteries.
   Do not meddle with matters that are beyond you;
   what you have been taught already exceeds
   the scope of the human mind.　　　　　　　　　　　　▶

C. Morality, Religion, Philosophy

8. This coded warning is directed against intellectual curiosity and questioning. Such questioning would typically have been encouraged by Greek influences, but there was a native tradition of it too, as the books of Job and Ecclesiastes show. For the wise young man the Torah should suffice. This passage is unique in the OT, though Ps 73.16 comes close.

C. Morality, Religion, Philosophy (cont.)

9. The government of the earth is in the hands of the Lord,
      he sets the right leader over it at the right time.
   Sovereignty passes from nation to nation
      because of injustice, arrogance and money.   (NJB)

10. Do not envy the wicked their achievements;
       trust the Lord and stick to your job,
    for it is very easy for the Lord
       to make the poor rich all in a moment.
    Even on the day a person dies it is easy for the Lord
       to give him what he deserves.
    Call no one happy before he dies,
       for not until death is a person known for what he is.   (REB)

11. My son, treat yourself well if you can afford it,
       and present worthy sacrifices to the Lord.
    Remember that death will not tarry;
       the hour of your appointment with the grave is undisclosed.
    Before you die, treat your friend well;
       reach out as far as you can to help him.
    Do not miss a day's enjoyment
       or forgo your share of innocent pleasure.

12. Forgive your neighbour any wrong he has done you;
       then, when you pray, your sins will be forgiven.
    If anyone harbours anger against another,
       can he expect help from the Lord?
    If he refuses mercy to his fellow,
       can he ask forgiveness for his own sins?

C. Morality, Religion, Philosophy (cont.)

9. For 400 years after the destruction of Jerusalem by Nebuchadnezzar the Jews abandoned any hope of national resurgence. To compensate, they insisted that the power of each world empire was conferred upon it by God – for a period. That idea is here set out generally. A little later, in the book of Daniel, it was given unconvincing elaboration; see esp. Ch.7.

10. To buttress orthodox teaching about God's justice, ben Sira here offers a consideration of no great weight. He is not thinking of a deathbed repentance, for he did not believe in any after-life, nor of a stoical facing of death: only that a man's fortunes may be reversed at the very end of his life. The classic formulation of the point was by the Greek Solon; his actual words, as recorded by Herodotus, are quoted in the penultimate line here, but with ben Sira's reason appended.

11. This is a theme which the Preacher had made his own (Eccl 2.24 etc.). The two authors, so unlike in many ways, drew the same conclusion from the finality of *death*. But ben Sira adds a recommendation to *sacrifice* and so gives it a small twist in a more orthodox direction.

12. Ben Sira's teaching on forgiveness is close to that of the gospels.

C. Morality, Religion, Philosophy (cont.)

13. Human beings come from the ground,
        Adam himself was formed out of earth;
    in the fullness of his wisdom
        the Lord has made distinctions between them,
        and diversified their conditions.
    Some of them he has blessed,
        hallowing and setting them near him;
    others he has cursed and humiliated
        by degrading them from their positions.
    Opposite evil stands good, opposite death, life;
        so too opposite the devout stands the sinner.
    Contemplate all the works of the Most High,
        you will find they go in pairs, by opposites.   (REB)

C. Morality, Religion, Philosophy (cont.)

13. Here he seems to be making an original contribution to the usual Wisdom debate about theodicy*. He starts off along orthodox lines: God's distribution of pleasures and pains is not to be questioned. But then he appears to make a point of substance.

Logically it is impossible for there to be – and for people to feel – pleasure without pain; therefore God cannot be blamed for the existence of pain in his world. However the passage may only be a fancy justification for the existing class structure.

Wisdom Identified with the Torah

4. 1   Hear the praise of Wisdom from her own mouth,
            as she speaks with pride among her people,

2   before the assembly of the Most High
        and in the presence of the heavenly host:

3   'I am the word spoken by the Most High;
        it was I who covered the earth like a mist.

4   My dwelling-place was in high heaven;
        my throne was in a pillar of cloud.

5   Alone I made a circuit of the sky
        and traversed the depths of the abyss.

6   The waves of the sea, the whole earth,
        every people and nation were under my sway.   ▸

Wisdom Identified with the Torah

Wisdom's self-praise falls into two parts. The first (1-6) is closely modelled upon Proverbs Ch. 8. Here, as there, Wisdom is presented as having a cosmic role, existing *before time* (9) and sharing with God in the work of creation (implied by v.3, with its echoes of Gen 1). But already in this first part there are hints of the surprise to come in the second.

In Proverbs Wisdom addressed 'all mankind', here *she speaks among her people* i.e. the Jews – and in Hebrew fashion v.1 is picked up by v.12, thus framing the unit. Likewise the *pillar of cloud* (4), referring to God's appearances during the exodus (esp. Ex 33.9), prepares us for the bold idea put forward in vv.7-12.

Wisdom Identified with the Torah (cont.)

24.7 Among them all I sought where I might come to rest:
in whose territory was I to settle?

8 Then the Creator of all things laid a command on me;
he who created me decreed where I should dwell.
He said, 'Make your home in Jacob;
enter on your heritage in Israel.'

9 Before time began he created me,
and until the end of time I shall endure.

10 In the sacred tent I ministered in his presence,
and thus I came to be established in Zion.

11 He settled me in the city he loved
and gave me authority in Jerusalem.

12 I took root among the people whom the Lord had honoured
by choosing them to be his own portion.

13 There I grew like a cedar of Lebanon,
like a cypress on the slopes of Hermon,

14 like a date-palm at En-gedi,
like roses at Jericho.

19 Come to me, all you who desire me,
and eat your fill of my fruit.'

23 All this is the book of the covenant of God Most High,
the law laid on us by Moses,
a possession for the assemblies of Jacob.   (REB)

Wisdom Identified with the Torah (cont.)

Throughout their history thinking Jews had reflected upon the relation between their own traditions and those of the gentile world around them. The dominant view of the OT is that of prophets before the exile and priests after it, that the Jews were God's *own portion* (12) and should glory in their separation. The opposite extreme view is not mentioned except to be castigated e.g. in 2 Macc 4.15. It is only in the Wisdom books that we find anything approaching an accommodation. For Wisdom was undeniably international and syncretistic* – which is why the author of Proverbs had to insist that 'the fear of YHWH is the foundation of Wisdom'. But that was too simple to satisfy indefinitely. Ben Sira offers a more sophisticated analysis. Civilisation is indeed indivisible, he says, but it all comes from God, and its finest flower is to be found in Jerusalem, in the Temple worship (10) and in the *law* of *Moses* (23, added as the author's comment at the end of Wisdom's speech). The claim which he here expresses in theological language was repeated, more plausibly if more prosaically, in his grandson's preface.

The Art of Medicine

.1   Treat the doctor with the honour that is his due,
       in consideration of his services;
       for he too has been created by the Lord.

2   Healing itself comes from the Most High,
       like a gift received from a king.

3   The doctor's learning keeps his head high,
       and the great regard him with awe.

4   The Lord has brought forth medicinal herbs from the ground,
       and no one sensible will despise them.

7   He uses these for healing and relieving pain;
       the druggist makes up a mixture from them.

8   Thus, there is no end to his activities;
       thanks to him, well-being exists throughout the world.

9   My child, when you are ill, do not rebel,
       but pray to the Lord and he will heal you.

10   Renounce your faults, keep your hands unsoiled,
       and cleanse your heart from all sin.

11   Offer incense and a memorial of fine flour,
       make as rich an offering as you can afford.

12   Then let the doctor take over – the Lord created him too –
       do not let him leave you, for you need him.   (NJB)

The Art of Medicine

An important branch of Wisdom was medical science. Ancient medicine was most advanced in Greece and Egypt, and doctors had high standing in both countries: v.2b should be translated with REB 'and he is rewarded by kings'. In Israel however illness was traditionally seen as punishment for sin; hence e.g. the criticism [2 Chron 16.12] of King Asa for consulting not the LORD but the doctors. Ben Sira's theology of medicine begins by conforming to what he had said about Wisdom in general. *The Lord created* both *the doctor* (1) and medicines (4), his work in creation being continued by his care for people's health (8). Then (9-11) the author seems to remember that indeed there is also illness which is caused by *sin*, so that religion still has a part to play in healing. But he ends with a framing echo of v.1: the doctor's skill is as dear to God as a *rich offering*.

The Tradesmen and the Scribe

38.24
A scholar's wisdom comes of ample leisure;
  to be wise he must be relieved of other tasks.

25
How can one become wise who follows the plough,
  whose pride is in wielding the goad,
who is absorbed in the task of driving oxen,
  whose talk is all about cattle?

26
He concentrates on ploughing his furrows,
  and toils late to give the heifers their fodder.

27
So it is with every craftsman
  and designer working both day and night.
Such are those who make engravings
  on signets and patiently vary the design;
they concentrate on making an exact likeness
  and stay up to all hours to finish their task.

28
So it is with the smith, sitting by his anvil,
  intent on his ironwork.
The fiery vapours shrivel his flesh
  as he wrestles in the heat of the furnace;
the hammer rings in his ears again and again,
  and his eyes are on the pattern he is copying.
He concentrates on completing the task
  and stays up late to give it a perfect finish.

The Tradesmen and the Scribe

The section 38.24-39.11 is a fascinating example of how OT writers adapted foreign material for their own purposes. About 2000 BC an Egyptian scribe, i.e. civil servant, wrote a short work, known to us as the *Satire on the Trades*, which praises his own profession at the expense of others. The *Satire* came to be used as a text in the education of scribes, and various copies survive from c.1300 BC onwards, often mangled by schoolboy copyists (*ANET* 432). The author of it took some seventeen 'trades' in turn, including all those treated by ben Sira, and pointed out their disadvantages. Many of these are physical. The mason's 'sides ache', the smith's fingers are 'somewhat like crocodiles', i.e. horny – a simile which ben Sira dropped, though he kept the point (38.28).

The Tradesmen and the Scribe (cont.)

29   So it is with the potter, sitting at his work,
              turning the wheel with his feet,
              always engrossed in the task of making up his tally of vessels;
30   he moulds the clay with his arm,
              crouching forward to exert his strength.
          He concentrates on finishing the glazing,
              and stays up to clean out the furnace.

31   All those rely on their hands,
              and each is skilful at his own craft.
32   Without them a city would have no inhabitants;
              no settlers or travellers would come to it.
33   Yet they are not in demand at public discussions,
              nor do they attain to high office in the assembly.
          They do not sit on the judge's bench
              or understand the decisions of the courts.
          They cannot expound moral or legal principles
              and are not ready with maxims.
34   But they maintain the fabric of this world,
              and the practice of their craft is their prayer.   ▸

The Tradesmen and the Scribe (cont.)

Ben Sira also dropped the personal disparagements which earn the Egyptian work its title of *Satire*, e.g. that the builder is 'dirtier than pigs' or that the embalmer smells of corpses. Indeed the general assessment with which ben Sira concludes his individual comments is, for the ancient world, outstandingly fair. Admittedly, 'tradesmen' do not *attain to high office in the assembly* (33); cp. the *Satire*, 'I have never seen a sculptor on an errand' i.e. on an embassy. *But they maintain the fabric of this world* (34) – high praise and far removed from the *Satire*.

One minor motif of the *Satire* becomes major in ben Sira. This is the idea that tradesmen work late at night, e.g. 'the barber is still shaving at the end of dusk'. Ben Sira takes up this point in the refrain which concludes each of his four trades. (He actually uses the identical word for *stays up* in each verse of the Greek (26, 27, 28, 30), though REB sees fit to offer four variants.) For him this marks an important difference between tradesman and scribe. The scribe needs *ample leisure* (38.24), a concept found here only in the OT. Lacking leisure, the tradesman has to *concentrate*, i.e. specialise, whereas the scribe takes *all* knowledge as his province (39.1, 4d).

The Tradesmen and the Scribe (cont.)

39. 1 How different it is with one who devotes
      himself to reflecting on the law of the Most High,
who explores all the wisdom of the past
      and occupies himself with the study of prophecies!

2 He preserves the sayings of the famous
      and penetrates the subtleties of parables.

3 He explores the hidden meaning of proverbs
      and knows his way among enigmatic parables.

4 The great avail themselves of his services,
      and he appears in the presence of rulers.
He travels in foreign countries,
      learning at first hand human good and human evil.

5 He makes a point of rising early to seek the Lord, his Maker;
      he prays to the Most High,
      asking pardon for his sins.

8 In his teaching he will reveal his learning,
      and his pride will be in the law of the Lord's covenant.

9 Many will praise his intelligence,
      and it will never be forgotten.

11 If he lives long, he will leave a name in a thousand;
      when he goes to his long rest, his reputation is secure.   (REB)

The Tradesmen and the Scribe (cont.)

When it comes to praising the scribe, the *Satire* is concerned only with the wordly success which awaits him. 'There is no profession free of a boss – except for the scribe: he is the boss.' Ben Sira is not unmoved by such rewards. His scribe has influence with *the great*, *he travels* abroad (39.4), he earns *praise* (9) during his life and a posthumous *reputation* (11). But to that secular picture, derived from international Wisdom, ben Sira adds his own note of Jewish piety. The literature he studies includes not only *all the Wisdom of the past* but also *the law* and the *prophecies* (1). Nor is it simply a question of study: there is a particular emphasis on *prayer* (5). In a mirror image of the tradesman's late hours, the scribe *makes a point of rising early* to pray. It is all a little wordy, even smug, for (as in the *Satire*) the picture of the scribe doubles as an idealised self-portrait. But like the praise of the doctor the whole section illustrates the general theology of culture sketched out in Ch. 24.

The Roll of Honour

.1 Let us now praise famous men,
and our fathers that begat us.

2 The Lord manifested in them great glory,
even his mighty power from the beginning.

3 Such as did bear rule in their kingdoms,
and were men renowned for their power,

4 Leaders of the people by their counsels,
and by their understanding men of learning for the people;

5 Such as sought out musical tunes,
and set forth verses in writing:

6 Rich men furnished with ability,
living peaceably in their habitations:

7 All these were honoured in their generations,
and were a glory in their days.

8 There be of them, that have left a name behind them,
to declare their praises.

9 And some there be, which have no memorial;
who are perished as though they had not been,
And are become as though they had not been born;
and their children after them.

10 But these were men of mercy,
whose righteous deeds have not been forgotten.

13 Their seed shall remain for ever,
and their glory shall not be blotted out.

14 Their bodies were buried in peace,
and their name liveth to all generations.

15 Peoples will declare their wisdom,
and the congregation telleth out their praise.   (RV)

The Roll of Honour

The last part of ben Sira's book (Chs 44-50) is a roll-call of the heroes of Israel's past, from Enoch [Gen 5] to Simon who was high priest c.220-195 BC. His choice of individual names and the reasons he gives for it are of interest to hebraists, but his general introduction has a wider appeal. In the AV it is often read at Christian services of commemoration, whether for the famous or (because of v.9) for ordinary people. The Revised Version is here preferred, as retaining most of the sonority but correcting some of the errors of the Authorised Version.

The wording of both Versions in v.10 is a source of confusion. *These* cannot possibly refer back to those *who have no memorial*. It must look forward to the roll-call of national heroes, which begins in [v.16] and lasts right through to [Ch.50]. NJB translates v.10a 'But here is a list of illustrious men'.

Surprisingly, there creeps into the Jewish terminology here a frequent mention of hellenistic concepts like 'honour'. Of Abraham, for example, ben Sira says that 'there was none found equal to him in glory' [v.19] – a very different Abraham from the figure portrayed in Genesis.

SUSANNA

Introduction

The story of Daniel and Susanna is found with the Greek text of Daniel. It was not highly regarded by the Jews, and there is no trace of it at Qumran. But Christian mss preserve two versions of it, of which the longer has always been preferred by the Church. This is a translation made in the C1st AD by Theodotion (Theo), who seems to have taken the LXX translation and revised it with the aid of a now lost Semitic original. Theo's version is easier to follow than that of the LXX. It is written in a good but rather stilted Greek, to which REB is closer than NJB (see v.20).

The story itself combines two folk-tales: that of the innocent woman accused and that of the wise young judge. It was natural for the Jews to attach it to Daniel, a traditional wise man whose name means 'God is my judge'. The main characters form a skilfully composed triangle, with the corrupt elders acting as foils to the hero and heroine in three different respects. On the judicial axis they are not only perjured witnesses but judges who have long abused their office (53, 57), while Daniel, though only a layman (50), is both honest and clever. On the erotic axis, the elders are lecherous and crafty, Susanna pure, if a little naive; as for Daniel, the author avoids the least hint of romantic involvement. On the axis of age, Daniel's youth is explicit (45), Susanna's implicit (30). In Daniel's case it links with another folk-tale motif, that of the hero's early demonstration of the virtue for which he later becomes renowned. That motif is used to round off the story (64) and to locate it in time before the other stories recorded in the canonical book of Daniel.

The whole tale is thus thoroughly Jewish and pious. Its message, that fidelity will be rewarded, is underlined by the words which frame it (3, 62): *according to the law of Moses*. But the story itself made its greatest appeal to Christian Europe in late medieval and renaissance times. It was a favourite subject not only of art (Rubens, Rembrandt, etc.) but also of drama and oratorio.

Susanna Framed by the Elders

1 In Babylon there lived a man named Joakim, • who had married Susanna daughter of Hilkiah, a very beautiful and devout woman. • Her parents were godfearing people who had brought up their daughter according to the law of Moses. • Joakim was very rich, and his house had adjoining it a fine garden; this was a regular meeting-place for the Jews, because he was the man of greatest distinction

5 among them. • Now that year the judges appointed were two of the community's elders; of such the Lord had said, 'Wickedness came forth from Babylon, from elders who were judges and were supposed to guide my people.' • These men were constantly at Joakim's house, and everyone who had a case to be tried came to them there.

• At noon, when the people went away, Susanna would go and walk in her husband's garden. • Every day the two elders used to see her entering the garden for her walk, and they were inflamed with lust. • Their minds were perverted; their thoughts went astray and were no longer turned to God, and they did not

10 keep in mind the demands of justice. • Both were infatuated with her; but they did not disclose to each other what torments they suffered, because they were ashamed to confess they wanted to seduce her. • Day after day they watched eagerly for a sight of her.   ▶

Susanna Framed by the Elders (cont.)

• One day, having said, 'Let us go home; it is time to eat,' • they left and went off in different directions; but turning back they found themselves face to face, and on questioning each other about this, they admitted their passion. Then they agreed on a time when they might find her alone.

15 • While they were watching for an opportune moment, Susanna went into the garden as usual, accompanied only by her two maids; it was very hot, and she felt a desire to bathe in the garden. • No one else was there apart from the two elders, who had hidden and were spying on her. • She said to the maids, 'Bring me olive oil and unguents, and shut the garden doors so that I may bathe.' • They did as she said: they made fast the garden doors and went out by the side entrance for the things they had been told to bring; they did not see the elders, because they were in hiding.

• As soon as the maids had gone, the two elders got up and ran to Susanna. 20 • 'Look, the garden doors are shut,' they said, 'and no one can see us! We are overcome with desire for you; consent, and yield to us. • If you refuse, we shall swear in evidence there was a young man with you and that was why you sent your maids away.' • Susanna groaned and said: 'It is a desperate plight I am in! If I do this, the penalty is death; if I do not, you will have me at your mercy. • My choice is made: I will not do it! Better to be at your mercy than to sin against the Lord!' • With that she called out at the top of her voice, but the two elders 25 shouted her down, • and one of them ran and opened the garden door. • The household, hearing the uproar in the garden, rushed in through the side entrance to see what had happened to her. • When the elders had told their story, the servants were deeply shocked, for no such allegation had ever been made against Susanna. (REB)

Susanna Framed by the Elders

The story is well introduced. First we meet the two main parties separately: Susanna and her family (1-4) and the two elders (v.5, where the quotation cannot be placed in the OT we have). Then we learn of the connections between the two, general (6) and immediate (7-14).

With v.15 we move to the story proper: Scene 1, in the walled garden. The LXX has Susanna take her walk in the early morning, but Theo changes it to siesta time. This allows him to introduce the erotic motif of the woman bathing, which was popular in hellenistic* literature, but cp. also Bathsheba in 2 Sam 11.2. And he makes the most of it in a novelettish manner. The detail of vv.15-21 and vv.24-27 is entirely missing from the LXX, including the device for getting *the maids* out of the way and the *garden doors shut*. The Greek verb in v.20a betrays the voyeur: literally, it is '*no one* is watching *us*'. The dialogue is artificial, and NJB's translation of v.20b is much too simple: 'we want to have you, so give in and let us'. Jewish law imposed the death penalty for adultery by a married woman. Susanna's cry in v.24 was required in order to establish her innocence [Dt 22.24], which is why *the elders shouted her down*.

Susanna Saved by Daniel

28 Next day, when the people gathered at her husband Joakim's house, the two elders arrived, intent on their criminal design to have Susanna put to death. • In the presence of the people they said, 'Send for Susanna daughter of Hilkiah,
30 Joakim's wife.' She was summoned, • and came with her parents and children and all her relatives. • Now Susanna was a woman of great beauty and delicate feeling. • She was closely veiled, but those scoundrels ordered her to be unveiled so that they might feast their eyes on her beauty. • Her family and all who saw her were in tears.

• Then the two elders stood up before the people and put their hands on her
35 head, • she meanwhile looking towards heaven through her tears, for her trust was in the Lord. • The elders said: 'As we were walking by ourselves in the garden, this woman came in with her two maids. She shut the garden doors and dismissed her maids, • and then a young man, who had been in hiding, came and lay with her. • We were in a corner of the garden, and when we saw this wickedness we ran towards them. • We saw them in the act, but we could not hold the man; he was
40 too strong for us, he opened the door and got clean away. • We seized the woman and asked who the young man was, but she would not tell us. That is our evidence.'

• Because they were elders of the people and judges, the assembly believed them and condemned her to death. • Then raising her voice Susanna cried: 'Eternal God, you know all secrets and foresee all things, • you know that their evidence against me is false. And now I am to die, innocent though I am of the charges these wicked men have brought against me.'

45 • The Lord heard her cry, • and as she was being led off to execution, God inspired a devout young man named Daniel to protest. • He shouted out, 'I will not have this woman's blood on my hands.' • At this the people all turned towards him and demanded, 'What do you mean?' • He stepped forward and said: 'Are you such fools, you Israelites, as to condemn a woman of Israel, without making careful
49 enquiry and finding out the truth? • Reopen the trial; the evidence these men have given against her is false.'   ▸

Susanna Saved by Daniel

For Scene 2, the trial *at Joakim's house*, Theo keeps much closer to LXX. Two further items of Jewish legal procedure are referred to here. A woman suspected of adultery had her hair let down and, according to rabbinic sources, might be required by the court to strip to the waist – the voyeur motif again (32). In a capital case, witnesses *put their hands on* the *head* of the accused. The verdict and sentence were formally pronounced by the whole people. Susanna remained passive throughout, except for her prayer after the verdict.

Rabbinic sources also help us to understand the context of Scene 3, the re-trial. Two things might happen on the way from the court to the place of execution. On the one hand pressure was brought on the accused to confess: this Susanna refuses to do (42-3). On the other hand a herald went ahead inviting any last-minute evidence of innocence. It is to that invitation that Daniel responds, which is why he appears so late in the story. The court then reconvenes for the re-trial.

But already since v.42, if not earlier, we have moved into a new kind of narrative. Gone is the realism, such as it was, of Scene 1 or even of Scene 2.

Susanna Saved by Daniel (cont.)

53   • Everyone hurried back, and the rest of the elders said to Daniel, 'Come, take your place among us and state your case, for God has given you the standing of an elder.' • He said, 'Separate these men and keep them at a distance from each other, and I shall examine them.' • When they had been separated, Daniel summoned one of them. 'You hardened reprobate,' he began, 'the sins of your past have now come home to you. • You have given unjust decisions, condemning the innocent and acquitting the guilty, although the Lord has said, "You must not cause the death of the innocent and guiltless." • Now, if you really saw this woman, then tell us, under what tree did you see them together?' He answered, 'Under a clove

55   tree.' • Daniel retorted, 'Very good! This lie has cost you your life, for already God's angel has received your sentence from God, and he will cleave you in two.' • He ordered him to stand aside, and told them to bring forward the other.

He said to him: 'Spawn of Canaan, no son of Judah, beauty has been your undoing and lust has perverted your heart! • So this is how the two of you have been treating the women of Israel, terrifying them into yielding to you! But here is a woman of Judah who would not submit to your villainy. • Now tell me, under what tree did you surprise them together?' 'Under a yew tree,' he replied. • Daniel said to him, 'Very good! This lie has cost you also your life, for the angel of God is waiting sword in hand to hew you down and destroy the pair of you.'

60   • At that the whole assembly shouted aloud, praising God, the Saviour of those who trust in him. • They turned on the two elders, for out of their own mouths Daniel had convicted them of giving false evidence; • they dealt with them according to the law of Moses, putting them to death as they in their wickedness had intended to do to their neighbour. So an innocent life was saved that day. • Then Hilkiah and his wife gave praise for their daughter Susanna, as did also her husband Joakim and all her relatives, because she was found innocent of a shameful deed.

   • From that day forward Daniel was held in great esteem among the people.

(REB)

Susanna Saved by Daniel (cont.)

The legal framework of Scene 3 is more apparent than real. True, witnesses certainly ought to be examined separately. But the key question put to each of them in this case, and answered with gratifying brevity, was hardly enough to destroy their evidence. It would help if we could suppose that the re-trial took place in the garden and that, in answer to the question *under what tree did you see them together*, the elders had each to point to a specific tree. But in the text as we have it Daniel behaves less like a judge unravelling truth than a prophet exposing sin.

He is inspired by God (50) and knows what *God's angel* will do (55, 59). He denounces the wicked (52-7) like Jeremiah [29.22f.] and delivers a punning sentence like Amos (8.1-3). REB's *clove . . . cleave* and *yew . . . hew* are used, as in the Greek, purely for the sake of the pun: there is no other significance either in the identity of the tree or in the nature of the punishment foretold. In the event the elders are punished according to the Torah: 'if he be proved to be giving false witness against his fellow, you shall treat him as he intended to treat his fellow' [Dt 19.19], i.e. the whole community stone him to death. The story ends by celebrating the triumph of virtue and the defeat of vice.

THE BOOKS OF THE MACCABEES

Introduction

The two books of Maccabees constitute a unique 'double' to conclude the historical books of the OT. They both tell of a brief but crucial period in the history of Israel, roughly 175-135 BC, during which (i) the Jewish way of life was subjected to an unprecedented frontal and flanking assault, but then (ii) the people fought back, under the leadership of the Maccabees, so vigorously that they won a brief period of independence – the only such period between the fall of Jerusalem in 587 BC and the establishment of the state of Israel in 1948 AD.

Viewed as historical sources, the two books corroborate each other. Together they enable an historian for the first time to form a picture not only of events in Judaea itself but also of the relation of those events to the international politics of the time. From a literary point of view, they complement each other. 1M was written in Judaea, and its affinities are with e.g. the books of Kings. It is strongly nationalist in tone, and its theology is correspondingly simple. In style, as far as one can tell from the Greek translation of the lost Hebrew original, it was straightforward – dull but dignified.

The author of 2 M by contrast regarded himself as a man of the world. Living in the Greek city of Alexandria, he had one eye on a wider public. True, he had no doubts of the rightness of the Maccabean cause – indeed he wished to awaken the sympathy of Alexandrian Jews for their brethren in Judaea – and his theology, though much more sophisticated than that of 1 M, was orthodox. But at the same time he is writing for an educated cosmopolitan readership. He writes in Greek, the language of education, and he displays a detailed knowledge of the Greek way of life. More remarkably – and more regrettably – he adopts a highly coloured style of history writing such as was popular in the hellenistic* period. In a way which is characteristic of that age, he writes self-consciously of his aims, high among which is entertainment. The result is, by modern standards, a tasteless mixture of the pious with the sentimental, of Gothic horror with legalistic documentation. But that very hybrid inadvertently provides a striking illustration of the enemy against which the Maccabees were fighting.

That enemy, in a word, was hellenism, the civilisation which had spread, in the wake of Alexander's conquering troops, right across the ANE and was also now dominating the Mediterranean, including the rising power of Rome. Hellenism was as attractive in its day as western civilisation has been in the modern period to the emergent nations, and for much the same reasons. With the Greek language came a whole range of benefits: first, science – medicine, agriculture, engineering, architecture; second, civic democracy, with the buildings that represented it (e.g. the gymnasium); third, high culture including art, drama and the potentially corroding philosophy. The author of 2 M understands what 1M does not, namely the powerful attraction exerted on many Jews by this international civilisation, even though his own style reveals how far its culture had declined since the great days of C 5th BC Athens and even C 3rd BC Alexandria.

In one important respect the threat of hellenism resembled the earlier threat of Baal-worship. The victory of either would have obliterated the distinctiveness of Judaism. But hellenism was more alien, more insidious and much stronger: it very nearly won. What then if Jerusalem *had* been permanently converted into a Greek city? Jesus of Nazareth would doubtless have been 'tolerated' – and Christianity still-born. That is part of the reason why Toynbee described the confrontation chronicled in 1M and 2 M as 'the most portentous event in the history of hellenism'. On that occasion it ended in bloodshed: 200 years later Paul of Tarsus acted as broker to a marriage between the two, whose offspring was European civilisation.

THE FIRST BOOK OF MACCABEES

Antiochus the Helleniser

.1 Alexander of Macedon, the son of Philip, marched from the land of Kittim, defeated Darius, king of Persia and Media, and seized his throne, being already king of Greece. • During the course of many campaigns, in which he captured strongholds and put kings to death, • he traversed the earth to its remotest bounds and plundered countless nations. When at last the world lay quiet under his sway, his pride knew no limits; • he built up an extremely powerful army and ruled over countries, nations, and princedoms, all of which rendered him tribute.

5 • The time came when Alexander fell ill, and, realising that he was dying, • he summoned his generals, nobles who had been brought up with him from childhood, and divided his empire among them while he was yet alive. • At his death he had reigned for twelve years. • His generals took over the government, each in his own province, • and, when Alexander died, they all assumed royal crowns, and for many years the succession passed to their descendants. They brought untold miseries on the world.

10 • An offshoot of this stock was that impious man, Antiochus Epiphanes, son of King Antiochus. He had been a hostage in Rome before he succeeded to the throne in the year 137 of the Greek era.

• At that time there emerged in Israel a group of renegade Jews, who inveigled many by saying, 'We should go and make an agreement with the Gentiles round about; nothing but disaster has been our lot since we cut ourselves off from them.' • This proposal was widely approved, • and some of the people in their enthusiasm went to the king and received authority to introduce pagan laws and customs. ▸

Antiochus the Helleniser

1 M rightly begins his brief account of the hellenistic age with *Alexander* the Great (356-323 BC), whose conquests set it off. When he died at the age of 33, he had left no appointed heir (the contrary statement in v.6 is one of a number of errors here, which however do not affect the story the author is telling) and for over a decade his marshals disputed the succession between them. In 312 BC the dust settled: Ptolemy took Egypt, while Seleucus took Babylon and established effective control over the greater part of Alexander's empire. For nearly two centuries thereafter the political map of the ANE looked more or less unchanged, except that Rome gradually extended her influence eastwards until in the end she swallowed it all. But for much of that time

the Seleucids i.e. descendants of Seleucus managed the great land empire previously controlled by Assyria, Babylon and Persia. And for the Jews the age-old problem remained, of being ground between Seleucids to the north and Ptolemaic Egypt to the south – though now the alien culture was the same on both sides of them.

1 M then boldly skips 137 years from the accession of Seleucus I to that of his descendant *Antiochus* IV in 175 BC. (The Seleucid or *Greek era* is used for dating purposes throughout 1M and 2M). Although the new king was *impious*, the proposal for change came from *renegade* i.e. hellenising *Jews*. These were the richer class, but initially they enjoyed some popular support (11-12). Their motives

---

Antiochus the Helleniser (cont.)

1. 14 • They built a gymnasium in the gentile style at Jerusalem; • they removed their marks of circumcision and repudiated the holy covenant; they intermarried with Gentiles and sold themselves to evil.

41 • The king issued an edict throughout his empire: his subjects were all to become one people • and abandon their own customs. Everywhere the nations complied with the royal command, • and many in Israel willingly adopted the foreign cult, sacrificing to idols and profaning the sabbath. • The king sent agents to Jerusalem and the towns of Judaea with written orders that ways and customs 45 foreign to the country should be introduced. • Whole-offerings, sacrifices, and drink-offerings were forbidden in the temple; sabbaths and feast days were to be profaned.

54 • On the fifteenth day of the month of Kislev in the year 145, 'the abomination of desolation' was set up on the altar of the Lord. In the towns throughout Judaea pagan altars were built; • incense was offered at the doors of houses and in the streets. • Every scroll of the law that was found was torn up and consigned to the flames, • and anyone discovered in possession of a Book of the Covenant or conforming to the law was by sentence of the king condemned to die. • Thus month after month these wicked men used their power against the Israelites 59 whom they found in their towns. • On the twenty-fifth day of each month they offered sacrifice on the pagan altar which was on top of the altar of whole-offering.   (REB)

Antiochus the Helleniser (cont.)

may have been as much commercial as cultural. For the *gymnasium* see on 2 M 4.12. Antiochus' motives on the other hand were political: his declining empire would be safer if the border province abandoned its exclusiveness. The supposedly universal *edict* of vv.41-2 is unhistorical but typical of 1 M's perspective (cp. 2.18-19).

In December 167 BC, as the climax of his measures, Antiochus brought the worship of the Temple into line with that of the rest of his empire. The term *abomination of desolation* (v.54, taken from Dan 11.31) is a typically Jewish abusive pun on the title of a pagan deity (see p.32). The deity in question was Baalshamaim, the Lord of Heaven, who was worshipped under a variety of titles in the ANE and also represented by a variety of cult objects – here actually by an altar-stone. Technically therefore the proposal was not to replace but to assimilate the worship of YHWH. As before, gentiles could not understand why Jews should object to a syncretism* which everyone else accepted. As before, many Jews would die rather than conform.

Mattathias Raises the Standard of Revolt

.1 It was in those days that a certain Mattathias son of John, son of Symeon, came on the scene. He was a priest of the Joarib family from Jerusalem, now settled at Modin, • and he had five sons: John called Gaddis, • Simon called Thassis, • Judas called Maccabaeus, • Eleazar called Avaran, and Jonathan called Apphus.

15 • The king's officers who were enforcing apostasy came to the town of Modin to see that sacrifice was offered. • Many Israelites went over to them, but Mattathias and all his sons stood apart. • The officers addressed Mattathias: 'You are a leader here, a man of mark and influence in this town, with your sons and brothers at your back. • Now you be the first to come forward; carry out the king's decree as all the nations have done, as well as the leading men in Judaea and the people left in Jerusalem. Then you and your sons will be enrolled among the king's Friends; you will all receive high honours, rich rewards of silver and gold, and many further benefits.'

• In a ringing voice Mattathias replied: 'Though every nation within the king's dominions obeys and forsakes its ancestral worship, though all have chosen to
20 submit to his commands, • yet I and my sons and my brothers will follow the covenant made with our forefathers. • Heaven forbid we should ever abandon the law and its statutes! • We will not obey the king's command, nor will we deviate one step from our way of worship.'

• As he finished speaking, a Jew came forward in full view of all to offer sacrifice on the pagan altar at Modin, in obedience to the royal decree. • The sight aroused the zeal of Mattathias, and, shaking with passion and in a fury of righteous
25 anger, he rushed forward and cut him down on the very altar. • At the same time he killed the officer sent by the king to enforce sacrifice, and demolished the pagan altar.• He shouted for the whole town to hear, 'Follow me, all who are zealous for the law and stand by the covenant!'   ▶

Mattathias Raises the Standard of Revolt

The family of *Mattathias* was destined not only to achieve independence but also (later) to establish a dynasty, known as Hasmoneans. Mattathias himself was a country *priest*: he lived 17 miles NW of Jerusalem but went to the capital when his family's turn came for a week's duty in the Temple. Of the five brothers, two became high priests, and all met a violent death. The meaning of their nicknames is unclear: *Maccabaeus*, the only one of consequence, probably means 'hammer'.

The scene of the confrontation is quite well depicted. *The king's officers* worked on Mattathias with flattery, pressure and bribery: *the king's Friends* (18) was an honorific order which the hellenistic monarchies had taken over from Persia.The drama is heightened by the parallelism, which is weaker in the speech of the officers, stronger in Mattathias' rejoinder.

Mattathias Raises the Standard of Revolt (cont.)

2. 28 • Then he and his sons took to the hills, leaving behind in the town all they possessed. • At that time many who sought to maintain their religion and law went down to live in the desert, • taking their children and their wives and their livestock with them, for their miseries were more than they could bear. • They were joined by a group of Hasidaeans, stalwarts of Israel, every one of them a volunteer in the cause of the law; • and all who were refugees from the troubles

44 came to swell their numbers and add to their strength. • Now that they had an organised force, they turned the fierceness of their wrath on the guilty men and renegades.   (REB)

Mattathias Raises the Standard of Revolt (cont.)

As often in Jewish history, outlaws took refuge in the *hills*, and even in the *desert* (29) west of the Dead Sea, like the later sect which owned the Dead Sea Scrolls. *Hasidaeans* (42) is the Greek form of *Hasidim*, the Loyalists, a group with a long future before them.

The Successes of the Resistance

3. 1 Judas Maccabaeus came forward to take his father's place. • He had the support of all his brothers and his father's followers, and they carried on Israel's campaign

25 with zest. • Judas and his brothers came to be regarded with fear, and alarm spread among the Gentiles round about . . .

4.12 • When the foreigners saw them advancing to the attack, • they moved out from their camp to give battle. Sounding their trumpets, Judas and his men • closed with them, and the Gentiles broke and fled into the plain . . .

36 • Judas and his brothers said: 'Now that our enemies have been crushed, let us go up to cleanse and rededicate the temple.' • When the whole army had

41 assembled, they went up to Mount Zion. • Then Judas detailed men to engage the citadel garrison while the temple was being cleansed. • They took unhewn stones,

50 as the law directs, and built a new altar on the model of the previous one. • They burnt incense on the altar, and they lit the lamps on the lampstand to shine within the temple.

52 • Early on the twenty-fifth day of the ninth month, the month of Kislev, in the year 148, • sacrifice was offered, as laid down by the law, on the newly constructed altar of whole-offerings.• On the anniversary of the day of its desecration by the Gentiles, on that very day it was dedicated with hymns of thanksgiving, to the music of harps and lutes and cymbals. • All the people prostrated themselves in worship and gave praise to Heaven for prospering their cause.

59 • Judas, his brothers, and the whole congregation of Israel decreed that, at the same season each year, the dedication of the altar should be observed with joy and gladness for eight days, beginning on the twenty-fifth of Kislev.   (REB)

The Successes of the Resistance

Mattathias died about a year later, in 166 BC. It took *Judas* only two years to turn the tables on the enemy. The records of his campaigns in 1M and 2M are fuller and more convincing than most military narratives in the OT and, though not of interest to the general reader, they allow Judas to be seen as a great guerrilla commander. His first objective was to restore Jewish worship in *the Temple*, and this he boldly set about even while there was still a hostile garrison occupying the *citadel* (41) which overlooked the Temple Mount from somewhere to the west. The date of the new *dedication* (4.56) was 14 December 164 BC, and it has indeed been celebrated ever since by Jews as the feast of *Hanukkah* (= Dedication) or Lights (see 4.50). It has been calculated recently that Halley's comet was visible over Jerusalem in the last few weeks of 164 BC. If so, it would certainly have been taken as a sign, and may possibly be commemorated in the term 'Lights'.

Judas's Embassy to Rome

3. 1   Judas had had reports about the Romans: that they were renowned for their military power and for the favour they showed to those who became their allies, and that any who joined them could be sure of their friendship • and strong military support. He was told of the campaigns they had fought, and the valour they had shown in their conquest of the Gauls, whom they had laid under tribute.

5   • Philip, and Perseus king of Kittim, and all who had set themselves in opposition to the Romans had been crushed in battle and conquered. • Antiochus the Great, king of Asia, had advanced against them with one hundred and twenty elephants, with cavalry and chariots and an immense force, only to be totally defeated.

12   • Thus they overcame rulers near and far, and all who heard of their reputation went in dread of them. • Yet for all this, not one of them ever gave himself the airs

16   of a prince, assuming a crown or putting on the purple. • Every year they entrusted their government and the rule of all their dominions to one of their number, all obeying this one man without jealousy or envy.

    • So Judas chose Eupolemus son of John, son of Accos, and Jason son of Eleazar, and sent them to Rome to make a treaty of friendship and alliance.   (REB)

Judas's Embassy to Rome

Culturally, Rome was already part of the hellenistic world. Politically, she had been extending her influence into the eastern Mediterranean for at least half a century. She had defeated *Philip* V and *Perseus* kings of Macedon (*Kittim*) and the Seleucid *Antiochus* III *the Great*, for whose good behaviour his son Antiochus had been taken hostage to Rome (1.10). Her military power was clearly irresistible; her republican customs (there were actually two consuls, not *one* – v.16) compared favourably with those of the hellenistic monarchies; and at this stage it was still possible to see her as benevolent and trustworthy. She was in fact a natural ally for someone in Judas's position. Of the representatives sent by him to Rome, the father's name is in each case Hebrew, the son's Greek – a further sign of the silent spread of hellenism.

Rome in turn had nothing to lose by a nominal *alliance*. But if she gave any support, material or even moral, to the Jewish resistance, it came too late to save Judas.

The Death of Judas

Within months of the signing of the treaty, yet another Seleucid army was in Judaea, based on the citadel in *Jerusalem*, with instructions to crush the revolt for good and all. (The topographical details are obscure in IM.) Judas was heavily outnumbered, but he characteristically decided to attack first. His brief speech before the battle uses a concept more Greek than Hebrew, that of *honour* (9.10). But the aftermath of his death is told in the best OT tradition.

The Death of Judas

9. 3 In the first month of the year 152, they moved camp to Jerusalem, • and from there they marched to Berea with twenty thousand infantry and two thousand cavalry. • Judas had established his camp at Alasa. He had with him three thousand picked troops, • but, when his men saw the size of the enemy forces, their courage failed and many deserted, until a mere eight hundred remained.

7 • Aware that his army had melted away and the campaign was going against him, Judas was greatly disheartened, for there was not time to reassemble his forces. Though himself despondent, • he said to those who were left, 'Let us take the offensive and see if we can defeat the enemy.' • His men tried to dissuade him: 'Impossible!' they said. 'No, we are too few. Let us save our lives now, and come back later to fight them when we have our comrades with us.' • But Judas replied: 'Heaven forbid that I should do such a thing as run away! If our time has come, let us die bravely for our fellow-countrymen, and leave no stain on our

17 honour.' • The fighting became very heavy, and many fell on both sides. • Judas was among the fallen; the rest of the Jews fled. • Jonathan and Simon carried Judas their brother away and laid him in the family tomb at Modin, • and there they wept over him. There was great grief throughout Israel, and the people mourned him for many days, saying,

21 How is our champion fallen,
the saviour of Israel!

• The rest of the history of Judas, his wars, exploits, and achievements – these were so numerous that they have not been recorded.   (REB)

Simon and the Dawn of Independence

33 Simon rebuilt the fortresses of Judaea, furnishing them with high towers and with massive walls and barred gates; he also stocked the fortresses with provisions. • He selected delegates and sent them to King Demetrius to negotiate

35 a remission of taxes for the country. • In reply to this request Demetrius sent a letter in the following terms:

> • From King Demetrius to Simon the High Priest and Friend of kings, and to the elders and nation of the Jews. Greeting.
> • We have received the gold crown and the palm branch which you sent, and we are prepared to make a lasting peace with you and to instruct the revenue officers to grant you remissions of tax. • All our agreements with you stand confirmed, and the strongholds which you built shall remain yours.
> • For any errors of omission or commission we grant a free pardon, to take effect from the date of this letter. We remit the crown-levy which you owed us, and every other tax formerly exacted in Jerusalem is henceforth
40 cancelled. • Any of you who are suitable for enrolment in our retinue shall be so enrolled. Let there be peace between us.

• In the year 170, Israel was released from the gentile yoke; • the people began to write on their contracts and agreements: 'In the first year of Simon, the great high priest, general, and leader of the Jews'.   ▶

Simon and the Dawn of Independence

Judas was succeeded by Jonathan, who became High Priest as well as military commander; and Jonathan by *Simon* in both roles. By now (142 BC) the Seleucid throne has been further weakened, and the new king *Demetrius* II is minded to come to terms with the rebels. Even though for the moment he retained his garrison in the citadel of Jerusalem, the concessions he made went far to justify the author's claim for *Israel* in 13.41. Simon himself was appointed to the order of the *Friends* (36, cp. 2.18).

Simon and the Dawn of Independence (cont.)

14.4   • As long as Simon ruled, Judaea was undisturbed. He sought his nation's good, and they lived happily all through the glorious days of his reign. • Notable among his achievements was his capture of the port of Joppa to secure his communications overseas. • He extended his nation's borders and made himself master of the land.

8   • The people farmed the land in peace; it produced its crops, and the trees in the plains their fruit. • Old men sat in the streets, talking together of their blessings;

10   and the young men arrayed themselves in splendid military style. • Simon supplied the towns with food in plenty and equipped them with weapons for defence, so that his renown spread to the ends of the earth. • Peace was restored to the land, and throughout Israel there was great rejoicing. • Everyone sat under his own vine and fig tree, and there was none to cause alarm. • Those were days when no enemy was seen in the land and every hostile king was crushed. • Simon gave his protection to the poor among the people; he fulfilled the demands of the law, and

15   rid the country of renegades and evil men. • He enhanced the splendour of the temple and furnished it with a wealth of sacred vessels.   (REB)

Simon and the Dawn of Independence (cont.)

The praise of Simon in Ch.14, which NJB prints as verse, contains a fascinating blend of features. Hellenistic influence is visible in the reference to *communications overseas* (5) and *splendid military style* (9b). Particularly Hebrew on the other hand are the idyllic motifs of vv.8-9a and 12 (cp. [Zech 8.4] and Mic 4.4 respectively) and the implicit equation in v.14 of *poor* with virtuous.

THE SECOND BOOK OF MACCABEES

The Author's Preface

19 • The story of Judas Maccabaeus and his brothers, the purification of the great Temple, the dedication of the altar, • together with the wars against Antiochus Epiphanes, • and the celestial manifestations that came to hearten the brave champions of Judaism, so that, few though they were, they pillaged the whole country, routed the barbarian hordes, • recovered the sanctuary renowned the whole world over, liberated the city and re-established the laws by then all but abolished, the Lord showing his favour by all his gracious help to them – • all this, already related in five books by Jason of Cyrene, we shall attempt to condense into a single work. • Considering the spate of figures and the difficulty encountered, because of the mass of material, by those who wish to immerse them-
25 selves in historical records, • we have aimed at providing diversion for those who merely want something to read, a saving of labour for those who enjoy committing things to memory, and profit for each and all. • For us who have undertaken the drudgery of this abridgement, it has been no easy task but a matter of sweat and midnight oil, • comparable to the exacting task of someone organising a banquet, whose aim is to satisfy a variety of tastes. Nevertheless, for the sake of rendering a general service, we remain glad to endure this drudgery, • leaving accuracy of detail to the historian, and concentrating our effort on tracing the outlines in this condensed version. • Just as the architect of a new house is responsible for the construction as a whole, while the man undertaking the ceramic painting has to take into consideration only the decorative requirements,
30 so, I think, it is with us. • To make the subject his own, to explore its byways, to be meticulous about details, is the business of the original historian, • but the person making the adaptation must be allowed to aim at conciseness of expression and to forgo any exhaustive treatment of his subject.

• So now let us begin our narrative, without adding any more to what has been said above; there would be no sense in expanding the preface to the history and curtailing the history itself.   (NJB)

The Author's Preface

This preface of 2M is typically hellenistic* in form and (except v.22) in content. Only in Ecclus do we get a similar self-consciousness on the part of an OT author (but cp. Luke's preface to his Gospel and Acts). More specifically, 2 M is a product of the Egyptian dispersion. Alexandria was the centre of hellenistic literature and of aesthetic criticism. Characteristically Alexandrian is the setting out of the author's purpose (25), the reference to *the midnight oil* (26), the simile of the *banquet* (27), the comparison of literature with a visual art (29), and the final dig at long-winded competitors (32) expressed in a neat antithesis. More specifically, the relation between writer and reader has changed: readers are divided into three classes, each looking for something different, but none of them serious in the traditional sense, whether Hebrew or Greek. They want it tabloid, i.e. short, easy and entertaining.

The Author's Preface (cont.)

Yet the author himself does have a serious purpose. Generally, he wishes to record for posterity the deeds of the *brave champions of Judaism* – the typically Greek terms 'Judaism' and 'Hellenism' make their first biblical appearance in 2 M. Specifically he seeks to do honour to the Temple in Jerusalem, and to encourage his fellow Alexandrian Jews to do likewise. Unfortunately some of his efforts *to satisfy a variety of tastes* (27) merely serve to detract from his potentially inspiring theme.

The Hellenising Movement

4.7 When, on the death of Seleucus, Antiochus known as Epiphanes succeeded to the throne, Jason, Onias's brother, procured for himself the office of high priest by underhand means. • In a petition to the king he promised him three hundred and sixty talents in silver coin immediately, and eighty talents from future revenue; • further, he undertook to pay an additional hundred and fifty talents if authority were given him to set up a gymnasium for the physical education of young men, and to enrol the inhabitants of Jerusalem as citizens of Antioch. • The king gave his assent; and Jason, as soon as he had secured the high-priesthood, made his fellow-Jews conform to the Greek way of life.

10 • He lost no time in establishing a gymnasium at the foot of the citadel itself, and he made the most outstanding of the young men adopt the hat worn by Greek athletes. • So with the introduction of foreign customs Hellenism reached a high point through the inordinate wickedness of Jason, an apostate and no true high priest. • As a result, the priests no longer showed any enthusiasm for their duties at the altar; they treated the temple with disdain, they neglected the sacrifices, and whenever the opening gong called them they hurried to join in the sports at the wrestling school in defiance of the law. • They placed no

15 value on dignities prized by their forefathers, but cared above everything for Hellenic honours. • This brought misfortune upon them from every side, and the very people whose way of life they admired and tried so hard to emulate turned out to be vindictive enemies.   (REB)

The Hellenising Movement

2 M here adds much detail to the austere narrative of 1 M 1.11-15. He reveals that the hellenising movement in Jerusalem was actually centred in the high priesthood. After the exile the *high priest* gradually became political as well as religious head of state; as such he had the contacts with the wider world, and would most easily fall victim to its glitter. *Jason's* Hebrew name was Joshua, but like many of his fellows he preferred the nearest Greek equivalent.

The *gymnasium* (12) and the *wrestling school* (14) were an important feature of Greek city life. They formed a centre not only of physical but also of more general Greek education e.g. in music and the recitation of Homer. Constitutionally also the first step was taken towards the conversion of Jerusalem into a hellenistic city. The Seleucids, like Alexander, were great founders of cities, which were mostly given the two dynastic names of Seleuceia or Antioch. Here it seems that the inhabitants of *the citadel* – the hellenising Jews and the foreign garrison –

The Hellenising Movement (cont.)

were allowed to call themselves '*citizens of Antioch-in-Jerusalem*'. Had things gone on in the direction of hellenism (13), the citizen body would have been given a new status as a city-*state* i.e. a city with a con-siderable degree of political and economic independence, including the right to mint its own coinage – a development which to Jason and his friends was well worth the substantial investment of vv. 8-9.

The Conflict Grows Sharper

27 But Judas, also called Maccabaeus, escaped with about nine others into the desert, where he and his companions lived in the mountains, fending for themselves like the wild animals, and all the while feeding on what vegetation they found there, so as to have no share in the pollution.

.1 • Not long afterwards King Antiochus sent an elderly Athenian to compel the Jews to give up their ancestral customs and to cease regulating their lives by the laws of God. • He was commissioned also to pollute the temple at Jerusalem and dedicate it to Olympian Zeus. . . .

.1 • Another incident concerned the arrest of seven brothers along with their mother. They were being tortured by the king with whips and thongs to force them to eat pork, contrary to the law. • But one of them, speaking for all, said: 'What do you expect to learn by interrogating us? Rather than break our ancestral laws we are prepared to die.' • In fury the king ordered great pans and cauldrons to be heated. • This was attended to without delay; meanwhile he gave orders that the spokesman's tongue should be cut out and that he should be scalped

5 and mutilated before the eyes of his mother and six brothers. • A wreck of a man, but still breathing, he was taken at the king's direction to the fire and roasted in one of the pans. As the smoke from it streamed out, the mother and her sons encouraged each other to die nobly. • 'The Lord God is looking on,' they said, 'and we may be sure he has compassion on us.' ▸

The Conflict Grows Sharper

2 M says nothing of Mattathias, and places the beginning of the resistance *before* the regulations requiring the Jews to abandon the Torah. The *elderly Athenian* (if the translation of 6.1 is correct) is not otherwise known. *Olympian Zeus* of 6.2 is merely the Greek equivalent of the Semitic 'Lord of Heaven' (see note on 1M 1.54).

Most of 2M's description of the persecution is taken up with stories of martyrdom. Unpleasing as the narrative is (it is a hellenistic literary equivalent of Roman gladiatorial shows), it contains material of some importance in the history of theology and indeed literature. In the full story seven brothers and their mother are martyred in succession; this selection retains only the first four.

Theologically, it may well have been out of the sufferings of those years that the idea of resurrection came (see Daniel 12): it seemed the only way to reconcile the sufferings of the righteous with the belief in a loving God. Here the doctrine is developed, as it were, point by point in the four speeches.

The Conflict Grows Sharper (cont.)

7.7   • After the first brother had died in this way, the second was subjected to the same indignities. The skin and hair of his head were torn off, and he was asked: 'Will you eat, or must we tear you limb from limb?' • 'Eat? Never!' he replied in his native language, and so he in turn underwent torture like the first. • With his final breath he said: 'Fiend though you are, you are setting us free from this present life, and the King of the universe will raise us up to a life everlastingly made new, since it is for his laws that we are dying.'

10   • After him the third was tortured. When the question was put to him, he at once showed his tongue, courageously held out his hands, • and spoke nobly: 'The God of heaven gave these to me, but his laws mean far more to me than they do, and it is from him that I trust to receive them again.' • Both the king himself and those with him were astounded at the young man's spirit and his utter disregard for suffering.

• When he too was dead, they tortured the fourth in the same cruel manner. • At the point of death, he uttered these words: 'Better to be killed by men and to cherish God's promise to raise us again! But for you there will be no resurrection.'

(REB)

The Conflict Grows Sharper (cont.)

The first speaks generally of God's *compassion* (6); *the second* foresees a *new* and everlasting *life* (9); *the third* adds that the resurrection will be physical (11); *the fourth* makes clear that only the righteous will be raised (14).

Why is this narrative so distasteful? It is not so much the detailed description of the atrocities – for since the Holocaust no one can doubt that such things happen – as the rhetorical packaging. The old OT tradition allowed deathbed speeches, but would have known that in such a context there is no place for anything but a noble simplicity. The doctrine of resurrection may be apposite and comforting – and even true; but its incremental exposition here is an insult to the heroism which the author wishes to portray. (Contrast the sensitive handling of the same theme in another Alexandrian Jewish work, Wisd Sol 3.) It is especially unfortunate that these stories, with a number of other similar ones in 2 M, formed a literary model for later Christian martyrologies.

Judas and the Purification of the Temple

. 1 | Meanwhile Judas, who was called Maccabaeus, and his companions were making their way into the villages unobserved, summoning their kinsmen to their side and recruiting others who had remained faithful to the Jewish religion, until they had collected up to six thousand men.

5 | • Once his band of partisans was organised, the Gentiles found Maccabaeus invincible, now that the Lord's anger had changed to mercy. • Maccabaeus came on towns and villages without warning and burnt them down; he recaptured strategic positions, and inflicted many reverses on the enemy, • choosing the night-time as being especially favourable for these attacks. Everywhere there was talk of his heroism.

. 1 | • Under the Lord's guidance, Maccabaeus and his followers recovered the temple and city of Jerusalem, • and demolished the altars erected by the heathen in the public square, together with their sacred precincts. • When they had purified the sanctuary, they made another altar, and striking fire with flints they offered sacrifice for the first time in two whole years; they restored the incense, the lamps, and the Bread of the Presence. • This done, they prostrated themselves and prayed to the Lord that he would never again allow them to fall into such disasters but, were they ever to sin, would discipline them himself with clem-

5 | ency rather than hand them over to blasphemous and barbarous Gentiles. • The sanctuary was purified on the twenty-fifth of Kislev, the same day of the same month as that on which foreigners had profaned it. • The joyful celebration lasted for eight days, like the feast of Tabernacles, and they recalled how, only a short time before, they had kept that feast while living like wild animals in the mountains and caves. • So carrying garlanded wands and flowering branches, as well as palm-fronds, they chanted hymns to the One who had so triumphantly achieved the purification of his own temple. • A decree was passed by the public assembly that every year the entire Jewish nation should keep these days holy.

37 | • At this point I shall bring my work to an end. • If it is found to be well written and aptly composed, that is what I myself aimed at; if superficial and mediocre, it was the best I could do. • For, just as it is disagreeable to drink wine by itself or water by itself, whereas the mixing of the two produces a pleasant and delightful taste, so too variety of style in a literary work charms the ear of the reader. Let this, then, be my final word.   (REB)

Judas and the Purification of the Temple

2 M's narrative of the purification of the Temple differs from that of 1M both in a number of historical details and in its religious emphasis. The author is much concerned for the purity of the cult – hence the *fire* struck *with flints* (10.3).

He also has a theology of the tribulations: as he puts it elsewhere [6.16], 'though he may discipline his people by disaster, he does not desert them'.

2M ends when it has taken the story down as far as 1M 7.

APPENDIX A:
HEBREW LITERATURE IN ITS ANE CONTEXT

Hebrew literature was born and grew to maturity in the close-knit cultural context of the Ancient Near East (ANE). The closeness of that culture in terms of literature is shown by its common use of parallelism (see p.21+) as its chief verse-form.

Two other peoples of the ANE produced bodies of literature comparable to that of the Jews: the Egyptians and the nations who occupied the Tigris and Euphrates valleys, here arbitrarily referred to as Babylonians. Two others, the Hittites and the people of Ugarit, have left us a literature which is smaller but still throws considerable light on the OT. Since the writings of all these four peoples precede the OT by many centuries, any literary *influence* can have been exerted in only one direction. But it is more prudent to speak of the ANE context, allowing that a context may operate unconsciously or even provoke to dissent.

The discovery of these texts (apart from some inscriptions) and their decipherment is the work of little over a century at most. Most of the longer texts are incomplete, some merely fragments, and the translation and interpretation is often fraught with great difficulties, even more than that of the OT. Certain points may, however, be made with confidence.

By and large the kinds of writing that are found in the OT are also found in one or more of the others, the range of Egyptian literature being broader than the OT, the Babylonian narrower. Now it may at first sight seem that, outside the OT, survival is due to chance. But most of the finds have been in palace or temple archives, i.e. they come from collections which must in some sense have been 'the best'. Moreover a number of works keep cropping up, at different times and places and in different versions. It appears that we can speak not merely of certain 'popular' works but even of something approaching a canon, certainly a canon of Babylonian psalms. We do therefore have the material for a rough comparison of the OT with the ANE literature which forms its context.

1. ANE Literature by Countries

Ancient **Egyptian** literature covers the period from c.2500 BC down to the Greek occupation c.300 BC. The Egyptian language was only a distant cousin of Hebrew but the cultural ties were always close, e.g. the shared practice of circumcision. Table 1 sets out what are, from the point of view of the OT, the most interesting works of Egyptian literature, together with their closest Hebrew parallels. The date is added, although in a civilisation as static as that of Egypt it makes relatively little difference. 'On' means that the text continued to be copied for a long time.

A few subjective judgements may be ventured on Egyptian literature. The most prized kind of writing in all periods was Wisdom, with *The Man Weary of Life* (*ANET* 405) the finest of all in that category. Equally fine is the best of the poetry, especially the love poems (*ANET* 467). In prose, Egypt was 'the home of the short story' (Peet). The *Adventures of Sinuhe* (*ANET* 18) is a splendid yarn, well up to the general standard of the OT. It has no exact OT parallel, however, because it is told purely for entertainment without religious or moralistic colouring. Egyptian myths are altogether inferior to those of the OT or Babylon. Indeed except for the hymn to the Aten (*ANET* 369), the best Egyptian writing was not religious. It was however the most consciously literary in the ANE, and so could range from the delicately sophisticated to the mannered and decadent. For Egyptian prophecy and history see pp.773+.

Table 1: Egyptian Literature

1. History	Campaign of Thutmose III against Megiddo	c.1450	Jg 4-5
2. Story	Adventures of Sinuhe	1800 on	
3. Poetry	Hymn to the Aten	c.1400	Ps 104
	Love poems	1400 – 1100	Song of Songs
	Songs of the Harper	1300 on	Ecclesiastes
4. Prophecy	Neferti	c.1500	prophets
5. Wisdom	Instructions/Admonitions	2300 on	Proverbs etc.
	'The Man Weary of Life'	c.2000	Job
	'The Satire on the Trades'	2000 on	Ecclus 24

The body of literature here called **Babylonian** comes from a succession of peoples who dominated the Tigris and Euphrates valleys from the third millennium BC onwards. First came the Sumerians, a non-Semitic people who invented cuneiform writing. They were conquered c.2350 BC by the Akkadians, a Semitic people whose language, written in cuneiform, was the lingua franca of the whole Asiatic ANE from c.1500-500 BC. Akkadians fell to Assyrians and Babylonians, all 'east Semites', who disputed control of the same region down to the Persian conquest in 539 BC.

Almost all the extant works of Babylonian literature come from the palace of Nineveh, where Asshurbanipal of Assyria collected them c. 650 BC. Those texts are clearly later copies of much earlier works, but is not always easy to determine the date of the original composition. The most striking works of Babylonian literature are shown in Table 2.

Of all these works – and indeed of all ANE literature – the epic of *Gilgamesh* stands out. 'The scope and sweep of the epic and its sheer poetic power give it a timeless appeal' (*ANET*). Its influence extended not only to the OT but to Homer. *Gilgamesh* is a secular epic, though in some versions it contains paradise and flood myths. The creation myth however was a cultic work, being recited annually at the Babylonian New Year festival. Of the other works, the two Wisdom dialogues are particularly interesting (see Afterword to Job). For prophecy and history see pp.773+.

There remain the law codes, which are important social documents both for themselves and for the light they throw on the OT. The most famous of them is the *Code* of king Hammurabi. Like many other law codes it has a long prologue and epilogue, in the high style i.e. with much parallelism. The skeleton of the introduction is as follows (*ANET* 164+):

Table 2: Babylonian Literature

1. Myth and Epic	The Creation Myth	? 1750 on	Gen 1
	Gilgamesh	2000 on	Gen 2+, 6+
	Atrahasis	? 1750 on	Gen 6+
2. Religious poetry	Hymns and psalms .	all periods	Psalms
3. Wisdom	'I will praise the Lord of wisdom'	c.1300	Job
	The Babylonian Theodicy	c.1400	Job
4. Prophecy	The Curse of Agade	c.2000	Is 34
5. Laws	The Code of Hammurabi	c.1800	Ex 21-22

When Anum and Enlil called Babylon by its exalted name, they named me to cause justice to prevail in the land, that the strong might not oppress the weak. Hammurabi the shepherd am I ... the king who has made the four quarters of the world subservient; the favourite of Inanna am I. When Marduk commissioned me, I established law and justice in the language of the land.

The epilogue repeats the purpose:

In order that the strong might not oppress the weak, that justice might be dealt to the orphan and the widow, I wrote my precious words on my stele ... Let any oppressed man who has a cause ... read carefully my inscribed stele.

The *Code* ends with 270 lines of curses on anyone who rescinds his laws or alters the text in any way.

There is one obvious feature here shared with the OT laws *and prophets*, viz. the especial care for the weak. Another is less obvious. The whole inscription takes the form of demonstration, almost a boast, to the gods that the king has carried out his function as a lawgiver. Modern scholars therefore do not suppose that all its provisions were necessarily implemented. That interpretation is helpful when we come to certain provisions in Deuteronomy, especially those of the sabbath-year (Ch.15).

The code itself has 282 clauses, all cast in the conditional form 'If/when ... he/she shall ...'. All are concerned solely with social matters; cultic affairs in the ANE were the province of the priests. The specific provisions are generally very close to those of the OT, but there are some interesting differences. Hammurabi's laws vary the punishment according to the social status of the parties involved, e.g. 'If a seignior struck a seignior's daughter and caused her to have a miscarriage, he shall pay ten shekels of silver'; but if the seignior's victim is a commoner's daughter it costs him five shekels, if a slave only two. The same section shows a second difference. If the pregnant woman dies,

being the daughter of another seignior, 'they shall put his daughter to death'. But the death of a commoner's daughter costs half a mina of silver (= 30 shekels), that of a female slave one third of a mina. OT law by contrast rarely admits the civilised principle of compensation, and never the barbarous one of vicarious punishment.

Ugarit is the ancient name of a town in N. Syria which was discovered in 1921. The texts found there were all written down c.1350 BC in a West Semitic tongue very close to Hebrew, Phoenician and Aramaic. That north-eastern corner of the Mediterranean was a node of ancient trade routes, and Ugarit played an im-portant role in spreading Babylonian myths and epics not only to Mycenaean Greece but also to the cities of Canaan and through them to the Hebrews.

The main works of Ugaritic literature are grouped in *ANET* under the heading of 'myths, epics and legends'. Of these the most important for the OT is the Baal epic or myth (*ANET* 129), which describes the struggle among the gods when El, the supreme deity, began to decline. The favourite is the fertility god Baal, but he must first overcome two contenders. One of these was the Sea (*Yam*), who was supported by various monsters, including a dragon (*Lotan*). The other is Death (*Mot*). In the course of the struggle Baal is overcome by *Mot*, but is then resurrected, like many another vegetation god. Parts of this story appear in many places in the OT – not taken seriously as religion but much used as a source of poetic imagery (see p.27+).

Another notable work of Ugaritic literature is known to us as the *Legend of King Keret*, of which these are the last surviving lines:

Yassib the lad departs,
enters his father's presence,
and lifts up his voice and cries:
'Hearken, I pray thee, Keret the noble,
list and incline thine ear ...
Thou hast let thy hand fall into mischief.

Thou judgest not the cause of the widow . . .
feedest not the fatherless before thee,
the widow behind thy back.
Descend from the kingship – I'll reign;
from thine authority – I'll sit enthroned.'
And Keret the noble makes answer:
'May Horon [god of the underworld] break,
    O my son,
may Horon break thy head,
Ashtoreth thy pate.'   (*ANET* 149)

The *Legend of King Keret* shares some features with the Court History of David. Generally it is ready to criticise a (possibly historical) king. It also shares specific motifs, e.g. his son's attempted usurpation and the argument about the administration of justice (cp. 2 Sam 15.1-6).

One other body of literature deserves a mention, that of the **Hittites**. The Hittites were actually Indo-Europeans, the first of those peoples to come down into the Mediterranean world. But when they entered Asia Minor (modern Turkey) in the second millennium BC they were soon absorbed into the dominant ANE culture based on Semitic languages and cuneiform writing. Like everyone else, they had their religious literature: myths, rituals, prayers. These are of no great interest except that the (prose) prayers contain a higher proportion of argument, including self-justification, than others in the ANE. In that respect they stand closer to Wisdom writings (e.g. Job), a category which is otherwise absent from the Hittite corpus. Of Hittite secular literature, the most important for the OT are the historical texts, dealt with below. Hittite power and literature, like those of Ugarit, came to a sudden end c.1200 BC.

2. ANE Literature by Kinds

Many individual works of ANE literature are quoted and discussed elsewhere in this book in the commentary on their nearest OT parallel (see tables on p.771). Similarly, certain kinds of writing are considered in the Introductions to the corresponding Hebrew kind, viz. Psalms and Wisdom literature; also in the Introductions to

Proverbs and the Song of Songs, and in the Afterword to Job. There remain two kinds, which are often claimed as especial contributions of the Jews: prophecy (poetry) and history (prose). These two are theologically linked, since both of them depended in the ancient world upon the conviction that the gods control human events in accordance with a plan of their own which men can sometimes discern but hardly ever divert.

To that extent there *are* some ANE parallels to Hebrew **prophecy**. Most of them however are more apparent than real, being pseudo-prophecies like those of Daniel 7-11. From Egypt the most plausible is the *Prophecy of Neferti* (*ANET* 444f.), which has a narrative setting. The Pharaoh sends for a wise man to entertain the court, and a prophet-priest called Neferti is brought in. He begins rather surprisingly, by saying: 'I shall speak of what is before my face; I cannot foretell what has not yet come.' He then launches into a social and moral critique of the country, partly in the present tense and partly in the future: 'I show thee the land topsy-turvy' and 'a man will sit still crooking his back [i.e. hunching his shoulders] while one man kills another'. He then forecasts that 'a king will come. . . . Ameni the triumphant his name', who will restore the country, 'and justice will come into its place'. But Ameni was the abbreviated name of Amenemhet III; most scholars regard the work as a pseudo-prophecy emanating from his court.

Babylonian literature has little more to offer. There are 'prophecies' which open in the stereotyped form 'A ruler [unnamed] will arise, he will rule for X years', and go on to link his attitude towards 'the temples of the gods' with the country's prosperity. At best these are like the summary judgements on the later kings in the OT, at worst they are an ancient equivalent of Old Moore's Almanac. Concepts of prophecy closer to the OT are found in the Mari letters of the C18th BC. (Closer still is the Deir Alla inscription of c.800 BC, for which see p.517; but the date and provenance of that text put it on the OT, not the ANE, side of the equation.)

Much more impressive as literature is the Babylonian *Curse of Agade*. This splendid poem tries to account for a national calamity, the destruction of the Sumerian capital Agade. He finds the cause in the se-quence of events which his poem records. The king of Agade, Naram-Sin, had in-curred the anger of the supreme god Enlil by despoiling his temple at Nippur. Enlil thereupon brought in some savage in-vaders, Gutians, who threatened to over-run the whole country. The threat was only averted by sacrificing Naram-Sin's own city to them. The other gods persuaded Enlil to curse Agade, and he did so in powerful language which has much in common with a long prophetic curse like that of Isaiah 34:

> Of that city, may skulls fill its wells,
> May no sympathising friends be found there. . . .
> May the oxen-slaughterer slaughter his wife instead,
> May your sheep-butcher butcher his child instead. . . .
> May your palace, built in joy, fall to ruins in anguish,
> May the evil ones, the ghosts of silent places, howl there evermore. . . .
> May your canal-boat towpaths grow tall grass. . . .
> Agade, instead of your sweet-flowing water may salt water flow.   (*ANET* 650)

The poem ends with the fulfilment of the curse, for this again is history rather than prophecy. Nevertheless it can be said that Babylonian literature, taken as a whole, contains many of the raw materials of prophecy as we know it in the OT. The *Curse of Agade* shows the theology of God's punishment for national sins, and expresses it in high dramatic poetry. The law codes of Hammurabi and others show the gods' demand for justice and for mercy to the weak. Mari knows the figure of the inspired prophet who announces a punishment to come for breach of religious or moral duty. Yet when the Hebrew prophets wrote roughly 1,000 years later, it could be seen how much greater was the whole than the sum of its parts.

The final kind of writing to be considered is **history**. In the judgement of some scholars, the Jews vied with the Greeks for the honour of inventing the writing of history. A closer look suggests that the Jews were as far behind the Greeks as they were ahead of the ANE.

One point must be got out of the way at once. Virtually everyone in the ancient world believed that the gods, in exercising their control of human affairs, could intervene between the intention and the action, and most believed also that they could intervene between the act and its consequences. Those beliefs lasted from the beginning of civilisation until well into modern times. The only change was that gradually in the ancient world human causation came to be admitted alongside divine causation – never in its place.

The Egyptians, with their static cosmos and their god-king, could have little idea of history. The inscriptions which record the victories of a Thutmose III or Rameses II, though quite readable, are almost unusable as historical documents. Kings could be criticised only after their deaths and then only for cultic offences. The Babylonians had a little more to offer. Their royal inscriptions have been described as 'egotistical boasts with pious overtones' (Grayson). But they do have some value as historical sources (e.g. they sometimes admit defeats), and the court scribes disposed of a lively style, marked by an abundance of similes. Moreover the king, being not a god but only the representative of God, was less autocratic than the Pharaoh: he had to pay some attention to his nobles and even, as the publication of the law codes shows, to his ordinary subjects. There are also plenty of lists surviving from Babylon, of kings and events and dates. But it seems that such lists were compiled, like observation of the stars, for purposes of divination, i.e. so that later generations could tell which were 'lucky' and which 'unlucky' days. In sum, most Babylonian historiography is tendentious.

It is only when we come to the Hittites that a clear step forward is made. Two inscriptions from c.1325 BC show a new approach. Both are the work of king Mursilis II and concern his father. The first marks a development in the philosophy of history. In a series of prayers to the supreme god (*ANET* 394+), the king asks how his country, 'the Hatti land', may be rid of a plague, i.e. of an epidemic which has been raging for some years. The king has made – and continues to make throughout the series – every effort, by consulting archives and oracles and diviners, to find out what the country has done wrong. Eventually he finds that the fault was his father's, for invading Egypt in breach of a treaty. The god had allowed him to defeat the Egyptian army and take prisoners, but 'when they moved the prisoners to the Hatti land, these prisoners carried the plague. From that day on people have been dying in the Hatti land.' Here the two kinds of causation are clearly treated as separate but complementary.

Mursilis also wrote a history of his father's reign – a remarkable document, with no apparent political axe to grind. *ANET* 319 contains the part of it in which he records his father's negotiations with the widow of Tutankhamun. She

> sent an envoy to my father and wrote him as follows: 'My husband died and I have no son. People say that you have many sons. If you were to send me one of your sons, he might become my husband. I am loth to take a servant [i.e. subject] of mine and make him my husband . . .'. When my father heard that, he called the great into council, saying: 'Since of old such a thing has never happened'. He proceeded to dispatch the chamberlain, saying: 'Go, bring reliable information back to me. They may try to deceive me. Perhaps they have a prince . . .'. The Egyptian queen answered my father in a letter as follows: 'Why do you say "they may try to deceive me"? If I had a son, would I write to a foreign country in a manner which is humiliating to myself and my country. . . . I have written only to you. Give me one of your sons, and he is my husband and king in the land of Egypt.' Because my father was generous, he complied with the lady's wishes and decided for sending the son.

This is an entirely new voice in ANE historiography. For the first time we are dealing with real people, and the expression matches the subtlety of their thoughts. We enjoy the narrative, and we have no reason to doubt its historicity. The only reser-vation we may have is that the *dramatis personae* are still confined to the royal families.

And so we come at last to the OT and to its masterpiece, the Court History of David. Why is it that its author seems an even greater artist and historian than Mursilis? As artist, first, he has at his disposal a repertoire of even greater subtlety. Nothing in ANE literature matches the delicate irony of the verses which open the narrative of David's great sin, the turning point of his reign: 'At the turn of the year, when kings take the field, David sent Joab out with his other officers. . . . One evening [i.e. late afternoon] David got up from his couch. . . . ' As history, too, this marks an advance even upon the Hittites, in three respects.

First, the OT writer enjoys a much longer perspective, provided for him by the concept of the covenant. This gives him both a chronological framework and a theology of history which extend far beyond a single reign. Second, while recognising the existence of the two levels of causality, the author has learned to leave the theology implicit. Thirdly, his analysis of human events is more democratic. The spotlight is still on the royal family, but 'the people' are always there in the background, and sometimes in the foreground (2 Sam 15.1-6; 1 K 12). And that is not just because Hebrew society was more democratic in itself. It seems clear that in many places the historian has, in addition to his sources at court, others which derive from clans and families. Hence, even when he is giving full rein to his imagination, his work always appears earthed in real life. If one looks for a genesis of genius, one could perhaps say that Hittite historiography has here been wedded to Egyptian story-telling.

But we must not be carried away. There is still a gap between the best Hebrew and Greek historians. It is not just the continued interweaving in the OT of 'pure' history with myth, legend and folk-tale; that criticism may still be made of Herodotus, if not of Thucydides. It is rather a lack of any critical evaluation of the sources (see p.782). And at that point we are talking of something much wider than the writing of history, namely a whole cultural cast of mind.

Conclusion

ANE literature provides more of an illumination than a challenge to the OT. Only a few works of the former rank with the best of the latter: *Gilgamesh* and *I will praise the Lord of Wisdom* from Babylonia, the love poems and *The Man Weary of Life* from Egypt. There is nothing in the ANE to rival the charm and subtlety of the stories in Genesis or 2 Samuel, the power and pathos of the prophets, the personal devotion of the psalms of trust, the intellectual and poetic force of Job. If this superiority is conceded, how can it be accounted for? To that question there are two possible answers – which turn out to be two sides of the same coin.

Mention has already been made of the greater democracy of Hebrew society. Neither the countryside itself nor its geographical position were suited to the kind of settled monarchy which prevailed elsewhere in the ANE. Solomon may have imposed one for a time, but it certainly never stuck. Efforts at centralisation and exploitation were repeatedly challenged by prophets and undone by invaders. Traditionally, kings were suspect (see Jg 9 and 1 Sam 8), and they and all other leaders were subject to severe criticism. Throughout the national literature, figures who elsewhere in the ANE would have been either heroes or villains – the patriarchs, Moses, Saul, David, Solomon – are painted in the mixed colours of humanity itself. They are not types but individuals.

A similar point emerges if one looks at the religion of the Jews. The monotheism that marked them out left no room for external limitations upon the supreme deity. There were no other gods to overrule him, nor was he bound by the stars to fate. The one God was restrained by his own nature (Hos 11.9) embodied in a covenant with creatures made in his own image. In the OT only humans could stand up to God, and that is precisely what we find them doing. Moreover those who do so are not just the great names like Abraham (Gen 18), Moses (Ex 32), Jeremiah (Ch.20) and Job, but the anonymous authors and users of many psalms (e.g. 8 and 73). At the same time Hebrew religion rejected the otherwise universal apparatus of magic. God could not be coerced, only persuaded.

So the Jews, as represented by and in the best of the OT, held their heads high before both God and kings – higher than any of their predecessors in the ANE. If that is the reason why their literature surpassed that of the ANE, it would also account for the respects in which they were themselves overtaken by the Greeks. For it was not until Greece that we can speak of democracy in any strict sense, and it was in Greece that science and philosophy were born. Hebrew thought and writing thus stand midway between those of the ANE and Greece.

APPENDIX B:
HEBREW AND GREEK LITERATURE : CONTACTS AND COMPARISONS

If one looks for other literatures to throw light on the OT, one must look in the first instance to the ANE. But by the criterion of influence upon European civilisation – and particularly European thought – a more fruitful comparison is with Greek (and Latin) literature.

It was Matthew Arnold who popularised the contrast between the Hebrew and the Hellene as exerting an equal and opposite pull upon the European imagination, being as it were the mother and father respectively of our mental inheritance. Other C19th scholars noted rather the similarities, and searched for parallels of thought and expression between the two bodies of literature. So the first question that arises is whether there were any ancient contacts between the two: specifically, can either have influenced the other?

As far as considerations of time and place go, it is perfectly possible. Greek and Hebrew literature began at roughly the same time, in the C8th BC (see date chart on p.791). Enterprising Greeks, who had been known as traders in the ANE for centuries before that, extended their activities across the region throughout the period during which most of the Hebrew Bible was being written, viz. down to the C4th BC. Yet there is no extant evidence of any influence either way between the two bodies of literature. All the parallels – and they are quite numerous – can be convincingly ascribed to the common influence of earlier ANE writings, of which the epic of Gilgamesh is outstanding (see M.L.West's book quoted on p.795).

After Alexander's conquests, of course, it is another matter. By c.250 BC many Jews must have been reading Homer etc., and conversely Greek readers had access to the Hebrew Bible in the LXX translation. It is quite possible that the authors of Job and Ecclesiastes knew some Greek literature; it is certain that the author of the Wisdom of Solomon did so. Yet even then we have to wait for the turn of the era to find a Jewish author explicitly quoting a Greek work or vice versa. Seen from the European perspective, it is astonishing how independent from each other were the Hebrew and the Hellene.

In spite of that the two bodies of literature have features in common. Many of these features derive from social and economic factors which they shared with all the literatures of antiquity.

1. The Tradition
Until the C3rd BC writing materials were expensive and literacy limited. In the ANE only the royal houses and the temples run by them could afford to train a school of scribes in copying and composition, and so to maintain a library. Among the Greeks wealth gradually became more widely distributed but literature still remained essentially a leisure pursuit.

Certain consequences followed. The readership and most of the *dramatis personae* came from the upper classes. Subject matter was largely confined to topics which in one way or another deserved to be called serious. Style, especially diction, was suited to subject matter. In the Greco-Roman tradition, certain words were regarded as appropriate only to poetry, certain others only to prose, while others again were suitable only to popular literature (what there was of it) or to plebeian characters appearing in patrician literature. (We cannot be certain how far the same linguistic convention operated in Hebrew and ANE literatures, since not enough of them survives.)

Moreover the tradition was not *felt* to be restrictive. In the ANE the same works were copied, albeit with variations, and recopied for centuries, even millennia. In Greece and Rome imitation was honourable, originality suspect. Homer was followed by Herodotus, Herodotus by Thucydides. Vergil too was praised for having emulated Homer (the reviewer actually said he had surpassed him, but nobody believed that), and he himself in turn became an exemplar for Renaissance and Augustan poets in Europe. The observance of the tradition guaranteed full membership of the literary community.

In the case of all ancient literature a further restrictive factor has been at work. What has survived is in effect an anthology. For the OT it was the rabbis who decided which works should be admitted to the canon. We know the kind of criteria they applied, and even in some cases how those criteria were met or circumvented (see Glossary s.v. canon). Classical Greek mss, in order to survive, had to pass two scrutinies, the first by Alexandrian scholars, the second by medieval monks. The criteria applied by them were certainly broader than those of the rabbis, but edification was not disregarded. Indeed the power of teachers to select certain texts for classroom use, and thus unwittingly to condemn others to oblivion, can be documented from pharaonic Egypt through hellenistic Alexandria down to modern examination syllabuses.

2. The Distinctive Ideas of the OT

To a modern reader coming fresh to the OT, what must strike most forcibly is the dominance of 'a definitive myth, a single archetypal structure' (Northrop Frye). That myth – the theme of 'disaster followed by restoration' – has the shape of an ellipse round two foci: the nation and God. Does not that differentiate it sharply from other literatures, including Greek?

Well, not as much as might be supposed. Much traditional literature has a national purpose, whether explicit or not. This is most obviously true of the epic: in George Lukács' words, the theme of the epic 'is not a personal destiny but the destiny of a community'. Frye has written similarly of Elizabethan historical drama that its 'central theme . . . is the unifying of the nation and the building of the audience into the myth as the inheritors of that unity, set over against the disasters of civil war and weak leadership'. This judgement is uncannily appropriate to most of the OT. It could also apply to a great deal of Greek and Roman literature.

Nor did the Jews have any monopoly of chauvinism. There is of course plenty of xenophobia in the OT. But the Greeks invented the more pervasive concept of barbarian. The Romans incorporated it into their own imperial myth, a myth which could lead even Vergil to write that Rome's destiny was 'to rule over other people, showing mercy to the humble and putting down the mighty from their seat'. And the voice of racial tolerance, rare in the ancient world, was as audible in the OT as in Greek and Roman literature taken as a whole. Witness in particular two stories: that of the Moabite heroine Ruth, where the punchline reveals that she was an ancestress of King David; and that of the anti-hero Jonah, whose childish sulks, when God spared the repentant Ninevites, are ridiculed by God himself.

Which brings us to God, and to the proper question: is not the OT hobbled as literature by the dominance of its belief in God? Once again it is worth pointing out that such a belief is not peculiar to the OT. If the distinction between God and gods is overlooked for the moment, all ancient literature (and most European literature down to 1900 AD) assumes the existence of God. And much of it is explicit: the fifth line of the *Iliad* says that it all happened 'in fulfilment of the will of Zeus'. The important difference is that only among the Jews was such a belief made a criterion of selection for the corpus of approved literature.

For *within* the OT that belief is much less restrictive than might be expected. It is only in the prophets and psalms that God dominates, as it were, from the foreground. There are, it is true, other places where he dominates from the background, viz the book of Job, the Priestly sections of the Pentateuch and much of the deuteronomic history. But in the rest of the OT, both narrative and Wisdom literature, as well as in most of the Apocrypha, God's presence in the background is such that a reader can easily suspend disbelief. Finally, his presence in Ecclesiastes is ironical, he is not mentioned at all in Esther, and he is totally absent from the Song of Songs.

Nevertheless, apart from these last two, he is always present in one way or another, even if it is only like the *manus dei* in a medieval painting. A modern reader might therefore expect various adverse effects upon the suspense and realism of the narrative and upon the free will of the characters. In practice, that is not how it works out. Suspense, first, is transferred from the outcome to the process, which can be equally absorbing. As to realism, the supernatural element in the OT is paradoxically less than in much ancient literature: God's presence virtually banishes omens, magic, demons and other spirits, and relegates angels and miracles to a minor place.

As to free will, only rarely does the providence of God determine the actions of men and women. In general, the OT is much more a record of the crimes and follies of mankind than of virtue and piety. Nor does God pre-empt the role of hero. On the contrary, the great heroes of the OT are precisely those who stand up against him in deliberate challenge, whether in direct clash of wills (Abraham, Moses, Job) or in disobedience (Samson, Saul, David). D.H. Lawrence saw it: 'The Bible is a great confused novel. You say, it is about God. But it is really about man alive.'

3. The Range of OT Literature

Whatever limitations the dominance of the 'great myth' may or may not have imposed upon the existing text of the OT, it certainly operated to limit the kinds of writing which the rabbis thought worthy of inclusion in their anthology. Extant Hebrew literature is patently narrower in range than classical Greek literature. Yet here also the difference between the two is less than is sometimes supposed – especially when the colossal disparity in size (1:1000?) is taken into account.

Common to both bodies are epic, history, lyric and what in OT studies is called Wisdom literature. But certain important kinds of Greek literature have no analogue in the Hebrew.

First is philosophy. The absence of philosophy, particularly ethics, is most noticeable because the Hebrews were passionately concerned with issues of right and wrong. But in their extant literature they never treated them in the systematic abstract way which is philosophical. Nor is it at all likely that philosophical works were written by Jewish authors but excluded from the canon of the Bible. For nowhere within the Hebrew Bible do we find the tools of philosophy. There is no sustained systematic argument in the OT before the Wisdom of Solomon, written in the first century BC under Greek influence. There is no sentence in it which recognises the balance of pros and cons as it is recognised by so many thousands of Greek sentences built upon the structure of 'on the one hand . . . on the other hand', or by sentences in any language containing the sequence ' . . . because, although . . . '. (Num 5.13 REB seems an exception, but the two English conjunctions both translate Heb 'and'.) Indeed the very particles which mark such logical connections were themselves not clear enough in their denotation to be usable for a strict process of argument. 'His argumentation', says Pedersen of the ancient Hebrew, 'consists in assurance and repetition'. The same applies to the composition of books. The books of Job and Ecclesiastes both obviously contain within them a set of considerations for and against certain conclusions. But neither of them reveals any logical progression in their argument. Philosophy lay outside the Hebrew genius as it lay outside all ANE literature. So did oratory, at least in the Greek sense of a logically articulated case.

Another absentee from the Bible is drama – tragedy and comedy – in the sense of plays written for entertainment. Like sculpture and painting, theatre was disapproved of in ancient Israel and is nowhere even mentioned in the OT. But the dramatic and the tragic are powerfully present, and the comic is not absent.

The dramatic is seen in various ways. To start with, all the OT poetry consists of speeches. Most is soliloquy, but there is a good deal of dialogue as well – the whole of Job, much of the Song of Songs, some psalms and a number of prophetic poems. The (prose) stories also çontains a high proportion of dialogue – often up to 50%, and as much as 60% in the case of Ruth – so that at a superficial level it is easy to recast them in dramatic form.

But that is not all. The OT stories are themselves 'scenic', i.e. they progress through a succession of scenes, each with its own place and time, stage props, actors and action. Character and motive are shown by visible action and audible speech rather than by authorial comment or stage direction. Moreover in reading them one finds the words time and again leading the mind's eye from the periphery to the centre, to the point of crisis or denouement (often marked in Hebrew by 'behold'), as if the camera were focusing in (e.g. Jael and Sisera, Ehud and Eglon in Jg 3-5). Indeed many stories in the OT are even more easily adaptable to film than to the stage.

Tragedy in the OT is to be seen most obviously in individuals. The stories of the great and representative figures in it fall mostly into the tragic pattern of greatness→sin→fall. There are variations on the classic Aristotelian schema e.g. Adam was not 'great', Job did not 'sin'. But Moses, Saul and David can all be regarded as tragic heroes.

There is also a tragic aspect to the nation's collective history. The OT writers discerned in that history the analogous sequence of covenant→breach (apostasy)→punishment (exile). But their belief in God's providence led some of them to extend the sequence two stages further: punishment→repentance→ restoration. Literary critics have argued that the extended trajectory then becomes that of comedy rather than tragedy. Other critics have observed its resemblance to the Marxist sequence of thesis→antithesis→synthesis, and recalled Marx's familiarity with the OT.

Comedy in the sense of the humorous is certainly present in the OT, but it needs to be looked for. There is the quiet humour which is seen especially in descriptions of domestic situations, such as Abraham's reception of the three unknown visitors in Gen 18, or the scene where Tobit and his wife blame each other for their poverty. There is the grim humour of dramatic irony in e.g. Esther or Judith. There is, thirdly, a gentler irony used at the expense of antiheroes like Adam and Jonah. But there is no sustained piece of Hebrew comic writing within the Bible. Whether there was any such outside it, we do not know.

Finally, Hebrew literature contains virtually nothing in the way of personal or 'occasional' lyric. There are love poems in the Song of Songs, and a number of poignant poems of despair in the Psalms and Jeremiah. There are also a few anonymous songs for special recurrent situations: victory songs, harvest songs, taunt songs. But there is scarcely anything recording the light and passing fancies of an identifiable individual: Is 22.15-18 is a rare exception.

As against this, there are certain kinds of literature which are either peculiar to the OT or represent a special development there, as compared with Greek literature. Most obvious is prophecy. Hebrew prophecy is unique. Its nearest parallels are in the ANE from which it sprang, and they are not very close (see pp.773+). Greek parallels are even remoter. But the versatile Aristophanes was similar in one important respect. He took it upon himself to make public criticisms of his own countrymen, on moral as well as political grounds, and incurred their resentment for doing so, as Jeremiah did for his Temple sermon (Jer 7). Roman satirists later played a somewhat similar role.

Hebrew psalms are also sometimes thought to be unique. In fact hymns and prayers are to be found in all literatures, Greek as well as ANE, though very few rise to the level of the finest psalms.

More surprisingly there is one secular kind of literature where the Hebrews have the priority, at least in time, over the Greeks. This is the short story or novella*, where the Hebrews could draw on an Egyptian tradition going back before 2,000 BC (see p.771). The OT contains many examples of the novella. Some are self-contained e.g. Ruth, Jonah, Esther. Others are embedded in larger works, like the Joseph story in Genesis (which incidentally has an Egyptian setting and, in part, an Egyptian source). Greece knew the embedded kind, e.g. the story of Bellerophon in Homer or that of Cambyses in Herodotus (Egypt again). But it was not until the Greeks went east after Alexander that they began to develop the self-contained novella.

There remains one other major kind of writing, that of history. Here everything depends on what counts as history-writing. If history is only 'the way in which a nation renders account to itself of its own past' (Huizinga), then the Pentateuch and the 'deuteronomic history' count. Both of them understand the interplay of human character, speech and action. Both of them take a mass of material and organise it into a coherent whole, in which events do not merely succeed one another in time but conform to a detectable pattern of cause and effect. In these respects they certainly stand comparison with the 'father of history', Herodotus. What they lack however is fundamental. It is his critical approach to his sources, that intellectual autonomy in virtue of which he can write: 'The Greeks say X and the Persians say Y, but I think Z'. And that contrast between two different casts of mind is one which underlies any general comparison between Greek literature and the OT *as we have it*.

4. Realism and Sublimity

It was said above that the corpus of extant Hebrew literature shares with extant Greek literature a basic seriousness of purpose. But in the case of the OT the purpose is more specifically focused upon the national-religious myth. The effect of this is that the tone of the OT is fundamentally unlike that of Greek literature.

One can put the point briefly by saying that, whereas most Greek authors speak in a conversational tone, Hebrew authors are inclined to shout. In Auerbach's words,

> the Scripture stories do not, like Homer's, court our favour, they do not flatter us that they may please and enchant us – they seek to subject us, and if we refuse to be subjected we are rebels.

For the claim of the biblical writers is an exclusive claim. There is nothing in Hebrew corresponding to another phrase one meets in Herodotus: 'that is my view, but everyone must make up his own mind about the question'. Indeed it could be said that Greek is a literature of questions, Hebrew of answers.

This might appear to raise a problem

for those who would read the Bible without submitting to the claim. In Graham Hough's words,

> the normal habit of literature is the non-Christian attitude, in which myths are impartially entertained. Those who maintain that the Christian myth is different from others are right – not because it is 'truer' than any other but because it was believed in a different way. And some critics have thought it unsuitable for literary purposes on that account. Yet the natural tendency of literature is to slip back into the older mode of symbolic acceptance.

And the OT does contain large parts where the author is indeed wooing us, not demanding acceptance: the J narratives in Genesis, the Court History of David, the Wisdom literature, Ruth, Jonah, Tobit. It is no accident that those parts are disproportionately represented in this anthology. But that does not invalidate Auerbach's general point.

The dominance of 'the great myth' in Hebrew literature has thus led its anthologists to admit a narrower range of works, whose authors adopt a more dogmatic tone, than their Greek counterparts. Is there in Greek and Roman literature any corresponding tradition among authors or anthologists which has likewise imposed limits and restrictions? Auerbach himself convincingly argued that there is one, the tradition already referred to about the nature of the sublime in literature.

It is a commonplace of criticism that Greco-Roman literature employed a 'separation of styles'. This is seen in various ways. Take Aristotle's insistence that the heroes of tragedy must be men of position in the land, and remember by comparison the humble birth of Moses, Samson, David, etc. And even where we have to do with personages of the court, can one imagine anything in Greek history or tragedy comparable to the scene in the cave where Saul went in to relieve himself and David cut off part of his cloak while he was doing so? As to diction, can one conceive anything in high poetry (say Pindar) like the image in Isaiah where the moral turpitude of Israel is compared to a 'menstruous rag'? If we instinctively recoil from that, it is because our conception of taste is formed on the Greek model. More important, the leading characters in Hebrew literature can fall much lower in dignity. Adam blaming Eve for giving him the apple; Saul relieving himself in the cave; the lustful David's impotence in old age; Job scraping his sores with shards; Jeremiah at the bottom of the well – all these are in positions where they have fallen far below Aristotle's conception of tragedy and Longinus's of sublimity. But they are the more human for it.

All this is characteristic of a literature in much of which 'poor' is synonymous with 'virtuous' and 'rich' with 'wicked'. It is no surprise that it was this literature and this culture from which sprang the gospels, the first books in western literature, and for long the only ones, which were written about the poor for the poor. Nietzsche called Christianity 'a religion for slaves'; he meant it as a gibe, but it can be taken as a compliment to much Hebrew literature.

Auerbach sums up his judgement of this matter as follows. The OT

> has a different conception of the elevated style . . . the sublime, tragic and problematic take shape primarily in the domestic and commonplace . . . The two realms of the sublime and the everyday are not only unseparated but basically inseparable.

That judgement is not only literary but theological. I believe it is correct. In the OT, God not only created the world but made humans in his own image; in the New Testament he became man; therefore nothing human – indeed nothing created – could be alien from God.

In this respect therefore it is the Greek tradition which imposes the greater restriction upon its authors – and upon its anthologists who shared the same conception of sublimity. Whether their 'social' blinkers were more restrictive than the 'religious' blinkers worn by the Hebrew authors, modern readers will decide for themselves.

There is one final difference between the two bodies of writing. The concept of literature itself, as of poetry and of most literary genres (tragedy, lyric, history etc.), was unknown to the Hebrew writers before Greek influence reached them in the third century BC. The result is that Hebrew literature is much less self-conscious than Greek. Greek authors not merely give their names but explain the nature and purpose of their writing. Herodotus, for example, announces his purpose as being 'to preserve the memory of the past, by putting on record the astonishing achievements both of our own and of other [i.e. the Asiatic] peoples'. This, being the convention we are used to, makes them seem more modern. We feel they are more likely to reveal themselves or speak in a personal tone of voice. But against that a writer who sees himself as a writer may be led into posturings such as those of which Aristophanes accused Euripides. Nor is there any connection between the convention and the tone of voice. Of biblical authors ben Sira is the one who tells us most, in his prologue, about how and why he came to write his book (known to us as Ecclesiasticus); but his personality comes across very palely beside that of an earlier author who hid behind a conventional pseudonymity in writing his book (known to us as Ecclesiastes). Similarly in Greek literature the anonymous 'Homer' is more human as a personality than Aeschylus or Sophocles of whom we know many biographical details.

Here again, therefore, the difference between Greek and Hebrew literature – in this case, a difference of self-consciousness – is of less significance than at first sight appears.

Conclusion

A recent writer on Homer has claimed that: 'The replacing of the colossal, the vague and the bestial with the human image and the human scale is perhaps the most vital and the most lasting of all the achievements of Greece, both in literature and in art'. As an implicit criticism of Egyptian literature and art this is valid; of Babylon it is weaker; of the OT it is false. It was precisely in its concern with the human image and the human scale that the OT moved decisively in what might be called the Greek direction; and it is that movement which has enabled the two together to exert their lasting influence on Europe.

APPENDIX C:
SOME OBJECTIONS ANSWERED

The kind of enterprise which this book represents is open to various objections. I distinguish five such. Some of them are mutually compatible, others not.

1. That the Old Testament is the word of God, every part of it inspired, and therefore that it is presumptuous to choose some parts of it while rejecting others. This is an objection typically made by a fundamentalist Christian or Jew.

But in the first place the Bible is itself an anthology, a selection made from a much larger body of literature, most of which was rejected when part was chosen. It is hard to see therefore what logical objection can lie to the extension of the principle of anthology. It is particularly strange to find Christians employing this argument about the OT, for two reasons. First, the judges who originally chose those books and rejected others were not Christians but Jewish rabbis. Second, the Christian Church has always made a selection *within* the Bible for purposes of ordinary worship.

But is it more constructive to consider the key concept here, namely inspiration. If we say that a work of art is inspired, we may be referring to its origin or to its quality. We may mean that it came into being through the influence of a power outside the author, especially God or (in the case of Greek literature) the Muses. Or we may mean that it is of sublime quality. These two meanings are related but distinct. The correlation between origin and quality may be quite low and, when it is, the quality matters more. It is self-evident that the quality of the OT is very variable. I also believe that even the best of it is still not different in kind from the best of Aeschylus, Shakespeare or Goethe. Readers offended by that judgement may find Coleridge's formulation helpful: 'Whatever finds me, bears witness

for itself that it has proceeded from a Holy Spirit'. He went on: 'In the Bible there is more that finds me than in all the other books I know'. Perhaps 'inspiring' is a more useful concept than 'inspired'.

2. That the books of the OT were not written as literature, and therefore it is fundamentally inappropriate to treat them as such. This is another religious objection, put vehemently by T.S. Eliot: 'I could fulminate against the men of letters who have gone into ecstasies over "the Bible as literature", the Bible as "the noblest monument of English prose".' Faithfully W.H. Auden echoed Eliot:

Thou shalt not be a friend to those
who read the Bible for its prose.

These are forceful judgements, but it is not easy to discern the logic of the argument upon which they rest. The implication seems to be that there are two sorts of writing, religious and secular, each with its own criteria of merit. That distinction admittedly is implicit in much of the OT. It also occasionally becomes explicit: see the different emphases of the Hebrew Ez 33.31f. and the Greek 2 Macc 2.25 and [15.38f.], reconciled in Eccl 12.10. But a modern reader, though aware of the distinction, is not bound by it. An author's intention cannot limit the reader's response.

Nevertheless the Eliot-Auden position contains a valid warning against a *purely aesthetic* approach to the OT, as sometimes practised nowadays. Such an approach seems a pale and reductionist activity, unable to handle either the passion or the truth-claims of the biblical authors. A good critic of religious literature must take into account the religious attitudes of the authors and the religious points they are making. It is just possible for a theological criticism to exclude literary questions, but literary criticism (of religious literature) cannot exclude theological questions.

For these reasons I assent to the judgement of Barr that 'the recognition of the Bible as a religious text is no obstacle to the reading of it as literature'. 'The Bible', it has been said, 'may be *more* than literature; it is certainly not less.' It can therefore be both 'holy ground' to believers and 'common ground' between believers and others (Barton).

3. *That a work of literature, a text, must be read as a whole and not (arbitrarily) excerpted.* This is a literary objection, derived from certain principles of modern literary criticism, but it chimes well with the religious objection no.1 above. It is an objection to taking sections of books – or even whole books – of the OT and reading them out of context.

When not pressed to extremes, this has been salutary, correcting a previous tendency to excessive fragmentation of texts. Much is gained from reading an episode in the context of 'its' book, though less from reading a book in the context of the books on either side of it in the canon. For a scholar, that gain may be very precious. But from the ordinary reader it is imprudent to demand 'all or nothing'.

The objection however is not as bland as that. It incorporates a sharp attack upon the analytical procedures used by previous scholars. The attack has two prongs. First, that whereas we can be (relatively) certain of the whole text, we cannot identify with certainty any of its supposed components. In fact however we *can* be certain in the case of most of the poetry in the OT: almost all the psalms and many of the prophetic oracles have audible limits. In the case of the prose narratives it is harder to be equally certain. But few scholars, even of the 'holistic' persuasion, challenge the identification of many components of the Pentateuch, and in the DtH the same goes for e.g. the Court History of David.

Secondly, analysis takes its start from the perception of incoherences in the 'whole' text. When it finds them, of whatever form, it tends to lay them at the door not of the author* or narrator* but of a (subsequent) editor*. A recent critic objects to this tendency: 'You can't solve the conundrum of a narrator's idiocy by attributing it to a supposed editor'. No, indeed. But there is no compelling reason to regard either author or editor as infallible. To take an example, the tale of Tamar in Genesis 38 interrupts the story of Joseph in Chs 37-49. To call the interruption anything less than a defect is pusillanimous. To ascribe it to the author of that otherwise admirably coherent story is obtuse.

But some of the objectors deploy an even more radical argument in favour of 'holistic' reading. It may be put like this, that to excerpt the OT is to misrepresent it fundamentally, rather like bowdlerising Shakespeare. Just as Shakespeare's bawdy was integral to his world-view, so some of the apparent weaknesses of the OT text – not merely its inconcinnities and anfractuosities but its contradictions and absurdities – are fundamental to its (realistic) view of human nature and the human condition. On this argument the absurdity of the psalm put in Jonah's mouth is to be admired as pointing up the absurdity of his character, and the dissonance in Job between the central poem and the surrounding folk-tale is to be welcomed as expressing the dissonance in his tormented spirit.

At this point every reader, whether scholar or not, has to take a stand. My own reaction is to feel that enough is enough. With critical tools like that , with 'multi-layered irony' and 'the device of a less-than-reliable narrator' (Brichto), it seems that anything can be explained. Even the great Alter can write that 'apparently conflicting versions of the same event set side by side may have been perfectly justified in a kind of logic which we no longer apprehend'. Well, they may.

But one would like more evidence of this logic than the contradictions which it is brought in to excuse.

4. *That the concept of God is so central to the books of the OT that they can be appreciated only by a reader who believes in God.* This objection also looks powerful. The Bible without God is like Hamlet without the Prince of Denmark; how then can unbelievers make sense of it?

One may distinguish two senses of 'unbelievers'. First, there are straight atheists. But the God in whom atheists do not believe is precisely the God of parts of the OT. Their unbelief does not usually derive from an inability to form a clear picture of God. Rather they have all *too* clear a picture (often a childhood picture) of a being whom, however, they reject as unworthy of allegiance. Thus paradoxically they can enter without excessive difficulty into much of the thought-world of the biblical writers.

Second there are agnostics. They too may well reject the picture of God as portrayed in parts of the OT. On the other hand they understand and even entertain the possibility that there may exist, if not a person, at least a purpose in the universe. And it is not necessary, in order to appreciate an author, to believe in everything that he believes in. What is necessary is to be willing to enter imaginatively into his world.

It is true that much of the thought-world of the OT has in the last century or two come to seem very remote. But for this very reason belief is no longer *expected* of most of us. Freed therefore from inhibitions and guilt in our approach to the literature, we are in a position to suspend disbelief more lightly than our grandparents.

5. *That it is impossible to make a valid criticism of literature in translation.* Inevitably there is some truth in this objection. One would not go all the way

with Eliot and define poetry as precisely that which is lost in translation. But we all know that e.g. a Greekless reader cannot fully appreciate Homer; and in the case of the OT there are further difficulties which must not be glossed over.

First, the text is often uncertain, as also is the pronunciation of the ancient language. Second, so little of the literature survives that often we cannot be sure of the denotations of the words, let alone their connotations. We know little of the literary conventions within which the authors operated, and have scarcely any controls in the non-literary use of the language.

All this presents a formidable handicap. Two considerations may however cut it down to size. First, a number of English scholars and writers have claimed that *less* is lost in the translation of Hebrew to English than in other translations. Any truth in this claim must be due partly to the great concision of the two languages – it is said that only Chinese is more concise. Bishop Lowth's judgement is perhaps more prudent:

> Our constant use of a close verbal translation [AV/KJV] has by degrees moulded our language into such a conformity with that of the original scriptures that it can upon occasion assume the Hebrew character without appearing altogether forced and unnatural

– a splendidly *non*-Hebraic sentence!

Second, one may admit that ignorance of Hebrew is a considerable handicap in appreciating the OT but still insist, against the purists, that half a loaf is better than no bread. How many English lovers of Dostoevsky or Tolstoy know Russian? Yet they would maintain with passion that their lives would have been infinitely the poorer without the translations they have read.

But in reply to this, as to the other objections, no counter-argument can be final. This book must, for better or worse, supply the answer itself.

GLOSSARY

(If an obscure word used in the book is not in this glossary, it may be in the index.)

Aetiology: an explanation of a cause. In the OT this usually takes the form of a narrative which purports to explain the origin of a custom or of a name. See also **Etymology**.

Akkadian: the language and literature of the first Semitic people to occupy Mesopotamia.

Amalekites: a nomadic or semi-nomadic people, traditional enemies of the Israelites, but not mentioned outside the OT.

ANE: Ancient Near East(ern); see Appx A.

Aniconic: lacking religious images (an epithet used of religions like Judaism).

Apocalyptic: (adjective, 'revelatory'). The noun belonging to it is 'an apocalypse', and 'The (New Testament) Apocalypse' is a learned name for the Book of Revelation. But 'apocalyptic' is also used as a noun by modern scholars to designate the kind of writing which distinguishes that book and the book of Daniel (see Postscript to Daniel, p. 646). The most striking feature of apocalyptic is its **Eschatology**, a picture of 'the last things' painted in highly coloured language, poetic, symbolic and mythical. Its scenario is not merely international but cosmic, its time-scale often worked out down to the last detail.

Apocrypha: a category of books rejected from the Hebrew **canon** but given a qualified approval by Christians and generally preserved in the **Septuagint**. Most of them were originally composed in Hebrew, though the Hebrew text of all but Ecclesiasticus is lost. The Roman Catholic Church recognises these books as part of the OT and knows them as deutero-canonical, i.e. added later to the **canon**. The Church of England, whose practice is followed here, accords them an uncertain status, but it does require them to be included in the text of the Bible as used at the coronation of a monarch.

Apostasy: the abandonment of one religion for another.

Atonement: reconciliation to God (see commentary on Leviticus 16).

Author: a term used in this book to denote the writer or composer of a substantial work which bears the impress of a single mind. This may be a whole book (e.g. Ruth, Job or the Song of Songs) or part of a book (e.g. Gen 37 with 39-45 or Is 40-55) or a body of now separated units like those of 'J' in the Pentateuch. See also **Editor**; **Narrator**.

Canaan: as used outside the OT from C15th BC on, a geographical term of imprecise reference, corresponding roughly to our 'Levant', and including the territory later designated 'Israel'. In the OT it is used, normally with pejorative overtones, of all Israel's neighbours except Philistines and Egyptians.

Canon: an approved body of literature. The canon of the Hebrew Bible gradually crystallised, in three phases. First came the **Torah** and the 'Former Prophets' (Joshua–Kings, less Ruth); then the Latter Prophets (Isaiah–Malachi, less Daniel); finally the Writings, i.e. the rest. The prologue to Ecclesiasticus, written c.120 BC, refers to 'the law and the prophets and the remainder of the books which have come down from the fathers', which shows that three groups of books already had canonical status. But there were still then in circulation a number of books of uncertain status, as is shown by the **Dead Sea Scrolls** and the mss of the **Septuagint**. Eventually, some time about AD100, the rabbis decided to draw up an exclusive list of approved works with an approved text. They did this for two main reasons. First, with the destruction of the Temple in AD 70 the Book became even more important. Second, orthodox Judaism needed to be protected against the doctrines of sects like that of **Qumran** and, more particularly, the Christians. There was in fact some debate before approval was given to certain books now in the canon (Ecclesiastes, the Song of Songs, and Esther), partly because they contain no mention of the holy name of **YHWH**. The somewhat lower status of Ruth, Daniel, Ezra-Nehemiah and [Chronicles] is also shown by their demotion to the third division. Later the Christian Church took a more favourable view of some books which had been excluded from the Hebrew canon and gave them an intermediate status – see **Apocrypha**.

Chiasmus: a sequence of words of the form ABB'A'. This kind of chiastic sequence is extremely frequent in the OT, especially in poetry. It is often used for the sake of neatness, but also in three special cases:

    1. to express completeness, e.g. Ps 19.1:

        The heavens are telling the glory of God;

the wonder of his works proclaims the firmament
2. to make a contrast, e.g. Jg 5.25:
   He asked water; milk she gave
3. to illustrate retribution, e.g. Gen 9.6:
   Whoever sheds the blood of man,
   by man shall his blood be shed.

Cosmogony: a theory or myth of the origin of the cosmos or universe.

Covenant: agreement. Covenant is a very important word in the OT – indeed in the whole Bible, since the word 'testament' is an English synonym for it. The Hebrew *berith*, of which it is the usual translation, has the fundamental meaning of a solemn undertaking or promise such as God made to Noah in Gen 9.12. But it came to be used of a reciprocal agreement, as between God and Israel. In that sense it is formulated succinctly in Ex 19.5 and at much greater length elsewhere in Ex and Dt. Later Jeremiah (31.31), regarding the 'old' covenant as broken, foretold the establishment of a new one.

Cycle: a collection of stories, loosely strung together, about a single person.

Dead Sea Scrolls: the collective name given to various ancient Heb. mss found since 1947 in caves near the Dead Sea. The most important ones were found at **Qumran**, where a religious community existed from C2nd BC to C1st AD. Texts have been found there of all books of the OT except Esther, ranging in length from a complete scroll of Isaiah to a few words. Because of their antiquity – the oldest were copied c.250 BC – the scrolls are of great interest to scholars seeking to establish the best text of the OT. But the readings they give vary in value. Some agree with the **Masoretic Text**, some with the **Septuagint** (notably in Jeremiah), some with neither. Apart from a few cases where a scroll alone preserves the correct reading (e.g. Is 40.6), their chief use is in providing Palestinian support for a reading of LXX where it differs from MT, e.g. Dt 32.8.

Debt-slave/slavery: a notorious social abuse in the **ANE**. The slavery was the end-state of the farmer whose holding was too small or too infertile to sustain his family. First he borrowed from a rich neighbour on the security of his land and house. When he could not repay, the neighbour took the property, while he himself became a tenant, tilling it on payment of an exorbitant share of the produce. If his fortunes declined further, he had to sell first his children and then his wife and himself into slavery. The prophets denounced this practice (e.g. Mic 2.2), and the Torah sought to alleviate it in various ways (Lev 25, Dt 15); see also Jer 34 and Neh 5.

Editor: a term used in this book to denote a person who takes one or more pieces of writing and modifies or arranges/rearranges them for literary or ideological purposes. Most of the OT went through a process of editing which involved many hands over many centuries.

Endogamy: marriage within a restricted group.

Eschatology: the theory of the 'last things'. These included the day of the Lord, the last judgement, the establishment of the messianic kingdom and the conversion of the gentiles.

Etymology: an explanation of the origin of a word (see also **Aetiology**).

Formula: a phrase which is regularly used in a given context, e.g. 'Thus saith the Lord' to introduce a prophetic oracle. Most formulae are specific to a certain kind or form of literature, but some are more widely used. For example, the polite 'abasement' formula 'Who am I, that . . .' is found in narrative, e.g. 1 Sam 18.18, but also in worship, e.g. Ps 8.4.

Framing: a device extremely common in Hebrew literature, whereby a word or phrase from the beginning of a poem or story is repeated at the end to round it off. It may be purely formal, but often it implies the fulfilment of God's plan, perhaps with overtones of **irony**. In its most elaborate form it is developed as a **pedimental** structure.

Gloss: words found in a ms which scholars believe not to have been in the original text but to have crept in during the process of copying and recopying, often having started life as a marginal comment or explanation.

Hellenistic: chronologically, the centuries between Alexander's conquest of the **ANE** and the end of the OT period, say 330 BC -100 AD; culturally, the Greek civilisation centred on Alexandria during that period.

Hesedh: a Hebrew word for which there is no English equivalent. The older versions render it 'tender mercy' or 'loving kindness', more modern ones 'love'. But it connotes rather more in the nature of obligation that any of these: hence sometimes 'loyalty'.

Holy: see Introd. to Leviticus.

Irony: the OT makes much use of irony in a variety of forms for theological purposes:

1. the irony of retribution, of 'the enginer hoist with his own petard' e.g. Haman's gallows in Esther.
2. the irony of pretensions exposed. The pretensions may be to knowledge (Adam) or status (Naaman) or power (Babylon in Is 47), but essentially they constitute a challenge to God. The symbol of the exposure is nakedness.
3. the irony of human ignorance before God's providence. The symbol of the ignorance is blindness, e.g. Tobit. When the author shares God's fore-knowledge, it becomes dramatic or tragic irony.

Legend: see p.18.

Liturgy: a formal act of public religious worship.

LXX: see **Septuagint**

Masoretic Text (MT): the text of the Hebrew Bible as set in order by the Masoretes, Jewish scholars of the C8th-C9th AD, and preserved in mss of the same period and later. The mss are an astonishingly faithful reproduction of the text as it was agreed by the rabbis when the Hebrew **canon** was finally established. The text contains a few variant readings, noted as such, but otherwise the different mss are remarkable for their identity, even of layout on the page. The care with which the sacred text was treated is shown e.g. by the calculation that a *waw* in Lev 11.42 is the middle letter of the **Torah**. The verse numberings of Hebrew bibles often differ by one or two from those of Christian bibles, as sometimes does the allocation of verses to chapters. For an example of the MT see the Leningrad Codex on p.36

Merismus: a form of expression used in Hebrew and other languages, whereby the two extreme terms of a sequence are used to denote the whole of it, as if we were to say 'A and Z' to mean the whole alphabet. So 'thou hast fashioned me behind and before' (Ps 139.5) means 'entirely', and when Lot did not know 'when his daughter lay down and when she got up' (Gen 19.33), the reference is clearly to what went on in between.

Messianic: a term with a wide range of meanings, distinguished in the note on p.532.

Midianites: a semi-nomadic people, based from C13th onwards in towns south-east of the Arabah (see Map 1), but capable of appearing further west. Important as relatives of Moses and enemies of Gideon, they gradually fade out of the pages of the OT.

Midrash: a homiletic commentary on a biblical text by later rabbis.

Mishnah: a record of rabbinic discussions about the law in the period 70-c.200 AD.

Motif: the smallest element in a story or description which has power to persist in the tradition or to recur within a single work, e.g. the sending out of the dove from the ark in the Flood story, which is found twice in Genesis but also in the Babylonian flood myth.

M T: see **Masoretic Text**.

Myth: see p.18.

Narrator: a term used in this book to denote the writer of a single story-unit (commonly a chapter), without any implication about who wrote the adjacent story-units. Narrator and **Author** may thus be the same person.

Novella: a 'short story' of a certain length. In the OT the term is used of an independent book like Ruth or Jonah or Judith, or of a similar self-contained unit within a larger book e.g. the Joseph story in Gen 37-48. The term **romance** is also used of these stories, with special reference to their contents and tone; see p.349.

Pantheon: a group of gods worshipped in a given religion, e.g. the Olympian pantheon of the Greeks and Romans.

Papyri: texts written on papyrus, the writing material made out of a particular kind of reed growing in the Nile.

Parallelism: the distinctive structural feature of Hebrew poetry; see p.21+.

Pedimental: a term used to describe the structure of a passage of prose or poetry in which the key-words of the first half are repeated in reverse order in the second half e.g. Isaiah 14. The term derives from the pediment of a Greek temple, where the architectural shape throws the emphasis upon the sculptures in the centre.

Pentateuch: the Greek name for the first five books of the OT.

Peripeteia: sometimes englished as 'peripety': a reversal of fortune.

Proselyte: a gentile convert to Judaism.

Qumran: see **Dead Sea Scrolls**.

Redeemer (Heb *gō'ēl*): a technical term for the next of kin who by Hebrew family law was charged with certain important responsibilities towards a deceased male relative. The responsibilities are variously described in different OT books: see Gen 38, Lev 25, Dt 25 and Ruth 4. The term was also applied metaphorically to God by Job (19.25) and Second Isaiah.

Romance: see **Novella**.

Septuagint (LXX): the Greek translation of the OT, made c.250 - 100 BC by the Greek-speaking Jews of Alexandria for their own use. By tradition the translators numbered 70 (Lat. *septuaginta*) – hence the name and its abbreviation. Our mss of the LXX go back to C4th AD. *Codex Sinaiticus*, for which see p.690, is the oldest and best. The mss contain the whole of the Hebrew **canon**, together with certain other books (see **Apocrypha**). All begin with the **Pentateuch**, which was translated first and with especial care. For the rest they vary somewhat among themselves in the additional books they contain and in the order of them all. In places the LXX offers an earlier and shorter text than the MT. For this reason Christian (especially Roman Catholic) scholars have tended to make considerable use of it in trying to establish the most faithful text of the OT, whereas Jewish scholars place most or even all of their reliance on the **Masoretic Text**.

Stairlike: a special kind of **parallelism**, where words from the first line of the couplet are repeated in the second, as in Ps 29.1+.

Stele: a standing stone inscribed with a text and/or a low-relief sculpture.

Sumerian: the non-Semitic people who occupied Mesopotamia before the **Akkadians**.

Syncretism: a fusing of two religions (see p.32).

Tabernacles, Feast of: the last of the three harvest festivals, which marked the end of the Jewish year. It was the most important of all the feasts down to the exile, when it was superseded by the Passover.

Theodicy: the doctrine of God's justice, which seeks 'to justify the ways of God to men', especially to explain the apparent lack of reward for virtue. In the OT the problem of theodicy is addressed above all in the book of Job.

Theophany: an appearance of a god to a human.

Theophoric names: those which incorporate the name or title of a god.

Topos (pl. **topoi**): a term of Greek literary criticism: a stock idea used in rhetoric to make or emphasise a point. Examples of topoi in the OT are:
1. the topos of impossibles, often used by prophets to lead into an exhortation e.g. 'Can the leopard change his spots?' (Jer 13.23). It is brilliantly inverted by Isaiah 49.15
2. the topos of opposites or 'the world upside-down', used with great versatility by the prophets e.g. Is 3.5; 11.6
3. the topos of inescapability, expressed in a list of failed attempts at escape e.g. Joel 1.4; Amos 5.19.

Torah: the Hebrew name for the first five books of the Bible (see p.36).

Ugaritic: the language and literature of a West Semitic people of north Syria in the second millennium BC (see p.772+).

Vicarious Suffering: suffering on behalf of others, as most notably on the part of the servant of the Lord in Isaiah 52-3.

Vow: a promise to a god to perform a certain action in return for the granting of a certain petition.

Wilderness: used to translate Heb. *midbar*, meaning uncultivated land to which herdsmen drive their flocks for pasture.

Wisdom: in OT studies a technical term for a certain kind of literature (see p.364+).

YHWH: the name of the God of Israel (see p.34).

DATE CHART

	The Nations	Israel and Judah	The OT
c.1300	**EGYPT** dominant		
	Rameses II 1290-1224		
	Merneptah 1224-1204	'Israel is laid waste'	
c.1200	Philistines settle	Exodus (?)	
	on coast	Battle of Taanach c.1100	Song of Deborah
		Saul c.1020	
		David c.1000	
	Shishak 945-925	Solomon c.950	
		Jeroboam c.925	
		Rehoboam c.925	
c.880	**ASSYRIA** dominant	Omri 885-874	
		Ahab 874-853	Elijah
		Jehu 841-814	Elisha
		Uzziah 781-740	Amos, Hosea
	Sargon II 721-705	Fall of Samaria 721	
		Hezekiah 716-687	Isaiah of
			Jerusalem
	Sennacherib 704-681	Siege of Jerusalem 701	
	Assurbanipal 669-630	Josiah 640-609	Deuteronomy
606	**BABYLON** dominant		
	Nebuchadnezzar 605-562	Fall of Jerusalem 597;	Jeremiah
		first deportation	
		Destruction of Jer. 587;	
		second deportation	
539	**PERSIANS** conquer		
	Babylon		Second Isaiah
	Cyrus 555-530	Return authorised	Ezra, Nehemiah
			Job, Eccl, Esther
333	**GREEKS** conquer Persia		
300-200	Ptolemies control Judaea		The Septuagint
200-142	Seleucids control Judaea		Ecclus
	Antiochus Epiphanes	Maccabean Revolt 167	Daniel
		Judas recovers Temple 164	
141	**(INDEPENDENCE)**	High Priest Simon	Tobit
		Qumran community	1M, 2M, Judith
6 3	**ROMANS** dominant: Pompey takes Jerusalem		Wisdom of
			Solomon
AD 30		Crucifixion of Jesus	
70		Destruction of Jerusalem	2 Esdras
			Hebrew canon*
			closed

MAPS

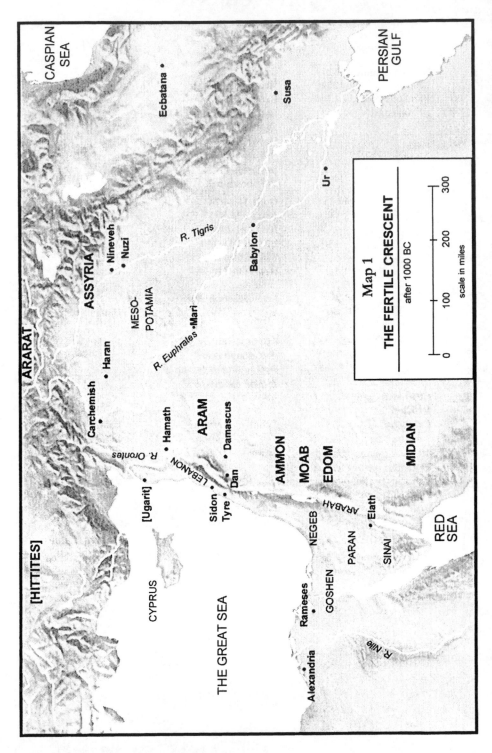

Map 1
THE FERTILE CRESCENT
after 1000 BC

scale in miles

0   100   200   300

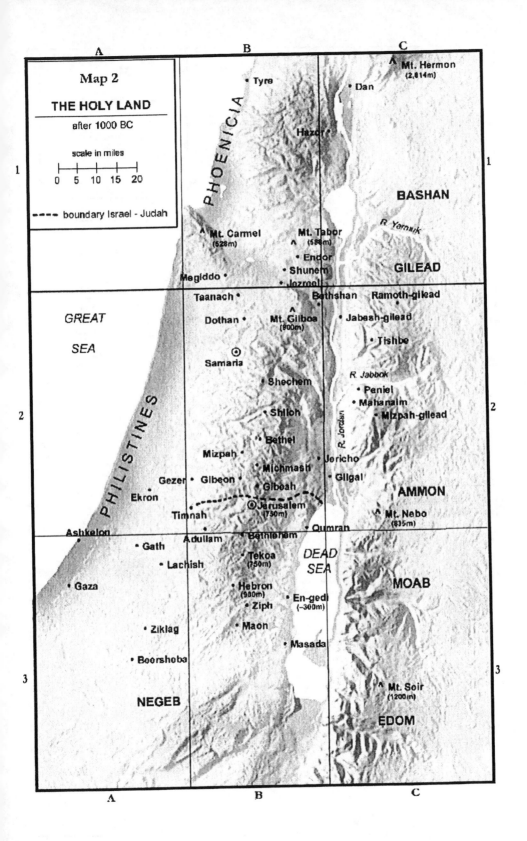

Map 2

THE HOLY LAND

after 1000 BC

scale in miles

0 5 10 15 20

---- boundary Israel - Judah

PHOENICIA

^ Mt. Hermon
(2,814m)

• Tyre

• Dan

Hazor •

BASHAN

R. Yarmuk

^ Mt. Carmel
(528m)

Mt. Tabor
^ (588m)

GILEAD

• Endor

• Shunem

Megiddo •

• Jezreel

Taanach •

Bethshan •   Ramoth-gilead

GREAT

SEA

Dothan •

^
Mt. Gilboa
(500m)

• Jabesh-gilead

• Tishbe

⊙
Samaria

R. Jabbok

• Shechem

• Peniel

• Mahanaim

• Shiloh

• Mizpah-gilead

R. Jordan

• Bethel

Mizpah •

• Michmash

Jericho •

Gezer •   Gibeon •

• Gilgal

Ekron •

• Gibeah

AMMON

Timnah •

⊙ Jerusalem
(750m)

^ Mt. Nebo
(835m)

Ashkelon •

• Qumran

Adullam •   • Bethlehem

• Gath

• Tekoa
(750m)

DEAD
SEA

MOAB

• Lachish

• Hebron
(980m)

• En-gedi
(−300m)

• Gaza

• Ziph

PHILISTINES

• Maon

• Ziklag

• Masada

• Beersheba

^ Mt. Seir
(1200m)

NEGEB

EDOM

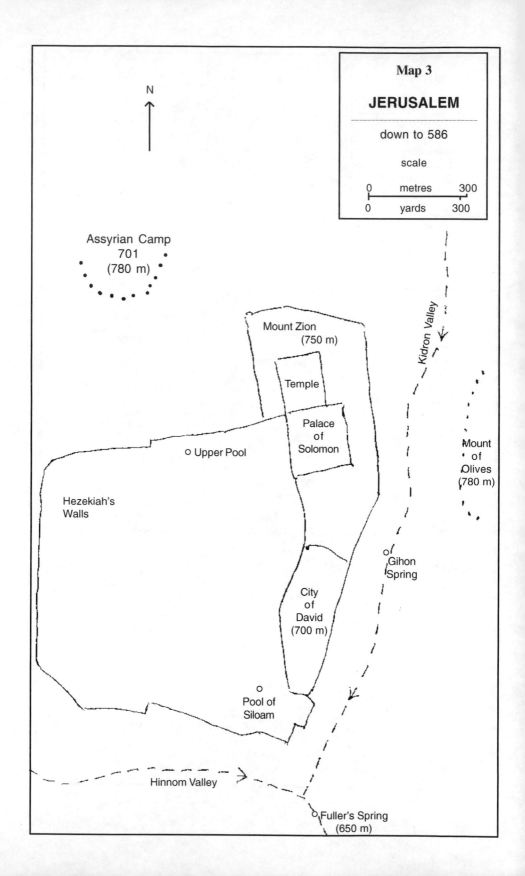

N

Map 3

JERUSALEM

down to 586

scale

| 0 | metres | 300 |
| 0 | yards | 300 |

Assyrian Camp
701
(780 m)

Mount Zion
(750 m)

Temple

Palace
of
Solomon

Upper Pool

Hezekiah's
Walls

Kidron Valley

Mount
of
Olives
(780 m)

Gihon
Spring

City
of
David
(700 m)

Pool of
Siloam

Hinnom Valley

Fuller's Spring
(650 m)

BOOKS FOR FURTHER READING

Three classics in the reading of the OT as literature are:
> R. Lowth, *Lectures on the Sacred Poetry of the Hebrews*, translated by C. Gregory London, 1787
> H. Gunkel, *Commentary on Genesis*, translated by M. E. Biddle, Mercer University Press, 1998
> E. Auerbach, *Mimesis*, 1946, translated by Willard Trask, Princeton University Press, 1953, Ch.1

More recent general works are:
> R. Alter, *The Art of Biblical Narrative*, Allen and Unwin, 1981
> R. Alter, *The Art of Biblical Poetry*, Basic Books, 1985
> J. Barton, *Reading the Old Testament*, Darton, Longman and Todd, 2nd edition, 1996
> H. Fisch, *Poetry with a Purpose*, Indiana University Press, 1988

Of individual books of the OT there are a number of readable modern studies, e.g.
> M. V. Fox, *The Song of Songs and the Ancient Egyptian Love Poetry*, University of Wisconsin Press, 1988
> M. V. Fox, *Character and Ideology in the Book of Esther*, University of South Carolina Press, 1991
> D. M. Gunn, *The Story of King David*, Society for Old Testament Studies, 1978
> D. M. Gunn, *The Fate of King Saul*, Society for Old Testament Studies, 1980

Parallels from ANE literature are mostly quoted from:
> *Ancient Near Eastern Texts Relating to the Old Testament*, Princeton University Press, 3rd edition with supplement, 1969. The translations in *ANET* are reasonably authoritative but not always easy reading. More readable is:
> A. George, *The Epic of Gilgamesh*, Penguin, 1999

Parallels from early Greek poetry are considered in:
> M. L. West, *The East Face of Helicon*, Oxford University Press, 1997

GENERAL INDEX

Asterisked entries are to be found also in the Glossary. Most entries are illustrative rather than exhaustive. Bold type is used for the most important reference under that head.

adultery, *see* women in the OT

Alexandria, 502, 646, 727, 738, 756, 765+, 778, Map 1

Alter, Robert, 94+, 238+, 413, 785

*Amalekites, 233++, 254, 354

angels, 65, 67, 72, 83, 206+, 550+, 645+, 695++, 703+, 708+, 715

animals, 47, 55, 58, 147+, 164, **399**+, 453, 536, 679, 710

anthropology, 32, 146+, 312 (*see also* Bedouin; ordeal; unclean)

*apocalyptic, 542+, 545, 640, **646**, 658, 695, 701 (*see also* New Jerusalem)

*apocrypha, 11, 691++

Arabs, 508, 515 (*see also* Bedouin, *wasf*)

*Aram/Aramaean, 31, 264, 311, 327, Map 1 (*see also* Damascus *in place index*)

Aramaic, 331, 517, 626, 704

archaeology, **29**+, 109+, 165, 222, 309, 311, 332, 334+, 340+, 517

Ark of the Covenant, *see* religion of the OT

assonance, **14**, 496, 513, 537, 540, 542, 685

Assyria: history, 311, 333, 335-39, 684 (*see also* Nineveh *in place index*)
    inscriptions, 178, 333, 336-38, 534+, 546

astral religion, 340, 395, 423, 453, 492, 553, 561

Atonement, Day of, *see under* religion of the OT

Auerbach, Eric, 72, 85, 781+

*author, 72, 245, 292, 369, 487++, 548+, 625, 737, 765, 783 (*see also* *editor; *narrator)

Baal, 32+, 35, 311+, 315++, 647++ (*see also* syncretism; Ugaritic Literature)

Babylon:
    history, 59, 339++, 557+, 577, 635
    literature, 25, 39, 110, 407+, 415, 418, 553, 635, **771**++ (*see also* creation myth; Gilgamesh)
    religion, 83, 151, 408, 482, 553, 557+ (*see also* Ishtar, Marduk *in names index*)

Bedouin, 128, 162, 196, 198, 268

blessing, **79**+, 88, 155, 164+, 177 (*see also* curse)

*Canaan/ites, 29+, 127, 139

*canon, 350, 409, 487, 503, 704, 716

Chaldaeans, 60, 602+, 627

*chiasmus, 81, 301, 444, 513 etc

Christianity, 131, 386, 414, 517, 568, 631, 782, 784 (*see also* gospels; Jesus;

New Testament; Paul)

circumcision, *see* religion of the OT

clean, *see* unclean

comedy, 65, 68, 163, 352, 363, 674++, 704, 719, 780

concubines, *see* women in the OT

Court History of David, 19, 265, 298+, 775

covenant, *see* religion of the OT

creation myth, ANE, **27**, 41, 43-46, 125, 375, 390, 397, 410 (*see also* Leviathan *in names index*)

cult, *see* religion of the OT

curse, 49, 165, 177+, 298, 369+, 394, 414, 463, 774

David, king, 221, 236-97, 331, 409, 419+, 532, 682

*Dead Sea Scrolls, 223, 409, 522, 551, 578, 608, 635, 645

*debt-slaves, 134, 153, 172, 348, 529, 601, 665, 680 (*see also* poor)

deuteronomic history, 39, 166, **184**, 222, 300+, 578

Deuteronomy, book of, **166**, 307, 339, 578

dispersion, 59, 179, 333, 345, 355, 363, 563, 607, 702, 704 (*see also* exile)

doublet, **18**, 56, 61+, 91, 238, 325, 602

Ecclesiastes, Book of, 487

Ecclesiasticus, Book of, 737

*editor, 38, 46, 56+, 91+, 94, 468, 499+, 521+, 578, 785

Edom, 31, 79, 81, 265, 463, 545+, 574, 664, Map 2 C3

Egypt:
    customs, 94, 97+, 103, 111, 116
    history, 29++, 98+, 106, 109, 115, 300, 310, 341+, 644 (*see also* Alexandria; Nile *in place index*)
    literature, 95, 364+, 415, 467+, 488, 501-06, 514-16, 540, 748+, **770**+, 773
    religion, 300, 416, 453+, 467+, 481, 491

*endogamy, 33, 74, 82, 92, 99, 208, 214, 707+

English translations of OT, **12**, 34+, 47, 121, 150, 427, 503+, 527, 534, 589

Ephraim (tribe), 199, 205, 308, 310, 651+

euphemism, 34, 204, 218, 315, 492, 502

exile, 333, 342++, 462, 568, 571, 600 (*see also* dispersion)

exodus, the, 31, 109+, 123++, 183

Exodus, Book of, 109

INDEX OF NAMES OF INDIVIDUALS AND BOOKS

Some names are to be found rather in the General Index

INDEX OF PLACES

Some place-names are to be found rather in the General Index